Strategic Management

Strategic Management
Awareness and Change

Third edition

John L Thompson
University of Huddersfield

INTERNATIONAL THOMSON BUSINESS PRESS
I ⓣ P An International Thomson Publishing Company

London • Bonn • Boston • Johannesburg • Madrid • Melbourne • Mexico City • New York • Paris
Singapore • Tokyo • Toronto • Albany, NY • Belmont, CA • Cincinnati, OH • Detroit, MI

Strategic Management: Awareness and Change, third edition

Copyright ©1997 John L Thompson

First Published by International Thomson Business Press

The Thomson Learning logo is a registered trademark used herein under license.

British Library Cataloguing-in-Publication Data
A catalogue record for this book is available from the British Library

First edition 1990
Second edition 1993
Third edition 1997, reprinted 1997, 1999 and 2001

Produced by Gray Publishing, Tunbridge Wells, Kent
Printed in China

ISBN 1-86152-100-6

Thomson Learning
Berkshire House
168–173 High Holborn
London WC1V 7AA
UK

http://www.thomsonlearning.co.uk

Contents

Part III   The Content of Competitive Strategies   306

10   Competitive Advantage Through Products, Processes and Service   309

11   Competitive Advantage Through People   356

12   Financial Strategy   377

Contents

Preface

This preface outlines the content and approach of this book and explains how it is appropriate both for managers and for students who will become future managers.

There are suggestions about how different types of reader might make effective use of the material.

Strategic awareness and change

This book is about strategic awareness and the management of strategic change. It looks at how managers can become strategically aware of their company's position and opportunities for change; at how changes often happen in reality; and at how the process might be managed more effectively.

It is in five parts. The first part looks at the strategy process as a whole and includes in Chapter 2 a comprehensive framework of the process, around which the book is structured. This part also includes chapters on strategic leadership and decision making and on culture and values as these are forces which determine how strategy is managed within organizations.

Part II concerns strategic awareness. Chapters on the organizational mission and objectives, strategic success and strategic failure are followed by an examination of the business and competitive environments. The section finishes with a discussion on competitive positioning and advantage.

Parts III and IV separate competitive and corporate level strategies. Corporate strategy issues concern the overall portfolio of activities undertaken by an organization, and their relatedness; competitive strategy is about how an organization might achieve and sustain competitive advantage in each activity in the corporate whole.

Part III, on **competitive** strategies, looks at how marketing, operations, human resource, financial and information strategies can all be an important source of, and support for, competitive advantage.

Part IV is a consideration of how changes in **corporate** strategy are formulated, followed by a study of the various strategic alternatives which a firm might consider and the determinants of a good choice.

The issues involved in strategy implementation are evaluated in Part V. Organization structures, resource management and the complexities of managing change are included. Pressures to change are always present in the form of opportunities and threats. At any point in time the significance of these pressures will vary markedly from industry to industry and from organization to

---

The manager's job is change. It is what we live with. It is what we are to create. If we cannot do that, then we are not good at the job. It is our basic job to have the nerve to keep changing and changing and changing again.

Sir Peter Parker, Executive Chairman, Rockware Group, speaking at a BIM Workshop in London, February 1986

organization. Managers may be aware of them and seek to respond positively; they may recognize opportunities and threats and choose to do little about them other than perhaps to avert crises; or they may be totally unaware of them. A lack of awareness can mean that potentially good opportunities are also lost; it may mean businesses fail if they are not able to react and respond to the threats and problems when they arise. Whilst all businesses must react to pressures from the environment such as supply shortages, new products from competitors or new retailing opportunities, some will be very proactive and thereby seek to manage their environment.

Finally, a new feature of this third edition is a selection of long cases, covering large and small businesses, both national and international in scope, manufacturing and service and the private, public and non-profit sectors. Some of these cases have been published before in the lecturers' manual which accompanies earlier editions of this book, but all of them have been either updated or rewritten for this publication.

It must be emphasized that no single approach, model or theory can explain the realities of strategic change in practice for all organizations; different organizations and managers will find certain approaches much more relevant to their circumstances and style. All approaches will have both supporters and critics. It is therefore important to study the various approaches within a sound intellectual framework so that they can be evaluated by readers and students.

Practising managers and students of business and management must work out for themselves the intricacies and difficulties of managing organizations at the corporate level and of managing strategic change. It is no good being told how to be prescriptive when it is patently obvious that there is no universal model. Observations of practice in isolation are equally limited in their usefulness. However, an attempt to find explanations which can be utilized does make sense. Testing and evaluating reality against a theoretical framework helps this process.

Changes for the third edition

Strategic management is a complex and dynamic subject, and since the first two editions of this book were published a number of new ideas have emerged. In addition, certain practices and priorities have changed to reflect developments around the world. These changes have been incorporated into this third edition. The whole text has been reviewed, and some chapters substantially rewritten and consolidated, but the basic structure of the book has remained the same.

Major changes for this edition are:

❏ There is a more extensive discussion of certain important strategic themes, particularly adding value, competency and capability and competitiveness (Chapter 1 plus subsequent chapters)
❏ Strategic management is discussed in terms of specific organizational competencies in content, process (change) and learning (again introduced in Chapter 1)
❏ A number of important strategic dilemmas upon which organizations must make decisions are presented in Chapter 2 and debated throughout the book

❑ The sections on effective strategic leadership and the visionary aspects of strategy creation have been strengthened (Chapter 3)

❑ A new framework for examining corporate culture is included in Chapter 4

❑ In Chapter 5 there is a clearer distinction between the corporate mission and vision, together with stronger sections on stakeholders, ethics and social responsibility

❑ Performance measurement is treated in a wider context than before; non-financial measures (previously scattered through various chapters) are consolidated with financial measures in Chapter 6

❑ Unlike previous editions, we look at the wider business environment issues before our more detailed study of the competitive environment (Chapters 8 and 9). Chapter 8 contains a new section on scenario planning. Our discussion of competitive advantage, again more scattered in the first two editions, is consolidated in Chapter 9, where there is also a more extensive treatment of competitive positioning, competitive strategy and competitor benchmarking

❑ The section on synergy has been extended

❑ Chapter 10 synthesizes marketing, operations and supply chain management. We focus on the strategic elements, leaving out much of the tactical material we included in previous editions

❑ Issues of empowerment and learning organizations are brought into a lengthier chapter on human resource strategy (Chapter 11)

❑ In the financial strategy chapter we pay more attention to cash management issues (Chapter 12)

❑ Chapter 13 has a stronger focus on strategic information and now discusses the need for both single-loop and double-loop learning to support continuous and discontinuous change

❑ Chapter 14 is stronger on strategy creation, contemporary aspects of strategic planning and strategic issues.

❑ There is new material on international strategy in Chapter 15

❑ Hostile takeovers, strategic alliances and network management are debated at greater length in Chapter 16

❑ In previous editions management buy-outs were the subject on a single chapter; this time they are consolidated in Chapter 17 on consolidation and recovery strategies

❑ Organizational structures and corporate management style were previously included in a single chapter. They now comprise two, Chapters 19 and 20, with the management style material strengthened. We also include more debate on the critical issue of focus versus diversity (Chapter 20)

❑ Chapter 21 looks in more detail at the important topics of crisis aversion and crisis proneness in organizations. Here we cross refer to the single- and double-loop learning issues from Chapter 13

❑ The final chapter of the book recaps the main themes and relates them to a number of the most recently published ideas on strategy – up-to-date to late 1996.

Inevitably many of the short, single-page cases included in the second edition have become dated. Some of these have been amended to make them more contemporary; a large proportion have been replaced with new examples. In addition a number of the figures have been recrafted to make them easier to understand and use.

A new **Lecturer's Resource Manual** has been developed to accompany the text. This book, available from the publishers and free to lecturers adopting the text, includes an additional selection of full-length cases together with teaching notes on all the cases in the main text. A new bank of self-test questions has been prepared for each chapter; students can use this to check their understanding of the key points and issues.

A note-form summary of the main chapters provides a source of possible hand-out materials for lecturers who might adopt this edition of the book for the first time.

OHP slide masters for the most important diagrams are also provided.

An innovative feature of the third edition is the *Strategic Management Website*. The website can be found at http://www.itbp.com. This new resource makes use of the enormous potential of the Internet as a learning tool. The website includes material for students and lecturers, links to other sites containing material which will be useful in illustrating the subject matter of this book, and an opportunity for users of the book to communicate directly with the author and other users, and to receive updated information and new case study and other learning materials as these become available. *Strategic Management: Awareness and Change, third edition*, is currently the only major strategy textbook to offer this valuable resource to its users.

The strategy website is an entirely optional supplement. Lecturers who choose not to rely on Internet-related material can still utilize in full all other features of the textbook, and resource manual. However, there is much new support which can be provided via the Internet which cannot be offered in print. For example, the website offers students the option to explore resources on the World Wide Web which are linked to key concepts in each chapter. These links have been selected because of their relevance to the subject matter and interest to students. The resources will be updated regularly so that the website is current and accurate and will remain the most relevant starting point on the Internet for students of strategic management.

A further benefit is the opportunity to provide case study updates and new learning materials after publication of the textbook. This will mean that the book can be kept fully up-to-date throughout its life – a valuable advantage to students and lecturers. Users can send comments back to the author about both the book and the website. There is also a new discussion group for lecturers which will serve as a forum for users to discuss ways of using the book and related materials on strategy courses, and to debate issues of current interest in the field of strategic management.

The strategy webiste is a valuable new resource which highlights the commitment of *Strategic Management: Awareness and Change* to remain at the forefront of both teaching and debate. Visit the site on the World Wide Web and see for yourself.

The audience for this book

The main purpose of the book is to help managers, and students who aim to become managers, (a) to develop their strategic awareness, (b) to increase their understanding of how the functional areas of management (in which they are most likely to work) contribute to strategic management and to strategic changes within organizations and (c) to appreciate how strategic change is managed in organizations.

The content is broad and the treatment is both academic and practical, in order to provide value for practising managers as well as full- and part-time students. The subject matter included is taught in a wide variety of courses including courses for the MBA and other postgraduate master's degrees, courses for the DMS and other post-experience management courses, courses for a number of professional qualifications, undergraduate courses in business studies and related areas and BTEC Higher National Diploma courses. The subject can be entitled strategic management, business policy, corporate strategy or business planning.

The material is relevant for all types of organizations: large and small businesses, manufacturing and service organizations, and both the public and private sectors. The examples included relate to all of these. Although the topics discussed are broadly applicable, there are certain issues which are sector-specific, and these are discussed individually.

Key features of the book

Learning objectives. At the beginning of each chapter I have listed the main tasks which you should have mastered by the end of the chapter.

Key concepts. The most significant concepts which underpin an understanding of strategic management and change are featured separately within the relevant chapter for special emphasis and easy reference.

Key readings. A selection of important ideas from leading writers on strategy have been summarized and presented separately as key readings.

Cases. In addition to numerous references in the main text to organizations and events, over 100 short case examples are included. These relate to a wide variety of organization types from throughout the world. Inevitably some of the cases will 'date' in the sense that the strategies and fortunes of the companies featured in the examples will change. Strategies have life cycles, and strategies which prove effective at certain times will not always remain so. Companies who fail to change their strategies at the right time are likely to experience declining fortunes. Occasionally I have included questions at the ends of chapters which encourage you to research and analyse the subsequent fortunes of companies included as cases. The cases are designed to illustrate points in the main text. They are also intended to supplement your own experiences and reading.

Quotations. Short and pithy quotations from a variety of senior managers in the private and the public sectors are sprinkled throughout the text to illustrate a spectrum of opinions. These are useful for provoking class discussion and examination questions.

Checklist of key terms and concepts. At the end of every chapter there is a summary of the chapter content and a checklist of key terms and concepts. This is included to enable you to evaluate whether you under stand the main points covered in the chapter before moving on.

Questions and research assignments. These questions relate to the ideas contained in the text and the illustrative cases, and some are examples of the type that feature in non-case study examinations of this subject. A number of research assignments, mostly library based, are included to encourage you to develop your knowledge and understanding further. The library-based assignments assume access to a library in the UK. Lecturers in other countries will be able to advise students on similar, more local, companies which can be substituted and researched.

How to use the book

Strategic management is concerned with understanding, as well as choosing and implementing, the strategy or strategies that an organization follows. It is a complex process which can be considered from a number of different perspectives. For example one can design prescriptive models based upon a series of logical stages which look at how to choose and implement strategies aimed at achieving some form of long-term success for the organization. This is a systematic approach designed to bring about optimum results. An alternative paradigm, or conceptual framework, is a systemic approach which concerns understanding what is happening in reality and thinking about how things might be improved. The emphasis is on learning about how strategic management is practised by looking at what organizations actually do and by examining the decisions they make and carry out.

In this book we consider both these perspectives, linking them together. Whilst it is always useful to develop models which attempt to provide optimizing solutions, this approach is inadequate if it fails to explain reality. Strategic management and strategic change are dynamic, often the result of responses to environmental pressures, and frequently not the product of extensive deliberations involving all affected managers.

Managers should be aware of the issues and questions which must be addressed if changes in strategy are to be formulated and implemented effectively. At the same time they should be aware of the managerial and behavioural processes which take place within organizations in order that they can understand how changes actually come about.

Prescriptive models are in fact found quite frequently in business and management teaching. For example, there are models for rational decision making built around the clear recognition and definition of a problem and the careful and objective analysis and evaluation of the alternative solutions. There are economic models of various market structures showing how an organization can maximize profit. However, decision making invariably involves subjectivity

---

I believe the single most important contribution to competitiveness is the ability of managers and management to think strategically about the business or businesses they are in. Although this capability is vital for general management, functional management should also be encouraged and trained in this approach at an early stage in their careers so that they can both contribute to the overall strategic assessment of a business or group of businesses and understand the key objectives.

Sir Trevor Holdsworth, when Group Chairman, Guest Keen & Nettlefolds plc
Quoted in *Improving Managerial Performance*,
BIM and Professional Publishing, 1985

and short cutting; and organizations do not always seek profit maximization as their top priority. Although organizations and individuals rarely follow these models slavishly – quite often they cannot, and sometimes they choose not to – this does not render them worthless. Far from it; they provide an excellent framework or yardstick for evaluating how people reach their decisions, what objectives are being pursued and how situations might be improved. The argument is that if managers observe what is happening and seek to explain it and evaluate it against some more ideal state then they will see ways of managing things more effectively. In this way managerial performance can be improved. Note the use of the expression 'more effectively'. For a whole variety of reasons situations cannot be managed 'perfectly'.

You will probably have personal experience of organizations, management and change. This experience might be limited or extensive, broad or specialized. You should use this experience to complement the examples and cases described in the book. Ideally the experience and the cases will be used jointly to evaluate the theories and concepts discussed. There is no universal approach to the management of strategy and strategic change. You must establish for yourself what approaches and decisions are likely to prove most effective in particular circumstances, and why. This is a learning experience which can be enhanced (a) by evaluating the theoretical and conceptual contributions of various authors, (b) by considering practical examples of what has proved successful and unsuccessful for organizations and (c) by examining these two aspects in combination to see which theories and concepts best help an understanding of reality.

Managers perform a number of activities, including planning and organizing the work of their subordinates, motivating them, con trolling what happens and evaluating results. All managers are planners to some degree; and it is extremely useful if they can develop an ability to observe clearly what is really happening in organizations and reflect on how things might be improved. Kolb (1979) calls this the learning cycle, and it can be usefully applied to a study of strategic management and change. Managers and students build on their own experiences when they read about theories and concepts and think about case study examples. They should reflect upon all these experiences continually and seek to develop personal concepts which best explain for them what happens in practice. Wherever appropriate they should experiment with, and test out, these concepts to establish how robust they are. This, of course, constitutes added experience for further reflection. In other words:

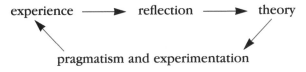

Experience is a wonderful thing, but not a useful one; when you are young, you don't trust others' experience, and if you trust it, this paralyses you; when you get old, it is too late to use it, and you cannot transmit it for the reasons quoted before.

Jacques Calvet, Le President du Directoire,
PSA Peugeot Citroën

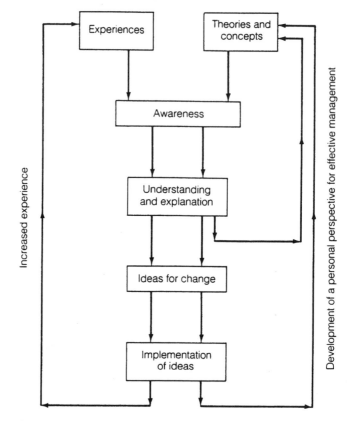

Figure 1   A learning cycle for strategic management.

This approach is illustrated in more detail in Figure 1. Experiences, theories and concepts generate awareness. This, with reflection, improves understanding. Constant evaluation helps develop a personal perspective of effective management. This process is enhanced by trying out ideas which generate new experiences.

Finally it is important to point out that students of strategic management may not be, or may not become, key strategic decision makers in their organizations but instead may specialize in one particular function, perhaps marketing, perhaps production or finance. Similarly their experience may be with only one product or one division of a multi-product or multi-divisional organization. Nevertheless the decisions they make or contribute to can affect the strategy for a particular product or service and in turn affect the organization. It is vital that they appreciate exactly how their function operates within an organizational context, and how decisions made in their area of interest can affect both other functions and the organization as a whole.

Reference

Kolb, D A (1979) *Organizational Psychology*, Prentice Hall.

Acknowledgements

It is impossible to acknowledge individually everyone who has contributed to this book; and I am indebted to numerous teachers, colleagues and past and present students for providing me with ideas and for helping me to develop the perspective for, and revise the content of, *Strategic Management: Awareness and Change*.

I would especially like to thank the following people. My friend and colleague, Bill Richardson, who died suddenly in October 1995; our discussions and joint research projects have made an important contribution to a number of the changes for this edition; Steven Reed, and earlier, Mark Wellings, from International Thomson Business Press, for their long-term help and support; and finally, as always, my wife Hilary for her encouragement and for tolerating the long hours I seem to spend sat at a word processor.

PART I

I think one of our problems as a nation is that we are apt to be somewhat complacent. We have been content with things as they are and have not been aware sufficiently early of progress and changes taking place in other countries which are going to result in their over-taking us if we don't change ourselves. In business one has constantly to be looking at ways of adapting to change in terms of technology, marketing, and possibly also financial structure. We need to see opportunities developing and take bold steps to ensure that we are in the vanguard of change. This requires vision and courage, and good communication with shopfloor people so that they understand the benefits of change, and welcome new technology and new working practices with enthusiasm.

Sir Hector Laing, when Chairman,
United Biscuits plc

Strategic Management

Organizations, their strategies, their structures and the management of them become ever more complex. Among the reasons for this are the increasing turbulence and propensity to change in the business environment, and the tendency for multi-product multi-national organizations to become commonplace. Organizations need to know where they are, where they are going and how to manage the changes. Managers in these organizations need to know where their roles fit in relation to the whole and how they can contribute to strategic developments and changes. These are the issues addressed by a study of strategic management.

This first part is designed to provide a broad appreciation of strategic management and to develop the framework used in the book. Specifically the objectives are:

❑ to outline the scope and complexity of the study area
❑ to provide an initial overview of some major contributors to the subject in order to illustrate what is meant by, and included in, strategic management, and to show that there is no single universally accepted approach
❑ to develop a framework which will provide a model for the structure and content of the book
❑ to illustrate and discuss the importance of strategic leadership and decision making, and culture and values, in every aspect of strategic management.

A number of issues and topics will be raised and discussed in brief in Chapters 1 and 2 and will then be explored in greater depth in the following chapters.

1

Exploring Strategic Management

In this chapter we develop an understanding of the subject and scope of strategic management and explore what is involved in managing the strategies of an organization.

Learning objectives

After studying this chapter you should be able to:

- define strategic management and strategic change
- distinguish between corporate, competitive and functional strategies
- define key success factors and give examples of these
- explain the term competitive advantage
- appreciate the significance of adding value, core competencies, strategic capabilities and strategic architecture
- explain what is meant by E–V–R congruence
- summarize briefly the views of a number of strategy authors on the process of strategic change
- identify a simple framework for an outline strategy statement.

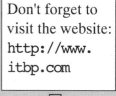

Don't forget to visit the website: `http://www.itbp.com`

Introducing strategy and strategic management

The need for all managers to be able to think strategically was stressed in the Preface, and the approach taken in this book concentrates on the development of strategic awareness. While strategic management incorporates major changes of direction, such as diversification and growth overseas, for the whole business, it also involves smaller changes in the strategies for individual products and services and in particular functions such as marketing and operations. Decisions by managers in relation to their particular areas of product or functional responsibility have a strategic impact and contribute to strategic change.

To some extent all managers are strategy makers.

Strategic management is a complex and fascinating subject with straightforward underlying principles but no 'right answers'.

Companies succeed if their strategies are appropriate for the circumstances they face, feasible in respect of their resources, skills and capabilities, and desirable to their important stakeholders – those individuals and groups, both internal and external, who have a stake in, and an influence over, the business.

Companies fail when their strategies fail to meet the expectations of these stakeholders or produce outcomes which are undesirable to them.

To succeed long term, companies must compete effectively and out-perform their rivals in a dynamic, and often turbulent, environment. To accomplish this they must find suitable ways for creating and adding value for their customers. A culture of internal co-operation and customer orientation, together with a willingness to learn, adapt and change, is ideal. Alliances and good working relationships with suppliers, distributors and customers are often critically important as well.

Whilst strategy is a complex topic, the underlying principles are essentially simple. There is, though, no 'one best way' of managing strategic change; and no single technique or model can provide either the right answer concerning what an organization should do, or superior and crystal-clear insight into a situation. Instead managers should utilize the range of theories and concepts which are available, adapting them to meet their own situation and circumstances.

At the same time, a study of strategic changes in a variety of different organizations is valuable. An examination of outcomes, followed by an analysis of the decisions which led to these relative successes and failures, is rich in learning potential. Examples should not be confined to just one sector. Manufacturing and service businesses, the private and public sectors and not-for-profit organizations are all relevant.

Box 1.1
KEY TERMS

Mission. The essential purpose of the organization, concerning particularly why it is in existence, the nature of the business(es) it is in, and the customers it seeks to serve and satisfy.

Objectives (or goals) are desired states or results linked to particular time scales and concerning such things as size or type of organization, the nature and variety of the areas of interest and levels of success.

Strategies are means to ends, and these ends concern the purpose and objectives of the organization. They are the things that businesses do, the paths they follow, and the decisions they take, in order to reach certain points and levels of success.

Strategic management is a process which needs to be understood more than it is a discipline which can be taught. It is the process by which organizations determine their purpose, objectives and desired levels of attainment; decide on actions for achieving these objectives in an appropriate timescale, and frequently in a changing environment; implement the actions; and assess progress and results. Whenever and wherever necessary the actions may be changed or modified. The magnitude of these changes can be dramatic and revolutionary, or more gradual and evolutionary.

Strategic change concerns changes which take place over time to the strategies and objectives of the organization. Change can be gradual or evolutionary; or more dramatic, even revolutionary.

Strategic awareness is the understanding of managers within the organization about: (a) the strategies being followed by the organization and its competitors, (b) how the effectiveness of these strategies might be improved and (c) the need for, and suitability of, opportunities for change.

Synergy is the term used for the added value or additional benefits which ideally accrue from the linkage or fusion of two businesses, or from increased co-operation between either different parts of the same organization or between a company and its suppliers, distributors and customers. Internal co-operation may represent linkages between either different divisions or different functions.

Box 1.2
EXAMPLES OF STRATEGY CHANGES

Lex service group, sizeable distributor of Rover, Rolls Royce and Volvo cars in the main, felt too dependent on one area of business and sought to find suitable diversification opportunities. Lex chose four and five star hotels in the UK and USA but later chose to sell them when the results were below those desired. This took place in the 1970s and 1980s, since when Lex entered and exited the distribution of electronics parts. More recently Lex has acquired related businesses to become the UK's largest car distribution and leasing company. In 1995 Lex bought Multipart, a distributor of commercial vehicle parts.

W H Smith, desiring growth beyond the scope offered from its current business lines (wholesaling and retailing newspapers and magazines, stationery, books and sounds) diversified into do-it-yourself with a chain of Do-It-All stores, introduced travel agencies into a number of its existing stores and acquired related interests in Canada and America. Travel was later divested, along with investments in cable television, to enable greater concentration on sounds, videos and consumer and office stationery. Important acquisitions have included the Our Price and Virgin music stores and the Waterstone's chain of specialist booksellers. Do-It-All became a joint venture with Boots, but it struggled to be profitable with strong competition from B & Q (owned by Kingfisher) and Texas, acquired by Sainsbury's in the mid-1990s. In 1996 WH Smith divested Do-It-All and its office stationery businesses. These are all examples of corporate strategic change.

In October 1995 WH Smith, responding to the willingness of the leading supermarket chains to sell newspapers, magazines and a carefully selected range of books – with discounted prices for current best-sellers – began to discount books from a number of publishers. This was an important change of competitive strategy as, previously, Smiths had been a staunch supporter of the Net

Book Agreement. This long-standing agreement between publishers and booksellers was designed to prevent intense price competition.

The Burton Group sold the last of its manufacturing interests in 1988. Once one of the leading men's clothing manufacturers in Europe the group, by a series of acquisitions and divestments, has become essentially a major retailer of fashion goods for both men and women.

Building societies restrained by legislation until the mid-1980s expanded their financial services to include current accounts with cheque books and cash-dispensing machines – to compete more aggressively with the high street banks – and diversified into such linked activities as estate agencies and insurance. Mergers have taken place between, for example, the Halifax and Leeds Permanent societies and Abbey National and National & Provincial, to strengthen their positions as diversified financial institutions. Moreover, the largest ones have given up their mutual status and become quoted companies.

In a quite different (and more evolutionary way) the decision by high street banks to open on Saturdays for a limited range of services was strategic change. Here the banks were copying the building societies.

National Bus Company was privatized during the mid-1980s mostly by splitting it up into small local or regional companies which were bought out by their existing management teams. The sector has since become more concentrated as certain growth-oriented operators such as Stagecoach and First Bus (a name change from Badgerline) have bought out other smaller companies. One major challenge for these aggressive companies has been to try and avoid intervention from the UK regulatory authorities, concerned with competition in the industry.

Everyone who can make or influence decisions which impact on the strategic effectiveness of the business should have at least a basic understanding of the concepts and processes of strategy. The processes will often be informal, and the outcomes not documented clearly. But they still exist, and managing the processes effectively determines the organization's future.

Without this understanding people often fail to appreciate the impact of their decisions and actions for other people within the business. They are less likely to be able to learn from observing and reflecting upon the actions of others. They are also more likely to miss or misjudge new opportunities and growing threats in the organization's environment.

Box 1.1 features definitions of key terms used in this book and Box 1.2 illustrates strategic change in a number of different organizations.

There are a number of aspects to strategic management. First, the strategy itself, which is concerned with the establishment of a clear direction for the organization and for every business, product and service, and a means for getting there, and which requires the creation of strong competitive positions. Second, excellence in the implementation of strategies in order to yield effective performance. Together these relate to the content of the organization's strategies. Third, innovation to ensure that the organization is responsive to pressures for change, and that strategies are improved and renewed. Four, the ability to manage strategic change, both continuous, gradual, incremental changes and more dramatic, discontinuous changes. Innovation and change concern the strategy process in an organization. Excellence and innovation should enable an organization to thrive and prosper in a dynamic, global environment, but in turn they depend on competencies in strategic awareness and learning. Organizations must understand the strategic value of the resources they employ and deploy, and how they can be used to satisfy the needs and expectations of customers and other stakeholders whilst outperforming competitors.

Table 1.1 illustrates these points as a set of competencies and their outcomes which ideally will result in competitive and strategic success.

We shall look behind the content and process aspects of strategic management in this chapter and then develop a more comprehensive framework, using these themes, in Chapter 2.

It is, however, important to realize that in many organizations, certain parts may be 'world class' and highly profitable whilst other businesses are not. Good practices in the strong businesses could be discerned, transferred and learned, but this may not be enough. Some industries and competitive environments are simply less 'friendly' and premium profits are unlikely. The

Table 1.1
Strategic competencies

Strategic competencies	Competency outcomes
Awareness and learning	
Strategy content	Effective corporate, competitive and functional strategies
Strategy process	Innovation Effective management of strategic changes
	The ultimate outcome: strategic and competitive success

real danger occurs if the weaker businesses threaten to bring down the strong ones which are forced to subsidize them. It is, of course, an irony that companies in real difficulty, possibly through strategic weaknesses, need to turn in an excellent performance if they are to survive.

Marks and Spencer (Case 1.4) is recognized as one of the UK's most successful retailers. Over a period of years M & S has gradually expanded overseas, opening stores in other European countries and in Hong Kong, for example. Their six stores in Hong Kong have become very profitable; the 15 in France have also succeeded and sell a wide range of English goods. The chain of Brooks Brothers up-market mens' fashion stores in the USA has proved more challenging and their performance has never equalled that of a traditional M & S store.

Strategic management builds upon studies of individual management functions, seeking to integrate them so that managers in one part of the business consider the implications of their decisions for other activities and managers. Strategic management is normally taught as a capstone subject on a variety of business and management courses, drawing widely upon other subject areas, studied previously, and seeking to integrate them.

Important themes, introduced here and developed later in the book are:

- ❏ strategic leadership and organization culture
- ❏ environmental fit
- ❏ corporate, competitive and functional strategies
- ❏ competitive advantage
- ❏ key success factors and core competencies
- ❏ E–V–R (environment–values–resources) congruence
- ❏ the management of strategic change.

Strategic thinking

It is worth mentioning that strategic management is not something that British companies are thought to be very good at. In the last 40 or so years, Britain has performed less well industrially than many of her major competitors in a number of key sectors. This conclusion has been reached by measuring such factors as relative world and European market shares won by British companies, investment expenditure, productivity and the proportion of revenue allocated for research and development. A lack of marketing skills, low productivity, inadequate investment and poor management generally have all been identified as causes, but in many cases these have clearly improved in recent years. Another important aspect is the general failure to assess properly how to compete best.

Discussing this theme, a few years ago Peter Beck, the Chairman of the British Strategic Planning Society during 1984–1986, was critical of British companies as a whole:

> *Far too many companies either have no goals at all, other than cost reduction, or their boss hides them in his head. There's no hope for companies in Britain unless more top managements accept the need for a widely communicated set of clear objectives.*
>
> (Beck, 1987)

Many of Beck's points are still pertinent. Strategic clarity is absent, Beck argues, for essentially three reasons: the difficulties of forecasting in today's business environment (but difficulty is no excuse for not trying!); the lack of managerial competence in many companies; and above all the frequent absence of strong leadership from the top.

Part of the problem is the distinction between established views hostile towards the formal and elaborate strategic planning systems that were in vogue during the 1960s and 1970s, but which failed to work in many cases, and the idea of 'strategic thinking'. It is perfectly possible for any organization to address a number of key questions about how well the company is doing, and why, and where it should seek to develop in the future, and how. It will be argued in this book that the most successful companies strategically are likely to be those that are aware of where they are and of what lies ahead, those that understand their environment and those that seek to achieve and maintain competitive advantage. By way of illustration the following points have been developed from a *Financial Times* article (Morrison and Lee, 1979).

Whatever their strategy, companies that are adept at strategic thinking seem to be distinguished from their less successful competitors by a common pattern of management practices.

- ❏ First, they identify more effectively than their competitors the key success factors inherent in the economics of each business. For example, in the airline industry, with its high fixed costs and relatively inflexible route allocations, a high load factor is critical to success. It is important, though, that high load factors are not at the expense of healthy sales of more expensive seats; and this requires skilful marketing.
- ❏ Second, they segment their markets so as to gain decisive competitive advantage. The strategic thinker bases his or her market segmentation on competitive analysis and thus may separate segments according to the strengths and weaknesses of different competitors. This enables him or her to concentrate on segments where he or she can both maximize their own competitive advantage and avoid head-on competition with stronger competitors.

Visit the website: http://www. itbp.com

- ❏ Third, successful companies base their strategies on the measurement and analysis of competitive advantage. Essential to this is a sound basis for assessing a company's advantages relative to its competitors.
- ❏ Fourth, they anticipate their competitors' responses. Good strategic thinking also implies an understanding of how situations will change over time. Business strategy, like military strategy, is a matter of manoeuvring for superior position and anticipating how competitors will respond, and with what measure of success.
- ❏ Fifth, they exploit more, or different, degrees of freedom than do their competitors. They seek to stay ahead of their rivals by looking for new competitive opportunities. Whilst innovation and constant improvement are essential, there are also potentially huge rewards for those organizations which are first to reach the new 'competitive high ground' by changing the currently practised 'rules of competition'.
- ❏ Finally, they give investment priority to businesses (or areas) that promise a competitive advantage.

Strategic success

In order to be successful, organizations must be strategically aware. They must understand how changes in their competitive environment – some of which they may have started and others to which they will have to react – are unfolding. The implied and simultaneous proactivity and reactivity requires strong and appropriate resources which continue to ensure the organization is able to meet the needs and expectations of its external stakeholders, including customers, suppliers and shareholders. Employees are both a key resource for delivering this satisfaction and an important internal stakeholder.

Satisfying the changing needs of stakeholders in a dynamic environment demands flexibility and sound control measures. Employees should be empowered to make and carry out decisions, but, to be strategically effective, this must be within a clear and co-ordinated framework which provides direction. Hamel and Prahalad (1989) use the term strategic intent to describe this directional vision. Coca-Cola, for example, intend to 'put a Coke within arms' reach of every consumer in the world', whilst the growth of Canon in the photocopying market was driven by a desire to 'beat Xerox'. Taking up an earlier point, Canon successfully rewrote the rules of competition. Xerox had become the market leader with a strategy based on large, high-capability machines which organizations leased from them; Canon sold smaller machines designed for the individual office.

Later in the chapter we will see how these three themes of environment, resources and organizational management and control can be synthesized into a useful model.

The UK Department of Trade and Industry has carried out a research project in an attempt to clarify the 'winning characteristics' of the most successful British companies. The findings, published in 1985, are summarized in Table 1.2.

Case 1.1(A) describes the success of the US company, Rubbermaid. We shall see in later chapters how success can easily prove to be relatively short-lived for companies which are insufficiently flexible and fail to change in a dynamic environment. In 1995 a set of poor results encouraged analysts to look for possible weaknesses in Rubbermaid's strategy; these are summarized in Case 1.1(B).

Functional, competitive and corporate strategies

Figure 1.1 shows that there are three distinct but inter-related levels of strategy.

Organizations choose to produce one or more related or unrelated products or services for one or more markets or market segments. The organization itself should be structured to encompass this range of product markets or service markets. As the number and diversity of products increases the structure is likely to be centred on divisions which are typically referred to as strategic

---

The flame of competition has changed from smokey yellow to intense white heat. For companies to survive and prosper they will have to have a vision, a mission and strategy. They will pursue the action arising from that strategy with entrepreneurial skill and total dedication and commitment to win.

Peter B Ellwood, Chief Executive, Lloyds TSB Group

Table 1.2

Ingredients for strategic success

Characteristics	Requirements
The most successful UK companies are:	
Led by visionary, enthusiastic champions of change	Communicated vision
Able to use the potential of employees ❑ in a customer-focused culture ❑ in a flattened structure	Empowerment Benchmarking good practice Team working
Aware of customer needs and expectations ❑ by constant learning and ❑ innovating in response to competitive pressures	Aware of key success factors Networking Competitor awareness
Constantly introducing new, differentiated products and services ❑ because they understand their competitors ❑ because they are innovative and ❑ because they use strategic alliances to enable them to focus on core businesses	Total quality management Supplier alliances
Able to exceed their customers' expectations with these new products and services	

Source: *Competitiveness – How The Best UK Companies Are Winning*, Department of Trade and Industry, London, 1995.

business units (SBUs). SBUs are responsible individually for developing, manufacturing and marketing their own product or group of products. Each SBU will therefore have a strategy, which Porter (1980) calls a competitive strategy. Competitive strategy is concerned with 'creating and maintaining a competitive advantage in each and every area of business' (Porter, 1980). It can be achieved through any one function. For each functional area of the business,

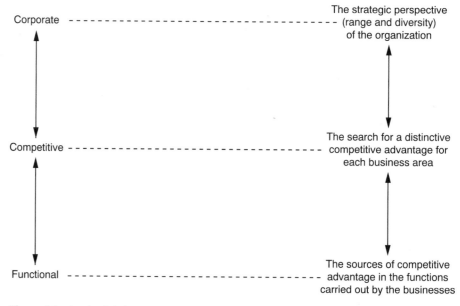

Figure 1.1 Levels of strategy.

Part A

In the 1994 and 1995 Fortune rankings, Rubbermaid was deemed to be the USA's *most admired company*. This award is based on a range of performance measures and indicators, not simply financial measures. It is both subjective and objective – managers in a number of industries are asked to evaluate other companies in their own industry. The company had been amongst the contenders for the title in several previous years.

IBM, dominant in computers for many years, was the USA's most admired company every year from 1982 to 1985. Subsequently, IBM has been faced with the need to regenerate strategically, highlighting just how transient success can sometimes be.

Rubbermaid, based in Ohio, manufactures over 5000 different household goods, including plastic buckets, sandwich boxes, dustpans, mops and washing-up brushes. All low-technology products in an industry with few entry barriers and competition from low labour cost countries. It has very ambitious financial objectives of 15% annual increases in both revenues and profits.

Behind the success

❑ Rubbermaid introduces new products at the rate of more than one a day.
❑ Competition is fierce – Rubbermaid recognizes innovation to be a 'do-or-die affair'.
❑ The company is very strongly customer focused. Its buckets are designed to hold their shape (and not spill their contents) when completely full; laundry baskets are hip-contoured for easier carrying; food storage boxes have extra wide protrusions for easy opening.
❑ In addition to constant product improvements there are genuine new product ideas. Rubbermaid pioneered a step-stool with an incorporated tool box, for example. This idea sprung from the drive to develop products for smaller households. 'The company looks for opportunities in every trend, be it fashion-led, sociological, demographic or global.'

❑ Rubbermaid has 20 business teams, each dedicated to a product line, and comprising people from marketing, manufacturing, finance, R & D and sales. Each team has responsibility for product developments and profitability — emphasizing the search for product improvements to improve profitability.
❑ Ideas are sought from 'everywhere'. Certainly employees and suppliers. One supplier provided a new type of plastic for easier-to-use ice cube trays – the cubes come out more readily; and because of the material's flexibility, the trays last longer. Ideas in one product area are frequently plagiarized and adapted for other products. Best practices are being shared.
❑ There is no formal product testing. Instead, and because speed is essential, the company uses specialist critiquing.

> We don't want to be copied. It's not that much riskier to just roll it out. Plus it puts pressure on us to do it right first time.

❑ Rubbermaid has a target of 33% of revenue from products introduced in the last 5 years.
❑ Poorly performing products are dropped almost as quickly as new ones are introduced. Constant renewal.

> Innovation is ingrained in the culture. That is the one thing that is not going to change.

Part B

In 1994 the price of resins, an essential raw material for almost all of Rubbermaid's products, began to rise, eventually doubling. When Rubbermaid announced a deterioration in its financial results for one quarter in 1995 its prominence and reputation provoked a critical appraisal from external analysts. Were there flaws in the strategy? The following weaknesses were suggested.

❑ Poor customer relations – passing on raw material cost increases in an arbitrary manner.

Continued overleaf

❑ Slow progress in improving manufacturing technologies and systems to keep up with product innovations.

❑ Over-ambitious and unrealistic growth targets have pushed managers too hard and many have lost their edge.

❑ At the same time, Rubbermaid has under-estimated the extent of the progress its competitors have been making. The company has been losing important customers.

❑ Rubbermaid has needed to strengthen its position in overseas markets; again progress has been slower than the desired rate.

Rubbermaid responded by claiming the poorer results were temporary and that the company would soon resume its normal growth path.

References: Farnham, A (1994) America's Most Admired Company, *Fortune*, 7 February; Smith, L (1995) Rubbermaid Goes Thump, *Fortune*, 2 October.

such as production, marketing and human resources the company will have a functional strategy. It is important that functional strategies are designed and managed in a co-ordinated way so that they inter-relate with each other and at the same time collectively allow the competitive strategy to be implemented properly.

Successful competitive and functional strategies add value in ways which are perceived to be important by the company's stakeholders, especially its customers, and which helps distinguish the company from its competitors. Adding value is discussed later in the chapter.

Corporate strategy, essentially and simply, is deciding what businesses the organization should be in and how the overall group of activities should be structured and managed. It has been described by Porter as 'the overall plan for a diversified business', although it is perfectly acceptable for a business to elect to stay with only one product or service. This does happen in many companies, especially small businesses. In this case the corporate and competitive strategies are synonymous.

Corporate strategy for a multi-business group is concerned with maintaining or improving overall growth and profit performance through acquisition, organic investment (internally funded growth), divestment and closure.

The term **strategic perspective** is often used to describe the range and diversity of activities, in other words the corporate strategy. Each activity then has a **competitive position** or strategy.

The linkages and inter-dependencies between the levels of strategy can be seen in the following example. In September 1995 the retail chain Sears announced a set of disappointing results; a number of its subsidiaries had experienced difficult trading conditions. One, Miss Selfridge, had found itself with inappropriate product lines for the prevailing weather conditions. Mini-skirts and midriff-revealing T-shirts stayed on the racks during the wind and rain of the first half of the summer. The buyers had arguably been unlucky, but nevertheless they misjudged what people would be interested in buying; marketing and sales efforts could not redeem the situation.

Synergy (defined in Box 1.1) is a critical aspect of both corporate and competitive strategies. It is important that the functions and businesses within an organization work collectively and support each other to improve effectiveness and outcomes. People are often naturally competitive; their competitive energy should be directed against external rivals rather than members of their own organization – although, carefully managed, internal competition for scarce resources can sharpen managerial skills. Individual businesses should benefit from being part of the organization; membership should reduce their costs or help provide other competitive advantages. At the same time, the organization as a whole should derive benefit from the particular mix of businesses, which should, in some way, complement each other. There may be inter-group trading, for example, with one business unit supplying another; equally, skills could be transferred, factory units could be shared, or the businesses could join together to purchase common requirements with substantial discounts.

Visit the website: http://www.itbp.com

Major changes to the corporate perspective will invariably be board-level decisions and actively involve the organization's strategic leader. Changes at the corporate and functional levels are more likely to be delegated to other managers in the business. The nature and extent of such delegation will vary from organization to organization and should reflect a careful balance between, on the one hand, the need to maintain effective control and integrate the businesses to create synergy, and, on the other hand, the benefits which can be gained from empowering those managers who are most aware of environmental changes and new competitive opportunities.

Strategic management: awareness and change

Traditionally courses in strategic management have been built around three important elements:

❑ strategic **analysis**
❑ strategy **creation and choice**
❑ strategy **implementation**.

These elements are important, and they feature clearly in this book, but they must not be seen simplistically as a set of sequential decisions taken at specific and prescribed times. As we have seen, strategic management is dynamic; strategies need to be reviewed and revised all the time. Figure 1.2 provides an interpretation of these elements, and the following commentary relates them to the key issues of content and process introduced earlier. In Chapter 2 we will use these ideas to develop and explain the framework around which this book has been written.

Strategic management involves **awareness** of how successful and strong the organization and its strategies are, and of how circumstances are changing. At any time, previously sound products, services and strategies are likely to be in decline, or threatened by competition. As this happens, new 'windows of opportunity' are opening for the vigilant and proactive companies.

New strategies must be created. These may be changes to the corporate portfolio or changes at the competitive level. Sometimes these strategic ideas will emerge from formal planning processes; at other times, and particularly in the case of functional and competitive strategies, changes will emerge as managers throughout the organization try out new ideas.

The actual strategies being pursued at any time reflect the organization's *strategy content*, and the important issues are:

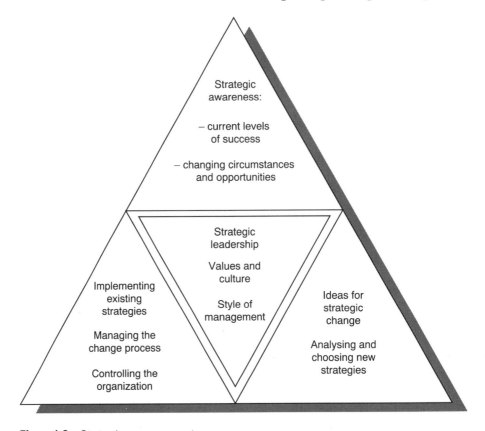

Figure 1.2 Strategic management.

❑ the ability of the organization to add value in meaningful ways, which
❑ exploit organizational resources to achieve synergy and at the same time
❑ satisfy the needs of the organization's major stakeholders, particularly its
shareholders and customers.

The selection of new strategies must take account of these criteria.

Existing and new strategies must be implemented. Effective implementation and the creation of new strategies concerns *process*. The processes involved in designing and carrying through any changes must be managed, monitored and controlled.

The remaining sections of this chapter will look at the underlying content and process issues in greater detail. However, at this point, it is important to explain why **strategic leadership**, **values**, **culture and style of management** are shown at the heart of Figure 1.2, dictating both content and process elements.

Strategic leadership

It has been pointed out that a major aim of this book is to encourage readers to be more strategically aware. Long-term strategic success requires that the efforts of managers are co-ordinated. This is the task of the chief executive or managing director of the whole organization and in turn of general managers of subsidiaries or divisions in the case of large complex organizations. For simplicity in this book we shall use the term strategic leader to refer to this role.

The theme of strategic leadership is the subject of Chapter 3, whilst Chapter 20 considers the specific role of general managers of subsidiaries and divisions.

The role is analogous to that of the captain of a ship. In a sailing race, for example, the captain must sail the ship possibly in uncertain or dangerous waters, with one or more clear goals in sight. The chosen strategy or strategies will be decided upon in the light of these goals, and the risks of any actions will be assessed. Nevertheless the captain's success will depend on the crew. It is essential that the crew act in a co-ordinated way, and therefore it is crucial that the strategies are communicated and understood.

Lee Iacocca, who became chairman of the Chrysler Corporation in the USA in the early 1980s and succeeded in turning it round, provides a useful example. Chrysler, faced with competition from General Motors, Ford and Japan, was nearly bankrupt and had lost its way. Iacocca changed some of his crew, but essentially his success lay in persuading his managers to think about how to succeed in the 1980s and to forget the strategies of the 1960s and 1970s. Cars were redesigned, marketing was improved, labour costs were lowered, productivity and quality were improved and government support was obtained. Chrysler recovered.

The strategic leader must build and lead a team of managers – and establish the goals or objectives. Styles will vary enormously, as will the scope of the objectives. Some leaders will be autocratic, others entrepreneurial. Some, arguably like Henry Ford of Ford Motor Company and Ray Kroc who started McDonald's, will be visionaries; others will set more modest goals.

The leader and his or her managers should be clear about where the organization is going, where they want to go and how they are going to get there. This requires an appreciation of the environment and an understanding of the organization's resources.

Culture and values

The organization culture, defined in Key Concept 1.1, and the associated values, dictate the way decisions are made, the objectives of the organization, the type of competitive advantage sought, the organization structure and systems of management, functional strategies and policies, attitudes towards managing people, and information systems. Many of these are inter-related.

In the late 1980s, Woolworths (the high street retailers now part of the Kingfisher Group) identified their customer service as being a weakness, particularly compared with their main rivals. People, they argued, are a major strategic resource, and they reflect the values of the organization. In common with many other service organizations, Woolworths introduced a customer-care training programme entitled 'Excellence', and linked it to staff rewards. There have been two achievements. First, customer perception of staff helpfulness has increased, and second, there have been financial gains.

For these reasons, styles of corporate decision making, leadership and values are a central driving force in the model in Figure 1.2. They are always important, and they are not easily changed without the appointment of a new chief executive.

Because they act as a driving force and affect all aspects of strategic management, leadership and culture are explored fully in the early part of the book, in Chapters 3 and 4, respectively.

CULTURE

Culture is 'the deeper level of **basic assumptions** and **beliefs** that are shared by members of an organization, that operate unconsciously, and that define in a basic 'taken for granted' fashion an organization's view of itself and its environment'.

Culture is 'learned, evolves with new experiences, and can be changed if one understands the dynamics of the learning process'.

Culture is 'a pattern of basic assumptions that works well enough to be considered valid, and therefore is taught to new [organization] members as the correct way to perceive, think and feel in relation to problems of external adaptation and internal integration'.

In the very simplest terms it is the way organizational members behave and the values that are important to them.

Culture is considered further in Chapter 4.

Quotations from Schein, EH (1985) *Organization Culture and Leadership*, Jossey Bass.

The next two sections of this introductory chapter summarize the main content and process aspects in strategic management. We are not looking here at the merit and logic of particular strategies, but rather at those content issues which underpin and determine the relative strategic value of the actual strategies.

Strategy content

Environmental fit

Several authors have defined strategy in terms of the relationship between an organization and its environment. One such definition is:

> The positioning and relating of the firm/organization to its environment in a way which will assure its continued success and make it secure from surprises.
>
> (Ansoff, 1984)

Figure 1.3 which takes an open systems perspective and considers the organization in the context of its environment, illustrates the implications. The organization draws its resources (employees, managers, plant, supplies, finance, etc.) from a competitive business environment. It has to compete with other firms for labour, supplies, loans, etc. It must then use these inputs in some organized way to produce products and services which can be marketed effectively and in many cases profitably. It must succeed in a competitive marketplace. As well as appreciating market demand and the strengths, weaknesses and strategies of its competitors, it must also respond to fundamental changes in society and the economy. Over time people's tastes change, their discretionary purchasing power rises and falls, luxuries can become necessities and previously popular products can become unfashionable. The economy is not static, and it is strongly affected by government policy. Whilst some companies influence government policy, many do not.

Therefore strategic management involves the following:

❏ a clear awareness of environmental forces and the ways in which they are changing
❏ an appreciation of potential and future threats and opportunities

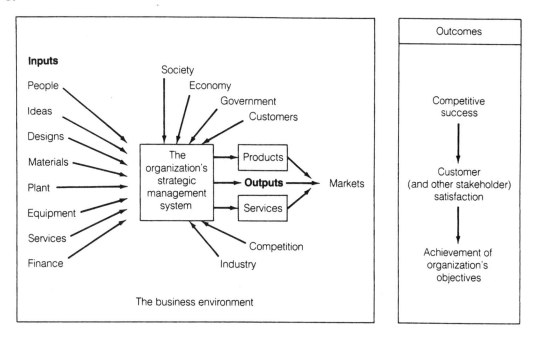

Figure 1.3   The strategic perspective. This model has been adapted from one used by the General Electric Co., USA.

❑ decisions on appropriate products and services for clearly defined markets
❑ the effective management of resources to develop and produce these products for the market – achieving the right quality for the right price at the right time.

Innovation is an important element in maintaining fit as environmental forces and competitor strategies change. An innovative organization fosters learning which leads to continuous, managed change to products, services and processes. In turn this demands an organization-wide commitment to improvement and change, together with the ability and willingness of managers to spot and seize change opportunities, factors again dependent upon leadership and cultural issues.

Key success factors

Strategic management is effective when resources match stakeholder needs and expectations and change to maintain a fit in a turbulent environment. As we have seen, the external environment consists of suppliers, distributors and customers as well as bankers and other financial institutions and shareholders. It also includes competitors and sometimes the government. These stakeholders all expect something from a business in return for their support. If organizations are to be successful – and in many cases, profitable – they have to meet the needs and expectations of their stakeholders. Their relative demands determine what it is that a business must do well.

A company will have to produce to high and consistent quality levels and meet delivery promises to **customers**. Delivery times have been reducing gradually in very competitive industries. **Suppliers and sub-contractors** expect regular orders and accurate forecasting when very quick deliveries are demanded from them. Without such support just-in-time production systems are impractical. Just-in-time systems rely on regular and reliable deliveries from suppliers in order to maintain constant production without the need for high parts inventories.

Companies will try to minimize their stockholding because this helps both cash flow and costs. Conglomerate subsidiaries will have to generate a positive cash flow in order to meet the financial expectations of the **parent company** who, in effect, act as its bankers. Costs have to be controlled so that companies remain price competitive, although low prices are not always a marketing weapon.

These stakeholder requirements represent **key success factors**, those things an organization must do well if it is to be an effective competitor and thrive. In addition many companies have to be innovative and improve both their product range and their customer service if they are to remain a leading competitor in a changing industry.

Some key success factors will be industry and sector specific. For example, successful consumer goods manufacturers will need skills in brand management. Charities need skills in fund raising and public relations. There is intense competition between charities for donations, and consequently they must be run as businesses. They can only spend what they can raise. It is also essential that they use their money appropriately, are seen to be doing so and are recognized for their efforts. The differing demands of fund raising and aid provision lead to complex cultures and organizations.

BUPA, the private medicine organization has a similar dilemma. The business comprises two parts, insurance, with a strong commercial culture and orientation, and hospitals, which are naturally more of a caring community.

Resources must be managed with stakeholder needs in mind. Consequently it is important that everyone in the organization recognizes and is committed to meeting key success factors, and is additionally responsive to change pressures in a dynamic and competitive environment. Without this commitment companies will be unable to sustain a match with the environment as it changes.

Figure 1.4 illustrates that if organizations are to satisfy their stakeholders, especially their customers, whilst outperforming their rivals, their competitive offering should comprise:

❑ the ability to meet the recognized key success factors for the relevant industry or market
❑ distinctive competencies and capabilities which yield some form of competitive advantage, and
❑ the ability and willingness to deploy these competencies and capabilities to satisfy the special requirements of individual customers, for which a premium price can often be charged.

Visit the website:
http://www.
itbp.com

Competitive advantage

Competitive advantage implies a distinct, and ideally sustainable, edge over competitors. It is more than the idea of a competitive strategy, which may or may not prove distinctive. See Key Concept 1.2.

Porter (1985) has shown how companies can seek broad advantage within an industry or focus on one or a number of distinct segments. He argues that advantage can accrue from:

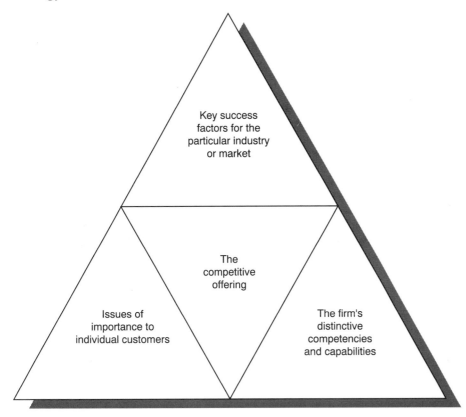

Figure 1.4 The competitive offering: criteria for effectiveness.

(i) **cost leadership**, whereby a company prices around the average for the market (with a 'middle-of-the-road' product or service) and enjoys superior profits because its costs are lower than those of its rivals

(ii) **differentiation**, where value is added in areas of real significance for customers, who are then willing to pay a premium price for the distinctiveness. A range of differentiated products (or services), each designed to appeal to a different segment, is possible, as is focus on just one segment.

Speed (say quicker new product development) and fast reaction to opportunities and threats can provide advantage, essentially by reducing costs and differentiating.

Real competitive advantage implies companies are able to satisfy customer needs more effectively than their competitors. Because few individual sources of advantage are sustainable in the long-run, the most successful companies innovate and continually seek new forms of advantage in order to open up a competitive gap and then maintain their lead. Successfully achieving this is a cultural issue, as we have seen.

Kenichi Ohmae (1982) offers an alternative, but clearly related, view of competitive advantage, highlighting three Cs – customers, competitors and the corporation.

❏ **Customers** will ultimately decide whether or not the business is successful by buying or not buying the product or service. But customers cannot be

COMPETITIVE ADVANTAGE

Business strategy is all about competitive advantage. Without competitors there would be no need for strategy, for the sole purpose of strategic management is to enable the company to gain, as effectively as possible, a sustainable edge over its competitors – to alter a company's strength relative to that of its competitors in the most efficient way. Actions affecting the health of a business (value engineering or improved cash flow which improve profitability) widen the range of alternative strategies the company may choose to adopt *vis-à-vis* its competitors.

A good strategy is one by which a company can gain significant ground on its competitors at an acceptable cost to itself. There are basically four ways.

❏ Identify the key success factors in an industry and concentrate resources in a particular area where the company sees an opportunity to gain the most significant strategic advantage over its competitors.
❏ Exploit any area where a company enjoys relative superiority. This could include using technology or the sales network developed elsewhere in the organization for other products or services.
❏ Aggressively attempt to change the key success factors by challenging the accepted assumptions concerning the ways business is conducted in the industry or market.
❏ Innovate. Open up new markets or develop new products.

The principal concern is to avoid doing the same thing, on the same battleground, as competition

The aim is to attain a competitive situation in which your company can (a) gain a relative advantage through measures its competitors will find hard to follow and (b) extend that advantage further.

Taken from Ohmae, K (1982) *The Mind of the Strategist*, McGraw-Hill.

---

treated *en masse*. Specific preferences should be sought and targeted. Products should be differentiated to appeal to defined market segments.
❏ **Corporations** are organized around particular functions (production, marketing, etc.). The way that they are structured and managed determines the cost of the product or service.

There are opportunities to create competitive advantage in several areas of business, such as product design, packaging, delivery, service and customizing. Such opportunities achieve differentiation, but they can increase costs. Costs must be related to the price that customers are willing to pay for the particular product, based to some extent upon how they perceive its qualities – again in relation to competitors.
❏ **Competitors** will similarly differentiate their products, goods and services, and again incur costs in doing so.

Competition can be based upon price, image, reputation, proven quality, particular performance characteristics, distribution or after-sales service, for example.

Strategic success, in the end, requires a clear understanding of the needs of the market, especially its segments, and the satisfaction of targeted customers more effectively and more profitably than by competitors.

Achieving competitive advantage

Competitive advantage, then, does not come from simply being different. It is achieved if and when real value is added for customers. This often requires companies to **stretch their resources** to achieve higher returns (Hamel and Prahalad, 1993, and discussed later in this section). Improved productivity may be involved; ideally employees will come up with innovations, new and better ways of doing things for customers.

This innovation can result in lower costs, differentiation or a faster response to opportunities and threats, the bases of competitive advantage; and it is most likely to happen when the organization succeeds in harnessing and exploiting its core competencies and capabilities.

It also requires that employees are **empowered**. Authority, responsibility and accountability will be decentralized, *allowing employees to make decisions for themselves*. They should be able and willing to look for improvements. When this is managed well, a company may succeed in changing the rules of competition. Basically organizations should seek to encourage **ordinary people to achieve extraordinary results**.

This will only happen if achievement is properly recognized, and initiative and success rewarded. Some people, though, are naturally reticent about taking risks.

3M (Post-It Notes), Sony, Hewlett-Packard and Motorola are four organizations which are recognized as being highly creative and innovative. In each case employees are actively encouraged to look for, and try out, new ideas. In such businesses the majority of products in the corporate portfolio will have only existed for a few years. Effective empowerment can bring continual growth to successful companies and also provide ideas for turning around companies in decline.

Competitive advantage is also facilitated by good internal and external communications – achieving one of the potential benefits of linkages. Without this businesses cannot share and **learn** best practice. Moreover information is a fundamental aspect of organizational control. Companies can learn from suppliers, from distributors, from customers, from other members of a large organization – and from competitors.

Companies should never overlook opportunities for communicating their achievements, strengths and successes. Image and reputation are vitally important; they help to retain business.

Adding value

A business must add value if it is to be successful. As supply potential has grown to exceed global demand in the majority of industries adding value has become increasingly important. In simple terms the extent of the value added is the difference between the value of the outputs from an organization and the cost of the inputs or resources used.

The traditional paradigm, based on the accountancy measure, is that prices reflect costs plus a profit margin. The lack of differentiation, for which a higher price can be charged, implies enormous downward pressures on costs. Performance measurement is then based upon *economy* (low input costs) and *efficiency* (minimizing the actual and attributed costs of the resources used for adding further value).

While it is important to use all resources efficiently and properly; it is also critical to ensure that the potential value of the outputs is maximized by ensuring they fully meet the needs of the customers for whom they are intended. An organization achieves this when it sees its customers' objectives as its own objectives and *enables its customers to easily add more value or, in the case of final consumers, feel they are gaining true value for money*.

The new paradigm is as follows. The key is value for the customer; if resources are used to provide real value for customers, they will pay a price which reflects its worth to them.

John Kay (1993) researched the most successful European companies during the 1980s, measured by their average costs per unit of net output. Six of the ten leading companies are featured in mini-cases in this book. Each company has an individual strategy for adding value and creating competitive success. Glaxo (number one in the ten) successfully exploited the international potential for its patented anti-ulcer drug Zantac. LVMH (Louis Vuitton, Moët Hennessy), sixth in the list, generates synergy from the global distribution of a diverse range of high quality, premium-brand products. Benetton, second, enjoys beneficially close links with its suppliers and distributors, again world-wide. Marks and Spencer (tenth, and Case 1.4 in this chapter) is also expert at supply chain management and further benefits from its value-for-money image and reputation. In contrast, low-price food retailer Kwik Save, fifth in the list, sells its products with a low margin but enjoys a relatively very high turnover to capital employed. BTR (number nine) has expertise in the management of a diversified conglomerate.

The important elements in adding value are:

❏ understanding and being close to customers, in particular understanding their perception of value
❏ a commitment to quality
❏ a high level of all-round service
❏ speedy reaction to competitive opportunities and threats
❏ innovation.

Organizations can seek to add value by, first, adding positive features, such as air conditioning, comfortable bucket seats and CD players in cars, and, second, by removing any features perceived as negatives or drawbacks. Anti-lock braking systems and four-wheel drive gearboxes reduce the concerns that some people have about driving in bad weather; extended warranty schemes remove the fear of unknown future repair costs. Each of these additions has a value for which some customers, not all, will pay a premium.

It is, of course, quite conceivable that organizations are pursuing strategies or policies which make life harder for their customers. Minimum order quantities, and, possibly, volume discounts, may force or encourage customers to buy more than they need or can afford to stock. Obsolescence can then become an issue. Organizations could evaluate the merit of discounts based on annual sales rather than only on individual orders. Simply, organizations should be looking to ensure they follow the top loop of Figure 1.5 and not the bottom one.

Organizations which truly understand their customers can create competitive advantage and thereby benefit from higher prices and loyalty. High capacity utilization can then help to reduce costs.

As an example, the prices of airline seats are related to the value they have for customers, the benefits they offer, not simply the airline's cost for providing the seat and the associated service. The first class cabin offers space, comfortable seats which can be reclined almost to the horizontal, and high-quality food and service. Business class is based on similar principles but to a more limited degree. Both classes are quieter than the economy section, offering some opportunity for business travellers to work; and reservations can be changed. Economy seats at full-fare allow for late bookings, open tickets to

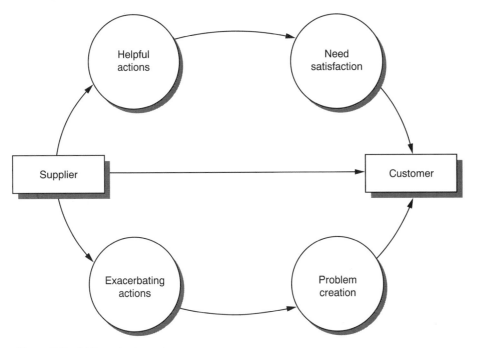

Figure 1.5   Adding value for customers.

allow for flexible return schedules, upstairs seats on Boeing 747's with some airlines and, clearly, more chance of an upgrade when a flight is not fully booked. Reduced apex fares can be very good value for money, but they are inflexible. Travellers must stay for a prescribed period, flights and tickets cannot be altered and sometimes payment must be made early and in full.

One important key success factor for an airline is the ability to sell the right mix of tickets to maximize the revenue potential from every flight. Empty seats imply lost revenue; at the same time, if every ticket is sold at a discounted price, the flight is unlikely to be profitable.

Consequently the airline performance measures include: load factors; passenger kilometres (the numbers of passengers multiplied by the distance flown); and the revenue per passenger kilometre.

Opportunities for adding value which attracts customers must be sought and exploited. Numerous possible opportunities exist at corporate, competitive and functional strategy levels, and these are listed in Table 1.3 cross-referenced to the relevant chapters in the text. Resources must be deployed to exploit these opportunities. Pümpin (1991), argues that multiplication – strategic consistency and performance improvement by concentrating on certain important strategies and learning how to implement them more effectively – promotes growth. The matching process is led and championed by the strategic leader, who is responsible for establishing the key values. Whilst striving to improve performance with existing strategies the organization must constantly search for new windows of opportunity. McDonald's, which is featured in Case 1.5 later in this chapter, provides an excellent example. Ray Kroc spotted an opportunity in the growing fast-food market and exploited it by concentrating on new product ideas and franchised outlets, supported by a culture which promoted 'quality, service, cleanliness and value'.

Table 1.3

The opportunities for adding value

	Chapter
❏ Opportunities from changes in industry regulation	9
❏ Marketing (segmentation; globalization)	10
❏ Operations (technology → cost reduction	10
→ service and quality	10
procurement and linkages with suppliers)	10
❏ People (exploiting expertise; encouraging innovation)	11
❏ Finance (globalization of financial markets; better use of assets)	12
❏ Information (exploiting the potential of information technology)	13
❏ Acquisition and restructuring strategies	16
❏ Co-operation strategies	16
❏ Cost-cutting and concentration	17
❏ Synergy – greater return from assets	Various
❏ Organizational changes (restructuring; new processes)	19

Core competencies

In order to meet their key success factors organizations must develop core competencies (Prahalad and Hamel, 1990). These are distinctive skills which yield competitive advantage, and ideally they:

(a) provide access to important market areas or segments
(b) make a significant contribution to the perceived customer benefits of the product or service; and
(c) prove difficult for competitors to imitate.

Once developed they should be exploited, as, for example, Honda have exploited their skills at engine design and technology. Core competencies must, however, be flexible and responsive to changing customer demands and expectations. Canon have developed core competencies in precision mechanics, fibre optics and microelectronics, and these are spread across a range of products, including cameras, calculators, printers and photocopiers. There is constant product innovation.

Successful products and services, then, are the manifestation of important, underlying core competencies; and the true competition between organizations is at this competency level.

Prahalad and Hamel acknowledge that there are three strands to core competency:

❏ technologies
❏ processes and
❏ strategic architecture.

Strategic capabilities

Stalk *et al*. (1992) argue that strategic success is based on capabilities – processes which enable the company to be an effective competitor. Distribution networks which achieve both high service levels (effectiveness) and low costs (efficiency) would be an example. Typically these processes will cut across whole organizations, rather than be product-specific, and they will rely heavily on information systems and technology.

Retailers like Boots (high street department stores, specialist pharmacies, optical retailing, Halfords car products and service bays, Fads and Homestyle) operate a number of different retail formats, capitalizing on their expertise in supply chain, information and service management.

Visit the website: http://www. itbp.com

Hamel and Prahalad (1993) concur that understanding processes should generate intelligence which can be used to create added or greater value from resources, in order to strengthen or enhance competitiveness. They refer to this as *stretching resources*. The ability to stretch resources is very dependent on strategic architecture, which we discuss next.

Kay (1993) stresses that, to be beneficial, both core competencies and strategic capabilities must be capable of exploitation and be *appropriable*. In other words, the firm must be able to realize the benefits of the competencies and capabilities for the company itself, rather than the main beneficiaries being its suppliers, customers or competitors.

Strategic architecture competencies

Competitive advantage further requires:

❑ the organization to behave in a co-ordinated, synergy creating manner, integrating functions and businesses
❑ the value adding network (links between manufacturers, retailers, suppliers and intermediate distributors) to be managed as an effective, integrated, system.

Kay (1993) refers to the ability to achieve these demands as strategic architecture. The ability to build and control a successful architecture is facilitated by strong technological competency and effective functional process competencies.

Honda, for example, is renowned for its expertise in engine design and technology; its success as an international company has also been dependent upon its ability to establish an effective distribution (dealer) network for all its products; this is enhanced by sound, IT-supported, communications and control systems. As another example, Marks and Spencer's functional competencies and brand technology create both an image and a capability which enable it to trade in clothes, foods, cosmetics, household furnishings and credit. These competencies also bestow on the company the power to demand and obtain from its suppliers world-wide both a strict adherence to Marks' technological specifications and very keen prices.

The important themes in architecture are:

(a) 'systemic thinking', which leads to synergy from the fostering of inter-dependencies between people, functions and divisions in organizations and
(b) the establishment of linkages or even alliances between organizations at different stages of the added value chain.

Respectively these refer to internal and external architecture.

Successful internal architecture requires that managers think 'organizationally' rather than put themselves first or promote their particular part of the organization to the detriment of other parts. Synergy from internal architecture also depends on the ability of the divisions or businesses in a conglomerate to support each other, transferring skills, competencies and capabilities and sometimes sharing common resources. This, in turn, is partially dependent on the ability of the organization to learn, and share learning. It is also affected by the actual portfolio of businesses managed by a corporation. Goold *et al.* (1994) use the term **heartland** to describe that range of businesses to which a corporate head office can add value, rather than see value destroyed through too much complexity and diversity.

Alliances enable companies to focus on their core skills and competencies. Nike, for example, a leading company in sporting and leisure footwear, focuses on product design, marketing and personality endorsements; it avoids manufacturing, which it sub-contracts to specialists world-wide. Partners have to support each other, though, and understand each other's various needs and expectations. The main benefits will come from sharing information, which in turn should enable companies to respond more quickly to new opportunities and threats. Alliance partners can also be an excellent means of overcoming relative weaknesses.

Leveraging resources

Hamel and Prahalad (1993) also emphasize the need to manage the organization's strategic resources to achieve ambitious, stretching objectives. Productivity can be improved by gaining the same output from fewer resources – this is downsizing (sometimes called rightsizing) – and by leveraging, achieving more output from given resources.

Clearly internal and external architecture are both important for leveraging resources. In addition, organizations can benefit by ensuring there is a clear and understood focus for the efforts. This could take the form of a properly communicated mission or purpose, which is acknowledged and understood. British Airways would claim that much of its success is based around a commitment to the slogan 'The World's Favourite Airline'. This example again emphasizes the significance of corporate image.

Figure 1.6 draws together the important themes of this section.

E–V–R congruence

If one wished to claim that an organization was being managed effectively from a strategic point of view, one would have to show, first, that its managers appreciated fully the dynamics, opportunities and threats present in their competitive environment, and that they were paying due regard to wider societal issues; and, second, that the organization's resources (inputs) were being managed strategically, taking into account its strengths and weaknesses, and that the organization was taking advantage of its opportunities. Key success factors and core competencies would be matched. This will not just happen, it needs to be managed. Moreover, potential new opportunities need to be sought and resources developed. It is also important, therefore, that the values

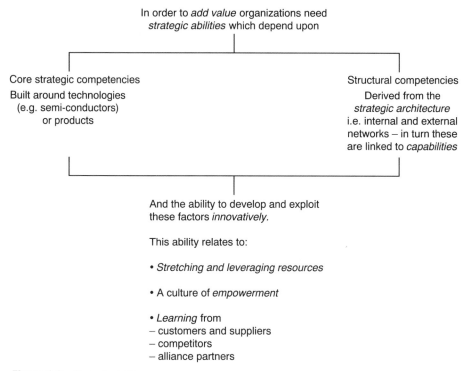

In order to *add value* organizations need
strategic abilities which depend upon

Core strategic competencies
Built around technologies
(e.g. semi-conductors)
or products

Structural competencies
Derived from the
strategic architecture
i.e. internal and external
networks – in turn these
are linked to *capabilities*

And the ability to develop and exploit
these factors *innovatively.*

This ability relates to:

• *Stretching and leveraging resources*

• A culture of *empowerment*

• *Learning* from
– customers and suppliers
– competitors
– alliance partners

Figure 1.6   Strategic abilities.

of the organization match the needs of the environment and the key success factors. It is the values and culture which determine whether the environment and resources are currently matched, and whether they stay congruent in changing circumstances. Values are traditionally subsumed as a resource in a SWOT (strengths, weaknesses, opportunities, threats) analysis, but I believe they need to be separated out. This notion of E–V–R (environment–values–resources) congruence is illustrated in Figure 1.7 and Case 1.2 on The National Trust.

An article by Peter Drucker (1994) complements these arguments when he states that all organizations have implicit or explicit 'theories' for their business, incorporating:

(a) assumptions about the environment, specifically markets, customers and important technologies
(b) assumptions about its mission or purpose and
(c) assumptions about the core (content) competencies required to fulfil the mission.

These assumptions, at any time, must be realistic, congruent, communicated and understood; to achieve this they must be evaluated regularly and rigorously.

Pümpin (1987) uses the term strategic excellence positions (SEP's) to describe 'capabilities which enable an organization to produce better-than-average results over the longer term compared with its competitors'. SEP's imply that organizations appreciate the views of customers and develop the capabilities required to satisfy these needs. Moreover, they are perceived by their customers to be a superior competitor because of their skills and accomplishments.

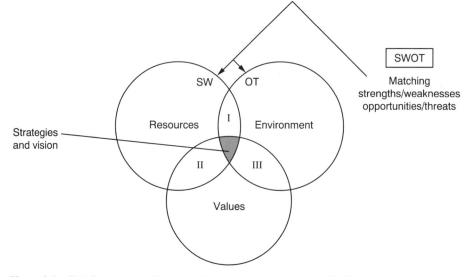

Figure 1.7   E–V–R congruence. The greater the congruence the greater the likelihood that the organization is managing its resources effectively to match the key success factors dictated by the environment.

It is important to deploy resources and to focus the drive for excellence (an aspect of the organization's culture) on issues which matter to customers. IBM, for example, have succeeded historically by concentrating on service, Rolls Royce (Motor Cars) on image and quality, and Procter and Gamble on advertising and branding.

Businesses should seek to develop competitive advantage and a strategic excellence position for each product and service. Overall E–V–R congruence then depends upon these SEPs together with any corporate benefits from linkages and inter-relationships.

Strategic excellence positions are represented by the overlap of environment and resources, area I in Figure 1.7.

The development of SEP's and E–V–R congruence takes time, and requires that all the functional areas of the business appreciate which factors are most significant to customers. Once achieved, though, it cannot be assumed that long-term success is guaranteed. Situations change, and new windows of opportunity open (Abell, 1978). The demand for guaranteed overnight parcel deliveries anywhere in the country, and immediate services within cities, opened up the opportunity for couriers; new technologies used in lap top computers and facsimile machines have created demand changes. Competitors may behave unexpectedly, and consequently there is a need for strategic awareness and for monitoring potential change situations.

Handy (1994) also stresses that timing plays a crucial role in the management of strategic change. He uses the Sigmoid Curve (Figure 1.8) to illustrate that organizations must change when they are successful, not when it is too late. Change should be at Point A not Point B; the shaded area represents a period of uncertainty and turbulence.

Vigilance should help an organization ·decide where it should be concentrating its resources at the moment, how it might usefully invest for the

Case 1.2
THE NATIONAL TRUST

The National Trust acquires and preserves countryside and historic places of interest 'for the benefit of us all', generally allowing access to members and fee-paying visitors. At the end of 1995 the National Trust was responsible for over half a million acres of land, 550 miles of coastline and some 250 houses and gardens. The Trust relies heavily on members' subscriptions to help fund its various activities; and gifts and endowments, together with some (limited) government funding, enable new acquisitions. Maintenance standards are high (and expensive) and conservation is seen as more important than commercial exploitation, and, where necessary, access. On occasions, but not very often, the numbers of visitors will be restricted either directly or indirectly, by, for example, limiting the parking facilities.

Stakeholders and interested parties – those whose interests the Trust must serve.

❑ National Trust members and visitors
❑ Donors of properties
❑ Conservation agencies and ramblers' associations
❑ Financial benefactors
❑ NT employees
❑ Government, and
❑ The nation as a whole.

Skills required
❑ Property management – both upkeep of the buildings and the management of land resources. Large areas of farmland are leased

❑ Expertise in arts and furnishings
❑ Public relations and marketing
❑ Financial skills – the Trust has substantial funds invested to yield income streams.

Values
The National Trust has proved successful in developing and deploying resources to meet the needs and expectations of its stakeholders. Staff are typically more 'property management' oriented than they are marketing oriented, but they are knowledgeable and expert. Preservation and the presentation of the properties to the standard maintained by their original owners are seen as important aspects of the service by both the Trust employees and its members. Theme parks and activities have no place in the National Trust; and there is a high moral tone to every activity, including the National Trust shops which tend to sell high-quality selected products at premium prices.

In addition, Trust staff appear to share an ethos (typically shared by people who work for other charities) which combines the feeling of working for a good cause, clear identification with its purpose and principles, and a certain readiness to accept lower rewards than those normally earned in manufacturing and service businesses.

National Trust membership doubled from 1 million to 2 million during the 1980s. A dilemma and a new challenge for the National Trust would arise if a more commercial orientation became necessary in order to fund desired activities.

future, and where it needs to divest as existing windows of opportunity start to close. New market needs may imply a change of values, and this again will take time and prove challenging. It is not easy, for instance, to change a strong cost culture into one which is more innovatory.

Area II of Figure 1.7 represents innovatory, continuous change as organizations add new, positive benefits for their customers, eradicate any problem creators and thus maintain or improve E–V–R congruence. Sometimes, though,

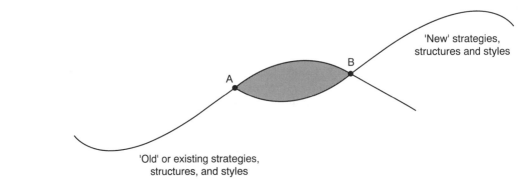

Figure 1.8   Timing strategic change.

continuous change is inadequate; more radical, discontinuous change or strategic regeneration (discussed in detail later in the chapter) is required. This takes us into Area III of Figure 1.7.

Bettis and Prahalad (1995) argue that business decisions are affected by a 'dominant logic', championed by the strategic leader and communicated through the organization. This could be an articulated vision or a culturally-integrated paradigm concerning 'what the business is about and how things get done'. Strategic regeneration implies this logic needs to be changed. IBM's growth and early industry dominance was built on a belief that mainframe computers were essential for organizations. Competitors such as Microsoft, which concentrated on software, highlighted that IBM's logic was outdated and it needed to be 'unlearned'. New products and new processes alone would prove inadequate. The new logic is one of decentralized personal computers in the hands of knowledgeable workers.

Organizations, therefore, should build on their past successes whilst always realizing that the past may not be the best guide to the future. At this point it is now appropriate to examine the process of strategic change in greater detail.

The strategy process

Opportunities for change

It is therefore vital that managers are strategically aware both of potentially threatening developments and of opportunities for profitable change, and that they seek to match and improve the fit between the environment and the organization's resources.

> *A wise man will make more opportunities than he finds.*
>
> (Francis Bacon)

There is no single recommended approach for seeking out and pursuing new opportunities. There is a broad spectrum ranging from what might be termed entrepreneurial opportunism to what Quinn (1980) calls 'logical incremental-ism'. These are analogous to the Bird and Squirrel approaches described in Box 1.3.

Strategic change can be relatively evolutionary or gradual, or much more dramatic or revolutionary. The nature of the opportunities (and threats) is

Box 1.3
APPROACHES TO STRATEGIC MANAGEMENT

The bird approach

Start with the entire world – scan it for opportunities to seize upon, trying to make the best of what you find.

You will resemble a bird, searching for a branch to land on in a large tree. You will see more opportunities than you can think of. You will have an almost unlimited choice. But your decision, because you cannot stay up in the air for ever, is likely to be arbitrary, and because arbitrary, it will be risky.

The squirrel approach

Start with yourself and your company – where you are at with the skills and the experience you have – and what you can do best.

In this approach you will resemble a squirrel climbing that same large tree. But this time you are starting from the trunk, from familiar territory, working your way up cautiously, treefork by treefork, deciding on each fork the branch that suits you best.

You will only have one or two alternatives to choose from at a time – but your decision, because it is made on a limited number of options, is likely to be more informed and less risky.

In contrast with the bird who makes single big decisions, the squirrel makes many small ones. The squirrel may never become aware of some of the opportunities the bird sees, but he is more likely to know where he is going.

Adapted from Cohen, P (1974) *The Gospel According to the Harvard Business School*, Penguin. Originally published by Doubleday, New York, 1973.

directly related to both the general and the specific industry environments; and the approach that particular organizations take in seeking to match resources to the environment is dependent on the basic values of the organization and the style of the strategic leader. However, as will be seen, it does not follow that the strategic leader is the sole manager of strategic change.

Effectively managed change requires a vision of the future – where the organization is heading or wants to go – together with the means for creating and reaching this future. Planning a way forward from where the organization is now may not be enough to create the future vision; at the same time, when there is a vision, it is illogical to set off in pursuit without the appropriate 'equipment'. There must, then, be a clear vision of a route, and this requires planning; on the way, managers should stay alert for dangers and opportunity (see Figure 1.9). Well-tracked routes (strategies which have proved successful in the past) and experience can both be beneficial, but in a dynamic environment, there will always be an element of the unknown.

Strategy creation

All managers plan. They plan how they might achieve objectives. Planning is essential to provide direction and to help ensure that the appropriate resources are available where and when they are needed for the pursuit of objectives. Sometimes the planning process is detailed and formal; on other occasions planning may be informal, unstructured and essentially 'in the mind'. In the context of strategy formulation a clear distinction needs to be made between the cerebral activity of informal planning and formalized planning systems.

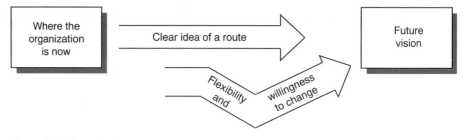

Figure 1.9 Strategic change.

Formal strategic planning systems are most useful in stable conditions. Environmental opportunities and threats are forecast, and then strategies are planned and implemented. Strategies which are appropriate, feasible and desirable are most likely to help the organization achieve its mission and objectives.

Where the environment is more turbulent and less predictable, strategic success requires flexibility, and the ability to learn about new opportunities and introduce appropriate changes continuously. Planning systems can still make a valuable contribution but the plans themselves must not be inflexible.

In addition it is important not to discount the contribution of visionary strategic leaders who become aware of opportunities – and on occasions, create new opportunities – and take risks based on their awareness and insight of markets and customers.

Formally planned strategies

Formal planning implies determined actions for achieving stated and desired objectives. For many organizations these objectives will focus on sales growth and profitability. A detailed analysis of the strategic situation will be used to create a number of strategic alternatives, and then certain options will be chosen and implemented.

Planning systems are useful, and arguably essential, for complex or diversified organizations with a large number of businesses which need integrating. There are, though, a number of possible approaches. Head office can delegate the detailed planning to each division, offering advice and making sure the plans can be co-ordinated into a sensible total package. Alternatively the planning system can be controlled centrally in order to establish priorities for resource allocation.

Whilst the discipline of planning and setting priorities is valuable, the plans must not be inflexible and incapable of being changed in a dynamic competitive environment. During implementation it is quite likely that some plans will be discarded and others modified.

Visionary leadership

Planning systems imply that strategies are selected carefully and systematically from an analytical process. In other instances major strategic changes will be decided upon without lengthy formal analysis. Typically such changes will reflect strong, entrepreneurial leadership and be visionary and discontinuous – 'I have seen the future and this is it!'.

To an outsider it can often appear that the organization is pursuing growth with high-risk strategies, which are more reliant on luck than serious thought. This can underestimate the thinking that is involved, because quite often these visionary leaders have an instinctive feel for the products, services and markets involved, and enjoy a clear awareness and insight of the opportunities and risks.

This mode of strategy creation is most viable when the strategic leader has the full confidence of the organization, and he or she can persuade others to follow his or her ideas and implement the strategies successfully. Implementation requires more detailed planning and incremental changes with learning – initially it is the broad strategic idea that is formulated entrepreneurially.

Formal planning and/or visionary leadership will invariably determine important changes to corporate strategies; competitive and functional level changes are more likely to involve adaptive and incremental strategy creation. The implementation of corporate level decisions is also likely to be incremental.

Adaptive strategic change

Some organizations will be characterized by extensive decentralization, empowerment and accountability. Here, managers throughout the organization are being encouraged to look for opportunities and threats and to innovate. The underlying argument is that managers 'at the coal face' are closest to the key changes in the organization's environment and should, therefore, be in a position where they can, on the one hand, react quickly, and, on the other hand, be proactive or intrapreneurial in attempting to change or manage the external environment. Managers will be encouraged and empowered to make changes in their areas of responsibility, and, ideally, rewarded for their initiatives. The implication is that functional changes will impact upon competitive strategies in a positive way as the organization adapts to its changing environment. Conceptually this is similar to incremental change.

Proponents of chaos theory such as Ralph Stacey (1993) argue that intentional strategies are, *per se*, 'too inflexible for unknown futures'. Relying on this approach is a 'recipe for stagnation and failure because of the extent of the complexity'. Companies must seek to 'achieve a state of creative tension on the edge of instability'. These theorists accept that organizational hierarchies and planning are needed to control day-to-day operations, but, long-term, strategies must be allowed to emerge from the 'self-organizing activities of loose, informal, destabilizing networks'.

Incremental strategic change

In dynamic and turbulent competitive environments detailed formal planning is problematical. The plans are only as good as any forecasts, which must be uncertain. It can make sense, therefore, not to rely on detailed plans, but instead just plan broad strategies within a clearly defined mission and purpose.

Having provided this direction the strategic leader will allow strategies to emerge in a decentralized organization structure. Managers will meet regularly, both formally and informally, to discuss progress and changing trends; they will plan new courses of action and then try them out – a form of 'real-time planning'. See Key Concept 1.3.

LOGICAL INCREMENTALISM

When I was younger I always conceived of a room where all these [strategic] concepts were worked out for the whole company. Later I didn't find any such room. ... The strategy [of the company] may not even exist in the mind of one man. I certainly don't know where it is written down. It is simply transmitted in the series of decisions made.

(James B Quinn, 1980)

Quinn argues that organizations test out relatively small changes and develop with this approach rather than go for major changes. An example would be Marks and Spencer testing a proposed new line in a selected and limited number of stores before deciding to launch it nationally. Lex Group (mentioned in Box 1.2) followed an incremental approach when it diversified into hotels, building and buying properties one by one rather than acquiring a chain of hotels.

An organization can, of course, use more than one means of bringing about strategic changes at any one time. During the 1980s, for example, Asda, the major food retailer, acquired, and later sold, the kitchen furniture group MFI. At the same time it developed and pursued strategies of opening new stores, re-designing and refurbishing existing stores, developing own label goods, introducing more fresh foods and non-food items, using information technology and stream lining the distribution system.

Strategy, therefore, can result from a stream of decisions and information fed upwards from the lower management levels of the organization. Quinn contends that this is sensible, logical and positive. ...

The most effective strategies of major enterprises tend to emerge step by step from an iterative process in which the organization probes the future, experiments and learns from a series of partial (incremental) commitments rather than through global formulations of total strategies. Good managers are aware of this process and they consciously intervene in it. They use it to improve the information available for decisions and to build the psychological identification essential to successful strategies. The process is both logical and incremental. Such logical incrementalism is not 'muddling' as most people understand that word. Properly managed it is a conscious, purposeful, proactive, executive practice.

Teamworking and learning are at the heart of these two modes. Managers must learn about new opportunities and threats; they should also learn from the successes and mistakes of other managers. Managers must be willing to take measured risks; for this to happen understandable mistakes and errors of judgement should not be sanctioned harshly.

Change is gradual and comes from experimentation; new strategies involve an element of trial and error. Success is very dependent upon communications. Managers must know of opportunities and threats facing them; the organization must be able to synthesize all the changes into a meaningful pattern, and spread learning and best practice.

Mintzberg (1989) argues that organizations should be structured and managed to ensure that formulators of strategies (managers whose decisions lead to strategic changes) have information, and that the implementers of strategies and changes have the appropriate degree of power to ensure that the desired changes are brought about.

It is quite normal to find all these modes in evidence simultaneously in an organization, although, of course, there is likely to be one dominant mode. *Moreover different managers in the same organization will not necessarily agree on the relative significance of each mode; their perceptions of what is actually happening will vary.*

The place of corporate planning

A number of books have been written on the subject of corporate planning, where it is generally agreed that strategic change is the outcome of objective, systematic decision making which establishes objectives and then seeks and chooses ways of achieving them. Change is a planned activity.

Corporate planning is therefore prescriptive in its approach. It would be churlish to argue that formal planning has no role to play in strategic management but, quite simply, there is more to strategic management and strategic change than planning.

Planning activity will consider opportunities and threats (although this is not the only way they should be spotted); it will allow a thorough evaluation of strengths and weaknesses; it will allow an assessment of where competitive advantage is or is not and how it might be achieved; and future scenarios can be tested. Planning can be used to help decide where the organization's scarce resources (for example, future investment capital) should be concentrated; and it can be used to establish tactics (actions) for carrying out strategies.

There are a number of useful planning techniques and these will be considered in a later chapter. But the overall role and relative importance of planning remains a controversial and disputed issue. As mentioned by Mintzberg (1982), strategy 'need not always be a conscious and precise plan'.

Bruce Henderson, founder of the technique-oriented Boston Consulting Group, has defended planning with the following argument:

> *Most companies don't have a strategy. They just talk about it, like they do about the weather.*
>
> *Companies need more tools and techniques if they are to survive and prosper. If companies really had been able to produce sophisticated strategies, would so many of them all have jumped together into the computer business? Many of the entrants who are now fighting for their lives had not even worked out relatively simple things ... how they were going to secure their technical talent, develop their software and so on. If they wanted to have a strategy worth the name they would have to go very much further than that. For instance, into highly complex mapping of competitor strengths and weaknesses.*
>
> (Henderson, 1983)

Finally it is quite plausible to argue that the outcome of planning need not be a plan. Rather than trying to produce a watertight document covering the next ten years, planning, as an exercise, should concentrate on identifying and evaluating alternative courses of action for the business, so that more opportunities are created. Planning therefore increases awareness.

In this section we have outlined the views of a number of contributors on strategy. It can usefully be summarized as follows. Strategic management is concerned with

❑ deciding the future direction and scope of the business, in line with perceived opportunities and threats. This will clearly require awareness and planning. The planning, however, may be more cerebral and visionary than detailed, formal and quantitative.

❑ ensuring that the required resources are, or will be, available in order that the chosen strategies can be implemented.

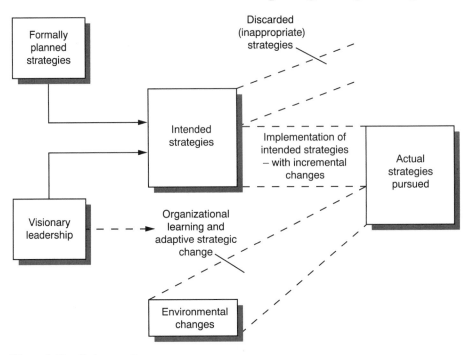

Figure 1.10   Strategy creation.

❑ ensuring that there is innovation and change. These changes can be in relation to corporate, competitive or functional strategies. Equally, innovation can take place throughout the organization. If this is to happen then an appropriate organization structure and culture must be in place.

Figure 1.10 summarizes these ideas and Case 1.3 applies them to Virgin Atlantic Airways.

The figure indicates that intended strategies can be the outcome of both a formal planning process and visionary leadership. On implementation some of these intended strategies will be discarded – they turn out to be based on misjudgements, or changing circumstances make them less viable. Meanwhile, in this changing environment, the organization does two other things as a result of learning. First, it incrementally changes the intended strategies as they are implemented. Second, it introduces new adaptive strategies when fresh opportunities are spotted. Consequently the actual strategies pursued will relate to, but differ from, the intended strategies.

Strategic regeneration

Organizations have to deal with dynamic and uncertain environments, as we have seen already. They should actively and continuously look for opportunities to exploit their competencies and strategic abilities, adapt and seek improvements in every area of the business – gradual change, building on an awareness and understanding of current strategies and successes. One difficulty is the fact that organizations are not always able to clarify exactly why they are successful.

Case 1.3
VIRGIN ATLANTIC AIRWAYS

Richard Branson is a well-known entrepreneurial businessman. He became prominent through the growth and success of his Virgin record label and music stores during the 1970s and 80s.

He decided to begin a trans-Atlantic airline in 1984. The move had been prompted by an American who approached him with an idea, and Branson took just a few weeks to make his decision. In this short period Branson analysed why small airlines had previously failed with similar ventures. In particular he focused on Freddie Laker's Skytrain which had competed with a basic service and low prices. When the major airlines reduced their prices Skytrain was driven from the market – it had no other competitive advantage. Virgin Atlantic Airways would offer added value and superior service at competitive prices, and concentrate on a limited number of the most lucrative routes. Branson had both a vision and many critics, who argued he lacked the requisite skills.

More detailed planning came later after he began recruiting people with expertise in the industry. In this case the planning concentrated on the implementation of a visionary strategy. The airline has grown steadily over a 12-year period, and won a number of awards for the quality of its service. Additional aircraft have been leased and new routes added. The growth has been in limited, incremental steps as Virgin Atlantic has learnt from experience in a very dynamic environment. The major carriers such as British Airways have clearly seen Virgin as a threat, and the whole industry has been affected in the 1990s by the Gulf War and the world-wide economic recession. When Virgin broke into the trans-Atlantic market with its innovative new service, it took the existing carriers by surprise; this was competition from an unexpected source.

A successful holiday business has also been developed alongside the airline.

At the same time it is also valuable if they can think ahead discontinuously, trying to understand future demand, needs and expectations. By doing this they will be aiming to be the first competitor with solutions. Enormous benefits are available to the companies which succeed.

In a sense this process is an attempt to invent the future, and the resources of the organization, its people and technologies, will need to be applied creatively. Companies should 'imagine new product opportunities' and strive to develop new products and services because they believe that customers will value them if they are available (Hamel and Prahalad, 1991). Sony, for example, developed a sketch pad for children, allowing them to project their drawings directly onto a TV screen as they do them. Developments like this are based on ideas and 'dreams' rather than merely attempting to improve existing products. Asking customers is not enough – companies must be able to both understand them and think at least one jump ahead. There is a danger when companies 'follow their nose' but fail to truly understand their markets. In such cases, research and development may drive product development down an inappropriate track. In addition, caution is necessary when ideas are implemented because markets and customers are likely to resist changes which seem too radical.

To minimize the risk, expeditionary marketing – low risk incursions into the market to test out new features or new performances – can be useful. Here organizations are really attempting to create markets ahead of competitors and just slightly ahead of customers.

In summary, organizations are searching for:

❏ long-term product or service leadership, which is dictated by the **environment**
❏ long-term cost leadership, which is **resource dependent**
❏ product and service excellence, doing things faster than competitors without sacrificing quality-essential **values**.

Strategic regeneration refers to simultaneous changes to strategies and structures (organizational processes) in this search.

Strategies have to be re-invented. New products and services should be created by questioning how and why existing ones are popular and successful, and looking for new ways of adding extra value. Electronic publishing and CD-Rom technology, for example, have enormous potential for dramatically changing the ways people learn. Rewards are available for those companies which learn how to exploit these *environmental opportunities*.

Visit the website:
http://www.
itbp.com

In thinking ahead, companies should consider both products (or services) and core competencies. Concentrating on products encourages a search for new competitive opportunities; thinking creatively about competencies (which transcend individual products and businesses) can generate radically new opportunities for adding value and establishing a different, future 'competitive high ground'.

Structural changes are designed to improve *resource efficiency and effectiveness*. The current trends are:

(a) downsizing – splitting the organization into small, autonomous, decentralized units
(b) delayering – using the power and potential of information technology for reducing the number of layers of managers, in order to speed up decision making; and
(c) process re-engineering – reviewing and redesigning processes in order that tasks can be performed better and quicker.

Simply, changes are required to the structure of the organization, the nature and scope of jobs and the network of communications.

Empowerment and teamworking are also seen as essential for creating the values necessary to enable this degree of change.

On paper the idea of strategic regeneration can be justified as essential, exciting and rewarding, but, not unexpectedly, there are likely to be major barriers when applying the ideas. The most obvious hurdles are:

❏ the quality of leadership required to provide the necessary drive and direction
❏ an inability to create an internal culture of change – the most powerful inhibitors will be experienced, established managers who have become out-of-date
❏ uncertainty about changing needs and competitor activities.

Pascale (1992) uses the word *transformational* to describe organizations which succeed with simultaneous strategic and structural change. They become **learning organizations** which 'encourage continuous learning and knowledge generation at all levels, have processes which can move knowledge around the organization easily to where it is needed, and can translate that knowledge quickly into changes in the way the organization acts, both internally and externally' (Senge, 1991).

The content and process aspects we have discussed in the last two sections will be re-examined in Chapter 2 when we develop a more robust framework for examining strategic management.

Strategy statements

We are now at a point where we can realize that strategies can be interpreted in a number of ways. Strategies can be planned, intentional and forward looking; at the same time, they can be an emergent pattern which has evolved over a period of time with learning and experimentation. Strategies can be stated in relatively broad terms, a visionary perspective for the future; again they can be much more short-term and tactical. It can also be valuable to summarize the strategies being pursued now. A summary statement of this nature can help managers throughout the organization, together with its external stakeholders, appreciate the current situation. This will enable managers to understand where they fit, and how the decisions they make can have a wider impact. The framework illustrated in Figure 1.11 should not be seen as definitive and inflexible, but rather as an attempt to synthesize the important strategic issues and provide insight.

The chart begins at the top with the corporate mission statement. In the context of this companies should evaluate E, V and R (environment, values, resources) in order to tease out any important and current strategic issues which need attention.

Strategic issues facing British Airways in the 1990s, for example, include:

❑ European deregulation in a global environment of increasing deregulation
❑ Global supply in excess of global demand, leading to intense price competition and a vital need to provide a consistently high level of customer service. The situation is exacerbated by certain governments subsidizing their national airlines
❑ For the leading carriers, the need for global route coverage, achievable in part with strategic alliances
❑ The potential of information technology to yield greater efficiencies and control over prices and seat sales.

In the light of current and projected future issues corporate, competitive and functional strategies can be reviewed in order to establish short-term objectives (or milestones), action plans and performance targets.

Figure 1.11 thus provides both a broad outline framework for thinking and planning and a set of headings for summarizing and explaining current strategies. It would be valuable if all the managers in any organization could express the current strategic situation in this way.

This type of analysis will help determine whether current strategies are the right ones, and highlight where businesses might look to make changes. Written down and given to managers it flags where they should be vigilant and on the look-out for new opportunities and threats.

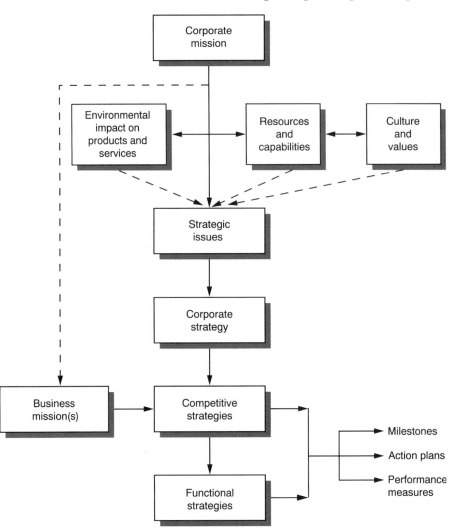

Figure 1.11   An outline strategy statement.

Strategic management in practice

Two short cases complete this introductory chapter. They feature instantly recognizable companies – Marks and Spencer and McDonald's – and describe aspects of their strategy content and processes. In both cases, incremental, innovatory changes can be seen against the background of a clear set of values and principles. It is fair to claim that in both companies these values are recognized and understood throughout the organization.

Marks & Spencer (M & S) is a major high street retailer of clothing (UK market leader), food, cosmetics and homewear.

M & S strategy is concerned with diversification of their product ranges within these broad product groups, but at the same time seeking to specialize where their St Michael label can be used effectively. All M & S products carry their own brand label. They seek to innovate whilst upgrading and adding value to their existing ranges.

M & S have found that many of their long-established stores in town and city centres are simply too small. An expansion programme has therefore developed along several lines. Adjacent units have been acquired when practical and new larger stores created; if land has been available, buildings have been extended; and new sales floors have been opened up by converting stockrooms and moving stock to outside warehouses. This brings its own logistics problems, of course. Satellite stores – smaller branches some distance away from the main branch – have been opened in certain towns. These satellites carry complete ranges – it might be mens' fashions, ladies' clothes, or children's items. The choice depends on the square footage available and the local prospects for particular lines. In similar vein, in towns considered too small to support a full branch, specialist stores, perhaps just for food, have been opened. Finally, new, larger, edge-of-town stores for car-bound customers have also been built. The selection of products within the whole M & S range varies between stores.

Other strategic changes are:

❏ Constant improvements in displays, partly to present products better, and also to get more items into the stores. 'Sales per square foot' is a vital measure of success.
❏ Electronic point-of-sale. Information technology has been harnessed to improve productivity and to enable M & S to respond faster to market changes – particularly relevant for fashion items. Thanks in part to technology, M & S staff costs as a percentage of their turnover are less than those of their competitors, but the quality of service has remained high.
❏ The development of support financial services, such as unit trusts, building upon the success of the M & S Chargecard, the third most popular credit card in the UK.
❏ International growth in France, Belgium, Canada, America and Hong Kong. The development has been gradual, with one of the objectives being to introduce new types of competition. Some mistakes have been made as part of the learning process, but the risks have been contained in order not to threaten the UK interests.

M & S possesses a number of identifiable strategic resources which have been instrumental in meeting customer key success factors, and thereby providing long-term profitable returns for shareholders. They include:

Physical resources	❏ The wide range of value-for-money St. Michael products
	❏ The sites and store displays
Intangible resources	❏ Image and reputation
	❏ Staff knowledge, expertise and commitment to service
Capabilities/ processes	❏ Supply chain management.

The foundation for the unique (St Michael) products and competitive prices is the M & S system of supply chain relationships, a considerable proportion of these being with UK manufacturers. Generally, where they are successful, they are long-term and non-contractual. They are based on mutual trust and common understanding. M & S is actively involved in product specification, input management (to their suppliers), quality control and production scheduling. M & S

Continued overleaf

is frequently the supplier's most important customer. Why does it work so effectively? The M & S reputation for fair dealing – with its suppliers, customers and employees – is too valuable to put at risk.

Whilst there have been, and continue to be, strategic changes, the fundamental principles or values of the business have remained constant. These are:

- ❏ High-quality, dependable products, styled conservatively and offering good value for money.
- ❏ Good relations with employees, customers, suppliers and other stakeholders.
- ❏ Simple operations.
- ❏ Comfortable stores.
- ❏ Financial prudence. Most properties, for example, are freehold – they have not been sold and leased back to fund the expansion.

Case 1.5
McDONALD'S

McDonald's, begun by a visionary, the late Ray Kroc, has become a very successful international company, popular with large numbers of customers, and certainly not just children. There are now over 18,000 branches worldwide, up to 3000 are added each year, and the formula works as well in Moscow and Beijing as it does in the USA. Although the products available are broadly similar in the USA and Europe, menus are seen as flexible in other parts of the world. Japanese stores, for example, feature Teriyaki Burgers, sausage patties with teriyaki sauce. 9500 stores are franchises, 2500 are company-owned and the rest are joint ventures.

The growth and success in an industry where 'fast food is a by-word for low wages and an unskilled temporary workforce' is not accidental. It has been very carefully planned and managed, although McDonald's relies a lot on the people at the sharp end. Employees are often young; they work a closely prescribed system, operating internationally established rules and procedures for preparing, storing and selling food. Various incentive schemes are practised. Labour turnover is high, however, and consequently McDonald's has its critics as well as its supporters. Nevertheless it is obvious that some competitors seek to emulate McDonald's in a number of ways – products, systems and employee attitudes.

Our competitors can copy many of our secrets, but they cannot duplicate our pride, our enthusiasm and our dedication for this business.

Ever since it began in 1955 McDonald's has been driven by a simple vision, known internally as Q, S, C and V – quality food; fast, friendly service; restaurants known for their cleanliness; and menus which provide value for money.

McDonald's is profitable because it is efficient and productive; and it stays ahead of its competitors by being innovative and looking for new opportunities.

A lot of the developments are planned and imaginative. McDonald's does not move into new countries without thorough investigation of the potential; the same is true for new locations. There are now McDonald's branches in American hospitals, military bases and zoos; worldwide they can be found in airport terminals, motorway service stations, supermarkets (Tesco), and on board cruise ships and Swiss trains.

McDonald's relies heavily on its suppliers for fresh food; again arrangements are carefully planned, monitored and controlled. The in-store systems for cooking and running branches are very tight – to ensure that products and service standards are the same world-wide.

New product development has utilized all the group's resources. The Big Mac, which was introduced nationally in the USA in 1968, was the idea of a Pittsburgh franchisee who had seen a similar product elsewhere. The aim was to broaden the customer base and make McDonald's more adult oriented. The company allowed the franchisee to try the product in his restaurant in 1967, although there was some initial resistance amongst executives who wished to retain a narrow product line, and it proved highly successful.

Egg McMuffins in the early 1970s were a response to a perceived opportunity – a breakfast menu and earlier opening times. Previously the restaurants opened at 11.00 am. Although the opportunity was appreciated the development of the product took place over four years, and the final launch version was created by a Santa Barbara franchisee who had to invent a new cooking utensil.

When Chicken McNuggets were launched in 1982 it was the first time that small boneless pieces of chicken had been mass produced. The difficult development of the product was carried out in conjunction with a supplier and there was immediate competitive advantage. The product was not readily copied. From being essentially a hamburger chain McDonald's quickly became Number 2 to Kentucky Fried for fast food chicken meals.

McDonald's continually tries out new menus, such as pizzas, in order to extend its share of the overall fast food market, but it has never diversified or sought to offer any different 'food concept'. To enhance its image of good value, and to compete in a very dynamic industry, McDonald's offers 'extra value meals', special combinations at low prices. There is innovation and the ability to create and adapt strategies to capitalize on opportunities.

In addition, McDonald's is a 'penny profit' business. It takes hard work and attention to detail to be financially successful. Store managers must do two things well: control costs and increase sales. Increased sales come from the products, certainly, but also from service. Cost control is vital, but it must not be achieved by compromising product quality, customer service or restaurant appearance. Instead, it requires a focus on productivity and attention to detail. Success with these strategies has been achieved partly through serious attempts to share learning and best practice throughout the global network.

The company is an industry leader and contends there are five main reasons behind this:

❏ Visibility: to this end substantial resources are devoted to marketing. The golden arches symbol is instantly recognizable.
❏ Ownership or control of real-estate sites; McDonald's argues that this factor differentiates it from its competitors who lease more.
❏ The commitment to franchising.
❏ It is world-wide, with restaurants in some 70 countries.
❏ It is a growth company.

Summary

In this chapter we have:

- outlined the scope of the subject area of strategic management relating it to the themes of content and process
- mentioned the factors required for strategic success
- introduced the idea of E–V–R congruence by reference to environmental fit and key success factors
- discussed the importance of organization culture as a feature of strategic management, and the need for strategic leadership

- defined competitive advantage, and shown the relationship between corporate, competitive and functional strategies
- explained the strategic significance of adding value and organizational competence
- summarized the different approaches, definitions and models that are relevant for our study of the subject
- argued that strategic change can be the result of a prescriptive planning process, or emerge from the decisions and actions of managers.

Questions and research assignments

Text related

1 How do Marks and Spencer seek to attain and maintain competitive advantage? What do you think their objectives might be?
2 Assess McDonald's in terms of E–V–R congruence.
3 From your background knowledge what might be the key success factors required in the popular music and airline businesses? How do you feel Virgin embraced these? How important a factor is 'risk taking'?

Library based

4 Sainsbury's first became market leader for 'packaged groceries' in 1983, with some 16% market share. Tesco and the Co-op each had 14.5% and Asda 8%.
   - ❏ In ten years the company's share price had risen by 900% against 175% for the FT All Shares index.
   - ❏ The performance combines 'profitability, productivity and a sense of social purpose' (*Financial Times* comment).
   - ❏ There was no 'grand strategy'.

We did not sit down in the early 70s and work out any corporate plan, or say that by a particular time we intended to be in a particular business, or to be of a particular size.
                    Roy Griffiths, Managing Director

- ❏ Rather, Sainsbury's has identified and 'obsessively pursued' opportunities that fitted the company's corporate values, the 'basics of the business'. These are:
- ❏ selling quality products at competitive (though not necessarily the cheapest) prices
- ❏ exacting quality control standards
- ❏ extensive research of competitors and customers
- ❏ strict financial management
- ❏ tight control of suppliers
- ❏ planned staff involvement

From your own observations and/or library research:
- ❏ How successful, strategically, do you believe Sainsbury's is?
- ❏ What is their competitive strategy?
- ❏ What changes have they made since 1983, and how successful have they been?

Checklist of key terms and concepts

At this stage you should feel confident that you have a basic understanding of the following terms and ideas:

- ★ Objectives (at this stage only as an idea)
- ★ Strategic management
- ★ Strategic change
- ★ Environmental fit
- ★ Key success factors
- ★ Adding value
- ★ Core competencies and strategic capabilities
- ★ Strategic excellence positions

- ★ Strategic leadership
- ★ Culture
- ★ Competitive advantage
- ★ Strategic architecture
- ★ E–V–R congruence
- ★ SWOT analysis
- ★ Corporate, competitive and functional strategies
- ★ Logical incrementalism
- ★ Corporate planning
- ★ Synergy

References

Abell, DF (1978) Strategic windows, *Journal of Marketing*, 42 (July).

Ansoff, HI (1984) *Implanting Strategic Management*, Prentice Hall.

Beck, P, quoted in Lorenz, C (1987) Crusading for a clear strategy, *Financial Times*, 25 February.

Bettis, R and Prahalad, CK (1995) The dominant logic: retrospective and extension, *Strategic Management Journal*, Volume 16, January.

Burns, T and Stalker, GM (1961) *The Management of Innovation*, Tavistock.

Drucker, PF (1994) The theory of business, *Harvard Business Review*, September–October.

Goold, M, Campbell, A and Alexander, M (1994) *Corporate Level Strategy*, John Wiley.

Hamel, G and Prahalad, CK (1989) Strategic intent, *Harvard Business Review*, May–June.

Hamel, G and Prahalad, CK (1991) Corporate imagination and expeditionary marketing, *Harvard Business Review*, July–August.

Hamel, G and Prahalad, CK (1993) Strategy as stretch and leverage, *Harvard Business Review*, March–April.

Handy, C (1994) *The Empty Raincoat*, Hutchinson.

Henderson, B (1983) *Lecture to the Annual Conference of the Strategic Management Society*, Paris, October.

Mintzberg, H, quoted in Lorenz, C (1982) Strategic doctrine under fire, *Financial Times*, 15 October. The themes are developed extensively in Quinn, JB, Mintzberg, H and James, RM (1987) *The Strategy Process*, Prentice-Hall.

Kay, JA (1993) *Foundations Of Corporate Success*, Oxford University Press.

Mintzberg, H (1989) *Mintzberg on Management*, Free Press.

Morrison, R and Lee, J (1979) From planning to clearer strategic thinking, *Financial Times*, 27 July.

Ohmae, K (1982) *The Mind Of The Strategist*, McGraw-Hill.

Pascale, R T (1992) Paper presented at the *Strategic Renaissance Conference*, Strategic Planning Society, London, October.

Porter, M E (1980) *Competitive Strategy*, Free Press.

Prahalad, CK and Hamel, G (1990) The core competence of the corporation, *Harvard Business Review*, May/June.

Pümpin, C (1987) *The Essence of Corporate Strategy*, Gower.

Pümpin, C (1991) *Corporate Dynamism*, Gower.

Quinn, JB (1980) *Strategies for Change: Logical Incrementalism*, Irwin.

Senge, P (1991) *The Fifth Discipline: The Art and Practise of the Learning Organization*, Doubleday

Stacey, RD (1993) *Strategic Management and Organizational Dynamics*, Pitman.

Stalk, G, Evans, P and Shulman, LE (1992) Competing on capabilities: the new rules of corporate strategy, *Harvard Business Review*, March–April.

2
A Strategic Management Framework

Learning objectives

After studying this chapter you should be able to:

- summarize **strategic management** in terms of three inter-related aspects: awareness, choice and implementation
- identify a series of questions concerning strategic awareness and decisions about strategic change and
- apply these to the outline framework around which this book has been structured
- appreciate that **strategic effectiveness** is based on awareness, strategy content and the process of strategic change, and that these elements relate to important organizational competencies
- explain why the **strategic challenge** for organizations concerns decisions about content and process within the context of a set of important issues and dilemmas.

In this chapter we explore strategic management by expanding and explaining Figure 1.2, which has been used to provide a framework for the order and content of the book. We then develop two additional frameworks of strategic effectiveness and the strategic challenge facing organizations in the 1990s.

Introduction

Models of strategic management have traditionally been built around three themes: analysis, choice and implementation. The model for the present text relates specifically to strategic awareness and change, but the compatibility between the two approaches is obvious.

Effective strategic management requires that managers address a number of important issues continuously and simultaneously. This can be achieved by constantly seeking answers to a number of questions. The questions are included in this chapter and applied to a simple example.

All strategic decisions are affected by the nature and style of strategic leadership in the organization, together with the prevailing culture and values, and this is reflected in the framework we use.

After re-examining the **strategic management** framework first presented in Figure 1.2 we develop two further frameworks. First, we consider the constituent elements of **strategic effectiveness and success** from the perspective of organizational competency, and then we explore the **challenges** facing organizations if they are to remain effective and successful in the dynamic, turbulent and competitive environments of the 1990s. Whilst different, the three frameworks are clearly related.

Don't forget to visit the website: http://www. itbp.com

While it is the first framework which has been used to provide an under-pinning structure for the book, all the elements of the other frameworks are discussed at various stages in the text.

Models of strategic management

Various models of strategic management already exist and, whilst there are differences between them, many tend to follow a pattern based on the following outline:

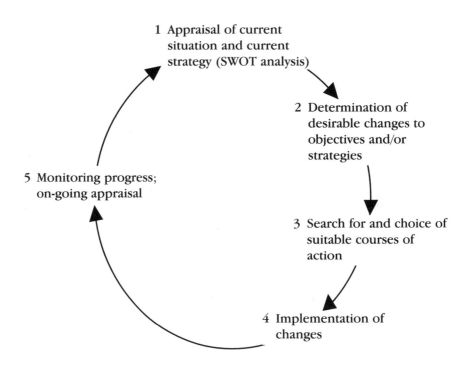

The basic proposal is that by a series of analyses and decisions an organization can determine the directions that its future strategy should follow. This approach is adequate on a prescriptive basis, but realistically it will fail to explain all that happens in practice. For example, in Chapter 1 the notion of incrementalism was introduced. Strategy changes which are gradual cannot be encapsulated into the above model. The process of strategic management should not be thought of as having a linear form exclusively.

Hence an alternative way of modelling the process is to base it upon three areas of decision – strategic analysis (or strategic awareness), strategic choice and strategy implementation – which should be seen as inter-related and linked to a monitoring and information system. The functional change discussed above would constitute both evaluation and implementation at the same time, for in many respects the manager is actually trying out something to see whether it works. He progresses in gradual steps, learning from experience all the time.

Strategic analysis: If an organization understands the nature of its market and is generally aware of, and responsive to, changes in the environment as a whole, it can be a successful competitor and achieve profit and growth. The levels of success that it is achieving with current strategies should be assessed, and future targets, which may imply more or even less of the same, or activities which are different, determined.

This requires an analysis of current results, an evaluation of current resources (strengths and weaknesses) and an assessment of opportunities and threats present and developing in the environment. The values held by the organization and its key managers are a crucial factor to include in this.

Strategic choice is concerned with establishing just what courses of strategic action are available to an organization and how these might be evaluated and one or more selected. Whilst strategic choice decisions are important for determining future courses of action, other strategic changes may emerge from a more gradual process of trial and error.

Additionally, managers may not be able to identify a feasible course of action. Competition might be too intense; legislation may prevent it; pressure groups may mount an effective opposition to the proposals; or the necessary resources may not be available. It would then be necessary for the organization to re-appraise its target objectives and set new ones.

Strategy implementation: a strategy is only useful when it has been implemented, and hence the organization must have an appropriate structure, clear and contributory functional strategies and systems which ensure that the organization behaves in a cohesive rather than a fragmented way. The larger, or more diverse the organization becomes, the more likely it is that this becomes a problem. In multi-product multi-national organizations with considerable inter-dependence between the products or services and between subsidiaries, for example, divisions may become competitive with each other and not pull together.

The way that an organization is structured into divisions and/or functions, and the amount of authority that is delegated to individual managers must inevitably influence day-to-day decision making. These 'coal-face' decisions determine (as suggested in Chapter 1) the actual strategies pursued and the levels of success. The objectives that an organization is pursuing in reality therefore stem from strategy implementation. In order to appreciate properly just how well an organization is doing relative to both its objectives and its competitors, to explore opportunities and threats, to appraise strengths and weaknesses, to evaluate alternative courses of action and so on, it is vital to have an effective information system. How an organization gathers and uses information is therefore another important aspect of strategic management.

The most important management technique is to understand the real situation in which you are operating.

Sir Paul Girolami, Chairman, Glaxo, 1987

The best way to predict the future is to invent it.

John Sculley, when Chairman, Apple Computers

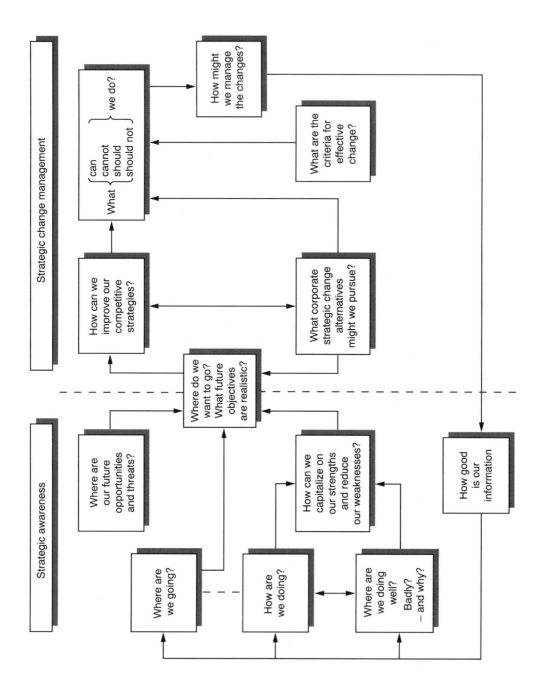

Figure 2.1 A strategy framework based on a series of questions.

Strategic management: a framework of questions

We have already established that this book is written around the themes of strategic awareness and strategic change. Figure 2.1 presents these themes in the form of a set of 12 questions.

Moving from left to right, the questions follow a logical sequence. If an organization needs to take stock of just where it is placed at the moment, evaluate emerging opportunities and threats before clarifying a set of objectives for which strategies, both corporate and competitive, can be evaluated, selected and implemented, then the model can be used in a sequential, and possibly iterative, way. It will, of course, be seen that information (the bottom box) implies monitoring and continuity.

However, I prefer to think of these questions as a set of important issues that managers everywhere in the organization should be addressing all the time in a turbulent environment. Nevertheless, they still need to be presented in a clear framework to ensure that any issues emerging can be placed in context, and any proposed changes assessed for their impact on other issues.

If managers seek answers to these questions continuously, and make and carry out appropriate strategic decisions, they will improve the performance and effectiveness of their organization by

❑ generating increased strategic awareness;
❑ ensuring that functional managers appreciate the strategic environment and the implications of decisions concerning individual products, services and markets; as well as
❑ making decisions about the need for, and appropriateness of, particular change opportunities.

Applying the framework of questions

Case 2.1 is a very simple example of a small service business, and it is included to illustrate how the framework of questions might be applied. It demands a consideration of various change opportunities developing from a clear awareness of the current situation.

Self-assessment questions

1 Where is Margaret Brooke going?
2 How is she doing?
3 Where and why is she doing well? Badly?
4 What are the opportunities and threats?
5 How might she capitalize on her strengths and reduce her weaknesses?
6 Where is her competitive advantage? Where might it be?

7 What might/should her future objectives be? What is realistic?
8 What choices does she have?
9 What would constitute a good choice?
10 What are the implementation aspects?

Case 2.1
MARGARET BROOKE

Mrs Margaret Brooke, the wife of a successful American businessman resident in the UK, loved buying and collecting antiques from auction sales. Unfortunately by early 1985 her house in Henley-on-Thames was 'overflowing' and beginning to look like a museum. She was restless for something to do and her husband was pressurizing her into getting rid of at least some of her antiques.

A friend gave her an idea. A converted derelict building in the West End of London was home for a large number of antique dealers (some 40 in all) who were able to rent small stalls (150 square foot floor area) for £30 per week. Arguing that she already had stock, would enjoy going out and buying more and that the rent was cheap, Margaret Brooke went into business.

After six months Mrs Brooke was unsure about her next move. She was certainly enjoying herself, she had learnt a lot about the antique trade, and her house was more orderly. But she felt that she should at least be breaking even and she did not know whether she was or not. For one thing she could not remember all the purchase prices of antiques she had owned before 1985. Additionally she had bought items she simply could not sell – but all the time she was doing less of this.

In future, she promised her husband, she would employ clear policies rather than simply buying and selling opportunistically as she had been doing.

So far she had taken few real risks. By concentrating on relatively inexpensive Victoriana she overcame her inexperience to a great extent. Unlike the scarce Queen Anne period furniture, for example, Victorian antiques were plentiful and there were very few 'fakes' on the market. For this reason she was not really in competition with the major dealers; but neither had she the opportunity for substantial profits. She never spent very much on any one article, and felt she could afford to make the odd mistake.

Margaret Brooke worked most days of the week and although she enjoyed selling she preferred spending her time at small auction sales. Her neighbour in the market frequently looked after her stall while she was away. Quite often Mrs Brooke sold her goods (furniture, pictures and other *objets d'art*) to other dealers in the market for a fast turnover, but this meant low mark-ups. For sales to non-dealers she tended to price halfway between the price she would happily pay for an article at auction and the amount she felt was the maximum a keen customer would pay. This represented a mark-up of around 100%.

At the end of six months she knew enough dealers to feel confident that she could sell on virtually all the furniture and oil paintings she might buy. However, she got very little satisfaction from dealing in articles that she herself did not like.

About one-third of the other stall holders seemed to be extremely knowledgeable; they specialized far more than Margaret Brooke did, and they appeared to be making a lot of money. Two, in particular, concentrated on renovated grandfather clocks and Georgian silver. The majority seemed not unlike Mrs Brooke – enthusiastic but not expert.

This analysis has been adapted from a short case written originally by Mr Kenneth Ambrose.

Suggested answers are provided below for the ten questions. Before studying these you should attempt to answer the questions yourself.

1 Where is Margaret Brooke going?

Mrs Brooke appears to be developing her business incrementally, learning about marketing opportunities and prices as she goes along. She has not properly sorted out how to divide her time between buying and selling, and as a result of this she seems happy to sell goods on at low margins rather than to hold stock longer for greater gains. She chooses to deal in antiques that she herself likes – and whilst this must result in profitable opportunities being lost, it also means that she would probably keep any articles she failed to sell in her own home.

2 How is she doing?

Her house is emptier and less cluttered, and she is enjoying herself and learning more about antiques and the antique trade all the time. She has almost certainly achieved all she originally set out to do.

However, she is not sure how well she is doing financially. As one of the major reasons for this is that she has been selling antiques that she originally bought to keep and cannot remember all the purchase prices, it seems likely that by simple record keeping she can quickly overcome this as she buys more and more for the business.

3 Where and why is she doing well? Badly?

She is making fewer mistakes as she learns more, and she seems to be reaching a stage where she understands certain lines well enough to know that she can sell on all she buys, albeit at limited profit. Mark-ups of 100% seem satisfactory, and her concentration on 'safe' Victoriana has probably been wise.

However, she must be limited in what she can handle by physical and transportation constraints. By relying on other stall holders to watch her stall and sell for her on an ad hoc basis she is neglecting a major aspect of her business. She also does not appear to put a realistic value on her time.

4 Where are her opportunities and threats?

She is in a market full of opportunities, but one that is competitive because there are few barriers to entry. She could expand ... but might require assistance. She could specialize more and consider the more profitable segments – but this would require more professionalism and imply greater risks.

At the moment she faces very few threats. But maybe she really wants to develop the business, and if so she could face threats from more knowledgeable dealers, from 'fake' antiques and from customers who might have greater knowledge and expertise than she has herself. Her husband, or bank manager, might constitute a threat if she starts investing more money in expensive specialized stock.

5 How might she capitalize on her strengths and reduce her weaknesses?

The areas she could look at are the following:

❏ Products   extending her knowledge
❏ Stock control   clearly deciding whether she is buying to sell to customers or to other dealers, and how long she should hold on to articles
❏ Pricing   related to the above
❏ Financial records   including valuing her time for profit calculations

More particularly, she must assess how effectively she is using her time – and how she wants to use it. If she wants to concentrate on buying and still run something of a successful profitable business she will need either a partner or an assistant ... and this would bring a new dimension to the business.

6 Where is her competitive advantage? Where might it be?

At the moment she really has none. She would not appear to have many prospects with either products, service or delivery.

She might consider using low prices, especially if the financial side is of secondary importance to her. But she then runs the risk of antagonizing the other stall holders, one of whom she is dependent upon.

As she seems to prefer buying to selling, could she seek competitive advantage by looking to 'buy to order' in some way? (Developed below.)

7 What might/should her future objectives be? What is realistic?

To determine these she will have to address the following issues:

- ❑ How much does she want to develop a 'real' business?
- ❑ How much time is she happy/willing to devote to it on a long-term basis?
- ❑ How profitable does she want it to be? Would she be happy to just break even?
- ❑ How much risk is she willing (and able) to take on products, money and other people?
- ❑ Where does she want to concentrate her effort?

Less ambitious objectives would seem to be more realistic.

8 What choices does she have?

- ❑ She could give it all up! After all, her house is emptier.
- ❑ She could stay roughly as she is, making sure she keeps proper records and assesses just how well she is doing financially.
- ❑ She could look to expand whilst staying in relatively safe Victoriana. Maybe she could join forces with another dealer, concentrating herself on buying. As partners they might be able to operate a larger stall. They might also be able to increase profits by better marketing – display, selling effort and pricing.
- ❑ She could specialize more, either in antiques with a higher profit margin or in just one type of good.
- ❑ She could act as essentially a buying agent – buying for other dealers who prefer to concentrate on selling or buying for individual clients. To accomplish the latter she would have to build an order book for particular customers and then go around the auctions buying for them.
- ❑ Finally, she could think of opening an antique shop, although for a number of reasons this would seem improbable.

9 What would constitute a good choice?

Simplistically, a good choice would be one which would achieve her objectives.

It will be seen, at this stage, how important her values are in this evaluation. Margaret Brooke started buying and selling antiques for a number of reasons, none of them apparently concerned with making substantial profits from a

Visit the website: http://www.itbp.com

commercial venture. She has enjoyed the experience and has done things in a relatively informal ad hoc way. If she wishes to continue in much the same way her likely choice of direction will be very different from the one she might select if she decides that now is the time to view the business as a real business.

Her ability is a constraint, but it is becoming less of one. She has a number of opportunities with varying degrees of risk. Arguably her choice must be acceptable to her, her husband and, possibly, the bank manager.

10 What are the implementation aspects?

These must centre upon knowledge and any need for new knowledge; money if expansion is planned; the amount of time involved; and possibly the need for additional assistance with the business.

There could well be implications for the fundamental values if outside help and/or commercial finance is introduced into the business.

Strategic management: awareness and change

Figure 2.2 is an annotated reproduction of Figure 1.2 from the first chapter. The driving forces of strategic management are strategic leadership, culture and values, and they are at the heart of the diagram. Proposals for changes to corporate strategies will always involve the strategic leader in some way, either as originator of the idea or someone who must ratify and take overall responsibility for the decision. Changes to competitive and functional strategies will reflect the structure of the organization and styles of managing it. These again stem from choices made by the strategic leader and the prevailing culture which the leader drives or accepts. Change proposals at every level should take account of the existing culture and values, as they will affect the implementation of new strategies, and consequently their feasibility.

Addressing how well the organization is doing involves a number of themes. If the organization is meeting the needs and expectations of its stakeholders, and achieving its objectives, then arguably it is successful. When it does not meet objectives and expectations, then it is failing. Good strategic awareness also involves a clear appreciation of events and trends in the external environment, and the overall competitive situation. Companies should monitor and benchmark competitors to ensure they create and sustain some form of competitive edge.

From this awareness should come new strategies. Ideas must be generated and evaluated; as we have seen, this process is multi-stranded as is likely to be different at the corporate and competitive strategy levels. We must understand how competitive advantage can be created and sustained for each business or activity – through a variety of functional strategies and opportunities for adding customer value – and how each business must add value for the organization if the portfolio of activities is to generate beneficial synergies.

The creation and implementation of strategy are both linked irrevocably to the structure of the organization and the way it operates in practice.

We have seen that there is a variety of ways in which the process of strategic change can be managed. No two organizations are completely alike in their behaviour; at the same time, there is no 'single best way' of managing strategic

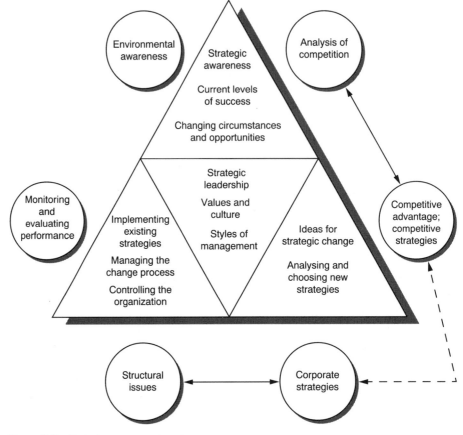

Figure 2.2 Strategic management.

Theme	Chapter
Strategic management	1, 2
Leadership, culture and values	3, 4
Strategic awareness	5, (6), 7
Monitoring and evaluating performance	6
Environmental analysis	8
Analysis of competition	9
Competitive advantage and strategy	10, 11, 12, 13
Ideas for change; strategic alternatives	14, 18
Corporate strategy	15, 16, 17
Structural issues	19, 20
Control and change	21, 22

change. What is essential is that the processes are co-ordinated and managed, and this requires sound monitoring systems, and the necessary information to sustain these systems.

Table 2.1 summarizes how these various themes are developed through the book.

All newly-appointed chief executives should ask five key questions:

❏ What are the basic goals of the company?
❏ What is the strategy for achieving these goals?
❏ What are the fundamental issues facing the company?
❏ What is its culture?
❏ And is the company organized in a way to support the goals, issues and culture?

Bob Bauman, ex-chief executive of SmithKline Beecham

Strategic effectiveness and success

This section, and our second framework, prescribes that strategists should view their organizations as portfolios of competencies which need to be continually developed and deployed in ways which enhance the organization's competitive position. Figure 2.3 shows how strategic effectiveness, strategic and competitive success in a dynamic and competitive environment, is dependent upon three groups of competencies: the *content* of the actual strategies; strategic *change* competencies; and strategic *learning* competencies.

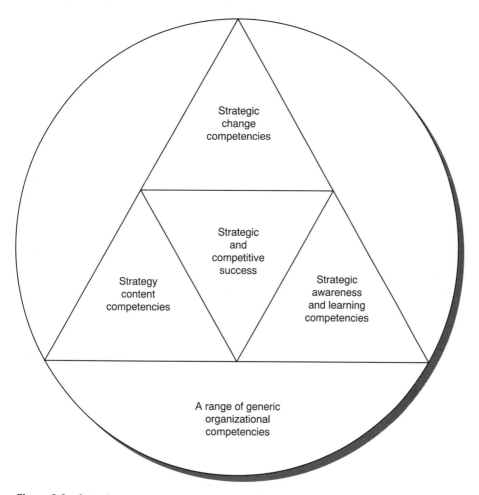

Figure 2.3 Strategic success; a competency perspective.

Strong and appropriate content competencies, as we have seen, will enable the organization to add value, innovate and exploit internal and external architecture to gain benefit from its technological competencies and strategic capabilities. From these will come distinct product and service advantages (differentiation) and controlled costs, yielding competitive advantage.

However the organization must be able to manage both continuous and discontinuous change in a dynamic environment, which in turn demands that it understands its environment. The organization can *learn* from several stakeholders, including its suppliers, distributors and customers as well as from its competitors, and it must seek to stay fully aware.

The outer circle of Figure 2.3 shows a range or 'bank' of generic competencies upon which organizations must be able to draw. Richardson and Thompson (1994) have identified 30 key competencies and grouped them into eight themes. The complete list is provided in Table 2.2. A strategically successful organization will require a large number, if not all, of these competencies. The relative significance of each competency will vary from organization to organization and over time. There is no magic formula; every organizational situation is unique. One important role of an effective strategic leader is to ensure the organization possesses the competencies it needs in the appropriate mix and measure. It is from this set of generic competencies that organizations derive their content, process and learning competencies. These competencies are all considered at various stages throughout the book.

Figure 2.4 draws together these layers of competency as an inter-dependent circular process. Organizations must be able to understand the complexity and trends of the changing environment. Some of the changes will be the result of external forces; others will be the outcomes of actions taken by the organization itself. From this learning, organizations must be able to manage change successfully, changing technologies, processes and architecture to maintain a successful match with the environment. In turn this should create positive and beneficial competitive outcomes.

The extent of the organization's success is partially dependent upon its ability to be proactive as well as reactive to the environment. To merely *survive*, the organization must be aware of the shocks and surprises being generated in its environment, and be able to co-ordinate information and effort throughout the organization in order to deal with any potential threats. Businesses will fail if they cannot accomplish this successfully.

Growth and prosperity, however, requires more. The organization must spot and create competitive opportunities ahead of its rivals and capitalize on these. In turn this necessitates an ability of managers in the various parts of the business to work in harmony, sharing information and capabilities and creating synergy. Architectural competency may well extend this sharing outside the organization to encapsulate the whole value chain.

The strategic challenge

This section, and our third framework, argues that organizations must manage and change their strategies within the context of a set of strategic issues and dilemmas. The stances they choose to deal with these issues and dilemmas, and the strategies, structures and styles that result from their decisions, will determine their overall effectiveness.

Table 2.2
Strategic effectiveness

Thirty critical organizational competency needs

Strategic awareness and control abilities

1 Maintain an awareness of environmental changes and their implications and *think strategically*
2 Design and operationalize a 'fitting' organization, the structures and systems of which match its environment(s) and, *through learning*, stay matched in a changing environment
3 Establish and maintain a portfolio of activities/businesses to which the organization can add value and foster synergies
4 Avoid the trap of self-enacted reality (whereby the organization drifts into problems because it has an unrealistic view of its position) and to reach more objectively, environmentally aware, informed decisions

Stakeholder satisfaction abilities

5 Understand and manage the organization as a stakeholder (political) interaction, and goal setting/attaining system
6 Diagnose organizational strategic standing, core content competencies and strategic abilities – its strength in its market place(s), its resource strengths and weaknesses and the opportunities and threats in its present and future environments

Competitive strategy

7 Understand competitive situations and to choose where and how to compete
8 Get closer to the customer – to understand, attract and satisfy him/her better than competitors by adding value more effectively
9 Choose winning product/market developments

Strategy implementation

10 Implement strategy throughout the organization
11 Create, share and implement a winning vision
12 Empower personnel and motivate them towards continuous organizational improvement
13 Foster internally-generated synergy through co-operation and sharing
14 Collaborate in strategic alliances for competitive advantage

Quality and customer care

15 Provide excellent quality as perceived by the customer
16 Continuously achieve states of greater organizational productivity
17 Invoke a creative, innovative and self-organizing climate in the organization

Functional competencies

18 Utilize research and development to help create a future for the business
19 Develop new products and services and bring them to market both effectively and in the appropriate timescale
20 Reach and satisfy customers with effective distribution of products and services nationally and/or internationally
21 Harness the potential of information technology for fast, efficient and effective information processing and sharing
22 Maintain financial control of the business and access capital for future investment programmes

Failure and crisis avoidance

23 Avoid business-failure situations
24 Plan for when things go wrong
25 Avoid socio-technical (life-threatening) disasters
26 Manage business-failure turnaround situations
27 Manage socio-technical disaster situations

Ethics and social responsibility

28 Manage 'green' issues
29 Manage socially responsibly
30 Become more ethically aware and manage with an ethical underpinning.

Source: Richardson, B and Thompson, J (1994) Strategic competency in the 1990s, *Administrator*, July.

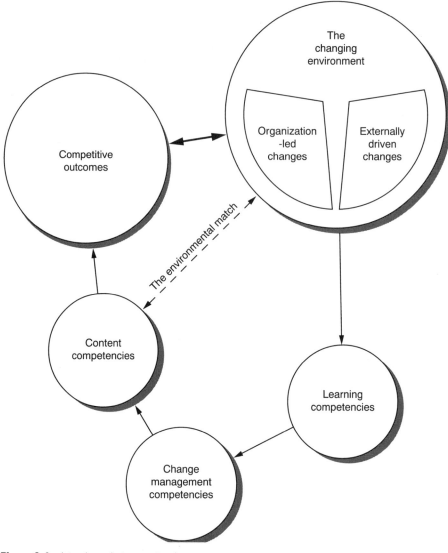

Figure 2.4 Inter-dependent competencies.

Consequently, Figure 2.5 again features strategy content and strategy pro-cesses; the third element of the model is the issues and dilemmas.

Strategic issues and dilemmas

This discussion introduces the topic; it is not intended to be fully comprehensive of all the issues and dilemmas that an organization faces.

A first and crucial issue is **size**. It is now quite normal to read that 'big is no longer beautiful', that it implies too much diversity and complexity. However, the issue of diversity is itself complex. Clearly, many large, diverse conglomerates have chosen to divest and focus, or, in cases such as ICI, split the organization into separate 'medium-sized' parts. The question remains: is a strategy of conglomerate diversification by nature a poor choice, or is it that many organizations are unable to *implement* the strategy and create a structure

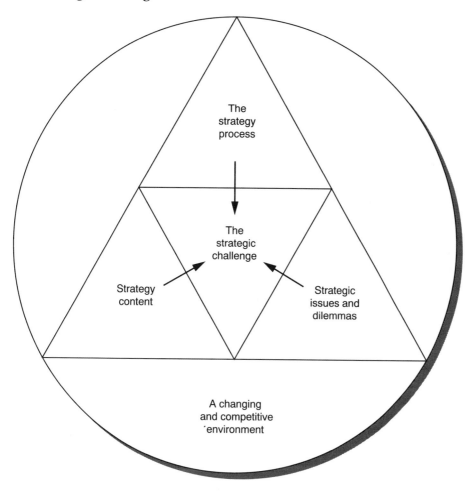

Figure 2.5   The strategic challenge.

whereby corporate headquarters can add value and foster the synergies which they believe exist? BTR and Hanson are successful, large, diversified conglomerates; they both adopt a financial control (Goold and Campbell, 1988) holding company style of corporate management. Styles of corporate management are discussed in depth in Chapter 20.

Focus can be achieved by concentrating on a limited number of clearly related (by marketing or technology) businesses. Some organizations are choosing to go further and divest activities and processes which are seen as non-core or non-essential. This is unlikely to mean they are no longer required at all, and consequently this strategy implies a need to develop a capability in managing networks and alliances.

'Small' meanwhile is dubbed innovative, creative and entrepreneurial. Small companies, though, are often fragile financially, often (not always) using low technology and featuring relatively poor working conditions. Successful ones, of course, grow to again become 'medium-sized'.

A second challenge is the attempt to **balance** and satisfy **the needs** and expectations **of** all the **stakeholders**. Shareholders, customers and employees have requirements which may conflict; moreover they can sometimes sharpen the tension between the short- and long-term perspectives. Most people would agree that a business must ensure it looks after its shareholders' investments and financial interests, but it would appear that organizations which balance the needs of all their stakeholders perform better (for their shareholders) in the long run. Whilst thinking about the various internal and external stakeholders, the organization, of course, must never lose sight of what competitors are doing.

Other tensions concern the marketing issues of **mass or niche** markets, and, in the case of larger businesses, how to balance **global and local** issues. Here, one challenge for larger companies concerns the potential benefits to be gained from thinking and behaving like fast-moving, flexible small organizations whilst obtaining the scale and synergy benefits which can accrue from size.

Many businesses need to develop a **culture of change orientation** without losing internal **cohesion and stability**. This implies an explicit and shared vision of where the organization is heading.

There is also a need to **decentralize** and give managers more delegated authority whilst not losing sight (at chief executive level) of the changes they are introducing. This involves a difficult trade-off between such empowerment (delegating real responsibility in order to make the business more effective in its relations with all its stakeholders) and the greater efficiencies often yielded by **centralized control** and systems which harness the latest information technology.

Visit the website: http://www. itbp.com

The revelation, in September 1995, that the estate agency subsidiary of the Halifax Building Society was paying its staff a bonus if they could sell houses by persuading clients to accept reduced prices, sparked an outcry. It was commented that the incident provoked an internal investigation and that the outcome was likely to lead to changes in the autonomy given to subsidiaries or stronger guidance on policy making.

Organizations must be able to **act quickly** in response to opportunities and threats, but not at the expense of product and service **quality** – achieving high quality at the same time as cutting costs and improving efficiencies.

In the early 1990s there was also the **dilemma of the recession.** Organizations must cut back, control their costs and accept lower margins when supply potential exceeds demand in an economic downturn. Profits fall. Paradoxically those competitors which are able to consolidate and invest strategically during a recession will be best prepared for the economic up-turn.

Finally, we are looking for the organization to be simultaneously **reactive and proactive**, planned and flexible, able to deal with pressures for both continuous and discontinuous change. These issues reinforce the paradox of **stability and instability**. Stability concerns running existing businesses efficiently and effectively, exploiting strategic abilities and continually looking to create higher returns from the committed resources. Instability refers to the search for the new competitive high ground ahead of one's rivals.

Dealing with these issues and dilemmas in a dynamic and unpredictable environment is clearly difficult; there are no easy answers and the situation is always fluid. Achieving success, therefore, again implies the creation and exploitation of key strategic competencies.

Collins and Porras (1995) have analysed a number of American companies which have proved to be resilient to the problems which hit them from time to time. Many Western companies have a life expectancy of less than 50 years; a select minority not only survive but thrive on change pressures. We appear to be able to take for granted that successful companies will be dedicated to customer service and all-round quality; they also typically feature an open culture with 'restless enquiry, learning and constant innovation'. Underpinning this is a strategic leader who is able to build an organization with appropriate values, principles and ways of thinking that will last through generations of shifting strategies. He or she need not be individually charismatic, though some clearly are.

Collins and Porras cite Walt Disney Corporation as a leading example. Walt Disney himself was charismatic, but the organization has survived and prospered since his death. The success of its theme parks, box office blockbusters such as The Lion King (1994) and Pocahontas (1995) and the 1995 acquisition of ABC, one of the USA's leading three television networks, are testimony to this. But there have been major setbacks at the same time, which Disney has had to weather. Jeffrey Katzenberg, head of the studios and the man responsible for several major film successes, left in 1994 when he was passed over for a promotion; he sought the number two post of President, vacant after the incumbent was killed in a helicopter accident. This happened shortly after the chief executive, Michael Eisner, had major heart surgery. In 1995 Disney abandoned its plans for a new Civil War theme park in Virginia, following an intensive protest campaign by environmentalists. During the early 1990s EuroDisney experienced severe financial difficulties.

Disney, according to Collins and Porras, relies more on experimentation than formal strategic planning; moreover, it effectively balances stability and change, integration and autonomy.

The issues and dilemmas we have introduced in this section will be examined in detail at various stages throughout the book.

Strategic success, failure and competency

The top part of Figure 2.6 synthesizes our arguments so far. Corporate strategic success, reflected in E–V–R congruence, is dependent upon the strategy content, the change process and dilemma management. A failure to control, change or innovate in a dynamic environment will engender a degree of incongruency and ultimately lead to corporate failure. It is, of course, conceivable that an new business will never establish a successful content–process–dilemma mix and consequently never enjoy congruency and success. The bottom part of the chart shows the range of generic strategic competencies centred around strategic leadership.

To ensure the existence of strategic competency, and to foster improvements, Richardson and Thompson further argue that organizations should seek to measure their competencies. Ideally these measures will be robust and objective and not simply subjective opinion or soundings. It is often argued that the introduction of measurement leads to improvement by focusing attention. However, caution is needed. Some of the competencies can be measured more readily than others; some can only be evaluated by more subjective performance indicators rather than by objective measures. Where attention is being focused by the demands of measurement, this attention should be on the factors which are most significant for strategic success rather than those which are easiest to measure.

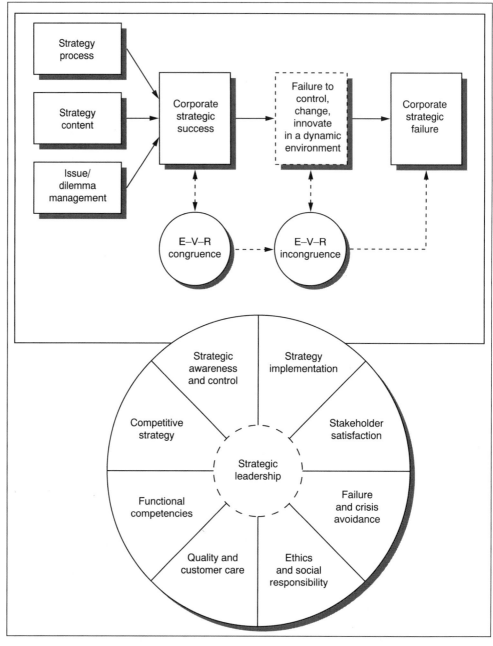

Figure 2.6   Success, failure and competency.

Summary

In this chapter we have:

- illustrated how strategic management can be seen as three inter-related aspects: strategic analysis (or awareness), strategic choice and strategy implementation
- developed a series of questions designed to provide insight into strategic awareness and strategic decision making – emphasizing that organizations should be addressing some or all of these on an on-going basis
- worked through a simple example using the questions
- examined a second framework which shows strategic success being dependent upon competencies in learning, strategy content and strategic change
- considered how the strategic challenge for organizations in the 1990s requires them to craft their strategy content and processes within the context of a set of key issues and dilemmas.

Research assignment

Library based

Take any organization that you are reasonably familiar with, for example the one you work for, one you have worked for, or maybe one that a member of your family works for, and:

either apply to it the ten questions provided with Case 2.1

or write down what you already know and can find out about it under the headings: environment, values and resources.

References and further reading

Collins, J and Porras, J (1995) *Built to Last*, Century Business.

Goold, M and Campbell, A (1988) *Strategies and Styles*, Blackwell.

Bartlett, CA and Ghoshal, S (1994) Beyond strategy to purpose, *Harvard Business Review*, November–December looks at how a study of strategic management has moved away from a focus on strategies, derived from planning, formal structures and systems which support structures, to an analysis of corporate purpose, processes and people who develop capabilities and competencies.

Much of the material included in this chapter is derived from earlier publications by Bill Richardson and John Thompson, including, in particular:

Strategic competency in the 1990s, *Administrator*, July 1994.

Strategy evaluation in powerful environments: A multi-competence approach, *Leadership and Organizational Development Journal*, **16**(4), July 1995.

Strategic and competitive success: Towards a model of the comprehensively competent organization, *Management Decision*, **34**(1), 1996.

3

Strategic Leadership and Decision Making

This is the first of two chapters which concentrate on the central core of the strategy framework (Figure 2.2). The nature, role and significance of strategic leadership are discussed, and issues of risk and entrepreneurship are explored. In addition we consider how decisions might be made in an organization.

Learning objectives

After studying this chapter you should be able to:

- define strategic leadership and identify the key roles of a strategic leader in the creation and implementation of strategy
- identify factors which contribute towards effective strategic leadership
- explain visionary leadership
- summarize a number of alternative theories of decision making
- define risk; and describe why different strategic leaders will have varying perceptions of what is an acceptable level of risk
- explain the significance of entrepreneurship, and describe entrepreneurial strategy making.

Don't forget to visit the website: http://www.itbp.com

Introduction

> The task of leadership, as well as providing the framework, values and motivation of people, and allocation of financial and other resources, is to set the overall direction which enables choices to be made so that the efforts of the company can be focused.

In this quotation, Sir John Harvey-Jones emphasizes the need for a clear direction for the organization.

It is the responsibility of the chief executive to clarify the mission and objectives of the organization, to define the corporate strategy which is intended to achieve these and to establish and manage the organization's structure. 'Mission' means the long-term objectives of the organization related to the strategic leader's vision of the nature and scope of the business or businesses that he or she feels would be appropriate and desirable.

The corporate strategy will be implemented within the structure, and this will introduce changes in competitive and functional strategies. The chief executive will also be a major influence on the organization's culture and values, which are key determinants of the ways in which strategies are created and implemented.

However, the chief executive is not the only creator of strategic change. Managers who are in charge of divisions or strategic business units (normally referred to as 'general managers') are also responsible for strategic changes concerning their own products, services or geographic territories. Functional managers will make and carry out decisions which result in strategic change. In many firms the chief executive will also act as chairman of the board, but in others he or she will be supported by a part-time, non-executive chairman who will contribute actively to corporate strategy decisions and external relations. In a limited number of large companies, particularly those which are diverse and multi-national, a chief operating officer will report directly to the chief executive. He or she will be responsible for ensuring that the operating parts of the business perform effectively, and consequently will influence changes in competitive and functional strategies. Throughout this book the term **strategic leader** is used to describe the managers who head the organization and who are primarily responsible for creating and implementing strategic change.

Whilst the strategic leader has overall responsibility for managing strategy in the organization it should not be thought that he or she is the sole source of thoughts and ideas. All employees can make a contribution, and should be encouraged to do so. The more that people are invited to participate in debate and discussions concerning products, services, markets and the future the more likely they are to accept changes.

The strategic leader, however, is in a unique position to gather and receive information about all aspects of the business, and it is encumbent on him or her to monitor the environment and the organization and watch for opportunities and threats. He or she will need both analytical skills and insight (or 'awareness') to provide an intuitive grasp of the situation that faces the organization. The way the organization manages to grasp opportunities and overcome potential threats will be very dependent on the personal qualities and values of the strategic leader.

Strategic leadership

The role of the strategic leader

The strategic leader is responsible directly to the Board of Directors of the organization, and, through the Board, to the stakeholders in the business. The responsibilities of the Board, and, in effect, the strategic leader, are featured in Box 3.1.

The strategic leader must **direct** the organization. He or she must ensure that long-term objectives and strategies have been determined and that they are understood and supported by managers within the organization who will be responsible for implementing them. The more feasible and achievable the objectives and strategies seem, the more likely they are to be supported.

These intended strategies will be implemented through the **organization structure** the strategic leader adopts. Some intended strategies will prove not to be feasible – the assumptions on which they are based may be wrong, and circumstances can change – and they will be discarded or postponed. Decisions taken by general and functional managers within a decentralized structure will lead to new, incremental and adaptive changes in competitive and functional strategies. A third major responsibility of the strategic leader is a system of **communications** which firstly enables managers throughout the organization to be strategically aware, and secondly ensures that the strategic leader stays informed of the changes that are taking place.

Box 3.1
The responsibilities of the board of directors

1. Manage the business on behalf of all the stakeholders (or interested parties)
2. Provide direction in the form of a mission or purpose
3. Formulate and implement changes to corporate strategies
4. Monitor and control operations with special reference to financial results, productivity, quality, customer service, innovation and new products and services and staff development

5. Provide policies and guidelines for other managers to facilitate both the management of operations and changes in competitive and functional strategies.

Responsibility 5 is achieved through the organization structure; 2 and 4 are dependent on an effective communications network.

I believe that increasing shareholder value is the key to profitable industrial growth. The choice, motivation and direction of management is crucial. Leaders should not be slow constantly to encourage change. They should see all problems as solvable and all questions as answerable.

Lord Hanson, founder and executive chairman of the renowned and very successful Hanson plc, who believes that he has personally been a successful strategic leader because he has:

❑ *ensured he has stayed informed*
❑ *wanted to actually do things in business*
❑ *deployed his not inconsiderable energy into making things happen*
❑ *been able to inspire others to do things*
❑ *stayed responsive to change pressures.*

Figure 3.1 extends these three contributions into seven themes which are discussed below.

Strategic vision

At the heart of this is a clear, understood and supported mission for the organization. Employees must appreciate the fundamental purpose and be committed to its achievement; the mission will provide guidance and direction when managers make decisions and implement strategies determined by others. The mission may be the vision of the current strategic leader; equally it may have been established by a predecessor. Similarly, the actual strategies – corporate and competitive – for achieving long-term objectives may be created personally by a strong or visionary strategic leader, or they may be ideas from anywhere inside the organization.

Pragmatism

This is the ability to make things happen and bring positive results. This implies that the organization's resources are managed efficiently and effectively, issues we develop in Chapter 6. Some strategic leaders will be *doers*, active in carrying strategies through; others will be delegators who rely instead on their skills for

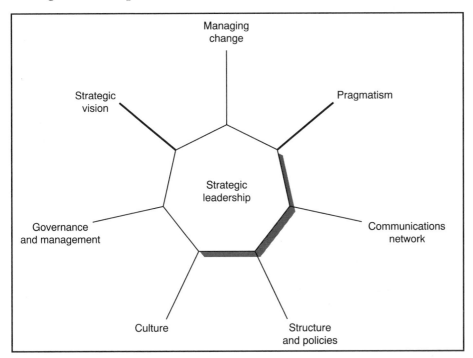

Figure 3.1   Strategic leadership.

motivating and inspiring. Control systems for monitoring results and strategic effectiveness are also important.

Some corporate leaders, then, will be strategic visionaries who are also active in operations; others will contribute ideas and leadership but be happy to devolve operational responsibility. It is possible for pragmatic but non-visionary leaders to be highly effective as long as they ensure the organization has a clear and appropriate purpose and direction. The dangers here are, first, that short-term success can sometimes be the result of efficient management against a background of friendly market forces (which can, of course, quickly become less friendly) and, second, that when previously successful strategies are in need of renewal, a non-visionary may fail to provide the appropriate leadership and champion the necessary changes. Consequently, Bennis (1988) suggests that vision is crucial and that the most effective leaders are those with ideas. This accords with the view of Sir Winston Churchill who believed that the 'emperor of the future will be the emperor of ideas'.

The strategic leader's vision and his or her record of achievement are critical for obtaining and maintaining the confidence and support of influential stake-holders, especially the very important institutional shareholders. The willing-ness of large shareholders to hold or sell their shares, and their expressed support for company strategies, are essential for maintaining a healthy share price and reducing the likelihood of a takeover. Their confidence in the ability of the leader is a major determinant; on occasions it is shareholder pressure which forces a change of leadership.

As well as vision and pragmatism it is necessary for the leader to build a structure and culture which captures the abilities and contributions of other managers and employees.

Governance and management

Corporate governance relates to the location and exercise of power and responsibility at the head of the organization, and it is discussed in detail later in the chapter. In simple terms, it is vital that the strategic leader ensures that there is a strong, competent and balanced executive team at the head of the organization.

Structure and policies

It is the strategic leader who decides on the appropriate structure for carrying out existing strategies and ensuring there is proper momentum for change.
  The issues are:

❑ Should the organization be relatively flat and informal or have several layers of management and more formality?
❑ Should it be split into individual businesses or divisions?
❑ How much power and responsibility should be delegated and decentralized?
❑ What is the appropriate role for the corporate headquarters?
❑ How might planning systems be used to direct and co-ordinate the various parts of the organization?
❑ To what extent should managers and other employees be empowered to take more responsibility?
❑ What structures and mechanisms are required to ensure that managers in different business areas and different functions integrate and plan how they can help each other? In other words, planning synergies through effective organizational teamworking.
❑ What policies are necessary and appropriate for guiding and directing decision making?

These issues are explored in greater detail in later chapters.

The communications network

Effective communication systems, both formal and informal, are required to share the strategic vision and inform people of priorities and strategies and to ensure strategies and tasks are carried out expeditiously. Where the organization is decentralized an effective communications network is vital for feeding information *upwards and laterally* inside the organization; without this control will be lost. In quite different ways, both 'managing by wandering around'

A lot of people want to be led; there are very few leaders in life. When people have a good leader who instills team spirit, and they live in an environment that demands excellence, energy and the keeping up of momentum in order to achieve a goal, then they want to stay, or, if they leave, they want to come back.

Linda J Wachner, CEO, Warnaco (US)

To be effective, leadership has to be seen, and it is best seen in action. Leadership must be communicated in words, but even more importantly in deeds, by example. Leaders must be seen to be up-front, up-to-date, up to their jobs and up early in the morning.
Lord Sieff of Brimpton, Chairman, Marks and Spencer, 1972–1984. See: Marcus Sieff on Management, Weidenfeld and Nicholson, 1990

and budgetary control systems can help achieve this co-ordination. Good lateral communications also help managers to learn from other parts of the business; this in turn can lead to 'best pratices' being shared.

In addition the strategic leader must champion the relationships between the organization and its important stakeholders, particularly its financiers, suppliers and major customers. Effective communications with government agencies and the media may also prove to be critically important.

Culture

To a great extent the culture of the organization is dictated by the strategic leader. The attitudes and behaviours of people are affected as well as their willingness to accept responsibility and take measured risks.

The strategic leader may have very clear or specific values which influence his or her style, and the culture of the organization. For example if the leader has a financial background and orientation, this may prove important. Financial targets and analysis may be crucial elements in the management of strategy. Similarly if the leader has a marketing background this could result in a different style of leadership, with perhaps more concentration on consumers and competition. An engineer may be very committed to product design and quality. These comments are generalizations, and will not always prove to be true; clearly, over a period of time a strategic leader is likely to become more of a generalist and less of a specialist. If a new strategic leader is appointed from another company it is inevitable he or she will bring values which have been learned elsewhere, and these may involve change. Logically the person will be chosen because of his or her successful record in one or more previous companies; and the newcomer may be determined to establish his or her presence by introducing changes.

Visit the website:
http://www.
itbp.com

Managing change

The importance attached to formal planning processes and emergent strategy creation in an organization will depend upon the personal preferences and the styles of management adopted by the strategic leader. Simply, the organization must be able to respond to the change pressures of a competitive environment. Curiosity, creativity and innovation become critically important values, and it is important for the strategic leader to ensure they become part of the corporate culture. However, whilst learning and incremental change is crucially important it may not be sufficient. As we saw in Chapter 1, *discontinuous change* and **strategic regeneration** will be necessary for organizations at certain stages in their life cycles. When this is the case, and strategies, structures and styles of management need re-inventing simultaneously, an effective, visionary leader will be essential.

The importance of an *effective* strategic leader cannot be stressed too highly, but of course an individual leader cannot and should not attempt to 'do everything'. An important skill is the ability to understand personal strengths and limitations and appreciate the most appropriate ways of contributing.

There is no single, recommended style for effective strategic leadership. Some leaders are autocratic, others democratic in the way they make decisions. Some rely on planning and analysis, others are more intuitive and visionary. Leaders vary in the degree of risk they will accept willingly. Some look for consistency as far as is practicable in today's dynamic environments; others are constantly opportunistic and driving change. Some pursue growth through efficiency and cost savings, others by adding new values in an innovatory climate. Some set very ambitious growth objectives; others are more modest. All of these styles can prove effective; the challenge lies in creating and maintaining E–V–R congruence.

It is always important to evaluate the leader's position and situation. A strategic leader may be the founder of an organization and still in control; he or she may be a later family generation. The leader may have 'risen through the ranks' to take control, or he or she may have been brought in specially, possibly to turn around a company in difficulty. The leader may be relatively new or have been in post for some time. The style of leadership adopted will depend upon the leader's preferred style, his or her background and the situational circumstances.

Box 3.2
EFFECTIVE AND INEFFECTIVE LEADERSHIP

Qualities and skills for effective leadership

❏ A vision – articulated through the culture and value systems.

❏ The ability to build and control an effective team of managers.

❏ Belief in success and in corporate strengths and competencies which can be exploited.

❏ The ability to recognize and synthesize important developments, both inside and outside the organization. This requires strategic awareness, the ability to judge the significance of an observed event, and conceptualization skills.

❏ Effective decentralization, delegation and motivation (the appropriate extent will vary).

❏ Credibility and competence. 'Knowing what you are doing' and having this recognized. This requires the abilities to exercise power and influence and to create change.

❏ Implementation skills; getting things done, which requires drive, decisiveness and dynamism.

❏ Perseverance and persistence in pursuing the mission or vision, plus mental and physical stamina.

❏ Flexibility; recognizing the need (on occasions) to change strategies, structures and style. Some leaders, of course, are single style and inflexible.

Characteristics of ineffective leadership

After some period of time in office some leaders appear to coast, enjoying their power and status, but no longer adding any real value to the organization. Specifically:

❏ There are few new initiatives; instead there is a reliance on tinkering with existing strategies to try and update past successes.

❏ Good new products and services are not developed.

❏ The leader surrounds himself or herself with loyal supporters, rather than enjoying the stimulus of newcomers with fresh mind-sets.

❏ Moreover, discordant views are either ignored or not tolerated.

❏ Cash reserves, beyond those needed to sustain a period of depressed sales, are allowed to accrue.

❏ The leader becomes out of touch with the views of customers and the activities of competitors.

❏ Too much time is spent by the leader on external activities, without ensuring other managers are dealing with important organizational issues.

Sources: Bennis, W, Interview recorded in Crainer, S (1988), Doing the right thing, *Director*, October; Boyle, D and Braddick, B (1981) *The Challenge of Change: Business Leaders for the 1980s*, Gower in association with Ashridge Management College; Kets de Vries, MFR (1989) *Prisoners of Leadership*, John Wiley; Kets de Vries, MFR (1994) CEOs also have the blues, *European Management Journal*, 12, 3; The author.

Box 3.2 provides a summary of the qualities and skills required for effective leadership, together with a list of the factors which typically characterize ineffective leadership.

A number of these themes are illustrated in Case 3.1 on Tom Farmer, founder of Kwik Fit. Tom Farmer imported his vision for Kwik Fit from America; success has involved opportunism and innovation backed up by sound business sense.

Case 3.1
TOM FARMER, KWIK FIT

Tom Farmer was born into a working-class family in Edinburgh in 1940; he was the seventh child. He left school at the age of 15 and began working in a tyre company. In 1964 he set up his own business, retailing tyres at discount prices. He quickly expanded from one to four outlets, and after four years sold the whole business for £450,000 to Albany Tyres. He 'retired' and went to live in California. Within three years he and his wife were bored. He returned to Scotland, but, because of his agreement with Albany, he could not start a new tyre retailing business.

Instead he brought over an idea he had seen in the USA: a fast-change exhaust shop. Again he quickly expanded from one to four outlets – so that he could re-employ a number of his old friends! As for the Kwik Fit name – he just dreamed it up.

Farmer is a workaholic, very committed to his business and his 5000 employees. Private garages and repair shops are often thought to involve dubious commercial practices; one of Tom Farmer's major achievements has been to bring a high level of perceived (and real) integrity into the industry. He places a strong emphasis on good customer service and friendliness, attributes which are featured in distinctive Kwik Fit advertisements.

By the early 1980s there were 200 depots; arguably the business grew too quickly. Inadequate management control left the company vulnerable to takeover for a while, but it has managed to retain its independence. For 29 years the company grew organically and stayed focused. There has been some geographic expansion – successfully in Belgium and Holland, but Kwik Fit has withdrawn from France. 'There are cultural differences. The French want to close for lunch. French managers are reluctant to bond with their employees. These are key Kwik Fit values.'

In 1994 Kwik Fit acquired 125 Superdrive Motoring Centres from Shell; a related business. In 1995 Kwik Fit Insurance was launched. Farmer argues it is based on the same principles: high service using someone else's products.

All of Tom Farmer's employees are on profit-share schemes; half are individual shareholders in the business.

In an interview with *Management Today* (August 1995) Tom Farmer made the following comments.

> If the customer is king, the staff are emperors.

> We don't have a head office; we have a support office. We don't have senior management; we have support management.

Yet Farmer is seen as a demanding man to work for – many employees are 'rather frightened of him'.

> All sound businesses are built on good Christian ethics: don't steal, don't exploit your customers or your people, always use your profits for the benefit of your people and the community.

None of these beliefs mean, of course, that an entrepreneur cannot live comfortably. Farmer has a large house, a corporate jet and a helicopter.

> We are in business to make a profit and we should not be ashamed of that, provided we stick to sound principles, and, at the end of the day, do proper things with that profit.

Footnote: Culture and values are the subject of Chapter 4; the profit objective is debated in Chapter 5.

Visionary leadership and strategy creation

Visionary leadership implies a strategic leader with a personal vision for the future of the organization and at least a broad idea of the strategies for pursuing the vision. Such leadership often appears to be based on intuition and possibly experience rather than detailed analysis, but truly visionary leaders possess strategic awareness and insight and do not require extensive analyses to understand key success factors and how the organization can use its abilities and competencies to satisfy needs and expectations. There is a 'feel' for which strategies will be appropriate and feasible and for the potential of the opportunity.

When a visionary leader pursues new opportunities and introduces changes the detailed plans for implementing the new strategies are unlikely to be in place; instead there will be a reliance on incremental learning, flexibility and adaption. For the approach to succeed, the leader must be able to inspire others and persuade them of the logic and merits of the new strategies. This is true for all important strategic changes, of course, but when new proposals have emerged from a more formal strategic planning system there will be substantive detail and analysis to justify the case instead of a strong reliance on vision and intuition.

Where major changes to the corporate strategy are being considered it may be necessary for the strategic leader to convince other members of the Board of Directors and, if new funding is needed, the institutional shareholders and bankers.

The strategy cannot be successful until it has been implemented and has brought the desired results and rewards. Such outcomes require the support and commitment of other managers, and consequently effective visionaries are often articulate, communicative and persuasive leaders.

In simple terms, then, visionary strategic leadership implies three steps: step one is the vision; step two is selling it to other stakeholders and managers; and step three is making sure it happens. Aspects of vision, communication and pragmatism.

Richardson (1994) suggests the following factors are typical of visionary leadership:

- ❑ 'covert' planning – planning is often cerebral rather than formal and systematic, such that planning *systems* are not a major aspect of strategy creation
- ❑ a passion about what they are doing and their business
- ❑ they are instrumental in creating and fostering a particular culture
- ❑ they are highly persuasive when encouraging others to implement their ideas and strategies
- ❑ they rely on charisma and personal power.

Founders of successful, fast-growing businesses are frequently visionary. Bill Gates, founder of Microsoft, had a vision of a computer on 'every' desktop in every office, providing timely information; he was the first to truly capitalize on the software opportunity this vision provided. In contrast, Alan Sugar (Amstrad) has built a business around a vision of imaginatively-designed but low-price electronics products, marketed aggressively to the consumer mass market. Anita Roddick's vision for the Body Shop is based on natural, environmentally-friendly cosmetics and related products.

These three leaders represent different backgrounds, styles and strategies; they can also justifiably be called **entrepreneurs**. An entrepreneur, basically, is someone who starts and develops a business, but we normally associate the term with businesses which grow, rather than stay small and localized.

In this book a *visionary* strategic leader is seen, typically, as someone who is an agent of change, either starting a new, differentiated business which takes off, or changing the direction and corporate strategy of a business in order to maintain or improve its rate of growth. Major, discontinuous change is implied. Whilst entrepreneurship again implies growth, the growth need not be visionary or discontinuous.

However, we need to be careful. A strategic leader who succeeds in turning around a company in crisis and *restores growth* can be a visionary. At the same time, it does not follow that visionary leadership is necessary for either new ventures or turnaround situations. When a company is in trouble, a good, analytical 'company doctor' who can restructure, rationalize and refocus the business can be very effective.

Individual managers, responsible for competitive and functional strategies, can be *entrepreneurial* and lead incremental or adaptive changes on a relatively small scale. Again, they are agents of change in a *decentralized* organization. For clarity, this is often described as *intrapreneurship* and it is something we will consider in more detail towards the end of the chapter, when we also consider the underlying economic importance of entrepreneurship.

Corporate governance

Box 3.1 earlier summarized the main responsibilities of the Board of Directors of an organization. The execution of these responsibilities is normally through the appointment of a chief executive; but the Board will also have a chairman to oversee decision making and operations. The chairman will additionally be responsible for ensuring that the structure and composition of the Board is appropriate.

There are two contentious issues. First: should the roles of chairman and chief executive be separated or combined? This is debated in Box 3.3. Second, what contribution should be made by non-executive directors, i.e. members of the Board who are not employed as executives within the firm? There are conflicting opinions on these issues, and no straightforward answers. The challenge is to ensure that there is effective leadership and control, and objectivity. This requires strong and capable leaders, but also opportunities for debate amongst the key executives who are responsible for both the creation and implementation of strategic change. Objectivity can often be improved by the appointment of outside non-executive directors with the ability to contribute particular skills and expertise. The Guinness affair in the mid-1980s, which concerned illegal share support operations during an acquisition, has been partially blamed on a Board which was not properly informed and objective. Strong and independent non-executive directors might have alleviated the difficulties.

A 1992 report by the Committee on Financial Aspects of Corporate Governance (chaired by Sir Adrian Cadbury) recommended that

❑ Board authority should be divided between a chairman and chief executive – but if Boards chose to combine the roles they should ensure 'the presence of a strong independent element with an appointed leader'

Box 3.3
CORPORATE GOVERNANCE

The topic for debate: *Should organizations separate the roles of chairman and chief executive, or combine them?*

If they are separated the chairman could be either executive (full-time) or non-executive (part-time). Typically a non-executive chairman would act as a sounding board for the chief executive, manage Board meetings and liaise with institutional shareholders. The chief executive would be in charge of both strategy and control. An executive chairman would accept responsibility for corporate strategy, with the chief executive controlling the business.

The majority of institutional shareholders in the UK favour a split in the roles for public companies; but not all large companies agree. Over 25% of the largest 100 UK companies combine the roles, many of them, including BOC, Grand Metropolitan and Kingfisher (Woolworths), successfully.

The case for the combined role
❑ Allows for clear, strong and accountable leadership
❑ Part-time, non-executive, chairmen are unsuitable for large, complex, multi-national businesses – the job is too demanding
❑ A non-executive deputy chairman is an ideal compromise
❑ The strength of the Board as a whole, in terms of both executive and non-executive directors, is a more critical issue

❑ The executive workload can be spread amongst all the executive directors, allowing for greater cohesion.

However: It is important to ensure that the strategic leader does not become lonely and isolated.

The case for splitting the roles
❑ More likely to guarantee proper checks and balances
❑ Ideal way of tightening control over strategic decision making without placing it in the hands of one person – large Boards are not always going to agree
❑ Allows for complementary skills, with each role requiring different expertise
❑ Succession issues are likely to be less complicated.

However: It is critical that the two people involved generally agree with each other and can work together.

Clearly there is no single answer which is appropriate for all companies. Strategic demands vary and individual abilities differ. The challenge is to establish both clear leadership and objectivity.

Adapted from: Morrison, R (1991) Two views on a split personality, *Financial Times*, 4 October.

The role of management is to maximize within a given environment. The role of the Board is to change the environment to the benefit of the company.

The best Boards have a mix of experiences, backgrounds, qualifications and ages, giving the strength of the mongrel, rather than the weakness of the pedigree.

Roy Watts, Chairman, Thames Water

❑ more decisions should be deferred to non-executive directors – who should also constitute an audit and remuneration committee
❑ more information should be given to shareholders.

The Committee and its findings are supported by the Confederation of British Industry, the Stock Exchange and the Institutional Shareholders Committee, but the recommendations are voluntary.

The importance of good governance has been highlighted in the early 1990s with a number of controversies surrounding the pay levels and share option schemes for senior managers in the privatized utility companies.

Corporate governance varies between countries, and it could impact increasingly on corporate strategies as companies become more global, and seek to acquire businesses, or set up joint ventures, more widely. Germany, for example, employs a two-tier Board structure to introduce checks and balances and ensure that employees, as well as shareholders, are properly represented. In France and Italy executives wield significant power and are rarely challenged by shareholders. In Japan, shareholders again tend to be passive, and the Board, essentially an extension of management, has no independent powers.

The contribution of non-executive directors

In thinking about the future direction of the organization, strategic leaders can, and will, seek advice and ideas from a variety of people, including fellow managers, outside contacts and non-executive directors.

Historically there has been some tendency to regard non-executive directors as people who contribute little more than their actual presence at Board meetings. However, I believe that this represents a wasted opportunity. It can prove useful, for example, to appoint an external director who understands the mood and mentality of the City, in addition to having contacts who might help with financing arrangements. The potentially significant role of City analysts and institutional investors is discussed later in the book.

Smaller companies, who may not employ experts in every functional area, can obtain their expertise from non-executives. New businesses, run by young managers, can obtain experience by appointing older or even retired businessmen who understand their products, services and markets. Most companies, in fact, could benefit from fresh insights from people whose perspective is different from that of the executive directors and managers. However, it will be important for the strategic leader to make use of their expertise by keeping

---

The traditional British unitary board structure is at its least effective in the strategy debate. It is essential for non-executive directors to play a positive and leading role when the issue of 'change' and 'response to change' is, or should be, on the agenda. Non-executive directors often prefer to remain low-key in the face of executive self-assurance. This is fundamentally wrong, since it is in the areas of broad-brush strategy, economic overviews, political evolution and the like, that experienced non-executive directors can offer most; while executives may have a narrower focus.

Moral: More non-executives and ensure that they speak their minds.

Alick Rankin, when Chairman, Scottish & Newcastle Breweries plc

Table 3.1
The Composition of UK Boards
of Directors, 1995

	All PLCs	Financial Times 100 Share Index Companies
Average number of directors	7	12
Percentage of these who are non-executive	51%	50%
Companies with a combined chairman/chief executive role	11%	6%*
Companies with a non-executive chairman	84%	84%†

*25 years ago this was 50%.
†21%, 25 years ago.
Source: *Hemmington Scott*.

them informed and discussing matters with them, rather than simply inviting them along to Board meetings.

Ideally there will be only limited interference from non-executives when things are progressing well, but they will be there when they are needed. A final essential contribution they can make is to stand aside and appraise the performance of the strategic leader and the other executive directors more objectively than they can do it themselves.

Finally, it is important to emphasize that whilst non-executive directors provide checks and balances on senior management teams, the performance of the non-executives should also be appraised.

Table 3.1 provides a brief summary of the composition of UK Boards in 1995.

Issues in strategic leadership

Finite shelf lives?

All leaders, including the most successful, have finite shelf lives, periods of time when they can contribute effectively to an organization. Some know when to step down and either retire or move on – before they cease to be effective. Others stay too long and risk being remembered for their later shortcomings rather than their earlier successes. Churchill was at his peak at the end of World War II; Margaret Thatcher achieved her zenith once the main planks of Thatcherite reform were in place. When she stayed on, opposition to her later policies began to ferment; the details of her downfall will be remembered at least as much as her achievements. Case 3.2 looks at another long-standing strategic leader who eventually lost the confidence of his Board.

Kets de Vries (1994) argues that chief executives who fail to make a timely exit go through a three-phase life cycle. As we progress through the 1990s, the length of this life cycle is shortening. The first stage is the entry of a new strategic leader into the organization, which is followed by experimentation

One certain way to ensure that your advice is rejected, is to prescribe exactly how the problem should be dealt with.

Sir John Harvey-Jones commenting on the role of non-executive directors

Case 3.2
Volvo

Volvo was led from 1971 to 1993 by Pehr Gyllenhammar, a lawyer who was married to the daughter of the previous chief executive. Gyllenhammar has been credited as a visionary leader who failed to implement many critical strategic proposals.

In the early 1970s he realized Volvo was reliant on a limited product range (essentially large cars, trucks and buses) and constrained by Sweden not being a member of the European Community. He acquired Daf from the Dutch government; a prolonged learning curve was required before Volvo's subsequent range of small cars proved successful. He began to build the first foreign-owned car assembly plant in the USA; production never started. He opened the revolutionary Kalmar assembly plant in Sweden in 1974, based on autonomous work groups rather than the traditional assembly line; the idea was successful, but not outstandingly so, and Kalmar was closed in 1993. In 1977 a proposed merger with Saab-Scania was abandoned when Saab had second thoughts. In 1978 Gyllenhammar agreed to sell 40% of Volvo to the Norwegian government in exchange for oil rights; Volvo's shareholders revolted.

In the 1980s Volvo acquired a US truck business and diversified into the food and drug industries in Sweden, but not without some friction with the Swedish government. Throughout this period Volvo's car subsidiary enjoyed continuing success, albeit with its relatively staid image and reputation.

In 1989 Volvo and Renault cemented a strategic alliance with the exchange of minority shareholdings; and in 1993 a full merger was proposed. Fearing the future role of the French government (Renault was nationalized but due for privatization), Volvo's shareholders again refused to back Gyllenhammar. After this defeat he resigned. Despite all the setbacks, Volvo has proved to be robust and, under Gyllenhammar, has grown into one of Sweden's leading businesses.

The diversification strategies have been focused on less cyclical industries to offset the uneven cash flow characteristics of car manufacturing, but a new corporate strategy was announced in April 1994. Non-vehicle interests would be divested systematically. Vehicle joint ventures with a series of companies world-wide would be sought.

Gyllenhammar's successor as chief executive, Sören Gyll, appears to be more of a team player. The new strategy for cars has been the responsibility of a new divisional head. In 1995 Volvo changed the marketing strategy for its cars, attempting to shift away from an image built wholly on safety, reliability and (more recently) environmental friendliness, to one of 'safe but sexy'. Advertisements claimed that (when accelerating in top gear) a Volvo 850 can outpace a Ferrari. The aim is to attract younger 'pre-family' and older 'post-family' buyers without losing the core 'family' customers and increase output by one third.

In addition, Volvo has entered into a new joint venture with Britain's TWR (sports car manufacturer) to produce coupé and cabriolet versions of the top-of-the-range Volvo 850.

with new strategies. Downsizing, acquisitions, re-engineering and a drive for improved service and quality are likely. The newcomers make their mark; results improve, certainly in the short-term. This becomes the second stage of consolidation, when it is likely that the changes are cemented in a new culture. If an organization was in crisis, the risks are now perceived to have fallen back; and herein can lie the seeds of a new crisis. The third stage, then, is one of decline and a new crisis.

The appropriate style

Visionary leadership is frequently associated with entrepreneurial strategies for companies enjoying prosperity in growth markets. As the organization continues to grow a more formal structure, together with robust control systems, will be required. The leader must therefore be flexible, capable of adapting and willing to relinquish some personal control. Ideally other managers will be empowered and encouraged to also be entrepreneurial and visionary.

This will not always happen – some visionary leaders tend to be inflexible. In such circumstances a change of leader would benefit the organization.

Similarly, companies in trouble, facing a strategic crisis or which need rationalizing require a leader who is skilled at managing detail and resources to generate, productivity improvements – again different characteristics from the visionary. However, as we highlighted earlier, once such an organization has been successfully rationalized, fresh growth requires vision, and here a more visionary leader can again prove ideal.

Succeeding a visionary

Unless proper plans are made, succession can be a critical issue. Unfortunately, many visionary leaders are driven by personal ambition and a personal vision; they are difficult to work with and they do not share their 'game plan'. As a consequence, they fail to build a pipeline of managers ready for succession. This raises a number of possible problem scenarios:

❑ owner-managed businesses may need to be sold, but once an entrepreneurial leader has left, what is the true value of the remaining assets?
❑ on a visionary's retirement a complete outsider may be needed, implying major change
❑ the leader could have an accident or illness, leaving a yawning gap which cannot be filled in time to prevent a crisis.

Grand Metropolitan, which has had four chief executives since it was created in 1957, provides an example of a company which has managed succession effectively. The first strategic leader was the founder, Sir Maxwell Joseph, who ran the business for 23 years. He started with hotels, later diversifying into restaurants, brewing, spirits, foods and leisure. When he retired in 1980 Grand Met was 90% dependent on the UK; and his successor, Sir Stanley Grinstead, was determined to reduce this. Grand Met began to invest in the USA. Sir Allen Sheppard took over for ten years in 1986 and his strategy was to focus where Grand Met could attain world leadership. This would be selected branded foods – Pillsbury (Green Giant foods, Burger King and Häagen Dazs ice cream) was acquired – and spirits. Remaining non-core businesses have been divested. In recent years Grand Met has been increasingly decentralized to speed up decision making. See Case 15.8

Leadership and corporate failure

Businesses 'fail' when they fail to meet the needs and expectations of their key stakeholders, or when decisions they take lead to outcomes which are unacceptable to the stakeholders. These 'failings' may generate crises which the business is able to deal with, usually at a cost; they may also lead to the ultimate collapse of the organization. The outcomes can take a variety of different forms, but authors such as Slatter (1984) have clearly identified three main, direct causes of corporate failure and collapse:

❑ weak or inappropriate strategic leadership
❑ marketing and competitive failings
❑ poor financial management and control.

It can be seen how these failings imply an *incongruency*, or lack of fit, between environment, values and resources, resulting from a lack of strategic awareness. Leadership issues obviously also underpin the marketing and financial weaknesses.

Richardson *et al.* (1994) have identified a number of discrete failure crisis situations, against which we can consider strategic leadership.

A ***niche becomes a tomb*** when a small company, locked into a successful product or service, 'lives in the past' and fails to change. This is invariably a sign of poor leadership, and quite frequently it will be tied in to succession problems. When ***markets are not understood*** small companies will fail to establish a position in the market they have targeted and simply not take-off and grow. Sometimes this will be the result of attention being concentrated on the production aspects of the business, where the entrepreneur may have expertise, at the expense of customer needs and expectations. Equally sales may be achieved, but not in sufficient volume. In a similar way, larger companies can misjudge markets. The innovative Clive Sinclair, with his ill-fated C5 electric car, is an example of this point.

Strategic drift with larger organizations is the result of introversion and inertia in a changing environment. Complacency from past success, or a concentration on day-to-day reactive or crisis management, can lead to a failure situation. The company does not spot emerging threats until it is too late to deal with them easily. By the early 1980s the once very successful ICI was under-performing in markets threatened by new, strong competitors; the company was top heavy, inward-looking and partially reliant on outmoded capacity. Sir John Harvey-Jones became chairman and proceeded to turn ICI around, but at the cost of lost capacity and lost jobs. Nevertheless, after Harvey-Jones retired, ICI was still vulnerable to threat. The acquisition of a block of shares by Hanson drew attention to the fact that ICI comprised two very different businesses with different cultures and key success factors, mature bulk chemicals and pharmaceuticals. The company was subsequently split in two: ICI and Zeneca.

Over-ambition can be seen in the guise of the failed entrepreneur and the failed conglomerate kingmaker. The former enjoys early success and rapid growth on the back of a good product or service, but the desire to maintain high growth encourages the entrepreneur to diversify into less profitable areas. A downward spiral begins. The conglomerate kingmaker wants to build a large and powerful corporation and is tempted to acquire businesses which cannot be justified financially. Specifically they pay a price which either over-values the assets or which cannot be recouped from earnings, or they over-estimate the potential for synergy with the existing businesses.

Good examples of this type of failure are provided by George Davies at Next and John Ashcroft at Coloroll; both businesses diversified, grew too rapidly in the 1980s and were financially embarrassed when trading conditions worsened. Both strategic leaders left. George Walker, founder of property development and leisure company, Brent Walker, suffered a similar fate. Brent Walker acquired the William Hill chain of betting shops from Grand

Visit the website:
`http://www.itbp.com`

Metropolitan, a diversification demanding completely new skills which again overstretched the company financially.

Failures of this nature are frequently characterized by strong, powerful strategic leaders and inadequate attention to critical financial measures and controls. In some instances the result is ***inadequate governance***. The business does not appear to be looking after the interests of all its stakeholders, but instead is driven by the strong, selfish and personal motives of the leader. Small businessmen will sometimes borrow money on the strength of the business and then milk it dry. Because they enjoy total control, their judgement is not questioned. Some leaders of large corporations, Robert Maxwell was an example, rule by fear and coercion, and as a result their actions are largely unchecked. Maxwell was driven by the desire to build a global empire and to receive recognition and acceptance.

Disagreements with the City

Earlier in this chapter we debated the topic of corporate governance, where there is an argument that individual strategic leaders should not be allowed to become so powerful that there are no effective checks and balances on their activities. A similar argument is often made for the role of the stock market and, in particular, institutional block shareholders. Institutional shareholders own over two-thirds of all UK shares, with private shareholdings amounting to some 20%. In the early 1970s, the respective percentages were 39 and 54. Institutions have their own shareholders, and consequently they pay close attention to the performance of the businesses in which they have invested.

Supporters of the stock market claim that institutional restrictions on management behaviour are a positive benefit for a company in terms of discipline and performance measurement. Critics suggest that the constant fluctuation in share prices, resulting from changes to both short-term performance and future expectations, is a deterrent to the long-term investment that is vital for future growth and success. This particular debate is continued in Chapter 5.

Although almost all of Britain's largest companies are quoted on the stock exchange, in large part due to their need for equity funding at certain stages of their development, some of the country's most dynamic entrepreneurs find this to be an uncomfortable state. They perceive the price of being a public company too high. Richard Branson (Virgin) and Andrew Lloyd Webber (The Really Useful Group) both bought back and reprivatized the successful companies they had developed. Fortunes in the entertainment business can fluctuate upwards and downwards quickly and dramatically; consequently some believe the stock market will be tempted to underestimate the true long-term value of the business and mark down the share price accordingly. The company is then undervalued.

Alan Sugar has also tried to privatize Amstrad but so far he has not been successful. The Body Shop, featured later in Case 4.3, began to explore the feasibility of privatization in 1995.

Falls from grace

Institutional pressures, then, can ensure that the strategic leader is held accountable for his or her strategic decisions and the performance of the company. Three years after the Stock Market crash of 1987, only one chief executive from the ten worst performing companies (measured by their share price movements) was still in post. Visible 'losers' included Sir Ralph Halpern of Burton (Halpern had earlier been responsible for turning Burton around after a poor performance during the 1970s), George Davies, the creator of Next, and Tony Berry who had built Blue Arrow into the world's largest employment agency. The lone survivor was Brian Beazer of Beazer (Construction) which was acquired by Hanson in 1991.

In the early 1990s David O'Brien, who had a 'strikingly unconventional style of management for a sector characterized by tradition', promoted a new, open, team based, customer-focused empowered culture at the National & Provincial Building Society. Profits increased dramatically in a Society which had been struggling, but costs also rose and staff found some of the changes to be quite stressful. 'Consolidation of the achievement', and a slowing down of the pace of change, was required, but the institutional shareholders felt this would be better achieved by the Society's financial director; O'Brien was forced out in 1994. Within a year it was announced that the National & Provincial was to be acquired by Abbey National.

Another colourful leader to lose shareholder support – and his job – was Gerald Ratner, who had been largely responsible for the rapid growth of the Ratner's jewellery chain after the acquisition of H Samuel. At an Institute of Directors conference in 1991 he claimed his company was able to sell sherry decanters at really low prices because they were 'total crap'. The tabloid newspapers were very critical and the company's previously strong image was damaged. The group name has subsequently been changed to Signet.

Although sometimes described as 'losers', many such chief executives resign and receive generous golden handshakes. The real losers are the employees who also lose their jobs in the contraction, and sometimes the shareholders.

Decision making

It has already been emphasized that strategies can **form** or **emerge** as well as be **formulated** or **prescribed**. The role of the strategic leader must be examined in this context.

Strategic change results from decisions taken and implemented in response to perceived opportunities or threats. The management of change therefore requires strategic awareness and strategic learning, which implies the ability to recognize and interpret signals from the environment. Signals from the environment come into the organization all the time and in numerous ways. It is essential that they are monitored and filtered in such a way that the important messages reach decision makers. If strategic change is to some degree dependent on a planning system, then that planning system must gather the appropriate data. Equally, if there is greater reliance on strategic change emerging from decisions taken within the organization by managers who are close to the market, their suppliers and so on, these managers must feel that they have the authority to make change decisions. In both cases appropriate strategic leadership is required to direct activity.

In this section we shall look at decision making in practice, at how decisions are taken and might be taken, and at why some bad decisions are made.

Decision making and problem solving

Decision making is a process related to the existence of a problem, and it is often talked about in terms of problem solving. A problem, in simple terms, exists when an undesirable situation has arisen which requires action to change it. In other words a problem exists for someone if the situation that they perceive exists is unsatisfactory for them. They would like to see something different or better happening and achieving different results.

However, in many instances the problem situation is very complex and can only be partially understood or controlled, and therefore decisions are not so much designed to find ideal or perfect answers but to improve the problem situation. In other instances, managers may find themselves with so many problems at any time that they can at best reduce the intensity of the problem rather than systematically search for a so-called right answer.

Russell Ackoff (1978) distinguishes between solving, resolving, dissolving and absolving problems. A **solution** is the optimum answer, the best choice or alternative, and rational decision making (developed below) is an attempt to find it. A **resolution** is a satisfactory answer or choice, not necessarily the best available, but one that is contingent upon circumstances, such as time limitations, or lack of real significance of the problem. This will again be developed below. A **dissolution** occurs when objectives are changed in such a way that the problem no longer seems to be a problem. Feelings about what should be happening are changed to bring them in line with what is happening; current realities are accepted. If problems are **absolved** they are ignored in the hope that they will disappear.

Visit the website: http://www.itbp.com

The notion of rational decision making

The outcome of the rational model for decision making is the optimum solution. In reality, or in terms of explaining what happens in practice, the model can only be hypothetical because of the assumptions it makes: the problem can be stated clearly and unambiguously; the decision maker has all the information he or she needs to make the optimum decision; a complete list of possible alternatives can be drawn up and evaluated against the objectives; the decision maker has the time and inclination to search for the ideal solution. However, whilst it does not explain decision making in reality, the rational model does provide a very useful framework for examining reality and seeking explanations for how managers do make decisions.

The alternative theories of decision making which follow are based on the premise that in reality there is more subjectivity and irrationality present. Simplification is used to reduce the complexity of problems and lessen the information handling.

Alternative theories

Satisficing behaviour
Herbert Simon (1976) contends that satisficing consists of finding a course of action that is acceptable in the light of the intended objective. A satisfactory rather than an optimal course of action is chosen because of internal and external constraints: time pressure, lack of information, the influence of other interested parties, and so on. A satisfactory course exists, according to Simon,

when there are criteria present which describe minimally satisfactory alternatives and when the alternative in question meets or exceeds all those criteria. It follows that rather than evaluate and select from a range of alternatives, only one need be considered if it meets the minimally satisfactory criteria. Simon argues that this approach is in fact rational within specified limits. Using the term **bounded rationality** he argues that the decision is bounded by three factors: the skills, habits and reflexes of the decision maker, which may no longer be conscious acts; the decision maker's values and motives; and his or her knowledge of issues relevant to the job. This approach therefore allows for limitations on information gathering and bias or focus on particular values. Simon does argue that in the case of extremely important or far-reaching decisions time will be found to make the evaluation of alternatives as exhaustive as possible.

It is easy to see how this could be reflected in certain strategic decisions. If, for example, the objective was to increase sales of a particular product by 5% in real terms, there would probably be a number of ways of achieving this. Increased advertising would be one; a new bonus scheme for the sales force might be another; a price reduction may work; and marketing the product through additional channels of distribution could also achieve the objective. There may or may not be a profitability constraint in the decision. In the rational approach all four and possibly more would be evaluated. In Simon's approach only one need be considered and chosen if it is predicted to yield the desired result.

Bounded discretion

Shull and his associates (1970) have developed Simon's concept of bounded rationality to encompass what they call bounded discretion. Decision makers, they argue, are bounded by a discretionary area comprising social norms, formal rules and policies, moral and ethical norms and legal restrictions. The decision maker accepts these restrictions and perceives that 'certain alternatives will be judged acceptable, whereas other activities will be deemed illegitimate and inappropriate'.

The basic values and culture of the organization, and the personal values of the decision maker, are essential aspects of both these approaches.

The science of muddling through

Lindblom (1959) describes an incremental approach to decision making, and he has subtitled it 'muddling through'. Contrast James Quinn's (1980) idea that incrementalism can be perfectly logical.

Lindblom's research was concerned with policy decision making in the public sector, but the lessons have a wider application. He differentiates between what he terms the **root** and the **branch** approaches. The former can be likened to the rational model, as the decision maker starts from fresh and stated assumptions (objectives) each time that he evaluates alternatives and seeks to make a decision. However, Lindblom argues that this approach is unworkable for complex issues where various interested parties are involved and where there is no clear agreement amongst them on objectives.

The branch approach, in contrast, looks at alternative policies in terms of their various implications without any stated and pre-determined objectives. The interested parties reach agreement on one particular policy, although for each of them the reasons for the choice may be different. The choice is one which receives a wide measure of agreement rather than one which clearly meets stated objectives.

Implicit in this approach are firstly that the evaluation is likely to concentrate on options that are most closely related to those already being followed, as they will already be enjoying some measure of support, secondly that a number of possible alternatives may never be considered, especially if they involve radical change, and thirdly that certain consequences will be ignored if they are not significant for the decision makers, however much they might affect some outsider.

Hence, over a period of time groups of managers will make minor and incremental changes to the way that certain tasks are managed and so on. Minor adjustments apparently carry little immediate threat to working practices, and so this approach is also useful for busy managers who, at any time, are faced with several problematical issues and have a number of relatively minor decisions to make. The decisions, being limited in scope, may not work if the problem has been misjudged or underestimated, and they may have certain adverse effects as they have not been thought through in detail. But they can be corrected quickly by further minor changes. Hence there is incremental progress towards an optimum solution.

In summary, as far as strategic management is concerned, Lindblom's approach helps explain how new competitive and functional strategies will emerge over time through minor incremental changes, as managers make a series of low risk decisions when problems arise or environmental changes are noted. It also highlights the need for clear and strong strategic leadership if major changes are to be managed effectively.

The mixed scanning model

Etzioni (1967) has tried to reconcile the rigid formality of the rational approach with the more undisciplined approach of the incrementalists. Features of his model are as follows.

❏ When decisions have to be made concerning new courses of action, prior decisions will be made to determine how much time, money and effort should be devoted to the search and evaluation. This takes place within the context of a ranking of objectives.
❏ Alternatives are evaluated by sequentially rejecting those which contain some 'crippling objection'.
❏ When the selected alternative is implemented it should be a planned process such that the least costly and most reversible aspects are introduced first, and the most costly and least reversible last. Such incremental changes can be monitored appropriately.

Fundamental to the model is the ranking of objectives, and so again its relevance for a particular organization will be related to the issue of strategic leadership and whether or not there are clearly stated, understood and supported objectives.

The above theories help us to understand how decisions are actually made in reality; in part they also explain why some organizations and managers make bad decisions, i.e. decisions which cause undesirable results which may be detrimental to the organization as a whole. A bad decision may be made if the problem is wrongly diagnosed or misunderstood, or if available and relevant

Box 3.4

POSSIBLE REASONS FOR BAD DECISIONS

❏ Tunnel vision; restricting the scope of analysis

❏ Personal, even selfish, objectives or ambitions

❏ No real framework; and the consequent grasp of the first or easy alternative

❏ Lack of information

❏ Deliberately ignoring information

❏ Failure to consider or generate alternatives; lack of creativity; insufficient time

❏ Inability or reluctance to appreciate consequences of certain actions

❏ Failure of a group to reach or agree a decision; or reaching a decision which no individual really supports, but which nobody fundamentally objects to

❏ Indecisiveness

Notes

A bad decision can arise at any stage within the overall process.

The more widely people think and consider implications in relation to their effect on other people the less likely it is that the above factors will be present.

information is ignored, or if personal objectives are allowed to take precedence over the real interests of the organization.

Box 3.4 is an extended list of possible reasons for poor or bad decision making.

Implementing decisions

Decision making involves both **information** and **people**. Whilst the strategic leader must develop an appropriate information system, he or she must also ensure that a good team of people has been gathered and manage them well.

> *The conductor is only as good as his orchestra.*
>
> (André Previn)

Considerable research has been carried out into group behaviour and it is not within the scope of this book to examine it in detail. But no leadership style is universally better than the others. Much depends on the personality, power and charisma of the leader.

The **implementation aspects** of the decision are also of vital importance. Simply, a decision can only be effective if it is implemented successfully and yields desirable or acceptable results. It may prove very sensible to spend time arriving at a decision by, say, involving the people who must implement it, aiming to generate a commitment at this stage even though it may be time consuming. Such a decision is likely to be implemented smoothly. One alternative to this, the speedy decisive approach, may prove to be less effective. If it is not supported, the alternative chosen may result in controversy and reluctance on the part of others to implement it. Vroom and Yetton (1973) have developed a model of five alternative ways of decision making.

Vroom and Yetton's model

A short summary of the five approaches is as follows.

❏ The leader solves the problem or makes the decision him or herself using information available at the time.

❑ The leader obtains necessary information from subordinates and then decides on the solution to the problem himself or herself. Subordinates are not involved in generating or evaluating alternative solutions.

❑ The leader shares the problem with relevant subordinates individually, obtaining their ideas and suggestions without bringing them together as a group. Then the leader makes the decision, which may or may not reflect the influence of subordinates.

❑ The leader shares the problem with the subordinates as a group, collectively obtaining their ideas and suggestions. Then he or she makes the decision, which again may or may not reflect their influence.

❑ The leader shares the problem with the subordinates as a group, and together the leader and subordinates generate and evaluate alternatives and attempt to reach an agreement on a solution.

(Vroom and Yetton use the expression 'solve' throughout.) Vroom and Yetton contend that the choice of style should relate to the particular problem faced, and their model includes a series of questions which can be used diagnostically to select the most appropriate style.

Whilst the model is useful for highlighting the different styles and emphasizing that a single style will not always prove to be the most appropriate, it is essentially a normative theory ('this is what you should do') and in this respect should be treated with caution.

Communicating the decisions

Box 3.5 includes a number of quotations from strategic leaders, all of which emphasize the need for good internal communications to enable effective decision making.

Risk

Certain business environments involve higher risks than others. High-technology industries, where there is constant innovation and technological change, involve high levels of risk. In pharmaceuticals it takes a number of years to develop and test a new drug before it can be introduced on to the market, and for much of this time there will be a real possibility that the new drug may never become a commercial success. Again, therefore, there is a high level of risk. A third example is oil exploration. The oil companies drilling in the North Sea, for example, have had to invest several million pounds in the hope of finding oil. Whilst they can reduce their risk with sophisticated geological surveys before full exploration is embarked upon, there is again a risk of failure and loss of investment.

What then is risk? Risk occurs whenever anyone must make a choice and the potential outcomes involve uncertainty. In other words if a manager is faced with a decision and the alternative choices involve estimated potential gains and losses which are not certainties, the situation involves risk. The outcome of a typical decision will be dependent on a number of factors, such as customer reaction, levels of demand and competitor reactions. Some managers will understand the situation better than others might, and partly for this reason be happier to accept the risk involved in a particular choice. Personality also affects the willingness to accept and take a particular risk.

Successful companies have a consensus from top to bottom on a set of overall goals. The most brilliant management strategy will fail if that consensus is missing.

John Young, Hewlett-Packard

The problem is not to get people to work. It is to get them working together for the same damn thing.

Sir John Harvey-Jones

Faced with the question of how to improve their competitiveness a dozen heads of business would, more than likely, provide a dozen different answers. But, whatever their preferred solutions, the fact is there would be no hope of success unless the management team was wholeheartedly committed to its objective.

That, I believe, is a fundamental truth in any business. There is no progress without leadership, and that has to come from the very top.

Sir John Egan, when Chairman, Jaguar plc

Two-way communication is at the heart of successful management of change. Top management must beware of the conceit that it has all the answers. Having identified a problem, it will often be very rewarding to put to those in middle management a challenge to suggest a solution. Being nearer to the 'sharp-end' of the business in practical terms, it is surprising how frequently and rapidly they will provide an answer; and, since it comes from the heartland of the business, its implementation will find easier acceptance.

Peter Smith OBE, Chairman, Securicor Group plc

Strategic awareness and change involves: becoming aware – listening, being on the shop floor more than in the office, and, most important of all, staying humble.

Taking action – sharing with others.

Michel Bon, PDG, Carrefour SA

As a strategic leader

… One must organize oneself to have as much time as possible to see colleagues in the firm, and to be known to be available to them, for talking face-to-face is more valuable than a long memo. One must go and see others in their offices. This is the only way to stay in touch with what is going on and to ensure that an agreed plan is being carried out.

Francois Michelin, PDG, Michelin et Cie

It is important that there is compatibility between the strategic leader's attitude towards risk and the demands of the industry. A risk-averse strategic leader in a high risk industry may miss valuable opportunities.

Risk increases as the amount of potential loss increases. For example a person might be offered a ticket in a raffle which costs £1.00, and the chance of winning the first prize of £150 might be 1 in 200. Another person might be offered the opportunity to invest £100 with a 1 in 200 chance of winning £15,000. Although the odds of winning and losing are identical, the risk involved in each situation is different. The potential loss in the second case is 100 times greater than in the first, and it consequently involves greater risk.

The following criteria are important in the decision:

❏ the attractiveness of each option to the decision maker
❏ the extent to which he or she is prepared to accept the potential loss in each alternative
❏ the estimated probabilities of success and failure

❏ the degree to which the decision maker is likely to affect the success or failure.

Hence in considering risk and strategic leadership in an organization a number of factors are worth investigating. It may well have an effect if the strategic leader is a significant shareholder rather than a minor one. Similarly, in the case of managers throughout the organization who are involved in strategic decisions in various ways, the culture and values of the organization with regard to reward for success and sanction for failure will be important. So too will be the personality of the managers and their **awareness** of the relative pay-offs and probabilities of success and failure.

Attitudes towards risk also affects the way managers make decisions.

Dunnette and Taylor (1975), whose research involved industrial managers, concluded: 'high risk takers tended to make more rapid decisions, based on less information than low risk takers, but they tended to process each piece of information more slowly ... although risk-prone decision makers reach rapid decisions by the expedient of restricting their information search, they give careful attention to the information they acquire.'

Environmental factors may prove significant. The availability and cost of finance, forecasts of market opportunities and market buoyancy, and feelings about the strengths and suitability of internal resources will all be important. For other managers within the organization the overall culture and styles of leadership and the reward systems will influence their risk taking.

Visit the website:
http://www.
itbp.com

Managing risk

Organizations will often pursue strategies which seek to manage or minimize risk. Hanson, an extremely successful and profitable company which is discussed in detail later, has always investigated 'the down side' in any strategy or proposed deal. Lord Hanson has said of his late partner, Lord White: 'We would actually have done a lot more deals if Gordon did not have so many worries. He is constantly looking for the potential trouble in a deal'. When Richard Branson started Virgin Atlantic Airways, clearly a high-risk venture, he was cautious. He began with just one Boeing plane on sale or return for one year. Issues of risk in the airline industry are featured in Case 3.3: GPA – Guinness Peat Aviation.

Entrepreneurship

It was argued in Chapter 1 that strategic management is concerned with environmental fit. It is important to achieve congruence between environment, values and resources for both existing and potential future products and services.

The management of existing businesses focuses attention on costs and prices (as they determine profits) and on ways of reducing costs by improving productivity. Technology changes, and new operating systems, may reduce costs; equally they may improve product quality for which premium prices might be charged.

GPA – GUINNESS PEAT AVIATION

GPA is an unquoted company based in the low-tax zone of Shannon in Ireland. Its original owners included airlines such as Aer Lingus and Air Canada, together with various banks and financial institutions from around the world. The majority shareholder (with 12%) was Mitsubishi; GPA's Chairman and founder, Tony Ryan, held 8%.

The company was founded in 1975 to 'act as a broker, hiring out one airline's surplus jets to other operators short of aircraft'. GPA bought its first aeroplane in 1979, its first new aeroplane in 1984; in the mid-1980s the strategy was changing. The company started to speculate in aircraft 'futures', paying for new aircraft delivery slots from manufacturers – with no firm orders. Fundamentally this is very risky. In the early 1990s analysts estimated that every 0.5% variation in the growth of demand for aircraft between 1990 and 2000 would lead to a variation in the world-wide fleet, needed to satisfy that demand, of 700 aircraft. This is out of a total fleet of 8300. GPA's profits and solvency now hinged on accurate judgements about the balance of supply and demand.

GPA has been described as a supermarket for aircraft. By mid-1991 the company owned over 300 commercial aircraft, which it leased to airlines around the world. One hundred more were due for delivery before mid-1992. GPA had firm orders and options for a further 700 planes (10% of world manufacturing capacity) with deliveries scheduled into the next century. The penalties for any postponements or cancellations varied between deals. This level of ordering involved huge sums of money. In 1991 a Boeing 737 cost $33 million and a 747 between $125 and $145 million depending on the specification. GPA conducts all its business in US dollars.

During the boom years of the late 1980s GPA was very successful. Profits increased tenfold from $25 to $250 million over five years, but they slumped when the impact of the Gulf War was felt on travel and tourism. Simply, GPA misread the extent of the downturn in its market.

The GPA strategy was to buy planes in bulk for price discounts of up to 25%, lease them on normally five- to seven-year non-cancellable agreements, and then sell used aircraft once the lease expired. The business is inevitably high risk, but GPA attempted to manage the downside in a number of ways.

❑ GPA became skilled at re-leasing aircraft which are returned from airlines in liquidation or receivership.

❑ The customer base is diverse. It soon included some 88 airlines in 45 countries world-wide, and continued to grow; both state-owned carriers and smaller, private companies with low credit ratings, who are both required and prepared to pay higher lease charges, are included. This still does not guarantee that leases will not collapse.

❑ Most of the planes are modern and fuel-efficient, ideal for when fuel prices are rising or uncertain.

One dilemma is that in an air travel recession the value of used aircraft falls, and most of GPA's profits are from sales rather than lease charges. Moreover airlines often delay or cancel new purchases – but at the same time, when planes have to be replaced, they may well switch to leasing instead of buying. GPA really needed a substantial cushion of equity to help minimize these risks; instead it became very highly geared. Over 75 banks lent money to GPA, and some would argue that they were too generous. It has been commented that the banking system could not afford for GPA to collapse.

The risk inherent in GPA was illustrated when a planned global flotation of a minority of the shares (in June 1992) collapsed. Share prices were falling and institutional demand in the USA simply did not materialize. Further attempts to sell new equity to existing shareholders – at prices which were still falling – also failed. In the troubles some attention was focused on the boardroom roles of two prominent non-executive directors: Sir John Harvey-Jones (a substantial investor himself) and Lord Nigel Lawson (who held no shares). An early attempt by middle managers to oust Tony Ryan also failed; the board rallied behind the founder.

In 1993 General Electric Aviation (a subsidiary of the American General Electric) acquired 65% of the equity for a knock-down bargain price and took over operational control of GPA's fleet. All shareholders lost heavily. There had been 'a surfeit of confidence and greed over prudence and caution'. Ryan was ousted from his position as Chairman and Chief Executive of GPA but he has a role within GE Aviation.

Future developments might concern new products (or services) or new markets or both, and they might involve diversification. For different alternatives the magnitude of the change implied and the risk involved will vary.

For both areas the changes which take place can be gradual or incremental, or they can be more dynamic or individually significant. Real innovation can be costly in terms of investment required, and consequently can involve a high level of risk, but sometimes it is necessary.

Figure 3.2 shows alternative development paths for a business. Entrepreneurs develop new ideas and new businesses, but there are different views on the implications of an entrepreneurial start-up. Schumpeter (1949) argues that entrepreneurs bring innovative ideas into a situation of some stability and create disequilibrium; the so-called Austrian School of economists suggest that entrepreneurs actually create equilibrium (in the form of E–V–R congruence) by matching demand and supply in a creative way. However, it is the path of future progress that really matters.

From its initial position the business could at first be successful but then fade away without further innovation and renewal – Path I. The original window of opportunity closes and the business fails to find or capitalize on a new one.

Some businesses never really improve and grow (Path II) – sometimes by deliberate choice, sometimes through lack of insight and awareness – but they survive whilst ever they can satisfy a particular niche or localized market. If one window of opportunity closes they find a new one, but in this respect they are more likely to be reactive rather than proactive. It is quite feasible for Path II businesses to *expand* as distinct from true growth based on improvement and excellence.

Paths III and IV feature more proactive entrepreneurial businesses which *grow* via productivity improvements and/or by leveraging their resources to develop new products and service opportunities. Sometimes, but certainly not always, such businesses will be decentralized, empowered and *intrapreneurial*.

Path V implies discontinuous change and requires visionary leadership, which Mintzberg (1973) summarizes as follows:

❑ Strategy making is dominated by the active search for new opportunities.
❑ Power is centralized in the hands of the chief executive – certainly as far as corporate strategy changes are concerned.
❑ Strategic change is characterized by dramatic leaps forward in the face of uncertainty.
❑ Growth is the dominant goal of the organization.

Implicit is an attempt to be proactive and manage the environment. Paths III, IV and V are clearly not mutually exclusive; they can all be present simultaneously in an organization.

Sustained entrepreneurial behaviour is required for a successful economy; organizations must innovate and search for opportunities to re-write the rules of competition. In this way home industries can succeed against foreign competitors (whose products and services may be differentiated successfully or priced very competitively because of cost advantages such as low wages) and find overseas markets. Paths I and II are not entrepreneurial businesses; in a different way, nor is an organization which grows via acquisitions but then fails to add new values and drive improvements along either Paths III or IV. Ironically the nature of the strategic changes and the increases in size and

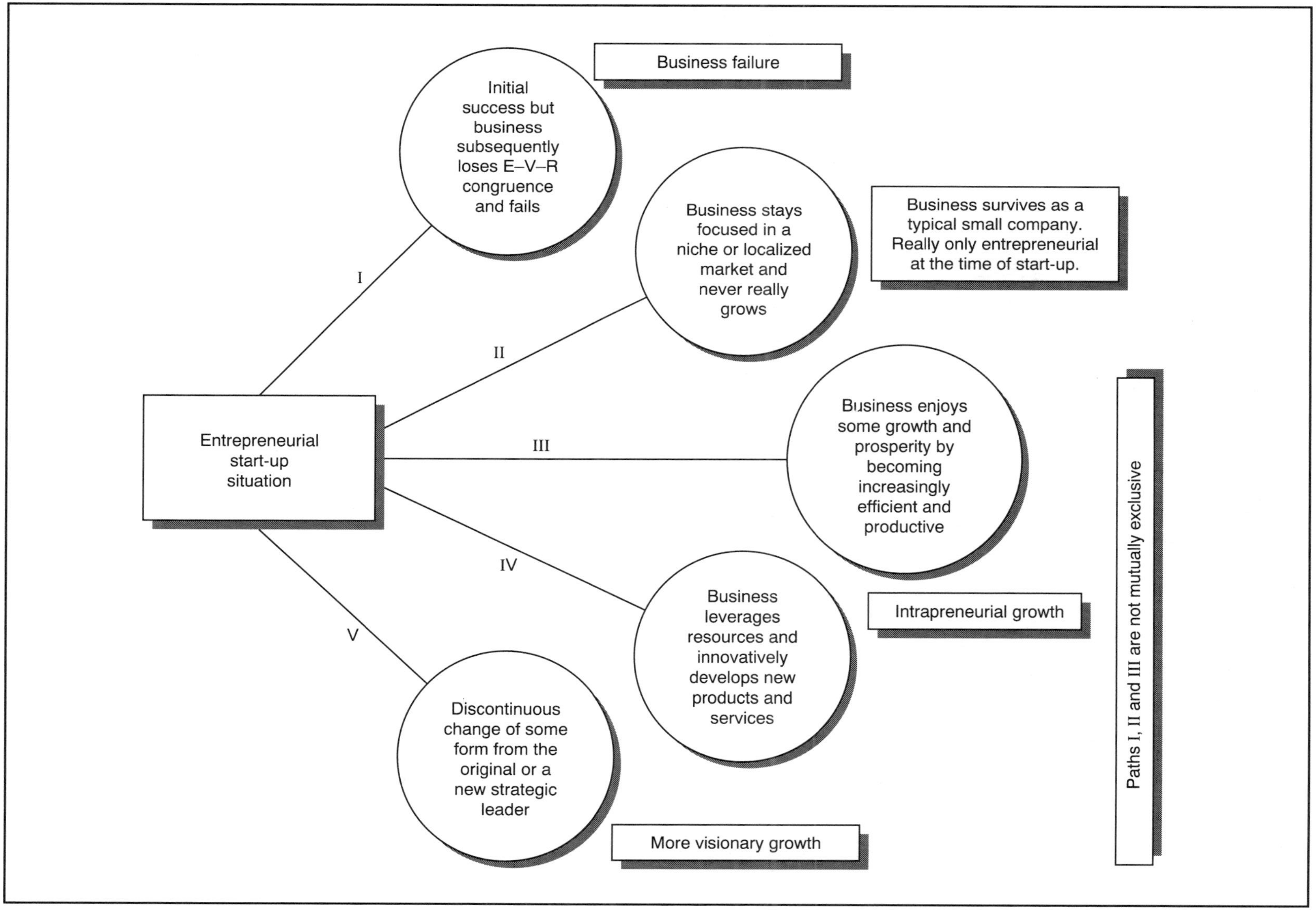

Figure 3.2 Business development paths.

revenue can suggest that these organizations are visionary and on Path V. However, where an organization which has been following Paths II, III or IV merges with, or is taken over by, another organization, there is likely to be a change of strategy, culture and possibly leadership. The acquired business may therefore experience a Path V change.

As well as sustained entrepreneurial behaviour, new entrepreneurs are required to start new businesses to replace the jobs which are lost when other companies collapse and certain industries decline – as have coal mining, steel making and shipbuilding, for example. Typically a different type of business, with dissimilar labour requirements, will emerge. In general in the UK, the problem is not so much in stimulating business start-ups, but in encouraging them to grow. However, as we have seen, growth demands changes in structure and style and requires the owner-manager to relinquish some power and control. Growing too quickly often implies problems with cash flow and co-ordination. Case 3.4 features an interesting example of a visionary entrepreneur who grew a successful business, sold it and began afresh.

It is, therefore, important for us to understand the motivation of entrepreneurs.

Achievement and power motivation

McClelland and Winter (1971) have argued since the 1950s that all managers, in fact all workers, are influenced and motivated by three desires: the desire to achieve, the desire for power, and the desire for affiliation at work. The relative strength of each of these three desires or motives will vary from individual to individual, and what matters as far as management is concerned is to understand what does motivate people rather than to believe that all people can be motivated in the same way.

Entrepreneurial behaviour is characterized by high achievement motivation, supported by a power motive, and with affiliation very much third.

Achievement motivation is characterized by concern to do a job well, or better than others, with the accomplishment of something unusual or important, and with advancement. Such managers thrive where they have personal responsibility for finding answers to problems, and they tend to set moderate achievable goals and take calculated risks. If the targets are too modest, there is little challenge and little satisfaction, but if they are too high they are too risky.

Actually achieving the goal is important. They also prefer constant feedback concerning progress. Achievement motivation is closely linked to the desire to create something.

Entrepreneurial behaviour also features a desire for power, influence and independence.

Ettinger (1983) has developed this thesis, and argues that there are two types of entrepreneur (Fig. 3.3). Independent entrepreneurs are intent on creating and developing their own organization and retaining control, as they are more concerned with independence than power. Where power is stronger, organization makers are looking for growth opportunities, because growth and size yields power. Arguably they will accept a loss of independence if they can build something important.

In March 1988 Midsummer Leisure, an expanding public house, snooker club and discotheque business with some 130 outlets, bought Bruce's Brewery, comprising 11 outlets and one site for development, from David Bruce for £6.6 million in cash.

David Bruce was in his late twenties when he opened his first pub-brewery in 1979. He had previously worked for such companies as Courage and Theakstons and felt that there was a market opportunity for a pub which brewed its own beer on site. He bought the lease on a site at the Elephant and Castle in London, an existing pub which was being closed down, and renamed it the Goose and Firkin. The pub was completely re-modelled with one large bar with wooden seats, bare floor boards and several decorations such as a stuffed goose. The aim was to re-create a traditional drinking house. Brewing took place in the cellar, which had a production capacity of 5000 pints per week. Additionally other real ales were sold. Lloyds Bank lent £10,000 for this new venture, but Bruce was turned down by others he approached. He had to take a second mortgage on his house to provide collateral for his overdraft and he borrowed some money from a friend of his wife.

Three types of real ale were brewed and sold, all with individual brand names and varying in strength. These were Bruce's Borough Bitter, Bruce's Dog Bolter and Bruce's Earth Stopper, which at o.g. 1075 was claimed to be the strongest draught beer in Britain. Traditional food of high quality supplemented the beer. Success came instantaneously and the turnover was into the thousands of pounds within weeks of opening. It quickly reached an annual quarter of a million pounds. A manager and a team of seven, including a brewer, were employed to run the pub.

A second outlet was opened in 1980; by 1985 there were seven, with the total reaching 11 in 1987. All 11 were in the Greater London area, and nine of them had in-house breweries. The last two were called the Fuzzock and Firkin and the Flamingo and Firkin. By the mid-1980s Bruce was the fifth largest operator of breweries in the UK. All the pubs had Firkin in the name, and by this time a number of new real ale brands had been introduced including Spook, brewed exclusively in the Phantom and Firkin. Bruce had also developed a reputation for promotional slogans for each pub. The Flounder and Firkin was a 'plaice worth whiting home about' and at the Phantom and Firkin you could 'spectre good pint when you ghost to the Phantom'.

Sales in 1986–7, with eight outlets operating, were £4 million. Bruce had sold 10% of the equity to Investors in Industry for £120,000, and they also provided additional loan facilities.

There had been difficulties, however. In 1982 Bruce had obtained a pub-brewery with additional warehouse capacity in Bristol. His aim was to distribute his real ales to West Country pubs. But the company was already experiencing problems from the rapid growth. Beer quality was inconsistent; there were cash flow problems; and David Bruce's own role was unclear. A microbiologist and an accountant were brought into the business, which relieved the first two of these. But Bruce still faced the problem that, whilst there were managers in every outlet, he was personally responsible for ensuring that his original success formula at the Goose and Firkin was implemented and maintained in all the pubs and at the same time was seeking new opportunities for growth and development. Once the company spread outside London Bruce felt that he was no longer able to give sufficient attention to detail throughout the organization. Essentially the problem was one of managing growth and at the same time retaining the 'personal touch', a key success factor for this type of service business.

The Bristol site was sold.

Bruce had hoped to take the company to the Unlisted Securities Market in 1987, but this never happened. Further growth, he felt, was inhibited by a lack of equity capital and the problems of interest charges on loans.

After paying off loans and capital gains tax, Bruce was left with £1 million, part of which he used to establish a charitable trust to provide canal holidays for disabled people.

In 1990 David Bruce started brewing again. Two pubs, both named The Hedgehog and Hogshead, and offering beers such as Hogbolter and Prickletickler, were opened in Hove and Southampton. The conditions of sale of Bruce's Brewery prevented Bruce from opening in Greater London. Key staff were recruited back from Midsummer Leisure (later acquired by Stakis); the sites were leased rather than freehold; and borrowing was kept to a minimum. Bruce personally invested £500,000.

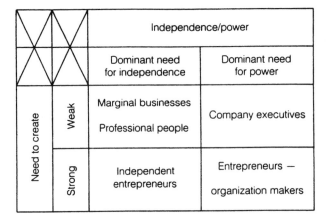

Figure 3.3 Typology of the entrepreneur. Adapted from Ettinger, J C (1983) Some Belgian evidence on entrepreneurial personality, *European Small Business Journal*, 1(2). Reproduced with permission.

Obviously some strategic leaders will exhibit more entrepreneurialism than others. The management style, the nature of objectives set and chased, and the type and magnitude of change within the organization will all be influenced.

Entrepreneurs need both creativity and confidence if they are to seek out and exploit new ideas; and they must be willing to take risks. Whilst McClelland and Winter describe achievement-motivated people as those who take very measured risks, there are some entrepreneurs who thrive on uncertainty and are successful because they take chances and opportunities that others would and do reject. They will not always succeed of course.

Intrapreneurship

Entrepreneurial activity, innovation and growth is affected greatly by the ambition and style of the strategic leader, his or her values, and the culture he or she creates, but arguably it should be spread throughout the organization.

Intrapreneurship is the term given to the establishment and fostering of entrepreneurial activity within large organizations. Many new ideas for innovation, for product or service developments, can come from managers within organizations if the structure and climate encourages and allows them to contribute. There are a number of ways. Special task forces and development groups are one alternative. Allowing individual managers the opportunity, freedom and, if necessary, the capital to try new ideas is another.

Success requires that change is perceived more as an opportunity than a threat, that the company is aware of market opportunities and is customer oriented and that the financial implications are thought through.

Summary

The strategic leader of an organization affects both strategy creation and strategy implementation. He or she is responsible for establishing the basic direction of the organization, the communications system and the structure. These influence the nature and style of decision making within the firm. In addition decision making and change is affected by the personal ambitions of the strategic leader, his or her personal qualities such as entrepreneurialism and willingness to take risks, the style of management adopted and the management systems used.

Specifically in this chapter we have:

- considered the role of the strategic leader as a creator and an implementor of strategy, emphasizing the need for direction, an appropriate organization structure and effective communications

- explained how visionary leaders have a vision for the future and a commitment to making it happen
- introduced the topical debate on corporate governance
- introduced a number of important issues such as shelf-life, succession and the implications of growth and change
- explained why some leaders fail
- introduced the rational model of decision making and compared it with other approaches to provide some insight into how decisions concerning strategy might be reached in practice
- emphasized that decision making involves both information and people, and by reference to Vroom and Yetton's model shown that there are a number of approaches for handling this
- discussed how bad decisions might be reached
- defined risk and looked at risk in relation to strategies
- examined entrepreneurship in relation to economic aspects and particularly decisions concerning strategic change.

Checklist of key terms and concepts

You should feel confident that you understand the following terms and ideas:

- ✯ Visionary leadership
- ✯ Styles of leadership
- ✯ Corporate governance
- ✯ The rational model of decision making
- ✯ Alternative satisficing and incremental approaches
- ✯ Risk
- ✯ Entrepreneurship and intrapreneurship.

Questions and research assignments

Text related

1 Using the Volvo case (Case 3.2) as a background, discuss why effective leadership involves both strategy creation and strategy implementation. From your experience and reading, which other well-known strategic leaders do you believe are strong on
   (i)   creation
   (ii) implementation
   (iii) both.

2 Case 3.4 David Bruce.
   (a) Do you think David Bruce's approach to growth and change was appropriate for the business he was in? Do you see it as opportunistic or incremental or planned?
   (b) Why do you think Bruce's breweries have been successful?
   (c) Do you think David Bruce's style of managing the organization was also appropriate?

Library based

3 What has happened to David Bruce since 1990?
   To what extent do you think the opportunities he identified provided a springboard for the successful, independent microbreweries which are enjoying success and prosperity in the 1990s?

4 Select at least one well-established large corporation which is quoted on the Stock Exchange, together with one of the companies privatized during the 1980s.

(a) Examine the composition of the Board of Directors in terms of executive and non-executive members.
(b) Determine whether the roles of chairman and chief executive are split or combined.
(c) What conclusions might you draw concerning strategic leadership and corporate governance in these organizations?

5 The following facts relate to Alan Sugar founder and chief executive of Amstrad, and one of Britain's richest businessmen. You are required to research the growth and success of Amstrad in the consumer electronics and microcomputers markets in order to answer the same questions as Questions 2(a), 2(b) and 2(c) above.

1947 Born Hackney, East London
1963 Left school
1966 Began selling car aerials from a van
1968 Founded Amstrad to sell plastic covers for record players. Involvement in televisions, video receivers and CB radio led to
1985 Launch of a low-cost word-processor and compact disc player
1986 Acquisition of the intellectual property rights of Sinclair computers from Clive Sinclair and launch of an IBM-compatible microcomputer
1988 Entered satellite dish market
1991 Entered laptop computer market.

Recommended further reading

Bennis has written a number of useful books on leadership. Bennis, W and Nanus, B (1985) *Leaders: The Strategies of Taking Charge*, Harper & Row (which is not his latest book) provides a useful introduction.

The semi-autobiographical books on business written by such British authors as Sir John Harvey-Jones (past Chairman, ICI), Lord Sieff (past Chairman, Marks and Spencer), George Davies (Next) and Debbie Moore (Pineapple), together with a biography of Alan Sugar by David Thomas, all provide insight into the perspective and strategies of individual leaders. Similar American books include ones by Lee Iacocca (Chrysler) and Victor Kiam (Remington). Swedish authors Borgström and Haag have written a biography of Volvo's Pehr Gyllenhammar.

Readers interested in leadership and strategic regeneration are referred to: Goss, T, Pascale, R and Athos A (1993), The reinvention roller coaster: risking the present for a powerful future, *Harvard Business Review*, November–December.

Harrison, EF (1981) *The Managerial Decision Making Process*, Houghton Mifflin, provides a comprehensive summary of the theories and concepts introduced in this chapter; the managerial perspective is covered well in Heirs, B and Farrell, P (1987) *The Professional Decision Thinker,* Sidgwick & Jackson.

References

Ackoff, R (1978) *The Art of Problem Solving,* John Wiley.

Bennis, W, Interview recorded in Crainer, S (1988) Doing the right thing, *The Director,* October.

Dunnette, MD and Taylor, RN (1975) Influence of dogmatism, risk taking propensity and intelligence on decision making strategy for a sample of industrial managers, *Journal of Applied Psychology,* **59** (4).

Ettinger, JC (1983) Some Belgian evidence on entrepreneurial personality, *European Small Business Journal*, 1(2).

Etzioni, A (1967) Mixed scanning: a third approach to decision making, *Public Administration Review*, 27, December.

Kets De Vries, MFR (1994) CEO's also have the blues, *European Journal of Management*, September.

Lindblom, CE (1959) *The Science of Muddling Through*; 2nd edn, reprinted in Pugh, D S (ed.) (1987) *Organization Theory*, Penguin.

McClelland, D and Winter, D (1971) *Motivating Economic Achievement*, Free Press.

Mintzberg, H (1973) Strategy making in three modes, *California Management Review,* **16**(2), Winter.

Quinn, J B (1980) *Strategies for Change: Logical Incrementalism*, Richard D Irwin.

Richardson, B (1994) Towards a profile of the visionary leader, *Small Business Enterprise and Development*, 1, 1, Spring.

Richardson, B, Nwanko, S and Richardson, S (1994) Understanding the causes of business failure crises, *Management Decision*, 32, 4.

Schumpeter, J (1949) *The Theory of Economic Development*, Harvard University Press, original German edition, 1911

Shull, FA, Delbecq, AL and Cummings, LL (1970) *Organizational Decision Making*, McGraw-Hill.

Simon, HA (1976) *Administrative Behavior: A Study of Decision Making Processes in Administrative Organizations,* 3rd edn, Free Press.

Slatter, S (1994) *Corporate Recovery: Successful Turnaround Strategies and their Implementation*, Penguin.

Vroom, V and Yetton, P (1973) *Leadership and Decision Making,* University of Pittsburgh Press.

4

Culture and Values

This chapter explores the role of organizational culture in strategic management since (i) the prevailing culture is a major influence on current strategies and future changes and (ii) any decisions to make major strategic changes may require a change in the culture. Culture is therefore a vital element in both strategy creation and strategy implementation.

Learning objectives

After studying this chapter you should be able to:

■ explain the impact of corporate culture on the management of an organization, and on managers and other employees
■ discuss the manifestations of culture in an organization
■ define Handy's four organizational cultures and list and define different sources of power
■ assess the conclusions of normative researchers concerning 'excellence'
■ appreciate important aspects of the Japanese business culture.

Introduction

When any group of people live and work together for any length of time, they form and share certain beliefs about what is right and proper. They establish behaviour patterns based on their beliefs, and their actions often become matters of habit which they follow routinely. These beliefs and ways of behaving constitute the organization's **culture**.

Culture is reflected in the way people in an organization perform tasks, set objectives and administer resources to achieve them. It affects the way that they make decisions, think, feel and act in response to opportunities and threats. Culture also influences the selection of people for particular jobs, which in turn affects the way that tasks are carried out and decisions are made. Culture is so fundamental that it affects behaviour unconsciously. Managers do things in particular ways because it is expected behaviour.

The culture of an organization is therefore related to the people, their behaviour and the operation of the structure. It is encapsulated in beliefs, customs and values and manifested in a number of symbolic ways.

The formation of, and any changes to, the culture of an organization is dependent on the leadership and example of particular individuals, and their ability to control or influence situations. This is itself dependent on a person's ability to obtain and use **power**.

Culture and power affect the choice, incidence and application of the modes of strategy creation, which will also reflect the values and preferences of the strategic leader. The preferred mode must, though, be appropriate for the organization's strategic needs, which are, of course, affected by competition. Moreover, culture and power are such strong forces that, if the prevailing culture is overlooked, implementation may not happen. Strong cultures can

Don't forget to visit the website: http://www. itbp.com

obstruct strategic change, particularly if companies are in decline and people feel vulnerable.

Quite simply, culture is at the heart of all strategy creation and implementation. Organizations are seeking to respond to perceived strategic issues. Resources must be deployed and committed, but successful change also requires the 'right' attitude, approach and commitment from people. This mind set, which might, for example, reflect a strong customer and service focus, could imply further empowerment and consequently cultural change.

In the early 1980s, Berry (1983) claimed that after some 20 years of emphasis on analytical techniques in strategic management, the concentration switched to the softer aspect of culture. The emphasis was no longer on the marketplace, but on what managers could do to resolve internal problems; by using culture, companies could become more strategically effective. The perspective of this book is that both the hard and soft aspects of strategy have important roles to play in strategic management.

Strong cultures, then, are an important strategic asset. Internalized beliefs can motivate people to exceptional levels of performance. An effective strategic leader will understand and mould the culture in order that a vision can be pursued and intended strategies implemented. Most successful companies develop strong cultures; the major doubt concerns an organization's ability to change the culture.

Moreover, large organizations formed by a series of acquisitions will frequently exhibit different cultures in the various divisions or businesses; in many international businesses this is inevitable. The challenge for corporate headquarters is to ensure that certain critically important values are reflected in all branches of the corporation and cultural differences do not inhibit internal architecture and synergy.

At the same time, cross-border mergers and alliances offer real opportunities to claim the best features of different cultures. For example, the acquisition of Rover by BMW and UK investments by other leading German companies such as Siemens, BASF and Bayer could bring together the longer-term German perspective on investment, training and employee consultation and the UK's flexibility in working practices and lower manufacturing costs.

Aspects of culture

The points discussed in this section are summarized in Figure 4.1.

Manifestations of culture

Edgar Schein (1985) contends that it is important to consider culture as having a number of levels, some of which are essentially manifestations of underlying beliefs.

The first and most visible level Schein terms 'artefacts'. These include the physical and social environment and the outputs of the organization. Written communications, advertisements and the reception that visitors receive are all included.

Values are the second level, and they represent a sense of 'what ought to be' based on convictions held by certain key people. For example if an organization has a problem such as low sales or a high level of rejections in production,

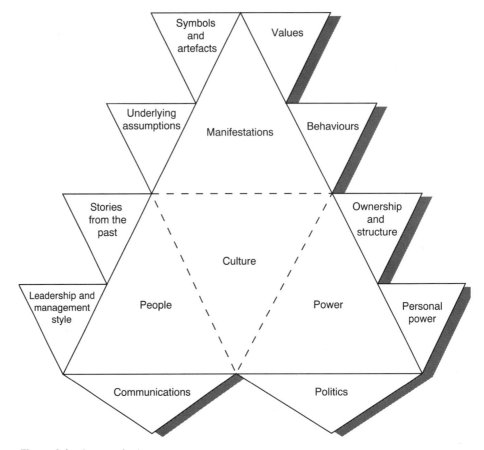

Figure 4.1 Aspects of culture.

decisions might be made to advertise more aggressively or to use high quality but more expensive raw materials. These are seen initially as the decision maker's values, which can be debated or questioned. Many of the strategies followed by organizations start in this way, and many will reflect values held by the strategic leader.

If the alternative is successful it may well be tried again and again until it becomes common practice. In this way the value becomes a belief and ultimately an assumption about behaviour practised by the organization. These basic underlying assumptions are Schein's third level, and they represent the 'taken-for-granted ways of doing things or solutions to problems'.

One belief accepted by employees within a bank might be that all lending must be secure. A football team could be committed to always playing attractive, open football. A university might be expected to have clear beliefs about the relative importance of research and teaching, but this is likely to be an issue where employees 'agree to disagree' leading to a fragmented culture. Examples of **behaviours** are speedy new product development, long working hours, formal management meetings and regular informal meetings or contacts with colleagues, suppliers and customers.

It is also important to appreciate that certain organizations may state that they have particular values but in reality these will be little more than verbal or written statements or aspirations for the future.

Schein argues that cultural paradigms are formed which determine 'how organization members perceive, think about, feel about, and judge situations and relationships' and these are based on a number of underlying assumptions.

People and culture

For Schwartz and Davis (1981) culture is 'a pattern of beliefs and expectations shared by the organization's members, and which produce norms that powerfully shape the behaviour of individuals and groups in the organization'. They argue that the beliefs held by the company are seen as major aspects of corporate policy as they evolve from interactions with, and in turn form policy towards, the marketplace. As a result rules or norms for internal and external behaviour are developed and eventually both performance and reward systems will be affected.

Success is measured by, and culture therefore becomes based on, past activities. Current decisions by managers reflect the values, beliefs and norms that have proved beneficial in the past and in the development and growth of the organization. Moreover they reinforce the corporate culture and expected behaviour throughout the organization.

The culture affects suppliers and customers, and their reactions are important. They will feed back impressions about the organization, and their views should be sought. Successful organizations will ensure that there is congruence between these environmental influences and the organization culture. In this way key success factors can be met if resources are administered, controlled and developed appropriately.

Organizations need a cohesive blend of the philosophies introduced earlier. A cohesive culture would exhibit strong leadership, whereby the strategic leader is sensitive to the degrees of decentralization and informality necessary for satisfying customer needs efficiently – and managing change pressures – in order to keep the business strong and profitable. At the same time a centralized information network will ensure that communications are effective and that managers are both kept aware and rewarded properly for their contributions. A fragmented culture, on the other hand, would suggest that the needs of certain stakeholders were perhaps not being satisfied adequately, or that strategies and changes were not being co-ordinated, or that managers or business units were in conflict and working against each other, or that the most deserving people were not being rewarded.

Case 4.1 describes how British Airways has attempted to become more cohesive.

Linked to this is **communication**, an essential aspect of culture. The organization might be seen as open or closed, formal or informal. Ideally employees from different parts of the business, and at different levels in the hierarchy, will feel willing and able to talk openly with each other, sharing problems, ideas and learning. 'Doors should be left open.' Employees should also be trusted and empowered to the appropriate degree. Good communications can 'stop nasty surprises'. It is helpful if employees know how well competitors are performing, where they are particularly strong, so they can commit themselves to high levels of achievement in order to out-perform their rivals.

BRITISH AIRWAYS

Prior to privatization British Airways was fragmented. Leadership was, to some considerable extent, 'military', with strict rules and procedures, and top-down communications. Cabin staff were essentially powerless and insufficiently customer oriented. Customer attitudes and reactions were not fed back into the organization, and BA was seen as less friendly than many of its rivals.

When Colin Marshall (now Sir Colin) became Chief Executive in 1983 he set 'giving the best service' as a key objective. He argued that this involved:

❏ appreciating what the market wants
❏ being able to respond quickly to changes in customer demand and expectations by
❏ having an appropriate organization structure and
❏ being adequately resourced.

These were to be achieved by ensuring that employees throughout BA were committed to providing a high level of customer service and that managers were equally aware of the needs and expectations of employees. Marshall sought to change the culture of BA to one of service orientation by:

❏ Issuing a new mission statement reflecting the revised objectives and values.
❏ A management training programme entitled 'Managing People First', designed to 'substantially enhance the participant's personal performance as a manager of others' by concentrating on developing a sense of urgency, vision, motivation, trust and a willingness to take responsibility.
❏ Improving both performance appraisal and a linked reward system.

❏ Customer service training for all employees who dealt directly with customers – entitled 'Putting People First'.
❏ Establishing 'Customer First' teams where groups of staff meet regularly to discuss their learning.

Front-line staff have been given more authority to use initiative, on the assumption they will behave more warmly to passengers. Positive and negative responses (complaints) are now fed through formalized channels, aided by increased use of information technology. Staff became more professional, and the organization more effective and more profitable.

New, revised service campaigns – 'Winning for Customers' and 'Managing Winners' – have been introduced in the 1990s, after the Gulf War caused a slump in air travel and airline profits. The 'Leadership 2000' programme aims to develop skills among BA's top 200 managers.

BA is very serious about the need to maintain strategic awareness and manage change effectively. As an illustration of this, in 1995, the company created the post of 'Corporate Jester'. A long-serving but energetic and enthusiastic manager, who has worked in a wide range of different functions, was charged with 'roaming around and asking questions'. The job is about 'creativity and challenge'.

Any highly successful business is in danger of over-confidence – success is probably the most dangerous time.

The purpose of the role is to try and ensure the company never starts to believe it can do no wrong, with nobody questioning the strategic leader.

Communication is clearly essential for creating effective internal and external architecture.

Hampden-Turner (1990) argues that culture is based on communication and learning. The strategic leader's vision for the organization must be communicated and understood; events and changes affecting the organization also need to be communicated widely. Managers should be encouraged to seek out new opportunities by learning about new technology and customer expectations, and to innovate. The organization should help them to share their experiences and their learning.

Power and culture

Power is reflected in the **ownership** of the business. It may be a family company with strong, concentrated power. A small group of institutional shareholders could control the business, in which case it is conceivable that short-term financial targets will dictate strategies. **Structural issues** include the extent to which the organization is centralized or decentralized, the role and contribution of corporate headquarters, and control and reward systems. **Personal** power is discussed later in this chapter; **politics** refers to the ways in which managers use power and influence to affect decisions and actions.

Determinants of culture

Deal and Kennedy (1982) have conducted research into US companies in an attempt to ascertain what factors lead to consistently outstanding (above average for the industry) performance. They found that over the long term the companies that are the most successful are those **that believe in something** and those where the belief or beliefs have permeated through the whole organization, i.e. they are communicated and understood. Examples quoted are progress via innovation and technology and 'excellence' in something that customers value, say service or delivery on time.

Deal and Kennedy argue that employees must be rewarded for compliance with the essential cultural aspects if these values are to be developed and retained over time; and they conclude that people who build, develop and run successful companies invariably work hard to create strong cultures within their organizations.

From their research Deal and Kennedy isolated five key elements or determinants of culture.

❏ The environment and key success factors: what the organization must do well if it is to be an effective competitor. Innovation and fast delivery are examples quoted.
❏ The values that the strategic leader considers important and wishes to see adopted and followed in the organization. These should relate to the key success factors, and to employee reward systems.
❏ Heroes: the visionaries who create the culture. They can come from any background and could be, for example, product or service innovators, engineers who build the appropriate quality into the product, or creative marketing people who provide the slogans which make the product or brand name a household word.
❏ Rites and rituals: the behaviour patterns in which the culture is manifest. Again there are any number of ways that this can happen, including employees helping each other out when there are difficulties, the way sales people deal with customers, and the care and attention that goes into production.

❏ The cultural network: the communications system around which the culture revolves and which determines just how aware employees are about the essential issues.

When the culture is strong, people know what is expected of them and they understand how to act and decide in particular circumstances. They appreciate the issues that are important. When it is weak time can be wasted in trying to decide what should be done and how. Moreover it is argued that employees feel better about their companies if they are recognized, known about and regarded as successful, and these aspects will be reflected in the culture.

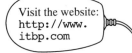

Visit the website: http://www. itbp.com

There can be a number of separate strands to the culture in any organization, which should complement each other. For example there can be aspects relating to the strategic leader, the environment and the employees. There could be a strong power culture related to an influential strategic leader who is firmly in charge of the organization and whose values are widely understood and followed. This could be linked to a culture of market orientation, which ensures that customer needs are considered and satisfied, and to a work culture if employees feel committed to the organization and wish to help achieve success.

Implications of culture

Pümpin (1987) suggests that seven aspects comprise the culture of an organization, and that the relative significance of each of these will vary from industry to industry. The seven aspects are:

1. The extent to which the organization is marketing oriented, giving customers high priority.
2. The relationships between management and staff, manifested through communication and participation systems, for example.
3. The extent to which people are target oriented, and committed to achieving agreed levels of performance.
4. Attitudes towards innovation. It is particularly important that the risks associated with failure are perceived as acceptable by all levels of management if innovation and entrepreneurship is to be fostered.
5. Attitudes towards costs and cost reduction.
6. The commitment and loyalty to the organization felt, and shown, by staff.
7. The impact of, and reaction to, technology and technological change and development. One major issue concerns whether or not the opportunities offered by information technology are being harnessed by the firm.

Many of these aspects are developed further in later chapters of the book.

Hampden-Turner (1990) believes that the culture is a manifestation of how the organization has chosen to deal with specific dilemmas and conflicts. Each of these can be viewed as a continuum, and the organization needs a clear position on each one. As we saw in Chapter 2, one dilemma might be the conflict between, on the one hand, the need to develop new products and services quickly and ahead of competitors, and, on the other hand, the need for thorough development and planning to ensure adequate quality and safety. Another dilemma is the need for managers to be adaptive and responsive in a

IKEA was started in Sweden by Ingvar Kamprad, who pioneered the idea of self-assembly furniture in handy packs. His vision of 'a better, more beautiful, everyday life for the many' led to 'a wide range of home furnishings, of good function and style, at low prices, for mass consumer markets'. Kamprad began with a mail-order business in 1943; the first IKEA store was opened in 1958. By the early 1990s, IKEA had some 125 shops in 26 countries. IKEA's strategy has always involved high quality merchandise at prices which undercut the competition. In 1993–4 IKEA's turnover approached $5 billion; after tax profits were *estimated* to be between six and seven per cent of revenue. IKEA has always been reticent about the financial data it releases.

IKEA stores focus on sales of self-assembly packs which customers take away themselves. IKEA will, however, deliver fully assembled pieces for a premium price. The stores have a wide range of facilities, typically including restaurants and games and video rooms for children; these are normally on the top floor, which is where customers come in. People are then routed carefully through a series of display areas to the downstairs purchase points which resemble a typical discount warehouse.

The furniture packs are *commissioned* from over 2300 suppliers in some 70 countries, many of them low labour countries in the Far East and Eastern Europe. IKEA designs all its own products and aims to lead customer taste. There is just one range of products for the global market; not every country and store stocks the full range, though. IKEA chooses not to have mini-ranges for specific countries and prides itself on an ability to respond to local fashion and opportunities by quickly adjusting the range in any one store. Sales per square foot invariably exceed industry averages.

Growth has been carefully regulated. IKEA waited seven years before opening a second branch; the first branch outside Sweden was in the early 1970s; the first US store opened in 1985, with typically one new store being added every year. This approach allows IKEA to properly establish local supply networks and ensures it does not become stretched financially. IKEA does not have a large market share in any single country; instead it has a global brand and an intriguing reputation which draws customers from substantial distances away.

Manifestations of IKEA's distinctive culture
The **artefacts** clearly include the stores, the products and the prices. There are (like Marks and Spencer) no brands other than IKEA's own. There are no annual or seasonal sales; prices stay valid for a whole year. There is a plethora of in-store information and communications, but no commissioned sales people.

Values. IKEA use the word 'prosumers' to imply that value is added by both IKEA and their customers in partnership. Employees are empowered to be innovative and helpful and challenged to 'dare to be different'. IKEA recognizes that always offering prices substantially below those of its competitors places considerable pressure on its staff.

Underlying assumptions can be summarized in the following quotes:

> We do not need to do things in traditional ways (window manufacturers have been approached to make table frames; shirt manufacturers for seat cushions).

> Break your chains and you are free; cut your roots and you die. IKEA should look for constant renewal. Experiments matter; mistakes (within reason) will be tolerated.

Behaviours. Every IKEA manager flies economy class and uses taxis only if there is no suitable alternative. In Holland, managers have been encouraged to actually stay with typical IKEA customer families to learn more about their needs.

People
A variety of **stories** permeate the IKEA culture. Initially customers in the US stores were simply not buying any beds – there had been no market research into US tastes; it was IKEA's global product. Eventually it was realized that Americans sleep in bigger beds than Swedes. Similarly

Continued overleaf

kitchen units had to be adjusted to handle extra large pizza plates.

Leadership and management style. Kamprad himself 'rarely shows his face to the public'. At one stage there was some adverse publicity concerning alleged wartime allegiances, but no lasting damage. The lack of published financial information reinforces this hidden aspect of IKEA.

The organization is structured as an inverted pyramid – employees are there to serve customers – and based on managers and co-workers. There are no directors, no formal titles and 'no dining rooms or reserved parking spaces for executives'. Managers are quite likely to switch between functions and countries. The organization is fundamentally informal with 'few instructions'. Every year there is an 'anti-bureaucracy' week when everyone dresses casually.

Communications. Both customers and employees are encouraged to provide ideas and suggestions, which may be translated into new products. 'Information enters the system from several points.'

Ownership and structural issues

IKEA remains a private company which owns all its sites. It pays for new sites in cash, which limits the pace of growth. 'We don't like to be in the hands of the banks.'

Inevitably the close-knit, informal style and values must be threatened by growth. At the end of the 1980s costs were approximately 30% of sales revenue; by early 1985 they had risen to nearer 40%.

Sources: Carnegy, H (1995), Struggle to save the soul of IKEA, *Financial Times*, 27 March; McGarrigle, I (1993), Daring to be different, *Retail Week*, 26 March; Summary in *Strategic Direction*, September 1992, pp. 4–7.

changing environment, but not at the expense of organization-wide communication and awareness. Such change-orientation may also conflict with a desire for continuity and consistency of strategy and policy.

IKEA (Case 4.2) focuses on being a low cost competitor and achieves this whilst maintaining a complex supply chain network. IKEA also has an ability to be flexible in response to local opportunities, which could easily add costs as well as value. The company is product- and production-driven, but able to capture and use ideas from customers and employees. The IKEA case draws together a number of points from this section.

Culture and strategy creation

We have already seen that the essential cultural characteristics will dictate the preferred mode of strategy creation in an organization; all the modes are likely to be present to some degree.

The culture will influence the ability of a strategic visionary to 'sell' his or her ideas to other members of the organization and gain their support and commitment to change. The planning mode is most suitable in a reasonably stable and predictable environment, but a reliance on it in a more unstable situation can lead to missed opportunities. It is an ideal mode for a conservative, risk-averse, slow-to-change organization.

Where environmental opportunities and threats arise continuously in a situation of competitive chaos an organization must be able to deal with them if it is to survive. It is the culture, with its amalgam of attitudes, values, perceptions and experiences, which determines the outcomes and relative success.

The structure must facilitate awareness, sharing and learning and people must be willing and able to act. People 'learn by doing' and they must be able to learn from mistakes. Peters (1988) states that 'managers have to learn how to make mistakes faster'. The reward system is critical here. Managers and employees should be praised and rewarded for exercising initiative and taking risks which prove successful; failures should not be sanctioned too harshly – as long as they are not repeated!

Berry (1983) argues that if a strategic leader really understands the company culture he or she must, by definition, be better equipped to make wise decisions. He or she might conclude that 'cultural change will be so difficult we had better be sure to select a business or strategy that our kind of company can handle well'. This is just as valid, and perhaps more useful, than believing that one can accomplish cultural change in order to shift the firm towards a new strategy.

Moreover, if business strategies and culture are intertwined, the ability to analyse and construct strategies and the ability to manage and inspire people are also intertwined. Hence a good strategy acknowledges 'where we are, what we have got, and what therefore managerially helps us to get where we want to be' and this is substantially different from selecting business options exclusively on their product/market dynamics. In other words developing and implementing strategy is a human and political process that starts as much with the visions, hopes and aspirations of a company's leaders as it does with market or business analysis. Ideas drive organizations.

With ever-shortening product life cycles, intense global competition and unstable economies and currencies the future is going to require organizations that are ready to commit themselves to change. Strategy is going to be about intertwining analysis and adaptation. The challenge is to develop more effective organizations.

Miles and Snow (1978), whose research has been used to develop Table 4.1, have suggested a typology of organizations which can be looked at in relation to culture and strategy formation. The typology distinguishes organizations in terms of their values and objectives, and different types will typically prefer particular approaches to strategy creation. Defenders, prospectors and analysers are all regarded by Miles and Snow as positive organizations; reactors must ultimately adopt one of the other three approaches or suffer long-term decline.

Strategic analysis on its own may improve the perception of leadership but have little influence on the nature, pace and direction of corporate decisions, since there is a natural tendency for corporate behaviour to follow the past momentum.

The power of 'corporate culture' should not be underestimated, both for a company's success, and, if it is inappropriate, in frustrating change. Values, strategies, systems, organization and accountabilities – the components of culture – are a very strong mix which can either make a company successful or alternatively, lead to its decline.

The task of corporate leadership is to apply energy and judgement to the corporate culture to ensure its continued relevance. And the art of Strategic Management is to bring forward, at the very least, the same energy that arises at times of crisis, and to address the potential culture barriers to renewal, early enough, whilst options are still available, before the trend of performance turns downwards. Typically this requires clear leadership signals, reinforced by changes in organization, systems and people.

Sir Allen Sheppard, Chairman, Grand Metropolitan plc

Table 4.1

Organizations, values and
strategies

Type	Characteristics	Strategy formation
Defenders	Conservative beliefs Low risk strategies Secure markets Concentration on narrow segments Considerable expertise in narrow areas of specialism Preference for well-tried resolutions to problems Little search for anything really 'new' Attention given to improving efficiency of present operations	Emphasis on planning
Prospectors	Innovative Looking to break new ground High risk strategies Search for new opportunities Can create change and uncertainty, forcing a response from competitors More attention given to market changes than to improving internal efficiency	Visionary mode
Analysers	Two aspects: stable and changing Stable: formal structures and search for efficiencies Changing: competitors monitored and strategies amended as promising ideas seen (followers)	Planning mode Adaptive/Incremental mode
Reactors	Characterized by an inability to respond effectively to change pressures Adjustments are therefore forced on the firm in order to avert crises	Adaptive mode

As examples of each type, I suggest that GEC, despite being in high technology industries, is relatively conservative and a defender. The risk-oriented innovative Amstrad is a prospector. The respective strategic leaders of these organizations, Lord Weinstock (until 1996) and Alan Sugar have adopted different styles of management and exhibited different corporate values. Historically many public sector bureaucracies have been stable analysers, whilst Marks and Spencer is a changing analyser. Prior to its decline and acquisition by BTR, Dunlop, in the 1970s, exhibited many of the characteristics of a reactor organization, and failed to change sufficiently in line with environmental changes.

Miles and Snow argue that, as well as being a classification, their typology can be used to predict behaviour. For example, a defender organization, in a search for greater operating efficiency, might consider investing in the latest technology, but reject the strategy if it has high risk attached.

Culture, structure and styles of management

Charles Handy (1976), building on earlier work by Harrison (1972) has developed an alternative classification of organizations based on cultural differences, and this is illustrated in Figure 4.2.

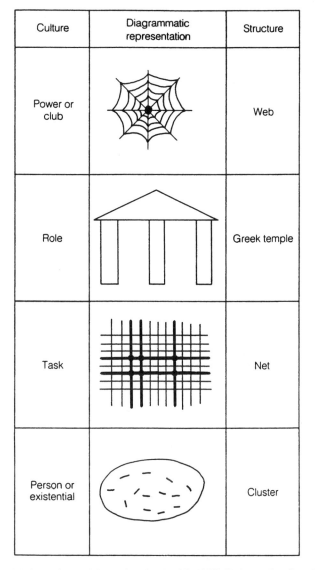

Culture	Diagrammatic representation	Structure
Power or club		Web
Role		Greek temple
Task		Net
Person or existential		Cluster

Figure 4.2 Handy's four cultures. Adapted from Handy, CB (1976) *Understanding Organizations,* Penguin.

The club culture or power culture

In the club culture type of organization, work is divided by function or product and a diagram of the organization structure would be quite traditional. There would be departments for sales, production, finance and so on, and possibly product-based divisions or strategic business units if the organization was larger. However, this structure is mostly found in smaller firms.

These functions or departments are represented in Handy's figure by the lines radiating out from the centre; but the essential point is that there are also concentric lines representing communications and power. The further away from the centre, the weaker is the power and influence. This structure is dominated from the centre and therefore is typical for small entrepreneurial organizations. Decisions can be taken quickly, but the quality of the decisions is very dependent upon the abilities of managers in the inner circle.

Hanson has been described by a former director as a 'solar system, with everyone circling around the sun in the middle, Lord Hanson' (see Leadbeater and Rudd, 1991). This analogy suggests both movement and dependency.

Decisions depend a great deal on empathy, affinity and trust both within the organization and with suppliers, customers and other key influences.

People learn to do instinctively what their boss and the organization expect and require. Consequently they will prove reliable even if they are allowed to exercise a degree of initiative. Foreign exchange dealers provide an illustration of this point.

For this reason the culture can be designated either 'club' or 'power'. Employees are rewarded for effort, success and compliance with essential values; and change is very much led from the centre in an entrepreneurial style.

A culture such as this may prevent individual managers from speaking their minds, but decisions are unlikely to get lost in committees.

The role culture

The role culture is the more typical 'organization' as the culture is built around defined jobs, rules and procedures and not personalities. People fit into jobs, and are recruited for this purpose. Hence rationality and logic are at the heart of the culture, which is designed to be stable and predictable.

The design is the Greek temple because the strengths of the organization are deemed to lie in the pillars, which are joined managerially at the top. One essential role of top management is to co-ordinate activity, and consequently it will be seen that both planning systems and incremental changes can be a feature of this culture. Although the strength of the organization is in the pillars, power lies at the top.

As well as being designed for stability the structure is also designed to allow for continuity and changes of personnel, and for this reason dramatic changes are less likely than more gradual ones.

High efficiency is possible in stable environments, but the structure can be slow to change and is therefore less suitable for dynamic situations.

Aspects of this culture can prove beneficial for transport businesses such as railways and airlines, where reliability and time-keeping are essential. Unfortunately it is not by nature a flexible, service-oriented culture. Intrapreneurship or elements of the task culture are also required for effectiveness.

The task culture

Management in the task culture is concerned with the continuous and successful solution of problems, and performance is judged by the success of the outcomes.

The challenge is more important than the routine.

The culture is shown as a net, because for particular problem situations people and other resources can be drawn from various parts of the organization on a temporary basis. Once the problem is dealt with people will move on to other tasks, and consequently discontinuity is a key element. Expertise is the major source of individual power and it will determine a person's relative power in a given situation. Power basically lies in the interstices of the net, because of the reliance on task forces.

The culture is ideal for consultancies, advertising agencies, and for research and development departments. It can also be useful within the role culture for tackling particularly difficult or unusual problem situations.

In dynamic environments a major challenge for large organizations is the design of a structure and systems which allow for proper management and integration without losing the spirit and excitement typical of small, entrepreneurial businesses. Elements of the task culture superimposed over formal roles can help by widening communications and engendering greater commitment within the organization. One feature is cost. This culture is expensive as there is a reliance on talking and discussion, experimentation and learning by trial. Although Handy uses the expression problem solving, there can be problem resolutions or moves towards a solution along more incremental lines, as well as decisions concerning major changes. If successful changes are implemented the expense can often be justified.

Visit the website:
http://www.
itbp.com

The person culture or existential culture

The person culture is completely different from the other three, for here the organization exists to help the individual rather than the other way round. Groups of professional people, such as doctors, architects, dentists and solicitors, provide excellent examples. The organization with secretarial help, printing and telephone facilities and so on provides a service for individual specialists and reduces the need for costly duplication. If a member of the circle leaves or retires, he or she is replaced by another who may have to buy in.

Some professional groups exhibit inter-dependencies and collaboration, allocating work amongst the members, although management of such an organization is difficult because of individual expertise and because the rewards and sanctions are different from those found in most other situations.

However, in an environment where government is attempting to increase competition between professional organizations, and in some cases to reduce barriers to entering the profession, it is arguable that effective management, particularly at the strategic level, will become increasingly necessary. Efforts will need co-ordinating and harnessing if organizations are to become strong competitors.

Management philosophies

Press (1990) suggests that the culture of an organization is based upon one or more philosophies. I have developed his ideas into Figure 4.3. The specific philosophies are related to the various stakeholders in the business, and are determined by two intersecting axes. One relates to whether the business is focused more internally or externally; the other is based on performance measures. Do they concentrate more on resource management and efficiency, or outcomes and effectiveness? This creates four discrete philosophies:

❑ **the resource focus** which concentrates on internal efficiencies and cost management
❑ **the shareholder focus** which sees the business as a portfolio of activities which should be managed to maximize the value of the business for its shareholders

Figure 4.3 Organizational philosophies. Adapted from Press, G (1990) Assessing competitors' business philosophies, *Long Range Planning*, **23,** 5.

❑ **the people focus** which emphasizes the skills and contribution of employees, and their needs and expectations
❑ **the market focus** which stresses the importance of satisfying customers by adding value and differentiating products and services.

All of these are important; none of them can be ignored. The culture can be analysed in terms of how these four philosophies are perceived and prioritized.

A company which relies heavily upon formal strategic planning, for example, is likely to concentrate more upon shareholders and resources. Hanson at a corporate level is, I would argue, similarly inclined; the individual subsidiary businesses will have a resource focus supported by people and market philosophies. (The Hanson strategy is explained in more detail later in the book.) General Electric (GE) of the USA (see Chapter 22) is another diversified conglomerate but with a different policy from Hanson on empowerment and decentralization. GE places most emphasis upon people and shareholders. Japanese companies, discussed later in this chapter, exhibit a particular blend of people, markets and resources.

Styles of management

Styles of management were described in Chapter 3 when the important role of strategic leadership was discussed. It is important to emphasize that the style adopted by the strategic leader can have a strong influence on the culture of the organization.

Everyone in the business feels (and is) involved. Everyone also feels (and is) accountable, especially those at the top.

Top management are given lots of freedom to determine and change strategy, but they can be questioned on anything by the rank-and-file partners ... this ... makes people think ahead and consider the consequences of their actions.

Stuart Hampson, Chairman, John Lewis Partnership since 1993.
Hampson is only the fourth Chairman since the Partnership was formed in 1929.

Styles which differ from the 'normal and traditional' can prove to be very effective in particular circumstances.

The John Lewis Partnership, Britain's third largest department store chain after Debenhams and House of Fraser, practises worker participation and democracy. John Lewis is also diversified into supermarkets with its Waitrose chain. The company has a chairman, a board of directors and a management structure, as do most companies, but parallel to this commercial structure stands a second structure which represents the interests of the ordinary worker who is also a partner in John Lewis. Whilst a partner working in a department in a store cannot directly influence management decisions, as a result of the partnership and its constitution the ordinary workers are again in ultimate control of the company they work for. This is supplemented by a profit-sharing scheme.

Decision making and communications within the organization must be affected by high levels of participation. John Lewis's motto of 'never knowingly undersold' is based on value for money which is helped by employee involvement. Through its workforce the company can relate well to its customers.

Culture and power

In Charles Handy's classification of organizations in terms of their culture, power is an important element which needs further consideration. While an introduction to the topic is included here, the subject of power is explored more fully in Chapter 22 when its impact on strategy implementation and strategic change are considered.

Power is related to the potential or ability to do something. Consequently strategic change will be strongly influenced by the bases of power within an organization and by the power of the organization in relation to its environment.

Internal power

Change is brought about if the necessary resources can be harnessed and if people can be persuaded to behave in a particular way. Both of these require power. Power results in part from the structure of the organization, and it needs exercising in different ways in different cultures if it is to be used effectively. At the same time power can be a feature of an individual manager's personality, and managers who are personally powerful will be in a position to influence change.

The ways in which managers apply power are known as 'power levers'; Box 4.1 describes seven major sources of power. The classifications of power bases produced by a number of authors differ only slightly. Box 4.1 has been developed from a classification by Andrew Kakabadse (1982), who has built on the earlier work of French and Raven (1959).

In order to understand the reality of change in an organization and to examine how change might be managed, it is important to consider where power lies, which managers are powerful, and where their sources of power are. Whilst a visible, powerful and influential strategic leader is often a feature of an entrepreneurial organization, the nature and direction of incremental change will be influenced significantly by which managers are powerful and how they choose to exercise their power.

❏ **Reward power** is the ability to influence the rewards given to others. These can be tangible (money) or intangible (status). Owner managers enjoy considerable reward power, managers in larger public sector organizations very little. For reward power to be useful, the rewards being offered must be important to the potential recipients.

❏ **Coercive power** is power based on the threat of punishment for non-compliance, and the ability to impose the punishment. The source can be the person's role or position in the organization, or physical attributes and personality.

❏ **Legitimate power** is synonymous with authority, and relates to an individual manager's position within the structure of the organization. It is an entitlement from the role a person occupies. The effective use of legitimate power is dependent upon three things: access to relevant information; access to other people and communication networks inside the organization; and approaches to setting priorities – this determines what is asked of others.

❏ **Personal power** depends on individual characteristics (personality) and physical characteristics. Charm, charisma and flair are terms used to describe people with personality-based power. Physical attributes such as height, size, weight and strength also affect personal power.

❏ **Expert power** is held by a person with specialist knowledge or skills in a particular field. It is particularly useful for tackling complex problem areas. It is possible for people to be attributed expert power through reputation rather than proven ability.

❏ **Information power** is the ability to access and use information to defend a stance or viewpoint – or to question an alternative view held by someone else – and is important as it can affect strategic choices.

❏ **Connection power** results from personal and professional access to key people inside and outside the organization, who themselves can influence what happens. This relates particularly to information power.

A power culture has strong central leadership as a key feature and power lies with the individual or small group at the centre who control most of the activity in the organization. In contrast, role cultures are based on the legitimacy of rules and procedures and individual managers are expected to work within these. Task cultures are dependent upon the expertise of individuals, and their success, in some part, depends upon the ability of the individuals to share their power and work as a team. Managers are expected to apply power levers in ways that are acceptable to the predominant culture of the organization, and at the same time the manner in which power levers are actually used affects what happens in the organization. Power is required for change; change results from the application of power. Hence the implementation of desired changes to strategies requires the effective use of power bases; but other strategic changes will result from the exercise of power by individual managers. It is important for the organization to monitor such activity and ensure that such emergent changes and strategies are desirable or acceptable.

The relative power of the organization

The ability of an organization to effect change within its environment will similarly depend on the exercise of power. A strong competitor with, say, a very distinctive product or service, or with substantial market share, may be more powerful than its rivals. A manufacturer who is able to influence distributors or suppliers will be similarly powerful. The issue is the relative power in relation to those other individuals, organizations and institutions on whom it relies, with whom it trades, or which influence it in some way. These other influences are known as stakeholders, and their impact is discussed in Chapter 5.

The search for excellence

Research into US companies

McKinsey and Company, well-known US management consultants, initiated an investigation in the 1970s into why certain companies were more successful than their rivals. The findings were published in 1980 in a *Business Week* article and they eventually became the basis for the book *In Search of Excellence* (Peters and Waterman, 1982). The research emphasizes the important contribution of culture and values to organizational success.

At successful companies, strong cultures are clearly a strategic asset as internalized beliefs motivate people to unusual performance levels. We must, however, be cautious. Whilst much may be known about the culture of a successful organization, we may not learn 'how to get it'. *In Search of Excellence* (in common with similar books) is descriptive, not prescriptive.

Some 40 companies were surveyed in a cross-section of industries and included IBM, Texas Instruments, Hewlett-Packard, 3M, Procter and Gamble, Johnson and Johnson, and McDonald's. The companies were selected for being 'well-run and successful organizations'. Most of the companies were well established and large. In the selection process 20 years of financial data were analysed and the companies under consideration were evaluated relative to competitors in their industry. In addition a subjective assessment of their innovation records was used as a final screen. The research concluded that the most successful companies exhibited eight common attributes, which are featured in Table 4.2, and that their success was based primarily on good management practice. Managers had invested time, energy and thought into doing certain important things well and those activities and values were understood by employees and appreciated by customers. In other words they had become part of the culture of the organization.

In most companies the role of one or more strategic leaders had proved to be very influential in establishing and developing the values, and in many cases the values had been established early in the company's history. In other words growth had been assisted by the culture. Peters and Waterman conclude that 'the real role of the chief executive is to manage the **values** of the organization' (see Chapter 3).

Peters and Waterman argue that 'excellent' companies are successful in their management of the basic fundamentals with respect to their environment: customer service; low cost manufacturing; productivity improvement; innovation; and risk taking. In order to ensure that the key values are understood and practised throughout the organization there is an emphasis on simplicity: simple organization structures; simple strategies; simple goals; and simple communications systems.

The attributes featured in Table 4.2 are essentially quite basic rather than startling, and they are very much related to the contribution made by people. 'The excellent companies live their commitment to people.' Not all the attributes were visible in each of the companies studied, nor were they given the same priority in different organizations, but in every case there was a preponderance of the attributes and they were both visible and distinctive. In less successful companies, argue Peters and Waterman, 'far too many managers have lost sight of the basics: quick action, service to customers, practical innovation, and the fact that you can't get any of these without virtually everyone's commitment'.

Since the book was published some of the 'excellent' companies, notably People Express, IBM and Caterpillar Tractor, have been less successful and so the findings of *In Search of Excellence* should be treated carefully. Basically the research found a number of common attributes to be present in the organizations studied rather than providing a set of recommendations concerning how unsuccessful companies could be transformed. It provided food for thought rather than answers.

In a more recent book Robert Waterman (1988), writing independently, argues that in order to become and remain successful organizations must

Table 4.2

In search of excellence: characteristics of the most successful organizations

A bias for action	Greater emphasis on trying things rather than talking about them and seeking 'solutions' rather than 'resolutions' Avoidance of long complicated business plans Use of task forces to tackle special problems (Handy's task culture)
Close to the customer	Companies are 'customer-driven, not technology-driven, not product-driven, not strategy-driven' They 'know what the customer wants, and provide it – better than competitors'
Autonomy and entrepreneurship	Managers are authorized to act entrepreneurially rather than be tied too rigidly by rules and systems
Productivity through people	Productivity improvements by motivating and stimulating employees, using involvement and communications 'Corny merit awards, like badges and stars work' if they are properly managed and not just used as a gimmick
Hands on, value driven	Values are established with good communications People must 'believe' The power and personality of the strategic leader is crucial
Stick to the knitting	Successful companies know what they do well and concentrate on doing it well
Simple form, lean staff	Simple structures
Simultaneous loose–tight properties	An effective combination of central direction and individual autonomy Certain control variables, such as a particular financial return measure or the number of employees, are managed tightly; for other things managers are encouraged to be flexible

Summarized from Peters, TJ and Waterman, RH Jr (1982) *In Search of Excellence*, Harper & Row.

master the management of change. As will be seen later in this book, there is often a fear of change and hostility towards it. These must be overcome, claims Waterman, because competition changes too quickly to allow companies to fall into what he calls the 'habit trap'. He further argues that strategies should be based on 'informed opportunism', developing from effective information systems which ensure that customers, suppliers and other key influences are consulted. Waterman emphasizes that for an information system to be effective it should not be allowed to become too rigid or bureaucratic.

Peters (1988) asserts that there are no long-term excellent companies. 'The pace of change has become far too rapid to make any enterprise secure. Tomorrow's winners will have to view chaos, external and internal, not as a problem, but as a prime source of competitive advantage.' Peters quotes Ford of Europe as an example of a company which has dealt successfully with the challenge of change by stressing a new set of basic values: world-class quality and service; greater flexibility and responsiveness; continuous and rapid product and service innovation. Arguably, however, the change was forced on Ford by strong Japanese competition.

The limits to excellence

To summarize, some firms do appear to obtain superior financial performance from their cultures, but it does not follow that firms who succeed in copying these cultural attributes will necessarily also achieve superior financial results. Organizations which pursue the excellence factors must surely improve their chances of success, but clearly there can be no guarantees. Ignoring these issues will increase the chances of failure.

But the need to maintain E–V–R congruence in a dynamic, competitive environment must never be forgotten.

During the early 1980s Jan Carlzon turned around the struggling SAS (Scandinavian Airlines System) by focusing on improvements in service and communications. Profits were restored with improved revenues, but costs later increased as well. As a driving philosophy, the service culture had to give way to a focus strategy and rationalization.

> Everything that does not further the competitiveness of our airline activities must be removed, sold or turned into separate entities.
>
> *(Jan Carlzon)*

BA, which followed SAS with a service culture, has been more successful in simultaneously controlling costs, and has consequently maintained its growth to become one of the world's most successful and admired airlines.

In my opinion effective strategic management requires:

1. A sound strategy, which implies an effective match between the resources and the environment.

Visit the website: http://www.itbp.com

I produce the show. I think I am a strategic person. But how do I get people to grab the strategy, to get it under their skin, to get a feel for it, to **get** it? I can't write it in a manual. I must make a show of it. I motivate people through the show. Communication. And it is not manipulating – it is a way of getting the message across.

Jan Carlzon, President and Chief Executive Officer, Scandinavian Airlines System

2. A well-managed execution and implementation of the strategy.
3. Appropriate strategic change. Whilst it can be important to 'stick to the knitting', firms must watch for signs indicating that strategies need to be improved or changed.

Culture and competitive advantage

Barney (1986) has examined further the relationship between culture and 'superior financial performance'. He has used microeconomics for his definition of superior financial performance, arguing that firms record either below-normal returns (insufficient for long-term survival in the industry), normal returns (enough for survival, but no more) or superior results, which are more than those required for long-term survival. Superior results, which result from some form of competitive advantage, attract competitors who seek to copy whatever is thought to be the source of competitive advantage and generating the success. This in turn affects supply and margins and can reduce profitability to only normal returns and, in some cases, below normal. Therefore **sustained** superior financial performance requires **sustained** competitive advantage.

Barney concluded that culture can, and does, generate sustained competitive advantage, and hence long-term superior financial performance, when three conditions are met.

❑ The culture is valuable. The culture must enable things to happen which themselves result in high sales, low costs or high margins.
❑ The culture is rare.
❑ The culture is imperfectly imitable, i.e. it cannot be copied easily by competitors.

Hence if the cultural factors identified by Peters and Waterman are in fact transferable easily to other organizations, can they be the source of superior financial performance? Barney contends that valuable and rare cultures may be difficult, if not impossible, to imitate. For one thing it is very difficult to define culture clearly, particularly in respect of how it adds value to the product or service. For another culture is often tied to historical aspects of company development and to the beliefs, personality and charisma of a particular strategic leader.

Cases 4.3 and 4.4, Body Shop and Club Méditerranée, provide examples of companies which have gained success and renown with a culture-based competitive advantage. Whilst maintaining the underlying principles and values, both companies have had to rethink their strategies to remain competitive.

Changing culture

The culture of an organization may appear to be in need of change for any one of a number of reasons. It could be that the culture does not fit well with the needs of the environment or with the organization's resources, or that the company is not performing well and needs major strategic changes, or even that the company is growing rapidly in a changing environment and needs to adapt.

Body Shop, which sources, manufactures and retails (mainly through franchises) natural lotions and cosmetics, has been a highly successful business with a price to earnings ratio which stayed well above the retail sector average throughout the 1980s. Body Shop was started in England in 1976, and for many years it enjoyed revenue and profits growth of some 50% per year. The business was founded by Anita Roddick and her husband, Gordon, who shortly afterwards took a sabbatical leave and rode a horse from Buenos Aires to New York. At this time the Roddicks had two young daughters. Stores have been opened in over 40 countries – there are now over 1200 – but over half the profits are still made in the UK. Body Shop was floated on the UK Stock Exchange in 1984.

Body Shop arouses enthusiasm, commitment and loyalty amongst those involved with it. Much of this has developed from the ethical beliefs and values of Anita Roddick, which have become manifested in a variety of distinctive policies. Gordon Roddick is now responsible for the highly efficient operational aspects of the business.

❑ Body Shop is very strong on environmental issues, offering only biodegradable products and refillable containers. Shops have been used to campaign, amongst other things, to save whales and to stop the burning of rain forests.
❑ Packaging is plain, but the shops are characterized by strong and distinctive aromas. The packages, together with posters and shelf cards, provide comprehensive information about the products and their origins and ingredients. This has created a competitive advantage which rivals have found difficult to replicate. The logo and packaging were redesigned in 1995.
❑ The sales staff are knowledgeable, but they are not forceful and do not sell aggressively, offering advice only if it is requested.
❑ Marketing themes concern 'health rather than glamour, and reality rather than instant rejuvenation'.

❑ Body Shop chose to avoid advertising for many years, preferring in-store information to attempts at persuasion. More recently, and especially in the USA, informative advertising has been used. In 1995 in the UK Body Shop introduced an in-store radio station, transmitted by satellite.
❑ Ingredients are either natural or have been used by humans for years. There is no testing on animals.
❑ Employees are provided with regular newsletters, videos and training packages. Anita Roddick contributes regularly to the newsletters, which concentrate on Body Shop campaigns. Employees and franchisees can attend the Body Shop training centre in London free of charge. All the courses are product centred and informative – they do not focus on selling, marketing or how to make more money.
❑ Employees are given time off, and franchisees encouraged to take time off, during working hours, to do voluntary work for the community.
❑ Body Shop has integrated manufacturing and retailing and is efficient and operationally strong. Fresh supplies are typically delivered with a 24-hour lead time. As a result of acquisitions, Body Shop has the capacity to manufacture most of its product range.
❑ 'Profits are perceived as boring, business as exciting.'
❑ 'The company must never let itself become anything other than a human enterprise.'

These strategies, policies and beliefs have, of course, generated substantial growth and profits. In the year ended 28 February 1991 turnover exceeded £100 million with trading profits of some £22 million. When these results were announced the UK share price exceeded 350 pence. Between 1984 and 1991, against the Financial Times All Share index of 100, Body Shop shares rose from an index figure of 100 to 5500. By mid-1995 the share price had fallen to 150 pence. Profits had fallen; new professional
Continued overleaf

senior managers had been brought in to add strength. One dilemma concerned whether the culture and quirky management style was still wholly appropriate as Body Shop became a much bigger multi-national business. Global scale brings global competition.

In the UK Body Shop had attracted more and more competition. Retailers such as Boots, Marks and Spencer and Sainsburys introduced natural products in their own label ranges; a further threat was posed by the US *Bath and Body Works*, whose early trial stores were a joint venture with Next. Bath and Body Works is renowned as a fast-moving organization, quick to innovate new ideas – and aggressive at advertising and promotion. Amongst its responses in the UK, Body Shop began trials of a party plan operation.

The Bath and Body Works chain was also growing faster than Body Shop in the USA, and that prompted the Roddicks to expand rapidly, opening new stores very quickly. The costs had a dramatic impact on profitability. UK retailers are generally perceived to be less slick than their US competitors at managing rapid change; Body Shop was no exception.

In 1994 Body Shop also began to face criticism concerning the reality behind its ethical stance; a full publication of its social audit – then being commissioned – was promised.

In October 1995 Body Shop announced its intention to reprivatize the company by buying back shares at a price of 200 pence. The objective was to escape the constraints of the City institutions, which Anita Roddick had earlier called 'the pinstriped dinosaurs'. The shares would then be placed in a charitable trust, which would be able to make donations to humanitarian and environmental causes. The plan was abandoned in March 1996 because of its loan implications; Body Shop would have had to borrow heavily to finance the plan, arguably leaving it too exposed.

Ideally the culture and strategies being pursued will complement each other, and, again ideally, the organization will be flexible and adaptable to change when it is appropriate. But these ideals will not always be achieved.

The culture of an organization can be changed, but it may not be easy. Strong leadership and vision is always required to champion the change process. If an organization is in real difficulty, and the threat to its survival is clearly recognized, behaviour can be changed through fear and necessity. However, people may not feel comfortable and committed to the changes they accept. Behaviour may change, but not attitudes and beliefs. When an organization is basically successful the process of change again needs careful management – changing attitudes and beliefs does not itself guarantee a change of behaviour.

The potential for changing the culture is affected by:

(i)   the strength and history of the existing culture
(ii)   how well the culture is understood
(iii) the personality and beliefs of the strategic leader and
(iv)   the extent of the strategic need.

Lewin (1947) contends that there are three important stages in the process of change: unfreezing existing behaviour, changing attitudes and behaviour, and refreezing the new behaviour as accepted common practice.

The first steps in changing culture are recognizing and diagnosing the existing culture, highlighting any weaknesses and stressing the magnitude of the need to change.

CLUB MÉDITERRANÉE

Club Med, founded in 1950 in France, is Europe's largest tour operator with a clearly distinguished product.

Club Med represents 'beautiful people playing all sorts of sports, white sand beaches, azure sky and sea, Polynesian thatched huts, free and flowing wine at meals, simple yet superb food' (*Economist*, 12 July 1986). It is an 'organized melange of hedonism and back to nature'.

The organization is spread around the world, with some 100 holiday villages and over 60 holiday residences (hotel/sports complexes) for both summer and winter vacations. Organizers are present in a ratio of 1:5 with guests, for whom they provide sports tuition and organize evening entertainment. All tuition, food and drinks with meals are paid for in advance in the holiday cost, and guests are provided with beads which they use as they choose to buy extra drinks and so on. Clothing is permanently casual.

Club Med has traditionally charged prices above the average for package holidays, its clientele have been mainly above-average income earners, and the organization has enjoyed a reputation for delivering customer service and satisfaction. The strategy has been developed and maintained by the founder of the business, Gilbert Trigano, who was 70 years old in 1991. Although Triagano was always an influential strategic leader, Club Med is a public company, with most of its equity held by institutional shareholders.

A culture of creativity and teamworking is encouraged at all levels in Club Med. Gilbert Trigano always saw the organization as 'one big, happy family'. No employee should feel as if they are simply a pawn; promotions are typically from within. The loyalty of Club Med staff is very high, making it difficult for outsiders to come in as managers. Trigano set up Club Med as an organization 'without rules – in a world where most companies operate with fixed rules and structures. Everyone is under an obligation to create, but, of course, not every idea is a success'.

The company grew successfully for over 30 years with little change to the basic strategy. By the mid-1980s, however, occupancy rates had fallen, and profits declined and then stagnated. While the underlying concept was still sound, people's tastes were changing. Holidaymakers increasingly sought higher quality facilities than the straw huts provided. Many Americans wanted televisions and telephones – 'it was the absence of these which helped make Club Med unique'.

Building on the original concept and strategy Club Med developed new products in order to better satisfy selected audiences around the world. In the early 1990s, one-third of Club Med's one million customers took their holidays outside France. In addition to the traditional villages, where in some cases straw huts have been replaced by bungalows, there are now both cheaper, half-board holidays available in newly acquired hotels and villages, as well as more expensive properties. This latter development was pioneered at Opio, near Cannes, which opened in 1989. Opio has expensive rooms with facilities, and, unusually, is open 12 months of the year. The international conference trade is being targeted. A limited number of villages now have a multi-lingual staffing policy to ensure that visitors from different European countries can all be greeted in their own language. Attempts are being made to attract more American visitors, but there is some scepticism. Americans are more puritanical in their tastes and expectations, and 'Club Med's sexy image' has not proved as successful in the USA.

There have been problems with certain other strategic developments:

❏ In the early 1990s profitability at the Vienna City Hotel and from the two cruise ships was inadequate.
❏ New developments in Japan were delayed.
❏ In 1991 Club Med bought a controlling stake in a second charter airline – its first airline came when Club Med acquired a competitor in the 1980s. Combined the two could fly to 100 destinations spread over 20 countries on four continents. In reality, Club Med had too much capacity and ended up selling 80% stakes in both airlines.

Continued overleaf

In 1993, with European occupancy rates depressed, Club Med recorded its worst ever results. Gilbert Triagno partially retired and was succeeded by his son, Serge, who was determined to:

❏ accelerate developments in new territories such as Asia and

❏ reduce costs to allow for more competitive prices, still with quality and innovation – it was 'time to realize people would not always come just because it is Club Med'.

'It is by focusing on our core business that we will return to profit.'

Nevertheless, Rosemary Astles, Marketing Director at Thomson Holidays, has been quoted as saying 'Club Med has a reasonably unique formula that has worked well in a number of markets ... but there will be [only] limited growth for the club concept in the future. It's a fairly mature market'.

Sources: Annual Reports; Club Med: The Bourgeois Holiday Camp, *The Economist*, 12 July 1986; Nash, T (1992), Club Med's Creative Family, *The Director*, October; Wood, S (1990) A New Life for Club Med, *Business*, January.

One way of changing behaviour would be the establishment of internal groups to study and benchmark competitors and set new performance standards. This would lead to wider discussion throughout the organization, supported by skills training – possibly including communication, motivation and financial awareness skills. People must become committed to the changes, which requires persistence by those who are championing the change and an emphasis on the significance and the desired outcomes.

Unless the changes become established and part of the culture, there will be a steady drift back to the previous pattern. Whilst critical aspects of the culture should remain rock-solid and generate strategic consistency, this must not mean the organization becomes resistant to change without some major upheaval. Competitive pressures require organizations to be vigilant, aware and constantly change-oriented, not change resistant.

Resistance to change should always be expected. People may simply be afraid because they do not understand all the reasons behind the proposed changes; they may mistrust colleagues or management because of previous experiences; communications may be poor; motivation and commitment may be missing; internal architecture may be weak, causing internal conflict and hostility; and the organization may simply not be good at sharing best practice and learning. We will return to this topic in Chapter 22, Managing Change.

The Japanese culture

Without question, Japanese companies have become formidable competitors in several industries. For many years they have been the 'principal challengers of Western firms serious about world markets'. More recently domestic recession, a high yen and intensifying competition from other Pacific Rim countries (many with lower wages) have restrained Japan's global expansion. However, a study of the philosophies, strategies and tactics adopted by Japanese companies will yield a number of valuable insights into competitive strategy, even though it is impractical to suggest that Western businesses could simply learn to copy their

Japanese rivals. This section looks at some of the reasons for Japan's success; it has to be acknowledged that in the l990s some of the practices are changing. 'In the long-run the only feasible response is to do better what the Japanese are doing well already – developing management systems that motivate employees from top to bottom to pursue growth-oriented, innovation-focused competitive strategies' (Pucik and Hatvany, 1983).

Deal and Kennedy (1982) have argued that 'Japan Inc.' is a culture, with considerable co-operation between industry, the banking systems and government. For this reason certain aspects of the Japanese culture are difficult to imitate. For example banks in the UK are public companies with their own shareholders and they borrow and lend money in order to make profit; this is their basic 'mission'.

Another key structural feature historically has been the *keiretsu*, or corporate families, whereby a unique mix of ownerships and alliances makes hostile take-overs very unlikely. At its height, for example, the powerful Mitsubishi *keiretsu* represented 216,000 employees in 29 organizations as diverse as banking, brewing, shipping, shipbuilding, property, oil, aerospace and textiles. The companies held, on average, 38% of each other's shares; directors were exchanged; and the fact that 15 of the companies were located together in one district of Tokyo facilitated linkages of various forms, including inter-trading wherever this was practical. The *keiretsu* influence is beginning to fade as Japanese companies are locating more and more production overseas in their search for lower manufacturing costs. Mitsubishi's shipping company, for instance, has begun to buy vessels manufactured in Korean yards; Japanese shipbuilders are no longer an automatic low-price competitor.

Culture plays a significant role at the heart of the Japanese strategy process.

In Japan the historic focus has been on human resources (Pucik and Hatvany, 1983) and this becomes the basis for three key strategic thrusts which are expressed as a number of management techniques. These act as key determinants of the actual strategies pursued (Figure 4.4). The three strategic thrusts are the notion of an internal labour market within the organization, a unique company philosophy, and intensive socialization throughout the working life.

The internal labour market is based on the tradition of lifetime employment whereby young men (not females) who join large companies after school or university are expected to remain with them for life and in return are offered job security. Commitment and loyalty to the employer result. With recession in recent years this practice has been less widespread.

The articulated and enacted unique philosophy is again designed to generate commitment and loyalty with the argument that familiarity with the goals of a company helps establish values and provides direction for effort and behaviour. YKK's 'Cycle of Goodness' (Box 4.2) is an excellent example.

The core of management is the art of mobilizing every ounce of intelligence in the organization and pulling together the intellectual resources of all employees in the service of the firm. We know that the intelligence of a handful of technocrats, however brilliant and smart they may be, is no longer enough. Only by drawing on the combined brain power of all its employees can a firm face up to the turbulence and constraints of today's environment.

Mr Konosuke Matsushita, Matsushita Electrical Industrial Company Ltd

---

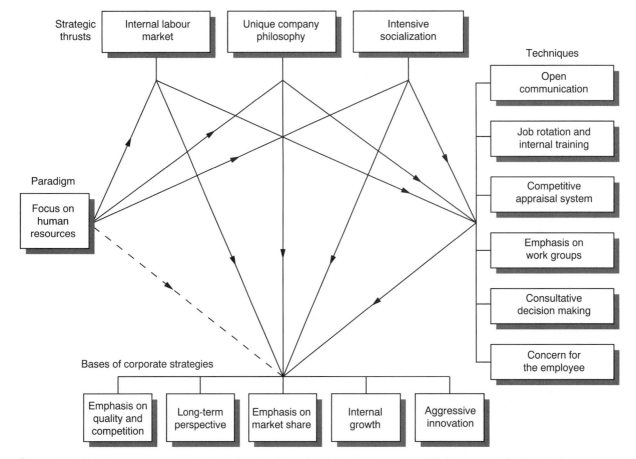

Figure 4.4 The Japanese management system. Developed from Pucik, V and Hatvany, N (1983) *Management Practices in Japan and their Impact on Business Strategy*, JAI Press.

The potential benefits of a company philosophy will only be gained if the philosophy is communicated to employees and demonstrated by managers. Hence this is a key aspect of company socialization in Japan, which starts with initial training and continues with further training throughout the working life.

These three strategic thrusts are closely linked to six management techniques used extensively in Japanese firms.

Open communication and sharing information across departmental boundaries aims to develop a climate of trust and a team spirit within the organization. This is enhanced by close integration between managers and employees. Job rotation and the internal training programmes supplement this communication system because through them employees become more aware of what happens throughout the organization. Because of very low labour turnover, promotion opportunities are very limited and advancement is slow and often

They [the Japanese] are relentless. Relentless. If you tell them the mountain is this high, and they have to run up it, they run up it. If you then say 'I'm sorry, but it's ten times the height', they don't say 'Hey; that wasn't the deal!' – they run up that too.

James Cannavino, when Senior Vice-President, Strategy and Development, IBM

Box 4.2
THE CYCLE OF GOODNESS

Attributed to Tadeo Yoshida, President, YKK

YKK is the world's leading manufacturer of zip fasteners. YKK produces and markets zips throughout the world, and is vertically integrated, designing and manufacturing much of its own machinery.

I firmly believe in the spirit of social service.

Wages alone are not sufficient to assure our employees of a stable life and a rising standard of living. For this reason we return to them a large share of the fruits of their labour, so that they may also participate in capital accumulation and share in the profits of the firm. Each employee, depending on his means, deposits with the company at least ten per cent of his wages and monthly allowances, and 50 per cent of his bonus; the company, in turn, pays interest on these savings. Moreover, as this increases capital, the employees benefit further as stockholders of the firm. It is said that the accumulation of savings distinguishes man from animals. Yet, if the receipts of a day are spent within that day, there can be no such cycle of saving.

The savings of all YKK employees are used to improve production facilities, and contribute directly to the prosperity of the firm. Superior production facilities improve the quality of the goods produced. Lower prices increase demand. And both factors contribute to the prosperity of other industries that use our products.

As society prospers, the need for raw materials and machinery of all sorts increases, and the benefits of this cycle spread out not just to this firm, but to all related industries. Thus the savings of our employees, by enhancing the prosperity of the firm, are returned to them as dividends that enrich their lives. This results in increased savings which further advance the firm. Higher incomes mean higher tax payments, and higher tax payments enrich the lives of every citizen. In this manner, business income directly affects the prosperity of society; for businesses are not mere seekers after profit, but vital instruments for the improvement of society.

This cycle enriches our free society and contributes to the happiness of those who work within it. The perpetual working of this cycle produces perpetual prosperity for all. This is the cycle of goodness.

based on seniority. However, performance is essential, and employees are carefully and regularly appraised in their abilities to get things done and to co-operate with others.

This is particularly important as Japanese companies revolve around groups rather than individuals, with work being assigned to teams of employees. This, together with the use of quality circles (whereby groups of employees are encouraged to discuss issues and problems and suggest improvements), is seen as a key motivator. There is considerable emphasis on consultative decision making, involving these working groups, and a desire for consensus decisions. This generates greater loyalty to the decisions and to implementation. Finally, managers are encouraged to spend time with employees discussing both performance and personal problems. Companies also provide housing and various other services for employees.

A number of Japanese companies have invested in manufacturing plants in the UK (as well as in the USA and other countries in Europe) in recent years. In a number of cases they have selected industries where the UK had already ceased to manufacture products because of an inability to compete (e.g. television sets and video recorders) or where the competitive edge had declined. Motor vehicles is an example of the latter. The British car industry fell

---

Case 4.5
NISSAN UK

Milestones	Key human resources aspects of the strategy

Milestones

1984 Agreement with UK Government concerning location and development incentives.

1985 Wearside (Sunderland) factory completed on schedule.

1986 First Bluebird cars sold.

1987 Production and sales both ahead of targets.

1988 Decision to develop additional engine and body shops. Left-hand drive models exported into Europe.

1990 Target of 80,000 cars per year set – with an 80% local content (i.e. British components and materials).

1992 Expansion announced. New target: 300,000 cars per year – approaching the output levels of the long-established companies.

Key human resources aspects of the strategy

❑ Single union agreement – with the AEU.

❑ All employees (including managers) have the same conditions of employment, and wear similar blue overalls at work.

❑ There are no (inflexible) written job descriptions.

❑ There is no clocking on and no privileged parking.

❑ Absenteeism has remained very low.

❑ There are daily communications meetings – searching for continuous improvement.

❑ Employees often go to Japan for training – skilled workers learn both operational and maintenance skills.

❑ The training budget, equivalent to 14% of sales revenue, is exceptionally high for a British company. A typical employee will receive nine days on-the-job and 12 days off-the-job training each year.

❑ Supervisors are empowered managers. They recruit and select their own staff (individually they are responsible for about 20 employees), and they control the layout and operation of their own part of the production line.

Source: Hill, R (1990) Nissan and the art of people management, *Director*, March.

behind the Japanese and German producers in terms of quality and productivity and has struggled to catch up. The first Japanese car plant was built by Nissan, and Case 4.5 describes the human resources strategies which have contributed markedly to its early success.

Company directors should be optimistic. But they should also be realistic. I agree with Michael Crozier who said in his *Day-to-day Management* (InterEditions) that the greatest danger for managing directors is the 'temptation to run on' and to completely lose touch with reality.

Common denominator in all this is pragmatism. The common thread running through the advice given is the paramount importance of everyday concerns and of the care given to detail.

Bernard Arnault, Group Chairman, LVMH, Moët Hennessy. Louis Vuitton

Quality and Competition

Although there are close supporting links between companies, government and the banking system, there is intense and aggressive competition between the individual firms in an industry, fostered by growth objectives and the loyalty of employees to their firm.

Prahalad and Hamel (1985) have suggested that the Japanese 'rewrite the rules of the game to take their competitors by surprise'. Through technology, design, production costs, distribution and selling arrangements, pricing and service they seek to build 'layers of competitive advantage' rather than concentrate on just one aspect. Many competitors in the West think more narrowly. Prahalad and Hamel suggest that Japanese companies are successful in part because they have a clear mission and statement of strategic intent, and a culture which provides both opportunity and encouragement to change things incrementally. Getting things right first time and every time – total quality management – is endemic in the culture.

Internationally Japanese companies may not be consistent with their strategies; instead they will seek the best competitive opportunities in different places and they will change continually as new opportunities arise and are created.

Japanese companies benchmark against the best in the world and willingly customize their products to meet local market demand.

Long-term perspective

We shall consider this further in Chapter 5 when we look at objectives. Whilst many Western companies concentrate on short-term strategies, influenced often by financial pressures, the Japanese take a long-term perspective.

Emphasis on market share

Visit the website:
http://www.itbp.com

Japanese companies are competitive, growth oriented and anxious to build and sustain high market shares in world markets. This will enable them to provide the job security that is a fundamental aspect of the culture. They often use their experience curve (which we shall examine in detail later) to develop strategies aimed at market dominance with a long-term view of costs and prices.

Internal growth

Mergers, acquisitions and divestitures are relatively uncommon in Japan – the Japanese favour the internal production system and innovation.

In a book on Japanese manufacturing techniques Schonberger (1984) argues that a major reason for Japan's success is their ability to use their resources well, better in fact than many Western competitors. In many factories, he contends, the equipment is no better than that used elsewhere in the world, but wherever they can Japanese companies invest in the best equipment available. Managerial skills are used in improvement drives, a search for simple solutions and, in particular, a meticulous attention to detail. Simplicity is important since management and shopfloor can relate better to each other; and flexible techniques and workforces result in low stock production systems, efficiency and lower costs.

The ability to trust and establish close links with other companies in the supply chain allows focused specialization and just-in-time manufacturing with low inventories. However, this type of dependency can act as a hindrance to global expansion until comparative supplier links can be established.

Innovation

Research and development is deemed important and funded appropriately. As a result much of Japan's technology is advancing quickly, and firms who fail to innovate go out of business. Ohmae (1985) has described Japan as a 'very unforgiving economy', with thousands of corporations destroyed every year through bankruptcy. He points out that Japan is selective about the industries in which research and development will be concentrated. Japan spends a relatively high proportion of its research and development money in ceramics and steel and as a result of past (and continuing) expenditure it has become a world leader in fibre optics, ceramics and mass-produced large-scale integrated circuits. For similar reasons the USA is world leader in bio-technology and specialized semiconductors, and Europe in chemicals and pharmaceuticals.

Product innovation in Japan is fast and competitive. For example, Sony launched the first miniaturized camcorder (hand-held video camera and recorder) in June 1989. Weighing 1.5 lb it was one-quarter of the size of existing camcorders. Within six months Matsushita and JVC had introduced lighter models. Within a further six months there was additional competition from Canon, Sanyo, Ricoh and Hitachi. Sony itself introduced two new models in Summer 1990. One was the lightest then available; the other had superior technical features. More recent models feature larger viewfinders and allow the user to hold the camcorder at arm's length instead of up-to-the-eye.

This faster model replacement is linked to an ability to break-even financially with fewer sales of each model. Japan has achieved this with efficient and flexible manufacturing systems and a greater willingness to utilize common, rather than model-specific, components.

Individual Western companies have proved that it is possible, with determination and distinctive products, to successfully penetrate Japanese markets, but contenders can expect fierce resistance and defensive competition.

Summary

It has been argued in this chapter that the organizational culture and the values held by managers and other employees within the organization are key influences on strategies and change. In turn the values and culture are influenced markedly by the values and style of the strategic leader. Decision making with regard to major changes, and adaptive changes, is influenced by culture and values, and equally the culture and values affect the decision makers.

Specifically we have:

- recapped (from Chapters 1 and 2) how culture and values influence a number of essential elements of the strategy process and are therefore a central driving consideration in strategy creation and change

- illustrated the typologies of organizations developed by Handy and by Miles and Snow in relation to cultural aspects
- emphasized the relationship between culture and strategic leadership
- looked at the relationship between culture and power
- considered the determinants and levels of culture;
- summarized normative research work into successful companies, emphasizing the role of culture, and pointing out the limitations of this work
- briefly looked at the relationship between culture and long-term sustained competitive advantage
- discussed the difficulties involved in changing culture
- looked at the strategies of typical Japanese companies, emphasizing how they are culture based, and considering the possible lessons for Western organizations.

Checklist of key terms and concepts

You should feel confident that you understand the following terms and ideas:

* ★ Visionary, planning and adaptive modes of strategy creation, and their relationship with culture

* ★ Power, role, task and person cultures, and their influence on strategy and strategic change
* ★ Power levers – how they affect culture, and the links with strategic leadership
* ★ Normative 'excellence' factors.

Recommended further reading

Deal and Kennedy (1982) is an ideal introduction to the subject of culture, whilst Schein (1985) provides a more comprehensive treatment. Frost, PJ, Moore, LF, Louis, MR, Lundberg, CC and Martin, J (1985) *Organizational Culture*, Sage, contains a number of relevant readings. Hampden-Turner (1990) is also very thought provoking.

It would also be useful to read one of the books written by Tom Peters either as an individual author (*Thriving on Chaos*, 1988, or *Liberation Management: Necessary Disorganization for the Nanosecond Nineties*, Macmillan, 1992) or in conjunction with Robert Waterman (*In Search of Excellence*, 1982) or Nancy Austin (*A Passion for Excellence*, Collins, 1985), in order to study the normative aspects of excellence in organizations.

Readers who are particularly interested in Japanese management are referred to Schonberger (1984).

References

Barney, JB (1986) Organization culture: can it be a source of sustained competitive advantage? *Academy of Management Review*, **11** (3).

Berry, D (1983) The perils of trying to change corporate culture, *Financial Times*, 14 December.

Deal, T and Kennedy, A (1982) *Corporate Cultures. The Rites and Rituals of Corporate Life*, Addison-Wesley.

French, JRP and Raven, B (1959) The bases of social power. In *Studies in Social Power* (ed. D Cartwright), University of Michigan Press.

Hampen-Turner, C (1990) Corporate culture – from vicious to virtuous circles, *Economist*.

Handy, CB (1976) *Understanding Organizations*, Penguin. The ideas are elaborated in Handy, CB *Gods of Management*, Souvenir Press.

Harrison, R (1972) Understanding your Organization's Character, *Harvard Business Review*, May/June.

Kakabadse, A (1982) *Culture of the Social Services*, Gower.

Leadbeater, C and Rudd, R (1991) What drives the lords of the deal? *Financial Times*, 20 July.

Lewin, K (1947) Frontiers in group dynamics: concept, method and reality in social science, *Human Relations*, 1.

Miles, RE and Snow, CC (1978) *Organization Strategy, Structure and Process*, McGraw-Hill.

Ohmae, K (1985) *Triad Power*, Free Press.

Peters, TJ (1988) *Thriving on Chaos*, Knopf.

Peters, TJ and Waterman, RH Jr (1982) *In Search of Excellence: Lessons from America's Best Run Companies*, Harper and Row. Original article, Peters, TJ (1980) Putting excellence into management, *Business Week*, 21 July.

Prahalad, CK and Hamel, G (1985) Address to the Annual Conference of the Strategic Management Society, Barcelona, October.

Press, G (1990) Assessing competitors' business philosophies, *Long Range Planning*, **23**, 5.

Pucik, V and Hatvany, N (1983) *Management Practices in Japan and Their Impact on Business Strategy*, Advances in Strategic Management, Vol. 1, JAI Press.

Pümpin, C (1987) *The Essence of Corporate Strategy*, Gower.

Schein, EH (1985) *Organizational Culture and Leadership*, Jossey Bass.

Schonberger, RJ (1984) *Japanese Manufacturing Techniques*, Free Press.

Schwartz, H and Davis, SM (1981) Matching corporate culture and business strategy, *Organizational Dynamics*, Summer.

Waterman, RH Jr (1988) *The Renewal Factor*, Bantam.

Questions and research assignments

Text related

1 Take an organization with which you are familiar and evaluate it in terms of Handy's and Miles and Snow's typologies.

2 List other organizations that you know which would fit into the categories not covered in your answer to Question 1.

For both Questions 1 and 2 you should comment on whether or not you feel your categorization is appropriate.

3 Considering the organization that you used for Question 1 assess the power levers of the strategic leader and other identifiable managers.

Library and assignment based

4 Find out where your nearest John Lewis or Waitrose store is and if possible visit it. Can you detect any differences in attitude between the John Lewis staff and those who work in similar stores?

Research how profitable John Lewis and Waitrose have been in comparison with their major competitors in the 1990s. What conclusions can you draw?

5 Our Price, part of WH Smith, is a leading specialist retailer of music and video products, including computer games – markets where the majority of competing *products* are identical. At the end of the 1980s, following years of growth, this market had flattened out. Our Price was acknowledged to be a company which provided excellent service but its stores were seen as 'dull, drab, boring and intimidating'.

WH Smith was determined to 're-position the brand' to revitalize it whilst ensuring it was easily distinguishable from its major competitors, especially the informal Virgin Megastores and the mainstream WH Smith stores, which are more formal and traditional. It was thought necessary to change the ways in which products are displayed and sold, media and in-store promotions, aspects of the service, and, especially, staff attitudes and behaviour.

A new *vision and values* was defined 'to build an attitude and way of behaving in all that we do in the business that will support ... the re-positioning of the brand'.

The Our Price vision

❏ The first place everybody thinks of for music
❏ The place its customers keep coming back to
❏ The place where the involvement and fulfilment of its people creates commercial success.

The required values

To pursue the vision effectively Our Price would need:

❏ To 'delight' its customers, who need to feel satisfied even if they leave the store without purchasing
❏ To empower its people
❏ To drive itself forward and embrace change ... whilst recognizing the need to be commercially successful.

Visit your nearest Our Price store and evaluate the impact of the vision and values. Compare and contrast Our Price with competing HMV stores and sounds departments within WH Smith high street stores. Do they seem and feel to be different? What are the implications of any differences?

PART

II

This part of the book questions where the organization is at present, what objectives and strategies are being pursued, how well the organization is performing and how effective it is as a competitor. Chapter 5 explores objectives, and the need for organizations and managers to be clear about the current objectives being pursued; their origins and their justification are discussed. Chapter 6 looks at measures of performance, concentrating on financial ratios. The advantages and limitations of such quantitative measures are discussed.

In Chapter 7 we consider the major causes of poor performance and company failure.

Strategic Awareness

I have always liked AN Whitehead's comment: 'The habit of foreseeing is elicited by the habit of understanding. We require such an understanding of the present conditions as may give us some grasp of the novelty which is about to produce a measurable influence on the immediate future'.

Sir Adrian Cadbury, Chairman,
Cadbury Schweppes plc (retired May 1989)

5

The Organizational Mission and Objectives

Learning objectives

After studying this chapter you should be able to:

- explain the terms vision, mission and objectives
- identify the various stakeholders of the organization and assess their impact on objectives
- summarize a number of economic theories of the firm which help explain objectives and direction
- discuss the significance of profits
- explain the possible objectives of certain not-for-profit organizations
- differentiate between official and operative objectives, and assess the impact of personal objectives
- define policies and explain how they are used to help achieve objectives
- identify the key issues involved in social responsibility and business ethics.

In this chapter we consider the objectives of the organization: their nature, how they might be established, and the influence of the stakeholders in the business. Social responsibility and business ethics are also discussed.

Introduction

A voyage of a thousand miles begins with a single step. It is important that that step is in the right direction.

(Old Chinese saying, updated)

Life can only be understood backward, but it must be lived forward.

(S Kierkegaard)

How can we go forward when we don't know which way we are facing?

(John Lennon, 1972)

Don't forget to visit the website: http://www.itbp.com

This chapter is about **objectives**. Objectives should be set and communicated so that people know where the strategic leader wants the organization to be at some time in the future. At the same time it is essential that the objectives currently being pursued are clearly understood. Because of incremental changes in strategies the actual or implicit objectives may have changed from those which were established and made explicit sometime in the past. Objectives, therefore, establish direction, and in some cases set specific end points. They should have time-scales attached to them. The attainment of them should be measurable in some way, and ideally they will encourage and motivate people.

If you don't know where you are going, any road will take you there.
Raymond G Viault, Chief Executive Officer, Jacobs Suchard, Switzerland

It is important, however, to distinguish between the idea of a broad purpose and specific, measurable, milestones. The organization needs direction in terms of where the strategic leader wants it to go, and how he or she would wish it to develop. This is really the 'mission' of the organization, a visionary statement concerning the future. This mission is likely to be stated broadly and generally, and it is unlikely that it can ever be achieved completely. Thus the organization pursues the mission, looking for new opportunities, dealing with problems and seeking to progress continually in the chosen direction. Improvements in the overall situation towards the stated mission are the appropriate measure of performance.

Managers at all levels are likely to be set specific objectives to achieve. These, logically, are quantifiable targets for sales, profit, productivity or output, and performance against them is measured and evaluated. Objectives then become measurable points which indicate how the organization is making definite progress towards its broad purpose or 'mission'.

Strategies are developed from the mission and the desired objectives as they are the means of achieving them. Hence a change of objectives is likely to result in changes of strategy. At the same time it is important to realize that incremental and emergent changes in strategy, whether the result of internal or external pressure, affect the levels of performance of the organization, i.e. the growth, profit or market share, and these performance levels should be related to the objectives actually being pursued.

The central theme of the chapter is that it is essential that the most senior managers in an organization understand clearly where their company is going, and why. Ideally all managers will appreciate the overall mission and how their own role contributes to its attainment. The strategies being followed may be different from those that were originally stated, and there may be good reasons for this. Thus the situation should be reviewed constantly and the strategic leader should seek to remain informed and aware of what is happening.

Definitions, terminology and examples

Box 5.1 defines the terms *vision, mission* and *objectives* and provides a range of examples from the private and public sectors. Figure 5.1 shows the relationships between these terms, highlighting their key constituents. This figure can usefully be related to the strategy statement framework introduced in Chapter 1 (Figure 1.11).

Strategy development is like driving around a roundabout. The signposts are only useful if you know where you want to go. Some exits lead uphill, some downhill – most are one-way streets and some have very heavy traffic indeed. The trick is in picking the journey's end before you set out – otherwise you go around in circles or pick the wrong road.

Gerry M Murphy, Chief Executive Officer, Greencore plc, Ireland

Box 5.1

Examples of vision, mission and objectives statements

Vision statements
A **vision statement** *describes what the company is to become in the (long-term) future.*

The Sony spirit
Sony is a trail blazer, always a seeker of the unknown. Sony will never follow old trails, yet to be trod. Through this progress Sony wants to serve mankind.

WH Smith (1995)
There's nowhere quite like WH Smith. It's full of energy and colour and excitement.

Just when you think you know them, they surprise you. Everywhere you look there are fresh, inspired ideas.

Smith's is an essential part of life. It's a unique blend of information, inspiration and just plain fun.

Everything is chosen with thought, designed with care and presented with imagination.

Customer service is instinctive. It's the right help at the right time, by people who know what they're saying and love what they're doing.

Smith's builds its reputation day by day, product by product and customer by customer.

Always in Front.

We can see represented here: adding new values, innovation, products which match customer needs, effective presentation, service and constant improvement.

British Airways
The world's favourite airline.

This vision focuses on employees and customers. The related mission emphasizes BA's desire to be the world's first truly global airline, which in turn has generated a corporate strategy of carefully selected alliances.

Mission statements
The **mission** *reflects the essential purpose of the organization, concerning particularly why it is in existence, the nature of the business(es) it is in, and the customers it seeks to serve and satisfy.*

Financial Times Conferences
The mission of the FTC is to organize conferences on subjects of interest to the international business community, using the highest calibre speakers and providing attending delegates with the finest service, thereby providing a low cost and time efficient means of obtaining both impartial quality information and making senior level industry contacts.

We can see a clear definition of the business, a formulation of objectives, delivery strategies, means of differentiating the service and stakeholder relevance.

BhS – British Home Stores (1990)
The BhS mission is to be the first choice store for dressing the modern woman and family. We are committed to service, quality, harmony, innovation and excitement in all that we do. We will succeed by being a focused organization in dynamic partnership with our customers and suppliers.

The impact of the mission on new strategies and BhS employees is examined in Chapter 11.

The Treasury
The Treasury's overall aim is to promote rising prosperity based on sustained economic growth.

In seeking to meet this aim we will:
- ❑ maintain a stable macroeconomic environment
- ❑ improve the long-term performance of the economy and the outlook for jobs, in strategic partnership with others
- ❑ maintain a professional, well-motivated and outward-looking organization, committed to continuous improvement.

Long-term objectives
Objectives *are desired states or results linked to particular time scales and concerning such things as size or type of organization, the nature and variety of the areas of interest and levels of success.*

BAA – British Airports Authority – Open objectives
BAA aims to enhance the value of the shareholders' investments by achieving steady and remunerative long-term growth. Its strategy for developing and operating world-class international airports that are safe, secure, efficient and profitable is based on a commitment to continuously enhancing the quality of service to passengers and business partners alike. This process of constant improvement includes cost-effective investment in new airport facilities closely matched to customer demand.

Kirin Brewery (Japan) – Closed objectives
For the decade of the 1990s:
- ❑ Increase sales from 1250 billion yen (1990) to 1700 billion (2000)
- ❑ Increase sales of non-beer products to 60% of total revenue by
- ❑ Diversifying (further) into biotechnology, construction engineering, information systems and service industries
- ❑ Become a global corporation.

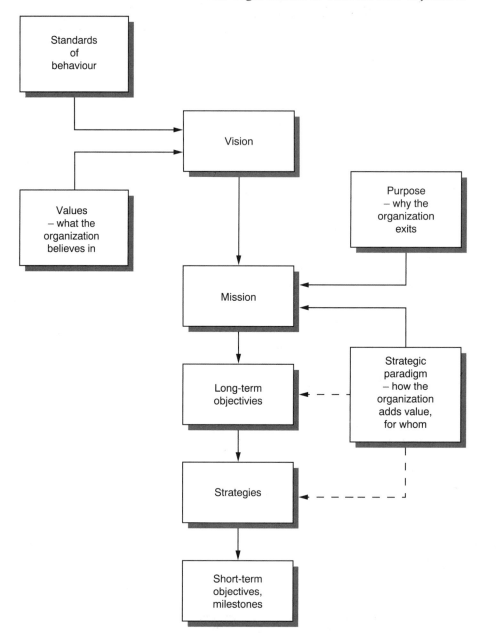

Figure 5.1   Vision and mission statements and objectives.

The examples in Box 5.1 were selected to illustrate the relevant points, not because they are superior to those of other organizations; they should be evaluated in this light.

The expression **aims** is sometimes used as an alternative to mission. The term **goals** is seen as synonymous with objectives, and in this book the terms are used interchangeably. Specifically, where other works are being referred to and those authors have used the term goal as opposed to objective, their terminology is retained. It is also important to distinguish between long-term and short-term objectives or goals. Thompson and Strickland (1980) provide a

Arne Ness said, when he climbed Everest, 'I had a dream. I reached it. I lost the dream, and I miss it.'

When we reached our dream we didn't have another long-term objective. So people started to produce their own new objectives, not a common objective, but different objectives depending on where they were in the organization.

I learned that before you reach an objective you must be ready with a new one, and you must start to communicate it to the organization. But it is not the goal itself that is important ... it is the fight to get there.

Jan Carlzon, Chairman and Chief Executive Officer, Scandinavian Airlines System

useful distinction. They argue that objectives overall define the specific kinds of performance and results which the organization seeks to produce through its activities. The **long-term objectives** relate to the desired performance and results on an on-going basis; **short-term objectives** are concerned with the near-term performance targets that the organization desires to reach in progressing towards its long-term objectives. Making use of such techniques as management by objectives, discussed in Chapter 11, these performance targets can be agreed with individual managers, who are then given responsibility for their attainment, and held accountable.

Measurement can be straightforward for an objective such as 'the achievement of a minimum return of 20% of net capital employed in the business, but with a target of 25%, in the next 12 months'. If the objective is less specific, for example, 'continued customer satisfaction, a competitive return on capital employed and real growth in earnings per share next year', measurement is still possible but requires a comparison of competitor returns and the monitoring of customer satisfaction through, say, the number of complaints received. Richards (1978) uses the terms 'open' and 'closed' to distinguish between objectives which are clearly measurable and typically finance based (closed) and those which are less specific and essentially continuing.

Vision statements

Whilst mission statements have become increasingly popular for organizations, vision *statements* are less prevalent. The lack of a published statement, of course, is not necessarily an indication of a lack of vision. Where they exist they reflect the company's vision of some future state – which ideally the organization will achieve. Terminology and themes such as a world class manufacturer, a quality organization, a provider of legendary service and a stimulating, rewarding place to work might well appear. The essential elements focus on those values to which the organization is committed and appropriate standards of behaviour for all employees. Possible improvement paths, employee development programmes and measures or indicators of progress should be established for each element of the vision.

Mission statements

The corporate mission is the over-riding *raison d'être* for the business. Ackoff (1986), however, has claimed that historically many corporate mission statements have proved worthless, one reason being that they consist of expressions like 'maximize growth potential' or 'provide products of the highest quality'. How, he queries, can a company determine whether it has attained its maximum growth potential or highest quality? Primarily the mission statement should not address what an organization must do in order to survive, but what it has chosen to do in order to thrive. It should be positive, visionary and motivating.

Ackoff suggests that a good mission statement has five characteristics.

❑ It will contain a formulation of objectives that enables progress towards them to be measured.
❑ It differentiates the company from its competitors.
❑ It defines the business(es) that the company wants to be in, not necessarily is in.
❑ It is relevant to all the stakeholders in the firm, not just shareholders and managers.
❑ It is exciting and inspiring.

Campbell (1989) argues that to be valuable mission statements must reflect corporate values, and the strategic leader and the organization as a whole should be visibly pursuing the mission. He takes a wider perspective than Ackoff by including aspects of the corporate vision and arguing that there are four key issues involved in developing a useful mission:

❑ It is important to clarify the purpose of the organization – why it exists. Hanson plc, for example, which is referred to at various stages in this book, is led by Lord Hanson who has said:

> It is the central tenet of my faith that the shareholder is king. My aim is to advance the shareholder's interest by increasing earnings per share.

By contrast Lex Service has stated:

> We will exercise responsibility in o\ur dealings with all our stakeholders and, in the case of conflict, balance the interest of the employees and shareholders on an equal basis over time.

The implications of these contrasting perspectives are discussed in the next section of this chapter.

❑ The mission statement should describe the business and its activities, and the position that it wants to achieve in its field.
❑ The organization's values should be stated. How does the company intend to treat its employees, customers and suppliers, for example?
❑ Finally it is important to ensure that the organization behaves in the way that it promises it will. This is important because it can inspire trust in employees and others who significantly influence the organization.

It is generally accepted that in successful British companies middle and junior managers know where the strategic leaders are taking the company and why. In less successful organizations there is often confusion about this.

Mission statements, like vision statements, can all-too-easily just 'state the obvious' and as a result have little real value. The secret lies in clarifying what makes a company different and a more effective competitor, rather than simply restating those requirements that are essential for meeting key success factors. Companies which succeed long-term are those which create competitive advantages and sustain their strong positions with flexibility and improvement. The vision and mission should support this.

The principal purpose of these statements is communication, both externally and internally, and, arguably, a major benefit for organizations is the thinking they are forced to do to establish sound statements.

The mission clearly corresponds closely to the basic philosophy or vision underlying the business, and if there is a sound philosophy, strategies which generate success will be derived from it. Sock Shop was founded in 1983, with a simple vision. One newspaper has summarized it as 'shopping in big stores for basic items like stockings is a fag, but nipping into an attractive kiosk at an Underground station, British Rail concourse or busy high street is quick, convenient and can be fun'. From this has emerged six key marketing features or strategies, which have become the foundations of the company's success and rapid growth:

❑ shops located within areas of heavy pedestrian traffic
❑ easily accessible products
❑ friendly and efficient service
❑ a wide range of quality products designed to meet the needs of customers
❑ attractive presentations
❑ competitive selling prices.

In 1989, after a number of years of growth and success, Sock Shop began to lose money. The hot summer weather and the London Underground strikes were blamed for falling sales. Increasing interest rates caused additional financial problems. Moreover Sock Shop expanded into the USA and this had proved costly. However in February 1990 Sock Shop founder, Sophie Mirman, commented: '... our concept remains sound. Our merchandise continues to be not merely "lifestyle". We provide everyday necessities in a fashionable manner'.

Sophie Mirman has since lost control of Sock Shop but her vision prevails.

Visit the website: http://www.itbp.com

Objectives: what should they be; what are they?

A full consideration of objectives incorporates three aspects:

❑ an appreciation of the objectives that the organization is actually pursuing and achieving – where it is going and why
❑ the objectives that it might pursue, and the freedom and opportunity it has to make changes
❑ specific objectives for the future.

In this chapter we look at the issues which affect and determine the first two of these.

Decisions about specific future objectives are considered further in Chapter 14.

As a background to the consideration of these points it is useful to look briefly at a number of theories of business organizations and to consider the role and importance of stakeholders.

Table 5.1 Structural characteristics of four market models

Market model	Number of firms	Type of product	Control over price by supplier	Entry conditions	Non-price competition*	Examples†
Pure competition	Large	Standardized Identical or almost identical	None	Free	None	Agricultural products; some chemicals, printing; laundry services
Monopolistic competition	Large	Differentiated	Some	Relatively easy	Yes	Clothing; furniture; soft drinks; plumbers; restaurants.
Oligopoly‡	Few or a few dominant	Standardized or differentiated	Limited by mutual interdependence. Considerable if collusion takes place	Difficult	Yes	Standardized: cement; sugar; fertilizers. Differentiated: margarine; soaps; detergents.
Pure monopoly	One	Unique	Considerable	Blocked	Yes	British Gas (domestic consumers); water companies in their regions; local bus companies in certain towns.

*Non-price competition occurs in many ways, e.g. by attempts to increase the extent of product differentiation and buyer preference through advertising, brand names, trade marks, promotions, distribution outlets; by new product launch and innovation, etc.
†Useful further reading: Doyle, P and Gidengil, ZB (1977) An empirical study of market structures, *Journal of Management Studies*, **14**(3), October, pp. 316–28. Some of the examples are taken from this.
‡There are many oligopoly models of collusive and non-collusive type. They make varying behavioural and structural assumptions.

Market models

Basic microeconomic theory states that firms should seek to maximize profits and that this is achieved where marginal revenue is equal to marginal cost. A number of assumptions under-pin this theory, including the assumptions that firms clearly understand the nature of the demand for their products, and why people buy, and that they are willing and able to control production and sales as the model demands. In reality decision makers do not have perfect knowledge and production and sales are affected by suppliers and distributors.

However, this basic theory has resulted in the development of four market models (Table 5.1) and the characteristics of these in respect of barriers to entry into the industry and the marketing opportunities (differentiation potential; price and non-price competition) determine whether or not there is a real opportunity to achieve significant profits.

Management of change for profit is what distinguishes businessmen from bureaucrats. In bureaucracies change can be the occasion for industrial unrest, higher costs and cutbacks in customer service. In business change should be an opportunity for improved working patterns, productivity increase and enhanced customer service. The profit motive conditions the business approach to managing change. Profit is earned through a proper balance between the interests of customers, employees and shareholders.

Peter Morgan, when Director General, The Institute of Directors

---

In markets which approach pure competition (pure competition as such is theoretical), firms will only make 'normal' profits, the amount required for them to stay in the industry. Products are not differentiated, and so premium prices for certain brands are not possible. There are no major barriers to entry into the industry and so new suppliers are attracted if there are profits to be made. Competition results, and if supply exceeds demand the ruling market price is forced down and only the efficient firms survive.

In monopolistic competition there are again several suppliers, some large, many small, but products are differentiated. However, as there are once more no major barriers to entry the above situation concerning profits applies. Newcomers increase supply and although those firms with distinctive products can charge some premium they will still have to move in line with market prices generally, and this will have a dampening effect on profits.

Only in oligopoly and monopoly markets is there real opportunity for 'super-normal' profits, in excess of what is required to stay in business. However, in oligopoly the small number of large firms tend to be wary of each other and prices are held back to some extent for fear of losing market share. Suppliers are inter-dependent and fear that a price decrease will be met by competitors (thus reducing profits) and price increases will not (hence market share will be threatened). There are two types of oligopoly, depending on whether opportunities exist for significant differentiation. In all these models competition is a major determinant of profit potential and therefore objectives must be set with competitors in mind. In a monopoly (again somewhat theoretical in a pure sense) excess profits could be made if government did not act as a restraint. Although such public sector organizations as British Gas and British Telecom have been privatized their actions in terms of supply and pricing are monitored (see Chapter 9).

Stakeholder theory

The influence of external stakeholders will be examined again in Chapter 8, which looks at the environment, but it is important to introduce the topic at this stage. A further assumption of profit-maximizing theory is that share-holders in the business should be given first priority and be the major consideration in decision making, and this arose because early economic theorists saw owners and managers as being synonymous. But this assumption no longer holds. As we have already seen, a study of market models demonstrates the important role played by competitors and by government as a restraining force, and it was also suggested that organizations must pay some regard to their suppliers and distributors. In addition, managers and employees must be considered. The decisions taken by managers which create incremental change will be influenced by the objectives and values that they believe are important. Managers are paid employees, and whilst concerned about profits, they will also regard growth and security as important.

These are all **stakeholders**. Freeman (1984) defines stakeholders as any group or individual who can affect, or is affected by, the performance of the organization.

Newbould and Luffman (1979) argue that current and future strategies are affected by

❑ external pressures from the marketplace, including competitors, buyers and suppliers; shareholders; pressure groups; and government
❑ internal pressures from existing commitments, managers, employees and their trade unions
❑ the personal ethical and moral perspectives of senior managers.

Stakeholder theory postulates that the objectives of an organization will take account of the various needs of these different interested parties who will represent some type of informal coalition. Their relative power will be a key variable, and the organization will on occasions 'trade-off' one against the other, establishing a hierarchy of relative importance. Stakeholders see different things as being important and receive benefits or rewards in a variety of ways, as featured in Table 5.2.

Stakeholder interests are not always consistent. For example, investment in new technology might improve product quality and as a result lead to increased profits. Whilst customers who are shareholders might perceptively benefit, if the investment implies lost jobs then employees, possibly managers, and their trade unions may be dissatisfied. If the scale of redundancy is large and results in militant resistance, the government may become involved.

The various stakeholders are not affected in the same way by every strategic decision, and consequently their relative influence will vary from decision to decision.

In 1995 Shell, one of Europe's most successful and respected companies, was forced to change an important strategic decision following a high-profile

Table 5.2 Examples of stakeholder interests		
	Shareholders	Annual dividends; increasing the value of their investment in the company as the share price increases. Both are affected by growth and profits Institutional shareholders may balance high-risk investments and their anticipated high returns with more stable investments in their portfolio
	Managers	Salaries and bonuses; perks; status from working for a well-known and successful organization; responsibility; challenge; security
	Employees	Wages; holidays; conditions and job satisfaction; security – influenced by trade union involvement
	Consumers	Desirable and quality products; competitive prices – very much in relation to competition; new products at appropriate times
	Distributors	On-time and reliable deliveries
	Suppliers	Consistent orders; payment on time
	Financiers	Interest payments and loan repayments; like payment for supplies, affected by cash flow
	Government	Payment of taxes and provision of employment; contribution to the nation's exports
	Society in general	Socially responsible actions – sometimes reflected in pressure groups

Note. This is not intended to constitute a complete list.

The investor and the employee are in the same position, but sometimes the employee is more important, because he will be there a long time, whereas an investor will often get in and out on a whim in order to make a profit. The worker's mission is to contribute to the company's welfare, and his own, every day. All of his working life he is really needed.

Akio Morita, Joint Founder, Sony

campaign by a leading pressure group. Shell wanted to sink its redundant Brent Spar oil platform in deep seas some 150 miles west of Scotland. It had reached an agreement with the UK government that, scientifically, this was the most appropriate means of disposal for the platform. Greenpeace objected and protesters boarded the platform, claiming it still contained 5000 tonnes of oil which would eventually be released to pollute the sea. The ensuing and professionally orchestrated publicity fuelled public opinion, and there were protests in a number of European countries, including attacks on petrol stations in Germany. Shell backed down and agreed to investigate other possibilities for disposal. The UK government expressed both anger and disappointment with this decision. Independent inspectors later proved that Greenpeace's claims were gross exaggerations – the residual oil was much, much less than 5000 tonnes. The press concluded: 'Shell went wrong in spending too much time convincing government of the case for sea-bed dumping, but not attaching enough importance to consulting other stakeholder groups'.

Shell had been made to appear socially irresponsible, yet the ethics of the Greenpeace campaign are questionable; these issues are explored further at the end of this chapter.

Waterman (1994) contends that today's most successful companies do not automatically make shareholders their first priority. Instead they pay primary attention to employees and customers, and as a result, they perform more effectively than their rivals. The outcome is superior profits and wealth creation for the shareholders.

Figure 5.2 shows that shareholders, employees and customers are the three key stakeholders the organization must satisfy; if they fail with any group long-term they will place the organization in jeopardy through a spiral of decline.

Whilst these arguments are, in themselves, convincing, many organizations do fail to satisfy their stakeholders long term. The theories which follow provide some insight into this reality.

Cyert and March's behavioural theory

Stakeholder theory is closely related to the ideas in Cyert and March's *A Behavioural Theory of the Firm* (1963). Cyert and March argue that the goals of an organization are a **compromise** between members of a coalition comprising the parties affecting an organization. The word compromise is used as the actual choice is linked to relative power and there are inevitably conflicts of interest. Cyert and March argue that there are essentially five directional pulls to consider:

❏ production related, and encapsulating stable employment, ease of control and scheduling
❏ inventory related – customers and sales staff push for high stocks and wide choice, management accountants complain about the cost of too much stock

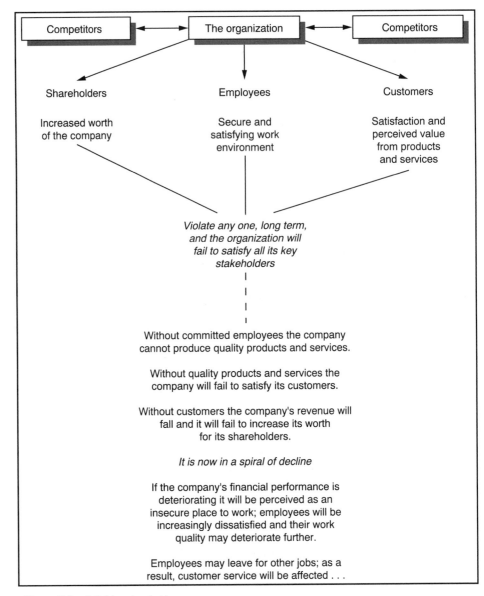

Figure 5.2 Satisfying shareholders.

- ❏ sales related – obtaining and satisfying orders
- ❏ market share, which yields power relative to competitors
- ❏ profit, which concerns shareholders senior management and the providers of loan capital.

This theory stresses the perceived importance of the short term, as opposed to the long term, because issues are more tangible and because decisions have to be taken as situations change. Organizations adapt over time and it is likely that changes will be limited unless it is necessary to change things more radically. In other words, once a compromise situation is reached there is a tendency to seek to retain it rather than change it; and the goals will change as the values and relative importance of coalition members change. As a result 'organizational slack' develops. This is 'payments to members of the coalition in excess of what is required to keep them in the coalition'. It is difficult, for example, to determine the minimum acceptable reward for employees; assets are generally under-exploited since it is difficult to know the maximum productivity of a person or machine; and uncertainties mean that less-than-optimal price, product and promotional policies will be pursued. The existence of slack does allow for extra effort in times of emergency. This theory can be usefully considered alongside Herbert Simon's theory of satisficing which was introduced in Chapter 3.

Developing these themes Herbert Simon (1964) makes an important distinction between objectives and constraints. For example an animal food company might wish to offer low priced feeds for livestock but be constrained by dietary requirements, which, by determining ingredients, influence costs and hence prices.

In recent years, many of the world's leading drug companies have changed their strategies as a result of external constraints. Governments have been increasingly reluctant to fund expensive drugs and treatments. Some companies have closed plants; others have relocated for lower costs. There has been an increased research focus on treatments which are most likely to receive funding, arguably at the expense of potential breakthroughs in other areas.

Simon further contends that one of the main reasons for an organization's collapse is a failure to incorporate the important motivational concerns of key stakeholders. Small businesses, for example, are generally weak in relation to their suppliers, especially if these are larger well-established concerns; and if they neglect managing their cash flow and fail to pay their accounts on time they will find their deliveries stopped. For any organization, if new products or services fail to provide consumers with what they are looking for, however well produced or low priced they might be, they will not sell.

Other theories of the firm

A number of other authors have offered theories in an attempt to explain the behaviour of organizations and the objectives they seek.

Baumol: sales maximization

Baumol (1959) argues that firms seek to maximize sales rather than profits, but within the constraint of a minimum acceptable profit level. It can be demonstrated that profit maximizing is achieved at a level of output below that which would maximize sales revenue and that, as sales and revenue increase beyond profit maximizing, profits are sacrificed. Firms will increase sales and revenue as long as they are making profits in excess of what they regard as an acceptable minimum. Businessmen, Baumol argues, attach great importance to sales as salaries are often linked to the scale of operations. 'Whenever executives are asked 'How's business?', the typical reply is that sales have been increasing or decreasing.'

Williamson's model of managerial discretion

Williamson (1964) argues that managers can set their own objectives, that these will be different from those of shareholders and that managerial satisfaction is the key. Satisfaction increases if a manager has a large staff reporting to him or her, if there are 'lavish perks' and if profits exceed the level required for the essential development of the business and the necessary replacement of equipment. This extra profit can be used for pet projects or the pursuit of non-profit objectives. The manner in which managers reward themselves for success is discretionary.

Marris's theory of managerial capitalism

Marris (1964) again postulates growth as a key concern, as managers derive utility from growth in the form of enhanced salaries, power and status. The constraint is one of security. If, as a result of growth strategies pursued by the firm, profits are held down, say because of interest charges, the market value of the firm's shares may fall relative to the book value of the assets. In such a case the firm may become increasingly vulnerable to take-over, and managers wish to avoid this situation.

Penrose's theory of growth

Penrose (1959) has offered another growth theory, arguing that an organization will seek to achieve the full potential from all its resources. Firms grow as long as there are unused resources, diversifying when they can no longer grow with existing products, services and markets. Growth continues until it is halted. A major limit, for example, could be production facilities either in terms of total output or because of a bottleneck in one part of the operation. Changes can free the limit, and growth continues until the next limiting factor appears. Another limit is the capacity of managers to plan and implement growth strategies. If managers are stretched, extra people can be employed, but the remedy is not immediate. New people have to be trained and integrated, and this takes up some of the time of existing managers. Penrose refers to this issue as the 'receding managerial limit' because again the limiting factor decreases over a period of time. In a climate of reasonably constant growth and change managers learn how to cope with the dynamics of change; and properly managed, given that over-ambition is constrained and that market opportunities exist, firms can enjoy steady and continuous growth.

Visit the website: http://www. itbp.com

Galbraith's views on technocracy

Finally, Galbraith (1969) has highlighted the particular role of large corporations, whose pursuit of size requires very large investments associated with long-term commitments. Because of these financial commitments the corporations seek to control their environment as far as they possibly can, influencing both government and consumer, and they in turn are controlled by what Galbraith calls 'technocrats' – teams of powerful experts and specialists. Their purposes are, first, to protect as well as control the organization, and hence they seek financial security and profit, and, second, to 'affirm' the organization through growth, expansion and market share. As is typical of oligopolists, price competition is not seen to be in their interests, and hence aggressive marketing and non-price competition is stressed. Additionally such firms will seek to influence or even control (by acquisition) suppliers and distributors, and they may well see the world as their market rather than just the UK. These issues are all explored later in the book.

Galbraith (1963) has also identified the growth of 'countervailing power' to limit this technocracy. The growth of trade unions in the past is an example of this, as is the increasing power of large retailers to counter the product manufacturers in individual countries. The increasing size and power of grocery retailers such as Sainsbury and Tesco, and their success with own-label brands, has put pressure on all product manufacturers, especially those whose products are not the brand leader. However, retailing across Europe is far more fragmented; the three leading retailers control just 15% of the total grocery market. In contrast, the three leading manufacturers of nappies control 66% of the market; in chocolate the percentage is 50, with 40% for crisps and snacks. As a consequence, many leading retailers are now forming various cross-border alliances in an attempt to strengthen their bargaining position.

As a result the potential for consumer exploitation is checked, and available profits are shared more widely.

Profit as an objective

Box 5.2 discusses whether profit is the ultimate objective of profit-seeking business organizations or whether it is merely a means to other ends, which themselves constitute the real objectives. (Not-for-profit organizations are considered separately later in this chapter.)

Ackoff (1986) argues that both profit and growth are means to other ends rather than objectives in themselves. He argues that profit is necessary for the survival of a business enterprise but is neither the reason for which the business is formed nor the reason why it stays in existence. Instead Ackoff contends 'those who manage organizations do so primarily to provide themselves with the quality of work life and standard of living they desire ... their behaviour can be better understood by assuming this than by assuming that their objective is to maximize profit or growth'.

However, it is also important to consider the 'quality of life' of investors (shareholders), customers, suppliers and distributors, as well as other employees of the firm who are not involved in decision making. Developing

Box 5.2
PROFIT

A business school is likely to teach that an organization must be good to people because then they will work harder. And if they work harder the business will make a profit.

They will also teach that a firm should strive to produce better products and services, because with better products the firm will make greater profits.

What if they told the story the other way round?

What if they taught managers: You have got to make a profit, because if you do not make a profit you cannot build offices that are pleasant to be in. Without profit you cannot pay decent wages. Without profit you cannot satisfy a lot of the needs of your employees. You have got to make a profit because without a profit you will never be able to develop a better product.

The profit would still be made. People would still get decent wages. Most employers would still make an effort to improve their products as they do now.

'But you would have a whole new ball game.'

Adapted from Cohen, P (1974) *The Gospel According to the Harvard Business School*, Penguin. Originally published by Doubleday, New York, 1973.

earlier points, it can be argued that employees are the major stakeholders, because if the firm goes out of business they incur the greatest losses.

In many respects it does not matter whether profit is seen as an objective or as a means of providing service and satisfaction to stakeholders, as long as both are considered and not seen as mutually exclusive. Chapter 6 addresses the question of how success is measured. In simple terms an organization will succeed if it survives and meets the expectations of its stakeholders. If its objectives relate to the stakeholders, it is successful if it attains its objectives.

The influence of shareholders

The view is widely held by Constable (1980) and others that too many British companies are encouraged to seek short-term profits in order to please their major shareholders, and that it is only by considering the long term and the interests of all stakeholders that British companies will become more effective competitors in world markets. Constable states: 'Britain's steady relative industrial decline over the past 30 years is related to an insistence on setting purely financial objectives which have been operated in relatively short time scales'. This is also reflected in the summary of the article by Sir Hector Laing in Key Reading 5.1. Although these comments were made some years ago, the general sentiments are still valid.

Key Reading 5.1
THE BALANCE OF RESPONSIBILITY: OWNERS AND MANAGERS

Ownership of United Biscuits in 1987 lies overwhelmingly with financial institutions, and they are inevitably remote. Where owners and managers are the same people, the goals and the means of achieving them are not in conflict; but institutional fund managers, themselves under pressure to perform in the short term, put pressure on public companies to pursue strategies which may be incompatible with sound long-term management.

The first priority for a business is to establish and sustain a long-term profitability level which satisfies the needs of both the business and its shareholders. If, however, a manufacturing business seeks to boost short-term profits and earnings per share for reasons of expedience, it may well reduce quality and service and fail to invest adequately for the future. The price for this is inevitable decline. This tendency is worsened if the company is under threat of take over. Countries like Germany and Japan take a longer term view and the 'Damoclean sword of hostile take-overs is still virtually unknown'.

Managers must not be discouraged by their owners, their shareholders, from taking risks, from undertaking research, and from investing in innovation..

Fund managers cannot consult their members (quite typically employees of the manufacturing organizations in question) and they need not take a company's employees into consideration when they buy and sell shares. This is potentially dangerous.

I am seeking to encourage a change in the climate of opinion in which institutional owners of companies accept the responsibility of ownership and take a rational, informed and reasonably long-term proprietorial view.

Instead of selling shares if they feel management is under-achieving, they should seek to offer help and advice.

Future growth, future jobs and future wealth sometimes means sacrificing immediate reward for the welfare of generations to come.

Summarized from an article by Sir Hector Laing, Chairman of United Biscuits plc, in *First*, **1**(2), 1987.

> The purpose of industry is to serve the public by creating services to meet their needs. It is not to make profits for shareholders, nor to create salaries and wages for the industrial community. These are necessary conditions for success, but not its purpose.
>
> *Dr George Carey, Archbishop of Canterbury*

> The responsibility of business is not to create profits but to create live, vibrant, honourable organizations with a real commitment to the community.
>
> *Anita Roddick, The Body Shop*

The issue of short-termism is complex, however, and achieving the ideals of Sir Hector Laing will prove difficult. Box 5.3 investigates the debate. Companies, obviously, cannot disregard powerful institutional shareholders.

Table 5.3 shows how a small minority of large and powerful shareholders – typically institutions – effectively control the UK's largest companies. In the mid-1990s there has been a drive to increase the 'transparency' of these large shareholder blocks; companies have been required to publish more information.

What is crucial is to ensure that there is dialogue and mutual understanding and agreement concerning the best interests of the company, its shareholders and other stakeholders.

In his debate on the short- and long-term perspective, Constable, in Table 5.4, contrasts two sets of objectives, ranked in order of priority. He contends that company B is likely to grow at the expense of company A, and that these objective sets, A and B, are essentially those adopted by large UK and Japanese companies respectively for much of the period since World War II. To suggest that Japanese success rests solely on a particular set of objectives is over simplifying reality, but it has certainly contributed.

In Japan and Germany, however, shareholders do not exert pressure in the same way as they do in the UK. Cross shareholding between companies in

Company	Year	Percentage of total number of shareholders holding 1 million plus shares	Percentage of total company shares held
Boots	1994	0.12	55.6
British Aerospace	1994	0.1	58.4
Lex Service	1994	0.25	43.6
Marks and Spencer	1993	0.1	57.9
Thorn EMI	1994	0.2	55.4

Table 5.3
Analysis of company shareholdings

Company	Year	Percentage of total company shares held by			
		Private individuals	Banks and nominee companies	Insurance, investment companies and pension funds	Other companies
British Aerospace	1994	4.7	82.0	5.1	8.2
Lex Service	1994	5.6	66.6	19.1	8.7
W H Smith	1995	12.4	66.6	16.1	4.9

Box 5.3
LONG- AND SHORT-TERMISM: THE DEBATE

It is generally acknowledged that companies must pursue strategies which increase the long-term value of the business for its shareholders, or eventually they are likely to be under threat of acquisition. Many companies also believe they are likely to be under threat from powerful institutional shareholders if short-term performance is poor, i.e. if sales and profits fail to grow. The result can be a reluctance to undertake costly and risky investments, say, in research and development, if the payback is uncertain. It is, however, disputed that there is a correlation between high spending on R & D and the likelihood of hostile take-overs.

Institutional shareholders clearly want to be able to exercise some control or influence over large companies where they have substantial equity interests. One dilemma is that whilst they want to rein in powerful and risk-oriented strategic leaders, they do not want to foresake the potential benefits of strong, entrepreneurial leadership. They can exert influence by:

❏ pushing for the roles of chairman and chief executive to be separated, and arguing for a high proportion of carefully selected non-executive directors
❏ attempting to replace senior managers whose performance is poor or lacklustre, but this can be difficult (it is often argued that shareholders are too passive about this option)
❏ selling their shares to predatory bidders.

Whilst this final option is a perpetual threat, and the biggest fear of many strategic leaders, not all companies are prevented from investing in R & D. ICI, Glaxo and 'others which are well-managed and in command of where they are going' invest. In addition, institutions argue that they are objective about their investments and turn down more offers for their shares than they accept. In 1989, for instance, the Prudential (the largest institutional investor in the UK) received 84 bids for companies in which they held shares. They accepted five.

Undoubtedly more **communication** between directors and their shareholders concerning results, plans and philosophies, would be desirable in many cases. Would this resolve the difficulties, or is something more drastic required?

Lipton (1990) has suggested that Boards should be subject to quinquennial reviews of their performance (partially conducted by independent outsiders) and their plans for the next five years. Hostile bids could be considered at the same time, but not between reviews. Boards may or may not be re-elected, depending upon their relative performance. The idea is to generate more stability and to 'unite directors and shareholders behind the goal of maximizing long-term profits'.

The late Lord White of Hanson plc (1990) disagreed. He argued that if institutional shareholders are willing to sell their shares it is usually the result of poor management generally, and not merely a reluctance to invest in R & D. 'Under-performing companies are frequently typified by high top salaries, share options confined to a handful of apparatchiks and generous golden parachutes.' Such companies are often legitimate take-over targets, and inevitably the bids are likely to be perceived as hostile.

Long-term success requires that companies and their strategic leaders are properly accountable for their performance, and, for many businesses, this really has to be to their shareholders. At the same time, shareholders must be objective and take a long-term perspective, and they must be active, not passive, about replacing poor managers and about intervening when they feel the corporate strategy is wrong.

The dilemmas relate to the implementation of these ideas and to the issue of whether institutions have advisers with enough detailed, industry-specific, knowledge to make an objective judgement.

Sources: Lipton, M (1990) An end to hostile takeovers and short-termism, *Financial Times*, 27 June; White, G (1990) Why management must be accountable, *Financial Times*, 12 July.

Company A	Company B	
1. Return on net assets, 1–3 year time horizon	1. Maintenance and growth of market share	**Table 5.4**
2. Cash flow	2. Maintenance and growth of employment	Contrasting company objectives
3. Maintenance and growth of market share	3. Cash flow	
4. Maintenance and growth of employment.	4. Return on net assets	

Japan means that only 25% of shares in Japanese businesses are for trading and speculation, and this generates greater stability. In Germany the companies themselves hold a higher proportion of their own shares, and banks act as proxy voters for private investors. Banks thereby control some 60% of the tradable shares, again generating stability. German companies also adopt a two-tier Board structure. A supervisory board has overall control and reports to shareholders and employee unions; reporting to this board is a management board, elected for up to five years.

In 1989 the UK electronics company Plessey was split up controversially by its then owners, GEC and Siemens of Germany. Since this time, Siemens has been willing to invest in long-term research and development; for a number of years its Plessey subsidiaries have consequently not been profitable. Plessey managers have stated their belief that this investment would not have happened under British ownership.

One long-serving senior manager claims: 'Neither Plessey nor GEC would have had the commitment to building a global market position, including the willingness to price accordingly and carry losses for a time. Plessey *talked* about being a global player, but was amateurish. It was doing things on a shoestring, without any realistic expectation that they would work'. (See Lorenz, 1994.)

We have introduced and discussed the notion of multiple objectives which can potentially be in conflict. Implicitly they suggest the need for an explicit statement of a wide range of objectives by the organization. If objectives are not stated clearly they are likely to be forgotten when the organization is under pressure. Stakeholders should be considered and consulted; priorities should be expressed; and crucially the objectives should be disseminated throughout the organization. Given this, the objectives can help resolve conflicts within the organization as there is clarity about where the organization is going.

An example is provided in Box 5.4, the stated objectives of HP Bulmer Holdings plc. The company's main business is cider; it is still under family control and it has invested in employee participation and share-ownership schemes.

The importance of the strategic leader

To conclude this section it is useful to emphasize the key role of the strategic leader, and his or her values, in establishing the main objectives and the direction in which they take the organization. Personal ambitions to build a large conglomerate or a multi-national company may fuel growth; a determination to be socially responsible may restrain certain activities that other organizations would undertake; a commitment to high quality will influence the design, cost and marketing approach for products. A strong orientation towards employee welfare, as is illustrated in the John Lewis example quoted in Chapter 4, will again influence objectives quite markedly.

Box 5.4
HP BULMER HOLDINGS PLC

Statement of company objectives

Our mission is to remain the world's most successful cider company. We will continue to measure our success in terms of market leadership, product quality, increasing shareholder value, and rewarding employment opportunities for our employees.

This will be achieved by attaining the following objectives:

1. Lead and grow the UK and international cider markets through meeting consumer needs by superior marketing and sustained high levels of customer service.
2. Maintain lowest industry costs and ensure the most economical supply of essential and quality raw materials.
3. Be dedicated to fulfilling the requirements of all our customers through achieving excellence in our products, operations and service.
4. Adopt best practice across all of our activities through an innovative approach to product, process development and information technology.
5. Foster a culture of continuous improvement through self-motivation, team work and acceptance of change.

6. Provide competitive pay, employee share ownership and single status employment while achieving a link between performance. reward and shareholder interests.
7. Give all employees the opportunity to develop skills and potential through actively improving their own and the company's performance. Promote from within whenever appropriate.
8. Keep employees informed of policy, plans and performance. Invite comments and feedback and, through employee involvement, show how individual and team efforts contribute towards the company's success.
9. Provide a high quality working environment taking all appropriate steps to ensure the health and safety of our employees, customers and the community.
10. Preserve the quality of life and environment in our everyday work and to benefit our local communities whenever an affordable opportunity arises.

Reproduced with permission.

The objectives and values of the strategic leader are a particularly important consideration in the case of small firms. Whilst it is possible for small firms to enjoy competitive advantage, say by providing products or services with values added to appeal to local customers in a limited geographical area, many are not distinctive in any marked way. Where this is the case, and where competition is strong, small firms will be price takers, and their profits and growth will be influenced substantially by external forces. Some small firm owners will be entrepreneurial, willing to take risks and determined to build a bigger business; others will be content to stay small. Some small businesses are started by people who essentially want to work for themselves rather than for a larger corporation, and their objectives could well be concerned with survival and the establishment of a sound business which can be passed on to the next generation of their family.

Each of the ideas and theories discussed in this section provides food for thought, but individually none of them explains fully what happens, or what should happen, in organizations. In my experience certain organizations are highly growth oriented, willing to diversify and take risks, whilst others, constrained by the difficulties of coping with rapid growth and implementing diversification strategies (discussed at some length in Chapter 16) are less ambitious in this respect. Each can be appropriate in certain circumstances and lead to high performance; in different circumstances they might be the wrong strategy.

Stakeholder theory is extremely relevant conceptually, but organizations are affected by the stakeholders in a variety of ways. Priorities must be decided for companies on an individual basis. Moreover the strategic leader, and in turn the organization, will seek to satisfy particular stakeholders rather than others because of their personal backgrounds and values. There is no right or wrong list of priorities. However, whilst priorities can and will be established, all stakeholders must be satisfied to some minimum level. In the final analysis the essential requirement is congruence between environment, values and resources.

So far in this chapter we have concentrated on profit-seeking organizations and considered just how important the profit motive might be. Not-for-profit organizations may be growth conscious, quality conscious or committed to employee welfare in the same way as profit seekers, but there are certain differences which require that they are considered separately.

Objectives of not-for-profit organizations

If we are to understand the objectives of not-for-profit organizations and appreciate where they are aiming to go, a number of points need to be considered.

❑ Stakeholders are important, particularly those who are providers of financial support.
❑ There will be a number of potentially conflicting objectives, and quite typically the financial ones will not be seen as the most essential in terms of the mission.
❑ Whilst there will be a mix of quantitative (financial) and qualitative objectives, the former will be easier to measure, although the latter relate more closely to the mission of the organization.
❑ For this reason the efficient use of resources becomes an important objective.

These points will now be examined in greater depth, making reference to Cases 5.1 and 5.2 (The National Theatre and London Zoo) together with a number of other examples, as not-for-profit organizations are many and varied.

At one extreme, at least in terms of size, **nationalized industries** with essentially monopoly markets have been seen as non-profit, and throughout their existence different governments have strived to establish acceptable and effective measures of performance for them. At various times both breakeven and return on capital employed have been stressed. There is an in-built objectives conflict between social needs (many of them provide essential services) and a requirement that the very substantial resources are managed commercially in order to avoid waste. The Conservative government of the 1980s followed a policy of privatizing certain nationalized industries partly on the grounds that in some cases more competition will be stimulating and create greater efficiency.

Case 5.1
THE NATIONAL THEATRE

The National Theatre is in fact three theatres in one building on the south bank of the Thames in London. A substantial proportion of revenue has to be allocated to cover the overheads on the building. The specially built theatre opened in 1976, and for 12 years it had only one Director, Sir Peter Hall. Richard Eyre became Director in 1988. Despite its name, and although it does at times tour the country, it does not attract a national audience. The plays it offers are generally different from those in the more commercial non-subsidized theatres in London's West End, and it attracts a mixture of regular theatre goers from the southeast, foreign tourists and occasional visitors.

The National receives a grant from the Arts Council (itself funded by the Treasury). At certain times during the 1980s the grant increased at less than the rate of inflation, a reflection of government policy concerning support for the arts and their belief that more private support is required. In addition the National receives private sponsorship and earns money from the box office, catering and other front-of-house sales. Sponsorship and subsidies allow ticket prices to be less than they otherwise would.

Some stakeholders, such as directors and actors, might hold the view that as the National is prestigious it should seek to offer the 'best of everything' – plays, actors, costumes, and scenery – and that it should experiment and seek to be innovative. At the same time it has to at least break even, although the types of play and musical which earn the most revenue at the box office are not necessarily those the National will seek to produce.

Sir Peter Hall has said that his main aim was to provide working conditions where actors can be at their most creative. Audiences and money matter, but they are not the primary goal.

How, then, is success measured? Audiences and revenue can certainly be measured, but 'success is something you can feel and smell when you are with an audience'.

The National Health Service can be viewed similarly. Fundamentally its purpose relates to the health and well-being of the nation, and attention can be focused on both prevention and cure. The role of the police in terms of crime prevention and the solution of crimes that have taken place can be seen as synonymous. The health service can spend any money it is offered, as science continually improves what can be done for people. In a sense it is a chicken-and-egg situation. Resources improve treatments and open up new opportunities for prevention; and these in turn stimulate demand, particularly where they concern illnesses or diseases which historically have not been easily treated. However, these developments are often very expensive, and decisions have then to be made about where funds should be allocated. Quite simply the decisions relate to priorities.

Customers of the health service are concerned with such things as the waiting time for admission to hospital and for operations, the quality of care as affected by staff attitudes and numbers, and arguably privacy in small wards, cleanliness and food. Doctors are concerned with the amount of resources and their ability to cope with demand; and administrators must ensure that resources are used efficiently.

There are a number of key points in this highly simplistic summary. The government funds the National Health Service, and as the major source of funds is a key influence. Pfeffer (1981) has argued that the relative power of influencers is related to the funds they provide. The less funding that is provided

London Zoo, in Regent's Park, is one of two zoological gardens which are controlled and administered by the Zoological Society of London. The other is Whipsnade Park, near Dunstable in Bedfordshire, and this covers 600 acres compared with 34 acres in London.

The Society's charter lays down its primary purpose as 'the advancement of zoology and animal physiology, and the introduction of new and curious subjects of the animal kingdom'. Given this scientific orientation, what should be the objectives of London Zoo? Who are the other stakeholders, and how important are they? The basic dilemma concerns how much zoos are places of entertainment and relaxation, with customers paramount, and how much they are organizations with primarily educational and scientific purposes. One constraint is the fact that Regent's Park is a Royal Park, and that bye-laws restrict certain activities such as on-site advertising.

Since 1985 the zoo has received a series of annual grants from the Department of the Environment, and in 1988 it was given £10 million as a one-off payment 'to put it on a firm financial footing'. It remains 'the only national collection in the world not publically funded on a regular basis'. Without these subsidies the zoo has a surplus of expenditure over income.

Income is essentially from visitors, the majority of whom live in comfortable travelling distance of London, and private sponsorship. Many of the visitors are on organized school trips; and weather conditions are very important in attracting or deterring people.

Many visitors are attracted by big animals, as evidenced by the commercial success of safari parks, but they are costly and dangerous, as well as well researched and relatively safe as far as endangered species go. Quite often the most endangered species are relatively unattractive. Whipsnade is regarded as more ideal for big animals; and London Zoo has had no hippos (since the 1960s) and no bears (since 1986). Whipsnade has both. Visitors can drive around Whipsnade, parking in various places en route, but it is not a safari park.

Critics have argued that London Zoo's management has failed to exploit the zoo's conservation work by featuring it in informative displays and that much of the zoo's important (and scientifically renowned) research is not recognized by the general public. This is correct, but the fact remains that much of the important conservation work involves species which are relatively uninteresting for many public visitors. Such an example is the rare Rodriguez Fruit Bat.

The Department of the Environment paid for a report by independent consultants (1987–1988), and they concluded that 'management at London Zoo did not reflect the commercial emphasis which was essential for survival and prosperity without a permanent subsidy'. They recommended the establishment of a new company to manage London and Whipsnade Zoos, separate from the scientific research of the Zoological Society. This company was established in October 1988, with the aim of reversing the falling trend in admissions and returning the zoo to profit in three years.

The numbers of visitors did increase in 1989 and 1990, but below the level required to break even. In April 1991 newspapers first reported that London Zoo might have to close, with some animals destroyed and others moved to Whipsnade. The Government refused further financial assistance, not wholly convinced of the need for urban zoos. Cost reduction, *per se*, was ruled out as this was likely to provoke a new fall in admissions. Instead rescue plans concentrated on a smaller zoo with a new concept – natural habitats such as an African rain forest complete with gorillas, and a Chinese mountain featuring the pandas. There would be less emphasis on caged animals.

Changes were made but attendances fell. The zoo's closure was announced formally in June 1992. New external funding has since provided a reprieve.

Since 1992 the Zoo has secured its survival by emphasizing its role as a conservation centre, breeding endangered species and returning them to the wild. It breaks even (1995), using publicity more effectively to attract some 1 million visitors a year.

by customers, the weaker is their influence over decisions. Hence a not-for-profit organization like the National Health Service may be less customer oriented than a private competitive firm. Some would argue that the private medical sector is more marketing conscious.

All organizations will seek to measure performance in some way. It was stated earlier in the chapter that performance against quantitative objectives can be measured directly whereas performance against qualitative objectives is typically indirect and more difficult. If attention is focused on the aspects that are most easily measured there is a danger that these come to be perceived as the most important objectives. Hospital administrators can easily measure the number of admissions, the utilization of beds and theatres, the cost of laundry and food and so on. Fundamentally more important is who is being treated relative to the real needs of the community. Are the most urgent and needy cases receiving the priorities they deserve? How is this measured? Performance measures therefore tend to concentrate on the **efficient use of resources** rather than the **effectiveness** of the organization. Although profit may not be an important consideration, costs are. In addition these measures may well be a source of conflict between medical and administrative staff and this is a reflection of the fact that there is likely to be disagreement and confusion about what the key objectives are.

Given this the objectives that are perceived as important and are pursued at any time are very dependent upon the relative power of the influencers and their ability to exercise power. Linked to this point is the relationship between hospitals and area and regional health authorities. Similarly where not-for-profit organizations have advisory bodies, or Boards of trustees, the relationship and relative power is important.

Tourist attractions such as London Zoo (Case 5.2) and the country's leading museums (including the British Museum, the Natural History Museum and the Victoria and Albert, which is the National Museum of Art and Design) have a potential conflict of objectives concerning their inevitable educational and scientific orientations and the requirement that they address commercial issues. Museums can earn money from shops and cafeterias and they receive some private funding, but to a great extent they are reliant on government grants. In the 1980s these grants did not keep pace with their monetary demands and hence it has been necessary for them to seek additional revenue as well as manage resources and costs more efficiently. Admission charges to museums have become a controversial issue. In November 1985 the Victoria and Albert Museum introduced voluntary admission charges, and in April 1987 the Natural History Museum started charging for entry. Some potential visitors are lost as they refuse to pay, and this has implications for the educational objective. It has been reported that by 1987 admissions to the Victoria and Albert had fallen to one million a year from a peak of 1.75 million in 1983, but they were increasing again after 1988. However, the museum was criticized by some arts lovers for a poster campaign describing it as 'an ace caff with quite a nice museum attached', although museum staff claimed that this was a major reason for the increase in attendances. Some museums, including the British Museum, adamantly opposed charging.

At The National Theatre (Case 5.1) the issue addresses art and finance. Subsidized theatres perceive their role to be different from that of commercial theatres and a number of them, including the Royal Shakespeare Company,

English National Opera and the Royal Opera House, Covent Garden, all compete for a percentage of Arts Council funding. When the Arts Council, as a major stakeholder and provider of funds, attempts to influence the strategies of the theatres they are often accused of meddling. Again there is a potential chicken-and-egg situation. If the theatres, under pressure from reduced subsidies (in real terms), raise more revenue and reduce their costs, they may find that this results in permanently reduced subsidies. Hence, as an alternative, they may choose to restrain their commercial orientation.

Cathedrals face a similar dilemma. The costs of repairs and maintenance are forcing some to charge visitors fixed amounts rather than rely on voluntary donations. Their mission is concerned with religion and charity but they are not immune from commercial realities.

Charities like Oxfam have sets of inter-dependent commercial and non-commercial objectives. Oxfam's mission concerns the provision of relief and the provision of aid where it is most needed throughout the world. Additional objectives relate to teaching people how to look after themselves better through, say, irrigation and better farming techniques and to obtaining publicity to draw public attention to the plight of the needy. Their ability to pursue these is constrained by resource availability. Consequently Oxfam have fund-raising objectives, and strategies (including retailing through Oxfam shops) to achieve them. It is difficult to say which receives most priority as they are so inter-dependent.

We have discussed the issue of the displacement of objectives in not-for-profit organizations. Attention is centred on quantitative measures as they are relatively easily carried out. The efficient use of resources replaces profit as the commercial objective, and whilst this may not be an essential aspect of the mission, it will be seen as important by certain stakeholders. In reality attention has switched from evaluating outputs (the real objectives) to measuring inputs (resources) because it easier to do. Where the stakeholders are major sponsors, and particularly in the case of government departments, there will be an insistence upon cost effectiveness. Many of the organizations mentioned in this section are managed by people whose training and natural orientation is towards arts or science, and this can result in feelings of conflict with regard to objectives. Quite typically the organization will pursue certain objectives for a period of time, satisfying the most influential stakeholders in the coalition, and then change as the preferences of stakeholders – or their relative power and influence – change.

Whilst profit-seeking and not-for-profit organizations have essentially different missions, the issue of profit making is complex. As we have seen, some not-for-profit organizations rely on subsidies and these enable prices to be kept below what they would otherwise be. In nationalized industries the element of customer service has been seen to be important with prices controlled or at least influenced by government. An independent regulator has been appointed when nationalized businesses have been privatized (see Chapter 9). However, unless the providers of grants and subsidies are willing to bear commercial trading losses and at the same time finance any necessary investment, there is a necessity for the organizations to generate revenue at least equal to the costs incurred. Where investment finance also needs to be generated a surplus of income over expenditure is important. This basically is profit. Whilst profit may not therefore be an essential part of the mission it is still required.

Visit the website:
http://www.
itbp.com

The following comments of Ackoff (1986) relating to the objectives of US universities usefully round off this section and act as an introduction to the next section on personal objectives.

> The objectives pursued by organizations frequently differ from those proclaimed. Some years ago I assumed that the principal objective of universities was the education of students. Armed with this assumption I could make no sense of their behaviour. I learned that education, like profit, is a requirement not an objective and that the principal objective is to provide their faculties with the quality of work life and the standard of living they desire. That's why professors do so little teaching, give the same courses over and over again, arrange classes at their convenience, not that of their students, teach subjects they want to teach rather than students want to learn and skip classes to give lectures for a fee.

These comments, interestingly, relate to an education system where students pay their own fees rather than enjoy government funding, as is the case in the UK. One might expect consumer resistance if students felt that their interests were not being satisfied.

British universities, of course, have become subject to tighter financial controls in the 1990s, resource utilization and cost efficiency have become increasingly important, and personal objectives along the lines of those above must cause conflict.

The impact of personal objectives

It has already been established that organizations are generally too large and complex to have only one objective. As a result, and influenced by stakeholders, there are typically several objectives with varying degrees of relative importance. It is now appropriate to consider why organizations cannot be treated separately from the people who work in them.

Objectives can be set (and changed) in any one of three ways.

- ❑ The strategic leader decides.
- ❑ Managers throughout the organization are either consulted or influence the objectives by their decisions and actions.
- ❑ All or some relevant stakeholders influence the organization in some way.

It is the second of these which is addressed in this section. Some organizations will have planning systems (which will be studied in a later chapter) which involve a wide range of managers throughout the organization, and they

---

You must provide a framework in which people can act. For example, we have said that our first priority is safety, second is punctuality, and third is other services. So if you risk flight safety by leaving on time, you have acted outside the framework of your authority. The same is true if you don't leave on time because you are missing two catering boxes of meat. That's what I mean by a framework. You give people a framework, and within the framework you let people act.

Jan Carlzon, President and Chief Executive Officer, Scandinavian Airlines System

therefore have up-to-date information about products, services and competitors fed in from those managers closest to the market. This can influence the objectives and strategies that the organization states it wishes to achieve and implement respectively.

At the same time the decisions made by managers determine the actual strategies pursued, and in turn revised, implicit, objectives replace the explicit ones. The incidence or likelihood of this is affected by the culture of the organization, the relative power bases of managers, communication systems, and whether or not there are rigid policies and procedures or more informal management processes that allow managers considerable freedom. Key Concept 5.1 defines **policies** and discusses their role in strategy implementation. The following brief example illustrates the impact of policies. Consider a multiple store that sells records as one of its products and has nearby a small independent competitor that appeals to different customers. If the small store closed down there could be new opportunities for the manager of the multiple store if he changed his competitive strategy for records by changing his displays, improved his stock levels and supported these moves with window displays promoting the changes. Head office merchandising policies concerning stocks and displays may or may not allow him this freedom.

Figure 5.3 charts the process outlined above. The strategic leader determines and states the objectives, strategies and proposed changes for the organization. In arriving at decisions he or she may be influenced in a minor or major way by stakeholders outside the organization and the managers consulted. In order to ensure that the strategies are implemented (and the objectives achieved) the strategic leader will design and build an organization structure – which may

---

KEY CONCEPT 5.1

Policies

- 'Policies' are guidelines relating to decisions and approaches which support organizational efforts to achieve stated objectives.
- They are basically guides to thoughts (about how things might or should be done) and actions.
- They are therefore guides to decision making. For example a policy which states that for supplies of a particular item three quotations should be sought and the cheapest selected, or a policy not to advertise in certain newspapers, or a policy not to trade with particular countries – all influence decisions. Policies are particularly useful for routine repetitive decisions.

- Policies can be at corporate, divisional (or strategic business unit (SBU)) or functional level; and they are normally stated in terms of management (of people), marketing, production, finance and research and development.
- If stated objectives are to be achieved, and the strategies designed to accomplish this implemented, the appropriate policies must be there in support. In other words the behaviour of managers and the decisions they take should be supportive of what the organization is seeking to achieve. Policies guide and constrain their actions.

- Policies can be mandatory (rules which allow little freedom for original thought or action) or advisory. The more rigid they are the less freedom managers have to change things with delegated authority; and this can be good or bad depending upon change pressures from the environment.
- It is vital to balance consistency and co-ordination (between the various divisions, SBUs and departments in the organization) with flexibility.
- Policies need not be written down. They can be passed on verbally as part of the culture.
- Policies must be widely understood if they are to be useful.

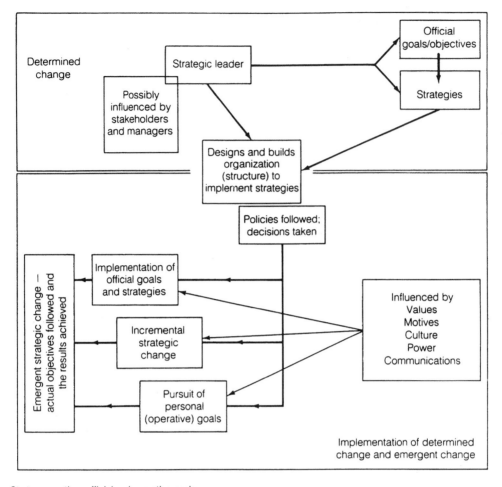

Figure 5.3 Strategy creation: official and operative goals.

restrict managers or allow them considerable freedom – and will determine policies which may be mandatory or advisory. This will tie in to the culture of the organization and will be influenced by the style and values of the strategic leader, both of which we discussed earlier. This process is reflected in the top part of Figure 5.3,

The bottom section considers what happens in reality. The types of policy and the authority and freedom delegated to managers guides, influences and constrains decision making. The motives, values and relative power of individual managers, the relative importance of particular functions, divisions or strategic business units in the organization, and the system of communications are also influential. The stated or *official objectives* may or may not be achieved; there may be appropriate incremental decisions which reflect changes in the environment; or managers may be pursuing personal objectives, which Perrow (1961) has termed *operative goals.* This is happening when the behaviour taking place cannot be accounted for by official company objectives and policies. The aggregation of these various decisions determines the emergent strategic changes, the actual objectives followed and the results achieved.

Type of organization	Typical official goals	Possible operative goals
Private sector firm	Profit Return on capital Customer service	Favouring certain suppliers (not lowest cost or best delivery) or customers (priority on low profit orders)
Hospital	Promotion of community health via cure and prevention	Personal ambitions of certain consultants (arguably wrong priorities) Use of more, but cheaper, unqualified nursing staff
Employment agency	Bring two interested (and ideally well-suited) parties together	Racial or other prejudice

Table 5.5

Examples of official and operative goals

Developed from ideas contained in Perrow, C (1961) The analysis of goals in complex organizations, *American Sociological Review,* **26,** December.

Official and operative goals

Perrow defines official goals as 'the general purposes of the organization, as put forth in the charter, annual reports, public statements by key executives and other authoritative announcements'. But, he argues, there are numerous ways of achieving official goals which cannot easily be accounted for; and groups and individuals may pursue unofficial goals. Operative goals, then, 'designate the ends sought through the actual operating policies of the organization; they tell us what the organization actually is trying to do, regardless of what the official goals say are the aims'.

Operative goals may complement official goals or they may conflict. A complementary situation would exist if the stated objective was in terms of a target return on capital employed, and if this was achieved through operative goals of managers and decisions taken by them regarding delivery times, quality and so on. If, however, a sales manager was favouring particular customers with discounts or priority deliveries on low profit orders, or a production manager was setting unnecessarily high quality standards (as far as customers are concerned) which resulted in substantial rejections and high operating costs, profits would be threatened. In such cases operative goals would conflict with official goals. Table 5.5 gives examples of potential conflict in different types of organization.

Social responsibility and business ethics

Having looked at some of the theories which are relevant for a study of objectives, and at typical objectives that organizations pursue and why, it is appropriate to conclude this chapter with a consideration of wider societal aspects. Objectives which relate to social responsibility may be affected by stakeholders; in some cases they result from legislation, but often they are voluntary actions. The issue is one of how responsible a firm might choose to be, and why. Again the particular values of the strategic leader will be very influential.

There are numerous ways that a firm can behave responsibly in the interests of society, and examples are given below. It should not be thought, though, that social responsibility is a one-way process; organizations can benefit considerably from it.

❑ **Product safety:** This can be the result of design or production and includes aspects of supply and supplier selection to obtain safe materials or components. Product safety will be influenced to an extent by legislation, but an organization can build in more safety features than the law requires. Some cars are an example of this. Volvo, for example, is promoted and perceived as a relatively safe car. Product safety will have cost implications. Sometimes the safety is reflected in perceived higher quality, which adds value that the customer is willing to pay a premium for, but at other times it will be the result of the organization's choosing to sacrifice some potential profit.

❑ **Working conditions:** Linked to the previous point, these can include safety at work, which again is affected by legislation which sets minimum standards. Aspects of job design to improve working conditions and training to improve employees' prospects are further examples.

❑ **Honesty,** including not offering or accepting bribes.

❑ **Avoiding pollution.**

❑ **Avoiding discrimination.**

The above points are all subject to some legislation.

❑ **Community action:** This is a very broad category with numerous opportunities, ranging from charitable activities to concerted action to promote industry and jobs in areas which have suffered from the economic recession. Many large organizations release executives on a temporary basis to help with specific community projects.

❑ **Industry location:** Organizations may locate new plants in areas of high unemployment for a variety of reasons. Whilst aspects of social responsibility may be involved the decision may well be more economic. Grants and rate concessions may be important.

❑ **Other environmental concerns** such as recycling, waste disposal, protecting the ozone layer and energy efficiency. Box 5.5 illustrates a number of specific examples.

Porter (1995) contends that many companies mistakenly see environmental legislation as a threat, something to be resisted. Instead, he argues, they should

---

Managers of today, and those who seek to succeed in the future, must have a highly-developed sense of responsibility to society and the environment. This is especially true of the chemical industry. We must understand and respond to public anxiety; debate, explain and listen. In Bayer's case we seek to communicate the fact that we are not only experts in what to do, but that we use our expertise in full awareness of our responsibilities towards the environment, our employees and neighbours, our customers and our shareholders. For us, environmental protection and safety have the same priority as high product quality and commercial success. Every one of our managers is expected to share in communicating these principles.

Hermann J. Strenger, Chairman of the Board of Management,
Bayer AG, Leverkusen

Box 5.5
EXAMPLES OF ENVIRONMENTAL STRATEGIES

'The 1990s will be the decade of the environment' (The President of the Petroleum Marketers Association of America quoted in *Fortune*, 12 February 1990, p. 24)

1. **McDonald's** took an equity stake in a new venture for recycling the waste collected at their restaurants. Some plastic containers which cannot be recycled have been withdrawn; food scraps are used for making compost. **Sainsbury's** give a one penny refund for every plastic carrier that customers re-use. This saves the retailer the cost of providing a new bag; it also reduces the amount of waste plastic.

2. **Electricity generating** has gradually switched to gas and cleaner coal (with a low sulphur content) because coal has been shown to cause acid rain.

3. **Packaging.** Smaller, lighter packages use fewer raw materials and they are cheaper to transport. Procter and Gamble and Unilever have both introduced more concentrated versions of their detergent brands – which, ironically, many consumers have seen as poor value for money because they have been unconvinced by the instructions to use less of the product! Soft drinks manufacturers have switched to fully recyclable aluminium cans and plastic bottles.

4. **ICI** is a leading contender in the challenge to find a replacement for chlorofluorocarbons (CFCs), gases which are used extensively in aerosols and refrigeration equipment, and which are widely blamed for depleting the ozone layer.

5. **Body Shop** produces a comprehensive, externally audited, environmental report, its *Green Book*. The emphasis on such factors as energy waste and product stewardship drives improvements. Amongst other initiatives, Body Shop has sought to eliminate its use of PVC because of the environmental impact of such packaging.

4. **The motor vehicle industry**. Historically car manufacturers exploited an opportunity very successfully – increased affluence and the desire for individual freedom had generated a demand for private cars. Their success in increasing levels of ownership created a number of threats: traffic density; pollution from exhaust emissions; material waste through obsolescence; the 'waste' of scarce resources in high-consumption, inefficient, engines; and safety problems arising from the sheer volume of traffic, congestion and hurry.

A response was needed, and this has involved both manufacturers and government.

❏ Legislation has made catalytic converters compulsory on all new cars after January 1993.

❏ New models invariably feature improvements in design and technology which reduce waste and increase fuel efficiency.

❏ New concept vehicles, including electric cars and others which mix the traditionally contradictory high performance with environmental friendliness. These have a long-term time scale.

❏ Links between different forms of transport (road, rail, air and water) are being strengthened. BMW, for example, has pioneered co-operative ventures in Munich, where research has shown that in one square kilometer of the city centre in busy periods 50% of the cars on the move are driving round looking for parking spaces.

❏ Old parts are being recycled. In France both Peugeot and Renault opened plants for this, followed by other European manufacturers, but these initiatives remain small ventures in relation to the total numbers of cars being scrapped. BMW opened a recycling plant in the UK at the end of 1992, a joint venture with a salvage specialist, to enable the recycling and reselling of parts and the reconditioning of engines. A typical BMW could be fully dismantled for £175.

❏ In 1995 Vauxhall was the first UK car manufacturer to be awarded the new BS7750 for environmental management; it had successfully eliminated some packaging, segregated waste, reduced energy consumption and improved its waste water management.

see regulation as an indication the company is not using its resources efficiently. Toxic materials and discarded packaging are waste. The costs incurred in eliminating a number of environmental problems can be more than offset by other savings and improvements in product quality. Companies should be innovative and not reluctantly just complying with their legal requirements.

On the other hand, the European chemical industry argues that bulk chemical manufacture is being driven out of EC countries by the costs of complying with environmental regulation. Standards in many Far Eastern countries are less restrictive.

❑ **The attitude of food retailers** towards, for example, accurate labelling (country of origin), free-range eggs, organic vegetables, biodegradable packaging, CFC-free aerosols and products containing certain dubious E-number additives. It is a moot point whether retailers or consumers should decide on these issues.

Examples of social responsibility can appear in other ways.

Securicor, the UK's leading security company, has a number of stated aims which reflect both a concern for employees and wider social responsibilities. The philosophy was introduced by chief executive Keith Erskine, previously a 'lawyer concerned with justice'; it resulted in the slogan 'Securicor Cares' and advertising on the theme 'Securicor Cares for Customers, Co-workers and the Common Good', and it remained intact after Erskine's death in 1974. In the 1972 Chairman's review Erskine detailed the following aims (these are selected from a longer list):

❑ to observe the highest code of business conduct
❑ to devolve and involve; to enrich both jobs and lives; to combine private enterprise with social justice; to care for the individual
❑ to ignore class or race; to judge only by merit; to work in comradeship.

Obviously objectives of this nature become part of the organization culture. Social responsibility is at the heart of activities and objectives because it is felt that the organization has an obligation both to the community and to society in general. However, it must not be assumed that the approach receives universal support. Milton Friedman (1979), the economist, argues that 'the business of business is business ... the organization's only social responsibility is to increase its profit'. Friedman also comments that donations to charity and sponsorship of the arts are 'fundamentally subversive' and not in the best interests of the shareholders. Social responsibility would then be the result of legislation. Drucker (1974) argues businesses have a role in society which is 'to supply goods and services to customers and an economic surplus to society ... rather than to supply jobs to workers and managers, or even dividends to shareholders'. The latter, he argues, are means not ends. Drucker contends that it is mismanagement to forget that a hospital exists for its patients and a university for its students. This contrasts with the comments by Russell Ackoff about university academics quoted earlier.

The topic is complex, and although the outcome of certain decisions can be seen to be bringing benefit to the community or employees the decision may have been influenced by legislation or perceived organizational benefit (enlightened self-interest) rather than a social conscience. One could argue that the organization will benefit if it looks after its employees; equally one could argue that it will suffer if it fails to consider employee welfare. The two approaches are philosophically different, but they may generate similar results. Some organizations feature their community role extensively in corporate advertising campaigns designed to bring them recognition and develop a caring responsible image.

Business ethics

Disasters like the explosion at the chemical plant in Bhopal, India, raise the question of how far companies should go in pursuit of profits. Ethics is defined as 'the discipline dealing with what is good and bad and right and wrong or with moral duty and obligation' (*Webster's Third New International Dictionary*). Houlden (1988) suggests that business ethics encompasses the views of people throughout society concerning the morality of business, and not just the views of the particular business and the people who work in it.

Issues such as golden handshakes, insider dealing and very substantial salary increases for company chairmen and chief executives are topical and controversial.

The high-profile case of British Airways and Virgin Atlantic, where BA was accused of using privileged information to evaluate Virgin's route profitability and to persuade Virgin customers to switch airlines, suggested BA acted unethically. In contrast, Hewlett-Packard, the US electronics multi-national which is widely regarded as being highly ethical, operates an internal ban on the use of improper means for obtaining competitor information. Additionally the company insists that any statements about its competitors must be fair, factual and complete.

Public attention is drawn to these issues, and people's perceptions of businesses generally and individually are affected. However, their responses differ markedly. Some people feel disgruntled but do nothing; others take more positive actions. Managers, however, should not ignore the potential for resistance or opposition by their customers, say through refusing to buy their products or use their services.

Another ethical concern is individual managers or employees who adopt practices which senior managers or the strategic leader would consider unethical. These need to be identified and stopped. If they remain unchecked they are likely to spread, with the argument that 'everyone does it'. Sales staff using questionable methods of persuasion, even lying, would be an example.

However, it does not follow that such practices would always be seen as unethical by senior managers – in some organizations they will be at least condoned, and possibly even encouraged.

Case 5.3 on the Co-operative Bank highlights how one organization has used an ethical stance to create a competitive advantage.

Ethical dilemmas

One classic ethical dilemma concerns the employee who works for a competitor, is interviewed for a job, and who promises to bring confidential information if he is offered the post. Should the proposition be accepted or not? The issue, featured at the beginning of this section, is how far companies should go in pursuit of profits. In such a case as this, of course, long-term considerations are important as well as potential short-term benefits. If the

Visit the website: http://www. itbp.com

Case 5.3
THE CO-OPERATIVE BANK

Retail banking in the UK has become extremely competitive as traditional building societies and foreign banks have entered the sector. To compete, charges have been kept relatively low, leaving the banks with too many unprofitable accounts. Their challenge: attracting the 'right customers', those who will retain a sizeable current account balance and also purchase other products such as insurance policies. A typical 'good customer' would be 25–40 years old and a member of the ABC1 social groupings.

The Co-op Bank, owned by the Co-operative Wholesale Society, began an advertising campaign in the early 1990s which concentrated on the bank's ethical stance towards business. The bank stated it would not deal with tobacco companies, cosmetics companies which used animals for testing, companies involved in blood sports, factory farming and animal fur products, and any business which caused pollution. Some corporate accounts were closed.

Almost immediately the volume of retail deposits increased by over 10%, with new customers actively citing the advertising campaign. Profits accrued after two years of losses. Many customers also took out the bank's new gold credit card.

The bank has developed a customer profile which features a disproportionate percentage of ABC1s. Managing Director, Terry Thomas, commented: 'After all, what bank would want to attract low income, badly-educated, ignorant people?'

competitor who loses the confidential information realizes what has happened it may seek to retaliate in some way. Arguably the best interests of the industry as a whole should be considered.

Another example is the company with a plant which is surplus to requirements and which it would like to sell. The company knows the land beneath the plant contains radioactive waste. Legally it need not disclose this fact to prospective buyers, but is it ethical to keep quiet? Petfood manufacturers, looking to expand their sales, would logically seek to differentiate their products by featuring particular benefits and satisfied, friendly pets, but they will also hope to persuade more people to become owners. Given the publicity on potentially dangerous breeds of dog, and the numbers of abandoned pets, particularly after Christmas, what would constitute an ethical approach to promotion? In 1991 a small number of ministers in the Church of England questioned whether the Church Commissioners, with £3 billion to invest to cover the future salaries and pensions of clergy, should be free to invest the money anywhere (in an attempt to maximize earnings) or whether they should be restricted to organizations which were known to be ethical in their business dealings.

Badaracco and Webb (1995) also highlight how internal decisions can be influenced by unethical practices. They quote instances of invented market research findings, and fudged investment returns which imply, erroneously, that the organization is meeting its published targets. They distinguish between 'expedient actions' and 'right actions'.

In contrast, a serious dilemma faces individuals in an organization who feel that their managers are pursuing unethical practices. There are several examples of individuals who have acted and suffered as a result of their actions. An accountant with an insurance company exposed a case of tax evasion by his bosses and jeopardized his career. Stanley Adams, an employee of Hoffman la

Roche, the Swiss drug company, believed that his firm was making excessive profits and divulged commercially sensitive information to the European Commission. He also lost his career and suffered financially. There are similar examples of engineers who felt that design compromises were threatening consumer safety, complained, and lost their jobs.

Many of the ethical issues which affect strategic decisions are regulated directly by legislation. Equally, many companies do not operate in sensitive environments where serious ethical issues require thought and attention. However, some companies and their strategic leaders do need a clear policy regarding business ethics. Quite often they have to decide whether to increase costs in the short run, say to improve safety factors, on the assumption that this will bring longer-term benefits. Short-term profitability, important to shareholders, could be affected. Increased safety beyond minimum legal requirements, for example, would increase the construction costs of a new chemical plant. If safety was compromised to save money, nothing might actually go wrong and profits would be higher. However, an explosion or other disaster results in loss of life, personal injury, compensation and legal costs, lost production, adverse publicity and tension between the business and local community. The long-term losses can be substantial.

Reidenbach and Robin (1994) have produced a spectrum of five ethical/unethical responses.

- ❏ *Amoral companies* seek to 'win at all costs'; anything is seen as acceptable. The secret lies in not being found out.
- ❏ *Legalistic companies* obey the law and no more. There is no code of ethics; companies act only when it is essential.
- ❏ *Responsive companies* accept that being ethical can pay off.
- ❏ *Ethically engaged companies* actively want to 'do the right thing' and to be seen to be doing so. Ethical codes will exist, but ethical behaviour will not necessarily be a planned activity and fully integrated into the culture.
- ❏ *Ethical companies* such as Body Shop have ethics as a core value, supported by appropriate strategies and actions which permeate the whole organization.

Because ethical standards and beliefs are aspects of the corporate culture, they are influenced markedly by the lead set by the strategic leader and his or her awareness of behaviour throughout the organization. If a proper lead is not provided, managers will be left to 'second guess' what would be seen as appropriate behaviour. Power, then, can be used ethically or unethically by individual managers.

Frederick (1988) contends that the corporate culture is the main source of any ethical problems. He argues that managers are encouraged to focus their professional energies on productivity, efficiency and leadership, and that their corporate values lead them to act in ways which place the company interests ahead of those of consumers or society

To guard against this it can be useful for a company to publish a corporate code of ethics, which all managers are expected to follow. Typically large US companies have been more progressive with such codes than those in the UK. In the early 1990s, some 30% of large companies in the UK had published codes, but the number has been growing all the time.

The typical issues covered in an ethics code include relationships with employees (the most prevalent factor in the UK codes of ethics), government (more important in the USA), the community and the environment.

Drawing on earlier points, attitudes towards bribery and inducement, and the use of privileged information, could also be incorporated in any code. Attention might also be paid to practices which are commonplace but arguably unethical. Examples would include a deliberate policy not to pay invoices on time, and creative accounting, presenting information in the most favourable light. The extent to which audited company accounts can be wholly relied upon is another interesting issue.

In my opinion business ethics is important and worthy of serious attention. However, a consideration of ethical issues in strategic decisions typically requires that a long-term perspective is adopted. Objectives and strategies should be realistic and achievable rather than over-ambitious and very difficult to attain. In the latter case individual managers may be set high targets which encourage them to behave unethically, possibly making them feel uneasy. Results may be massaged, for instance, or deliberately presented with inaccuracies. Such practices spread quickly and dishonesty becomes acceptable. The longer-term perspective can reduce the need for immediate results and targets which managers feel have to be met at all costs. However, pressure from certain stakeholders, particularly institutional shareholders, may focus attention on the short term and on results which surpass those of the previous year. The longer-term perspective additionally allows for concern with processes and behaviour, and with how the results are obtained. The drive for results is not allowed to override ethical and behavioural concerns.

Houlden (1988) concludes that strategic leaders should be objective about how society views their company and its products, and wherever possible should avoid actions which can damage its image. If an action or decision which certain stakeholders might view as unethical is unavoidable, such as the closure of a plant, it is important to use public relations to explain fully why the decision has been taken. The need for a good corporate image should not be underestimated.

In later chapters we discuss how organizations might achieve competitive advantage. Ethical considerations can make a significant contribution to this. A commitment to keeping promises about quality standards and delivery times, or not making promises which cannot be met, would be one example. If employees are honest and committed, and rewarded appropriately for this, then costs are likely to be contained and the overall level of customer service high, thereby improving profits.

Checklist of key terms and concepts

You should feel confident that you understand the following terms and ideas:

★ Vision
★ Mission
★ Objectives (or goals)

★ Stakeholder theory
★ Official and operative goals
★ Social responsibility and business ethics.

You should also appreciate how different market models provide opportunities for, and constraints on, competition.

Summary

In this chapter we have explored objectives, looking at where the organization is going and considering why. We shall return to the subject in Chapter 14, when we consider the process of reviewing objectives and possibly setting new objectives as part of strategic decision making.

Specifically we have

- differentiated between the vision, the mission and objectives, and explained that aims and goals are frequently used as alternative expressions
- considered what is required for a mission statement to be useful
- recapped, from microeconomics, the four key market models
- introduced the notion of stakeholder theory, and examined how this can lead to multiple objectives and priorities

- briefly summarized a number of theories of the firm based upon the premise that ownership and management are separated
- discussed whether profit is a means to other ends or an end (objective) in itself
- considered typical objectives of UK companies, especially those influenced by shareholders, and contrasted them with those of Japanese companies
- highlighted the differences between profit-seeking and not-for-profit organizations, and emphasized that for the latter it is likely that inputs (resources) will be a key measure of performance
- reviewed Perrow's work on official and operative goals, and posed the question: is the organization going where it intended to go?
- looked at the subject of social responsibility and business ethics.

Questions and research assignments

Text related

1 Consider how the objectives of HP Bulmer Holdings, detailed in Box 5.4 might be ranked in order of priority.

   Is there a difference between an ideal ranking and the likely ranking in practice? Note: Members of the Bulmer family hold over 50% of the ordinary shares.

2 What key issues do you believe should be incorporated in a company statement on ethics?

Library based

3 When Tottenham Hotspur became the first English Football League club with a stock exchange listing (in 1983) the issue prospectus said: The Directors intend to ensure that the Club remains one of the leading football clubs in the country. They will seek to increase the Group's income by improving the return from existing assets and by establishing new sources of revenue in the leisure field.

   (a) Research the strategies followed by Tottenham Hotspur plc since 1983. Do you believe the interests of a plc and a professional football club are compatible or inevitably conflicting?

   (b) In view of the comments about social responsibility how do you view the fact that football clubs generally invest far more money in players (wages and transfer fees) than they do in their grounds (amenities and safety)?

4 Have the objectives (in particular the order of priorities) of the Natural History Museum changed since the introduction of compulsory admission charges in April 1987?

5 In view of the findings after the *Herald of Free Enterprise* disaster at Zeebrugge in March 1987 and the *Estonia* disaster in 1994, how does a company like P & O (the owners of the *Herald*) balance the extra costs involved in additional safety measures with the need to be competitive internationally, and the time added on to voyages by more rigorous safety procedures with customer irritation if they are delayed unnecessarily?

Recommended further reading

Richards (1978) is a useful short book devoted to the subject of goals and objectives. Newbould and Luffman (1979) provides a suitable introduction to stakeholder theory; Freeman (1984) is a text on strategic management from the perspective of stakeholders.

Drucker, PF (1990) *Managing the Non-profit Organization,* Butterworth-Heinemann, is a useful text.

Simon's article (1964) contains a number of valuable ideas and themes.

Readers interested in business ethics will find the following text provides a stimulating anecdotal discussion of the main issues: Blanchard, K and Peale, NV (1988) *The Power of Ethical Management,* Heinemann.

References

Ackoff, RL (1986) *Management in Small Doses,* John Wiley.

Badaracco, JL and Webb, A (1995) Business ethics: a view from the trenches, *California Management Review,* 37.2, Winter.

Baumol, WJ (1959) *Business Behaviour, Value and Growth,* Macmillan.

Campbell, A (1989) Research findings discussed in Skapinker, M (1989) Mission accomplished or ignored? *Financial Times,* 11 January. See also: Campbell, A and Nash, L (1992) *A Sense of Mission: Defining Direction for the Large Corporation,* Addison-Wesley.

Constable, J (1980) The nature of company objectives. Unpublished paper, Cranfield School of Management.

Cyert, RM and March, JG (1963) *A Behavioural Theory of the Firm,* Prentice-Hall.

Drucker, PF (1974) *Management: Tasks, Responsibilities, Practices,* Harper & Row.

Frederick, WC (1988) An ethics roundtable: the culprit is culture, *Management Review,* August.

Freeman, RE (1984) *Strategic Management: A Stakeholder Approach,* Pitman.

Friedman, M (1979) The social responsibility of business is to increase its profits. In *Business Policy and Strategy* (eds DJ McCarthy, RJ Minichiello and JR Curran), Irwin.

Galbraith, JK (1963) *American Capitalism. The Concept of Countervailing Power,* Penguin.

Galbraith, JK (1969) *The New Industrial State,* Penguin.

Houlden, B (1988) The corporate conscience, *Management Today,* August.

Lorenz, C (1994) Does nationality really matter? *Financial Times,* 13 April.

Marris, R (1964) *The Economic Theory of Managerial Capitalism,* Macmillan.

Newbould, GD and Luffman, GA (1979) *Successful Business Policies,* Gower.

Penrose, E (1959) *The Theory of the Growth of the Firm,* Blackwell.

Perrow, C (1961) The analysis of goals in complex organizations, *American Sociological Review,* **26,** December.

Pfeffer, J (1981) *Power in Organizations,* Pitman.

Porter, M.E. (1995) Interviewed for the Green Management letter, *Euromanagement,* June.

Reidenbach, E and Robin, D (1995) Quoted in Drummond, J: Saints and sinners, *Financial Times,* 23 March.

Richards, MD (1978) *Organizational Goal Structures,* West.

Simon, HA (1964) On the concept of organizational goal, *Administrative Science Quarterly,* 9(1), June, pp. 1–22.

Thompson, AA and Strickland, AJ (1980) *Strategy Formulation and Implementation,* Irwin.

Waterman, R (1994) *The Frontiers of Excellence: Learning From Companies That Put People First,* Nicholas Brealey Publishing.

Williamson, OE (1964) *Economics of Discretionary Behaviour: Managerial Objectives in a Theory of the Firm,* Kershaw.

6

Strategic Success: How Are We Doing?

In this chapter we look at how the performance of a company might be measured and assessed. Important links between results, objectives and the aspirations of stake-holders are considered. The role and significance of financial ratios is discussed.

Learning objectives

After studying this chapter you should be able to:

- explain how success might be measured and assessed
- evaluate the significance of financial measures of performance
- describe the key parts of a balance sheet, profit and loss account and cash flow statement;
- calculate and evaluate a number of ratios relating to investment, performance and financial status
- discuss how profitability might be improved
- identify the difficulties involved in measuring the effective performance of many not-for-profit organizations.

Introduction

The performance of a company, the outcomes of the strategies it is pursuing, is typically measured by financial ratios but an appreciation of a company's strategic success also requires consideration of the following:

- actual achievement against stated or official objectives
- the relative success of the organization in implementing its stated strategies
- the effect of adaptive and incremental changes and the impact of any operative objectives on the organization
- the expectations and aspirations of stakeholders.

The progress and relative success of the organization should also be evaluated against the competition. Strategies and successes of competitors could pose threats if the organization fails to react or respond. Equally, this type of evaluation can reveal new opportunities. We will examine this particular issue in greater depth in Chapter 9.

In this chapter, then, we will concentrate on how the strategic success of an organization might be evaluated, focusing on outcomes. We are tackling the question: how are we doing? It is important to remember that in Chapter 2 we argued that the creation of successful outcomes is itself dependent upon the possession of appropriate competencies in strategic awareness, change management and strategy content, which also need to be measured and evaluated.

Don't forget to visit the website: http://www.itbp.com

How are we doing?

Financial measures

An analysis of financial ratios is useful for a number of reasons.

❏ It enables a study of trends and progress over a number of years to be made.
❏ Comparisons with competitors and with general industry trends are possible.
❏ It can point the way towards possible or necessary improvements – necessary if the organization is performing less and less well than competitors, useful if new opportunities are spotted.
❏ It can reveal lost profit and growth potential.
❏ It can emphasize possible dangers – for example if stock turnover is decreasing or ratios affecting cash flow are moving adversely.

However, financial analysis concentrates on **efficiency** rather than **effectiveness** unless the objectives are essentially financial or economic ones. The real measure of success, as far as the strategic leader and the various stakeholders are concerned, is whether or not the objectives *they* perceive as important are being achieved. (See Key Concept 6.1.)

Outside analysts, such as students and interested readers, can gain some insight into the apparent objectives of an organization by reading annual reports, articles, press releases and so on, but only the people involved in decision making know the real objectives. Financial analysis from the published (and easily obtained) results can be very informative and lead to conclusions about how well a company is performing, but certain aspects remain hidden. Decision makers inside an organization use financial analysis as part of the wider picture, but outsiders are more restricted. Financial analysis, then, is a very useful form of analysis, and it should be used, but the wider aspects should not be overlooked.

The achievement of objectives

Financial analysis may show that a particular organization is growing at a slower rate than its major competitors but that its profitability is considerably higher (the indices and ratios in question are considered later in this chapter). One might conclude that this is perfectly satisfactory or that the declining market share is a cause for concern. It is satisfactory if profitability is a central objective; it is worrying if the organization is seeking to grow and strengthen market share in its particular industry.

Major customers and suppliers are important stakeholders, and their expectations cannot be ignored. A supplier might grant extended credit in return for regular and guaranteed orders; a different supplier might agree to substantial discounts for fast payment of invoices. Whilst one can calculate the creditor turnover ratio and look at trends over a period, one may not know the causes behind the figures.

The analysis may disclose substantial investments in research and development, or in fixed assets, and these changes will affect certain ratios in the short term. The long-term implications and expectations of these investments may not be known outside the organization, but they may relate to important long-term objectives.

Efficiency and effectiveness

There are three important measures of performance:

☐ **Economy**, which means 'doing things cost effectively'. Resources should be managed at the lowest possible cost consistent with achieving quantity and quality targets.

☐ **Efficiency**, which implies 'doing things right'. Resources should be deployed and utilized to maximize the returns from them.

Economy and efficiency measures are essentially quantitative and objective.

☐ **Effectiveness**, or 'doing the right things'. Resources should be allocated to those activities which satisfy the needs, expectations and priorities of the various stakeholders in the business.

Effectiveness relates to outcomes and need satisfaction, and consequently the measures are often qualitative and subjective.

Where economy, efficiency and effectiveness can be measured accurately and unambiguously it is appropriate to use the expression 'performance measures'. However if, as is frequently the case with effectiveness, precise measures are not possible, it can be more useful to utilize the term 'performance indicators'.

As the following chart indicates only efficient and effective organizations will grow and prosper. Effective but inefficient businesses will survive but under-achieve because they are not using minimum resources; efficient but ineffective companies will decline as they cease to meet the expectations of their stakeholders – simply, the things they are doing are wrong, however well they might be doing them.

	Ineffective	Effective
Inefficient	Corporate collapse	Survival
Efficient	Gradual decline	Growth and Prosperity

Mazda: efficient but not effective

Yoshihiro Wada, President of Mazda since 1991, has concluded that car companies must have a strong core product range before they seek to add on speciality cars, and the latter should never be allowed to take precedence over the core as far as attention and resource allocations are concerned. This was the mistake that Wada believed Mazda had made, causing it to lose money in the early 1990s. A new range of up-market cars had monopolized managers' time and attention, but sales and revenue did not reflect this prioritization. An industry analyst commented: 'Mazda has become a company that is really good at making cars but bad at judging what kind of cars to make'.

Mazda cars are recognized for their very high quality, and in terms of sales, Mazda is Japan's fourth largest car producer. But it attempted to grow quickly without truly understanding the potential demand for its cars. Elegant, high-performance cars simply do not command a wide market appeal; people will not buy expensive cars just because they look good. Moreover, Japanese customers tend to be brand loyal. In addition, the new Mazda range was expensive because their engineers had been allowed considerable freedom. Critically, whilst focusing attention on the high added-value, differentiated cars, Mazda neglected to improve two important mass-market models, which were allowed to languish.

The company remained efficient, but it ceased to be effective. As a result, 24.5% of the equity was sold to Ford, a very unusual step for a Japanese company. Mazda was hoping to benefit from Ford's expertise in marketing.

Charities: a paradox

If a charity seeks to save money by minimizing administration and promotion expenditures it is focusing on short-term efficiency. If it concentrates on long-term effectiveness it may well be able to justify investing in marketing and administration in order to raise even more money.

A charity which spends some 60% of its current income on administration and marketing (and the rest on its directly charitable activities) could well, in the long run, be more effective than one which spends only 20% in this way.

The aim is to establish the most appropriate structure, administration network and promotional expenditure to achieve the purpose – and then run it efficiently.

Reference for Mazda: Nakamoto, M (1995) Mazda tries to put its house in order, *Financial Times*, 23 January.

If the organization is paying increased attention to quality or service, or adding value to the product or service in some other way, this may be reflected in better performance figures through lower costs, higher profits or increased profitability. These figures may not reflect the long-term value of any strengthening of competitive advantage.

Case 6.1
British Tourist Authority (BTA)

The mission of the BTA is 'to strengthen the performance of Britain's tourist industry in international markets by encouraging people to visit Britain and encouraging the improvement and provision of tourist amenities and facilities'.

BTA objectives
The BTA has agreed the following long-term objectives:

1 Maximize the benefit to the economy of tourism to Britain from abroad.
2 Ensure that the Authority makes the most cost-effective use of resources in pursuing its objectives.

  Resources, of course, are constrained by grants and the ability to agree joint venture projects; and therefore the benefits generated are inevitably limited. With more money benefits could be increased – but when do they become less cost-effective to create?
3 Identify what visitors want and stimulate improvements in products and services to meet their needs.
4 Encourage off-peak tourism.
5 Spread the economic benefit of tourism more widely, and particularly to areas with tourism potential and higher-than-average levels of unemployment.

Objectives 3, 4 and 5 may well prove contradictory. Moreover there will always be considerable elements of subjectivity and value judgement in establishing priority areas.

Measures of corporate performance
BTA could be judged to be successful if visitors (business people and tourists) come to Britain, if

they come both off-season as well as in season (Objective 4), if they spend increasing amounts of money whilst they are here, if they spend in the preferred places (Objective 5), and if they go home and tell other people to come – and over a period this increases the number of visitors and their expenditure (Objective 1 explicitly and Objective 3 implicitly).

These are all measures of effectiveness, whilst Objective 2 addresses resource efficiency. However there is a problem of cause and effect. Whilst the criteria listed above can all be measured, the net contribution of the BTA cannot be so easily ascertained. Tourists and business people would still come, regardless of the existence of the BTA. In addition, many of the reasons for them choosing to come – or not to come – are outside both the control and influence of the BTA. The cause and effect of BTA initiatives is consequently very difficult to ascertain without extensive tracking studies which, on occasions, can be prohibitively expensive. However research in the early 1990s showed that at that time 27% of all visitors to the UK had visited a BTA office abroad.

It is believed implicitly that the activities undertaken around the world contribute to corporate objectives and performance, but often it is the activities (efficiencies) which are measured rather than the outcomes. Are particular promotions actually implemented? Are planned brochures published? Are desirable workshops and seminars attended? In fairness, despite the difficulties, BTA does attempt to measure the impact of the special promotions it undertakes on the numbers of visitors to the UK.

Where a company has important and identifiable shareholders with a sub-stantial or significant shareholding in the organization, an effective strategic leader will ensure that he or she fully understands their expectations. The shareholders may be more concerned with short-term earnings than long-term growth in the value of their investment, or vice versa. It is important to know. Ratios will indicate where the company is performing well or badly in this res-pect, and by using the share price one can judge how the stock market (and in turn the shareholders) view the company at the moment; but again outside analysts cannot be absolutely clear as to whether the organization is fully meet-ing shareholder expectations.

Whilst it is feasible to measure outcomes and results, and compare them with stated objectives, it may not follow that the strategies pursued by the company have themselves generated the results. Case 6.1, British Tourist Authority, ex-plores this issue.

The implementation of stated strategies

Another measure of how well the organization is doing concerns whether the strategies it decided to pursue are in fact being implemented. Linked to this is the issue of how strategic change is taking place, the incidence of incremental change and the impact of operative objectives. This relates back to Chapter 5, (Figure 5.3). The important issue is one of management and control. How aware is the strategic leader, and is he or she satisfied with what is happening? Is the change process being managed effectively? The information system has a crucial role to play if managers are to be kept informed and aware.

Visit the website: http://www. itbp.com

If this analysis suggests that the change process is not being managed effec-tively – prescribed strategies are not being implemented; incremental adaptive changes are not felt to be resulting in acceptable outcomes – there should be an examination of the causes. It could be that the organization has failed to appre-ciate or forecast certain changes in the environment, or has been caught out by changes in competitor strategies, or has experienced difficulties in implementing strategies because appropriate resources were not available. As a result the strate-gies themselves may need changing, or the implementation may need rethinking.

This situation assessment and evaluation of the possible need to change should be seen as a definite learning process by the strategic leader, who should seek to be constantly aware of changes taking place and changes that might be needed.

The need for change

Constant vigilance in this respect, then, supported by an effective information system will indicate where strategies need review. If decision makers in the organization are aware of how well it is doing and of environmental threats and opportunities and internal strengths and weaknesses, they can also address the

---

The most important facts are not always the obvious ones. It is a key attribute of the successful manager that he can assimilate a lot of information, and identify instinctively which particular items indicate that the business may be in danger of losing its direction.

Tom W Cain, ex-Director, Human Resources, The Channel Tunnel Group Ltd

important question: what is likely to happen if we carry on with present strategies? Is change needed?

Answering this question requires insight into competitive strategies, the relative success of competitors, changes in the environment, how good the organization's resources are, and how well they are being managed. These issues are the subject of the next chapters.

Stakeholder expectations

Chapter 5 showed that the organization is influenced by a number of stakeholders whose aspirations and expectations for the business may conflict. The organization's objectives should balance the interests of all the stakeholders as effectively as possible. In achieving this, such aspects as product quality, availability and delivery, reliability, productivity and company image are important measures of success, in addition to purely financial criteria. Striving for success in any area, and achieving it, may result in poor performance in another. As a result, some stakeholders are satisfied but others are less satisfied.

The balanced scorecard

In an attempt to encompass the needs and expectations of all the company's main stakeholders, Kaplan and Norton (1992) suggest that organizations should focus their efforts on a limited number of specific, critical performance measures which reflect stakeholders' key success factors. In this way managers can readily concentrate on those issues which are essential for corporate and competitive success.

Kaplan and Norton use the term 'balanced scorecard' to describe a framework of four groups of measures, and argue that organizations should select critical measures for each one of these areas. The four groups, and examples of possible measures, are:

❏ **Financial**   Return on capital employed
                                   Cash flow
❏ **Customers**   Perceived value for money
                                   Competitive prices
❏ **Internal processes**   Enquiry response time
                                   Enquiry → order conversion rate
❏ **Growth and improvement**   Number of new products/services
                                   Extent of employee empowerment

It can be seen that these measures encapsulate both efficiency and effectiveness.

Different perceptions of quality

Measuring effectiveness requires a recognition that *quality* does not mean the same things for every customer. Organizations must determine what will generate repeat business and seek to provide it. Supermarkets, for example, can offer service in the form of a wide range of products, brand choice for each product in the range, low prices, fast check-out and ample car parking. Stores can focus aggressively on one or more of these or seek a balanced profile. The major chains will have a basic competitive posture and then tailor each store to meet local conditions.

Performance measurement and E–V–R congruence

It was stated in Chapter 2 that congruency between environment, values and resources is a *reflection* of strategic success, and that it represents an appropriate mix of the generic competencies. How, then, might we measure E–V–R congruence?

Figure 6.1 illustrates the implications and requirements. Whilst environment, values and resources are separated within the diamond, rather than overlaid, the need for congruence is implicit. There are two premises to this model:

❑ Corporate success is concerned with the mission and purpose of the organization, but frequently it will be assessed by financial measures of some form. Commercial businesses are judged on profitability and growth, although profits, *per se*, are really a means, not an end. Not-for-profit organizations must be commercially viable, for they can only spend what they can raise. Reinforcing points made in Chapter 5 and Key Concept 6.1, charities are dependent on their fund raising, and consequently will measure their success on their ability to raise increasing amounts of money. Long-term success is built around a cycle comprising the ability to raise money, to spend it wisely and effectively, to be seen to be doing this and to be doing it efficiently, and on the strength of this to raise even more money.

❑ Long-term strategic success therefore requires that the interests of stakeholders are met, and are seen to be met; that this is accomplished efficiently with capable resources; and that there is a commitment to the mission reflected in organizational values.

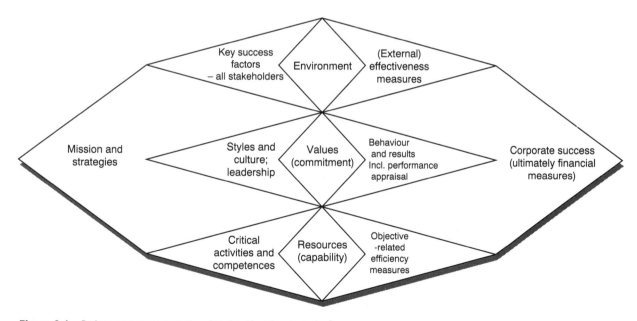

Figure 6.1 Performance measurement – what should we be measuring?

The implication is that in addition to resource efficiency and stakeholder satisfaction, organizations should also attempt to **measure values** to ensure the culture is appropriate.

Organizations which attempt this will firstly need to clarify which values and behaviours are critical for carrying out corporate and competitive strategies, and pursuing the mission, both now and in the future. In 1991, for example, Yorkshire Water determined that their key values were: trust, loyalty, pride, honesty, integrity, endeavour, quality, service/excellence and competitiveness. Adherence to these values would be manifested in a number of behaviour traits. It was seen as important that employees were committed to, and confident about, their roles, and that they were suitably empowered and rewarded. Effective communications networks were also thought to be vital.

Research can capture a snapshot of currently held values and the extent to which particular behaviours are being manifested. Some organizations will prefer to use volunteers from amongst the workforce rather than select a sample. The findings should be evaluated against a set of expectancies, and follow-up research can track both positive and negative developments. The organization must then decide what action to take if there is any deterioration or the initial absence of a critical value or behaviour pattern. Changing the culture of the organization, introduced in Chapter 4, is dealt with in greater detail in Chapter 22.

Admired companies

Sound profits and a strong balance sheet are very important, but alone they will not necessarily lead to a company being 'admired' (*Economist*, 1991). Admiration encourages customers to buy more and to stay loyal, employees to work harder, suppliers to be more supportive and shareholders to also remain loyal. In the 1980s, the *Economist* initiated a research project to establish which companies are most admired by other businesses, particularly those with whom they compete directly. The research replicated a similar survey by *Fortune* in the USA. More recently, *Management Today* has taken over the project in the UK. Business people are asked to allocate marks against certain criteria for their main rivals. The criteria used are as follows: quality of management; financial soundness; value as a long-term investment; quality of products and services; the ability to attract, develop and retain top talent; capacity to innovate; quality of marketing; and community and environmental responsibility.

Polling takes place every year, and the overall winning company in 1995 was Cadbury Schweppes, which also topped two sub-categories: quality of management and quality of marketing. The runner-up was Unilever, despite adverse publicity resulting from the problematical launch of two new detergents products in 1994. The 1994 winner, Rentokil, dropped to 11th place; and Glaxo, second in 1994, disappeared out of the top 12 after the acquisition of

Visit the website:
http://www.
itbp.com

I wrote 'The 12 Objectives for Managing Goodyear Successfully in the '90s'. They include having a leadership position in costs, quality, customer service and innovation.
Stanley Gault, Chief Executive, Goodyear Tire and Rubber

Wellcome. Three retailers, Tesco (fourth), Marks and Spencer (seventh) and Sainsbury (ninth) were very highly regarded (see Hasell, 1994 and 1995).

In a parallel vote, business people were asked for their views on all companies, not just those in their own industry sector. Here the clear winner was Marks and Spencer, followed by Glaxo Wellcome, Hanson and British Airways. This admiration and popularity is confirmed by a *Financial Times/ Price Waterhouse* survey of Europe's most respected companies, which uses very similar evaluation criteria and methods (see *Financial Times*, 1995). British companies led in five categories:

❑ diversified holding companies   — Hanson
❑ media businesses and publishing   — Reuters
❑ retailing and distribution   — Marks and Spencer
❑ telecommunications   — British Telecom
❑ transport   — British Airways.

Significantly, the manufacturing sections were dominated by German, Swedish and Swiss companies. The most respected company overall was ABB (Asea Brown Boveri), followed by Nestlé, BA, BMW, Royal Dutch Shell and Marks and Spencer.

We saw in Chapter 1 how Rubbermaid has dominated the *Fortune* poll in the USA in recent years, with companies such as Coca-Cola, Microsoft, 3M and Walt Disney close behind.

Another survey in the UK by BMRB/Mintel (see Summers, 1995) has asked a sample of consumers which companies they perceive offer good value for money, understand their market, are trustworthy and care about the environment. Boots won every category except environmental concern, where it came second to the Body Shop. Inevitably the winning companies in a poll such as this will be those with high visibility and presence, especially retailing organizations, reflecting the value of a good corporate image. Ironically, Marks and Spencer does not appear in the top ten in any category.

Financial success alone does not guarantee admiration from competitors and popularity with all the stakeholders; at the same time, as evidenced by the Body Shop, deteriorating financial returns will bother shareholders far more than customers!

Financial analysis

The published financial accounts of a company, as long as they are interpreted carefully, can tell a good deal about the company's activities and about how well it is doing. We shall concentrate on three main aspects, examining the financial measures and what they can tell us, and consider the strategic implications. The three aspects are as follows.

❑ **Investment:** How do the results relate to shareholders and the funds they have provided, and to the company's share price?
❑ **Performance**: How successfully is the business being run as a trading concern? Here we are not so much concerned with profit as with profitability. How well is the company using the capital it employs to generate sales and in turn profits?
❑ **Financial status**: Is the company solvent and liquid? Is it financially sound?

The ratios calculated in each of these categories have relevance for different stakeholders. Shareholders, and potential investors, are particularly concerned with the investment ratios. Performance ratios tell the strategic leader how well the company is doing as a business. Bankers and other providers of loan capital will want to know that the business is solvent and liquid in addition to how well it is performing. These points will be developed throughout this chapter.

This form of analysis is most relevant for profit-seeking businesses, although some of the measures can prove quite enlightening when applied to not-for-profit organizations.

Ratios are calculated from the published accounts of organizations, but an analysis of just one set of results will only be partly helpful. Trends are particularly important, and therefore the changes in results over a number of years should be evaluated. Care should be taken to ensure that the results are not considered in isolation of external trends in the economy or industry. For example the company's sales may be growing quickly, but how do they compare with those of their competitors and the industry as a whole? Similarly, slow growth may be explained by industry contraction, although in turn this might indicate the need for diversification.

Hence industry averages and competitor performance should be used for comparisons. One problem here is that different companies may present their accounts in different ways and the figures will have to be interpreted before any meaningful comparisons can be made. Furthermore the industry may be composed of companies of varying sizes and various degrees of conglomeration and diversification. For this reason certain companies may be expected to behave differently from their competitors.

In addition it can be useful to compare the actual results with forecasts, although these will not normally be available to people outside the organization. The usefulness is dependent on how well the forecasts and budgets were prepared.

Financial statements

The two most important statements which are used for calculating ratios are the profit and loss account and the balance sheet, simplified versions of which are illustrated in Tables 6.1 and 6.2. The full accounts may be required in order to make certain adjustments.

From the **profit and loss account** (Table 6.1) we wish to extract a number of figures. **Gross profit** is the trading profit before overheads are allocated. It is the difference between the value of sales (or turnover) and the direct costs involved in producing the product(s) or service(s), which is known as the **contribution.** In the case of multi-product or multi-service organizations, where it may be difficult to attribute overheads to different products and services accurately, comparison should be made between the contributions from different divisions or strategic business units.

When depreciation and selling and administrative overheads are subtracted from gross profit the remainder is **profit before interest and before tax**. This is the net profit that the organization has achieved from its trading activities; no account has yet been taken of the cost of funding. This figure is not normally shown in published accounts; it has to be calculated by adding interest back onto profit before tax.

		£
	Sales/turnover	
less:	Cost of goods sold	
	equals	Gross profit
less:	Depreciation	
	Selling costs	
	Administration costs	
	equals	Profit before interest and tax*
less:	Interest on loans	
	equals	Profit before tax
less:	Tax	
	equals	Profit after tax
less:	Dividends	
	equals	Retained earnings (transferred to balance sheet)

Table 6.1
Simplified profit and loss account

*In published accounts this figure will not normally be shown. It is required, however, for the calculation of certain ratios.

Information required for ratio calculations			Conventional presentation of figures in published accounts	
	Fixed assets	(Land; property, buildings; plant and equipment)		**Fixed assets**
plus	**Current assets**	(Stock; debtors; cash and investments)	plus	**Current assets**
less	**Current liabilities**	(Creditors: amounts falling due within one year; specifically trade creditors; overdraft; taxation not yet paid)	less	**Current liabilities**
equals	**Net assets**		equals	**Total assets** less **Current liabilities**
	Long-term loans	Generally termed creditors: amounts falling due after more than one year)	plus	**Long-term loans**
			equals	**Total net assets**
plus	**Shareholders' funds**	(Called-up share capital; share premium account; revaluation reserve; profit and loss account)		**Shareholders' funds**
equals	**Total capital employed**			
Net assets	equals	**Total capital employed**		**Total net assets = Shareholders' funds**

Table 6.2
Simplified balance sheet

Profit before tax is the figure resulting when interest charges have been removed. Tax is levied on this profit figure, and when this is deducted **profit after tax** remains. This represents the profits left for shareholders, and a proportion will be paid over to them immediately in the form of dividends; the remainder will be re-invested in the future growth of the company. It will be transferred to the balance sheet as retained earnings (or profit and loss) and shown as a reserve attributable to shareholders.

This simplified outline excludes the need to, and value of, clearly separating the revenue and profits from ongoing businesses or continuing activities, recent acquisitions and discontinued activities.

Balance sheets are now normally laid out in the format illustrated in Table 6.2. Assets are shown at the top and the capital employed to finance the assets below.

Fixed assets comprise all the land, property, plant and equipment owned by the business. These will be depreciated annually at varying rates. Balance sheets generally reflect historical costs (the preferred accounting convention), but occasionally assets may be revalued to account for inflation (land and property values can increase significantly over a number of years) and any ratios calculated from an asset figure will be affected by this issue of up-to-date valuations.

Current assets, assets which are passing through the business rather than more permanent features and which comprise stocks (raw materials, work-in-progress and finished goods), debtors (customers who are allowed to buy on credit rather than for cash), investments and cash, are added on. **Current liabilities,** short-term financial commitments, are deducted. These include the overdraft, tax payments due and trade creditors (suppliers who have yet to be paid for goods and services supplied).

The left-hand column of Table 6.2 shows the resultant figure as net assets, which is equal to the **total capital employed in the business**, or the sum of long-term loans and shareholders' funds. The right-hand column differs slightly and presents net assets as total assets minus the sum of current liabilities and long-term loans – and therefore equal to shareholders' funds. This is the normal way in which a company will present its accounts, leaving us to calculate a figure for total capital employed.

Long-term loans are typically called 'creditors: amounts falling due after more than one year'. **Shareholders' funds** are made up of the called up share capital (the face value of the shares issued), the share premium account (money accrued as shareholders have bought shares for more than their face value, dependent on stock market prices at the time of sale), any revaluation reserve (resulting from revaluation of assets) and retained earnings (past profits re-invested in the business).

Balance sheets balance. Net assets are equal to the capital employed to finance them.

Investment ratios

The five key investment ratios are explained in Table 6.3, and the linkages between four of them are illustrated in Figure 6.2.

The **return on shareholders' funds** deals with the profit available for ordinary shareholders after all other commitments (including preference share dividends) have been met; and it is divided by all the funds provided both

Ratio	Calculation	Comments	
Return on shareholders' funds (%)	$\dfrac{\text{profit after tax}}{\text{total shareholders' funds}}$	Measures the return on investment by shareholders in the company. The more unstable the industry and the company, the higher this will be expected to be	**Table 6.3** Investment ratios
Earnings per share (pence)	$\dfrac{\text{profit after tax}}{\text{number of ordinary shares issued}}$	Profit after tax represents earnings for the shareholders. It can be returned to them immediately as dividends or re-invested as additional shareholders' funds (retained earnings)	
Price-to-earnings ratio *P/E*	$\dfrac{\text{current market price of ordinary shares}}{\text{earnings per share}}$	Indicates the multiple of earnings that investors are willing to pay for shares in the stock market. The higher the ratio, the more favourably the company is perceived	
Dividend yield (%)	$\dfrac{\text{dividend per share}}{\text{market price per share}}$	Equivalent to rate of interest per cent paid on the investment. Shareholders will not expect it to equal say building society rates – re-invested profits should generate longer-term increases in the share price.	
Dividend cover (number of times)	$\dfrac{\text{earnings per share}}{\text{dividend per share}}$	The number of times the dividends *could* have been paid from the earnings. The higher the better	

directly and indirectly by ordinary shareholders. 'The return on shareholders' funds is probably the most important single measure of all. It takes into account the return on net assets, the company's tax position, and the extent to which capital employed has been supplied other than by the ordinary shareholders (for example by loans)' (Reid and Myddelton, 1974).

Earnings per share indicates how much money the company has earned in relation to the number of ordinary shares. Taken in isolation this measure is useful if considered over a number of years. Companies can be compared with each other if the ratio is linked to the current market price of shares. This calculation provides the price-to-earnings ratio *P/E*.

Table 6.4 illustrates the *P/E* ratios for a number of major retailers at the end of 1991 and late in 1995. Generally they have fallen slightly, illustrating the lasting impact of the recession of the early 1990s, but two stand out. Asda has recovered from a point of very low confidence – we shall look at Asda's turnaround strategy later in the book – whilst the Body Shop's collapsing *P/E* reflects the changes and pressures described in Case 4.3.

The *P/E* ratio indicates the amount (how many times the current earnings figure) that potential shareholders are willing to pay in order to buy shares in the company at a particular time. It is affected by previous success and profits, but really it is an indication of expectations. The more confidence the market has in a company, generally the higher will be its *P/E*. It can also indicate relatively how expensive borrowing is for the company. If the company opts to raise money from existing shareholders by offering new shares in a rights issue (the shareholders are invited to buy new shares in fixed proportion to those they

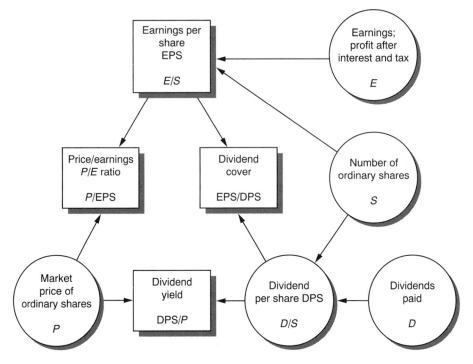

Figure 6.2   Linkages between four investment ratios: the squares represent the investment ratios; the circles the figures required for calculating ratios. (Note: The two figures required to calculate each ratio are shown leading into the box.)

Table 6.4
Major retailers: price-to-earnings ratios

	P/E ratios	
	Late 1995	**End 1991**
Asda	16.4	4.4
Body Shop	8.7	43.8
Boots	15.2	16.7
Kwik Save	10.9	12.7
Marks and Spencer	17.9	18.1
Sainsbury	13.0	14.7
Tesco	13.4	13.8
WH Smith	13.9	13.0

Source: *Financial Times.*

already hold) the higher the *P/E* is, the cheaper is the capital. A high *P/E* implies that shareholders will pay many times current earnings to obtain shares.

The *P/E* ratio is also very important in acquisition situations. Consider two companies as an example. Company A has issued 500,000 ordinary shares with a face value of 25p and their current market price is 600p. Current earnings per share are 20p (£100,000 in total). Hence the *P/E* is 600/20 = 30.

Company A looks attractive to the shareholders of company B when it makes a bid for their shares. B also has 500,000 shares issued, again with a face value of 25p, but they are trading at only 150p as company B has been relatively sleepy of late and growth has been below the average for the industry. With earnings per share of 10p (£50,000 in total) the *P/E* is 15.

A offers one new share in company A for every three shares in B (perhaps more generous than it need be), and the shareholders in B accept. A–B now has 666,667 shares issued; at the moment the combined earnings are £150,000. If the stock market, and the shareholders, are confident that A can turn B round and increase earnings significantly the current *P/E* of 30 could remain. If so the new price of shares in the combined A–B is 675p. Earnings per share are 22.5p (£150,000/666,667 shares).

A's share price has in effect risen, possibly making it appear an even more successful company. Any company wishing to acquire A will now have to pay more. Equally A's ability to acquire further companies on the lines above has been enhanced.

The price-to-earnings ratio and earnings per share are measures which are most applicable to companies whose shares are traded on the stock market.

Two dividend ratios

The **dividend yield** provides the rate of interest that shareholders are receiving in relation to the current market price for shares. It must be used cautiously as it takes no account of the price that people actually paid (historically) to buy their shares; and in any case shareholders are often more interested in long-term capital growth.

The **dividend cover** indicates the proportion of earnings paid out in dividends and the proportion re-invested. Company dividend policies will vary between companies, and, for example, a decision to maintain or reduce dividends in the face of reduced earnings will be influenced by the predicted effect on share prices and in turn the valuation of the company, which as we saw above can be an issue in acquisitions.

Quoted companies can also be analysed by considering the movement of their share price against the Financial Times 100 Shares Index or the All Shares Index, and against the index of shares for their particular industry. Under- and over-performance of the shares is a further reflection of investors' confidence and expectations.

Performance ratios

Tables 6.5 and 6.7 (overleaf) explain the various performance ratios.

Profitability

The **return on net assets** or the **return on capital employed** uses profit before interest and before tax and compares it with the assets, or capital employed, used in the business to create the profit. Actual profit is important as it determines the amount of money that a company has available for paying dividends (once interest and tax are deducted) and for re-investment. But it is also important to examine how well the money invested in the business is being used – this is **profitability**. This particular ratio ignores how the business is actually funded, making it a measure of how well the business is performing as a trading concern. It was mentioned earlier that contributions from different products or strategic business units should be compared in the case of multi-product organizations. The return on net assets should also be used to compare the profitabilities of products and strategic business units. In this way

Table 6.5
Performance ratios

Ratio	Calculation	Comments
Return on net assets Return on capital employed (%)	$$\frac{\text{Profit before interest and before tax}}{\text{Total capital employed in the business}}$$	Measures the relative success of the business as a trading concern. Trading profit less overheads is divided by shareholders' funds and other long-term loans. Useful for measuring and comparing the relative performance of different divisions/strategic business units
Profit margin (%)	$$\frac{\text{Profit before interest and before tax}}{\text{Sales (turnover)}}$$	Shows trading profit less overheads as a percentage of turnover. Again useful for comparing divisions, products, markets
Net asset turnover (number of times)	$$\frac{\text{Sales}}{\text{Total net assets or capital employed in the business}}$$	It measures the number of times the capital is 'turned over' in a year. Or: the number of pounds of sales generated for every pound invested in the company

the ratio can be used for evaluating particular competitive strategies and the relative importance to the business of different products. However, this measure should not be used in isolation from an assessment of the relative importance of different products in terms of turnover. High volume products or divisions may be less profitable than smaller volume ones for a variety of reasons, which we shall examine when we look at portfolio analysis.

This ratio is particularly useful when it is examined in the light of the two ratios which comprise it. The top of Table 6.6 shows how the return on net assets is equal to the profit margin times the net asset turnover.

Table 6.6
Performance ratios for different companies and Industries

Sector	Company	Results	Return on net assets (%) =	Profit margin (%) ×	Net asset turnover
			$\dfrac{\text{Profit}}{\text{Net assets}}$ =	$\dfrac{\text{Profit}}{\text{Sales}}$ ×	$\dfrac{\text{Sales}}{\text{Net assets}}$
Retailing	Kwik Save	1994	30.6	= 4.9 ×	6.3
	WH Smith	1995	17.6	= 4.75 ×	3.7
Foods	Dalgety	1995	19.2	= 3.0 ×	6.4
Rest'nts	Harry Ramsden's	1994	12.76	= 23.3 ×	0.55
Manufacturing	Courtaulds Textiles	1994	14.1	= 5.2 ×	2.69
	HP Bulmer (Cider)	1995	23.1	= 11.6 ×	1.99
	Sony	1994	3.48	= 2.67 ×	1.3
Energy	British Nuclear Fuels	1995	1.6	= 6.6 ×	0.24

The **profit margin** is the proportion of sales revenue represented by profits (before interest and tax); the **net asset turnover** illustrates how well the company is utilizing its assets in order to generate sales. It can be seen from Table 6.6 that different companies and industries exhibit different patterns.

Case 6.2 highlights the significance of net asset turnover for the relatively high profitability of Kwik Save in the past.

Certain companies will adopt strategies which are designed to yield good profit margins on every item sold, and as a result probably add value into the product or service in such a way that their assets are not producing the same

---

Case 6.2
KWIK SAVE

Kwik Save compete with grocery giants like Sainsbury and Tesco, but they have an individual strategy. Whilst Asda, Sainsbury and Tesco (together with other competitors) have built ever bigger stores, developed own-brand alternatives, and introduced non-food items, Kwik Save concentrated on having a large number of smaller well-located units selling mainly a limited range of branded products at competitive prices. Choice is therefore more limited than in some other stores, and less is invested in shopper comforts, but this is compensated for in the prices. The basic message is 'Everything is kept simple'.

The end result is lower overheads, which reduces the break-even level in every store. Historically Kwik Save have turned over their assets approximately six times per year, more times than their main rivals. Combined with a profit margin of some 5% (which compares quite favourably with other grocery supermarket chains) this yields a profitability of 30%. This is higher than most of their rivals.

In comparison, in a typical year, Marks and Spencers will have a profit margin much higher than that of Kwik Save, but, because they invest far more in their stores and offer a wide range of products (albeit under only one brand name), their net asset turnover will be around 2.0 times.

Whilst the strategy has proved very successful, Kwik Save have been aware of a number of drawbacks. By concentrating on selling only food they were vulnerable to the introduction of Sunday trading. Stores offering a wider range of products are likely to benefit far more than food stores. In addition, their success attracted direct competition from rivals like Aldi, the German supermarket chain which has opened a number of stores in the UK. Whilst Kwik Save offer some 4000 product lines (Sainsbury and Tesco have over 20,000) and price between 5% and 10% lower than the giants, Aldi offer just 600 lines and discounts of over 20%.

In 1993 Sainsbury and Tesco both reduced the prices of their own-label products to widen the price gap between own-label and brand leader; this move put real pressure on Kwik Save's discounted prices for the leading brands. As a counter-measure, Kwik Save introduced own-label products for the first time. The extent was limited to some 15% of total shelf space, whereas Sainsbury and Tesco would each feature at least 30%, but the amount of discount was huge. Shoppers could save around 50% of the main brand price.

In 1994 Kwik Save acquired the Scottish discount chain, Shoprite; its 90 stores gave Kwik Save a much stronger presence in the north of Britain.

Strong profits continued through 1994, but in 1995 Kwik Save suffered its first ever profits fall. The accumulated pressures from European discounters, stronger discounting by the giants, the need to substantially re-vamp its older stores and the investment required in Shoprite were all blamed. Further difficulties in 1996 led to shop closures

amount of sales per pound sterling as is the case for a company which uses assets more aggressively, adds less value, and makes a lower profit margin. Particular industries and businesses may offer little choice in this respect; others offer considerable choice.

If a decision is reached that for the business as a whole, or some part of it, the return on net assets (profitability) must be improved, there are two approaches. Either profits must be increased, or assets reduced, or both. Figure 6.3 illustrates the alternatives available to the organization, and at the bottom the functional responsibilities. Hence a corporate or competitive strategy change will result in changes to functional strategies. This will be developed further in Chapter 17 when we consider turnaround strategies for companies experiencing difficulties.

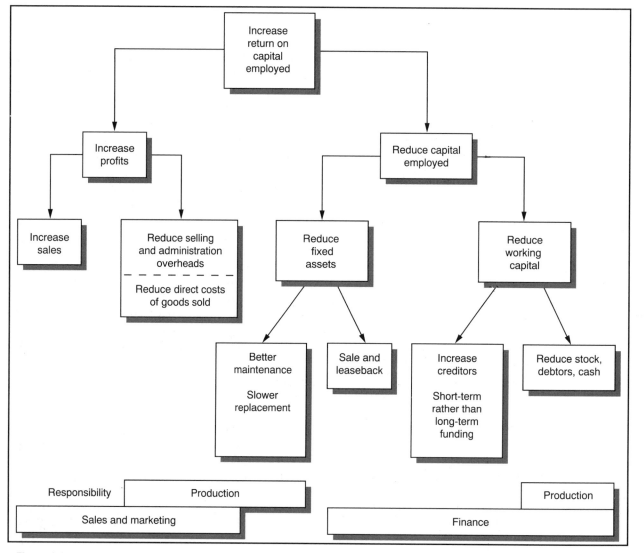

Figure 6.3   Improving profitability.

Other useful performance ratios

Table 6.7 explains **stock turnover** and **debtor turnover** which both indicate how well the company is managing two of its current assets. The stock turnover will depend on how the company is managing its operations – different strategies will lead to higher or lower stocks. Low stocks (high stock turnover) save costs, but they can make the business vulnerable if they are reduced to too low a level in order to save money and result in production delays. Debtor turnover, for certain types of business, looked at over a period can show whether the company is successful at persuading credit customers to pay quickly. This can affect the marketing strategy if decisions have to be taken not to supply certain customers who are slow payers.

The **gross profit margin** and the **selling and administration costs to sales ratio** are useful for indicating the percentage of turnover attributable to overheads. If a company has a high gross profit margin but is relatively unprofitable after accounting for overheads it is a sign of poor management. The product or service is able to command a price comfortably in excess of direct costs (direct labour and materials) but this contribution is being swallowed by overheads which are possibly too high and in need of reduction. Such a company is appropriate for restructuring and perhaps acquisition. Again these ratios should be examined over a period of years to ensure that the overhead burden is not creeping up without just cause. In terms of increasing profits (to improve profitability (Figure 6.3)) it may be easier to reduce overheads than to reduce direct costs.

Ratio	Calculation	Comments
Stock turnover (number of times)	$\dfrac{\text{Turnover}}{\text{Stock}}$	Shows how quickly stocks move through the business. Logically the quicker the better – as long as it does not result in stock shortages. Most accurate measurement from *average* stock level over the year rather than the balance sheet figure
Debtor turnover (number of times; or days of credit given)	$\dfrac{\text{Turnover}}{\text{Debtors}}$ $\dfrac{\text{Debtors}}{\text{Turnover}} \times 365$	Shows how quickly credit customers pay. Again use *average* debtors. Retail organizations, like Marks and Spencer, sell mostly for cash, or charge interest for credit through their credit cards. A similar measure, credit purchases/average creditors, shows how much credit time is received by the company.
Gross profit margin (%) and	$\dfrac{\text{Gross profit}}{\text{Turnover (sales)}}$	Indicates percentage profit before overheads
Selling and administration costs to sales (%)	$\dfrac{\text{Selling and administration costs}}{\text{Turnover (sales)}}$	Shows overheads (indirect costs) in relation to turnover

Table 6.7
Other useful performance ratios

Table 6.8

Measures of financial status

Ratio	Calculation	Comments
Solvency Debt ratio (%)	$\dfrac{\text{Long-term loans}}{\text{Total capital employed}}$	The lower the debt ratio the more the company is cushioned against fluctuations in trading profits
Interest cover (number of times)	$\dfrac{\text{Profit before interest}\atop\text{and before tax}}{\text{Interest on}\atop\text{long-term loans}}$	Indicates how many times the interest is covered by earnings Sometimes argued banks expect a figure of at least three times
Liquidity Current ratio (ratio *x*:1) (also known as working capital ratio)	$\dfrac{\text{Current assets}}{\text{Current liabilities}}$	Shows the extent to which short-term assets are able to meet short-term liabilities 1.5:1 and 2:1 both suggested as indicative targets. Also suggested that working capital (current assets minus current liabilities) should exceed stock
Liquidity or acid test ratio (ratio *x*:1)	$\dfrac{\text{Liquid assets (i.e.}\atop\text{current assets less stock)}}{\text{Current liabilities}}$	This shows how liquid the company is relative to short-term liabilities. Stock is excluded as it can take months to turn into cash

Measures of financial status

Measures of financial status can be divided into two groups: solvency and liquidity. The ratios are explained in Table 6.8.

Solvency

The major ratios are the **debt ratio** and **interest cover.** The debt ratio relates to the company's gearing – how much it is funded by equity capital (shareholders' funds) and how much by long-term loans. Loans generally carry fixed interest payments, and these must be met regardless of any profit fluctuations; a company can elect not to pay dividends to shareholders if profits collapse, which gives it more flexibility.

Managers and investors will both be wary of the debt ratio creeping up, as it does when companies borrow money from the banking system to finance investment or acquisitions. In fact acquisitive companies must relate their acquisition strategies to their ability to finance them. Sometimes money can be raised from shareholders, but the company must be confident that shareholders will subscribe to rights issues. If not, and the shares have to be sold to the banks who underwrite the issue (who then sell them when the price is appropriate), blocks of shares can be bought up by other acquisitive companies and this can pose a threat. The alternative is long-term loans, and the higher the proportion these constitute, the more stable profits need to be. This is taken up later in the book.

Interest cover shows by how much the interest payments are covered by profits.

Liquidity

The two main liquidity ratios, the **current ratio** and the **acid test (liquidity) ratio**, relate to working capital. Has the company sufficient money available to meet its short-term commitments? They are determined by the flow of cash in and out of the business. A shortage of cash, and commitments to meet, will push the company towards increased borrowings (say a larger overdraft), and this will increase interest commitments.

Whilst targets of 1.5:1 and 2.0:1 are sometimes quoted for the current ratio, these should be treated with some caution. Companies who trade mainly in cash, rather than allow credit, are likely to have a ratio much nearer 1:1 and still be perfectly liquid. Retailers and breweries are cases in point.

A company will experience liquidity problems if it invests in stock and then fails to win orders or if it fails to control its debtors. Conversely a successful company can have cash problems. Success at winning orders may require investment in machinery or stocks and labour, and these may have to be paid for before and during production and before the goods are delivered and paid for by customers. This can lead to temporary illiquidity, and is known as over-trading.

Cash flow, therefore, can be just as important as profitability. Where demand is seasonal for certain products production may take place when sales are low, in advance of peak demand. This puts pressure on cash flow in the way outlined above. A perfect example of this is Standard Fireworks, a largely focused business, whose sales are concentrated in the weeks before bonfire night, but who produce all through the year.

Cash reserves built up in good years can be run down to finance a company during lean years or a recession.

Cash flow issues affect corporate strategy in terms of the range of products, services and businesses selected, competitive strategies in terms of the way they are marketed (to avoid the worst implications of seasonal fluctuations) and functional production, marketing and financial strategies.

It is not unusual for companies to be slow in paying their bills when their performance is poor. This impacts upon their customers, and highlights the importance of cash flow, particularly in a recession. Table 6.9 shows how cash is generated and spent.

> Visit the website:
> http://www.
> itbp.com

Cash generated by operating activities (including operating profits, changes in stocks, debtors, and creditors and depreciation charged in the accounts).		
Add:	interest from investments proceeds from any share issues receipts from any asset sales new loans taken out	
Deduct:	interest paid on loans loans repaid tax paid dividends paid fixed assets purchased	
Leaving:	money available for further investment	

Table 6.9
A typical cash flow statement

Cash flow can be improved in a number of ways, for example, by

❏ increased turnover – but only if linked to
❏ effective management of debtors and creditors
❏ higher operating profit margins
❏ reduced tax payments
❏ reduced investment in working capital and/or fixed assets
❏ improved gearing to reduce interest payments.

Simply, a company must be able to produce cash in order to finance future investments and acquisitions, meet outstanding payments on earlier acquisitions and cover any unexpected events requiring extraordinary charges. The engineering company, T & N (Turner and Newall), is now having to find substantial funds to meet its liabilities from many years ago when it dealt in asbestos. Legal actions against the company are taking place in the USA as well as in the UK.

Accounting for inflation

It is an accounting convention to use historical costs and within the accountancy profession there is on-going debate and disagreement about how best to treat inflation. This topic is outside the scope of this book. However, it is important to take some account of inflation when looking at growth rates for actual data such as turnover and profits as otherwise companies appear to be doing far better than in reality they are.

A simple example is featured in Table 6.10. In making adjustments of this type the actual turnover (or profit) figures must be reduced by in effect taking a constant value of the pound (or other relevant currency). A 1994 pound was worth less than a 1983 pound (the base year for this comparison) as a result of inflation.

Table 6.10
Marks and Spencer plc –
turnover adjusted for inflation

Year ended 31 March	Turnover (£ million)	Index of growth (1983 =100)	Annual year-on-year growth (%)	Value of 1983 (pence)	Adjusted index of growth (1983=100)	Annual year-on-year growth after inflation (%)
1995	6807	271	4.1			
1994	6541	261	9.9	59.0	154	8.5
1993	5951	237	2.7	60.0	142	0.7
1992	5793	231	0.3	61.0	141	(4.0)
1991	5775	230	3.0	64.0	147	(1.4)
1990	5608	223	9.5	67.0	149	(2.0)
1989	5122	204	11.9	74.4	152	4.8
1988	4578	182	8.5	79.9	145	4.3
1987	4221	168	13.0	82.6	139	8.6
1986	3735	149	16.0	85.8	128	10.0
1985	3208	128	12.0	90.6	116	7.0
1984	2863	114	14.0	95.1	108.4	8.4
1983	2510	100		100	100	

Other quantitative performance indicators

In addition to all these financial ratios, businesses will typically collect and evaluate information concerning the performance of all the activities being undertaken. For each functional area there will be a number of measures, such as the value of orders acquired by every salesperson, machine utilization, turnover at every retail outlet, output per shift, productivity per employee and absenteeism. Performance will be evaluated against targets or objectives agreed with individual managers who should be held accountable. These are measures of resource efficiency. They are important control measures which evaluate the efficiency of each functional area of the business.

Similarly, individual sectors will favour particular measures. Retailers will typically consider sales per square foot of trading space, sales per employee, average shopping spend per trip and the number of new store openings or refits.

Improvements can strengthen the company's competitive capability. In isolation, however, these measures do not indicate how successful the company is strategically. This particular issue is very significant for not-for-profit organizations which cannot use the traditional profitability ratios sensibly and at the same time cannot readily measure their effectiveness in relation to their fundamental purpose. Consequently they often rely more on quantitative measures of efficiency. This is the subject of the next section.

Service businesses

In addition to the above measures, the ability to retain customers is a key requirement for service businesses. Retention implies customer satisfaction and probably word-of-mouth recommendation. It is likely to result in higher profits because of the high costs incurred in attracting new business. Moreover, customers are likely to increase their level of spending over time. For insurance companies the cost of processing renewals is far cheaper than the cost of finding new clients; and many people will take out additional policies with a company they feel they can rely on.

Key performance measures for solicitors are their ability to achieve results for their clients, and the service they offer, measurable by, for instance, the speed with which they respond to letters and telephone calls.

The measurement of success in not-for-profit organizations

It was suggested in Chapter 5 that the objectives of not-for-profit organizations are often stated in terms of resource efficiency because of the difficulty of quantifying their real purpose. As a result, the measures of their success that are utilized in practice may not be closely related to their real mission and purpose. Where this happens, financial and other quantitative measures are being used as the measures of performance, and efficiency not effectiveness is being evaluated. In other words, performance and success is being measured, but despite the usefulness of, and need for, the measures being used, they may not be assessing strategic performance directly in relation to the mission. These points are expanded below.

Drucker (1989) comments that many not-for-profit organizations are in fact more money conscious than business enterprises are because the funding they need is hard to raise. Moreover, they could invariably use more money than they have available. Money, though, is less likely to be the key element of their mission and strategic thinking than are the provision of services and the satisfaction of client needs. Given this premise, the successful performance of a not-for-profit organization should be measured in terms of outcomes and need satisfaction. Money then becomes a major constraint upon what can be accomplished and the appropriate level of expectations.

The outcomes, in turn, must be analysed against the expectations of the important stakeholders. For many organizations in this sector this involves both beneficiaries of the service and volunteer helpers as well as financial supporters and paid employees. Typically their personal objectives and expectations will differ.

But what is the case in reality? How difficult is it to measure performance and success in this way? Fundamentally the Boy Scout and Girl Guide organizations are concerned with helping youngsters develop and grow into confident and capable young men and women. But do they evaluate their success in this respect or in terms of, say, membership and monetary income which, being essentially quantitative, are far easier to measure? Similarly, it would be inadequate to claim success because of a general feeling that good was being done and that young people must be benefiting from their membership. The real measures of success concern the changes that take place outside the organization as a result of the organization's efforts.

As another example, the success of local meals-on-wheels services is related to their impact on the health and life expectancy of the elderly rather than to the number of meals served or the cost per meal.

The performance and effectiveness of the education system relates to the impact on pupils after they leave the system, their parents, the taxpayers who fund education and future employers. Their perspectives will differ, and their individual aspirations and expectations will be difficult to quantify and measure. It is far easier to measure efficiency in the way that resources are utilized – for example by class sizes, staff–student or staff–pupil ratios, building occupancy and examination performance.

Visit the website: http://www.itbp.com

Similarly, local authorities exist to serve local residents, and their mission is concerned with making the area a better place to live. Would all the residents agree on what is implied by 'a better place to live', and could changes be objectively measured and evaluated? Because of the difficulties, value for money from the resources invested is more likely to be considered, and improvements in the efficiency of service provision sought.

The not-for-profit sector is increasingly attempting to measure effectiveness in terms of impacts and outcomes rather than efficiency alone. The task is not straightforward.

Value for money looks at the relationship between the perceived value of the output (by the stakeholders involved) and the cost of inputs. Essentially it is used as a comparative measure. There are too many uncertainties for there to be any true agreement on the magnitude of 'very best value', and consequently one is seeking to ensure that good value is being provided, when measured against that of other similar, or competitive, providers.

If we consider both inputs and outcomes then we are considering the efficiency and effectiveness of the organization's transformation processes, its ability to add value.

Case 6.3 considers changes in two privatized industries, both of which are subject to external regulation, and in the National Health Service (NHS). With the NHS it is also tempting to make international comparisons. How much per head of the population is spent on health care? What percentage of gross domestic product does this represent? Again, these are input measures when it is outcomes that matter. The life expectancy of British people and the infant mortality rate are critically important outcomes, but, whilst health care makes an important contribution, it is not the only causal factor.

Jackson and Palmer (1989) emphasize that if performance is to be measured more effectively in the public sector, then the implicit cultural and change issues must also be addressed. The climate must be right, with managers committed to thinking clearly about what activities should be measured and what the objectives of these activities are. This may well involve different reward systems linked to revised expectations. This approach, they suggest, leads managers to move on from measuring the numbers of passengers on British Rail to analysing how many had seats and how punctual the trains were; and measuring and analysing the numbers of patients re-admitted to hospital after treatment, rather than just the numbers of patients who are admitted and the rate of usage of hospital beds. Jackson and Palmer also emphasize the importance of asking users about how effective they perceive organizations to be.

A final comment

Measurement and analysis is critical if performance is to be evaluated and improved. Measurement focuses attention on an issue, and by doing this can often help to bring about improvement. However there is almost no limit to the number of factors that could be measured in some way or another. It is therefore important to stress that organizations need to clarify which factors are critical for their competitive success, concentrate attention on these, measuring performance objectively and resolutely. Their selection of factors must not simply be those which are most readily measured.

Where an organization concentrates on the 'wrong' measures, those that are not critical for competitive success, and uses them to drive performance improvements, their efforts will really be wasted and possibly even harmful. Moreover, attention and effort may be drawn away from those measures and issues that do matter; gaps will be left.

Generally, where organizations pay too much attention to the 'wrong' issues and overlook more critical ones, they will be favouring quantitative, resource measures at the expense of more subjective, non-cost measures.

Privatized water companies

Since privatization in 1989, the privatized water companies have had to report annually to external regulators on the service levels provided to customers. These relate to:

❑ the availability of water resources to meet supply demands
❑ the reliability and adequacy of the water supply distribution system – i.e. water pressures, leakages and interruptions to supply
❑ the adequacy of the sewerage system; and
❑ the speed of response to customer queries and complaints.

There are a number of specified measures and achievement targets for these service issues. Additional restraints on price changes ensure that these effectiveness targets are not met by simply spending money, ignoring efficiencies and passing the burden on to customers.

British Gas

British Gas was privatized in 1986, since when the Director General of OFGAS (Office of Gas Supply) has set standards for, amongst other things:

❑ the time it takes to respond to gas leaks; and
❑ how soon new customers can be connected.

If British Gas consistently fails to achieve its service targets a price cut can be imposed.

In addition there is a price formula for domestic prices, agreed between British Gas and OFGAS. Annual price changes are to be $X\%$ percentage points less than the current rate of inflation. If inflation is below $X\%$ prices should be reduced. This formula is designed to drive efficiency and productivity.

The National Health Service

Prime Minister John Major announced a new Citizen's Charter in July 1991. This implied a change of attitude for the NHS – patients should be seen as customers with rights, rather than people who should be grateful for treatment, however long the wait. From April 1992 hospitals would have to set standards for maximum waiting times.

This followed on from the 1989 NHS White Paper: *Working for Patients*, which was designed to achieve:

(a) raising the performance of all hospitals and GPs to the level of the best (significant differences existed in measured performances)
(b) patients receiving better health care and a greater choice of services through improved efficiencies and effectiveness in the use of NHS resources
(c) greater satisfaction and rewards for NHS staff.

To achieve these, a number of structural changes have since been introduced.

❑ Individual hospitals have been able to become autonomous self-governing trusts (within the NHS) instead of being administered by health authorities. They are required to at least break-even. There is less centralized bureaucracy. But the changes have not all proved easy for all concerned; new tensions have arisen. It was believed that hospitals (health care providers) needed stronger management with a defined input from clinicians, but clinicians and hospital administrators are not always in agreement.
❑ Hospitals are free to treat any patient and GPs are free to book treatment at any hospital. Arrangements depend on the prices charged by individual hospitals for the treatment, and the ability and willingness of health authorities or GPs to pay.

These changes imply:

❑ the separation of the providers and purchasers of health care
❑ a need for health authorities to determine clear priorities within specified budgets
❑ the role of purchasers is to monitor the health needs of communities, prioritize and ensure a provision of supply to meet needs
❑ competition between hospitals in respect of services (available beds and staff) and prices
❑ the opportunity for patients and their doctors to select a preferred hospital.

Continued

❏ Certain General Practices (primary care producers), depending on the number of patients, can apply for their own NHS budget, which they can then spend as they deem most appropriate. This also assumes that in the long run, GPs will be able to offer a better service because it will be easier for patients to change their GPs.

In addition:

❏ Hospitals are required to give patients individual and reliable appointment times, and generally more and speedier information.

❏ Future investments have to be properly justified.

❏ There is pressure to reduce further the cost of drugs, by, say, using generic rather than branded products.

❏ Local pay arrangements have been made more flexible to provide better reward systems.

In short, hospitals and GPs have been made more accountable, and at the same time, given more responsibility and authority to encourage them to provide a better overall service for their customers. The ultimate aim: 'the best value for money'.

Checklist of key terms and concepts

You should be confident that you can calculate the major financial ratios and that you understand their meaning. The question on British Airways overleaf includes a list of the main ratios; you should work them out before checking your answers with those provided.

Summary

In this chapter we considered the question: How are we doing? It has been emphasized that success should really be measured in relation to the achievement of objectives. Companies can be regarded as successful if they are achieving the objectives set by the key stakeholders. It is also important to consider the implementation of strategies created to achieve the objectives, together with the control and understanding that the strategic leader has of incremental changes.

The need for the strategic leader to be aware of what is happening and the learning process involved in evaluating the need for change were emphasized, together with the importance of considering what might happen if the organization continues with present strategies.

It has been pointed out, though, that financial measures are normally used to evaluate performance. As these may not refer to objectives held by stakeholders they may be a measure of efficiency rather than effectiveness. Specifically:

- a simplified profit and loss account, balance sheet and cash flow statement, have been outlined and analysed
- major investment, performance and financial status ratios have been explained and examples have been provided
- the need to consider several years, rather than one in isolation, has been emphasized and the value of inter-company comparisons (within the same industry) and inter-divisional evaluations have been considered
- the importance of share prices and the *P/E* ratio for quoted companies has been emphasized
- the importance of profitability measures (rather than profit alone) has been highlighted and it has been pointed out that cash flow can be just as important as profitability
- a number of issues and difficulties in measuring the performance of not-for-profit organizations have been discussed.

Questions and research assignments

1(a) Calculate the following ratios for British Airways from the financial data provided in the table below

Investment ratios:
Return on shareholders' funds
Earnings per share
Price/Earnings ratio
Dividend yield
Dividend cover

Performance ratios:
Return on net assets
Profit margin
Net asset turnover
Stock turnover
Debtor turnover
Gross profit margin

Solvency ratios:
Debt ratio
Interest cover

Liquidity ratios:
Current ratio
Liquidity ratio

(b) List other possible performance measures for BA in respect of economy, efficiency and effectiveness. What measurement issues and difficulties are raised by your list? Which of the factors/measures do you believe to be the most critical.

A worked ratio analysis and a list of possible additional measures are given overleaf.

Additional library questions

(c) Compare your results in (a) with those for the three previous years and for subsequent years.

2 'The purpose of the Metropolitan Police Service is to uphold the law fairly and firmly; to prevent crime; to pursue and bring to justice those who break the law; to keep the Queen's peace; to protect, help and reassure people in London; and to be seen to do all this with integrity, common sense and sound judgement.' How might they measure their success?

3 The Royal Charter for the Royal National Institute for the Blind (RNIB), granted originally in 1949, states that the RNIB exists in order to:

❏ promote the better education, training, employment and welfare of the blind
❏ protect the interests of the blind; and
❏ prevent blindness.'

How might they assess how well they are doing?

British Airways
Extracts from profit & loss account and balance sheet, 31 March 1995

	£million		£million	£million
Turnover	7177	Fixed assets	6163	
		Investments	471	
Cost of sales	6436			6634
Gross profit	741	Current assets		
		Stock	70	
Overheads/administration	123	Debtors	1182	
		Short-term loans	1099	
Operating Profit	618	Cash	64	
Other Income/Provisions	(76)			2415
Interest	215	Current liabilities		2320
Tax	77	Working capital		95
Profit after interest and tax	250	Total net assets		6729
Dividend paid	119			
Retained profit	131	Long-term loans	4582	
		Provisions for charges	57	
Number of ordinary shares	954,605,000	Shareholders' funds	2090	
Year end share price	402 pence	Total capital employed		6729

Recommended further reading

In addition to Reid and Myddelton the following books provide a more detailed insight into financial ratios:

Parker, RH (1972) *Understanding Company Financial Statements*, Pelican.
Sizer, J (1989) *An Insight into Management Accounting*, 3rd edn, Penguin.

The *Financial Times* publishes a comprehensive daily summary of share prices, and the following publication provides a clear explanation of all FT statistics: *A Guide to Financial Times Statistics* (regularly updated).

Company Financial Information is also available from Extel, Datastream and MicroExstat. Most university libraries subscribe to Extel which provides information sheets periodically, updated whenever companies publish interim and end-of-year results. Datastream is a computer service and may also be available; it is particularly useful for graphs of share movements and share index comparisons as well as ratio calculations. McCarthy's, if available, provides summaries of articles in major newspapers that relate to companies.

Annual reports of public companies are normally provided by the company on request. In the case of private companies the data have to be purchased from Companies' House (Cardiff and London).

A wider treatment of performance measurement can be found in: Dixon, JR, Nanni, AJ and Vollman, TE (1990) *The New Performance Challenge: Measuring Operations for World-class Competition*, Irwin.

References

Drucker, PF (1989) What businesses can learn from nonprofits, *Harvard Business Review*, July–August.

Economist (1991) Britain's most admired companies, 26 January.

Financial Times (1995) Europe's most respected companies, special survey, 19 September.

Hasell, N (1994, 1995) Britain's most admired companies, *Management Today*, December.

Jackson, P and Palmer, R (1989) *First Steps in Measuring Performance in the Public Sector*, Public Finance Foundation, London.

Kaplan, RS and Norton, DP (1992) The balanced scorecard – measures that drive performance, *Harvard Business Review*, January–February.

London, S (1991) Repairing the balance sheet, *Financial Times*, 22 November.

Summers, D (1995) Boots comes top in corporate image poll, *Financial Times*, 23 October.

Reid, W and Myddelton, DR (1974) *The Meaning of Company Accounts*, 2nd edn, Gower. The quotation was taken from the second edition; there are later editions.

Appendix: possible performance measures for British Airways

British airways: worked ratio analysis

Investment ratios

Return on shareholders' funds $= \dfrac{250}{2090} =$ 11.96%

Earnings per share $= \dfrac{250}{954.605} =$ 26.2 pence

Price/earnings ratio $= \dfrac{402}{26.2} =$ 15.34

Dividend yield $= \dfrac{12.46}{402} =$ 3.1%

Dividend cover $= \dfrac{26.2}{12.46} =$ 2.1 times

Performance ratios

Return on net assets $= \dfrac{618}{6279} =$ 9.2%

Profit margin $= \dfrac{618}{7177} =$ 8.6%

Net asset turnover $= \dfrac{7177}{6729} =$ 1.07 times

Stock turnover $= \dfrac{7177}{70} =$ 102 times

Debtor turnover $= \dfrac{7177}{1182} =$ 6.1 times (or 60 days)

Gross profit margin $= \dfrac{741}{7177} =$ 10.3%

Solvency ratios

Debt ratio $= \dfrac{4582}{6729} =$ 68%

Interest cover $= \dfrac{542}{215} =$ 2.5 times

Liquidity ratios

Current ratio $=$ 2415:2320 $=$ 1.04:1

Liquidity ratio $=$ 2345:2320 $=$ 1.01:1

An airline is a people-dependent service business. Unquestionably its revenue, profits, profitability, liquidity and market share are all important. But alone they are inadequate for assessing the overall performance.

The following list contains examples of appropriate measures which might also be used.

Economy measures

❑ Costs – e.g. the cost of fuel
❑ The cost of leasing aircraft
❑ Staff levels and costs – slimming these is acceptable as long as the appropriate quality of service is maintained. This could be measured as an overhead cost per passenger.

Efficiency measures

❑ Time keeping/punctuality (*In the case of British Airways, this has increased from 73% within 15 minutes in 1991 to 84% in 1995*)
❑ Revenue passenger kilometres (RPK), the number of passengers carried multiplied by the distances flown
❑ Available seat kilometres (ASK), the number of seats available for sale multiplied by the distances flown
❑ The overall load factor = RPK/ASK
   For BA in the 1990s: RPK has increased by 35%, ASK by 32%, giving an increase in the load factor from 70.1% to 71.6%. (Similar measures for freight are also relevant)
❑ Solid performance with these measures is essential if the airline is to run at all profitably, but increasing them really requires the airline to be more **effective** in persuading more customers to fly, utilizing marketing and consistently good service
❑ A related measure is: Passenger revenue per RPK. Improving this implies increasing the return from each flight, given that on any aircraft there are likely to be several pricing schemes in operation. *In the 1990s BA's revenue per RPK has fluctuated between a minimum of 6.13 pence and a maximum of 6.50 pence, highlighting the difficulties involved in driving this up in a competitive industry*
❑ Income (from all sources) related to the numbers of employees
❑ Reliability of the aircraft, i.e. continuous flying without breakdown (as a result of efficient maintenance – see below)
❑ The average age of the aircraft in the fleet

Effectiveness

❑ Ability to meet all legislative requirements
❑ Image – which is based on several of the factors listed in this section
❑ Staff attitudes and contributions – both on the ground and on board the aircraft – care, courtesy, enthusiasm, friendliness, respect and efficiency
❑ The aeroplane itself – does it look and feel new and properly looked after?
❑ Other aspects of the on-board service, such as the cleanliness of the seating and toilet areas, food and entertainment
❑ Innovation – new standards of passenger comfort
❑ Safety record
❑ The number of routes offered, the timing of flights and the general availability of seats (this requires good links with travel agents)
❑ Recognition of, and rewards for, regular and loyal customers – reflected in the accumulation of air miles by passengers and the numbers of passengers who become 'gold card' holders in regular flier schemes

- ❏ Having seats available for all people with tickets who check-in. Whilst airlines, like hotels, often overbook deliberately they must ensure they are not 'bumping' people onto the next available flight at a level which is causing ill-will and a poor reputation
- ❏ The compensation package when people are delayed
- ❏ Time taken at check-in
- ❏ Reliability of baggage service – particularly making sure bags go on the right flight. This also involves the issue of bags being switched from one flight to another for transit passengers
- ❏ The time for baggage to be unloaded (this is partially in the hands of the airport management)
- ❏ The absence of any damage to luggage
- ❏ The systems for allocating particular seats in advance of the flight and at check-in
- ❏ The number of complaints; the number in relation to the number of passengers
- ❏ The way complaints are handled
- ❏ The ability to balance the cost of maintenance with the costs incurred if things go wrong. If there is inadequate maintenance there are likely to be incidents or accidents which are costly in lost revenue and goodwill. At the same time airlines could 'over-maintain' to a level where they are no longer able to compete because of too-high costs
- ❏ The additional factors below are not wholly the responsibility of airlines as they also involve the airport owners:
- ❏ Terminal provisions and comfort – seating, escalators, restaurants, duty-free shopping and toilets
- ❏ Security – evidence of security and perception that it is being taken seriously
- ❏ Availability of trolleys

Endnotes

It is also important to consider how all these factors might be measured and evaluated.

Observation, passenger surveys, complaints and comparisons with other airlines are all possibilities.

The distinction between **indicators** (aspects of service which are actually difficult to measure), **measures** and **performance targets** (standards to measure against) needs to be recognized.

The following points are also worth noting:

- ❏ it is sensible not to be over-ambitious with both measures and targets
- ❏ if something cannot be measured it is perhaps better to leave it out
- ❏ the chosen measures must be relevant and easily understood; hopefully the very act of measurement will foster improvements.

7

Company Failure

This chapter describes the main causes of decline and failure. These are usually financial and competitive weaknesses. Recovery strategies for companies in trouble are developed later (Chapter 17).

Learning objectives

After studying this chapter you should be able to:

- explain what is meant by corporate decline and failure
- identify the main symptoms of decline
- describe the most likely causes of decline
- calculate a Z-score, a possible predictor of potential failure.

Don't forget to visit the website:
http://www.itbp.com

Introduction

We have discussed objectives and the importance of stakeholders, and looked at how one might measure success. Although it is common to use financial ratios to measure relative success, the key issue concerns whether the organization is meeting the objectives set for it by its stakeholders. The crucial role played by the strategic leader has been discussed and the importance of creating and sustaining competitive advantage has been raised. In this chapter we shall see that poor strategic leadership, insufficient control of the essential aspects of financial management and the failure to be competitive are the key issues behind corporate failure.

In broad terms it could be argued that a company is unsuccessful if it fails to meet the objectives set for it by its stakeholders, or if it produces outputs which are considered undesirable by those associated with it. A company which polluted or harmed the natural environment in some way would be classified as unsuccessful by certain stakeholders but it would not necessarily fail financially and go out of business. Companies sometimes develop and launch new products which fail because very few people buy them – the Ford Edsel car and Strand cigarettes are well-quoted examples. In this respect the companies are unsuccessful with particular competitive strategies, but again they may not necessarily experience corporate failure as a result.

Corporate failure and the lack of success should not be seen as synonymous terms. A private sector, profit-seeking, organization would be classified as a failure if it ended up in liquidation and was closed down with its assets sold off piecemeal. A similar company might be unsuccessful and in decline, but able to avoid failure. Appropriate strategic action which addresses the causes of the decline may generate recovery. For example, the major shareholders might insist upon the appointment of a new strategic leader, or the financial or competitive weaknesses might be acted upon. Such a company might also be acquired by another, and this may be because the shareholders are happy to sell their shares or because the company has been placed in receivership and the receiver has arranged the sale of the business as a going concern. Receivership occurs when a business is unable to pay its creditors, for example its suppliers or bank-loan interest. The receiver is normally a professional accountant and is charged with saving the business if it is possible to do so. In a similar way a non-profit-seeking organization could be closed down or provided with new leadership and direction on the insistence of its major financial stakeholders or trustees.

A company might be relatively unsuccessful compared with its competitors for a prolonged period of time if the key stakeholders allow it. For example a small private company whose shares are not quoted on the stock exchange might be making only very limited profits and growing at a rate slower than its industry, but its owners may be happy for it to stay in existence whilst it is solvent. In the English football league a large number of clubs, particularly outside the Premier League, fail to make any profit on their footballing activities because their crowds are too low, but other commercial activities, sponsorship, sales of players and benevolent directors keep them in business. However, such a lack of success consistently will weaken the company, cause it to exhibit symptoms of decline (discussed below) and may ultimately lead to failure.

In this chapter we look at what factors typically lead to corporate failure and at how managers might realize that their company is heading for failure unless remedial action is taken. Turnaround strategies for companies in trouble will be considered in detail in Chapter 17.

Symptoms of decline

Symptoms of decline are not the causes of failure but indicators that a company might be heading for failure. They will show when a company is performing unsuccessfully relative to what might be expected by an objective outsider or analyst. As mentioned above they will indicate the outcome of poor strategic leadership, inadequate financial management or a lack of competitiveness. Slatter (1984), building on the earlier work of Argenti (1976), has analysed 40 UK companies in decline situations which have either been turned around or have failed. He concludes that there are ten major symptoms. In the same way that relative success can be evaluated from financial analysis, a number of these symptoms of decline are finance based:

❑ falling profitability
❑ reduced dividends, because the firm is reinvesting a greater percentage of profits
❑ falling sales, measured by volume or revenue after accounting for inflation
❑ increasing debt
❑ decreasing liquidity
❑ delays in publishing financial results, a typical indicator that something is wrong

- ❏ declining market share
- ❏ high turnover of managers
- ❏ top management fear, such that essential tasks and pressing problems are ignored
- ❏ lack of planning or strategic thinking, reflecting a lack of clear direction.

If any of these symptoms are perceived it will be necessary to identify the underlying causes before any remedial action might be attempted. Slatter concluded that a number of causal factors recurred on several occasions in the companies he studied, and these are summarized below, but categorized in terms of issues of leadership, finance and competitiveness.

Whilst Slatter's work is over ten years old, more recent research by the Society of Practitioners of Insolvency (1995) reaffirms his arguments. An investigation of 1000 insolvencies in 1994 determined that the greatest single cause of business failure was loss of market, which was responsible for 29% of the insolvencies. Inadequate cashflow accounted for a further 25% and leadership failings 16%. Earlier analyses by the SPI placed greater emphasis on inadequacies in the financial structure of organizations.

Causes of decline

Inadequate strategic leadership

Poor management

Ineffective management concerning key strategic issues can be manifested in a number of ways. The company could be controlled or dominated by one person whose pursuit of particular personal objectives or style of leadership might create problems or lead to inadequate performance. The organization might fail to develop new corporate or competitive strategies such that previous levels of performance and success are not maintained when particular products, services or strategies go into decline. This issue can be compounded or alleviated by weak or strong managers respectively supporting the strategic leader, and by the quality of non-executive directors on the Board. Poor strategic leadership in terms of building an appropriate organization might mean that key issues or key success factors are ignored or are not given the attention they deserve. A company that is dominated by accountants or engineers might, for example, fail to pay sufficient attention to changing customer requirements and competition. Equally a company without adequate financial management might ignore aspects of cost and cash flow management – a factor which will be explored later in this chapter. Similarly a company which is undergoing rapid change and possibly diversification might concentrate its resources in the areas of development and neglect the core businesses which should be providing strong foundations for the growth.

Acquisitions which fail to match expectations

This particular point will be explored in detail in Chapter 16, but the significance is worthy of mention here. Companies seeking growth or diversification may take over other companies or merge with them. Research, which will be discussed later, suggests that in many cases the profits and successes anticipated from the acquisition fail to materialize. This can be the result of a poor choice by the strategic leader who overestimates the potential or an inability to manage the larger organization effectively because the problems are under-estimated. It is not unusual for companies which fail to have sought fast growth, often following strategies involving major acquisitions. Examples include: Blue Arrow which acquired the US company Manpower to create the largest employment agency business in the world, funded by a major rights issue which over-stretched the company; Next, which failed to integrate a series of acquisitions effectively; Storehouse, formed when Habitat/ Mothercare acquired British Home Stores; and leisure group Brent Walker, which borrowed heavily to fund the purchase of pubs, casinos and the William Hill chain of 1600 betting shops.

Mismanagement of big projects

This is related to the previous point, but incorporates a number of other possible strategic decisions. By big projects is meant any really new venture for an organization, including developing new and different products and entering new markets, possibly abroad. It is essential to forecast potential revenues without being unrealistically optimistic, and to control expenditures and costs, but this does not always happen. It seems that companies often

❑ underestimate the capital requirements, through poor planning, design changes once the project is underway, and inaccurate estimations of the development time that will be required
❑ experience unforeseen start-up difficulties, sometimes resulting from lack of foresight and sometimes from misfortune
❑ misjudge the costs of market entry because of customer hostility or hesitation, or the actions of competitors.

Companies should be careful not to stretch their financial and managerial resources with big projects as they can cause other healthier parts of the business to suffer.

The link between strategic leadership and failure crisis situations was explored in Chapter 3.

Poor financial management

Poor financial control

This again can manifest itself in a number of ways. Particularly important are the failure to manage cash flow and the incidence of temporary illiquidity as a result of overtrading, which were discussed in Chapter 6. Inadequate costing systems can mean that companies are not properly aware of the costs of the different products and services they produce, and as a result they can move from profit to loss if the mix of products they produce and sell is changed. If an organization invests in expensive equipment for potentially lower costs or product differentiation, then it automatically increases its fixed costs or overheads. This will increase the breakeven point and consequently make the company more volume sensitive. Investments of this nature should not be undertaken lightly and without a thorough and objective assessment of market potential; but some companies do invest without adequate analysis and create financial problems for themselves. Finally some companies in decline situations appear not to budget properly. Budgets are short-term financial plans which forecast potential demand and sales revenue, the costs which will be incurred in meeting this demand, and the flow of cash in and out of the business. If budgeted targets are not being met it is essential to investigate why and take any steps necessary to improve the situation. Without proper budgeting companies cannot estimate profits and cash needs adequately and can therefore experience unexpected financial difficulties.

Cost disadvantages

In addition to the problem of breaking even and covering overheads, described above, companies can experience other cost disadvantages which result in decline.

Companies without scale economies can be at a cost disadvantage relative to larger competitors and suffer in terms of low profit or a failure to win orders because their prices are higher. Companies which are vertically integrated and able to exercise control over their supplies, or which are located in areas where labour or service costs are relatively low, can enjoy an absolute cost advantage over their rivals and thereby put pressure upon them. Company structure can yield both cost advantages and cost disadvantages. Large multi-product companies can subsidize the cost of certain products and again put pressure on their rivals; or conversely they can find that their costs are higher than their smaller competitors because of the overhead costs of the organization structure, say through an expensive head office. Finally poor operating management can mean low productivity and higher costs than ought to be incurred, and thereby cause decline. These cost problems all affect competitiveness and they are therefore linked to the additional competition factors discussed below.

Visit the website:
http://www.
itbp.com

Other issues

It was mentioned in Chapter 6 that the debt ratio should be controlled so that companies did not risk embarrassment through not being able to pay interest charges because of low profits. Companies which rely on loan capital may find that in years of low profits they are unable to invest sufficiently and this may lead to decline. Conversely other companies may decline because they have not invested as a result of conservatism rather than financial inability. This reflects another weakness of strategic leadership.

Competitive forces

Porter's model of the forces which determine industry profitability is discussed in Chapter 9. Whilst all the relevant forces can be managed to create competitive advantage, each of them could cause a weak competitor to be in a decline situation.

The effect of competitive changes

Primarily companies can find themselves in decline situations if their products or services cease to be competitive. Their effective life and attractiveness to customers might be ending; or their competitors might have improved their product or introduced some thing new, thereby strengthening their product differentiation and competitive edge and inevitably causing demand for other products to fall. In other words decline can result from a loss of clear differentiation and in turn a failure to maintain competitive advantage.

If costs increase, say because of increased labour costs which competitors manage to avoid, then pressure will be put on prices or profit margins, and it may no longer be worthwhile manufacturing the product or service.

Resource problems

It was mentioned above that increased labour costs can render a company uncompetitive; other resources controlled by strong suppliers can have a similar effect. In addition a company can experience cost problems as a result of currency fluctuations if it fails to buy forward appropriately to offset any risk and with property rents if leases expire and need renegotiating in a period of inflation.

Inadequate or badly directed marketing

This factor relates to issues of rivalry between competitors. Companies whose competitive strategies rely on differentiation must ensure that customers recognize and value the source of the differentiation. This requires creative and effective advertising and promotion targeted to the appropriate segments and can be very expensive, especially if the industry is characterized by high advertising budgets. Companies who fail to market their products or services effectively may decline because they are failing to achieve adequate sales.

Case 7.1, Laker Airways, illustrates a number of the above points. Freddie Laker, when he launched his Skytrain, undercut the prices of the major airlines and appealed to a distinct sector of the market, but he was overconfident and committed too many resources on his new venture and on possible growth which did not materialize. His financial arrangements constituted his downfall. The case also illustrates the importance of understanding and not underestimating the environmental forces which influence the organization. This is the theme of Chapter 8.

In a decline situation a number of the factors above may be present and interlinked; and it may not be easy to distinguish between cause and effect. For example a company may be losing market share or sales and experiencing a decline in profits because its product or service is no longer competitive. It may have a cost disadvantage or its competitors may have more effective sources of differentiation. Is the cause of this situation poor management internally which has failed to contain costs or create and sustain competitive advantage, or the result of external competitive forces to some extent outside the control of the organization? If the company is to be turned around, then both the symptoms of decline and the underlying causes need to be acted upon.

In simple terms, when a company is in real trouble the strategic leader, who may be new and brought in specially, might be expected to perform one of a number of alternative roles. He or she may have to act as firstly an undertaker and liquidate the company, secondly a pathologist, carrying out major surgery such as divesting poorly performing parts of the business or cutting their size, or thirdly a health clinic doctor, restoring the company's fortunes. Prices might be increased to generate more revenue or improve the gross margin. Variable costs, and if possible fixed costs, might well be reduced, again to improve margins and also to reduce the need for working capital. Divestment is one way of reducing assets and generating revenue. Attempts are also likely to be made to improve stock and debtor turnover in order to improve the cash flow. The alternative strategies will be explored in detail in Chapter 17.

Freddie Laker, who became Sir Freddie in 1978, was an entrepreneur and a pioneer in the competitive international air transport industry. He was a well-quoted self-publicist whose commercial exploits brought him fame and recognition. He introduced cheap transatlantic air travel, providing travel opportunities for many people who previously had not been able to afford the fares; but his business collapsed in the early 1980s.

In the 1960s Laker Airways was a small independent company 'operated on a shoestring' which offered a number of inclusive package holidays and provided charter flights for organizations who could book all the seats on a plane and flights for tour companies who did not own their own airline. Laker's stated intention was to stay small: 'If we get any bigger than six planes you can kick my arse'.

In the 1970s his ambitions changed and he became determined to 'try a new market and offer transport to a lot more people'. At this time the only cheap air fares across the Atlantic were charter flights, whereby travellers had to be a member of some sponsoring organization for at least six months before flying. The international carriers operated a price-fixing cartel organized by the International Air Transport Association (IATA) with the connivance of all governments concerned. Charter flight regulations tended to be abused, and consequently the major carriers fought for stricter monitoring which brought about a decline. Laker conceived Skytrain, a 'no booking, no frills' operation with prices significantly below those offered by the major airlines, who naturally opposed his idea.

Laker applied to the Civil Aviation Authority (CAA) for a licence first in 1971 and was refused. In late 1972 he was given permission as long as he flew out of Stansted, although his base was at Gatwick. Delaying tactics involving British and US airlines, the UK Labour government, the US government and the American equivalent of the CAA meant that the first flight did not take place until September 1977 when Skytrain was launched with enormous publicity, this time from Gatwick. In this period oil prices had increased dramatically and Skytrain, although still

under £100 for a single fare, was double the price estimated in 1971. In turn the Skytrain fare was well under half the cost of the cheapest fare offered by IATA carriers who subsequently had to reduce their fares in the face of this new competition.

Although they did this reluctantly, it had a devastating impact on Laker. Skytrain's competitive advantage was its low price resulting from its low cost base; its service package was clearly inferior to that of the major carriers. When the price gap was narrowed, Skytrain became less attractive to customers; its early competitive advantage was not sustainable.

Skytrain made £2 million profits in its first year of operation, but difficulties experienced when it was extended to Los Angeles in 1978 effectively wiped out the profitability. In 1979 Laker became a fully licensed transatlantic carrier and for the first time was able to pre-sell reserved seats. Laker's confidence grew, and anticipating that he would be given permission to fly more routes around the world he ordered ten Airbus A-300s and five McDonnell Douglas DC10s at a total cost of £300 million. Eventually this was to bring his downfall. Laker was already using DC10s for Skytrain and when the US government grounded all DC10s for checks in 1979 Laker lost £13 million in revenue. In 1980 he failed to win licences to fly Skytrain in Europe and to Hong Kong, although he did begin services from Prestwick and Manchester and to Miami.

Profits of £2.2 million were reported for 1980–1981, but significantly three-quarters of this came from favourable currency movements. By 1981 the pound was falling against the dollar, demand was declining, revenue was down, but the debt interest payments, mostly in dollars, were rising. There were, in effect, too many planes and not enough passengers flying the Atlantic. The major airlines wanted fares to rise, but Skytrain remained the force which kept them low. Laker did manage to renegotiate some interest payments and a cash injection from McDonnell Douglas, but he also had to increase fares and sell his Airbuses. He was left with a

Continued overleaf

break-even level of virtually all the seats on every Skytrain, but was able to fill only one-third of them. When the receiver was called in (February 1982) Laker had debts of some £270 million.

Laker had pioneered cheap transatlantic airfares, which have stayed in different guises since his collapse, but he made the mistake of becoming over-confident. The man who originally intended to stay small went for growth. At the same time he was determined to retain total control of his company and therefore raised loan capital against very limited assets rather than seeking outside equity funding. The interest payments brought him down, particularly as he raised most of the money in dollars without ade-

quate cover against currency fluctuations. Finally, as something of a buccaneering character described by one airline executive as a man who 'a few hundred years ago would have brass earrings, a beard and a cutlass', he underestimated the power of the vested interests who opposed him. Had their opposition not delayed the introduction of Skytrain by six years maybe things would have turned out differently.

Source: Monkton, C and Fallon, I (1982) *The Laker Story*, Christensen Press and Sunday Telegraph.

Endnote: Laker started another transatlantic airline in 1996.

Predicting a failure

Financial databases, such as Datastream, typically provide an index known as a Z-score, which was devised by Edward Altman (1968) and which purports to predict potential corporate failure as a result of insolvency. Altman's research in the USA in the 1960s found the Z-score to be a good indicator of potential bankruptcy, but further research in the UK by Argenti (1976) and others suggests that the index should be used cautiously. The Z-score, which is explained in Key Concept 7.1, tends to be more appropriate in the last two years before bankruptcy when it could be argued that a good financial analyst should be able to see clearly that a company is experiencing difficulties and is in decline. Argenti argues that managers rarely look for symptoms of decline, and consequently the Z-score can be a useful indicator of when such an analysis might be appropriate. If a company appears to be in decline and the trend is identified soon enough, then recovery strategies can be initiated.

Visit the website: http://www. itbp.com

KEY CONCEPT 7.1

Z-SCORES

The original Z-score of Altman (1968) is:

$$Z = 1.2 \times X^1 + 1.4 \times X^2 + 3.3 \times X^3 + 0.6 \times X^4 + 1.0 \times X^5$$

where

X^1 = is working capital divided by total assets

X^2 = is retained earnings divided by total assets

X^3 = is earnings before interest and tax divided by total assets

X^4 = is market value of equity divided by book value of total debt

X^5 = sales divided by total assets

and

❏ working capital is current assets less current liabilities
❏ total assets is fixed assets plus all current assets
❏ retained earnings is accumulated profits in the business
❏ market value of equity is the number of ordinary shares × their current market price + the value of preference shares

❏ book value of total debt is long-, medium- and short-term debt, including overdraft

For US companies, Altman argued that if Z is less than 1.8 they are 'certain to go bust' and if it exceeds 3.0 they are 'almost certain not to'. Argenti suggests the appropriate UK figures are more of the order of 1.5 and 2.0 respectively.

Companies with a strong asset base will tend to have a high Z-score under the Altman formula, but such businesses do fail, generally then being sold as going concerns.

Taffler (1977) has devised an alternative formula which places greater emphasis on liquidity:

$$Z = 0.53 \times X^1 + 0.13 \times X^2 + 0.18 \times X^3 + 0.16 \times X^4$$

where

X^1 = profit before tax divided by current liabilities (incorporating profitability)

X^2 = current assets divided by total debts (working capital)

X^3 = current liabilities divided by total assets (financial risk)

X^4 = the no credit interval (liquidity)

and the 'no credit interval' is defined as:

$$\frac{\text{Immediate assets} - \text{current liabilities}}{\text{Operating costs} - \text{depreciation}}$$

Using Taffler's formula a score in excess of 0.2, and certainly 0.3, indicates a company with good long-term prospects; below 0.2, and definitely below 0.0, is a score characteristic of companies which have failed in the past.

Sources: Altman, El (1968) Financial ratios, discriminant analysis, and the prediction of corporate bankruptcy, *Journal of Finance*, **23**(4), September. Taffler, RJ (1977), Going, going, gone, *Accountancy*, March.

Summary

In this chapter we have attempted to draw together a number of topics considered earlier in the book and discussed how they can affect corporate decline. Specifically these issues are strategic leadership, financial management and competition.

In addition the distinction between a lack of success and decline and failure has been explored, and a number of symptoms of decline have been listed. The Z-score, an index of corporate well being or decline, has been illustrated briefly.

Questions and research assignments

Text related

1 Do the causes discussed in this chapter provide an adequate explanation for any corporate failure with which you are familiar?

Library based

2 In 1983 Z-scores provided by Datastream suggested that the following companies (amongst others) were in decline:

❏ Rover Group (then British Leyland)
❏ British Aluminium
❏ Renold (chainmakers)
❏ Acrow (cranemakers)
❏ Dunlop
❏ Lucas
❏ Tube Investments.

A number of other companies (including those listed below) were considered vulnerable to acquisition because their share prices were low in comparison with the book value of their assets:

❏ Lonrho
❏ P&O
❏ House of Fraser
❏ Debenhams
❏ Tootal Group
❏ Coats Patons
❏ British Aerospace
❏ Vickers.

Having studied this chapter, and before reading Chapter 17 on turnaround strategies, ascertain what has happened to these companies since 1983.

Recommended further reading

Readers who want more information on company failure are referred to Slatter's book.

References

Altman, EI (1968) Financial ratios, discriminant analysis and the prediction of corporate bankruptcy, *Journal of Finance*, **23**(4), September. The Z-score is explored further in Altman, EI (1971) *Corporate Bankruptcy in America*, Heath.

Argenti, J (1976) *Corporate Collapse*, McGraw-Hill.

Slatter, S (1984) *Corporate Recovery: Successful Turnaround Strategies and their Implementation*, Penguin.

Society of Practitioners in Insolvency (1995) *Personal Insolvency in the UK*, SPI, London.

Taffler, RJ (1977) Going, going, gone, *Accountancy*, March.

INTERLUDE

Environmental and Resource Analysis; Synergy

Figure II.l presents an outline of how the next six chapters fit together. We are primarily concerned with the sustained fit between environment and resources to achieve and maintain E–V–R congruence. This implies a changing but on-going match between environmental opportunities and threats and the organization's resource strengths and weaknesses.

The environment will be discussed in general terms in Chapter 8; the competitive environment, a critically important sub-set, is incorporated into Chapter 9. The environment presents organizations with a set of issues, challenges, opportunities and requirements; their success is dependent upon how they deal with them. These demands are considered in this interlude.

To achieve and sustain competitive advantage (Chapter 9) the organization must harness its resources effectively. Businesses, activities and functional areas need to support each other to deliver synergies (explained in Key Concept II.l). The organization's key strategic resources, and their contributions to competitive advantage and success, are examined in four chapters:

Chapter 10 – Products, processes and services, when we also look at the whole value chain
Chapter 11 – People
Chapter 12 – Finance
Chapter 13 – Information.

The traditional way of summarizing environmental opportunities and threats and organizational strengths and weaknesses is a SWOT analysis, which we discuss below.

In addition to the SWOT framework, we will consider (in Chapters 8 and 9) four additional frameworks which are valuable for analysing the strategic situation facing a company. These are:

❑ A PEST or STEP analysis for examining the environment
❑ Porter's framework for industry analysis
❑ Competitor gap analysis
❑ Porter's model of competitive advantage.

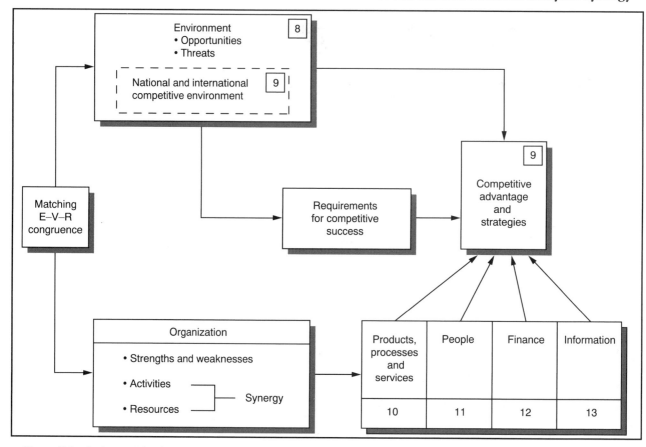

Figure II.1   Environmental and resource analysis.

Environmental awareness and management

It is essential for managers throughout the organization, whatever function or business unit they might have responsibility for, firstly to understand the environment as it affects them and as it affects other parts of the organization, and secondly to appreciate how the various parts of the organization are interdependent.

The environment changes as events take place (for example a change in legislation or innovation by a competitor) and as the relative power and influence of the constituent parts changes (for example two key buyers merge and demand more preferential trading arrangements in line with their new buying power). The organization can influence events, and should seek to do so in order to achieve favourable results; but not everything can be influenced or forecast. Hence the organization must be flexible enough to adapt and change as necessary in the face of external changes. This is affected, as we have seen, by the culture and the role of strategic leadership. The strategic leader may establish a broad strategic direction and delegate considerable responsibilities to business units and functions, to enable them to respond quickly to new opportunities and threats. These managers may work within reasonably tight policy guidelines or have greater individual freedom. Tighter objectives and more central control by the strategic leader is an alternative approach which is generally more suitable for stable environments and less diversified firms. It was emphasized earlier that it is necessary for the strategic leader to understand what is happening and what changes are taking place whatever the structure and culture of the organization. Changes can then be stimulated by reactions to external events, or a determination to influence events outside the organization. Many of these will be relatively small incremental changes; occasionally they will be major events. Acquisition of another company can be a determined major change of strategic direction, possibly involving considerable risks; acquisition by another company can be the result of previous failures to respond to environmental pressures, resulting in decline.

Some organizations and strategic leaders will seek to avoid taking high risk decisions and major changes of direction; most organizations will surely want to avoid having revolutionary changes forced on them by stronger external forces. The alternative in both cases is gradual evolutionary change by the organization which monitors the environment for new opportunities and takes those which are most desirable and appropriate. As indicated above this requires awareness throughout the organization of changes and trends in the environment, flexible resources which can be used to capitalize on the opportunities, and an ability to co-ordinate the resources in order to implement the desired changes effectively.

However, as we saw in Chapter 1, continuous, emergent change, whilst *always* valuable, may sometimes not be enough. Discontinuous change and strategic regeneration is required to deal with the pressures of competition and changing customer demands.

As will be seen later, when the management of change is discussed in Chapter 22, changes may often be resisted by people unless they clearly appreciate the reasons why the changes are necessary and share the objectives. This is again an issue of culture.

SWOT analysis

Environmental opportunities are only potential opportunities unless the organization can utilize resources to take advantage of them and until the strategic leader decides it is appropriate to pursue the opportunity. It is therefore important to evaluate environmental opportunities in relation to the strengths and weaknesses of the organization's resources, and in relation to the organizational culture. Real opportunities exist when there is a close fit between environment, values and resources. Similarly the resources and culture will determine the extent to which any potential threat becomes a real threat. This is E–V–R congruence.

All the resources at the disposal of the organization can be deployed strategically, including strategic leadership. It is therefore useful to consider the resources in terms of where they are strong and where they are weak as this will provide an indication of their strategic value. However, this should not be seen as a list of absolute strengths and weaknesses seen from an internal perspective; rather, the evaluation should consider the strengths and weaknesses in relation to the needs of the environment and in relation to competition. The views of external stakeholders may differ from those of internal managers (who in turn may disagree amongst themselves) when evaluating the relative strength of a particular product, resource or skill. Resources should be evaluated for their relative strengths and weaknesses in the light of key success factors.

Even though an organization may be strong or weak in a particular function, the corresponding position of its major competitors must also be taken into account. For example, it might have sophisticated computer-controlled machine tools in its factory, but if its competitors have the same or even better equipment, the plant should not be seen as a relative strength. This issue refers to distinctive competences – relative strengths which can be used to create competitive advantage. As any resource can be deployed strategically, competitive advantage can be gained from any area of the total business.

An evaluation of an organization's strengths and weaknesses in relation to environmental opportunities and threats is generally referred to as a SWOT analysis.

As mentioned above, a mere list of absolute factors is of little use. The opportunities which matter are those which can be capitalized on because they fit the organization's values and resources; the threats which matter are those that the organization must deal with and which it is not well equipped to deal with; the key strengths are those where the organization enjoys a relatively strong competitive position and which relate to key success factors; the key weaknesses are those which prevent the organization from attaining competitive advantage.

Again, to be useful the lists of factors should be limited to those which matter the most, so that attention can be concentrated on them. In arriving at such a summary SWOT statement it can therefore be useful to start by drawing up a large grid and using it for assessing relative importances.

Figure II.2 illustrates a popular and useful framework for a SWOT analysis applied to Asda earlier in the 1990s, before the introduction of new strategies focusing on the product ranges, in-store layouts and a clear distinction between large Asda superstores and smaller units with a limited range and discounted prices (called Dales). The chart highlights how certain issues can be considered as either a strength or a weakness, an opportunity or a threat, depending upon how they are managed in the future.

Once all the important **strategic issues** have been teased out from a long list of strengths, weaknesses, opportunities and threats, the following questions should be asked:

❑ How can we either neutralize critical weaknesses or convert them into strengths?
❑ Similarly: can we neutralize critical threats or even build them into new opportunities?
❑ How can we best exploit our strengths in relation to our opportunities?
❑ What new markets and market segments might be suitable for our existing strengths and capabilities?
❑ Given the (changing) demands of our existing markets, what changes do we need to make to our products, processes and services?

Alongside a general SWOT analysis, it is essential to evaluate the relative strengths and weaknesses of the company's leading competitors. Appropriate frameworks for this are included in Chapter 9.

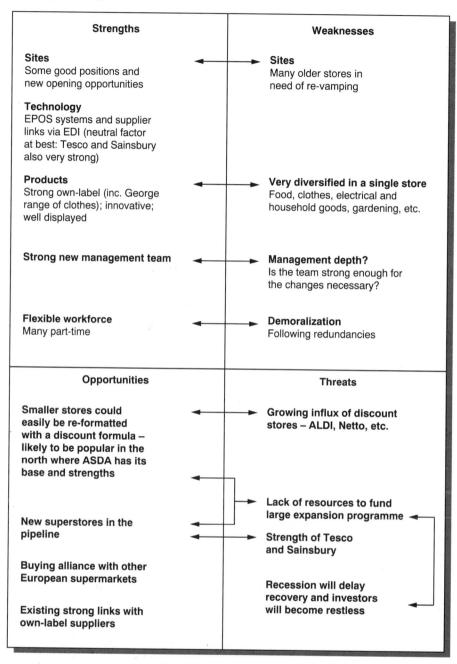

Figure II.2 ASDA plc SWOT analysis, early 1990s.

Auditing strategic resources

In a SWOT analysis the strengths and weaknesses of resources must be considered in relative and not absolute terms. It is important to consider whether they are being managed effectively as well as efficiently. Resources, therefore, are not strong or weak purely because they exist or do not exist. Rather, their value depends on how they are being managed, controlled and used.

Table II.1

Aspects of the resource audit

Resource/function	Key considerations
Marketing	Products and services
	– range
	– brand names
	– stage in life cycle
	Patents
	Strength of salesforce
	Distribution channels
Operations	Location and plant
	Capital equipment
	Planning and manufacturing systems
	Quality control
	Supplies
Research and development	Annual budget
	Technology support
	Quality of researchers
	Record of success and reputation
Finance	Capital structure
	Working capital
	Cash flow
	Costing systems and variances
	Nature of shareholders
	Relations with bankers
Human resources	Numbers and qualifications
	Skills and experience
	Age profile
	Labour turnover and absenteeism
	Flexibility
	Development and training record and policies
	Motivation and culture

In auditing resources we consider the functional areas of the business, as this is where the human, financial and physical resources are deployed. These areas might include finance, production, marketing, research and development, procurement, personnel and administration. However, it is also important to consider how they are related together in the organization's structure and control systems. A brilliant and successful marketing manager, for example, might seem to represent a strength; however, if there is no adequate cover for him and he or she leaves or falls ill, it is arguable that the firm has a marketing weakness.

Control systems, such as production and financial control, and the ways in which managers co-operate within the organization influence how well resources are managed for efficiency and effectiveness. Table II.1, which is not meant to be fully comprehensive, provides a sample of key resource considerations. In completing such an audit the various resources should be evaluated: their existence, the ways that they are deployed and utilized, and the control systems that are used to manage them.

Using Table II.1 as an example, efficiency measures of the salesforce might include sales per person or sales per region, but the effectiveness of the salesforce relates to their ability to sell the most profitable products or those products or services which the organization is keen to promote at a particular

Resource/ function	Areas of strength	Areas of weakness	Significance of strength	Significance of weakness	Table II.2
Marketing					
Operations, etc.					

time, perhaps to reduce a high level of stocks. The efficiency of individual distribution outlets can be measured by sales revenue in a similar way. But the effectiveness of the distribution activity relates to exactly which products are being sold and to whom, whether they are available where customers expect them, and how much investment in stock is required to maintain the outlets. The efficiency of plant and equipment is linked to percentage utilization. The effectiveness involves an assessment of which products are being manufactured in relation to orders and delivery requirements, to what quality and with what rejection levels.

It is also important to assess the relative strengths and weaknesses in relation to competition. Thus each of the designated areas of consideration included in Table II.1 might be analysed with the chart shown in Table II.2.

The theme of these chapters on the organization's resources is that managers must be aware of and must address strategic issues if the resources are to be used for creating and sustaining competitive advantage. Marketing can be looked at from the point of view of managing the activities which comprise the marketing function. Product design and pricing, advertising, selling and distribution would be included here. But if an organization is marketing oriented there is an implication that employees throughout the organization are aware of consumers and customers, their needs, and how they might be satisfied effectively whilst enabling the organization to achieve its objectives. Consumer concern becomes part of the culture and values. Consumers and customers are mentioned separately because for many organizations, particularly the manufacturers of products for consumer markets, their customers are distributors and their ultimate consumers are customers of the retailers they supply.

Innovation and quality can be seen as aspects of production or operations management. Again it is helpful if these factors become part of the culture. An innovatory organization is ready for change, and looking to make positive changes, in order to get ahead and stay ahead of competition. A concern for quality in all activities will affect both costs and consumer satisfaction.

In human resources management values are communicated and spread throughout the organization.

Financial management includes the control of costs so that profit is achieved and value is added to products and services primarily in areas which matter to consumers. This should provide differentiation and competitive advantage.

Lower costs and differentiation are the basic sources of competitive advantage. These relate to both an awareness of consumer needs and the management of resources to satisfy these needs effectively and, where relevant, profitably. Marketing orientation and the effective management of production and operations, people and finance are all essential aspects of the creation and maintenance of competitive advantage.

Whilst these chapters on functional and competitive strategies are important for an understanding of strategic management in all types of organization, they are especially important for a large proportion of small businesses and many not-for-profit organizations. Corporate strategic changes such as major diversification and acquisition, divestment of business units which are under-performing or international expansion may not be relevant for small firms with a limited range of products or services and a primarily local market, or for not-for-profit organizations with very specific missions. However, these organizations must compete effectively, operate efficiently and provide their customers and clients with products and services which satisfy their needs. Competitive and functional strategies are therefore the relevant issue.

Synergy

It is also vital that the functions discussed in the previous section are co-ordinated because they are interdependent. Decisions taken for one function will affect other functions and other managers in the organization. The communication of decisions, and an understanding of what is happening throughout the organization, depend on information flows and information systems (the subject of Chapter 13). By examining organizational value chains, Chapter 10 considers how resources overall can be managed to create competitive advantage.

Just as individual functions must work in harmony, it is also necessary that the various parts of the business be co-ordinated. These parts could be represented by different products or various strategic business units. Depending on the degree of diversification the links between them may be relatively strong or relatively weak. What matters is that their efforts are co-ordinated in order to achieve synergy (Ansoff, 1968). Synergy is defined in Key Concept II.1. Ansoff describes synergy as the $2 + 2 = 5$ effect: the combination of the parts produces results of greater magnitude than would be the case if the parts operated independently. If functions, products or business units were not co-ordinated efforts may well be duplicated, or delays might be built into the organization system because of a lack of understanding. Where several products or services are produced some common experiences or activities might well be shared.

Synergy is more likely to occur if all these strategies are linked in such a way that the organization as a whole is managed effectively, which Drucker (1973) has defined as 'doing the right things'. Individual business units and functions must themselves be managed efficiently or, as Drucker would say, they must be 'doing things right'. As we saw in Chapter 6 resource efficiency considers how well resources are being utilized and the returns being obtained from them. Effectiveness incorporates an evaluation of whether the resources are being deployed in the most beneficial manner.

SYNERGY

Synergy is concerned with the returns that are obtained from resources. The argument is that resources should be combined and managed in such a way that the benefits which accrue exceed those which would result if the parts were kept separate. In other words, if an organization manufactures and markets six different products, the organization should be structured to yield the benefits which might be possible from combining these different interests. For example, central purchasing for all products might yield economies of scale; factory rationalization might increase productivity or lower production costs; sales staff might be able to obtain more or larger orders if they are selling more than one product; each product might gain from name association with the others; and distributors might be more satisfied than if the company offered only a very limited range or a single product. Some of the benefits are clearly measurable; others are more subjective.

There are three basic synergy opportunities:

❑ functional – sharing facilities and competences
❑ strategic – complementary competitive strategies
❑ managerial – compatible styles of management and values.

Where an organization is considering increasing its range of products and services, or merging with or acquiring another company, synergy is an important consideration. In the case of an acquisition the combination of the companies should produce greater returns than the two on their own. Adding new products or services should not affect existing products or services in any adverse way, unless they are intended to be replacements. When such strategic changes take place the deployment of resources should be re-evaluated to ensure that they are being utilized both efficiently and effectively.

In just the same way the existing deployment and management of resources, the way they are combined, and the structure and management systems within the organization should be such that synergy is being obtained; i.e. that opportunities for greater returns are not being ignored as a result of poor resource management.

This may well imply the sharing of knowledge and other resources between divisions or business units, possibly attempting to disseminate best practice. This is only feasible if resource efficiencies are measured and compared in order to identify which practices are best. Internal rivalries may prevent the attainment of the potential benefits from sharing.

Benefits might also be gained by offering important skills to other organizations. The logistics of distribution and product support are critical success factors for Caterpillar, the world's largest producer of construction equipment. Caterpillar formed a new service business to capitalize on the expertise they had developed, offering warehousing, transport management and other support services world-wide. They now distribute products as diverse as bathroom fittings, air compressors, vehicle parts and sportswear.

It will be suggested later in the book that anticipated synergy from strategic changes is easily overestimated and that it may not accrue. Potential benefits from adding new activities may be misjudged. In Box 1.2 one diversification by the Lex Service Group in the 1970s was mentioned briefly. Lex were successful and profitable with essentially car distribution and felt that their resources and skills would be ideally suitable for transfer into hotel management. They anticipated synergy because of their management skills. Their level of success from the change, however, was below their expectations and they withdrew from this industry.

Searching for synergy
Sony

A number of Japanese electronics companies (manufacturers of televisions, videos and hi-fi equipment) have sought links with the US makers of music and films, arguing that there is potential synergy from merging hardware and software. New products are technologically feasible – the manufacturers want to secure their commercial exploitation. Such developments include high definition televisions, flat screen TVs (both large and small for mounting on walls [like a picture] and carrying around), personal video disc players the same size as personal cassette players and miniaturized CDs and CD players. Films can also be the basis for computer games. The large film companies have huge film libraries for video and games exploitation, both growth markets at the end of the 1980s. The strategy is similar to that of the manufacturers of razors who have derived benefits and synergy from also manufacturing razor blades.

Sony acquired CBS Records 1987 and Columbia Pictures from Coca-Cola in 1989. Previously Coca-Cola had anticipated synergy from linking soft drinks and entertainment, but it had not accrued. Matsushita acquired MCA (Universal Pictures, record labels and part-ownership of a network TV station) in 1990. Toshiba negotiated a joint venture with Time Warner. Earlier Rupert Murdoch had bought Twentieth Century Fox to exploit the film library on his cable and satellite TV networks worldwide.

Continued overleaf

The strategy has been defended with logical arguments. It has been suggested that if Sony had owned Columbia in the 1970s their Betamax video format would have proved more successful because more pre-recorded videos would have been available on this format rather than the successful VHS – developed by Matsushita who were more resourceful in striking agreements with video makers. Similarly, CBS would prove a useful vehicle for forcing the pace of the switch from records to compact discs.

Sceptics argue the synergy will not accrue, arguing that the typical Japanese company and Hollywood film makers have dramatically different cultures which may not prove compatible. Moreover, Japan itself is not noted for creativity in entertainment. Interestingly record companies have been reluctant to release music in the new high-technology DAT (digital audio tape) format. Whilst Sony have pioneered the hardware, CBS have chosen not to break industry ranks.

In 1995 Matsushita divested MCA, selling it to Seagram. At this time, Sony was still not in a position to claim it had effectively integrated its entertainments subsidiaries to deliver the anticipated benefits, profits and synergies.

Sears
Sears, like Burton, Next and Storehouse (British Home Stores, Mothercare and previously Habitat), is a retail chain which ran into difficulties with the recession of the early 1990s. Sears was 'sprawling and unwieldy', comprising the British Shoe Corporation (including Dolcis and Shoe Express), Wallis, Warehouse, Richards, Olympus and Milletts chains, as well as Selfridges department store in London. Menswear, sportswear and leisure products accompanied the shoes. During the 1990s, BSC has been rationalized and certain brands, such as Curtess, largely discontinued; Richards and Olympus have been divested.

A new chief executive (Liam Strong, recruited from British Airways) joined Sears in 1992, and quickly set about trying to integrate the businesses more effectively. Project teams looked for inter-group savings in buying, merchandising and marketing; some £8 million (10% of profits at that time) was found in a matter of months. Training events have been used to bring together both functional and store managers from the various chains, and ideas have been 'stolen' and shared.

LVMH – Moët Hennessy. Louis Vuitton LVMH, which describes itself as the world's leading luxury products group, "brings together a unique collection of crafts and brands well known in prestige circles: champagne, cognac, luggage, perfumes and haute couture". Haute couture accounts for just 3% of world-wide revenue; the other four areas each provide a roughly equal contribution. LVMH brands include: Moët and Chandon, Veuve Clicquot, Hennessy, Hine, Christian Dior, Givenchy and Christian Lacroix as well as the Louis Vuitton leather products. LVMH and Guinness jointly own a world-wide wine and spirits distribution network. In 1993 LVMH sold its Roc Skincare subsidiary to Johnson and Johnson; its products did not fit properly as they sell exclusively through pharmacies.

These are all products with a global appeal, albeit to relatively limited market niches. For such products, the marketing/selling network has to be extensive or it cannot support the global distribution; consequently there can be major benefits from linking together an appropriate range of products and brands. LVMH's synergistic benefits are:

❏ name association, particularly with fashion and perfumes
❏ advertising – savings by advertising several brands in the same magazines
❏ distribution – although there are specialist outlets for different products, large department stores sell many LVMH brands. Because the LVMH range as a whole is vital for these stores, LVMH can command premium positions and displays
❏ sales – a world-wide sales force and network yields savings.

Sustained competitiveness

We have already seen that maintaining E–V–R congruence over time requires adaptation and change and that many firms, however successful they may be at certain times in their history, become takeover targets or go out of business. Strong and profitable companies can become crisis prone in a short space of time if their strategies become outdated through fashion or competition. Yesterday's key success factors may not be relevant today, let alone tomorrow.

Of the 30 companies in the Financial Times share index for 1935, only nine still exist in their own right. These include Blue Circle (then known as Associated Portland Cement), Bass, GEC, GKN and Tate and Lyle; most of these have changed markedly over the 60 years, sometimes acquiring other businesses. The remaining businesses have mostly been acquired, although some were nationalized. Imperial Tobacco and London Brick were both acquired by Hanson; BTR bought Dunlop and Hawker Siddeley. Two other companies, ICI and Courtaulds, still exist but both have been split into two separate businesses.

The 'best' UK companies are clearly amongst the world leaders in their relevant industry sectors, as we saw in Chapter 6; the problem is the large number of businesses which are not innovative, truly competitive and world class. Product markets, supply chains, capital markets and communications are now typically global; companies must, therefore, think globally and benchmark (or evaluate) themselves against the best companies in the world.

Competitive advantage, a superior competitive position, can be manifested by differentiation, lower costs than competitors and the speed at which a company can change. Behind these *what factors* are a *why* (essential requirements) and a *how* (the means). The requirements relate to the corporate culture and values, the ability of the organization to learn and change and the relative strength of key processes and technological competencies. The means concern the ability to add value, innovate, leverage and stretch resources and manage supply chain linkages effectively, which, in many cases are in turn dependent upon the ability to empower people and harness their true potential contribution. The *what* factors may have short time scales; the *why* issues are long-term and deep rooted. The *how* factors blend the short and long terms and enable the necessary changes.

A number of these issues, which were first explained in Chapters 1 and 2, are explored in detail in the next six chapters.

Today's profitable companies are finding that success depends more and more on providing a flexible response to rapidly changing customer demands. British companies must learn to adapt their resources, skills and knowledge to changing market environments. Part of the secret of doing this is to be constantly alert to what both competitors and customers – at home and abroad – are thinking and doing.
Eric Forth MP, previously Under Secretary of State for Industry and Consumer Affairs

---

References

Ansoff, HI (1968) *Corporate Strategy*, Penguin (originally published by McGraw-Hill in New York in 1965).
Drucker, PF (1973) *Management*, Harper & Row.

8

The Business Environment

In this chapter we explore the relationship between the organization and its environment. Environmental opportunities and threats must be appreciated and evaluated for their potential impact on the organization. In addition, the organization's resources must be managed and developed in such a way that they match the needs of the environment.

Learning objectives

After studying this chapter you should be able to:

■ explain issues of complexity, dynamism and uncertainty in relation to the organization's environment
■ identify how changes might be forecast
■ discuss the organization as an open system and assess the impact of a number of environmental forces
■ construct a focal zone diagram to illustrate the relative importance of the various stakeholders and other influences
■ describe certain changes taking place currently in the international and UK environments.

Introduction: managing in an increasingly turbulent world

In this chapter we examine in detail the environment in which the organization operates and consider how the forces present in the environment pose both opportunities and threats. The topic of stakeholders, which was introduced in Chapter 5, is developed further as a number of the environmental forces which affect the organization clearly have a stake in the business. Competitors inevitably constitute a major influence on corporate, competitive and functional strategies and they are the subject of Chapter 9.

If a firm is to control its growth, change and development it must seek to control the forces which provide the opportunities for growth and change, and those which pose threats and demand responses. Not only must managers be aware of environmental forces and environmental change, they must manage the organization's resources to take advantage of opportunities and counter threats. In turn the strategic leader should ensure that this happens and that the values and culture of the organization are appropriate for satisfying the key success factors. Quite simply, the environment delivers shocks to an organization, and the way in which resources are deployed and managed determines the ability to handle these shocks. This relates to E–V–R congruence.

Over time, paradigms concerning 'what will work' to bring about success in a particular industry or competitive environment will be created and maintained. However, as environmental and competitive forces change, the current reality (at any time) of what is required for competitive success may be drifting away

Don't forget to visit the website: http://www. itbp.com

from the organization's paradigm; consequently a new paradigm will be essential. In an age of discontinuity, paradigms will need changing more frequently and more dramatically; expediting these changes is a key managerial task.

Put another way, in a turbulent environment, the organization must change its strategies and possibly its beliefs if it is to maintain E–V–R congruence. Case 8.1 illustrates an important change of paradigm in UK agriculture. Farmers are now looking at their farms as potentially diversified businesses and not simply farms.

A number of key themes underpin the issues discussed in this chapter:

❑ Traditional industries such as steel, coal and shipbuilding have given way to new, more technological – and frequently electronics-based – industries which demand new labour skills, and where 'knowledge workers' are of prime importance.

❑ In addition to changing skills demands, there have been other changes in the labour markets of developed countries. Many families have joint wage earners and more women are working.

❑ Manufacturers from the UK, USA, Germany, Japan, and from other nations with a long-standing tradition in manufacturing, have been willing to relocate factories in developing countries with lower wage costs. Technology, which allows increasing levels of output from the same-size factory, has facilitated these changes.

Case 8.1
DIVERSIFICATION IN UK AGRICULTURE

Essentially the problem is one of overcapacity. Increasing surpluses of staple commodities such as grain, butter, milk and meat have developed as demand for many products has been static and the consumption of animal fats has declined. Prices have been forced down, costs have risen, and government and European Union support is being reduced. To remain viable many farmers must seek alternative uses for their resources, comprising land, labour and capital equipment.

There are limited opportunities for adding value to existing products and for producing alternative and unusual crops, but increasingly farmers are establishing non-farming enterprises to yield revenue, profit and employment. A number of opportunities exist, but many require skills which are different from those which are essential in farming. Farmers therefore need to be more strategically aware and take a wider view of the essential purpose of their enterprises.

The opportunities available include the following.

❑ Forestry: there is a large demand in the UK for wood and wood products, much of which is currently satisfied through imports

❑ Tourism: bed and breakfast accommodation, self-catering cottages, caravanning and camping facilities

❑ Retailing direct to the public through farm shops and garden centres

❑ Sport and recreation: ponds and gravel pits for fishing or growing fish to sell to angling clubs; shooting either game or clay pigeons, and possibly including gun hire; sailing facilities; equestrian opportunities including horses for trekking and hunting, and stabling; golf courses on surplus land; and using rough terrain and woodland for simulated war games

❑ Engineering, woodworking and craft workshops.

❏ Consequently, the competitive arena has been changing, with, recently, the highest economic growth being enjoyed by the Pacific Rim countries. In many industries, global supply potential exceeds demand, placing downward pressures on real prices.

❏ Product and service markets, supply chains, capital markets and communication systems have become global in nature.

❏ Governments have masterminded increasing degrees of deregulation. Other countries have followed the UK's lead and privatized public sector utilities; air travel and telecommunications markets have been opened up to more competition.

❏ Consumers are more aware and more knowledgeable; environmental groups have begun to wield increasing influence.

Simply, environments are more turbulent; managing them and managing **in** them demands more flexibility and more discontinuity than in the past.

The competitive future for the UK does not lie in reducing wages to compete with the Far East and Eastern Europe, and thus creating a downward spiral of expectation; rather it lies in finding new ways of innovating, adding value, differentiating and *leading* consumers. Notwithstanding this, some cutting back to create and maintain trim and efficient organizations will always be essential.

There are several frameworks for studying the environment of an organization. In addition to considering the company's **stakeholders** in terms of their relative power, influence, needs and expectations, a **PEST analysis** can also prove useful. This is an objective and straightforward consideration of changing political, economic, social and technological influences. This review should help to clarify changing opportunities and threats.

Figure 8.1 summarizes these points and also highlights that the *nature* of the stakeholders and the environmental forces is a useful indicator of the most appropriate strategic approach for the organization to take. Where the environment is *complex, turbulent and uncertain* it will be necessary for the organization to be vigilant and speedily *reactive*. A carefully *planned approach* is ideal in *stable and predictable* circumstances; and a positive and *proactive approach* should be adopted where the environment can be changed or influenced.

Understanding the environment

Although the constituent forces of the environment can be listed and assessed for opportunities and threats, and the forecasting of possible changes can be attempted, of most importance for managers is on-going insight and awareness. The important issues might well be listed as part of a SWOT analysis: they constitute an essential part of the planning process and can be used for developing and evaluating possible strategic changes. Managers, however, should always be attentive to changes and their decisions and actions should be both reactive and proactive as appropriate. In other words their awareness should result from constant vigilance and attentiveness rather than from any isolated clinical analysis. This will in turn be dependent on the information system within the organization, sources of external information and the uses made of it, and the ability of individual managers to evaluate the importance

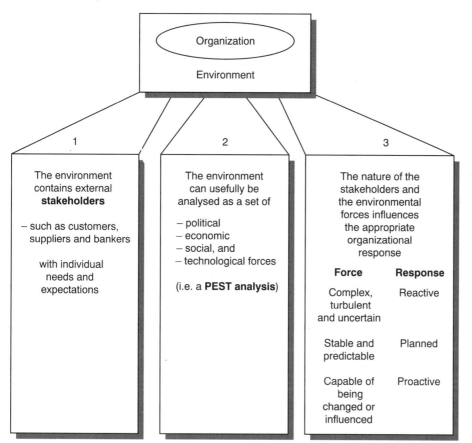

Figure 8.1 The organization and the environment.

and potential significance of events they become aware of. Whilst environmental forces and influences clearly exist and change, what matters is the perception managers place on their observations and experiences, i.e. the meaning they attribute to information. The information aspects are the subject of Chapter 13; manager capabilities are dependent on experience and basic understanding of the overall strategic process. It is particularly useful if managers are able to take a strategic perspective rather than a functional one because then they may perceive opportunities and threats in areas outside their own particular specialisms.

In a fast-changing world where businesses are buffeted by external forces, managers need to be nimble to respond capably, to keep the company on track and to meet its objectives. They must be outwardly focused, aware of important trends that will impact on business or industry. They need to be opportunity-aware, without losing the more usual inward-looking focus on doing things better and responding to threats.

Neville Bain, Group Chief Executive, Coats Viyella

Uncertainty, complexity and dynamism

Duncan (1972) argues that the environment is more uncertain the more complex it is or the more dynamic it is. An often used example of an organization facing a generally stable, non-dynamic and hence fairly certain environment is a small rural village post office. Whilst most organizations face far more uncertainty, their managers also enjoy more challenges. Moreover, in recent years, the position of small village post offices has become more uncertain!

The dynamic environment

Dynamism can be increased by a number of factors. Rapid technological change involving either products, processes or uses will mean that changes are likely to occur quickly and that organizations must stay aware of the activities of their suppliers and potential suppliers, customers and competitors. Where competition is on a global scale the pace of change may vary in different markets, and competition may be harder to monitor. In such cases the future is likely to be uncertain. Risk taking and creative entrepreneurial leadership may well be required as strategies pursued in the past, or modifications of them, may no longer be appropriate.

The complex environment

An environment is complex where the forces and the changes involving them are difficult to understand. Quite often complexity and dynamism occur together. Technology-based industries are an excellent example of this. The structure of the organization, the degree of decentralization and the responsibility and authority delegated to managers throughout the organization, and information systems can render complexity more manageable. Managers will need to be open and responsive to the need for change and flexible in their approach if they are to handle complexity successfully.

Managerial awareness and the approach to the management of change are therefore key issues in uncertain environments. If managers are strategically aware, and flexible and responsive concerning change, then they will perceive the complex and dynamic conditions as manageable. Other less aware managers may find the conditions so uncertain that they are always responding to pressures placed on the organization rather than appearing to be in control and managing the environment. Hence a crucial aspect of strategic management is understanding and negotiating with the environment in order to influence and ideally to control events.

Environmental influences

Systems thinking

Figure 8.2, which illustrates how the organization might usefully be seen as part of an open system, is really an elaboration of part of Chapter 1, Figure 1.3. Figure 1.3 looks at how the organization processes inputs into outputs within the constraints imposed by external environmental forces. Figure 8.2 looks at

---

One thing is clear. Even if you're on the right track you'll get run over if you just sit there!

Sir Allen Sheppard, Chairman Grand Metropolitan plc

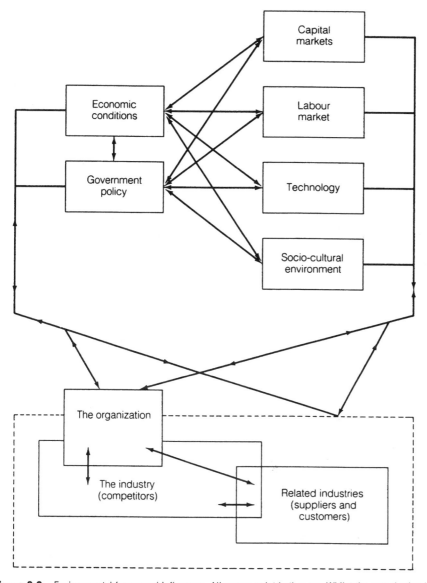

Figure 8.2 Environmental forces and influences. All arrows point both ways. Whilst the organization is influenced by the environment it must also seek to manage the environment.

these forces in greater detail. The organization is shown as one of a number of competitors in an industry; and to a greater or lesser degree these competitors will be affected by the decisions, competitive strategies and innovation of the others. These inter-dependencies are crucial and consequently strategic decisions should always involve some assessment of their impact on other companies, and their likely reaction. Equally a company should seek to be fully aware of what competitors are doing at any time.

Furthermore this industry will be linked to, and dependent on, other industries: industries from which it buys supplies, and industries to which it markets products and services. Essentially this relates to Porter's model of the forces which determine industry profitability that we will consider in Chapter 9.

The relationships between a firm and its buyers and suppliers are again crucial for a number of reasons. Suppliers might be performing badly and as a result future supplies might be threatened; equally they might be working on innovations which will impact on organizations they supply to. Buyers might be under pressure from competitors to switch suppliers. It is important to be strategically aware, and to seek to exert influence over organizations where there are dependencies.

Visit the website:
http://www.
itbp.com

These industries and the firms which comprise them are additionally part of a wider environment. This environment is composed of forces which influence the organizations, and which in turn can be influenced by them. Particular forces will be more or less important for individual organizations and in certain circumstances. It is important that managers appreciate the existence of these forces, how they might influence the organization, and how they might be influenced. This relates to stakeholder theory. This systems approach, which considers the organization in relation to its environment, is useful for two main reasons. First, it can help managers to understand and explain the decisions and behaviour that can be observed throughout the organization. Individual managers may be aware of what is happening in their management area or business unit within the organization; it is also useful if they understand activities elsewhere in the corporation. Second, it enables greater insight into the changing equilibrium situation concerning the firm and its environment. As environmental forces change and as the organization adapts through incremental changes the equilibrium situation is in fact changing and managers should be aware of this.

Mintzberg (1987) has used the term 'crafting strategy' to explain how managers learn by experience and by doing and adapt strategies to environmental needs. He sees the process as being analogous to a potter moulding clay and creating a finished object. If an organization embarks upon a determined change of strategy certain aspects of implementation will be changed as it becomes increasingly clear with experience how best to manage the environmental forces. Equally managers adapt existing competitive and functional strategies as they see opportunities and threats and gradually change things. In each case the aim is to ensure that the organization's resources and values are matched with the changing environment.

External forces

Economic conditions affect how easy or how difficult it is to be successful and profitable at any time because they affect both capital availability and cost, and demand. If demand is buoyant, for example, and the cost of capital is low, it will be attractive for firms to invest and grow with expectations of being profitable. In opposite circumstances firms might find that profitability throughout the industry is low. The timing and relative success of particular strategies can be influenced by economic conditions. When the economy as a whole or certain sectors of the economy are growing, demand may exist for a product or service which would not be in demand in more depressed circumstances. Similarly the opportunity to exploit a particular strategy successfully may depend on demand which exists in growth conditions and does not in recession. Although a depressed economy will generally be a threat which results in a number of organizations going out of business, it can provide opportunities for some. When we consider turnaround strategies later in the book we shall consider appropriate strategies for depressed industries.

Economic conditions are influenced by **government policy**; equally they are a major influence affecting government decisions. There are numerous ways, however, that government decisions will affect organizations both directly and indirectly as they provide both opportunities and threats. Whilst economic conditions and government policy are closely related, they both influence a number of other environmental forces which can affect organizations. **Capital markets** determine the conditions for alternative types of funding for organizations; they can be subject to government controls, and they will be guided by the prevailing economic conditions. The rate of interest charged for loans, for example, will be affected by inflation and by international economics, and will be government led. Government spending can increase the money supply and make capital markets more buoyant. The expectations of shareholders with regard to company performance, their willingness to provide more equity funding or their willingness to sell their shares will also be affected.

The **labour market** reflects the availability of particular skills at national and regional levels; this is affected by training, which is influenced by government and the TECs. Labour costs will be influenced by inflation and by general trends in other industries, and by the role and power of trade unions.

Technology in one respect is part of the organization and the industry half of the model as it is used for the creation of competitive advantage. However, technology external to the industry can also be captured and used, and this again can be influenced by government support and encouragement. Technological breakthroughs can create new industries which might prove a threat to existing organizations whose products or services might be rendered redundant, and those firms which might be affected in this way should be alert to the possibility. Equally, new technology could provide a useful input, perhaps in manufacturing, but in turn its purchase will require funding and possibly employee training before it can be used.

The **sociocultural environment** encapsulates demand and tastes, which vary with fashion and disposable income, and general changes can again provide both opportunities and threats for particular firms. Organizations should be aware of demographic changes as the structure of the population by ages, affluence, regions, numbers working and so on can have an important bearing on demand as a whole and on demand for particular products and services. Threats to existing products might be increasing; opportunities for differentiation and market segmentation might be emerging.

The examples referred to here are only a sample of many, and individual managers should appreciate how these general forces affect their organization in particular ways. Table 8.1 provides a list of environmental influences and forces, but again it is general. Readers should use this outline framework to evaluate which forces influence their organization, how they exert influence, and how important relatively each of them is. This issue will be explored in greater detail later when we consider actual environmental changes in the mid-1990s. Case 8.2 looks at how environmental forces have affected the European pharmaceutical industry.

For any organization certain environmental influences will constitute powerful forces which affect decision making significantly. For some manufacturing and service businesses the most powerful force will be customers; for others it may be competition.

Table 8.1

Environmental influences

Influence	Examples of threats and opportunities
The economy	The strength of the economy influences the availability of credit and the willingness of people to borrow. This affects the level of demand. Interest rates and currency fluctuations affect both the cost and demand of imports and exports
Capital markets	This includes shareholders, and their satisfaction with company success. Are they willing to buy more shares if offered them to increase equity funding? Would they willingly sell if someone bid for the organization? Also included is the banking system, the cost and availability of loan capital
Labour market	Changes in structure with an ageing population and more women seeking work. Availability of skills, possibly in particular regions. The influence of trade unions. The contribution of government training schemes
Technology	Robotics in manufacturing in such industries as car assembly. Computers for design and manufacturing. Information technology such as electronic point of sale in retailing
Sociocultural environment	Pressure groups affecting demand or industry location Changing tastes and values
Government	Regional aid policies Special industry initiatives, say where high technology is involved The legal environment is part of this, including the regulation of competition. Restraints on car exhaust emissions (pollution control) and labelling requirements would be other examples
Suppliers	The availability and cost of supplies, possibly involving vertical integration and decisions concerning whether to make or buy in essential components.
Customers	Changes in preferences and purchasing power Changes in the distribution system
Competitors	Changes in competitive strategies Innovation
The media	The effect of good and bad publicity, drawing attention to companies, products and services

In some situations suppliers can be crucial. In the case of some small businesses external forces can dictate whether the business stays solvent or not. A major problem for many small businesses concerns the management of cash flow – being able to pay bills when they are due for payment and being strong enough to persuade customers to pay their invoices on time. A small sub-contract metal working business which works mostly for the large car manufacturers and whose main supplier is British Steel will have little power of persuasion. Payments may be delayed, and the customers will be too large and important to be threatened in any meaningful way, such as by the refusal to do any more work for them; meanwhile the supplies will have to be paid for or future deliveries are likely to be suspended. Whilst it is essential for all managers to have some insight into how their organization is affected by the environment, it is also desirable for them to consider how some of the environmental forces might be influenced and managed to gain benefits for the organization. This is less possible generally in the case of small businesses as they are relatively less powerful. However, small companies should examine

Past, and inevitable, government interest and involvement makes drugs a politically sensitive industry. Individual consumers have relatively little influence on the choice of a particular drug, which is prescribed by doctors who are often working under constraints or limitations imposed by their respective governments. This affects the research and marketing strategies of the drug manufacturers. Governments across Europe have frequently agreed favourable prices with international companies who locate and invest in their countries, which has led to the establishment of more plants than are really needed and some loss of production efficiencies. The total spend on prescription drugs rose throughout Western Europe in the 1980s and early 1990s. Between 1989 and 1992 it grew by nearly 50% in real terms. Almost all of the cost is borne by the public purse. The main reasons for the growth are ageing populations and medical advances.

However, in the economic recession, governments have become less and less willing to meet an ever-increasing bill; and in 1993 drug spending was deliberately curbed. The pharmaceutical companies have been forced to respond, and they have reacted in a number of ways:

❑ Workforces have been reduced and sites closed. Hoechst and Bayer (German), Glaxo Wellcome and Fisons (British) and Ciba (Swiss) have all followed this strategy

❑ In addition there have been a number of strategic acquisitions and divestments. Two of the UK's leading companies were sold, Fisons to Rhône-Poulenc Rorer and Boots (manufacturing interests only) to BASF. Wellcome was taken over by Glaxo, following a contested bid. Glaxo Wellcome, now the world's largest drug company with just under 5% world market share, Zeneca and SmithKline Beecham dominate the UK industry, and, following rationalizations, are performing strongly. In 1996 two Swiss companies, Sandoz and CIBA, merged to create the second largest company in the world

❑ As a form of industry restructuring both Smith-Kline Beecham (Anglo-American) and Merck (US) have acquired leading American drugs wholesalers

❑ New marketing strategies have been developed, actively promoting to doctors and hospitals those drugs that governments are still willing to pay for. This applies particularly to drugs which are differentiated, protected by patent and not subject to intense competition. Sales forces have also been rationalized

❑ Research and development has been redirected to focus on:

(i) programmes which could lead to innovative and high-revenue drugs. The development of 'me-too' brands, which must be sold with lower margins in more competitive markets, is now seen as only low priority

(ii) *generic* (unbranded) drugs where patents have expired. Margins are low but generic drugs are popular with governments

❑ European companies have forged alliances with US companies to obtain their greater expertise in cost management and in the research and development of generic products.

In 1995 the UK retained 40% of those employed in contract research in Europe and was attracting new investment by overseas companies. When Sweden's Pharmacia merged with Upjohn of the USA in 1995, a new corporate head office was opened in London. There are four main reasons why 'London is the centre of the globe in terms of the pharmaceutical industry':

❑ UK scientists are as good as those in France, Germany, Switzerland and the USA, but the total cost of employing them is lower

❑ the UK government's regulatory scheme differs from those of certain other countries and allows the drug companies to make between 17% and 21% return on capital employed, thus encouraging more investment

❑ strong UK capital markets have supported the blossoming biotechnology industry and

❑ the UK is home to the European Medicines Evaluation Agency which issues drug licences for the whole EU.

their environment for opportunities and threats in order to establish where they can gain competitive advantage and where their resources might most usefully be concentrated. For many not-for-profit organizations such as the National Theatre and London's major museums the government constitutes a major environmental force because each of these organizations is dependent in different ways on government grants. The National Health Service is similarly very dependent upon government policies which affect all decision areas. Consultants' salaries, nurses' pay, new hospitals and wards, and new equipment are substantially determined by government decisions, which they will seek to influence.

Forecasting the environment

A complex and dynamic modern environment is inevitably difficult to forecast; the inherent uncertainties can make it highly unpredictable and potentially chaotic. External events and competitor activities can trigger a chain reaction of responses and new scenarios. But Handy (1989) contends that 'those who know why changes come waste less effort in protecting themselves or in fighting the inevitable'. Consequently, however difficult it may be to actually forecast environmental change, organizations must attempt to stay strategically aware.

In analysing the environment managers should seek to do the following.

❑ Identify which forces are most important, and why they are critical. This will reflect opportunities and threats.
❑ Forecast how these forces might change in the future, using whatever methods are appropriate.
❑ Incorporate these expectations and predictions into decision making and management thinking. Fahey and King (1983) have emphasized the usefulness of including line managers from the whole organization in any teams which are specifically charged with environmental analysis, as this can lead to more effective dissemination of information to enable it to be used in decision making. Managers will be individually aware of many changes in the environment. Where strategic change takes place incrementally through managers with delegated authority, this information can be easily incorporated in decisions. But where major strategic change is being considered centrally by the strategic leader it is important to gather the relevant data together.
❑ Be honest and realistic when evaluating strengths and weaknesses relative to competitors, and when considering the organization's ability to respond to opportunities and threats. The environment should be managed wherever possible, and managers should seek to ensure that their resources are compatible with the organization's environment and the factors and forces that will influence and determine success.

In recruiting and appointing key staff, it is essential to recognize not only the needs of the organization as it is today, but to try to identify what its needs will be in the future and the skills which will take it there.

David Collischon, previously Chairman, Filofax plc

This last factor implies that forecasts should be as realistic as possible; they should be used in decision making and for the determination of future strategy; and the implications of changes in the environment should be acted upon and not ignored.

Individual managers will develop their environmental and strategic awareness through experience and perception, and by thinking about their observations and experiences. It is particularly important to assess the significance of what happens and what can be observed to be happening. However, in considering future strategic changes there will be an additional need to forecast the changes which might take place in the environment concerning supplies, customers, competitors, demand, technology, government legislation and so on. Some of the future changes may be forecast through straightforward extrapolation of past events; many will not. Some of the environmental forces can be better quantified than others, and consequently some subjectivity will be involved. Hogarth and Makridakis (1981) have argued that the overall performance of organizations in predicting future changes is poor, and that the most sophisticated methods of forecasting are not necessarily the best. However, despite the difficulties, forecasting is important. Managers who are encouraged to think about future changes, to ask questions and to query assumptions will increase their insight and awareness and this should help decision making.

Visit the website: http://www.itbp.com

What, then, do managers need to forecast, and how might the forecasting be carried out?

The economy and the possible impact of economic changes can be assessed in a number of ways. Economic growth, inflation, government spending, interest rates, exchange rates, the money supply, investment and taxation may all be influential. The Treasury provides forecasts periodically, based on its own econometric model. A number of universities and business schools also publish predictions based on their econometric models. Sometimes they are in agreement, but often they are not. Analysts from City institutions are regularly quoted on television and radio news programmes, and again there is often disagreement. The problem lies in the number of inter-relationships and inter-dependences amongst the economic variables and in imperfect understanding of all the cause and effect relationships. Additionally economic forces and changes around the world, such as changes in the exchange value of key currencies, inflation rates in major markets such as the USA and balances of payments in different countries can all affect the UK and organizations based in the UK, especially those with overseas interests. Although all the changes cannot be forecast with great accuracy, managers should be aware of what is happening at the moment and the implications of any trends that can be observed.

Demographic influences include some which can be forecast reasonably well and some which are more unpredictable. Changes in population structure can be readily forecast; changes in tastes and values are more difficult. Again it is essential to be able to appreciate the significance of observed events and changes. The government does provide statistics on social trends, which give some insight, but organizations need to be continually aware rather than rely on statistics which are a little dated when published.

At one level this issue is relatively clear: there is a general breakdown of two-parent families, a growth in the number of 45–54-year-olds and a decline in those 15–24. But what are the implications? Categorizing people into socio-economic or house-type groupings has often been used to try and understand demand patterns, but the situation remains complex. Individual firms must conduct attitude and behavioural research. Why, for example, does a friend of the author drive a £30,000 car but wear a £20 wristwatch? Why does his wife buy premium-price luxury ice cream and the cheapest own-label toilet paper?

Political influences relate to changes in governments and their priorities and legislation programmes. Opinion polls help in forecasting the former, and indications of the latter are readily available. However, planned legislation is not always passed for various reasons.

Developing from this is the need to forecast how certain laws and regulations might be implemented. Organizations considering mergers or acquisitions have to try and predict whether a referral to the Monopolies and Mergers Commission is likely before mounting their bid. Contacts within the so-called corridors of power can be of great benefit.

Demographic and political forecasting often relies on expert opinion, which can be obtained through personal contacts, commissioned research or published information in journals and newspapers. Outside opinions may well be biased or prejudiced because of strong views on certain issues or because of political perspectives, and this must be taken into account. Wilson (1977) has shown how probability-diffusion matrices can be useful here. Where opinions concerning the likelihood or probability of certain events are being gathered it is useful to plot both the strength of feeling (high or low probability of occurrence) and the diffusion of opinion (consistency or dispersion) amongst the sources or experts.

Scenario planning is often used in strategic management to explore future possibilities. Possible happenings and events are considered by looking at potential outcomes from particular causes and seeking to explain why things might occur. The value is in increased awareness by exploring possibilities and asking and attempting to answer 'what if' questions. Although scenario planning can be predictive and can be used to plan strategic changes, it can also help decision making by providing managers with insight so that they can react better when things happen or change. It can also be helpful for conceptualizing possible new competitive paradigms. See Box 8.1.

Technological forecasting covers changes in technology generally, and the possible impact of innovations which result from research and development by an organization, by its competitors, and by other firms with which it is involved in some way. Expert opinion through scenario planning and from technical journals can be useful. Technological changes can have an impact throughout an organization and consequently it is useful for managers in various functions to consider the possible effects on them.

Key success factors

Key success factors were explained in Chapter 1, when it was pointed out that the environment dictates which factors an organization really needs to address if it is to secure long-term competitive advantage and strategic success. We distinguished between:

❑ Industry-specific factors which apply to all competitors in the industry.
   Airlines experience high fixed costs through their investment in expensive

Box 8.1
SCENARIO PLANNING

Don't try to eliminate uncertainty – embrace it....
despite overwhelming evidence to the contrary, many
of us still view the future as an extension of the past.
Clem Sunter, Anglo American Corporation of
South Africa (the world's largest mining group)

Three central themes underpin effective scenario planning:

❑ It is important to clarify just what a business can and cannot change. Small farmers, for example, cannot enjoy the scale economies of large farms, nor can they affect the climate. They can, within reason, improve their soil, and they can change their crops.

❑ What seems trivial or a pipe-dream today could be crucial in the future. In 1874, Western Union in America turned down Alexander Graham Bell's prototype telephone!

❑ Multiple scenarios need to be explored and held as real possibilities. Shell, which pioneered scenario planning, is arguably ready to respond quickly to shocks which affect supply or prevailing prices.

British Airways: an application

BA believes that annual planning meetings (which are valuable and have a role to play) 'do not help people think about what might happen a decade from now'. Moreover, 'people have difficulty envisaging dramatic change'.

Consequently, BA has created two scenarios for the period to 2005, which it has used in management meetings to provoke discussion about the implications of possible changes. These are known as *Wild Gardens* and *New Structures*.

Wild Gardens postulates a world where market forces are unleashed. Asian markets in particular grow rapidly; and, early in the next century, after a period of strong growth, the US falls into a long recession. The 1996/7 general election in the UK is won for a fifth consecutive time by the Conservatives; the country remains divided over Europe. The EU is enlarged to bring in more Eastern countries, but there is no single currency. The European Commission takes over negotiation of airline agreements from member governments, and concludes an Atlantic open skies agreement which gives free access to transatlantic routes to carriers from both Europe and the USA. Access to domestic airports in Europe and the USA is widened.

The *New Structures* scenario is more stable, and gives greater control to individual governments. Asia's rise proves to be slower than initially anticipated, and Asian investment is reduced. Labour comes to power in the UK and joins France and Germany in promoting stronger European integration. A single currency (the Euromarque) is agreed, together with integrated air traffic control and a European high-speed rail network. There is increased commitment to the environment. President Clinton remains in power and reaches agreement with the Republicans to work together to increase investment and productivity. Taxes are increased; defence expenditure is reduced. North Korea provokes a security crisis in Asia and China suffers unrest after the death of Deng Xiaoping.

In discussions, BA managers believed that *New Structures* implied greater emphasis on ethical issues and customers who demand increased personal attention. *Wild Gardens* could mean English ceases to be **the** international language and that fluency in Asian languages would inevitably be more important. As outcomes:

❑ BA decided to trial interactive television screens in airport lounges, allowing travellers to raise issues with an employee whose face they can see

❑ BA is investigating a single database covering its customers around the world

❑ there are discussions with partner airlines, Qantas and US Air concerning the implications of Wild Gardens. Even if Asia develops more slowly, the language implications will not disappear.

Sources: Dickson, T (1995) Scenarios at the Ready, *Financial Times*, 5 May and Skapinker, M (1995) Plane talking, *Financial Times*, 24 February.

aeroplanes and the inflexible routes and schedules which are allocated by the Civil Aviation Authority. As a result the load factor becomes critical, and strategies must concentrate on ensuring that planes fly with as many seats filled as possible.

In a similar way it is crucial for hotels to fill their bedrooms as often as possible. This need is evidenced in the high promotional activity of many hotels and their desire to acquire conference trade in non-tourist seasons. Restaurants and other services help acquire business and achieve repeat stays, but the rooms must be used if overheads are to be met.

❏ Individual company success factors.

An obvious example is the Body Shop chain which now operates in over 40 countries and which has exploited a desire for natural cosmetics. It is, of course, a point of debate about how much of the demand has been created by the existence of the products and how much the products were introduced to meet a demand that already existed.

❏ Factors which appeal to particular customers and provide competitive advantage for an organization.

Success in a changing environment

Professor Roland Smith, ex-Chairman of British Aerospace, has argued that, whatever the industry, success lies in the management and marketing of innovation and risk (Smith, 1987). Innovation, he contends, is at the heart of marketing, and without innovation businesses become sterile and decline. In today's increasingly global environment the need for innovation is becoming stronger, because the sources of innovation world-wide, and hence the sources of competition, are more widespread than was the case 20 years ago. Smith cites the Far East in particular as a source of innovation. If UK organizations are to compete and grow they will need to be more entrepreneurial or change oriented and more willing to take risks. The relationship between innovation and entrepreneurship was introduced in Chapter 3 and will be explored in greater detail in Chapter 10.

Strategic leadership, according to Smith, will need to balance technical expertise with strategic and marketing insights, as high-quality research will need to complement an awareness of customer needs around the world. The speed of response to environmental changes, in particular to the actions of competitors, will be vital. There is already spare capacity in many industries, and hence no room to lag behind changes.

To be successful, companies must address four central themes:

❏ They must recognize that change is continuous. Change is all around us, it is fast-moving and accelerating and it will continue indefinitely.
❏ Strategy is fundamental. A business needs clear goals and a plan of how to reach them.
❏ There is a dependency on people. Committed and talented people are essential for superior performance.
❏ Leadership is essential at all levels.

Neville Bain, Group Chief Executive, Coats Viyella

In certain industries Japan has clearly set the competitive agenda for many years. But there are exceptions, such as computer software. To succeed here Japan would need to learn the kind of creative skills traditionally associated with the USA, and Silicon Valley in particular ...

The Japanese have seen the religion of creativity, just as we've seen the religion of total quality management. But the cultural factors inhibiting them are much more powerful. TQM is a mechanical process. You have to understand it, engineer it and instil it in your organization, and none of that is trivial. But it's not rocket science. Creative thinking is much more deep-seated.

Harvey Jones, CEO, Synopsis (a Californian software company)

Sadler (1988) suggests that successful organizations in the 1990s must be able to:

❑ deliver high levels of service to customers – 'service' here means the total package of product and associated services;
❑ use information and information technology both to improve efficiencies and to obtain competitive advantage;
❑ motivate and develop a knowledgeable workforce – 'knowledge and talent are emerging as the only scarce resources' and;
❑ manage cultural change.

Kanter (1991) has concluded that the leading competitive nations have different priorities for achieving competitive success, and that these differences stem from national cultures. Her research indicated the following priorities:

Japan	1. Product development
	2. Management
	3. Product quality

USA	1. Customer service
	2. Product quality
	3. Technology

Germany	1. Workforce skills
	2. Problem solving
	3. Management

Managing the environment

If an organization is to manage its environment it will seek to be proactive rather than reactive. To achieve this managers must clearly appreciate the relative importance of the various stakeholders, and seek to influence them rather than be predominantly influenced by them. An organization will never be able to predict everything that might happen and avoid ever having to react to unexpected events, but some will be more in control of the situation than their rivals, who might find themselves always responding to changes instituted by others.

Aware organizations will seek to ensure that their interests are appreciated and supported by their local authority and that their local Member of Parliament is supporting them wherever government policy might affect them;

they are active in the local community in a positive way; their employees are satisfied with wages and conditions of employment; industrial relations are more friendly than hostile; suppliers regard them as good reliable customers; and buyers regard them as competitive and reliable suppliers. In this situation it will be easier to implement changes when they become either desirable or necessary.

So far in this chapter we have considered the impact of environmental forces on the whole organization. In the case of organizations which are multi-product or multi-national the various forces may exert different influences upon particular business units and in different countries. Additionally individual functions within an organization will be affected by certain forces which have little impact on other areas of the business. It may well be necessary for the strategic leader to collate the information available concerning how the various stakeholders affect the various parts of the business in relation to the specific functions and business units, rather than in holistic or overall terms. If, for example, a major supplier to the organization has been acquired recently by one of the firm's competitors, this will have an impact on the particular business units which buy from this supplier. However, this may well become a corporate issue if, say, the strategic leader feels that it would be worthwhile considering the establishment of a closer relationship with an alternative supplier, perhaps through acquisition, merger or joint venture. If customer tastes for a particular product or service produced by the organization change favourably, perhaps because of innovation or the development of a new form of differentiation, or because of supply difficulties on the part of a competitor, the impact is most relevant for the competitive strategy of the product or business unit in question. The contribution of this part of the business can be expected to increase. There is correspondingly an impact upon the marketing function, as opportunities to increase market share may be provided if a new advertising campaign is launched.

Visit the website:
http://www.
itbp.com

It is important for managers to appreciate just where the greatest opportunities and threats lie at any time. Jauch and Glueck (1988) suggest that organizations might usefully examine the various forces along the lines of the map featured in Figure 8.3. The forces are each allocated a section of the circle and the extent to which the segment is shaded indicates the relative importance of the force at a particular time. The example represents a situation where the competitive sector is active and changing, with new entrants to the market and the need for strategic changes. There is greater focus on this sector than any other, indicated by the extent to which it is shaded. The cause lies mainly in new technologies which can be applied to the industry. The capital market is important because of the need for investment funding to utilize the technology. The supply situation is seen as stable, and the government is regarded as relatively unconcerned, perhaps because of the in-built competitiveness. This type of diagram is particularly useful for focusing attention on those areas which are currently affecting the organization and which require strategic attention.

Ideally changes in the environment will be seen more as opportunities for positive organizational change than as threats which force changes upon the organization which they were not ready for and which may be difficult to implement. Aware organizations will see changes as opportunities; others may see them as potential threats. Some companies may be unaware of environmental changes and be threatened to the extent that they are driven out of business. In 1987 legal practices were allowed to advertise in the UK for the first time. It was also made possible for them to use direct mail for promoting their services, to run seminars and to be present at exhibitions. Was this an opportunity or a threat? In addition independent conveyancers had been legalized, providing a new form of competition, particularly for those practices which rely heavily on property transactions. It has been suggested that the culture gap between the legal profession, which is essentially reactive, waiting for customers to bring business in, and marketing, which looks outwards and seeks both to create and to influence demand, could be a threat and an opportunity. Practices have responded differently, with some benefiting enormously and other less successful ones being acquired by more successful practices (Rock, 1987).

Ansoff's model

Ansoff (1987) contends that 'to survive and succeed in an industry, the firm must match the aggressiveness of its operating and strategic behaviours to the changeability of demands and opportunities in the market-place'. The extent to which the environment is changeable or turbulent depends on six factors:

❑ changeability of the market environment
❑ speed of change
❑ intensity of competition

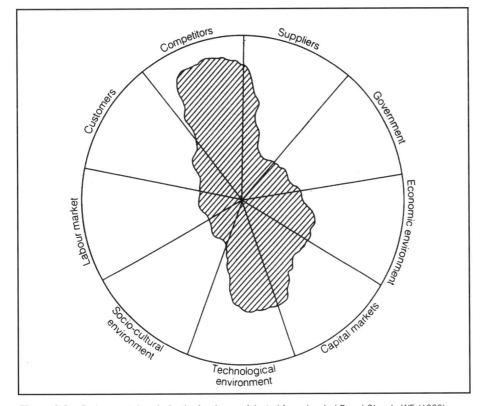

Figure 8.3   Environmental analysis: the focal zone. Adapted from Jauch, LR and Glueck, WF (1988) *Strategic Management and Business Policy*, 3rd edn, McGraw-Hill.

❏ fertility of technology
❏ discrimination by customers
❏ pressures from governments and influence groups.

Ansoff suggests that the more turbulent the environment is, the more aggressive the firm must be in terms of competitive strategies and entrepreneurialism or change orientation if it is to succeed. The firms in an industry will be distributed such that a small number are insufficiently aggressive for the requirements of the industry, and as a result they are unprofitable or go out of business. Another small number will be above average in terms of success because they are best able to match the demands of the environment. Many will achieve results about average; and some others may also fail because they are too aggressive and try to change things too quickly again through lack of awareness.

Where an organization is multi-product or multi-national the various parts of the business are likely to experience some common environmental influences and some which are distinctive, which reinforces the need for managers who are closest to the market and to competitors to be able to change things.

Ansoff suggests that the environment should be analysed in terms of competition and entrepreneurship or change. By attributing scores to various factors the degree of competitive and entrepreneurial turbulence can be calculated. The competitive environment is affected by market structure and profitability; the intensity of competitive rivalry and the degree of differentiation; market growth; the stage in the life of the products or services in question and the frequency of new product launches; capital intensity; and economies of scale. Certain of these factors, namely market growth, the stage in the life of the product and profitability, also help to determine the extent to which the environment is entrepreneurial. Changes in structure and technology, social pressures and innovation are also influential.

The culture of the organization and managerial competencies should then be examined to see whether they match and changed as appropriate if they do not. Again scores are attributed to various factors. Culture encompasses factors such as values, reaction and response to change and risk orientation. Problem-solving approaches, information systems, environmental forecasting and surveillance, and management systems are included in the competencies. He is really arguing that the resources of the organization and the values must be congruent with the needs of the environment.

Systems thinking

Checkland (1981) suggests that when organizations are considered as human activity systems the key issues are structure, emergent properties, communication and control. Essentially the organization is a collection of components or subsystems and as such can be most readily analysed by looking at structures based on functions or business units. These component parts interact, and decisions made in one part of the organization have effects which are felt more widely. Consequently if decision makers are able and encouraged to take a holistic view such that the implications of their decisions on others are considered, then there is likely to be greater integration between the parts. This becomes increasingly important where the component parts are interdependent. Although certain business units in an organization might be substantially independent, functions rarely are. Marketing decisions often affect production management, for example. Financial decisions and decisions concerning human resources may have widespread implications. To achieve the appropriate integration, communication and control systems are important. Emergent properties relate to behaviour that results from the way the component parts interact and behave and are 'properties which are only meaningful when attributed to the whole and not the parts'. Rivalries and co-operation result in particular decisions and behaviours which will differ from those which would emerge if departments or units were to consider themselves as being isolated. Ideally the emergent properties should result in synergy and therefore bring benefits to the organization.

The basic argument is that the organization is likely to be both reactive and proactive towards environmental forces in a more effective manner if resources internally are co-ordinated. This co-ordination requires awareness of the contribution of other departments and units and a commitment to helping them. A holistic or systemic organization-wide perspective rather than a narrower functional or divisional one is implied. Additionally a sense of common purpose is necessary rather than the pursuit of the personal objectives which were discussed in Chapter 5.

The relationship between environmental forces and internal resources is at the heart of Figure 8.4 which has been adapted from the Harvard Business

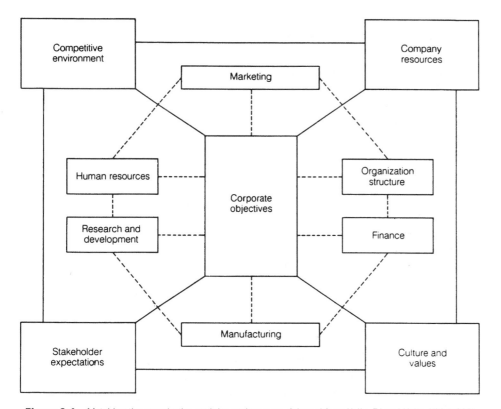

Figure 8.4 Matching the organization and the environment. Adapted from Kelly, FJ and Kelly, HM (1987) *What They Really Teach You at the Harvard Business School,* Piatkus.

School approach to strategy (Kelly and Kelly, 1987). The strategy statement framework included in Chapter 1 (Figure 1.11) showed resources and capabilities, products services and markets, and culture and values linked to corporate objectives and strategy. Figure 8.4 is essentially the same. The selected products, services and markets are environment driven and, here the competitive environment and stakeholders are shown with resources and values as four key strategic elements, again linked to corporate objectives. Resources should be viewed as strengths and weaknesses *relative* to those of competitors. These elements can be changed, but in many cases not readily and not quickly, and consequently at any point in time they are reasonably fixed.

Six operating elements are also incorporated. **Marketing** relates to how the various products and services are positioned in relation to competitors, and how they are priced, advertised and distributed. **Manufacturing** involves the types of production process, location issues and technology utilization. **Finance** incorporates both performance targets and sources of funding. **Research and development** considers how much to spend on research and development and whether the perspective is short or long term. **Human resources** relates to the types of people utilized and how they are rewarded. The **organization structure** encompasses how these functions are co-ordinated and controlled.

These operating elements determine whether or not the corporate objectives are achieved. It was mentioned earlier in this section that the different functions in the organization were affected to varying degrees by different stakeholders, and that certain stakeholders who have a significant impact on certain functions may have little direct importance for others. Equally the specific stakeholders may influence individual functions in quite different ways. Their impact upon the whole organization is therefore affected by the organization structure and relative power and influence within the firm. This table also highlights the strategic value of functional managers taking a more holistic view of the organization and their role and contribution.

The behaviour of the operating elements, together with any emergent properties, also influences the objectives attained, as explained in Chapter 5, Figure 5.3. Policies for each of the functions, and control systems built into the structure, may be relatively rigid or relatively flexible. The greater the flexibility the more opportunity there is for managers to effect changes and ensure that the organization responds to any perceived changes in environmental opportunities and threats. However, there is also more opportunity for managers to pursue personal objectives when policies are flexible. This reinforces the need for both strategic awareness and holistic or systemic thinking to ensure that there is some degree of commitment to a common purpose, the corporate objectives of the organization.

There is no doubt that the world is becoming one marketplace. Capital markets, products and services, management and manufacturing techniques have all become global in nature. As a result, companies increasingly find that they must compete all over the world – in the global marketplace.

Maurice Saatchi, when Chairman, Saatchi and Saatchi Company plc

The business environment for UK companies

Now that we have considered the relationship between an organization and its environment in a conceptual way, it is appropriate to look at specific changes affecting the UK business environment.

The global environment

Ohmae (1985) has described a number of changes which have taken place as industries and competition have become increasingly global in nature. Economies of scale, market shares and forms of differentiation must be considered in the light of the world market if competition stems from organizations based in different countries or from multi-national firms with plants in more than one country. However, as Box 8.2 shows, tastes and preferences can vary between countries, affecting the strategies of different competitors.

Where industries have become truly international, as is the case with cars, then organizations have developed inter-relationships and joint ventures. The joint venture between Rover and Honda whereby Rover has manufactured an essentially Japanese car under licence is one example. Similarly, Peugeot has supplied diesel engines to Chrysler; Volvo and Renault worked together for a number of years.

Late in 1995, Volvo and Mitsubishi opened a new plant in Holland where two different models would be produced together on one production line.

This issue will be explored in greater detail as a strategic option later. The effect has been that different countries have concentrated their research efforts on specific aspects of car design and thereby have become expert in, say, fuel

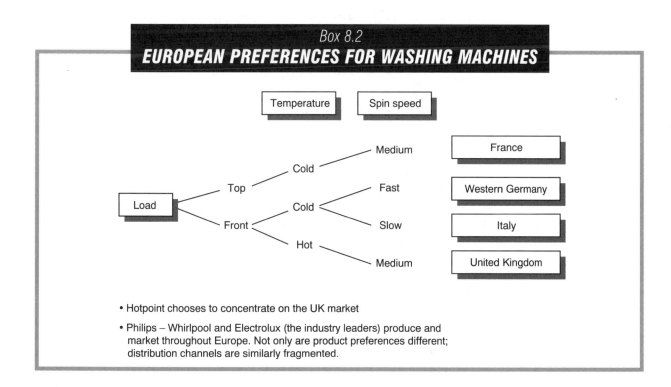

Box 8.2

EUROPEAN PREFERENCES FOR WASHING MACHINES

- Hotpoint chooses to concentrate on the UK market

- Philips – Whirlpool and Electrolux (the industry leaders) produce and market throughout Europe. Not only are product preferences different; distribution channels are similarly fragmented.

The world's changing. People in the US and Europe aren't going to live the way they do 100 years from now unless they do a lot of things differently. Who says that because we have 240 million people on this big piece of land [USA] we should have two cars and second homes, while 800 million people in India and 1 billion in China should live the way they live? We've only been wealthy in this country for 70 years. Who said we ought to have all this? Is it ordained?

John F. Welch, Chairman and CEO, General Electric

usage, electronics or ceramic engines. In a similar way different countries have concentrated their overall research and development expenditure on selected industries rather than attempting to cover everything. Ohmae suggests that Japan and Japanese businesses have concentrated on ceramics, automobiles and steel, plus electronics to a lesser extent; the USA on aerospace and electronics; West Germany on chemicals; and the UK on chemicals and aerospace. Defence electronics and pharmaceuticals might also be added to the UK list. These concentrations have led to positions of power or dominance in the different industries. Ohmae specifically comments that the UK has not invested as heavily in automobiles and machine tools, both of which have undergone a relative decline. Where research expenditure is limited or specialized UK companies are likely to concentrate on specific market segments rather than maintaining a broad presence in world industries and markets.

Parallel with this has been a gradual switch from steel-based industries to electronics-based industries and the emergence of Japan as a major international competitor. Ohmae argues the existence of a business triad of the USA, Europe and Japan as inter-dependent developed commercial nations which must seek to work together. Other areas of the world, Latin America, Africa and Asia, are still developing industrially and are behind the triad. However, for this reason they often enjoy lower labour costs which pose a threat.

Not only have electronics-based industries replaced steel-based ones, some are now forecast to converge to create new industry definitions and, in turn, further upheaval. Telecommunications, computers and video may well join forces to create a single, global multi-media industry, serving many new markets. The time is forseen when consumers with wire-less, hand-held devices will be able to talk to each other, see each other in video images, exchange faxes and communicate directly with their computers.

As countries become richer and per capita incomes increase, demand and tastes change. Also when countries are relatively wealthy the markets for certain products become saturated and demand is transferred to newer items. Consequently new products such as video recorders and compact disc players to supplement existing televisions and hi-fi units were initially successful in the richest countries. Over time, and especially when prices came down through the experience curve effect, they spread into other countries. At any time, therefore, the market for a product may be reaching saturation level in one country, growing in a less rich country and just taking off in a poorer country. This has implications for the way that products with potentially international demand are marketed world-wide. Ohmae argues that the lag between the take-off times in different countries decreases continually, and therefore companies cannot simply aim to spread products around the world gradually and sequentially.

Whilst an international strategy of bringing the cheapest materials to the cheapest labour for manufacture before selling to the most expensive market seems to be logical, it may not happen. For one thing it can often be advantageous to be located close to markets; for another there may be benefits in capital intensity which uses few workers who are all very highly skilled and not available in certain developing countries.

Companies migrate over time, seeking locations where costs are lower or which are nearer to markets, depending on the benefits they are seeking. Numerous US, European and Japanese companies have opened plants in countries with cheaper labour in order to reduce costs, partly to obtain higher profit margins. They have also opened subsidiaries near to international markets, even though there may not be cost savings. When Nissan started building cars on Tyneside it was to provide ready access to the British and European markets. It required government pressure to ensure that British-made components comprise a certain percentage of the total input value and that the plant is not simply assembling components imported from cheap labour countries.

Examples of German companies which have moved production from Germany to low-cost labour countries in order to remain competitive include Daimler Benz (diesel engines to South Korea), Bosch (car loudspeakers to Mexico and Malaysia) and Siemens (car-wiring systems to Turkey and Czechoslovakia). BASF has switched its fertilizer manufacturing to Belgium to reduce costs. Case 8.3 evaluates Siemens' decision to locate a new semi-conductor factory in the UK.

Proactive strategic changes of this nature transform the nature of competition in a country and force a reaction from existing competitors, who need to concentrate on their own competitive advantage and also ensure that government is sufficiently protective. British companies that are affected also need to try and persuade British consumers to buy British goods; and this in turn requires that they are genuinely competitive in terms of design, quality, price and availability.

Visit the website: http://www.itbp.com

Capital intensity requires significant investment and access to capital markets. Furthermore it creates barriers to entry. Research and development expenditures, the cost of modern computer-controlled production facilities, the potential benefits from sophisticated information technology, the need to maintain a strong sales network around the world, and the need to advertise heavily to establish brand identity and differentiation all create barriers to entry. At the same time they increase fixed costs and make firms volume sensitive, thereby emphasizing the need for global marketing.

In a global company such as ours it is essential to have managers who think and operate internationally. International experience is a 'sine qua non' for anyone aspiring to top managerial posts. This is one of the key principles of our international guidelines on human resource policy.

International experience helps managers both professionally and personally as they work in a totally different business and cultural environment, use their skills at the 'sharp end' and adapt to unfamiliar circumstances. Facing the challenge of working abroad, learning new languages, living in unfamiliar societies – these mould character and are enriching experiences.

Hermann J. Strenger, Chairman of the Board of Management, Bayer AG, Leverkusen

Case 8.3
THE SIEMENS SEMICONDUCTOR PLANT

In August 1995 Siemens announced that it was to build the 'world's most advanced semi-conductor plant' on the outskirts of North Shields, Tyneside. The investment would total 1 billion Deutschmarks (almost a half million pounds sterling) and create 2000 jobs. The plant would produce high added value ASICS, application-specific integrated circuits, such as those used in multi-media applications in computers, digital mobile telephones and smart cards and for controlling air bags in cars. ASICS are not commodity products and consequently they are not part of the industry sector where 'copy and cut the price' prevails.

Why had Tyneside been chosen?

❑ national and local grants
❑ a flexible workforce who are willing to work a three-shift system seven days a week
❑ some relevant skills
❑ a proven track record; Nissan, Fujitsu (semi-conductors) and Samsung (electronics) have all established successful factories in the area
❑ the UK is not affected by the European Social Chapter, holding down the total costs
❑ four nearby universities provide a solid educational infrastructure.

Five 'losers' were clearly identified. First, Germany, Siemens' home base, simply because the costs were too high. Second, Silicon Glen in Scotland on the grounds that there were already 'too many' electronics firms competing for the skilled workforce, potentially pushing up costs again. Third, Ireland. An alternative site had been identified in Cork, alongside an established electrical and industrial complex. There were substantial grants available and the area had proved it can make semiconductors; Intel has a successful plant there. Fourth, Austria, next to Siemens' existing semiconductor plant. The area offered a suitable infrastructure, grants and a skilled workforce. Additionally the site was well-positioned for European-wide distribution. Finally, Portugal, which could provide grants and relatively cheap labour. However the infra-structure was limited, with a poor local supply network and a lack of key labour skills.

Within four months, Siemens had obtained planning permission, a local office, employees and building contractors. Work was underway. The company's challenge was to build a state-of-the-art plant quickly and efficiently, but, because of the pace of technological change, retain flexibility concerning the operational aspects for as long as possible.

British manufacturing industry in perspective

The Confederation of British Industry (CBI) (1991) highlighted that 'contrary to popular opinion, Britain's manufacturing industries made big strides throughout the 1980s, but, because they started so far behind their biggest competitors, they face another 10 year struggle – at least – to catch up'. Output rose 25% in ten years, and the UK's share of world exports began to rise after years of decline. Throughout the 1980s productivity rose faster than in any other country except Japan, partly because of an increased emphasis on quality, innovation and training. Nevertheless Britain's productivity still lags behind that of Germany, America and Japan; and the situation has been complicated by a world recession which resulted in overcapacity and reduced investment.

Dodsworth and Garnett (1987) comment that Britain's recovery from earlier recessions involved major problems and unusual opportunities, and argue that four crucial factors underlie the strategic changes which have taken place.

❑ Capacity has been reduced so much in certain industries that investment is not likely to take place on a scale which will return Britain's earlier market shares. Motor vehicles is one example of this.

❑ Companies in certain other industries are successful and profitable but concentrated only in specific sectors as a result of effective differentiation strategies. Textiles is an example, and as a result the country is a net importer of textiles.

❑ The UK has retained positions in declining industries more effectively than it has invested in new growth industries. The world economy has switched from steel-based to electronics-based industries but the UK has not been a leader.

❑ Internationally the UK does not have a reputation for being well organized in relation to markets and demand. Where this is the case organizations are more likely to be reactive to changes than proactive globally.

In considering the relative success of manufacturing companies in the UK it is important to distinguish between British companies and foreign-owned subsidiaries which compete in the same industries. Evidence suggests that, although improvements were taking place in British industry in the late 1980s and early 1990s, the lead was often coming from US and Japanese multinationals based here.

The changing environment in the United Kingdom

Rather than merely listing a number of environmental changes which have taken place in the UK, the following selective list has been applied to retailing to show something of the cause–effect relationship between environmental changes and organization strategies.

❑ *Political*: Changing policies concerning new shopping centre developments; tighter controls over certain products; new trading standards; the legalization of Sunday trading and extended opening hours.

❑ *Economic*: Generally increased purchasing power.

❑ *Social*: Increased car ownership and mobility for many; more knowledgeable consumers; changing population structure with more older people.

❑ *Technological*: Electronic point-of-sale systems in stores; electronic data inter-change links with suppliers; the growing potential for consumers to buy via IT rather than necessarily visiting stores.

The overall effects of these environmental forces and changes on retailing include the following:

❑ more competition
❑ more capital investment in new bigger stores, fixtures and fittings

---

In my experience, corporate life-threatening problems in large manufacturing companies have developed over a long period. These problems should never have been permitted to grow so large, but they were allowed to do so by top management who were lethargic and self-satisfied, who engaged in self-delusion and congratulated themselves on their exalted status. In short, the managements were the problem.

Eugene Anderson, ex-Chairman and Chief Executive, Ferranti International plc

- ❏ more merger activity, not all of which has succeeded (Asda merged with MFI for instance, but MFI was later bought back by its managers)
- ❏ increased concentration with fewer small shops
- ❏ innovation, such as Body Shop and Sock Shop sometimes linked to
- ❏ segmentation and specialization
- ❏ greater diversification of product ranges
- ❏ diversification overseas by such majors as Marks and Spencer and WH Smith, following the successful example of such companies as Benetton
- ❏ more professional management
- ❏ higher occupation costs (increased overheads) as a result of competition for prime sites
- ❏ increasing percentage of products with retailers' own brand names, as retailers have become increasingly powerful relative to their suppliers
- ❏ relative decline of the high street, replaced by out-of-town shopping centres.

In the 1990s customer care and high levels of service are increasingly important in the search for competitive advantage. This service is primarily delivered at branch level. The roles of branch managers and staff, which changed during the 1980s with the growth of information technology and centralized buying, continues to change. The major challenge for many large retailers lies in finding the right ways to empower, motivate and reward their branch staff, allowing them to use their initiative for improving service, without losing the efficiency benefits of the centralized systems.

Conclusion: competitive success

In many industries the competitive environment is dynamic and uncertain. Changes by any single competitor at any time impact on rival organizations who may be forced to react. Their reactions introduce further changes to the competitive environment, which may be in a state of perpetual flux. Figure 8.5 summarizes this idea, and the significance is debated at greater length in Chapter 9. Clearly some competitors will be more proactive than their rivals, attempting to *manage their competitive environment*; and some will be in a position to react more quickly and positively to threatening changes.

If companies are to out-perform their competitors they must first identify who they are and how and why they are successful. Organizations which appreciate the competitive structure of their industries and markets will be in a better position to clarify competitive threats and opportunities.

Competitive success requires organizations to control their costs and to differentiate their products and services in order to add value. A strategy of **cost leadership** necessitates the management of essential cost drivers (*efficiency*) and the avoidance of unnecessary costs, by eliminating product or service benefits which are not required for efficacy, and not seen as important by customers (*effectiveness*). **Differentiation** is achieved by concentrating on features which do matter to certain customer segments, if not to all customers, especially those features which competitors cannot copy easily, and for which customers will pay a premium price (*effectiveness*). At the same time it is important to manage the operations *efficiently*.

These themes are the subject of the next chapter.

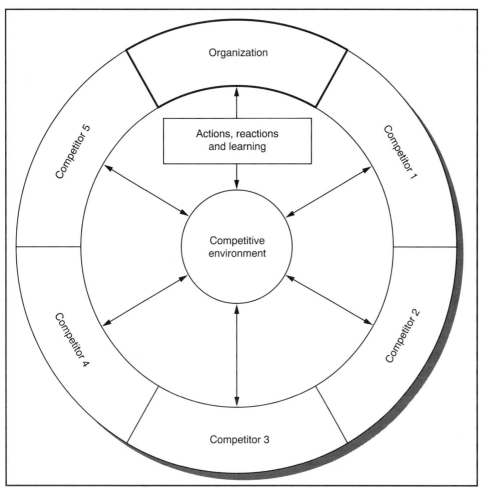

Figure 8.5 Dynamic competition.

Summary

In this chapter we emphasized the importance of analysing the environment in terms of opportunities and threats and the need for managers in organizations to seek to manage their environment as well as understand how the organization is influenced. This requires matching the organization's resources and values with the environment.

Specifically we have:

- considered the complex, dynamic and uncertain aspects of the environment, and how changes might be forecast
- introduced the concept of the organization as part of an open system whereby environmental forces impact upon the organization and in turn the organization can seek to influence or manage the environment, with functions within the organization seen as inter-dependent sub-systems whose inter-relationships create emergent properties
- reviewed the concept of key success factors, and looked at those factors which affect all competitors in an industry, those which can lead to the achievement of competitive advantage for individual companies and those which could be important for a variety of industries in the future
- considered the need to evaluate the relative power of different stakeholders in terms of managing the environment, and used the idea of the focal zone diagram for this
- briefly described Ansoff's model which aims to match resources with the dynamics of the environment
- emphasized that the various influences and stakeholders may not affect every business unit or function in the organization in quite the same way, making it important for managers to take a holistic view of the whole firm
- considered current changes taking place in the international and UK environment.

Checklist of key terms and concepts

You should feel confident that you understand the following terms and ideas:

★ The organization as part of an open system

★ SWOT analysis
★ Key success factors
★ Scenario planning.

Questions and research assignments

Questions and research assignments
Text related

1 Draw a diagram incorporating the environmental influences and stakeholders for one of the pubs featured in the Bruce's Brewery case (Chapter 3, Case 3.4). Do the same for London Zoo (Chapter 5, Case 5.2).

2 Evaluate the threats and opportunities faced by any organization with which you are familiar.

3 From this evaluation, develop a SWOT analysis and consider the strategic implications.

4 Possibly in a group discussion build a scenario relevant for the motor vehicle industry in ten years time. How will people be using their cars? What will they expect in terms of size, performance and external and interior design?

Library based

5 How have changes in competition from around the world affected the UK footwear industry? What are the strategies of the leading, remaining manufacturers?

You may wish to focus on C & J Clark and British Shoe Corporation as well as one or more specialist manufacturers. You might also investigate the source of your personal wardrobe of shoes, boots and trainers.

6 In 1991 Thames Television lost its franchise to broadcast services in the London area. As a result, it has had to re-think its strategies in order to survive. Investigate the background to this event and Thames' reactions and subsequent success.

Recommended further reading

Environmental analysis usually constitutes one topic in every text on strategic management, and few books concentrate exclusively on this subject area. However, Freeman, RE (1984) *Strategic Management*, Pitman, provides a useful analysis of strategic decisions from the point of view of stakeholders.

Lynch, R (1990), *European Business Strategies,* Kogan Page, describes the development of several large European companies.

References

Ansoff, HI (1987) *Corporate Strategy*, Penguin.

Checkland, PB (1981) *Systems Thinking, Systems Practice*, John Wiley.

Confederation of British Industry (1991) *Competing with the World's Best,* CBI.

Dodsworth, T and Garnett, N (1987) British manufacturing: a wealth of contradictions, *Financial Times,* 23 November.

Duncan, R (1972) Characteristics of organizational environments and perceived environmental uncertainty, *Administrative Science Quarterly*, 313–27.

Fahey, L and King, R (1983) Environmental scanning for corporate planning. In *Business Policy and Strategy: Concepts and Readings*, 3rd edn (eds D J McCarthy *et al.*), Irwin.

Handy, C (1989) *The Age Of Unreason*, Hutchinson.

Hogarth, RM and Makridakis, S (1981) Forecasting and planning: an evaluation, *Management Science*, **27**, 115–38.

Jauch, LR and Glueck, WF (1988) *Strategic Management and Business Policy*, 3rd edn, McGraw-Hill.

Kanter, RM (1991) Transcending business boundaries: 12,000 world managers view change, *Harvard Business Review*, May–June.

Kelly, FJ and Kelly, HM (1987) *What They Really Teach You at the Harvard Business School,* Piatkus.

Mintzberg, H (1987) Crafting strategy, *Harvard Business Review,* July–August.

Ohmae, K (1985) *Triad Power: The Coming Shape of Global Competition,* Free Press.

PA Consulting Group and the Confederation of British Industry (1988) *UK Productivity – Closing the Gap*, PA Consulting Group, London, September.

Rock, S (1987) The law learns to solicit for business, *The Director*, November.

Sadler, P (1988) *Managerial Leadership in the Post Industrial Society*, Gower.

Smith, R (1987) The marketing challenge, *First,* **1**(2).

Wilson, IH (1977) Forecasting social and political trends. In *Corporate Strategy and Planning* (eds B Taylor and J Sparkes), Heinemann.

9

The Competitive Environment and Competitive Advantage

In this chapter we analyse the nature of the competitive environment by considering the structure of industry in the UK and the regulation of competition by government; and by exploring the concept of competitive advantage in greater detail. The need to understand the competitive environment and to seek opportunities to strengthen competitiveness is paramount for every business.

Learning objectives

After studying this chapter you should be able to:

- explain the notion of strategic life cycles and the importance of timing
- define industrial concentration and describe the structure of industries in the UK
- construct an experience curve and explain its significance
- summarize the competition policy of the UK government
- analyse two analytical models designed by Michael Porter relating to industry structure and competitive advantage
- define product differentiation
- explain the linkage between cost structures, break even and profits
- show how an organization can evaluate its competitive strategies against those of its competitors.

Don't forget to visit the website: http://www.itbp.com

In Chapter 1 we said that strategy is 'all about competitive advantage ... the sole purpose of strategic management is to enable the company to gain, as effectively as possible, a sustainable edge over its competitors' (Ohmae, 1982). In the main part of this chapter we shall consider what is meant by 'doing well' in relation to competitors and look at how one might evaluate the nature of an industry. From this we shall examine how competitive strategies might be developed.

It is important here to reinforce that **corporate strategy** refers to the range of products and services offered by an organization, and the number of different industries and markets in which it competes. The company should aim to develop a distinctive competitive advantage in every area of activity. These constitute **competitive strategies**. Corporate competitiveness can sometimes be enhanced by synergy (see Key Concept II.1), and by transferring skills, sharing activities and creating effective linkages between the parts of the organization responsible for the different products and services.

When considering the appropriateness of current strategies and the need for change, managers must take account of the passage of time if their decisions are to be effective. Environmental pressures may mean that the organization needs to act quickly in response to some opportunity or threat. Equally a strategy that has been successful in the past may no longer be appropriate. This issue will be considered early in the chapter. There is a brief look at the overall business structure of the UK, and at government control of the competitive environment. Both these factors present opportunities and threats to individual organizations.

Competition: an introduction

According to Michael Porter (1980) effective strategic management is the positioning of an organization, relative to its competitors, in such a way that it outperforms them. Marketing, operations and personnel, in fact all aspects of the business, are capable of providing a competitive edge – an advantage which leads to superior performance and superior profits for profit-oriented firms.

Two aspects of the current position of an organization are important: (1) the nature and structure of the industry and (2) the position of the organization within the industry.

1. The number of firms, their sizes and relative power, the ways they compete, and the rate of growth must be considered. An industry may be attractive or unattractive for an organization. This will depend upon the prospects for the industry and what it can offer in terms of profit potential and growth potential. Different organizations have different objectives, and therefore where it is able an organization should be looking to compete in industries where it is able to achieve its objectives. In turn its objectives and strategies are influenced by the nature of the industries in which it does compete. Porter has developed a model for analysing the structure of an industry. This is examined later in the chapter.
2. The position of a firm involves its size and market share, how it competes, whether it enjoys specific and recognized competitive advantage, and whether it has particular appeal to selected segments of the market.

An effective and superior organization will be in the right industry and in the right position within that industry. Obviously, an organization is unlikely to be successful if it chooses to compete in a particular industry because it is an attractive industry which offers both profit and growth potential but for which the organization has no means of obtaining competitive advantage. Equally a company should not concentrate only on creating competitive advantage without assessing the prospects for the industry. With competitive advantage a company can be profitable in an unattractive industry, but there may be very few growth opportunities if the industry is growing at a slower rate than the economy generally. Much depends upon objectives and expectations.

In the economy profit is the reward for creating value for consumers; and in individual businesses profits are earned by being more successful than competitors in creating and delivering that value. Profit may or may not be an end in itself, but profits are important for achieving other objectives and for helping finance growth. We showed (Chapter 6) that the profit remaining after interest and tax can be paid in dividends or re-invested in the firm. Obviously a firm will be healthier in the long run if it can invest as it wishes and finance the investments without building up too substantial a debt. In the same way a not-for-profit organization may not have a profit-oriented mission, but it must generate revenue to stay viable and a surplus over expenditure to develop the organization.

The most successful competitors will

❑ create value
❑ create competitive advantage in delivering that value and
❑ operate the business effectively and efficiently.

For above-average performance all three are required. It is possible to run a business well – efficiently – but never create competitive advantage. Certain products and services may have competitive advantage and yet be produced by organizations that are not run well. In both, potential is not fully exploited. Moreover, competitive advantage must be sustained. A good new product, for example, may offer the consumer something new, something different, and thus add value. But if it is easily imitated by competitors there is no sustainable competitive advantage. For example, Freddie Laker pioneered cheap transatlantic air travel but went out of business in the face of competition and management weaknesses.

In my experience sustaining competitive advantage, rather than creating it initially, presents the real challenge. Competitive advantage cannot be sustained for ever and probably not for very long without changes in products, services and strategies which take account of market demand, market saturation and competitor activity. People's tastes change, the size of markets is limited not infinite, and competitors will seek to imitate successful products, services and strategies. Competitive advantage can be sustained by constant innovation. Companies that are change oriented and seek to stay ahead of their competitors through innovatory ideas develop new forms of advantage. Case 9.1 considers how Coca-Cola retains global leadership of the soft drinks market.

The importance of timing

Products and services have finite lives, and broadly speaking they follow a life-cycle pattern. Strategies also have life cycles. Strategies which deliver value and competitive advantage will bring benefits to the organization in terms of success, growth and profits. However, if consumer preferences change, and the factors creating the advantage are no longer perceived as valuable, the advantage is lost. A change of competitive strategy is required. Similarly if the advantage is cost based and the factors generating the cost advantage change, such that the advantage is lost, a new strategy is required. Again any advantage is potentially vulnerable to copying or improvements in some way by competitors, particularly if it is seen to be generating success.

Referring back to E–V–R congruence, at times particular strategies reflect a congruence between resources and the environment. However, demand can change, or investment resources to strengthen competitive advantage may not be available. The congruence may disappear and withdrawal or divestment may well be appropriate.

Towards the end of 1992 it was being claimed that Porsche sports cars had become 'an extravagance which increasingly few people are able to afford'. Sales were around half those of the mid-1980s. Production costs had to be slashed and the company rationalized. Fortunately Porsche was a family company with no debt and a strong cash base; it was therefore able to survive on its reserves until a new range of sports models was ready (in 1996). Referring back to the Sigmoid curve (Figure 1.8), Porsche's timing was flawed; it was not ready to change at the most appropriate time.

Although it is typically priced higher than many competing products, Coca-Cola remains the world's best-selling soft drink. The Coca-Cola company was founded over 100 years ago, and today it remains largely focused; Columbia Pictures was acquired some years ago, but later sold to Sony. Seventy per cent of Coke's sales and 80% of its operating profits are now earned outside the USA. The company has a 45% share of the world market for carbonated drinks, some 40% of the US market and 50% on average of markets outside the USA.

Over the years critics have predicted that something would happen to stem the continual and successful growth of the business, possibly changing tastes, stronger competition or market saturation. This has not happened; Coca-Cola has continued to increase world-wide sales through clever marketing and occasional new products. In 1996 Coca-Cola was America's most admired company in the *Fortune* rankings. In terms of increases in shareholder wealth, Coca-Cola has been unrivalled in the USA throughout the leadership of the present chief executive, Roberto Goizueta. Goizueta has been the strategic leader since 1981. Nevertheless, Coca-Cola has made a number of strategic misjudgements.

Competitive strategies

Coke had successfully established Fanta (the fizzy orange drink launched in 1960) and Tab (sugar-free Coca-Cola, 1963) when Goizueta took over. In 1982 Diet Coke was launched. Diet products are particularly important for the American market, but generally less significant elsewhere. However, in 1985, New Coke was launched to replace the original blending, but subsequently withdrawn after a consumer outcry. The Fresca range has also been launched.

Coke became popular overseas when it was shipped out to GIs during World War II, and systematically it has been introduced to more and more countries. Soft drinks are very much a local product. *I'd love for the Chinese to arrive in New York and say: My goodness, they have Coca-Cola here too* (Goizueta).

Coca-Cola control production of the concentrated syrup from Atlanta; mixing, bottling/canning and distribution is franchised to independent businesses world-wide. Goizueta inherited a distribution network which was underperforming and he set about strengthening it with proper joint venture agreements and tight controls. Effective supply management is absolutely vital for the business.

Coca-Cola has always advertised heavily and prominently; and Goizueta has also negotiated a number of important promotional agreements. Coca-Cola have special aisles in Wal-Mart stores; Coke's Hi-C orange juice is supplied to McDonald's, for example. In recent years there has been increased emphasis on branding and packaging at the expense of pure advertising. *We had really lost focus on who our customer was. We felt our customer was the bottler, as opposed to the McDonald's and the Wal-Marts* (Goizueta).

Faced with increased competition from retail own-label brands sold mainly through supermarket chains, Coca-Cola has carefully defended and strengthened its other distribution outlets such as convenience stores, fast-food restaurants and vending machines.

Competition

Coca-Cola's main rival is Pepsi Cola, which has a 30% share of the US market and 20% of the world market. Its share has been growing since the 1993 introduction of Pepsi Max, a sugar-free product with the taste of the original Pepsi. Pepsi is diversified into snack foods (Frito-Lay in the USA, Walkers and Smiths crisps in the UK) and restaurants (Pizza Hut, Taco Bell and Kentucky Fried in the USA); just one third of global profits come from soft drinks. Pepsi also owns much of its bottling network. In 1996 the Pepsi brand was relaunched with a massive international promotional campaign. The new Pepsi colours, predominantly blue, were chosen to appeal to the younger buyer. Also significant is Cott of Canada, which produces discounted colas with acceptable alternative tastes. Cott produces concentrate for Wal-Mart in the USA and for Sainsbury and Virgin in the UK.

The two classic cases from the 1960s, featured in Case 9.2, involve well-known companies which also illustrate the above point extremely well. Although dated they are still relevant examples.

One further message in these examples is that all strengths are potential weaknesses. Both Tizer and Lesney had failed to appreciate when the effective life of a particular strategy was coming to an end, as much as anything because it had proved so successful in the past. As a result the strategy became a weakness.

The dynamic, competitive environment

Causes generate effects. Actions lead to outcomes. On occasions companies may attempt to seize the competitive initiative and introduce an innovatory change. An action by one competitor which affects the relative success of rivals provokes responses. One action can therefore provoke several reactions, depending upon the extent of the impact and the general nature of competition. Each reaction in turn further affects the other rival competitors in the industry. New responses will again follow. What we have in many markets and industries is a form of

---

Case 9.2
TIZER AND LESNEY: THE IMPORTANCE OF STRATEGIC LIFE CYCLES

Tizer

Tizer was some 30 years old in the 1960s and it had become successful by producing its well-known fizzy drink in a number of regional plants and selling it direct to small corner shops and off-licences. Van driver salesmen collected returnable empty bottles as they sold new ones. But customer shopping habits were changing with the growth of self-service stores and supermarkets; corner shops were in decline. In addition breweries were acquiring off-licences and insisting that they stocked only brewery products. The new retailers were often part of a national chain with central rather than local buying. In addition, returnable bottles were seen as out-dated. Tizer's strategy, which had brought success to the company, was no longer appropriate; change was needed.

Lesney

Lesney was one of the fastest growing companies in the UK in the 1960s as a result of the success of Matchbox toys. Large quantities of the small die-cast scale models of cars were produced cost effectively by using sophisticated production equipment and systems. They were priced very competitively and distributed widely through a variety of outlets rather than only toy shops. Buyers collected them, purchasing new models when they were introduced. Lesney was so busy meeting demand that they failed to innovate. An American competitor, Mattel, saw an opportunity based on how children played with the cars, and introduced a range of small cars with friction-free wheels on plastic bearings. These cars rolled further when pushed; they behaved differently in use and allowed such things as looping-the-loop. Mattel charged 30p for their cars (Matchbox cost $12\frac{1}{2}$p) and they sold. Lesney's competitive strategy, similar to that of Tizer, was no longer appropriate and it needed replacement. Lesney succeeded in responding to the competition, but early in the 1980s they went into receivership. As with many UK toy producers they had been unable to withstand foreign competition.

These examples have been developed from the Tizer (A) case, written by JM Stopford and P Edmonds, and the Lesney Products and Company Ltd (A) case, written by CJ Constable. Copies of both cases are available from the European Case Clearing House, Cranfield.

competitive chaos, a competitive business environment which is permanently fluid and unpredictable. For example, the Post Office continues to experience new forms of competition from cheaper telephone calls, courier services and fax machines; it must adapt and respond to defend its place in the market.

This dynamism is illustrated in Figure 9.1. It is important to differentiate between two sets of similar, but nevertheless different, decisions. First, some

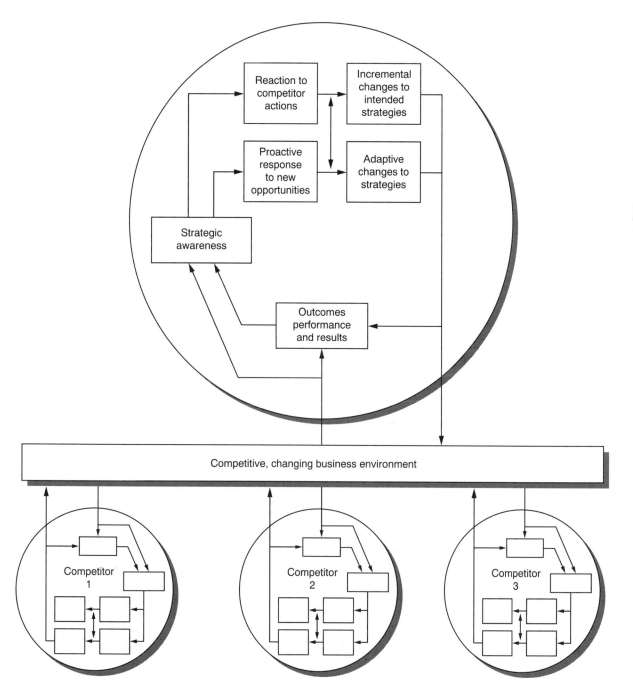

Figure 9.1 Strategic change in a competitive environment.

actions are innovatory and represent one competitor acting upon a perceived opportunity ahead of its rivals; other actions constitute reactions to these competitive initiatives. Second, some decisions imply **incremental change** to existing, intended strategies; on different occasions companies are adapting their strategies (**adaptive change**) as they see new opportunities which they can seize early, or possible future threats which they are seeking to avoid. The process is about *learning and flexibility.*

The skills required by organizations are:

❑ the ability to discern patterns in this dynamic environment and competitive chaos, and spot opportunities ahead of their rivals;
❑ the ability to anticipate competitor actions and reactions;
❑ the ability to use this intelligence and insight to lead customer opinion and out-perform competitors.

Post-It notes are one instance where a manufacturer, 3M, 'knew' there was a demand before consumers realized it themselves. This awareness and insight clearly requires more than simple market research.

Ocean Spray has been cited by Rosabeth Moss Kanter (1990) as another US company which spotted a potentially lucrative competitive opportunity missed by its rivals. Small 'paper bottles' for soft drinks were being used in Europe, but the leading US manufacturers did not see them taking off in America and were not enthusiastic. Ocean Spray, who manufacture a range of products, including drinks, from cranberries (sometimes mixed with other fruits) had empowered a middle manager from *engineering* to look for new ideas for the company – an aspect of their planned strategy – and he saw the potential. The result was an 18-month exclusive rights agreement. The packaging concept proved attractive and the final outcome was a substantial increase in the popularity of cranberry juice drinks. Simply children liked the package and came to love the drink. Ocean Spray products are now much more evident around the world.

The Ocean Spray example illustrates how competition can come from un-expected sources. It is dangerous for any organization to assume that future competitive threats will only come from rivals, products and services they already know and understand; in reality, it can be the unrecognized, unexpec-ted newcomers which pose the real threat, because, in an attempt to break into an established market, they may introduce some new way of adding value and 'rewrite the rules of competition'.

Bill Gates' 'view of the future', based on personal computers on every desk, was radically different from that of long-time industry leader, IBM, and it enabled Microsoft to enter and dominate the computer industry. British Air-ways was surprised by the entry and success of Virgin Atlantic Airways on profit-able trans-Atlantic routes, as it perceived its main competition to come from the leading US carriers. Virgin was adding new values, offering high and differ-

Visit the website: http://www. itbp.com

One advantage when you're No. 1 or 2 in an industry is that you can really have a hell of a lot of say in what the future's going to be like by what you do. I'm not a believer in always forecasting the future. But if you take actions that can create that future, at least shape it, then you can benefit from it.

Roberto Goizueta, Chief Executive Officer, Coca-Cola Corporation

entiated levels of service at very competitive prices. The success of Direct Line, with telephone insurance services at very competitive prices, has provoked a response from existing companies; telephone banking is having a similar effect. In both cases the nature of the service has been changed dramatically – and improved for many customers.

Competition and the structure and regulation of industry in the United Kingdom

The four economic models of pure or perfect competition, monopolistic competition, oligopoly and monopoly were introduced in Chapter 5, when it was pointed out that the opportunity for substantial profits was most likely to be found in oligopoly and monopoly structures. Competition in the other models, resulting mainly from lower barriers to entry, has the effect of reducing profit margins. It is now useful to consider which models are dominant in the UK as this influences the ways firms compete. Specifically it affects the opportunities for differentiation and for the achievement of cost advantages which, as will be seen later in this chapter, are major determinants of competitive advantage.

Monopoly power

Also later in this chapter we shall consider the role of government in monitoring, policing and controlling competition. It is important to point out here that as far as the regulatory authorities are concerned a 25% market share offers opportunities for a company to exploit monopoly power. Hence, although the model of pure monopoly assumes only one producer with absolute power in the marketplace, a large producer with a substantial share will be regarded as having monopoly power. It does not follow that such power will be used against the consumer; on the contrary it can be to the consumer's advantage. Large companies with market shares in excess of their rivals may be able to produce at lower cost for any one of several reasons including the ability to invest in high output, low unit cost technology; the ability to buy supplies in bulk and receive discounts; the ability to achieve distribution savings; and the opportunity to improve productivity as more and more units are produced. In fact savings are possible in every area of the business. Economists call these savings economies of scale, and they are related to the notion of the experience or learning curve which is explained in Key Concept 9.1.

A cost advantage, then, can be a major source of competitive advantage, and this point will be developed in greater detail later. The producer who is able to produce at a lower cost than his or her rivals may choose to price very competitively with a view to driving competitors out of the market and thereby increasing market share. Equally he or she may not; and by charging a higher price can make a greater profit per unit and thereby seek profit in preference to market share. In the first case the consumer benefits from lower prices and therefore monopoly power is not being used against the consumer. However, once a firm has built up a truly dominant market share it might seek to change its strategy and exploit its power more. This is when government needs to intervene in some way.

The experience curve

A large size, relative to competitors, can bring benefits. In particular, if a company has a market share substantially greater than its competitors it has opportunities to achieve greater profitability. Lower costs can be achieved if the company is managed well and takes advantage of the opportunities offered by being larger. These lower costs can be passed on to the consumer in the form of lower prices, which in turn puts pressure on competitors' profit margins and strengthens the position of the market leader.

Lower costs are achieved through economies of scale and the experience or learning effect. In the 1960s the Boston Consulting Group in the USA estimated that the cost of production decreases by between 10% and 30% each time that a company's experience in producing the product or service doubles as long as the company is managed well. In other words as cumulative production increases over time there is a potential cost reduction at a predictable rate. The company learns how to do things better. The savings are spread across all value-added costs: manufacturing, administration, sales, marketing and distribution. In addition the cost

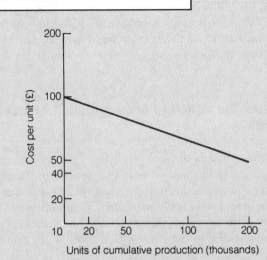

Exhibit 2 The same 85% experience curve plotted in log-log form.

of supplies decreases as suppliers experience the same learning benefits.

The experience effect has been observed in high and low technology industries, in new and mature industries, in both manufacturing and service businesses, and in relation to consumer and industrial markets. Specific examples are cars, semi-conductors, petrochemicals, long distance telephone calls, synthetic fibres, airline transportation, crushed limestone and the cost of administering life insurance.

The experience curve is illustrated by plotting on a graph the cumulative number of units produced over time (the horizontal axis) and the cost per unit (the vertical axis). Exhibit 1 does this. This particular curve is called an '85% experience curve' as every time output is doubled the cost per unit falls to 85% of what it was. In reality the plot will be of a least squares line but the trend will be clear. However, it is more common to plot the data on logarithmic scales on both axes, and this shows the straight line effect illustrated in Exhibit 2.

Sources of the experience effect

❏ Increased labour efficiency through learning and consequent skills improvement
❏ The opportunity for greater specialization in production methods
❏ Innovations in the production process
❏ Greater productivity from equipment as people learn how to use it more efficiently
❏ Improved resource mix as products are redesigned with cost savings in mind

This is not an exhaustive list, and the savings will not occur naturally. They result from good management.

(Continued overleaf)

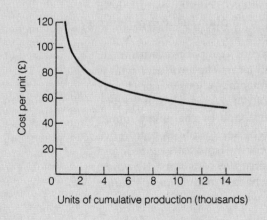

Exhibit 1 An 85% experience curve plotted on a normal scale.

Pricing decisions and the experience effect

A market leader or other large producer who enjoys a cost advantage as a result of accumulated experience will use this as the basis for a pricing strategy linked to his or her objectives, which might be profit or growth and market share oriented. Exhibit 3 illustrates one way that industry prices might be forced down (in real terms, after accounting for inflation) as the market leader benefits from lower costs. Initially prices are below costs incurred because of the cost of development. As demand, sales and production increase prices fall, but at a slower rate than costs; the producer is enjoying a higher profit margin. This will be attractive to any competitors or potential competitors who feel that they can compete at this price even if their costs are higher. If competition becomes intensive and the major producer(s) wish to assert authority over the market they will decrease prices quickly and force out manufacturers whose costs are substantially above theirs. Stability might then be restored.

Companies with large market shares can therefore dictate what happens in a market, but there is a need for caution. If a company ruthlessly chases a cost advantage via the experience effect the implication could be ever increasing efficiency as a result of less flexibility. The whole operating system is geared towards efficiency and cost savings. If demand changes or competitors innovate unexpectedly the strategy will have run out of time as we have already seen. Companies should ensure that they are flexible enough to respond.

This material has mainly been summarized from Abell, DF and Hammond, JS (1979) *Strategic Market Planning: Problems, and Analytical Approaches*, Prentice-Hall.

Exhibit 3 is adapted from *Perspectives on Experience*, The Boston Consulting Group, 1972.

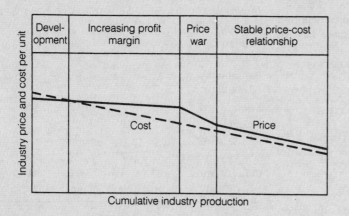

| Development | Increasing profit margin | Price war | Stable price-cost relationship |

Industry price and cost per unit

Cost

Price

Cumulative industry production

Exhibit 3 Pricing in relation to costs and the experience effect.

Concentration

Concentration is the measure of control exercised by organizations. There are two types.

Aggregate concentration, which we shall mention only briefly, considers the power of the largest privately owned manufacturing firms in the economy as a whole.

Sectoral or market concentration traditionally considers the percentage of net output or employment (assets, sales or profits can also be measured) controlled by the largest firms in a particular industry, be it manufacturing or

---

It is not acceptable for those in charge of companies trading worldwide simply to be better than their UK rivals. In all the areas that matter – research and development, product quality, price and after-sales service and support – we have to be better than our best *international* competitors. For me, that also means we have to be able to succeed in Japan.

Sir David Plastow, when Chairman and Chief Executive, Vickers plc. (Historically Vickers have manufactured Rolls Royce cars as well as defence products.)

Box 9.1
FOUR CONCENTRATED INDUSTRIES

1 Trainers and Sports Shoes

In recent years this has been the fastest growing sector of the global footwear industry, driven by creative marketing and product development which has encouraged people to pay high prices for perceived high added value, differentiated, fashionable products. Manufacturers have been innovative (air pumps), they have clinically segmented the market by designing specialized products (running shoes, tennis shoes, basketball shoes), and obtained celebrity endorsements from sporting superstars. At the same time they have reduced their costs by establishing production in low labour cost countries in the Far East, Eastern Europe and South America.

Global market shares in 1993 (in percent) were:-

Nike	24.1	
Reebok	19.1	53.5
Adidas	10.3	

Seven companies each had a share between 2.5% and 5%, leaving 20% for a large number of smaller companies.

2 Batteries

The popularity of portable stereo systems and games machines and the increasing sales of products such as smoke alarms means some half billion batteries are sold each year in the UK. The market comprises the standard zinc batteries (such as Ever Ready Silver Seal) which account for over one-third of sales; long-life alkaline batteries (Duracell and Ever Ready Energizer) which account for some 60% and are growing at the expense of zinc batteries. Rechargeable NiCad batteries constitute a very small percentage.

The leading companies are Duracell (American) and Ever Ready, sold recently to Ralston Purina of the USA by Hanson. Rayovak Vidor is the only British manufacturer remaining. Vidor manufacture retailer own-label batteries, as do Varta of Germany and Philips, who produce for IKEA and Sainsbury's.

UK market shares in 1993:

	Total	Zinc	Alkaline
Duracell	30	–	51
Ever Ready	26	49	20
Other known brands	29	41	18
Retail own-label	15	10	11

Duracell first became the overall market leader in 1993, but its 51% share of the growth sector in the market reinforces its overall strength.

3 Soups

UK Market Shares in 1993 (in percent) were as follows:

	Total	Canned	Instant mixes	Packet/ bowl soups
Heinz (American)	39	57		
Batchelors (Unilever, Anglo-Dutch)	10		40	25
Campbells (Canadian)	7	10		
Knorr	7		18	43
Baxters	7	10		
Crosse and Blackwell (Nestlé)	2	2		6
Other Brands	7	4	12	1
Own Label	20	17	30	25

Canned soups account for 69% of the total market, instant mixes 18% and packet/bowl soups 10%. The final 3% comprises the growing fresh chilled segment, dominated at the moment by the New Covent Garden Soup company.

4 Chocolate

Three companies dominate the market in the UK, Cadbury, Nestlé-Rowntree, and Mars, with shares of 29, 26 and 21% respectively (1994). Cadbury, who own Trebor, Bassett, Pascall and Murray, also lead the confectionery market, and through Schweppes are an important player in the soft drinks market. Nestlé-Rowntree, whose Kit Kat product is the leading brand, is an international food conglomerate; Mars (US) is the dominant company in the pet foods market.

The fourth company, with a 5% share, is Terry's Suchard, owned by Philip Morris, whose other brands include Marlboro cigarettes, Miller Beer and Maxwell House coffee.

service. High concentration figures tend to encourage monopoly or oligopoly behaviour, most probably the latter, which implies substantial emphasis on differentiation and non-price competition, with rivals seeing themselves as inter-dependent.

In Box 9.1 we examine three industries which exhibit high concentration ratios and consider the importance of diversification and market segments. There may well be marketing and distribution advantages for companies which belong to conglomerates and this could increase their relative market power. Similarly products which dominate particular market segments will yield advantages.

Many industries in the UK are essentially oligopolistic in structure, with a limited number of major competitors and barriers to entry.

Generally competition will be non-price rather than price, but price competition will be seen in situations where supply exceeds demand and there is aggressive competition for market share.

There is still opportunity for smaller companies to compete successfully in certain oligopoly markets, especially if they can differentiate their product so that it has appeal for particular segments of the market.

In the chocolate industry Thornton's has been successful with a limited range of high quality products distributed through the company's own specialist outlets. In contrast, there are certain industries which exhibit very low concentration. Ladies' dresses are one example, and they are very much affected by fashion and the nature of the businesses which involve large numbers of part-time workers; leather goods are another, and here the barriers to entry are very low.

The UK exhibits higher concentration overall than is found in rival countries such as the USA and Germany. However, UK companies generally compete in world markets, and therefore size is an important issue. However, few British companies are dominant producers when considered in world terms.

The dilemma for government is to encourage firms to grow in size and become powerful competitive forces in world markets but at the same time to ensure that such size and power is not used to exploit consumers in the UK.

The regulation of monopoly power

In the UK it is generally accepted that it is the state's role to monitor the forces of competition, to minimize any waste of resources due to economic inefficiency, to guard against any exploitation of relatively weak buyers or suppliers, and to ensure that powerful companies do not seek to eliminate their competitors purely to gain monopoly power.

Restrictive practices
Restrictive practices are controlled by the Restrictive Practices Court, and the basic presumption is that they are against the public interest. A restrictive practice is defined as 'an agreement under which two or more persons accept restrictions relating to the price of goods, conditions of supply, qualities or descriptions, processes, or areas and persons supplied'. A practice may be allowed if it can be demonstrated that there is a consumer benefit, that it is being used to promote exports, or that it is necessary to counteract anticompetitive measures being taken by others.

Merger investigations

The Monopolies and Mergers Commission is empowered to look at the way monopoly power is exercised in particular cases that are referred to it by the Director General of Fair Trading or an appropriate Minister of State. Similarly the Commission can be asked to investigate proposed mergers where either £30 million of assets are involved or where market share in excess of 25% would result. Each case is considered on merit, and this time the presumption is not automatically that monopoly power is against the public interest. High profitability is considered acceptable if it reflects efficiency, but not if it is sustained by artificial barriers to entry.

The delay involved in an investigation can be important strategically. The process is likely to take at least six months and in that time a company which opposes the take-over bid against it will work hard to improve its performance and prospects. If this results in a substantial increase in the share price the acquisitive company may withdraw on the grounds that the cost has become too high. A new bill was introduced in 1989, which amongst other things, speeded up the clearance for proposals if companies notified the Office of Fair Trading of their intentions in advance and allowed companies formally to seek to prevent a reference by undertaking to sell off part of the businesses involved in an acquisition if competition concerns are raised.

When the conglomerate Williams Holdings bid for Racal in 1991 they undertook to sell the Chubb lock and safe businesses owned by Racal if they were successful. Williams already owned two competing businesses, Yale and Valor.

Anticompetitive behaviour

The 1980 Competition Act gave the Director General of Fair Trading powers to investigate the conduct of individual firms in order to determine whether specific practices such as discriminatory prices, predatory prices and refusal to supply non-appointed distributors were anticompetitive. If the Office of Fair Trading concludes that a firm is behaving anticompetitively reference can be made to the Monopolies and Mergers Commission for further investigation.

Since September 1990 the European Commission has also been able to influence the growing number of corporate mergers and acquisitions in the European Union.

Mergers are exempted, though, if each company has more than two-thirds of its EU-wide turnover in any one EU country.

Box 9.2 provides several recent examples of competition policy in action.

Analysing an industry

Porter (1980) argues that five forces determine the profitability of an industry. They are featured in Figure 9.2. At the heart of the industry are rivals and their competitive strategies linked to, say, pricing or advertising; but, he contends, it is important to look beyond one's immediate competitors as there are other determinants of profitability. Specifically there might be competition from substitute products or services. These alternatives may be perceived as substitutes

Box 9.2
RECENT EXAMPLES OF COMPETITION POLICY IN ACTION

Restrictive practices

Concrete manufacture, like other parts of the building materials industry, has a poor record. Several price rings and market share agreements have been exposed. In 1995, for example, eight producers were fined for price fixing, when it was commented that because the main market for large concrete sections is public works, it was the public at large that was being exploited.

Mergers

In 1995, the government had to assess the implications of competing bids by defence companies British Aerospace and GEC for VSEL, the Barrow-based submarine manufacturer. GEC already owned rival facilities; BAe did not. The government could refer the GEC bid, or even both, to the Monopolies and Mergers Commission (MMC). In the event, both bids were allowed, and GEC won control of VSEL.

Anticompetitive behaviour

Pre-recorded compact discs cost no more to manufacture than audio cassettes, yet they retail at higher prices. Moreover, European CD prices are higher than those generally prevailing in the USA. Critics argue that music companies exploit the willingness of consumers to pay higher prices because they perceive CDs to be a superior product. The producers accept they cross-subsidize and argue their profits are re-invested to nurture and develop new performers. The MMC determined that the pricing strategy was not against the public interest.

In 1989, the MMC concluded that no brewer should own more than 2000 on-licensed premises, known as tied houses. After lobbying,

the government increased this number, but it still provoked a restructuring of the industry. Some brewers have chosen to concentrate more on brewing and divest retail activities; others have increased their retailing and related restaurant activities.

Stagecoach, which, through a series of acquisitions, is the UK's largest and most aggressive bus operator – and the first outside company to acquire a rail franchise with privatization – has been criticized by the MMC on more than one occasion. Typical issues have involved low fares and even free services to drive other competitors out of business, and thereby establish local monopolies.

Predatory pricing in 1993 by News International, when it slashed the prices of the *Sun, Times* and *Sunday Times*, was, however, allowed. Using profits from BSkyB, its satellite broadcasting business, News International was aiming to drive rivals out of the market and then, having increased its market share, restore higher prices. In the event, consumers benefited for a period; rival newspaper prices were also reduced. *The Independent* changed hands, but the only paper to be closed was *Today* (in 1995). *Today* was owned by News International.

In 1993, the MMC agreed that it was not against the public interest for manufacturers of fine fragrances to control the distribution of their products by limiting them to department stores and specialist outlets which would provide expert advice to customers. Discounted supplies through supermarkets and outlets such as Superdrug could be restrained. The MMC ruled that consumers value the prestige brand image and that this should be defendable.

by buyers even though they are part of a different industry. An example would be plastic bottles, cans and glass bottles for packaging soft drinks. There may also be a potential threat of new entrants, although some competitors will see this as an opportunity to strengthen their position in the market by ensuring, as far as they can, customer loyalty. Finally it is important to appreciate that companies purchase from suppliers and sell to buyers. If they are powerful they

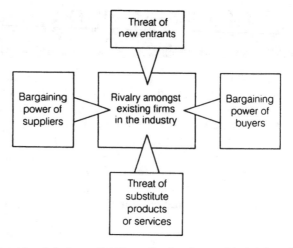

Figure 9.2 Determining industry profitability – the five forces. Adapted from Porter, ME (1980) *Competitive Strategy: Techniques for Analysing Industries and Competitors*, Free Press.

are in a position to bargain profits away through reduced margins, by forcing either cost increases or price decreases. This relates to the strategic option of vertical integration which will be considered in detail later in the book. Vertical integration occurs where a company acquires, or merges with, a supplier or customer and thereby gains greater control over the chain of activities which leads from basic materials through to final consumption.

Any company must seek to understand the nature of its competitive environment if it is to be successful in achieving its objectives and in establishing appropriate strategies. If a company fully understands the nature of the five forces, and particularly appreciates which one is the most important, it will be in a stronger position to defend itself against any threats and to influence the forces with its strategy. The situation, of course, is fluid, and the nature and relative power of the forces will change. Consequently the need to monitor and stay aware is continuous.

The threat of new entrants: barriers to entry

Where barriers to entry are high new entrants are likely to be deterred, and if they do attempt entry they are likely to provoke a quick reaction from existing competitors. Low barriers generally mean that responses will be slower, offering more opportunities. A number of factors can create barriers:

❏ **Economies of scale:** Some of the possible ways of achieving economies of scale were considered earlier in this chapter. In addition the experience curve can be important. If there is a need for substantial investment to allow a new entrant to achieve cost parity with existing firms this may well be a deterrent. In such a case if a newcomer enters the market with only limited investment and is not able to achieve comparable economies of scale, he or she will be at a cost disadvantage from the start, in which case substantial differentiation will be required, but this introduces another issue.

❏ **Product differentiation:** If consumers perceive rival products or services to be clearly differentiated then newcomers must also seek to establish a distinct identity. Differentiation is explained in Key Concept 9.2. Newcomers will therefore have to invest in advertising and promotion to establish their new brand, and this may be expensive. The major brewers and chocolate manufacturers, for example, spend millions of pounds each year promoting specific products and brands.

❑ **Capital requirements:** Any requirement for substantial investment capital in order to enter a market is a barrier to entry. The investment may be on capital equipment, research and development, or advertising to establish a market presence, and it may deter many aspiring competitors. However, large multi-product companies who wish to break into a market may finance the necessary investment with profits from other areas of the business.

KEY CONCEPT 9.2

PRODUCT DIFFERENTIATION

A product or service is said to be **differentiated** if consumers perceive it to have properties which make it distinct from rival products or services, and ideally unique in some particular way. Differentiation is most beneficial when consumers value the cause of the difference and will pay a premium price to obtain it, and where competitors are unable to emulate it.

Differentiation recognizes that customers are too numerous and widely scattered, and with heterogeneous needs and adequate spending power, for them all to prefer exactly the same product or service. Hence competitors will distinguish their brand, product or service in some way, perhaps size, quality or style, to give it greater appeal for certain customers. Those customers who value the difference will be willing to pay a premium price for it and ideally buy it consistently in preference to the alternatives.

Consequently, effective organizations will be both customer-driven (responsive) and customer-driving (innovative).

Sources of differentiation

❑ *Speed*. High street opticians and photo developers compete on their speed of service; courier businesses are successful because of the speed at which they can move items.

❑ *Reliability*. Consistent quality and the ability to keep promises – providing what customers want, where, when and how. One example is McDonald's.

❑ *Service*. Adding extra values to augment the service and thereby satisfy customers. Staff in certain hotels illustrate this point; Xerox provided a new level of service by incorporating a self-diagnostic computer chip in its copying machines.

❑ *Design* – both in the product itself (Bang and Olufsen hi-fi equipment, for instance) and in its repairability. This also relates to:

❑ *Features* such as *cordless* irons, kettles and drills. The balance, though, is critical; some video cassette recorders now have too many features for most customers.

❑ *Technology*, which, say, led to the development of laser printers.

❑ *Corporate personality*. There is a value in certain corporate names and images, such as the Body Shop.

❑ *Relationships with customers* through effective supply chain management.

Market segmentation

The differentiation need not be clearly tangible as long as customers believe that it exists.

Where specific groups of customers with broadly similar needs can be identified and targeted they are known as **market segments**, and often products and services are differentiated to appeal to specific segments. The segmentation might be based on ages, socioeconomic groups, life-style, income, benefits sought or usage rate for consumer markets, and size of buyer and reasons for buying in the case of industrial markets. To be viable the segment must be clearly identifiable, separated from other segments, easily reached with advertising and large enough to be profitable. Given these factors and a differentiated product, prices, distribution and advertising can all be targeted specifically at the segment.

Successful differentiation and segmentation require that products and services are clearly *positioned*. Toyota, for example, wanted to appeal to the lucrative executive market with a car that offered the 'ultimate in quality' and succeeded against BMW, Mercedes and Volvo. The car needed to be differentiated from the main Toyota brand and consequently it was named Lexus.

❑ **Switching costs:** These are not costs incurred by the company wishing to enter the market but by the existing customers.

If a buyer were to change his supplier from an established manufacturer to a newcomer costs may be incurred in a number of ways. New handling equipment and employee training are examples. Buyers may not be willing to change their suppliers because of these costs, thereby making it very difficult for any newcomer to poach existing business.

❑ **Access to distribution channels:** Existing relationships and agreements between manufacturers and the key distributors in a market may also create barriers to entry. Some manufacturers may be vertically integrated and own or control their distributors. Other distributors may have established and successful working relationships with particular manufacturers and have little incentive to change. Companies aspiring to enter a market may look for unique distribution opportunities to provide both access and immediate differentiation.

❑ **Cost advantages independent of scale:** This represents factors which are valuable to existing companies in an industry and which newcomers may not be able to replicate. Essential technology may be protected by patent; the supply of necessary raw materials may be controlled; or favourable locations near to supplies or markets may not be accessible. Government restrictions on competition may apply in certain circumstances.

Case 9.3 overleaf features the powerful barriers to entry in three completely different industries.

Potential entrants, attracted by high margins in an industry and not detracted by any of the above barriers, must try and gauge any likely retaliation by existing manufacturers; and Porter argues that this can be assessed by examining

❑ past behaviour when newcomers have entered or tried to enter the market;
❑ the resource capabilities of existing companies which will affect their ability to retaliate;
❑ the investment and commitment of existing companies which may make retaliation inevitable if they are to protect their investment and position;
❑ the rate of growth of the industry – the faster it is the more possibilities for a newcomer to be absorbed.

Existing firms may be prepared to reduce prices to deter entry and protect their market shares, especially if supply already exceeds demand. As a result, even in an oligopoly, profitability can be contained.

The bargaining power of suppliers

The behaviour of suppliers, and their relative power, can squeeze industry profits. Equally the ability of a firm to control its supplies by vertical integration (acquiring its suppliers) or long-term supply arrangements can be very beneficial. The relative power is affected by five major factors.

❑ Concentration amongst suppliers *vis-à-vis* the industry they sell to: if the supply industry is very concentrated then buyers have little opportunity for bargaining on prices and deliveries as suppliers recognize that their opportunities for switching suppliers are limited.

❑ The degree of substitutability between the products of various suppliers and the amount of product differentiation: a buyer could be tied to a particular supplier if his or her requirements cannot be met by other suppliers.

❑ The amount of, and potential for, vertical integration which might be initiated by either the supplier or the buyer: again government regulation on competition may prevent this.

❑ The extent to which the buyer is important to the supplier: if a buyer is regarded as a key customer he or she may well receive preferential treatment.

❑ Any switching costs that might be incurred by buyers will strengthen the position of suppliers.

The bargaining power of buyers

Any competitive action by buyers will act to depress industry profits, but specific arrangements with distributors or customers can be mutually beneficial. Vertical integration is again a possibility. The major supermarket grocery stores with their multiple outlets nationwide are in a very strong bargaining position with most of their suppliers.

This power has been strengthened by the success of private label brands, whose prices can be up to 60% below those for the recognized major brands. Private labels now account for some 33% of UK retail food sales. They have proved most successful with chilled meals, frozen vegetables, fruit juices and cheese; and least successful with pet foods, sugar, coffee and breakfast cereals. Barriers against private label products are provided by innovation and aggressive marketing and promotion.

Visit the website: http://www. itbp.com

As the market for overseas travel grew in the UK, the power of the leading travel agency groups also grew *vis-à-vis* the tour operators – it is, after all, the travel agency that actually sells the holiday and has direct contact with customers, who they are able to influence. As a consequence the leading tour operators sought to acquire their own agencies and exercise greater control over the supply chain. Thomson bought Lunn Poly (the largest tour operator bought the leading agency) and Pickfords was acquired by Airtours. At the same time, industry rationalization has meant that a small number of tour operators (all of whom also own their own airline) dominate the market.

In 1994 Boeing indicated that it had begun a review of its world-wide purchasing policies and that it intended to match future parts contracts with aircraft orders from specific countries. This implied that new contracts may not be awarded to countries whose governments had selected European Airbus planes in preference to Boeing.

The bargaining power of buyers is determined by

❑ the concentration and size of buyer

❑ the importance to the buyer of the purchase in terms of both cost and quality (the more important it is the more he or she must ensure good relations with the supplier)

❑ the degree of product standardization, which affects substitutability

❑ the costs, practicability and opportunity for buyers to switch supplier

❑ the possibility of vertical integration, initiated by either the supplier or the buyer.

Case 9.3
BARRIERS TO ENTRY: ZANTAC, CHAMPAGNE AND PERFUMES

Zantac

Sir Paul Girolami became the chief executive of Glaxo in 1980, and sequentially divested the non-pharmaceutical businesses: specialized chemicals and food, agricultural and horticultural products. In 1985 Glaxo was not in the leading ten world pharmaceutical companies; in 1988 it was number 2 to Merck. In 1990 half of Glaxo's world-wide revenue was contributed by Zantac, its anti-ulcer drug whose chemical name is Ranitidin. Zantac enjoyed one important competitive advantage over its main rival Tagamet (SmithKline Beecham) – it is a twice daily treatment rather than four times a day.

Glaxo exploited the product successfully with two unusual strategies. Firstly it registered Ranitidin simultaneously in all major markets – typically drugs are registered first in their home market, followed by other countries sequentially. Secondly Glaxo uniquely used other companies for manufacturing and distributing the product (including three separate companies in the USA), rather than building a world sales force. Turnover tripled in 1983/1984 and then quadrupled during the next five years. As a result of these factors, Zantac has been able to command a premium price and still become the world's biggest selling prescription medicine.

By 1995, after Glaxo's takeover of Wellcome, Zantac still accounted for 30% of the group's sales, but key patents were beginning to expire. Originally thought to be protected until 2002, basic Zantac now appeared to come fully out of patent in 1997. Generic versions were appearing in Europe, causing sales to fall.

Glaxo, however, began to patent new versions, including a superior reformulation known as Tritec. Nevertheless, this itself was under some threat. In the USA, the previously preferred treatment programme of 12 months of an anti-ulcer drug was giving way to a one-month programme supported by a critical, new antibiotic.

Moreover, Glaxo received approval to market a non-prescription, over-the-counter version (Zantac 75) as a treatment for heartburn, thus opening up a huge new market opportunity.

Champagne

Several barriers to entry have acted to preserve the exclusiveness of the champagne industry. In most countries, and with the notable exceptions of the USA and Russia, the term champagne can be applied only to wines made from grapes grown in one area, Champagne, in northwest France. The best grapes for champagne are grown on a particular type of chalky soil found only in this region. In addition strict (and enforced) French government rules require that only three varieties of grape may be used; and after the first fermentation the wine must be matured in the bottle for at least a year to generate the bubbles.

The business is carefully regulated, generally in favour of the 19,000 growers. Growers, who operate in co-operatives, historically have accounted for approximately one-third of the champagne that is manufactured; the rest has been produced by merchants who buy the grapes from the growers at prices fixed contractually every six years.

During the early and mid-1980s demand and sales grew by some 70%. As a result grape prices rose and growers particularly started to manufacture more. These events attracted competitors who looked for ways of overcoming the entry barriers. The real threat came from other premium quality sparkling wines manufactured in countries such as Spain. The grower/merchant price agreement broke down in 1990, roughly at the time demand fell back. In an attempt to reinforce the image of superiority and exclusivity, and in response to the competition from other sparkling wines, champagne prices were increased deliberately. 'Quality and image is more important than quantity.'

The most influential company in the industry is LVMH (Louis Vuitton Moët Hennessy) whose brands (including Moët & Chandon, Dom Perignon, Veuve Clicquot, Mercier and Pommery [very popular in Japan]) command a 24% market share. LVMH own 1500 prime hectares out of the region's total of 35,000 hectares.

Continued

Perfumes

LVMH (with the Christian Dior, Givenchy and Christian Lacroix brands) is also a major competitor in the fine fragrances sector of the perfumes market, along with Estée Lauder (which includes Aramis), L'Oréal (Anais Anais, Cacharel, Fidji, Giorgio Armani and Ralph Lauren Polo) and Unilever (Brut, Fabergé and Calvin Klein). It is estimated to cost **at least** $40 million to develop and launch world-wide a new fragrance, and clearly this is only feasible for sizeable, international organizations. LVMH and L'Oréal are French companies, Estee Lauder is American and Unilever is Anglo-Dutch.

The threat of product substitutes

The existence or non-existence of close substitutes helps to determine the elasticity of demand for a product or service. In simple terms this is price sensitivity. If there are close substitutes, demand for a particular brand will increase or decrease as its price moves downwards or upwards relative to competitors. Price changes can be initiated by any firm, but other competitors will be affected and forced to react. If products are not seen as close substitutes then they will be less price sensitive to competitor price changes.

For this reason firms will seek to establish clear product or service differentiation in order to create customer preference and loyalty and thereby make their product or service less price sensitive. Where this is accomplished industry profits are likely to rise, which of course may be attractive to prospective newcomers who will seek to create further differentiation in order to encourage customers to switch to them and enable them to establish a presence in the market.

Rivalry amongst existing competitors

Porter terms rivalry amongst existing competitors 'jockeying for position'. Competition may take the form of price competition, advertising and promotion, innovation, or service during and after sale. Where competitive firms are mutually inter-dependent retaliation is a key issue. Before deciding upon aggressive competitive actions firms must attempt to predict how their competitors will react; when other firms are proactive an organization must at least be defensive in order to protect market share and profitability. The intensity of competition is affected by the market structure and depends on the following:

❑ the number of competitors and the degree of concentration
❑ the rate of growth of the industry – slow growth increases the pressure upon competitors to fight for market share
❑ the degree of differentiation – the less there is the more likely is price competition
❑ cost structures – where fixed costs are high relative to variable costs companies are very sensitive around the breakeven point. Profits are very dependent upon volume. This is illustrated in Figure 9.3 which contrasts the position for companies with high and low fixed costs.

As passenger aircraft become larger and more technologically sophisticated, the cost of buying (or leasing) and insuring them grows. The operating cost per

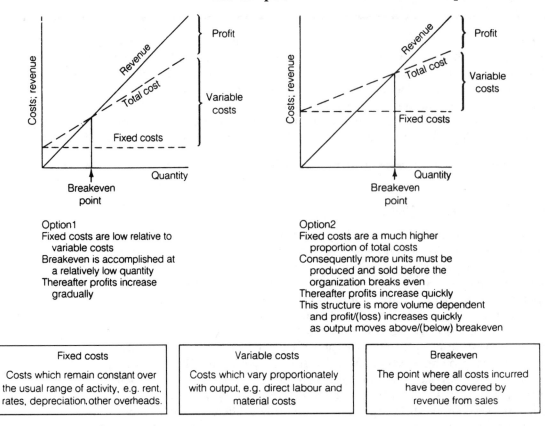

Option1
Fixed costs are low relative to
   variable costs
Breakeven is accomplished at
   a relatively low quantity
Thereafter profits increase
   gradually

Option2
Fixed costs are a much higher
   proportion of total costs
Consequently more units must be
   produced and sold before the
   organization breaks even
Thereafter profits increase quickly
This structure is more volume dependent
   and profit/(loss) increases quickly
   as output moves above/(below) breakeven

Fixed costs	Variable costs	Breakeven
Costs which remain constant over the usual range of activity, e.g. rent, rates, depreciation, other overheads.	Costs which vary proportionately with output, e.g. direct labour and material costs	The point where all costs incurred have been covered by revenue from sales

Note: On the two graphs the revenue and cost schedules are shown as straight lines for simple illustration

Figure 9.3   Cost structures, breakeven points and profits.

seat mile – and break-even loadings – increases steadily, but with international over-capacity and competition, the revenue per seat mile has been falling. Some airlines have closed or been acquired; others have had to reduce salaries and employees.

❑ The implications of changing size or supply capability through investment: although demand may be increasing at a relatively gradual and consistent rate, supply provision may increase in sizeable blocks as a result of the necessary investment. If a firm wishes to increase output and it has exhausted the possibilities from increased usage of existing plant it will have to invest in new plant. When this is commissioned it may increase supply potential substantially and affect competitors as the company seeks orders to utilize its new capacity. Consider as examples a small charter airline which has three freight aeroplanes. If it buys a fourth it increases its capacity by 25% overnight. Similarly if there are two three-star hotels in a medium-sized town and a third is opened, the competitive situation changes markedly.

❑ The extent to which competitors are aware of the strategies of their rivals: one issue in this is the relative importance of the product or service to the various competitors. If a product is a by-product of another more important operation, for example, then the company concerned may compete very aggressively for sales and be far more concerned with volume than profits.

❑ The objectives of the competing firms – what matters to them. Are they more interested in profit, turnover or percentage market share? The objectives determine the strategies.

❑ Exit barriers, and the costs of leaving the industry: if these are high for any reason firms may be willing to accept low margins and limited profit opportunities in order to remain in the industry. The types of factor which determine exit costs are dedicated assets which have no profitable alternative use; the costs of redundancy; inter-relationships within a conglomerate, whereby a product may be either a by-product or an essential component for another division; emotional ties related to the history of the product and its association with the business; and pressure from government not to close down.

An example of dedicated assets which have no alternative use would be multiplex cinema complexes. As the number of these grows cinema audiences will have to increase if they are all to be viable. If this increase fails to materialize, the cinemas should close. But what is the alternative use for a building containing, say, ten small cinemas?

Manufacturers of consumer electronics products have to invest continually to maintain the technology required for the necessary product improvements. To generate revenues to fund further investment they need volume sales; to create these they price with low, competitive margins. Profits are very slim, but the sunk costs are such that the cycle continues; it is too costly to come out of the industry. The cycle is reinforced by consumer purchasing behaviour. Consumers know which brands they are happy to consider, their short-list depending upon the quality and differentiation they are seeking. They then buy on price, seeing certain brands as inter-changeable. Inevitably, the retailers also earn only low margins.

Box 9.3 provides a summary checklist of factors for industry analysis, and Box 9.4 analyses the supermarket industry against Porter's model of five forces.

The rivalry factors discussed above, and the rivalry strategies, are both affected by any slowing down in the rate of industry growth, by acquisitions, and by changes in the marketing strategy of any one competitor resulting from the perception of new opportunities for differentiation or segmentation.

To be an effective competitor, a company must

❑ appreciate which of the five forces is the most significant (it can be different for different industries) and concentrate strategic attention in this area

❑ position itself for the best possible defence against any threats from rivals

❑ influence the forces detailed above through its own corporate and competitive strategies

❑ anticipate changes or shifts in the forces – the factors that are generating success in the short term may not succeed long term.

Much will depend upon the strategic leader, the quality of management in the organization and the prevailing culture.

Many companies spend a lot of time and money researching customers' views, but most spend nothing like enough on observing competitors. The main reason for change is to keep ahead of competitors or to catch up on the complacent market leaders. Companies must invest in development – it's a case of 'duck or no dinner'.

Sir Simon Hornby, ex-chairman, W H Smith Group plc

Box 9.3
A CHECKLIST FOR INDUSTRY ANALYSIS

❏ How many firms are in the industry, and what size are they?
❏ How concentrated is the industry?
❏ To what degree are products substitutes?
❏ Is the industry growing or contracting?
❏ What are the relative powers of suppliers? buyers? competitors?
❏ What are the prevailing competitive strategies?

❏ What entry barriers exist?
❏ What economies of scale are present?
❏ What experience/learning curve effects are important?
❏ What exit barriers exist (if any)?
❏ What important external factors affect competition?

Box 9.4
INDUSTRY ANALYSIS – SUPERMARKETS

Threat of new entrants
Barriers to entry are very high, because of the necessary supply network and distribution infrastructure. The continual investment in EPOS (electronic point-of-sale) and EDI (electronic data inter-change) systems creates further barriers. In addition, it is very difficult and very expensive to acquire new sites in prime positions. It is possible, given financial reserves, to build a position in selected market niches.

Relative strength of suppliers
Supply agreements with major retail chains, using EDI, make the leading suppliers and supermarkets more and more inter-dependent. Ownership of a leading brand yields power, but secondary and tertiary brands must be more vulnerable. Further inter-dependency with own-label supply agreements.

Relative strength of buyers
Invariably buyers will have more than one supermarket that they can access, especially if they are car owners. There will be some loyalty, but only if prices and service are competitive.

Threat of substitutes
Small independent stores have a niche and a role, but the supermarkets are dominant. However, they are vulnerable on price for those products/brands offered by smaller, discount stores, especially where customers are willing to multi-shop. Home shopping via IT presents a future threat, and arguably it is a sector of the market the supermarkets must develop rather than relinquish.

Existing rivalries
The industry is very competitive, with four or five chains competing for the family shopping budget. Sainsbury, Tesco, Asda and Safeway have different competitive strategies (product ranges, pricing strategies, etc.) and have differing appeals, but they remain largely inter-changeable.

Summary:

Barriers to entry	high
Power of suppliers	medium
Power of buyers	medium/high
Threat of substitutes	medium
Existing rivalries	intense

The role of government

Rather than incorporation as a separate sixth factor, Porter maintains the importance of government lies in an ability to affect the other five forces through changes in policy and new legislation. The examples below are not exhaustive.

1. The introduction of competition into the National Health Service with the establishment of independent Hospital Trusts – outlined in Case 6.3.
2. A series of privatizations during the 1980s, including British Aerospace, Rolls Royce, British Airways and British Steel, along with the critically important utilities: British Telecom, British Gas and the water and electricity industries.

To prevent these utilities becoming national or local monopolies in private ownership, with enormous potential to exploit their customers, industry regulators have been appointed, again as outlined in Case 6.3. The regulators and the newly privatized businesses have at times disagreed over important strategic issues.

Individual regulators are given freedom to establish specific guidelines with-in clear broad principles, and some would argue that this makes conflict between them and the regulated businesses inevitable. One of the reasons for, the diversification strategies by privatized companies is that they create business activities which are outside the direct control of the regulator. Given a general trend away from diversification to a concentration on core businesses and competencies (see Chapter 16), this may prove to be risky. Maybe the impact of the regulators also needs regulating.

Another control element affecting gas, electricity and telecommunications is the legislated permission for certain new businesses to compete on specified terms. Kinetica, for example, buys gas from producers in the spot market (typically at prices below those British Gas is paying on long-term contracts) and pipes it through British Gas' pipeline infrastructure to industrial and commercial buyers, paying British Gas an agreed proportion of its revenue. Kinetica is essentially a telephone sales operation, using the electricity-users database supplied by its owner, Power Gen. Through similar arrangements, electricity from one regional company can be moved and sold to industrial users in other regions. These controls clearly have a regulatory effect on prices, and in time they are to be extended to domestic markets – as has been the case with Mercury and telephone calls.

3. Deregulation of particular industries, such as air transport – see Case 9.4.

The lessening of restrictions and regulations unleashes new competitive forces and changes the nature of the industry. Some competitors will benefit; others will suffer.

In the UK the changes in air transport have created an interesting dilemma. BAA (British Airports Authority), who run most of the major airports in the UK (the exception is Manchester), was privatized in 1987. Airport charges are regulated by the Civil Aviation Authority (CAA) who have insisted on a new five-year formula covering the period April 1992 to March 1997. In Years 1 and 2 charges would change by a figure 8% below RPI (retail price index); in Year 3 by RPI less 4%; and in Years 4 and 5 by RPI less 1%. These imply a need for cost savings, together with greater efficiency and productivity. At the same time the

Case 9.4

DEREGULATION AND THE INTERNATIONAL AIRLINE INDUSTRY

When governments regulated their airline industries, in order to control both national and international competition, new airlines were prevented from entering markets, existing companies could not simply offer flights into or out of any airport of their choice, routes could not be poached and prices for specified routes were fixed.

This regulation has been systematically reduced since the late 1970s. At this time in the **USA**, where flying is as commonplace as bus and train journeys, and airline seats are perceived as essentially a commodity product, domestic competition was opened up. This has unleashed the underlying competitive nature of the industry with dramatic effects. The industry is characterized by chaos.

It is relatively easy to break into the industry once companies are allowed to do so. Planes can be leased and funded from revenue; maintenance can be bought in. Normally both fuel and planes are easily obtained. A company can enter by offering a limited service and concentrating on particular cities. Deregulation in the USA attracted such companies; and existing large airlines sought to expand their routes. Buyers were generally willing to fly with the airline which offered a flight at the time they wanted to travel, not differentiating, rather than building their arrangements around the schedule of their first-choice airline.

The **British government** has sought competition rather than monopoly control in the UK, privatizing British Airways in 1987. In 1991 the CAA (Civil Aviation Authority) relaxed certain rules, allowing new airlines to fly into and out of Heathrow for the first time since 1977. This intensified transatlantic competition as two strong US airlines (American and United, the two largest airlines in the world), which were restricted to Gatwick, acquired Heathrow/America routes from two weaker competitors, TWA and Pan Am respectively. At the same time Virgin Atlantic was: allowed to operate from Heathrow as well as Gatwick; allowed to fly to more American destinations; and given a number of BA's slots on the lucrative Heathrow to Tokyo route. All of these changes increased the competition for BA.

In 1992 European Union transport ministers agreed plans for a new 'open skies' policy, eventually featuring:

❑ Freer access for airlines to new routes throughout Europe. Previously many routes have been protected by governments to prevent competition with their national carriers. One difficulty in implementing this is the ability of air traffic controllers to cope with more flights; European air traffic control is not fully co-ordinated and is overstretched.
❑ Greater freedom for airlines to set their own seat prices, within certain protective safeguards. This did not imply that prices would fall quickly because operating costs are already high, with many flights operating below capacity.
❑ Lower barriers to entry for new carriers.

Deregulation began in **Australia** in 1990, when controls on prices and schedules were removed, resulting in domestic price warfare, cost cutting measures and the entry of a new national airline, 'the first for decades'. British Airways was allowed to buy a substantial shareholding in Qantas, Australia's leading international airline.

Effects
❑ New route strategies based on a 'hub and spokes' – flights are concentrated around particular regional centres. American control 65% of the slots at Dallas; United own 68% of the slots at Washington National and 48% of Chicago; and Delta 70% of Atlanta. Internationally carriers expect the same control at the major airport in their home country, but many are now seeking to establish further hubs around the world.
❑ Company winners and losers. In 1991 in the USA, for example, two previously major competitors, Eastern and Pan Am, went out of business. Earlier People Express, founded in the USA in the early 1980s (following deregulation) to offer cheaper price flights,

Continued

also failed after rapid growth and profitability. Companies such as American, United and Delta, less well-known before deregulation, have grown dramatically.

❏ New, small, focused airlines have also proved successful. Southwest Air, based in Dallas, flies point-to-point (not hub-and-spoke) on short-haul routes, offering low fares, no pre-assigned seating and calling at secondary airports. Empowered employees deliver high service – founder Herb Kelleher has 'made working in this business an adventure for the employees'. The company uses only one type of aircraft, Boeing 737s, and avoids computer reservation systems in travel agencies; it prefers direct sales to its customers. Southwest has been consistently profitable; its operating ratios confirm that it out-performs most other US airlines.

❏ New joint venture agreements and cross-shareholdings. In July 1992 BA reached an agreement with financially-troubled US Air (the fourth largest US carrier) to acquire a shareholding, and thereby gain access to US domestic routes. This arrangement is threatened now that BA and American are discussing a strategic alliance.

❏ Increased competitiveness with job losses during recession. The 1991 Gulf War had a major impact as many people were deterred from flying.

❏ Greater reliance on information technology to allow pricing flexibility in order to maximize load factors. However, the increasing number of 'price wars' and special low-fare promotions has led to non-optimum fare mixes and unprofitable flights. In 1994 in the USA, for example, 92% of passengers flew on discount tickets and the average fare paid was just 35% of the published full fare. At the same time …

❏ Greater emphasis on service quality, especially punctuality and reliability, to try and establish customer loyalty.

❏ The introduction of frequent flyer promotions (free flights on particular airlines for regular travellers who accumulate points for miles). This is also aimed at generating more loyalty.

The end result has been a potent mix of poor profits, leading to corporate failures, disgruntled employees who are either laid off or forced to accept pay cuts, and unhappy passengers who are affected by the inevitable overbooking as airlines try to ensure every plane flies full.

❏ The industry has exhibited one aspect of classic oligopoly behaviour with deregulation. In 1992 American tried to lead fares back up – and failed.

Why, then, deregulate? Simply, governments are impressed by the seductive cost savings for passengers. But, would some regulation be more sensible? Whether it would or would not, it would prove very difficult to reintroduce strict controls.

need grows for both a fifth runway in the London area (to add to two at Heathrow and one each at Gatwick and Stansted) and a fifth terminal at Heathrow. BAA will be the developers, assuming their finances are sufficiently robust.

The forces described above determine the profitability of an industry, and hence the attractiveness of the industry for companies already competing in it and for companies who might wish to enter it. As well as understanding the nature and structure of the industry it is important for organizations to decide how best to compete. In other words, firms must appreciate the opportunities for creating and sustaining competitive advantage.

Competitive advantage

Porter (1985) has developed his work on industry analysis to examine how a company might compete in the industry in order to create and sustain competitive advantage. In simple terms there are two basic choices.

❑ Choice one: Is the company seeking to compete
  • by achieving lower costs than its rivals and, by charging comparable prices for its products or services, creating a superior position through superior profitability?
  or
  • through differentiation, adding value in an area that the customer regards as important, charging a premium price, and again creating a superior position through superior profitablity?
❑ Choice two: In what arena is the company seeking competitive advantage? In a broad range of segments or a narrow range, perhaps just one?

Three generic strategies

These two choices lead to the three generic strategies illustrated in Figure 9.4. **Cost leadership** is where the company achieves lower costs than its rivals and competes across a broad range of segments. **Differentiation** occurs when the company has a range of clearly differentiated products which appeal to different segments of the market. **Focus strategies** are where a company chooses to concentrate on only one segment or a limited range of segments. With this approach it can again seek either lower costs or differentiation.

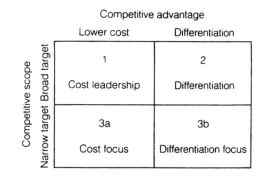

Figure 9.4   Porter's model of competitive advantage – the generic strategies. Adapted with permission of the Free Press, a division of Macmillan Inc., from *Competitive Advantage: Creating and Sustaining Superior Performance*, Porter, ME, Copyright 1985 ME Porter. (Source: Porter, ME (1985) *Competitive Advantage: Creating and Sustaining Superior Performance*, Free Press.)

Motor vehicles and retailing: applications of the generic strategies

Before considering these generic strategies in greater detail it is useful to apply them to a particular industry. Porter argues that in the motor vehicle industry (Figure 9.5) Toyota became the overall cost leader. The company is successful in a number of segments with a full range of cars, and its mission is to be a low cost producer. In contrast General Motors also competes in most segments of

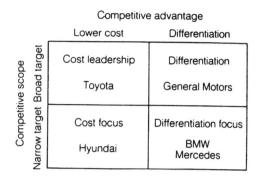

Figure 9.5 Porter's model of competitive advantage applied to the world motor industry.

the market but seeks to differentiate each of its products with better styling and better features. GM also offers a wider choice of models for each car in its range.

Hyundai is successful around the world with a restricted range of four small and medium size cars which it produces at low cost and prices competitively. It should be noted that neither Toyota nor Hyundai market the **cheapest** cars available.

BMW and Mercedes have both succeeded by producing a narrow line of more exclusive cars for the price-insensitive quality conscious customer. There are a number of cars available from both companies but they are clearly targeted at people who are willing to pay premium prices for perceived higher quality.

Retailers similarly seek to compete on either image or cost. Image-based retailers add value to either or both the product and the service provided to customers. Success in differentiating generates customer loyalty and premium prices. Cost-based retailers operate with competitive margins, searching for strategies which balance high turnover with low costs resulting from operating efficiencies.

Visit the website:
http://www.
itbp.com

The cost leadership strategy of Toyota is discussed in Case 9.5; Case 9.6 looks at differentiation strategies.

Porter argues that a company cannot achieve superior profitability if it is 'stuck in the middle' with no clear strategy for competitive advantage.

Moreover, competitors seeking cost advantages should not lose sight of the need to maintain distinctiveness; and competitive differentiators should be vigilant in managing their costs. Otherwise, the potential for superior profits is lost.

Cost leadership

To achieve substantial rewards from this strategy Porter argues that the organization must be **the** cost leader, and unchallenged in this position. There is room for only one; and if there is competition for market leadership based on this strategy there will be price competition.

Cost leadership as a generic strategy does not imply that the company will market the lowest price product or service in the industry. Quite often the lowest price products are perceived as inferior, and as such appeal to only a proportion of the market. Consequently low price related to lower quality is a

Case 9.5
TOYOTA'S COST LEADERSHIP STRATEGY

- Toyota historically has enjoyed a 40% plus market share in Japan, supplemented by 7.5% of the US market (where it also manufactures) and 3% of Europe – Toyota has followed Nissan in manufacturing in the UK.
- Toyota has sought to sell a range of cars at prices marginally below those of comparable Ford and General Motors cars. Ford and GM both sell more cars than Toyota world-wide. However, Toyota's operating profits have exceeded those of its rivals because it has ruthlessly controlled its costs.
- Production systems, based on JIT (just-in-time supply of components), are very efficient. Toyota claims fewer defects than any other manufacturer, resulting from the vigilance of each worker on the assembly lines. The Lexus range of top-quality cars requires one-sixth of the labour hours used to build a Mercedes. The best Toyota plant assembles a car in 13 man hours, whereas Ford, Honda and Nissan all require 20.
- 'Toyota does not indulge in expensive executive facilities'.
- Toyota also spends 5% of sales revenue on research and development (as high as any major competitor), concentrating on a search for continuous improvements 'to inch apart from competitors', rather than major breakthroughs.
- There is a policy of fast new model development. In the early 1990s Toyota models had an average age of two years; Ford and GM cars averaged five years.

Revenues, however, fell back in 1995. Sales of Toyota's new, revamped version of its best-selling Corolla saloon had been disappointing. 'In its hot pursuit of cost savings, Toyota has produced a car that lacks character.'

Overall cost leaders, slicing through the competitive middle market, must still produce distinctive, differentiated products to justify their near-market-average pricing policy.

In addition, the growing popularity of 4-wheel drive recreational vehicles has affected saloon car sales.

In America, Chrysler, the third largest producer, has been striving hard to achieve world-class operating margins. Improved capacity utilization, flexible manufacturing systems and successful new models with bold designs and shorter life cycles have all contributed. In addition, Chrysler dominates the important minivan and multi-purpose vehicles segments. Chrysler's objective: *To be the premier auto company in the world by the year 2000.*

differentiation strategy. Low cost therefore does not necessarily mean 'cheap' and low-cost companies can have upmarket rather than downmarket appeal. Equally low cost does not imply lower rewards for employees or other stakeholders as successful cost leaders can be very profitable. Their aim is to secure a cost advantage over their rivals, price competitively and relative to how their product is perceived by customers, and achieve a high profit margin. Where this applies across a broad range of segments turnover and market share should also be high for the industry. They are seeking above-average profits with industry average prices.

Cost focus strategies can be based on finding a distinct group of customers whose needs are slightly below average. Costs are saved by meeting their needs specifically and avoiding unnecessary additional costs.

Figure 9.6 illustrates the above points and relates competitive advantage to efficiency and effectiveness.

Case 9.6
THREE DIFFERENTIATION STRATEGIES: BMW, LAURA ASHLEY AND JAMES PURDEY

BMW

BMW follows a number of strategies designed to protect its market niche, especially from Japanese competition. Notably these cover both the cars and the overall service package provided by BMW for its customers.

- Cars can be tailored and customized substantially. Customers can choose any colour they want, a benefit normally restricted to Rolls Royce and Aston Martin; and there is a wide range of interior options and 'performance extras'.
- Safety, environment, economy and comfort are featured and stressed in every model.
- National BMW sales companies are wholly-owned together with strategically located parts warehouses. The independent distributors place their orders directly into BMW's central computer.
- There are fleets of specially equipped cars to go and help BMW motorists who break down.
- BMW has stated that it intends to stay independent, and, unlike many car companies, avoid joint ventures with competitors.
- In 1994 BMW became the first European car manufacturer to produce in the USA.
- Historically, BMW has chosen to ignore sports cars and hatchbacks, which it has seen as downmarket from luxury saloon cars. However, the 1994 BMW Compact was a hatchback version of the successful 3-series, a BMW sports model was used for the James Bond film, Goldeneye, and, of course, the acquisition of Rover gave BMW a range of successful, smaller hatchbacks – along with Land Rover recreational and multi-purpose vehicles.

BMW is seeking to derive synergy from this acquisition in a number of ways. Rover engines, developed from Rover's joint venture with Honda, are to be used for BMWs. Rover cars will be used to open up new market opportunities in the Far East, with the more expensive BMW models added on afterwards. Land Rover Discovery models have made a limited impact in the US market, but there is a shortage of dedicated distributors; consequently a new Discovery model, to be built in both the UK and USA, will be branded BMW to provide access to the more substantial BMW distribution network.

These recent moves indicate that BMW has realized that without development, and maybe a move into new segments, a niche can all-too-readily become a tomb. Mercedes, at the same time, has formed a joint venture with SMH, the maker of Swatch watches, to develop a radically new micro compact car, and is developing a smaller family car and a range of multi-purpose vehicles.

Laura Ashley

Laura Ashley was started in the 1950s by the late Laura Ashley and her husband, Bernard. The company was very successful with an instinctive approach to designs for fashions and fabrics. Laura Ashley designed, manufactured and retailed mostly clothes and furnishings. The company later diversified with a chain of perfume stores, leather goods stores and a knitwear business in Scotland. The company fared badly in the recession, and by 1991 was losing money.

The company's success has always depended upon the strength of the Laura Ashley name and brand, but the company has struggled after the death of Laura Ashley herself. In 1995 American Ann Iverson became the fourth chief executive of the decade. She inherited a company which was still clearly differentiated and popular with customers but where costs had escalated, resulting in margins of just 2%.

Ann Iverson declared she would tackle the cost base whilst 'preserving the mood and emotion, the countryside feeling' of the brand.

Continued overleaf

Her strategies have involved:

❏ Selected store closures around the world, in particular in the USA.
❏ A consolidation of the design, buying and merchandising functions.
❏ A slimming of the product range.

The need for the company to actually manufacture, rather than focus on its core strengths of design and retailing, has been questioned.

James Purdey
Purdey firearms would be classified as a super luxury product; they retail at 'prices more normally associated with small houses'. The company manufactures something in the order of 60 guns per year, 90% of which are sold abroad.

It goes without saying that there is close attention to detail, and quality control is incredibly tight. Every order is perceived as a special; nothing is seen as standard. The stocks are oil polished rather than varnished in a lengthy, labour-intensive process; and buyers can choose almost any special, idiosyncratic feature as long as they are happy to pay the appropriate premium. Typically orders are placed two years in advance of delivery.

Because they appeal to a very limited market segment, and because they literally last a lifetime (and sometimes longer), growth potential for James Purdey, without diversification, is clearly limited.

There is little advantage in being only one of a number of low cost producers. The advantage is gained by superior management, concentrating on cost-saving opportunities, minimizing waste, and not adding values which customers regard as unimportant to the product or service. Many products do have values added which are not regarded as necessary by the market. Cost savings can generally be achieved in any and every area of the business; and quite often they begin with the strategic leader. Senior executives who enjoy substantial perks are unlikely to pursue a cost leadership strategy. Porter suggests that it is a mistake to believe that cost savings are only possible in the manufacturing function and that this strategy is only applicable to the largest producers in an industry. However, where cost leadership generates market share and volume production opportunities, economies of scale in manufacturing do apply. Key Concept 9.1, the experience curve, emphasizes that the effect is only achieved if it is managed; it is not automatic.

Differentiation

Cost leadership is usually traded off against differentiation, with the two regarded as pulling in opposite directions. Differentiation adds costs in order to add value for which customers are willing to pay premium prices. For a differentiation focus strategy to be successful the market must be capable of clear segmentation, and the requirements for this were highlighted in Key Concept 9.2.

Although cost leadership and differentiation may be mutually exclusive, successful strategies can be based on a mix of the two. YKK, the Japanese zip manufacturer and world market leader, achieves both cost leadership and significant differentiation. This case is explored in detail in Chapter 10. Sainsbury's argue that their strategy is based on providing good food at low cost for the broad middle ground in the market. They do not offer the cheapest food; equally they do not offer the choice or range of a specialist delicatessen. Consequently the ideas of Michael Porter can be questioned. However, they do

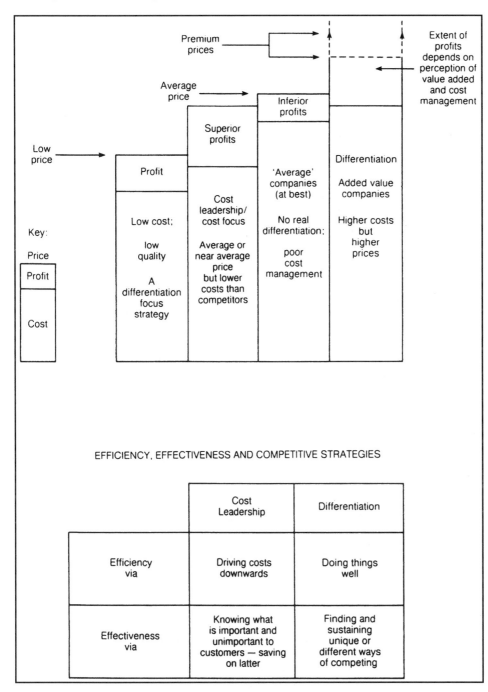

Figure 9.6 Competitive strategies.

provide an extremely useful framework for analysing industries and competitive advantage.

With differentiation superior performance is achieved by serving customer needs differently, ideally uniquely. The more unique the difference, the more sustainable is the advantage. Differentiation must inevitably add costs, which can only be recouped if the market is willing to pay the necessary premium prices. It is crucial that costs are only added in areas that customers perceive as important; and again this can relate to any area of the operation. A solicitors' practice, for example, might find competitive advantage in the manner and promptness in which customer queries are dealt with, both over the telephone and in person. A fuller list might include the following possibilities:

- ❑ quality of materials used (related to purchasing)
- ❑ superior performance (design)
- ❑ high quality (production; inspection)
- ❑ superior packaging (distribution)
- ❑ delivery (sales; production)
- ❑ prompt answer of queries (customer relations; sales)
- ❑ efficient paperwork (administration).

Furthermore it is insufficient merely to add value; customers must recognize and appreciate the difference. If it cannot be seen easily it should be communicated, perhaps through advertising. Communication between manufacturer and customer is vital, for it is only by understanding customer needs that the most appropriate value can be added. Take as an example the supplier of a component to an assembly company. At face value the supplier will seek to help the assembler lower his or her costs, or enhance the quality of his or her product, the choice depending upon the competitive strategy of the assembler. But this level of thinking alone might overlook further worthwhile opportunities. How does the assembler handle and store the components? And so on. If a supplier understands fully his or her customers' operations he might find new ways of adding value.

The differentiation strategy can be easily misjudged, however, for a number of reasons, including

- ❑ by choosing something that buyers fail to recognize, appreciate or value
- ❑ by over-fulfilling needs and as a consequence failing to achieve cost-effectiveness
- ❑ by selecting something that competitors can either improve on or undercut
- ❑ by attempting to overcharge for the differentiation
- ❑ by thinking too narrowly, missing opportunities and being outflanked by competitors.

When I'm on a plane, I prowl around and talk to passengers and ask the staff about everything. I normally come back with a hundred notes in my pocket scribbled on little pieces of paper. Direct feedback is far better than market research.
Richard Branson, Chairman, Virgin Group, quoted in Ferry, I,. Branson's misunderstood Midas touch, Business, November (1989)

The strategy of Virgin Atlantic Airways is built around quality service and differentiation. Virgin's 'Upper Class' aims to offer a first-class-equivalent service at business-class prices and provides, for example, electrostatic headphones which customers can keep afterwards, a selection of 30 films to watch on personal mini video-cassette players, and chauffeur-driven rides to and from airports.

Successful competitive strategies

Competitor benchmarking

Summarizing key points from the previous section, a true cost leader will also enjoy some form of differentiation, and successful differentiators will be effective cost managers. Differentiation and cost control are compatible. All companies should continually search for innovatory differentiation opportunities and for ways of improving their cost efficiencies. We have seen in earlier chapters that leveraging resources and setting stretching targets for employees can help bring about innovation and savings; benchmarking best practice in other organizations (a process of measurement and comparison) can also provide new ideas and suggestions for reducing costs and improving efficiency. Organizations from different sectors and industries can be a useful source of ideas if they have developed a high level of expertise. It should be stressed that this process is a search for ideas that can be customized for a different organization rather than an exercise in simply copying.

At the same time, it is vital for an organization to clearly understand its position relative to its competitors. Table 9.1 provides a general framework for considering competitive strategies and Figure 9.7 shows how we might benchmark competitors for comparison with an organization and with customer preferences. The key order criteria – key success factors – are listed down the left-hand side and ranked in order of their importance to customers. Their relative significance is plotted against the horizontal axis. The ability of different competitors to meet these key success factors is illustrated by the dotted lines. Competitor A is clearly relying on its quality and technical back-up, for which it has a good reputation, but is it truly satisfying customer needs? Competitor B seems to offer an all-round better service, and in a number of areas is providing a service beyond that demanded. Given the areas, this actually may be good as it will indicate a reliable supplier.

Visit the website:
http://www.
itbp.com

How would our customers rank our products/services in relation to those of our competitors?

Not as good as. We must improve!

No worse than. This implies a general dissatisfaction, so there must be real opportunities to benefit from improvement and differentiation.

As good as the others, no better, no worse. Again opportunity to benefit if new values can be added and real differentiation perceived.

Better than. We must still work hard to retain our lead!

I subscribe absolutely to the concept of stealing shamelessly! Wherever you come across a good idea, if it's likely to work, pinch it. There's nothing wrong with that. There is a quite respectable word – benchmarking – which is the same thing if you think about it.

Bill Cockburn, Group Chief Executive, WH Smith

Table 9.1
A framework for evaluating
competitive strategies

Scope	Global; industry-wide; niche Single or multi-product/service Focused or diversified Vertical linkages with suppliers/distributors
Objectives	Ambitious for market or segment leadership Market presence just to support other (more important) activities
Success	Market share Image and reputation Profitability
Commitment	Aggressive: willing to acquire to grow Passive survivor Willing to divest if opportunity arises
Approach	Offensive – attacking other competitors Defending a strong position (Note: the same strategy [new products, price cuts] can be used both offensively and defensively) Risk taking or risk averse Teasing out new segments or niches
Strategy	High quality – perhaps with technological support High service Low price
Position	Cost advantage or even cost leadership enjoyed Clearly differentiated
Competitive resources	High technology base; modern plant Location relative to markets Quality of people (ability to add value) Reputation

The examples provided for each of the eight criteria are not offered as an exhaustive list.

Competitive positioning

A successful competitive position implies a match between customers' perceptions of the relative quality or value of a product or service – in comparison to rival offerings – and its price, again in relation to the prices of competing products or services. The relevant area of analysis is the segment or segments in which an organization chooses to compete; and, in addition, the 'total price' should be used for comparison purposes. Customers, for example, may willingly pay a premium purchase price initially for a particular brand of, say, an electrical good or car if they believe that over its life it will incur lower maintenance and service costs than competing brands. Products offered at initially lower prices may be perceived to be more expensive overall.

Figure 9.8 features a competitive positioning grid. Three basic positions are shown by Sectors 1,2 and 3. Sector 6, high perceived prices but only average (at best) quality is an untenable position in the long-run. Sector 4 illustrates a company competing on price, which can be a successful strategy, but it can provoke competitive responses. In which case, it may only serve in driving

Significance of factor

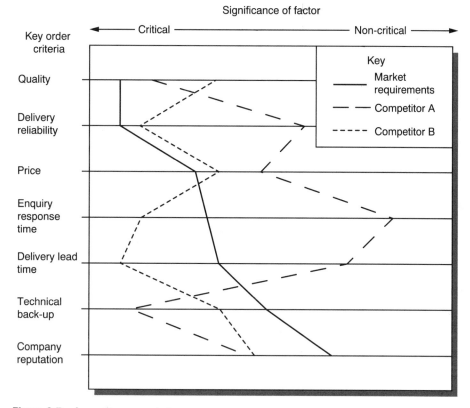

Figure 9.7 Competitor gap analysis.

down all prices and making all competitors less profitable. Do-it-yourself chains, such as B&Q, for example, are now starting to believe that the key to survival – in a crowded market – is to offer permanently competitive prices as well as developing a unique identity. Sporadic high discounts are being replaced by 'everyday low prices'; success is more dependent on volume sales than the actual margins on individual products.

Effective differentiators, commanding premium prices and earning superior profits with high margins, are shown as Sector 5. Their success is partially dependent upon sound cost management, as we have seen.

Figure 9.9 illustrates a number of possible competitive strategy changes for companies in selected positions in the matrix.

Concluding comments

This chapter has concentrated on how an organization can gain a deeper understanding of its competitive environment with a view to becoming a stronger more effective competitor through creating and sustaining competitive advantage. The closer a business is to its customers, the more it will understand the market and the industry. Competitive strategy, essential for every product and service that the organization makes and markets, involves a

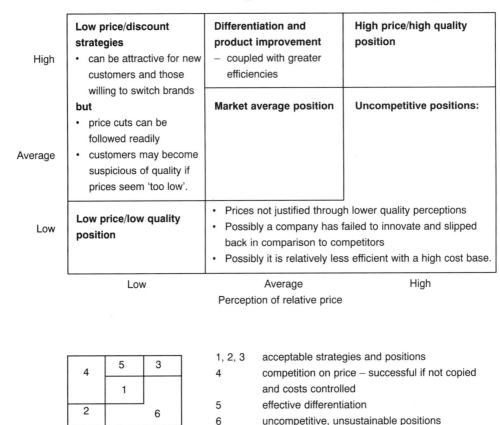

Figure 9.8   A competitive position matrix.

vision about how best to compete. There are a number of ways to generate competitive advantage, and the process is both logical and creative. The choice will also be influenced by the strategic leader and by the organization's culture. However, every employee contributes in some way to both lower costs and uniqueness, and therefore it is important that the competitive strategy is communicated and understood throughout the organization.

Table 9.2 summarizes a number of the points covered in this chapter and shows how individual functions can contribute to competitive advantage. These issues will be explored further in the next three chapters.

In the end, the most successful companies will be those with:

❑ differentiated products and services which are recognized for their ability to add value, and are
❑ produced efficiently
❑ upgraded over time through innovation and improvement, and which
❑ prove relevant for international markets.

Porter contends that competitors can be viewed as 'good' or 'bad'. Good ones differentiate, innovate and help to develop an industry; bad ones just cut prices in an attempt to drive others out of business. Good competitors should be encouraged as they sharpen their rivals and help to set up barriers against bad

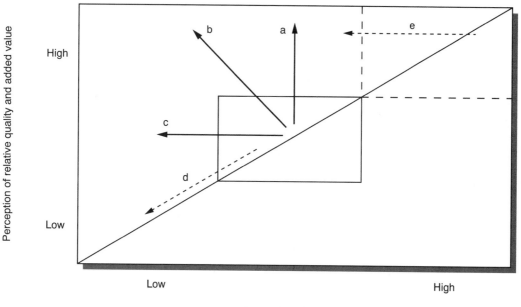

Figure 9.9 Possible competitive strategy changes. Strategies a, b and c – obvious improvement strategies from an average position. Strategy d – possible switch from an average to a low price/lower quality segment. Strategy e – price reduction for market share from a high-quality competitor. Competitors in area 6 (Fig. 9.8) right of the diagonal line need new strategies to move to the left of the diagonal.

competitors. A good competitor seeks to increase the market by improving products, not by cutting prices. An interesting example is Polaroid who invented and patented the instant picture camera. Kodak introduced a rival product but Polaroid eventually succeeded in establishing that it broke their patent illegally. Whilst both products were in competition Polaroid became a much more effective competitor as they were unable to rely on their barrier to entry. By contrast it has been argued that certain large Japanese companies have literally bought themselves into segments of the computer and semiconductor industries by accepting very low prices until volume sales have been achieved. Where this has the effect of driving rivals out of business, as has been the experience in random access memory (RAM) chips, the question arises whether it is in the best long-term interests of consumers. Much depends upon the strategies of companies when they reach a stage of market domination.

These points are expanded further in Key Reading 9.1.

New windows of competitive opportunity are always opening.

❑ Products and services can be improved to open up new markets and segments, as was the case with organizers which competed for the market pioneered by Filofax.

❑ New technologies change behaviour and demand, e.g. personal computers, personal cassette players such as the Sony Walkman, and hole-in-the-wall cash dispensers.

❑ Changes in attitude. Concern for the environment created the opportunity for unleaded petrol; acceptance of fast foods led to the growth of McDonald's and Pizza Hut.

Table 9.2

Functional strategies and competitive advantage

Functional strategy	Competitive strategy	
	Low cost	Differentiation
Marketing	Large companies can obtain media discounts	Image – reinforced by well-known strategic leader
Operations	Efficient plant management and utilization (productivity) Re-engineered processes which reduce costs	Low defect rate and high quality Re-engineered processes which add extra value
Human resources	Training to achieve low rejections and high quality. Policies which keep turnover low	Incentives to encourage innovation
Research and development	Reformulated processes which reduce costs	New, patented breakthroughs
Finance	Low cost loans (improves profit after interest and before tax)	Ability to finance corporate strategic change, investments and acquisitions
Information technology	Faster decision making in flatter organization structure	Creative use of information to understand customer needs, meet them and out-perform competitors
Distribution/ logistics	Lower stock-holding costs	Alliances with suppliers and/or distributors which are long-term mutually supportive

This list of examples is indicative only, and not an exhaustive set of possibilities.

They say: 'Do you sleep well at night with all the competition?' I say: 'I sleep like a baby'. They say: 'That's wonderful'. I say: 'No, no. I wake up every two hours and cry!' Because its true, you know. You have to feel that restlessness.

Roberto Goizueta, Chief Executive, Coca-Cola Corporation

How can we expect to succeed when we are playing cricket and the rest of the world is practising karate?

Sir Edwin Nixon, Chairman, Amersham International

International competitiveness

National competitiveness is not associated with factor costs, economies of scale and government protectionism. Rather it is associated with the ability to innovate – using the term in its widest sense. The search for new technologies and new ways of doing things – and this requires investment. Investment in research and development, in information technology and in marketing – and very much in people. A change in culture is implied for countries like Britain.

Sustained competitive advantage at a national level can only come about if firms are committed to change and to shifting the base of their competitive edge. The Japanese did this with motor cars, starting with basic, low-cost vehicles, progressing through mass market production to technically advanced products. Companies gain international competitive advantage, succeeding against the 'best' rivals, because they respond positively to pressure and challenge – they benefit heavily from having strong domestic rivals, aggressive home-based suppliers and demanding local customers.

The creation of this competitive advantage by certain firms in certain industries does not happen by chance. According to Porter (1990) there are four key attributes which together constitute the 'diamond of national advantage'. The term 'diamond' is used to emphasize the inter-relationships and inter-dependencies between the factors.

The diamond of national advantage

The four constituent parts are as follows:

1. **Factor conditions**, such as the availability of skilled labour. These factors, however, are not inherited, but consciously created often as a response to scarce resources. The Japanese, for example, enjoy competitive advantage in terms of delivery lead times and low costs, through JIT (just-in-time) systems, which they invented mainly as a response to the scarcity and high cost of land and space in Japan. The most valuable factor advantages tend to be specialized and require sustained investment. In fact, quite often they must be specialized in order to be sustainable – a generally well-educated workforce, for instance, is not a source of long-term advantage, but particular specialized skills may well be.

   Frequently the creation of suitable factor conditions is a function of the other three forces, which facilitate the investment needed.

2. **Demand conditions**, especially in the home market. Porter argues strongly that global competitiveness actually increases the significance of the home market. A demanding clientele at home will often force firms to innovate if they are to compete successfully; and it is this which provides the basis for sustainable international advantage. If the nation's values and culture are also being exported – as has been the case with particular aspects of the USA to Europe, such as fast foods and credit cards – the advantage is reinforced.

3. **Related and supporting industries**, which themselves are internationally competitive. This ensures ready access to the raw materials and skills necessary to create advantage through either low costs or differentiation. The close proximity of related industries can ensure a quicker response to market trends and changes, and facilitate rapid innovation. At the same time suppliers should not be locked in irrevocably and exclusively to manufacturers, and producers should be free to resource abroad if necessary or appropriate.

   Italian leather goods are an example of this. Manufacturers of different types of shoes (often specializing in a limited product range), producers of gloves and handbags, machinery suppliers and the leather manufacturers themselves are located in a closely linked cluster which is mutually advantageous and self-reinforcing.

4. **Firm strategy, structure and rivalry in the domestic market**. There is no one single universal management style which guarantees competitive success. Whilst the Italians have developed flexible networks which meet their need to compete in fast moving fashion markets, the medium-sized German companies which dominate the European engineering industry, by contrast, succeed because of their well-defined management hierarchies and working practices which emphasize quality, precision and reliability.

   Rivalry amongst domestic producers acts as a powerful competitive stimulus. Hoffman-La Roche, Ciba-Geigy and Sandoz, the three main Swiss pharmaceutical companies, are a case in point. In industres

(Continued overleaf)

where the Japanese have achieved domination, there are several rivals; Porter's research team identified 112 machine tool manufacturers, 34 in semi-conductors, 25 in audio equipment and 15 in cameras. The more this rivalry is concentrated geographically, the greater the intensity of the effect. Italian jewellery, Swiss pharmaceuticals and Japanese motorcycles have all benefited from geographic concentration.

A commentary

Porter's central message in *The Competitive Advantage of Nations* is that competition is good for nations, and that anything which departs from or undermines competition is, by definition, bad. This could appear to be inconsistent with arguments put forward in his earlier books. To be fair he has always stressed the value of 'good' competition which forces rivals to strive for ever-higher standards. But he also emphasizes the importance of assessing industry attractiveness before seeking to establish sustainable competitive advantage. Industry attractiveness is related to the ability to make above-average profits. An industry with intense rivalry between competitors, powerful suppliers and demanding buyers, and possibly with stagnant or declining sales, may offer only low profit potential to even the most effective and efficient business. Rationalization, and the exit of certain producers, will be required to make the

industry more attractive. Once this has happened, companies which find ways of creating and sustaining competitive advantage can be profitable.

Porter believes that the source of competitiveness is the national home base. However, for many companies operating in Europe the home base has already become too small. Electrolux derives competitive advantage from a European base rather than its home base of Sweden.

Consistent with other work on the relative success of diversification and acquisition strategies in the USA (see Chapter 16) Porter argues 'companies should be narrowing their focus to build international strength in core businesses'. This may well be true in a number of cases, but some diversification may be inevitable for companies whose core products are experiencing long-term, even terminal, decline. Diversification may be tricky to implement successfully and be a high-risk strategy, but it may be the only realistic alternative to prevent decline.

Writing in *The Economist* (1990) Porter invoked European companies 'to compete and not collaborate' with too many cross border mergers or strategic alliances. The benefits of the 1992 single market were most likely to be gained 'if competition is encouraged and collusive behaviour curtailed'. The trend towards alliances and cross-border mergers will not make firms more competitive: 'dominant firms, or ones

caught in a web of links with rivals, will not innovate and upgrade. Supposed efficiencies from mergers will prove elusive in practice. Companies depending on collaborative activity will become mired in problems of co-ordination'.

Porter may be correct to point out the dangers of cross-national mergers, such as those in the European airline industry, stifling competition. His arguments about the difficulties involved in implementing alliances, similar to those involved in making acquisitions work effectively, are also well founded. Other researchers have reached similar conclusions. But alternative evidence clearly supports the contention that economies of scale do exist in industries like telecommunications, aircraft manufacture and semiconductors which have expanded beyond national borders. Equally the European car industry, where six manufacturers each enjoy market shares between 10 and 15%, is unlikely to be sustainable in its existing form when national barriers are removed. Some cross-national mergers, and/or a strengthening of existing alliances, seems inevitable. Indeed, the leading German and Japanese companies have already embarked on a series of alliances, and Ford of America has joined them.

Based on: Porter, ME (1990) *The Competitive Advantage of Nations*, Free Press; and a summary of the conclusions in *The Economist* (1990), 9–15 June, pp. 23–6. A useful critique can be found in *Management Update*, **2**(1), Autumn, 1990.

Summary

In this chapter we have explored the issues behind competitive strategy, concentrating on the nature and structure of the industry and the position of the firm in the industry.

Specifically we have:

- emphasized the importance of timing in competitive strategy – there are push forces for change from competitor actions, and pull forces from the market; the organization must respond to these by recognizing that strategies have life cycles and that at times they need replacing
- considered the structure of industry in the UK – the meaning of monopoly power has been explored in relation to the experience curve and economies of scale; concentration ratios have been defined and examples of industries exhibiting high concentration have been analysed
- described the policy of the UK government towards competition in terms of structure, conduct and performance; and considered how this might affect strategic decision making – in particular the roles of the Office of Fair Trading, the Restrictive Practices Court and the Monopolies and Mergers Commission have been featured
- analysed the model proposed by Michael Porter which contends that an industry can be analysed in terms of five key forces: the threat of new entrants; the relative power of both suppliers and buyers; the threat of substitute products or services; and rivalry amongst the existing firms in the industry – these forces determine industry profitability
- linked to the above model, defined product differentiation and explored the linkage between cost structures, breakeven and profits
- analysed a second Porter model of competitive advantage which argues that three generic competitive strategies of cost leadership, differentiation and focusing can be based on lower costs and differentiation
- developed a grid and a checklist for evaluating a company's competitive strategy and comparing it with the competition
- reviewed Porter's work on international competitiveness.

Checklist of key terms and concepts

You should feel confident that you understand the following terms and ideas:

- ☆ Monopoly power
- ☆ Concentration ratios
- ☆ Competition policy in the UK
- ☆ Economies of scale; the experience curve
- ☆ Porter's model of five forces which determine industry profitability
- ☆ Product differentiation
- ☆ The relationship between cost structures, breakeven and profits
- ☆ Porter's model of competitive advantage
- ☆ Cost leadership, differentiation and focus strategies
- ☆ Competitor benchmarking
- ☆ The diamond of national advantage.

Questions and research assignments

Text related

1 From your own experience, and from news-paper and other articles you have read or seen, list examples of where monopoly power and restrictive practices have been investigated, and where proposed mergers have been considered by the Monopolies and Mergers Commission. (If you wish to follow up any of these investigations, all the reports are published by HMSO.)

2 Study Figure 9.5 and consider where you would place other major car manufacturers and why. Where should Rover be categorized? Which companies appear to be 'struck in the middle' without a clear strategy for competitive advantage?

Library based

3 Take an industry of your choice, perhaps the one you work for, and assess it in terms of
(a) concentration
(b) Porter's model of five forces.
From this analyse one or more of the major competitors in terms of their chosen competitive strategies.

The following might prove useful sources of information:

❏ Business Monitors (PA and PQ series)
❏ Annual Report of the Director General of Fair Trading (as a source of ideas)
❏ Monopolies and Mergers Commission reports, which usually feature a comprehensive industry analysis
❏ McCarthy's Index (press cutting service for firms and industries).

4 In 1994 the Office of Fair Trading was examining the supply chain for Wall's Ice Cream, a Unilever subsidiary. The MMC had earlier agreed that it was in order for Unilever to insist that retailers stock only Wall's ice cream if they are using freezer cabinets Unilever has supplied. However, the company cannot insist that retailers buy their ice cream only from certain specified wholesalers. What was the outcome of this investigation?

5 How successful has Porsche been since the introduction of its new models? Do you believe the size of its niche is viable, or might the company have to extend its range?

6 Trace the major strategic changes (and changes of ownership) in the brewing industry since the MMC report in 1989.

Recommended further reading

Ohmae (1982) provides a pithy and anecdotal introduction to competitiveness, and Michael Porter's two books (1980 and 1985) are valuable works of reference on industry structure and competitive advantage.

It would also prove fruitful to read at least one report of the Monopolies and Mergers Commission which analyses competition in a particular industry.

References

Kanter, RM (1990) Strategic alliances and new ventures, Harvard Business School Video Series.

Ohmae, K (1982) *The Mind of the Strategist*, McGraw-Hill.

Porter, ME (1980) *Competitive Strategy: Techniques for Analysing Industries and Competitors*, Free Press.

Porter, ME (1985) *Competitive Advantage: Creating and Sustaining Superior Performance*, Free Press.

Prowse, M (1986) Competition policy: how the UK got left behind, *Financial Times*, 11 June.

PART III

In this part we consider how the
organization might add value through
products, processes, service, people,
information and financial management in
order to create and sustain competitive
advantage. People and information are
critical strategic resources required to
underpin the strategic processes through
which products and services are
designed, created, promoted and
delivered to customers. Some of the
material will already be familiar to many
readers; it is for this reason that we select
those topics which have important
strategic implications.

The Content of Competitive Strategies

Figure III.1 shows how organizational resources need to be used to drive the competitive cycle. Constant or ideally growing, sales and market share can lead to economies of scale and learning, and, in turn, cost reductions and improved profits. The profits could, in a particularly competitive situation, be passed back to customers in the form of lower prices, but, more normally they will be reinvested in the organization. This can generate productivity improvements, sometimes with new capacity, and, then, lower prices and/or further cost reductions. The investment can also bring about new sources of added value and differentiation, possibly allowing higher prices and further profit growth. The improved competitiveness should also increase sales and market share and drive the cycle round again. These changes might take the form of gradual, continuous improvements or radical changes to establish new rules of competition.

To drive the cycle continuously, organizations will need a mix of steady state managers to maintain efficiencies and more creative change agents to develop new initiatives.

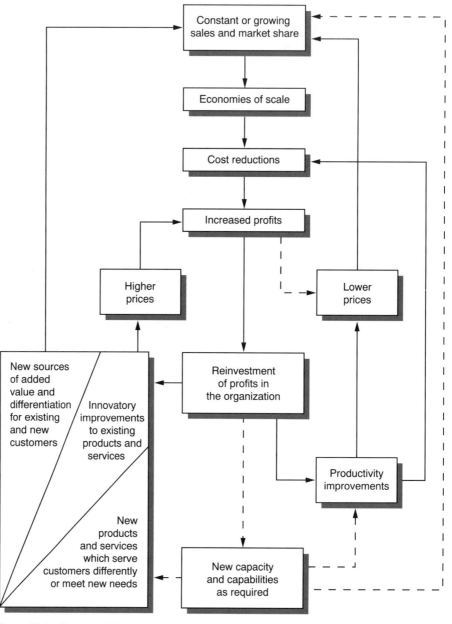

Figure III.1 The competitive cycle.

10

Competitive Advantage Through Products, Processes and Service

This chapter develops a framework for understanding how value and competitive advantage can be created and measured in every functional area of the business. The strategic contribution of marketing, operations, research and development, innovation and total quality management are discussed.

Learning objectives

After studying this chapter you should be able to:

■ Demonstrate how competitive advantage might be created through adding value in any functional area of the business
■ Describe an organizational value chain and explain how it might be used for evaluating competitive advantage
■ Explain the strategic significance of market positioning, segmentation, branding and customer management
■ Discuss the importance of research and development and how innovation might be fostered in an organization
■ Assess the contribution of operations management in satisfying customer needs profitably
■ Identify marketing and operations issues which are particular to service, not-for-profit and small businesses
■ Explain the strategic significance of effective linkages with suppliers and distributors
■ Define total quality management and assess its significance as an aspect of organization culture.

Introduction

Organizations add value through a series of processes, including research and new product development, manufacturing and marketing activities. In order to create and sustain competitive advantage from this value (in the form of effective differentiation and/or cost savings) organizations need the help of their suppliers and distributors. As well as a manufacturing infrastructure, two key organizational resources – people and information – make a valuable contribution. People and information are the subject of separate chapters; the other issues are discussed here.

We look first at the concept of an organizational value chain, which provides an excellent framework for clarifying how an organization might create differentiation and effectively manage its costs. We then consider selected aspects of marketing strategy, highlighting how careful positioning and branding can foster important links between an organization and its customers. The creation of new values, new products, new services and new levels of customer service are discussed before we examine the strategic contribution of operations

Don't forget to visit the website: http://www. itbp.com

management. After looking at the importance of a linked supply chain, we conclude by examining how issues of quality and service underpin the whole process.

Clearly, on occasions, it is vital that organizations review, and, where necessary, change or 're-engineer' their processes. Quite often major process changes require changes to the structure and style of the organization. Consequently a discussion of business process re-engineering is deferred to Chapter 19 when we look at issues of structure.

Figure 10.1 draws these themes together. The most important points are:

- ❑ Value creation requires co-operation between suppliers, manufacturers, distributors and customers.
- ❑ Manufacturers must understand their customers' needs and organize to satisfy these needs creatively, innovatively and effectively in a changing and competitive environment.
- ❑ Cost management and constant improvement are always important, as are a high level of service delivery and 'total quality management'.
- ❑ This implies well thought-out, effectively controlled processes, whose performance is evaluated and measured.
- ❑ There is a fundamental reliance on the contribution of people.

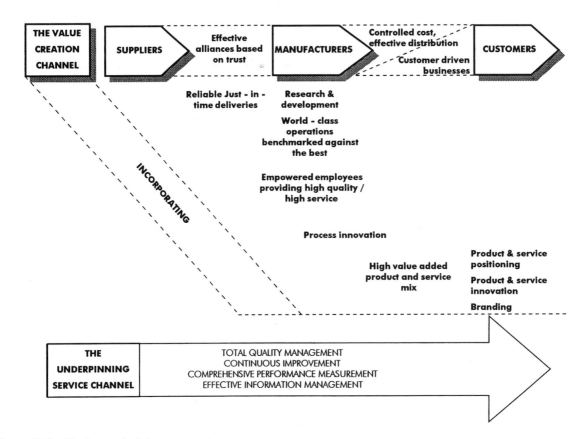

Figure 10.1 Effective supply chain management.

Excellence and quality were perceived to be vital strategic issues during the 1980s, as British companies strove to close the gap between themselves and their competitors, particularly the Japanese. These factors are now seen as 'givens'; simply, they are essential requirements for competitiveness rather than opportunities for distinctiveness. The strategic challenge now is to find ways of adding new values distinctively. A competitive marketing stance is crucial; synergistic links between operations and marketing are critical. Gemini Consulting (1994) contend that many multi-national organizations have yet to fully appreciate the implications of this. They are less globally-minded than they think or claim, less customer-focused and insufficiently flexible to dominate world markets. Parallel research by London Business School and IBM (IBM, 1994) concludes that only one in 50 manufacturing sites in Europe is genuinely 'world class', although 75% of the companies involved believed they were strong enough to compete with the best of their international rivals.

The first subject of this chapter is the role of the value chain in diagnosing competitive advantage by

❏ generating an understanding of the behaviour of costs and the implications for strategy
❏ identifying a firm's actual and potential sources of differentiation.

However, as Ohmae (1988) argues, it is important to remember that competitive advantage is being sought for one major purpose – to serve customers' real needs. It is not simply to beat competition, although clearly an organization is seeking to be more effective, competitively, than its rivals.

In addition to ensuring that resources are concentrated on creating and sustaining core competencies which meet today's key success factors, there must be some investment in the future. Hamel and Prahalad (1989) cite the Japanese approach of 'strategic-intent' strategies concerned with changing the competitive environment and using customer-oriented innovations to weaken those competitors who are currently strong and, at the same time, develop new key success factors.

The organization's value chain

Whilst strategic success depends upon the way the organization as a whole behaves, and the ways managers and functions are integrated, competitive advantage stems from the individual and discrete activities that a firm performs. A cost advantage can arise from low cost distribution, efficient production or an

---

A manager's ability to initiate and manage change will be critical in determining the success of his business. He must monitor the competitive environment constantly and be prepared to react quickly to changes in market conditions. More importantly, though, he must also be seeking to take the initiative by building up and using competitive advantage through innovation; not just through new products but through pursuing an innovative approach to production, marketing, personnel policies, control systems and every other aspect of the business. Efficient management is essential, but it is innovative management that is the real key to success.

Patrick Sheehy, when Chairman, BAT Industries plc

excellent salesforce who succeed in winning the most appropriate orders. Differentiation can be the result of having an excellent design team or being able to source high-quality materials or high-quality production. Value chain analysis is a systematic way of studying the direct and support activities undertaken by a firm. From this analysis should arise greater awareness concerning costs and the potential for lower costs and for differentiation. Quite simply, argues Porter (1985), competitive advantage is created and sustained when a firm performs the most critical functions either more cheaply or better than its competitors. But what are the most critical factors? Why? How and where might costs be reduced? How and where might differentiation be created?

Activities in the value chain

The value chain developed by Michael Porter is illustrated in Figure 10.2. There are five primary activities, namely inbound logistics, operations, outbound logistics, marketing and sales, and service. In the diagram they are illustrated as a chain moving from left to right, and they represent activities of physically creating the product or service and transferring it to the buyer, together with any necessary after-sale service. They are linked to four support activities: procurement, technology development, human resource management, and the firm's infrastructure. The support activities are drawn laterally as they can affect any one or more of the primary activities, although the firm's infrastructure generally supports the whole value chain. Every one of the primary and support activities incurs costs and should add value to the product or service in excess of these costs. It is important always to look for ways of reducing costs sensibly; cost reductions should not be at the expense of lost quality in areas which matter to customers and consumers. Equally costs can be added justifiably if they add qualities which the customer values and is willing to pay for. The difference between the total costs and the selling price is the margin. The margin is increased by widening the gap between costs and price. The activities are described in greater depth below.

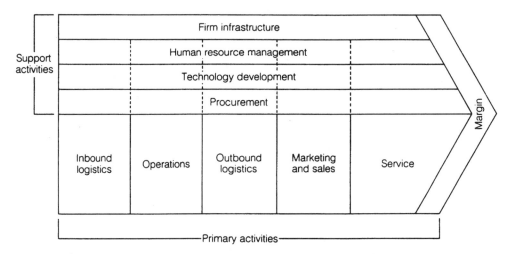

Figure 10.2   The value chain. (*Source*: Porter, ME (1985) *Competitive Advantage: Creating and Sustaining Superior Performance*, Free Press.) Copyright Michael E Porter, © 1985. Adapted with permission of the Free Press.

Primary activities

- ❏ **Inbound logistics** are activities relating to receiving, storing and distributing internally the inputs to the product or service. They include warehousing, stock control and internal transportation systems.
- ❏ **Operations** are activities relating to the transformation of inputs into finished products and services. Operations includes machining, assembly and packaging.
- ❏ **Outbound logistics** are activities relating to the distribution of finished goods and services to customers.
- ❏ **Marketing and sales**: includes such activities as advertising and promotion, pricing, and salesforce activity.
- ❏ **Service** relates to the provision of any necessary service with a product, such as installation, repair, extended warranty or training in how to use it.

Each of these might be crucial for competitive advantage. The nature of the industry will determine which factors are the most significant.

Support activities

- ❏ **Procurement** refers to the function or process of purchasing any inputs used in the value chain, as distinct from issues of their application. Procurement may take place within defined policies or procedures, and it might be evidenced within a number of functional areas. Production managers and engineers, for example, are very important in many purchasing decisions to ensure that the specification and quality is appropriate.
- ❏ **Technology development:** technology is defined here in its broadest sense to include know-how, research and development, product design and process improvement.
- ❏ **Human resource management** involves all activities relating to recruiting, training, developing and rewarding people throughout the organization, issues discussed in Chapter 11.
- ❏ **The firm's infrastructure** includes the structure of the organization, planning, financial controls and quality management designed to support the whole of the value chain.

Again, each of these support activities can be very important in creating and sustaining competitive advantage.

Sub-activities

Porter argues that it can often be valuable to subdivide the primary and support activities into their component parts when analysing costs and opportunities

---

Ours is a business which is judged by the quality of service, attention to detail and a consistent level of personal commitment by all those engaged in it. This can only be achieved by dedication, training and perceptive management. The good manager endeavours to solve problems before they arise and to anticipate the needs of guests. He must think today what he does tomorrow and learn from the lessons of yesterday.

Lord Forte of Ripley, when Chairman, Forte plc

for differentiation. For example it is less meaningful to argue that an organization provides good service than to explain it in terms of installation, repair or
training. The competitive advantage is likely to result from a sub-activity specifically. Similarly, the marketing mix comprises a set of linked activities which
should be managed to complement each other. However, competitive advantage can arise from just one activity in the mix, possibly the product design, its
price or advertising, technical support literature, or from the skills and activities
of the salesforce.

Linkages within the value chain

Although competitive advantage arises from one or more sub-activities within
the primary and support activities comprising the value chain, it is important
not to think of the chain merely as a set of independent activities. Rather it is a
system of inter-dependent activities. Linkages in the value chain, which are relationships between the activities, are very important. Behaviour in one part of
the organization can affect the costs and performance of other business units
and functions, and this quite frequently involves trade-off decisions. For example, more expensive materials and more stringent inspection will increase costs
in the inbound logistics and operations activities, but the savings in service
costs resulting from these strategies may be greater. The choice of functional
strategies and where to concentrate efforts will relate to the organization's
competitive and corporate strategies concerning competitive advantage.

Visit the website:
http://www.
itbp.com

Similarly a number of activities and sub-activities depend on each other. The
extent to which operations, outbound logistics and installation are co-ordinated can be a source of competitive advantage through lower costs (reduced
stockholding) or differentiation (high quality, customer-oriented service). This
last example uses linkages between primary activities, but there are also clear
linkages between primary and support activities. Product design affects manufacturing costs; purchasing policies affect operations and production costs; and
so on.

In addition the firm can benefit from establishing linkages between activities
in its business units only, and no realistic case could be made for a merger. In
addition some of the cultural problems involved in takeovers and mergers,
which are also discussed in Chapter 16, can be avoided.

We have introduced and discussed the concept of the value chain and it is
now important to consider how it might be applied in the evaluation of costs
and differentiation opportunities.

The value chain and competitive advantage

Cost leadership and differentiation strategies

Cost leadership
We discussed in Chapter 9 the argument of Porter (1985) that the lowest cost
producer in either a broad or narrow competitive scope

❑ delivers acceptable quality but produces the product or service with lower
   costs than competitors
❑ sustains this cost gap

❏ achieves above-average profits from industry average prices.

This cost advantage will be achieved by the effective management of the key determinants of costs.

The differentiation strategy

Similarly Porter argues that the successful application of a differentiation strategy involves

❏ the selection of one or more key characteristics which are widely valued by buyers (there are any number of opportunities relating to different needs and market segments)
❏ adding costs selectively in the areas perceived to be important to buyers, and charging a premium price in excess of the added costs.

The success of this strategy lies in finding opportunities for differentiation which cannot be matched easily by competitors, and being clear about the costs involved and the price potential. Costs in areas not perceived to be significant to buyers must be controlled, and in line with competitor costs, for otherwise above-average profits will not be achieved.

The successful implementation of both these strategies therefore requires an understanding of where costs are incurred throughout the organization. Understanding costs and the search for appropriate cost reductions involves an appreciation of how costs should be attributed to the various discrete activities which comprise the value chain. Table 10.1 compares a possible cost breakdown for a manufacturing firm with that for a firm of professional accountants. If an analysis of the value chain is to be meaningful, it is important that the costs are genuinely attributed to the activities which generate them – and not simply apportioned in some convenient way – however difficult this might prove in practice. Given the figures in Table 10.1 one might question

	Manufacturing firm (% of total)	Professional firm of accountants (% of total)	
Primary activities			
Inbound logistics	4	8	(data collection for audits)
Operations	64	26	(actual auditing)
Outbound logistics	1	5	(report writing and presentations)
Marketing and sales	7	21	(getting new business)
Service	1	3	(general client liaison)
	77	63	
Support activities			
Procurement	1	1	
Technology development	10	8	(IT development)
Human resources management	2	16	
Firm's infrastructure	10	12	
	100	100	

Table 10.1
Indicative cost breakdown of a manufacturing and a service business

These figures are only indicative, and should not be seen as targets for any particular firm.

whether the manufacturing firm is spending enough on human resources management and marketing, and the accountancy practice too much.

Cost drivers

It is important to appreciate which cost drivers are the most significant. The following cost drivers can all influence the value chain.

- ❏ Economies of scale and potential experience and learning curve benefits.
- ❏ Capacity utilization, linked to production control and the existence of bottlenecks.
- ❏ Linkages. Time spent liaising with other departments can incur costs, but at the same time create savings and differentiation through inter-relationships and shared activities.
- ❏ Inter-relationships and shared activities. Shared activities, possibly a shared sales force, shared advertising or shared plant, can generate savings. Close links between activities or departments can increase quality and ensure that the needs of customers are matched more effectively.
- ❏ Integration. This incorporates the extent to which the organization is vertically integrated, say manufacturing its own component parts instead of simply assembling bought-in components, or even designing and manufacturing its own machinery. This again can influence costs and differentiation, and is an important element of the strategy of YKK which is featured as an example later in this chapter.
- ❏ Timing – buying and selling at the appropriate time. It is important to invest in stocks to ensure deliveries when customers want them, but at the same time stockholding costs must be monitored and controlled.
- ❏ Policies. Policy standards for procurement or production may be wrong. If they are set too low, quality may be lost and prove detrimental. If they are too high in relation to the actual needs of the market, costs are incurred unnecessarily.
- ❏ Location issues. This includes wage costs, which can vary between different regions, and the costs of supporting a particular organization structure.
- ❏ Institutional factors. Specific regulations concerning materials content or usage would be an example.

Porter argues that sustained competitive advantage requires effective control of the cost drivers, and that scale economies, learning, linkages, inter-relationships and timing provide the key opportunities for creating advantage. In the case of a low-cost leadership strategy, the cost advantage is relative to the costs of competitors, and over time these could change if competitors concentrate on their cost drivers. Consequently it is useful to attempt to monitor and predict how competitor costs might change in the future linked to any changes in their competitive and functional strategies.

Common problems in cost control through the value chain

It was mentioned above that it can prove difficult to assign costs to activities properly, and this is one of the difficulties which are likely to be encountered in using value chain analysis as a basis for more effective cost management. Porter contends that there are several common pitfalls in managing costs for competitive advantage:

❑ Misunderstanding of actual costs and misperceptions of the key cost drivers.
❑ Concentrating on manufacturing when cost savings are required. Quite frequently it is not the area to cut if quality is to be maintained, especially once a certain level of manufacturing efficiency has been achieved.
❑ Failing to take advantage of the potential gains from linkages.
❑ Ignoring competitor behaviour.
❑ Relying on small incremental cost savings when needs arise rather than introducing a long-term permanently installed cost management programme.

Differentiation opportunities

It has been mentioned on a number of occasions that competitive advantage through differentiation can arise from any and every area of the business. In relation to the component parts of the value chain, the following are examples of where differentiation might originate.

Primary activities

❑ **Inbound logistics:** careful and thoughtful handling to ensure that incoming materials are not damaged and are easily accessed when necessary, and the linking of purchases to production requirements, especially important in the case of just-in-time (JIT) manufacturing systems.
❑ **Operations:** high quality; high-output levels and few rejections; and delivery on time.
❑ **Outbound logistics**: rapid delivery when and where customers need the product or service.
❑ **Marketing and sales:** advertising closely tied to defined market segments; a well-trained, knowledgeable and motivated salesforce; and good technical literature, especially for industrial products.
❑ **Service**: rapid installation; speedy after-sales service and repair; and immediate availability of spare parts.

Support activities

❑ **Procurement:** purchasing high-quality materials (to assist operations); regional warehousing of finished products (to enable speedy delivery to customers).
❑ **Technology development**: the development of unique features, and new products and services; the use of information technology to manage inbound and outbound logistics most effectively; and sophisticated market analyses to enable segmentation, targeting and positioning for differentiation.
❑ **Human resources management:** high-quality training and development; recruitment of the right people; and appropriate reward systems which help motivate people.
❑ **Firm's infrastructure:** support from senior executives in customer relations; investment in suitable physical facilities to improve working conditions; and investment in carefully designed information technology systems.

In searching for the most appropriate means of differentiating for competitive advantage it is important to look at which activities are the most essential as far as consumers and customers are concerned, and to isolate the key success factors. It is a search for opportunities to be different from competitors in ways which matter, and through this the creation of a superior competitive position.

The Japanese zip manufacturer YKK, the world market leader, grew to enjoy a superior competitive position, and the company's strategy is analysed against the value chain in the next section. The underlying philosophy of YKK, the cycle of goodness, was illustrated in Chapter 4, Box 4.2.

An application of the value chain

YKK have arguably succeeded in creating both cost leadership and substantial differentiation with their corporate, competitive and functional strategies, and these have resulted in effective barriers to entry into the industry and close relationships with customers. The idea might be illustrated as follows:

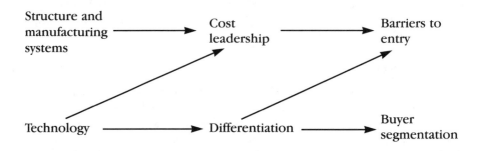

The essential components of the strategy, summarized below, are illustrated in Figure 10.3, which places them in the context of the value chain and highlights the linkages.

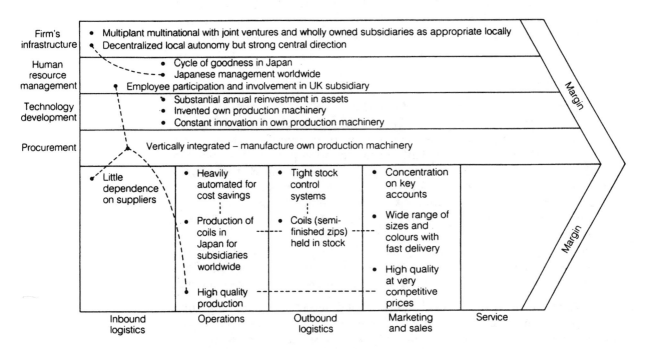

Figure 10.3 YKK's competitive advantage and the value chain. Developed from Channon, DF and Mayeda, K, *Yoshida Kogyo KK 'A' and 'B' Case Studies*. Available from The European Case Clearing House. The dotted lines (– – –) illustrate the linkages.

YKK is structured as a multi-plant multi-national company with both wholly owned subsidiary companies and joint ventures throughout the world. The latter organizations are primarily the result of local politics, particularly in low labour cost countries in the Far East. Whilst the subsidiaries are decentralized and enjoy some local autonomy, they are invariably managed at the top by Japanese executives on a period of secondment. Consequently there is substantial influence from the Japanese parent.

YKK invests a significant percentage of after tax profits back in the business, and as a result is heavily automated and able to enjoy the benefits of the experience/learning curve. Moreover YKK prices its finished products very competitively both to generate customer satisfaction and to create barriers to entry. The company is vertically integrated, designing and manufacturing its own production machinery, and this gives it a unique competitive edge. It is also particularly innovative as far as both machinery and finished products are concerned.

Coils of semi-finished zips are produced in the Far East, particularly Japan, and exported to such countries as the UK, where they are cut to size and finished in response to customer orders. This results in both cost advantages and speedy deliveries from semi-finished stocks. A wide range of colours and sizes is kept ready for finishing. In the UK the key garment manufacturers and the retail outlets they serve are targeted by YKK and are given special service.

The cycle of goodness philosophy has not been exported in its complete form, but employee relations are an important aspect of the human resources strategy. Participation and involvement are essential features, and total quality management is a key feature.

Conceptually the value chain is a useful way of analysing resources and functions within the organization in the context of how they might individually contribute to competitive advantage. At the same time the linkages between them should be assessed, because it is from these inter-relationships and linkages that synergy in the form of additional cost savings or differentiation is created. To apply the value chain properly it is important also to allocate costs to activities and to evaluate whether costs could be saved in various areas or whether additional spending on certain activities might yield additional benefits by adding value in ways which are important to consumers. In practice it can be difficult to assign costs accurately. In this respect the actual application, rather than the concept, of the value chain is more applicable for managers than for students of this subject. In my experience, applications of the value chain do pose difficulties for managers, primarily because the management accounting systems in many organizations do not readily provide the data in the form required. Developing this theme, Johnson and Kaplan (1987) contend that certain costs are extremely difficult to allocate to certain

---

Corporate restructuring to improve international competitiveness is a vital priority for British and European businesses in the 1990s. However, such restructuring must be a continual process of change and revitalization if we are to consistently satisfy the consumer's need for the highest quality products and services at the most competitive cost. The leadership of this process is the primary role of management in the modern company.

Ian G McAllister, when Chairman and Managing
Director, Ford Motor Company Limited, UK

individual products, but they are the costs of activities which are very significant in relation to total quality and in turn competitive advantage. Machine failures are one example, and they affect a number of products and can mean that deliveries are late and possibly priorities are changed. But how should the costs be allocated? As production systems become increasingly sophisticated, overheads, as a proportion of total costs, increase relative to the direct costs of labour and materials. Genuinely allocating these production overheads is difficult.

Nevertheless the value chain can provide an extremely useful framework for considering the activities involved in producing products and services and considering their significance for customers.

In the next section of this chapter we look at the importance of customers, and how organizations might exploit marketing ideas and policies to add value for customers in a competitive environment.

Marketing strategy

We have stated earlier, in Chapters 8 and 9, that industries and markets are generally becoming more competitive and international. Companies which are unable to differentiate clearly will be forced to compete on price; even effective differentiators will find they need to price carefully. Moreover the need for improved levels of service can never be fully satisfied. Companies, therefore, must understand the needs and expectations of their customers and seek to satisfy these – with support from their suppliers and distributors – more effectively than their rivals. Existing customers must be retained and new business won. In a competitive environment, product and service development and innovation are essential for both of these objectives.

Some organizations, targeting new customers, may be tempted to neglect their existing accounts. This is wrong. It will invariably cost less to retain a customer than to win a new one. In addition, it has been estimated that in terms of profit, a 2% increase in customer retention is equivalent to a 7% cost reduction.

In this chapter we consider:

❑ market positioning strategies and
❑ branding, and later
❑ new product and service development and innovation
❑ total quality management to ensure a high level of customer service.

Satisfying consumer needs

> *Marketing is not a specialized activity at all. It encompasses the entire business. It is the whole business seen from the point of view of its final result, that is from the customer's point of view. Concern and responsibility for marketing must therefore permeate all areas of enterprise.*
>
> (Peter Drucker, 1954)

Thus marketing is a concept, and as such it is an important aspect of organizational culture. Marketing links selling organizations with buyers. Selling, however, is concerned with converting finished products and services into cash; marketing involves decisions about what that product should be, how it should be promoted, and where and how it should be made available.

If an organization is marketing oriented, then decisions about products and services will clearly relate to the needs of the market. Product design, specification, quality and packaging will be designed to customer and consumer preferences. Prices will be influenced by competition and consumer perceptions of quality relative to alternative products or services, as well as by costs. Advertising and promotion will seek to show how the product or service meets consumer needs and will target the product to specific segments of the market; and the product will be made available where customers would expect to find it. These four decision areas (product, price, promotion and place) comprise what is known as the **marketing mix**, and the management of them lies within the marketing function. However, there is also an implicit need for production, financial and other managers in the organization to regard consumers as vital stakeholders in the business because if their needs are not met they may well buy from the company's competitors. Customers buy products and services because they believe that they will satisfy particular needs and wants, not simply because they are available. Acceptance of the marketing concept means that all the functions within the business work together to sense, serve and satisfy customers.

Each of the marketing mix activities provides an opportunity for a company to differentiate, create and sustain competitive advantage; and some organizations are renowned for their expertise in a particular area. Avon, for example, created a distinct competitive advantage through distributing direct to customers in their homes. However, the most successful competitors appear to differentiate in a variety of ways simultaneously and thus add multiple values for their customers. Case 10.1 considers how Benetton differentiates, manages its costs very soundly and networks closely with its suppliers and distributors to add value in a number of distinctive, winning ways. To achieve this level of success, organizations need to:

❏ keep in close touch with their customers to monitor their changing needs and expectations
❏ at the same time, monitor and evaluate competitor activity, and also
❏ use their own resources to come up with new ideas which might interest or excite customers ahead of their rivals.

Visit the website:
http://www.
itbp.com

The marketplace decides the extent of our success. Hoechst sets its sights on a partnership with customers based on a spirit of mutual interest. We aim to recognize our customers' needs swiftly, and satisfy them promptly in a cost-effective manner. We respect the power of the marketplace.

Professor Wolfgang Hilger, Chairman, Hoechst AG

One important element of both the marketing mix and an organization's production strategy is the product range, encapsulating issues of range size and variety. The bulk of an organization's sales and profits will typically be generated by a minority of the products in the range.

In 1996, to save costs and drive turnover, WH Smith decided to reduce the size of its total product range from 49,000 to 35,000 lines. To give one example, WH Smith concluded that 95% of the profits it earned from pens came from 275 pens out of a total range of 700.

Case 10.1
BENETTON

Benetton was founded in Italy in 1965 by a brother and sister to distribute homemade sweaters to retailers. Luciano Benetton had wholesaling experience, and his sister, Guiliana, design skills. Two other brothers joined later. The first Benetton store was opened in 1968. By 1978 there were 1000, and by 1988 5000, franchised outlets world-wide. After 1978 more and more manufacturing was subcontracted. Benetton has also diversified into related goods like shirts, jeans, gloves, shoes and perfume. The business is still run from a headquarters in Italy.

Europe is seen as the home market, with production and marketing in both the West and East. However Benetton is well established in the USA and Canada, and growing in Japan and the Pacific rim.

In 1972 Benetton started dyeing assembled garments rather than just the yarn; and this has enabled it to develop competitive advantage through a speedier response to fashion changes. If an item is selling unexpectedly well in one particular shop, and additional stocks are wanted, Benetton aims to provide the additional stocks faster than its competitors could. Requests are relayed through terminals to Benetton's mainframe computer, which also carries comprehensive product details and production requirements – the benefit of using CAD and CAM extensively. Production requirements can therefore be fed quickly into the manufacturing system, even though a lot of work is sub-contracted. Finished products are stored in one central warehouse, run by robots and just a handful of people. A quarter of a million items can be handled daily. Benetton aims to replenish their shops with popular items in one week ex-stock, four weeks including production. Production costs are increased by dyeing finished goods, but stock management overall (raw materials, semifinished and finished items) is efficient.

> Much has changed in the world since Benetton was started in 1965, but not our mission: to satisfy people's needs with young, colourful, comfortable and easy-to-wear products. This has been our route to world leadership in the design, production and distribution of clothing, accessories and footwear for men, women and children. Our range has been constantly enriched over time by intensive research into new materials and designs – and further additions will follow.

Benetton is an international company with a global brand image, which has been built around the theme 'The United Colors of Benetton'. This international image is boosted by a strong association with motor racing. Benetton won both the Formula 1 drivers' and constructors' championships in 1995.

> Colour makes Benetton unique. The secret lies in presenting a broad spectrum of shades, creatively mixed and matched – new and different every time. The study of colour is our greatest research commitment as we constantly seek out new tones.

Advertising features the same central message and choice of media throughout the world, although the actual themes of the advertisements vary. This is based on the premise that customers in different countries use clothing and accessories to express personal lifestyle preferences, with a tendency to demand increasingly higher quality goods. Advertising campaigns 'feature simplified, unambiguous images that convey meaning to the largest possible number of people and cultures throughout the world'.

(Quotations extracted from
Benetton Annual Reports)

Simply they must be *responsive* in a dynamic environment: reactive to customers and competitors as appropriate, and proactive in finding new ways of adding value.

Marketing must therefore relate closely to innovation. New products or services may result from a search to find better ways of satisfying needs; equally they may result from technical developments which create something new and different. In both cases there will be a need to persuade the market to change behaviour, in the first case by highlighting exactly how needs can be better satisfied, and in the second possibly by attempting to change needs and tastes. Some organizations will be more innovative than their competitors and willing to take greater risks. Davidson (1972) used the expression offensive marketing to 'describe a set of attitudes and techniques designed to exploit the marketing approach fully'. Companies, he argues, should innovate and respond to competition by counterattack and not by imitation. Offensive marketing companies are

- ❑ **profitable**: they achieve an appropriate balance between the firm's and the consumers' needs
- ❑ **offensive**: they seek to lead the market and make competitors followers
- ❑ **integrated**: the marketing concept permeates throughout the organization
- ❑ **strategic:** the marketing effort is directed towards long-term competitive advantage
- ❑ **effective at implementing the strategy.**

Figure 10.4 summarizes four important evaluative frameworks which are discussed briefly below

The product life cycle

Sales of a product or service follow a pattern – they grow slowly, then more quickly, peak and then decline. The time scale for different products can vary markedly, some staying in existence for over 100 years and others appearing and disappearing in just one year. The life cycle illustrated could represent a successful product in aggregate terms or individual competing brands of the same product or service. Conceptually the pattern is the same. However, the time scale, the steepness of the growth and decline, and the maximum sales achieved will vary between competing brands, with some being launched after others and some disappearing before their competitors.

The product or service is not profitable until the growth stage, and it is most profitable during the maturity and saturation stages. Profits peak before sales revenue is maximized, and then fall away to zero during the decline phase.

I am convinced that well-balanced, well-managed companies who are alive to their customers' needs and able to take action efficiently and quickly to meet them, will move ahead of others.

Geoffrey Mulcahy, Chairman and Chief Executive,
Kingfisher Plc

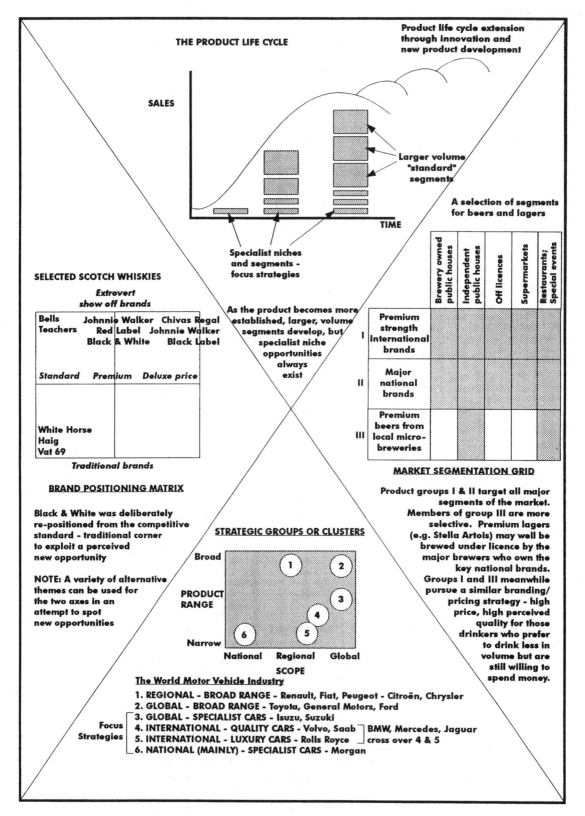

THE PRODUCT LIFE CYCLE

SALES

Product life cycle extension through innovation and new product development

Larger volume "standard" segments

TIME

Specialist niches and segments - focus strategies

As the product becomes more established, larger, volume segments develop, but specialist niche opportunities always exist

A selection of segments for beers and lagers

	Brewery owned public houses	Independent public houses	Off licences	Supermarkets	Restaurants; Special events
I Premium strength International brands					
II Major national brands					
III Premium beers from local micro-breweries					

MARKET SEGMENTATION GRID

SELECTED SCOTCH WHISKIES

Extrovert show off brands

Bells Teachers	Johnnie Walker Red Label Black & White	Chivas Regal Johnnie Walker Black Label	
Standard	*Premium*	*Deluxe price*	
White Horse Haig Vat 69			

Traditional brands

BRAND POSITIONING MATRIX

Black & White was deliberately re-positioned from the competitive standard - traditional corner to exploit a perceived new opportunity

NOTE: A variety of alternative themes can be used for the two axes in an attempt to spot new opportunities

Product groups I & II target all major segments of the market. Members of group III are more selective. Premium lagers (e.g. Stella Artois) may well be brewed under licence by the major brewers who own the key national brands. Groups I and III meanwhile pursue a similar branding/ pricing strategy - high price, high perceived quality for those drinkers who prefer to drink less in volume but are still willing to spend money.

STRATEGIC GROUPS OR CLUSTERS

Broad

PRODUCT RANGE

Narrow

National   Regional   Global

SCOPE

Focus Strategies

The World Motor Vehicle Industry
1. **REGIONAL - BROAD RANGE -** Renault, Fiat, Peugeot - Citroën, Chrysler
2. **GLOBAL - BROAD RANGE -** Toyota, General Motors, Ford
3. **GLOBAL - SPECIALIST CARS -** Isuzu, Suzuki
4. **INTERNATIONAL - QUALITY CARS -** Volvo, Saab ⎤ BMW, Mercedes, Jaguar
5. **INTERNATIONAL - LUXURY CARS -** Rolls Royce ⎦ cross over 4 & 5
6. **NATIONAL (MAINLY) - SPECIALIST CARS -** Morgan

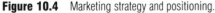

Figure 10.4 Marketing strategy and positioning.

Once products start declining it becomes increasingly necessary for companies to replace them with something else if they are to remain viable. However, it is possible to extend the life cycle by continually finding new users or new uses for the product once the existing situation reaches saturation point. Nylon is an example which is often quoted to illustrate a product that has continually been applied to new uses. Radio is another. Originally radios were essentially non-portable and exclusively mains operated. Over the years portable versions have been developed, followed by battery-operated transistor radios, and more recently radio cassette players, stereo radio cassette players, car radios, ultrathin radios, 'Walkman's' with radios and clock radios. Throughout these developments which have made listening easier and more convenient, there has been an increase in the number of stations which can be obtained and better reception. As a result owners of one type of radio have replaced them with the newer better models, and in many cases have increased their ownership to more than one radio per household.

It is important, therefore, that companies are aware of the stage in the product life cycle that their various products and services are at: first, because this provides an indication of the most appropriate competitive and marketing strategies; second, because it is an important determinant of profitability; and, third, because it helps highlight the need for new products or services if the company is to grow, or at least not decline. The product life cycle is not predictive in the sense that companies can easily forecast when the product will move from one stage to another, but a clear appreciation of the current situation is helpful. It increases awareness and at times indicates the need for change.

Ohmae (1982) points out that the length of the product life cycle is decreasing for an increasing number of products, particularly those affected by microelectronics. Primarily there are three reasons:

- technological changes in materials and processes
- changing tastes of customers
- competitive activity aimed at increasing market share in order to gain greater benefit from the experience effect.

Particular models of electronic calculators, watches, stereo products and computer peripherals are examples of products whose life cycles have shortened. At the same time the development costs and times of the newer versions have increased, requiring companies to make early decisions concerning the commitment of time and resources for research and development, which itself must be applied and consumer oriented.

No business, however modest its aspirations, can safely assume that the way it serves its customers today will be sufficient for tomorrow. New competitors are always on the horizon, potentially offering a better deal. Customers' tastes change, and so do the means of satisfying them, be it through advances in product and process technology or new ideas on the organization and motivation of the workforce, whose own aspirations and aptitudes in turn are rapidly altering. In such a climate, mere survival demands at least a response to change; competitive success requires that change is anticipated, exploited, and at best originated.

John Banham, previously Director-General,
Confederation of British Industry

Market analysis and segmentation

It is important for managers in an organization to understand how large in aggregate terms the market or markets in which they compete are, and how quickly they are growing. It is also vital that they appreciate how the market is segmented, how it might be segmented, and how segment and niche opportunities are constantly changing.

The product life cycle chart in Figure 10.4 illustrates that whilst niche opportunities always exist, larger, volume segments emerge as the product or service becomes more and more popular. Proactive organizations will seek to create new niche opportunities which have the potential to grow into larger and profitable segments in which they are the leading competitor.

In simple terms, not every customer seeks exactly the same specification, levels of performance, looks or availability from a product or service. Some will be more concerned with price than others; some will be loyal to particular brands whilst others will readily substitute. In other words they seek different satisfactions. Where these differences can be identified, and customers can be grouped and reached through specially targeted advertising and promotion, products can be tailored to suit particular needs; and this concentration on the special needs of a segment can make a product particularly attractive to certain customers.

Figure 10.4 provides a very simple segmentation grid to show how different beers can be seen as mass market or niched products. The 'standard' beers of the major brewers and the leading international lagers (typically brewed under licence) are widely available, although their popularity and promotional support may vary markedly between the different segments. Some premium brands will be distributed much more selectively, as are the products of the smaller regional breweries. Very small micro-brewers focus on a limited number of pubs and restaurants within their targeted segments.

Consequently further levels of analysis are required if we are to understand the complexities of this market. Public houses, for example, are differentiated by their owners (often the leading brewers) to appeal to distinctive groups of customers – groups separated by age, social class and drinking habits. Some pubs are primarily 'drinking houses' with a wide range of different beers, whilst others will feature pool tables, games machines and juke boxes. Many have been refurbished as pub-restaurants for older couples and families. Again the various products/brands will enjoy differing popularity in the different types of outlet.

The leading hotel groups often manage a range of different format properties, each designed to appeal to a separate market segment or buyer need. Crowne Plaza hotels, for example, owned by Holiday Inn, are high-rise rather than three or four storeys and offer above average facilities. Some hotels in the group feature Holidomes, which are indoor recreation centres. Holiday Inn also have Holiday Inn Select (business hotels), Holiday Inn Suites (for longer stay customers), Garden Court hotels (high service levels, but few frills such as the moderately expensive restaurants found in standard Holiday Inns), and Express hotels and motels (budget prices and no restaurants).

Competitor analysis

Analysing the market in terms of customer preferences and segments can reveal new opportunities for creating competitive advantage, but organizations may not be able to take advantage of every opportunity they spot. The decision to try and take advantage of an opportunity should be related to the particular strengths of the organization and the closeness of fit between these and the preferences of the market. An organization should seek to define any distinctive competencies it may have which will enable it to add value in particular ways and thus differentiate a product or service such that it is not easily copied by competitors. The distinctive competence could relate to product or service design or quality, distribution coverage, advertising and image or price.

In a competitive environment a firm will want its product or service to be clearly differentiated, attractive to the customers it is targeting and relatively more profitable than its competitors. This is the price–quality relationship. Where a number of products or brands compete with each other and where the market perceives them as substitutes, profitability is determined by both costs and market perceptions. The attractiveness of an individual product or brand to buyers will depend upon how it is priced relative to the alternatives and the perception of its relative quality. Customers will expect the alternative they perceive as being the best quality to be priced higher than the perceived lower quality alternatives. Conversely a manufacturer of a product or service which the market perceives as being inferior to competition, regardless of whether it is actually inferior, must price below those alternatives that the market perceives as being superior if it is to achieve any significant sales. A manufacturer in this position might well seek to add value in some new way in order to improve the perceived quality or seek to ensure that the costs attributable to the product are below those incurred by competitors.

A brand positioning matrix like the one shown on the left of Figure 10.4 can be useful for this. A number of brands of Scotch whisky, including Bells, Teachers and Black & White, have been deliberately repositioned, using new promotions, as a result of this type of analysis. Younger drinkers were identified as a growing target market, but they prefer whiskies with an 'extrovert' rather than a 'traditional' image.

Strategic groups

Market segmentation analyses markets by customer and preference differences; brand positioning analysis considers the position of a brand, relative to competing brands, from the perspective of the customer. Ideally the matrix will concentrate on those factors of greatest significance to the market. A third useful chart is a strategic group, or cluster, analysis which focuses on identifying exactly which brands compete with which other brands and follow broadly similar strategies. The chart in Figure 10.4 identifies six distinct groups in the world motor car industry.

It is important to realize that in any one market segment there can be competitors from more than one cluster. Renault and Peugeot (Cluster 1) compete with Ford and General Motors (Cluster 2) in selected segments; the Lexus models from Toyota (Cluster 2) compete with models from Cluster 4.

In reality, in the market segmentation grid for beers and lagers (Figure 10.4), a selection of segments (by type of outlet) is shown across the top and clusters of competitors are shown down the side.

In the end these various analyses enable manufacturers to better appreciate the nature of the market place in terms of customer demands and expectations, and the relative magnitude of their direct competition. They can also identify valuable new opportunities.

Branding

Many differentiated products, and some services, are identified by brand names. These brand names, and/or the identity of the companies which own them, convey an image to customers. Simply, brands are reputations; and advertising is often used to create and reinforce this image and reputation. As competition intensfies, more and more products are perceived as commodities, sold essentially on price. When this happens, differentiation and branding become increasingly significant. The product itself needs a clear brand identity; a supportive corporate image, a company brand, is also valuable.

Brands add value, possibly the promise of some particular satisfaction or experience, a 'guarantee' of a specific level of quality, or reliability. Consequently a brand can be seen as an actual product or service augmented by some additional added value. Branding is important and valuable; the drive to establish and maintain a recognized brand image can bring about differentiation and innovation. Nescafé, for example, has had several variants and improvements over the years. However, the value added must be real; informed customers in the 1990s will quickly see through any marketing hype. Moreover, the distinctiveness will not be achieved without investment, in both research and development and advertising, issues we will take up later.

Ideally, successful branding will generate customer loyalty and repeat purchases, enable higher prices and margins, and provide a springboard for additional products and services. Customers expect to find the leading brand names widely available in distribution outlets, but, in the case of, say, grocery products, the supermarkets will typically only offer the Number One and Number Two brands alongside their own-label competitor. In the case of groceries, strong branding has been essential for enabling the leading manufacturers to contain the growing power of the leading supermarket chains. Nevertheless, branding has not exempted them from tight pricing strategies. Edwin Artzt, until recently the Chief Executive of Procter and Gamble, has stated that 'winning companies offer lower prices, better quality, continuous improvement and/or high profits to retailers'. The quality of own-label products has increased, and consequently the magnitude of the premium that customers will pay for the leading manufacturer brand has declined in recent years. Procter and Gamble, which is not alone in this strategy, has adopted perpetual 'everyday low prices' for all its products. Marlboro, the world's leading cigarette brand, has been reduced in price dramatically in the mid-1990s. In the competitive food sector, product innovation, quality, specific features and, to a lesser extent, packaging are seen as the most effective means of distinguishing brands from own-label alternatives.

Examples:

❑ *Persil* and *Pampers*: brand names not used in conjunction with the manufacturer's name – they are produced by Unilever and Procter and Gamble respectively.
❑ *Coca-Cola*: manufacturer's name attributed to a product.
❑ *Cadbury's Dairy Milk* and *Barclaycard Visa*: the first is a combination of a company and a product name, the second a combination of an organization and a service.

Visit the website:
http://www.
itbp.com

❏ *St Michael*: the personalized brand name used on all products sold by Marks and Spencer.

❏ *Hoover*: A company name which has become irrevocably associated with a particular product, although it is just one of a range of products produced by Hoover.

A number of large organizations have, through strategic acquisitions and investments in brands, established themselves as global corporations. Examples include:

❏ *Unilever*: now own a variety of food (Bird's Eye, Batchelors, Walls, John West, Boursin, Blue Band, Flora), household goods (Shield soap, Persil, Lux and Surf detergents) and cosmetics (Brut, Fabergé and Calvin Klein) brands.

❏ *Philip Morris*: US tobacco company which has acquired General Foods (US; Maxwell House coffee) and Jacobs Suchard (Switzerland; confectionery and coffee).

❏ *Nestlé*: including Chambourcy (France), Rowntree (UK) and Buitoni (Italy).

❏ *LVMH*: Discussed earlier, in the introduction to Part II.

These companies can afford substantial investments in research and development to innovate and:

❏ strengthen the brand, say by extending the range of products carrying the name

❏ develop new opportunities. For example, Mars Bars Ice Cream, which was launched simultaneously in 15 European countries and priced at a premium over normal ice cream bars

❏ transform competition in the market. Pampers disposable nappies have been developed into a very successful range of segmented products selling throughout the USA and Europe.

Brand names are clearly an asset for an organization. The value of the brand, the so-called brand equity, relates to the totality of all the stored beliefs, likes/dislikes and behaviours associated with it. Customer attitudes are critical; so too are those of distributors. The fact that a brand can command a certain amount of shelf space in all leading stores carries a value. However, creating and maintaining the image is expensive. It has been estimated that manufacturers spend on average 7% of sales revenue to support the top ten leading brands, covering all product groups; this percentage increases as the brand recognition factor decreases. Because of this, manufacturers need to control the number of brands they market at any time; Procter and Gamble have withdrawn 25% of their brands in recent years. Similarly, new product launches need to be managed effectively. Case 10.2 considers some of the threats to Kellogg's, the world's leading manufacturer of breakfast cereals.

There is a so far unresolved debate concerning how these assets might be properly valued in a company balance sheet. The US magazine, *Financial Week*, has postulated that the world's most valuable brand name is Marlboro (owned by Philip Morris) and that it must be worth in excess of $30 million. In terms of monetary value, Coca-Cola is perceived to be second. The most valuable European brand is Nestlé's Nescafé; the three leading British brands (worldwide) are Johnnie Walker Red Label whisky (owned by Guinness), Guinness itself and Smirnoff Vodka (Grand Metropolitan). Where the most recognized

At the end of the 1970s and into the early 1980s Kellogg was the clear market leader for breakfast cereals throughout the world, but with a declining market share in the USA. Between 1979 and 1983 share fell from 42% to 38% in a market which was growing at only 2% per year, compared with 7% a decade earlier. One issue was public pressure against foods with a high sugar content.

It was anticipated that Kellogg like their main rivals in the cereals market, would diversify into other foods. Kellogg has diversified on a relatively small scale, but essentially has chosen to concentrate on grain-based products, in particular cereals, 'which it knows best'. New products have been developed and launched on a regular basis, some featuring artificial sweeteners. Additionally, because of the declining birth rate, new products have been aimed at adults as well as children. Fibre content has been seen as important for this. Kellogg are careful not to target products too narrowly on the grounds that once they are in a house any member of the family is likely to eat them. There have been a number of successes, and some failures.

As a result Kellogg's market share of 42% was restored in 1985, and generally since then they have out-performed their main rivals who have not been too successful with their diversification strategies.

Breakfast cereals in Europe

Kellogg is again market leader with a 50% market share and six out of the ten best selling brands. British consumers eat more cereal per head than any other country, including the USA, but other European countries, which have tended to prefer breads, meats and cheeses for breakfast, provide a real opportunity as people are becoming more health conscious. In the 1990s, for example, the French market for breakfast cereals has been growing at over 20% per year.

Weetabix has traditionally held second place, but no more. The market has become more competitive and Kellogg has faced an important challenge from a joint venture between Nestlé and General Mills of the USA, known as Cereal Partners, who are seeking a 20% market share. They currently have around 10%. General Mills has provided the brands – particularly Cheerio's, an oat cereal which helps reduce cholesterol, and Golden Grahams, which compete with (and preceded) Kellogg's Golden Crackles – and Nestlé the distribution network. At the same time, private label brands have been enjoying the fastest rate of growth, especially for mueslis and bran products, which are particularly popular with adult consumers.

The challenge for Kellogg lies in creating new product ideas, and the generation of a strong enough cash flow to fund the necessary advertising budgets, both for supporting existing brands and launching the new cereal products. Each cereal product needs to be promoted individually.

brand names are tied to high market shares and above-average margins, they are typically valued at over twice their annual revenues.

Relationship marketing

Branding helps to establish, build and cement relationships between manufacturers, their customers and their distributors. The term relationship marketing is used to reinforce the argument that marketing should be perceived as the management of a network of relationships between the brand and its various customers. Marketing, therefore, aims to enhance brand equity and thus ensure continued satisfaction for customers and increased profits for the brand owner. Implicit in this is the realization that new customers are harder, and more expensive, to find than existing ones are to retain. This potent mix of brand identity and customer care is clearly related to the whole service package offered by manufacturers to their customers, and to total quality management, which we discuss later in this chapter.

Global products

Conventional marketing wisdom suggests that individual countries exhibit different needs and that the same product cannot be sold throughout the world. Modifications of varying degrees must be made to suit individual tastes. Specifically the marketing mix will be unique for each separate market. Levitt (1984) argued that these differences would narrow and that opportunities for products to be more global in their market coverage would increase. He emphasized that although the same product may be sold in a variety of countries it does not follow that the branding, positioning, promotion and selling need be the same, although in certain instances they are. As a result manufacturers should examine both the similarities and differences in needs and tastes in their target markets. Globalization does not imply that tastes will become homogeneous throughout the world, but that market segments will expand across frontiers.

Manufacturers will benefit considerably in terms of cost savings if they can make their products global and market them in a similar way throughout the world; and a number of products have illustrated that this is possible. Coca-Cola, Levi jeans, Marlboro cigarettes, Kodak film, McDonald's and many electrical and electronic products are examples. See also Case 10.1, Benetton.

Certain McDonald's products such as the Big Mac and hot apple pies are available ubiquitously world-wide; in addition, individual country products are sold selectively. Norwegians can buy MacLaks (salmon sandwiches), whilst branches in Italy are the only ones in Europe to feature salad bars. None the less the style and ambience of the restaurants, and the distinctive golden arches sign, are the same world-wide.

Kotler (1988), however, argues that less than 10% of the world's products will lend themselves to global branding, and that many new life-styles are emerging that lead to the opening up of many new differentiated markets.

Research and development, innovation and new products

New product development

Hamel and Prahalad (1991) claim that the most profitable companies will be those that create and dominate new markets, looking for opportunities to further exploit key skills and competencies. They will take measured risks, innovate and launch new products and services, some of which may fail. Such companies will learn from their experiences.

New products are also needed to replace existing ones at appropriate stages in the life cycle and as additional products to foster growth. Where new products are additional to those the company already markets, rather than replacements, there should be an analysis of where synergy might be obtained. New products will be aimed at generating new revenue, and they may boost the sales of existing products if they strengthen the overall line or mix, but they will also generate additional costs. Synergy can be obtained where such costs are not entirely new ones but where certain of them can be shared amongst an increasing number of products. Too diverse a range of unrelated products could lead to organizational problems because of the different skills required in manufacturing and marketing and key success factors which are different for each business area.

Cooper (1987), whose research work has concentrated on industrial products, argues that new innovatory products have a far greater chance of market success than 'me too' variants of existing competitive products, and that without realized competitive advantage the likelihood of success with new products is reduced. Cooper contends that the most important determinants of new product success, in order of importance, are as follows.

❑ The product is superior to competing products in meeting customers' needs.
❑ The product has unique features for the customer.
❑ The product is of a higher quality than competing products.
❑ The product performs a unique task for customers.
❑ The product is highly innovative, new to the market.
❑ The product reduces customers' costs.

The emphasis in these factors is perceived competitive advantage.

Research and development and innovation

In some industries, such as pharmaceuticals research and development, as well as investment in manufacturing technology, is essential for long-term survival and growth. However, Pearson (1988) argues that outstanding companies are consistently innovating in every area of the business, pursuing changes which create value for their customers and consumers. Their approach is to search for new opportunities and package or present them in such a way that they deliver consumer satisfaction. The meaning of innovation is explored in Key Concept 10.1.

There are two distinct but inter-dependent themes:

❑ the acquisition of new technologies through Research and Development (R & D) or buying a new business and
❑ exploiting existing and new technologies innovatively in an entrepreneurial culture.

Intense international competition in many markets means that customers now expect excellent service at very tight prices; manufacturers find it more and more difficult to pass on to customers the full extent of inflationary cost increases. There is, therefore, a constant pressure to improve productivity in manufacturing and distribution, whilst attempting to steal a competitive lead with new products which 'change the basis or rules of competition'.

Innovation may result from internal developments which arise from R & D programmes, and from managers and other employees thinking about how activities might be carried out more efficiently or effectively. Innovation may

---

KEY CONCEPT 10.1

INNOVATION

Innovation takes place when an organization makes a technical change, e.g. produces a product or service which is new to it, or uses a method or input which is new and which is original.

If a direct competitor has already introduced the product or method then it is imitation, not innovation. However, introducing a practice from a different country or industry rather than a direct competitor would constitute innovation.

Innovation implies change and the introduction of something new. Creating the idea, or inventing something, is not innovation but a part of the total process. Whilst at one level it can relate to new or novel products, it may also be related to production processes, approaches to marketing a product

or service, or the way jobs are carried out within the organization. The aim is to add value for the consumer or customer by reducing costs or differentiating the product or total service in some sustainable way. In other words, innovation relates to the creation of competitive advantage. In summary there are four main forms of innovation:

❑ new products, which are either radically new or which extend the product life cycle
❑ process innovation leading to reduced production costs, and affected partially by the learning and experience effect
❑ innovations within the umbrella of marketing, which increase differentiation

❑ organizational changes which reduce costs or improve total quality.

Where the innovation reflects continuous improvement, product or service *enhancement*, and only minor changes in established patterns of consumer behaviour, the likelihood of success is greater than for those changes which demand new patterns of usage and consumption. Examples of the latter include personal computers and compact disc players. Discontinuous innovations such as these are more risky for manufacturers, but if they are successful, the financial payoffs can be huge. By contrast, continuous improvements – which, realistically, are essential in a dynamic, competitive environment – have much lower revenue potential.

---

also be driven by outside forces, such as changes in the nature of competition. Nayak (1991) argues that most good ideas do not come from marketing, sales or competitors, but from customers. It is therefore a function of R&D strategies and of the overall strategic awareness of people. In the latter respect it is cultural. In the case of large complex organizations comprising a number of divisions or business units, decisions have to be taken concerning whether R&D is primarily a centralized or a decentralized activity. At the same time, the extent to which authority and responsibility generally is decentralized affects the freedom and willingness of managers to be innovative. Organizations need strategies for their R & D activities because

❑ R & D constitutes an investment for which the appropriate level of funding must be found;
❑ R & D efforts should be directed towards supporting other strategies concerning improvements in products, services and their manufacture and creation, or the development of new products and services to meet future needs.

It is significant that R & D generally in the UK has received lower priority status than is the case for most other major industrialized countries. Statistics show that whilst R & D spending (as a percentage of sales) by UK companies generally increased during the 1980s, it still lags behind comparable figures for the USA, Germany and Japan.

It is important to allocate R & D funds between invention (technical research) and innovation (applications in manufacturing and marketing). It has been argued that in many industries, such as electronics, both governments and companies in Europe have concentrated on technical research and failed to exploit the inventions. The more marketing-oriented Japanese companies have therefore been able to establish their strong market positions.

Case 10.3 features a British invention which has been exploited abroad and innovation by Gillette.

Innovation and new products

Innovation can take place in any and every area of the business, but at times it will relate specifically to the introduction of a new product or service. New product innovations such as chilled prepared meals (Marks and Spencer), the compact disc (Philips) and the anti-lock braking system for cars (Bosch) took place in companies with established R & D strategies. As a set of activities major product changes and innovations involve idea generation; idea screening; concept definition; development; testing; trial; and launch. These activities are creative, developmental and analytical. Ideas can arise from talking to customers and researching their requirements, from searching internally for better ways of doing things, and by examining competitor activity. Developing a concept through to a stage of market acceptance is likely to be an incremental iterative process characterized by learning. Creativity is an essential requirement, together with entrepreneurial leadership within the organization to champion the changes involved. This need not be the strategic leader personally, as was pointed out in Chapter 3, but it will be important for the strategic leader to encourage entrepreneurship and provide innovatory managers with the necessary encouragement, support and freedom to implement changes.

Visit the website: http://www. itbp.com

The US company 3M is renowned for its ability to empower employees and produce innovatory new products. Masking tape is one such product, Post-It Notes another. Laboratory staff, for example, are free to devote 15% of their time on developing personal ideas; moreover they are free to work in their own preferred way. Technicians are encouraged to talk with customers; internal networking is fostered. Audit teams, which have an official function to evaluate the commercial potential of new technical ideas, cross business boundaries and spread both ideas and good practices.

Innovation and entrepreneurship

There is, then, a clear link between entrepreneurship, which was introduced in Chapter 3, and innovation. Drucker (1985) argues that innovation is the tool of entrepreneurs.

The expression entrepreneurship is being used here to describe a culture oriented towards improvement and change, but the term intrapreneurship, introduced in Chapter 3, could be used instead.

Changes in the service provided to customers and the development of new products and services imply changes in operating systems and in the work of employees, and some of the proposed changes may well be the result of ideas generated internally. But many of the ideas for innovations come from outside the organization, from changes in the environment. This emphasizes the crucial importance of linking together marketing and operations and harnessing the contribution of people.

Case 10.3
THE BAYGEN RADIO AND GILLETTE

The BayGen Radio

The BayGen Radio was invented by English inventor, Trevor Baylis in the early 1990s. Unlike other portable radios, the BayGen does not use batteries; it is powered by clockwork. Its main target market is the Third World, where the cost of batteries is often prohibitively expensive.

Baylis developed the idea after watching a television documentary on the spread of AIDS in Africa, where it was stated that important information was not being made available to people because they could not afford radios. Baylis felt there must be enough power in a spring to drive a small generator, and experimented until he had one which worked.

His prototype radio was featured on the BBC's Tomorrow's World programme, which in turn was seen by Christopher Staines, who at the time was a director of mergers and acquisitions with a leading accountancy firm. Staines was motivated to work through the night on a business plan proposal which he faxed to Baylis. Within 48 hours Staines had the world-wide development rights; Baylis realized he needed external support to exploit the potential of his invention.

Staines raised £143,000 from the Overseas Development Agency and took the idea to South Africa, where he had family connections. He succeeded in raising start-up capital of £600,000; and the publicity generated brought endorsement from President Nelson Mandela. A new factory with a capacity to build 20,000 radios a month was ready in September 1995. The generator has been improved and refined to yield 40 minutes of listening from 20 seconds winding. The secret lies in a special spring which releases energy at a constant rate; by contrast, the spring used for a toy train releases energy with a decreasing flow. Many of the employees are disabled, and early customers included the Red Cross and Unicef. The generator clearly has the potential to be adapted for use in other products.

The first radios were sold to the aid agencies at a wholesale price of $30 (£19). The agencies are free to subsidize them, and sell on at lower prices. The objective is to market the radio at a price lower than the cost of a normal radio and a one year supply of batteries.

In January 1996 the radio was available in the UK by mail order at a price of £65.

Gillette

Gillette dominates the world market for wet shave products, specifically razors and razor blades; a series of timely innovations has kept the company ahead of its rivals. The market is segmentable into three: shaving systems, disposable blades and double edge blades. Gillette dominates systems; Wilkinson Sword is particularly strong in double edge blades, but this is very much the smallest segment.

The growth product in the 1980s was disposable razors, driven by the success of Bic (France) which became a very strong Number 2 to Gillette in this segment. Although Gillette retained its lead, the switch to disposables was a problem. They are relatively low margin products. The company was forced to rationalize and jobs were lost.

However, in 1989, Gillette launched a new product which had been conceived years earlier in its British research laboratory. The Sensor features spring-mounted twin blades which follow the contours of the face to provide a closer, more comfortable shave. This higher margin product immediately built a healthy market share. More recently Sensor for Women and the premium price SensorExcel (with an improved handle and skin guard) have been launched successfully.

Footnote: Braun, featured in Case 10.4, is a subsidiary of Gillette.

Ford in the USA realized some years ago that a number of its engineers had a tendency to 'over-engineer' solutions to relatively simple problems. As a result, its costs were higher than those of its rivals, particularly Japanese and Korean companies, and its new product development times were considerably longer. Instead the company needed 'creative engineers' with a fresh perspective and greater realization of customer expectations.

Moreover innovation and change is an investment, and consequently the financial implications are also an essential consideration.

To summarize this section, the theme of entrepreneurship is that change is normal but need not involve high risk. Entrepreneurs thrive on uncertainty and are involved in the search for innovatory changes in the ways things are done. Successful entrepreneurs are clear decision makers who take calculated risks rather than high risks. Entrepreneurial innovative organizations perceive change as an opportunity, not a threat; expectation of change and improvement is part of the culture; employees expect changes and are supportive; and the financial implications are also properly thought through.

If the culture is change resistant rather than change oriented then proposed changes in systems, technology and ways of doing things may be resisted. In this case it will be necessary either to fit the approach to innovation into the existing culture or to seek to change the culture – ideally the latter.

Speed and competitive advantage

Companies, however successful they might be, are likely to be knocked over by innovative competitors if they stand still and ignore a changing environment. They must adapt and improve if they are to retain their position. To sustain any competitive advantage and grow they must innovate more quickly than their rivals. Consequently, speed is becoming an increasingly important factor in the search for competitive advantage.

The world recession at the end of the 1980s, coupled with the continued economic progress of such Third World countries as Taiwan and Korea, increased world-wide competition. The results are greater cost pressures, new global marketing and production opportunities, the tendency for competitors to copy each other's innovations, and the launching of new products almost simultaneously throughout the world – previously launches tended to be staged over a number of months or even years.

Technological developments in electronics are leading to shorter life cycles for many products and growing difficulties in establishing sustainable competitive advantage. Increasing research and development costs are focusing attention on the strategic value of innovation and incremental change – the constant search for gradual improvements. This is enhanced by the possibilities

---

We are students of Japan here in General Electric. We think they're marvellous, marvellous industrialists. We like their new product development, we like their speed, we like their quality focus. I put them at the pinnacle, and we're working every day to learn everything we can from them.

John F. Welch, Chairman and CEO, General Electric

of computer-aided design and manufacturing, and, in turn, just-in-time systems.

The emergence of global markets and competition is opening up new segmentation opportunities. Companies who can capitalize on these through innovation and product and market development are often able to differentiate their products and services.

Shorter product development times, just-in-time manufacturing, together with the benefits of learning and incremental improvements, can all lead to lower costs. Hence cost leadership and differentiation remain key sources of competitive advantage – speed can enhance their potential.

Speed can, therefore, be manifested in a number of ways. Product development times can be reduced; deliveries from suppliers can be speeded up through just-in-time; and, by utilizing information technology, distributor and retail stocks can be replenished faster. Speed can relate to the whole of the value chain. However, obtaining the competitive benefits of speed is likely to involve more than improved efficiencies through cutting the time taken to do things. A change of attitude towards providing faster, better and customized service is also required. All activities in the value chain need reviewing in an attempt to improve effectiveness.

Competitive advantage through speed will only be feasible if the organization structure facilitates the changes implied, rather than constrains them. Ideas and information must be able to permeate quickly through the organization; and managers at the operational level must be empowered to make decisions. This implies decentralization and possibly fewer levels of management in the hierarchy.

Successful organizations will become fast learners, ideally finding out about changing customer preferences and expectations ahead of their competitors. They will also need to be able to respond quickly to changes in competitor strategies. This again emphasizes the importance of decentralization.

When speed was less important it was quite normal for products to be developed and tested in advance of any investment in the new plant which would eventually be required to produce them in volume. These must now be seen as parallel, not sequential, activities. This necessitates close co-operation between the various functional areas of the business, perhaps using special project teams. As we shall see in Chapter 19, such changes can prove difficult to implement.

Finally, the notion of speed must be considered very carefully in certain industries. The design and development of new drugs and new aeroplanes, for example, should not be hurried if safety and reliability could be compromised.

Operations management

Operations management involves the design, planning and control of the production function, and the decisions which relate to the use of materials, people and machines.

Manufacturing or operations management is concerned with having the right product or service ready at the right time, produced to the right quality, but also at the right cost to ensure that profits are earned. Competitive advantage can be achieved by low costs and by differentiation (which normally adds on costs). Profits are the difference between selling prices and costs. There is an obvious need to control costs, which is a key objective of operations management. But it is also essential to build quality into the product or service, and this is another key objective of operations.

The link between marketing and operations

In this section we look at the relationship between marketing and operations and the need for the two functional strategies to be co-ordinated. Marketing and demand generate opportunities and expectations for the production and operations function; at the same time operational limitations can constrain marketing. Hill (1991) contends that operations management can contribute to the achievement of competitive and corporate objectives in a number of ways, and these are detailed below. The significance of each factor for any organization will depend upon the key success factors.

❏ Capacity and capability: Can the organization produce and provide the goods or services demanded? We must consider dependability and quality. Dependability is the ability to meet delivery and cost targets and promises, and as a result of just-in-time systems it is becoming increasingly important. Quality issues include the ability to maintain a reliable and consistent product quality, the quality of customer service both before and after sale, and the speed of delivery offered and achieved. It is important to understand which quality issues and measures customers and consumers regard as most crucial and to achieve these.

   Organizations must identify and distinguish between order qualifiers (things they have to be able to do to compete in a market) and order winners (distinctive skills and activities which create competitive advantage). When one competitor opens up a competitive gap, say with an innovation, and this is attractive to customers, it becomes an order qualifier for rivals. The lead competitor must then search for a new competitive advantage to sustain its lead.

❏ Efficiency: The effectiveness of the production process, essentially costs, is determined by such measures as cost per unit produced and profit or turnover per employee.

❏ Adaptability: We must consider the flexibility in the short term to respond to changes in demand, and strategies for investing in the future through innovation and research and development. In some industries, as mentioned in the previous section, product life cycles are shortening, and this emphasizes the need for adaptability and a willingness and readiness to change in line with demand.

The driving force in all the world's markets is competition. And the most aggressive drivers are the Japanese. Their competitive strength and ambitions are apparent around the world. Ultimately the only way to succeed is to be fully competitive in the marketplace. Fundamentally this means offering products with utility, style and value that the buyers want, making them with world-class productivity and quality, and serving the customers better than anyone else.

John F Smith Jr, Vice Chairman (International Operations),
General Motors Corporation

Wild (1984) contends that manufacturing decisions should lead automatically from marketing decisions concerning the products or services to be offered, the markets to be served, and the form and level of service which is required or desirable.

In the 1980s Ford redesigned a number of their cars to fit in with consumer preferences. Wheels were moved closer to the corners to improve road holding; and the designers' preference for streamlined rear ends (to enhance the aerodynamic performance) was constrained in order to provide adequate storage space.

These marketing decisions affect, first, the choice of the appropriate operating system and production process. Manufacturing plants can be designed to produce products individually; to produce in batches whereby a range of different products are produced on the same equipment, although not necessarily following the same process route; to produce on assembly lines, which are designed to handle large volumes of the same product, utilizing either labour or robots to assemble parts; or to produce continuously, whereby a capital-intensive plant produces large volumes, again of one product, with labour used to supervise the equipment rather than to do the work. The choice of process is determined by the nature and volume of demand – how many and how similar – and the need for flexibility. In turn the process selected affects both costs and delivery lead times. Continuous plants tend to be the lowest cost and offer the shortest lead times, with individual production at the opposite end of the scale, but they require very large volumes to be viable and they can be very inflexible as far as changing the product is concerned.

Second, the market factors determine the objectives for the operating system. The objectives will concern the service required by customers (differentiation opportunities) and targets for resource utilization (which affects costs). Third, the operating strategies concerning the capacity of the plant or operation, the scheduling of production and inventory (or stock) to be held in the system are involved. As a simple illustration of different objectives and strategies one might compare a department store, a supermarket and a mail-order company. They all buy goods in, stock them, and then sell them on to customers, but the nature of the service they offer, customer expectations and the key success factors all differ. Consequently the operating systems, objectives and strategies will also differ. Department stores offer a wide range of goods which customers can see and handle, which means high stocks, and generally they are not low priced. Staff offer personal service. Supermarkets offer a more limited choice, and staff concentrate on maintaining full shelves and checking people out quickly. For some, low prices may be part of their strategy. A mail order company may offer the same goods as a department store and be able to control their stocks much more efficiently as they are all held in one place rather than in several stores. But the products cannot be seen or tried, and as a result returns may be high.

Holding stock at various parts of the production system can ensure that there is little likelihood of the organization running out. Raw material stocks can be useful to ensure that production can start if an order is received. Semi-finished goods might offer flexibility if they can be used in more than one final product, with the final choice depending again on orders received. Finished goods stock can mean quick deliveries. But all these stocks are a cost, and generally there will be financial pressure to reduce stocks as much as possible. Stocks should

Case 10.4
BRAUN

Braun (Germany) manufacture consumer electrical goods which they market world-wide. Products are designed, produced and marketed in the light of seven strategic principles:

1. Every Braun product is Braun designed; and marketing, technology and cost aspects are considered jointly.
2. The basic strategy is based on small electrical appliances for global markets. Braun target the mainstream market rather than specialist niches.
3. There is a concentration on known production technologies in plastics, metal working and electronics, and a reluctance to diversify away from these.
4. Braun looks to design innovative products with innovative features, and not imitate competitors. Products are constantly improved wherever they can be 'made more useful' for consumers. Half of Braun's products are under three years old.
5. Product quality standards exceed both the industry average and those that marketing stipulate.
6. Braun invests in manufacturing technology and automation to obtain better control and higher returns than are typical of low labour cost countries.
7. Braun looks for high vertical integration, sourcing strategic parts in-house.

The aim of these principles is to build in competitive advantage which other competitors find hard to replicate.

The principles applied

Braun manufacture toasters for which there is a huge market world-wide. Some 10 million per year are bought in the USA alone. The toasters incorporate heating elements which are also used in their hair dryers and coffee makers, and an innovative infra-red sensor (which is a bought-in component contrary to Principle 7). Braun alarm clocks again sell in a large international market. They are all black and flatter than most rival products. Braun have developed the ability to manufacture the clock workings, and they have introduced innovatory voice-control and infra-red hand movement mechanisms for switching off the alarm. Both products are based on known technologies supported by high investment and automation.

Source: Presentation by Bernhard Wild, 'Practical manufacturing strategy: The neglected competitive weapon' conference, Strategic Planning Society, London, 26 November 1990.

really be considered from a strategic point of view. The amount of investment in stocks throughout the production system should relate to the importance of their possible contribution to the organization's marketing effort and needs. Case 10.4, describes how Braun products are based on seven strategic principles which embrace both marketing and manufacturing. However, whilst demand and market opportunities will influence the appropriate operating system and strategies, operational aspects may constrain the marketing strategy. Case 10.5, which considers the marketing–operations link for McDonald's, illustrates that the appropriate level of service from the chosen system can only be met if the product range, and consumer choice, is limited. Without this low prices and fast service would not be possible. Manufacturing strategy involves a number of trade-offs of this nature, and decisions should consider both customer and company needs.

Case 10.5
MCDONALD'S: THE MARKETING AND OPERATIONS LINK

Aspects of the marketing strategy

The product	A variety of fast foods, soft drinks and coffee for eating in and taking away
	Inexpensive relative to restaurants
Markets	Families with young children
	Teenagers
	Shoppers
	Office workers (at lunchtime)
	Children's parties
Service required	Rapid service; no waiting
	Busy and clean image
	Rapid turnover of customers, to maximize use of limited seating space

Aspects of the operations strategy

The operating system

The operating system is a joint kitchen and counter-service system, with co-ordinated staffing, designed to have products cooked and ready for use when they are demanded. Popular products are always cooked ready for immediate sale; for others there is a limited waiting time. The aim is to minimize both waiting time and waste – cooked products not sold after a certain time are thrown away. All cooking and serving operations are consistent in every McDonald's, and training in the systems is extensive. This controls costs, service, quality and reliability.

Objectives

Customer service	Reliable and consistent quality
	Low cost/price
	Rapid service and little waiting
Resource utilization	High for low cost. This imposes a constraint – minimum waiting means food is ready or prepared ready to cook which can only be achieved with a limited product range

Strategies

❏ Capacity must be linked to fluctuating demand (peaks and troughs throughout the day) and therefore part-time employees are utilized extensively.

❏ Scheduling depends upon demand forecasts for individual products, when to produce how many of which, in anticipation of demand.

❏ Inventories: because the product is food, and to save space (and costs), stocks will be maintained as low as possible but not so low as to risk running out of particular items. The significance of this is sharpened by the fact that suppliers are strictly controlled and food can only be obtained from certain sources.

For more detail see Love, JF (1986)
McDonald's: Behind the Arches, Bantam.

The product range

No two consumers have identical needs, and market segmentation and product differentiation opportunities arise from this. However, the more a manufacturer tries to cater for all the different needs expressed by the market, the more his or her production costs will rise. Similarly the more the product or product range is standardized and limited to contain costs, the less perceived differentiation is likely to exist as far as the consumer is concerned. The appropriate product design, and the appropriate product range, are those which balance the need to differentiate, create and sustain competitive advantage with the need to manage costs in order to earn profits.

Caulkin (1988) argues that the manufacturing requirements for international competitiveness are changing. In the past it may have been adequate to argue that meeting and beating rivals on cost and product quality were the essential issues. Now, however, successful companies are also competing on two additional dimensions: variety and time. Variety is the ability to switch production quickly between numerous different items to meet the flexible needs of customers; time is the delivery lead time, which needs to be short despite the necessary flexibility. Satisfying these needs makes use of automated manufacturing technology (AMT) and just-in-time (JIT) production systems, respectively.

The Foundation for Manufacturing and Industry (FMI, 1995) similarly argue that British companies need to develop abilities in 'mass customization', production units which can be altered to meet individual customer needs, thus combining the benefits of scale economies with products designed for specific customers. The real answer for British companies competing against low wage countries does not lie in slashing costs; customizing designs that satisfy increasingly sophisticated consumers offers more opportunity for distinctiveness and competitive advantage.

Traditionally cost, product quality, flexibility and responsiveness to consumer demands have been seen as conflicting objectives, with trade-offs between themselves and with volume production. They must all be achieved in some significant measure now, because of world over-capacity in many industries, competition which is becoming increasingly global, and new standards of manufacturing efficiency, many of which are being set by Japan. This is not purely a question of automation. Bad practice can be automated. Caulkin argues that instead manufacturing must be viewed strategically and not as a support service to marketing and financial decisions. The factory is a source of competitive advantage and it must be viewed and managed in this light.

Manufacturing (too often) is seen as a reactive function supporting marketing. Instead it should be seen as supporting markets, and very evident in product/market decisions. In turn this requires that the contribution of individual employees is encouraged and maximized. International competitiveness results from a process of continuous improvement in every aspect of a firm's activities, and this is now referred to as **total quality management**. This point will be developed later in this chapter.

Capacity and capability

Production capacity is designed to link supply and demand. Demand for a product or service may grow steadily, or growth may be less predictable and affected by seasonal or cyclical fluctuations. It may not be easy to alter supply potential in the same pattern. For example the demand for three-star hotel accommodation may be growing at 10% per year in a town where there are already three such hotels. Say these are occupied at nearly full capacity most weeks and as a result a fourth hotel is opened. Supply then exceeds demand as, depending on the size of the new hotel, the number of rooms available has increased by perhaps a third overall. The new hotel may find it difficult to obtain business if the competing hotels enjoy customer loyalty; conversely, if it is better equipped the existing hotels may find themselves threatened. As a result marketing strategies might be expected to change.

Hence at any time demand and supply capability may be at odds. A manufacturer faced with this dilemma may have to choose between not investing and expanding, and thereby losing potential sales and market share, and investing in temporarily excess capacity which will increase total production costs. Where operating systems have some flexibility built in, say because they can produce different products which can be switched around, or because overtime working is a possibility, incremental changes up and down in line with market demand are possible. However, at other times major strategic decisions concerning investment will be required.

Service, not-for-profit and small businesses

Service businesses

Armistead (1985) suggests that service businesses have two essential characteristics. First, they are heavily dependent on people. Kotler (1988) argues that in service businesses people actually become a fifth element in the marketing mix, along with the product, its price, promotion and place (distribution). Second, the service is often transient.

Quite often it cannot be stored, as in the case of hotel bedrooms, airline seats, and time-slots at dentists and hairdressers. If a bedroom or aircraft seat is left empty for a particular night or flight the lost revenue can never be recovered. A dentist or hairdresser can recoup some financial losses by working longer hours than were otherwise intended, but the time has still been spent unproductively.

People

Invariably in service businesses close contacts are established between the providers and the users of the service. This contrasts with manufacturing where the people who actually make the product are far less likely to meet the consumers. In a service business something is done directly for the consumer (for example dental work or a hair cut) or indirectly, such as a taxi taking them from A to B, or a retailer selling them something manufactured elsewhere. Additionally services must normally be capable of dealing with a large number of customers whose particular needs are different in a variety of ways and who may be similar in only one respect – they want the basic service.

Understanding the various preferences and catering for individual needs is a major source of competitive advantage.

As a result it is essential to train and develop staff if customer needs are to be satisfied effectively, because staff are in constant contact with the customers. McDonald's (Chapter 1, Case 1.5) emphasizes the importance of staff in this very successful service business. Pope (1979) argues that a major reason behind the success of Walt Disney Enterprises is an emphasis on 'positive customer attitudes' amongst all their staff.

Disney now practise a number of policies to achieve this.

❑ New staff are properly welcomed to the corporation, and they undertake an induction programme with other new recruits.
❑ They are fully briefed, using high-quality audiovisual presentations, concerning the Disney philosophy and all the operations, and are introduced to the excellent staff facilities.

Visit the website:
http://www.
itbp.com

❑ There is on-the-job training, with emphasis on how to handle customer questions and queries.

❑ Managers spend one week per year in non-managerial 'front-line' jobs, to ensure that they stay in touch with customers.

❑ There is significant use of staff newspapers and feedback questionnaires.

As a result, attentiveness to customers and their needs has pervaded the culture and values of the company and this has resulted in excellent word-of-mouth recommendations, repeat visits to Disney theme parks and a world-wide reputation for excellence.

Transient services

Where services are transient or perishable and cannot be stored, matching demand and supply is absolutely crucial. If demand is misjudged and over-provided for, then additional costs will be incurred. This will be reflected in higher prices or lower profits. Sometimes the transient nature of the service may be reflected in the competitive strategy, which might be aimed at boosting off-peak demand. Special weekend packages in hotels which normally cater for business people, or winter rates in summer resorts, are examples. The use of railway saver tickets and rail cards is another. There is need for care where price discrimination of this nature is involved, however. If existing customers of the service are able to switch their usage times so that they obtain the cheaper rates when they might otherwise pay higher prices, lost revenue will result.

Marketing and service businesses

The more complex and customized the service (see Figure 10.5) the greater the opportunities for differentiation and adding value.

A number of service businesses such as airlines, hotels, insurance, banking and building societies are already very active and visible in their use of marketing. They target and segment their markets, they differentiate their products and they advertise heavily. However, a number of others have not yet applied marketing with the same enthusiasm, some because they are very small businesses, such as hairdressers, plumbers and jobbing builders who rely on word of mouth more than advertising and who may or may not specialize; others, such as the education sector have not felt it necessary as demand for their services has been obtained readily, and such professional practices as solicitors and accountants have regarded advertising and promotion as unprofessional.

Not-for-profit organizations

Most not-for-profit organizations are services, and in addition they are often highly visible as far as the public is concerned. Consequently the points discussed above concerning the importance of people and customer orientation apply again. But the situation is perhaps more complex. When the objectives of not-for-profit organizations were considered in Chapter 5, the importance of a variety of different stakeholders that resulted in multiple and potentially conflicting objectives was emphasized. Consequently, in addition to appreciating and satisfying the needs of customers, the needs of other stakeholders, particularly providers of funds, must also be satisfied. Marketing in this case concerns an appreciation of the needs of all key stakeholders, and the manage-

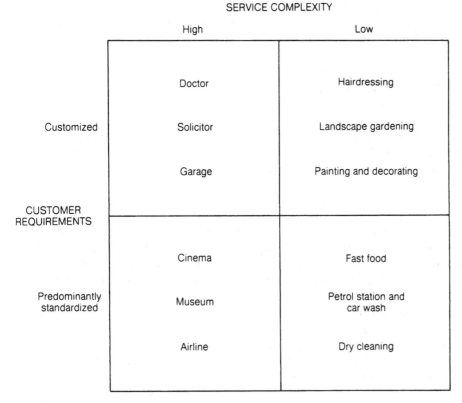

Figure 10.5 Categorizing service business.

ment of all the resources to satisfy these needs as effectively as possible. The image of the organization, influenced by any advertising and publicity, can be particularly important, and it should be managed.

Small businesses

Small companies exist in both manufacturing and service industries, and whilst an appreciation of the marketing concept is as important as it is for any large business, the implementation of the marketing mix activities must inevitably be different.

Small companies have only limited resources. As a result their distribution might be restricted because of the cost of transport and the necessary investment in stock for large-scale availability; and advertising expenditure is likely to be severely constrained. However, they should use market analysis to search for strategic opportunities. Small segments with particular needs might be identified and targeted, and these might well be concentrated geographically. With such an approach a small business can create loyal customers through effective differentiation related to needs.

The technology involved in a small manufacturing firm is unlikely to be state-of-the-art; moreover the size is unlikely to yield economies of scale. This implies higher production costs in comparison to the largest and most efficient firms. However, careful targeting and differentiation, together with flexibility and very high service, can help overcome these weaknesses.

Despite the restrictions it is very important for small businesses to develop established relationships with both suppliers and customers, based on an appreciation of needs and preferences, issues we explore in the next section.

Supply chain architecture

Developing his earlier work on industry structure (Porter, 1980), where he highlights the significance of the relative power of buyers and suppliers, Porter (1985) argues that in the search for competitive advantage a firm must be considered as part of a wider system:

suppliers → firm → distributors → consumers

As well as seeking improvements in its own activities, a firm should assess the opportunities and potential benefits from improving its links with other organizations. A firm is linked to the marketing and selling activities of its suppliers, and to the purchasing and materials handling activities of its distributors or customers.

The supply chain, then, is a process, and managing it is a key strategic capability. Cost savings and service differentiation can be achieved.

Organizations can create synergy, and enjoy the appropriate benefits, if they can successfully link their value chain with those of their suppliers and distributors. Just-in-time (JIT) deliveries, for example, integrate a supplier's outbound logistics with the organization's inbound logistics. Stock and costs can be reduced for the manufacturer, whose delivery lead time and reliability should also be improved. Set up properly, a JIT system can enable suppliers to plan their work more effectively and reduce their uncertainty. This requires an open exchange of reliable, up-to-date information and medium- to long-term supply arrangements. When Nissan was developing the supply chain for its UK manufacturing plant in Sunderland, it deliberately forged links with its suppliers' suppliers in its search to control costs without sacrificing quality and service. A retail bookseller, taking orders for non-stock items, needs to be sure of the delivery lead time from his publishers or wholesaler before quoting a date to his customer. This again demands accurate information – supported by reliable supply.

Organizations looking to launch a new product need to ensure their supply and distribution networks are properly in place; given this, all interested parties can benefit. Retailers will need to be convinced of a new product's viability and potential before they agree to stock it – normally at the expense of taking something else off their shelves. Manufacturers must be sure that stocks are

---

ICI Explosives Division, who manufacture a range of explosive products, have also developed expertise in detonating explosions; quarry managers, who buy the products, really want stones and rocks on a quarry floor rather than the explosives. As a consequence ICI will now produce a three-dimensional map of a quarry for their customers, indicate where the charges need to be placed, and then, when suitable holes have been drilled in the quarry face (by the quarry owners), carry out controlled explosions. In this way they add value for their customers and link the two value chains.

available where customers expect to find them before they proceed with launch advertising.

The key lies in an integrated network, where all members of the supply chain see themselves as mutual beneficiaries from an effective total system. This does not always happen. Buyers and suppliers often see their relationships as confrontational; they enter negotiations with an 'I win; you lose' philosophy when a 'win–win' is required.

Supply chain management issues become increasingly important where organizations seek to reduce the number of their suppliers, buying as many items as possible from each selected supplier. It is quite feasible that these major suppliers will have to buy-in products they do not make themselves in order to create the 'basket' of items demanded by their customer. This strategy has been adopted by the leading oil companies and car manufacturers. In 1994 Ford in the USA included components from 700 US suppliers in its Tempo model; in 1995 the company's equivalent Mercury Mystique used 227 suppliers world-wide. One supplier, for example, will now be required to provide a fully-assembled dashboard, ready for immediate installation; it is likely that the electronic instrumentation will be bought-in.

Preece *et al.* (1995) use the value chain to explain how Levi Strauss, producer of the internationally successful Levi's jeans, has created value and used its value-creating activities to carefully establish a distinctive corporate reputation, which, as we have already seen, is a form of competitive advantage. Key aspects include:

❏ established links with suppliers from around the world
❏ team manufacturing (underpinned by training and empowerment) and linked to high technology equipment and sophisticated information support
❏ global advertising and branding
❏ alliances with retailers who concentrate on Levi jeans and do not stock competitor products
❏ a programme of 'marketing revitalization' designed to reduce lead times and improve the availability of the products.

Strengthening the processes involved in managing the supply chain relates to the level of service companies are able to offer their customers and to total quality management, the subject of our last section.

Service and total quality management

The **effective** satisfaction of the needs of the final consumer of a product or service involves everyone in the supply chain. Marketing must recognize opportunities for adding value; operations personnel must supply that value. This implies widespread awareness of consumer needs and expectations, and effective co-operation between marketing and operations. However, if this is also to be achieved efficiently everyone in the supply chain must be committed

---

There is no conflict between good customer service and good returns to shareholders.
John J Wilson, Chairman, London Electricity plc

to helping their personal customers. To accomplish this, manufacturing can learn from service businesses. External suppliers must be linked in to manufacturing; people at each stage of the manufacturing process should see the next stage as their customers and seek to provide them with quality and service. Manufacturers who do not sell directly to the final consumer must also work closely with their distributors. This systemic awareness comes from asking: 'Who is my customer, and who are my customer's customers?'.

Consumer satisfaction can lead to loyalty and superior profits. If this profit is used in part to reward employees and to further improve quality and service, a cycle of improvement can be instigated. Peters and Austin (1985) state: 'It is hard to distinguish customer satisfaction from employee satisfaction. You can't have one without the other'.

Winning companies compete by delivering a product that supplies superior value to customers rather than one that costs less. Many strategists have believed that business winners are those that capture commanding market share through lower costs and prices. The winning midsize companies compete on the value of their products and services and usually enjoy premium prices.

Quality is thus a key source of differentiation and competitive advantage. Customers value quality and are willing to pay a premium for it.

In this context quality implies more than the quality of the product itself although this obviously is important. It incorporates the organization's ability to meet the specific needs and requirements of customers, such as delivery on time of exactly the right quantity, packaged appropriately. This is an area of constant change as competing organizations strive to find new opportunities to create differentiation and to satisfy their customers' needs better. In turn this increases customer expectations, placing greater demands on supplying organizations. Case 10.6 examines the service challenge to Sainsbury's.

Moreover, improving the quality of the way activities are managed and carried out in organizations invariably leads to lower costs through less waste and through 'getting it right first time', a central theme of total quality management.

Successful organizations will also strive to 'get it right every time'. Company reputations for good quality and service are quickly lost when customers start telling stories of their (possibly isolated) bad experience. Clearly this impinges on the management of people, and will be discussed further in Chapter 11. The expression 'total quality management' therefore relates to everything which happens in an organization and which can lead to lower costs and particularly the improvement of customer service. The speed of response to queries, the way in which telephone calls are dealt with, accurate delivery notes and invoices are all examples outside the direct production activity. They all reflect a concern for getting it right. All these activities should aim to provide customer satisfaction at a profit.

Visit the website: http://www.itbp.com

Quality is not a label you can put on a product afterwards. Quality is a way of life that must apply to everything within the company and all its external relations. Quality is in essence a question of leadership. Only a minor part of errors are attributable to the shop floor. Quality is created by the attitude and action of management. It is something that must be part of corporate objectives and strategies.

Georg Karnsund, President, Saab-Scania AB

Case 10.6

THE SERVICE CHALLENGE FOR SAINSBURY'S

Sainsbury's vies with Tesco for market leadership of the UK retail grocery industry. In the early 1990s Tesco increased its market share through a series of initiatives, including a loyalty card scheme, and both retailers reduced the prices of a large number of 'everyday' products. During the 1980s Sainsbury, again like Tesco, had invested heavily in new superstores. A key challenge, critical for competitive advantage in the 1990s, is customer service.

> Our strategy is about giving better quality, about value for money. Our customers come in every week, perhaps twice a week, and buy a huge range of products. If we are not performing, that is seen very quickly.
>
> (David Sainsbury, Chairman)

Sainsbury began to address service more aggressively in the early 1990s. Head office jobs were cut, but the number of staff in the stores was increased. Advertising was strengthened. A more extensive customer research programme revealed that shoppers were happy with Sainsbury's products but not its service. The major irritant was 'wonky' trolleys which prove difficult to steer in a straight line, followed by a lack of tills,

the consequential long queues at the tills, product locations being changed too frequently, flimsy carrier bags and fruit and vegetable bags which are difficult to open when they are removed from a roll. There were also complaints that check-out operators were scanning items more quickly than customers could pack them.

Sainsbury introduced new policies. Once a check-out queue reached a certain size, another till would be opened. Customers asking about the location of a product were to be taken personally to the shelf rather than merely told where an item could be found. Staff were asked to cut the scanning speed from 22 to 18 items a minute.

Staff were involved extensively in the changes and £9 million was spent on retraining over an 18-month period.

> We realized that the staff themselves were actually best placed to offer solutions to customers' problems. Many of our regulations and procedures were actually hindering staff from serving customers in the way they wanted to.
>
> (Anthony Rees, Director of Strategic Marketing)

Endnote: None of these changes has given Sainsbury a sustainable competitive edge.

The background to total quality management

The strategic opportunity and value of total quality was really recognized by the Japanese in the 1960s. It happened when certain leading companies realized that policies they were following, designed to improve product quality, were also resulting in lower costs, and they looked for further ways of improving the overall quality of the service they offered their customers. US companies responded in the 1970s after a number of their key markets had been eroded by Japanese competitors. Britain and the rest of Europe has lagged behind, and it is only in the 1980s that total quality became a major strategic issue.

We always travel with our teddy bears. When we got back to our room at the hotel we saw that the maid had arranged our bears very comfortably in a chair. The bears were holding hands.

I needed a few more minutes to decide on dinner. The waitress said: 'If you would read the menu and not the road map, you would know what you want to order'.

Binter, MJ, Booms, B and Tetreault, MS (1990) The service encounter: diagnosing favourable and unfavourable incide nts, Journal of Marketing, 54, January

Total quality management can usefully be viewed as a cycle, as featured in Figure 10.6. First of all customer needs must be identified and addressed. Their needs are basically what they say they are, not necessarily what a manufacturer would like them to be; and manufacturers should seek to provide their customers with exactly what they want, delivering the right number at the right time, neither early nor late. Suppliers should create a reputation for reliability.

In satisfying these needs manufacturers should seek to improve the quality of their operations in terms of people, systems and technology. Improving people can be relatively inexpensive, but it requires that they are seen and treated as a key resource. Training is essential, and the ways in which employees might improve the quality of their individual contribution should be discussed with them. Most people know how they could perform more effectively, but quite often they are never asked. Systems should reflect clear policies and standards, and communication systems should keep people aware of how well or badly

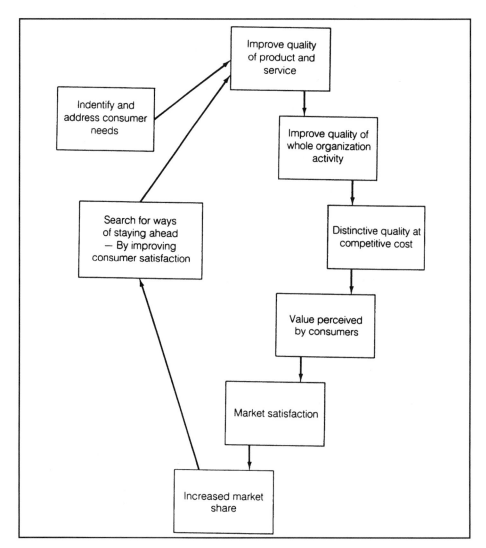

Figure 10.6 The quality cycle.

the company is doing at any time. Technology can improve quality through increased productivity and through eliminating human error, but it can be very expensive.

The organization needs to be recognized for the quality and value that it is building into its products and customer service if it is to benefit. Customer satisfaction and loyalty should be sought, resulting in a stronger market position. But then the process continues as organizations should strive to improve the quality of their products and services continually. Gradually costs should be reduced, and services and customer satisfaction should be improved as the quality improvements are sustained. Total quality becomes both a philosophy, which should be an essential value of the organization, and activities designed to deliver customer satisfaction profitably.

Total quality management therefore should start with the strategic leader who must emphasize a commitment to it, but it must spread throughout the company. Everybody in the organization is responsible for quality. The basic philosophy is that prevention (getting things right first time) is better than detection (finding out through expensive inspection systems or customer complaints). The underlying aim is continuous improvement. By focusing on quality, costs can be reduced and service improved. Other employees within the organization should be seen as internal customers, and their needs should be recognized and satisfied. It was mentioned earlier that JIT systems similarly reinforce these inter-dependences. It is very likely that organizations who are quality minded, especially if they are operating JIT systems, will increase the pressure on their external suppliers to improve their quality.

The benefits of total quality management

PA Consultants (1987) contend that companies who have pursued total quality have been able to benefit in a number of ways. Specifically they have:

❏ improved the company image (British Airways, for example, believe that they have been able to increase their passenger volumes as a result of training all their employees to fulfil the interests of their customers, thereby improving their image and reputation)
❏ improved productivity
❏ reduced costs
❏ created greater certainty in their operations (by reducing conflicts within the operating system they have improved the speed of delivery and their flexibility in responding to changes in customer requirements)
❏ improved morale (employees have shown greater concern and commitment where they have seen that there is an emphasis on things being done well and that high standards have been encouraged, valued and rewarded)
❏ committed customers.

People feel the best about their work when they do a high-quality job! Getting a job done quickly is satisfying. Getting a job done at low cost is rewarding. But getting a job done quickly, at low cost and with high quality is exciting!

Robert C Stempel, Chairman,
General Motors Corporation

Organizational needs for total quality management

Peters (1988) argues that if an organization is committed to total quality management there are a number of issues which must be addressed.

First, the necessary commitment to getting things right first time must be encouraged and developed throughout the organization. Moreover, employees must be trained about how they can measure quality and quality improvements. Second, there must be a guiding system or ideology stemming from the strategic leader; continual quality improvements must be managed. To this end, and third, there need to be clear targets and measures of success. Numbers of rejects, repeats and returns from customers, and the cost of after-sales servicing are all examples. Results should be communicated. Fourth, quality improvements should be rewarded, as should new ideas for further improvement. This helps maintain a momentum. Fifth, quality issues should be communicated laterally throughout the organization as problems can span several areas of the business. Finally, relationships with both buyers and suppliers should be developed. The organization is seeking to satisfy the needs and requirements of their customers; suppliers should be seeking to meet the requirements and needs of the organization. They are all linked in a chain of inter-dependences.

Research by consultants AT Kearney (1992) concludes that 80% of companies with TQM programmes do not encapsulate all these issues, and, as a result, fail to obtain any marked improvement in performance. Their research also showed that companies with the most successful programmes objectively 'benchmark' their competitors to identify and understand 'best current practice' for adding and delivering value. Peters also suggests that opportunities to improve will never dry up and that organizations who seek to innovate and find new and better ways of doing things are more likely to create differentiation and reduce their costs.

Summary

Porter's value chain analysis has been introduced and considered as a framework for evaluating the activities of the business in the context of competitive advantage.

We have considered the importance of the marketing concept and consumer orientation for a variety of businesses, not only manufacturing, and highlighted how marketing can be used to create and sustain competitive advantage. We have also discussed the important strategic contribution of operations in ensuring that the right product is available at the right time in the right place, produced to the right quality to meet consumer needs satisfactorily, and at a cost that ensures that the organization can earn profits. Operations strategies must be derived from marketing strategies; but in turn operational considerations may constrain marketing.

Specifically we have:

- introduced the notion of the value chain and described its component primary and support activities
- discussed the importance of linkages between the activities, highlighting that they can be a major source of synergy
- recapped on the essential aspects of cost leadership and differentiation strategies
- highlighted the need to attribute costs to activities if the value chain is to be useful for decision making, emphasizing that this may not be straightforward;
- discussed the various cost drivers and some common problems in controlling costs as a result of value chain analysis
- summarized how differentiation might be created anywhere within the organization
- used the Japanese zip manufacturer, YKK, as an illustration of the value chain
- looked at the increasing importance of speed as a competitive weapon
- defined the marketing concept in relation to culture and values, and the marketing mix in relation to competitive and functional strategies
- discussed product differentiation, branding, market segmentation and the usefulness of positioning analysis and targeting
- considered the concept of the product life cycle and how the appropriate marketing strategies vary between the different stages in the cycle
- looked at the importance and management of new products, emphasizing the value of synergy
- considered how innovation, linked to quality and entrepreneurship, can be a key value
- emphasized the links between research and development, design, marketing, production and costs
- considered the importance of capacity (the relationship between demand and supply at any time), capability (the ability to meet customer and consumer needs and key success factors) and adaptability (flexibility to change)
- looked at service businesses from the point of view of their dependence on people and the problems caused by the transience of many services
- emphasized that total quality management is a key organizational value which can contribute significantly towards the achievement of consumer satisfaction and lower costs – the importance of getting things right first time.

Checklist of key terms and concepts

You should feel confident that you understand the following terms and ideas:

- ☆ The value chain
- ☆ The product life cycle
- ☆ Market segmentation and product positioning
- ☆ Branding
- ☆ Innovation and new product development
- ☆ The significance of capacity
- ☆ Supply chain management
- ☆ Total quality management.

Questions and research assignments

Text related

1 Draw a brand positioning chart for motor vehicles. You might wish to use the following as axes:
   - ❏ lowest price → highest price
   - ❏ British made → foreign made

   or you could select any criteria that you feel are important.

2 Using Case 10.5 (McDonald's) as a framework, derive the possible marketing and operations strategies for a specialist high-quality restaurant located in the country.

3 Place the following service businesses on the grid illustrated in Figure 10.5:
   - ❏ A dental practice
   - ❏ A plumber
   - ❏ A Haute cuisine restaurant
   - ❏ A taxi service
   - ❏ A zoo
   - ❏ A private school
   - ❏ Refuse collection
   - ❏ A local bus service.

4 Take any product you have bought recently and consider exactly what constitutes quality as far as you as a consumer are concerned. What issues and difficulties will have been encountered in building in that quality?

Library based

5 Take an organization of your choice, research its strategy and again draw up a value chain. If you are able to gain access to the costs of the firm, allocate them to the value chain following the principles incorporated in Table 10.1.

6 In 1991 Trusthouse Forte (THF) changed the company name to Forte and regrouped their various hotels into five brands:
   - ❏ Forte Travelodges
   - ❏ Forte Posthouses
   - ❏ Forte Crest
   - ❏ Forte Heritage
   - ❏ Forte Grand.

   Determine the target markets for each of these brands and comment on Forte's segmentation strategy.

   What has happened to Forte since 1991?

7 It has been argued that during the 1980s the market for blue denim jeans has moved into the decline phase of the product life cycle. Given this, what strategies are open to manufacturers of jeans, and what strategies have been pursued by the major manufacturers such as Levi Strauss?

8 By visiting one or more supermarkets and looking at breakfast cereals on the shelves, consider the product and segmentation strategies of Kellogg. How does their apparent product strategy compare with that of their main rivals?

9 Take a product of your choice and answer the following questions:
   (a) How many competing brands of the product are there, who manufactures them, and what are the major market shares?
   (b) Where is the product in terms of the product life cycle? Position each major competing brand in relation to this.
   (c) What are the differentiation and segmentation strategies of the leading competitors?
   (d) How is advertising used?

   (Some marketing research data can be obtained from Mintel reports and similar analyses; advertising expenditures are available in Meal reports.)

10 Take a manufacturing organization of your choice, and determine the range of products produced. What do you feel might be the objectives and tasks of the operations manager (or whatever he or she might actually be called) in this organizations? Where do you envisage the manager will encounter most problems? What difficulties might be involved in introducing new products into the organization?

References

Armistead, CG (1985) In *Operations Management in the Service Industries and the Public Sector* (eds C Voss, C G Armistead, B Johnston and B Morris), John Wiley.

Caulkin, S (1988) Manufacturing excellence. Britain's best factories, *Management Today*. September.

Cooper, RG (1987) *Winning at New Products*, Gage Educational Publishing, Toronto.

Davidson, JH (1972) *Offensive Marketing*, Cassell.

Drucker, PF (1954) *The Practice of Management*, Harper & Row.

Drucker, PF (1985) *Innovation and Entrepreneurship*, Heinemann.

FMI (1995) *Tomorrow's Best Practice*. A joint research programme between the Department of Trade and Industry, IBM and the Foundation for Manufacturing and Industry.

Gemini Consulting (1994) *Champions of Change*. A joint research programme by Gemini and the International Consortium for Executive Development Research.

Hamel, G and Prahalad, CK (1989) Strategic intent, *Harvard Business Review*, May–June.

Hamel, G and Prahalad, CK (1991) Corporate imagination and expeditionary marketing, *Harvard Business Review*. July–August.

Hill, T (1991) *Production/Operations Management*, 2nd edn, Prentice-Hall.

IBM/London Business School (1994) Made in Europe, Report, IBM.

Johnson, HT and Kaplan, RS (1987) *Relevance Lost: The Rise and Fall of Management Accounting*, Harvard Business School Press.

Kearney, AT (1992) Research findings, quoted in Taylor, P (1992) Such an elusive quality, *Financial Times*, 14 February.

Kotler, P (1988) *Marketing Management: Analysis, Planning and Control*, 6th edn, Prentice-Hall.

Levitt, T (1984) *The Marketing Imagination*, Free Press.

Nayak, PR (1991) Technological change (Report), Arthur D Little.

Ohmae, K (1982) *The Mind of the Strategist*, McGraw-Hill

Ohmae, K (1988) Getting back to strategy, *Harvard Business Review*, November–December.

PA Consultants (1987) *How to Take Part in the Quality Revolution – A Management Guide*, Dr Steve Smith, PA Management Consultants.

Pearson, EA (1988) Tough minded ways to get innovative, *Harvard Business Review*, May–June.

Peters, TJ (1988) *Thriving on Chaos*, Knopf.

Peters, TJ and Austin, N (1985) *A Passion for Excellence*, Collins.

Pope, NW (1979) Mickey Mouse marketing, *American Banker*, 25 July, and More Mickey Mouse marketing, *American Banker*, 12 September.

Porter, ME (1980) *Competitive Strategy: Techniques for Analysing Industries and Competitors*, Free Press.

Porter, ME (1985) *Competitive Advantage: Creating and Sustaining Superior Performance*, Free Press.

Preece, S, Fleisher, C and Toccacelli, J (1995) Building a reputation along the value chain at Levi Strauss, *Long Range Planning*, 28, 6.

Wild, R (1984) *Production and Operations Management. Principles and Techniques*, 3rd edn, Holt, Rinehart & Winston.

11

Competitive Advantage Through People

People are a strategic resource. They make an essential contribution to strategy creation and strategy implementation. There is a need for clear strategies for developing managers and for allocating authority and responsibility to them.

Learning objectives

After studying this chapter you should be able to:

- discuss the critical strategic contribution of people
- identify a number of important policy areas concerning the effective management of human resources
- discuss the key aspects and implications of employee empowerment
- explain the links between objectives, appraisal, reward and motivation
- assess the importance of management teams and leadership behaviour
- describe what is meant by a learning organization.

Don't forget to visit the website: http://www. itbp.com

Introduction

Successful organizations meet the needs and expectations of their customers more effectively than their competitors; at the same time, they generate acceptable financial returns. Achieving these outcomes requires competent and committed people.

Human resources – people – are an essential strategic resource. Everything an organization does, in the end, depends on people. Although technology and information technology can make a major strategic impact, it is people who exploit their potential. Managers and employees are needed to implement strategies and to this end they must understand and share the values of the organization. They must be committed to the organization and they must work together well. At the same time, where an organization is decentralized and operating in a turbulent environment, the strategic leader will rely on people to spot opportunities and threats, to adapt and create new strategies.

Consequently it is people who ultimately determine whether or not competitive advantage is created and sustained. Adding new values with innovation, they can be an opportunity and a source of competitive advantage; equally, unenthusiastic, uncommitted, untrained employees can act as a constraint. People's capabilities are infinite and resourceful in the *appropriate organizational climate*.

Achieving the highest level of outcomes that people are capable of producing will therefore depend upon the human resource practices adopted by the organization. Whilst the issues are clear and straightforward – they involve selection, training, rewards and work organization – there is no single 'best approach' to the challenge. A relatively formal, 'hard' approach can prove very successful in certain circumstances; other organizations will derive significant benefits from a 'softer', more empowered style. One issue here is whether the business is being driven by a small number of identifiable, key decision makers or by the employees collectively.

To bring out the best in people, they have to be managed well, and this requires leadership. A useful metaphor is that of an orchestra. Every member (manager/employee) is a specialist, with some making a unique contribution, which, on occasions, can take the form of a solo performance. Nevertheless, all the contributions must be synthesized to create harmony (synergy), which is the role of the conductor (strategic leader). A single musician (weak link) can destroy a performance; a chain is only as strong as its weakest link.

We have argued earlier that distinctive competitive advantage is driven by organization-specific competencies and capabilities. These embrace skills and relationships, the ability to change and to manage change, and the extent to which the organization as a whole can stay environmentally aware and learn. These competencies and capabilities are manifested in the culture and style of management – driven, in turn, by strategic leadership.

A successful organization, therefore, needs people with appropriate skills and competencies who can work together effectively. People must be:

❏ committed (commitment can be improved)
❏ competent (competencies can be developed; and can bring improved product quality and productivity)
❏ cost-effective (ideally costs should be low and performance high, although this does not imply low rewards for success)
❏ in sympathy with the aims of the organization (are the values and expectations of all parties in agreement?).

The executives and employees who go to make up a total work force are the most important assets of the company. They always have been and always will be. The real issue is how to maximize the value from those assets and that is why all senior executives irrespective of function have an obligation to contribute to people development at every level.

Unattributed quotation from a manufacturing company director. Taken from Coulson-Thomas, C and Brown, R. (1989) The Responsive Organisation. People Management: The Challenge of the 1990s, *British Institute of Management*

In times of discontinuity and accelerated change, survival depends on flexibility, on our ability to learn to adapt. Organizations which learn fast will survive. Management must take the lead. We must mobilize our greatest asset, our people, invest in their training and orchestrate their talents, skills and expertise. Their commitment, dedication, quality and care will build the competitive advantage of a winning team. Only they can provide our customers with the best product and service in the industry. The management of change takes tenacity, time, talent and training.

JFA de Soet, President, KLM Royal Dutch Airlines

In this chapter we will compare the hard and soft approaches to human resource management, discuss issues of management competency, briefly consider a number of the important issues involved in managing people and highlight the importance of leadership behaviour. The key topics of empowerment and learning organizations are discussed.

Human resource strategy

People, then, are critically important strategic resources. Successful companies will be able to attract, motivate, develop, reward and keep skilled and competent managers and other employees. They will be able to create and implement strategic changes in a supportive culture. However, even successful companies have lean periods, and when these occur, they will again be able to retain their most important people. There is no 'one best way' of achieving this.

Box 11.1, which contrasts the hard and soft approaches to human resource management, gives an example of two companies in the same industry which are both successful with quite different styles. Companies can, of course, be hard on certain aspects, soft on others. In addition, the style may alter with the strategic demands placed on an organization. When times are difficult and a company must rationalize and downsize, a hard approach may prove to be appropriate for driving through the changes quickly. However, a softer, more empowered style may be required to rejuvenate the company and bring new sources of competitive advantage.

The key tension or dilemma that is being addressed is the balance between centralization for control and decentralization for greater empowerment. The relative advantages and disadvantages of centralized and decentralized structures are discussed later in Chapter 19; the implications of empowerment are explored in Key Concept 11.1. Many writers, including, for example, Handy (1984), argue that in future organizations will increasingly become federations of decentralized units, bound together by effective communication systems and a shared vision. Professional, knowledge-based workers will be prominent, and many of them will be paid negotiated fees rather than offered 'permanent' contracts and salaries. This will enable both companies and people to focus and specialize on their core competencies rather than be diversified when technologies and competition are changing rapidly. Success will very much depend on internal linkages within the organizational federation and strong external alliances with suppliers and distributors. Empowered employees are in a strong position to find new ways of adding value and innovating.

In 1994, the employees of United Airlines in the USA, the largest airline in the world, agreed to accept paycuts in exchange for majority control of the company, which was experiencing financial difficulties. As an outcome, decision making was decentralized more. One example was the bringing together of 350 pilots, flight attendants, mechanics and other employees to plan the development of a new, low-cost, short-haul shuttle service on the West Coast. United had to achieve very high service levels and low prices to compete with SouthWest Airlines. The new venture was established reportedly 'without a single flaw'.

In an instance such as this, people who normally deal with problems and 'fire-fight', with a tactical perspective, are being encouraged to think more operationally and strategically – designing a service and the necessary systems

Box 11.1

HARD VERSUS SOFT HUMAN RESOURCE MANAGEMENT

Hard HRM assumes:

❏ people are viewed as a resource and, like all resources, companies gain competitive advantage by using them efficiently and effectively

❏ the deployment and development of employees – who are essentially there to implement corporate and competitive strategies – is delegated to line managers who are responsible for groups of people

❏ scientific management principles and systems can be useful but should be used cautiously.

Soft HRM assumes:

❏ workers are most productive if they are committed to the company, informed about its mission, strategies and current levels of success; and

❏ involved in teams which collectively decide how things are to be done

❏ employees have to be trusted to take the right decisions rather than be controlled at every stage by managers above them.

Soft HRM argues that people are different from other resources (and often more costly) but they can create added value and **sustainable** competitive advantage from the other resources. Therefore soft HRM places greater emphasis on control through review and evaluation of outcomes, such that employees are led rather than managed.

An example

Federal Express (FedEx) and UPS are two leading international overnight courier services. FedEx is not unionized and adopts soft HRM strategies. There is, for example, a successful pay-for-suggestions system together with a number of other empowerment initiatives. Employees have been involved in discussions and decisions concerning restructuring and the use of technology, and they are seen to be highly motivated.

UPS employees, by contrast, have no direct involvement in work organization issues. Time and motion engineers design jobs, and employee performance is measured daily against company standards. UPS, however, pays the highest wages and benefits in the industry and offers share options to employees. Promotion is invariably from within and successful employees can rise quickly. Again people are highly motivated and loyal. The productivity of UPS drivers – drivers are the key front-line employees – is claimed to be three times that of FedEx drivers. UPS argues that its network and scheduling is so complex that there have to be regimented systems and standardized jobs.

whereby, ideally, many of the problems they are familiar with are eliminated at the design stage.

Many organizations, however, still prefer more rigid controls from the centre, even though they may have reduced the number of layers in the organizational hierarchy and widened managers' spans of control. This, they believe, is the way to achieve efficiency and managed costs. Tighter systems inevitably constrain innovation and employee development; but, they assume, new ideas and people can be bought-in or recruited.

Simply, some companies will seek to develop their employees and managers, invariably promoting from within. A strong culture and vision should foster both commitment and continuous, emergent change. Necessary new competencies are *learned*. In such organizations, team-working and networking are likely to be prominent. Other organizations prefer to search for the best people

KEY CONCEPT 11.1

EMPOWERMENT

Empowerment means freeing employees from instructions and controls and allowing them to take decisions themselves. Total quality management implies constant improvement; to achieve this employees should be contributing to the best of their ability. Proponents argue that rules stifle innovation and that future success relies not on past results but on the continuing ability to manage change pressures. Managers must be free to make appropriate changes in a decentralized structure.

There are three main **objectives** of empowerment:

- ❏ to make organizations more responsive to external pressures.
- ❏ to 'delayer' organizations in order to make them more cost effective. British Airways, for example, now has five layers of management between the chief executive and the front line who interface with customers. It used to be nine.

  Managers become responsible for more employees who they are expected to coach and support rather than direct.
- ❏ to create employee networks featuring teamworking, collaboration and horizontal communications. This implies changes in the ways decisions are made.

The important questions are why, how and when. The leading retailers, for example, benefited from increasing centralization throughout the 1980s. Information technology has enabled cost savings and efficiencies from centrally controlled buying, store and shelf layouts, stocking policies and reordering. In the 1990s there is little support for changing this in any marked way and delegating these decisions to store level. At the same time individual stores will be judged in part on the quality of service they provide to their customers; and it is in this area that there is considerable scope for empowering managers.

As empowerment is increased it is important that employees are adequately informed and knowledgeable, that they are motivated to exercise power, and that they are rewarded for successful outcomes. In flatter organization structures there are fewer opportunities for promotion.

There are **three basic empowerment options**:

- ❏ Employees can be encouraged to contribute ideas. As we have seen earlier, several new product ideas for McDonald's have come from individual franchisees. In reality this may represent only token empowerment.
- ❏ Employees work in teams which share and manage their own work, but within clearly defined policies and limits. This should increase both efficiency and job satisfaction.
- ❏ More extensive decentralization where individuals are much freer to change certain parameters and strategies. Evaluating outcomes is seen as the important control mechanism rather than rules and guidelines. An important distinction here is between making people accountable for their individual actions and making them accountable for the overall result. Constructive accountability gives people freedom to make decisions and demands that they accept responsibility for the consequences. This requires strong leadership, a clear mission and effective communications, rewards and sanc-

tions. Information must flow openly upwards and sideways as well as down. In many organizations there is a tendency for 'bad news' to be selectively hidden, with perhaps two-thirds not flowing up to the next layer. Many potential threats are thereby not shared within the company. This would be unacceptable in an empowered organization.

An example: Banc One

Banc One, whose headquarters are in Columbus, Ohio, has quickly grown into one of the USA's leading banks by acquiring several other banks. The company deliberately avoids the property sector and concentrates on personal accounts. Strategy implementation blends decentralized decision making with group-wide guidance and advice. Individual managers cannot choose their own product portfolio, but they are free to set their own marketing and pricing strategies. There is an elaborate reporting system and IT is harnessed to share relative successes and results amongst the 1300 plus branches. Managers can quickly compare their own performances. In addition a team of internal consultants visits the branches to provide support and advice, and spread best practices.

For many organizations empowerment implies that the core organization strategies are decided centrally, with individual managers delegated a discretionary layer around the core (as shown in the diagram opposite).

It is crucial firstly to find the right balance between the core and discretionary elements, and secondly to ensure that managers support and own the core strategy.

(Continued)

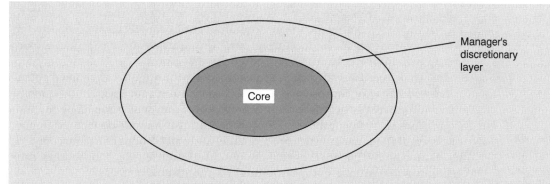

Manager's
discretionary
layer

Core

The deciding factors

❏ The competitive strategies and the relative importance of close linkages with customers in order to differentiate and provide high levels of service. When this becomes essential empowerment may imply an inverted pyramid structure. The structure exists to support front-line managers, as shown in the diagram below.

Successful empowerment means putting the 'right' people in place and ensuring they are able to do their job – which they understand and own. In this way they feel important.

❏ The extent to which the environment is turbulent and decisions are varied rather than routine.

❏ The expectations and preferences of managers and employees, and their ability and willingness to accept responsibility. Not everyone wants accountability and high visibility. If empowerment is mishandled it is possible that work will be simply pushed down a shorter hierarchy as managers seek to avoid responsibility.

Successful empowerment requires appropriate skills, which in turn frequently implies training. The appropriate style of management is coaching. Moreover it is important to link in monitoring systems together with rewards and sanctions. Finally empowerment must be

taken seriously and not simply limited to non-essential decisions. Empowerment implies risk taking, and any mistakes, whilst not overlooked, must be handled carefully.

Empowerment is a powerful motivator as long as it does not suddenly stop when the really important and interesting decisions have to be taken.
(Jeremy Soper, ex Retail Sales Director, WH Smith)

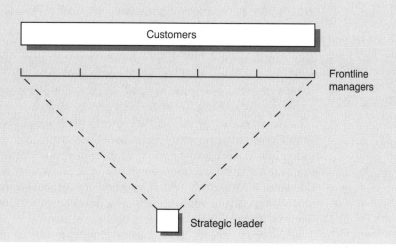

Customers

Frontline
managers

Strategic leader

who might be available; they willingly recruit outsiders. They are seeking to *buy-in* the new competencies they require. People may feel less committed to such organizations in the long term, and consequently there will be a greater reliance on individualism and individual contributions.

The challenge for companies growing from within is that they need to become and stay very aware strategically if they are to remain ahead of their rivals; they will actively benchmark and look for new ideas which might be helpful. Companies securing new skills and competencies from outside face a different dilemma. If the competencies are available, and can be bought by any competitor, how can they ensure they find the best ideas and people, and how can they generate some unique competency and competitive advantage?

Some companies, of course, will look to do both, finding, in the process, an appropriate balance. An analogy would be a leading football club which buys expensive, talented players in the transfer market whilst, at the same time, nurturing young players. There are many instances where highly skilled, experienced players do not fit in at a new club, certainly not at first; and when several arrive at once, it can be very disruptive until they are moulded into an effective team.

Capelli and Crocker-Hefter (1995) further distinguish between companies that seek to compete by moving quickly, perhaps by necessity, responding speedily to new opportunities, and those that have developed a more sustainable advantage in a long-standing market. They conclude that organizations competing on flexibility will typically find it more appropriate to recruit from outside. A reliance on developing new competencies internally may mean they are too slow to gain early advantage from new opportunities. By contrast, organizations competing in established markets with long-standing relationships are more likely to rely on internally developed, organization-specific skills and strong internal and external architecture.

Case 9.1 contrasted Coca-Cola and PepsiCo. Coke is the entrenched market leader; in recent years it has remained focused and relied on strengthening its competitive position and distribution network. Pepsi, on the other hand, has sought to narrow the gap between the two. It has diversified and actively sought new, exploitable niches around the world. Capelli and Crocker-Hefter confirm that Coca-Cola has relied heavily on developing its own future managers whilst Pepsi hires aggressively and offers fast-track promotion for high individual performance.

These points are shown diagrammatically in Figure 11.1. There are, inevitably, implications. We have already argued that, generally, industries and markets are becoming more dynamic and turbulent, demanding that companies develop new product and market niche opportunities. This appears to imply an increasing reliance on recruiting strong, competent people from outside. In turn this means that internal relationships and the culture may be under constant pressure to change. Companies are recruiting and rewarding individual experts; at the same time, synergistic opportunities demand strong internal architecture and co-operation. Clearly this is another organizational dilemma. Companies which succeed in establishing a strong, cohesive and motivating culture whilst developing new competencies flexibly and quickly are likely to be the future high performers.

Reinforcing points from earlier chapters, this demands effective strategic leadership and a shared, understood vision for the organization. The extent to

Visit the website: http://www.itbp.com

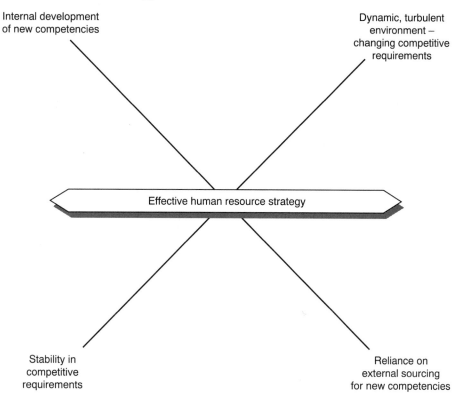

Internal development
of new competencies

Dynamic, turbulent
environment –
changing competitive
requirements

Effective human resource strategy

Stability in
competitive
requirements

Reliance on
external sourcing
for new competencies

Figure 11.1   Effective human resource strategy.

which an organization can become a 'learning organization', discussed towards the end of this chapter, is of great significance. In terms of Figure 11.1, one important challenge lies in finding ways of internally developing the necessary new competencies to compete in a turbulent environment sufficiently quickly and cost-advantageously. It implies a move from either of the two side sectors to the top part of the chart.

Managerial competency

It is necessary, therefore, for the managers in an organization, individually and collectively, to possess particular skills and competencies which relate to the competitive demands faced by the organization. But what should they be? And: how might organizations find answers to this question?

At a base level, it is clear that managers must be able to:

❏ **think** and decide, embracing the latest ideas
❏ **act** and make things happen, and
❏ **network** to bring about change.

There is a simple rule for success in business: get the people you need in the right numbers with the right skills and competencies to do the job.

Sir Bob Reid, ex-Chairman, British Railways Board

A more comprehensive framework has been provided by Skapinker (1989) based on human resource practices at Cadbury Schweppes.

Cadbury Schweppes appraise their managers in terms of 50 skills and competencies, broken down into the following six groups:

❑ **Strategy:** the ability to think critically and to challenge conventional wisdom; environmental awareness, being well informed on the economic, social and political environment in which the business operates.
❑ **Drive:** self-motivation.
❑ **Influence:** the ability to communicate, both verbally and in writing; the ability to develop subordinates.
❑ **Analysis:** being able to draw out information during meetings with colleagues; the ability to analyse, organize and present numerical data.
❑ **Implementation:** the ability to understand the impact of decisions on other parts of the organization.
❑ **Personal factors:** readiness to take unpopular or difficult decisions.

Adopting the theme that managers must be both learned and learning, Figure 11.2 repackages these ideas as five distinct mindsets. Managers, in different degrees, will and must possess all these abilities. The issues concern the balance and the opportunity. Some managers will be extremely competent in certain areas, but their profile, approach and style may not be appropriate for the demands placed on them. Additionally, and given the way managers work with constant interruptions, and performing a series of short, pragmatic tasks, it can be difficult for them to find time to think, reflect and challenge. Short-termism and 'more-of-the-same' can all-too-readily be the result.

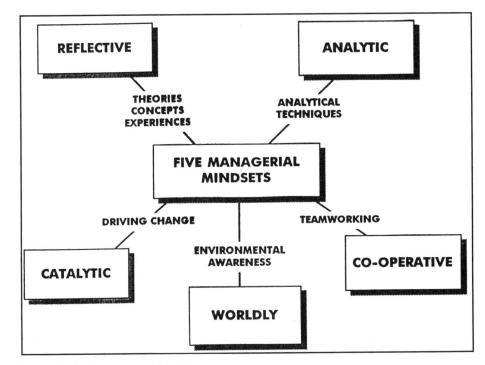

Figure 11.2 Five managerial mindsets.

Many books have been written – and continue to be written – describing the behaviour patterns and practices of successful organizations. Whilst there is inevitably some element of idiosyncrasy and uniqueness, this approach is interesting and valuable. It can be a rich source of ideas. However it is not the same as identifying those competencies which have been shown empirically to be associated with the creation of superior performance.

It is because these questions are complex that some organizations will adopt and build human resource practices which help create and sustain competitive advantage. They are peculiar to that organization's environmental matching challenge. Such organizations enjoy strong E–V–R (environment–values–resources) congruence. The competitive value of their competencies lies in the fact that whilst the general approach may be transferable, the specifics are not.

Managing human resources

Figure 11.3 summarizes a number of the key elements in the management of human resources. Appropriate people with the required and desired competencies, and/or the potential for growth and development, need to be recruited. They require clear objectives to give them both direction and performance yardsticks, backed by training and development opportunities. Outcomes should be measured, and performance reviewed and rewarded as appropriate. Underperformance or failure should be sanctioned in some way.

In this section we look briefly at a number of these issues; we also consider the importance of motivating employees, team building and succession planning.

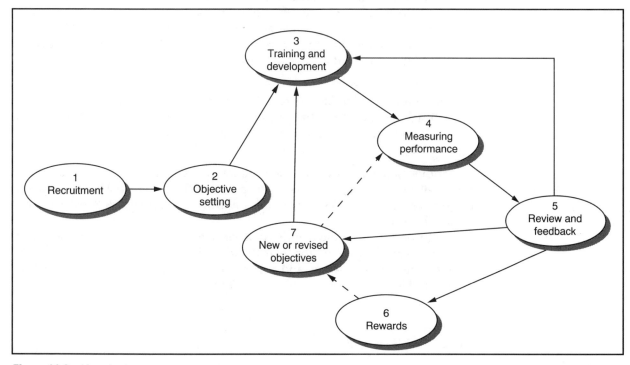

Figure 11.3   Managing human resources.

A lot of a company's success has to do with the sort of people you've got in the company. I say to the people, 'If you don't want to compete, if you won't confront change and competition, I really don't think you're right for the company'.

My point is, let's not run away from the fact that we're a performance-oriented organization. And that does create uncertainty and challenge and hyperventilation in a lot of people, but we've got to address it. So we give them development, we explain what we're doing, we try to train them to a greater degree of readiness. And when we win we celebrate.

David Johnson, Chief Executive Officer, Campbell Soup.

Managers' objectives

Hersey and Blanchard (1982) contend that organizational success and performance is affected by the congruence between the objectives of managers and those of their subordinates. They argue that the organization can only accomplish its objectives if those of managers and subordinates are supportive of each other and of the organization. Moreover, McGregor (1960) has argued that people need objectives to direct their efforts, and that if objectives are not provided by the organization they will create their own. This may not necessarily be disadvantageous for the organization as Schein (1983) has suggested that managers are generally oriented towards economic goals and see profit as being important. But personal objectives, which were discussed in Chapter 5, are likely to be allowed more freedom if managers are not given clear objectives. Porter *et al.* (1975) contend that individual behaviour is affected by people's perceptions of what is expected of them; and hence it could be argued that objectives pursued by managers will be dependent on

❑ personal motives;
❑ their understanding and perception of what the strategic leader and their colleagues expect them to contribute (expectations, although still subject to some interpretation, may or may not be made clear to managers);
❑ the culture of the organization.

Various systems and policies for setting and agreeing managers' objectives are available, but they are outside the scope of this book. Ideally the resultant objectives will be 'SMART', **specific**, **measurable**, **achievable**, **realistic** and with a **timescale**.

Whilst objective setting is important for dealing with tasks and priorities, it should never be forgotten that managing people effectively also involves communicating and interacting, and making sure there is always time and opportunity available for dealing with unexpected events.

Where people grow, profits grow.

Dr Alex Krauer, Chairman and Managing Director, Ciba-Geigy

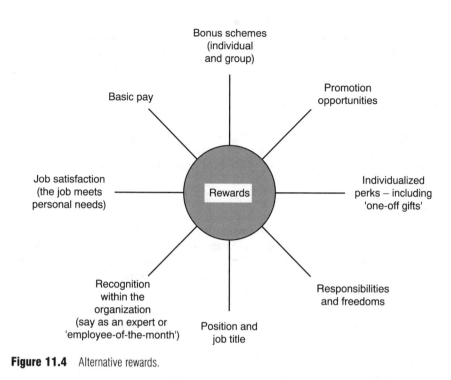

Figure 11.4   Alternative rewards.

Rewards

Rewards are an important motivator, but it is important to appreciate that an individual may feel rewarded by things other than money or promotion. See Figure 11.4. The demands and responsibilities of a job, and the freedom people are given to decide how to do things, can be rewarding. Additionally, working with a particular group of people, especially if they are seen to be successful, can be rewarding. If people feel that their efforts are being rewarded and that future efforts will also be rewarded, their quality of work is likely to improve. In this way total quality can be improved. Moreover where incremental strategic change is dependent on individual managers seeing, and acting upon, opportunities and threats, the reward system must be appropriate and motivating.

Sooner or later you'll hear about someone who made a decision that you think was very good in terms of the company's strategy. When you do, make sure you give that person many strokes, and do it as officially as possible, so other people will learn from it. A positive example is the best way to create the right atmosphere.

Of course, if you think someone made a wrong decision, let him know, but tell him when you are alone – and don't let him view it as a punishment.

Over time you give people the security to take responsibility by measuring and rewarding performance. For a year or two you can motivate people through emotion and showbiz, but, for the long run, people must know they will be measured in an accurate way in relation to the responsibility they have been given.

Jan Carlzon, when President and Chief Executive Officer,
Scandinavian Airlines System

An increasing number of organizations, including BP, WH Smith and Federal Express, are adopting formalized upward feedback as well as manager/subordinate appraisal. Although difficult to implement successfully, such systems can be very useful for increasing managers' awareness concerning their style and effectiveness.

It is crucial that any performance evaluation systems which influence or determine rewards are open and fair, and perceived as such.

Rewards, of course, depend upon the success of the organization as a whole as well as individual contributions. Hence we next look at individual motivation and the issues involved in building successful management teams.

Involving and motivating people

If people are to be committed to the organization, and to the achievement of key objectives, they must be involved. Employees at the so-called grass roots level are likely to know the details of the business and what really happens better than their superiors and managers. If they are involved and encouraged to contribute their ideas for improvements, the result can be innovation or quality improvement.

Moreover, if managers and other employees are to make effective strategic contributions it is important that they feel motivated. Whilst money and position in the organization can motivate, there are other essential factors. Hertzberg (1968) emphasized the importance of the following:

❑ the potential to contribute and achieve through the job
❑ recognition for effort and success
❑ promotion opportunities
❑ interesting work
❑ responsibility.

David McClelland (McClelland and Winter, 1971) emphasizes the importance of knowing colleagues and subordinates and understanding what does in fact motivate them. He contends that people have three needs in varying proportions – achievement, power and affiliation – and individual profiles of the balance between these needs vary. He argues that managers should attempt to understand how much their subordinates desire power, look for opportunities where they can achieve, and want close or friendly working relationships, manifested, say, by not working in isolation. If managers then seek to meet these needs, subordinates can and will be motivated.

One major motivational challenge concerns downsizing. When organizations are cutting back, and people are being made redundant, it is both essential and difficult to maintain the commitment of those remaining. After all, they are the people upon whom new competitive advantages will depend, and without this the company cannot successfully rejuvenate. These points are illustrated in Case 11.1 on Bhs.

Research by Roffey Park Management Centre (1995) established that whilst there is considerable enthusiasm amongst authors, consultants and senior managers for teamworking, empowerment and flexibility, many employees remain 'cynical, over-worked, insecure and despondent' about the impact of flatter organization structures and the consequent reduction in promotion prospects. Employees frequently perceive delayering to be a cost-cutting exercise

Visit the website:
http://www.
itbp.com

Bhs is the renamed high street retailer British Home Stores. Since 1986 Bhs has been part of Storehouse, along with Mothercare and Blazer; Bhs contributes 75% of the group's turnover. Towards the end of the 1980s, the financial performance deteriorated rapidly and Bhs appointed a new chief executive. David Dworkin was an American with some radical new ideas.

In January 1990, two months after his arrival, Dworkin arranged a three-day seminar with 15 of the most senior managers in the group, when they essentially talked about problems and strategic issues.

We discovered very few strengths and lots of weaknesses.

A new mission statement was crafted and subsequently used as a basis for a number of major changes.

The Bhs mission is to be the first choice store for dressing the modern woman and family. We are committed to service, quality, harmony, innovation and excitement in all that we do. We will succeed by being a focused organization in dynamic partnership with our customers, suppliers and each one of us.

Dworkin restructured Bhs, removing several layers of management, including ten of the 15 managers from the 1990 seminar. This saved £10 million. The main losses were from back offices, with the proportion of sales floor staff increasing from 60 to 80% of all employees. In addition there were new incentive schemes for those remaining with the company and a number of 'fresh thinkers' were recruited. New performance targets were to be established, with bonuses for achievement. In 1995 profit-related pay schemes replaced the traditional annual pay increase – with full staff agreement.

People must become the company's greatest source of competitive advantage. Bhs employees must be flexible in their approach to change.

The company's director of human resources arranged a series of meetings to explain the implications of the new mission to managers throughout the organization who were then required to discuss it with other employees; and a change action programme was introduced. Known as Activity Value Analysis, every activity in the group was scrutinized and, where appropriate, redesigned. Responsibility for the change programme was handed over to 12 carefully selected 'change agents' and they sought to involve people from every-where in the business. Some 5000 ideas for improvement were generated from amongst the existing staff. During the 1990s there have been major changes concerning products, branding, displays and supplier relationships.

Training was provided to support the change process, and this helped to minimize subsequent staff turnover. Previously, in the 1980s, turnover had been high.

The intention was to establish a learning organization whereby continuous daily improvements could be made. We challenged every aspect of what we did. We made people think that everything we did in the past was wrong and everything we were going to do in the future was right.

Sales per square foot quickly improved, but, in fairness, they were improving from a very low base. Perhaps predictably, some employees were not truly comfortable with the magnitude of change and felt the company was being run with a culture of fear. Dworkin left Bhs in the early 1990s; Keith Edelman, who came to the group from Carlton Communications, has been chief executive since 1993.

The financial results reflect a change in fortunes for the group. Although sales growth has been sluggish during the recession of the early 1990s, profits have grown strongly.

Bhs

Financial results for trading years to the end of March, using 1991 figures as a base index.

Year	Turnover	Operating profits
1991	100	100
1992	103	117
1993	113	272
1994	121	354
1995	123	447

For a group which has undergone as much change as Storehouse in its nine-year existence, developing a culture which drives the business – its values and beliefs – takes time. It requires managerial stability, consistent leadership and direction, effective communication. And above all, the right people and the right operational processes.

(1995 Annual Report)

Source: Thornhill, J (1992) Battle to rebuild family store, *Financial Times*, 4 November.

which actually reduces morale. When such rationalization is essential – and often it is – the real challenge comes afterwards, in encouraging the remaining managers to look for innovative new ways of adding value and to take risks, albeit limited and measured risks. This reinforces the critical importance of finding the most appropriate reward systems, together with mechanisms for involving, managing and leading people to achieve superior levels of performance.

Team building

Both formal and informal teams exist within organizations. Formal teams comprise sections or departments of people who work directly together on a continuous basis and in pursuit of particular specified objectives, and teams of senior managers who meet on a regular basis with an agreed agenda. Informal teams can relate to managers from different departments, or even divisions, who agree informally to meet to discuss and deal with a particular issue, or who are charged with forming a temporary group to handle an organization-wide problem. In both cases relationships determine effectiveness. Ideally all members will contribute and support each other, and synergy will result from their interactions. Simply putting a group of people together in a meeting, however, does not ensure that they will necessarily work well together and form an effective and successful team.

A successful team needs:

❑ shared and agreed objectives
❑ a working language, or effective communications
❑ the ability to manage both the tasks and the relationships.

Cummings (1981) contends that individual contributions to the overall team effort are determined by personal growth needs (for achievement and personal development) and social needs – perceived benefits from working with others to complete tasks, rather than working alone.

Within any team, therefore, there will be a variety of skills, abilities and commitments. Some people will be natural hard workers who need little supervision or external motivation; others, who may be diligent and committed, may need all aspects of their task spelt out clearly; the major contribution of particular members might be in terms of their creativity and ideas. Meredith Belbin (1981) argues that a good team of people will have compensating strengths and weaknesses, and that as a group they will be able to perform a series of necessary and related tasks.

Specifically they will

❑ create useful ideas
❑ analyse problems effectively
❑ get things done
❑ communicate effectively
❑ have leadership qualities
❑ evaluate problems and options logically
❑ handle the technical aspects
❑ control their work; and
❑ report back effectively either verbally or in writing.

Belbin has identified a number of characteristics or contributions which individuals make to teams. They relate to the provision of ideas, leadership, the resolution of conflict, the gathering and analysing of data and information, carrying out certain detailed work which might be regarded as boring by certain members, organizing people to make their most useful contributions, and developing relationships within the group. Individuals will obviously contribute in a number of areas, not just one or two, but they will often be particularly strong in some and weak in others. A balance is required if the team is to work well together and complete the task satisfactorily.

Whoever is responsible for leading the team – it might be the strategic leader and his or her team of senior managers, or department managers – should consider the various strengths and weaknesses of people and seek to develop them into an effective and cohesive team. If any essential areas of contribution are missing this should be dealt with; and any potential conflicts of strong personalities should be determined early.

Succession issues

Succession problems can concern both strategic leadership and managerial positions throughout the organization. Small firms whose growth and success have been dependent upon one person, most probably the founder, often experience problems when he or she retires, especially where there has been a failure to develop a successor in readiness. Some very large organizations also experience problems when particularly charismatic and influential strategic leaders resign or retire. Although they may be replaced by other strong leaders there may be changes to either or both the strategy or culture which do not prove successful.

However, succession problems can be seen with key people in any specialism and at any level of the organization. Firms need management in depth in order to cope with growth and with people leaving or being promoted. This implies that people are being developed constantly in line with, and in readiness for, strategic change; and this relates back to appraisal and reward systems. ICI, for example, deliberately move managers between countries and product groups as part of their management planning. This, they claim, opens the company up to 'different ideas and outside perceptions'.

To summarize the management of the flow of people, and their development, relates to ensuring that people with the necessary skills are recruited, trained and available in relation to the managerial and other tasks which have to be carried out. However, it is also necessary that people are motivated and integrated if their performance is to be effective.

Management and leadership

As well as integrating managerial efforts it is also important to consider what approach managers take to their jobs and towards innovation and opportunities for change and improvement. Mintzberg (1975) contends that managers do not spend a great deal of their working time planning work. Rather, they respond to situations and needs as they arise. Time management is vital for them and most tasks take only a limited amount of time each. Although information is available and mostly obtained informally, emphasizing the value of close working relationships and team development, judgement and intuition are vital. It therefore follows that underlying values and general strategic awareness are likely to be vital considerations and significant influences on the decisions they reach.

Zaleznik (1977) develops this theme further, suggesting that management is basically about problem solving, producing results, and controlling tasks in complex organizations. Leadership, he argues, is about managing the work other people do, and involves organizing people and delegating tasks. Zaleznik contends that managers should ideally exercise leadership qualities. Managers who fail to exercise leadership will aim to preserve the *status quo* and not change things; managers who are leaders are likely to be more effective in changing behaviour patterns. It follows that constant innovation, entrepreneurship and quality improvement are more likely to happen where managers, both at the strategic leader level and throughout the organization, exercise leadership qualities. Kotter (1990) expresses the distinction slightly differently, arguing that management is concerned with coping with complexity and achieving order and consistency, whilst leadership is about coping with change. Organizations need to do both. Kotter says that ideally individual managers will be able to achieve both, but recognizes that only some are able to. This is not material as long as the organization can build an effective team with both managerial and leadership skills.

Developing leadership qualities

Peters and Austin (1985) have suggested that leadership involves vision, enthusiasm, passion and consistency, and that these qualities should be evident

---

A **real manager** has to be a good leader in the sense that he has to embody an open-minded attitude of leadership in himself, in his fellow managers and even in the heads of each employee of his organization. **Leadership**, therefore, means to enable and help people to act as individual entrepreneurs within the frame of a commonly born vision of the business. A **bad manager**, on the other hand, is more an administrator who follows severe rules and customs within a stiff bureaucratical hierarchy.

Dr Hugo M Sekyra, CEO and Chairman, Austrian Industries

It is crucial to recognize how critical in a service business is the performance and attitude of the very large numbers of relatively junior staff who are the ones that have contact with the customer. The care that all these staff show in dealing with customers will exactly match the care shown by their management in dealing with them. Not only must they be well trained and know what is expected of them, but they need to be supervised, coached and counselled effectively. They need to be listened to, their concerns addressed and their motivation sustained in their jobs, many of which are repetitive. Management achieve the quality of customer care they deserve.

Ultimately the achievement of quality is in the mind of the customer.

David A Quarmby, when Joint Managing Director, J Sainsbury plc

throughout the organization. Such leadership is accomplished and demonstrated through the following.

❑ **Caring for customers and constant innovation:** Awareness of needs is increased by seeing and listening to customers and, where possible, consumers, and monitoring competitors. Innovation is the result of being constantly adaptive to these needs and competitive pressures.
❑ **People**: Quality comes from employees; it is not a technique. Managers should talk to employees, solicit their ideas, listen to their contributions, encourage their greater involvement in decisions and their implementation, find out what motivates them, and counsel and generally encourage them.

Successful companies are often innovative and deliver total quality by involving the whole workforce. Many such organizations, jobs and people have been made more flexible through decentralization.

Peters and Austin use the expression 'management by wandering around (MBWA)' to emphasize the importance of keeping in touch with customers, people and opportunities to innovate.

Charles Handy (1989) argues that leadership must become endemic and fashionable, not exceptional, amongst managers. He defines a leader as someone 'who shapes and shares a vision which gives point to the work of others', and contends that:

Visit the website:
http://www.
itbp.com

❑ the vision must be different from what everyone else is doing
❑ it must be clear, understandable, and capable of making a vivid impression
❑ it must make sense to people, and relate to the work they do
❑ the leader must 'live the vision' and be seen to believe in it
❑ the leader must develop a team of people who share the vision and who are committed to its achievement.

Developing the contentions of Peters and Austin, Kotter and Handy, it becomes apparent that it is necessary for organizations, and strategic leaders in particular, to ensure that their managers are capable of being leaders. This involves:

❑ recruiting people with leadership potential
❑ giving people challenges which involve taking measured risks, especially in the early stages of their managerial careers – success should be rewarded and failure should used as a basis for learning. This should contribute to the development of a change-oriented 'learning organization' which succeeds in keeping up with, or ahead of, changes in its environment
❑ job switching between functions, divisions and countries to broaden people's perspectives.

The idea of a learning organization is explored further in Key Concept 11.2. A learning organization can appear attractive from a theoretical and a conceptual viewpoint, but creating one is certainly not easy. It implies changes which will not be acceptable and feasible for many strategic leaders and managers.

KEY CONCEPT 11.2

THE LEARNING ORGANIZATION

The basic arguments:

- ❏ In a decade when quality, technology and product/service variety are all becoming widely available at relatively low cost, speed of change is essential for sustained competitive advantage.
- ❏ If an organization, therefore, fails to keep up with, or ahead of, the rate of change in its environment it will either be destroyed by stronger competitors, or lapse into sudden death or slow decline. The ideal is to be marginally ahead of competitors – opening up too wide a gap might unsettle customers.
- ❏ An organization can only adapt if it is first able to learn, and this learning must be cross-functional as well as specialist.

Hence a learning organization encourages continuous learning and knowledge generation at all levels, has processes which can move knowledge around the organization easily to where it is needed, and can translate that knowledge quickly into changes in the way the organization acts, both internally and externally.
(Senge, 1991)

Strategically important information, together with lessons and best practice, will thus be spread around; and ideally this learning will also be protected from competitors.

Essential requirements
- ❏ Systemic thinking, such that decision makers will be able to use the perspective of the whole organization; and there will be significant environmental awareness and internal co-operation.

  For many organizations the systemic perspective will be widened to incorporate collaboration and strategic alliances with other organizations in the added value chain.
- ❏ Management development and personal growth – to enable effective empowerment and leadership throughout the organization, and in turn allow managers to respond to perceived environmental changes and opportunities.
- ❏ A shared vision and clarity about both core competencies and key success factors. Changes should be consistent through strategic and operational levels.

- ❏ Appropriate values and corporate culture – to fully exploit core competencies and satisfy key success factors.
- ❏ A commitment to customer service, quality and continuous improvement.

  Kotter and Heskett (1992) argue that the appropriate culture is one which is capable of constant adaptation as the needs of customers, shareholders and employees change.
- ❏ Team learning within the organization through problem sharing and discussion.

These points have been used to develop the following matrix which draws together a number of points discussed in this chapter and relates them to key issues of change management.

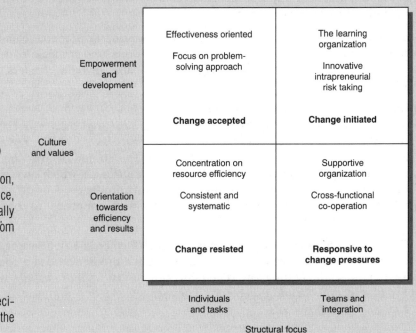

	Individuals and tasks	Teams and integration
Empowerment and development	Effectiveness oriented / Focus on problem-solving approach / **Change accepted**	The learning organization / Innovative intrapreneurial risk taking / **Change initiated**
Orientation towards efficiency and results	Concentration on resource efficiency / Consistent and systematic / **Change resisted**	Supportive organization / Cross-functional co-operation / **Responsive to change pressures**

Culture and values

Structural focus

Summary

This chapter has been based on the premise that people are an essential strategic resource. Through quality, innovation, entrepreneurship and leadership they can create and sustain competitive advantage. Equally, a shortage of skills and expertise can constrain an organization strategically. Consequently the key issues of integrating and leading human resources have been considered.

Specifically we have:

- discussed key issues in human resource strategy, defining the hard and soft approaches, and concluding there is no single best approach
- examined the implications of empowering managers and employees

- considered the competencies required by managers, emphasizing that specific competencies which generate competitive advantage may not be readily transferable between organizations
- discussed aspects of human resource management, in particular objectives, rewards, motivation, team building and succession planning
- highlighted the strategic value of managers exercising leadership characteristics and behaviour, mentioning that leadership qualities must be developed in managers, and suggesting that this is again an issue of organizational culture
- described what is meant by a learning organization

Checklist of key terms and concepts

You should be confident that you understand the following terms and ideas:

★ Hard and soft human resource management

★ Empowerment
★ Managerial competency
★ A learning organization.

Questions and research assignments

Text related

1 Consider how strategic changes in one retail sector, from an emphasis on hardware stores that specialize in personal service and expert advice to customers from all employees, to a predominance of do-it-yourself supermarkets, might have affected issues of staff motivation, personal development needs and appropriate reward systems.

2 Albeit by rule of thumb, take a team of people with whom you associate closely and evaluate their behaviour characteristics Where is the team strong? Weak? Do you believe it is balanced? If not, what might be done to change things?

Activity based

3 Observe a discussion or decision situation involving a leader and a group of subordinates. This need not be in an organizational setting – it could involve a group of scouts or guides or something similar. Evaluate the leader's behaviour in terms of task accomplishment, team involvement and the development of individuals.

4 Obtain the latest accounts for Bhs and visit one of the high street stores. Can you see evidence that the changes discussed in Case 11.1 have had a real impact on consumers? How would you compare and contrast (benchmark) Bhs with its main competitors?

References

Belbin, RM (1981) *Management Terms: Why They Succeed or Fail*. Heinemann.

Capelli, P and Crocker-Hefter, A (1995) HRM: The key to competitive advantage, *Financial Times Mastering Management series, Number 6*, 1 December.

Cummings, TG (1981) Designing effective work groups. In *Handbook of Organizational Design* (eds PC Nystrom and WH Starbuck), Oxford University Press.

Handy, C (1984), *The Future of Work*, Blackwell.

Handy, C (1989) *The Age of Unreason*, Hutchinson.

Hersey, P and Blanchard, K (1982) *The Management of Organisational Behaviour*, 4th edn, Prentice-Hall.

Hertzberg, F (1968) One more time how do you motivate employees? *Harvard Business Review*, January–February.

Kotter, JP (1990) What leaders really do, *Harvard Business Review*, May–June.

Kotter, JP and Heskett, JL (1992) *Corporate Culture and Performance*, Free Press.

McClelland, D and Winter, D (1971) *Motivating Economic Achievement*, Free Press.

McGregor, DM (1960) *The Human Side of Enterprise*, McGraw-Hill.

Mintzberg, H (1975) The manager's job – folklore and fact, *Harvard Business Review*, July–August.

Peters, T and Austin, N (1985) *A Passion for Excellence*, Collins.

Porter, LW, Lawler, EE and Hackman, JR (1975) *Behaviour in Organisations*. McGraw-Hill.

Roffey Park Management Centre (1995) *Career Development in Flatter Structures* Research report.

Schein, EH (1983) The role of the founder in creating organizational culture, *Organisational Dynamics*, Summer.

Skapinker, M (1989) Making the best of many moulds, *Financial Times*, 8 February.

Tyson, S and York, A (1982) *Personnel Management Made Simple*. Heinemann

Zaleznik, A (1977) Managers and leaders: are they different?, *Harvard Business Review*, May–June.

12
Financial Strategy

Learning objectives

After reading this chapter you should be able to

- assess the significance of financial objectives for organizations, and discuss examples of companies for whom these are of paramount importance
- discuss the advantages and disadvantages of different sources of investment capital
- apply a number of different investment appraisal techniques, and evaluate their contribution to investment decisions
- calculate the optimal capital structure for a firm and its weighted average cost of capital
- describe the capital asset pricing model
- explain how a company might be valued, say for acquisition purposes
- identify how financial strategies might yield competitive advantage.

Financial strategy is an important component of both competitive and corporate strategy. Financial considerations can either provide opportunities for development or act as major constraints.

Introduction

Financial measures of performance were introduced and discussed in Chapter 6, and in Chapter 7 the significance of poor financial management in corporate failure was shown. In this chapter we consider financial opportunities for and threats to growth and change.

Whilst poor financial management can be a cause of failure, sound financial management is often crucial for success. Figure 12.1 illustrates how financial management and strategy can be both a source of competitive advantage and a key determinant of the ability to manage corporate strategic change effectively.

The top half shows that a positive approach to financial matters can create differentiation and lower costs. Resources can be leveraged to increase the returns from them; companies which generate more revenue by increases in efficiency should increase their profits. Efficiency improvements also result in lower costs, as we have already seen. Finance itself, though, can be a direct source of competitive advantage:

Don't forget to visit the website:
http://www.itbp.com

- ❏ companies which manage their stocks, debtors and creditors will improve their cash flow and reduce both operating and borrowing costs
- ❏ some companies, particularly large corporations, can reduce their borrowing costs by negotiating lower rates of interest. This improves their figure for profit after interest and before tax
- ❏ some companies, again often large, international corporations, will be expert at minimizing their tax payments, thus improving profits after interest and tax.

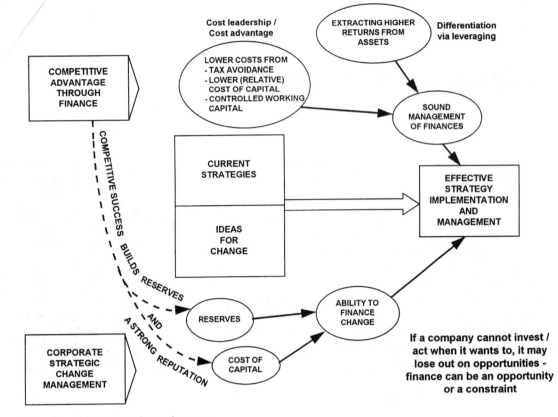

Figure 12.1 Financial strategy and strategic success.

These bottom line profit increases can be used to pay higher dividends to shareholders and for reinvestment in the business. Highly profitable companies will also strengthen their reputation with all the stakeholders.

If changes to corporate strategies are to be managed effectively, a company must be able to act decisively to seize an opportunity ahead of its competitors. This means that access to finance must be available, either from reserves, shareholders or banks. The actual cost of borrowing is then a key determinant of future competitiveness. These points are shown in the bottom half of Figure 12.1. The various issues raised by these arguments are explored in this chapter.

We consider, first, whether the organization is able to pursue the investment strategies that it would like to follow and needs to follow for survival.

Can it afford them? Is finance available? From where? Second, we discuss the risk and costs involved compared with potential returns. If an investment opportunity exists and the potential returns can be forecast, the lower the cost of borrowing money, the higher the profits that are available.

❑ Is the company profitable and able to pay its interest and dividend commitments? Is it performing well enough for its shares to have a valuation above the market average, providing some security from external predators and giving it strategic flexibility?

❑ How do shareholders, bankers and other investors and potential investors view the company's performance? Are they willing to lend more money for future growth and development, and at what cost to the company? What rate of return do they expect from their investment?

❏ How is the company financed in terms of debt and equity? Does this represent an opportunity or a threat?

❏ What investment opportunities are available, and how might they be evaluated?

❏ How can finance be a source of competitive advantage?

Financial strategy

Financial strategy involves:

❏ providing the firm with the appropriate financial structure and funds to achieve its overall objectives

❏ examining the financial implications of various strategic alternatives such as acquisition, or investment in new products or new plants, and identifying the most lucrative ones (financial aspects may or may not be the only factor involved in the selection)

❏ providing competitive advantage through cheaper funding and a flexible ability to raise capital (Clarke, 1988).

Financial performance

The central objective of a strategic leader may be growth in profits. Relative success will be determined by how well assets and shareholders' funds are being used to earn profits and increase the value of the business. Such an orientation regards shareholders as the most important stakeholder in the organization, and has been practised very successfully by, for example, Hanson plc. Hanson's approach is described later, but it is based on the acquisition of companies and their assets and the use of those assets in the most profitable manner, which usually involves quick sales of parts of the acquired businesses. In a different way it might be argued that GEC, which showed over £1 billion of investments in the balance sheet in the late 1980s, is choosing to earn money by careful speculation rather than investing to create jobs, and is thereby oriented towards its shareholders.

However, when companies compete in notoriously cyclical industries, as does GEC, cash reserves are essential to see a company through periods of recession. These reserves allow the company to hang on to parts of the business which cannot pay their way in the short term but which are essential for long-term success, and to invest strategically in anticipation of renewed growth.

If other objectives such as growth are central, profitability is still an essential requirement.

Managers throughout the organization may be concerned with the survival of the organization as an independent entity in order to provide themselves with some personal security. Sound or above-average financial performance is likely to boost share prices. Long-term, consistent, above-average performance should keep the company's valuation relatively high, making it less vulnerable to a predator, and also making it easier for the company to raise money for further expansion. Financial performance objectives are therefore likely to be seen as important by managers. This theme is supported by research by Schein (1983) which was mentioned in Chapter 11 and which suggests that managers are generally oriented towards economic goals and see profit as being important.

Fund raising

Finance is needed in order to maintain an adequate cash flow to keep the business operating and for development. For the latter the right amount is needed at the right time and at the right cost. Lesney (Matchbox) Toys was discussed briefly in Chapter 9, Case 9.1. During the 1960s Lesney was regarded as 'blue chip' as it experienced rapid growth and high profits. The share price and earnings growth were above average. By the early 1970s, as a result of competition and a downturn in demand in the USA, profits had shown a fall. Lesney, which found it easy to raise money in the 1960s, was unable to raise finance to buy part of another toy company, Lines Brothers, which was in liquidation. A lack of finance constrained strategic development at that time.

Investments should yield more than the cost of the capital used to fund them. The profits earned should be greater than the money needed to finance a loan or increased equity funding. Similarly, from a financial perspective, if a company already has the funds and does not need to borrow, the returns from the investment should exceed the potential earnings from using the money for financial speculation.

Visit the website: http://www. itbp.com

Companies, then, should be able to raise money when they need it or potentially valuable strategic opportunities may be lost. The nature of the funding, equity or loan, which is discussed in the next section, should relate to both costs and risks. Loan funding requires regular and fixed interest payments, whilst equity offers more flexibility. However, equity is generally more expensive. The decision therefore is influenced by the consistency of profits as inconsistency makes loan funding more risky. In addition the cost of the funding can lead to competitive advantage through lower costs, and this point is taken up at the end of the chapter.

Financing the business

Sources of funds

Table 12.1 gives the sources of funds for large UK companies during the 1980s, broken down into equity, borrowing and retained earnings, and comparative percentages for the UK and other developed countries in the early 1990s. The statistics indicate that most funds used by established UK organizations are normally generated internally through retained profits, but from time to time it is necessary to raise funds externally. This conclusion applies to both the public and the private sectors. Generally loan capital or borrowing has been used more extensively than equity, which might take the form of new equity issued openly or rights issues to existing shareholders.

Now in the UK and USA, equity funding is proving more significant than borrowing; the reverse is the case for Germany, France and Japan, partially the result of different regulations. In the 1990s recession, we can see UK companies using new equity to compensate for reduced cash flows and retained

Financing the business

(a) Large UK companies, 1983–1989

Table 12.1
Sources of funding

	1983	**1984**	**1986**	**1989**
Sources				
Capital issues	1	9	17	14
Borrowing	31	22	13	33
Retained earnings	66	62	69	52
Other sources	2	7	1	1
(e.g. exchange differences)				

Source: Annual abstract of statistics, HMSO.

(b) Selected developed countries, early 1990s

	Equity	**Borrowing**	**Retained earnings**
UK	40	29	31
USA	(14)	76	38
Japan	10	72	18
Germany	6	48	46
France	34	52	14
Italy	14	52	34

Source: OECD.
All figures shown as percentages of total funds raised.

earnings, and US companies buying back shares and returning funds to their shareholders. This strategy is a form of defence against possible unwelcome bids. Regulations reduce the likelihood of German, French and Japanese companies being acquired by unwelcome predators.

Investment funding, then, is available through borrowing or increased equity, but assets can be increased without investing to the same extent. This is accomplished by leasing them rather than purchasing them. Table 12.2 summarizes the major advantages and disadvantages of equity and loan capital and all three sources are discussed below.

	Advantages	**Disadvantages**
Share capital; equity	Dividends can be reduced or waived if profits low or there is a need to retain more money. No fixed repayment date. New equity increases creditworthiness.	Can change shareholder register and voting rights. Issue costs. Dividends are not tax-deductible, interest is. Can increase cost of capital.
Borrowing; loan capital	Fixed cost; often lower than equity. No dilution of equity. Interest payments are tax-deductible.	Increased risk for company, which can affect equity value. Agreed repayment date. Can be limited by willingness of people to lend.

Table 12.2
Advantages and disadvantages of equity and loan funding

Equity capital

Generally equity capital would be increased by a rights issue of ordinary shares to existing shareholders. As an example, holders of ordinary shares might be offered one new share for every two or three they already own, at a price equal to or below the current market price. At a higher price people would be unlikely to purchase. If all shareholders take up the offer then the percentage breakdown of the shareholders' register will remain the same; if they are not taken up by existing shareholders they will be offered to the market by the institutional underwriters, and the share register profile may change. Blocks of shares could be built up quite readily, and at a price below the current market price; and depending upon who was buying them threats to the organization from powerful shareholders could emerge.

Potential takeover threats might also emerge, but these would normally be within the strictly enforced City Code of Practice on Takeovers. Any holding of 4.9% of ordinary shares must be declared. Once a holding of 14.9% has been obtained a buyer must wait at least a week before buying any more to allow both the company and other shareholders to assess the changing position. When a potential bidder acquires 30% of the shares he must automatically offer to buy the rest at a price not less than the highest price paid in the market over the previous 12 months.

Rights issues will not be successful without the support of institutional shareholders. This requires investor confidence in the company's strategy and strategic leadership.

Although many shareholders buy and retain shares with a view to a long-term capital gain, resulting from their sale at a price higher than the one they were bought at, dividend policy is important. Dividends represent a rate of return on shareholders' investments and they are discussed in greater detail below. Although dividends are not fixed and can theoretically be raised or lowered freely and in relation to increases or decreases in profits, and to any changing need for retained earnings for investment, companies generally seek stability.

Loan capital

There are various forms of loan capital, but they all have one essential characteristic. They do not carry ownership which ordinary shares do. Loans might well be for a definite period of time, after which they are repayable, and with a fixed rate of interest for each year of the loan. Hence interest payments come out of profits, but they cannot be reduced if profits decline through unfavourable trading conditions. Overdrafts provide flexible short-term funding up to an agreed limit, and their cost will vary both up and down as the prevailing market rate of interest changes. Loans are invariably secured against assets, which reduces the risk for the lender. If interest payments are not met, the bank, or whoever has loaned the money, is free to appoint a receiver and effectively take over day-to-day control of the company. Interest is paid out of profits before they are assessed for taxation, and they can thereby reduce the company's tax burden; dividends for ordinary shareholders are paid after tax.

Generalizing, the cost of borrowing can be expected to rise as the degree of risk for the lender increases. Lenders will expect higher returns from higher risk investments. Government securities are considered very safe, for example, and consequently the anticipated rate of return will typically be lower than for other investments. Secured loans are safer than ordinary shares, as mentioned above, and therefore borrowing should normally prove cheaper than equity.

The ability to obtain either – and the cost – are likely to be dependent on how well the company has been performing, and how well it has been perceived by the market to have been performing. Opportunity, ability and cost are therefore essential criteria in deciding upon a preference between equity and loan funding, but this decision should be related to the decision concerning whether to invest at all. Investments, which are discussed later in the chapter, should be analysed by comparing their returns, discounted for the period they are earned, with the cost of financing them, or the opportunity cost of the money being used. The viability of an investment is therefore dependent upon the cost of the capital used. The cheaper the cost of capital, the more likely it is that an investment is viable and profitable. Hence if the cost of obtaining investment funding is high, opportunities might be lost.

Moreover, the capital structure of the company determines the impact of profit fluctuations on the money available after tax for paying dividends and for reinvestment. Large loans and high interest payments absorb profits, and this can be crucial if profits fluctuate significantly for any reason. The more that is paid out in dividends, the less that is available for re-investing, and vice versa. In turn dividend payments are likely to affect the view that shareholders and the market have of the company's performance, and this will affect their willingness to lend more.

Leasing

In many cases organizations are more concerned with using assets than actually owning them. Leasing assets is one way of acquiring them without paying their full price at any one time; the popularity of leasing has grown since the late 1970s.

When an asset is leased there will normally be an agreed annual charge for a fixed number of years, and possibly there will be an arrangement whereby the company obtains ownership of the asset for a residual price at the end of the period of the lease. In aggregate terms leasing is unlikely to be cheap, but it can have a significant effect on cash flow. Additionally there have been advantageous tax regulations. Leasing is generally low risk for the lessor, who retains legal ownership of the asset and can reclaim it if the lease payments are not met.

Leasing has offered strategic opportunities, as well as financial benefits, for certain organizations. Some companies have chosen to sell and lease back property they owned, for example, finding willing partners in property companies and institutional investors. The funds released have then been available for other investments.

Dividends

Dividends are the part of profits (after interest and tax) which are paid out to shareholders. The rest is retained and re-invested in the business. Dividend policy therefore influences the extent to which these retained funds must be supplemented with external capital. From the mid-1970s to the mid-1990s UK companies have, on average, retained some 45% of their after-tax profits for reinvestment. The comparable figure for the USA is 54%. Japan achieved 63% and Germany 67%.

Dividend policy in the UK is also affected by tax regulations. Companies are required to pay 20% of their dividend figure as ACT (advance corporation tax), which can later be reclaimed against corporation tax created by future profits. However, where a large multi-national does not make enough of its profits in the UK, it may not be able to reclaim all its dividend-related ACT, thus increasing its effective rate of tax. In 1994 the engineering and car components group GKN made a hostile bid for Westland Helicopters. Analysts declared that there was no synergy potential in the proposed acquisition; rather it was designed to allow GKN to build up its UK profits and thereby reduce its taxes. GKN had been having to write off ACT it could not reclaim.

Gitman (1982) contends that in deciding upon their dividend policy companies should consider two inter-related objectives: first, the need to maximize owners' wealth in the long term and, second, the need for continued investment funding. In reality firms generally pursue an essentially stable dividend policy despite fluctuating profits, and increases are expected to take account of inflation. Figure 12.2 illustrates a stable dividend policy by Thorn-EMI plc during the 1980s and 1990s despite substantial changes in the earnings per share.

Stable dividends – even during a recession, when they may not be covered fully by earnings – are justified as a reward to shareholders for their loyalty. Moreover, in relation to total reserves, the amount involved is often quite small. Unstable dividends are frequently perceived to represent inconsistency by the board of directors and a lack of board confidence in the future.

Although some large companies have reduced their dividends in the recession of the early 1990s many have resisted, such that the average dividend cover for companies quoted in the *Financial Times* has fallen below 2 times. In 1980 the average dividend cover was nearly 3 times. When earnings rise more steeply after the recession it is unlikely that dividends will track them upwards, and instead, like Thorn-EMI continue to increase gradually.

Weston and Brigham (1979) argue that stable dividends tend to lead to higher share prices because investors are more favourably disposed towards companies whose shares provide dividends 'they are sure of receiving' than they are towards less reliable companies who are regarded as more risky. The logic is that some shareholders rely on dividend income and are therefore

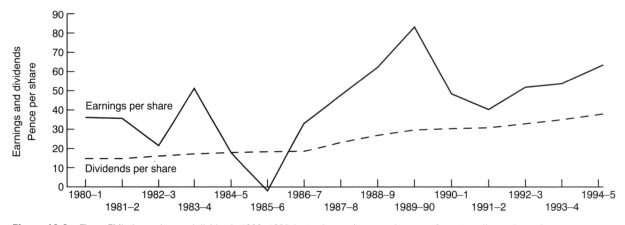

Figure 12.2   Thorn-EMI plc earnings and dividends 1980–1995 (note: the earnings per share are after extraordinary charges).

willing to pay a premium for those shares they consider to carry least risk. Higher share prices are also to some extent a defence against acquisition as they make the company more expensive to buy, and consequently they are very significant to managers as employees.

Stable dividends and variable earnings must mean either that the company is unable to pursue a consistent investment policy or that in some years it has to raise additional capital through the issue of new equity or through borrowing. Both earnings and dividends will affect the willingness of shareholders to provide increased equity funding. It is very important that shareholders understand why companies are following a particular dividend policy in order that they can react objectively. The onus is on companies to explain their decisions. This is particularly important if capital is required for future investments which should increase the shareholders' wealth in the long term. If dividends are not being increased at the same rate as earnings, this is one way of funding the investment.

Thus, to summarize, loans and equity both offer advantages and disadvantages in providing additional investment funding. One key point is that debt capital is usually cheaper as it carries less risk for the lender. Moreover, as debt capital increases, the company's cash value to its owners (shareholders) increases as the interest payments are tax deductible. But a company with high gearing may not be able to afford low profit years because of the risk of receivership and the impact on dividends and retained earnings. Increased debt capital adjusts the capital structure in such a way that any fluctuations in earnings before interest and tax are exacerbated, affecting the money available for dividends and retentions. Retained earnings are the major source of investment capital for UK companies. Dividends affect the perceptions of shareholders and in turn both the potential to raise more equity and the overall share value of the company. If profits are declining this issue can present a dilemma. Maintaining dividends in the face of reduced profit means lower retained earnings and possibly a greater need for external financing. Increased loan capital for future investment can make the problem worse.

Companies in particular industries might usefully be analysed to check whether their capital structure and the percentage of debt reflects their overall stability. One would expect companies in stable industries to have a higher percentage of debt than those in more unstable dynamic industries.

Having looked at different types of funding and their implications for the business we shall next consider the cost of capital and how this might affect investment decisions.

The cost of capital

The optimal capital structure

In theory there is an optimal capital structure (OCS) in terms of debt and equity for any firm, and it will depend on:

❏ the amount of risk in the industry
❏ the riskiness of the company's corporate and competitive strategies, and their potential impact on profits
❏ the typical capital structure for the industry, and what competitors are doing – the cost of funding can provide competitive advantage as we shall examine later

❏ management's ability to pay interest without too serious an impact on dividends and future investment

❏ both the owners' and the strategic leader's preference for risk, or aversion to it.

The weighted average cost of capital

In considering, or attempting to decide, the optimal capital structure it is important to evaluate the **weighted average cost of capital** (WACC). The WACC, again in theory, is the average rate of return that investors expect the company to earn. In practice it is the average cost of raising additional investment funding. If a company used only loan funding the WACC would be the after-tax cost of borrowing more. But most organizations have a complex structure of debt and equity, each of which carries a different cost. The WACC is therefore an attempt to approximate what more funding would cost if it were raised proportionately to the percentages of debt and equity in the optimal capital structure. In practice it will relate to the current capital structure.

Determining the weighted average cost of capital

The formula is

$$\text{WACC} = (\text{Percentage of long-term debt in the OCS} \times \text{After-tax cost of debt})$$
$$\text{plus}$$
$$(\text{Percentage of ordinary shares in the OCS} \times \text{After-tax cost of equity})$$

As mentioned above, the WACC will normally be calculated in terms of the firm's current capital structure rather than the theoretical OCS.

The **cost of long-term debt is** the weighted average of the various interest rates incurred on existing loans – after accounting for tax. Hence for a company which pays 10% interest on 40% of its loans, 12% on the other 60% and tax at an effective rate of 30%, the cost of long-term debt is

$$((10\% \times 40) + (12\% \times 60)) \times (1 - 0.3) = 7.84\%$$

The **cost of equity** is more difficult to calculate. One popular model for estimating it is the capital asset pricing model (CAPM), which is described here only in outline. Franks and Broyles (1979) provide a much more detailed explanation.

The capital asset pricing model

In theory the cost of equity for an individual company should equal the rate of return that shareholders expect to gain from investing in that company. This is based on their perception of the amount of risk involved. The CAPM attempts to capture this. The formula is

$$R = F + \text{beta}(M - F)$$

R is the expected earnings or return on a particular share and F represents the risk-free rate of return expected from the most secure investments such as government securities, where the likelihood of default is considered negligible. The expected risk-free rate is determined by the current interest rate on these securities and expected inflation. *M* is the average rate of return expected from all securities traded in the market and beta is a measure of risk based on the volatility of an individual company's shares compared with the market as a whole. A beta of 1.6 (empirically high) means that a company's share price fluctuates by 1.6 times the market average. In other words, if the market average rises or falls by 10%, the company's share price increases or decreases by 16%. A low beta might be 0.3. Low beta shares in a portfolio reduce risk, but in general high beta shares do little to reduce risk.

Dimson (1995) quotes research by London Business School which yields the following betas:

Hong Kong and Shanghai Bank   1.6
(includes Midland Bank)
Hanson   1.0
J. Sainsbury   0.6
Manchester United Football Club   0.4.

As an example, assume the risk-free rate is 10%, the market as a whole is returning 18%, and a company's beta is 1.2.

$$R = 10 + 1.2(18 - 10) = 19.6\%$$

In other words the market would be expecting the company to achieve 19.6% earnings on shareholders' funds. As explained in Chapter 6 this is earnings after interest and tax divided by total shareholders' funds, including reserves.

By contrast, if a company's beta was 0.5

$$R = 10 + 0.5(18 - 10) = 14\%$$

The CAPM is useful for estimating the cost of equity but there are certain problems in implementing it. Primarily all the data will be adjusted and extrapolated historical data, when really it is realistic forecasts of future earnings and returns that matter. *F* and *M* theoretically represent expected future returns, and beta should be based on expected future fluctuations, but normally historical data will be used in the model on the assumption that trends continue. The prevailing and predicted rates of interest in the economy will be used to increase or decrease past return figures.

Visit the website:
http://www.
itbp.com

The WACC can now be calculated. Assume that a company has £1.2 million equity funding and £800,000 in long-term debt, and that the relative costs of each are 16% and 8% respectively.

Source of funding	Total (£ million)	Percentage of total	Cost (%)	Weighted cost
Equity	1.2	60	16	9.6
Loans	0.8	40	8	3.2

Thus WACC = 12.8%.

Of course, retained earnings which can be re-invested in the company could alternatively be paid out as dividends, which shareholders could themselves invest wherever they chose. Consequently the return on such reinvestments in the company should be at least the same as that which investors expect from their existing shares. Given that all shareholders' funds are incorporated in the CAPM, this is taken into account.

This whole area is extremely complex, but nevertheless the cost of capital is an important consideration alongside availability. The cost of capital can affect the viability of a proposed investment, and it can affect the overall costs of producing a product or service and thereby influence competitive advantage. Investments, and how they might be evaluated, are the subject of the next section.

Investments and capital budgeting

Decisions concerning where a company's financial resources should be allocated are known as investment or capital budgeting decisions. The decision might concern the purchase of a new piece of equipment, the acquisition of another company, or financing the development and launch of a new product.

Competitive advantage and corporate strategic change are both relevant issues.

The ability to raise money, and the cost involved, are key influences, and should be considered alongside two other strategic issues:

❑ Does the proposed investment make sense strategically, given present objectives and strategies?
❑ Will the investment provide an adequate financial return?

The latter question is partly answered by the company's cost of capital and is explored in this section. Strategic fit is a broad issue and is addressed at various points in the book.

In simple terms, an investment represents the commitment of money now for gains or returns in the future. The financial returns are therefore measured over an appropriate period of time. Estimating these returns relies substantially on forecasts of demand in terms of both amount and timing; and generating the returns further relies upon the ability of managers to manage resources in such a way that the forecasts are met. Uncertainty is therefore an issue.

Generally any investment should be evaluated financially on at least the following two criteria:

❑ Individually, is it worth proceeding with?
❑ Is it the best alternative from the options the company has, or if money is reasonably freely available to the company, how does the proposal rank alongside other possibilities?

In the financial evaluation of a proposed investment which produces a cash flow over a period of time, it is necessary to incorporate some qualification for the fact that inflation and other factors generally ensure that a 'pound tomorrow' is worth less than its current value. This is achieved by discounting the cash flow, which is discussed below and illustrated in Box 12.1.

Box 12.1
ANALYSING PROPOSED INVESTMENTS

Discounted cash flows

Background explanation

If the prevailing rate of interest on bank deposit or building society accounts is 10% an individual or organization with money to invest could save and earn compound interest with relatively little risk. If the rate stayed constant £100 today would be worth £110 next year and £121 the year after if the interest was not withdrawn annually. To calculate future values simply multiply by $1 + r$ each year, where r is the rate of interest. Therefore in ten years' time £100 is worth $£100(1 + r)^{10}$.

Reversing the process enables a consideration of what money earned in the future is worth in today's terms. In other words, if a company invests now, at today's value of the pound, it is important to analyse the returns from the investment also in today's terms, although most if not all the returns from the investment will be earned in the future when the value of the pound has fallen. This is known as **discounting future values**. So £100 earned next year is worth $£100/(1 + r)$ today, i.e. £90.90.

Similarly £100 earned ten years hence would be worth in today's terms $£100/(1 + r)^{10}$. This is known as **net present value.**

In discounting cash flows and calculating net present value discount tables are used for simplicity.

An example

Assume that a company invests £1 million today and in return earns £250,000 each year for five years, starting next year. Earnings in total amount to £1.25 million, but they are spread over five years. The company's estimated cost of capital is 10%.

Year	Cash flow receipts (£ thousand)	Discount factor at 10%	Net present value (£ thousand)
1	250	0.909	227
2	250	0.826	206
3	250	0.751	188
4	250	0.683	171
5	250	0.621	153
			945

Hence £1 million is invested to earn £945,000 in today's terms – a loss of £55,000. Logically a positive figure is sought; and if the investment is required to show a return which is higher than the cost of capital, this target return rather than the cost of capital should be used as the discount rate and a positive net present value should be sought at this level.

Financially this investment would only be viable with a lower cost of capital. Logically all projects look increasingly viable with lower capital costs. The calculation below is of the cost of capital at which this particular project becomes viable.

The internal rate of return

The next step would be to discount at a lower rate, say 5%.

Year	Cash flow receipts (£ thousand)	Discount factor at 5%	Net present value (£ thousand)
1	250	0.952	238
2	250	0.907	227
3	250	0.864	216
4	250	0.823	206
5	250	0.784	196
			1083

This time a positive net present value of £83,000 is obtained.

The following formula is used to calculate the internal rate of return:

$$\frac{83,000}{138,000} \times \frac{5}{100} = 3\%$$

(£83,000 is the positive net present value at a 5% cost of capital, £138,000 is the difference in net present value between the 5% and 10% rates, and the 5/100 represents the percentage difference between the 5 and 10.)

This 3% is added to the 5% to give 8%, which is the yield or internal rate of return from this investment.

(Continued)

Check:

Year	Cash flow receipts (£ thousand)	Discount factor at 8%	Net present value (£ thousand)
1	250	0.926	232
2	250	0.857	214
3	250	0.794	198
4	250	0.735	184
5	250	0.681	170
			998

In other words this investment gives a yield of 8%. This is also known as the internal rate of return, the discount rate which makes the net present value of the receipts exactly equal to the cost of the investment. In the same way that one might look for a positive net present value, one would be looking for an internal rate of return that exceeded the cost of capital.

Payback

Payback is simply the length of time it takes to earn back the outlay; and obviously one can look at either absolute or discounted cash flows, normally the former. In the example above the payback is four years exactly. The outlay was £1 million, and the receipts amounted to £250,000 each year.

Payback is quite useful. For one thing it is relatively simple. For another it does take some account of the timing of returns, for returns can be re-invested in some way as soon as they are to hand.

Evaluating proposed investments

If an organization wishes to be thorough and objective investments could usefully be analysed against the six criteria listed below. The first three of these are essentially quantitative; the second three incorporate qualitative issues. Sometimes the strategic importance of a particular proposal may mean that, first, the most financially rewarding option is not selected or that, second, an investment is not necessarily timed for when the cost of capital would be lowest. As an example of the first point consider a firm in a growing industry which feels that it has to invest in order not to lose market share, although the current cost of capital may mean that the returns from the investment are less than it would wish for or that it could earn with a strategically less important option. An example of the second point would be a firm whose industry is in recession but predicted to grow, and where investment in capital in readiness for the upturn might result in future competitive advantage. At the moment the cost of capital might be relatively high, but the strategic significance of the investment might outweigh this.

The six criteria for evaluating a proposed investment are as follows:

❏ the discounted present value of all returns through the productive life of the investment
❏ the expected rate of return, which should exceed both the cost of capital (the cost of financing the investment) and the opportunity cost for the money (returns that might otherwise be earned with an alternative proposal)
❏ payback – the payout period and the investment's expected productive life – which is a popular measure as it is relatively easily calculated
❏ the risk involved in not making the investment or deferring it
❏ the cost and risk if it fails

❏ the opportunity cost – specifically, the potential gains from alternative uses of the money.

The three quantitative measures (the first three measures) are explained in Box 12.1.

Discounting techniques are theoretically attractive and used in many organizations, though more in the USA than Europe, and particularly where the proposal is capital intensive. But the technique must involve uncertainty if the cash flows cannot be forecast accurately, as is often the case. Additionally the net present value is dependent on the discount rate used, and this should relate to the weighted average cost of capital, which again may be uncertain. Research by Richard Pike (1982) concludes that payback is the technique used most widely because of its simplicity in both calculation and comprehension. The expected rate of return and the net present value are used less frequently as they are more complicated and of arguably less value if payback periods are relatively short. In his research Pike also determined that most respondents used a discount rate of 15% rather than a weighted average cost of capital specific to them.

There will always therefore be some important element of managerial judgement, and one might argue that this managerial intuition will be preferred in some smaller firms which place less emphasis on planning than do larger firms and in those companies that are more entrepreneurial and risk oriented. However, if the decision maker really understands the market and the strategic implications of the proposed investment, this may not be detrimental.

Large organizations evaluating possible investments for different divisions or business units should consider the estimated rate of return from each proposal, the current returns being obtained in each division and the company's average cost of capital – as well as any strategic issues. Take the following two possibilities:

	Division A	*Division B*
Rate of return on proposal	20%	13%
Current returns	25%	9%

Division A's proposal could seem unattractive as it offers a lower return than existing projects, whilst B's investment offers an improvement to current returns. If the company's cost of capital is 15%, A's proposal is profitable and B's proposal is not.

Issues in investment decisions

As we have seen, for financial analyses to be useful, cash flows need to be forecast and a suitable discount rate selected. It is quite typical for companies not to inflate future cash flows, but to think in terms of today's values, and instead use a discount rate which incorporates an inflation factor. Critics argue that this causes companies to underestimate the true discounted value of a cash flow. In the same way as selecting an arbitrary discount figure, such as the 15% mentioned above, this approach can encourage companies to underinvest. The same critics argue that companies should be consistent and ideally select non-inflated cash flows and discount rates which, likewise, ignore inflation. The discount rate, then, should be the actual interest rate (which has fallen dramatically during the 1990s) supplemented by a risk premium. Moreover, different projects carry different elements of risk and should, therefore, be assessed individually. A discount rate appropriate for the particular project should be selected, rather than the same one used repetitively and regardless of the nature of the project.

Grundy and Ward (1994) further argue that it is vital to also consider the underlying 'drivers of value' in any investment. Is the opportunity strategically attractive, and will any advantage gained be sustainable? Are there synergies with other parts of the business? Whilst it is not an excuse for avoiding careful assessment, it is clear that some of these synergies may be unpredictable in advance. They may emerge with learning and experience. Parallel and future changes and investments can additionally mean that the proposed cash flows, if they are examined in isolation, may again be underestimates. They might later be boosted by synergistic benefits not yet realisable.

Tackling these strategic issues, they argue, will help put the numerical analysis into a proper perspective. After all, every investment proposal involves uncertainty (a constantly changing environment, the ability of the company to actually implement the strategy and generate the proposed returns) and intangibles (competitor reactions).

The evaluation of a proposed investment then depends on forecasts of the revenue which might be generated and the ability of managers to ensure that the anticipated earnings do accrue. Risk and uncertainty are important issues. Sensitivity analysis is one way of incorporating a consideration of risk into investment decisions. Another way would be to increase the discount rate, implying that the cost of capital might realistically be higher than the value being used, but this will effectively reduce the present value of future earnings and make an investment seem less attractive than it would at a lower discount rate. However, research in both the USA and the UK by Donaldson and Lorsch (1983) and Pike (1982) respectively suggests that many managers do not specifically include risk in their investment decisions.

Visit the website: http://www.itbp.com

In simple terms sensitivity analysis involves changing certain parameters and assessing their implications. For example an investment might be forecast to yield cash flows over six years as follows: £500,000; £750,000; £1.2 million; £1.4 million; £1.5 million; and £1 million in Year 6, to give a total of £6.35 million in absolute terms. If the cost of the investment is £4 million, payback comes very early in the fifth year. The effect of extending the payback period by slowing down the build-up but without reducing the overall total might be evaluated by comparing the two net present values. An appropriate absolute flow might be £400,000; £600,000; £800,000; £1 million; £1.2 million; and £2.35 million in Year 6. Payback this time takes five years and more of the revenues are earned in later years when they will be discounted more heavily. This second flow will not only take longer to pay back, but the net present value and the internal rate of return will also both be lower.

Finally the sensitivity of a reduced overall cash flow might be evaluated: £500,000; £750,000; £1.1 million; £1.3 million; £1.4 million; and £800,000 in Year 6. Payback again is early in Year 5, but the absolute cash flow and in turn the net present value are lower.

These flow changes could result from changing the parameters of market growth rate, market share achieved, prices or costs incurred. Sensitivity analysis tests the robustness of proposed investments to any changes in the essential component variables.

Valuing a company

Acquisition of another company constitutes an investment, and similarly one major strategic objective might be to avoid being taken over by another firm. In both cases the current value of an organization is important. A company can be acquired by buying an appropriate percentage of its shares, and the likely purchase price of these in a bidding situation will be influenced substantially by their current market price in trading. However, the market price at any time may or may not reflect the value of the organization.

Rule of thumb

A typical rule of thumb valuation of a company would be to multiply the most recent annual profits (or an average of the last few years) times an x factor. Relatively small xs will be selected for small companies (which have fewer customers and fewer key people) and service businesses, where it is easier for key people to be lost during or after the acquisition. The x factor might vary from three up to 13 for large, established manufacturing businesses.

The balance sheet valuation

The balance sheet value of a company is normally taken from the value of the net assets. Divided by the number of ordinary shares issued this yields the asset value behind every ordinary share, and it can therefore be useful in assessing what an appropriate bid price for the ordinary shares might be. However, caution is needed because the balance sheet traditionally records historic costs rather than present values, and this can be misleading in the case of property. In addition, although some companies do account for this, the value of such intangible assets as brand names is rarely reflected in the balance sheet.

The market valuation

The market valuation of a company is the number of ordinary shares issued multiplied by their present price plus the inherited debt. This will reflect the likely lowest cost to a buyer, as any bid for shares at a price below their existing price is unlikely to succeed. In reality the price of shares is likely to increase during the period between when current shareholders realize that a bid is likely, or when one is announced, and when control is finally achieved by the bidder.

The current share price and the asset value of shares should be looked at together.

Earnings potential

Allen (1988) contends that it is future earnings potential that determines how valuable a company is, not historical results. An analysis of past and current performance is therefore limited in its usefulness. In isolation a high return on capital employed, for example, can hide the reality of an asset base which is declining in real terms. Therefore one should estimate the future cash flows which the company is capable of generating and discount these by the cost of capital. The current value of the company is determined by this net present value calculation.

The decision to acquire a company, however, will not be based solely on the discounted future earnings, nor the purchase price, but both these are very important. Acquisition strategies will be explored in greater depth in Chapter 16, but here it is important to stress the need to consider both strategic and financial issues. Future earnings potential for both the acquiring and the acquired companies could be improved with a merger if valuable synergy of some form is derived, and for this potential a premium price might be justified.

Consequently, Copeland *et al.* (1990) recommend a five-level valuation approach. The first level is the current market value, described above. The second level is the earnings potential, the value of the projected cash flow, discounted. The third level projects a value once internal improvements have been undertaken. New business processes, for example, could improve the cash flow. The fourth level is the value after restructuring, when non-core or poorly performing activities have been sold or divested. The fifth level combines level three and four benefits. Significantly, the improvements implied in these three levels may require a fresh management team and style.

Financial objectives and strategies

Acquisitive companies like Hanson have sought to acquire companies whose potential is high but whose overheads and other indirect costs such as interest payments are also high. Such companies will show a high gross margin, which indicates that the market is willing to pay a price much higher than the direct labour and materials costs of producing the product or service, and relatively low profitability, or even losses, when overheads, interest and tax are deducted. Profits should be improved by appropriate rationalization and cost cutting. Quite often the acquirer is able to reduce the cost of loan capital, which also increases profits. Additionally the purchase price can be offset by the sale of parts of the company which do not fit the strategic objectives of the acquirer. Case 12.1 details the sale by Hanson of parts of Imperial Group after the company was acquired in a hostile and competitive takeover in 1986. Hanson's strategy is summarized as part of the case. Other, similar, Hanson acquisitions are explored in the full case study on the company.

In such takeovers financial objectives and issues are often predominant, and a key objective for the companies is the increase in the value of the company for the shareholders. The constant need for achievement in financial performance measures will be an essential feature of the organization culture. Senior executives, often known as tracking teams, are likely to devote time and energy looking for strategic acquisition opportunities which can be used for financial gain through the input of more effective management and appropriate divestment. However, whilst such acquisitions can provide real growth opportunities the ability to finance them can prove to be a constraint, and once the acquisition activity and growth slows down the companies look vulnerable.

We will return to the subject of acquisitive conglomerates in Chapter 16.

Finance and competitive advantage

Michael Porter (1985), whose work was discussed in Chapter 9, argues that companies achieve competitive advantage through lower costs and differentiation. Low cost finance (a cost of capital lower than one's competitors), cost-effective production and high quality through low wastage can all lower costs.

THE ACQUISITION OF IMPERIAL GROUP BY HANSON

In 1986 Hanson won control of Imperial Group for £2.8 billion. The bid was unwelcome to the Imperial Directors who supported a rival bid from United Biscuits.

In the financial year which ended in October 1985 Imperial Group sales were £4.92 billion with pre-tax profits of £235.7 million. Approximately half of the sales and half of the profits arose from the tobacco interests, but Imperial was diversified as follows:

Tobacco	Players, Embassy, Golden Virginia, St Bruno
Foods	Ross Frozen Foods, Youngs Seafoods, Golden Wonder Crisps, HP and Lea and Perrin Sauces
Brewing	Courage (incl. John Smith and Harp Lager)
Hotels	Anchor Hotels (in 1985 Imperial had sold the Howard Johnson chain of American hotels)
Restaurants	Happy Eater Roadhouses, Welcome Break Motorway service areas
Shops	Finlays Newsagents.

Divestments

In 1986 the hotels and restaurants were sold to Trusthouse Forte for £186 million. The sale was subject to approval by the Monopolies and Mergers Commission which investigated the effect of linking the Happy Eater chain and Welcome Break services with THF's Little Chef group.

Also in 1986 Courage was sold to Elders IXL (Australia) for £1.4 billion. Since this sale Elders has sold Courage's public houses for £1 billion, retaining the breweries.

Golden Wonder was sold to Dalgety for £87 million in 1986.

£1.7 billion out of a buying price of £2.8 billion was thus recouped in the year of purchase.

In 1988 HP and Lea and Perrins were sold to BSN (France) for £199 million and Ross Frozen Foods and Young Seafoods were sold for a further £335 million.

After two years Hanson had recouped over £2 billion and still retained the tobacco interests, which, as mentioned above, constituted some 50% of Imperial turnover and profits.

This success was matched in the USA – where Hanson also has substantial interests – with the acquisition of SCM, again in 1986. After paying $1 billion to buy SCM, disposals recouped $1.3 billion and Hanson still retained Smith-Corona typewriters and a profitable chemical business.

Rationalization

Imperial Tobacco was rationalized by reducing the number of factories from five to two and cutting both the workforce and the number of brands. Productivity and profits improved. Significantly Hanson treated Imperial Tobacco as one business and looked for synergies – before the acquisition the old Players and Wills companies, despite being merged, had operated with separate headquarters in Nottingham and Bristol.

This approach was similar to Hanson's management of Ever Ready batteries which it had acquired in 1981. Profits, poor at the time of the acquisition, were again improved by rationalization and concentration in the UK – factories overseas were closed. In addition expenditure on research and development was cut back such that Ever Ready has been perceived to be less innovative than its main rival, Duracell. Ever Ready has, however, developed and introduced Gold Seal batteries to compete successfully with Duracell. Ever Ready was sold in April 1992 'to help finance further acquisitions'.

The Hanson strategy

This strategy was based on three essential principles:

❑ The key objective is to maximize shareholder value.
❑ Many companies do not do this and are therefore run badly.
❑ Such companies are good buys because their assets can be made to create more value for shareholders.

The strategy can be applied successfully in any industry, and Hanson has diversified into a number of unrelated areas including construction, bricks, textiles, animal foods and meat processing, pulp, coal, gold and chemicals. Hanson has

Continued overleaf

not always stayed in the industry, but divested companies and business units when appropriate for its strategy.

In the main businesses in competitive industries, and which require investment, are sold, and mature, slow-growth companies retained. Cyclical businesses are also attractive targets for Hanson. In the early 1990s some 90% of Hanson's profits were from mature industries. Despite the lack of growth potential in these businesses the Hanson restructuring strategies have generated a high and consistent growth in group profits.

Earnings per share are maximized when business units achieve the highest possible sustainable return on capital employed. Earnings per share can be improved by increasing returns from existing capital or by reducing capital and maintaining earnings. The latter theme encapsulates divestments.

Although it does not always happen it could be argued that in an organization such as this, which is not primarily concerned with staying in particular industries, business units should be sold when their earnings cannot be increased further and should be replaced by others with greater potential.

Shareholders who support such organizations expect the increased returns to be generated quickly, and consequently Hanson is not thought to be interested in companies which cannot be improved within three to four years.

Although earnings per share can be improved by investing and using debt financing, rather than equity, Hanson are basically risk averse and seek to constrain their gearing.

The company also benefits from low-cost finance and astute tax management.

Business units are decentralized and given strict targets to achieve, but all capital investments are carefully scrutinized at Board level. Within these financial constraints businesses can adapt their competitive and functional strategies.

Investments which can create new differentiation opportunities are also influenced by the company's financial strength – the ability to raise the necessary funding from appropriate sources and the cost. The cost of raising the money influences the prospects for the investment. Proposed investments by companies in the UK have often had to appear more profitable than similar proposals elsewhere because the cost of capital has been higher. Table 12.3 shows that in the early 1990s lower investment costs in Germany and Japan provided opportunities for competitive advantage. Differentiation strategies are designed to add value which matters to consumers and for which they will pay a premium price. The lower the cost of adding the value, the greater is the profit opportunity.

Clarke (1988) argues that companies can also achieve competitive advantage through 'strategic mobility' which involves such factors as

❏ knowing clearly the current and future value of all parts of the business, so as to know whether they are worth keeping or whether any offers for any part might be worth accepting

Table 12.3

Comparative costs of capital – early 1990s. Ranking: 1 = lowest cost of capital; 4 = highest cost.

	USA	Japan	Germany	UK
Research and development (10-year payback)	3	1	2	4
Equipment and machinery (20-year life)	4	2	1	3
Expensed items (three-year life)	4	2	1	3

Source: Federal Reserve Bank of New York.

  Whilst banking systems are different, the key is the success of respective governments in containing inflation.

❏ knowing which companies are available for purchase and what the costs and values are

❏ being able to raise the money to acquire them.

Strategic mobility of this nature is obviously a more relevant benefit for some companies than others. It is particularly applicable for companies with several business units, and those whose willingness to consider buying and selling businesses is derived from strong financial objectives.

Working capital and competitive advantage

Pass and Pike (1987) emphasize the value of managing working capital effectively as a way of reducing costs and contributing to competitive advantage. Working capital is measured as the difference between current assets and current liabilities.

Current assets include stock (raw materials, work in progress and finished goods), debtors (unpaid bills for goods and services supplied to customers), cash in hand, and short-term investments.

Current liabilities include monies owed to trade creditors (for raw materials, etc.), bank overdraft and other short-term loans, and outstanding tax, dividend and interest obligations.

As a **flow of money** working capital is related to the movement of funds in, through and out of the business. If there is better management of stock levels, debtors (days of credit given) and creditors (days of credit taken) then overdrafts can be reduced or cash available increased. Given this there is either a saving of interest payments, which corresponds to a reduction in costs, or potential earnings from short-term investments.

Astute multi-national companies will seek to minimize their tax payments by moving profits and funds between countries and businesses and making use of tax havens. This will lead to higher after-tax profits which enable higher dividend payments to share holders, higher retentions and lower cost investments. Hanson, for example, have recently paid taxes equivalent to 22% of pre-tax profits, well below the prevailing corporation tax rates for the UK and the USA – 35 and 34%, respectively.

Checklist of key terms and concepts

You should feel confident that you understand the following terms and ideas:

★ Gearing
★ The optimal capital structure
★ The weighted average cost of capital
★ The capital asset pricing model
  (In each case a conceptual understanding primarily)
★ Investment appraisal
★ Sensitivity analysis
★ Company valuations.

Summary

In this chapter we have considered financial strategy in terms of the cost and availability of capital and the implications for the firm of different types of funding. These issues have been shown to influence the ability of the company to pursue certain strategies and the opportunity to gain competitive advantage through effective financial management. Additionally the financial evaluation of proposed investments has been examined, but it has been pointed out that other strategic issues are also important in deciding whether or not to pursue an investment.

Specifically we have:

- ❑ considered the significance of financial objectives for organizations
- ❑ discussed the advantages and disadvantages of equity and loan capital, and the impact of high debt funding or high gearing especially when profits are prone to fluctuate
- ❑ looked at the importance of dividend policy and the typical policies pursued by UK companies
- ❑ summarized the techniques for calculating the optimal capital structure and the weighted average cost of capital and discussed the thinking behind the capital asset pricing model
- ❑ considered how investments might be evaluated both in terms of strategic fit and financially, and described three quantitative techniques, namely net present value, the internal rate of return and payback
- ❑ highlighted the potential value of carrying out a sensitivity analysis
- ❑ discussed how a company might be valued, say for acquisition purposes
- ❑ looked briefly at strategies pursued by companies for whom financial objectives are arguably central
- ❑ evaluated how financial strategies might yield competitive advantage.

References

Allen, D (1988) *Long Term Financial Health – A Structure for Strategic Financial Management*, Institute of Management Accountants.

Clarke, CJ (1988) Using finance for competitive advantage, *Long Range Planning*, **21**(2).

Copeland, T, Kotter T and Murrin J (1990) *Valuation: Measuring and Managing the Value of Companies*, John Wiley.

Dimson, E (1995) The Capital Asset Pricing Model *Financial Times Mastering Management series*, Number 4, 17 November.

Donaldson, G and Lorsch, JW (1983) *Decision Making At The Top*, Basic Books.

Franks, JR and Broyles, JE (1979) *Modern Managerial Finance,* John Wiley.

Gitman, LJ (1982) *Principles of Managerial Finance*, 3rd edn, Harper and Row.

Grundy, T and Ward K (1994) Beyond the numbers game, *Financial Times*, 28 December.

Pass, C and Pike, RH (1987) Management of working capital: a neglected subject, *Management Decision*, **25**(1).

Pike, RH (1982) *Capital Budgeting in the 1980s*, Institute of Cost and Management Accountants Occasional Paper.

Porter, ME (1985) *Competitive Advantage: Creating and Sustaining Superior Performance*, Free Press.

Schein, EH (1983) The role of the founder in creating organizational culture, *Organisational Dynamics*, Summer.

Weston, JF and Brigham, EF (1979) *Managerial Finance*, 6th edn, Holt, Rinehart & Winston.

Questions and research assignments

Text related

1 Calculate the weighted average cost of capital given the following information:

Optimal capital structure 50:50

Debt funding: half is at 10% interest, half at 12%

Effective tax rate 30%

Risk-free rate 8%

Return expected in the stock market 12%

Company's beta 1.2

2 A firm has two investment opportunities, each costing £100,000 and each having the expected net cash flows shown in the table. Whilst the cost of each project is certain, the cash flow projections for project B are more uncertain than those for A because of additional inherent risks. Those shown in both cases can be assumed to be maxima. It has therefore been suggested that whilst the company's cost of capital is of the order of 10%, B might usefully be discounted at 15%.

(a) For each alternative calculate the net present value, the internal rate of return and the payback.

(b) On the data available what would you advise the firm to do?

(c) How limited do you feel this analysis is?

	Expected cash flows	
	Project A (£)	Project B (£)
Year 1	50,000	20,000
Year 2	40,000	40,000
Year 3	30,000	50,000
Year 4	10,000	60,000

Library based

3 Obtain the accounts for a number of competitors in the same industry (using the annual reports, Extel or Datastream). Evaluate the capital structure and dividend policy of each company. How have recent investments been funded: retained earnings, debt, equity or leasing? Consider why the differences you have found might have arisen. Considering the capital structure and profit trends of each company, which of the competitors do you feel best matches the risk and uncertainty of the industry?

4 Take a small company and a large company in an industry you consider to be relatively low risk and in one you consider much higher risk. Compare and evaluate the respective capital structures and the implications. Do the figures confirm your expectations of how the companies might be expected to be funded?

5 In 1989 a financial consortium (known as Hoylake) was formed for the specific purpose of acquiring the diversified conglomerate, BAT (British American Tobacco), which it intended to split into parts and sell. In the event the bid failed, largely because of legal complications in America, where BAT owned insurance businesses.

Evaluate the 1989 bid for BAT by Hoylake and BAT's reaction and defence. Was BAT vulnerable because it had failed to look after the interests of its shareholders as effectively as it might? Do you feel the shareholders have benefited from the outcome?

13

Competitive Advantage and Information

In this chapter we consider the vital role of information in strategic decision making at all levels, and some of the difficulties involved in ensuring that decision makers have the information which they need at the time decisions need to be made. The increasing contribution of information technology is discussed.

Learning objectives

After studying this chapter you should be able to:

- identify the importance of information for strategic awareness and for decisions relating to strategic change
- explain how misinterpretation can lead to what is known as counter-intuitive behaviour
- define information technology and management information systems
- explain the strategic information challenge facing organizations in the context of both continuous and discontinuous change
- describe a number of cases where information technology has been used to create competitive advantage

Don't forget to visit the website: http://www. itbp.com

Introduction

Information is needed for, and used in, decision making. Information, information systems and information technology are all aids to decision making. The more information managers and other employees have about what is happening in the organization, and in its environment the more strategically aware they are likely to be. Information about other functional areas and business units can be particularly helpful in this respect.

However, decisions and decision making involve both facts and people. While the right information available at the right time can be extremely useful, the real value of information relates to how it is used by decision makers, particularly for generating and evaluating alternative possible courses of action. In designing and introducing information technology and management information systems into organizations it is necessary to consider the likely reaction of people as well as the potential benefits which can accrue from having more up-to-date and accurate information available. Information gathering should never become an end in itself, for the expertise and experience in people's heads can be more useful than facts on paper.

Moreover it is important to evaluate who actually needs the information, rather than who might find it useful for increasing awareness, and to ensure that those people receive it. Hence the structure and culture of the organization should ensure that managers who need information receive it, and at the right time. Information can lead to more effective decision making, but it is a manifestation of power within the organization, and this aspect needs monitoring. If information which could prove useful is withheld from decision makers, negligently or deliberately by political managers pursuing personal objectives, the effectiveness of decision making is reduced. This theme will be developed in greater depth when we consider strategy implementation towards the end of the book.

Information is used through a filter of experience and judgement in decision making, and its relative value varies between one decision maker and another. In certain instances the available information will be accurate, reliable and up-to-date. In other circumstances the information provided may already be biased because it is the result of the interpretation of a situation by someone who may have introduced subjectivity. Some managers, perhaps those who are less experienced, will rely more heavily on specific information than others, for whom experience, general awareness and insight into the situation are more important.

In this chapter information and information technology will be examined in relation to strategic change, decision making, planning, control and people. Although information technology and information systems can be expensive to introduce, those organizations which receive information, analyse and distribute it to the appropriate decision makers faster than their competitors can achieve a competitive edge, particularly in a turbulent environment.

Information, information systems and information technology

Information

Information has been defined as 'some tangible or intangible entity that reduces uncertainty about a state or event' (Lucas, 1976), which is a way of saying that information increases knowledge in a particular situation. When information is received, some degree of order can be imposed on a previously less well-ordered situation. Davis and Olsen (1985) define information more rigidly as 'data that has been processed into a form that is meaningful to the recipient, and is of real perceived value in current or prospective decisions'. Information, then, must be received by those who need it, although the channels through which it flows can be either formal or informal. Computer analyses, written and oral reports, telephone conversations and lunchtime chats can all provide information. The grapevine or word of mouth in an organization can be extremely important. Bias might be introduced at any stage where interpretation of data is an issue, and some sources may in fact be unreliable. Data can be misinterpreted quite innocently and cause misunderstanding, and decision makers can handle only so much information. Hence the availability of information does not mean that it will lead to more effective decisions. Information technology and systems should contribute towards making the provision of information more useful for decision makers.

Decision making and interpretation of information
Spear (1980) argues that when information systems and the provision of information for managers are being considered it is important to bear in mind

how people make decisions, interpret data and information, and give meaning to them. In decision making managers sometimes behave in a stereotyped way and follow past courses of action; sometimes they are relatively unconcerned with the particular decision and may behave inconsistently. In each case they may ignore information which is available and which if used objectively would lead to a different conclusion and decision. At other times information is used selectively and ignored if it conflicts with strongly held beliefs or views about certain things. In other words information may be either misused or not used effectively.

Moreover when considering a problem situation managers have to interpret the events they are able to observe and draw certain conclusions about what they believe is happening. The question is: do managers perceive reality? The following example will explain the point. Worker-directors have always been a controversial issue amongst managers and trade union officials in the UK, with some of them supportive and others, in reality a majority, strongly opposed to their introduction. Managers who oppose them argue that they will reduce managerial power to run an organization; union opponents argue they would increase managerial power because the directors would be carefully selected or co-opted to include mainly those who were antagonistic to many of the aims of the union. These views represent meaning systems. The idea of worker-directors, and what they are, is definite and agreed; their meaning and the implications of using them are subjective and interpretative.

A parallel situation would concern the interpretation of economic data. If, say, interest rates are rising, share prices are falling or the value of the pound is strengthening, would a supporter of monetarist economics draw the same conclusions about the possible future impact on his or her business as would someone who opposed monetarism in favour of demand management?

Information needs are also related to meaning systems. A prison, for example, is concerned with both punishing and rehabilitating offenders, and different interested parties will have conflicting views on which of the two is more important. The measurement of the success of the strategies derived from these objectives can be related to the behaviour of prisoners both during their period in prison and afterwards. Information collection should relate to this, and then it is subject to interpretation. At the same time prison officers may be most concerned with making sure that potential trouble is contained and possible protests against, say, overcrowding are avoided. Their information needs relate to intelligence about potential trouble.

In large complex firms it is useful if managers understand what is happening elsewhere in the organization at any time. The importance of this always applies to managers in the various functions of a business unit, and an appreciation of progress and performance in other business units increases in value if the business units are inter-dependent in some way. However, unless the

---

Swift, accurate and relevant information will be ever more at a premium in the years ahead, and the sources will proliferate. But information is not knowledge, and there will be an even greater premium on knowledge: informed comment, new ideas, fresh perceptions about facts.

Jason McManus, Time Warner Inc. Quoted in
Fortune, *26 March 1990, p. 86.*

information systems, both formal and informal, are successful in providing an objective picture, meaning systems are likely to play a significant role. Given this, there may well be misunderstandings about other parts of the firm.

One problem for decision makers is how to react to information received from a source which is viewed sceptically and not trusted. People who design new information systems need to take some account of the way the information might be received, interpreted and used if decision-making effectiveness is to be improved.

Counter-intuitive behaviour

A failure to think through the implications of certain decisions on other managers, departments or business units can have effects that are unwelcome. The same can happen if there is an inability to appreciate the consequences because of a lack of information, or if there is a misunderstanding resulting from the wrong interpretation of information. This relates to meaning systems, which were described above. Such an event is known as counter-intuitive behaviour, and it often creates a new set of problems which may be more serious than those which existed originally.

Jay Forrester, in his book *Urban Dynamics* (1969), discusses how a strategy of building low-cost housing by the US equivalent of a local authority in order to improve living conditions for low-income earners in inner city areas has done more harm than good. The new houses draw in more low-income people who need jobs, but at the same time they make the area less attractive for those employers who might create employment. General social conditions decline. The area becomes even more destitute, creating again more pressure for low-cost housing. 'The consequence is a downward spiral that draws in the low-income population, depresses their condition, prevents escape and reduces hope. All of this done with the best of intentions.'

Related problems occur with misinterpretation of information. Consider the example of an independent retailer who finds that he is selling more of a particular item than normal and more than he expected to sell. Deliveries from his wholesaler or other suppliers require a waiting period. Does he simply replace his stock, or increase his stockholding levels? How does he forecast or interpret future demand? When he starts ordering and buying more, or buying more frequently, how do his suppliers, and ultimately the manufacturer, respond? On what do they base their stockholding and production decisions, given that there will be penalties for misunderstanding the situation? Such problems are made worse by time lags or delays. The use of information technology by major retail organizations lessens the impact of this dilemma.

Summarizing, the fact that information is available does not necessarily mean that more effective decisions will result.

Information technology

Information technology (IT) can be regarded as 'the application of hardware (machinery) and software (systems and techniques) to methods of processing and presenting data into a meaningful form which helps reduce uncertainty and is of real perceived value in current or future decisions'.

An OECD report (1989) suggested that the real impact of IT has yet to be realized. The report contends that IT has so far failed to produce the major spur to economic growth normally associated with major technological change, but suggests it will happen in the 1990s. The report draws a parallel with the development of electricity and transmission systems between 1860 and 1900, pointing out that it was in the early twentieth century that manufacturers properly realized and benefited from its potential for increasing productivity. This required changes in machine tooling, plant design and attitudes. If organizations are to benefit from the potential of IT work practices and organization cultures will again have to change; the potential is not achieved simply by investing in computers. This point will be developed later.

Management information systems

While computers and IT might be an essential feature of a management information system (MIS), the basic ideas behind an information system have little concern with computers. A management information system collects, processes and distributes the information which is required for managers to make decisions. It should be designed to be cost effective, in that the additional revenue or profits generated by more effective decisions exceed the cost of designing, introducing and running the system, or that the value of management time saved is greater than the cost of the system. Additionally the information provided should be valid, reliable and up-to-date for the decisions concerned.

Ackoff (1967) suggested that management information systems can easily be based on erroneous assumptions.

❑ Managers are short of information. In many cases managers have too much irrelevant information.
❑ Managers know the information they require for a decision. However, when asked what information they might need, managers play safe and ask for everything which might be relevant, and thereby contribute to the overabundance of irrelevant information.
❑ If a manager is provided with the information required for a decision he or she will have no further problem in using it effectively. How information is used depends on perceptions of the issues involved. Moreover, if any additional quantitative analysis or interpretation is required, many managers are weak in these skills.

As a result management information systems may fail to fulfil their promises and not prove beneficial in terms of generating more effective decisions. Information systems serve decision makers, and really should not be designed and introduced without a clear and objective appreciation of the information needs of the decision makers. However, the potential of IT and information systems to create competitive advantage should not be overlooked.

Visit the website:
http://www.
itbp.com

Information, information technology and decision making

It was noted above that a number of researchers, including Ackoff, contend that many formalized information systems fail to meet expectations. This applies to those which are particularly dependent upon the application of computers and IT. Lorsch and Allen (1973) have suggested that this is because when information systems become increasingly complex they facilitate upward but not downward information flows. This might result in increased information and strategic awareness for the strategic leader and senior executives but not for those who manage competitive and functional strategies lower down the organization and who adapt strategic changes in the light of environmental trends. In contrast Mintzberg (1972) argues that it results from top managers selecting and preferring personal contact and informal information processing in much of their work and decision making.

Earl and Hopwood (1980) point out that there is a tendency for the potential of IT to lead to an increasingly technological perspective on the way information is processed by managers. This leads to increasingly formal systems and bureaucratic procedures which 'neither fit nor suit the realities of organizational activity'.

Sometimes informally exchanged information between managers who trust and respect each other is extremely important; and in some organizations political activity and power is important in certain decisions. In a seminal article, Drucker (1988) pulled a number of these themes together and considered their potential impact on organizations. His arguments are summarized in Key Reading 13.1. With the complexities we have discussed above as a backcloth, it is now important to examine the strategic information challenge facing organizations.

The strategic information challenge

Why do some organizations, which are currently enjoying success and high profits, fail to realize when products, services or strategies are about to lose customer support? Why do they fail to anticipate competitor initiatives? And: why are others able to be more proactive?

Being close to customers, and in touch with new developments in a dynamic and possibly chaotic marketplace, requires information, intelligence and learning. Successful organizations monitor the activities of their customers, suppliers and competitors; they ask questions and test out new ideas. They express a willingness to learn and to change both their perspective on competition – their mindset concerning which factors determine competitive success – and the things they actually do. Sophisticated analyses and models of past and current results and behaviour patterns make an important contribution, but, as Day (1996) argues, it is also necessary to think through how a market might respond to actions designed to retain existing customers and win new business, whilst out-flanking and out-performing competitors. One of the reasons for Canon's continued success has been its ability to spot new market opportunities for its advanced technologies and exploit them early. Canon is also adept at reducing its dependency on products/markets as competition intensifies and demand plateaus. In the 1970s, for example, Canon successfully switched emphasis away from cameras (whilst remaining active and innovatory in the market) to photocopiers and more recently to computer printers.

We have already argued that in order to become and remain strategically successful, organizations must create and sustain competitive advantage. They must continue to enjoy E–V–R (environment–values–resources) congruence, frequently in a dynamic and turbulent environment. In Chapters 1 and 2 we showed how successful competitive outcomes depend on content competencies, which embrace technologies, processes and networking abilities. Figures 2.3 and 2.4 further showed how content competency must be under-

THE FUTURE ORGANIZATION

Large businesses, 20 years hence, will typically have half the levels of management compared with organizations in the late 1980s and about one-third of the managers. The structure will be based essentially on knowledge and will be composed of specialists who will enjoy considerable independence and will discipline their performance through organized feedback from colleagues. These changes will result from the greater need for innovation and entrepreneurship, and from the implications of IT. The amount of data available will increase, and IT will need to be utilized increasingly to analyse it. IT, though, must not be seen merely as an opportunity to process data or crunch numbers faster than can be done manually.

Currently a number of management posts exist primarily to relay data around the organization; the managers concerned are neither decision makers nor leaders. Applied properly, IT will allow more effective data processing to generate better information. In other words, and bearing in mind comments made earlier in this chapter, developments in IT will enable managers to enjoy greater strategic awareness and to contribute more reliable information concerning strategic change decisions. Managers can then be responsible for business units or functions in the organization and manage them

as independent units, much in line with the web structure and power culture (Handy, 1978) which was discussed in Chapter 4. Competitive and functional strategies will therefore continually be adapted as circumstances change.

Strategic developments which affect a number of parts of the organization will stem from special project groups and task forces composed of seconded members of business units and functional departments.

The strategic leader will have access to more information, provided in an appropriate form and quickly, and will therefore be able to direct the whole organization with fewer managers to relay information to and from the business units and functions. In this respect Drucker compares the organization with a symphony orchestra, where over 100 specialist musicians all respond to one leader. The conductor can control the whole orchestra without assistance as he can see and hear everyone and be seen by the musicians. IT will simulate this effect.

As another example, Drucker praises the way in which, from the middle of the eighteenth century, the British Government administered the whole of the Indian subcontinent with just 1000 civil servants. Many of these lived in isolated outposts and operated as individuals, with four clearly delineated tasks to perform. In

total there were nine provinces, each with a political secretary, and some 100 people reporting directly to him. The system worked, despite limited communications, because it was designed to enable people to have the information they needed to do their job. Each of the 1000 district officers wrote a comprehensive monthly report detailing what he had expected would happen in the previous month, what had happened and, if there were discrepancies, why. This was followed by comments on what he expected to happen in the next month, together with perceived opportunities, threats and needs. In return he received a comprehensive reply from the political secretary.

Drucker argues that in information-based organizations it will be necessary that

❑ there are clear, simple and few common objectives that translate into particular actions;
❑ managers are allowed the freedom to operate, rather than being told in detail how to do things, but are given expected targets and measures;
❑ all managers accept responsibility for information.

In other words, managers will appreciate who they depend on, and for what, and who depends on them. In addition a

Continued

manager will understand clearly the information needed for a particular decision and the information needs of other managers if they are to perform effectively. This implies a breakthrough from the notion that the more data there are available, the better it is for decision makers. When this happens IT can begin to be really useful. However, it does imply major change, including a change in culture, to switch from a situation where managers do not appreciate precisely the information they need to make decisions. This was first highlighted by Ackoff (1967) and commented upon earlier in the chapter.

Drucker contends that the information-based organization will have four critical problem areas to deal with:

❏ developing rewards, recognition and career opportunities for specialist
❏ creating a unified vision where every manager is a specialist
❏ devising an effective structure to encompass the task forces (this relates to the problems encountered with matrix organizations, which are discussed later in Chapter 19)
❏ ensuring the development of managers for strategic leadership.

Whilst the problems can be identified, the solutions are less obvious. Hence, Drucker concludes, the information-based organization is the managerial challenge of the future.

Based on Drucker, PF (1988) The coming of the new organization, *Harvard Business Review*, January–February.

pinned by competency in change management, which, in turn, depends upon awareness and learning competencies. Clearly information must support this web of competencies if they are to be integrated effectively. Information must be gathered and shared, but this is not merely a question of designing a new information system.

Day (1996) contends that many organizations 'do not know what they know' either because data and signals are misinterpreted or because the flows are inadequate. Decision makers do not receive the information they need, or they fail to learn about things that might prove useful. Organizations which prioritize vertical channels and ignore horizontal flows are the ones most likely to fail to learn. The important elements are:

❏ Tracking events in the market and the environment, choosing responses (both proactively and reactively) and monitoring the outcomes of the actions which follow. Competitor initiatives must be dealt with; benchmarking best practices and general awareness can suggest new ideas.
❏ Making sure that important information from the questioning and learning from these emergent changes is disseminated effectively.
❏ Reflecting upon outcomes in the context of E–V–R congruence to ensure the organization can sustain an effective match with its environment.
❏ Where appropriate, adapting policies and procedures to better guide future decisions.

The implication is a constant willingness to be flexible and to change as necessary. Companies must work from the twin perspectives of opportunity and threat. First, a willingness to learn and grow, and, second, a realization that without appropriate and timely change a company is likely to face a crisis. Gilbert (1995) further argues that strategically successful organizations leverage their innovative competitive ideas with speed and act quickly.

They obtain market feedback continuously and rapidly and adapt to the feedback ahead of their rivals. They exploit the potential of strategic as well as competitive and operating information systems.

Three levels of information

Operating information systems

Cost accounting systems, sales analyses and production schedules are essential for efficiency and control. Used creatively, as, for example, is the case with airline reservation systems (see Case 13.2 later), they can create competitive advantage, but they are not designed to drive strategic change. Case 13.1 looks at how IT is used for control at Mrs. Fields' Cookies.

Competitive information systems

Important elements of the various operating systems need to be integrated and synthesized to ensure the organization is using its resources both efficiently and effectively. Specifically it is meeting the needs and expectations of important external stakeholders. Competitive information systems, therefore, relate to competitive advantage and E–V–R congruence. They require managers to think and work across functional boundaries and consider the total service package provided to customers, encapsulating all the ways in which an organization can add value in a co-ordinated way.

However, Gilbert (1995) argues that managers will not always be aware of the information they have used in arriving at a competitively successful formula. Where organizations do not fully understand why they are successful, that success may be fragile.

Case 13.1
MRS FIELDS' COOKIES

Mrs Fields' Cookies has used IT to gain the control benefits of centralization whilst maintaining a decentralized organization structure. The company operates soft cookie stores in most states in the USA and in selected countries world-wide. In the USA they are typically located in busy shopping areas but in the UK they are most likely to be seen at main railway stations and airports. A wide range of cookies are baked in the store and sold either individually or in small quantities.

IT is used for control and to instruct individual store managers direct from Utah in the USA. Whilst there is a regional sales network, Mrs Fields' has relatively few middle managers. See also Key Reading 13.1.

Each store has a computer built into the sales till. The computer analyses the latest sales patterns and provides an hourly baking schedule for cookies, which are baked throughout the day and only sold fresh. Sales data are also fed back to Mrs Fields' head office in Utah, where they are again analysed and projections revised. One argument for this system is that it allows staff more time to concentrate on customer service – interestingly the in-store computer also flags when sales are below estimated targets and instructs staff to introduce special promotions or hand out free samples. The company motto is 'Good Enough Never Is' and employees are encouraged to feed back their ideas for improving the business. The founder and Chief Executive, Mrs Debbi Fields, attempts to maintain some form of personal contact with every store, even if it is only pre-recorded messages.

Strategic information systems

Whilst competitive information systems will typically focus on existing competition, organizations must also be able to learn about the business environment in order that they can anticipate change and design future strategies. Marchand (1995a) stresses that strategic information management should not be confined to the level of the strategic leader, but rather dispersed throughout the whole organization. This implies an innovative culture and an organization structure which facilitates the sharing of information. The concept of a learning organization was introduced at the end of Chapter 11. A learning organization requires considerable decentralization and empowerment, which must not be at the expense of control. Centralized systems are often required for sound control and effective co-ordination, thus presenting organizations with a dilemma – how to obtain the speed and flexibility benefits of decentraliztion without sacrificing control.

It is important to stress that appreciating the significance of particular events, and assessing the potential significance of opportunities and threats which have been spotted, often requires judgement, which we will discuss at greater length in Chapter 18.

Hence as one moves up these three levels of decision making, the contribution of IT and information systems to decision making changes. Once operating systems are established, they can be used to make a number of decisions and drive the operations. By measuring performance, the systems can again make a valuable contribution and highlight when things are going wrong. For strategic decisions, however, IT is primarily an aid to decision making. Systems cannot realistically make the decisions, and consequently interpretation and meaning systems are particularly important. For such decisions the systems should be designed to provide information in a form which is useful to decision makers.

Information uses

Expanding this point, Marchand (1995b) distinguishes between four important and distinct uses for information at the operating, competitive and strategic decision-making levels.

- *Command and control* – the formal gathering of information to allow centralized control and decentralized accountability. Budgeting and resource allocations will typically be included. Command and control is valuable for managing resources efficiently, but, used in isolation, it does not drive rapid change. Many organizations, like Hanson, use tight financial targeting and monitoring as an essential driver of their competitiveness. Command and control invariably requires an organization to be broken down into sub-units, such as independent businesses, divisions or functional departments.
- *Improvement*. Here the emphasis is on integrating the functions to improve both efficiency and effectiveness through better all-round service. Processes which link the functions are often the focus of attention, and initiatives such as total quality management and business process improvement will be integral.
- *Opportunities for organizational synergy*. If complex multi-business organizations can find new opportunities for internal synergy, sharing and inter-dependency, they can clearly benefit. Team working and special project teams are one way of doing this. This can be particularly important if the organization acquires another business which needs to be integrated.

• *Environmental opportunities*. Market intelligence, competitor monitoring and benchmarking best practice can generate new ideas and opportunities, as we have seen. This requires that managers are vigilant and enquiring. Critically, ideas spotted by one part of an organization, and of no discernible use to that business, might be valuable for another business or division, and consequently the ability to share – based on an understanding of needs and a willingness to trust and co-operate – is essential.

Figure 13.1 illustrates that an organization must be able to manage all four information needs simultaneously and harmoniously if it is to benefit from improved efficiencies and manage change both continuously and discontinuously. Herein lies the real strategic information challenge. The deployment of organizational resources, the corresponding style of management and the cultural implications vary between the four information needs and the decision-making processes they support. Command and control management requires the organization to be separated into functions, businesses and/or divisions for clarity; the others demand different forms of integration, both formal and informal, to share both information and learning.

Figure 13.2 illustrates how organizations need to first, develop a perspective on how they can add value and create competitive advantage. Through monitoring, measurement, continuous improvement and innovation they should seek to become increasingly efficient and effective. This continual process represents *single-loop learning* and it is essential if competitive advantage is to be sustained in a dynamic environment. As we have seen earlier,

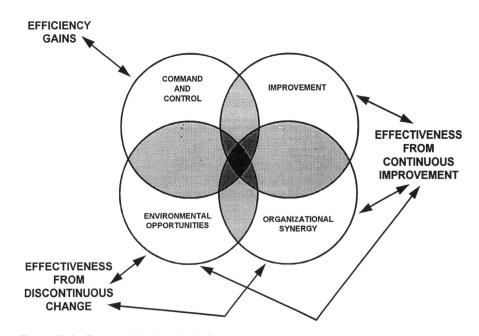

Figure 13.1 The strategic information challenge.

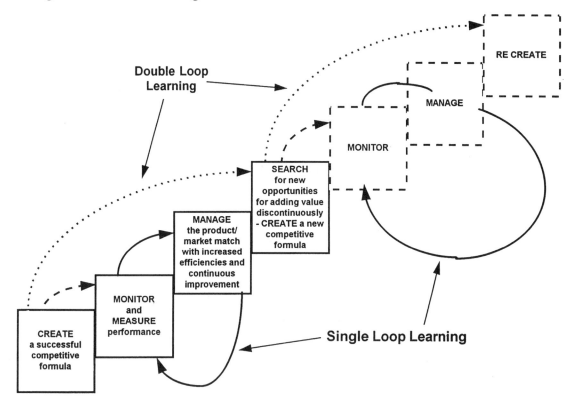

Figure 13.2 Single- and double-loop learning and strategic change.

this requires sound operating and competitive information systems. However, over time, on its own, this will not be enough. Organizations must always be looking for new competitive paradigms, really new ways of adding different values, ahead of competitors – both existing rivals and potential new entrants looking for an opportunity to break into the market. Effective strategic information systems, relying on informality, networking and learning, are required for this *double-loop learning*.

Clearly, fostering a culture of improvement and single-loop learning in an organization is more straightforward than the challenge of double-loop learning. Organizations which invest in strategic planning, research and development and new product/service programmes, are locked into the process, but the real benefits cannot be gained if these activities and the requisite learning is confined to head office departments and specialist functions. It must permeate the whole organization; it must become embedded in the culture. We can see how this reflects a key organizational tension and dilemma – the paradox of stability and instability – which we introduced in Chapter 2. Stability, we said, concerns running existing businesses efficiently and effectively, exploiting strategic abilities and continually looking to create higher returns from the committed resources. Instability refers to the search for the new competitive high ground ahead of one's rivals.

Information, then, is required to support the decision-making processes related to strategic change – both formally planned changes and emergent, adaptive, incremental change – at all levels of the organization. These processes are the subject of Chapter 14. Information, however, can also be a source of competitive advantage as we see next.

Information technology and competitive advantage

It is clear that IT offers many potential strategic opportunities which go beyond the notion of faster data processing, but that harnessing these opportunities involves changes of attitude and culture amongst managers. McFarlan (1984) claims that IT strategies should relate to two criteria:

❏ How dependent is the organization on IT systems which are reliable 24 hours a day, seven days a week? International banks and stock and currency dealers who trade around the clock, and who use IT to monitor price movements and record their transactions, need their systems to be wholly reliable.
❏ Is IT crucial if the organization is to meet key success factors? If it is, there is an implication that companies can benefit from harnessing the latest technological developments. An obvious example is the airline industry. Case 13.2 looks at IT in British Airways, but in fairness it reflects developments by all the leading airlines.

Major car manufacturers have similarly become increasingly dependent in IT which is used for:

❏ computer-aided design and engineering to speed up product development
❏ robotics on the assembly lines to reduce costs and increase productivity
❏ databases for gathering marketing intelligence and targeting promotional campaigns. As markets become increasingly segmented IT can help establish a database of potential customers who meet very specific criteria. Direct mail campaigns can then be targeted more effectively.

Rayport and Sviokla (1995) argue that competition is now based on two dimensions: the physical world of resources and a virtual world of information. Information clearly supports and enhances every activity in an organization, but, it can itself be a source of added value and consequently competitive advantage as long as organizations are able to extract that value.

Visit the website:
http://www.
itbp.com

Michael Porter (1985) further suggests that technological change, and in particular IT, is amongst the most prominent forces that can alter the rules of competition. This is because most activities in an organization create and use information. Porter and Millar (1985) contend that IT is affecting competition in three ways:

❏ IT can change the structure of an industry, and in so doing alter the rules of competition
❏ IT can be used to create sustainable competitive advantage and provide companies with new competitive weapons
❏ as a result of IT new businesses can be developed from within a company's existing activities.

These three themes are examined in greater detail below.

British Airways invests in excess of 3% of its gross revenue in IT, and expects this to rise to 5% by the end of the 1990s. IT was first utilized over 30 years ago to streamline the reservations systems. Subsequently it was used for aircraft scheduling and spares control and for crew rostering. Improved efficiencies in these areas are critical as cargo and passenger volumes grow, and continue to grow.

Increasingly, IT has also been used to add value and to improve BA's overall service and effectiveness in a very competitive industry. A number of the applications are described below.

Computerized reservation systems now link travel agencies directly with the airlines and provide instantaneous information on availability followed by reservations and tickets. There are a number of systems but the market is dominated by two, which carry up-to-date information on hundreds of airlines and their flight schedules. Sabre (owned by American Airlines) covers some 5–10% of European flights and 45% of the US market; Galileo/Apollo (two merged systems, owned by United Airlines and BA together with nine other airlines) covers 40% of Europe and 30% of the USA. These systems allow airlines to change prices and pricing policies frequently in their attempt to maximize their yield. In other words, fares for a particular flight can be adjusted in line with demand, and ticket prices can be discounted to try to fill the aeroplane if there are spare seats. The airlines want to sell seats at the highest prices they can obtain, but an empty seat means lost and irrecoverable revenue. This is complex as there are 30 different fares available on a typical transatlantic flight on a Boeing 747.

Travel agents, with access to substantial information, will often shop around for the lowest fares. Additionally, computer reservation systems allow passengers to be allocated specific seats well in advance of their flight rather than when they check in at the airport. Clearly both the airline and the passenger can benefit. The airlines further argue that these systems give them better control over their deliberate over-booking policies. An airline is often willing to sell more seats than they have available on a flight, assuming that some passengers with tickets will not travel, and balancing the cost of compensation and lost goodwill against the lost revenue from empty seats.

BA, like most major international airlines, has a frequent flyer programme with air miles and various other benefits. Air Miles are also available from organizations with whom BA has an alliance – these include other airlines, car rental companies and leading hotel chains. Without IT to record the relevant flight and fare details, such programmes would not be feasible.

New ticketing machines at airports enable passengers on domestic shuttle flights to buy their ticket and obtain their printed boarding card in 40 seconds. The technology also exists for machines to scan a passenger's thumbprint (assuming it has been previously verified), issue a ticket and debit that person's bank account. This is seen as more secure than the existing machines, which respond to credit and debit cards, and more likely to generate customer loyalty. Hand-held computers are available to speed up checking-in and reduce queuing.

ACARS (Aircraft Communications Addressing and Reporting System) allows fast transfer of information by radio waves between computers on the ground and computers on board aircraft. Data transmitted during a flight can help plan routine and extra ground maintenance and boarding delays can be reduced. Some of the ground time between flights is spent analysing and responding to information on load and balance.

Personal video players, which are typically standard in first class, can be adapted to enable passengers to book hotels and cars during their flights and possibly use their credit cards for mail-order shopping. (Hertz already have touch-panel machines with visual prompt screens at airports to enable passengers to reserve cars at their destination just before they fly. A printed confirmation takes 6 seconds.)

BA has also harnessed IT to improve its response to complaints. Only three customers in 1000 complain about anything, but this still represents several hundred letters every day. Most people are only looking for an explanation and an apology, but they expect it quickly. If they receive a satisfactory response, they tend to stay loyal to BA; we have already seen that customer retention is much less expensive than generating new business. Given that the customer's explanation must be checked carefully, it has proved beneficial to link the customer service system with BA's other information systems, such as bookings and flight information. New letters of complaint are scanned in and the relevant records checked quickly before a response is generated. Each letter is given a priority rating.

Industry structure

According to Porter (1980), the structure of an industry can be analysed in terms of five competitive forces: the threat of new entrants; the bargaining power of suppliers; the bargaining power of buyers; the threat of substitute products and services; and rivalry amongst existing competitors. These forces were discussed in detail in Chapter 9.

Porter and Millar (1985) suggest that IT can influence the nature of these forces, and thereby change the attractiveness and profitability of an industry. This is particularly applicable where the industry has a high information content, such as airlines, and financial and distribution services. In distribution, for example, the automation of order processing and invoicing may lead to an increase in fixed costs, and as a result encourage greater rivalry between competitors for additional business. Moreover, firms which are either slow or reluctant to introduce IT may be driven out of the industry, because they will be unable to offer a competitive service. Where the cost of the necessary IT, both hardware and software systems, is high it can increase the barriers to entry for potential new firms.

Case 13.3 explains how package holiday tour companies have made use of IT to lower costs and allow them to compete more aggressively on pricing. The result of all the competitive activity has been an increase in concentration, with the largest companies gaining market share at the expense of smaller rivals, many of whom have left the industry.

Porter and Millar show that IT can both improve and reduce the attractiveness and profitability of an industry, and that as a consequence manufacturers should analyse the potential implications of change very carefully.

IT has transformed such financial services as banking, enabling customers to carry out many of their financial transactions by telephone or machine without needing to queue for a cashier. However, there is the disadvantage that certain aspects of banking are being made more impersonal, and the personal service aspect is being reduced.

The creation of competitive advantage

Porter (1985) argues that competitive advantage results from lower costs or differentiation, and that these strategies can be applied with either a broad or a narrow market focus. This was discussed fully in Chapter 9.

Lower costs

If costs are reduced to a level below competitors' costs and this advantage is maintained, above-average profits and an increased market share can result. Porter and Millar suggest that whilst the impact of IT on lower costs has historically been confined to activities where repetitive information processing has been important, such restraints no longer apply. IT can lead to lower labour costs by reducing the need for certain production and clerical staff. As a result there should be both lower direct production costs and reduced overheads. IT applied to production systems can improve scheduling, thereby increasing the utilization of assets and reducing stocks, and in turn lowering production costs.

Case 13.4 on the application of IT at WH Smith illustrates the potential for improving stock turnover and increasing profitability with electronic point-of-sale (EPOS) systems.

Thomson Holidays – pioneering IT for competitive advantage

The package tour holiday industry is extremely competitive, with pricing an important weapon. The leading holiday companies are vertically integrated and own high street travel agency chains as well as their own airlines. Thomson which became the market leader several years ago, believes that much of its early competitive advantage derives from its pioneering of IT-based booking systems, and that further developments with IT have helped it to retain market leadership.

In general it is difficult to create and sustain competitive advantage in this industry. Package tour companies hire beds and airline seats, put them together, and by adding fringe services market them as a package holiday. Offering better service at airports or a wider range of tours in the various resorts can easily be copied by rivals, and so any competitive edge is quickly eroded.

Thomson first introduced computers in ten regional offices in 1976, allowing easier access for travel agents. Previously agents had to telephone one location; now they had access to ten linked centres. The computer generated management information and invoices as well as providing availability data for agents, but the agents still relied on the telephone, backed up by paperwork for confirming bookings.

Thomson recognized that what was needed was a terminal in every travel agent's office, but appreciated that if the system were exclusively Thomson it might be less popular than one which also allowed access to rival organizations. In 1979 they began experimenting with Prestel, and in 1982 introduced TOP or the Thomson Open-line Programme. Through TOP travel agents enjoy instant access to Thomson holiday information on their terminal screens, but their terminals also access rival, but less sophisticated, systems. The problem of customers having to wait whilst telephone calls to check availability ring unanswered because the system is congested has been largely eliminated. This has proved particularly valuable on busy Saturdays and has enabled Thomson to save on staff costs. The computer can handle both options and confirmed bookings, and customers are encouraged to book because more and better information can be made available to them. The system has been continually improved, and the effect has been reduced booking costs for both Thomson and the travel agents. In addition the role of the agent has been changed more towards selling than administration. Other operators have followed, but the time lag has proved beneficial to Thomson.

Thomson has also been able to obtain more control and planning information for future capacity planning; and the gradual introduction of terminals linked to the UK in their offices abroad has improved the total service in other ways.

Current IT applications

IT has had a major impact on the marketing and selling of holidays because at the booking stage it is information that is being exchanged. The actual service, the holiday itself, comes later. Customers, however, still prefer to visit a travel agent and deal directly with a sales person for the transaction. Nevertheless, for certain elements of the service, IT has had only limited impact – travel shop windows are invariably filled with handwritten signs for late booking holidays and prices.

Tour operators move the prices of holidays several times a day when they are chasing last minute bookings, based on the number of unsold holidays, the current levels of demand, and, most importantly, competitor prices for the equivalent holiday. Sophisticated IT systems are essential to facilitate this flexibility. From the customers' position, both Teletext and the Internet provide information on the availability of last minute holidays.

Some travel agencies provide self-service, touch-screen terminals which allow customers to access multimedia information about holidays and talk to sales people via a video-telephone link. Interactive televisions also offer information about hotels in audio, video and text forms.

Case 13.4
INFORMATION TECHNOLOGY AND WH SMITH

WH Smith (WHS) have applied IT to their retailing activities in two major ways. Firstly they began introducing electronic point of sale (EPOS) in the mid-1980s, and more recently they have applied computer-aided design (CAD) to store layouts. Amongst the retail leaders in both areas, they have the additional objective of linking the two applications 'to create a marketing advantage other retailers may find hard to match'.

EPOS improves profitability by speeding up replenishment times and by allowing better stock control in individual stores. Previously stock checking and re-ordering was normally on a three-week manual cycle. Since a large WHS branch would have 60,000 lines, three times the number in a large Sainsbury's, it was difficult for the head office to understand what was selling well at any particular time, and consequently branch managers and staff were responsible for stock management within availability constraints.

The objectives for EPOS were:

❏ increased profits through better sales and margins
❏ better staff utilization – stock counting is hardly challenging
❏ improved stock turn.

The relatively expensive system chosen by WHS links every store to a central computer and hence stock is now controlled from the centre. The increased centralization of buying and distribution, facilitated by IT and EPOS, also enables:

❏ bulk buying for lower prices

❏ lower warehousing and distribution costs by stock reduction in the system as a whole
❏ more flexibility through fast and accurate knowledge concerning which lines are selling well and which ones poorly.

The system also required co-operation from suppliers, as much of the potential benefits are lost if items are not bar-coded at source to enable the light pen to read them at the point of sale.

Many of the tills used for operating this system are also able to read credit and debit cards and print out the sales vouchers. This reduces the time required to serve those customers who prefer not to pay with cash, and also speeds up the money transfer from the customers' banks to WHS.

The computer-aided design link

Using information generated through EPOS, CAD enables the space and layout of stores to be adjusted to capitalize on the products which are selling well, particularly those with superior margins. High-value-added items can be placed in the most beneficial shelf spaces and bins. This will improve, and ideally maximize, sales per square foot, a key success factor for retailers. These developments were originally linked to a strategy of re-designing 20 stores every year, and commissioning 20 new ones. These targets have been reduced in the 1990s recession.

WHS need flexibility as the demand for their various lines can fluctuate significantly. Moreover new lines need different display stands, an excellent example in recent years being compact discs.

Major supermarkets like Sainsbury's use hand-held computers which allow staff to record the current stock levels each evening. Shelves can then be replenished overnight or the next day from regional warehouses. Sales representatives from say food manufacturers who sell extensively to small outlets can use similar hand-held computers for entering their orders. The computer can price the order immediately and a confirmation can be printed out. The stored information can be easily transferred to streamline the delivery. Cost saving is also possible where computer systems can be networked. If, for example, a manufacturer can establish a computer link with either his or her suppliers or buyers, there is considerable scope for both lowering costs and improving service. This would be particularly useful for supporting a just-in-time manufacturing system.

Similarly, Tesco has sought to establish closer linkages with their suppliers. Orders for immediate delivery are transmitted electronically, although projections based on the latest sales analyses will have been provided some weeks earlier. If supplier delivery notes are sent ahead of the actual delivery these can then be used to check the accuracy of the shipment and a confirmation returned. This represents a promissory note to pay by an agreed date, and no further invoicing is required. These points are explored further in the full case on Tesco.

Enhancing differentiation

Differentiation can be created in a number of ways including quality, design features, availability and special services that offer added value to the end consumer. McFarlan *et al.* (1983) contend that IT offers scope for differentiation where

❑ IT is a significant cost component in the provision of the product or service, as in banking, insurance and credit card operations
❑ IT is able to affect substantially the lead time for developing, producing or delivering the product (CAD/CAM systems play an important role in this)
❑ IT allows products or services to be specially customized to appeal to customers individually
❑ IT enables a visibly higher level of service to customers, say through regular and accurate progress and delivery information, which might be charged for
❑ more and better product information can be provided to consumers.

Most insurance companies quote rates for insuring property and cars partially based on specified postcode districts. To achieve this they need accurate information on the risks involved in different areas and how these are changing. This in turn requires close liaison and information exchanges with brokers. The insurers, brokers and ultimately customers can all benefit as premiums more accurately reflect risks.

Visit the website:
http://www.
itbp.com

The scope of competitive advantage in relation to a broad or narrow focus can also be affected by IT, which can be used to identify and satisfy the needs of specialized market niches. The technology is used to analyse company and industry databases to highlight unusual trends or developments. Porter and Millar suggest that large companies which differentiate their range of products or services to appeal to a broad group of segments can use IT to target niches more effectively and segment individual products in ways that previously were only feasible for smaller more focused companies.

New competitive opportunities

It appears that information technology is resulting in the creation of new businesses in three distinct ways.

❑ New businesses are made technologically feasible. Telecommunications technology, for example, led to the development of facsimile services and organizations that provide fax services. In a similar way microelectronics developments made personal computing possible.

❏ IT can create demand for new products such as high-speed data communications networks that were unavailable before IT caused the demand.
❏ New businesses can be created within established ones. A number of organizations have diversified into software provision stemming from the development of packages for their own use.

There are numerous examples of how competitive advantage has been derived specifically from information technology. Debit cards, such as Barclay's Connect, have replaced cash and cheques for many customers; similar to credit cards in format, they allow money to be debited immediately from a bank account. Because computers can store and process information very quickly, they allow the banks and building societies to offer rates of interest which increase and decrease directly in line with the size of a customer's deposit.

We have mentioned earlier how JIT systems improve supply chain management for both suppliers and customers; without IT they are not feasible. The US company, McKesson, which supplies over-the-counter pharmaceuticals to retail chemists, used its salesforce to record on a computer the counter and shelf layouts of their customers. This allowed McKesson to pack orders in such a way that customers could unpack them and display them quickly and sequentially.

Most newspapers now enjoy cost and differentiation benefits from computerized typesetting, whereby type is set directly by a journalist typing at a keyboard. In the case of national daily newspapers, and against some trade union resistance, computerized typesetting was pioneered by Eddie Shah, when he established the *Today* newspaper, which, after changes of ownership has now been closed down. For the *Financial Times*, IT supports all the share prices, charts and other information it includes every day.

Most large hotel chains, including, for example, Sheraton and Marriott, operate clubs or programmes for their regular visitors. Participants receive such benefits as free upgrades and free meals as well as the programme points which they can exchange later for free stays or Air Miles. It is quite normal for travellers to prioritize a particular chain because of the perceived benefits of programme membership. These hotel chains typically cover much of the world, and often include independent hotels in franchise arrangements. Loyalty programmes would simply not be feasible without IT.

An increasing number of restaurants are using terminals for keying in orders and relaying the information quickly to the kitchen. Some are beginning to provide waiters with hand-held sets and pagers which vibrate gently rather than beep – to minimize any disturbance. The pagers tell waiters when an order is ready for collection, allowing them to spend more time on the restaurant floor in direct contact with customers, instead of constantly checking whether an order is ready. The US retailer Wal-Mart issues pagers to customers waiting for prescriptions so they can continue shopping rather than either wait in line or come back speculatively to check if their package is ready.

The new engine housing for the Boeing 737 was designed in a computerized virtual environment. Wind tunnel testing has always been expensive and limited the number of options evaluated; IT enables far more designs to be tested at much lower cost and with much greater speed. Both Boeing and its airline customers benefit.

In summary, implementing IT for competitive advantage requires:

❏ an awareness of customer and consumer needs, changing needs, and how IT can improve the product's performance or create new services

❏ an awareness of operational opportunities to reduce costs and improve quality through IT

❏ an appreciation of how the organization could be more effective with improved information provision, and how any changes might be implemented. The impact upon people is very significant.

The argument is that competitive advantage can stem from any area of the organization.

Summary

This chapter has been based on the contention that strategic decision making and decision makers require information. The importance of the information reaching the appropriate decision makers has been highlighted, as has the significance of managers interpreting data and information. It has been suggested that managers can be more effective if they are aware strategically; and the contribution of IT to achieving this has been discussed. Finally, there has been consideration of how information and IT might create a competitive advantage.

Specifically we have:

• considered how managers interpret information and give meaning to it and how this might affect decisions, and following on from this shown that incorrect interpretation can lead to counter-intuitive behaviour

• defined information technology and management information systems

• considered the impact of IT on managers – arguing that greater utilization of IT is a cultural issue – and Peter Drucker's arguments concerning the future impact of IT on managers and organizations

• examined the strategic information challenge facing organizations by considering the various uses for information and the three levels of information system

• featured how IT can create and sustain competitive advantage by affecting the structure of an industry, reducing costs, enhancing differentiation and leading to the establishment of new businesses, products and services.

Checklist of key terms and concepts

You should feel confident that you understand the following terms and ideas:

★ Meaning systems and counter-intuitive behaviour

★ Decision making at the operational, competitive and strategic levels

★ The distinction between single- and double-loop learning in the context of continuous and discontinuous change.

Questions and research assignments

1 For an organization with which you are familiar identify an operational system which is heavily dependent on IT and assess its strategic impact.
   - ❏ In what ways does the system contribute towards competitive advantage?
   - ❏ How might this contribution be increased?
2 Consider how the increasing utilization of information technology in retailing has affected you as a customer. Do you feel that the major retail organizations who have introduced and benefited from the greater utilization of IT have attempted to ensure that the customer has also benefited and not suffered?
3 Consider why it is argued that the increasing utilization of IT by organizations is a cultural issue. How might managers be encouraged to make greater use of the technology which is available?

Library and assignment based

4 For an organization of your choice ascertain the range of products and services offered.
   - ❏ What are essential information needs from outside the organization (the environment) for managing these products and services both now and in the future?
   - ❏ Where are the limitations in availability?
   - ❏ What role might IT play in improving availability?
5 By visiting and talking to staff at an appropriate level, in both a travel agency and a retail store using an EPOS system, ascertain the effect that IT has had on their decision making. Do you feel the staff are more aware strategically? If so, has this proved valuable?

References

Ackoff, RL (1967) Management misinformation systems, *Management Science* (14), December.

Davis, GB and Olsen, M (1985) *Management Information Systems: Conceptual Foundations, Structure and Development*, 2nd edn, McGraw-Hill

Day, G (1996) How to learn about markets, *Financial Times Mastering Management Series*, No. 12, 26 January.

Drucker, P F (1988) The coming of the new organization, *Harvard Business Review*, January–February.

Earl, MJ and Hopwood, AG (1980) From management information to information management. In *The Information Systems Environment* (eds HC Lucas, FF Land, JJ Lincoln and K Supper), North-Holland.

Forrester, J (1969) *Urban Dynamics*, MIT Press.

Gilbert, X (1995) It's strategy that counts, *Financial Times Mastering Management Series No. 7*, 8 December

Handy, C (1978) *Gods of Management*, Souvenir Press.

Lorsch, J and Allen, S (1973) *Managing Diversity and Independence*, Harvard University Press.

Lucas, H (1976) *The Analysis, Design and Implementation of Information Systems*, McGraw-Hill

Marchand, DA (1995a) Managing strategic intelligence, *Financial Times Mastering Management Series*, No. 4, 17 November.

Marchand, DA (1995b) What is your company's information culture? *Financial Times Mastering Management Series No. 7*, 8 December.

McFarlan, FW (1984) Information technology changes the way you compete, *Harvard Business Review*, May–June.

McFarlan, FW, McKenney, JL and Pyburn, P(1983) The information archipelago – plotting a course, *Harvard Business Review*, January–February.

Mintzberg, H (1972) The myth of MIS, *California Management Review*, Fall.

OECD (1989) *New Technology in the 1990s – A Socioeconomic Strategy*, OECD.

Porter, ME (1980) *Competitive Strategy: Techniques for Analysing Industries and Competition*, Free Press.

Porter, ME (1985) *Competitive Advantage: Creating and Sustaining Superior Performance*, Free Press.

Porter, ME and Millar, VE (1985) How information gives you a competitive advantage, *Harvard Business Review*, July–August.

Rayport, JF and Sviokla, JJ (1995) Exploiting the virtual value chain, *Harvard Business Review*, November–December.

Spear, R (1980) *Systems Organization: The Management of Complexity*, Unit 8, *Information*, The Open University T243.

Figures 13.1 and 13.2 first appeared in Thompson, JL (1996) Strategic effectiveness and success: the learning challenge, Management Decision, 34, 7, MCB Publications.

PART
IV

The Content of Corporate Strategy

Early in the book we clarified that strategic management encapsulates both the formulation and implementation of strategies and the synergistic issues of linking corporate, competitive and functional strategies. We stated that organizations need to decide:

❏ What the overall strategic perspective of the organization should be – the extent to which the organization should be focused or diversified; the range of products, services, markets and territories to include – and
❏ How they might create and sustain competitive advantage for every distinct business, product, service and market.

In Part III we have examined the key issues in competitive strategy. We now widen our discussion and consider corporate strategic change. It will be appreciated that we are building on the competitive issues we have already discussed and that competitive advantage is an integral part of corporate strategy.

Part IV examines:

❏ How organizations might assess the need and opportunities for corporate strategic change (including planning techniques) and formulate new strategies (strategy creation) – Chapter 14.
❏ The framework of competitive and corporate strategies from which the organization can choose, accepting that at any time only a selected number of options will be feasible and realistic – Chapter 15.
❏ Issues and considerations in corporate growth strategies – Chapter 16.
❏ Issues in consolidation and recovery strategies – Chapter 17.
❏ Key criteria in the evaluation and selection of strategies – Chapter 18.

The final part of the book will then discuss strategy implementation and the management of strategic change.

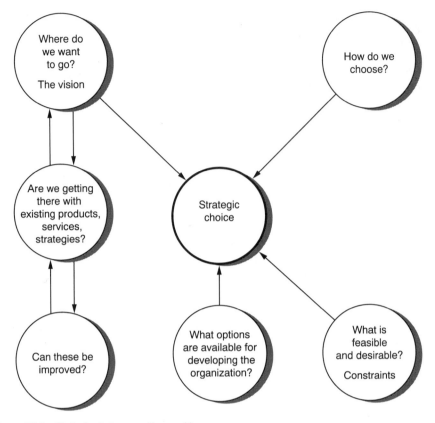

Figure IV.1 Strategic choice: questions and issues.

Figure IV.1 above summarizes the key questions and issues in strategic choice. First, a vision for the future is required. Companies must then consider whether, with improvement, but without major changes, existing strategies are adequate for pursuing the mission and achieving targets and stakeholder expectations. If they are not, then alternative strategies must be found. This process involves the clarification and assessment of strategic options at both the competitive and corporate levels.

It is important to appreciate that *strategic change* always involves

analysis   choice   implementation

but that the way in which these activities or stages are carried out, and the time and emphasis given to each, varies with the mode of strategy creation adopted.

14
Planning and Creating Corporate Strategy

This chapter is about strategy creation or formulation, planning and strategic planning systems. Planning is a cerebral activity: managers think about where the organization should be going, why and how. It can also be an established system which collects and evaluates data before future courses of action are determined. A number of strategic planning techniques are discussed.

Learning objectives

After studying this chapter you should be able to:

■ Distinguish between planning as a cerebral activity carried out by all managers and systematic corporate planning
■ Explain the role of corporate planning in strategy creation
■ Describe a number of approaches to corporate planning and in relation to these discuss who should be involved in planning
■ Explain the concept of the planning gap
■ Assess the contribution of a number of planning techniques, including directional policy matrices and PIMS
■ Discuss how corporate planning might be applied to local government and not-for-profit organizations.

Introduction

In this chapter we look at how decisions about future strategic change and areas for development are made. We examine the role of planning systems, and the contribution of planning techniques to the broad issue of which direction the organization should take in the future.

> *The planning era, if one may call it that, occurred some time ago, and has been discredited as we have moved on to the greater belief in the development of common values in the organization, and are rediscovering again today the necessity to be close to the market.*
>
> (Sir John Harvey-Jones, Past Chairman ICI, 1987)

> *Planning is one of the most complex and difficult intellectual activities in which man can engage. Not to do it well is not a sin; but to settle for doing it less than well is.*
>
> (Russell Ackoff, 1970)

Planning the future – **thinking** about the most appropriate strategies, and changes of strategic direction – is essential for organizations, particularly those experiencing turbulent environments. The above quotations and Key Reading 14.1 by Michael Porter remind us of the need for strategic thinking. Rigid systematic planning is no longer fashionable, nor is it the only way in which

Don't forget to visit the website: http://www.itbp.com

THE STATE OF STRATEGIC THINKING

Strategic planning, popular in the 1960s and 1970s, deservedly fell out of fashion. In most companies planning had not contributed to **strategic thinking**; but, because strategic thinking is essential, a new role should be found for planning.

Strategic planning became fashionable for two basic reasons.

❏ Short-term budgeting to control operations developed after World War II, and because many of the implications of current decisions have a long-term significance these essentially financial plans were stretched into longer-term plans.

❏ As firms grew increasingly complex it was recognized that the various functions and business units needed to be integrated. Strategic planning seemed an ideal way of setting corporate strategies systematically rather than intuitively.

The outcome for many organizations was formal planning systems, heavily reliant on financial data, and supported by thick planning manuals.

On the positive side planning can encourage managers to think about the need and opportunities for change, and to communicate strategy to those who must implement it. This was particularly important in the 1960s and early 1970s when there was an abundance of investment opportunities and a dearth of capital and key priorities needed to be established. In complex multi-activity organizations, decisions have to be made concerning where to concentrate investment capital in relation to future earnings potential, and this has generated a number of portfolio analysis techniques such as the Boston growth-share matrix. Rather than use these techniques for gaining greater awareness and insight, for which they are well suited, managers sought to use them prescriptively to determine future plans. (Techniques are limited in this respect; this issue is discussed in the main text.)

Planning had become unfashionable by the 1980s for a number of reasons.

❏ Planning was often carried out by planners, rather than the managers who would be affected by the resultant plans.

❏ As a result, the outcome of planning was often a plan which in reality had little impact on actual management decisions, and therefore was not implemented.

❏ The planning techniques used were criticized primarily because of the way in which they were used.

❏ The important elements of culture and total quality management were usually left out.

However, many industries have experienced turbulent environments caused by such factors as slower economic growth, globalization and technological change, and consequently strategic thinking is extremely important. The following questions must be addressed.

❏ what is the future direction of competition?
❏ what are the future needs of customers?
❏ how are competitors likely to behave?
❏ how might competitive advantage be gained and sustained?

Strategic planning should be rethought so that these questions are constantly addressed rather than addressed occasionally as part of an annual cycle. Line managers who implement plans must be involved throughout the process. 'Every executive needs to understand how to think strategically.' Rigorous frameworks and planning manuals are not necessary as long as the proper thinking takes place.

There should be a strategic plan for each business unit in a complex organization, i.e. clear competitive strategies built around an understanding of the nature of the industry in which the business competes, and sources of competitive advantage. Chosen strategies must have action plans for implementing them, including an assessment of the needs for finance and for staff training and development. This is generally less difficult than formulating a corporate strategy for the whole organization.

Summarized from Porter, ME (1987)
The state of strategic thinking,
The Economist, 23 May.

strategic change decisions are made. There are dangers if organizations become reliant upon professional planning and the only outcome is a plan. This may not allow for effective strategic thinking, and may not result in a clear direction for the future.

There are also dangers in thinking that all strategic changes can be planned systematically. Whether it is the result of formal and systematic planning, or much more informal and *ad hoc* management, an organization will have strategies and processes whereby these strategies are changed. The processes need to be understood, and in many cases improved. It is important to assess where and how the organization should change and develop in the light of market opportunities and competitive threats, but there are lessons to be learnt about their appropriateness to certain strategic opportunities. Managers should say clearly where the organization is, and where it might sensibly go, and start making appropriate changes. They should then monitor progress and be aware of changes in the environment; in this way they can be flexible and responsive.

Robinson (1986) argues that the role of the planner should not be to plan but to enable good managers to plan. It is not the task of the planner to state the objectives; rather he or she should elicit and clarify them. Planning should concentrate on **understanding the future**, which is, of course, uncertain and unpredictable, and helping managers to make decisions about strategic changes. Thus the aim of planning should be to force people to think and examine, not to produce a rigid plan.

We shall look at how organizations and managers might seek to address future issues. We consider what is meant by the term planning, and what is involved in the systematic planning cycle approach to the management of strategic change. The contribution of a number of planning techniques will be evaluated, and possible pitfalls and human issues in planning will be pinpointed.

Planning techniques, used carefully, can provide a valuable description and analysis of the current situation. But the future is not necessarily the past extrapolated forward, and whilst we can learn from past decisions, actions and events, companies must develop new competitive and corporate paradigms for managing the future and its inherent uncertainties. Vision and flexibility will be essential, alongside a clear direction and purpose. New thinking is essential for reaching the new competitive high ground first. Consequently the planning, visionary and emergent modes of strategy creation, introduced in Chapter 1, will first be explored in more detail.

Strategy formulation

In Chapter 1 we explained how strategy formulation involves three strands:

❑ *planning*, both systematic and formal strategic planning systems and informal, cerebral planning
❑ *vision* and visionary leadership, and
❑ *emergent strategies* – incremental changes to pre-determined, intended strategies and adaptive additions with learning and responsiveness to opportunities and threats.

If all strategies were planned formally, then organizations would be able to look back and review the decisions that they had made over a period of time. At some stage in the past there would have been a clear recorded statement of intent which matched these events closely. In reality stated plans and actual events are unlikely to match closely. In addition to strategies which have emerged and been introduced entrepreneurially, there are likely to have been expectations and planned possible strategies which have not proved to be viable. However, broad directions can be established and planned and then detailed strategies allowed to emerge as part of an on-going learning experience within the organization.

Idenburg (1993) presents these ideas in a slightly modified way, distinguishing between:

- ❏ Formal planning systems, through which clear objectives should lead to intended strategies.
- ❏ Learning or real-time planning, which represents a formal approach to adaptive strategy creation. Managers meet regularly, both formally and informally, and debate how key strategic issues are changing and emerging. Objectives and strategies will be changed in a turbulent environment.
- ❏ Incremental change and logical incrementalism. The organization will have a clear mission and directional objectives, and it will be recognized that pursuing these requires flexibility. Managers will be encouraged to experiment with new ideas and strategies, learning and adapting all the time. Internal politics and systems will play an important role in this mode.
- ❏ Emergent strategies. Specific objectives will not be set; instead, organizations will be seen as fully flexible, 'muddling through' environmental turbulence. Opportunism, being ready and able to 'seize the main chance' is critical.

Mintzberg and Waters (1985) and Bailey and Johnson (1992) have also shown how the simple three-mode categorization might be extended, but the underlying implications remain unchanged.

Figure 14.1 shows the three modes of strategy creation together. The diagram extends Figure 1.10, incorporates E–V–R (environment–values–resources)

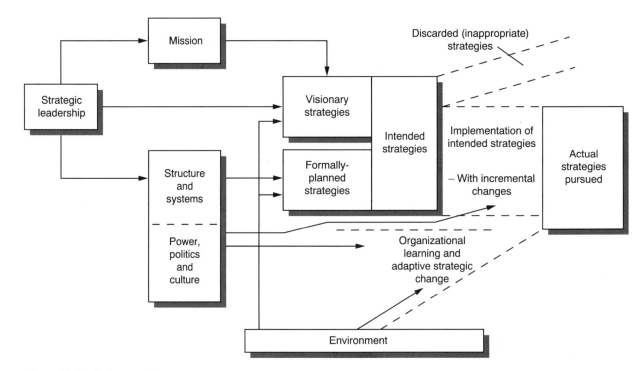

Figure 14.1 Strategy creation.

congruence and our earlier arguments about the importance of strategic leadership and culture. A number of points should be noted:

❑ Although it is not made explicit some strategies, especially those formulated by a visionary entrepreneur, attempt to shape and change the environment, rather than react to changing circumstances.

❑ The organization structure and the actual planning process will affect the nature of planned objectives and strategies. Wherever a group of managers are involved in planning, their personal values and relative power will be reflected. See Cyert and March's behavioural theory, Chapter 5.

❑ Adaptive changes will also reflect the values, power and influence of managers.

It is important to appreciate that the three modes described above are not mutually exclusive, that one mode frequently leads on from another. The implementation of visionary ideas and strategies typically requires careful planning, for example, and this will invariably bring about incremental changes. In Chapter 1 we also confirmed that all three modes will be found in an organization simultaneously, but the mix and prioritization will be particular to an individual company. We emphasized that individual managers, depending largely on their position within the organization, will not necessarily agree on the relative significance of each mode. It is essential that managers understand and support the processes.

The mixed approach is both sensible and justifiable. In some manufacturing industries the time taken from starting to plan a substantive innovatory change to peak profit performance can be ten years. This needs planning, although the concept may be visionary. Throughout the implementation there has to be adaptive and incremental learning and change. Where strategies are being changed in a dynamic environment it is also useful, on occasions, to evaluate the current situation and assess the implications. This could well be part of an annual planning cycle.

It is now appropriate to re-read Case 1.5 which looked at how the three modes can be seen in practice in McDonald's. McDonald's has a clear and understood vision which also embraces its thousands of franchisees world-wide. In 1995 its annual rate of global expansion grew to some 3000 new restaurants; this requires careful planning. This planning, together with arrangements with building contractors and suppliers, has also allowed McDonald's to cut 30% off the cost of opening every new restaurant – through the use of more efficient building systems, standardized equipment and global sourcing. As a consequence, it can now afford to open restaurants in locations which, in the past, have been seen as uneconomical. Given the intense competition in the fast-food industry, it is also essential for McDonald's to remain flexible and responsive, internationally, nationally and locally.

Figure 14.2 further relates these themes to the three levels of strategy: corporate, competitive and functional. In large organizations much of the responsibility for corporate strategic change will be centralized at the head office, although the businesses and divisions can be involved or consulted. Competitive and functional change decisions are more likely to be decentralized, but again, not exclusively. Corporate policies can require or constrain changes at these levels.

	Corporate strategy	Competitive strategies	Functional strategies
Planning	Formal planning systems	Planning the detail for implementing corporate strategies	
Visionary	Seizing opportunities – limited planning only	Innovation throughout the organization	
Adaptive/	Reacting to environmental opportunities and threats, e.g. businesses for sale; divestment opportunity	Reacting to competitor threats and new environmental opportunities	
Incremental		Learning and adjustment as planned and visionary strategies are implemented	

(left axis label: Modes of strategy creation)

Figure 14.2   Levels of strategy and modes of strategy creation.

Planning and strategy formulation

Mintzberg (1989) contends that the strategic leader should be the chief architect, in conjunction with planners, of corporate plans; the process should be explicit, conscious and controlled; and issues of implementation should be incorporated. Essentially analysis leads to choice, which leads on to implementation. The process is sequential:

$$\text{Analysis} \rightarrow \text{Choice} \rightarrow \text{Implementation}$$

Certain organizations might claim that detailed long-term planning is essential for them. An airline, for example, must plan capacity several years ahead because of the long delivery lead times for new aeroplanes and the related need to manage cash flow and funding. In addition resources must be co-ordinated on an international scale. Whilst planes are utilized most days and fly as many hours in the day as possible, crews work only limited hours, and typically finish a flight or series of flights in a location which is different from their starting point.

However, Mintzberg argues that this is planning the implications and consequences of the strategic perspective, not necessarily the perspective itself. Detailed planning of this type should not inhibit creativity concerning the perspective.

The visionary mode

A visionary strategic leader who formulates strategic change in his or her mind may only be semi-conscious of the process involved. He or she will clearly

---

You know me ... We're not necessarily great overall strategists. We often do things and then work out afterwards what the overall strategy was.

Richard Branson, Chairman, Virgin Atlantic

understand the current and desired strategic perspective, and ideally the culture of the organization will be one where other managers are receptive of the changes in perspective. The personality and charisma of the leader, and his or her ability to sell his/her ideas, will be crucial issues, and as speed of action, timing and commitment are typical features the strategy can prove highly successful.

The entrepreneurial approach suggests that the strategic leader is very aware of the strengths, weaknesses and capabilities of the organization; the current matching with the environment; a wide range of possibly diverse opportunities for change; and the likely reaction of managers to certain changes. Similar to the 'bird approach' described in Chapter 1, Box 1.3, the selection is made somewhat arbitrarily without careful and detailed planning, and therefore an element of risk is involved. This informality in the process is important to allow for creativity and flair. The strategic leader then sells the idea to other managers, and the strategy is implemented and adapted as experience is gained and learning takes place. In other words, the vision acts as an umbrella and within it specific decisions can be taken which lead to the emergence of more detailed strategies.

With this mode it is difficult to separate analysis and choice, so that

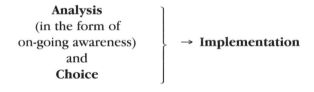

Dangers

The success of this mode in the long term depends on the continued strategic awareness and insight of the strategic leader, particularly if the organization revolves around a visionary leader and becomes heavily dependent upon him or her. People may be visionary for only a certain length of time, and then they become blinkered by the success of current strategies and adopt tunnel vision, or they somehow lose the ability to spot good new opportunities. It might also be argued that, if luck is involved, their luck runs out. The problems occur if the strategic leader has failed to develop a strong organization with other visionaries who can take over.

On a current basis the strategy requires management as well as leadership. In other words, managers within the organization must be able to capitalize on the new opportunities and develop successful competitive positions within the revised strategic perspective. This might involve an element of planning; equally it might rely more on the adaptive approach described below.

The adaptive and incremental modes

Under the adaptive and incremental modes strategies are formed and evolve as managers throughout the organization learn from their experiences and adapt to changing circumstances. They perceive how tasks might be performed, and products and services managed, more effectively, and they make changes. They also respond to pressures and new strategic issues. There will again be elements of semi-consciousness and informality in the process. Some changes will be gradual, others spontaneous, and they will act collectively to alter and improve competitive positions. As individual decisions will often involve only limited change, little risk, and possibly the opportunity to change back, this is essentially the 'squirrel approach' described in Chapter 1, Box 1.3. Managers learn whether their choice is successful or unsuccessful through implementation.

Hence this mode implies limited analysis preceding choice and implementation, which are intertwined and difficult to separate. A proper analysis follows in the form of an evaluation of the relative success

$$\text{Analysis (limited)} \rightarrow \left.\begin{array}{c}\textbf{Choice and}\\\textbf{implementation}\end{array}\right\} \rightarrow \textbf{Analysis}$$

Adaptive strategic change requires decentralization and clear support from the strategic leader, who also seeks to stay aware of progress and link the changes into an integrated pattern. It is often based on setting challenges for managers – challenging them to hit targets, improve competitiveness and stretch or exploit internal systems and policies to obtain the best possible returns. The greater the challenge, the more care needs to go into establishing a suitable reward system. When the structure enables effective adaptive change, then intrapreneurship can be fostered throughout the organization and individual managers can be allowed the necessary freedom. However, if adaptive changes are taking place in a highly centralized organization, and despite rigid policies, there is a problem which should be investigated. The major potential drawbacks concern the ability of the organization and the strategic leader to synthesize all the changes into a coherent pattern, and the willingness and ability of individual managers to take an organization-wide perspective. This latter point is examined later in the chapter.

Information technology provides opportunities for collecting and co-ordinating information and should be harnessed to support decentralization. In addition **team briefing** can prove useful. Here a strategic leader would regularly brief his or her senior executives, discussing progress, and any proposed changes to the corporate strategy and policies. On a cascading basis managers would quickly and systematically communicate this information downwards and throughout the organization by meeting with teams of people responsible to them. The secret lies in utilizing team briefing meetings to also communicate information upwards by reporting on new strategic issues and how they are being handled.

The key macro and micro variables of our business are so dynamic that poker becomes more predictable than planning and reactivity more profitable than rumination.
Dr John White, ex-Managing Director, BBA Group (many of whose customers are involved in the motor vehicle industry)

Planning and planning systems

What do we mean by planning?

All managers plan. They plan how they might achieve objectives. However, a clear distinction needs to be made between the cerebral activity of informal planning and formalized planning systems.

A visionary strategic leader, aware of strategic opportunities and convinced that they can be capitalized upon, may decide by himself where the organization should go and how the strategies are to be implemented. Very little needs to be recorded formally. Conversations between managers may result in plans which again exist only in individual managers' heads or in the form of scribbled notes. Equally, time, money and other resources may be invested by the organization in the production of elaborate and formally documented plans.

Visit the website:
http://www.itbp.com

In all cases planning is part of an on-going continuous activity which addresses where the organization as a whole, or individual parts of it, should be going. At one level a plan may simply describe the activities and tasks which must be carried out in the next day or week in order to meet specific targets. At a much higher level the plan may seek to define the mission and objectives, and establish guidelines, strategies and policies which will enable the organization to adapt to, and to shape and exploit, its environment over a period of years. In both cases, if events turn out to be different from those which were forecast, the plans will need to be changed.

The value of strategic planning

When managers and organizations plan strategies they are seeking to:

❏ be clearer about the business(es) that the organization is in, and should be in
❏ increase awareness about strengths and weaknesses
❏ be able to recognize and capitalize on opportunities, and to defend against threats
❏ be more effective in the allocation and use of resources.

Irrespective of the quality or format of the actual plans, engaging in the planning process can be valuable. It helps individual managers to establish priorities and address problems; it can bring managers together so that they can share their problems and perspectives. Ideally the result will be improved communication, co-ordination and commitment. Hence there can be real benefit from planning or thinking about the future. What form should the thinking and planning take? Should it be part of a formalized system making use of strategic planning techniques?

I have a saying 'Every plan made is an opportunity lost' because I feel that if you try to plan the way your business will go, down to the last detail, you are no longer open to seize any opportunity that may arise unexpectedly.

Debbie Moore, Founder Chairman, Pineapple Ltd

Corporate and functional plans

Corporate and strategic plans concern the number and variety of product markets and service markets that the organization will compete in, together with the development of the necessary resources (people, capacity, finance, research and so on) required to support the competitive strategies. Strategic plans, therefore, relate to the whole organization, cover several years and are generally not highly detailed. They are concerned with future needs and how to obtain and develop the desired businesses, products, services and resources. The actual time-scale involved will be affected by the nature of the industry and the number of years ahead that investments must be planned if growth and change is to be brought about.

Functional plans are derived from corporate strategy and strategic plans, and they relate to the implementation of functional strategies. They cover specific areas of the business; there can be plans relating to product development, production control and cash budgeting, for example. Functional plans will usually have shorter time horizons than is the case for strategic plans, and invariably they will incorporate greater detail. However, they will be reviewed and up-dated, and they may very well become on-going rolling plans. Whilst strategic plans are used to direct the whole organization, functional plans are used for the short-term management of parts of the organization.

Competitive strategies and functional strategies and plans are essential if products and services are to be managed effectively, but they should be flexible and capable of being changed if managers responsible for their implementation feel it necessary.

Ohmae (1982) emphasizes that individual products must be seen as part of wider systems or product groups/business units, and that although short-term plans must be drawn up for the effective management of individual products, it is important to ensure that thinking about the future is done at the appropriate level. As an example a particular brand or type of shampoo targeted at a specific market segment would constitute a product market. The company's range of shampoos should be produced and marketed in a co-ordinated way, and consequently they might constitute a strategic planning unit. The relevant strategic business unit might incorporate all the company's cosmetics products and there should be a competitive strategy which ensures that the various products are co-ordinated and support each other. In terms of strategic thinking Ohmae suggests that it is more important to consider listening devices as a whole than radios specifically, and that this type of thinking resulted in the Sony Walkman and similar products. In just the same way the Japanese realized a new opportunity for black and white television receivers in the form of small portable sets, when other manufacturers had switched all their attention to the development of colour sets. If the level of thinking is appropriate, resources are likely to be allocated more effectively

Alternative approaches to planning

Taylor and Hussey (1982) feature seven different approaches to planning which are detailed briefly below.

❑ **Informal planning** takes place in someone's head, and the decisions reached may not be written down in any extensive form. It is often practised by managers with real entrepreneurial flair, and it can be highly successful. It is less likely to be effective if used by managers who lack flair and creativity.

❏ **Extended budgeting** is rarely used as it is only feasible if the environment is stable and predictable. Extended budgeting is primarily financial planning based on the extrapolation of past trends.

❏ **Top-down planning** relates to decisions taken at the top of the organization and passed down to other managers for implementation. These managers will have had little or no input into the planning process. Major change decisions reached informally may be incorporated here, and then a great deal depends upon the strength and personality of the strategic leader in persuading other managers to accept the changes. At the other extreme, top-down plans may emanate from professional planners using planning techniques extensively and reporting directly to the strategic leader. These are the type of plans that Porter (1987) in Key Reading 14.1, suggests may not be implemented.

❏ **Strategic analysis/policy options** again uses planning techniques, and involves the creation and analytical evaluation of alternative options. Where future possible scenarios are explored for their implications, and possible courses of action are tested for sensitivity, this form of planning can be valuable for strategic thinking. It is an appropriate use of planning techniques, but it is important to consider the potential impact on people.

❏ **Bottom-up planning** involves managers throughout the organization, and therefore ensures that people who will be involved in implementing plans are consulted. Specifically functional and business unit managers are charged with evaluating the future potential for their areas of responsibility and are invited to make a case for future resources. All the detail is analysed and the future allocation of resources is decided. In an extreme form thick planning manuals will be involved, and the process may be slow and rigid. Necessary changes may be inhibited if managerial freedom to act outside the plan is constrained. A formal system of this nature is likely to involve an annual planning cycle, which we look at later.

❏ **Behavioural approaches** can take several forms, but essentially the behavioural approach requires that managers spend time discussing the future opportunities and threats and areas in which the organization might develop. The idea is that if managers are encouraged to discuss their problems and objectives for the business freely, and if they are able to reach agreement concerning future priorities and developments, then they will be committed to implementing the changes. However, it is quite likely that all the conflicts concerning resource allocation and priorities will not be resolved.

❏ The **strategic review** was developed to take the best features of the other six approaches and blend them together into a systematic and comprehensive planning system. A typical system is discussed in detail in the next section.

All of these approaches have individual advantages and disadvantages, and they are not mutually exclusive. The approach adopted will depend on the style and preferences of the strategic leader, who must, as we saw in Chapter 3:

❏ clarify the mission and corporate objectives and establish the extent and nature of changes to the corporate perspective

❏ approve competitive and functional strategies and plans for each part of the business, however they might be created and

❑ establish appropriate control mechanisms, which may or may not involve substantial decentralization.

It has been established that planning may be either informal or formal. Informal planning, as such, cannot be taught; but formal planning systems can. These are the subject of the next sections.

The planning gap

A number of essentially similar models of systematic planning have been developed by such authors as Argenti (1980), Hussey (1976), Cohen and Cyert (1973) and Glueck and Jauch (1984). All these models utilize the concept of gap analysis, which is extremely useful for strategic thinking purposes and which is featured as Key Concept 14.1.

The concept of the planning gap relates very closely to issues which were raised in Chapter 5 on objectives. It addresses the questions:

❑ where do we want to go?
❑ where can we go realistically?

When considering where and how an organization might develop in the future, both the desired and realistic objectives are essential considerations. Desired objectives relate to where the strategic leader and other decision makers would like to take the organization if it is possible to do so. Realistic objectives incorporate the influence of the various stakeholders in the business, and their expectations; the existence of suitable opportunities; and the availability of the necessary resources. The issue of the risk involved in the alternative courses of action which might be considered is crucial. The discussion of the planning gap in Key Concept 14.1 draws attention to the increasing risk which is typically associated with certain strategic alternatives, in particular diversification, which is often implemented through acquisition. Failure rates with diversification are high, as will be discussed in Chapter 16. However, diversification may be the only feasible route to the achievement of high growth targets or the maintenance of present rates of growth in profits and sales revenues. The strategic leader, perhaps under significant pressure from City investors, shareholders and analysts who expect growth rates to be at least maintained, may be forced to pursue high-risk strategies.

Whilst undue risk should be avoided wherever possible, it is always important to accept a certain level of risk and set stretching targets for managers and businesses.

(We do not discuss again in this chapter the types of objective – profit, growth, security, stakeholder satisfaction and so on – which the organization might set. Readers may wish to refer back to Chapter 5.)

A contemporary approach to strategic planning

In order to ensure that planning does not become an end in itself, and that planners do facilitate management thinking, many large companies have evolved personalized contemporary planning systems along the lines of the one illustrated in Figure 14.6.

The organization's culture and the expectations of the strategic leader and the key stakeholders influence the whole process of analysis and decision

KEY CONCEPT 14.1

THE PLANNING GAP

The planning gap should be seen as an idea which can be adapted to suit particular circumstances, although gap analysis could be regarded as a planning technique.

An example of the planning gap is illustrated in Figure 14.3. The horizontal axis represents the planning time horizon, stretching forward from the present day; either sales volume or revenue, or profits, could be used on the vertical axis as a measure of anticipated performance. The lowest solid line on the graph indicates expected sales or profits if the organization continues with present corporate, competitive and functional strategies; the top dashed line represents ideal objectives, which imply growth and which may

or may not ultimately be realized The difference between these two lines is the gap. Quite simply the gap is the difference between the results which the organization can expect to achieve from present strategies continued forward and the results that the strategic leader would like to attain.

The example illustrated in Figure 14.3 shows the gap filled in by a series of alternative courses of strategic action ordered in an ascending hierarchy of risk. Risk is constituted by the extent to which future products and markets are related to existing ones; and this idea of increased risk and strategic alternatives is developed further in Figures 14.4 and 14.5.

The least risk alternative is to seek to manage present products and services more effectively, aiming to sell more of them and to reduce their costs in order to generate increased sales and profits. This is termed market penetration in the simple growth vector developed by H Igor Ansoff and illustrated in Figure 14.4. It can be extended to strategies of market and product development, which imply respectively:

❏ New customers or even new market segments for existing products, which might be modified in some way to provide increased differentiation; and

(Continued)

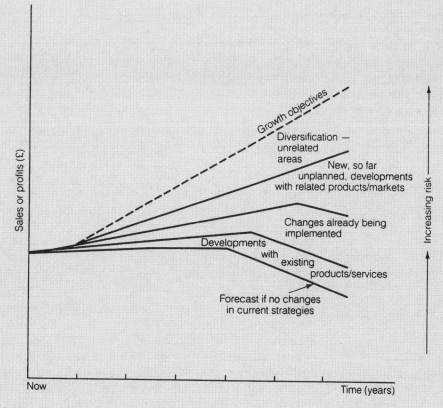

Figure 14.3   An example of the planning gap.

❑ New products, ideally using related technology and skills, for sale to existing markets.

(In this context 'new' implies new to the firm rather than something which is necessarily completely new and innovative, although it could well be this.) Figure 14.3 distinguishes between market and product development strategies which are already under way and those which have yet to be started.

The highest risk alternative is diversification because this involves both new products and new markets. Figure 14.5 develops these simple themes further and distinguishes between the following:

❑ Replacement products and product line extensions which are based on existing technologies and skills and which represent improved products for existing customers
❑ New products, based on new or unrelated technologies and skills, which constitute concentric diversification (these may be sold to either existing or new customers)

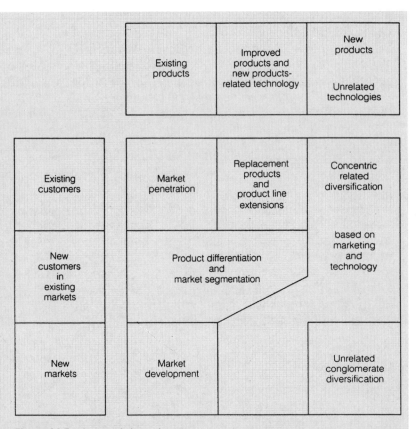

Figure 14.5   An extended growth vector.

❑ Completely new and unrelated products for sale to new customers. This is known as conglomerate diversification and is regarded as a high-risk strategic alternative.

Using the planning gap

Thinking about the extent of the initial gap between present strategies and ideal objectives enables managers to consider how much change and how much risk would be involved in closing the gap and achieving the target objectives. Some of the strategies considered might be neither feasible nor desirable, and consequently the gap might be too wide to close. Similarly the degree of risk, especially if a number of changes are involved, might be greater than the strategic leader is willing to accept. In these cases it will be necessary to revise the desired objectives downwards so that they finally represent realistic targets which should be achieved by strategic changes that are acceptable and achievable.

This type of thinking, of course, is related to specific objectives concerning growth and profitability. It does not follow, as was discussed in Chapter 5, that either growth or profitability maximization will be the major priority of the organization, or that the personal objectives of individual managers will not be an issue.

Product / Market	Present	New
Present	Market penetration	Product development
New	Market development	Diversification

Figure 14.4   Ansoff's growth vector. (Source: Ansoff, HI (1987) *Corporate Strategy*, revised edition, Penguin.)

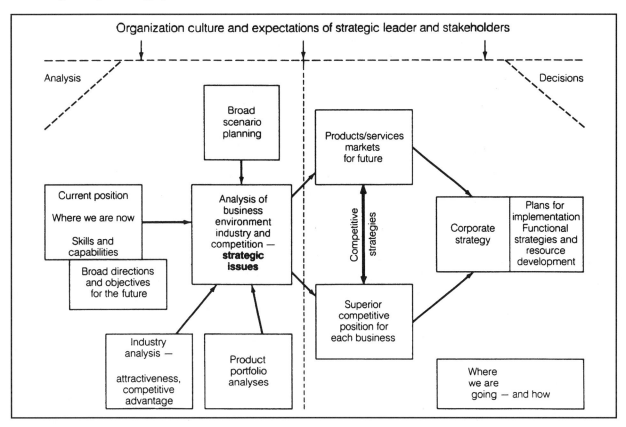

Figure 14.6 A contemporary approach to strategic planning.

making. The thinking starts with an assessment of the current position of the organization, its skills and resources, and an evaluation of whether there is a clear understanding of the 'mission', the broad objectives and directions for the future.

Then we analyse the business environment thoroughly, concentrating on the industries in which the organization currently competes and those in which it might apply its skills and resources. Feeding into this analysis are three other analyses:

❑ Broad scenario planning – conceptualizing a range of different futures which the organization might have to deal with, to ensure that the less likely possibilities, threats and opportunities are not overlooked, and to encourage a high level of flair and creativity in strategic thinking (see Chapter 8).
❑ Product portfolio analyses, which are discussed in greater detail in the next section; contingency and possible crisis planning considerations can be incorporated in this.
❑ Industry analyses, following the Porter criteria for judging attractiveness and opportunities for competitive advantage (discussed earlier).

This environmental analysis should focus on any **strategic issues** – current or forthcoming developments, inside or outside the organization, which will impact upon the ability of the organization to pursue its mission and meet its objectives. Ideally these would be opportunities related to organizational strengths. Wherever possible any unwelcome, but significant, potential threats should be turned into competitive opportunities.

Case 14.1 looks at the stategic issues facing high street banks in the 1990s and how they have affected strategic developments.

From these analyses competitive strategy decisions must be reached concerning:

❏ The reinforcement or establishment of a superior competitive position, or competitive advantage, for each business within the existing portfolio of products and services.
❏ Product markets and service markets for future development, and the appropriate functional strategies for establishing a superior competitive position.

Case 14.1
STRATEGIC ISSUES AND HIGH STREET BANKING

During the 1990s, and following the world-wide economic recession and the ensuing bad debts, the UK high street clearing banks have changed their strategies as a response to a number of key challenges and issues.

The strategic issues

❏ They faced a need to switch from a position of high overheads with an extensive branch infrastructure and the associated high-risk lending (required to cover the overheads) to one where their (lower) cost base is in equilibrium with the type and volume of lower risk business that can be more readily justified.
❏ Information technology, exploited effectively, offered new opportunities for providing more efficient services without sacrificing either quality or reliability.

Both of these issues implied restructuring and job losses, although there was always the possibility that once the banks had re-established strong controls and truly efficient systems they would reconsider taking higher risks again.

❏ A prediction that many personal customers would switch emphasis from borrowing to saving. The high street banks were not perceived to be good for savers, offering relatively low rates of interest in comparison to the building societies and PEP-linked unit trusts.

New strategies include

❏ Stronger credit controls for more effective loan management – implying both improved information and tracking and a reduction in the number of loans.
❏ Computerized credit and loan assessments to link charges with risks more closely than in the past. This has changed the role of individual bank managers, and, for some businesses, made borrowing more difficult.
❏ A tighter focus on specific market segments, looking for positions of strength, rather than 'being involved in everything'. In particular, UK banks have reviewed their overseas exposure.
❏ A search for more attractive savings products in an increasingly competitive environment.
❏ New forms of service. Following the pioneering work of First Direct (a subsidiary of the Midland) other clearing banks have introduced telephone banking services. This would not have been possible without information technology.

Source: Weyer, MV (1994) The banks find their balance, *Management Today*, November.

Amalgamated, these functional and competitive strategies constitute the corporate strategy for the future, which in turn needs to be broken down into resource development plans and any decisions relating to changes in the structure of the organization, i.e. decisions which reflect where the organization is going and how the inherent changes are to be managed.

It is important that new strategic issues are spotted and dealt with continuously, and the organization structure must enable this to happen, either by decentralization and empowerment or by effective communications.

An example of a systematic corporate planning system for a large organization

A corporate planning team for a large corporation, based at its head office, will typically comprise both planners and analysts. The analysts are responsible for monitoring the external environment, searching for new opportunities and threats. They also model the implications of possible future events and scenarios for the group. The planners consolidate the individual plans for every business in the group to create the overall corporate plan. Group progress against the plan is continuously monitored and evaluated by the planners.

A timetable for a typical planning system is included in Table 14.1. Say the company's financial year end is 31 March: around this time, when the relative success of the group for the year is becoming clear, the planners will produce a final review of progress towards corporate objectives. They evaluate where the group is doing well and where it is less successful, and the extent to which it is satisfying its major stakeholders. To this is added a rigorous internal

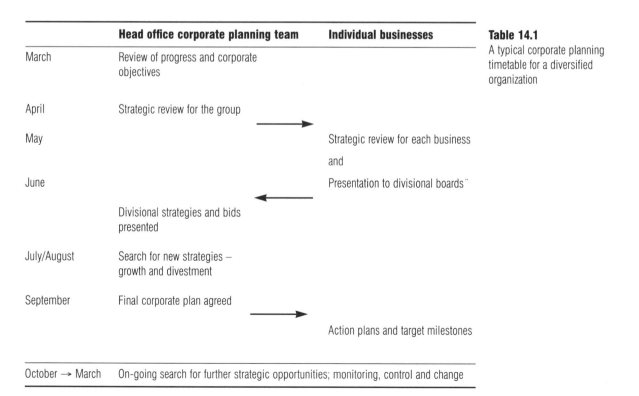

	Head office corporate planning team	Individual businesses
March	Review of progress and corporate objectives	
April	Strategic review for the group	
May		Strategic review for each business
		and
June		Presentation to divisional boards "
	Divisional strategies and bids presented	
July/August	Search for new strategies – growth and divestment	
September	Final corporate plan agreed	
		Action plans and target milestones
October → March	On-going search for further strategic opportunities; monitoring, control and change	

Table 14.1
A typical corporate planning timetable for a diversified organization

(corporate resources) and external (environmental developments) assessment of the group, provided by the analysts. They specifically highlight the important **strategic issues** facing the group – appropriate and feasible opportunities and critical threats – together with details about current and (if known) planned competitor strategies.

During April the group chief executive (the strategic leader) convenes his corporate strategy committee, which comprises senior Board members and the head of the corporate planning group. The divisional managing directors are not members, although on occasions they will be asked to attend. They are excluded on the grounds that when bids from the divisions for additional investment capital are being considered later in the year, they would all support each other's projects. Any opposition by one divisional head would provoke counter-hostility from the others.

The outcome of the April meeting is a preliminary statement of corporate objectives for the year ahead; these will normally re-affirm the company's mission statement, although it may be reviewed and amended. Typically the objectives will summarize:

❏ growth and profit aspirations
❏ the company's strategy for exploiting core competencies and capabilities and its willingness to diversify (possible acquisition targets and divestments may be discussed but not announced)
❏ international/geographic objectives
❏ the commitment to, and standards for, quality, service and customer care
❏ the resources available to support expansion.

Visit the website:
http://www.
itbp.com

This is broadly equivalent to the top line of the planning gap – see Key Concept 14.1.

During May and early June each business unit finalizes its own strategic review, which is presented to the relevant divisional board of directors. Each company is likely to carry out comprehensive SWOT, competitor and portfolio analyses (portfolio analysis is explained later in the chapter) and indicates:

(i)   The anticipated revenue and profit targets if there are no **major** changes to competitive and functional strategies.
(ii)   The requirements for the company to achieve or maintain competitive advantage.
(iii) Strategic changes it would like to make, the anticipated returns and the resource implications

       (Each business may be asked to submit proposals based on a range of financial assumptions, ranging from limitless resources to very tight funding. All significant investments will need to be justified in detail; the assistance of head office planners could be enlisted in formulating proposals.)

(i) and (ii) will be used immediately for up-dating the company's action plans and budgets, recognizing that these may have to be adjusted later.

The role of the divisional board is to question and challenge before reaching a set of recommendations for the chief executive. The strategy committee then meets for a second time at the end of June to discuss these recommendations, which may be accepted (and the necessary resources provided) or rejected. Portfolio analysis is again used to consider the current and emerging state of the group; and strategic opportunities for inter-divisional support and internally generated synergies are sought.

At the same time the committee compares the promised returns from all the businesses with their own initial growth objectives. If a gap remains, and further resources are available or can be found, the corporate analysts will be asked for costed options and recommendations. The strategic leader may, of course, have ideas of his or her own to input. In addition the analysts will be asked for recommendations concerning how the group might rationalize and achieve further cost savings, beyond those being offered by the divisions. Divisional boards may suggest the divestment of particular businesses, but this is unusual; such decisions are more likely to start with the strategic leader or the analysts.

This evaluation takes place throughout the summer, and the strategy committee meets for a third time in September to agree the corporate strategy. Final targets are issued to the divisions and business units, enabling them to review, and if necessary change, their current plans and budgets. It is these final plans which are co-ordinated by the head office planners into the corporate plan and used for committing and managing the group's strategic resources.

Different reactions will be provoked by these strategic decisions. Business units which are allocated resources and given support for their proposed strategies tend to be euphoric; those which see themselves as 'losers' are frequently demotivated, an inevitable drawback of this approach.

The divisions and individual businesses are not precluded from changing functional and competitive strategies at any time in response to competitive threats and opportunities, but if they require additional resources, outside their budgeted allocation, they have to apply to the chief executive.

A planning system along the lines of this example is basically a process which forces managers to address key questions and issues. Head office is likely to find that the detailed plan can be a useful document for explaining their basic intentions to the major institutional shareholders. The value of the finished plan to the individual subsidiaries – as distinct from the *process* of planning its content – is more questionable. They should see the document as a *summary of thinking* and a statement of intent, rather than a rigid plan that must be executed.

Analytical approaches should not inhibit organizations from spotting, creating and seizing opportunities:

In 1971 Marcus Sieff, when Deputy Chairman of Marks and Spencer, met Sandy Dewhirst. Chairman of Dewhirsts, the clothing manufacturers, by chance in an M & S store. Dewhirst commented that his company had strong cash reserves and wondered if they might be invested for the mutual benefit of the two businesses. Sieff commented that M & S was importing men's suits from Italy, Scandinavia and Israel; if any interested UK manufacturer could meet their quality requirements there would be an opportunity for them to supply M & S. (At one time UK companies had enjoyed a high level of expertise in men's tailoring, but the competencies had largely been lost.)

Dewhirst recruited a Swedish technologist, and began manufacture in Sunderland in 1973. Within 15 years it had opened two further factories. Turnover in men's suits was £45 million per year; 1000 people were employed

Source: *Sieff, M (1990),* Marcus Sieff on Management, *Weidenfeld & Nicolson*

The corporate strategy may also be changed by the strategic leader at any time during the year if new windows of opportunity become available; such changes may imply either a visionary approach to major strategy additions or more emergent, opportunistic responses to events.

In addition the planning exercise can be essential for providing a framework against which the strategic leader can monitor the commitment of resources and the emergent outcomes.

Commentary

This approach to corporate planning may well succeed in the essential task of co-ordinating the plans for all the divisions and businesses, enabling the strategic leader to exercise control over a conglomerate. In addition, the system should not prohibit vision and learning within the corporation, which is important as these are the two modes of strategy creation most likely to take the organization forward in a competitive and uncertain environment. Unfortunately the vision and learning may be concentrated within each division; ideally it will permeate the whole organization.

Typically strategic planning systems used to be very formal. All ideas from the individual businesses had to be supported by comprehensive, documented analyses. Now it is frequently accepted that many proposals cannot be fully justified quantitatively; instead the assumptions and justifications will be probed and challenged by divisional boards. Care must also be taken to ensure that the evaluation and resource allocation processes do not create too high a level of internal competition. Divisions and businesses should have to justify their intentions and proposals, and it is inevitable they will be competing for scarce resources. Nevertheless the 'real enemy' are external competitors, not other parts of the organization, and this must never be forgotten.

Additionally, some organizations still tend to use the performance targets as the primary means of control, which sometimes results in short-term thinking. Once a business drops below its target it is put under considerable pressure to reduce costs, and this may restrict its ability to be creative and innovative. Many strategic planning systems could be improved if the head office corporate planners had more contact and involvement with the businesses; they sometimes tend to be remote and detached.

In summary: formalized planning systems may be imperfect, but a system of some form remains essential for control and co-ordination. Alone it cannot enable the company to deal with competitive uncertainties and pressures. Vision and learning are essential. But planning must not be abandoned.

This section has considered the important role and contribution of strategic planning in large, and possibly diverse, organizations. In the next two sections we broaden our discussion and consider strategic planning in two very different contexts: local government and small businesses.

Strategy and local government

A typical local authority is likely to perceive the aim of the activities it carries out as the provision of more, and ideally better, services for the local community. These services fall into three broad categories: front-line (housing, education and leisure); regulatory (environmental health, planning and building control) and promotional (economic development and tourism).

Consequently many councils will want to increase spending wherever possible. In simple terms spending minus income (including grants from central government) equals the sum to be raised from householders and businesses, and generally more spending is likely to lead to higher local taxes. The freedom to increase these is constrained by central government. Borrowing is used primarily to fund capital programmes – for example, new council houses, the rent from which can help pay the interest on the loan – and for managing the cash flow on a temporary basis.

It is very difficult to measure quantitatively the benefits which accrue from certain services, such as parks and gardens for public recreation. Performance measures were discussed in Chapter 6. Information from the Audit Commission enables one authority to compare its costs and spending in total, and per head of the population, for individual services with those incurred by similar authorities in the UK. Where this is utilized it is basically a measure of efficiency, rather than an assessment of the overall effectiveness of the service provision.

In addition the growing incidence of competitive tendering is forcing a closer examination of the costs of providing particular services. Where services are put out for tender an authority will determine the specific level of service to be provided, and then seek quotations for this provision. Tendering organizations neither suggest nor influence the actual level of service. This power remains firmly with the local authority. As more and more services are compulsorily put out to tender local authorities will essentially become *purchasers* of services on behalf of the local community. Historically they have been the service providers, and it is quite feasible that this will continue if their employees win the contracts. Inevitably more attention will be focused on standards and community responsibilities. In the past such analyses of effectiveness have been rare.

Historically, in fixing a future budget a typical local authority is likely to have started with the existing service provision and extrapolated forward the costs of at least maintaining this service. To this will have been added the costs of providing new, additional services; and the selection of priorities amongst alternative options will have been heavily affected by the relative power and influence of certain councillors and sub-committees on what is typically called the Policy or Policy and Resources Committee. In addition there may have been one-off, non-recurring items such as special refurbishments or maintenance programmes. It is likely that the process has been incremental rather than the whole activity is viewed in a detached way whereby specific objectives are evaluated and re-stated. It is unlikely that there will have been any initial assessment of whether any existing services might be withdrawn, although this might have happened later.

Once a budget was established departments were able to amend the levels of service they provided with particular activities, and make changes as long as they operated within their spending limits. Unexpected needs for additional spending might be met from special contingency funds which were held back for this purpose.

Central government pressure is now forcing local authority executives to change their approach to corporate strategic management. Policies and service levels are evaluated and questioned, and priorities reviewed. Structures are being changed in a more serious attempt to co-ordinate the various services and achieve co-operation and synergy. In the past internal conflict has frequently been the norm.

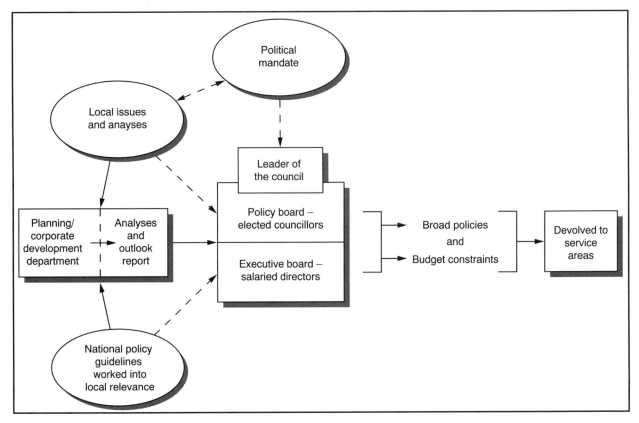

Figure 14.7 Strategy creation in local government.

Figure 14.7 illustrates a typical approach. Key strategic and policy decisions will involve both the elected councillors and senior salaried executives. Two strategic leaders must work together: the leader of the council and the chief executive. Analyses and reports will be fed in by professional planners and analysts, and the Policy and the Executive Boards will meet separately (and possibly jointly) to finalize broad policies and budget allocations. These will then be devolved to the various service areas for more detailed planning and implementation.

Strategic planning and small businesses

Many small companies stay focused and do not diversify or acquire another business. Their corporate perspective stays the same; but they still need to create some form of competitive advantage and develop and integrate functional plans. In this respect, small business planning is similar to that for an individual business inside a conglomerate. Aram and Cowen (1990) believe small businesses can improve their performance by limited investment in strategic planning and development – returns well in excess of costs can be generated. Unfortunately many small owner-managers misguidedly believe that:

❑ strategic planning is too expensive and only belongs in large organizations

❏ formalized processes, requiring expert planners, are essential
❏ the benefits are too long term and there are no immediate payoffs.

As a result they adopt a more seat-of-the-pants reactive approach. Clearly both vision and flexibility are important features of most successful small businesses, but these can be built on to provide greater strength and stability. Simply, and reinforcing points made earlier in the chapter, small companies can benefit in just the same way as large ones from discerning the important **strategic issues** and from involving managers from the various functions in deciding how they might best be tackled.

Aram and Cowen recommend that small companies should involve all relevant managers in discussions about priorities, opportunities, problems and preferences. They should look ahead and not just consider immediate problems and crises. Objective information and analyses (albeit limited in scope) are required to underpin the process, which must be actively and visibly supported by the owner-manager or strategic leader, who, in turn, must be willing to accept ideas from other managers. Adequate time must also be found; and sound financial systems should be in place to support the implementation of new strategies and plans.

Strategic planning issues

Who should plan?

Amongst the various authors on corporate planning who have been referred to earlier in this chapter, there is a consensus of opinion that strategic planning should not be undertaken by the chief executive alone, planning specialists divorced from operating managers, marketing executives or finance departments. An individual or specialist department may be biased and fail to produce a balanced plan. Instead it is important to involve, in some way, all managers who will be affected by the plan, and who will be charged with implementing it. However, all these managers together cannot constitute an effective working team, and therefore a small team which represents the whole organization should be constituted, and other managers consulted. This will require a schedule for the planning activities and a formalized system for carrying out the tasks. As discussed above, it is important that planning systems do not inhibit on-going strategic thinking by managers throughout the organization. Threats must still be spotted early and potential opportunities must not be lost.

Planning traps

Ringbakk (1971) and Steiner (1972) have documented several reasons why formal planning might fail and have discussed the potential traps to avoid. Amongst their conclusions are the following:

❏ Planning should not be left exclusively to planners who might see their job as being the production of a plan and who might also concentrate on procedures and detail at the expense of wide strategic thinking.
❏ Planning should be seen as a support activity in strategic decision making and not a once-a-year ritual.
❏ There must be a commitment and an allocation of time from the strategic leader. Without this managers lower down the organization might not feel that planning matters within the firm.

❏ Planning is not likely to prove effective unless the broad directional objectives for the firm are agreed and communicated widely.

❏ Implementors must be involved, both in drawing up the plan (or essential information might be missed) and afterwards. The plan should be communicated throughout the organization, and efforts should be made to ensure that managers appreciate what is expected of them.

❏ Targets, once established, should be used as a measure of performance and variances should be analysed properly. However, there can be a danger in over-concentrating on targets and financial data at the expense of more creative strategic thinking.

❏ The organizational climate must be appropriate for the planning system adopted, and consequently structural and cultural issues have an important role to play.

❏ Inflexibility in drawing up and using the plan can be a trap. Inflexibility in drawing up the plan might be reflected in tunnel vision, a lack of flair and creativity, and in assuming that past trends can be extrapolated forwards.

❏ If planning is seen as an exercise rather than a support to strategy creation, it is quite possible the plan will be ignored and not implemented.

The impact of planning on managers

Unless the above traps are avoided and the human aspects of planning are considered, the planning activity is unlikely to prove effective. Abell and Hammond (1979) and Mills (1985) highlight the following important people considerations.

❏ Ensure the support of senior executives.

❏ Ensure that every manager who is involved understands what is expected of him or her and that any required training in planning techniques is provided.

❏ Use specialist planners carefully.

❏ Keep planning simple, and ensure that techniques never become a doctrine.

❏ Particularly where detailed planning is involved, ensure that the time horizon is appropriate. It is harder to forecast and plan detail the further into the future one looks.

❏ Never plan for the sake of planning.

❏ Link managerial rewards and sanctions to any targets for achievement which are established.

❏ Allow managers of business units and functions some freedom to develop their own planning systems rather than impose rigid ones, especially if they produce the desired results.

In summary, planning activities can take a number of forms, and organizations should seek to develop systems which provide the results they want. Ideally these should encapsulate both strategic thinking and the establishment of realistic objectives and expectations and the strategies to achieve them. Planning techniques can be used supportively, and their potential contribution is evaluated in the next section. Systematic corporate planning, though, should not be seen as the only way in which strategic changes are formulated.

The role of planning and planners

In the light of the comments above on strategy formulation we conclude this section by considering further the role of planning and planners. Planning and strategy creation are different in the sense that planners may or may not be strategists but strategists might be found anywhere in the organization. Mintzberg suggests that planning activities are likely to involve a series of different and very useful analyses, but it does not follow that these must be synthesized into a systematic planning system. Planners can make a valuable contribution to the organization and to strategic thinking by:

❑ Programming strategies into finite detail to enable effective implementation (this will involve budgeting and ensuring that strategies are communicated properly, plus the establishment of monitoring and control processes).
❑ Formalizing on-going strategic awareness – carrying out SWOT analyses and establishing what strategic changes are emerging at any time.
❑ Using scenarios and planning techniques to stimulate and encourage thinking.
❑ Searching for new competitive opportunities and strategic alternatives, and scrutinizing and evaluating them.

In other words, all the activities incorporated in the planning systems discussed earlier in the chapter are seen to be making an important contribution, but they need not be component parts of a systematic model. Rather they are contributors towards strategic thinking, awareness and insight.

Johnson (1992) further points out that on occasions plans are documented in detail only because particular stakeholders, say institutional shareholders or bankers, expect to see them as justification for proposals. There is never any real intention that they should be implemented in full.

Figure 14.8 draws together a number of these themes and illustrates the

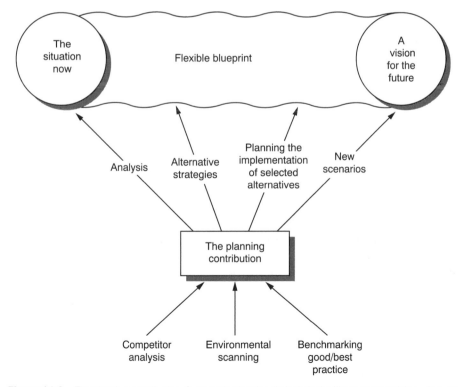

Figure 14.8 The planning contribution. Systematic planning (in isolation) will not create a vision – but you can plan your own way towards a vision. Ideas generated through planning may well change the vision.

various contributions that planning and planners can make. In conjunction with this, we next consider the relative value and contribution of selected planning techniques.

Strategic planning techniques

It has already been shown in Chapter 1 that different strategists and authors of strategy texts adopt different stances on the significance of vision, culture and strategic planning techniques in effective strategic planning.

In this book we take the view that the role of the strategic leader, styles of corporate decision making and organization culture are key driving forces in strategy creation and implementation. However, we accept that strategic planning techniques, which rely heavily on the collection and analysis of quantitative data, do have an important contribution to make. They help increase awareness, and thereby reduce the risk involved in certain decisions. They can indicate the incidence of potential threats and limitations which might reduce the future value and contribution of individual products and services. They can help in establishing priorities in large complex multi-product multi-national organizations. They can provide appropriate frameworks for evaluating the relative importance of very different businesses in a portfolio.

However, their value is dependent on the validity and reliability of the information fed into them. Where comparisons with competitors are involved, the data for other companies may well involve guesstimation.

Judgement is required for assessing the significance of events and competitor strategies; vision is essential in discontinuous change management.

In my opinion strategic planning techniques should be used to help and facilitate decision makers. They should not be used to make decisions without any necessary qualifications to the data and assumptions.

Portfolio analysis

The Boston Consulting Group growth-share matrix (Box 14.1) can be very useful for positioning products in relation to their stage in the product life cycle as long as one is both careful and honest in the use of data. It can provide insight into the likely cash needs and the potential for earnings generation. However, whilst a particular matrix position indicates potential needs and prospects it should not be seen as prescriptive for future strategy. In certain respects, all competitive positions are unique, and it is very important to consider the actual industry involved and the nature and behaviour of competitors. Business unit and product managers are likely to be able to do this with greater insight than specialist planners as they are in a better position to appreciate the peculiarities of the market.

The product portfolio suggests the following strategies for products or business units falling into certain categories:

- ❏ Cash cow   milk and redeploy the cash flow.
- ❏ Dog   liquidate or divest and redeploy the freed resources or proceeds
- ❏ Star   strengthen competitive position in growth industry.
- ❏ Question   invest as appropriate to secure and improve competitive position.

Given that a dog represents a product or service in a relatively low growth industry sector, one which does not enjoy market segment leadership, it follows that many companies will have a number of dogs in their portfolios. Liquidation or divestment will not always be justified. Products which have a strong market position, even though they are not the market leader, and which have a distinctive competitive advantage can have a healthy cash flow and profitability. Such products are sometimes referred to as cash dogs. Divestment is most appropriate when the market position is weak and when there is no real opportunity to create sustainable competitive advantage – as long as a buyer can be found. Turnaround strategies for products which are performing very poorly are examined further in Chapter 17.

According to Hamermesch (1986) many businesses which are classified as cash cows should be managed for innovation and growth, especially if the industry is dynamic or volatile, or can be made so. In other words, strategies which succeed in extending the product life cycle can move it from a state of maturity into further growth. One example quoted is coffee. This market experienced renewed growth when the success of automatic coffee makers increased demand for new varieties of fresh ground coffee.

At one time in the ballpoint-pen market Bic was the clear market leader and a cash cow when the market reached a stage of maturity. However, the introduction of roller-ball pens and erasable ball-point pens generated new growth and marketing opportunities for other competitors.

When 'milking' products care also has to be taken not to reduce capacity if there is a chance that demand and growth opportunities might return as a result of scarcities or changes in taste. When restrictions on the import of Scotch whisky into Japan were eased in the late 1980s, the product enjoyed star status even though it was seen as a cash cow in the UK.

Strategic decisions based on portfolio positions may also ignore crucial issues of inter-dependence and synergy. Business units may be treated as separate independent businesses for the purposes of planning, and this can increase the likelihood of the more qualitative contributions to other business units, and to the organization as a whole, being overlooked when decisions are made about possible liquidation or divestment.

Directional policy matrices

The best-known directional policy matrices were developed in the 1970s by Shell and General Electric and the management consultants McKinsey. They are broadly similar and aim to assist large complex multi-activity enterprises with decisions concerning investment and divestment priorities. A version of the Shell matrix is illustrated in Figure 14.10; further details can be found in Robinson *et al.* (1978).

Visit the website: http://www.itbp.com

In using such a matrix there is an assumption that resources are scarce, and that there never will be, or should be, enough financial and other resources for the implementation of all the project ideas and opportunities which can be conceived in a successful, creative and innovative organization. Choices will always have to be made about investment priorities. The development of an effective corporate strategy therefore involves an evaluation of the potential for existing businesses together with new possibilities in order to determine the priorities.

Box 14.1
THE BOSTON CONSULTING GROUP (BCG) GROWTH-SHARE MATRIX

Basic premises

Bruce Henderson (1970) of BCG has suggested firstly that the margins earned by a product, and the cash generated by it, are a function of market share. The higher the market share is, relative to competitors, the greater is the earnings potential; high margins and market share are correlated. A second premise is that sales and revenue growth requires investment. Sales of a product will only increase if there is appropriate expenditure on advertising, distribution and development; and the rate of market growth determines the required investment. Third, high market share must be earned or bought, which requires additional investment. Finally no business can grow indefinitely. As a result products will at times not be profitable because the amount of money being spent to develop them exceeds their earnings potential; at other times, and particularly where the company has a high relative market share, earnings exceed expenditure and products are profitable.

Profitability is therefore affected by market growth, market share, and the stage in the product life cycle. A company with a number of products might expect to have some which are profitable and some which are not. Generally mature products, where growth has slowed down and the required investment has decreased, are the most profitable, and the profits they earn should not be re-invested in them but used instead to finance growth products which offer future earnings potential.

The matrix

The matrix is illustrated in Figure 14.9. Chart (a) shows the composition of the axes and the names given to products or business units which fall in each of the four quadrants; chart (b) features 15 products or business units in a hypothetical company portfolio. The sterling-volume size of each product or business is proportional to the areas of the circles, and the positioning of each one is determined by its market growth rate and relative market share.

(Continued)

(a)

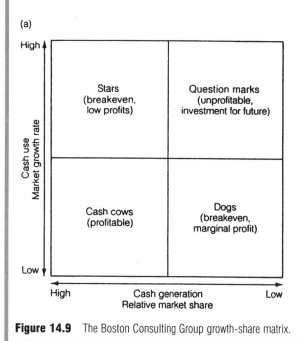

(b)

An example of a balanced portfolio

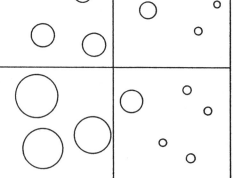

Figure 14.9   The Boston Consulting Group growth-share matrix.

The **market growth rate** on the vertical axis is the annual growth rate of the market in which the company competes, and really any range starting with zero could be used. The problem is where to draw the horizontal dividing line which separates high growth from low growth markets.

The **relative market share** on the horizontal axis indicates market share in relation to the largest competitor in the market. A relative market share of 0.25 would indicate a market share one-quarter of that of the market leader; a figure of 2.5 would represent a market leader with a market share that is 2.5 times as big as that of the nearest rival. The vertical dividing line is normally 1.0, so that market leadership is found to the left-hand side of the divider. It is important to consider market segmentation when deciding upon the market share figure to use, rather than using the share of the total market.

The growth-share matrix is thus divided into four cells or quadrants, each representing a particular type of business.

❏ **Question marks** are products or businesses which compete in high growth markets but where market share is relatively low. A new product launched into a high growth market and with an existing market leader would normally constitute a question mark. High expenditure is required to develop and launch the product, and consequently it is unlikely to be profitable and may instead require subsidy from more profitable products. Once the product is established, further investment will be required if the company attempts to claim market leadership.

❏ Successful question marks become **stars,** market leaders in growth markets. However, investment is still required to maintain the rate of growth and to defend the leadership position. Stars are marginally profitable only, but as they reach a more mature market position as growth slows down they will become increasingly profitable.

❏ **Cash cows** are therefore mature products which are well-established market leaders. As market growth slows down there is less need for high investment, and hence they are the most profitable products in the portfolio. This is boosted by any economies of scale resulting from the position of market leadership. Cash cows are used to fund the businesses in the other three quadrants.

❏ **Dogs** describe businesses which have low market shares in slower growth markets. They may well be previous cash cows, which still enjoy some loyal market support although they have been replaced as market leader by a newer rival. They should be marginally profitable, and should be withdrawn when they become loss makers if not before. The opportunity cost of the resources they tie up is an important issue in this decision.

The matrix is constructed within two axes: the horizontal axis represents industry attractiveness, or the prospects for profitable operation in the sector concerned; the vertical axis indicates the company's existing competitive position in relation to other companies in the industry. New possibilities can be evaluated initially along the vertical axis by considering their likely prospects for establishing competitive advantage. It will be appreciated that Michael Porter's work links closely to this.

In placing individual products in the matrix the factors shown in Table 14.2 are typical of those which might be used.

Each factor would be given a weighting relative to its perceived importance, and each product being evaluated would be given a score for every factor. The aggregate weighted scores for both axes determine the final position in the matrix.

Table 14.2
Factors in the directional policy
matrix

Industry attractiveness	Market growth
	Market quality, or the ability for new products to achieve higher or more stable profitability than other sectors
	Supplier pressure
	Customer pressure
	Substitute products
	Government action
	Entry barriers
	Competitive pressure
Competitive position and relative strength	Competition
	Relative market shares
	Competitive postures and opportunities
	Production capability
	Research and development record and strengths
	Success rate to date, measured in terms of market share and financial success (earnings in excess of the cost of capital)

Using the matrix

Figure 14.10 illustrates that the overall attractiveness of products diminishes as one moves diagonally from the bottom right-hand corner of the matrix to the top left. Priority products, in the bottom right-hand corner, are those which score highly on both axes. As a result they should receive priority for development, and the resources necessary for this should be allocated to them.

Products bordering on the priority box should receive the appropriate level of investment to ensure that at the very least market share is retained as the industry grows.

Products currently with a weak competitive position in an attractive industry are placed in the top right-hand corner of the matrix. They should be evaluated in respect of the potential to establish and sustain real competitive advantage. If the prospects seem good, then carefully targeted investment should be considered seriously. If the prospects are poor it is appropriate to withdraw from the market. A weak position in an attractive industry might be remedied by the acquisition of an appropriate competitor.

Products across the middle diagonal should receive custodial treatment. It is argued that a good proportion of products are likely to fall into this strategic category, which implies attempting to maximize cash generation with only a limited commitment of additional resources.

Currently profitable products with little future potential should be withdrawn gradually, but retained as long as they are profitable and the resources committed to them cannot be allocated more effectively elsewhere.

Products for divestment are likely already to be losing money if all their costs are properly assigned.

The directional policy matrix, like other matrices, is only a technique which assists in determining which industry and product sectors are most worthy of additional investment capital. Issues of synergy and overall strategic fit require further managerial judgement before final decisions are reached.

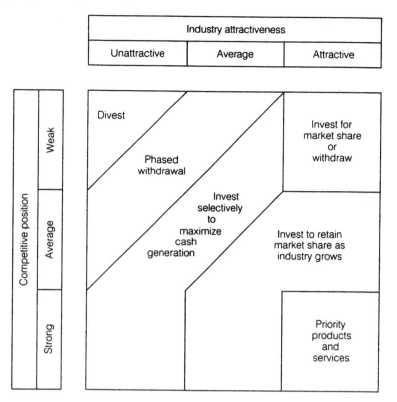

Figure 14.10 The directional policy matrix developed by Shell.

SPACE (Strategic Position and Action Evaluation)

Rowe *et al.* (1989) have developed a model based on four important variables:

❏ the relative stability/turbulence of the environment
❏ industry attractiveness
❏ the extent of any competitive advantage
❏ the company's financial strengths – incorporating profitability, liquidity and current exposure to risk.

Scores are awarded for each factor, and then diagrammed – see Box 14.2. This particular illustration features a financially strong company (or division or product) enjoying competitive advantage in an attractive industry with a relatively stable environment. The appropriate strategy is an aggressive one. The table shows the appropriate strategies for four clearly delineated positions, and judgement has to be applied when the situation is less clear cut.

This technique usefully incorporates finance, which will affect the feasibility of particular strategic alternatives and the ability of a company to implement them. It has similar limitations to directional policy matrices.

PIMS (Profit Impact of Market Strategy)

According to Buzzell and Gale (1987) the profit impact of market strategy (PIMS) approach is similar to portfolio analysis in that industry characteristics and strategic position are seen as important determinants of strategy and

Box 14.2
SPACE: STRATEGIC POSITION AND ACTION EVALUATION

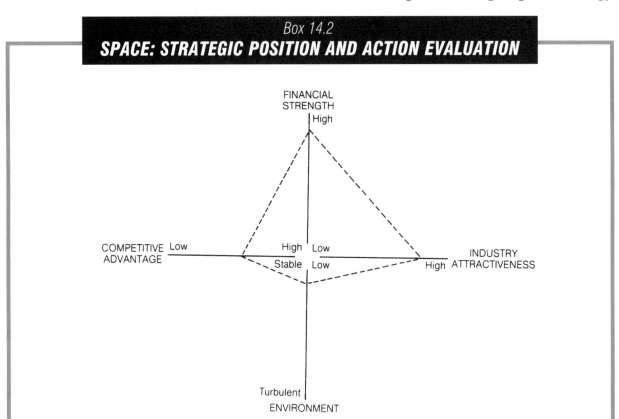

Strategic thrust	Aggressive	Competitive	Conservative	Defensive
Features:				
Environment	Stable	Unstable	Stable	Unstable
Industry	Attractive	Attractive	Unattractive	Unattractive
Competitiveness	Strong	Strong	Weak	Weak
Financial strength	High	Weak	High	Weak
Appropriate strategies	Growth – possibly by acquisition	Cost reduction, productivity improvement, raising more capital – to follow opportunities and strengthen competitiveness	Cost reduction and product/service rationalization	Rationalization
	Capitalize on opportunities		Invest in search for new products, services and competitive opportunities	Divestment as appropriate
	Innovate to sustain competitive advantage			
		Possibly merge with a less competitive but cash-rich company		

Source: Rowe, AJ, Mason, RO, Dickel, KE and Snyder, NH (1989) *Strategic Management: A Methodological Approach*, 3rd edn, Addison-Wesley.

strategic success. However, PIMS was designed to explore the impact of a wide variety of strategic and environmental issues on business performance, and to provide principles that will help managers to understand how market conditions and particular strategic choices might affect business performance.

PIMS was invented by General Electric in the 1960s as an internal analysis technique to identify which strategic factors most influence cash flow and investment needs and success. Its scope was extended by the Harvard Business School and eventually in 1975 the Strategic Planning Institute (SPI) was established to develop PIMS for a variety of clients.

PIMS is a very sophisticated computer model and its database is information submitted by clients. They provide about a hundred pieces of information about the business environment and the competitive position of each product, production processes, research and development, sales and marketing activities and financial performance. From an analysis of the data those elements which are most significant to the performance for each business are identified and the information is relayed to the client.

PIMS can be used for

❏ evaluating business performance relative to competitors and
❏ establishing targets for return on investment and cash flow.

The SPI claim that variables in the PIMS models are able to explain some 80% of the variations in performance of the businesses included.

Major findings

Amongst the most significant findings which have emerged from the PIMS models are the following.

❏ High investment intensity (investment as a percentage of sales) is associated with low profitability. Substantial investment creates additional production capacity which companies seek to use. Quite often this results in low prices and low margins for products. Japanese industry, in contrast, has been able to harness good management and labour practice with their high investment intensity, and this has resulted in high profitability. This links to the next conclusion from PIMS.
❏ High productivity (value added per employee) and high return on capital are associated. This appears to be an obvious conclusion, but the significance of the point is that, whilst the previous finding indicates that high investment

---

The management of change is both difficult and time-consuming, the more so if a company's leadership and strategies have been successful in the past. However, we have found at Grand Metropolitan that if time and resources are invested in developing a clear 'vision' – that is, in defining a company's ambition in terms of the role it will play, the geographic and market sectors in which it will compete, and the sustainable competitive advantage it has or can achieve, as well as the distinctive skills that will make it successful and resilient – then this creates a major integrating force which can help leadership overcome barriers to change, channels the energy of management to strive towards their highest aspirations, and positions the company to exploit strategic opportunities.

Sir Allen Sheppard, when Chairman, Grand Metropolitan plc

in capital and the corresponding reduction in labour intensity do not create profits, improvements in working practices have a more positive impact on profitability.

❑ Additional investment in products and industries which are currently performing well is not guaranteed to bring increased profits.

❑ High relative market share has a strong influence on profitability but is not the only factor.

❑ High industry growth rates absorb cash, and can have a harmful effect on cash flow – this is made worse by high capital intensity.

❑ High relative product quality is related to high return on investment. An element of managerial judgement is involved in the data substantiating this.

❑ High relative quality is said to exist when managers in the organization believe that they have a superior competitive position.

❑ Product innovation and differentiation lead to profitability, especially in mature markets, but relative market share also has a considerable influence on this factor.

❑ Vertical integration is more likely to prove successful in stable industries than in unstable ones. Vertical integration tends to increase fixed costs, making the firm more vulnerable if there is intense competition or technological change.

❑ The conclusion of the experience curve is sound in that unit cost reductions over time prove profitable for companies with high market share.

Visit the website:
http://www.itbp.com

Limitations of PIMS

It is important to appreciate that there are certain drawbacks which Constable (1980) amongst others have listed. These include the following.

❑ PIMS assumes that short-term profitability is the prime objective of the organization.

❑ The analysis is based on historical data and the model does not take account of future changes in the company's external environment.

❑ The model cannot take account of inter-dependences and potential synergy within organizations. Each business unit is analysed in isolation.

Planning techniques can be extremely useful, particularly as they force managers and organizations to ask themselves many relevant and searching questions and compile and analyse important information. But the techniques do not, and cannot, provide answers; they merely generate the questions. The danger is that some managers may perceive the output of a technique such as PIMS or a matrix analysis as answers to strategic issues.

Conclusion

To conclude this chapter it is useful to return to our opening comments concerning the crucial importance of **strategic thinking**. Whatever approaches are adopted, whichever techniques are utilized, the organization (corporately) must appreciate the totality of its strategic scene, as illustrated in Fig. 14.11. This encompasses:

- ❏ an appreciation of how past decisions and actions, reflecting how the organization has developed and exploited particular competencies, have brought the organization to its present position
- ❏ insight into the future although, looking forward, it will not be possible to predict future actions with any degree of certainty. Some future changes will reflect continuous improvement, others will be more discontinuous
- ❏ internal developments and changes with empowerment
- ❏ the competitive environment surrounding the organization.

In the next chapter we begin to examine in detail the types of strategic change the organization might introduce.

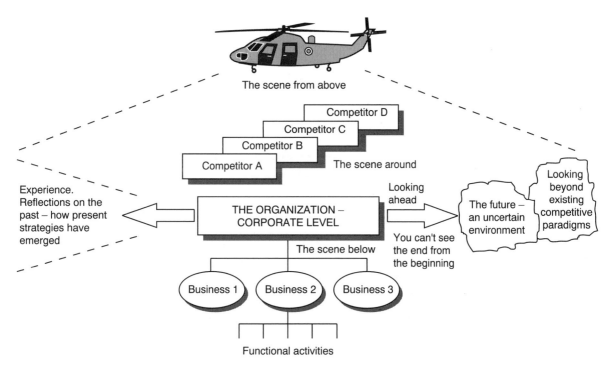

Figure 14.11   The strategic scene (based on ideas in Mintzberg, H (1995) Strategic thinking as seeing. In *Developing Strategic Thought* (ed. B Garrett), McGraw-Hill.

Summary

In this chapter we have considered the question of generally where the organization might go in the future, as a preamble to an evaluation of specific development paths. The role and contribution of planning and planning systems in relation to this decision have been discussed. The concept of gap analysis has been introduced and it has been emphasized that a variety of strategic alternatives can be assessed in terms of feasibility desirability and risk as means of closing the gap – the difference between where managers expect the organization to reach if they continue with present strategies and where they would like to reach. Alternative approaches to planning have been considered, and it has been emphasized that strategies are not necessarily created through a planning process. They can be established entrepreneurially with vision playing a more significant role than systematic planning, and they can emerge with learning and incremental change.

Specifically we have:

- considered the need for planning, and its relative importance in helping strategic thinking, given that rigid formal planning systems have become unfashionable
- distinguished between planning at the corporate and functional levels
- described seven basic approaches to planning, and an example of a comprehensive formal planning system
- examined the concept of the planning gap and, in outline, ways of closing the gap
- looked briefly at a more contemporary approach to planning
- discussed who should plan, planning pitfalls and the impact of planning on managers
- developed the theme of portfolio analysis considered directional policy matrices and SPACE, and in addition discussed the potential contribution of PIMS as a planning technique
- recapped on the key features of the planning, adaptive and entrepreneurial modes of strategy creation, examining these in terms of (a) analysis, choice and implementation issues and (b) strategic perspective and competitive position
- considered these modes in the light of strategic change in local government and small businesses.

Checklist of key terms and concepts

You should feel confident that you understand the following terms and ideas:

- ★ Strategic thinking and strategic planning
- ★ Systematic planning models
- ★ Strategic issues
- ★ The planning gap
- ★ Ansoff's growth vector
- ★ Directional policy matrices and SPACE
- ★ PIMS
- ★ Strategic perspective and competitive position
- ★ Planning, visionary and emergent modes of strategy creation.

Questions and research assignments

Text related

1 Mintzberg has distinguished between 'grass roots' strategies (which can take root anywhere in the organization but eventually proliferate once they become more widely adopted) and 'hothouse' strategies which are deliberately grown and cultured. What do you think he means?

2 Who should plan? What should they plan, how and when?

3 A manufacturer of industrial products is structured around five separate strategic business units (SBUs). Use the data below to construct a Boston matrix and assess how balanced the portfolio seems. Where are the strengths? Weaknesses?

SBU	Sales (£ million)	Number of competitors	Sales of three top companies (%)	Market growth rate
A	0.4	6	0.8, 0.7, 0.4	16
B	1.8	20	1.8, 1.8, 1.2	18
C	1.7	16	1.7, 1.3, 0.9	8
D	3.5	3	3.5, 1.0, 0.8	5
E	0.6	8	2.8, 2.0, 1.5	2

4 In the context of the Boston matrix, is the Big Mac a cash cow? What do you feel McDonald's competitive strategy for the Big Mac should be?

Library based

5 For an organization of your choice, ideally one with which you are familiar:

(a) Ascertain how the planning, entrepreneurial and adaptive modes might apply currently to strategic change in the organization. Which mode is predominant? Why do you think it is the preferred mode? How successful is it?

(b) What would be the opportunities and concerns from greater utilization of the other modes?

(c) As far as you are able, draw up a directional policy matrix for the products and services of the organization. (Use your own judgement in assigning weights to the various factors for assessing industry attractiveness and competitive position.)

6 In 1975 the Boston Consulting Group wrote a report for the British government concerning the penetration of Honda motorcycles in the USA. They concluded that the success was the result of meticulous staff work and planning.

Pascale (1984) disagrees and argues that the success was entirely due to learning and persistence, and that it was Honda's learning experience concerning operating in the USA that eventually led to a more rationally planned approach.

Both arguments are documented in Pascale, R (1984) Perspectives on strategy – the real story behind Honda's success, *California Management Review*, **26** (3). Read this article and assess the points Pascale makes.

Recommended further reading

Ansoff, HI (1987) is a comprehensive but easy-to-read book on strategic decision making.

Readers interested in corporate planning are recommended to read one of the several books written by either John Argenti or David Hussey. Those included in the references are both ideal.

Mintzberg, H. (1989) *Mintzberg on Management*, Free Press, provides a thorough analysis of planning, adaptive and entrepreneurial strategy creation.

Quinn, JB (1980) *Strategies for Change: Logical Incrementalism*, Richard D Irwin, is an excellent reference work on adaptive or incremental change.

Mintzberg, H (1994) *The Rise and Fall of Strategic Planning*, Prentice-Hall, examines the role and contribution of planning.

Rowe *et al.* (in the References) is a good introduction to techniques which are useful in strategic decision making.

References

Abell, DF and Hammond, JS (1979) *Strategic Market Planning*, Prentice-Hall.

Ackoff, RL (1970) *A Concept of Corporate Planning*, John Wiley.

Ansoff, HI (1987) *Corporate Strategy*, revised edition, Penguin.

Aram, JD and Cowen, SS (1990) Strategic planning for increased profit in the small business, *Long Range Planning*, **23**, 6.

Argenti, J (1980) *Practical Corporate Planning*, George Allen & Unwin.

Bailey, A and Johnson, G (1992) How strategies develop in organizations. In *The Challenge of Strategic Management* (eds G Johnson and D Faulkner), Kogan Page.

Buzzell, RD and Gale, BT (1987) *The PIMS Principles – Linking Strategy to Performance*, Free Press.

Cohen, KJ and Cyert, RM (1973) Strategy formulation, implementation and monitoring, *Journal of Business*, **46**(3), 349–67.

Constable, J (1980) Business strategy. Unpublished paper, Cranfield School of Management.

Glueck, WF and Jauch, LR (1984) *Business Policy and Strategic Management*, 4th edn, McGraw-Hill.

Hamermesch, R (1986) Making planning strategic, *Harvard Business Review*, July–August.

Harvey-Jones, JH (1987) In an introduction to Ansoff, HI, *Corporate Strategy*, Penguin.

Henderson, B (1970) *The Product Portfolio*, Boston Consulting Group.

Hussey, D (1976) *Corporate Planning – Theory and Practice*, Pergamon.

Idenburg, PJ (1993) Four styles of strategy development, *Long Range Planning*, **26**, 6.

Johnson, G (1992) Strategic direction and strategic decisions, presented at 'Managing Strategically: Gateways and Barriers', Strategic Planning Society conference, 12 February.

Mills, DQ (1985) Planning with people in mind, *Harvard Business Review*, July–August.

Mintzberg, H (1989) Presentation to the Strategic Planning Society, London, 2 February. (Further detail can be found in Mintzberg, H. (1973).)

Mintzberg, H (1973) Strategy making in three modes, *California Management Review*, **16**(2), Winter.

Mintzberg, H and Waters, JA (1985) Of strategy deliberate and emergent, *Strategic Management Journal*, **6**(3).

Ohmae, K (1982) *The Mind of the Strategist*, McGraw-Hill.

Porter, ME (1987) The state of strategic thinking, *The Economist*, 23 May.

Ringbakk, KA (1971) Why planning fails, *European Business*, Spring.

Robinson, J (1986) Paradoxes in planning, *Long Range Planning*, **19**(6).

Robinson, SJQ, Hitchens, RE and Wade, DP (1978) The directional policy matrix – tool for strategic planning, *Long Range Planning*, **21**, June.

Rowe, AJ, Mason, RO, Dickel, KE and Snyder, NH (1989) *Strategic Management: A Methodological Approach*, 3rd edn, Addison-Wesley.

Steiner, G (1972) *Pitfalls in Comprehensive Long Range Planning*, Planning Executives Institute.

Taylor, B and Hussey, DE (1982) *The Realities of Planning*, Pergamon.

15

Strategic Alternatives and Market Entry Strategies

As a preamble to a more detailed treatment of growth, recovery and divestment strategies, and management buy-outs, in this chapter we describe the various strategic alternatives that exist. Only some of them will be appropriate for an organization at a particular time. The international dimensions of strategy are explored.

Learning objectives

After studying this chapter you should be able to:

■ identify and describe a number of possible strategic alternatives
■ explain how selected strategies might be implemented through internal or external growth
■ discuss the important considerations involved in international strategies.

Introduction

In this chapter we outline the various strategic alternatives that might be available to an organization in thinking and deciding where it wants to go, and for helping to close the planning gap. The attractiveness of particular alternatives will be affected by the objectives of the organization. Whilst a whole range of options are discussed in this chapter, it does not follow that they will all be available to an organization at the same time. Because of the costs or risks involved, particular alternatives might be quickly rejected. Chapters 16 and 17 consider certain of the strategies in greater depth. In particular, in Chapter 16 I discuss diversification, acquisition and joint ventures. Retrenchment and turn-around strategies are the subject of Chapter 17. The factors which determine the attractiveness and wisdom of particular alternatives are explored in Chapter 18. The appropriate strategy always matches the environment, values and resources congruently.

For many organizations the appropriate strategies will have a global dimension, and consequently I have included a section on international issues in this chapter.

In their consideration of strategic alternatives, some organizations will be entrepreneurial and actively search for opportunities for change. Others will only consider change if circumstances dictate a need. Some organizations will already have sound and effective strategies which are producing results that they are satisfied with. Others may ignore the need to change. Some texts have quoted the example of the typewriter companies who knew instinctively that electric typewriters, let alone word processors, would never catch on.

Figure 15.1 provides a summary of the possible strategic alternatives. From origins in a single business concept, market penetration and product and market development are shown as level one growth strategies as they mainly affect competitive strategies rather than imply major corporate change.

Don't forget to visit the website: http://www.itbp.com

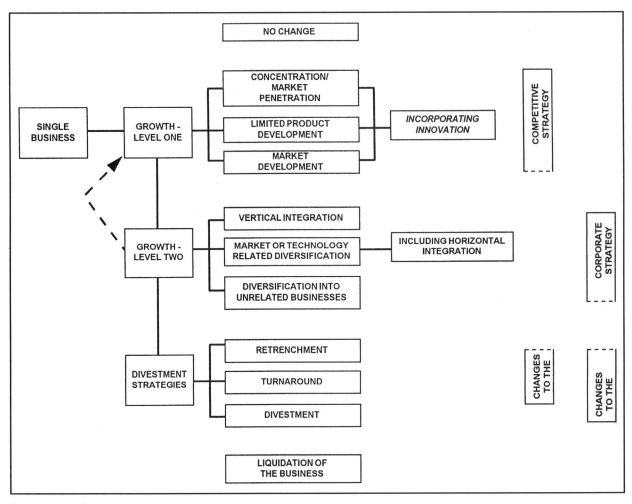

Figure 15.1   Strategic alternatives.

The level two growth strategies imply more ambitious and higher risk expansion which is likely to change the corporate perspective or strategy. These options, explained below, may involve either a strategic alliance or an acquisition, and these *strategic means* are discussed later in the chapter. We established in Chapter 1 that it is important for organizations to seek competitive advantage for each business in the portfolio. Consequently, once an organization has diversified, it will be necessary to look for new competitive opportunities – or level one growth strategies – for the various individual businesses. This is illustrated by the dotted line on the chart.

The bottom section of Figure 15.1 shows the main strategies for corporate reduction.

Figure 15.2, market entry strategies, summarizes the various ways in which an organization might implement its chosen strategies. It should be appreciated that any strategic alternative can be international in scope, rather than focused on a single country or market, and that as we move from the top to the bottom of the chart the inherent scope, risk and potential benefits all increase.

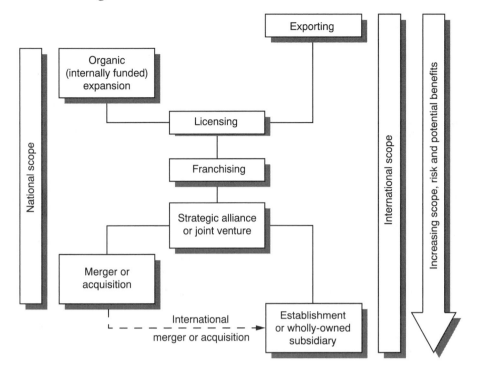

Figure 15.2 Market entry strategies.

The choice must take into account the risk that the strategic leader considers acceptable given any particular circumstances, and the ability of the organization to deal with the risk elements. Some organizations will not select the most challenging and exciting opportunities because they are too risky.

The options should not be thought of as being mutually exclusive – two or more may be combined into a composite strategy, and at any time a multi-product organization is likely to be pursuing several different competitive strategies.

The do-nothing alternative

This do-nothing alternative is a continuation of the existing corporate and competitive strategies, whatever they might be, and however unsuccessful the company might be. The decision to do nothing might be highly appropriate and justified, and the result of very careful thought and evaluation. However, it can also be the result of managers lacking awareness, being lazy or complacent or deluding themselves into believing that things are going well when in fact the company is in difficulties. Doing nothing when change is required is a dangerous strategy.

A company might appear to an outsider to be doing nothing when in reality it is very active. Some companies, for example, prefer not to be the first to launch new product developments, especially if they know that their competitors are innovating along similar lines. A product may be developed and ready to launch but be held back whilst another company introduces its version into the market. This allows the initial reaction of consumers to be monitored and evaluated and competitive and functional strategies reviewed before eventual launch. Timing is the key to success with this strategy. A company will want sufficient time to be sure that its approach is likely to prove successful; at the same time it must react sufficiently quickly that it is not perceived to be copying a competitor when that competitor has become firmly established.

In general the do-nothing alternative may be viable in the short term but is unlikely to prove beneficial or realistic in the long term as environmental factors change.

Level one growth strategies

Four internal growth strategies are discussed in this section. However, it should be appreciated that the strategies described are not fully discrete and independent of each other. The ideas behind them are closely linked, and it may be very difficult to classify a particular strategic change as one of these strategies rather than another. Consequently the important issue is the line of thought and the reasoning behind the strategy in question, and the objectives.

Concentration or specialization

This strategy implies what Peters and Waterman (1982) designate 'sticking to the knitting' in their book *In Search of Excellence*, which was discussed in Chapter 4. It involves concentrating on doing better what one is already doing well. Although it may seem similar to doing nothing, growth is an objective and there is an implicit search for ways of doing things more effectively. In this respect it overlaps with the ideas of market and product development described below.

Resources are directed towards the continued and profitable growth of a 'single' product in a 'single' market, using a 'single' technology. This is accomplished by attracting new users or consumers, increasing the consumption rate of existing users, and, wherever possible, stealing consumers and market share from competitors. The word 'single' needs careful interpretation, as companies like Kellogg (breakfast cereals) and Timex (watches) would be classified as organizations which have succeeded with specialization strategies. An extensive product line of differentiated brands designed to appeal to specific market segments would periodically have new additions and withdrawals.

The two main advantages are, first, that the strategy is based on known skills and capabilities and in this respect it is generally low risk. Second, because the organization's production and marketing skills are concentrated on specialized products and related consumers, and not diversified, these skills can be developed and improved to create competitive advantage. The company has the opportunity to be sensitive to consumer needs by being close to them, and may build a reputation for this.

Market penetration strategies generally have a high likelihood of success, greater in fact than most other alternatives. There are important limitations, however. First, alone they may be inadequate for closing an identified planning gap.

Whilst concentration is a growth strategy, the long-term growth is likely to be gradual rather than explosive. This should not be seen as a disadvantage, because steady growth can be more straightforward in managerial terms. Any firm pursuing this strategy is susceptible to changes in the growth rate or attractiveness of the industry in which it competes, and therefore the strategy can become high risk if the industry goes into recession. There is also a constant need to monitor competitors and ensure that any innovations do not constitute a major threat.

This strategic alternative is particularly applicable to small businesses which concentrate their efforts on specific market niches.

Market development

Market development, together with product development which is considered next, is very closely related to a strategy of specialization. All these strategies build on existing strengths, skills, competencies and capabilities. Market development is generally another relatively low-risk strategy; and the idea behind it is to market present products, with possible modifications and range increases, to customers in related market areas. Changes in distribution and advertising will typically support this strategy.

Visit the website: http://www.itbp.com

One example of a market development strategy would be a firm who decided to modify its product in some minor way to make it attractive to selected export markets where tastes and preferences are different. This would be supported by advertising and require the opening of new channels of distribution.

Product development

Product development implies substantial modifications or additions to present products in order to increase their market penetration within existing customer groups. It is often linked to an attempt to extend or prolong the product life cycle, and typical examples would include the second and revised edition of a successful textbook, or the re-launch of a range of cosmetics with built-in improvements which add value. Case 15.1, Lego, looks at product development.

Innovation

Innovation is linked to the three strategies described above but involves more significant changes to the product or service. The strategy implies the replacement of existing products with ones which are really new, as opposed to modified, and which imply a new product life cycle. The line which differentiates a really new product from a modification is extremely difficult to quantify. In the case of the new Ford Fiesta for example, there are a number of major changes. The car is very different from the existing model – but the name is the same.

Similarly, it is important to consider which product life cycle is being addressed. The Sony Walkman and similar personal cassette players have enjoyed their own successful life cycle; at the same time they have extended the product life cycle of cassette players generally.

It can be risky not to innovate in certain industries as a barrier against competition. Innovatory companies can stay ahead by introducing new products ahead of their rivals and concentrating on production and marketing to establish and consolidate a strong market position. All the time they will search for new opportunities to innovate and gain further advantage. A number of food manufacturers have utilized innovation to consolidate their market positions as

Case 15.1
LEGO

In a volatile and competitive environment we have concentrated and used our strength to go deeper into what we know about.

(Kjeld Kirk Kristiansen, President)

Lego, the brightly coloured plastic building bricks, were launched in 1949, and have always proved popular in an industry renowned for changing tastes and preferences and for innovation. Lego is Danish, family owned and secretive, hiding its actual sales and profit figures. Toy industry analysts estimate Lego's annual sales to be $1.4 billion.

The basic strategy is one of product development, with Lego developing an enormous number of variations on its basic product theme. At any time some 300 different kits (at a wide range of prices) are available world-wide. There are 1700 different parts, including bricks, shapes and miniature people, and children can use them to make almost anything from small cars to large, complex, working space stations with battery operated space trains. Brick colours are selected to appeal to both boys and girls; and the more complex Lego Technic sets are branded and promoted specially to make them attractive to the young teenage market. Over 100 billion plastic bricks and pieces have been produced since Lego was introduced.

In a typical year Lego replaces one-third of its product range, with many items having only a short life span. New ideas are developed over a two- to three-year period and backed by international consumer research and test marketing. Lego concentrates on global tastes and buying habits. The Pacific Rim is perceived to offer the highest growth potential. 'If you differentiate too much you start to make difficulties for yourself, especially in manufacturing.' Competition has forced Lego to act internationally and aggressively. One US company, Tyco, markets products which are almost indistinguishable from Lego. Lego has attempted unsuccessfully to sue for patent infringement and now views this competition as undesirable but stimulating. More recently new competition has come from another rival construction product, K'Mex, again American.

Lego manufactures in Switzerland, Germany, Brazil, South Korea and the USA as well as Denmark, making their own tools for the plastic injection moulding machines. Tool making could easily be concentrated in one plant, but takes place in three to engender competition and to emphasize quality. Lego deliberately maintains strong links with its machinery suppliers. In this and other respects Lego see themselves as being closer culturally to a Japanese company than a US one. Investments in production and improvements are thought to be in the region of £100 million per year.

Some years ago Lego diversified with a theme park – built with Lego bricks – in Denmark. This has been followed with a similar development on the site of the old Windsor Safari Park; a third is planned in San Diego.

Sources: Marsh, P (1991) Family continuity holds the key to longevity in a one-product company, *Financial Times*, 20 June. Marsh, P (1996) Lego plans involve a great many bricks, *Financial Times*, 13 March. Darwent, C (1995) Lego's billion dollar brickwork, *Management Today*, September.

the major food retail chains have increased in size and power. Not only were the retailers in an increasingly strong negotiating position concerning prices and trading arrangements, they were also beginning to market their own-brand alternatives at very competitive prices. Astute manufacturers have innovated and maintained a flow of new products to retain a competitive advantage by limiting the market potential for retailer own-brands.

Constant innovation is likely to prove expensive, and will require other products and strategies to be successful in order to provide the funding.

Case 15.2
SWISS WATCHES

In the early 1980s the Swiss watch industry was in deep trouble. Many firms had closed and numerous jobs had been lost. Only the select companies manufacturing expensive and high-quality watches were secure from competition from the Far East, particularly the low-labour-cost countries, and their digital electronic watches. The Swiss watch industry had effectively missed out on the early growth of electronic watches, although the first one was actually produced in Switzerland.

By the mid-1980s the situation had been transformed as a result of the Swatch, and similar analogue electronic watches. They were low priced, plastic, reliable and fashion oriented. It has been estimated that in 1985 output from the Swiss watch industry accounted for 45% of world output in value terms from 10% of the volume.

The corresponding figures for Japan were 35:35 and for the rest of Asia 14:50.

This required a change of culture in response to changes in consumer expectations. Although there are limited but highly profitable opportunities for expensive quality watches, in general watches are no longer expected to last a lifetime. They are now perceived as a fashion accessory, and consumers buy them more often and replace them periodically or when they go wrong. In the mid-1970s 274 watches were purchased for every 1000 Britons; ten years later the figure had risen to 370. In the USA the corresponding figures are 240 and 425.

Swatch watches are now so popular that at leading airports small concessionary units concentrate exclusively on them.

Case 15.2, The Swiss watch industry case might also be considered as a turn-around strategy because in the early 1980s the industry was in difficulty. But innovation, and the appeal to new market segments through repositioning the products, have proved extremely successful. Elements of market and product development are included.

Combination strategies

A firm with a number of products or business units will typically pursue a number of different competitive strategies at any time. Product development, market development and innovation may all be taking place.

The internal growth strategies discussed in this section are primarily concerned with improving competitive strategies for existing businesses. Such changes may not prove adequate for closing the planning gap, and consequently higher risk external growth strategies may also be considered. Such changes are likely to involve a new strategic perspective.

Case 15.3 looks at how Tube Investments changed from being a diversified company into one which specializes in engineering products for selected market segments. The change was implemented through the divestment of bicycles and domestic appliances, leaving a core of engineering businesses. External growth through the further acquisition of companies, particularly in the USA, which produce related engineering products has allowed Tube Investments to pursue strategies of product and market development in order to consolidate its position as a global competitor.

Case 15.3
TUBE INVESTMENTS

Christopher Lewington was recruited in 1986 to become the new Chief Executive and he quickly decided that Tube Investments (TI) needed a clear vision and strategy, in contrast with previous acquisition strategies which had been relatively haphazard.

It was stated in early 1987 that 'TI's strategic thrust is to become an international engineering group concentrating on specialized engineering businesses and operating in selected niches (particularly automotives) on a global basis. Key businesses must be able to command positions of sustained technological and market share leadership'.

In 1986 Raleigh cycles and a number of varied domestic appliance products constituted 42% of TI sales revenue, 30% of pre-tax profits and 45% of capital employed. These were the areas for divestment. Cycles, with their low technology, had been affected by foreign competition which compounded the problems caused by falls in demand in parts of Western Europe. Because different markets required specific product differences, and because of the emergence of defined niches such as those for BMX and mountain bikes, Raleigh 'needed marketing which TI could not provide'. Domestic appliances was an international industry and multi-nationals such as Philips and Electrolux were very powerful competitors. TI was too small.

Lewington felt that TI had neither the financial resources nor the breadth of management to run a company diversified across specialist engineering and consumer products and markets. Specialist engineering was where TI could add most value and gain the greatest benefit.

In 1987–1988 TI sold Raleigh to Derby International, a specially formed foreign-backed consortium who more recently acquired Royal Worcester pottery. Glow Worm and Parkray central heating systems were sold to Hepworth Ceramics; Creda and New World domestic appliances to GEC and Birmid Qualcast respectively; and Russell Hobbs kitchen equipment to Polly Peck. Machine tool interests and some welded tube products were also divested.

At the same time TI acquired companies, especially in the USA, including Bundy, the largest US manufacturer of small diameter tube for use in cars and refrigerators, and John Crane, a manufacturer of mechanical seals.

TI then specialized in a range of engineering products including aircraft piston rings, industrial furnaces, and tubes for specific market segments. For the automotive industry, silencers, suspension systems, car seats and seat slide mechanisms are manufactured.

In 1992 TI launched a successful but hostile bid for the Dowty Group. Dowty gave TI polymer engineering products, which link with Crane, and related aerospace businesses in landing gear and propellers. These latter activities became a joint venture with Snecma of France in 1993. The remaining Dowty businesses (modems, terminals and electronic systems) were quickly divested.

Since 1992 the corporate structure has remained largely unaltered. TI, instead, has sought growth from the better exploitation of the knowledge and service aspects of its businesses and from a stronger focus on anticipating and meeting customers' needs – competitive strategies.

Sales of £1.5 billion in 1995 were double those when Lewington arrived; profits increased fivefold in the same period. 'Newcomers' Bundy and Crane contributed some 80% of sales revenue; 40% of TI's business is now in the USA.

Level two growth strategies

Level two growth strategies are frequently implemented through acquisition, merger or joint venture rather than organic growth. Franchising can provide another means of generating external growth, but it is only likely to be applicable for certain types of business.

External growth can involve the purchase of, or an arrangement with, firms which are behind or ahead of a business in the added value channel which spans raw material to ultimate consumption. Similarly it can involve firms or activities which are indirectly related businesses or industries, those which are tangentially related through either technology or markets, and basically unrelated businesses. The key objectives are additional market share and the search for opportunities which can generate synergy. The outcome from this will be larger size and increased power, and ideally improved profitability from the synergy. In reality, as will be explored in greater depth in Chapter 16, the outcome is more likely to be increased size and power than improved profitability. Synergy often proves to be elusive.

Proposed acquisitions of organizations which would result in substantial market share and possible domination may well be subject to reference to the Monopolies and Mergers Commission which, as was discussed in Chapter 9, may act as a restraint on proposed corporate development. Certain avenues for growth may in effect be closed to an organization.

Horizontal integration

Horizontal integration occurs when a firm acquires or merges with a major competitor, or at least another firm operating at the same stage in the added value chain. The two organizations may well appeal to different market segments rather than compete directly. Market share will increase, and pooled skills and capabilities should generate synergy. Numerous examples exist. Rover Cars, now part of BMW and previously known as Austin Rover, and before that British Leyland, is the result of a series of amalgamations over many years. Such brand names as Austin, Morris, MG, Wolsley, Standard, Triumph and Rover, which were all originally independent car producers, are incorporated. Jaguar was also included until it was re-floated as an independent company in the mid-1980s.

In the financial services sector, the National Westminster Bank was created by the merger of the National Provincial Bank and Westminster Bank, and more recently a number of building society mergers have taken place. The Alliance and Leicester and Nationwide Anglia are typical examples.

Case 15.4 Electrolux, is an example of international horizontal integration.

Vertical integration

Vertical integration is the term used to describe the acquisition of a company which supplies a firm with inputs of raw materials or components, or serves as a customer for the firm's products or services (a distributor or assembler). If a shirt manufacturer acquired a cotton textile supplier this would be known as backward vertical integration; if the supplier bought the shirt manufacturer, its customer, this would constitute forward vertical integration.

Case 15.4
ELECTROLUX

In 1970 Electrolux was a Swedish-based manufacturer of mainly vacuum cleaners, supported by refrigerators. A new chief executive introduced a strategy of horizontal integration and acquisition, and within 20 years Electrolux became the world's leading manufacturer of white goods – refrigerators, freezers, washing machines, tumble dryers and dishwashers.

Major acquisitions include:

1984   Zanussi (Italy)
1986   White Consolidated (third largest US producer)
1987   Tricity (UK, from Thorn-EMI)
1988   Corbero/Domar (Spain)
1991   Lehel (largest producer of white goods in Hungary – providing a base for expansion in Eastern Europe)
1994   AEG

Electrolux bought 400 companies over 20 years, with unrelated businesses and surplus assets often being sold off to recoup part of the purchase price.

Production has been rationalized, with many parts standardized, in an attempt to reduce costs, but Electrolux remains a global manufacturer. Wherever possible the best practices from new acquisitions are shared across frontiers, and clearly Electrolux has faced a series of challenges in integrating the new businesses with their distinctive, national cultures. The integration strategy is based upon speed and the immediate input of a small task force to search for synergy and divestment opportunities.

The ultimate success will depend upon the ability of Electrolux to integrate its marketing, particularly in Europe, which accounts for some two-thirds of the sales. Product differentiation is possible, but the fact that competing white goods invariably look alike in many respects adds difficulties. In addition, tastes and preferences concerning particular features vary from country to country.

In 1991 products carrying the Electrolux brand name were re-launched as a pan-European upper mass market brand, with new design features and common advertising and promotion. A similar strategy, but with a more down-market image, was to follow for Zanussi-branded products. Local brands have also being retained, targeted at individual country preferences – for the UK this means Tricity and Bendix. This dualistic strategy, involving up to four distinct brands in most countries, differs from that of Whirlpool, the US company which acquired Philips' white goods business, and is Electrolux's main rival. Whirlpool is more reluctant to differentiate between countries.

In June 1992 Electrolux agreed a joint venture with AEG, a smaller European competitor and a subsidiary of Daimler-Benz. Electrolux acquired the whole AEG appliance business in 1994. This final acquisition gave Electrolux 30% of the European market, with individual country shares of some 35% in France, Germany, Italy and the UK. The AEG brand is particularly strong in Germany; Electrolux is most popular in Northern Europe, Zanussi in Southern Europe.

At times firms will reduce the extent to which they are vertically integrated if they are failing to obtain the appropriate benefits and synergy from the fusion of two sets of skills and capabilities. Early in 1988, for example, the Burton Group sold the last of its suitmaking factories in order to concentrate on retailing. At one time Burton had been one of the leading clothing manufacturers in Europe, but that was before made-to-measure suits were substantially replaced in popularity by ready-made suits.

Backward vertical integration aims to secure supplies at a lower cost than competitors, but after the merger or acquisition it becomes crucial to keep pace with technological developments and innovation on the supply side, or competitive advantage may be lost.

In 1987 Rover divested its parts distribution business, Unipart – an example of vertical disintegration. Eight years later, after its acquisition by BMW, Rover sought unsuccessfully to buy Unipart back, arguing that it needed to control its parts distribution to support its increasingly international role.

Forward vertical integration secures customers or outlets and guarantees product preference, and it can give a firm much greater control over its total marketing effort. At the consumer end of the chain, retailers generally are free to decide at what final price they sell particular products or services, and their views may not always accord with those of the manufacturer. However, greater control over distribution might mean complacency and a loss of competitive edge through less effective marketing overall. In addition, manufacturing and retailing, if these are the two activities involved, require separate and different skills, and for this reason synergy may again prove elusive.

With vertical integration there will always be uncertainty as the system of relationships amongst a group of suppliers and manufacturers, or a group of manufacturers and distributors, is changed. Generally it is argued that if there are only a few suppliers and several buyers vertical integration can have significant effects. Figure 15.3 features a system comprising three suppliers, five manufacturers and four retailers, all of whom are independent. The lines joining the boxes show the trading relationships. If supplier C acquired, or was acquired by, manufacturer 5 (option 1) then a number of issues have to be resolved. Currently manufacturer 5 relies exclusively on supplier C. Does it make sense for this to continue, or might it be useful to establish a trading relationship with another supplier (also now a competitor) to hedge against future possible difficulties such as technological change and innovation? At the moment, also, competing manufacturers 2, 3 and 4 all buy some of their supplies from supplier C. Will they continue to do so? If not, supplier C is likely to have substantial spare capacity. Similar issues would be raised by option 2, integration between manufacturer 1 and retailer W.

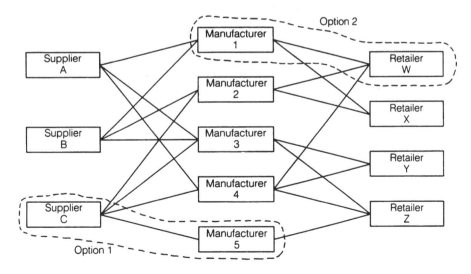

Figure 15.3 Vertical integration.

Many of the benefits of vertical integration can be achieved without merger or acquisition. Joint ventures, discussed later, are one option. In addition there may simply be agreements between companies who appreciate that there can be substantial gains from proper co-operation. Marks and Spencer provide an excellent example. Marks and Spencer benefit from long-term agreements with their suppliers with whom they work closely. Many suppliers of a wide variety of products sold by Marks and Spencer rely very heavily upon them, as they are their major customer. At the same time Marks and Spencer set exacting standards for cost, quality and delivery and guarantee to buy only when these standards are met continuously; and there will always be competitors who would like them as a customer.

The effect of vertical integration can be created organically, without merger or acquisition, but this is likely to be more risky. New skills have to be developed from scratch. Examples of this would be a manufacturer deciding to make components rather than buying them from specialist suppliers, or starting to distribute independently rather than relying on external distributors.

Because new and different skills are involved, vertical integration really implies diversification, but normally these strategic change options are considered separately. The growth and development of Airtours as a vertically integrated holiday company is outlined in Case 15.5.

Concentric diversification

Any form of diversification involves a departure from existing products and markets. The new products or services involved may relate to existing products or services through either technology or marketing; where this is the case, the diversification is known as concentric rather than conglomerate. A specialist manufacturer of ski clothing who diversified into summer leisure wear to offset seasonal sales would be an example. Potential consumers may or may not be the same; distribution may or may not change; the existing production expertise should prove beneficial.

Similarly, when retailers such as Boots and WH Smith add new and different lines and products they are seeking to exploit their resources and their retailing skills and expertise (core competencies) more effectively.

There is an assumption that synergy can be created from the two businesses or activities; and ideally the new, diversified, company enjoys strengths and opportunities which decrease its weaknesses and exposure to risks.

Any organization seeking concentric diversification will look for companies or opportunities where there are clearly related products or markets or distribution channels or technologies or resource requirements. The related benefits should be clear and genuinely capable of generating synergy. However, diversification might be adopted as a means of covering up weaknesses or previous poor decisions. Benefits will not be expected immediately, and the change involved may divert interest and attention away from existing problems or difficulties.

Conglomerate diversification

In the case of conglomerate diversification there is no discernible relationship between existing and new products, services and markets. The diversification is justified as a promising investment opportunity. Financial benefits and profits

Case 15.5
AIRTOURS

In 1990 Airtours was a relatively small but fast-growing package tour operator. Based in Lancashire it offered low-price holidays in cheaper resorts and for a while had a reputation for carrying rowdy youngsters. Most of its customers were based in the north, and Airtours benefited competitively when the impact of the recession was felt first in the south. When bookings fell dramatically before and during the Gulf War (in Airtours' case, by 40%), the company pulled out of selected markets, slowed down its planned move to new premises and froze capital expenditure on new information technology. Airtours was, however, building an airline, and was committed to taking delivery of five McDonnell Douglas aircraft (on lease) which would operate from Manchester (three planes), Birmingham and Stansted.

Airtours successfully predicted the collapse of International Leisure Group, which included Intasun, the second largest package tour operator. When ILG ceased trading in March 1991 Airtours had agents in place in targeted resorts (the Balearic and Canary Islands, Portugal and Greece) who were ready to buy up all the released Intasun beds. Striking early, and with the Gulf War still an issue, Airtours obtained good price deals. Within just one week Airtours booked 90,000 new holidays and quickly became the third largest package tour operator. The company had no debt. In 1992 Airtours bought Pickfords, the third largest travel agency in the UK with 333 branches, using its own cash reserves.

In 1993 Airtours narrowly failed to acquire Owners Abroad, then marginally the second largest UK package tour operator ahead of Airtours. Together the two businesses would have been bigger than the existing market leader, Thomson. However Airtours did buy the 214 Hogg Robinson travel agencies to add to Pickfords, giving it Number Two position in this sector of the market – the travel agency sector leader is Thomson subsidiary, Lunn Poly. Pickfords and Hogg Robinson have subsequently been combined and renamed Going Places.

Further acquisitions of small UK tour operators have now given Airtours second position in the package tour market; the company has also expanded in Europe by buying the leisure activities of SAS (Scandinavian Airline Systems). SAS Leisure owns or manages 14 resort hotels and also had a substantial interest in its own charter airline.

Airtours diversified into the cruise business in 1994 when it bought two cruise ships and began to provide its own holidays in the Mediterranean and Canaries. In 1996, Carnival, the leading US cruise company, set out to acquire a 29.6% stake in Airtours, firmly linking the two businesses.

should be available from the new investment, and any costs incurred will be more than offset. Financial synergy might be obtained in the form of greater borrowing capacity or acquired tax credits.

The strategy is regarded as high risk because the new technologies, new skills and new markets involved constitute unknowns and uncertainties. Moreover, because the change is uncertain and challenging, it can be tempting to switch resources and efforts away from existing businesses and areas of strength; and this compounds the element of risk involved.

Conglomerate diversification is often linked to portfolio analysis, and the search for businesses which might remedy any perceived weaknesses. A company with reserves of cash to invest, because it has a number of cash cow businesses, might seek to buy businesses with growth potential in new industries. Some acquisitive and financially oriented companies diversify in this way with a view to rationalizing the businesses they buy. Parts will be retained if they feel they can add value and benefit accordingly; other parts will be divested. Some companies diversify to reduce the likelihood of being acquired themselves by an unwelcome outsider.

Diversification and acquisition strategies and tests to establish whether or not a proposed diversification seems worthwhile will be considered in Chapter 16.

After considering both internal and external growth strategies, in the next section we describe a number of consolidation and reductionist strategies, primarily for companies experiencing difficulties. Quite often the problems arise because previous growth, diversification and acquisition strategies have been either poorly conceived or poorly implemented.

Visit the website:
http://www.
itbp.com

Disinvestment strategies

The term disinvestment strategies is used to represent strategic alternatives where money is not invested for growth purposes. However, the sale of assets or businesses may be involved and money raised from this may well be reinvested to develop or enhance competitive advantage and support those remaining areas of the business which are seen as essential. Where disinvestment strategies are successful, and businesses in difficulty are turned around, money may then be invested for future growth.

In 1990 ACT, UK manufacturers of Apricot computers, were in financial difficulties. The hardware business was sold to Mitsubishi and ACT focused on their remaining core competence: computer services. Some of the money from the sale was used to acquire a financial services software company. Rappaport and Halevi (1991) defend such a strategy, arguing that the best opportunities for adding value in computing in the 1990s lie in applications. Existing technology has created powerful machines whose potential consumers have yet to exploit.

Disinvestment strategies involve consolidation and repositioning strategies as well as the sale or closure of one or more parts of a business. They are applicable in certain circumstances, including

❑ where a firm is overextended in a particular market
❑ where it experiences an economic reversal because of competitor or other pressures
❑ when demand declines
❑ where the opportunity cost of resources being used is such that better returns could be earned elsewhere
❑ when the synergy expected from an acquisition proves elusive.

Case 15.6, which covers the de-merger of Asda and MFI in 1987, is an illustration of the last point. The two organizations merged in 1985 and used potential synergy as a justification. In the event the combined organizations were less successful than they had been individually before the merger. This case also illustrates the search (by Asda) for effective corporate and competitive strategies and links back to the SWOT analysis of Asda in the Interlude on Environmental and Resource Analysis.

Disinvestment can be accomplished through retrenchment, turnaround, divestment or liquidation, and the choice from these particular alternatives

Asda's real growth into one of the UK's largest food retail chains began in the mid-1960s when it first recognized the potential for out-of-town sites with large car parks. Asda are concentrated in the north of England; the head office is in Leeds. By the early 1990s Asda owned some 200 food stores, having acquired 60 supermarkets from Gateway in 1989. Asda's other main retailing activity in the 1980s was carpets and furnishings. Asda had tried unsuccessfully to divest Allied Carpets in the mid-1980s and instead boosted it by buying two-thirds of Waring & Gillow (furniture shops) and forming Allied Maples – again in 1989. Allied Maples was finally sold to Carpetland in 1993. Asda's success has been attributed to low overheads, cost control, high sales per square foot and low cost sites – but it has generally been less profitable than its main rivals, Sainsbury and Tesco.

In 1985, with a welcome bid, Asda acquired MFI, the nationwide retailer of self-assembly furniture. This represented concentric diversification as, although the products were different, the customer base was essentially the same. Synergy was expected between the food superstores and MFI rather than through the furniture links, as both were professional edge-of-town retailers in complementary businesses. Both were innovators and their management teams could learn from each other. There was an additional hidden motive. The Chairman of Asda, Sir Noel Stockdale, was approaching retirement and there was no natural successor. Derek Hunt of MFI was thought to be an ideal replacement. Hunt became Chief Executive of Asda–MFI in 1986, but retained his working base in the south of England where MFI headquarters had been.

The expected benefits and synergy did not accrue. In 1984 the return on net assets of Asda was 43% and of MFI 38%. In the three years that the companies were merged the relevant figures for the group dropped from 40% in 1985 to 27% in 1987.

In 1987 MFI was sold in a management buyout to a consortium led by Derek Hunt, but Asda retained a 25% interest. Since the de-merger MFI has acquired its main supplier of furniture packs,

Hygena, and this backward vertical integration appears to have brought some tangible financial benefits.

However, in the recession at the end of the 1980s/early 1990s MFI traded at a loss. Interest costs arising out of the buy-back and a reputation for poor quality compounded their trading difficulties.

At Asda, John Hardman took over as chairman in 1987, but he resigned in 1991 when Asda also started losing money. The losses continued in 1992. The company was trading profitably but exceptional charges were leading to pre-tax losses. Asda had paid too much for the Gateway sites and still owned 25% of the debt-ridden MFI. The MFI shares have since been sold, but the Gateway stores were valued in the balance sheet at just two-thirds of their acquisition price. Moreover Asda lacked an effective competitive identity and was perceived to be a less successful retailer than its main rivals, who were also proving more successful in obtaining the premium sites for new stores. Asda had centralized its distribution into a limited number of regional warehouses, but had been a follower rather than a leader in this key strategic development. In 1990 Asda formed a joint venture with George Davies (ex-Next) in an attempt to revive its non-food activities with a range of designer clothes.

The new chairman (Patrick Gillam) and youthful chief executive (Archie Norman, 37) embarked on a three-year programme which 'would not produce significant results in the immediate future'. Their aim was to turn back the clock and return to 'meeting the weekly shopping needs of ordinary working people and their families'. Asda sees itself positioned and differentiated as 'the store for ordinary working people who demand value'. The market has been carefully segmented and prices made keener; Asda aims to be some 5–7% below Sainsbury and Tesco to drive higher volumes. Productivity has been improved and service quality stressed; supplier arrangements have been strengthened; and there is an increased emphasis on fresh foods

Continued overleaf

and clothing, where Asda believes it has a relative strength. There are also regional variations in stocking policy. Norman perceived the increasing success of the discount-price food retailers to be a threat as Asda has retained a number of small stores in less affluent areas. Asda decided to convert 65 such stores to a discount format, branded Dales, and offer core food lines only. (This sector is already very competitive.) The remaining 140 stores would remain as multi-product supermarkets, but their layouts have been redesigned. The intention is a 'market hall atmosphere' with fresh food, bakery and butchery departments as well as George clothing areas. By continuing to stock a wide range of non-food items, Asda continues to differ from Sainsbury, Tesco and Safeway.

When Gillam and Norman took over, the *Financial Times* suggested that Asda's institutional investors 'would be persistently whisper-ing thoughts of mortality into the ears of Asda's new emperors'. In the event Asda has been successfully turned around. After exceptional charges the company recorded further pre-tax losses in 1992 and 1994, but it was healthy and profitable in 1995. Debts of £1 billion in 1991 have largely been eradicated and Asda has overtaken Argyll's Safeway to capture third place in the market.

The culture has also changed. Asda now has a huge open-plan head office and managers are asked to wear Asda baseball caps at their desks if they do not want to be disturbed. In its attempt to strengthen its customer focus, Asda has increasingly pushed head office managers out into the stores. Internal communications have been fostered and a 'Tell Archie' [Norman] suggestion scheme has proved particularly successful.

(The actual logic behind the MFI diversification is evaluated in a separate case in Chapter 16.)

determines whether the changes relate to functional, competitive or corporate strategies. Sometimes the term 'turnaround' is used to represent both the retrenchment and the turnaround strategies described in this section; and the expression 'recovery strategies' is also synonymous with both. Where part of a firm is sold to generate funds which can be channelled into areas or business units which are regarded as good future prospects, this too would be categorized as a recovery strategy.

The causes and symptoms of decline, which determine the need for such strategies, were discussed in Chapter 7 and whilst this chapter outlines the alternatives, recovery and divestment strategies are discussed further in Chapter 17.

Retrenchment

Remedial action is required when a company experiences declining profits as a result of economic recession, production inefficiency or competitor innovation. In such circumstances efforts should be concentrated on those activities and areas in which the company has distinctive competence or a superior competitive position. The assumption would be that the firm can survive.

In order to improve efficiency three aspects are involved, either individually or in combination:

❑ **cost reduction** through redundancies, leasing rather than buying new assets, not replacing machinery or reducing expenditure on such things as maintenance or training – the danger lies in cutting spending in areas where competitive advantage might be generated

❏ **asset reduction**, selling anything which is not essential
❏ **revenue generation,** by working on the debtor and stock turnover ratios.

Essentially the aim is to reduce the scale of operations to a position where the company has a solid, consolidated and competitive base. The key issue concerns how much reduction is needed, whether it is minor or drastic, and how quickly the company must act. Where any changes are regarded as temporary, it is important to ensure that there is the necessary flexibility to allow for renewal and growth.

Turnaround strategies

Turnaround strategies involve the adoption of a new strategic position for a product or service, and typically lead on from retrenchment. Resources which are freed up are re-allocated from one strategic thrust to another; particularly significant here is the re-allocation of managerial talent which can lead to an input of fresh ideas. Revenue-generating strategies, such as product modifications, advertising or lower prices designed to generate sales, are often involved; and in addition products and services may well be refocused into the niches which are thought to be most lucrative or defensible.

Retrenchment, cutting back, is relatively easily accomplished as long as managers are willing to take the necessary steps. As suggested above, the three key issues are:

❏ cutting in the 'right' areas and not destroying important competencies
❏ cutting back to a carefully determined core, and then
❏ creating new competitive advantages to build upon this core and generate new growth.

In 1990 Tony O'Reilly, the Irish businessman who is chief executive of Heinz in the USA, formed a group of investors to buy the struggling Waterford Wedgewood crystal and ceramic products group. Three years of further losses preceded three subsequent years of profit as the business was rationalized with the loss of 3000 jobs.

O'Reilly's ambitious target now is to double the size of the business in the next five years. Strategies put forward include:

❏ Expanding core businesses by targeting new markets. Younger buyers, attracted by lower price points, are seen as one possible opportunity, and a new brand, Marquis, has been developed to exploit it.
❏ Diversification into loosely related areas such as linen and leather products to exploit the company's competency in brand management.
❏ Developing the collectability of products such as Coalport figurines. This strategy opens international opportunities in the USA and the Far East.
❏ Increasing product availability, say through more specialist gift boutiques in large stores and mail order.
❏ Infill acquisitions such as the purchase of Stuart Crystal in 1995.

Divestment

Where retrenchment fails, or is not regarded as feasible, a part of the business is likely to be sold. Basically the organization is hoping to create a more effective and profitable portfolio of products and services. The key problem is finding a buyer if the business in question is in difficulties, and particularly a buyer who is willing to pay a premium price for the assets. This can happen where a prospective buyer feels that he or she has the appropriate skills to manage the business more effectively, or where there is potential synergy with the activities already managed by the acquirer. Management buy-outs relate to the first of these issues. Existing managers often feel they could manage their business more profitably if they were freed from any constraints imposed by the parent organization and were completely free to try out their ideas for change.

Divestment, then, is most likely when a company needs to raise money quickly, or when a business is seen as having a poor strategic fit with the rest of the portfolio and, as a result, is holding back the whole organization. Two special cases of divestment are

❏ The successful entrepreneur whose business has grown to a size where he or she has obtained all the benefits they sought and is seeking to sell out.
❏ Divestments of parts of the business following an acquisition. This strategy, usually designed to maximize the value of the business for shareholders, was discussed in Chapter 12.

Where a business is not contributing strategically to a parent organization, but there is no urgent need for cash, it may be floated off as an independent company rather than sold. Existing shareholders are simply given separate shares in the newly formed company, which needs to be strong enough to survive on its own. Organizations adopting this strategy hope to see the market value of their shares improve as the more concentrated business is perceived to be stronger.

Sometimes companies will swap assets with other organizations. In 1992 ICI swapped their fibres operations for the acrylics businesses of Du Pont, the US chemicals company. This is one aspect of ICI's current strategy of specializing in activities where it can achieve a strong global presence, and divesting others. Du Pont benefit by becoming the leading supplier of nylon in Europe, an area they had targeted for expansion; ICI moves from third place to world leadership in acrylics, which are used, for example, in windows and bathroom furniture.

Liquidation

Liquidation involves the sale of a complete business, either as a single going concern or piecemeal to different buyers, or sometimes by auctioning the assets. It is an unpopular choice as it represents an admission of failure by the present management team, but it may well be in the best long-term interests of the stakeholders as a whole.

Strategic means

The level one strategies described earlier in this chapter are most likely to be implemented through the re-investment of past profits, building on existing strengths and capabilities. This is generally known as organic growth, and it does not involve any formal arrangements with other organizations. However, certain forms of joint venture, together with franchise arrangements, can also be useful in bringing about market and product development.

Level two growth strategies, particularly concentric diversification which exploits existing competencies, could also be achieved through organic growth, but for the reasons outlined below, they are more likely to involve acquisition, merger or joint venture. These three strategic means are mentioned briefly in this section and given a more detailed treatment in Chapter 16.

Organic growth

Organic growth is an attractive option in that it can be controlled and the changes need not be sudden or traumatic as is typical of an acquisition or merger. In addition, there is no problem of different organizational cultures which have to be harmonized.

However, if organic growth is used to implement an external growth strategy, it may take considerable time; and whilst it is happening competitors may have more than enough opportunity to prepare their defences and possibly introduce strategies designed to create barriers to entry and thwart the potential success of the proposed changes. If diversification is involved, new skills and capabilities will be required, and these may be difficult to develop to a stage where there is competitive advantage. If existing management resources are allocated to the new development, there is an opportunity cost involved when they are removed from areas in which they are currently contributing. Finally it may be easier to raise money for an acquisition, as it happens more quickly and consequently the money invested starts to earn returns sooner.

Acquisition, merger and joint venture

An acquisition, merger or joint venture is likely to take place when an organization lacks a key success factor for a particular market. Joint ventures and strategic alliances are particularly useful where there are strong reasons against a full merger or acquisition. Joint ventures and strategic alliances can take a number of forms. When a group of oil companies collaborated in the development of the Alaskan pipeline to transport oil from the wells in the north of Alaska to the un-frozen ports in the south, it amounted to joint ownership. The strategy was logical; the pipeline was prohibitively expensive for one company alone, and the appropriate capacity was far in excess of the demand from any single company involved. Agreements could concern collaboration on design or rights to manufacture products designed by other companies. These types of joint venture are particularly popular with companies in different countries. Finally, if a manufacturer acquired a minority shareholding in a supplier, this would also constitute a form of joint venture aimed at achieving the advantages of vertical integration without a full merger and the need to fuse two cultures and sets of skills.

Joint ventures with local companies are essential for strategic development and growth in many Third World countries, who wish to limit foreign ownership, promote domestic employment and obtain some involvement in industries which operate multi-nationally.

Whatever the strategic means selected, there are likely to be problems in bringing together the interests, skills and managers of two companies and cultures. The managerial time required to make it work can compromise the value added and reduce profitability, and divert attention away from other important issues within existing businesses.

Franchising

Franchising again takes many forms, and it provides an opportunity for rapid growth for established businesses and a relatively low risk means of starting a small business. Service businesses are more common than manufacturing in franchising, and as the UK continues to switch from a manufacturing to a service economy they may become increasingly important. Tie Rack is one example of a retail organization which has concentrated on specific market segments and grown rapidly with franchising. Thornton's chocolate shops, Fastframe picture framing, Prontaprint printing and copying shops, Body Shop and the British School of Motoring are other examples. Although McDonald's is franchised throughout the USA, many restaurants in Britain are owned by the company. Kentucky Fried Chicken, Burger King and Spud-U-Like, however, are franchised.

A company which chooses franchising as a means of strategic growth enters into contractual arrangements with a number of small businesses, usually one in each selected geographical area. In return for a lump sum initial investment and on-going royalties the typical franchisor provides exclusive rights to supply a product or service under the franchisor's name in a designated area, know-how, equipment, materials, training, advice, and national support advertising. This allows the business in question to grow rapidly in a number of locations without the investment capital which would be required to fund organic growth of the same magnitude. Another advantage for the franchisor is the alleviation of some of the need for the development of the managers, skills and capabilities required to control a large, growing and dispersed organization. Instead efforts can be concentrated on expanding market share. It is essential, though, to establish effective monitoring and control systems to ensure that franchisees are providing the necessary level of quality and service.

The small business franchisee needs sufficient capital to buy into the franchise, but the risk is less than most independent starts because the business is already established. As a result a number of small independent businesses operate as part of a chain and can compete against larger organizations.

Licensing

Licensing is an arrangement whereby a company is allowed to manufacture a product or service which has been designed by someone else and is protected by a patent. Companies in different countries are often involved. Pilkington, for example, patented float glass and then licensed its production throughout the world. Pilkington earned money from the arrangements and established world leadership; they would not have been able to afford to establish production plants around the world. In contrast Mary Quant, designer of cosmetics, tights, footwear, beds and bed linen, has never manufactured the products she designs. They are all licensed; and some are marketed under the Quant name and some under the manufacturer's name (Myers beds and Dorma bed linen). One argument in favour of this arrangement has been that production and labour relations problems are avoided, enabling the business to concentrate on the areas in which it has expertise and competitive advantage.

International strategies

Internal growth, external growth and disinvestment strategies may all involve an international dimension with special complexities. Countries differ economically (variable growth rates), culturally (behaviours, tastes and preferences) and politically. National politics can dictate the appropriate strategy – some markets cannot be penetrated effectively without joint ventures with local companies.

Internal growth might involve exporting to new markets overseas and the development of special varieties of a product or service in order to target it to the specific needs and requirements of overseas customers. External growth can range from the creation of distribution or assembly bases abroad, to joint ventures and licensing agreements with foreign companies, to the establishment of a comprehensive multi-national organization.

Kay (1990) recommends that organizations should seek to determine the smallest area within which they can be a viable competitor. Whilst a retail newsagent can still succeed by concentrating on a local catchment area, most car manufacturers, in common with many other industries, now see their relevant market as a global one. The short cases on Tube Investments (Case 15.3) and Grand Metropolitan (Case 15.8 later in this chapter) and the full case on Thorn-EMI are illustrative of companies which have chosen to concentrate on products or services where they can be an internationally strong competitor. Such companies are hoping to create synergy by specializing in core skills and competencies and exploiting these as widely as possible.

Organizations which develop their corporate strategy internationally have to consider in particular:

- ❑ marketing and financial strategies
- ❑ the structure of the organization
- ❑ cultural and people issues.

Marketing

The question of how global products and services can be made, and the extent to which they have to be tailored to appeal to different markets, was introduced in Chapter 10. Markets vary from those termed multi-domestic (where the competitive dynamics of each separate country market are distinctive and idiosyncratic) to global (where competitive strategies are transferable across frontiers). Coca-Cola, Levi jeans and the expensive perfumes and leather goods marketed by LVMH, Moët Hennessy Louis Vuitton, do attract a global consumer with identical tastes, but they are more exceptional than normal. The challenge to design the 'world car', for example, remains unresolved. Honda initially hoped to achieve this when it began redesigning its Accord range in the mid-1980s, but concluded that international performance expectations, and in turn components, are irreconcilable. In Japan the Accord is seen as a status symbol car for congested roads where driving is restricted; in the USA it is a workaday vehicle for travelling long distances on open highways.

Clearly different competitors in the same industry adopt a variety of competitive strategies. Some owners of premium and speciality beer and lager brands elect to control the brewing of their product and rely on local, individual country brewers for distribution; others license the actual brewing to these national companies. Grolsch, recognizable by its distinctive bottles with metal

Visit the website:
http://www.
itbp.com

frame tops, is brewed and bottled in Holland and exported. Most UK premium beers which succeed in the USA are similarly exported to that country. Guinness is brewed in Dublin and exported for bottling in the USA, whilst Fosters and Budweiser are both brewed under license in the UK.

There is a follow-up issue concerning the appropriate range of products or services. The following framework could be a useful starting point for analysing both opportunities and competitor strategies:

	Product/service range	**Geographic scope**
1	Narrow	National
2	Broad	National
3	Narrow	Global
4	Broad	Global

Where organizations find it necessary to be located close to customers in order to provide the delivery and other services demanded, this can be achieved with strategic stockholding rather than manufacturing.

Finance

The management of currency transfers and exchange rates adds complexity. Floating exchange rates imply uncertainty, although companies can, and do, reduce their risk by buying ahead. The European Exchange Rate Mechanism is designed to minimize currency fluctuations, but economic pressures may still cause periodic devaluations. Predictable or fixed rates benefit, for example, a car manufacturer which produces engines and transmission systems in one country, transfers them to assembly plants in a second and third country, each specializing in different cars, and then finally sells them throughout Europe. Costs and estimated profits must be based on predicted currency movements, and any incorrect forecasting could result in either extra or lost profits.

Where such an organization structure is created, transfer pricing arrangements are required. If managers of the various divisions or business units are motivated or measured by their profitability figures there will be some disagreement about transfer prices which affect their value added figures. Equally the organization may be seeking to manage transfer arrangements for tax purposes, seeking to show most profit where taxes are lowest.

Companies with a main base in a country whose currency is strong and appreciating may find their international competitiveness weakened. Exported products will become relatively expensive, competing imports cheaper. Such companies may be tempted to invest and relocate elsewhere. In 1995, for example, Toyota, which already had a number of manufacturing plants around the world, began to seriously consider closing down plants in Japan

Globalization is now no longer an objective, but an imperative, as markets open and geographic barriers become increasingly blurred and even irrelevant. Corporate alliances, whether joint ventures or acquisitions, will increasingly be driven by competitive pressures and strategies rather than financial structuring.

John F Welch Jr, Chief Executive Officer, General Electric (US),
quoted in Fortune, *26 March 1990, p. 34*

because of the high yen. Companies must also see financial markets as global, seeking to borrow where loans are cheapest – as long as the source is not too risky.

Whilst both governments and companies would ideally like a strong local currency and to be able to export at high prices to earn substantial wealth internationally, this may not be practical. It certainly requires high added value and very clear differentiation.

Structure, culture and people

The two key questions are:

❑ where to make the various products and services to obtain the necessary people and other resources required, to be as close as appropriate to each defined geographic market, and to manage costs efficiently; and
❑ how best to structure the organization in order to control it effectively, but, at the same time, ensure it is sufficiently responsive to changing environments. The speed and nature of change pressures may be uneven. IT increasingly offers opportunities for more effective control of globally dispersed businesses.

The alternatives are:

❑ A globally centralized organization, remote from markets, and relying on exporting. This is likely to prove cost-efficient but possibly out-of-touch.
❑ Manufacturing plants located close to markets in order to satisfy local needs and preferences. This structure, known as both international and multi-domestic, could still be controlled centrally, or substantially decentralized into fully autonomous units, in which case the plants may be independent or co-operate in some way. This is a more expensive structure, but one which can offer higher levels of service. Unilever, which relies on localized manufacturing and marketing, is an example. Whilst cement is an international commodity product, companies are structured in this way because there is no benefit to be gained from transporting cement across frontiers.
❑ Centralized manufacture of key components, possibly in a low-wage country, with final assembly or finishing nearer to markets. Caterpillar Tractor utilize this strategy.
❑ An integrated global structure with production locations chosen on resource or cost grounds. Finished goods will be transported to markets. In this structure the organization will have an international presence, but in say Country X its sales could consist mainly of products imported from other locations, whilst most of Country X's production is exported. Marketing, production *control*, purchasing and research and development will all be co-ordinated globally if they are not centralized.

Centres of excellence may be established where cultural values and behaviours are most appropriate. Philips concentrate technology development in the Far East, where a long-term perspective is natural; IBM have established R & D facilities in Italy, which they regard as suitably intuitive and innovative. However, if national preferences and requirements are markedly different, there is an argument in favour of establishing dedicated R & D facilities in several countries. ICI has a technical centre in Japan for developing special chemicals and materials in collaboration with the major car and electronics manufacturers. The intention is to sell their products to Japanese plants throughout the world. 'Japanese companies prefer to collaborate with chemicals suppliers which have scientists and engineers in Japan, and a factory to produce material locally.' General Motors has strengthened its Opel technical development centre in Frankfurt to spearhead its expansion in all international markets outside the USA. Eastern Europe and the Pacific Rim are targets for growth in respect of both production and sales. Meanwhile Ford is trying to integrate product development globally in its search for a range of world cars.

This alternative has many strategic advantages, but it can be complex to control and costly in overheads. Typical companies are Sony and Coca-Cola (Case 9.1). Coca-Cola, based in Atlanta, commands 45% of the world's soft drinks market and 40% of the US domestic market. The key success factor is obtaining distribution and access to markets, and because Coca-Cola is mostly water this is decentralized. Branding and marketing is global and centralized. The strategy is to sell concentrate or syrup to local bottlers, be they independent businesses or joint venture partners. Pricing is based on what can be afforded locally, and a variety of support mechanisms are offered. Coke is frequently promoted with local endorsements, but marketing and advertising also features sponsorship of international sporting events. The evolving international strategy of Matsushita is described in Case 15.7.

The international location decision is affected by a number of key issues, including:

❏ The existence of any national resources which influence competitive advantage in any significant way. Nike and Reebok have built factories in China, Thailand and the Philippines for labour cost savings. A number of leading computer and semi-conductor businesses are located in California's silicon valley because of the pool of skilled labour and acquired expertise to support research and development. Consumer electronics and pharmaceuticals are further examples of industries where the headquarters of the leading companies are concentrated in one or a few countries.
❏ Scale economies from key resources in, say, production or technology. Toyota, Honda and Nissan preferred to produce in Japan and export for many years, but the strong yen eventually encouraged them to locate abroad.
❏ Transport considerations.
❏ The availability of a suitable supply chain.
❏ Political issues.

Whatever the structural format a truly international business must develop a global mission and core values (such as consistent quality world-wide), and achieve integration through effective communications. The corporate strategy must be centralized even if the company has a number of independent subsidiaries and operates in several multi-domestic markets. However, the organization must be able to embrace the different national cultural traits and behaviours, and this presents an important managerial challenge. Decisions have to be made concerning the balance of local managers and mobile 'international' managers who are easily transferable between divisions and countries.

Bartlett and Ghoshal (1989) summarize the above points as three potentially conflicting issues which must be reconciled. These are:

❏ the need for efficiency through global centralization

Matsushita, whose brands include Panasonic, National and Technics, is the world's largest consumer electronics company. JVC is a subsidiary business. The product range includes video and audio products, electronic components, batteries, home appliances and kitchen equipment.

In the early 1990s Matsushita operated 150 plants in 38 countries including Brazil, the USA, Austria, Tanzania, Malaysia and China. 'The sun never sets on its holdings.' Products are moved widely across frontiers, some even back to Japan, but 70% of Matsushita's employees still work in Japan.

Matsushita has become international for a variety of reasons, not least the strength of the yen, but its growth overseas has been measured and careful.

Initially a plant would be opened in a country to manufacture specifically for that market. The next stage during the 1980s was to move these plants away from merely replicating products designed and manufactured in Japan to the production of variants which had been adapted for local markets. Exporting from these overseas plants then followed. One example here was microwave ovens. European customers like their ovens to finish meat in different ways; the UK, for example, has a preference for crispy fat and consequently needs microwaves with extra strong heating elements. 'It is difficult for product engineers in Japan to understand all the differences and to respond accordingly.'

A further stage involved 'export centres' where all the design and development of a range of products is now based outside Japan, often using lower cost labour. Malaysia now produces 25% of all Matsushita's televisions, and 90% of that country's production is exported, mostly to other countries in South-east Asia and the Middle East. It is argued that Malaysian television plants outperform those back in Japan in terms of both quality and efficiency.

Matsushita remains strongly centralized. Subsidiaries cannot deposit or borrow money locally; all financial transactions are handled through a central treasury in Japan. One reason for the caution has been the difficulty of transferring important Japanese values to certain other countries. China is said to be relatively poor on punctuality; the Chinese are not natural team-workers and do not share their knowledge readily. Matsushita's US employees have very high technical skills, higher than their colleagues in Japan, but they are apparently less willing to take responsibility for changing things and to tinker with manufacturing processes.

Nevertheless, there have been problems and relative failures. Following the lead of Sony, which bought Columbia Pictures and CBS Records, Matsushita acquired MCA film studios and music interests. The deal did not prove successful because of the cultural differences and the real difficulty of trying to manage a business such as this, focused in Hollywood, from a base in Japan. MCA managers were refused investment money to buy either Virgin Records or a stake in NBC Television. The subsidiary was eventually sold to Seagram. Sony too experienced problems with this type of diversification but was willing to decentralize more power and responsibility to local managers.

Schlender (1994) offers six lessons from the international approach and experience of Matsushita:

- ❑ be a good corporate citizen in every country; respect local cultures, customs and languages
- ❑ export your best manufacturing technology to overseas subsidiaries, not second-hand equipment
- ❑ minimize the number of expatriate managers and groom local talent to take over
- ❑ allow plants to establish their own rules and procedures, fine tuning the manufacturing processes to match the skills of the local work-force
- ❑ invest in local R & D facilities to tailor products to markets
- ❑ encourage competition between those plants located overseas and those back home.

Reference: Schlender, BR (1994) Matsushita shows how to go global, *Fortune*, 11 July.

❏ the need to respond locally through decentralization

❏ the need to innovate and transfer learning internationally.

More recently Bartlett and Ghoshal (1992) have concluded:

❏ There can be no such thing as a 'universal international manager'. Large global companies will need functional specialists (such as production experts) and national managers (committed to one country and most familiar with that culture) as well as those executives who are able to switch readily between divisions and countries. International managers are responsible for corporate and competitive strategies within the organization, whilst national managers ensure that the needs of local customers, host governments and employees are satisfied effectively. The organizational challenge in respect of functional managers is to ensure that best practices are learned and spread throughout the organization.

❏ The attempts to integrate all the global operations (products, plants and countries) should be concentrated towards the top of the organizational hierarchy. At lower levels managers should have clear, single-line, responsibilities and reporting relationships. (This structural issue is discussed further in Chapter 19.).

One benefit of adopting these recommendations is a limited requirement for international managers, who, inevitably, are in short supply because of the qualities they are required to have. Some industrialists would argue that this supply constraint is the deciding force, and that a successful global matrix structure would be preferable. One such structure is described in a later case on ABB, Asea Brown Boveri. ABB's managers are encouraged to 'think globally but act locally'. Their key measure is profitability and this can be enhanced if managers respond effectively to local employee and customer needs, seeking to satisfy different aspirations and requirements, whilst thinking globally about, say, sourcing and supply flexibility to take advantage of price and currency opportunities.

Visit the website: http://www.itbp.com

Contrasting views on international strategy

We saw in Key Reading 9.1 that Porter (1990) believes global strategies essentially supplement the competitive advantage created in the home market. Firms must retain their national strengths when they cross over borders. Ohmae (1990) disagrees and argues that global firms should shake off their origins. Managers must take on an international perspective, avoiding the near-sightedness which often characterizes companies with centralized and powerful global headquarters. Markets, he says, are driven by the needs and desires of customers around the world, and managers must act as if they are equidistant from all these customers, wherever they might be located.

Ohmae is perhaps presenting a futuristic vision of how he believes things will be as global forces strengthen. At the moment, whilst world leaders like IBM, Sony and Nestlé, are spread around the world, and substantially dependent on non-domestic customers, their underlying cultures and competitiveness remain rooted in the USA, Japan and Switzerland, respectively.

Chandler (1990) stresses the continuing importance of economies of scale (cost advantages with large scale production) and economies of scope (the use of common materials and processes to make a variety of different products

In the industries that have changed the world, from fertilizers to machinery to computers, the firms that make the big capital investment early are the ones that survive. The cost advantages are tremendous for those who have scope and scale – the ability to make many products out of the same set of materials. If we continue to do what we did in the 1980s – look to make money on the deal and sacrifice long-term investment for dividends or interest – then the people who buy our companies will be foreigners ... You have to create a world-wide organization to compete, or you will be bought by someone.

Alfred D Chandler, Harvard Business School,
quoted in Fortune, *26 March 1990, p. 83*

profitably). This implies carefully targeted investment in large-scale operations and a search for international marketing opportunities.

The selection of a strategy

The issue of what constitutes a good strategic choice is the subject of Chapter 18, but it is important here to emphasize that the strategic choices described above may not be real options for an organization at any given time. Theoretically they may exist as alternatives; realistically they could not be implemented. Equally, certain alternatives may be forced on organizations.

Whilst internal or external growth strategies might be preferred to fulfil objectives and fill the planning gap, disinvestment strategies may be required because of competitor or other environmental pressures. Strategies are only feasible if they can be implemented; a desire to grow through horizontal or vertical integration, concentric or conglomerate diversification, may require a suitable acquisition to be available at a price the company can afford to pay. An inability to raise money for any reason can act as a constraint on a particular choice. If management skills are not available to manage a merger or acquisition it may prove sensible to avoid or delay such a choice, however desirable it might be. Penrose's (1959) argument that growth is limited by the organization's spare resources, particularly management, was discussed in Chapter 5. The ability to succeed with product or market development will be dependent on the firm's relative strength and power in relation to competition; there may be competitive barriers to successful implementation.

Whichever strategy is selected issues of competitive advantage and implementation become paramount. Chances of success increase if there is an opportunity to create and sustain competitive advantage.

The influence and preference of the strategic leader will be a major determinant of the strategy selected. The strategic leader will also build the organization structure, and ideally the strategy and structure will mould together to generate synergy from the various activities. This in turn will depend upon the organization culture. Hence there is a relationship between strategy, structure, leadership and culture. When there is a change of leadership there may well be a change of strategy and in turn of structure and culture; when strategies fail to meet up to expectations, there may be a change of leadership. Case 15.8, Grand Metropolitan, is an example of a company whose corporate strategies have undergone major changes of direction and focus. The developments can be linked to changes in strategic leadership.

Case 15.8
GRAND METROPOLITAN

By the early 1990s Grand Metropolitan (GM) had become the world's leading manufacturer and distributor of spirits, through its IDV subsidiary, and an important manufacturer of foods, particularly in the USA. GM own Pillsbury, the Jolly Green Giant foods company. The strategic perspective had changed dramatically in 25 years, influenced markedly by three strategic leaders. The changes are illustrated in Figure 15.4.

In the early 1960s, led by Sir Maxwell Joseph, GM, then known as Grand Metropolitan Hotels, was a leading hotel company and specialized. Through a series of acquisitions GM diversified into restaurants (Chef and Brewer, 1966 and Berni Inns, 1970), dairies and supermarkets (Express Dairies, including Eden Vale and Ski products, 1969), leisure activities (Mecca, 1970), brewing (Truman Hanbury Buxton, 1971 and

Watney Mann, 1972) and spirits (IDV, 1973). Additional hotel chains were also acquired. This external growth activity slowed down in the 1970s because GM had become highly geared and was affected by the international oil crisis and high interest rates. When Joseph retired in 1980 three strategic problems could be identified:

❑ GM was over-reliant on the UK (90% of turnover)
❑ IDV was inadequately represented in the USA, a key market for spirits
❑ many hotels needed upgrading if they were to capitalize upon the increase in tourism, especially from the USA.

The new chief executive, Stanley Grinstead, sought mainly to consolidate and build, concentrating on the USA. GM acquired its US spirits

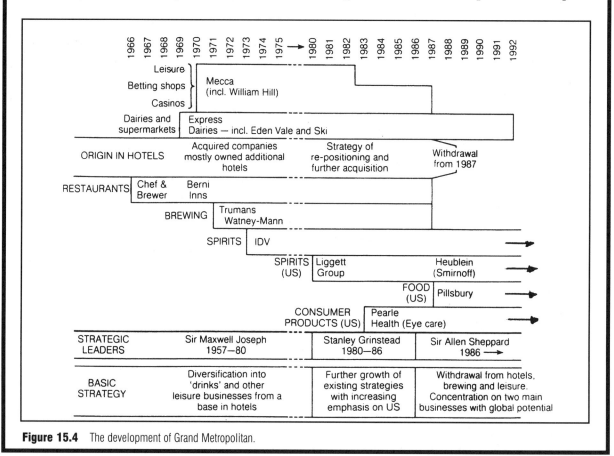

Figure 15.4 The development of Grand Metropolitan.

distributor, Liggett and Myers, in 1980. Liggett also manufactured cigarettes but the tobacco interests were quickly sold off. GM bought Inter-Continental hotels from Pan American and adopted a strategy of repositioning its hotels. Lower grade properties were divested. GM concentrated on exploiting its major brand names and also bought Pearle Health Products in the USA. By the mid-1980s hotels contributed 19% of turnover and 6% of profits. The breweries were suffering as lager became more popular at the expense of bitter beers.

Sir Allen Sheppard, who took over in 1986, chose to focus on those businesses where GM could obtain world market strength and divest everything else. The major acquisitions were Heublein (1987), owners of Smirnoff Vodka, the world's second largest spirits brand, Pillsbury, whose main brands are Green Giant, Burger King and Häagen Dazs ice cream, and Pet, which includes Old El Paso Foods (US) and Shippam pastes in the UK. Mexican food is an important growth sector in the USA. After divestments over half GM's revenue is now earned in the USA.

IDV boasts over ten of the leading spirits in the world and has approximately 10% of the world market. The brands include Smirnoff and Popov vodka, J&B whisky, Gilbey's Gin, Malibu, Croft and Bailey's Irish Cream, the result of a joint venture with Express Dairies. IDV also distributes wines, owning Piat d'Or, and retails wines and spirits through its Peter Dominic stores.

GM's structure is decentralized and it is traditional that managers are seen as transferable between companies in the group. Their success has always relied upon synergy and the sharing of skills and expertise. The true synergy potential of food and drinks remains debatable – whilst food is essentially a necessity, drinks are more aspirational – but both businesses feature strong, international brands. GM has developed competencies in people, management and control systems, and operational effectiveness, and uses these to add value to its businesses. Whilst the strategy has changed dramatically the structure and culture has been more consistent.

Sir Allen Sheppard retired as chief executive in 1996 and was replaced by George Bull, an internal promotion.

Summary

In this chapter we have outlined the strategic alternatives which firms select to meet objectives and constraints, and the means by which they might be implemented. It has been mentioned that at any particular time all the options will not be realistically available to an organization. A firm in real difficulties is less likely to be considering major growth options than disinvestment strategies, for example. It has also been shown how individual strategies can be combined, and how strategies are changed over time and with changes of strategic leadership.

Specifically we have:

- described briefly the no change, internal growth, external growth, disinvestment and combination strategies
- considered some of the special problems involved when the strategic change has an international dimension
- discussed how organic growth, acquisition, merger, joint venture, franchising and licensing can be used to implement the strategy
- emphasized the linkage between strategy, strategic leadership, structure and culture.

Checklist of key terms and concepts

You should refer back to Figures 15.1 and 15.2 and ensure that you understand conceptually all the strategic alternatives incorporated in the diagram.

References

Bartlett, C and Ghoshal, S (1989) *Managing Across Borders: The Transnational Solution*, Harvard Business School Press.

Bartlett, C and Ghoshal, S (1992) What is a global manager? *Harvard Business Review*, September–October.

Chandler, AD (1990) The enduring logic of industrial success, *Harvard Business Review*, March–April.

Kay, JA (1990) Identifying the strategic market, *Business Strategy Review*, Spring.

Ohmae, K (1990) *The Borderless World*, Harper.

Penrose, E (1959) *The Theory of the Growth of the Firm*, Blackwell.

Peters, TJ and Waterman, RH Jr (1982) *In Search of Excellence: Lessons from America's Best Run Companies*, Harper & Row.

Porter, ME (1990) *The Competitive Advantage of Nations*, Free Press.

Rappaport, AS and Halevi, S (1991) The computerless computer company, *Harvard Business Review*, July–August.

Questions and research assignments

Text related

1 For each of the following strategic alternatives, list why you think an organization might select this particular strategy, what they would expect to gain, and where the problems and limitations are. If you can, think of an example of each one from your own experience:
   - ❏ do nothing; no change
   - ❏ concentration
   - ❏ market development
   - ❏ product development
   - ❏ innovation
   - ❏ horizontal integration
   - ❏ vertical integration
   - ❏ concentric diversification
   - ❏ conglomerate diversification
   - ❏ retrenchment
   - ❏ turnaround
   - ❏ divestment
   - ❏ liquidation.

2 What are the relative advantages and disadvantages of organic growth as opposed to external growth strategies?

Library based

3 When MFI was bought back from Asda in 1987, considerable loan funding was involved. In the 1988–1989 financial year operating profits were £92 million but net interest payments took £50 million of this. During 1989 consumer spending on the types of products that MFI sells fell. Moreover, interest rates had risen.

   As far as MFI are concerned, do you feel the merger with Asda was a strategic error?

   Having up-dated the situation, describe what strategic decisions have been taken by MFI to counter their decreasing profits.

4 Trace the success of Tube Investments since the acquisition of Dowty? What impact has it had on TI as an aeroplane components supplier? Given the restructuring which has been taking place in this industry how significant do you believe the outcome was?

5 (a) What are the essential differences between an export, an international and a global organization?

   (b) What might be the most appropriate strategy for a sizeable UK-based company with international ambitions in the following industries? (assume your choice could be implemented)
   - steel
   - pharmaceuticals
   - civil aircraft
   - ladies' cosmetics.

6 For an organization of your choice, trace the changes of strategy and strategic direction over a period of time. Relate these changes to any changes of strategic leadership, structure and, wherever possible, culture.

7 Sony is renowned as an innovative company within the consumer electronics industry, and its success has depended substantially on televisions, videos and hi-fi equipment. In recent years Sony has followed a strategy of globalization and diversification – arguably in related product areas. The international strategy has been called global localization; Sony aims to be a global company presented locally, and this involves devolving authority away from Tokyo and expanding manufacturing and R & D around the world.

   How does Sony achieve this?

16

Issues in Strategic Growth

In this chapter we explore selected growth strategies: diversification, acquisition and joint ventures. The justifications for pursuing them are considered, together with research evidence about their relative success. In addition there is a section on effective acquisition strategies.

Learning objectives

After studying this chapter you should be able to:

- ■ identify the typical growth patterns of large companies
- ■ discuss the extent of diversification in the UK in relation to other countries
- ■ list why organizations might seek to diversify, often by acquisition
- ■ discuss the risk involved in this strategic alternative
- ■ explain why acquisitions often fail to bring the desired level of benefits
- ■ summarize the stages involved in designing an effective acquisition strategy
- ■ describe forms and examples of joint ventures and strategic alliances.

Introduction

Don't forget to visit the website: http://www. itbp.com

In this chapter we look at selected aspects of growth strategies, namely diversification, mergers and acquisitions, strategic alliances (agreements between two or more companies) and joint ventures (alliances involving minority ownerships or the establishment of a new, jointly owned company). The advantages and potential drawbacks of external growth strategies are compared with internal (or organic) growth in Table 16.1.

We have already established that one of the highest risk strategies is diversification through acquisition. Companies who wish to avoid this level of risk can consider alternatives. One possibility is to stay relatively focused rather than to diversify, although as we shall see this can leave an organization vulnerable; another option is diversification through organic growth, accepting that whilst this may seem safer it may be too slow to implement. A final alternative is to look for a suitable alliance partner, where the competencies of the two organizations can be combined for mutual benefit.

Figure 16.1 demonstrates that the growth challenge is to find opportunities for developing and deploying technologies, processes and competencies in ways which generate a more effective and beneficial match between the organization's products and services and its customers and markets. Some of the key themes are:

- ❏ the potential for synergy from internal and external linkages and alliances
- ❏ the diversification/focus dilemma

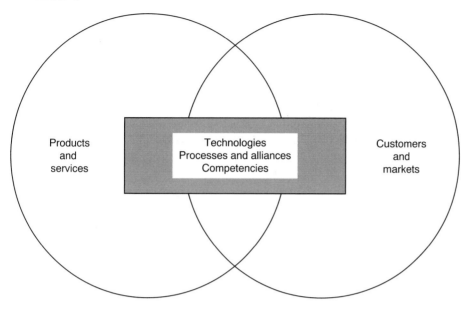

Figure 16.1 The growth challenge.

❏ opportunities for, and abilities in, transferring skills and competencies
❏ opportunities to benefit from the exploitation of a successful corporate brand name.

External growth strategies continue to be popular alternatives for many companies, particularly larger ones, but research suggests they often fail to meet expectations. Growth strategies need careful, thorough and objective analysis before they are pursued, and care and attention in implementation.

	Advantages	Possible drawbacks	
Organic growth	❏ Lower risk ❏ Allows for on-going learning ❏ More control	❏ Slow ❏ Lack of early knowledge – may be misjudgements	**Table 16.1** Alternative growth strategies
Acquisition	❏ Fast ❏ Buys presence, market share and expertise	❏ Premium price may have to be paid ❏ High risk if any misjudgement ❏ Preferred organization may not be available ❏ May be difficult to sell unwanted assets	
Strategic alliance	❏ Cheaper than takeover ❏ Access to market knowledge ❏ Useful if acquisition impractical	❏ Possible lack of control ❏ Potential managerial differences and problems	
Joint venture	As for strategic alliance plus ❏ greater incentive and closer contact ❏ can lock out other competitors better	As for strategic alliance	

Most diversification by UK companies since the 1960s has been through acquisition and merger rather than the internal creation of new activity. A merger of two organizations will always be agreed mutually, and in some cases acquisition of one firm by another is friendly and agreed. In other cases proposed acquisitions are opposed and fought bitterly by managers in the threatened firm who try to persuade their shareholders that the company would be better off remaining under their control. These are typically known as takeovers, and when the bid succeeds a premium price is often paid. Although not all acquisitions are aimed at bringing about diversification, the majority appear to represent some form of diversification.

However, many acquisitions and mergers lead to disappointing results – profitability is reduced; synergy does not emerge. It is difficult to predict success or failure in advance, as issues of both strategy creation and implementation are involved. Changes in corporate strategy are generally more unpredictable and risky than those which concentrate on improving competitive and functional strategies. However, growth opportunities for the present products and markets may be limited and insufficient to fill the planning gap. Few products and ideas cannot be copied and so a company must build and retain a superior competitive position. Experience, applied properly, is of great importance in this. Nevertheless, well-executed acquisitions and diversifications can be sound and very good strategic moves.

We shall explore diversification and acquisition strategies by UK companies, and consider the major reasons why a number are regarded as failures. In addition we shall consider how to manage these strategies effectively. At the end of the chapter joint ventures and strategic alliances, again strategies which are increasing in popularity but sometimes characterized by disappointing results, are evaluated.

Implementation is the subject of Chapters 19–22. However creative and imaginative strategies may be, they can only be regarded as effective if they can be implemented successfully.

Diversification and acquisition by UK companies

The increasing tendency to diversify

Channon (1983) has analysed the extent to which the largest firms in the UK have become increasingly diversified since 1950. He used the *Times* Top 200 companies as his database and categorized them as follows:

❑ *Single product companies*. Not less than 95% of sales derived from one basic business.
❑ *Dominant product companies*. More than 70%, but less than 95%, of sales from one major business.
❑ *Related product companies*. Companies whose sales are distributed amongst a series of **related** businesses, where no single business accounts for 70% of sales. This would include companies who had pursued strategies of vertical or horizontal integration or concentric diversification.
❑ *Conglomerate/unrelated product companies*. Companies whose sales are distributed amongst a series of **unrelated** businesses, again where no single business accounts for 70% of sales.

Channon contends that typically a company will start life as a single product enterprise and then graduate through the dominant product stage to become a related business, before finally emerging into a conglomerate. However, he emphasizes that companies do not have to follow this particular growth pattern. Some will miss one or more of the natural stages; others will choose to stay in one form and not change.

Table 16.2 illustrates the changes in the structure of the largest UK enterprises between 1950 and 1980, and compares the structural patterns with those of the largest 500 US companies in 1970 and 1980. Utilizing data from Dyas and Thanheiser (1976) some comparisons with French and German companies in 1970 are also provided.

In 1950 only 25% of the top 200 companies in the UK had become diversified to the related or unrelated stage, and of these only 5% were classified as conglomerates. By 1980 the respective percentages had increased steadily to 65 and 17% respectively. This compares with percentages of 78% and 24% for the largest 500 companies in the USA. Over the same period the number of concentrated single product companies had declined from 35 to 8%.

In contrast with 1970 UK figures of 60% (related and unrelated) and 11% (conglomerate/unrelated) the respective figures for France were 52 and 10%, and for Germany 56 and 18%.

During the late 1980s and early 1990s **conglomerate** diversification has decreased in popularity, and instead companies have sought to grow in related areas where skills and competencies are more clearly transferable. Acquirers now typically seek to avoid diversifications that are unrelated to their basic businesses on more than one of the following dimensions: geography, technology, type of product/market or service/market, and the style of corporate parenting required (i.e. cultural and leadership issues).

As markets and industries become increasingly global a certain minimum size and market share is often thought to be necessary for competitive viability. This is known as **critical mass** and it is one explanation for the growing incidence of mergers and alliances between related and competing organizations. Critical mass is important to ensure that

❏ there is sufficient investment in R & D to keep pace with the market leader

	United Kingdom percentage of top 200 companies				International comparisons			
					France, percentage of top 100	Germany, percentage of top 100	USA, percentage of top 500	
	1950	1960	1970	1980	1970	1970	1970	1980
Single	35	20	11	8	16	22	10	0
Dominant	40	43	29	27	32	22	41	22
Related	20	28	49	48	42	38	36	54
Conglomerate/ unrelated	5	9	11	17	10	18	13	24

Table 16.2
Diversification by UK and international companies

Sources: Channon, DF (1983) *Strategy and Structure in British Industry*, Macmillan; Dyas, GP and Thanheiser, HT (1976) *The Emerging European Enterprise: Strategy and Structure in French and German Industry*, Macmillan.

❑ the important cost benefits of the experience curve can be achieved
❑ marketing activities achieve visibility and a competitive presence. This might require a wide product range and good coverage globally.

Lloyds Bank has acquired fellow organizations TSB and the Cheltenham and Gloucester (C & G) Building Society to give it the most comprehensive geographic coverage in UK financial services; critical mass and cost-reduction opportunities were used to justify the acquisitions. The new company is one of the top three in all the financial services sectors it targets. Mortgages are now marketed through C & G; Lloyds was already strong in this segment. Lloyds is also a key player in the small business lending market and TSB is very popular with savers. TSB included an important insurance underwriting business to merge with Lloyds Abbey Life.

Two additional examples from the USA are, first, the merger in 1994 of defence contractors Lockheed and Martin Marietta to hedge against the world-wide recession in the defence industry. Combined they are the world's largest contractor in an over-supplied industry where costs and prices have become critical. In the same year the cable television company Viacom acquired Block-buster Video (distribution business) and Paramount (film studios) to establish a major new communications corporation.

Much of the growth and diversification by UK companies has been brought about by merger and acquisition. Some of this has been outside the UK, mostly in the USA. Statistics from JP Mervis, London-based corporate finance advisers, suggest that, of acquisitions by UK companies in Europe and the USA in the late 1980s, over 90% of the spending was in the USA. Acquisitions involved some well-known companies and brand names. Grand Metropolitan, the leisure and hotels group, took over Pillsbury (the Jolly Green Giant foods group) after an acrimonious battle; and Marks and Spencer bought Brooks Brothers, an up-market menswear retailer. Marks and Spencer have experienced implementation difficulties with this acquisition.

In the 1990s links with European companies have inevitably grown in popularity. Because of both competitive requirements and regulatory and cultural issues it seems likely that many of these links will be between existing competitors and take the form of joint ventures and strategic alliances rather than mergers or acquisitions. On occasions there will be clear arguments in favour of linking two organizations, but pressure from shareholders, managers or governments may mean acquisition is not feasible.

The diversification/focus debate

Although their popularity has waned in the 1990s, research evidence confirms that **_successful_** diversified conglomerates can be very profitable. Hanson and

---

Identify the strengths of your business and build on them. Do not diversify into unrelated areas. Find out what your managers can do and let them have a go.

It is a common fault of British companies to spend large amounts of money acquiring other companies, and remove from the budget those activities that increase costs and overheads in the short term, but which would build the existing business. Always find money to invest in the future by building on strengths.

Leslie Hill, Chairman and Chief Executive, Central Independent Television plc

BTR (whose portfolios are discussed in greater detail in Chapter 20) have been notable examples. They succeeded because they:

❑ carefully targeted their acquisitions
❑ avoided paying too much (normally)
❑ adopted an appropriately decentralized structure and control systems; and
❑ corporately added value.

Implementation is critical. Normally conglomerates will be structured as holding companies with very slim head offices; individual businesses will enjoy considerable autonomy; and tight financial control systems will prevail. Financial improvements take precedence over a search for skills transfer and synergies. Businesses are acquired (and divested) more on the logic of their financial contribution than arguments concerning strategic fit.

Head office capabilities and contributions for adding value typically include low cost financing for the subsidiaries and skills in trading assets and improving operating efficiencies. In simple terms, these organizations have developed a strategic expertise in running a diversified conglomerate, skills not matched by many organizations which choose this strategic alternative. The issues are also explored further when we discuss the control aspects of implementation in Chapter 20.

Goold *et al.* (1994) use the term ***heartland*** to describe a range of business activities to which a corporation can add value rather than destroy value by trying to manage a conglomerate which is too diverse. Key constituents are:

❑ common key success factors – often market driven
❑ related core competencies and strategic capabilities
❑ related technologies.

In defence of conglomerate diversification, Sir Owen Green, previously a successful chairman of BTR, has commented:

> *As soon as things go wrong, companies start talking about focus. Focus is the crutch of mediocre management ... If you are trained in the techniques of management ... you should be able to apply them across a range of companies. Diversified companies possess both defensive qualities in recession and a springboard for new ventures in more expansive times.*
> *(Management Today*, June 1994, p. 40)

Finally, it should not be forgotten that a strategy of focus is not immune from the risk of overdependency. Case 16.1 considers the different challenges faced by three focused organizations.

Causes and effects of diversification activity

An exploration of the UK trend

Constable (1986) argues that the UK has experienced the highest rate of diversification amongst the leading industrial nations since 1950, and as a result now has the most concentrated economic structure. Industrial concentration was defined in Chapter 9. Coincidentally this trend has been accompanied by a trend to the weakest small company sector.

The process of diversification has been achieved largely through acquisitions and mergers, which have taken place at a higher rate than that experienced in other countries, especially Japan where there are few large-scale acquisitions.

Constable contends that Japan, the USA and Germany have concentrated more on product and market development and on adding value to current areas of activity, and that partly as a result of this they have enjoyed greater economic prosperity. Hilton (1987) has suggested that one reason behind this is that in Germany and Japan there is a greater emphasis on the respective banking systems providing funding, rather than shareholders, and this has influenced both the number of takeover bids and expectations of performance.

As a result of the diversification, merger and acquisition activity the UK has developed a number of large companies with sizeable asset bases and domestic market shares, but few which are dominant in their industries or sectors at a world or even a European level. Constable argues that the high level of strategic energy devoted to these strategies has created an illusion of real growth, with an emphasis on the shorter-term financial aspects of strategic expertise as opposed to the operational and market-based aspects which, long term, are of great significance. Arguably too much top management time and effort has been spent on seeking and implementing acquisitions, and avoiding being acquired.

Although the nature of investment funding and stock market expectations have been significant influences behind the diversification and acquisition activity in the UK, there are other explanations. If a company has growth objectives and there are finite limits to the potential in existing markets, as well as barriers to becoming more international in order to penetrate related markets abroad, diversification may be an attractive option. However, there may already be intense competition in domestic markets which the company considers entering, especially if the industries involved are attractive and profitable. The competition may be both UK producers and imported products and services and may be compounded by active rivalry for share and dominance. In such circumstances, direct entry may seem less appropriate than acquisition of an existing competitor.

Visit the website: http://www.itbp.com

As acquisitions and mergers increase industrial concentration and the power of certain large organizations, government policy on competition may act as a restraint on particular lines of development for certain companies. Large firms may be encouraged to diversify into unrelated businesses where there is little apparent threat to the interests of consumers, rather than attempting horizontal integration which might be prevented by the intervention of the Monopolies and Mergers Commission. Joint ventures offer another way round this constraint.

A contrasting argument suggests that a company which has grown large, successful and profitable in a particular industry is likely to seek diversification whilst it is strong and has the resources to move into new business areas effectively. The benefits of such a move are likely to seem more realizable by the acquisition of an existing organization than by the slower build-up of new internal activities. This type of growth requires finance, which generally has been available for successful companies.

The minimum scale for effective survival is always rising. A niche can easily become a tomb.

Lord Weinstock, Managing Director, GEC

Rolls Royce

Rolls Royce had to be rescued with an injection of government funding early in the 1970s; the company had become too dependent financially on the success of one engine project, the RB211. In the mid-1990s the company is still focused on the design and manufacture of large, powerful aero engines. Rolls Royce's main two competitors are General Electric and Pratt and Whitney, both American and both more diverse. Not only is GE a diversified conglomerate, GE Finance controls GPA, the aircraft leasing company based in Ireland.

Most development funds are committed to high thrust engines whereby two engines can power large jets over increasingly long distances. Typically engines are customized for particular aeroplanes, and airline customers normally specify their engine preference from the alternatives available. Rolls Royce's Trent 700 has captured 40% of the engine orders for the Airbus A330, but it has so far been less successful with early orders for the Trent 800, designed specifically for the newest Boeing, the 777. Development work on the Trent 800 began in 1988, with an estimate of ten years' investment before any real payoff.

Kodak

Kodak's growth and success has been heavily dependent on photographic film and printing paper. During the 1980s Kodak realized that it faced a possible future threat from digital photography, which has the potential to make traditional film redundant. Half-hearted attempts to develop expertise in digital photography were relatively unsuccessful and consequently Kodak changed to a diversification strategy. In 1988 Kodak bought a pharmaceutical company, Sterling Drug.

Synergy was not forthcoming – the move was not seen as a success – and a new chief executive, George Fisher, was eventually recruited from the electronics company, Motorola. Fisher divested peripheral businesses to focus on those related to *imaging*. He rationalized that even when digital cameras were successful and popular, people would still want hard copies of their photographs. In fact, digital offered important new opportunities; customers could experiment alongside a technician who would be able to visibly enlarge and crop images before a final picture is printed. The technology now exists; the challenge is making it affordable for typical consumers.

Interestingly one Kodak disposal was L & F Household (cleaning products) to Reckitt and Colman of the UK, who already manufactured toiletries and household products. Reckitt's decided to sell Colman Foods (manufacturer of Robinson's Barley Water as well as the renowned mustards) to help finance the purchase, ending 185 years of tradition in food products. Reckitt and Colman would now be focused internationally on toiletries, household products and pharmaceuticals.

Nokia

In the early 1990s Nokia of Finland decided to focus on the telecommunications industry. Four key strategic themes were identified: telecommunications orientation; globalization; focus; and value-added products.

Nokia grew rapidly and profitably during 1992–1994 by concentrating on becoming a major player in mobile telecommunications (where it achieved a 20% share of the world market, second only to Motorola) and digital cellular equipment, where it became second to Ericsson of Sweden. Other Nokia products included televisions, tyres and power, but telecommunications grew from 14% to 60% of the total. Nokia was very successful with its small, lightweight portable telephones; one range competed with Japanese phones by including Japanese numerical characters.

In 1996 there was a profits warning and a collapsing share price. The growth in demand for mobile phones had led to production bottlenecks, compounded by component supply issues. Nokia was experiencing problems training its new recruits quickly enough. World prices for analogue phones were falling rapidly; even though market demand was growing healthily, new competitors such as Siemens and Alcatel (Germany and France) were causing supply to exceed demand.

Nokia undertook drastic cost reduction programmes and sought to become even more focused on telecommunications. Television manufacture was just one divested activity. The target is for 90% of sales to relate to telecommunications.

When companies are acquired then both sales and absolute profits increase quickly, and sometimes markedly. But does profitability also increase? Are assets being utilized more effectively in the combined organization? Is synergy really being obtained? Or are the increased sales and profits merely an illusion of growth?

Finally, Constable offers two further arguments to explain the strategic activity in the UK. First, strategic leaders of large organizations are typically aggressive in nature, and acquisition is an expression of aggression. Second, there is a commonly held belief that the larger a company becomes the less likely it is itself to be a victim of a takeover bid. Hence, whilst diversification is essentially offensive and designed to bring about expansion and growth, it could be argued that on occasions it is a defensive strategy.

Reasons for diversification and acquisition

There are then a number of sound and logical reasons why a firm might seek to diversify through acquisition. Some of these have been mentioned above; others are discussed below. Most are economic. The fact that diversification and acquisition strategies often prove less successful than the expectations for them is more likely to result from the choice of company to acquire and from issues and problems of implementation than the fact that the idea of diversification was misguided. This will be explored further later in the chapter.

Diversification may be chosen because the existing business is seen as being vulnerable in some way: growth potential may be limited; further investment in internal growth may not be justified; the business may be threatened by new technology. Some businesses are undervalued by the stock market, making them vulnerable to takeover if they do not diversify. Some products and businesses may currently be valuable cash generators, but with little prospect of future growth. In other words they may be cash cows generating funds which need to be re-invested elsewhere to build a future for the company. Leading on from this, the company may have growth objectives which stretch beyond the potential of existing businesses.

Diversification may occur because a company has developed a particular strength or expertise and feels it could benefit from transferring this asset into other, possibly unrelated, businesses. The strength might be financial (high cash reserves or borrowing capacity), marketing, technical or managerial. If genuine synergy potential exists, both the existing and newly acquired businesses can benefit from a merger or acquisition.

A company which has become stale or sleepy, or which has succession problems at the strategic leader level, may see an acquisition as a way of obtaining

---

There is a gin rummy school of management ... you pick up a few businesses here, discard a few there ...

The sad fact is that most major acquisitions display an egregious imbalance: they are a bonanza for the shareholders of the acquiree; they increase the income and status of the acquirer's management; and they are a honey pot for the investment bankers and other professionals on both sides. But, alas, they usually reduce the wealth of the acquirer's shareholders, often to a substantial extent.

Warren Buffett, Berkshire Hathaway

fresh ideas and new management, and this may seem more important than the extent to which the businesses are related.

Some diversification and acquisition decisions are concerned with reducing risk and establishing or restoring an acceptable balance of yesterday's, today's and tomorrow's products in a complex portfolio. This will be especially attractive where a company is relying currently on yesterday's products.

Some strategic changes in this category will result from the ego or the ambitions of the strategic leader, who may feel that he or she can run any type of business successfully, regardless of the degree of unrelatedness. Some may be very keen to grow quickly, possibly to avoid takeover, and acquisitions may happen because a company is available for purchase rather than as the outcome of a careful and detailed analysis.

It will be suggested later that the major beneficiaries of an acquisition are often the existing shareholders of the company being acquired. Consequently it is sometimes argued that the self-interest of the City and large institutional shareholders might be behind certain mergers and acquisitions.

Research into diversification and acquisition

The relative success of diversification and acquisition

A number of research studies have been carried out in both the UK and the USA on the relative success of diversification and acquisition strategies. There are some general conclusions as well as specific findings, and the major ones are documented here. In the main most of the findings are consistent.

It is important to emphasize, however, that this is a particularly difficult area to research because of problems with data availability. If, for example, one is attempting to study the change in a company's performance before and after an acquisition, then one needs several years of data to ensure that longer-term effects are studied once any teething problems of early implementation are overcome. However, company W may have acquired company X in, say, 1990 and as a result been included in a research study which began the same year. Ideally the performance of the combined WX would be compared with the previous performance of W and X as independent companies. If company W is naturally acquisitive it may divest some unattractive businesses from X during 1991 in order to raise money to help finance the purchase of company Y in 1992 and company Z in 1994. An on-going programme of this nature means that it is impossible to compare the long-term effects of one particular acquisition on an organization. The original sample continually reduces. In the same way a comparison of the performance over a period of time of companies which might be classified as single, dominant, related and unrelated product will be affected by firms which change category as a result of the strategies they follow.

General conclusions from the research suggest that no more than 50% of diversification through acquisition strategies are successful. Quite simply, the synergies which were considered to exist prior to acquisition are frequently not realized. There is also agreement that shareholders in a company which is taken over or acquired benefit from selling their shares to the bidder, who often pays an unwarranted premium. Shareholders who accept shares in the acquiring company instead of cash, together with the existing shareholders in that company, tend to be rewarded less in the longer term using share price appreciation as a measure. As mentioned earlier in the chapter, the research findings also support the contention that the profitability gains attributable to internal investments in companies are generally much greater than those accruing to acquisition investments.

Lorenz (1986) suggests that research in this field can be classified into four schools: accounting, economic, financial and managerial. The accounting school have concentrated on post-merger profitability in the 1970s, and their general conclusion, accepting sampling problems, is that few acquisitions resulted in increased profitability and for most the effect was neutral. Some had negative effects. Cowling *et al.* (1979), members of the economic school, concluded that there has been an increase in market power but no increase in economic efficiency.

The financial school have analysed share price movements and concluded that bid premiums are often as high as 20–40%. Many takeovers in both the UK and the USA are hostile and opposed aggressively, and this often leads to the payment of high premiums. Five years after acquisition, half of the US acquirers had out-performed the stock market; the other half had performed below average. The success rate is thought to be lower in the UK. One issue in this type of research concerns whether or not stock market prices and performance accurately reflect economic performance.

Kitching (1973), categorized in the managerial school, has concluded that the less related an acquisition is, the more risky it is. Additionally it is more risky to move into new markets than into new technology, assuming that the two are not achieved together. Critics of this conclusion argue that related acquisitions are more likely to be in attractive industries, and consequently more likely to succeed for this reason.

Specific research findings

British research

Reed and Luffman (1986) analysed the performance of 349 of the largest 1000 companies in the UK between 1970 and 1980. These 349 were selected because their product base did not change during the decade. They concluded that the more diversified companies grew fastest in terms of sales and earnings, and the capital value of their shares declined by the lowest amount. The respective figures, after accounting for inflation, were 2.1% average annual growth in sales and 1.3% average annual growth in earnings before interest and tax. The capital value of their shares declined by 3.44% per year on average. Dominant product companies were the next most successful group against these measures, followed by related companies and finally single product companies.

However, the return on capital employed ratios were not consistent with the growth figures. Dominant product companies were the most profitable (19.1% on average), followed by single product companies (18.1%), related product companies (16.9%) and finally unrelated product companies (16.7%). Reed and Luffman conclude that this is a result of the complexities of the inherent changes rather than of the strategy itself.

These findings replicated US research by Rumelt at the Harvard Business School (1974), and they suggest that the contention by Peters and Waterman (1982) that successful companies 'stick to the knitting' is justified.

Meeks (1977) looked at post-merger profitability during the late 1960s and early 1970s. He started with a sample of 213 firms, reducing the sample size annually as the organizations concerned changed their strategies again in some significant way. In four years the sample halved; and after seven years there were only 21 companies left from the original 213. Meeks looked at the percentage of remaining firms each year and considered whether their profitability had increased or decreased. In the first year after the merger 34% of the firms exhibited lower combined profitability than they had enjoyed previously as independent companies. This percentage increased during the first four years to a high of 66%, with half the original sample left. At the end of seven years of research, 62% of the remaining 21 companies were showing reduced profitability.

Meeks concluded that mergers which involved related businesses increased market power, but this was not the case for conglomerate mergers. All types experienced lower profitability and reflected reduced efficiency as a result of the merger activity. Greater size primarily yields higher salaries for executives, a generally more stable corporate performance and increased immunity from takeover.

US research

Salter and Weinhold (1982) studied 36 widely diversified US companies between 1967 and 1977 and concluded that 'diversification strategies designed to raise performance actually brought return on equity down'. In 1967 the companies concerned were producing returns which were 20% above the *Fortune* 500 average, and consequently they could afford to diversify. In 1977 they were 18% below average.

Porter (1987) analysed the strategies and performance of 33 large US conglomerates during the 1970s, and based his general conclusions upon the pattern of later divestment of the acquisitions. Well over half his sample divested at least some of their acquisitions, and a typical retention period seemed to average five to six years. Companies which moved into related activities generally performed better than those which diversified into unrelated areas. From this research Porter suggested three tests for successful diversification, and these are discussed later in this chapter.

McKinsey, in research published in 1988, have documented the performance of 116 large UK and US companies since 1972. Sixty per cent had failed to earn back the cost of capital on the funds invested in acquisitions, and this figure rose to 86% for large unrelated acquisitions.

Nesbitt and King (1989) examined the progress of 1800 US companies between 1978 and 1988 and concluded that corporate performance is dependent on strategy implementation rather than the strategy itself. The degree of diversification as opposed to specialization, taken in isolation, has little impact.

Burgman (1985) studied 600 US acquisitions which took place between 1974 and 1978 and concluded that:

❏ the higher the premium paid to acquire a company, the less likely it was to be successful
❏ prospects for success were greater where the acquirer had a functional appreciation of the business being acquired
❏ success depended upon the ability to retain key managers in the acquired company

❑ larger acquisitions were often more successful, possibly because the sheer size and financial commitment necessitated a thorough appraisal beforehand.

Further research, some of it more recent, confirms these key findings.

These research programmes and papers by Biggadike (1979) and Kitching (1967) suggest a number of reasons why acquisitions fail, and these are considered below.

Why acquisitions fail

It has been mentioned previously that a key reason why acquisitions fail is that they do not generate the synergy which was anticipated or at least hoped for. This is particularly true for conglomerate rather than concentric diversification. Case 16.2 looks at the search for synergy by Daimler-Benz. In general it is easier to gain synergy from production and operations than it is from marketing. It is difficult to gain real additional benefit from selling more than one product or service into one market.

Linked to this issue is the reality that in many cases the real weaknesses of the acquired company are hidden until after the acquisition, and consequently are underestimated. Also underestimated are the cultural and managerial problems of merging two companies and then running them as one. As a result insufficient managerial resources are devoted to the process of merging, and hence the hoped-for synergy remains elusive.

This problem typically arises because the acquiring company concludes that the skills which were to be transferred to the new acquisition in order to generate the synergy are in reality not available. They are already fully committed and in the end are not transferred.

Key managers who have been responsible for the past growth and success of the company being acquired may choose to leave rather than stay with the new conglomerate. Where this happens, and depending on the extent of the contribution of these managers, past successes may not be repeatable.

Further reasons concern the amount paid for the acquisition, and the extent of the premium. For a contested takeover in particular, the bidding company may become overenthusiastic and optimistic about the prospects, overstretch itself financially and then not be able to afford the necessary investment to generate benefits and growth in the new company. When a premium is paid the acquirer is likely to set high targets initially for the new company in order to try and recover the premium quickly. When these targets are missed, because they are unrealistic, enthusiasm is lost and feelings of hostility may develop. It can be argued that if synergy really is available, price is less significant as an issue, and a premium may well be justifiable. On the other hand, if an acquisition is fundamentally misconceived a low or a cheap price will not make it successful at the implementation stage.

Finally the reaction of competitors may be misjudged.

The difficulties apply in service businesses as well as manufacturing, as the following examples illustrate. General Accident acquired a related insurance business in New Zealand in 1988 and as part of the purchase inherited the NZI Bank. The loan book deteriorated in the world-wide recession, and, lacking the necessary turnaround skills, General Accident decided to close the bank. The Prudential similarly chose to exit estate agencies after incurring huge losses.

DAIMLER-BENZ – AN ELUSIVE SEARCH FOR SYNERGY

Daimler-Benz has long been renowned for engineering excellence, product quality and marketing. At the beginning of the 1990s it was Europe's largest manufacturing group, and comprised:

Mercedes-Benz – commercial vehicles
– passenger cars
AEG – electrical & electronic products
Dasa – aerospace
Debis – financial information services

Vehicles were responsible for two-thirds of annual sales revenue; AEG and Dasa each generated approximately 15%.

The majority of the non-vehicle businesses had been acquired systematically during the 1980s; the intention had been to create an 'integrated technology' group. Daimler-Benz's stated objectives for the acquisitions were, first, to offset stagnating vehicle sales by expanding into high-technology growth markets, and second, to strengthen the automotive businesses by applying advanced technologies from the new acquisitions. The challenge was always to achieve this potential synergy; the time-scale to realize the benefits was set at ten years, and the important institutional shareholders allegedly pledged their support for the strategy.

Initially vehicles had to subsidize the new businesses; and critics argued that the second of the two objectives did not require ownership and that in reality the synergy argument was being used as an afterthought to justify the diversification.

Daimler-Benz's strategic dilemma was that both AEG and Dasa required turning around at the same time that vehicles were under threat from Japanese car manufacturers, who were becoming increasingly competitive in the more up-market sectors. Mercedes needed new, more competitive models to prevent being squeezed into too small a niche. An alliance with Mitsubishi was mooted as one suitable way forward.

AEG, which Mercedes had rescued from near bankruptcy, was already diversified (including white goods, typewriters and traffic control systems) and was itself searching for synergies. Some business areas were losing money, and in 1994 AEG's appliance business was sold to Electrolux (see Case 15.4). AEG's railway equipment division became a 50:50 joint venture with ABB, Asea Brown Boveri. Daimler-Benz had to pay ABB as AEG's division was currently losing money and its new partner was profitable. The two businesses complemented each other well: ABB

focused on heavy locomotives, high-speed trains and signalling; AEG was concentrated on light and urban railways and airport transit systems.

Dasa (Deutsche Aerospace) comprised a number of separately acquired companies and there was some duplication of activities. Messerschmitt is a major supplier to the European Airbus project, but its contribution, rear fuselages, is technically less sophisticated than Aerospatiale's forward fuselages and flight decks and British Aerospace's wings. Further alliances with other members of the Airbus consortium – to develop commuter aircraft and helicopters – were discussed. In 1992 Daimler-Benz added to this division when it acquired a 78% shareholding in the Dutch aerospace company, Fokker. The Dutch government held the remaining shares; again the company was already in difficulty.

The promised synergies did not materialize as Germany suffered its deepest recession in manufacturing since 1945. Mercedes-Benz began to trade at a loss in 1993, and this led to job reductions and investment in plants outside Germany (to avoid the difficulties of high domestic wage rates and a strong Deutschmark). Development work on new four-wheel drive vehicles and a micro-car were already underway, the latter in conjunction with SMH of Switzerland, best known as the manufacturer of Swatch watches.

A new Chairman was appointed in Summer 1995 and later that year Daimler-Benz announced a trading loss equivalent to £2.7 billion, 'the worst non-fraudulent result ever recorded by a German company'. A leading analyst commented that the company was 'so bogged down with aerospace and AEG it had missed important opportunities in the automotive arena'. Drastic action was anticipated.

In January 1996 further AEG divisions were sold to Alcatel Alsthom (France); the remainder were to be fully absorbed into Mercedes-Benz. Daimler-Benz also announced the withdrawal of further financial support for Fokker, making its collapse seem inevitable unless a new buyer came forward.

Daimler-Benz redefined itself as a 'transportation group' and restructured into 25 operating units in seven main divisions. All operating units had to fit the core strategy and achieve a target return of 12% return on equity. Failure to achieve would result in sale or closure. The future of Dornier (manufacturer of regional aircraft) and MTU (Daimler aero engines) looked particularly precarious unless alliance partners could be found.

They had overpaid for their acquisitions and the anticipated learning and synergy was slow to materialize. Some would argue the strategy of linking insurance with estate agencies was misjudged; others that the problems were really those of implementation. In particular, the Prudential attempted to exercise central control over a disparate group of acquisitions.

In reality acquisition is an uncertain strategy. However sound the economic justification may appear to be, implementation or managerial issues ultimately determine success or failure. These issues are the subject of the next section.

Issues in diversification and acquisition

Visit the website:
http://www.
itbp.com

Where two companies choose to merge there is the opportunity for a reasonably comprehensive assessment of relative strengths and weaknesses, although it does not follow that one or both will not choose to hide certain significant weaknesses. In the case of a contested takeover only limited information will be available. Crucially the information which will affect the ease or difficulty of merging the two cultures and organizations, and implementing the changes, is less freely available than financial data. As a result financial analysis may be used to justify the acquisition, but it will not answer questions relating to implementation. Table 16.3 highlights the significant information which is unlikely to be available until after the acquisition.

The following list of questions and issues indicates the key considerations which should be addressed by a company before it acquires another:

❏ how the acquiring company should re-structure itself in order to absorb the new purchase, and what implications this will have for existing businesses and people
❏ what acceptable minimum and maximum sizes are for proposed diversifications in relation to present activities
❏ what degree of risk it is appropriate for the company to take
❏ how to value a proposed acquisition and how much to pay
❏ how to maintain good relationships with key managers during negotiations to try to ensure that they stay afterwards
❏ how to maintain momentum and interest in both companies after a successful offer
❏ how fast to move in merging organizational parts and sorting out problems
❏ reporting relationships and the degree of independence allowed to the acquired company, particularly where the business is unrelated
❏ whether and how to send in a new management team.

Some of these issues are considered in the next section where effective acquisition strategies are discussed, but many of them are taken up in later chapters which consider the implementation aspects of strategic change. Figure 16.2 illustrates that an effective strategy is one which is based upon good vision and sound implementation prospects. Vision is in relation to the organization's strengths and market opportunities, and an effective strategy will match these. In the context of diversification and acquisition, implementation relates to a consideration of how the two organizations will be merged together and the changes required to structures, cultures and systems in order to ensure that potential synergy is achieved. Poor vision and poor implementation will both cause strategic management to be less than effective. If the logic behind an

Before	After	
Organization charts	Inner philosophy and culture	**Table 16.3**
Data on salaries of top management	Real quality of staff in decision roles	Information available before and after an acquisition
Reasonably detailed information on board members and key executives – but only brief details on middle management	Salary and reward structures and systems	
	Decision process	
Products	Inter-relationships, power bases, hidden conflicts and organizational politics	
Plants	Individual objectives being pursued	
Corporate identity, image and reputation		
Past record, especially financial		

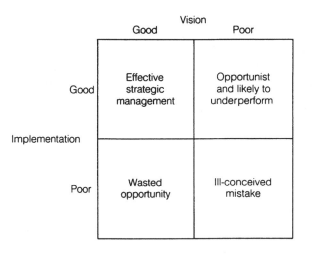

Figure 16.2 Strategy creation and implementation. Based on a matrix devised by Booz, Allen and Hamilton.

acquisition is poor, then the merged corporation is likely to underperform, however well the two companies might be managed as one corporate whole. If the vision is good but implementation is weak, underperformance is again likely because synergy will not be created.

If companies develop by a series of acquisitions it is quite typical for several banks to become involved. These could be spread world-wide; their cultures and lending philosophies may differ; their levels of exposure will vary; the assets securing the loans will not be the same; and certain banks may see themselves as lenders to just one company rather than the whole organization. Problems are likely to arise if one of the banks gets into financial difficulties or if the company seeks to extend a loan or adjust the terms.

Effective acquisition strategies

A number of authors have suggested ways of improving the effectiveness of acquisition strategies.

Drucker (1982) argues that there are five rules for successful acquisitions.

❏ It is essential for the acquiring company to determine exactly what contribution it can make to the acquired company. It must be more than money.

- ❏ It is important to search for a company with a 'common core of unity', say in technology, markets or production processes.
- ❏ The acquiring company should value the products, services and customers of the company that it is taking over.
- ❏ Top management cover for the acquired company should be available in case key managers choose to leave after the acquisition.
- ❏ Within a year managers should have been promoted across company boundaries.

In a report entitled *Making Acquisitions Work: Lessons from Companies' Successes and Mistakes*, Business International (1988) offer the following guidelines.

- ❏ **Plan first:** As a company, know exactly what you are going to do. Ascertain where the company being acquired has been, and maybe still is, successful, and ensure that it can be maintained – taking special account of any dependence on key people. Appreciate also where it is weak. It is quite possible that it will have good products but overheads which are too high.
- ❏ **Implement quickly:** People in the acquired company expect decisive action, and delay prolongs speculation. At the same time it is important not to act without thinking things through first.
- ❏ **Communicate frankly:** Explain the acquisition or merger, the expected benefits and the changes which will be required. In addition it is useful to ensure that there is an understanding of the values and expectations of the acquiring company.
- ❏ **Act correctly,** particularly as far as redundancy is concerned.

Ramsay (1987) argues that effective acquisition strategies have four stages, which are illustrated in Figure 16.3:

- ❏ the need to formulate a clear strategy
- ❏ the search for possible acquisitions
- ❏ the acquisition
- ❏ the merger of the organizations following acquisition.

The formulation of a clear strategy

An effective, well-thought-through diversification and acquisition can constitute real strategic growth by providing entry into a new market, a new opportunity to build on competitive strengths, an opportunity to create and benefit from synergy, and the possibility of removing some element of competition. This, however, implies more logic behind the acquisition than mere sales growth or the purchase of a profit stream. Hence there are a number of issues to consider in attempting to formulate an effective strategy for acquisition.

- ❏ First, the issue of how much to concentrate and how much to diversify must be examined. We mentioned earlier that research indicates that concentration is generally superior but that the opportunities available may not be sufficient to fill the planning gap. A major advantage of concentration, and a limit on diversification, is that experience is difficult to copy. Learning and experience can lead to superior competitive positions through an understanding of customers and how to satisfy their needs through production and service. Horizontal integration and concentric diversification can both provide opportunities to capitalize on learning and experience.

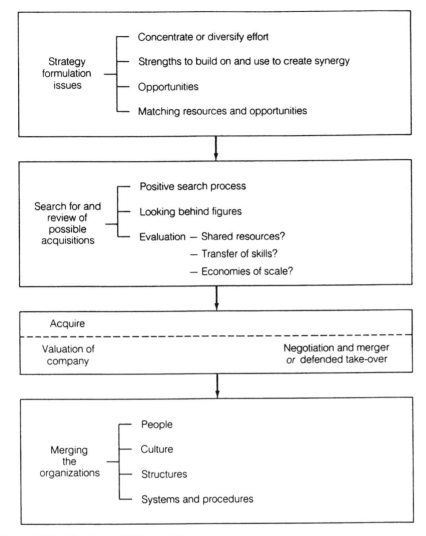

Figure 16.3 Effective acquisition strategies.

❑ Second, a good strategy will build on existing strengths and develop synergy around them. This requires an opportunity to transfer skills and competencies and achieve economies of scale. This issue is discussed further below.

❑ Third, it is important to be able to spot an opportunity and act quickly and decisively to capitalize on it. It has been argued, for example, that, once legislation permitted it in the mid-1980s, the building societies which moved quickly into estate agencies benefited far more than those who lagged behind, because the cost per site increased with the acquisition activity. Such a strategic move would be classified as vertical integration because an estate agency is really a channel of distribution for mortgages.

❑ Fourth, resources (strengths) and opportunities need to be matched. The ability to do this effectively relates to the way the company is managed, and to the culture and values.

The search for, and review of, possible acquisitions

❑ There should be an active and positive search process. Acquisitions are difficult, diversification is risky, and the decisions can prove expensive if they are wrong. Strategic leaders should track and carefully analyse possible acquisitions rather than rely on opportunities which might arise.

❑ It is essential to be realistic. Where there is a friendly merger, or the acquisition of a company in difficulties, it is possible that certain key weaknesses may be hidden; and in the case of a hostile bid situation it is important not to become unrealistic through determination and, as a result, pay too much.

❑ Before acquiring it is crucial to assess just how resources are going to be shared, where and how skills are going to be transferred, and where and how economies of scale are going to be obtained. If such an analysis is left until after an acquisition, synergy is likely to prove more elusive.

The price paid to acquire a company relative to its earning potential, and the ability to generate synergy through shared activities or transferred skills, are the key determinants of likely success.

Porter (1987) contends that a portfolio of unrelated companies is only a logical corporate strategy if the aim is restructuring. Restructuring is the strategy pursued by conglomerates like Hanson, and it requires the identification of companies which are underperforming and which can be transformed with new management skills. Ideally they are valued below their real potential when acquired. The new owner seeks to improve the competitive position of the organization and improve its profitability. Logically companies or business units are sold when they no longer have potential for increasing earnings further. The opportunity to pursue this strategy effectively lies in the ability to spot and acquire undervalued companies cheaply and to manage unfamiliar businesses better than the existing managers.

In any acquisition, Porter argues, three tests should be passed.

❑ The industry involved should be or could be made structurally attractive. In other words, the potential returns exceed the company's cost of capital.

❑ The entry cost should not be so high that future profit streams are compromised. As well as the purchase price, the cost must also take account of professional fees involved in the merger or acquisition.

Granada incurred professional fees exceeding £100 million for its takeover of Forte – Case 16.4 later. Forte's defence costs, post-acquisition divestment fees together with other payments and provisions built up an accumulated total of some £250 million. Granada paid £3.9 billion for Forte.

❑ One of the companies should be able to gain competitive advantage, and the newly acquired business should be better off in the new corporation than elsewhere. In other words the inter-relationships, based on shared activities and transferred skills, must give added value which outweighs the costs incurred. These benefits are often not gained for two main reasons. The new, more diverse, more complex, organization is likely to be decentralized, but the business units may be independent in practice rather than interdependent. Managers may not be able to understand and implement the inter-relationships.

Case 16.3 evaluates the Asda–MFI merger against these three tests and argues

---

Case 16.3
THE ASDA–MFI MERGER

The case considers whether the merger of Asda and MFI, described earlier in Case 15.6, met the criteria for successful diversification suggested by Porter.

The attractiveness of the kitchen furniture industry

Suppliers of kitchen furniture did not enjoy as strong a market profile as did MFI, and buyers individually had very little power. *En masse* they are influential. Any competitor wanting to enter the market on the MFI scale would require massive investment; substitute products were essentially units which were already assembled, such as those sold by Magnet Southern. Increases in disposable income might make these more attractive. There was intense rivalry for market share, however, as sales of kitchen furniture were flat in the 1980s.

On balance the industry was not unattractive, and MFI was a past 'winner'. Profits had grown 87% in real terms between 1980 and 1985.

The cost of entry

MFI cost Asda £570 million, which represented $5\frac{1}{2}$ times net assets and 14 times 1984 pre-tax profits. It was a 31% premium on the current market capitalization, and it measured MFI on a price-to-earnings ratio of 22 rather than the 18 that it had been before the bid. Debt and equity funding were both involved; and Asda's gearing increased from little more than zero to 40%.

Both sets of shareholders were supportive, but with hindsight it seems a high price.

Increased competitive advantage

There was no real benefit to be gained from common purchasing; no site sharing; and the two companies enjoyed different geographical concentrations. Asda was northern and MFI national.

After the merger the companies were run autonomously with few activities shared.

Prior to merging it had been argued that there would be intangible benefits from shared expertise. In the event there was little cross-flow of managers, product innovation, marketing or operations skills. The cultures remained separate; and Derek Hunt, who became Chief Executive, worked from London despite Asda's northern base.

Whilst Asda did compete with Sainsbury's, who have a chain of Homebase DIY stores, this was not seen as a threat which MFI would address, and in any case MFI was very narrowly focused within the DIY sector.

Whilst the industry was not unattractive the merger proved expensive for Asda, and the potential synergy used to justify the merger to shareholders seemed not to be there in reality.

---

that it did not pass them all. It was mentioned in Case 15.6, which described the merger and de-merger, that the expected synergy was not achieved.

Hence companies which are seeking to grow through acquisition and the consolidation of the acquired and existing businesses should ensure either that skills can be transferred or that activities can be shared, i.e. clear inter-relationships can be identified. These can relate to any part of the value chain. The aims are greater economies of scale, lower costs or enhanced differentiation through sharing activities, know-how or customers, or transferring skills and know-how. The research findings quoted earlier suggest that these opportunities are more likely to be found in industries which are in some way related. Tobacco companies in both the UK and the USA, for example, when faced with declining demand and hostile pressure groups realized that they would have to diversify if they were to avoid decline. They chose such industries as food, wine and brewing initially because they felt that they could transfer their skills and expertise in marketing consumer products.

Acquisitions are likely to prove disappointing if the opportunity for such synergy is not evaluated objectively in advance, or if the companies convince themselves that synergy must be possible without establishing where and how.

It is also vital to check carefully for any 'skeletons' prior to an acquisition. In 1990 ICI Explosives bought Atlas Powder in the USA. In the same year, a US rival of Atlas, Thermex Energy, was declared bankrupt, and when, some years later, Atlas was found guilty of conspiring to drive Thermex out of business, ICI was held responsible by the US courts. Substantial, but contested, damages were awarded against ICI.

Acquiring the company

The key issues involved in the acquisition itself have been discussed earlier. Valuations were considered in Chapter 12, and it was emphasized above that it is important to look for hidden weaknesses in friendly mergers and avoid paying too much in a contested takeover bid. It was mentioned earlier that if too high a premium is paid the acquisition is less likely to be successful (Burgman, 1985), and a vicious circle of disillusionment can easily be created. If the acquisition is overvalued or a substantial premium is paid, the expected early returns on the investment will be very high. An acquisition involves an investment which must be paid back by generating returns which exceed the cost of capital involved. If targets are missed the possible disillusionment and loss of confidence may mean that additional investment to develop the business, which really is needed, will not be forthcoming. Consequently, performance will deteriorate further and the business will run down. A likely outcome of this will be its sale at a discounted price, and the acquirer will have lost money from the acquisition. The payment of any premium should be related to the ability of the acquirer to add value by sharing activities or transferring skills.

Unwelcome bids

Organizations which find themselves the object of an unwelcome bid can defend themselves in a number of ways. A revised profit forecast, promising improvements, can prove effective – but subsequently the improvement must be delivered. This will sometimes be linked to a promise to restructure and divest parts of the business which are not core and not contributing synergy. An appeal to regulatory bodies may at least impose a delay; and finally, the company can seek a 'white knight', a preferred friendly bidder. Jenkinson and Mayer (1994) have shown, first, that white knight interventions normally succeed but, of course, the company's independence has still been lost, and, second that where there is no white knight cash bids are more difficult to defend against than equity bids.

These issues are explored further in Box 16.1 and Case 16.4.

Implementation issues

Ernst and Young (1995) argue that the nature of the post-acquisition challenge depends upon the type of acquisition and the objectives behind it. They identify four alternatives:

| Box 16.1 |
| **HOSTILE TAKEOVERS** |

In a research sample year (1989) in the UK there were 161 bids for publicly-listed companies; 35 of these were hostile takeover attempts as distinct from agreed or friendly acquisition bids. In one sense the year was seen as typical: some 70% of the *largest* acquisitions/takeovers were hostile. Of these about half will normally succeed; in the other cases the target company will be able to mount an effective defence strategy.

By contrast Germany had experienced just three hostile takeover bids since 1945. They are equally rare in France and almost unheard of in Japan. They remain popular in the USA, where a larger number of defence mechanisms are available than is the case in the UK.

Alternative defence strategies
(Listed in order of popularity in the UK)

Financial responses
Companies will hope to be able to announce forthcoming profit improvements – they have been targeted because, although fundamentally competitive and sound, recent profits have been disappointing. They may also seek to revalue their assets to make the bid appear to be undervaluing the true worth of the business.

Legal and political tactics
Political lobbying and attempts to get a bid referred to the competition authorities, the latter to, at the very least, buy time and allow a company to mount a stronger defence.

Attempted white knight bids
An alternative, preferred, outside bidder is sought.

Corporate restructuring
As we see in Case 16.4, disposals are announced. Bidders will claim that attempts to rationalize and downsize, whilst appropriate and desirable, have been provoked by the bid and are indicative of reactive senior management. Sometimes the strategic leadership will attempt to mount a management buy-out as an alternative to the outside bid.

Poison pills
This strategy, most popular in the USA, describes shareholder rights plans which effectively increase the price to the bidder. An example would be preferentially priced stock being available to existing shareholders, giving them a later right to new ordinary shares. Similarly the term *golden parachutes* describes special departure terms for directors in the event of an unwelcome acquisition.

Outcomes
Generally a well-formulated and strategically logical bid for a poor performer should succeed; a strong performer will clearly be in a stronger position to defend itself and its record. However, in isolation, a strong financial performance is not everything – simply, there may appear to be more strategic logic in the business being parented by the bidder instead of staying as it is.

Cash bids have the greatest likelihood of success. In 1989 21% of the 161 bids were equity based and just 11% of these succeeded; 43% were cash only with a 56% success rate; the remaining 36% were mixed cash/equity bids and 53% of these succeeded. Normally the value of a hostile bid will be increased once the nature and robustness of the defence is revealed.

Cash bids are most likely to fail if an alternative *white knight* bidder is found. The likelihood of the success of equity and mixed bids appears to depend upon the quality of the financial defence.

Source: Jenkinson, T and Mayer, C (1994) *Hostile Take-overs: Defence, Attack and Corporate Governance*, McGraw-Hill.

Case 16.4
GRANADA'S ACQUISITION OF FORTE

Hostile takeovers had become relatively rare during the recession of the 1990s when Granada launched its unwelcome bid for Forte in November 1995.

At this time Forte was the UK's largest hotel group with a number of divisions and activities. The hotels included Exclusive hotels around the world, the Méridien chain (bought from Air France), the Heritage, Posthouse and Travelodge brands and White Hart hotels. Little Chef-type restaurants and airport catering were the other main activities. Forte's strategic leader was Sir Rocco Forte, son of the chain's founder. He had been chief executive since 1982 and chairman since 1992. The company had recently been growing at a slower rate than Granada and was underperforming against the FTSE index.

Granada was mainly diversified into Granada Television, London Weekend TV, Granada rentals and Sutcliffe contract catering. Granada also operates motorway service stations with linked lodge accommodations. The strategic leader was Gerry Robinson, an Irish-born accountant whose first job had been as a cost clerk with Lesney products. Robinson has been described as instinctive and impatient and under his leadership Granada had outperformed the FTSE index. He was perceived as a success by Granada's institutional shareholders. Granada was run from a small, tight head office of 24 people; Forte's head office, by contrast, employed 290.

Granada stated that if the bid was successful it would seek buyers for a number of Forte businesses and that the intended retentions were Forte Posthouse hotels, Travelodges in the UK and the chain of Little Chef (364), Happy Eater (68) and Côte (30 in France) restaurants. This collection of assets was valued at £1.7 billion and it generated 80% of Forte's profits. Heritage and White Hart hotels might also be retained; a decision would be taken later. Forte's shareholding in the Savoy, a hotel it wished to acquire but where it had so far been thwarted, would also be sold.

Shortly after the bid, Forte sold its wine and spirits distribution business, Lillywhite's sports retail store and 490 Travelodges in the USA. It sought buyers for its Savoy shares, the airport catering and White Hart Hotels, and later agreed to sell the UK Travelodges and Little Chef-type restaurants to Whitbread if Forte's bid failed. Granada had applied to the UK Takeover Panel to restrain further asset sales during the period of the bid. Forte also announced Britain's largest ever share re-purchase, again if the bid failed. Forte was looking to re-focus on its core competency in hotels and retain the Exclusive, Méridien, Heritage and Posthouse brands. The company was credited with a creative and positive defence strategy, but maybe the divestments were coming too late.

Granada's initial bid was increased in January 1996 to a figure equivalent to a 35% premium on the share price prior to the initial bid. The offer was a mixture of shares and cash, fully underwritten by a cash alternative. The additional amount represented a special dividend to be paid out of Forte's own assets. The outcome depended upon the attitude of a number of City institutions, many of whom held shares in both organizations. A key player, and one of the last to announce its decision, was Mercury Asset Management (MAM), a shareholder in Granada which also owned 14% of Forte. MAM backed Granada and the bid succeeded.

Granada finally paid £3.9 billion to acquire Forte. Its new balance sheet showed £3.5 billion debt. Granada urgently needed to dispose of some Forte assets to raise cash and to then generate a positive cash flow from the businesses it retained.

Sir Rocco Forte immediately announced he was putting together a consortium to try and buy back Forte's Exclusive, Méridien and Heritage hotels. But he later withdrew.

- *Financial acquisitions* are companies brought into a holding company, sometimes for the purpose of re-structuring. The main objectives for the acquisition are the financial opportunities from cost (overhead) eradication, cost reduction and improved efficiencies. Those parts of the business which do not offer these opportunities are likely to be offered for sale; and, in fact, any part of the business is likely to be available for sale to a buyer offering a premium price. The critical implementation issues concern timing and decisiveness.
- *Geographic acquisitions* are intended to expand the acquirer's core business across new frontiers. Merging different country cultures is the key challenge, but this is generally regarded as manageable as long as the strategic logic for the merger is sound. One dilemma concerns cuts and job losses in the acquired business; alleged 'national bias' may well cause resentment.
- *Symbiotic acquisitions* describe situations where newly acquired products and competencies are absorbed into the parent's business but the acquired company retains some independence. Abbey National's purchase of Scottish Mutual is an example. The establishment of an appropriate new structure, culture and communications system are the implementation issues.
- *Absorbtion acquisitions* imply that the two businesses are fully integrated, with one effectively losing its identity. Such acquisitions are particularly challenging to implement as really everything changes.

Visit the website:
http://www.
itbp.com

For any acquiring company to gain financially, sales must be increased and costs reduced to a level which compensates for any price premium paid. Researchers suggest this is rarely less than 20%. Easy savings are rare, particularly in the case of many hostile bids, where the target is often a high, rather than a poor, performer. Too many companies, apparently, pursue the elusive synergistic opportunities and do not act on the cost base quickly and decisively. They also tend to postpone the difficult issues relating to culture and style. Successful acquisitive companies like Hanson and BTR do act quickly and do concentrate on cost eradication and reduction; they also impose their own style of management on their new business, top-down from the centre.

Clearly, the type of acquisition and the rationale behind it must influence the appropriate implementation strategy; Hanson and BTR are restructuring organizations. Where genuine synergy potential exists, a more participatory style is likely to prove appropriate and foster the necessary learning and skills transfer.

Merging the two organizations

Merging two organizations involves decisions about the integration of strategic capabilities, in particular:

❏ operating resources – salesforces, production facilities
❏ functional skills – product development, R & D
❏ general management skills – strategy development, financial control, human resource strategies.

The speed and pattern of the integration will be dependent on the desired inter-dependency of the businesses, and the opportunities for synergy. It is essential that there is a strategy for the implementation, and ideally this will be developed after the merger or acquisition when fuller details are available.

Moreover, important issues concerning people, culture, structure systems and procedures must be thought through.

❑ **People**: It is accepted that many chief executives and other senior managers leave acquired companies either immediately or within one to two years after the acquisition, especially where the acquisition was contested. This may or may not be significant, depending on the strengths of the acquiring company. In some cases it will prove crucial, particularly where the managers have been the major source of competitive advantage. The managers in the two organizations being merged may well have different values, ethics and beliefs in quality and service, and these will somehow have to be reconciled.

❑ **Culture:** It is quite possible that the two organizations will have different cultures, which also must be reconciled. One may be a large company and the other small, with typical role and power cultures respectively. Managers will be used to different levels of responsibility. One may be much more formal and procedural than the other. One may be entrepreneurial and risk oriented, and the other cost conscious and risk averse.

These cultural issues should be considered when the post-acquisition structure is designed, and in the new systems and procedures.

❑ **Structure systems and procedures:** Whilst mentioned here, this is the subject of Chapter 19, and it concerns the degree of decentralization. As companies become larger and more complex they must be broken down into business units, and managers must be given some degree of independence – to motivate them and to ensure that functional and competitive strategies can be adapted in response to environmental changes. However, if activities are to be shared, or skills transferred, it is essential to ensure that independence does not inhibit, or even prohibit, the implementation of the necessary inter-dependences.

McLean (1985) contends that six factors determine whether the integration of two or more companies is a success or a failure:

❑ first, active leadership by the strategic leader of the acquiring company in conveying objectives and expectations, and in redesigning the structure of the organizations

❑ second, the conscious development of shared values and a transfer of the important aspects of the culture of the acquiring firm

❑ third, an appropriate inter-change of managers between the firms, which can be one way of retaining valuable managers from the acquired company

❑ fourth, proceeding with caution (although some changes may have to be implemented quickly, say to reduce costs in certain areas, others will be less urgent; this provides an opportunity to learn about the underlying strengths of the new business which might be capitalized on)

❑ fifth, relationships with customers must be protected until decisions about future products and market priorities are taken

❑ sixth, rigid new systems, which might be inappropriate for the new business, should not be imposed too ruthlessly or too quickly. Where there are differences in, in particular, culture, technology and marketing needs, managers in the acquired company should be allowed the necessary freedom to manage the competitive and functional strategies and respond to market pressures.

To summarize this section, it could be argued that:

❑ the price paid for an acquisition should reflect the ability of the acquirer to add value, share resources and transfer skills
❑ the strategy for achieving this should be soundly based, and the potential synergy real rather than imagined
❑ post-acquisition management should recognize that, whilst changes will have to be made in order to add value, two cultures have to be integrated if the strategy is to be implemented effectively.

In this chapter so far we have concentrated on diversification and acquisition strategies.

Joint ventures and strategic alliances are an attempt to obtain the benefits of diversification and access to new competitive opportunities without the costs and implementation problems of acquisition or merger. They are not without problems of their own.

Joint ventures and strategic alliances

Whilst some form of partnership can be one of the quickest and cheapest ways to grow or develop a global strategy, it is also one of the toughest and most risky. Many alliances fail. The needs of both partners must be met, and consequently three important questions must be answered satisfactorily:

❑ **why** use an alliance?
❑ **who** to select as a partner?
❑ **how** to implement the agreement?

There is disagreement amongst authors concerning definitions of the terms 'joint venture' and 'strategic alliance'. I use strategic alliance to encapsulate all forms of agreement between partners, and joint venture for those agreements which involve either the establishment of a new, independent company owned jointly by the partners, or the minority ownership of the other party by one or both partners.

An alliance could involve direct competitors sharing a common skill, or related companies sharing different skills and competencies. These organizations might well be linked in the same added value chain (e.g. a manufacturer and either a supplier or a distributor). Such an alliance should generate synergy through co-operation, innovation and lower costs whilst allowing each partner to concentrate on its core competencies. The intention will be to increase competitive advantage without either merger or acquisition.

It is important to distinguish between alliances agreed by two manufacturers of competing or complementary products, perhaps to gain scale economies or wider geographic access, and alliances between organizations at different stages in the added value chain. As an example of the former, Toshiba (Japanese manufacturer of heavy electrical apparatus, electronic devices, information systems and consumer products such as televisions, videos, kitchen appliances and white goods) has a global network of allies for different products and technologies, including GEC Alsthom, Siemens, Ericsson, General Electric, Motorola, Time Warner and Apple. Toshiba sees this 'circle of friends' as an opportunity for sharing ideas to obtain the latest technology and to gain competitive advantage through learning. Benetton (Case 10.1) fits the latter category; its strong partnership sourcing agreements and network of retail franchisees yield economies, speed and competitive advantage. Here, the ability to manage a network of partners is a core competency and source of competitive advantage. Case 16.5 describes how Yorkshire Water has adopted an onion strategy to allow it to concentrate more on its core service competencies; as a result it has formed a network of partnerships.

Reasons for joint ventures and strategic alliances

❏ The cost of acquisition may be too high.
❏ Legislation may prevent acquisition, but the larger size is required for critical mass.
❏ Political or cultural differences could mean an alliance is more likely to facilitate integration than would a merger or acquisition.
❏ The increasing significance of a total customer service package suggests linkages through the added value chain – to secure supplies, customize distribution and control costs. At the same time individual organizations may prefer to specialize in those areas where they are most competent. An alliance provides a solution to this dilemma.
❏ The threat from Japanese competition has driven many competitors into closer collaboration – but they may not wish to merge.
❏ Covert protectionism in certain markets necessitates a joint venture with a local company.

Forms and examples of joint ventures and strategic alliances

Joint ventures and strategic alliances can take a number of forms. The six categories which follow should not be seen as mutually exclusive; some joint ventures will cover more than one.

❏ Component parts of two or more businesses might be merged.

GEC Alsthom is a 50:50 joint venture company formed in 1988 when the power systems divisions of GEC were merged with the Alsthom subsidiary of France's CGE. The company, the largest manufacturer of generating equipment in the EU, was created to allow GEC and CGE to compete more effectively with ABB, Asea Brown Boveri, the Swedish/Swiss multi-national and the world's biggest electrical engineering group. The companies compete directly in a number of sectors, such as railway equipment and rolling stock. More recently an alliance between GEC Alshtom and Siemens has been mooted – to develop the high speed trains of the future. The intention here would be to reduce risk in an industry bedevilled by political issues. Governments around the world are inevitably involved and projects are frequently delayed or even cancelled for both political and financial reasons.

Everywhere in Europe companies are giving up sovereignty because of the costs involved in research and development. The extent and speed of technological changes are such that no one thinks he is capable of doing it all on his own.

Lord Weinstock, when Managing Director, GEC

Since being privatized in 1989 most of the ten water companies in the UK have pursued diversification strategies. The core business activities are water supply and the management of waste water (i.e., sewage treatment). Prices and quality standards are closely regulated, and consequently the diversification is aimed at offsetting the perceived risks and constraints inherent in regulated businesses. The most popular activity has been waste management, the collection and disposal of industrial and domestic waste. For example, Severn Trent Water acquired Biffa, and Wessex formed a joint venture with Waste Management of the USA, one of the world's largest companies in the industry.

Yorkshire Water created two separate, but linked, businesses: Yorkshire Water Services to control the core businesses, and Yorkshire Water Enterprises for other commercial ventures.

Yorkshire Water Enterprises became active in:

Waste management – industrial effluents and clinical waste

Engineering consultancy and support – a joint venture with Babcock International. Since 1989 YW have been investing in treatment plants (mainly) and water distribution networks, the latter to free up engineering resources which the joint venture would seek to deploy and exploit

'Pipeline Products' – the sale of existing stores items to external customers

'Waterlink' – a network of approved sub-contractor plumbers. YW provide an arrangement service

Laboratory services – providing analytical services to a range of businesses and agencies

Management training – primarily exploiting existing markets and competencies

Property development – representing 'real' diversification.

The Director General of OFWAT, the industry regulator, emphasized that he was not going to ignore these strategic developments. 'Customers of core services must not be affected adversely.' For example, the water companies were prevented from selling services from the associated businesses to the core at contrived prices which benefited shareholders at the expense of captive water customers. Additionally 'the required investment funds for the water supply services must not be put at risk'.

Yorkshire Water Services
YW stated quite early that it did not intend to build and then manage a diversified corporation. Once the appropriate business had been constructed, with YW's resources deployed effectively, the layers would be peeled away systematically – an onion focus strategy – until only the core business remains. The defined core activity is *water delivery*, which incorporates the removal of sewage and water treatment. The pursuit of this strategy entails divesting certain non-core or support activities into either wholly owned subsidiaries or independent contractors (in properly negotiated alliances), and possibly more joint ventures, but only where there are providers able to deliver the range and quality of services.

Four alternative implementation approaches for this strategy are illustrated in Figure 16.4. The services divested by YW are also highlighted. Where there are agreements with multiple outside contractors (alternatives 2 and 3), separate geographic regions are typically the predominant logic. For example, the pipework to sewage treatment works is divested to individual local authorities.

This corporate onion strategy aims to improve a company's competitiveness with the premise that non-core services can invariably be acquired more effectively from an experienced outside provider, selected because it already has competitive advantage. It is essential to define the core carefully and to establish the appropriate

Continued overleaf

on-going relationships in order to minimize risk. The order and timing of each divestment is also an important issue.

The company benefits because it can concentrate on its core activities; it has access to a wider skill and resource base, which should promote best practice, enable greater service flexibility and lead to overall quality improvements. Resources should match needs more effectively. In addition, clearer accountability should foster cost reductions, and the introduction of controlled competition should enhance the quality of in-house service provision and act as a catalyst for change throughout the organization.

To implement the strategy successfully the central organization must develop competency in network management. Effective partnership sourcing such as this requires unambiguous long-term agreements, clear performance measures and shared risk. It is most appropriate where the service is a core activity for the contracted supplier. The partners should engage in on-going dialogue and maybe even exchange personnel periodically.

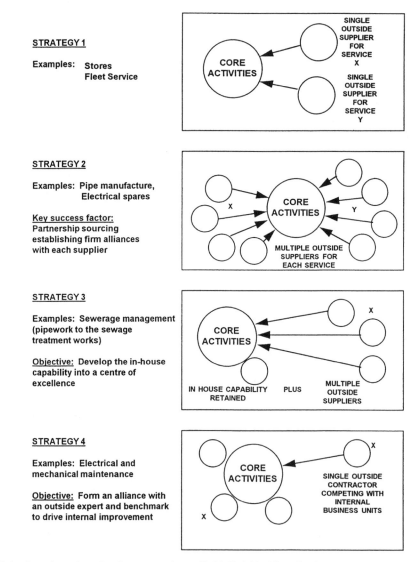

Figure 16.4   Four alternative onion-focus strategies applied in Yorkshire Water Services.

❏ Companies might agree to join forces to develop a new project.

Club Méditerranee and Carnival Cruise Lines (US) joined forces to provide cruise-based holiday packages for Europe and Asia. Philips and Nintendo have jointly developed a new generation of video games on compact discs compatible with Philips' CD-i – compact disc-interactive – players which link up to high-definition televisions. Airbus Industrie was formed because no partner alone could afford the development costs of large passenger aircraft, and because of pressure from European governments who wanted to reduce the predominance of the large US companies.

❏ Companies might agree to develop a new business jointly.

Sony of Japan and Apple (computers) of the USA formed a new multi-media company in 1991. The aim was to produce a 'palm-size, wire-less personal communication device with digital audio and visual functions'.

❏ There might be specific agreements between manufacturers and their suppliers.

Jaguar Cars and GKN reached an agreement in 1988 whereby GKN would become the sole supplier of car bodies to Jaguar. Since the privatization of Jaguar in the mid-1980s its bodies had been supplied by the Rover Group, its previous parent company, which was vertically integrated in this respect. Jaguar and GKN formed a new company, owned 50:50, and the aim to build a new plant and have it operative by 1991 was accomplished successfully.

❏ A company might make a strategic investment in another firm.

Guinness and LVMH have exchanged shareholdings and formed a whole series of distribution joint ventures around the world. There are efficiency savings and marketing advantages from combining, particularly, the spirits brands of the two companies. LVMH owns the world's leading cognac brand, Hennessy, as well as its leading champagnes; Guinness, through its Distillers subsidiary, owns a portfolio which includes Johnnie Walker, the world's best selling scotch whisky, and Gordon's gin, another international best-seller.

❏ Companies might form international trading partnerships.

Fujitsu of Japan now owns 80% of ICL, the UK computer manufacturer, but runs it as an independent subsidiary. However, they are allied in the form of joint retailing and servicing in North America and Australia.

Developing from these forms of joint venture and strategic alliance, Connell (1988) contends that companies collaborate strategically for primarily three reasons:

❏ First, to gain access to new markets and technologies as markets become increasingly international.

In 1989 Pilkington, the UK float glass manufacturer and world market leader, sold 20% of its US vehicle glass subsidiary to Nippon Sheet Glass of Japan. Pilkington had 17% of the world market for *vehicle glass*, Asahi of Japan 19%. Nippon already had 9% and manufactured float glass under licence from Pilkington. Nippon gained access to the US market; Pilkington were looking to build a customer base in Japan, arguing that as car manufacture becomes increasingly global they needed a presence in all major markets. Pilkington already supplied the Toyota plant in the USA.

❑ Second, to share the costs and risks of increasingly expensive research and development.

The alliance between Rover and Honda is an example of this. The agreement was started with an initiative from Sir Michael Edwardes in 1978 when he was Chief Executive of the Rover Group, then called British Leyland (BL). Edwardes considered that the new models being developed by BL were inadequate, particularly in the middle car range. He chose Honda because they were not too big to be interested in a deal with BL and because their technology was regarded as being very good. The Triumph Acclaim was the first car to emerge from the collaboration. BL enjoyed exclusive production and marketing rights to a Honda design and bought the necessary tooling from Honda. The first Rover 200 series was also developed jointly, with the 213 model having a Japanese engine. Later the agreement included the assembly of each other's related models – specifically the Rover 800 series and the Honda Legend.

During 1989 further progress was made. In July, having been acquired from the UK government by British Aerospace, Rover bought 20% of Honda (UK), which was to build a manufacturing plant in Swindon, Wiltshire. In return Honda acquired 20% of the Rover shares. In October Honda agreed that Rover's Longbridge plant in Birmingham would be the sole European source of its new model, the Concerto. The up-dated Rover 200 series was a comparable car.

Following this Honda agreed to help Rover raise its efficiency and productivity to world-class levels during the 1990s. Honda would also buy most of the body panels required for its European factories from Rover, but develop its new Swindon plant to produce more than one car. Rover would then cease to assemble for Honda.

The alliance has been systematically reduced since Rover was sold to BMW.

❑ Third, to manage innovation more effectively. This is important because of high R & D costs and greater globalization, which together often ensure that any competitive advantage gained from technology is relatively short-lived. Both the opportunities and threats require that companies are able to be flexible and change quickly.

In 1995 Motorola joined with IBM, Siemens, and Toshiba (an existing alliance) to develop the next generation of advanced memory chips, which are highly complex and extremely costly to develop and make. There is arguably a fourth reason – an attempt to regain lost competitiveness in a marketplace. This is thought to be the cause of a series of agreements amongst European electronics manufacturers, and links between them and Japanese and US competitors.

Whilst there are a number of reasons and justifications for such strategic alliances, they can again be difficult strategies to implement effectively.

Key issues in joint ventures and strategic alliances

Ohmae (1989) argues that the following issues are significant and help to determine whether the agreement is likely to prove effective.

❑ Successful collaboration requires commitment on both sides. Without sufficient management time, trust and respect the agreement is likely to fail.

Visit the website:
http://www.
itbp.com

In reality, all the required resources must be committed. Either for managing linkages, or for managing a new joint venture company, capable managers must be transferred or seconded. The outcome of the alliance will depend upon both the commitment of the partners and the emergent power and influence they exert.

❑ There must be mutual benefits, the attainment of which may well involve sacrifices on both sides. Both partners should appreciate clearly what the other party wants from the agreement, and their objectives.

If the commitment of each ally is uneven, the keener partner or the faster learner is likely to assume control. This might mean that the interests of the weaker partner are either bought out or simply taken over.

❑ If circumstances change during the period of the alliance, flexibility may be required as the objectives and priorities of either or both partners may change.
❑ Cultural differences, which might be either geographic or corporate in origin, will have to be reconciled.

In addition it is sensible if alliance partners see their joint involvement as an opportunity to learn new skills and good practices. Partners are not simply there to plug gaps or weaknesses. Analysts acknowledge that the Japanese have been very good at learning from their alliances, and that Western companies have been slower to exploit the learning opportunities.

Badaracco (1991) differentiates between

❑ migratory knowledge – easily transferred technical skills, and
❑ embedded knowledge about how a company does business, which is particularly useful for deepening insight into new markets.

Where companies do enter an alliance through weakness rather than strength, it is vital that they use the partnership for learning and development.

In 1991 Ford formed an alliance with Yamaha to develop a new engine for the Fiesta and Escort ranges. Whilst such high-performance engines as the Ford-Cosworth are the outcome of past joint ventures, this was the first incidence of an alliance for mainstream car engines. Analysts have commented that Ford needed an agreement because they had become weak in a rapidly changing industry, stimulated by new materials, higher fuel consumption expectations and tighter emission standards. 'Ford must learn from the deal, and not subcontract their engine technology for the long term.'

It was mentioned earlier that acquisitions should be evaluated in terms of their ability to generate synergy. Joint ventures and strategic alliances should be regarded in the same light. Devlin and Bleackley (1988) argue that the key issues are the strategic wisdom behind the decision to form an alliance in the first place, the choice of partner, and the management of the alliance once it has been agreed. The position of both parties to the agreement should be improved from the alliance. If there is a real opportunity for synergy, joint benefits and mutual trust and commitment by both parties, joint ventures can be an effective means of implementing strategic change. However, although some of the inherent difficulties of acquisition are avoided by this type of agreement, there will still be implementation issues. Unless these are tackled properly, the joint venture is likely to prove expensive and tie up resources which might be deployed more effectively.

Alliances can fail and/or be dismantled for a number of reasons – such as the acquisition of one of the partners by an outside organization (Rover/Honda after Rover was sold to BMW) – and consequently the extent to which any organization is dependent upon its alliances should be carefully monitored.

Summary

This chapter has concentrated on the specific growth strategies of diversification and acquisition, and we have also considered joint ventures. The emphases have been on why organizations might select such strategies, how they might be managed effectively and the key considerations and issues. It was emphasized that diversification and acquisition were being discussed together as diversification in the UK is more likely to be implemented through acquisition than through internal growth, and most acquisitions involve some degree of diversification. The issues and difficulties involved therefore relate to both.

Specifically we have:

- considered the typical growth pattern of large companies, and the extent of diversification by the largest firms in the UK, USA, France and Germany
- looked at the reasons behind the increasing diversification and industrial concentration in the UK, the effects and implications

- considered more generally why organizations might choose a strategy of diversification and acquisition, emphasizing the issues of growth and economic reasoning
- discussed a selection of research findings which conclude that diversification and acquisition strategies often fail to bring about the benefits which were forecast, and are therefore relatively high risk
- summarized the findings on why acquisitions fail, emphasizing that money and people are key aspects
- listed the major considerations and issues concerning diversification and acquisition
- discussed the components of an effective acquisition strategy, namely the logic underpinning the formulation of the strategy; the search for, and review of, possible acquisitions; the acquisition itself; and implementation aspects of merging the two organizations
- considered forms and examples of joint ventures and strategic alliances
- discussed briefly the key issues in formulating and implementing this strategy effectively.

Checklist of key terms and concepts

You should feel confident that you understand the following terms and ideas:

★ The distinction between single product, dominant product, related product, and unrelated product/conglomerate companies

★ The conclusions from the research by Reed and Luffman, Meeks, Salter and Weinhold, Porter, Nesbitt and King and Burgman

★ The key financial and people issues in diversification and acquisition

★ The key aspects of an effective acquisition strategy

★ Joint ventures and strategic alliances.

Questions and research assignments

Text related

1 From the various points and issues discussed in this chapter list the possible advantages and disadvantages of
   (a) acquisition strategies and
   (b) joint ventures and strategic alliances.
   From your experience list one successful and one unsuccessful example of each strategy. Why have you selected these particular cases?

2 What are the key arguments for and against strategies of unrelated diversification and focus? Again, from your own experience, list examples of each.

Library based

3 What has happened to Granada since the successful acquisition of Forte in 1996? Specifically: Has Granada been able to dispose of those businesses/activities it indicated it regarded as non-core during the bid? What has happened to Granada's profitability, share price and debt ratio?
   On balance, in your view, was the acquisition a sound strategic move for Granada?

4 Obtain statistics on either a selection of large companies which interest you, or, the largest 20 companies in the UK, and
   (a) ascertain the extent to which they are diversified and classify them as either single, dominant, related or conglomerate product companies
   (b) determine their relative size in relation to their competitors in the USA, Japan and Europe.

5 Develop a summary of the diversification and acquisition strategies of Trafalgar House plc. (A useful early summary can be found in Barber, L

(1986) Bruised Trafalgar struggles to regain its political touch, *Financial Times*, 19 May.)
   (a) Trafalgar bid for the P & O shipping line in 1983, but it was referred to the Monopolies and Mergers Commission. Although approval was granted, Trafalgar allowed the bid to lapse. Given they already owned Cunard, was this an appropriate strategic move?
   (b) Trafalgar acquired the Scott Lithgow (1984) and John Brown (1986) shipyards from British Shipbuilders. Where do you think they might have been able to add value in this declining industry?
   (c) Did the acquisition of Davy consolidate this move and offer real potential synergy?
   (d) Trafalgar bid unsuccessfully against Eurotunnel for the Channel tunnel, proposing a linked bridge and tunnel scheme. They were successful in a bid to build a bridge across the Thames at Dartford to relieve congestion in the existing Dartford tunnel. Trafalgar built the bridge with private investment money which will be recouped by tolls on traffic. Do you believe these developments could be justified strategically? Why? Why not?
   (e) Should Trafalgar House have divested its interests in passenger shipping and hotels?
   (f) What has happened since Hongkong Land acquired a minority shareholding early in October 1992?

6 Why did Woolworth Holdings change its name to Kingfisher in 1989? What was the reaction of the City to this proposal?
   How successful has Woolworth/Kingfisher been? Has its diversification been successful?

Recommended further reading

Channon (1983) provides a useful background to this chapter, and the articles by Constable (1986) and Reed and Luffman (1986) illustrate the problems of diversification and acquisition very effectively.

Ohmae's paper on strategic alliances (1989) is a valuable summary of the issues in this increasingly popular strategic alternative. Also useful is Lyons, MP (1991) Joint ventures as strategic choice – a literature survey, *Long Range Planning*, 24(4).

References

Badaracco, JL (1991) *The Knowledge Link: How Firms Compete Through Strategic Alliances*, Harvard Business School Press.

Biggadike, R (1979) The risky business of diversification, *Harvard Business Review*, May–June.

Burgman, R, Research findings quoted in McLean, RJ (1985) How to make acquisitions work, *Chief Executive*, April.

Business International (1988) *Making Acquisitions Work: Lessons from Companies' Successes and Mistakes*, Report published by Business International, Geneva.

Channon, DF (1983) *Strategy and Structure in British Industry*, Macmillan.

Connell, DC (1988) Strategic partnering and competitive advantage, Presented at the 8th Annual Strategic Management Society Conference, Amsterdam, October.

Constable, CJ (1986) Diversification as a factor in UK industrial strategy, *Long Range Planning*, 19(1).

Cowling, K, Stoneman, P and Cubbin, J (eds) (1979) *Mergers and Economic Performance*, Cambridge University Press.

Devlin, G and Bleackley, M (1988) Strategic alliances – guidelines for success, *Long Range Planning*, 21(5), October.

Drucker, PF (1982) Quoted in Drucker: The dangers of spoonfeeding, *Financial Times*, 15 October.

Dyas, GP and Thanheiser, HT (1976) *The Emerging European Enterprise: Strategy and Structure in French and German Industry*, Macmillan.

Ernst and Young (1995) Key success factors in acquisition management, research project with Warwick Business School, Ernst and Young, London.

Goold, M, Campbell, A and Alexander, M (1994) *Corporate Level Strategy*, John Wiley.

Hilton, A (1987) Presented at 'Growing Through Acquisition', conference organized by Arthur Young, London, 31 March.

Jenkinson, T and Mayer, C (1994) *Hostile Take-overs: Defence, Attack and Corporate Governance*, McGraw-Hill.

Kitching, J (1967) Why do mergers miscarry? *Harvard Business Review*, November–December.

Kitching, J (1973) Acquisitions in Europe: causes of corporate successes and failures, Report published by Business International, Geneva.

Lorenz, C (1986) Take-overs. At best an each way bet, *Financial Times*, 6 January.

McLean, RJ (1985) How to make acquisitions work, *Chief Executive*, April.

Meeks, J (1977) *Disappointing Marriage: A Study of the Gains from Merger*, Cambridge University Press.

Nesbitt, SL and King, RR (1989) Business diversification – has it taken a bad rap? *Mergers and Acquisitions*, November–December.

Ohmae, K (1989) The global logic of strategic alliances, *Harvard Business Review*, March–April.

Peters, TJ and Waterman, RH Jr (1982) *In Search of Excellence: Lessons from America's Best Run Companies*, Harper & Row.

Porter, ME (1987) From competitive advantage to corporate strategy, *Harvard Business Review*, May–June.

Ramsay, J (1987) The strategic focus: deciding your acquisition strategy, Paper presented at 'Growing Through Acquisition', conference organized by Arthur Young, London, 31 March.

Reed, R and Luffman, G (1986) Diversification: the growing confusion, *Strategic Management Journal*, 7(1), 29–35.

Rumelt, RP (1974) *Strategy, Structure and Economic Performance*, Division of Research, Harvard Business School.

Salter, MS and Weinhold, WA (1982) *Merger Trends and Prospects for the 1980s*, Division of Research, Harvard Business School; quoted in Thackray, J (1982) The American takeover war, *Management Today*, September.

17

Issues in Strategic Consolidation and Recovery

The causes and symptoms of decline were discussed in Chapter 7. In this chapter we examine the potential for recovery and alternative strategies that might be considered. We also look at strategies appropriate for a recession.

Learning objectives

After studying this chapter you should be able to:

■ identify the four possible outcomes of strategic change when companies are in difficulties
■ describe a number of retrenchment and turnaround strategies
■ discuss the thinking behind divestment strategies and the implementation issues involved
■ explain and debate the key issues behind the increasing popularity of management buyouts in the UK
■ explain which strategies are important during a recession
■ summarize the possible strategies for individual competitors in declining industries.

Don't forget to visit the website:
http://www.itbp.com

Introduction

At any given time certain industries will provide attractive growth prospects for those companies who already compete in them, and for potential newcomers. At the same time, however, other industries will be in terminal decline. This might be taking place slowly or rapidly. In the case of slow decline, profitable opportunities may still exist for those companies which can relate best to changing market needs. Where decline is rapid, prospects are likely to be very limited. A third group of industries might be undergoing significant change, and the companies which can adapt effectively will be able to survive and grow.

The motor cycle industry in the UK is an example of an industry which has collapsed. In 1950 Britain made 80% of the world's motor cycles. In the 1990s it makes less than 1%. Inefficient production, poor marketing and inadequate product development in the face of Japanese competition are the causes. By contrast certain shipbuilders in the UK and Europe have survived competition from the developing countries and Japan by adapting to changes in demand and adding value.

Japan and South Korea, with overall market shares of 45% and 21%, respectively, excel with 'run-of-the-mill' tankers and container ships. Western Europe cannot compete and has seen its shipbuilding yards decline. Some yards, however, have survived by focusing on high added value vessels such as gas and chemical carriers, ferries and cruise ships, which, together in any one year, amount to 10% of the global tonnage but represent 33% of total value.

The causes and symptoms of decline were discussed in Chapter 7. The most obvious **symptoms** are slower growth figures for sales or profits and a deterioration in the various financial measures of performance. The major **causes** are poor management and leadership, acquisitions which fail to provide synergy and meet expectations, the lack of effective financial controls, cost disadvantages, poor marketing, and a general inability to compete.

Any recovery from a difficult situation will be related to:

❑ improving marketing effectiveness and competitiveness, and hence increasing revenue
❑ managing the organization more efficiently, and thereby reducing costs.

Where these changes in functional and competitive strategies prove inadequate, something more drastic will be required. In the outline summary of strategic alternatives in Chapter 15, four disinvestment strategies were introduced:

❑ Retrenchment strategies aim to increase revenue and reduce costs by concentrating and consolidating. These involve changes in functional strategies.
❑ Turnaround strategies relate to changes in competitive strategies and frequently feature re-positioning for competitive advantage.

Retrenchment and turnaround strategies are often collectively called recovery strategies.

❑ Divestment.
❑ Liquidation.

These result in changes to the company's corporate strategy.

In this chapter we explore recovery and divestment strategies in greater detail, considering first the overall feasibility of recovery and different recovery situations. These issues are of primary concern to companies that are already experiencing difficulties and showing symptoms of decline. In the last section we look at strategic alternatives for declining industries, which is relevant for companies that may be currently successful or unsuccessful in a situation of change.

We also discuss management buy-outs, which are increasing in popularity and are one way of managing a divestment situation.

The feasibility of recovery

When sales or profits are declining because a company is uncompetitive or because an industry is in decline, recovery may or may not be possible. If a company is a single product firm, or heavily reliant on the industry in question, then it may be in real difficulties and in danger of liquidation unless it can diversify successfully. If profits are declining, such a strategy may be difficult to fund. Where the situation applies to one business unit in an already diversified company, the company as a whole may be less threatened. However, a change of strategy will be required, and the issue concerns whether or not a successful recovery can be brought about and sustained.

The likelihood of a possible recovery improves where:

❑ the causes of the decline in the firm's sales and profits can be tackled and the problems overcome – this depends upon how serious and deep-rooted they are

❑ the industry as a whole, or particular segments of the industry which might be targeted, remains attractive
❑ there is potential for creating or enhancing competitive advantage.

Recovery situations

Slatter (1984) has postulated that there are essentially four types of recovery situation, and these are illustrated in Figure 17.1. Once the profits of the firm or business unit have declined to a crisis stage, then a change in strategy is essential. However, the industry and competitive factors might be such that recovery simply is not feasible. Insolvency is inevitable, whatever alternative strategies might be tried. Successful retrenchment strategies might be implemented and profits improved to a non-crisis level again. However, unless the industry remains in some way attractive and potentially profitable, or the firm retains its competitive advantage, the retrenchment might subsequently fail. A third alternative is a successful turnaround but no real growth and sustained recovery. Possibly in a low-profit industry insufficient funds are generated to finance investment for further growth and diversification. A sustained recovery implies real growth, and possibly further changes in functional, competitive and corporate strategies.

Non-recoverable situations

Slatter argues that in situations where there is little chance of survival and the likelihood that both retrenchment and turnaround strategies will fail, a number of characteristics are likely to be present.

❑ The company is not competitive and the potential for improvement is low. This might be the result of a cost disadvantage which cannot be remedied. Certain businesses and industries which have declined in the face of foreign competition, especially from countries with low wage costs, are testament to this.
❑ The company is not diversified and lacks both the resources and access to resources to remedy this weakness.
❑ Demand for the basic product or service involved is in terminal decline.

Temporary recovery

Where a retrenchment strategy is implemented successfully it may or may not be sustained. If new forms of competitive advantage are found and sustained, or the product or service is effectively re-positioned, subsequent insolvency may be avoided. However, if costs are reduced or additional revenues are generated in an essentially unattractive and declining industry, the effect will be

---

We weren't making money at SAS (Scandinavian Airlines System) when I came here. We were in a desperate situation, and that's the worst time to focus on preventing mistakes and controlling costs. First, we had to increase revenues. We had to decide what business we were going to do – before you can start managing effectively you must know who is your customer and what is your product – and go to work on the revenue side. Then we could think about cutting costs, because only then would we know which costs could be cut without losing competitiveness.

Jan Carlzon, President and Chief Executive Officer, Scandinavian Airlines System

---

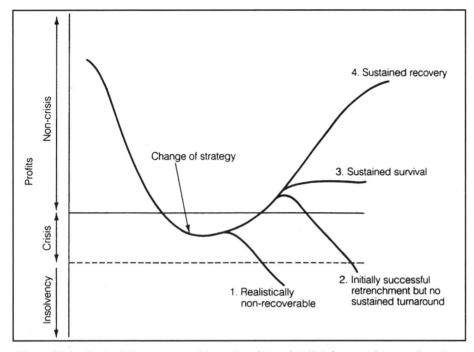

Figure 17.1 The feasibility of recovery. Adapted from Slatter, S (1984) *Corporate Recovery*, Penguin.

limited. In such cases it will become important for the company to invest the cash generated from the retrenchment to diversify if that is possible.

If an organization has captive customers who are in some way dependent and face high short-term exit costs – possibly because of agreed specifications – they can exploit them for a period by charging high prices. There will be a temporary profit improvement, but the customers will be lost in the medium- to long-term. Companies following this strategy need to use the extra revenue and the time they buy to develop new strategic opportunities.

Case 17.1 illustrates a temporarily successful turnaround by the Burton Group which was not sustained. Further retrenchment has been required.

Sustained survival

Sustained survival implies that a turnaround is achieved but there is little further growth. The industry may be in slow decline, or generally competitive and unprofitable. Survival potential and limited profit opportunities continue to exist, but little more. Sustained survival would also apply where a company failed to use its increased earnings effectively and did not diversify into new more profitable opportunities which could provide growth prospects.

Sustained recovery

A sustained recovery is likely to involve a genuine and successful turnaround – possibly new product development or market re-positioning. In addition the turnaround may well be followed by a growth strategy, perhaps acquisition and diversification.

The recovery is helped if the industry is strong and attractive and the company's decline has been caused by poor management rather than because the industry itself is in a decline.

Case 17.1
THE BURTON GROUP

The Burton Group is now primarily a retailer of fashionable clothing for men and women through a number of branded outlets.

The company was started as a single shop in 1901 by Montague Burton, who had built the company into a vertically integrated organization of factories and some 600 stores when he died in 1952. The main product area had been made-to-measure suits for men.

In the late 1960s the company had problems of management succession and it was basically stagnant with underutilized assets. Burton was also experiencing a number of specific problems.

❏ The menswear market was switching in preference from made-to-measure to ready-made suits.
❏ The company had a large manufacturing base in relation to the falling demand for its products. Moreover the factories were inefficient and insufficiently capital intensive.
❏ There was growing competition from such stores as Marks and Spencer.
❏ The company had an old-fashioned image, made worse by stores which were not designed or fitted for the growing market for ready-made clothes.

A new management team was appointed and their strategy was one of diversification. In the early 1970s Burton acquired five new businesses:

❏ Evans – outsize fashions for women with fuller figures
❏ Ryman's – office supplies
❏ St Remy – clothing stores in France
❏ Green's – cameras and hi-fi equipment
❏ Trumps – an employment agency.

Burton also opened a chain of womenswear shops with the Top Shop brand name.

The diversification strategy failed in overall terms, although parts did prove successful, and divestment began in the mid-1970s.

In addition:

❏ Branches were modernized, and some were enlarged. The aim was to make Burton stores more appealing to younger buyers. Some stores, though, were closed.
❏ A new chain of Top Man stores was opened to complement Top Shop.
❏ There was greater emphasis on the womenswear market, with more Top Shops and the acquisition of Dorothy Perkins.
❏ The Principles chain was developed.
❏ Manufacturing was pruned; and the final factory was disposed of in 1988.

Between 1976 and 1979 the number of employees was reduced from 21,400 to 11,000.

These changes were led by Ralph Halpern, who became Chief Executive in 1977 (and Executive Chairman in 1981), and the result was revitalization, new growth and profitability. The Burton Group built up a 12.5% share of the UK clothing market, second only to Marks and Spencer. Halpern was feted as a retailer of genius, and rewarded with a million pound salary, a knighthood and celebrity status. However, when this expansion required consolidation in the 1980s, a number of strategic misjudgements were made.

❏ In 1985 Burton took over Debenhams after a fierce battle. The new department stores required expensive revamping and the payback was slower than anticipated. Moreover, different retailing skills were involved.
❏ Burton diversified into shopping centre development, and was financially exposed when property prices fell.
❏ The growth led to over-expansion and the acquisition of new sites with very high rent and lease charges. These proved too expensive in the retail recession of the late 1980s.

Profits and the share price collapsed and Halpern departed in November 1990, to be replaced as Chief Executive by his deputy, Lawrence Cooklin. In mid-1991 Burton sought to raise money in a 'desperate rights issue', imposed a pay freeze

Continued

and looked to rationalize by reducing both the number of stores and head office administration.

The company traded at a loss during 1991–1992; a new, experimental, out-of-town discount format, branded IS, was introduced and the flagship Harvey Nichols department store was sold for £51 million in August 1991. (Harvey Nichols was floated on the stock exchange in 1996 with a valuation of £150 million.) Analysts commented that Burton was still searching for a retail format suitable for the 1990s and estimated the odds of a second successful recovery to be no better than 50:50. Cooklin was replaced in February 1992 by American John Hoerner from Debenhams.

Hoerner was determined to tackle two key strategic issues:

❏ The Burton brands/businesses saw themselves in competition with each other; they frequently targeted the same customers
❏ The company was too willing to discount its prices when trading levels were disappointing.

Three years later Burton was profitable again. What had happened? Initially:

❏ Hoerner initiated a cross-formats review of target markets, design, merchandising, pricing strategies, visual marketing and buying.

❏ The formats were then re-focused, some more than others, and new strategies trialled. Top Shop, for example, targeted 16–19-year-olds by experimenting with a 'funky, grungey' look. Those targeted loved the new image; unfortunately Top Shop's other customers did not, and they voted with their feet. Top Shop switched to a less radical look which had appeal for all ages up to 30.
❏ Locations were reviewed from a corporate perspective. Some sites were closed and replaced with new ones, although not as many. In addition some formats were exchanged for other Burton brands to try and achieve the most appropriate location for each one.
❏ The new but unprofitable IS format was abandoned in 1994.
❏ The head office was reduced in size and numbers. In the branches there was a programme of switching employees from full-time contracts to flexible part-time hours.

Hoerner later turned his attention to supplier relationships and to the links and inter-dependencies between the Burton formats. The future strategy will be based on building the strength of the various brand names.

Both a sustained survival and a sustained recovery may involve divestment of assets or part of the business to enable the company to concentrate on selected market segments or products.

Slatter (1984) studied a number of successful and unsuccessful attempts at turnaround, and concluded that there are three main features of a sustained recovery.

❏ Asset reduction is invariably required in order to generate cash. Quite frequently this will be achieved by divestment of part of the business.
❏ A new strategic leader is usually necessary. The new strategic leader will typically be associated with a re-structuring of the organization, the introduction of new strategies and a re-definition of roles and policies.
❏ Better financial control systems are also a normal feature.

Whilst retrenchment and initial survival can be achieved by concentrating on improving *efficiencies*, sustained survival and recovery will invariably require more *effective* competitive and corporate strategies. Case 17.2, Filofax, provides an example of a sustained recovery.

Case 17.2
FILOFAX

Although it has been in existence for many years, Filofax became prominent and grew rapidly in the early 1980s; its success was based on its range of personal organizers. Growth was maintained throughout the 1980s by extending the product life cycle for organizers. A number of distinct price points brought in new users; additional page sets facilitated new uses by adding extra value; a Deskfax business organizer was pioneered. In 1988 turnover was just under £15 million, with pre-tax profits of £2.75 million.

Filofax's success, however, attracted competition, most notably from lower-priced alternatives such as WH Smith's own-label range. Filofax products began to look overpriced, and the distribution network was seen as weak and fragmented. By 1990 the company was losing money. At the end of the decade, Robin Field, a management consultant who had been helping the company, became the new chief executive.

Filofax was immediately rationalized. Jobs were lost, prices cut and marketing expenditure reduced. The most popular organizer within the range was now selling at just half its 1985 price. If growth and prosperity was to be restored, however, new competitive advantages had to be found.

Filofax segmented and targeted its potential customers. Products were improved to appeal particularly to those people who have to organize their own lives without the assistance of a secretary; the armed forces and members of the clergy are keen buyers. The emphasis has stayed with domestic users, as distinct from business customers, to minimize the impact of electronic organizers; and a new budget range has been introduced. Thirty thousand organizers were sold in 1987; 80,000 in 1994.

In addition Field looked to acquire suitable distributors and manufacturers of related products. In 1992 Filofax bought Lefax, a US manufacturer of luxury organizers, and a French distributor. This was followed in 1993 by Drakes, which has a 90% share of the UK market for duplicate message books, and distribution businesses in Germany and Sweden. In 1994 Henry Ling was acquired. Ling produces greeting cards, a high-growth product which sells through the same outlets as organizers. In 1995 Filofax bought Topps, a UK manufacturer of leather and simulated leather goods; Topps already owned Microfile, a competitor of Filofax.

In 1995 turnover had grown to £20 million, with £2.9 million pre-tax profits. Organizers contributed 75% of revenue and profits.

To summarize this section, the opportunities for sustained recovery, or at least survival, improve where:

❏ there are fewer causes of the decline
❏ the crisis is not deep-rooted, perhaps because the decline is the result of poor management rather than an unattractive declining industry
❏ there is support from key stakeholders for the changes required (this may involve understanding by financiers and the commitment of managers and other employees to the necessary changes)
❏ strategic opportunities to differentiate, re-focus and create competitive advantage exist
❏ the company has the ability to reduce costs.

Having considered the background feasibility of recovery, we now examine the actual recovery strategies in greater detail.

Retrenchment strategies

In this section organizational and financial changes, cost and asset reduction, and strategies aimed at generating revenue are considered. Retrenchment strategies are essentially functional, rather than competitive or corporate, and are aimed at making the company more productive and profitable whilst retaining essentially the same products and services, although there might be some rationalization. By concentrating on financial issues, they often address major causes of the company's decline.

Organizational changes

It was emphasized above that a change in strategic leadership is frequently involved in recovery strategies. In addition there might be a need to strengthen the management team in other areas. The fact that there are personnel changes is not the important issue. The subsequent changes to strategies, structure and policies, and the effect on the existing staff and their motivation, are what matter. Re-organizations are likely to take place, involving new definitions of roles and responsibilities. Policies and management and control systems may also be changed to give managers new opportunities to achieve, and to convince them that recovery prospects are real.

Financial changes

Poor financial control systems, say a badly managed cash flow, are often a feature of companies in difficulties. In addition overheads may have been allowed to become too high in relation to direct production costs, and the company may not know the actual costs of producing particular products and services or be able to explain all expenditures. The establishment of an effective costing system, and greater control over the cash flow, can improve profitability and generate revenue.

Visit the website: http://www.itbp.com

Another retrenchment strategy is the restructuring of debt to reduce the financial burden of the company. Possibly repayment dates can be extended, or loan capital converted into preference shares or equity, thereby allowing the company more freedom through less pressure to pay interest. Changes by Eurotunnel provide an excellent example of this.

Cost reduction strategies

When the acquisition strategies of such companies as Hanson were discussed, it was emphasized that they looked for companies with high gross margins and relatively low after-tax profitability. These are indications of overheads which have been allowed to grow too much, thereby providing opportunities for improving profits by reducing organizational slack and waste. Companies could address the overheads issue for themselves, without being acquired, if they recognized the extent of the problem and were determined to reduce their costs in order to improve their competitiveness and profitability.

In terms of reducing costs, the normal starting place is labour costs. In many cases opportunities will exist to reduce labour costs and improve productivity, but if the reductions are too harsh there can be a real threat to the quality of both the product and the overall service offered to customers. One opportunity is to examine working patterns and attempt to manage overtime, part-time arrangements and extra shifts both to meet demand and to contain costs. Companies can slip easily into situations where overtime and weekend working are creating costs which cannot be recovered in competitive prices.

Redundancies may be required to reduce costs and bring capacity more into line with demand. Again this can be implemented well or poorly. In most cases the issue is not losing particular numbers of people and thereby saving on wages, but losing non-essential staff or those who fail to make an effective contribution. There is always the danger in a voluntary redundancy programme that good people will choose to leave or take early retirement.

Costs can be reduced anywhere and everywhere in the value chain. Better supply arrangements and terms can reduce costs; products can be redesigned to cost less without any loss in areas significant to customers; and certain activities, such as public relations, training, advertising, and research and development might be cut. The argument here is that these activities are non-essential, and this might be perfectly plausible in the short term. It may not be the case for the longer term, and therefore they would need to be reinstated when extra revenues had been regenerated.

Asset reduction strategies

Divestment of a business unit, or part of the business, is an asset reduction strategy but is considered in greater detail later. It is really more of a corporate than a functional strategy, and the decision should not be made on financial grounds alone. Whilst the sale of a business can raise money, this gain may be more than offset if there is existing synergy with other parts of the company which suffer in some way from the divestment.

Internal divestment or rationalization can take a number of forms. Plants might be closed and production concentrated in fewer places; production might be re-scheduled to generate increased economies of scale. The idea is both to reduce overheads and reduce direct costs.

Assets might be sold and leased back. As far as the balance sheet is concerned, assets have been reduced and in turn cash has been generated. The scope and capacity of the business may be unaffected; the changes are exclusively financial.

Revenue-generating strategies

The marketing strategies considered in the next section on turnarounds are essentially revenue-generating strategies, and they frequently involve changes in competitive strategies. However, revenue can also be generated by improving certain management control systems. If stocks are reduced by better stock management or by a review of the whole production system and a move towards just-in-time, cash is freed. In just the same way, if debtors can be persuaded to settle accounts more speedily, cash flow can be improved.

Turnaround strategies

Retrenchment strategies will usually have short time horizons and they will be designed to yield immediate results. Turnaround strategies are likely to address those areas which must be developed if there is to be a sustained recovery. They involve changes in the overall marketing effort, including the re-positioning or re-focusing of existing products and services, together with the development of new ones. They are designed to bring quick results and at the same time contribute towards longer-term growth. They overlap with the internal level one growth strategies outlined in Chapter 15, and they may also be a stepping stone to growth through diversification.

Retrenchment strategies do not affect customers directly but the following turnaround strategies are designed to improve the effectiveness of the company's marketing. Consequently they are addressing customers and consumers directly, and for this reason some degree of caution is required in implementing the changes involved.

Changing prices

Prices can be changed at very short notice, and price increases or decreases can result in increased revenue. Price rises can increase revenue as long as the elasticity of demand ensures that sales do not decline unacceptably with the price increase. Price decreases can improve demand and hence revenue – again depending on the elasticity of demand. Hence it is important to have an insight into the demand elasticity for individual products and services although forecasting the effect of price changes will be subject to some uncertainty. In general the opportunity to increase prices is related to the extent of existing differentiation, and the opportunity to differentiate further and create new competitive advantage.

It is important to remember that unless particular products and services are regarded as underpriced by customers in relation to their competition, a price rise should be accompanied by advertising support and possibly minor changes and improvements in the product or packaging. The price change must be justified.

It is also important to consider the likely reaction of competitors, which in turn will be influenced by the structure of the industry and the degree and type of competitive rivalry. Oligopoly markets, an essential feature of the UK industrial structure, were introduced in Chapter 5, when it was emphasized that oligopoly competitors tend to follow price decreases but not price rises.

In relation to the concept of price changes, discount structures might be altered to favour certain groups of customers at the expense of others. Such a strategic move can both raise revenue and improve the attractiveness of a company to certain market segments. Any negative effect on other customer groups should be monitored carefully.

Re-focusing

The idea behind re-focusing is to concentrate effort on specific customers and specific products, relating the two closely together. The strategy requires careful thought and attention in relation to why people buy and opportunities for differentiation, segmentation and competitive advantage. The selection of particular product/market and service/market niches for concentrating effort will depend upon revenue and growth potential, gross margins, the extent and type of competition for the segment or niche, and the potential to create a response to marketing activity, such as advertising.

In the short term products or services which sell quickly and generate cash quickly may be attractive opportunities even if their gross margin is small; and there may well be a group of customers for whom an appropriate package can be created.

New product development

The replacement of existing products with new ones, discussed earlier in the book, may be required to effect a turnaround if a company has been losing competitiveness in an attractive industry by falling behind competitors in terms of innovation and product improvement. Equally product improvements, designed to prolong the product life cycle, can be extremely useful in low growth or declining industries. They can be used to help a company concentrate on the particular segments of the market which are remaining relatively strong.

Rationalizing the product line

Variety reduction, can similarly be useful for concentrating efforts on the stronger market segments and opportunities, particularly where the industry overall is losing attractiveness. Such a strategy needs a proper understanding of costs, and which individual products and services are most and least profitable. In a multi-product organization, with inter-dependences between the business units, for example, transfer price arrangements can distort profitabilities. It has already been mentioned earlier that certain products and services can be vital contributors to overall synergy, but individually not very profitable, and care needs to be taken with these.

Emphasis on selling and advertising

An emphasis on selling and advertising might take the form of selected additional expenditure in order to generate greater revenue, or the examination of all current marketing expenditure in order to try and ascertain the best potential returns from the spending.

Expenditure on advertising, below-the-line promotions and the salesforce is used to promote products and services in order to generate sales revenue. However, all these activities are investments, and their potential returns should be considered. The increased revenue expected from any increased spending should certainly exceed the additional costs incurred, and there is an argument that the opportunity cost of the investment funds should also be assessed.

Whilst five alternative approaches to improving marketing effectiveness have been considered in this section, a number of them may be used in conjunction at any time. Moreover these turnaround strategies may also be combined with the retrenchment strategies discussed earlier, the aim being both to reduce costs and to improve revenue at the same time.

It has already been explained that the divestment of products or business units can be useful for reducing assets in retrenchment strategies. Divestments can also be used to rationalize the product line, as discussed above. They are the subject of the next section.

Divestment strategies

Divestment can be essentially **internal**, the closure of a plant as part of a rationalization programme, or **external**, the sale of part of the business. The justification will be similar for each, and any resources saved or generated should be re-allocated.

Davis (1974) argues that divestments are often sudden decisions rather than decisions reached as part of a continual evaluation process which reviews all the products and services in the firm's portfolio periodically. Companies who utilize portfolio analysis as part of their planning will be in a position to identify which parts of the business are the poorest performers and possible candidates for divestment. However, Devlin (1989) contends that effective divestment is a skill which few strategic leaders actually possess. This, he suggests, is a critical strategic issue, given that many acquisitions fail to achieve their expected returns. Divestment, though, suggests an admission of failure.

There will be an obvious reluctance to sell a business unit to another company, especially a competitor, who might succeed and transform the business into an effective performer. This will be particularly important if such success could pose a future threat to business units which have been retained. For these reasons divestments are often associated with a change of strategic leader as an outsider is less likely to feel any loyalty to past decisions.

Issues in selecting a divestment candidate

There are a number of possible considerations which might be relevant in selecting a product, service or business unit for divestment. Both financial and strategic aspects are important:

❑ the current position in the product life cycle, and the likely future potential for further growth and profitability
❑ the current market position, and opportunities for competitive advantage
❑ taking these two points further and considering portfolio analyses, the future potential for cash generation and future investment requirements in order to remain competitive (linked to this is the opportunity cost of the resources being utilized)
❑ identified alternative uses for the resources which could be freed up, and in certain cases the extent of the need to free up resources for relocation
❑ the ability to find a suitable buyer willing to pay an acceptable price.

In Case 16.2 we saw how Daimler-Benz decided to withdraw funding from its Fokker aircraft subsidiary. Realistically a new owner was required for Fokker. One possibility was Bombardier, the Canadian company which had already rescued Shorts (Belfast, and a major sub-contractor to Fokker), de Havilland and Learjet. Bombardier's post-acquisition strategy is to invest heavily to restructure, modernize and extend the product line. It weighs the turnaround chances carefully, looking for good management and stable employee relations, sound technologies, products with competitive advantage and long-term growth potential, component orders to offset cyclical downturns and tight cost management. In the event, Bombardier decided Fokker was not an appropriate purchase.

❑ in addition to these points, the strategic potential to divest some business or activity which is profitable in order to raise money to invest in something which is likely to be even more profitable (implicit in this might be a desire to limit the strategic perspective and scope of diversification, or a desire to contain borrowing)

❑ the issue of whether it is cheaper to close a business or plant or keep it running despite low returns, i.e. exit costs and barriers

❑ the contribution to existing synergy, and the overall value to the organization (certain businesses may be making a loss but be valuable to the organization because of their contribution to other activities, their past reputation, their significance to certain customers who are important to the organization and their general value as a competitive weapon)

❑ the opportunity to satisfy existing customers, which the organization would wish to retain, with alternative products and services

❑ the tangible and intangible benefits from specializing and reducing the extent to which the organization is diversified. In this context Tube Investments was discussed in Chapter 15. See also case 17.3, Philips.

Case 17.3
PHILIPS

Philips, the Dutch electricals and electronics group, has invented such everyday products as the cassette recorder, video recorder and compact disc, but invariably has failed to be the major beneficiary from their development. Late in the 1980s Philips was underperforming and in need of revised strategies and restructuring. There were 'too many managers and not enough management'. Arguably Philips was too diversified and involved in businesses where it had neither critical mass nor the resources to grow to the required size. Semi-conductors was one example.

In 1990 a new chief executive, Jan Timmer, determined that Philips would systematically focus on key areas. Interests in defence electronics and telecommunications were divested. In 1989 Philips had sold 53% of its domestic appliance division (refrigerators, cookers, and so on) to Whirlpool of the USA, the world's leading manufacturer; Whirlpool purchased the remaining 47% in 1991. At this time Philips was losing money and the sale helped reduce debts.

Strategically Philips could now concentrate on consumer electronics – it also owns the German manufacturer, Grundig – and lighting products. Although it is managed on a hands-off basis,

Philips owns over 70% of Polygram, one of the major competitors in the global recorded music business, and this supports its interests in consumer music products. Whilst Philips as a whole has become stronger and more profitable, there have been disappointments as well as successes. In 1992 Philips launched its new DCC (digital compact cassette) system to compete with Sony's new mini compact discs and players. Both of these systems offer high-quality recordings and reproduction in a reduced size format. Some experts were suggesting that Philips would have the advantage because the new DCC players would also play existing tape cassettes – mini-disc players are not compatible with any other system. Other commentators suggested the opposite result because the mini-disc could replace Walkmen. Neither format took off, but, at the same time, Philips' CD-i (compact disc-interactive) machines have become the industry standard.

In 1991 Philips launched a new light bulb, based on the principle of induction, and without either filaments or electrodes. The new bulb, although expensive, has an exceptionally long life of some 15 years and is very efficient. It is seen as ideal for certain uses such as tunnel lighting.

Issues in the divestment

Once the decision to divest has been taken, there are a number of further considerations.

First, there is the issue of how active and how secretive the search for a buyer should be. It can be argued that there should be an active search for an acceptable buyer who is willing to pay an appropriate premium, on the grounds that it is all too easy to sell a business cheaply. A low price might be expected where the sale is hurried, perhaps because there is a pressing need to raise money or where a first offer is accepted without an exploration of other options. There is also an argument in favour of secrecy and speed as opposed to prolonged and publicized negotiations. Employees may leave if they feel their company is no longer wanted by its existing parent; relationships with important suppliers and customers may also be affected.

In addition, simply offering a business for sale may not be productive. Sales must be negotiated and potential buyers must be vetted. The terms of the sale should be financially acceptable; and the buyer should not be an organization who can use the newly acquired business to create a competitive threat to retained activities.

Devlin (1989) suggests that, in general speed is of the essence. Long delays are likely to mean lost confidence. But some businesses may be difficult to sell.

Second, buyers can be categorized into different types, and the potential of the business for them needs careful consideration during negotiations.

❑ There are **sphere-of-influence buyers,** who might expect immediate synergy from the acquisition. These would include competitors for whom it would be horizontal integration, and buyers and suppliers for whom it would imply vertical integration. These are the buyers who are most likely to pose future threats unless the divestment removes any involvement in the industry in question.
❑ There are **related industry companies** who might not be current competitors but for whom it might be possible to share activities and transfer skills.
❑ There are **unconnected conglomerate acquirers.**
❑ There are **management buy-outs,** which we discuss in the next section.

Third, there is an argument that the cash raised from the sale should be deployed effectively and without undue delay. If a company is decreasing in size, building up reserves of cash, and can find no suitable investment opportunities, it might become vulnerable to acquisition. Ideally a use for the cash will be determined before the sale, but implementation of a combined sale and investment may prove difficult. Devlin argues that where these changes can be managed effectively, divestment can provide a source of new competitive advantage.

Having explored retrenchment, turnaround and divestment strategies, we later look at these strategies specifically in the context of an economic recession, and then conclude this chapter by considering alternative strategies for declining industries and how the most appropriate strategy might be selected.

Management buy-outs in the UK

Management buy-outs, described simply, involve the purchase of a business from its existing owners by the current managers in conjunction with one or more financial institutions.

Buy-outs first became significant in the USA in the 1970s, but prior to the early 1980s legislation in the UK restricted their potential. Until 1981 it was illegal for a company to finance the purchase of its own shares. Batchelor (1988) contends that the growth in popularity of management buy-outs in the UK has been founded on a different model to that popularized in the USA. In the UK the proposal to purchase a business from its existing owners has typically come from the managers; in the USA, where the investment banks play a more aggressive role, the idea has often originated with the financial institutions. In the USA the sales have often been associated with a need to reduce borrowing; in the UK this has been less of a necessity. Sales have been aimed at generating greater focus and concentration and divesting businesses which are not producing acceptable financial returns or generating synergy. One motive for this has been to reduce the prospect of a hostile takeover bid resulting from poor overall performance. Some buy-outs occur because family owners have no organized succession and a sale to the existing managers is seen as more desirable than sale to an unknown outsider who has no personal involvement in the company. In addition some businesses have been bought from the receivers after the original owners had got into difficulties, and some have been bought from the government as part of their privatization programme.

They have so far proved more popular in the UK than in the rest of Europe, but they are steadily growing in popularity throughout Europe. They have been assisted by governments who have made the conditions for them increasingly favourable through legislative and tax changes designed to encourage enterprise.

Management buy-outs generally involve three parties: managers (and on occasions other employees who may become equity holders); vendors; and external financiers, who provide both equity and loan capital. All have objectives and expectations. **Managers** acquire control of their own business, often with a substantial equity stake whilst investing only a small proportion of the total funding involved. This reverses the trend to divorce ownership and control, which was discussed in Chapter 5, and clearly influences the organizational culture and objectives. **Vendors** divest businesses which may be performing poorly or failing to create synergy with their other activities, and they frequently accomplish this amicably and profitably. **Financiers** are attracted to management buy-outs because they offer the potential to earn higher financial returns than investing in large companies and lower failure rates than traditional start-up businesses.

There are also **management buy-ins** whereby a group of outside managers are brought in to run a company which is sold to them and their backers rather than to existing managers. The disadvantage is the loss of continuity and the lack of insight and experience in the particular company; a possible advantage in certain circumstances is the influx of fresh ideas.

The term leveraged buy-out, which originated in the USA, is often used where the lead financiers take the lead role in large buy-outs (and buy-ins). The name refers to the high level of borrowing which the company takes on, using the assets being purchased as leverage.

Visit the website:
http://www.
itbp.com

Year	Total no. buy-outs and buy-ins	No. of large buy-outs/ buy-ins, i.e. exceeding £10m capital	Average value £ million	
1981–1985	1050		2.1	**Table 17.1**
1986	300	28	4.3	Management buy-outs and
1987	350	35	9.2	buy-ins in the UK
1988	400	54	12.7	
1989	500	71	13.1	
1990	550	61	5.2	
1991	500	45	5.3	
1992	520	54	5.8	
1993	510	51	5.5	
1994	550	81	6.5	
1995	560	115	12.0	

Source: KPMG Corporate Finance

The general conclusion from research over a number of years by the Centre for Management Buy-out Research at the University of Nottingham is that buy-out teams improve the performance of businesses and that, after an initial drop in employee numbers, they create jobs.

Table 17.1 illustrates how the number of buy-outs and buy-ins in the UK grew steadily during the 1980s and has been relatively stable during the 1990s. The average value, affected by the number of large buy-outs, peaked in 1989 and then fell back. Notable examples in the 1980s include Hornby Hobbies, the long-established toy company, Parker Pen and Premier Brands, the foods and confectionery arm of Cadbury Schweppes which produces Cadbury's drinking chocolate, biscuits, Smash instant mashed potato, Typhoo tea and Chivers and Hartley's products. Recent examples, featuring well-known companies, are Sweater Shop, Levington (horticultural products), Dolland and Aitchison (opticians), Charles Letts (diaries), Standard Fireworks and Shepperton Film Studios. We saw in an earlier chapter how Virgin and Andrew Lloyd Webber's Really Useful Group were management buy-backs of publicly quoted companies.

Objectives and key success factors

Whilst there are important issues of managers wanting to own their own businesses, and possibly preserve their jobs when their company is in difficulties, management buy-outs are characterized by important financial objectives and constraints. Buy-outs typically have unusual financial structures and high gearing, as will be illustrated later, and the financial institutions which back them have financial targets and expectations. Consequently management buy-outs are expected to prove to be profitable for their shareholders and other backers by earning out the debt assumed when the company is bought out and by improving the company's performance in comparison with the results achieved by the previous owners.

In order to meet these expectations, and in addition to the essential key success factors for the business and the industry, it is important that managers are able to make the business more competitive and overcome the constraints imposed by the high debt burden. In addition they must be able to generate a positive cash flow. Eustace (1988) suggests that this is easier where the technology involved is relatively stable and where the products or services are not affected significantly by seasonal demand.

The managers and employees involved in a buy-out are likely to have a number of objectives, as highlighted above. Where they have invested in the company, they will be seeking a return on that investment, and it is in this area that their objectives are closely related to those of their financial backers. However, the expectations of the institutional investors who have provided equity capital and the banks who have lent money on fixed interest terms may differ. Coopers and Lybrand (1989) suggest that banks are likely to regard buy-outs as a better alternative than many other lending opportunities: they will pay a higher rate of interest than large established companies are willing to pay; they are more likely to succeed than traditional start-ups; and they are generally safer than lending to the Third World. The banks will normally agree to a higher percentage of debt in relation to equity (gearing) or in relation to total capital employed (the debt ratio) than is conventional, and will look for a cash flow which can both pay the interest and repay the debt after an agreed number of years. Despite the flexibility of the banks, borrowers should be cautious about the debt burden they accept. The MFI buy-out from Asda, described earlier, is a useful example of the need for caution. The buy-out was highly geared and the downturn in demand for MFI products in 1989 made the interest payments increasingly problematical. Because the deteriorating results were seen as temporary rather than long term, the financial institutions were willing to exercise flexibility, and hence a possible crisis was averted.

Their confidence and flexibility was justified when MFI, after two difficult years (1990 and 1991) when interest payments turned respectable trading profits into pre-tax losses, was profitable again in 1992. Predicting further growth and success MFI sought to re-float the company late in 1992. The business, which was valued at £670 million, some £50 million less than the 1987 buy-back value, was a 'very different animal from the one it was in 1987'. Using information technology to link their shops with their warehouses and factories MFI had slashed stocks. Many products are now delivered direct to customers rather than everything being theoretically available for instant collection.

Institutions are frequently concerned about long-term growth prospects and the ultimate flotation of the company, but this is not always the ideal outcome. Some floated companies are later re-privatized.

Advantages and issues

The advantages to the vendor and to the managers buying out the business are featured in Box 17.1, and these relate to the objectives of both parties. The issues included also relate to the objectives and motives of the managers and the company selling the business. The second issue suggests that there might well be a conflict of interest as far as the vendor is concerned. It is important for the vendor to negotiate a good financial deal in selling the business, particularly as far as existing shareholders are concerned, but at the same time other motives may be important. The company may want to deal with the business once it has been bought out, and would trust the managers already involved; or the sale may be because of financial pressures and the strategic leader or owner of the parent might be concerned to ensure that managers and

Box 17.1
MANAGEMENT BUY-OUTS: ADVANTAGES AND ISSUES

Advantages to the vendor

❏ The cash is from a willing buyer who has knowledge of the business. If the price is acceptable, the cash is neither better nor worse than cash from elsewhere, but such a sale is good for the corporate image.

❏ It can reduce borrowings, divest a loss-making activity, or enable specialization and concentration.

❏ Because of the existing knowledge of the buyers, the negotiations will concentrate on the financial package rather than any possible hidden truths about the business.

❏ If there are any interrelationships or interdependences with activities which are being retained, continuity should be maintained.

Advantages to the managers

❏ There is continuity of employment, and also continuity of both management and trading relationships for suppliers and customers.

❏ There is commitment to the business because of personal financial involvement, providing real incentives to succeed. This is often used to justify the high gearing allowed by financiers.

❏ They know the problems, and probably how to improve productivity and reduce overheads.

The latter is often crucial for transforming a marginal business into a profitable operation.

❏ It could lead to real substantial long-term gains if a flotation results.

Issues and drawbacks

❏ A company or business unit which a vendor is willing to sell at a particular price may be seen as incapable of being turned round sufficiently to meet the needs of potential financiers.

❏ The vendor has the problem of ensuring that he or she obtains a good deal, if not the best deal, for existing shareholders, and at the same time takes appropriate account of other stakeholders. The managers may not be the only bidders.

❏ A company is possibly unwilling to sell a business to its existing managers and then watch them improve performance and thereby expose the previous failings. This is regarded as less of an issue than it used to be.

❏ There may be a negative effect on the motivation of managers who are not equity holders in the buy-out.

❏ There may be a negative effect on manager motivation again if the buy-out fails and the company is sold to another external buyer.

employees who have been loyal in the past are provided with a secure future. A sale to them rather than an outsider might seem a better guarantee of this. Consequently there might be a clear preference to sell to the managers rather than invite a number of bids and select the highest. It has been suggested that some companies would prefer not to sell the business to its existing managers and then see them succeed where previously the business has failed to meet expectations, but this is not thought to be generally a significant issue.

It has already been mentioned that financial institutions who provide equity and loan funding will have financial targets, and they will be reluctant to support a business which is not thought capable of meeting their specific financial expectations. A vendor may be willing to sell a business at a particular price, and the business may be commercially viable with a product or service which can be produced and sold profitably. However, if the financial returns are expected to be too low to meet the financiers' requirements, the transaction is unlikely to go ahead.

Success and failure

From points made earlier in this section, it is clear that a successful buy-out is likely to involve the purchase of predictable cash flows at an economical price. Coopers and Lybrand (1989) argue that for investors the ideal company would be one in a mature market, with established market share, low speculative research and development and a predictable cash flow. In reality the buy-out is more likely to involve a poorly performing business or division with an under-utilized asset base, which is seen as a non-core activity by its existing parent company.

The success rate, however, tends to be relatively high.

The parties involved and their expectations

The management team

Coopers and Lybrand contend that the financial backers will expect the management group involved in the buy-out to be a team. They will expect them to be competent in all the functional areas of the business and to have skills in those areas which are essential for competitive success. In the case of the purchase of a business unit from a large company, it is important to consider which functions were previously performed by the vendor's head office rather than by the managers involved in the buy-out, and how this will be dealt with. The appointment of a non-executive chairman from outside the company might prove valuable in the provision of new strategic ideas. The team of senior managers should be cohesive; and the level of management below them, those without an equity holding, should be motivated and committed to the new organization. The company may seem less secure to them, and consequently they might be tempted to consider leaving.

It is important that the management team, whatever their personal motives and expectations, appreciate the performance expectations of their backers and are willing to make the necessary changes to reduce costs and re-position the company's products as appropriate. Managers may conflict initially rather than agree on the future objectives for the company. Those who are most committed to existing products, services and practices may be less willing to support change than others who have less loyalty to the past. Certain managers, possibly any who are near to retirement, might be most concerned with security, and therefore look to minimize risks; others may be more growth and risk oriented. Such differences must be reconciled to agree future direction. The changes which are required may involve changes of culture as well as of products and services, particularly where growth and diversification into new areas is considered desirable.

Financial institutions

In putting together a proposed buy-out package it is important to seek a fit between the expectations of potential backers and the ability of the business to meet these expectations. Certain institutions might prefer a steady and regular return over a number of years; others might seek rapid growth and an early flotation, and as a result accept a higher level of risk with their investment. Coopers and Lybrand suggest that banks typically look for a rate of interest of 2% above base rate on loans secured against assets; and an interest cover (profit before interest and tax divided by interest payments) of at least a factor of two.

Form of exit	Investors leaving			Comments
	Management	**Employees**	**Financiers**	
Liquidation	X	X	X	Ideally all investments recovered in full
Sale to another organization	X	X	X	Again, all investments repaid, ideally. Managers and employees may remain with the new owners
Earn out – managers use profits to buy out financiers			X	Financiers cease to be owners
Managers use own money (or borrow) to purchase financiers' shares			X	As above
Private sale of shares by financiers			X	Financiers replaced by other financiers
Managers, employees trade shares amongst themselves	X	X		Individuals able to exit; newcomers may become owners
Stock market flotation	X	X	X	Full or partial exit by financiers; partial exit by managers, employees

Table 17.2
Exit from buy-outs

Batchelor (1988) suggests that the rate charged to very large companies would be perhaps 1% above base rate. Because of the need for assets and security it may be more difficult for a service business to organize a buy-out than a manufacturing company. Institutional providers of equity ideally seek a minimum rate of return on their investment of 30–40%, the actual expectation being influenced by the level of risk. This could be made up of interest or dividends together with any repayments and the growth in the value of their capital investment in the business. This in turn depends upon the percentage of the issued ordinary shares owned by them.

Exit routes

One important consideration for all parties investing in a buy-out is their ability to withdraw their money at any time. Exit routes are particularly important for financiers, who are likely to want some flexibility. Table 17.2 features seven different exit routes and shows which investors benefit from each alternative.

In summary, the important issue is the closeness of fit between the expectations of all the parties involved and the potential of the business to achieve certain targets. If the requirements of the parties, especially the investors, are not met, they are likely to seek an exit route.

Financing a buy-out

It has already been mentioned that management buy-outs are funded by a mixture of investment capital provided by managers (and possibly other employees) and institutional shareholders and by loans. The equity holdings can be composed of ordinary shares, preference shares and preferred ordinary shares with enhanced rights. The preference shares will carry a fixed annual dividend which might increase in amount annually unless the shares are redeemed by a certain date. The nature of the equity provision will be linked to the risk, the anticipated returns, and the ability of the investor to withdraw without financial loss.

The equity stake of the managers might vary through what is known as a **ratchet mechanism**. Where this applies the number of ordinary shares issued to managers increases if certain performance criteria (say profit or revenue targets, or a flotation by a certain date) are met. The aim is to provide an incentive for managers, particularly if their initial shareholding is only a very small percentage of the total because of the magnitude of the funding involved. One difficulty of ratchet mechanisms relates to the establishment of targets which are acceptable to all parties involved, and in addition there is the possibility that they will encourage the pursuit of short-term targets in preference to the longer-term interests of the business.

Loans are occasionally separated into mezzanine finance and senior debt. Mezzanine loans, usually unsecured, rank after senior (secured) debt but before equity in the event of a company failing. To compensate for the greater risk they typically carry interest one to three percentage points above secured loans.

A worked example

The buy-out illustrated in Table 17.3 is hypothetical but the figures and percentages are based on real examples.

The first decision would concern the amount of money required to capitalize and establish a viable business. The assumption is a figure of £3 million. The maximum amount of debt which could be secured against the assets of the business is illustrated as £1,750,000. The profit and loss calculation is based on a rate of interest of 17% per annum on this loan, which might be representative of 70% of the company's existing trade debtors, 60% of the property value, and 40% of plant and machinery and stocks. Hence £1,250,000 is required in equity. The institutional shareholders might accept an 80:20 preference:ordinary split, and the example illustrates preference shares yielding 15% per annum, a favourable rate for the company. The ordinary shares are again split 80:20, with the managers being required to invest a total of £50,000 for their 20%. This type of breakdown, with a debt ratio of nearly 60%, is very typical for a small buy out. The percentage of loan funding is higher than would normally be found in a more conventional situation.

The profit and loss account shows a profit before interest and tax of £900,000, interest of £300,000 (17% of the £1,750,000 loan), tax estimated at £250,000 and preference dividends of £150,000. The loan interest cover is a factor of three. The sum of £200,000 is therefore available for ordinary shareholders, and, if £100,000 is paid in dividends (a 40% return), £100,000 is available to reinvest in the business. It could be that the managers would reinvest their dividends as well. Whilst this might seem successful, it would have to be improved as the business developed if the preference shares were to be redeemed and the bank loan paid off.

Visit the website: http://www.itbp.com

Capitalization				Table 17.3
Ordinary shares	£ thousands	Ownership	Percentage of funding	A worked example of a successful
Management	50	(20%)	2	buy-out
Investors	200	(80%)	7	
	250			
Preference shares				
Investors	1000		33	
Debt				
Secured bank loan	1750			
	3000		58	

Profit and loss account

	Turnover	12000
Less:	Cost of sales	9500
Equals:	Gross profit	2500
Less:	Overheads	1600
Equals:	Profit before interest and taxation	900
Less:	Interest	300
	Tax	250
	Preference dividend	150
Equals:	Profit available for ordinary shareholders	200
Less:	Dividends	100
	Retained in the business	100

In conclusion, the following list summarizes the key factors and issues which are likely to determine the relative success of a buy-out:

❑ the ability to raise a significant amount of debt in relation to the assets and other sources of funding
❑ the strengths and abilities of the managers involved
❑ the ability of the business to generate a cash flow which is strong enough to pay the interest burden and subsequently pay off the loans
❑ the price negotiated with the vendor
❑ the exit opportunities for the investors.

Management buy-ins

Management buy-ins occur where an organization is established to buy-out a company.

There are certain features which are similar to management buy-outs. There are again investors who provide the bulk of the investment, and a management team who take an equity stake in the business. But this time the managers are not internal to the business and fully aware of the strengths and weaknesses.

Consequently their management skills and their ability to manage a new unfamiliar situation are crucial issues.

De Quervain, quoted in Batchelor (1987), argues that there are three essential characteristics of a successful buy-in.

❑ The management team are successful and experienced, ideally in the same or a similar industry, and they are familiar with the problems associated with independent companies. In other words their experience is not solely with subsidiaries of large conglomerates where head office performs a number of key strategic roles. It is particularly useful if they have previous experience of a buy-out or buy-in.
❑ The investors are willing to accept risks which are higher than those associated with buy-outs. The failure rate is likely to be higher, and consequently the investors must place considerable trust in the management team.
❑ The target company, which may already be independent or a subsidiary of a larger organization, is known to be underperforming and is capable of being turned around.

Issues of culture and change are particularly important where a new management team has ideas which are significantly different from those of existing managers. An example might be a relatively stable, possibly sleepy, family company which is taken over by professional managers who wish to introduce new systems, improve efficiencies and cut overheads. Some existing managers will feel threatened and seek to leave; others will not be required. Uncertainty will surround the changes. In relation to these issues, Batchelor suggests that agreed and fully supported deals are more likely to succeed than those which involve an external management team making a hostile bid. Particularly difficult are those situations where the existing managers make an unsuccessful counter-bid to buy out their company.

Management buy-ins have fallen in popularity during the early 1990s because of their relatively low success rate, and also because of the difficulties in matching keen and suitable managers with appropriate acquisitions. The failure rate is greatest in the case of small companies bought from private ownership. Case 17.4, David Brown, illustrates the successful acquisition and turnaround of a private company by two managers actively searching for a suitable buy-in opportunity.

Robbie *et al*. (1991) highlight three main problems with management buy-ins:

❑ Unknown difficulties which typically come to light after the buy-in. Often these are the result of poor control systems and are not fully appreciated by the vendor.
❑ Many buy-in managers have a large company background and consequently less appreciation of small companies and their particular problems.
❑ Where the buy-in is of a company in difficulty there may be problems with key stakeholders. Important suppliers may be owed money and see this as an opportunity to press for payment; despite redundancies employees may be hoping for pay rises to compensate for sacrifices during the decline.

To reduce the risk, some buy-in teams may try to negotiate staged payments based upon their relative success.

DAVID BROWN

In January 1990 David Brown, based in Huddersfield, was bought from its 87-year-old family owner, Sir David Brown, by two businessmen, Chris Brown (no family ties) and Chris Cook. The company had been owned by generations of the Brown family since it was founded in 1860, but in recent years it had declined and become unprofitable. Sir David was resident in the south of France and reliant on a management team. There was perceived to be a lack of drive and control. Brown and Cook had worked together previously and both had backgrounds in large engineering companies. They had joined forces to look for a suitable buy-in opportunity and they had support from Bankers Trust who organized the financing from banks and venture capitalists.

Essentially David Brown is an engineering business, with an international reputation for its gears. Earlier it had also been renowned for tractors – which it no longer produces. At one point during World War II Brown was the only available source of gears for the engines of Spitfires and Hurricanes. In 1947 David Brown acquired Aston Martin and Lagonda (later divested) and manufactured high-performance cars for some years. The company also diversified into manufacturing machine tools, particularly for producing gears, and fast ships – Vosper Thorneycroft was acquired. The company became increasingly dependent on defence business but was slow to adapt as demand changed and fell.

David Brown was bought for £46 million and financed as follows:

	£m
Ordinary shares	2.0
Preference shares	5.8
Total equity	7.8
Mezzanine debt	9.2
Senior loans	29.0

The company was quickly restructured after the buy-in. The existing head office staff was reduced dramatically, and new managers brought in. The workforce has also been cut; shop floor practices have been changed and productivity has risen. There have been new products and new information and financial control systems. The business became financially viable.

The company was separated into four discrete divisions to enable a strong focus on markets, customers and service. These were:

- standard gearboxes for electric motors
- customized, special gearboxes and machine tools
- vehicle transmissions, especially for tanks and trains
- pumps – for the oil and petrochemical industries.

Despite the recession David Brown has been profitable and the debt was soon reduced.

Nothing we did was particularly clever or unusual. It was just about managing a business properly – and buying the right one.
(Chris Brown, Joint Managing Director)

The original capital structure was due for review in January 1993 when the supporting institutions were free to take out their equity (75% of the total) if they wished. Were this to have happened Brown and Cook would have had four options:

1. reverse into an already listed company
2. increase borrowings again to buy out the investors
3. sell out
4. float.

In the event David Brown's strong cash flow enabled the managers to repay a £16 million loan five years ahead of schedule and maintain investment in the business. In April 1993 the company was successfully floated with a valuation of £90 million.

Later that year £11 was spent on acquiring a complementary hydraulics and transmissions business; and in 1995 David Brown bought four industrial gears businesses that had been retained by the Brown family at the time of the buy-in. Three of these were overseas, in Australia, South Africa and Zimbabwe, and they had become available after the death of Sir David Brown in 1993. These acquisitions were funded with a £15.6 million rights issue.

In October the company was restructured again, this time to provide a stronger focus on its three core activities. There were separate divisions for industrial gears, mobile equipment drives and pumps; a fourth division would develop sales (and eventually manufacturing) in the targeted Asia Pacific region.

Managing in a recession

The early 1990s has been characterized by an economic recession. The recession has been global and has affected most countries, industries and businesses, regardless of size or sector. In a recession retrenchment strategies are frequently required as demand falls and costs need containing; at the same time, there is a need, wherever practical, to invest and prepare the organization to benefit from the recovery when it comes.

Recession alone will not necessarily put a company into a crisis or turnaround situation; rather it highlights existing weaknesses either created in, or hidden in, boom conditions. The organizations which are best prepared to cope with a recession are those with relatively low borrowings. Highly geared companies may be forced to divest assets in order to raise cash to cover their interest and repayment needs.

Clifford (1977) has suggested that companies which survive a recession most successfully are characterized by superior management which emphasizes the protection of margins, the efficient use of capital, and a concentration on markets or segments where distinctive competitive advantage is possible. Such competitive advantage will result from more effective cost control, innovative differentiation, a focus on service and quality and speedy reaction and change in a dynamic environment. The recession of the late 1980s/early 1990s has forced organizations to be creative in their search for cost reductions – earlier productivity drives had eliminated many inefficiencies. Information technology has provided some valuable opportunities. Cost savings must then be controlled to ensure that they do not creep up again. The focus of the cost cutting is critical. Training and research and development, for example, should not be sacrificed unnecessarily because new ideas and service quality are increasingly important for adding value, helping customers find new competitive opportunities themselves and persuading consumers to buy when their spending power is limited. R & D, then, should be managed better rather than cut, and directed more towards short-term improvements. However, the long-term needs should not be wholly ignored. In particular the development time for new products and services should be speeded up.

Visit the website: http://www.itbp.com

Dividend payments and investment funding may have to be traded off against each other. Some organizations will reduce dividends when profits fall to conserve their resources; others will maintain them to appease shareholders. See Chapter 12.

Moreover, increasing global competition has forced companies to target markets and niches more effectively, and, in many cases, increase their marketing rather than cut expenditure. The emphasis has typically focused on efficiencies and savings rather than luxury – consumers with less discretionary purchasing power have been more selective.

Whittingham (1991) reinforces points made earlier in the book and contends that innovation and product and service improvement is a more effective use of scarce resources in a recession than is diversification, and that cutting back too much leaves companies exposed and under capacity for the recovery. Ideally organizations will consult and involve employees, looking to, say, negotiate pay freezes and reduce hours rather than make staff redundant. This provides greater flexibility to grow. Nevertheless, many firms will not have sufficient resources to pursue their preferred option.

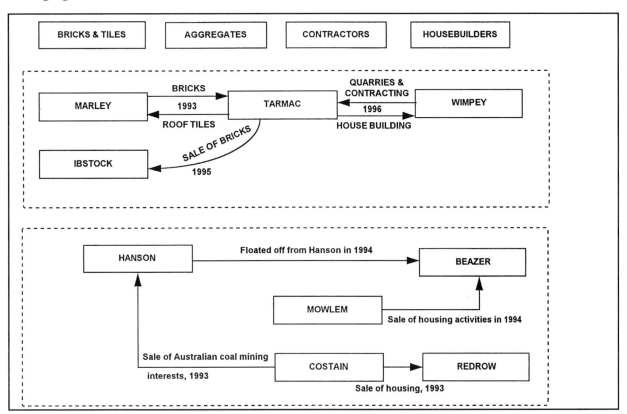

Figure 17.2 Two examples of restructuring in the UK construction and building materials industry during the recession of the 1990s. (Based on a chart in the *Financial Times*, 15 March 1996.)

When companies do emerge from a recession and attempt to satisfy increasing demand there is a fresh challenge – the need to control events, monitor the cash flow and guard against over-trading.

Finally, in a recession it is quite normal for individual company strategies to bring about industry restructuring, as we see illustrated in Figure 17.2, which looks at just two examples from the UK construction and building materials industry.

The top example shows how Tarmac, once the country's leading housebuilder, re-focused on aggregates and contracting. In 1993 Tarmac swapped its roof tiles business for Marley's bricks, which it later sold to Ibstock. In 1996 Tarmac then swapped its housebuilding interests for Wimpey's quarries and contracting businesses. Tarmac, with a 25% market share, is now the largest producer of crushed rock, sand and gravel.

We have used the recession as a time to bring new products out. It shows you're not demoralized, and its something new to go to customers with.

Being private has enabled us to plough our own furrow through the good and the bad times and not be swallowed up. All our capital investment would be looked at in a different way if we were a public company.

Sir Anthony Bamford, Chairman, JC Bamford (JCB Excavators),
quoted in the Financial Times, *2 June 1993.*

The second example shows how Mowlem and Costain have divested peripheral yet related activities to concentrate on contract construction. At the same time, Hanson, already the country's leading brick producer with a 30% market share and a major aggregates company (18% share) divested its housebuilding by floating Beazer as an independent company.

Strategies for declining industries

Rarely is an industry unattractive for every company competing in it; mature and declining industries can be made attractive for individual competitors if they can find appropriate and feasible opportunities for adding value and creating competitive advantage. Some firms experiencing decline in a mature industry will be the cause of their own demise, through their persistence with dated, inappropriate competitive strategies; and in some cases, an innovatory new strategy by one competitor can rejuvenate the whole industry.

Harrigan (1980) draws upon the themes outlined when portfolio analysis was discussed in Chapter 14 and considers whether retrenchment, turnaround or divestment is the most appropriate strategy for an individual competitor in a declining industry. Strategies of leadership and niche marketing (turnaround), exploiting or harvesting (retrenchment) and divestment are considered in the light of the overall attractiveness of the industry whilst it is declining and the opportunities for an individual competitor to create and sustain competitive advantage. These are illustrated and defined in Figure 17.3.

Harrigan contends that the most appropriate strategy is dependent on four factors:

❑ The nature of the decline, and the causes – the speed at which decline is taking place, and whether specific segments are still surviving and offering differentiation and niche marketing opportunities for companies who can create and sustain competitive advantage. These factors affect the attractiveness of the industry.

❑ The ability of a company to target these market segments effectively and create consumer preference. This is affected by company strengths and weaknesses.

❑ The **exit costs** for all competitors. Exit costs influence the degree of urgency that companies feel towards finding a way of remaining competitive rather than simply withdrawing. Exit costs relate to
   • the inability to find a buyer for the business, and the cost of closure;
   • the strategic significance for the company as a whole, particularly if vertical integration strategies are affected;
   • the possible effect upon key stakeholders, such as shareholders, managers and the strategic leader, especially if they have had a long-term commitment to the product service or business unit.

❑ Linked to all these, the opportunities or threats which exist as a result of competitor activities, what they choose to do and why. If the product is strategically significant, certain competitors may choose not to withdraw, accepting very low profits or even no profits, and thereby making it more difficult for others.

Figure 17.3 encapsulates the first two points above; the decision will also

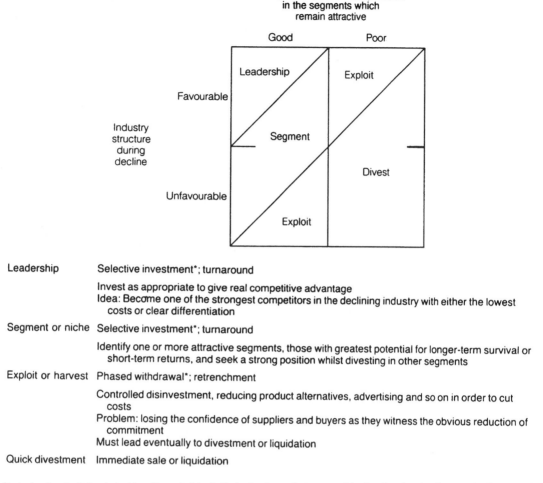

Competitive position and potential
in the segments which
remain attractive

Leadership	Selective investment*; turnaround
	Invest as appropriate to give real competitive advantage
	Idea: Become one of the strongest competitors in the declining industry with either the lowest costs or clear differentiation
Segment or niche	Selective investment*; turnaround
	Identify one or more attractive segments, those with greatest potential for longer-term survival or short-term returns, and seek a strong position whilst divesting in other segments
Exploit or harvest	Phased withdrawal*; retrenchment
	Controlled disinvestment, reducing product alternatives, advertising and so on in order to cut costs
	Problem: losing the confidence of suppliers and buyers as they witness the obvious reduction of commitment
	Must lead eventually to divestment or liquidation
Quick divestment	Immediate sale or liquidation

Figure 17.3 Strategies for declining industries. The asterisks indicate the terms that are used in the directional policy matrix discussed in Chapter 14 (Figure 14.10). Developed from Harrigan, KR (1980) *Strategies for Declining Businesses*, Heath; Harrigan, KR and Porter, ME (1983) End-game strategies for declining industries, *Harvard Business Review*, July–August.

involve the last two points.

Competitive advantage is likely to be attained by those companies who are aware early of the decline, and the opportunities present during the decline, and who seek to create the most advantageous positions ahead of their competitors. Companies who react when things have started to go wrong are less likely to succeed in creating an effective strategy.

Rejuventating mature businesses

Baden-Fuller and Stopford (1992) define a mature business as 'one whose managers believe themselves to be imprisoned by their environment and unable to succeed'. As a consequence they are invariably giving poor service to their customers and achieving financial returns that are barely adequate. Often, with a more creative, entrepreneurial, innovative approach, they can be rejuvenated. The challenge, simply, is to become a stronger competitor. This transformation is likely to require a number of developmental steps over an extended time period, rather than be achieved with a one-off major project; it implies a change of culture and style. Success will not be instantaneous; it will need building.

Baden-Fuller and Stopford have developed a four-stage model for rejuvenation.

- ❏ **Galvanization** comes when there is a clear recognition of the true state of the business and the establishment of an able management team which is committed to dealing with the problem. This may only need a change of strategic leader; on other occasions the changes will be more extensive. If those managers who are responsible for bringing about the crisis, through poor decisions and judgement, or negligently allowing the situation to deteriorate, stay, they will need to change.

  Progress then requires resources. Independent businesses are likely to require fresh capital and possibly new owners. Subsidiaries of larger organizations will have to justify new, corporate investment.

- ❏ **Simplification** follows, implying a clearer focus and the concentration of scarce resources on a smaller agenda to build a strong and sustainable core. Strategies, structures and styles may all have to change. This level of change is sometimes termed *strategic regeneration* and we will look further into the demands and implications in Chapter 22. The business must next

- ❏ **Build** new competencies and competitive advantages. Because of resource pressures this is again likely to take time and prove highly challenging. Finally, true rejuvenation requires it to

- ❏ **Exert leverage** to extend its new competencies and capabilities into new products, services, markets and opportunities.

Total quality management initiatives and business process re-engineering programmes can make a major contribution, but alone they will not make an organization more innovatory. The whole enterprise must become more customer focused, committed to efficiency and improvement, and responsive to environmental demands.

It would be useful at this point to return to Figure 13.2. Through double-loop learning an uncompetitive firm has found new opportunities for adding value and creating advantages; it has then used single-loop learning initially to leverage this new advantage.

Implementing recovery strategies

In the previous chapter we stressed that organizational issues and difficulties often result in failure of the diversification and acquisition strategies to yield the desired results. Organizational issues will again be important in the case of recovery strategies. Time is likely to be limited, and proposed changes will have to be implemented quickly. The support and co-operation of managers and other employees will be essential, particularly where redundancies, changes in organization structures or changes in working practices are required. Quite possibly changes in attitudes – an issue of organizational culture – will be involved. Although the gravity of the situation may be visible, and the dangers of failing to change clearly understood, the changes will need managing properly if they are to prove effective. The issues involved in managing change are discussed in Chapter 22.

Summary

At any time certain industries will be declining and others will be relatively unattractive as far as particular companies are concerned because of intense competition. Individual companies might be performing poorly and in need of either a recovery strategy or an appropriate divestment. These strategies have been discussed in this chapter, which has built on Chapter 7 where the symptoms and causes of decline were discussed.

Specifically we have:

- considered the feasibility of recovery in a particular situation, and the four possible outcomes of a change in strategy: a failure to recover, temporary recovery, sustained survival and sustained recovery
- discussed the retrenchment strategies of organization and financial change, cost and asset reduction, and revenue generation;

- examined how a number of strategies aimed at improving marketing effectiveness might bring about a turnaround
- looked at divestment strategies, in terms of the divestment decision itself, and the financial and strategic justifications, and the issues involved in implementing the strategy
- considered the growing incidence of buy-outs in the UK, and why they have become increasingly popular
- discussed the objectives and expectations of all the interested parties: vendor, managers, employees, and providers of both loan and equity funding
- explored the advantages for the various parties and the issues raised
- briefly considered buy-ins, and the similarities and differences
- analysed strategic management in a recession
- briefly considered mature and declining industries and the possible strategies for individual competitors.

Questions and research assignments

Text related

1 Why might a company wish to remain a competitor in an industry despite low or declining profitability?

Classify your reasons as objective or subjective. Can the subjective reasons be justified?

2 What factors do you feel would be most significant to all parties involved in a proposed buy-out during the negotiations? Where are the major areas of potential conflict?

3 Were the institutions supporting David Brown (Case 17.4) to have taken the unusual step of removing their equity, how would you rank the four options available to the buy-in team?

If they had decided to reverse into an already listed company (option 1) what selection criteria would you use in searching for a suitable partner?

Library based

4 Reed Elsevier's origins are not in publishing, where they now concentrate, but in paper and packaging. They became a force in publishing when they acquired IPC (International Printers Ltd) in the early 1970s.

❏ Why has Reed chosen to divest all non-publishing activities in recent years?

❏ What is Reed's current position in the publishing industry? How strong are they?

❏ What growth strategies in publishing do you feel would be appropriate? You may wish to include opportunities in electronic publishing.

5 Hornby is one of the few survivors in the UK toy industry, but it has experienced some dramatic changes of strategy and ownership. Hornby was acquired by Lines in 1964; in 1971 Lines was in liquidation. Dunbee-Combex-Marx then bought Hornby, but DCM itself collapsed in 1981. At this stage Hornby was bought-out by its managers. Its main products are still electric train sets and Scalextric; and they continue to be manufactured in the UK, although there is some foreign sourcing.

What has happened to the company since 1982? How successful has the MBO been? What are Hornby's current products and strategies?

Checklist of key terms and concepts

You should feel confident that you understand the following terms and ideas:

* ✭ The four possible recovery situations illustrated in Figure 17.1: non-recoverable, temporary, sustained survival and sustained recovery
* ✭ Retrenchment strategies
* ✭ Turnaround strategies
* ✭ Divestment strategies

* ✭ Management buy-outs
  * Why they happen
  * What they offer the parties involved
  * The unusual funding arrangements
* ✭ Management buy-ins
* ✭ Leadership, segment, exploit and divestment strategies in the context of a declining industry
* ✭ Strategic rejuvenation for a mature business.

Recommended further reading

Slatter (1984) is a very comprehensive study of turnaround strategies, but Harrigan (1980) provides useful insight into declining businesses.

Harrigan, KR and Porter, ME (1983) End-game strategies for declining industries, *Harvard Business Review*, July–August, combines Harrigan's research into declining businesses with Porter's work on competitive advantage.

Nelson, R and Clutterbuck, D (1988) *How Twenty Well-known Companies Came Back From The Brink*, Allen, contains a number of interesting case studies.

Baden-Fuller and Stopford (referenced below) also contains some valuable insights and cases in strategic rejuvenation.

The most substantial publications in the area of management buy-outs are by Wright and Coyne at the Centre for Management Buy-out Research at Nottingham University. In addition the *Financial Times* publishes a special supplement on this topic every twelve months, and these supplements contain both up-to-date statistics and case studies.

References

Baden-Fuller, C and Stopford, J (1992) *Rejuvenating the Mature Business: The Competitive Challenge*, Routledge.

Batchelor, C (1987) Revival of the fittest, *Financial Times*, 24 March.

Batchelor, C (1988) Where Britain leads the field, *Financial Times*, 12 July.

Clifford, DK (1977) Thriving in a recession, *Harvard Business Review*, July–August.

Coopers and Lybrand (1989) Presentation at Huddersfield Polytechnic, 21 February.

Davis, JV (1974) The strategic divestment decision, *Long Range Planning*, February.

Devlin, G (1989) Selling off not out, *Management Today*, April.

Eustace, P (1988) Britain's buyout boom. *The Engineer*, 4 February.

Harrigan, KR (1980) *Strategies for Declining Businesses*, Heath.

Robbie, K, Wright, M and Chiplin, B (1991) *Management Buy-ins: An Analysis of Initial Characteristics and Performance*, Centre for Management Buy-out Research.

Slatter, S (1984) *Corporate Recovery: Successful Turnaround Strategies and Their Implementation*, Penguin.

Whittingham, R (1991) Recession strategies and top management change, *Journal of General Management*, **16**(3), Spring.

18

Strategy Evaluation and Choice

In this chapter we summarize the criteria which might be used to assess whether or not existing strategies are effective, and to evaluate proposed future changes in strategy. Useful techniques described earlier in the book are recalled.

Learning objectives

After studying this chapter you should be able to:

■ define the key criteria for evaluating the appropriateness, feasibility and desirability of a particular strategic alternative
■ discuss why there may be a trade-off between these factors
■ explain the contribution to this evaluation of ten techniques described earlier in the book
■ list nine key strategic principles
■ argue the importance of strategy implementation
■ explain the role of judgement in strategic choice.

Introduction

There is no single evaluation technique or framework as such that will provide a definite answer to which strategy or strategies a company should select or follow at any given time. Particular techniques will prove helpful in particular circumstances. A number of frameworks and techniques which are often classi-fied as means of evaluating strategy have been discussed in earlier chapters; they are summarized in Table 18.1.

Don't forget to visit the website: http://www. itbp.com

Table 18.1   A summary of strategy evaluation techniques

Evaluation technique	Discussed in Chapter
SWOT analysis	Interlude between 7 and 8
Planning gap analysis	14
Porter's industry analysis and competitive advantage frameworks	9
Investment appraisal techniques using discounted cash flows	12
Net present value	
Internal rate of return	
Payback	
Plus cost–benefit analysis for public sector	
Cash flow implications	6
Breakeven analysis	9
Sensitivity analysis	12
Portfolio analyses	14
Scenario modelling	8 and 14
Simulations of future possibilities using PIMS	14

There are certain essential criteria, however, which should be considered in assessing the merits and viability of existing strategies and alternatives for future change. This chapter considers how one might assess whether or not a corporate, competitive or functional strategy is effective or likely to be effective. The issues concern **appropriateness, feasibility and desirability.** Some of the considerations are likely to conflict with each other, and consequently an element of judgement is required in making a choice. The most appropriate or feasible option for the firm may not be the one that its managers regard as most desirable, for example.

In many respects the key aspects of any proposed changes concern the **strategic logic,** basically the subject of this book so far, and the **ability to implement.** Implementation and change are the subject of the final chapters.

Strategic logic relates to:

❑ the relationship and fit between the strategies and the mission of the organization; and the current appropriateness of the mission, objectives and the strategies being pursued (synergy is an important concept in this)
❑ the ability of the organization to match and influence changes in the environment
❑ the availability of the necessary resources.

Figure 18.1, which restates the notion of E–V–R congruence, shows that organizations must seek and exploit opportunities for adding value in ways which are attractive to customers. This can be at both the corporate and competitive strategy levels. At the corporate level, the organization is looking to establish a heartland of related businesses and activities; at the competitive level, the challenge is to create and sustain competitive advantage. Resources must be deployed to exploit the new opportunities, and this is driven – or, in some cases, frustrated – by strategic leadership and the culture of the organization.

Implementation concerns the management of the resources to satisfy the needs of the organization's stakeholders. Implicit in this is the ability to satisfy customers better than competitors are able to do. Matching resources and environmental needs involves the culture and values of the organization; and decisions about future changes involve an assessment of risk. Relevant to both implementation and strategic logic is the role and preference of the strategic leader and other key decision makers in the organization.

In this chapter we address the following questions: What constitutes a good strategic choice? What can the organization do and what can it not do? What should the organization seek to do and what should it not seek to do?

When evaluating any corporate, competitive or functional strategy it is worth considering a number of key strategic principles, all of which are discussed in detail elsewhere in the book. Where these principles are evident, and particularly where they are strong and powerful forces, the likelihood of strategic success and effectiveness is enhanced.

Principles of strategy

❑ Market orientation
❑ Distinctiveness – relating to differentiation and competitive advantage
❑ Timeliness (appropriate for the current situation) and
❑ Flexibility (capable of change)

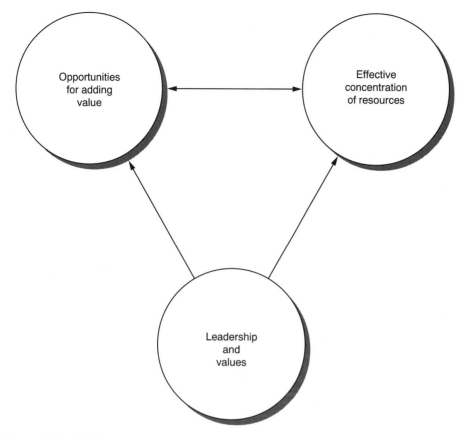

Figure 18.1 E–V–R congruence restated.

❑ Efficiency – relating to cost control and cost efficiency, particularly in production and operations
❑ Building on strengths
❑ Concentration and co-ordination of resources (rather than spreading them too widely) to achieve synergy
❑ Harmonization of strategy creation and implementation
❑ Understanding – if a strategy is to be supported by employees who are motivated and enthusiastic it must be communicated and understood.

Corporate strategy evaluation

Rumelt (1980) argues that corporate strategy evaluation at the widest level involves seeking answers to three questions:

❑ Are the current objectives of the organization appropriate?
❑ Are the strategies created previously, and which are currently being implemented to achieve these objectives, still appropriate?
❑ Do current results confirm or refute previous assumptions about the feasibility of achieving the objectives and the ability of the chosen strategies to achieve the desired results?

It is therefore important to look back and evaluate the outcomes and relative success of previous decisions, and also to look ahead at future opportunities and threats. In both cases strategies should be evaluated in relation to the objectives they are designed to achieve. A quantitative chart along the lines of Table 18.2 could be devised to facilitate this. In order to evaluate current and possible future strategies, and to help select alternatives for the future, the objectives are listed at the top of a series of columns. It will be appreciated from the examples provided that some of the objectives can have clear and objective measurement criteria and others are more subjective in nature. The alternatives, listed down the left-hand side, could be ranked in order of first to last preference in each column, or given a numerical score. In making a final decision based on the rankings or aggregate marks it may well prove appropriate to weight the objectives in the light of their relative importance.

In terms of assessing the suitability of strategic alternatives in particular circumstances Thompson and Strickland (1980) suggest that market growth and competitive position are important elements. Table 18.3 summarizes their argument. Concentration, for example, is seen as an appropriate strategy where market growth is high and the existing competitive position is strong. By contrast, where market growth is slow and the competitive position is weak, retrenchment is likely to be the most suitable strategy for the organization. Where 'not material' is listed in a column, the contention is that the strategy is appropriate for either high or low growth or strong or weak competitive positions.

Criteria for effective strategies

When assessing current strategies, and evaluating possible changes, it is important to emphasize that there is no such thing as a right or wrong strategy or choice in absolute terms. However, certain factors will influence the effectiveness

Table 18.2   Evaluating strategies in terms of objectives

Strategic alternative	Objectives*					
	Ability to achieve specific revenue or growth targets	Ability to return specific profitability targets	Ability to create and sustain competitive advantage	Synergy potential – relationship with other activities	Ability to utilize existing (spare) resources and skills	and so on
Existing competitive strategies for products, services, business units	Score out of say ten					
and	or					
Possible changes to corporate and competitive strategies	rank in order of preference					

*For evaluation purposes, each objective could be given a relative weighting.

Strategy	Market growth	Competitive position
Concentration	High	Strong
Horizontal integration	High	Weak
Vertical integration	High	Strong
Concentric diversification	Not material	Not material
Conglomerate diversification	Low	Not material
Joint ventures into new areas	Low	Not material
Retrenchment	Low	Weak
Turnaround	High	Weak
Divestment	Not material	Weak
Liquidation	Not material	Weak

Table 18.3
Strategic alternatives: their appropriateness in terms of market growth and competitive position

Developed from ideas in Thompson, AA and Strickland, AJ (1980) *Strategy Formulation and Implementation,* Irwin.

of strategies and the wisdom of following certain courses of action. These factors are considered in this chapter in three sections: **appropriateness; feasibility; desirability.** This categorization has been selected for convenience, and it will be appreciated that there is some overlap between the sections.

A number of authors, including Tilles (1963) and Hofer and Schendel (1978), have discussed the factors which determine the current and future possible effectiveness of particular strategies. The major issues are summarized in Figure 18.2 and are discussed below.

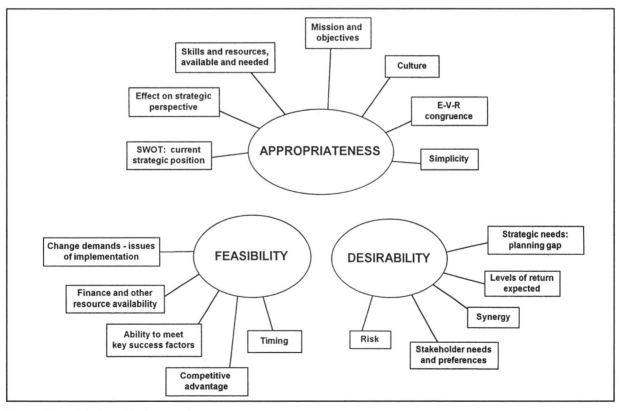

Figure 18.2   Criteria for effective strategies.

Appropriateness

In reviewing current strategies, assessing the impact of adaptive incremental changes that have taken place and considering strategic alternatives for the future it is important to check that strategies are consistent with the needs of the environment, the resources and values of the organization, and its current mission. These general points are elaborated below. For the rest of this section the term 'the strategy' is used to refer to each particular strategy being considered, be it a current one or a proposed change or addition.

SWOT; current strategic position

Is the strategy appropriate for the current economic and competitive environment?

Is the strategy able to capitalize and build on current strengths and opportunities, and avoid weaknesses and potential threats?

To what extent is the strategy able to take advantage of emerging trends in the environment, the market and the industry?

Effect on the strategic perspective

Does it have the potential for improving the strategic perspective and general competitive position of the organization?

The company, then, must be responsive to changes in the environment and it may wish to be proactive and influence its market and industry. All the time it should seek to become and remain an effective competitor.

Skills, competencies and resources: available and needed

Are the strategies being pursued and considered sufficiently consistent that skills, competencies and resources are not spread or stretched in any disadvantageous way?

Does any new proposal exploit key organizational competencies? For current businesses and strategies: can the organization effectively add value, or would a divestment strategy be more appropriate?

Mission and objectives

Does the strategy fit the current mission and objectives of the organization? Is it acceptable to the strategic leader and other influential stakeholders? (This issue is developed further in the desirability section below.)

The last two points above basically look at the relationship between ends and means.

Culture

Does the strategy fit the culture and values of the organization?

E–V–R congruence

Summarizing the above points, is there congruence between the environment, values and resources?

Simplicity

Is the strategy simple and understandable? Is the strategy one which could be communicated easily, and which people are likely to be enthusiastic about? These factors are also aspects of desirability.

Feasibility

Change demands – issues of implementation

Is the strategy feasible in resource terms? Can it be implemented effectively? Is it capable of achieving the objectives it addresses?

Can the organization cope with the extent and challenge of the change implied by the option?

Finance and other resource availability

A lack of any key resource can place a constraint on certain possible developments.

Ability to meet key success factors

A strategic alternative is not feasible if the key success factors dictated by the industry and customer demand, such as quality, price and service level, cannot be met.

Competitive advantage

The effectiveness of a strategy will be influenced by the ability of the organization to create and sustain competitive advantage. When formulating a strategy it is important to consider the likely response of existing competitors in order to ensure that the necessary flexibility is incorporated into the implementation plans. A company which breaks into a currently stable industry or market may well threaten the market shares and profitability of other companies and force them to respond with, say, price cuts, product improvements or aggressive promotion campaigns. The new entrant should be prepared for this and ready to counter it.

Visit the website:
http://www.
itbp.com

Timing

Timing is related to opportunity on the one hand and risk and vulnerability on the other. It may be important for an organization to act quickly and decisively once an opening window of opportunity is spotted. Competitors may attempt to seize the same opportunity.

At the same time managers should make sure that they allow themselves enough time to consider the implications of their actions and organize their resources properly. Adaptive incremental change in the implementation of strategy can be valuable here. An organization may look to pursue a new strategy, learn by experience and improve by modification once they have gone ahead.

Strategic leadership and the structure, culture and values of the organization are therefore important.

Timing is also an implementation issue; Case 18.1 provides one illustration of its significance. Next introduced a number of successful strategic changes which resulted in growth and increased profitability, but then overstretched themselves by pursuing strategies for which they had insufficient resources at the time. This theme relates to the theory of growth and the existence of the receding managerial limit suggested by Edith Penrose (1959), which was discussed in Chapter 5.

Desirability

Strategic needs; the planning gap

The ability of the strategy to satisfy the objectives of the organization and help close any identified planning gap are important considerations. Timing may again be an important issue. The ability of the strategy to produce results in either the short term or the longer term should be assessed in the light of the needs and priorities of the firm.

The level of returns expected

Synergy

Effective synergy should lead ideally to a superior concentration of resources in relation to competitors. The prospects for synergy should be evaluated alongside the implications for the firm's strategic perspective and culture, which were included in the section on appropriateness. These factors in combination affect the strategic fit of the proposal and its ability to complement existing strategies and bring an all-round improvement to the organization. Diversification into products and markets with which the organization has no experience, and which may require different skills, may fit poorly alongside existing strategies and fail to provide synergy.

Risk

It has already been pointed out that risk, vulnerability, opportunity and timing are linked. Where organizations, having spotted an opportunity, act quickly, there is always a danger that some important consideration will be overlooked. The risk lies in these other factors, many of which are discussed elsewhere, which need careful attention in strategy formulation.

❏ The likely effect on competition.
❏ The technology and production risks, linked to skills and key success factors. Can the organization cope with the production demands and meet market requirements profitably? Innovation often implies higher risks in this area, but offers higher rewards for success.
❏ The product/market diversification risk. The risk involved in overstretching resources through diversification has been considered earlier in this chapter.
❏ The financial risk. The cash flow and the firm's borrowing requirements are sensitive to the ability of the firm to forecast demand accurately and predict competitor responses.
❏ Managerial ability and competence. The risk here involves issues of whether skills can be transferred from one business to another when a firm diversifies, and whether key people stay or go after a take over.
❏ Environmental risks. It is also important to ensure that possible adverse effects or hostile public opinion are evaluated.

Many of these issues are qualitative rather than finite, and judgement will be required. The ability of the organization to harness and evaluate the appropriate information is crucial, but again there is a trade-off. The longer the time that the organization spends in considering the implications and assessing the

In my experience those who manage change most successfully are those who welcome it in their own lives and see it as an opportunity for stimulation and learning new things. Implicit is the willingness to take risks, including making intelligent mistakes. I am much more interested in important failures that prepare the way for future success than I am in cautious competence and maintaining the status quo.

Robert Fitzpatrick, when President Directeur Général, Euro Disneyland SA

At the end of 1988 George Davies lost the chairmanship of Next, the retail company he had built which had experienced rapid growth and success during the 1980s. Recent strategic changes had failed to provide the desired level of success. Arguably the speed of the growth and the extent of the diversification had been too great for Next's resources, and profits had fallen as a result.

Over four years and with a series of strategic moves, Davies had transformed the relatively dowdy menswear retailers J Hepworth into Next, a group which was innovative, design led and fashion oriented. Next segmented the retail market, selling fashionable clothing to younger men and women, as well as jewellery and furniture. In addition Next had diversified into general mail order by the acquisition of Grattan, one of the largest catalogue retail operations.

The moves which proved problematical occurred in 1987 and 1988. In 1987 Next took over Combined English Stores (CES), a large and already diversified retail group which included Biba (the West German fashion retailer), Zales (jewellery), Salisbury's (luggage, handbags and the like), a chain of chemist's shops, a carpet business and a holiday company. This gave Next a substantial high street presence, together with the problem and expense of converting a large number of stores to the fashionable Next image and format, which was regarded as a key factor in their record of success. Critics argued that Next had acquired too many stores, however, and Zales and Salisbury's were in fact sold to Ratners in autumn 1988. This reduced the extent of Next's diversification, and helped reduce the gearing from 125%.

In January 1988 the Next Directory, an exclusive mail-order catalogue, was **sold** to potential customers through advertising and direct mail. Catalogues are normally free. The product range in the Directory was designed to appeal to upmarket buyers, not the traditional mail order customers, who could specify when they wanted their goods delivered. The launch and the new concept proved less successful than forecasts and expectations. Moreover, in 1988 there was growing friction between Next and Grattan. Grattan disagreed with Next's plans to re-develop their product line. Davies has claimed that in October 1988 there were serious discussions about splitting Next and Grattan, as happened with Asda and MFI.

At the end of 1988 Next's profitability had declined, their strategy was not co-ordinated, and there were concerns about a fall in demand in 1989 as a result of increased interest charges and inflation

Had the diversification into mail order and the acquisition of Combined English Stores been appropriate and feasible?

Next were unable to provide all the necessary resources at the time they were required; and George Davies was quoted in the *Financial Times* on 5 December 1988 as saying, 'The lesson that I've learnt this year is that you must stick to the markets you know'.

Next, also, were a highly innovative company, but Davies was seen as an autocratic strategic leader who had failed to develop an appropriately supportive team of managers and an organization which was sufficiently decentralized.

After Davies' departure Next concentrated on two principal businesses:

❏ retailing ladies', men's and children's clothing, accessories and home furnishings; the remaining retail businesses were divested
❏ the Next Directory. Grattan was sold to Otto Versand, the German mail order company.

George Davies, whose collaborative alliance with Asda has been successful, was replaced as chief executive by David Jones, who had joined Next when it acquired Grattan. Jones has been described as a cautious, conservative accountant.

I probably gamble a little more than people think, but only when I have the information to ensure it is a safe bet.

David Jones

Jones' strategies for rationalizing and consolidating the business proved very successful and by the end of 1995 Next had been turned around. It was profitable and had accrued cash reserves of £150 million.

What strategies would be appropriate, desirable and feasible for utilizing these resources effectively? Possibilities included:

❏ The acquisition of another UK retail group
❏ Expansion of the Next concept in France, where one store had already been opened, or further growth in the USA, where Next had four stores.

risks, the greater the chance it has of reducing and controlling the risks. However, if managers take too long, the opportunity or the initiative may be lost to a competitor who is more willing to accept the risk.

Stakeholder needs and preferences

This relates to the expectations and hopes of key stakeholders, the ability of the organization to implement the strategy and achieve the desired results, and the willingness of stakeholders to accept the inherent risks in a particular strategy.

Strategic changes may affect existing resources and the strategies to which they are committed, gearing, liquidity, and organization structures, including management roles, functions and systems. Shareholders, bankers, managers, employees and customers can all be affected; and their relative power and influence will prove significant. The willingness of each party to accept particular risks may vary. Trade-offs may be required. The power and influence of the strategic leader will be very important in the choice of major strategic changes, and his or her ability to convince other stakeholders will be crucial.

Using the evaluation criteria

The criteria can be used in a number of ways in the search for an appropriate balance and trade-off; it is rare that one strategic option will be the most appropriate, most desirable and completely feasible.

A company might well discern just which option or options are highly appropriate and desirable and then evaluate or test their feasibility. Turner and Newall (T & N) have focused on automotive components for world markets in recent years and have sought to move away from asbestos-related products. Having acquired the German piston manufacturer, Goetze, T & N wanted to buy another German piston company, an acquisition which would make it the world leader. This acquisition faced two key feasibility tests. First, the targeted company was carrying high debts. T & N, forced to make provisions for on-going claims relating to asbestos in the USA and UK, would probably need to sell one or more existing non-core businesses to help fund the purchase – just how feasible would this be? Second, might the German or European competition authorities seek to block the acquisition?

Visit the website: http://www. itbp.com

An objective review of internal resources and relative strengths and competencies could flag options which are appropriate and internally feasible. These can then be evaluated for external feasibility and desirability. Is there a real market opportunity? Does it accord with the ambitions and preferences of the strategic leader?

Environmental scanning can be used to highlight opportunities which would be appropriate and externally feasible. These then need testing for internal feasibility and desirability, taking into account the risk element.

Sometimes a new window of opportunity will be spotted and all the criteria will need to be applied, possibly quite quickly.

The final choices and prioritization may be difficult. There might be two feasible alternatives, one of which is highly desirable to certain stakeholders but logically less appropriate than the other for the organization's overall strategy. Some organizations, particularly small companies and ones dominated by powerful, idiosyncratic leaders, may be tempted to place desirability first. A strategic leader may have personal ambitions to develop the organization in particular directions and in terms of growth targets. If the preferred strategy is implemented successfully, it will later be rationalized as highly appropriate.

Conversely, a risk-averse company may have an acquisition opportunity which is strategically appropriate and feasible, but for cultural reasons is seen as undesirable.

It is important to stress again that a strategy must be implemented before it can be considered effective. The formulation may be both analytical and creative, and the strategy may seem excellent on paper, but the organization must then activate it. The value of commitment and support from the strategic leader, managers and other employees should not be underestimated.

Case 18.2 presents three recent strategic changes pursued by the Walt Disney Corporation and invites readers to use the criteria we have discussed to evaluate their relative merit.

Whilst evaluation techniques can assist in strategic decision making, individual subjectivity and judgement will also be involved. Consequently we conclude this chapter by examining the role of judgement.

Judgement

Strategic changes can be selected by an individual manager, often the strategic leader, or a team of managers, and Vickers (1965) stresses that three contextual aspects have a critical impact on the decision:

- ❑ the decision makers' skills and values together with aspects of their personality *(personal factors)*
- ❑ their authority and accountability within the organization *(structural factors)*
- ❑ their understanding and awareness *(environmental factors)*.

Related to these, the decisions taken by managers are affected by their personal judgemental abilities, and understanding judgement can, therefore, help us explain why some managers appear to 'get things right' whilst others 'get things wrong'. Vickers suggests that there are three types of judgement:

- ❑ *Reality judgements* Strategic awareness of the organization and its environment and which is based upon interpretation and meaning systems.
- ❑ *Action judgements* What to do about perceived strategic issues.
- ❑ *Value judgements* concerning expected and desired results and outcomes from the decision.

Figure 18.3 shows how these are interconnected. Decision makers need to understand 'what is' (reality), 'what matters' (values) and 'what to do about it'

The judgement dilemma

Judgement, *per se*, cannot be taught or learned; instead it comes from experience. Experience is gained by making mistakes, which, of course, are the result of poor judgement! Managers exercise poor judgement because it cannot be taught or learned.

Case 18.2
Walt Disney Corporation

Walt Disney's fame and early success was based substantially upon films, books and comics featuring cartoon characters like Mickey Mouse and Donald Duck. To further exploit these characters, which Disney saw as resources, and to capitalize upon increased leisure spending (a window of opportunity) the first Disneyland theme park was opened in 1955 in Anaheim, California. Within one year Disneyland contributed 30% of the company's revenue.

Although Walt Disney himself died in 1966 his strategies were continued. The Magic Kingdom was opened in Florida in 1971, followed eleven years later by Epcot. These have proved immensely successful, but were not seen as 'really new'. In the 1980s the environment for leisure businesses was perceived to be changing dramatically, but Disney was no longer regarded as a trend setter. Revenues, profits and stock prices all fell.

Disney appointed a new strategic leader, Michael Eisner, in 1984, and he has successfully opened several new windows of opportunity for the corporation. He introduced more aggressive marketing (together with price increases) at the theme parks, and throughout the 1980s the numbers of visitors, including foreigners, grew steadily. Additional attractions, including the Disney-MGM film studio in 1989, were added, together with a support infrastructure including Disney resort hotels. New marketing and licensing opportunities for Disney characters have been sought. Disney has established a new film company, Touchstone Pictures, to enable it to make movies with more adult themes for restricted audiences without affecting the Disney name and family image. They have also invested in videos and satellite television. One key theme pervades most of the developments – the hidden wealth of the Disney name and characters. Disney is a successful, growing, profitable company, partially thanks to recent films such as Aladdin, The Lion King, Pocahontas and Toy Story.

Three strategic developments

In 1992 Disney opened EuroDisney, its new theme park outside Paris – the concept had already been moved successfully to Japan. However the initial visitor, revenue and profit targets had to be revised downwards after the first trading year. Drastic refinancing of the project was required. Whilst attendance levels were disappointing, the key problem was that visitors, affected by the recession, were not spending liberally. The recession was also affecting Disney's ability to sell associated properties in the theme park; the projected cash flows needed this extra income. High French interest rates then compounded the difficulties. However, it was also apparent that European employees were initially unable to replicate the enthusiasm of their US counterparts, and the overall service package was not the same. EuroDisney has since established itself and become profitable, but there was a steep learning curve.

In 1995, following a gradual downward trend in theme park attendances in Florida, Disney began to construct a new attraction – Disney's Wild Animal Kingdom – billed as 'a celebration of all animals that ever or never existed'. The live animals will (unusually) be presented in 'true-life adventure stories of mystery, danger and humour' rather than in zoo or safari park settings. Mechanical, mythical animals will be featured alongside. Interestingly, in 1994, environmentalists had forced Disney to abandon plans for a new park in Virginia (near Washington) which would have celebrated the main events in US history.

Also in 1995 Disney paid the equivalent of £12 billion to acquire Capital Cities/ABC, owner of ABC Television, to create the world's largest entertainment company. A major *content* company, Disney, was merging with a leading *distribution* company. The deal was justified with two arguments. One, Disney's valuable intellectual property would enjoy enhanced media access – ABC owns eight television stations, ESPN cable TV and an extensive radio network. ABC also publishes newspapers, books and magazines. Two, Disney's existing distribution network was ideally placed to exploit and syndicate ABC's programmes. On the other hand, having mainly concentrated on content and intellectual property, Disney was now diversifying into a new area with new strategic demands. It was moving away from direct competition with focused companies like Viacom to rival communications giants such as Time Warner.

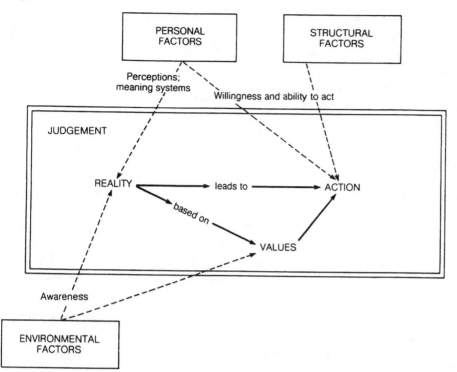

Figure 18.3 Judgement and strategic decision making.

(action). Their choice will be based upon a conceptualization of what might or what should be a better alternative to the current situation. Ideally it will incorporate a holistic perspective, implying either an understanding or a personal interpretation of the organization's purpose or mission, and it also requires an appreciation that what matters is a function of urgency and time horizons. A company with cash difficulties, for example, might need a strategy based upon immediate rationalization or consolidation; a liquid company evaluating growth options has greater flexibility. The choice will also be affected by managers' relative power and influence, their perception of the risks involved, and their willingness to pursue certain courses of action.

Having considered a number of possible frameworks through which organizations might formulate their strategies and changes in strategies (Chapter 14) and a variety of strategic alternatives in Chapters 15–17, in this chapter we have considered the criteria which determine the effectiveness of strategies. It has been emphasized that effective strategies take account of both formulation and implementation issues. Implementation is therefore the subject of the remaining chapters of the book.

Summary

In this chapter we have addressed the questions: What constitutes a good strategic choice? What can the organization do and what can it not do? What should the organization seek to do and what should it not seek to do?

In simple terms the effective strategy is the one which (a) meets the needs and preferences of the organization, its key decision makers and influencers – ideally better than any alternatives – and (b) can be implemented successfully.

A number of issues which determine the effectiveness of a strategy have been considered under the headings of appropriateness, feasibility and desirability.

Specifically we have:

- briefly looked at strategy evaluation in its widest context, how strategies might be measured in terms of their ability to meet the objectives they were designed to satisfy, and which strategic alternatives might be the most appropriate in particular circumstances
- reviewed ten evaluation techniques
- highlighted a number of key strategic principles which might usefully be sought in any strategy
- discussed effective strategies under three headings: appropriateness, feasibility and desirability
- emphasized that there are trade-offs between these factors, in that the most desirable strategy may not be the most feasible and so on
- concluded by commenting that the preference of the strategic leader will have a significant influence on the choice and by exploring the role of judgement in strategic decision making.

Checklist of key terms and concepts

You should feel confident that you understand the following terms and ideas:

⭑ The ten evaluation techniques summarized in Table 18.1
⭑ Key strategic principles
⭑ Evaluation criteria included under the headings of

- appropriateness
- feasibility
- desirability and the possible trade-offs involved

⭑ Judgement.

Questions and research assignments

Text related

1 Which of the evaluation techniques featured in Table 18.1 do you feel are most useful? Why? How would you use them? What are their limitations?

2 From your experience and reading, which evaluation criteria do you think are most significant in determining the effectiveness of strategies?

List examples of cases where the absence of these factors, or the wrong assessment of their importance, has led to problems.

Library based

3 In 1996 Walt Disney Corporation was thought by analysts to be a prospective buyer for EMI Music after its split from the Thorn Rentals part of Thorn-EMI. Would 'music' be an appropriate and desirable addition to the Disney portfolio? What in fact has happened?

4 In 1983 Tottenham Hotspur became the first English football club to be listed on the Stock Exchange. Subsequently the club diversified, acquiring a number of related leisure companies. The intention was to subsidize the football club with profits from the new businesses. Initially this happened, but in the recession of the late 1980s football had to prop up the other activities. Businesses were closed or divested, and the ownership of Tottenham Hotspur changed hands in 1991.

Research the various changes and evaluate the strategies. Was it appropriate and desirable for Tottenham to become a public limited company?

Recommended further reading

Hofer and Schendel (1978) and Tilles (1963) are both useful sources of further detail.

References

Hofer, CW and Schendel, D (1978) *Strategy Evaluation: Analytical Concepts,* West.

Penrose, E (1959) *The Theory* of *the Growth of the Firm,* Blackwell.

Rumelt, R (1980) The evaluation of business strategy. In *Business Policy and Strategic Management* (ed. WF Glueck), McGraw-Hill.

Thompson, AA and Strickland, AJ (1980) *Strategy Formulation and Implementation,* Richard D Irwin.

Tilles, S (1963) How to evaluate corporate strategy, *Harvard Business Review,* July–August.

Vickers, G (1965) *The Art of Judgement: A Study* of *Policy Making,* Chapman & Hall.

PART V

Strategy Implementation, Change and Control

INTERLUDE

Strategy Implementation

It was emphasized in the previous chapter that to be considered effective a chosen, intended strategy must be implemented successfully. The prospects for effective implementation are clearly dependent upon the appropriateness, feasibility and desirability of the strategy. Some strategies are not capable of implementation. At the same time, competency in implementation – the ability to translate ideas into actions and generate positive outcomes – can itself be a source of competitive advantage. Internal processes can add value by creating high levels of customer service and/or saving on costs by, say, removing any unnecessary delays or duplication of activities. In this last section of the book therefore we consider issues of strategy implementation and control. Reed and Buckley (1988) suggest that new strategies are selected because they offer opportunities and potential benefits, but that their implementation, because it involves change, implies risk. Implementation strategies should seek to maximize benefits and minimize risks. How might this be accomplished?

The major implementation themes concern organization structures, policies and control systems related to the management of resources; and the management of strategic change. The fundamental questions are as follows.

❏ How appropriate is the organization structure, given the diversity of the strategic perspective and the inter-relationships between the various business units, products and services?
❏ How effectively are we managing our resources? Are the various functions and activities co-ordinated and contributing towards clearly understood objectives?

This last question relates to both implementation and control, and the ability of the organization to answer it is determined by the effectiveness of the information system and the strategic awareness of managers.

❏ How do we manage changes in strategy, appreciating that cultural and behavioural changes may be required?

These questions provide the themes of the next four chapters, but before examining them in greater detail it is useful to consider a number of general aspects of implementation.

Strategy → structure or structure → strategy?

The structure of an organization is designed to break down the work to be carried out, the tasks, into discrete components, which might comprise business units and functional departments. People work within these divisions and functions, and their actions take place within a defined framework of objectives, plans and policies which are designed to direct and control their efforts. In designing the structure and making it operational it is important to consider the key aspects of empowerment, employee motivation and reward. Information and communication systems within the organization should ensure that efforts are co-ordinated to the appropriate and desired extent and that the strategic leader and other senior managers are aware of progress and results.

We have already established that in a competitively chaotic environment one essential contribution of the strategic leader is to provide and share a clear vision, direction and purpose for the organization. See Figure V.1. From this, and taking into account the various ways in which strategies might be created (incorporating the themes of vision, planning and emergence), actions and action plans need to be formalized. These strategies and proposals for change cannot be divorced from the implementation implications. Is the structure capable of implementing the ideas? Are resources deployed effectively? Are managers suitably empowered? Do organizational policies support the strategies? If the answers to these questions contain negatives, then either the strategic ideas themselves, the structure, organizational policies or aspects of resource management will need to be reviewed and rethought. The final decisions will either be determined or strongly influenced by the strategic leader, and affected by the culture of the organization. Case V.1 describes a number of strategic, structural and managerial changes at Amstrad; Amstrad has always been a strategically creative company but it has sometimes been constrained by implementation difficulties.

If appropriate, feasible and desirable strategies which **are** capable of effective implementation are selected and pursued, the organization should be able to establish some order and control in the environmental chaos and avoid major crises. This still requires that strategies, products and services are managed efficiently and effectively at the operational level. Responsibility for operations will normally be delegated, and consequently, to ensure that performance and outcomes are satisfactory, sound monitoring and control systems are essential.

It is important to appreciate that whilst structures are designed initially – and probably changed later at various times – to ensure that *determined* strategies can be implemented, it is the day-to-day decisions, actions and behaviours of people within the structure which leads to important *emergent* strategies. There is, therefore, a continual circular process in operation:

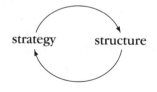

Consequently, whilst issues of structure and implementation are being considered at the end of this book, they should not be thought of as the end point in the strategy process. They may be the source of strategic change.

To summarize, the outcome, in terms of strategic management and organizational success, is dependent on:

Visit the website:
http://www.
itbp.com

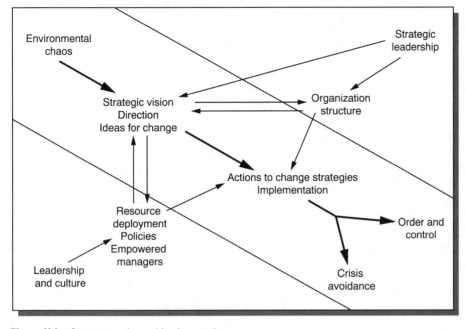

Figure V.1 Strategy creation and implementation.

☐ the direction provided by the strategic leader
☐ the culture of the organization
☐ the extent to which managers throughout the organization understand, support and **own** the mission and corporate strategy, and appreciate the significance of their individual contribution
☐ the willingness and ability of suitably empowered managers to be innovative, add value and take measured risks to deal with environmental opportunities and surprises
☐ the effectiveness of the information, monitoring and control systems.

Implementation and change

Implementation incorporates a number of aspects, some of which can be changed directly and some of which can only be changed indirectly. The latter aspects are more difficult for the strategic leadership to control and change. The success of the strategic leader in managing both the direct and indirect aspects influences the effectiveness of

☐ the implementation of strategies and strategic changes which are determined through the planning and visionary modes of strategy creation and
☐ the ability of the organization, and its managers, to respond to changes in the environment and adapt in line with perceived opportunities and threats.

Case V.1
AMSTRAD

Amstrad, the UK-based producer of personal computers and other electrical and electronic products, has been run since 1968 by its founder, entrepreneurial businessman Alan Sugar, who is also the Chairman and leading shareholder of Tottenham Hotspur football club. Amstrad was floated in 1980, but, when Sugar tried to buy it back some years later – offering investors a lower price per share than they had paid originally – he was frustrated by the company's institutional shareholders. Corporate and competitive strategies have changed creatively over the years, but Amstrad has experienced a number of implementational difficulties.

Amstrad's real success began when Sugar identified new electronics products with mass market potential, and designed cheaper models than his main rivals were producing. Manufacturing was to be by low-cost suppliers, mainly in the Far East, supported by aggressive marketing in the West. Expenditure on high profile marketing was possible because little or no capital was tied up in plant and machinery. Central overheads were kept low and potential suppliers were 'played off against each other in order to reduce direct costs'.

Sugar himself does not have a background in engineering, and when he bought Sir Clive Sinclair's computer business in 1986 he is reported to have said: 'For God's sake, Clive, I don't care if they have rubber bands in them as long as they work'. Instead Sugar has a flair for understanding the *external* design requirements of electronic products and the price points that will attract large numbers of customers.

In 1988 the flexibility which Amstrad had built into this strategy turned from a strength to a weakness. There were five main reasons for this:

❏ In 1987 there was a world-wide shortage of memory chips, essential components for Amstrad. Some chip prices were doubled and others trebled, and in order to maintain production Amstrad had to pay whatever suppliers asked. The production of certain products was cut back deliberately.

❏ The launch of a new personal computer was delayed because a sophisticated chip, designed by Amstrad, failed to work when full production began.

❏ Labour shortages in Taiwan led to a reduced supply of audio products.

❏ A joint venture with Funai of Japan for the production of videos in the UK took off more slowly than anticipated. Previously all Amstrad's videos had been manufactured for them in Japan, by Funai.

❏ Amstrad established its own distribution network in West Germany, replacing an existing agreement with a third party. However the previous distributor was left with surplus, unwanted, stock which it sold off cheaply, undercutting Amstrad's own price.

As a consequence Sugar began to move production to higher cost locations in Europe and Amstrad itself became a manufacturer. However, the recession of the early 1990s affected Amstrad's sales and the company traded at a loss for the first time in 1991–1992; it was to record three consecutive years of losses. Sales of personal computers suffered when manufacturers of higher quality and more expensive machines, including IBM and Compaq, slashed their prices to try and stimulate demand and Amstrad's competitive edge (its price advantage) was lost. Alan Sugar's dilemma was that if he withdrew from the market he had nothing really new to replace PCs.

Amstrad had earlier withdrawn from computer games, unable to compete successfully with the aggressive Nintendo. Satellite dishes (introduced in 1988), however, seemed safer with continental sales buoyant; and the increasing involvement of BSkyB in major sporting activities (exclusive coverage of the cricket world cup and live football from the Premier League) augured well for the 1990s. Amstrad's word processors and fax machines (introduced in 1989) were

Continued

continuing to sell satisfactorily; and although demand for VCRs (video cassette recorders) had fallen, Amstrad had successfully innovated a new double-decker machine which allows users to edit their own tapes and to record from two television channels at the same time. The company had launched a new lap-top computer in 1991.

Sugar's initial reaction was to consolidate and to minimize inventories in order to strengthen Amstrad's balance sheet. He commented: ' ... no intention of moving into technology-led businesses or the high end of the market. Our vocation is always in the lower end of the market'.

The appropriateness of the strategy for the 1990s was questionable. Although new electronics products were in the development pipeline, Amstrad's basic problem was that the markets in which it competed were already crowded. It needed to find new market niches with real growth potential.

Late in 1993 Amstrad acquired Viglen, a rival manufacturer of personal computers, but a company which focused on direct sales and corporate customers. Within a year Amstrad had reduced its high street sales by withdrawing its products from Dixons, whose margins, it claimed, were too low. To compensate Amstrad began a direct-selling operation, using the expertise it acquired with Viglen.

Amstrad bought two other businesses. First, it acquired the loss-making Danish manufacturer of cellular telephones, DanCall, and entered this fast-growth market. DanCall was a high technology business; Amstrad could offer complementary skills in mass production. Second was a controlling interest in Betacom, another telephone equipment company.

Also in 1994, Sugar recruited David Rogers from Philips to be his new chief executive and to take over some of the strategic leadership responsibilities. Rogers was mainly responsible for the new businesses, but his brief was to:

❏ help to introduce more robust management systems

❏ integrate the new acquisitions to achieve synergies

❏ help determine new growth areas, and

❏ foster new strategic alliances which would reduce Amstrad's dependency on personal computers. One alliance was with an IBM subsidiary which manufactured ink-jet printers, and which Amstrad later bought.

Amstrad was restructured into three divisions: ACE (Amstrad Consumer Electronics), personal computers and telecommunications. By early 1995 Amstrad was again profitable, but ACE was making losses. ACE was split into two divisions, one which would focus on buying-in and trading low-price products, mainly from South-east Asia, and one whose main role was to spot and develop new opportunities. ACE was cut back at the beginning of 1996 with a number of job losses.

Late in 1995, history also repeated itself in one respect – new DanCall products were delayed. At this time, after just 18 months with the company, Rogers resigned.

In June 1996 it was reported that Amstrad had been having discussions with Psion, and that Psion was likely to launch an acquisition bid. Psion, founded in 1980 by an academic turned entrepreneur, David Potter, is best known for its Psion Series 3 palm-held computer diary/organizer. Psion's products are typically high added value and high margin, and the real synergy is thought to be between Psion's data management competencies and DanCall's competencies in mobile telephone technology. New opportunities for combining data and voice technologies were believed to exist. Commentators assumed that Viglen would be retained as a stand-alone subsidiary but that ACE would be divested. David Potter commented: 'Psion has no interest in the consumer electronics side'. In the event, discussions foundered and no bid materialized.

Aspects of implementation which can be changed directly

❑ The organization structure (the actual, defined structure, not necessarily the way people behave within the structure).
❑ Management systems.
❑ Policies and procedures.
❑ Action plans and short-term budgets.
❑ Management information systems.

Aspects of implementation which are changed indirectly

Communication systems

While the management information system can affect formal information flows, the network of informal communications truly determines awareness. Such communications are affected by, and influence, the degree and spirit of co-operation between managers, functions and divisions.

Managing and developing quality and excellence

Attention to detail, production on time and to the appropriate quality, and the personal development of managers and other employees are all factors in this. As well as developing managers' skills and capabilities generally, it is important to consider the quality of management in particular areas and the cover for managers who leave or who are absent. The organization structure should provide opportunities for managers to grow and be promoted.

Manifested values and the organization culture

This involves the way things are done: standards and attitudes which are held and practised.

The fostering of innovation

The willingness of people to search for improvements and better ways of doing things, their encouragement and reward is very much influenced by the strategic leader, with leadership by example often proving significant.

Those aspects which can be changed directly generally imply physical changes in the way that resources are allocated. Behavioural aspects, which imply changes in beliefs and attitudes, can only be modified indirectly. Both are considered in the forthcoming chapters.

Problems of successful implementation

Owen (1982) contends that in practice there are four problem areas associated with the successful implementation of strategies.

❑ At any time strategy and structure need to be matched and supportive of each other. Products and services need to be managed independently, or in linked groups or business units, if they are to be matched closely and effectively with their environments. There may be good reasons for having a structure which does not separate the products, services and business units in this way. The strategic leader might prefer a centralized structure without delegated responsibilities, for example. The organization might possess certain key skills and enjoy a reputation for strength in a particular area, and this might be influential in the design of the structure. Equally, certain skills might be absent and have to be compensated for. Related to this might be the willingness or reluctance of managers to change jobs or location within the structure. Structures cannot be created and activated independently of the people involved; their individual skills may provide either opportunities or constraints. Changing attitudes and developing new skills is accomplished indirectly, as pointed out above, and takes time.

It is also possible that related products may be produced in various plants nationally or internationally, when a geography-oriented structure, which keeps the plants separate, is favoured for other sound reasons. In addition it may not prove feasible to change the structure markedly every time there is a change in corporate strategy, and instead, acceptable modifications to the existing structure are preferred to more significant changes.

❏ The information and communications systems are inadequate for reporting back and evaluating the adaptive changes which are taking place, and hence the strategic leader is not fully aware of what is happening. Hence the performance of the existing structure is not monitored properly, and as a result control mechanisms may be ineffective.

❏ Implementing strategy involves change, which in turn involves uncertainty and risk. New skills may have to be developed, for example. Whilst managers may agree in meetings to make changes, they may be more reluctant in practice to implement them. Motivating managers to make changes is therefore a key determinant.

❏ Management systems, such as compensation schemes, management development, communications systems and so on, which operate within the structural framework will have been developed to meet the needs of past strategies. They may not be ideal for the changes which are taking place currently, and again it is difficult to modify them continually.

Alexander (1985) argues that additional factors are also significant, especially:

❏ the failure to predict the time and problems which implementation will involve
❏ other activities and commitments that distract attention and possibly cause resources to be diverted
❏ the bases on which the strategy was formulated changed, or were forecast poorly, and insufficient flexibility has been built in.

All these problems presuppose that the formulated strategic change is sound and logical. A poorly thought-out strategy will create its own implementation problems.

Successful implementation

To counter these problems Owen suggests the following.

❏ Clear responsibility for the successful outcome of planned strategic change should be allocated.

❑ The number of strategies and changes being pursued at any time should be limited. The ability of the necessary resources to cope with the changes should be seen as a key determinant of strategy and should not be overlooked.

❑ Necessary actions to implement strategies should be identified and planned, and again responsibility should be allocated.

❑ 'Milestones', or progress measurement points, should be established.

❑ Measures of performance should be established, and appropriate monitoring and control mechanisms.

These, Owen argues, can all be achieved without necessarily changing the structural framework but rather changing the way people operate within it.

In addition, Alexander contends that the involvement and support of people who will be affected by the changes in strategy must be considered, and that the implications of the new strategies and changes should be communicated widely, awareness created, and commitment and involvement sought. Incentives and reward systems underpin this.

In just the same way that no single evaluation technique can select a best strategy, there is no best way of implementing strategic change. There are no right answers, as such. A number of lessons, considerations and arguments, however, can be incorporated into the thinking and planning; and these are the themes of the next four chapters.

Three final points need to be mentioned to conclude this introduction. First, although there are no right answers to either strategy formulation or strategy implementation, the two must be consistent if the organization is to be effective. Arguably, **how** the organization does things, and manages both strategy and change, is more important than the actual strategy or change proposed.

Second, the style of strategic leadership will be very influential. It was argued in the previous chapter that the preference of the strategic leader affects the desirability of particular strategic alternatives. The structure of the organization, the delegation of responsibilities, the freedom of managers to act, their willingness to exercise initiative, and the incentive and reward systems will all be determined and influenced by the strategic leader. These in turn determine the effectiveness of implementation. The strategic leader's choices and freedom to act, however, may be constrained by any resource limitations and certain environmental forces.

Third, the timing of when to act and make changes will also be important. In this context, for example, Mitchell (1988) points out that timing is particularly

---

In building societies we have moved from a situation in which 'change' was not the norm to one where it is. From being little changed from their formation to the late 1970s, over the next ten years societies changed immeasurably. We now expect change. Moving on from expecting change, we must desire it. It must be seen as necessary for competitive advantage and success. But to realize competitive success it will be necessary to manage the change – not just to react to it or even to be proactive – but actually to inspire and then manage the changes to ensure competitive success for the Halifax. In managing change, we must then ensure we remain in control – controlling change is an essential part of managing it.

Richard Hornby, when Chairman, Halifax Building Society

crucial in the implementation decisions and actions which follow acquisitions. Employees anticipate changes in the organization, especially at senior management level, and inaction, say beyond three months, causes uncertainty and fear. As a result, there is greater hostility to change when it does occur. The dangers of hasty action, such as destroying strengths before appreciating that they are strengths, are offset. Mitchell concludes that it is more important to be decisive than to be right, and then learn and adapt incrementally.

In the next two chapters we examine issues of structure, considering both the design of the framework and the management and control of the activities which operate within the framework. This is followed by an assessment of action plans, policies and control mechanisms, and finally an assessment of the issues involved in change and the management of change.

References

Alexander, LD (1985) Successfully implementing strategic decisions, *Long Range Planning,* **18**(3).

Mitchell, D (1988) *Making Acquisitions Work: Lessons from Companies' Successes and Mistakes,* Report published by Business International, Geneva.

Owen, AA (1982) How to implement strategy, *Management Today,* July.

Reed, R and Buckley MR (1988) Strategy in action – techniques for implementing strategy, *Long Range Planning,* **21**(3).

19

Issues in Organizational Structure

In this chapter we look at the linkages between strategy and structure by examining a number of alternative structural forms and by considering the key issue of centralization and decentralization. The forces which influence and determine the structure are discussed.

Learning objectives

After studying this chapter you should be able to:

- discuss the advantages and disadvantages of centralization and decentralization
- identify and describe five basic structural forms which an organization might adopt
- explain why structures evolve and change as organizations develop and grow
- summarize the main determinants of organization structure.

Don't forget to visit the website: http://www. itbp.com

Introduction

Lawrence and Lorsch (1967) have argued that the organization should be structured in such a way that it can respond to pressures for change from its environment and pursue any appropriate opportunities which are spotted. Given that strategies are concerned with relating the organization's resources and values with the environment, it follows that strategy and structure are linked. Structure in fact, is the **means** by which the organization seeks to achieve its strategic objectives and implement strategies and strategic changes. Strategies are formulated and implemented by managers operating within the current structure. Thompson and Strickland (1980) comment that whilst strategy formulation requires the abilities to conceptualize, analyse and judge, implementation involves working with and through other people and instituting change. Implementation poses the tougher management challenge.

The essential criteria underpinning the design of the organization structure are first, the extent to which decision making is **decentralized,** as opposed to centralized, and second, the extent to which policies and procedures are **formalized.** Decentralization to some degree is required if incremental and adaptive strategic change is to take place; and the issue of centralization/decentralization is explored as a key concept early in this chapter. Formality is linked to the extent to which tasks and jobs are specialized and defined, and their rigidity, i.e. the period of time over which jobs have remained roughly the same. The longer the period is, arguably, the greater will be the resistance to changing them.

Centralization and formality in the structure yield economies but at the same time remove initiative from managers who are most closely in touch with the organization's customers and competitors. This is likely to affect motivation and slow down the firm's sensitivity to changes in the environment. Decentralization therefore allows decisions to be made by the people who must implement the changes, and informality allows these managers to use their own initiative and change things in a dynamic turbulent environment.

These criteria create four extreme types of structure. First, those which are centralized and formal, which tend to be bureaucratic, slow to change and efficient in stable circumstances. Companies which are centralized and informal tend to be small, with power concentrated in the hands of one central figure. Decentralized formal organizations are typically large businesses divided up into divisions and business units. Power is devolved to allow adaptive change, but formal communication systems and performance measures are required for co-ordination. Finally decentralized and informal organizations tend to be groups or teams of people who are put together for a specific purpose and then abandoned once the task is accomplished. Film crews would be an example, as would special project groups within large firms.

The challenge for most organizations is to find the appropriate degrees of decentralization and informality to enable them to maintain control whilst innovating and managing change in a dynamic and turbulent environment. In turn this requires that managers are **empowered.** (Empowerment was explained in Chapter 11.)

These structural types will be evidenced in the organization frameworks and structural designs which are explored in detail in this chapter. It is important to appreciate that structure involves more than the organization chart or framework which is used for illustrative purposes and to explain where businesses, products, services and people fit in relation to each other. Charts are static; structures are dynamic and involve behaviour patterns.

Structural forms

There are a number of discrete structural forms which can be adapted by an organization when attempts are made to design an appropriate structure to satisfy its particular needs. The following are described in this section:

❏ the entrepreneurial structure
❏ the functional structure
❏ the divisional structure
❏ the holding company structure
❏ the matrix structure.

This is not an exhaustive coverage in the sense that personalized varieties of each of these alternatives can easily be developed.

In my experience, the key to growth is to pick good managers, involve them at the outset of discussions on strategy and objectives, and then devolve as much responsibility as they will accept. That's the only way you know if they are any good.
Michael Grade, Chief Executive, Channel Four Television

Autonomy is what you take, not what you are given.
Roy Watts, Chairman, Thames Water

Chandler (1962) and subsequent authors such as Salter (1970) have suggested that as firms grow from being a small business with a simple entrepreneurial structure, a more formal functional structure evolves to allow managers to cope with the increasing complexity and the demands of decision making. As the organization becomes diversified, with a multiplicity of products, services or operating bases, a different structure is again required, and initially this is likely to be based on simple divisionalization. In other words there are stages of structural development which evolve as strategies change and organizations grow. Chandler contends, though, that whilst strategy and structure develop together through a particular sequence, structures are not adapted until pressures force a change. The pressures tend to relate to growing inefficiency resulting from an inability to handle the increasing demands of decision making. Matrix organizations have been designed to cope with the complexities of multi-product, multi-national organizations with inter-dependences which must be accommodated if synergy is to be achieved. However, matrix organizations are difficult to manage and control.

It has been emphasized earlier that many organizations fail to achieve the anticipated synergy from strategies of diversification and acquisition, and as a result divest the businesses they cannot add value to. Implementation difficulties are often linked to a failure to absorb the new acquisition into the existing organization, and this is likely to involve changes in the structure.

It is important to appreciate that the structural forms described in this section are only a framework, and that the behavioural processes within the structure, the way that resources are managed and co-ordinated, really determines effectiveness. In turn this is related to the way that authority, power and responsibility is devolved throughout the organization, and whether generally the firm is centralized or decentralized. These themes are explored in Key Concept 19.1, where it is emphasized that decentralization and divisionalization are not synonymous. The establishment of a divisionalized structure does not necessarily imply that authority to adapt competitive and functional strategies is freely delegated; the firm could remain centralized.

The entrepreneurial structure

The entrepreneurial structure, built around the owner/manager and typically utilized by small companies in the early stages of their development, is illustrated in Figure 19.1. The structure is totally centralized. All key decisions are made by the strategic leader, and employees refer everything significant back to him or her. It is particularly useful for new businesses as it enables the founder, who normally will have some expertise with the product or service and whose investment is at risk, to control the growth and development.

Organisational flexibility is essential. Rates of change have speeded up. The hierarchical organisation is slow to respond. Decisions taken at the centre are too far away from the coal face. While the centre seeks local and relevant understanding, delays in decision making result.

In today's turbulent business environment speed of decision making is critically important ... decisions should be pushed down the organisation and as close to the customers as possible.

Sir John Harvey-Jones MBE, quoted in The Responsive Organisation, *BIM, 1989*

CENTRALIZATION AND DECENTRALIZATION

Centralization and decentralization relate to the degree to which the authority, power and responsibility for decision making is devolved through the organization. There are several options, including the following.

❏ All major strategic decisions are taken centrally, at head office, by the strategic leader or a group of senior strategists. The size of any team will depend upon the preference of the overall strategic leader together with the size, complexity and diversity of the organization. Strictly enforced policies and procedures will constrain the freedom of other managers responsible for business units, products, services and functional areas to change competitive and functional strategies. This is centralization.

❏ Changes in the strategic perspective are decided centrally, but then the organization is structured to enable managers to change competitive and functional strategies in line with perceived opportunities and threats.

❏ The organization is truly decentralized such that independent business units have general managers who are free to change their respective strategic perspectives. In effect they run a series of independent businesses with some co-ordination from the parent headquarters.

The role of general managers in charge of divisions and business units is explored in Chapter 20.

The extent to which true decentralization exists may be visible from the organization's charted structure. It is useful to examine the membership of the group and divisional/business unit boards, regardless of the number and delineation of divisions. The organization is likely to tend towards decentralization where there is a main board and a series of subsidiary boards, each chaired by a member of the main board. The chief executive/strategic leader, who is responsible for the performance of each subsidiary, will not necessarily have a seat on the main board. The organization will tend towards greater centralization where the main board comprises the chairmen/chief executives of certain subsidiaries, generally the largest ones, together with staff specialists. Hence decentralization and divisionalization are not synonymous terms.

The ten main determinants

❏ The size of the organization
❏ Geographical locations, together with the
  • homogeneity/heterogeneity of the products and services
  • technology of the tasks involved
  • inter-dependences
❏ The relative importance and stability of the external environment, and the possible need to react quickly
❏ Generally, how fast decisions need to be made
❏ The work load on decision makers
❏ Issues of motivation via delegation, together with the abilities and willingness of managers to make decisions and accept responsibility
❏ The location of competence and expertise in the organization. Are the managerial strengths in the divisions or at headquarters?
❏ The costs involved in making any changes
❏ The significance and impact of competitive and functional decisions and changes
❏ The status of the firm's planning, control and information systems.

Advantages and disadvantages

There are no right or wrong answers concerning the appropriate amount of centralization/decentralization. It is a question of balancing the potential advantages and disadvantages of each as they affect particular firms.

It has been suggested that companies which achieve and maintain high growth tend to be more decentralized, and those which are more concerned with profits than growth are more centralized. The highest performers in terms of both growth and profits tend to retain high degrees of central control as far as the overall strategic perspective is concerned. Child (1977) contends that the most essential issue is the degree of internal consistency.

Advantages of centralization

❏ Consistency of strategy
❏ Easier to co-ordinate activities (and handle the inter-dependences) and control changes
❏ Changes in the strategic perspective are more easily facilitated.

Disadvantages of centralization

❏ May be slow to respond to changes which affect subsidiaries individually rather than the organization as a whole, depending upon the remoteness of head office
❏ Easy to create an expensive head office who rely on management information systems and become detached from customers, and for whom there are too many diverse interests and complexities
❏ General managers with real strategic ability are not developed within the organization. Instead the organization is dependent on specialists and as a result the various functions may not be properly co-ordinated. Does this achieve a fit between the organization and its environment?

Advantages of decentralization

❏ Ability to change competitive and functional strategies more quickly
❏ Improved motivation
❏ Can develop better overall strategic awareness in a very complex organization which is too diverse for a head office to control effectively.

Disadvantages of decentralization

❏ May be problems in clarifying the role of head office central services which aim to co-ordinate the various divisions and business units and achieve certain economies through, and the centralization of, selected activities
❏ Problems of linking the power which general managers need and the responsibility which goes with the power. General managers must have the freedom to make decisions without referrals back.

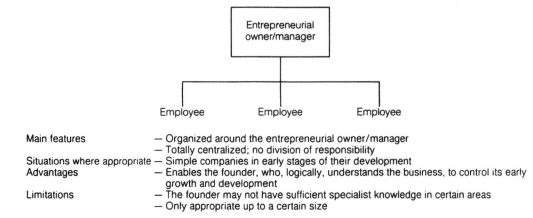

Main features	— Organized around the entrepreneurial owner/manager
	— Totally centralized; no division of responsibility
Situations where appropriate	— Simple companies in early stages of their development
Advantages	— Enables the founder, who, logically, understands the business, to control its early growth and development
Limitations	— The founder may not have sufficient specialist knowledge in certain areas
	— Only appropriate up to a certain size

Figure 19.1 The entrepeneurial structure.

There is an argument that this is not really a formal structure as all responsibility, power and authority lies with one person. However, in some small companies of this nature, selected employees will specialize and be given job titles and some limited responsibility for such activities as production, sales or accounting. In this respect the structure could be redrawn to appear more like the functional organization discussed below. The functional form only really emerges when **managers** are established with genuine delegated authority and responsibility for the functions and activities they control.

New firms with entrepreneurial structures are likely to be established because the owner/manager has contacts and expertise in a particular line of business and, for whatever reason, wishes to establish his or her own business. Whilst the entrepreneur will want to control the early stages of growth, it does not follow that he or she will have expertise in all aspects of the business. Many start-ups occur because the founder understands the technology and production or operational aspects of the business. Marketing, sales and financial control may well be areas of potential weakness with a consequent reliance on other people together with an element of learning as the business develops. This need can prove to be a limitation of the entrepreneurial structure.

Another limitation relates to growth. At some stage, dependent on both the business and the founder, the demands of decision making, both day-to-day problem decisions and longer-term planning decisions, will become too complex for one person, and there will be pressure to establish a more formal functional organization. The owner/manager relinquishes some responsibility for short-term decisions and has greater opportunity to concentrate on the more strategic aspects of the business. This can prove to be a dilemma for some entrepreneurs, however, particularly those who started their own business because they wanted total control over something, or because they were frustrated with the greater formality of larger companies.

The functional structure

The functional structure, illustrated in Figure 19.2, is commonplace in small firms which have outgrown the entrepreneurial structure and in larger firms which produce only a limited range of related products and services. It is also

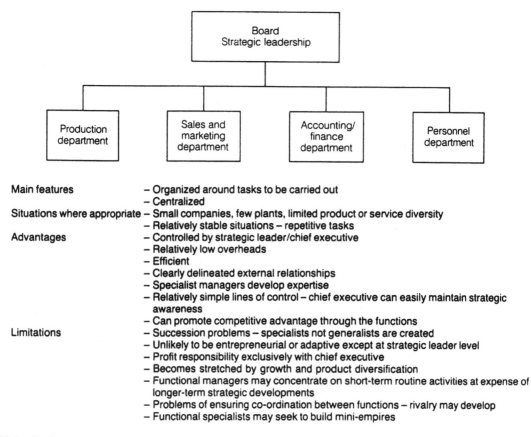

Main features — Organized around tasks to be carried out
— Centralized
Situations where appropriate — Small companies, few plants, limited product or service diversity
— Relatively stable situations – repetitive tasks
Advantages — Controlled by strategic leader/chief executive
— Relatively low overheads
— Efficient
— Clearly delineated external relationships
— Specialist managers develop expertise
— Relatively simple lines of control – chief executive can easily maintain strategic awareness
— Can promote competitive advantage through the functions
Limitations — Succession problems – specialists not generalists are created
— Unlikely to be entrepreneurial or adaptive except at strategic leader level
— Profit responsibility exclusively with chief executive
— Becomes stretched by growth and product diversification
— Functional managers may concentrate on short-term routine activities at expense of longer-term strategic developments
— Problems of ensuring co-ordination between functions – rivalry may develop
— Functional specialists may seek to build mini-empires

Figure 19.2 The functional structure.

the typical internal structure of the divisions and business units which comprise larger diversified organizations. It is more suitable in a stable environment than a turbulent one as it is generally centralized with corporate and competitive strategies again being controlled substantially by the strategic leader.

The structure is built around the tasks to be carried out, which tend to be split into specialist functional areas. Managers are placed in charge of departments which are responsible for these functions, and they may well have delegated authority to change functional strategies. Consequently the effectiveness of this structure is very dependent on the ability of these specialist managers to work together as a team and support each other and on the ability of the strategic leader to co-ordinate their efforts.

The functional structure can be highly efficient with low overheads in comparison with divisional structures, which have to address the issue of functions duplicated in the business units and at head office. Functional managers will develop valuable specialist expertise which can be used as a basis for the creation of competitive advantage, and the relatively simple lines of communication between these specialists and the strategic leader can facilitate a high degree of strategic awareness at the top of the organization.

There are a number of limitations, however. The concentration on the functions tends to lead to managers with greater specialist expertise rather than a more corporate perspective. General managers who can embrace all the functions are not developed, and consequently any internal successor to the chief executive is likely to have a particular specialist viewpoint, which may involve cultural change. This might conceivably mean a change from a financial orientation to a customer-led organization, for example, or vice versa.

Functional organizations are less likely to be entrepreneurial throughout the company than is the case in more decentralized forms, although the strategic leader could be personally dynamic and entrepreneurial. Because corporate and competitive strategy changes are generally the responsibility of the strategic leader, functional managers may concentrate on short-term issues at the expense of longer-term strategic needs. The tendency for profit responsibility to lie primarily with the strategic leader compounds this. Functional managers may seek to build mini-empires around their specialism, and this can lead to rivalry between departments for resources and status and make the task of co-ordination and team-building more difficult.

The structure is stretched and becomes more inefficient with growth and product or service diversification. As the firm grows from a limited range of related products to unrelated ones, co-ordination proves increasingly difficult. Hence a need grows for some form of divisionalization, together with a revised role for the strategic leader. The strategic leader is now responsible for co-ordinating the strategies of a series of business units or divisions, each with a general manager at their head, rather than co-ordinating specialist functional managers into a cohesive and supportive team. Financial management skills become increasingly necessary. Adaptive changes in competitive strategies are now likely to be delegated.

Once organizations reach the functional stage, their choice of future corporate growth strategy will have a major bearing upon the structural developments. Figure 19.3 shows the structures discussed in this section linked to relevant growth strategies. These linkages must be seen as indicative; it does not follow that organizations must follow these routes. Figure 19.3 additionally includes the global structure which we discussed in Chapter 15, and, for this reason only, is excluded from this chapter.

Visit the website: http://www. itbp.com

The divisional structure

One example of a divisional structure is illustrated in Figure 19.4, using product groups as the means of divisionalizing. Geographic regions are another means that are frequently used, and sometimes both geography and product groups are used in conjunction. Vertically integrated organizations might divisionalize into manufacturing, assembly and distribution activities.

The primary features are as follows:

❏ a set of divisions or business units which themselves are likely to contain a functional structure, and which can be regarded as profit centres
❏ each division will be headed by a general manager who is responsible for strategy implementation and to some extent strategy formulation within the division
❏ decentralization of limited power, authority and responsibility.

Divisional structures are found when complexity and diversity increases and where turbulent environmental conditions make it appropriate to decentralize

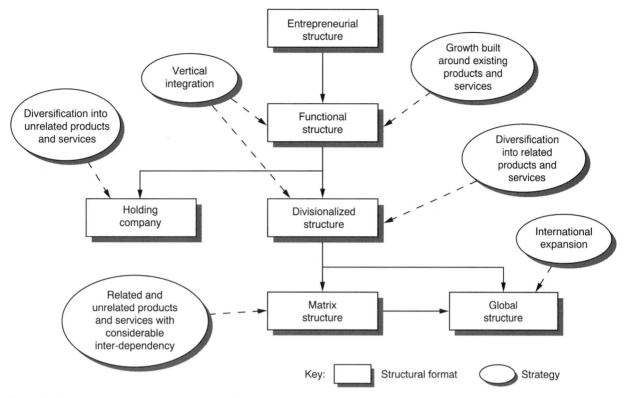

Figure 19.3   Growth strategies and related structural formats.

some responsibility for making sure that the organization is responsive and possibly proactive towards external forces in a variety of different industries. They are also useful where there are major differences in needs and tastes in the company's markets around the world.

The major advantage of this structure is that it can facilitate the ability of the organization to manage the strategies of a number of disparate products and markets effectively. The major difficulty lies in designing the most appropriate structure.

There is no one best way of dividing a business into divisions, especially if the composition of the whole corporation changes with acquisitions, divestments and closures. Large companies will change their structures periodically in an attempt to improve both efficiency and effectiveness. Structural changes of this nature imply changes in the power structure, the relative amount of decentralization and in managers' jobs, and for these reasons they may prove disruptive.

Martin Taylor joined Barclays Bank from Courtaulds in 1994 as its new chief executive and initiated a corporate restructuring programme. One element of this was the creation of a single division encapsulating all the bank's services for its large company customers. Medium-size and large organizations need to raise money in capital markets, which historically had led to the creation of investment banking activities distinct from the commercial lending business. Nat West had earlier incorporated corporate lending within investment banking; Midland had also integrated the activities but later decided to separate them again.

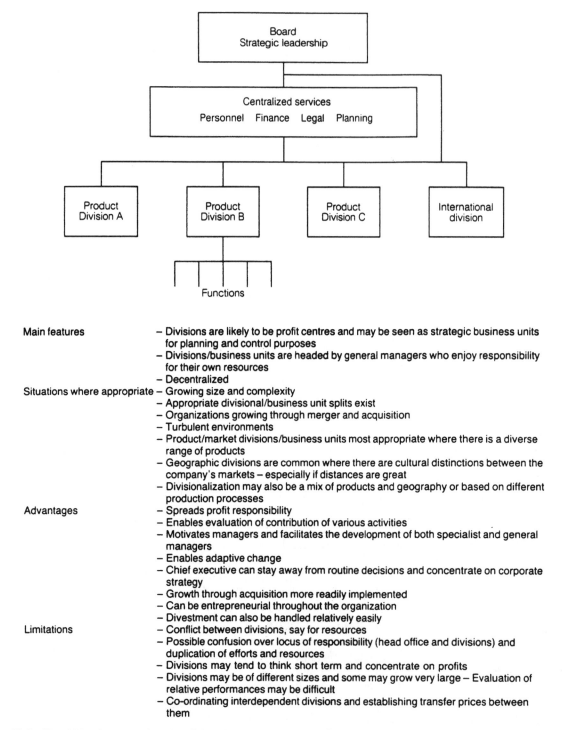

Main features — Divisions are likely to be profit centres and may be seen as strategic business units for planning and control purposes
— Divisions/business units are headed by general managers who enjoy responsibility for their own resources
— Decentralized

Situations where appropriate — Growing size and complexity
— Appropriate divisional/business unit splits exist
— Organizations growing through merger and acquisition
— Turbulent environments
— Product/market divisions/business units most appropriate where there is a diverse range of products
— Geographic divisions are common where there are cultural distinctions between the company's markets – especially if distances are great
— Divisionalization may also be a mix of products and geography or based on different production processes

Advantages — Spreads profit responsibility
— Enables evaluation of contribution of various activities
— Motivates managers and facilitates the development of both specialist and general managers
— Enables adaptive change
— Chief executive can stay away from routine decisions and concentrate on corporate strategy
— Growth through acquisition more readily implemented
— Can be entrepreneurial throughout the organization
— Divestment can also be handled relatively easily

Limitations — Conflict between divisions, say for resources
— Possible confusion over locus of responsibility (head office and divisions) and duplication of efforts and resources
— Divisions may tend to think short term and concentrate on profits
— Divisions may be of different sizes and some may grow very large – Evaluation of relative performances may be difficult
— Co-ordinating interdependent divisions and establishing transfer prices between them

Figure 19.4   The divisional structure. A product divisional structure is illustrated. Geographic divisions, or a mixture of the two, are also used.

Other advantages of divisional structures are that profit responsibilities are spread between the divisions or business units. This helps to motivate managers who can be given authority and responsibility for profit, and enables an evaluation of the contribution of each activity to the organization as a whole. Responsibility for changes in competitive and functional strategies can be delegated to the general managers in charge of each division or business unit; and it is feasible for these managers also to have responsibility for changes in the corporate strategy of their divisions. In this way the strategic leader of the corporation can concentrate substantially on corporate strategy and avoid involvement in routine decisions. Acquisitions and divestments can be handled so that only parts of the firm are affected directly. Finally this structure facilitates innovation and intrapreneurialism throughout the corporation if there is encouragement for this by the strategic leader.

In addition to the difficulty of designing an appropriate structure, there are also problems of implementation. It was highlighted above that divisions are normally seen as profit centres, and consequently their profit targets will be used as a basis for assessing performance and effectiveness. There may be problems in establishing profit targets which are seen as equitable, given that divisions (a) may well be of uneven sizes, (b) are likely to be operating in markets which differ in their attractiveness, (c) may have strong or weak relative market shares, (d) be inter-dependent upon each other and (e) have to compete with each other for scarce corporate resources. Where there are inter-dependences the corporate policy on transfer prices will favour certain divisions at the expense of others, which again can cause conflict. Wherever profits are a key measure, buying divisions will look for discounts and favourable treatment from within the corporation; selling divisions will expect other parts of the company to pay the going market price, or they will prefer to sell outside. Such profit orientation may also encourage divisions to think in terms of short-term financial measures rather than address more strategic issues.

Where an organization has a variety of different products, all of which depend on core skills and technologies, the challenge is to harness and improve the skills (which are, in effect, corporate resources) whilst ensuring competitiveness and operating efficiency for each product range. We saw in Chapter 1, for example, that Canon have developed a range of discrete products (cameras, copiers, printers, etc.) around three core competencies: precision mechanics, fibre optics and microelectronics.

Finally each division is likely to contain a functional structure, and there is also likely to be functional support from headquarters. The corporation as a whole may be able to negotiate better borrowing terms than an individual division could; personnel policies may need to be consistent throughout the firm; and head office planners may provide support to divisional planners. Reconciling any conflicts between these divisional and head office groups, together with the need to minimize the potential waste from duplicate resources, can be a limitation of this structural form. The problem can be more difficult to resolve where there are layers of divisions, as discussed below.

Where organizations grow very large, complex and diversified it may be necessary to establish a number of layers of divisions or business units within larger divisions. Each business unit or subdivision may also be a profit centre with its own general manager.

Table 19.1 shows how WH Smith has chosen to structure its various businesses. Whilst it would be possible to have several more divisions, instead of just four main ones, they would be of significantly different sizes. Clearly there are other alternatives to the chosen structural groupings: Waterstone's could be organized as a single world-wide business, for example. In addition, the retailing and distribution activities involve basically the same products. A few years earlier, when WH Smith owned travel agencies and specialist stationery stores, the structural challenge was more complex. The appropriate support and co-ordination roles for both head office and divisional staff will depend on the structure which is preferred. For example the purchasing of books, records and stationery for wholesale and retail could usefully be centralized, and the same electronic point-of-sale (EPOS) system could be relevant for all the retail activities. There is no one right answer to the WH Smith structure problem.

As organizations develop globally the structural issues are compounded. We saw in Chapter 15 that Porter (1990) and Ohmae (1990) disagree about how a company should transform itself into a successful global firm. Ohmae argues it should shake off its origins; Porter thinks they must be preserved. Should all the high added value activities (such as design, development and engineering) be centralized at a global company's home base (typified, for example, by Unilever) or spread around the world? Ohmae advocates decomposing the central head office into a number of regional headquarters, with the control of different functions (marketing, production, etc.) being dispersed to different extents and to different locations. The approaches of Ford and Nestlé are featured in Case 19.1; later, Case 19.3 discusses ABB, a company which has deliberately followed a strategy of devolution.

Table 19.1
WH Smith: group structure, 1995

1. Retailing: UK and Europe		
W H Smith Retail	–	High street stores – books, sounds, stationery
	–	Airports and stations
	–	Specialist Playhouse video stores
Virgin Our Price	–	Specialist sounds stores
	–	Virgin Megastores
Waterstone's	–	Specialist booksellers – large towns and cities
2. Retailing: USA		
WH Smith inc	–	Gift shops, typically in hotels and airports
The Wall inc	–	Specialist sounds stores – the amalgamation of acquisitions
Waterstone's	–	Specialist bookselling in major cities and airports
3. Distribution: UK and Europe		
WH Smith news and books	–	Newspaper and magazine wholesaling and distribution
	–	Book distribution to retailers, schools and libraries
WH Smith business supplies	–	Five acquired suppliers of commercial stationery and office products amalgamated under the Nice Day brand – and sold in 1996 to Guilbert of France
4. Do It All	–	DIY retailers, a 50:50 joint venture with Boots and sold to Boots in 1996

TWO TRANS-NATIONALS: FORD AND NESTLÉ – DECENTRALIZATION IN A DIVISIONALIZED STRUCTURE

The challenge for these multi-product, multi-national businesses is to design and implement a structure which enables them to be sensitive to different customer requirements whilst containing costs. The successful competitors, especially in a recession, are those which can deliver high service and quality at low cost.

Ford

In 1995 Ford decided to change from being a 'multi-national organized by geography, with regional profit centres, into a global car manufacturing business organized by product line'. Ford is smaller than General Motors and less profitable than Chrysler, its two main US rivals; it needed to be more efficient and more effective.

Ford elected to integrate its previously separate North American and European operations – it would later incorporate its businesses in Asia-Pacific, South America and Africa – to create a single global profit centre for all vehicle operations. The main aim was to remove duplication of the 'basic' elements of its various cars, including, for example, chassis, engines and transmissions. Even with these combined, Ford argued, the design and feel of a car can readily be customized to suit local tastes around the world. Cars which are essentially global should also emerge from the restructuring, together with speedier new product development processes.

The new structure would feature three distinct levels and responsibilities:

❑ A single product development organization, incorporating design and engineering, based in the USA and responsible for all Ford vehicles
❑ Five 'vehicle centres' (four located in the USA, one split between the UK and Germany) each of which would have responsibility for the world-wide development of a particular range of vehicles. The European centre would cover small and medium front-wheel drive cars such as the Fiesta, Escort and Mondeo and their equivalents. The other centres are: large front-wheel drive cars; rear-wheel drives, including Jaguar; personal use trucks; and commercial trucks.
❑ Production plants. The next generation Escort, due in either 1998 or 1999, will be produced in several countries – including the UK, Germany, the USA, Mexico, Brazil, Argentina and a plant somewhere in Asia.

Nestlé

Nestlé produces and sells in over 100 countries, many of which have strong local preferences. Its corporate headquarters was slimmed down in the early 1990s in an attempt to be more innovative and more customer-focused. There are now seven strategic business units (including coffee and beverages; foods, etc.) which have world-wide *strategic* responsibility. Operations in the various countries are co-ordinated through a regional network. Six business unit head offices are co-located at corporate headquarters in Switzerland; Nestlé's mineral water interests, including Perrier are run from Paris. There were plans to locate the global confectionery business in York (Nestlé acquired Rowntree in 1988) but these were abandoned because of the travel implications.

Each strategic business unit is free to operate in the most appropriate way – there is no longer a 'central way of doing things'. The style and approach appears to vary with the degree of novelty/maturity of the business, its market share and technological intensity, and the need to be localized. The intention is to establish the most appropriate cost structure and decision making procedures. The requirements for E–V–R congruence vary between the divisions. There are, however, in-built mechanisms to try and spread best practices and to overcome a past tendency to resist adopting ideas developed in other countries.

[Case 19.3 provides a useful contrast. ABB favours devolved business headquarters.]

ICI's strategic and structural problems were partially a result of the range and diversity of its products. These ranged from bulk chemicals (including chlorine and petro-chemicals [plastics from oil and gas]) to more sophisticated products such as pharmaceuticals and pesticides. The prospects for bulk chemicals are traditionally dependent on the world economic cycle, and consequently profits vary dramatically from year to year. Drugs are classically immune from the economic cycle, and they are also cash generative. ICI's dilemma concerned the utilization of its profits for research and development and capital investment, and whether to cross-subsidize or treat the businesses separately. During the boom years of the mid-1980s chemicals and related products were very profitable; but in the recession of 1991 they contributed just 30% of ICI's profits from 70% of the turnover.

Between 1980 and 1985, chaired by Sir Maurice Hodgson and later Sir John Harvey-Jones, ICI reduced its global workforce from 225,000 to 175,000 and purged its costs. The early 1980s were also recession years. ICI's competitive position strengthened. The company was also restructured into seven global product divisions co-ordinated through nine regional territories. Financial responsibilities were split amongst the divisions and the regions. UK inflation later in the 1980s meant ICI's costs started to rise again, and faster than those of its main competitors. The workforce was further reduced (to 132,000 in 1990) and productivity improved – but it was still not enough.

In 1990 ICI was restructured again in an attempt to place greater emphasis on the global nature of its businesses, increase the financial accountability of the divisional business managers, and focus greater attention on improving shareholders' wealth. The head office was slimmed down, and the number of regional chairmen was reduced to three. The regions lost any managerial responsibility over individual businesses. The product division heads became autonomous, and they could spend up to £10 million without reference to the main board. In comparison, business chiefs in Hanson have traditionally had to seek executive approval for all capital expenditures over £500 or $1000. When Hanson acquired 2.8% of ICI's shares in spring 1991, and raised the threat of a hostile takeover bid, the company was encouraged to evaluate again both its strategy and structure. No bid materialized, but Hanson and external analysts questioned whether ICI was effectively exploiting its assets.

ICI decided to concentrate on businesses where it could achieve a strong global position. The fibres operations were swapped for the acrylics businesses of Du Pont early in 1992, for instance.

In July 1992 ICI's board announced plans to split the company into two separate businesses in 1993 – ICI and ICI Bio, later renamed Zeneca. Shareholders in ICI would be given an equivalent shareholding in the new company. ICI would retain industrial chemicals, paints and explosives, it would have 88,000 employees world-wide and be the seventh largest chemical company in the world (relegated from fifth). These businesses are all high volume and capital intensive. Zeneca, geared more towards differentiated, high added value products, would comprise the drugs and agrochemicals businesses and be the ninth largest pharmaceutical company in the world. There would be 35,500 employees. It was assumed that most of ICI's cash reserves would remain with the bulk chemicals when it was announced that Zeneca would have an early rights issue. The opportunities for synergy really lay within the two product clusters, not between them.

Moreover, each business had different strategic needs. A successful split would enable the necessary further rationalization at ICI and foster new product investment in Zeneca. Both companies should now become better protected from hostile take-over. ICI might appear to be relatively unattractive; Zeneca would probably be very expensive whilst ever it remains successful and profitable. Since the split Zeneca shares have performed well when compared with those of other international drugs companies; ICI shares, by contrast, have been poor performers in the international chemicals industry.

ICI reached an agreement with Union Carbide of the USA to exchange information for benchmarking purposes; ICI realized that it was overstaffed and that its costs were still relatively high and had to be reduced further. In 1995 ICI appointed a new chief executive, a recruit from Unilever, Charles Miller-Smith. He found 'a traumatized organization of survivors from one of the world's most comprehensive management delayerings'. After extensive deliberation, Miller-Smith decided ICI needed to focus on intermediate (acrylic and polyester film products) and consumer-oriented products (including Dulux paints) and not bulk chemicals. Additionally ICI's future will be more dependent on investment and development in the USA and Asia than in Europe. High performance targets have been set for ICI's subsidiaries and managers.

The traditional divisionalized structure may prove inadequate for coping with the complexities of diversity and globalization. Whilst the holding company and matrix structures provide alternatives (the choice depending on interdependences and synergy needs) some organizations will eventually choose to split up into smaller, less diverse parts.

Courtaulds was split into its separate textiles and chemicals businesses in 1990. Both companies compete in the same industry, but they are at different stages of the supply chain. Case 19.2 describes the break-up of ICI in 1993.

The arguments for such splits are:

❑ the whole is worth less than the sum of the parts – the complexity is preventing individual businesses from achieving their true potential; and
❑ being part of a large organization prevents or delays important decisions.

The holding company structure

The holding company structure, illustrated in Figure 19.5, is ideal for diversified conglomerates where there are few inter-dependences between the businesses. The small head office acts largely as an investment company, acquiring and selling businesses and investing money as appropriate. The subsidiaries, which may or may not be wholly owned, are very independent, and their general managers are likely to have full responsibility for corporate strategy within any financial constraints or targets set by headquarters. It is quite common to

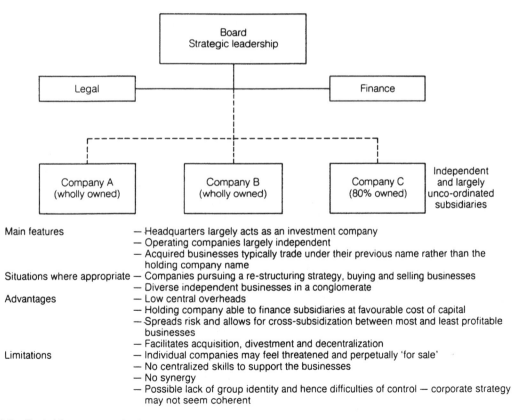

Main features	— Headquarters largely acts as an investment company
	— Operating companies largely independent
	— Acquired businesses typically trade under their previous name rather than the holding company name
Situations where appropriate	— Companies pursuing a re-structuring strategy, buying and selling businesses
	— Diverse independent businesses in a conglomerate
Advantages	— Low central overheads
	— Holding company able to finance subsidiaries at favourable cost of capital
	— Spreads risk and allows for cross-subsidization between most and least profitable businesses
	— Facilitates acquisition, divestment and decentralization
Limitations	— Individual companies may feel threatened and perpetually 'for sale'
	— No centralized skills to support the businesses
	— No synergy
	— Possible lack of group identity and hence difficulties of control — corporate strategy may not seem coherent

Figure 19.5 The holding company structure.

find that the subsidiaries trade under individual names rather than the name of the parent organization, especially where they are acquisitions who may at any time be sold again.

The holding company structure is particularly appropriate for companies pursuing restructuring strategies, buying, rationalizing and then selling businesses when they can no longer add further value.

We will look at a number of examples when we discuss diversified conglomerate organizations in the next chapter.

The advantages of this structural form are that it implies low central overheads and considerable decentralization but enables the head office to finance the subsidiaries at a favourable cost of capital. Risks are spread across a wide portfolio, and cross-subsidization is possible between the most and least profitable businesses. This again raises the issue of ascertaining a fair reward structure for the general managers.

The limitations relate, first, to the vulnerability that general managers may feel if they suspect that their business may always be for sale at the right price. There are fewer centralized skills and resources supporting the businesses, little co-ordination and therefore few opportunities for synergy. In addition there may be no group identity amongst the business units and a lack of coherence in the corporate strategy. The potential benefit to headquarters lies in their being able to earn revenue and profits from the businesses, ideally in excess of pre-acquisition earnings, and being able to sell for a real capital gain.

A number of control issues which face head offices of divisionalized and holding company structures have been mentioned in the above sections, and these will be explored in greater detail later in the chapter.

Visit the website:
http://www.
itbp.com

The matrix structure

Matrix structures are an attempt to combine the benefits of **decentralization** (motivation of identifiable management teams; closeness to the market; speedy decision making and implementation) with those of **co-ordination** (achieving economies and synergy across all the business units, territories and products). They require dual reporting by managers to, say, a mix of functional and business unit heads or geographic territory and business unit general managers.

The matrix structure is found typically in large multi-product, multi-national organizations where there are significant inter-relationships and inter-dependences as illustrated in Figure 19.6 and Case 19.3 and in small sophisticated service businesses such as a business school. The matrix structure in Figure 19.6 illustrates an organization which is split into a series of divisions, based on both products and geographic territories. The product groups would be responsible for co-ordinating the production and marketing of their particular products in a series of plants which might be based anywhere in the world. The geographic divisions would have responsibility for co-ordinating the sales, marketing and distribution of all the corporation's products, regardless of where they are manufactured, within their territorial area. The operating units would be the production plants, who were members of one or more product groups, depending upon the range of products manufactured in the plant, and whose products are marketed in more than one territory or geographic region. Consequently the general manager in charge of each operating unit is responsible in some way to a series of product and territory chiefs (four in the

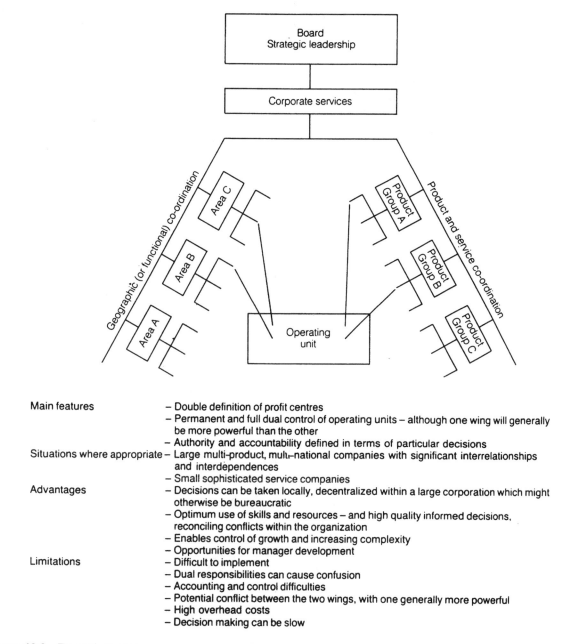

Figure 19.6 The matrix structure.

Main features	– Double definition of profit centres
	– Permanent and full dual control of operating units – although one wing will generally be more powerful than the other
	– Authority and accountability defined in terms of particular decisions
Situations where appropriate	– Large multi-product, multi-national companies with significant interrelationships and interdependences
	– Small sophisticated service companies
Advantages	– Decisions can be taken locally, decentralized within a large corporation which might otherwise be bureaucratic
	– Optimum use of skills and resources – and high quality informed decisions, reconciling conflicts within the organization
	– Enables control of growth and increasing complexity
	– Opportunities for manager development
Limitations	– Difficult to implement
	– Dual responsibilities can cause confusion
	– Accounting and control difficulties
	– Potential conflict between the two wings, with one generally more powerful
	– High overhead costs
	– Decision making can be slow

illustration), all of whom will have profit responsibility. The matrix is designed to co-ordinate resources and effort throughout the organization. Structures such as this evolved in the 1960s and 1970s because of the need to establish priorities in multi-product multi-national organizations. Should the resources and efforts be concentrated on the product groups or in the geographic territories? The ideal answer is both.

Figure 19.8 is a more straightforward illustration of how the staff in a business school might be organized. It is assumed that all the academic staff would

ABB was formed in 1988 when the Swedish company Asea merged with Brown Boveri of Switzerland to create a global electrical engineering giant. ABB has since acquired a series of smaller businesses. The chief executive is Percy Barnevik, and he sees a challenge in maintaining drive and dynamism whilst digesting large acquisitions. He is committed to a matrix structure and his aim is to make ABB the global low-cost competitor.

ABB has been divided up into 1300 identifiable companies and 5000 profit centres. These are aggregated into eight business segments and 59 business areas. There are 200,000 employees world-wide.

The eight segments are:

❑ Power plants, itself further sub-divided into
  – gas turbine plants
  – utility steam plants
  – industrial steam plants
  – hydro power plants
  – nuclear power plants
  – power plant controls
❑ Power transmission
❑ Power distribution
❑ Electrical equipment
❑ Transportation
❑ Environmental controls
❑ Financial services
❑ Other activities

The segments are responsible for organizing manufacture around the world and for product development. Horizontally ABB is divided up into a mix of countries and regions. Figure 19.7 summarizes the basics of the matrix. There is a 12 member executive board representing products, regions and corporate operations, and a slim head office (under 200 employees) in Zurich. It is not seen as essential that the divisional headquarters for the eight business segments are located in Zurich.

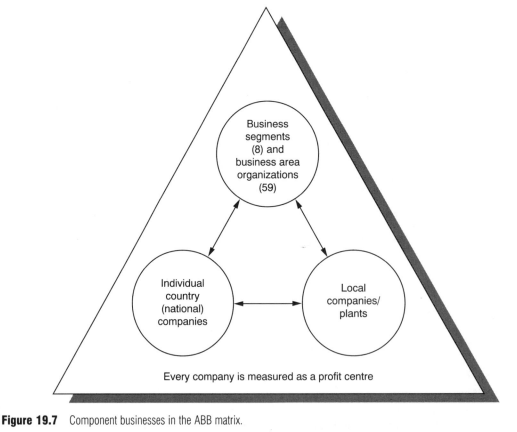

Figure 19.7 Component businesses in the ABB matrix.

ABB is a multi-national without a national identity.

Financial reporting and evaluation is on a monthly basis.

The basic structure, therefore, is based on small units (of 50 people each on average) supported by good communications and information technology. Although ABB comprises distinct businesses, both technology and products are exchanged. Every employee has a country manager and a business sector manager. Dual responsibilities such as this are often key issues in matrix structures which fail. However Barnevik insists that ABB's version is 'loose and decentralized' and that it is easily recognized that the two bosses are rarely of equal status.

Barnevik believes that if a large company is to manage internal communications effectively it must develop a *horizontal integration process.*

The role of **middle managers** – in a flatter structure – concerns coaching and technology and skill transfer. **Strategic leadership** is about creating purpose and challenging the status quo; it is not simply, as historically it was, to allocate corporate resources and resolve internal conflicts.

Barnevik has also commented that the biggest problem has been 'motivating middle and lower level managers and entrenching corporate values – particularly a customer and quality focus'. He believes that his executives should see the business as their number one priority and assumes that highfliers will spend up to 30 hours a week (in addition to their regular tasks) travelling, attending conferences and evening seminars and lectures.

It is the responsibility of every manager to network within the family of companies, developing informal relationships and looking for synergistic opportunities.

have a specialization which would fit into one of the six columns shown, and that expertise and development in their subject specialism would be important to the staff. At the same time the business school would offer a series of 'products' or services which are shown as four rows. Staff from each subject group would be allocated to each of these areas. Each product group, and possibly each course within the group, would have a leader with responsibility for delivering a quality product and earning revenue; each subject group would also have a leader responsible for allocating resources and ensuring that staff develop academically.

The potential advantages of a matrix are that responsibility and authority are delegated and spread throughout a complex organization and the stifling tendencies of a bureaucracy are avoided. Because of the flows of information, and the establishment of priorities, decisions are informed and quick. Conflicts between the various groups are reconciled within the structure by the establishment of the priorities and objectives. In addition there are numerous specialist and generalist development opportunities for managers.

Also in theory changes in priorities can be readily accommodated. A typical large accountancy practice, for example, will specialize in audit work, tax, consultancy, etc., and their work for different clients and industrial sectors will be co-ordinated. Some commentators believe that in the future 'clients must come first' and any internal, parochial boundaries built around specialisms must be destroyed.

However, the limitations have tended to ensure that these advantages have rarely been achieved. Dual responsibilities are difficult to handle; conflicts are not very easily reconciled; and as a result decision making can be slow. In

	Human resources	Marketing	Operations	Finance and accounting	Business policy/ strategy	Economics
Undergraduate courses						
Postgraduate and post-experience courses						
Research						
Executive courses						

Figure 19.8   Possible matrix structure for a business school.

addition the overhead costs can be quite high. It is also very difficult to establish the appropriate objectives and targets for the general managers, and to get priorities agreed. As a result it has often been the case that one wing of the matrix has enjoyed greater power than the other. A typical conflict might arise in the case of a special variant of a product for a particular market segment. The territory manager might be keen to market this product in order to offer a comprehensive range and support other, possibly completely different, products from other product groups within the corporation. The product chief, responsible for production of the product, might feel that the volume in question was too small and insignificant and that the product should not be produced. The locus of power within the matrix, together with any political activity by the managers concerned, would determine the decision reached.

Temporary matrices

As an alternative to the full matrix, and in an attempt to gain some of the benefits and avoid the drawbacks, some organizations make use of temporary project teams. In such cases groups or teams of managers are brought together from various parts of the organization to work on a particular project for a period of time before returning to their normal jobs. Such groups are very useful for the management of change, and they can be superimposed on any basic structure. Peters and Waterman (1982), in *In Search of Excellence*, pointed out that such teams are frequently in evidence in the most successful large corporations. The major advantage of these groups is that they are less costly than the complete matrix form, with its high overheads, but there are again limitations. There might be a tendency to seek to use the best managers quite frequently; and in such instances conflicts will be created within the organization when they are taken away from their other responsibilities.

Where there is a rigid hierarchy, specialization and narrow functional perspectives which prevent managers taking a holistic approach, the structure will inhibit managers from pursuing the organization's purpose effectively. Crises are likely to result. A typical response would be a task force to deal with the problem. As a result strong informal relationships will be formed, and these networks are likely to survive after the project team is disbanded and be used to overcome structural rigidities.

Alternatives to the matrix

In many cases, then, the matrix has proved to be too complicated to be effective. The primary reason has been the inability to deal with the issues of dual responsibility. Henri Fayol (1916) established a number of basic management principles, one of which was 'unity of command', the need to be responsible to only one manager; and the matrix has challenged this premise. Fayol's contention, however, has not been overturned. Decisions have been stifled by confusion, complexity and delay because managers have not been sufficiently sophisticated to operate effectively within this theoretically ideal structure. The need for a structural form which offers the potential advantages of the matrix to large complex multi-product, multi-national organizations, and which can be implemented, remains. If an organization is unable to design and operate a structure which enables the effective linking of a diverse range of related interests to achieve synergy, and at the same time permits the various business units to be responsive to environmental change, the organization may need to be split up.

Hunsicker (1982) quotes Philips, Ciba-Geigy and Texas Instruments as examples of multi-nationals which introduced and then retreated from the pure matrix structure. Hunsicker argues that matrices were designed to co-ordinate activities, and that the real strategic need has now become the development of new initiatives. This suggests a greater emphasis on temporary project teams, and the development and encouragement of managers within the organization so that they are more innovative and intrapreneurial. This implies that attention is focused more on changes in behaviour than on changes in the structural framework.

Visit the website: http://www. itbp.com

Pitts and Daniels (1984) list the following opportunities for obtaining the benefits of a matrix-type structure within more unitary forms:

❑ Strengthen corporate staffs to look after corporate strategic developments. They might, for example, search for new opportunities which existing business units could exploit.
❑ Rotate managers between functions, business units and locations. This increases their awareness and provides inputs of fresh ideas.
❑ Locate those executives responsible for product co-ordination in geographic territories physically closer to those managers responsible for production of the key products. Quite often such territory managers are based in their territories, close to their customers and somewhat divorced from manufacturing.
❑ Create some form of liaison groups which meet periodically and whose brief is to co-ordinate related issues. Such a group might attempt to co-ordinate the global strategies of a number of related products in a search for synergy and mutual benefits.
❑ Build the notion of agreed contributions between business units into both the management by objectives systems and the compensation schemes.
❑ Periodically review and amend the constitution of the divisions without restructuring the whole organization.

These suggestions again concentrate more on the processes within the structure than on the framework itself. We have therefore considered a number of basic structural forms and it is now appropriate to look in greater detail at the needs and considerations underpinning the design of a structure which is appropriate for both the strategies and the people who must implement these strategies.

Structure: determinants and design

In this section we draw together the key points concerning the determination and design of effective organization structures. Many of the points have been incorporated in the discussion of structural forms.

Determinants of structure

There are four main determinants of the design and effectiveness of an organization structure: size, tasks, environment and ideology.

Size

The previous section on alternative structural forms illustrated that, as the organization grows larger and becomes increasingly complex and diverse, the structure needs to change to allow for effective communication and co-ordination.

Tasks

The need for co-ordination is linked to the complexity, diversity and interdependence of the tasks that the organization must carry out. Where the businesses are unrelated, for example, the holding company structure can be appropriate. Where the business units are interdependent and particularly where there is considerable trading activity within the organization between the various activities, a divisional or matrix structure will be needed. The structure must take account of the information needs and exchanges which are required for effective decision making.

Environment

The key environmental issues concern the nature of the pressures for change and the speed at which the organization must be able to respond and act. These in turn relate to the nature of the industry, competition, and the general sensitivity of demand to environmental forces and changes. The extent of centralization/decentralization is therefore important in dealing with this issue, together with the readiness and willingness of managers to accept and implement change.

Ideology

Ideology can be either a driving force or a limiting force with regard to certain structural alternatives. It could be argued that, the longer an existing structure has existed, the more difficult it will be to make changes because people will be used to particular jobs and responsibilities. The preference of the strategic leader to retain a particular structure, or experiment with new forms, and his or her views on the appropriate amount of decentralization will also have a significant bearing.

The basic logic behind the design of the structure is to make the complexity manageable so that the organization can perform effectively with existing strategies and deal with the formulation and implementation of strategic change. Organization structures should be designed with this in mind, and the above four factors should be taken into consideration. It will not be possible, however, to predict whether a particular structural change will be more or less effective than the present structure. Much depends upon the reaction of managers and other employees to the changes implied, and their ability to deal with the communication and decision-making needs.

Structural design

Lorsch and Allen (1972), building on earlier work by Lawrence and Lorsch (1967), contend that the design of the structure must accommodate two requirements: the need to differentiate and separate the various groups which comprise the organization, and the need to integrate their respective contributions.

The need for differentiation is influenced by the different attitudes, values and behaviour of the various groups. Whilst total quality and consumer satisfaction are important considerations for all managers, the objectives of a production department, a sales department and the finance department could be expected to differ. Production might be concerned with simplifying the demands on production control and reducing costs through efficiency. Their flexibility would be increased if they were allowed to hold high levels of raw material and components stock, but this would increase costs and possibly cause conflicts with the accountants. A sales department might prefer to choose which customers and orders should receive priority, regardless of production costs, and suggest high levels of finished goods stock to allow instant deliveries. In a similar way the various product groups might operate in environments which place quite different pressures on them. The values and styles of management appropriate in each case might lead to inconsistencies of style within the organization as a whole.

Integration is concerned with the collaboration and co-ordination between the various activities, and conflict reduction. The various functions within a business unit must be integrated so that their differences are reconciled and objectives and priorities are agreed. The need for integration between business units will relate to inter-dependences.

Dividing and separating tasks

The division of work is normally achieved in two ways: first, by the way in which the tasks are separated and grouped into functions or divisions – the basic

---

The management style of the future is the flattened pyramid. It's not a trick, but a fantastic invention: you don't order people from the top, you lead them. You give them vision and help. You must let the manager do his own thing. If you do not, the company cannot run fast enough.

Jean-Marie Descarpentries, President, CMB Packaging

structural forms described earlier in this chapter – and, second, by the shape of the departmental and divisional structures within the organization. Shape is concerned with the number of levels in the management hierarchy and the span of control of each manager. Generally, as the number of levels increases the span of control decreases, and vice versa. These points are illustrated in Figure 19.9. The tall pyramid on the left could represent an organization with a number of divisional layers or a department with several levels of management. This shape can lead to delays and increasing formality as there is a greater separation of the top and bottom levels. However, it does offer an increased number of promotional opportunities for managers. The flatter shape on the right illustrates fewer layers of management, but greater demands on individual managers as their span of control, the numbers of people reporting directly to them, increases. Communications are likely to be easier and more informal, but there will be fewer promotional opportunities. Generally, there is a tendency for structures to become flatter, and as this happens individual jobs and roles are having to change.

Co-ordinating and integrating work

Communications are again an essential issue, together with the relationships between people, functions and businesses. Ideally team-working and cross-fertilization will strengthen the external architecture and generate synergy. A selection of alternative approaches is listed below:

❑ linking related profit centres into appropriate strategic business units
❑ partial centralization
❑ clearly defined policies
❑ special task forces and liaison groups

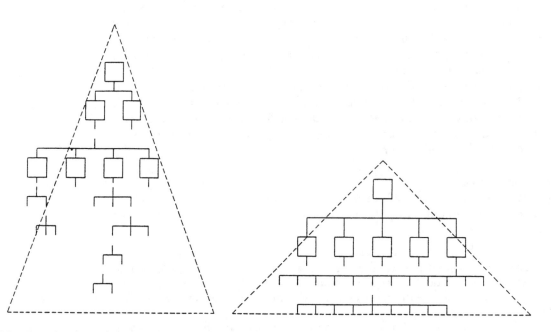

Figure 19.9 Alternative structural shapes.

❏ management by objectives and performance management
❏ team briefing
❏ manager rotation
❏ communicated mission and core values.

Some managers are by nature out-going and intrapreneurial; they will establish and nurture their own networks which share information and support organizational learning. The actual physical location of managers, functions and businesses can be an important element in achieving this. Where people are located close together, maybe in open-plan cross-functional offices, such networking is much easier. Where businesses are geographically separated, integration is inevitably more difficult, despite the opportunities provided by the latest developments in IT.

Case 19.4 summarizes aspects of the approach utilized by General Electric in the USA.

Mintzberg's co-ordinating mechanisms

Mintzberg (1979) also considers that it is necessary for an organization to divide the whole task into smaller subtasks in order to achieve the benefits of specialization and division of labour. In order to accomplish the total task Mintzberg agrees that the subtasks must then be co-ordinated and integrated, and argues that there are five main co-ordinating mechanisms:

❏ **mutual adjustment** – essentially informal communication systems
❏ **direct supervision** whereby managers take responsibility for the work of others, controlling and monitoring activity
❏ **standardized work processes** – the content of tasks is specified clearly, say through detailed job instructions
❏ **standardized outputs** – expected results are specified and manager performance is evaluated against these targets (this is a performance-oriented mechanism)
❏ **standardized skills** where the training and experience required to do jobs effectively is specified.

Standardized skills incorporate the notion of specific qualifications being required for particular specialist positions. Co-ordination is achieved through workers and managers understanding what is expected of each other and making effective contributions naturally. An anaesthetist and a surgeon, for example, appreciate each other's roles and contributions.

In addition there is a sixth mechanism which results from mutual adjustment and adaptive changes in strategy. Mintzberg refers to this as the **standardization of norms** where employees share a set of common beliefs. This is a cultural issue which evolves as mutual adjustment and informal communications lead to adaptive changes and the establishment of new norms of behaviour. The evolution of a road through a forest from a well-trodden path would constitute an analogy.

Mintzberg argues that small entrepreneurial firms rely mainly on direct supervision by the owner/manager, and that as the organization grows and becomes more complex standardized work processes, outputs and skills become increasingly popular in a sequential and ascending order. Mutual adjustment is the favoured mechanism in what Mintzberg terms adhocracies,

General Electric (GE) which manufactures aircraft engines, defence electronics and household consumer goods, provides financial services and owns NBC Television in the USA, has annual revenues in excess of $50 billion. Until 1994 GE also owned the Kidder Peabody Investment Bank.

The company is decentralized and employees are encouraged to speak out and pursue ideas. External contacts and sources are constantly monitored for new leads and opportunities. 'We'll go anywhere for an idea.' The chief executive officer, John F Welch, believes 'the winners of the 1990s will be those who can develop a culture that allows them to move faster, communicate more clearly, and involve everyone in a focused effort to serve ever more demanding customers'.

The decentralization aims to 'inject down the line the attitudes of a small fast-moving entrepreneurial business and thereby improve productivity continuously'. Integration strategies promote the sharing of ideas and best practices.

There is a developed strategy of moving managers between businesses and countries to transfer ideas and create internal synergy, together with a reliance on employee training. Welch regularly attends training courses to collect opinion and feedback. 'My job is to listen to, search for, think of and spread ideas, to expose people to good ideas and role models.' GE's *'work out'* programme involves senior managers presenting GE's vision and ideas to other managers and employees, and then later reconvening to obtain responses and feedback on perceived issues and difficulties. External advisers (such as university academics) monitor that communications are genuinely two-way.

Managers are actively encouraged to work closely with suppliers and customers, and they have '360 degree evaluations', with inputs from superiors, peers and subordinates. 'People hear things about themselves they have never heard before.'

Welch summarizes his philosophy as follows:

If we are to get the reflexes and speed we need, we've got to simplify and delegate more – simply trust more. We have to undo a 100-year-old concept and convince our managers that their role is not to control people and stay on top of things, but rather to guide, energize and excite. But with all this must come the intellectual tools, which will mean continuous education of every individual at every level of the company.

[Strategic regeneration at GE is examined in Chapter 22.]

and which are discussed later in this section. Each structural type and style of management has a most appropriate co-ordinating mechanism, and this is explored below.

Mintzberg's structural configurations

Mintzberg (1983) has described five structural configurations, each of which is suitable for organizations at certain stages of development and in particular environmental circumstances. Each structural configuration achieves co-ordination and congruence of environment, values and resources in different ways. Moreover, whilst each configuration comprises five basic parts or sets of resources, as outlined below, the relative size and importance of these parts varies between the configurations.

The five constituent parts of the organization
Mintzberg's five parts are illustrated in Figure 19.10 and are as follows.

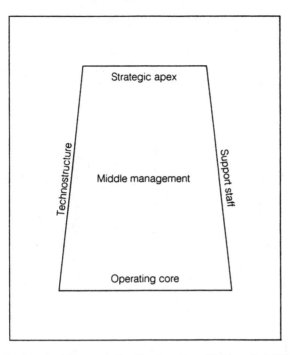

Figure 19.10   The basic parts of the organization. Developed from Mintzberg, H (1983) *Structure in Fives,* Prentice-Hall.

❏ The **operating core** relates to those employees who carry out the various tasks involved in the primary activities of the value chain, which include securing inputs, transforming the inputs into outputs by adding value and then distributing the outputs.

❏ The **strategic apex:** the strategic leader and his or her colleagues who are responsible for developing the corporate strategy, managing relations with the environment, designing the structure and allocating resources.

❏ The **middle management:** middle managers, with authority, link the strategic apex with the operating core. They manage the tasks carried out by the operating core, applying any policies and systems established by the strategic apex, and feed information up and down the organization.

❏ **Support staff:** support activities occur at various levels in the hierarchy and provide assistance to both middle managers and the operating core. Such activities would include research and development, public relations and certain aspects of the personnel function such as running the payroll.

❏ The **technostructure** comprises analysts who affect the work of others, such as work study analysts, planners and the training and recruitment staff in personnel. Galbraith (1969) uses the expression 'technocrats' to describe the experts and specialists who control much of the activity in large, powerful and growth-oriented corporations. Some of Galbraith's ideas were summarized in Chapter 5.

The five configurations

Mintzberg's five configurations are discussed below, and the salient points are compared in Table 19.2. These configurations do not match completely with the structural forms outlined earlier but they are clearly related.

Table 19.2 Selected features of Mintzberg's five configurations

	Simple structure	Machine bureaucracy	Professional bureaucracy	Divisionalized form	Adhocracy
Key co-ordinating mechanism	Direct supervision	Standardization of work	Standardization of skills	Standardization of outputs	Mutual adjustments
Key part of organization (resource concentration)	Strategic apex	Technostructure	Operating core	Middle management	Support staff
Roles of strategic apex/leadership in addition to responsibility for corporate strategy	All administration	Co-ordination and conflict resolution	External liaison and conflict resolution	Strategic perspective and control of performance	External liaison, conflict resolution and project monitoring
Centralization/decentralization	Centralized	Limited horizontal decentralization	Decentralized	Decentralized vertically	Decentralized
Environment	Simple and dynamic	Simple and stable	Complex and stable	Relatively simple and stable but diverse	Complex and dynamic
Power and values	Controlled by strategic leader – possibly owner/manager	Technocratic and sometimes external control	Professional manager control	Middle management control, i.e. general managers	Expert control
Typical examples	Small firms Young organizations	Processing companies Assembly companies	Hospital University	Diversified or multi-product organization	Management consultants

The simple structure Mintzberg's first configuration relates very closely to the entrepreneurial structure. It is typically small, and has no technostructure and little formal planning. Decision making is centralized with the chief executive or owner/manager, and performance is very dependent on the strategic leader.

The machine bureaucracy Machine bureaucracies are generally found where the work is routine, with standardized production processes. Jobs are tightly defined and regulated, and there is a powerful technostructure to search for efficiencies and cost control opportunities. This configuration is typical of mass production assembly systems.

Some power is decentralized to the specialist functional managers, but strategic change decisions are largely centralized. As the specialists implement the proposed changes, strategy formulation and implementation are separated. The machine bureaucracy is relatively slow to change, and therefore more suitable for stable environmental conditions. In a number of respects it is similar to the functional structure.

The professional bureaucracy The professional bureaucracy is typically found in organizations which rely heavily on administrators and administration systems, such as hospitals and universities. It is bureaucratic but not centralized, and power lies with specialist professionals and professional managers. Where professionals are in evidence they are likely to hold formal qualifications; and standardized skills will be the main co-ordinating mechanism. Support administrators are unlikely to be as well qualified as the professionals. However, in the 1980s and 1990s there has been an increasing tendency for administrators in some of these organizations to study for high-level management qualifications.

The polytechnics in the UK were examples of professional bureaucracies which had to change their structures. Until 1989 their administrative systems provided a link between the powerful academic structure, comprising highly qualified academics and heads of department, and the respective local authorities who controlled their financial affairs. Since the polytechnics were in effect privatized in April 1989, when they became independent higher education corporations with plc status, new administrative and financial structures have been introduced with additional layers of management. Because new funding arrangements have been introduced, commercial considerations and market orientation have also increased in significance. The polytechnics became 'new universities' in 1992 and it was necessary for them to review their distinctive mission and market niche.

Visit the website: http://www. itbp.com

Does this structural configuration encourage or inhibit change? Adaptive change is likely to be evident and influenced significantly by external professional organizations. Committee structures will restrict the freedom of the professionals to change things, but the changes will still prove difficult to co-ordinate in many instances. More substantial strategic changes are difficult to implement as the structure tends to be inflexible. Performance measures relating to effectiveness, rather than to the efficient utilization of resources, are difficult to establish and monitor because of the nature of the service.

The divisionalized structure This configuration represents any structure based on autonomous divisions or business units co-ordinated by a central administrative structure. It typically develops out of a machine bureaucracy when there is diversification. Power and responsibility is devolved to the divisions, creating a key strategic role for the general managers who head the divisions. These general managers, who comprise Mintzberg's middle line in this configuration, are responsible for changes in competitive strategies; but the extent of the decentralization in the organization as a whole may be restrained. General managers, for example, may centralize the power within their divisions.

Divisions will be expected to agree objectives and targets with the strategic leader; and measures of effective performance related to these will be used for monitoring and control purposes. Hence the standardization of outputs is the most appropriate co-ordination mechanism.

Recapping on points made previously, the overall strategic leader in a divisionalized structure is responsible for managing and co-ordinating a portfolio of businesses. General managers at lower levels in the hierarchy are responsible for portfolios of business units or product/markets. If they are to accomplish this effectively they must be able to reach informed decisions concerning resource allocation, especially finance. The technocracy therefore provides an important support function.

The adhocracy An adhocracy is an informal and innovative organization which features teams of specialists and decentralized power. An advertising agency or a management consultancy group would be a typical example. Liaison between groups of experts is very important, and some variant of the matrix structure, such as temporary project teams or liaison groups, is likely to be evident. Expertise lies throughout the organization, the operating core and support staff being particularly important.

Adaptive strategic changes, originating anywhere within the organization, are likely to be commonplace and encouraged as this configuration is attempting to deal with a complex and dynamic environment. The pursuit of personal objectives and organizational politics (considered in greater detail in Chapter 22) are facilitated and must be monitored and controlled. Decision making may be slowed down where people are very active politically. Linked to these issues, conflict will also be present, and resolving this will be a key role for the strategic leader.

It is quite possible to find more than one configuration present in an organization where diverse interests mean that E–V–R congruence cannot be achieved effectively with only one style of management. A newspaper, for example, may have an adhocracy for dealing with editorial aspects and a machine bureaucracy for printing. A university overall is likely to be a professional bureaucracy, but

---

The constituent companies [in LVMH, Moët Hennessy, Louis Vuitton] have asked for the following: simplified structures, autonomy for the operational units and a method of administration in keeping with their particular culture.

I am convinced that the success of our group and its subsidiaries is due to the fact that we trust the operational teams to carry out their own quest for quality.

We keep these companies autonomous at middle management level so that they can have the advantages of medium size companies as well as the advantage of belonging to a powerful group that can fund their development.

Bernard Arnault, Group Chairman, LVMH, Moët Hennessy, Louis Vuitton

the business school within it may well be more of an adhocracy and built around a matrix, as described earlier.

At this stage it would be useful to review the Key Reading 13.1, Chapter 13. Drucker (1988) argues that the organization of the future will have fewer managers and fewer layers in the management hierarchy. Information technology will lead to more autonomy for individual managers and more informed decision making when specialists have decentralized responsibility for key activities within the organization. Strategy co-ordination will still constitute a major challenge.

Business process re-engineering (BPR)

Because business process re-engineering can have a dramatic impact on organization structures, it is important to mention it at the end of this chapter. A detailed study and critique of BPR is, however, outside the scope of this book.

To be successful organizations must add value for their customers and other stakeholders in some distinctive way. Strategic capabilities are the means and *processes* through which value is added, as distinct from the products and services themselves and their competitive positioning. When managers are delegated responsibility for changing and improving the ways in which tasks are carried out it is these processes which are being changed incrementally and adapted.

Typical processes include:

❏ supply chain management – to fulfil orders, but also including administrative procedures for dealing with enquiries and orders
❏ developing new products and services
❏ providing service to customers
❏ managing people – including, for example, developing people
❏ managing finances – especially the cash flow.

Successful innovation in these internal processes can:

❏ lead to greater efficiency
❏ improve quality and service
❏ save time
❏ create or enhance differentiation and thus
❏ **add value for customers**.

Sometimes this gradual change may not be enough in a competitive environment. The existing processes – and their outcomes – may simply be inadequate or even unacceptable. Consequently a more radical review is necessary if the organization is to become or remain a leading competitor in an industry. Managers must systematically benchmark and evaluate best practice, using competitors and any other relevant organizations, and consider the extent to which the processes need redesigning. This objective appraisal, and the changes which result from it, can take the form of business process re-engineering, which is really another example of planned change. BPR implies that an organization completely rethinks how certain tasks are carried out, and searches for new ways through which performance can be improved.

US Air, British Airways' American partner, recently reviewed the process by which aeroplanes flying domestic routes are emptied, cleaned and the passengers and luggage loaded for the next flight. The outcome was a time reduction from 45 to 25 minutes for selected flights. As a result operating efficiencies are increased – the planes are in the air longer and on the ground less – without passengers being inconvenienced.

It is often found that radical process re-engineering requires the reduction or breaking down of functional and individual job boundaries as the new processes do not have to coincide with the existing departmental structure. People and departments will now be expected to be more supportive of each other and share information and best practices. These linkages and the greater flexibility in turn imply empowerment and learning.

BPR has undoubtedly enjoyed a period of popularity as organizations, sometimes using consultants, have initiated restructuring programmes. Invariably these have involved job losses and downsizing. Unfortunately, with hindsight, some organizations have realized that they have lost important skills and competencies in the exercise and also caused demoralization amongst those employees who stay. The downsizing has not resulted in the organization establishing the efficient and effective 'right size' from which new opportunities for adding value can be generated. Not unexpectedly, therefore, BPR has been widely criticized, but defended by its proponents who argue that too many organizations do not appreciate how to apply it properly.

In 1990 David O'Brien became the new chief executive of the National and Provincial Building Society. He quickly initiated a programme of change, designed to strengthen the society's customer focus and service. Eight levels and 20 grades of management were reduced to three and four, respectively; there was a dramatic increase in team-working and integration.

O'Brien's Director of Business and Organization Development commented: 'If managers are not convinced that robbing them of their traditional functional power – though not necessarily their jobs – is good for the future, the whole programme is jeopardized'.

The extent of the change had a traumatic impact on employees and resistance grew. In the end O'Brien left the society, which, some time later, was acquired by the Abbey National.

Checklist of key terms and concepts

You should feel confident that you understand the following terms and ideas:
* The strategy → structure, structure → strategy issue
* Centralization and decentralization
* The five structural forms: entrepreneurial, functional, divisional, holding company, matrix
* The division and integration of tasks in structural design
* Mintzberg's five co-ordinating mechanisms; five parts of the organization: operating core, strategic apex, middle management, support staff, technostructure
* Five structural configurations: simple structure, machine bureaucracy, professional bureaucracy, divisionalized, adhocracy
* Business process re-engineering – at a conceptual level only.

Summary

The introduction to this chapter emphasized that, whilst organization structures are designed to ensure that strategies can be implemented effectively, the processes within the structure affect the formulation of future strategies. Particularly significant is the location of power, responsibility and authority in the organization and the extent to which these are centralized and decentralized. In large organizations the relationship between head office and the business units relates to this issue. In this chapter we have explored the links between strategies and structure.

Specifically we have:

- looked at the determinants, advantages and disadvantages of centralization and decentralization
- examined five structural forms – the entrepreneurial structure, the functional structure, the divisional structure, the holding company structure and the matrix structure – in terms of (a) their main features, (b) where they are most appropriate, (c) their advantages and (d) their limitations

- within this section, highlighted (a) the alternative approaches to divisionalization, (b) why matrix organizations are difficult to implement and manage, despite being theoretically very attractive, and (c) that the behavioural processes within the structural framework are an essential consideration
- considered how structures might evolve and change as organizations grow larger, more complex and more diversified,
- discussed the four main determinants of structure: size, tasks, environment and ideology
- considered how the major requirements of the structure, namely that the tasks to be carried out can be effectively divided and integrated, might be accomplished
- described the five co-ordinating mechanisms, the five component parts of the organization and the five structural configurations identified by Mintzberg
- briefly mentioned that business process re-engineering can have a major impact on organization structures.

Questions and research assignments

Text related

1 It was stated in the text that decentralization and divisionalization are not synonymous. What factors determine the degree of decentralization in a divisionalized organization?

2 For an organization with which you are familiar, obtain or draft the organization structure. How does it accord with the structural forms described in the text. Given your knowledge of the company's strategies and people, is the structure appropriate? Why? Why not? If not, in what way would you change it?

3 'Sophisticated innovation requires a configuration that is able to fuse experts drawn from different disciplines into smoothly *ad hoc* project teams' (Henry Mintzberg discussing adhocracies).

Do you agree? Can innovation not be incorporated into the alternative structures?

Do you believe the adhocracy approach will overcome the perceived drawbacks of the matrix structure?

Library based

4 Obtain a current organization chart for the WH Smith Group, and consider how the various businesses featured in Table 19.1 are integrated. Do you feel that this is the most suitable structure?

5 Evaluate the divisionalized or holding company structure of a large diverse multi-product multinational, considering the main board status of the key general managers. Does this suggest centralization or decentralization?

If you are familiar with the company, do your findings accord with your knowledge of management styles within the organization?

6 How successful have the two Courtaulds businesses been since they were established in the 1990 corporate split?

Recommended further reading

The second edition (1984) of Child's book *Organization: A Guide To Problems and Practice* is an ideal source of further information.

Mintzberg (1979) contains more detail on structural forms.

The texts by Mintzberg (1983) and Thompson and Strickland (1980) are also worthy of further study.

The article by Drucker on 'The coming of the new organization' (1988) is provocative reading.

References

Chandler, AD (1962) *Strategy and Structure: Chapters in the History of the American Industrial Enterprise*, MIT Press.

Child, JA (1977) *Organization: A Guide to Problems and Practice*, Harper & Row. (A more recent edition is now available.)

Drucker, PF (1988) The coming of the new organization, *Harvard Business Review*, January–February.

Fayol, H (1916) *General and Industrial Administration*, Pitman, 1949 (translation of French original).

Galbraith, JK (1969) *The New Industrial State*, Penguin.

Hunsicker, JQ (1982) The matrix in retreat, *Financial Times*, 25 October.

Lawrence, PR and Lorsch, JW (1967) *Organization and Environment*, Richard D Irwin.

Lorsch, JW and Allen, SA (1972) *Managing Diversity and Interdependence*, Division of Research, Harvard Business School.

Mintzberg H (1979) *The Structuring of Organizations*, Prentice-Hall.

Mintzberg, H (1983) *Structure in Fives: Designing Effective Organizations*, Prentice-Hall.

Ohmae, K (1990) *The Borderless World*, Harper.

Peters, TJ and Waterman, RH Jr (1982) *In Search of Excellence: Lessons from America's Best Run Companies*, Harper & Row.

Pitts, RA and Daniels, JD (1984) Aftermath of the matrix mania, *Columbia Journal of World Business*, Summer.

Porter, ME (1990) *The Competitive Advantage of Nations*, Free Press.

Salter, MS (1970) Stages in corporate development, *Journal of Business Policy*, Spring.

Thompson, AA and Strickland, AJ (1980) *Strategy Formulation and Implementation*, Richard D Irwin.

20

Corporate Strategy and Corporate Management Style

In this chapter we explore the relationship between the corporate centre and the subsidiary businesses in large organizations. We look in particular at diverse, conglomerate businesses. Finally there is an assessment of the role of general managers in large, multi-divisional organizations.

Learning objectives

After studying this chapter you should be able to:

■ distinguish between the alternative control mechanisms which large, diverse organizations might use
■ discuss the strategic and control issues of diverse, conglomerate businesses
■ explain the role and contribution of corporate head offices to large, multi-business organizations
■ discuss the role and skills of general managers in these organizations.

Introduction

We have established that growth is often an important objective for organizations. Frequently this growth will involve diversification and acquisitions in either related or unrelated areas. In recent years the strategic logic of large, diversified conglomerates has been questioned as many organizations have instead chosen to focus on related businesses, technologies or core competencies – where they can more readily add value across the businesses and generate synergy. However, conglomerate, diversified businesses should not be automatically dismissed; they can be both successful and profitable if they can find new, suitable businesses to acquire and if their strategic control system is appropriate. Simply, the strategy can still be justified if it can be implemented successfully. In this chapter we first explore alternative approaches to strategic control and apply these issues to diversified conglomerates. We also discuss the role and contribution of corporate head offices, which, generally, in recent years, have been slimmed down. We examine the particular role of general managers and conclude with some short comments on organizations in the mid- to late 1990s.

Don't forget to visit the website: http://www. itbp.com

Styles of corporate management

The questions addressed in this section are the following: What is the appropriate role for corporate headquarters in divisionalized organizations? How much power should be centralized? How independent should the divisions and business units be? These relate to the difference between the divisional and the holding company structures and styles of management, and the themes of integration and behavioural processes within the structural framework are explored further.

In relation to these issues Goold and Campbell (1988) have contrasted the views of Sir Hector Laing, ex-Chairman of United Biscuits, with those of Lord Hanson. Laing contends that it takes a number of years to build a business, and that during this period corporate headquarters should help the general managers of business units to develop their strategies. Hanson argues that it is more appropriate for head office to remain detached from operations, and instead of involvement to set strict financial targets. All Hanson businesses are for sale at any time. Both approaches have been shown to work, but with different levels of overall performance and strategic growth patterns. These two approaches represent two ends of a spectrum – a third approach is a compromise between the two. Goold and Campbell have categorized large UK companies following these three approaches as follows.

Financial control companies

Financial control is seen as an ideal approach for a holding company where the businesses are independent and unrelated. Hanson and BTR, discussed later, are excellent examples of this style, which has also been preferred by the more focused GEC.

❑ Strategy creation is heavily decentralized to business unit managers. Within their agreed financial targets they are free to develop and change their competitive and functional strategies.
❑ Budgets and targets – and their achievement – are critically important control mechanisms.
❑ The small head office monitors financial returns closely and regularly, intervening when targets are missed – head office is a 'controller'.
❑ Head office also acts as a corporate investment banker for investment capital.
❑ Achievement is rewarded, and units are encouraged to put forward and chase ambitious targets. Underperforming managers are likely to be removed.
❑ The head office adds value by acquiring and improving underperforming businesses; if additional value cannot be added it may well sell-off businesses.
❑ There will, typically, be few inter-dependencies and links between the businesses.
❑ Growth is more likely to be by acquisition than organic investment, with many financial control companies taking a short-term view of each business and being reluctant to invest in speculative research and the development of longer-term strategies.

Strategic planning companies

Strategic planning tends to be adopted in organizations which focus on only a few, and preferably related, core businesses. Examples include Cadbury Schweppes, United Biscuits and BP. Historically it has been the favoured approach for most public sector organizations.

❏ Strategic plans are developed jointly by head office and the business units, with head office retaining the final say. Strategic planning is centralized.

❏ Day-to-day operations only are wholly decentralized.

❏ Head office sets priorities and co-ordinates strategies throughout the organization, possibly initiating cross-business strategies, and thereby acts as an 'orchestrator'.

❏ A long-term perspective is realistic, and the search for opportunities for linkages and sharing resources and best practice can be prioritized. This normally requires central control. Individually the businesses would tend to operate more independently; organization-wide synergies may involve sacrifices by individual businesses.

❏ Goold and Campbell conclude there are co-ordination problems if this approach is used in truly diversified organizations.

❏ Budgets are again used for measuring performance.

❏ The tight central control can become bureaucratic and demotivate managers, who may not feel *ownership* of their strategies.

Other dangers are, one, thinking may become too focused at the centre, with the potential contributions of divisional managers underutilized, and two, the organization may be slow to change in response to competitive pressures. Value can be added successfully if corporate managers stay aware and expert in the core businesses and if the competitive environment allows this style to work.

Strategic control companies

Financial control and strategic planning are appropriate for particular types of organization, but both styles, whilst having very positive advantages, also feature drawbacks. The strategic control style is an attempt to obtain the major benefits of the other two styles for organizations which are clearly diversified but with linkages and inter-dependencies. Value is added by balancing strategic and financial controls.

❏ Strategy creation involves decentralization to the business units, although head office still controls the overall *corporate* strategy.

❏ The role of head office is to review divisional and business plans, and approve strategic objectives and financial targets, accepting they may need to be changed in a competitive environment.

Performing a 'coaching' role, head office encourages businesses to achieve their potential by active involvement and by fostering the spreading of learning and good practice through the organization.

❏ Strategy creation and budgetary control can be separated, allowing for more creative performance measurement.

Sometimes competitive pressures and misjudgements mean strategies have to be changed, and hoped-for financial targets may be missed. A strategic control style can recognize this and deal with the implications.

❏ Head office does, however, monitor and control financial performance and success against strategic milestones and objectives.

Although decentralization is a feature, head office still requires considerable detail about the various businesses if it is to ensure the synergy potential is achieved and very short-term thinking is avoided. Political activity will be prevalent as individual businesses compete with each other for scarce corporate resources.

Two leading organizations which utilized this style – ICI and Courtaulds – concluded they were overdiversified. There were numerous businesses and some were clearly inter-linked. At the same time these 'clusters' had little in common and featured different strategic needs and cultures. Because of these differences, and the inevitable complexity, corporate headquarters could not add value with a single entity. Both companies split into two distinct parts to enable a stronger focus on core competencies and strategic capabilities.

Levels of success

Goold and Campbell studied 16 large UK companies, including those given as examples above, and concluded that each style has both advantages and disadvantages and that no one style is outstandingly the most successful.

Strategic planning companies proved to be consistently profitable during the 1980s, mainly through organic growth. Head office corporate staff tend to be a quite large group and differences of opinion with general managers sometimes cause frustration within the divisions and business units. **Financial control companies** exhibited the best financial performance. In a number of cases, particularly BTR and Hanson, this resulted from acquisition and divestment rather than organic growth. Short-term financial targets were felt to reduce the willingness of general managers to take risks. There were few trade-offs whereby short-term financial targets were sacrificed for long-term growth. A general manager, for example, might consider a programme of variety reduction and product rationalization with a view to developing a more consistent and effective portfolio. In the short term this would result in reduced revenue and profits before new orders and products improved overall profitability. This temporary fall might be unacceptable in the face of short-term financial targets. **Strategic control companies** also performed satisfactorily but experienced difficulties in establishing the appropriate mix of strategic and financial targets for general managers. Financial targets, being the more specific and measurable ones, were generally given priority.

Goold and Campbell concluded that whilst the style of management adopted within the structure determines the strategic changes which take place, the overall corporate strategy of the company very much influences the choice of style. Large diverse organizations, for example, will find it difficult to adopt a strategic planning approach. Equally, where the environment is turbulent and competitive, increasing the need for adaptive strategic change, the financial planning approach is less appropriate. Not unexpectedly Hanson's main acquisitions have been of companies in mature slow growth sectors.

Whilst companies may appreciate there is a mismatch between their corporate strategy and style, changing the style can be difficult. Moreover, many organizations will not be able to implement a new style as effectively as the one they are used to.

Goold *et al.* (1993) revisited the organizations and their research five years later, partly stimulated by the change of fortunes for some of the companies involved. This review reinforced the conclusion that financial control is ideally suited to a group of autonomous businesses in a conglomerate, but it is less suitable for a portfolio of core businesses or ones seeking to compete globally. In 1988 Goold and Campbell had argued that the adoption of a hands-off, financial control style by GEC and other electronics companies in the UK had hindered their development as globally competitive businesses. Global development demands synergy between a number of national businesses. BTR and Hanson had begun to focus more on selected core businesses, and their relative performance was deteriorating, an issue we take up later.

Strategic planning continued to add value as long as corporate managers have close knowledge and experience of their core businesses. Where their port-folio was arguably too diverse – although not so diverse they could be classified as diversified conglomerates – strategic control companies were experiencing difficulties. The researchers poured scorn on the idea that a decentralized structure, supported by a modern budgeting and planning system, will enable a competent management team to add value to almost any new business. Strategic control can only work with an effective mix of tight financial control and devolved authority to instigate emergent strategic changes; to achieve this successfully, head offices again need to appreciate the detail of competitive strategies in the subsidiaries.

Appreciating the specific problems and opportunities faced by subsidiary businesses is particularly important for establishing fair reward systems.

Reward systems are likely to be based on specific performance targets, but these could relate to growth in revenue, absolute profits or profitability ratios. Stonich (1982) has suggested that business units might be categorized as having high, medium or low growth potential. Four factors could be used in evaluating their relative performances: return on assets; cash flow; strategic development programmes; and increases in market share. The relative weighting attributed to each of these four factors would be changed to reflect their specific objectives and whether they were of high, medium or low growth potential. Return on assets and cash flow would be critical for low growth business units, and market share and strategic development programmes most important for those with high growth potential. The factors would be weighted equally for medium growth. This approach would be particularly relevant where general managers were changed around to reflect their particular styles of management and the current requirements of the business unit.

One question left unanswered concerns the extent to which the conclusions of Goold and Campbell are a result of British management strengths, weaknes-ses and preferences. Certain Japanese companies appear to grow organically at impressive rates whilst maintaining strict financial controls and directing corporate strategic change from the centre. This tendency, however, is affected by legislation which restricts the ability of Japanese companies to grow by acquisition and merger. Without this control Japanese firms may have followed different strategies.

Strategic management at the corporate level

In earlier chapters we saw how Burton (Case 17.1) and Next (Case 18.1) both experienced financial difficulties after they diversified outside their core competencies. Burton speculated in property development; Next grew too quickly and acquired mail order businesses to add to its high street retail stores.

They have since been turned around by new management teams who have divested the peripheral interests and refocused on a redefined core. Such focus strategies have become typical in the recession-hit 1990s, when shareholders have been more interested in performance than growth. For many commentators focus is a more logical strategy than diversity, particularly as companies like BTR and Hanson, very successful in the 1980s, have seen a deterioration in their performance and fortunes in the 1990s.

At the same time, General Electric (Case 19.4), with unrelated interests which range from aero-engine manufacturing to television broadcasting, has become the largest US company (by market value) thanks to a long period of consistently strong financial results. General Electric fosters constant improvement and changes discontinuously in a decentralized, empowered structure. Strategy implementation is again at the heart of the success, championed by the charismatic strategic leader, Jack Welch.

Recapitulating arguments we introduced briefly in Chapter 16, Sir Owen Green, retired Chairman of BTR, comments:

> *As soon as things go wrong, companies start talking about focus. Focus is the crutch of mediocre management. If you are trained in the techniques of management (and very few companies are) there is no reason why you should not be able to apply them across a range of companies.*
>
> (Quoted in *Management Today*, June 1994, page 40)

This view appears to conflict with the arguments of Goold *et al.* featured above. In an article in the *Financial Times*, Jackson (1995) states:

> *If the past couple of years have taught anything about corporate structure, it is that broad generalizations about integration versus specialization, or conglomeration versus focus, are worthless. Everything depends on the pressures affecting individual industries: and within them, the different circumstances of the companies themselves.*

The corporate portfolio

Porter (1987) argues that corporate strategy is that which makes the corporate whole add up to more than the sum of its parts, but further contends that the corporate strategies of too many companies dissipate rather than create shareholder value. He comments:

> *Moving from competitive strategy to corporate strategy is the business equivalent of passing through the Bermuda Triangle. The failure of corporate strategy reflects the fact that most diversified companies have failed to think in terms of how they really add value.*

Porter defines a strategy like that of Hanson as restructuring. Underperforming companies are bought for a sensible price and their assets are made to add

---

Here at head office, we don't go very deep into much of anything, but we have a smell of everything. Our job is capital allocation – intellectual and financial. Smell, feel, touch, listen, then allocate.

John F Welch, Chief Executive Officer, General Electric

more value. Rationalization is likely to be a feature; non-core businesses should be sold off quickly. Once any company in the corporation can no longer add any new value, it should be sold and the money reinvested in fresh acquisitions. Financial management is typically a key element. The head office can provide lower-cost finance than the subsidiary business would be able to obtain as an independent company; financial control systems drive performance. Long-term success depends on the timing of the divestments and, particularly, the ability to find suitable new acquisitions, again at the right time. When companies get larger and larger, each new acquisition has to be of a sizeable business to have any real impact on the whole corporation. As organizations have generally been tightened through the recession – simply to ensure they can survive and compete – a restructuring strategy has been more difficult to implement successfully.

Where acquisitive diversifiers are not pursuing a restructuring strategy, Porter argues they must look for opportunities where they can transfer skills and/or share activities.

Goold *et al.* (1994) reinforce Porter's arguments when they contend that acquisitions can be justified where the corporation can add value to the business, generating either synergy or valuable emergent properties. Any business must add value to its parent corporation; in turn, the corporation must add value to the subsidiary. The company is better-off with its existing parent than it would be with another parent or on its own. Parenting skills, therefore, relate to the ability of a head office and strategic leadership to manage a portfolio of businesses efficiently and effectively and to change the portfolio as and when it is necessary. It is, in fact, quite conceivable for head offices to destroy value if a subsidiary simply does not fit with the rest of the portfolio and is consequently held back. Parenting skills vary between countries and cultures.

As we saw in Chapter 16, Goold *et al.* use the term ***heartland*** to describe a range of businesses to which a corporation can add value and not destroy it. A heartland might be constituted by:

❏ common key success factors
❏ related core competencies and/or strategic capabilities
❏ a common or related industry or technology.

The relative success of conglomerate diversification is, therefore, largely an issue of strategy implementation, specifically the parenting skills of the acquirer, and the ability to add value for both the subsidiary and the parent. These implementation issues are explored in Case 20.1.

The role and contribution of corporate headquarters

In this section we draw together many of the above issues by considering the role and contribution of company head offices. Typically these will be larger and grander in centralized organizations; historically powerful centres are now being reduced in size – and their work distributed to subsidiaries – as corporations become more decentralized and adopt flatter organization structures.

There are two fundamental purposes of corporate headquarters:

❏ serving the global legal and financial needs of the business and
❏ supporting strategy making.

Visit the website:
http://www.
itbp.com

However, many head offices have historically provided a more extensive range of services to their constituent businesses, including, for example:

❏ marketing
❏ management development and personnel
❏ property management
❏ centralized research and development
❏ corporate public relations
❏ industrial relations.

There is a clear need for head offices to add value to the corporation and not simply 'spend the money earned by the businesses'. With the recent trend for organizations to slim down the size and scope of head offices, in many cases only corporate strategy, financial reporting and control and secretarial/legal services remain centralized. Some head offices retain a responsibility for *policies* but not the activities.

Summarizing points made earlier, large centralized head offices where all the key business heads are located in one place – Unilever is an example – can control the corporation *efficiently*, but strategies can easily become top-down and slow to change. Decentralized organizations such as ABB (Case 19.3) push profit responsibility down to the businesses and empower managers. The head office provides more of a support role with few discrete functions. The new challenge is one of co-ordination.

In considering how head offices can best add value to the business as a whole, four broad issues must be addressed:

❏ how to control and co-ordinate the constituent businesses – issues of structure, corporate leadership and internal communications and synergy
❏ how to advise the strategic leader and keep him or her strategically aware
❏ driving performance and improvement through effective reward systems
❏ deciding which activities should be
  • provided from head office – for which a fee should be levied
  • devolved to the individual businesses
  • bought-in from outside specialists.

The alternative approaches include the stand-alone holding company, financial control approach; centralizing specific functions and services; controlling strategic change at the corporate level; and fostering linkages, learning and sharing good practices. Case 20.2 describes how one company operates with a truly slimmed-down head office.

Head offices can destroy value if they:

❏ become established as **the** perceived centre for expertise in the corporation – they cannot understand all the important detail about competitiveness in their constituent businesses whose managers will become demoralized if their potential contribution is not acknowledged
❏ assume that potential linkages and synergy will happen automatically
❏ duplicate effort and costs unnecessarily
❏ buy and sell businesses at the wrong prices
❏ create or perpetuate a culture where internal competition takes precedence over the need to compete with external rivals.

FOUR DIVERSIFIED CONGLOMERATES: BTR, HANSON, TOMKINS AND WILLIAMS HOLDINGS

This case tracks the strategic development of four leading acquisitive UK diversified conglomerates. At different times all four companies have been very successful, typically using a 'hit squad' approach by a small team of turnaround specialists who are expert in evaluating recent acquisitions, setting demanding (financial) targets, rewarding success and dismissing managers who cannot perform. More recently Hanson has announced it is to be broken up and BTR and Williams have pursued more focused strategies. In every case two major challenges are the ability to find and fund a suitable acquisition at the appropriate time and stage of corporate development and then finding opportunities to add value. Diversified conglomerates typically concentrate on mature industries where the right competitive strategy can bring high rewards but where there is only limited growth potential.

BTR

BTR grew strongly in the 1980s under the strategic leadership of Sir Owen Green. By the early 1990s the company was diversified into control systems, polymers (including factories in Taiwan), electrical products (Hawker Siddeley motors as well as Newey and Eyre), construction (Tilcon,* Graham Builders Merchants,* Pilkington Tiles* and aggregate businesses in the USA), transportation (railway equipment), packaging (Rockware Glass), paper technology and consumer products (Dunlop Slazenger* and Pretty Polly lingerie).

Alan Jackson succeeded Sir Owen Green as chief executive in 1991 (Green remained as Chairman for some time afterwards) and instituted a strategy of withdrawal from non-manufacturing interests. The companies marked with an asterisk have since been sold to other parents or to their existing managers. At the same time Jackson made a number of acquisitions, including Varta, the German battery manufacturer and Gencorp, an US company which produces

vibration controls. Hawker Siddeley (1991) was the last *major* acquisition.

Goold *et al.* (1994) examined the parenting style of BTR. They concluded that the company's underlying belief or paradigm is that businesses can benefit from pressure on costs and productivity; focused, mature, businesses which are pushed to increase prices and margins (at the expense of market share and growth) can be made more profitable. BTR's parenting skills are intensive profit planning; the ability to manage a decentralized business with multiple profit centres; low central overheads; and skills in acquiring and turning around acquisitions. This last point includes the ability to introduce the BTR culture into the new business.

BTR's heartland is based on manufacturing businesses, industrial customers, low to moderate technology and capital intensity, relatively stable environments with only limited impact from economic cycles and niche markets.

Hanson

The development of Hanson, essentially a company which has pursued a restructuring strategy, is outlined in Case 12.1 and discussed in detail in the full case study. Over a period of some 20 years Hanson was involved in 35 agreed acquisitions, six hostile takeovers and 15 unsuccessful bids. Following the 41 acquisitions there were 40 business disposals. Hanson also bought sizeable stakes in 22 other companies. For many years Hanson was acknowledged to be a very successful company from which many other organizations could learn some important lessons. Up to the mid-1980s Hanson consistently out-performed the stock market. However once the acquisition trail became more difficult, with a series of well-publicized hostile bids failing to result in takeovers, the strategy was questioned. When Lord Hanson's partner, Lord White, died, Hanson himself was over 70-years-old and succession became a real issue of concern.

Continued overleaf

In 1995 it was announced that Hanson was to be split into four separate businesses; existing shareholders would receive stock in each of the new, more focused, companies. At the time of the announcement the main Hanson companies in the UK and the USA were as follows – a number have since been divested:

Tobacco   Imperial Tobacco (UK)
Chemicals   Quantum (USA and Hanson's most recent large acquisition) and SCM (also USA)
Energy   Peabody Coal and Suburban Propane (USA), Eastern Electricity (UK)
Construction ARC aggregates (UK) and Cavenham (forestry interests in the USA)
Industrial   Including cranes, bricks, electrical products and vitamins.

The new businesses will focus on tobacco, chemicals, energy and building materials.

Tomkins

This conglomerate grew out of a buckle manufacturing business based in Walsall; acquired businesses included Smith and Wesson handguns, lawnmowers, bicycles (in the USA) and a range of different industrial products. The chief executive, Greg Hutchings, is ex-Hanson. In 1992 Tomkins acquired Rank Hovis McDougall (the milling and baking business which owns the Bisto, Paxo and Mr Kipling brands), beating off a rival bid from Hanson. Four years later, after successfully absorbing RHM, Tomkins bought the US company, Gates Rubber, the world's largest manufacturer of power transmission belts and industrial hoses. RHM cost £93.5 million; Gates was roughly the same. There have been no major divestments.

Williams Holdings

Built by accountants Nigel Rudd (a deal-maker) and Brian McGowan (acknowledged to be good at handling City institutions) Williams grew during the 1980s from a Midlands base in foundries. McGowan left in 1993; Rudd remains as strategic leader. The acquisition strategy in the 1980s was based largely on good opportunities for restructuring, but Williams quickly realized the value of established brand names and concentrated on businesses where it could exploit its brand management skills.

Through the 1980s and early 1990s the acquisitions included: Fairey Engineering, Rawlplug, Polycell, Crown Berger paints, Smallbone (kitchen units), Amdega (conservatories), Dreamland (electric blankets), Kidde (from Hanson – aerospace and fire extinguishers), Yale (locks) and Valor (locks and heating). Several of these have since been sold as Williams chose to focus on three business areas: building products (including DIY), fire protection and security (locks). Other UK fire equipment companies were added to the portfolio: Angus, Rockwell and a Thorn-EMI subsidiary. These were followed by related fire and locks acquisitions in Italy and the USA, and in 1996 Williams bought Sicli and Siddes, the largest fire protection company in France. At £175 million, Sicli was its largest purchase for five years.

Williams claims to be Britain's first 'focused conglomerate' but some critics argue that focus requires more than the structural 'bundling of a number of businesses into separate divisions'. The fire and security businesses help offset the economic cycles of the construction and building industries, and Williams (with 12% of the world market) offers a wider range of fire protection products than any of its rivals. As fire regulations are tightened around the world, this industry also enjoys a high growth potential; it has yet to reach the maturity stage.

(Tomkins, Hanson, BTR and Williams) ... all started in the same place; buy what you can, sort it out and move on. Now our aspirations are to build businesses internationally.

(Roger Carr, Chief Executive, Williams, in 1996)

The relative success of conglomerates is typically measured in terms of their ability to add value for their shareholders by exploiting the assets

(Continued)

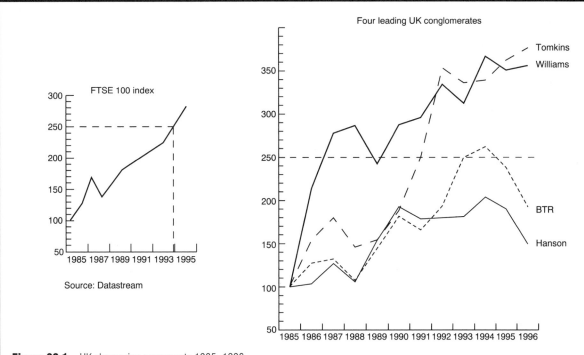

Figure 20.1 UK share price movements 1985–1996.

they own. The performance of these four conglomerates since 1985, charted against the Financial Times 100 share index, is shown in Figure 20.1. We can see that Tomkins and Williams have outperformed the index for most of this period; BTR and Hanson tracked the index reasonably well until 1994, since when they have fallen back.

The role of general managers

Basically general managers co-ordinate the work of subordinate specialist managers; they are responsible for the management of strategy implementation and, in certain cases; strategy formulation. Clearly the chief executive or managing director of the company, the overall strategic leader, is a general manager. So too are the heads of divisions and business units, and the heads of operating units in a matrix structure. Their task is to match effectively the resources they control with their particular environment and to achieve E–V–R congruence.

Divisionalized organizations were examined in the previous chapter, where it was shown that the degree of decentralization and the power, authority and responsibility enjoyed by general managers will be affected by their relationship with head office and headquarters corporate staff. Whatever the extent of the decentralization from head office to business units, the business units themselves might be highly centralized. It depends on the style of management adopted by the particular general manager in charge.

Each division or business unit is part of a larger organization and corporate structure, and consequently it is not fully autonomous. Whilst the organization

Case 20.2
RALEIGH AND ROYAL WORCESTER

In the late 1980s a UK accountant and ex-BTR manager, Alan Finden-Crofts, organized the purchase of the Royal Worcester and Spode ceramics businesses (from London International) and Raleigh Bicycles (from Tube Investments [see Case 15.3]). Both companies were losing money. Finden-Crofts created two shell companies, Exeter International and Derby International respectively, to be the new owners.

These businesses are markedly different in terms of both products and processes. Raleigh bicycles are assembled in subsidiary plants in the USA, Germany, Canada, South Africa and the Netherlands as well as the UK; bought-in components (many from the Far East, including China) comprise two-thirds of the finished costs. Bikes are also manufactured under license in a number of other countries. Critical for success is the ability to manage an integrated network of suppliers, assemblers and distributors across the globe. By contrast, Royal Worcester manufacture exclusively at two sites in the UK, and there is significant vertical integration. The main purchase is print transfers. Consequently there has been little emphasis on generating cross-business synergies.

However, both businesses have benefited from stronger supplier relationships and stock management systems introduced by the new owner. Production lead times have been reduced; internal communications have improved.

Finden-Crofts spends half his time working from an office in his home in Sussex; the other half is spent visiting plants and distributors. His main contribution is to monitor and manage the cash flow. His philosophy is that:

Companies waste a lot of time and money calling in other people to some grand head office; I'd rather spend my time going out to the subsidiaries to see what's going on.

as a whole has an external environment comprising customers, suppliers, competitors and shareholders amongst other influences, each division will have corporate headquarters as part of its environment. Business units may have both divisional headquarters and corporate head office in their environment. General managers in divisions and business units therefore do not have full responsibility for strategy creation and implementation. They can be pressurized by corporate headquarters, and they can turn to head office in their search for additional finance and other resources. The provision of finance within the organization may operate differently from the external market, but justification should still be required.

The relationship between general managers and head office will determine whether they are free to change their portfolios of business units and products or just adapt competitive and functional strategies. Performance measures and expectations will also affect this. Where specific short-term objectives and targets are set, and monitored strictly, general managers are less likely to focus on corporate changes and instead will concentrate on more immediate changes which can yield faster results. Their flexibility to make changes will increase as their targets become more vague and directional and less specific. Even though the general managers of business units may not be responsible for the formulation of changes in the corporate strategy which will affect their sphere of influence, they will invariably be responsible for the implementation of the changes.

General management skills and values

It has been established, then, that effective strategic management concerns issues of formulation and implementation. Strategic choices concern:

❑ the nature and orientation of the organization – the strategic perspective
❑ the deployment of its resources, ideally to achieve and sustain competitive advantage.

The strategic choice is implemented by the strategic leader, either the chief executive, the owner/manager in the case of a small business, or a general manager. It was pointed out in Chapter 3 that different strategic leaders (a) exhibit different patterns of behaviour and styles of management and (b) will have different technical skills and biases as a result of their background. Arguably alternative general managers would seek to implement basically the same strategy in different ways. The views of a number of authors concerning the relationship between general manager skills and particular strategies are discussed below.

Herbert and Deresky (1987) have examined the issue of match between the general manager and the strategy, concluding that the orientations and styles given below were important for particular strategies.

Strategy	*Styles and qualities required*
Development (start-up and growth)	Aggressive, competitive, innovative, creative and entrepreneurial
Stabilizing (maintaining competitive position)	Conservative, careful and analytical
Turnaround	Autonomous, risk and challenge oriented and entrepreneurial

Herbert and Deresky contend that financial skills are important for all strategies, with marketing skills being particularly important at the development stage and production and engineering skills invaluable for stabilizing strategies. This raises three issues. One: which specialist functional managers might be most appropriate for promotion to general management in particular circumstances? Recent research in the USA confirms that the most typical background for large company chief executives is finance; the same pattern applies in the UK. Marketing, technical and manufacturing specialisms also feature but it is rare for a manager with a human resources background to become the strategic leader. Two: is a change of general manager appropriate as products and businesses grow and decline and need changes in their strategies? Three: as strategies evolve and change should general managers adapt their styles of management accordingly?

Dixon (1989) suggests that **innovatory** general management skills are most required in the early and late stages of the life of a business or product in its present form. These skills are required to establish or recreate competitive advantage and, in the case of terminal decline, to find an alternative product, service or business. These changes are often best accomplished by outsiders with fresh ideas. Correspondingly the constant search for efficiencies and improvements whilst an established product or business is maturing is normally best carried out by specialists.

A major problem with this type of innovation lies in the fact that changes in senior management, structure or values may be involved. The outlook and styles of general managers are likely to be different, and their responses to different sets of expectations and performance targets will vary. Again this raises the issue of which managers are most appropriate for managing particular strategies.

Developing this argument further, Rosabeth Moss Kanter (1989) has researched the general management skills required to run businesses effectively in the competitive environment of the late 1980s and the 1990s. Large companies, she contends, must be able to match corporate discipline with entrepreneurial creativity in order to become 'leaner' and more efficient whilst being committed to both quality and innovation.

Visit the website: http://www. itbp.com

Three strategies are particularly important:

❑ re-structuring to improve synergy from diverse businesses
❑ the development of joint ventures and strategic alliances to input new ideas
❑ the encouragement of intrapreneurship within organizations.

These points are explained in greater detail in Key Reading 20.1.

Kanter's main conclusion is that **process is more important than structure.** She suggests that:

❑ general managers must be able to balance maintenance and entrepreneurial skills
❑ internal competition (typically fostered in organizations which are divided into discrete divisions and business units) can be harmful and impede synergy
❑ incentive and reward schemes should reflect the need for co-operation and support between business units
❑ the increasing incidence of joint ventures, which requires the forging of closer links with other external businesses, suggests that structures may need revision if the potential and desired synergy is to be achieved.

There are similarities and differences in these conclusions, reflecting again that there is no one best answer. The issue of match between general manager and strategy is important, and consequently one might expect that changes in one will lead to changes in the other.

Clearly as organizations become flatter and more decentralized skills in synthesis and integration are critically important.

Organizations in the late 1990s

Handy (1994 and 1995) contends that in order for companies to remain competitive internationally they must re-think their basic structures. 'Fewer key people at the heart of the organization, paid very well, producing far more value.' Handy acknowledges that it is quite feasible that corporations will continue to grow, either organically or through acquisition, but believes that either physically or behaviourally they need to be in small units, focused and closely networked to their suppliers and customers. More activities and components will be bought-in from specialists than is the case at the moment; internally they will also comprise networks characterized by subsidiarity, with

COMPETITIVENESS IN THE 1990S

Future success lies in the **capability** to change and to accomplish key tasks by using resources more efficiently and more effectively. Organizations must be innovative and, at the same time, control their costs. Sustainable competitive advantage, however, does not come from either low costs, or differentiation, or innovation alone. It needs the **whole organization** to be *focused, fast, flexible and friendly*.

Being **focused** requires investment in core skills and competencies, together with a search for new opportunities for applying the skills. Intrapreneurship should be fostered to constantly improve the skills; and managers throughout the organization should be strategically aware and innovative. They should own the organization's mission, which, by necessity, must be communicated widely and understood.

Fast companies move at the right time, and are not caught out by competitors. New ideas and opportunities from the environment will be seized first. Ideally they will be innovating constantly to open up and sustain a competitive gap, because gradual improvements are likely to be more popular with customers than are radical changes. But 'instant success takes time' – the organization culture must be appropriate.

Flexibility concerns the search for continual improvement. The implication is a 'learning organization' where ideas are shared and collaboration between functions and divisions generates internal synergy. This, in turn, suggests that performance and effectiveness measures – and rewards – concentrate on outcomes.

Internal synergy can be achieved with cross-functional teams and special projects, and by moving people around the organization in order to spread the best practices. General Motors allows components and assembly workers, who work in separate plants in different locations, to contact each other by telephone to sort out problems and faults without relying on either written communications or messages which go 'up, across and down again'. These workers see each other as 'colleagues in the *whole* organization'. It is important that internal constraints (imposed by other functions and divisions) and which restrain performance are highlighted and confronted. To be effective this requires a clear and shared vision and purpose for the organization, decentralization and empowerment.

Friendly organizations are closely linked to their suppliers and customers to generate synergy through the added value chain. Such external collaboration may be in the form of strategic alliances.

Summarized from: Kanter, RM (1989) *When Giants Learn To Dance*, Simon and Schuster.

the 'centre' (as distinct from a traditional head office) doing only what the parts cannot do themselves. The real power will switch from the top of the organization to the businesses, and consequently a co-ordinating mission and purpose will be essential. Handy favours 'federalism' or reverse delegation – the centre acts on the bidding of, and on agreement with, the parts.

Supported by sophisticated information technology and systems, people will become the most important strategic resource, and, because their expertise and intelligence is an intangible asset, largely unquantifiable, it will become harder to value the **real** assets of a business. Consequently the appropriate measures of performance must be carefully evaluated; and reward systems will have to be derived which motivate and keep those managers who are potentially the most mobile. The valuable managers will not all be at the most senior levels. Handy believes that switching jobs regularly and moving people between different parts of the organization, perhaps to other countries, can be dysfunctional. Simply they will not be in place long enough to become known, and, in the future, trust will be an essential element in management, strategic change and strategy implementation.

We have designed organizations based on distrust. We have designed organizations so that people will not make mistakes. And, of course, we now encourage people to make mistakes because that is how they learn.

(Handy)

Handy's arguments imply major changes to strategies, structures and styles of management for many organizations. Where these are simultaneous – ***strategic regeneration*** – the changes are dramatic, painful and often difficult to carry through. This is discussed further in Chapter 22.

Summary

The corporate strategies and structures of large organizations are clearly linked and inter-dependent. In fact, it is generally easier to change the strategy than it is the structure and style of management, an issue we develop further in Chapter 22. Different organizations adopt different corporate management styles, ideally choosing a style that matches the requirements and demands of their activity portfolio and corporate environment. The composition, role and contribution of the corporate head office is a key issue in effective strategy implementation at the corporate level.

Specifically we have:

- looked at the different control mechanisms and management styles in large companies, differentiating between the financial control, strategic planning and strategic control approaches
- explained the term 'heartland' of related businesses
- examined the particular control and strategy implementation problems of diversified conglomerates
- debated the role and contribution of corporate head offices
- discussed the role, skills and values of general managers.

Checklist of key terms and concepts

You should feel confident that you understand the following terms and ideas:

★ Financial control, strategic planning and strategic control as links between head office and business units

★ A heartland of businesses.

Questions and research assignments

Text related

1 For which (general) corporate strategies are the financial control, strategic planning and strategic control styles of corporate management most appropriate?

2 How do you think the need for general managers might have changed as organization structures have generally been flattened and delayered?

Library based

3 Update the material on any or all the four conglomerate businesses discussed in Case 20.1. Using this and details of the corporate strategies pursued by other large companies you are familiar with: Is conglomerate diversification increasingly giving way to focus strategies? Can focus generate sufficient growth to satisfy shareholders in buoyant economic conditions?

4 Take any large organization you are familiar with: How has its head office structure and roles changed in recent years. (You may wish to further examine the company you used for Question 5 in Chapter 19).

5 Investigate the role of:
   (a) general managers in the health service
   (b) the heads of financial services (whatever they might be called) in universities.

How has their role changed and developed in the last five years? How is, and how might, their performance be assessed? What are the most appropriate measures of effectiveness, and why? Are they rewarded in line with measures of performance?

References

Dixon, M (1989) The very model of a mythical manager, *Financial Times*, 10 May.

Goold, M and Campbell, A (1988) *Strategies and Styles,* Blackwell.

Goold, M, Campbell, A and Alexander, M (1994) *Corporate Level Strategy*, John Wiley.

Goold, M, Campbell, A and Luchs, K (1993) Strategies and styles revisited: Strategic planning and financial control, *Long Range Planning,* **26**, 5. And: Strategies and styles revisited: strategic control – is it tenable? *Long Range Planning,* **26**, 6.

Handy, C (1994) *The Empty Raincoat* Hutchinson.

Handy, C (1995) *Beyond Certainty: The Changing Worlds of Organizations*, Hutchinson.

Herbert, TT and Deresky, H (1987) Should general managers match their business strategies, *Organizational Dynamics,* **15**(3), 40–51.

Jackson, T (1995) Giant bows to colossal pressure, *Financial Times,* 22 September.

Kanter, RM (1989) *When Giants Learn to Dance,* Simon & Schuster.

Porter, ME (1987) From competitive advantage to corporate strategy, *Harvard Business Review,* May–June.

Stonich, PJ (1982) *Implementing Strategy,* Ballinger.

21

Issues in Strategic Resource Management

In this chapter we look at the operational aspects of strategy implementation, examining issues involved in the management and co-ordination of resources.

Learning objectives

After studying this chapter you should be able to:

■ define the operational aspects of strategy implementation
■ distinguish between resource allocation issues at corporate and business unit level
■ explain the importance of functional inter-relationships
■ describe different types of budget and explain their contribution to strategy implementation
■ list the important aspects of measurement and control systems
■ identify the main issues in crisis avoidance and management.

Don't forget to visit the website: http://www.itbp.com

Introduction

The implementation of intended strategies, and the ability of the organization to be responsive in a dynamic, competitive environment, require the organization's strategic resources to be deployed and managed both efficiently and effectively. It is also vital for the organization, on the one hand, to seek to be crisis-averse rather than crisis-prone, and, on the other hand, to be able to deal with crises if and when they do occur. These issues are the subject of this chapter.

Once intended strategies have been determined, either in broad outline or in greater detail, the organization must plan their implementation. This means, first, that the resources required for implementation – including capital equipment, people and finance – are available where and when they are needed. Resources need to be **allocated** to different managers, functions and businesses, and then **co-ordinated** to generate synergy. And second, the managers responsible for implementation understand what is expected of them and are empowered and motivated to take the necessary decisions and actions. In addition, **monitoring and control** systems are required.

At the corporate strategy level, we have already seen how organizations might establish priorities for different divisions and businesses using portfolio analysis, and evaluate the strategic and financial implications of alternative investments. Decisions may be taken within the constraints of existing capital, financial and human resources; if they demand new resources, then these must be obtained in an appropriate time-scale. Proposed acquisitions may require an organization to raise funding externally; organic development of new products may require new skills and competencies. Resources can, of course, be switched from one part of a business to another.

At the functional level, **policies** and procedures can guide managers and other employees in the utilization of these corporate resources to add value, create competitive advantage and achieve the desired objectives. These policies can be tightly defined to maintain strong, central control, or very loose and flexible to enable people to use their initiative and be flexible. The on-going management of the resources will then use action plans and budgets.

Action plans relate to the detailed strategies and plans for the various key functions, the activities which must be carried out if competitive and corporate strategies are to be implemented successfully; **budgets** add a crucial financial dimension to these plans. Together they attempt to integrate sales, supply potential, production activities and cash flow to ensure that resources are available to produce goods and services where and when they are required. The organization avoids a situation where it has booked orders, or has requests it would like to take, but no resources to enable production or supply; it also avoids situations where it has idle capacity and no orders, or instances where it is producing for stock rather than for customers. This planning process provides a useful check that the corporate and competitive strategies that have been formulated are both appropriate and feasible in the sense that they can be implemented.

At the same time, this planning and budgeting must not be so rigid that the organization is unable to be responsive. Forecasts and judgements will never be completely accurate; when intended strategies are implemented there will need to be incremental changes and revisions to plans. To respond to new environmental opportunities and competitor initiatives, the organization will need to be adaptive. Emergent strategic change of this nature demands resource flexibility, both at the corporate and functional levels.

The plans should incorporate clear milestones – target levels of achievement against a time-scale. By constant monitoring the organization can check whether it is booking sufficient business, whether it is producing the necessary quality on time, whether it is under- or over-producing, whether its costs and prices are different from those it forecast, and whether it is managing the movement of cash in and out of the business to the budgeted targets.

A review of progress can highlight potential deficiencies to either resource requirements or likely outcomes. If orders are exceeding expectations, then additional resources may be required if the organization is to properly satisfy the new level of demand. If these cannot be found, schedules will need to be changed and maybe future supplies rationed. If orders are below expectations, then either new business opportunities will need targeting at short notice – possibly implying very competitive prices and low margins – or end-of-year targets revised downwards. Vigilance and pragmatism here can help ensure the organization does not face unexpected crises. Effective communications and management information systems are essential for planning, monitoring and control.

Corporate resource planning

Corporate resource planning relates to the allocation of resources between the various parts of the organization together with corporate investment decisions concerning the acquisition of additional resources. If investment funds are limited their allocation will be based on the strategic importance of the various spending opportunities as well as financial evaluations of the viability of each project. If funds are not available and need to be borrowed to finance possible projects, the return on the investment should exceed the cost of capital.

Organizations should seek the best possible returns from investments because, as Seed (1983) suggests, they can be seen as an undesirable but necessary freezing of corporate funds. However, some general and functional managers, especially if they have a technical background, may see investments in new plant and equipment as a reflection of status, preferring the best and most modern technology. Where this happens there could be a suboptimal allocation of corporate resources. This argument can also be applied to the purchase of large luxurious city-centre head offices.

The organization structure, whichever form it might take, will form the basis for the allocations. Where the organization is multi-divisional, the extent to which power and responsibility are decentralized will determine how much freedom is given to general managers to allocate resources amongst their functional managers and departments. Where the power to change functional or competitive strategies is delegated to general managers, they will also require delegated authority to change resource allocations. This may imply moving resources within their area of responsibility. Equally it may necessitate the acquisition of additional resources from elsewhere within the organization or from outside. In functional organizations resources must be allocated to those areas that are most significant in the creation of competitive advantage.

Where any strategic resources are located centrally and used by the various divisions and business units their effectiveness will need to be carefully monitored. The extent of their use is an efficiency measure; effectiveness relates to their allocation to the areas in which they can yield most benefit for the organization.

The allocation of resources at a corporate level is closely tied in to the planning system through which priorities must be established. Portfolio analyses such as the directional policy matrix may well be used to help to determine which products and business units should receive priority for investment funding; and any new developments which are proposed will require resources. An acquisition, for example, will need to be financed, but the integration of the new business after the purchase may also involve the transfer of managers and other resources.

Corporate resource planning and organization growth

Corporate resources may be allocated in different ways in line with the speed of growth of the organization and the degree of instability in the environment.

Rapid growth

Where the business overall, or selected business units within it, are growing rapidly the resource allocation process must be able to accommodate this growth and the consequent and possibly continual demand for additional resources. The process could be either centralized or decentralized, or a mixture of the two, influenced by the management style of the overall strategic leader and the inter-dependences between the various parts of the organization.

If it is centralized priorities will be established by head office corporate staff using some formal planning system and periodic review of the potential of all business units. Business units will need to provide the necessary information. With a decentralized approach the priorities would again be decided centrally but after allowing all divisions and business units to formulate their own preferred strategies and make their case for the corporate resources that they would require to implement their preferences. A mixed approach would involve resources for continuing activities being allocated through centralized mechanisms and incremental additions funded through a bidding process.

In all cases the decisions should balance the potential financial gains with the strategic logic implied. Whilst divisions or business units may be making individual requests for resources to support certain programmes, the opportunities for synergy, sharing activities and transferring skills across activities should be assessed. In addition the desirability of the implications of the various proposals for the overall strategic perspective of the organization should be considered.

Limited change and stability

Where businesses are growing more steadily and in a relatively stable environment, resource allocation for continuing programmes could be a straightforward extrapolation of previous budgets, incorporating an allowance for inflation. However, a mere continuation of present strategies without evaluation and proper review may lead to ineffectiveness.

Established policies, such as fixing advertising budgets at an agreed percentage of projected sales revenue or maintaining particular levels of stocks, are likely to be a key feature of this approach.

Decline situations

Where businesses or business units are in decline some quite tough decisions often have to be taken. Where the organization as a whole is in difficulty the strategic leader must search for new opportunities for re-deploying resources. In the case of selected business units that are experiencing decline, unless there are opportunities for turnaround, resources should be transferred to activities with better growth and profit potential. In both cases the decisions are likely to be centralized, particularly as there may have to be structural changes to accommodate the rationalization, divestment or other strategic changes.

Once resources are allocated to divisions, business units and functions there will be further allocations to individual managers within each area; and this to a greater or lesser extent will be delegated to the general manager or functional manager in charge of each one. This is known as functional or operational resource planning; in the process it is important not to overlook any interdependences between the budget holders.

Functional resource planning

When resources are allocated to functions, and to particular activities within functions, there are a number of essential considerations.

❑ First, it is important to consider the relative importance of each function; the concept of the value chain, explained in Chapter 10, could prove helpful in establishing this.

❏ Second, competitive advantage is established within functional activities; consequently an appreciation of key success factors and competitive opportunities is crucial if the resource allocation is to lead to strategic effectiveness.

❏ Third, the important linkages between functions, which are the sources of potential synergy, should be considered. Any appropriate sharing of resources should be encouraged. To this end, activities should be complementary and supportive.

❏ Fourth, where there are sequential dependences, the whole resource allocation process must take account of these. For example, if activity Z is dependent upon activity X which precedes it, then it is both inefficient and ineffective to allocate resources to Z unless adequate resources are also given to X. An obvious application of this would be production activities which must be built around any bottlenecks. Similarly the capacity of hospital operating theatres should be consistent with the number of beds available for recuperation.

The marketing department of a large high street retail chain ran a series of promotions in the mid-1990s, whereby customers who spent a designated amount of money (on any goods) could then buy a particular item for a substantially reduced price. Success was dependent upon the company's buyers making sure that there was sufficient stock of the promoted item in all its branches on the appropriate days. This did not always happen, and qualifying customers had to be given vouchers which they could redeem once stocks were received.

Similarly, poor resource planning by Ford of Europe reduced its competitiveness. Done (1992) reports that Ford failed to equip its Halewood (Merseyside) plant with the facility to assemble left-hand-drive Escorts and Orions. During 1991 the recession in the UK led to a collapse in demand for right-hand drive models; but sales potential remained buoyant in Germany. Because Halewood could not satisfy the demand it was reduced to three-days-a-week working. At the same time German customers were reluctantly having to accept engines without catalytic converters because of supply problems.

Certain techniques, such as network analysis, can be very useful in planning a project and establishing the resource needs. The whole project should be managed for efficiency, with time and resources being saved wherever appropriate. Nevertheless, as Robert Burns said, 'The best laid schemes o' mice an' men ... Gang aft a-gley'. In the early 1960s it was decided to introduce into the UK a successful American car wax. The decision was made to launch the product initially within the Granada television region, using limited television advertising and concentrating distribution only in selected garages. The commercials were scheduled in the middle of a late-night magazine programme with a relatively small audience. However, in the event an important European football match featuring Manchester United was re-programmed at short notice and the car wax advertisements filled the half-time commercial break. A demand for the car wax was generated which the importers simply could not supply. The situation was made worse by people asking for the product in outlets other than garages.

Case 21.1 looks at the particular resource and co-ordination problems of Standard Fireworks, a company which manufactures fireworks for ten months of the year but delivers virtually all of its production during a one month period.

Standard began manufacturing fireworks in the UK in the 1890s. By the 1960s the number of UK producers had declined to 11, and Standard was one of the largest. In the 1990s, with factories in Huddersfield and Doncaster – as well as a joint venture in China – it is the only UK *manufacturer*. Standard (with its subsidiary, Brock) has some two thirds of the UK market; imported brands such as Astra and Black Cat, mostly from China, constitute the remainder. Europe has tighter regulatory standards than the Far East, where labour costs are also lower. Simply, UK manufacture is less profitable than production in China, but if offers more political stability. The quality of UK production is higher in the case of the more sophisticated fireworks; for lower-price items quality differences are not an issue. Quality control is always important.

Standard has 17,000 customers in the UK, many of them small, independent retailers, who buy over 80 million fireworks (worth £18 million to Standard) each year. Although Standard's team of eight salesmen collect provisional, indicative orders all through the year, confirmed orders tend to be placed during October for immediate delivery. Virtually all the deliveries are made in the 3 to 4 weeks which precede Bonfire Night on November 5; all payments are due in late November. The company is profitable, with pre-tax profits of £3.5 million.

The company was controlled by its founding family for over 90 years before it was acquired by the mini-conglomerate, Scottish Heritable Trust, in 1986. SHT's other businesses included hospital beds, golf clubs, sock manufacture and gravel pits. Standard acquired its competitor, Brock, in 1987, and now utilizes the Brock brand for the fireworks it manufactures in China. Standard was bought out by its managers in 1992.

Historically Standard decided what it would make in any one year, and essentially told its retail customers what they could have. This is no longer the case. Production takes place mainly between January and September; Standard does not manufacture any fireworks in November and December, the last two months of its financial year. The product mix, and the numbers of each firework, are initially based on the previous year's delivery pattern, and then adjusted in line with the indicative orders received. Production is constant, rather than loaded at the end of the period, and

there are no night shifts. Safety considerations rule out a last-minute rush. It is a 'one-shot' business, with little opportunity to alter the product mix at the end of the cycle if forecasting has been poor.

Fireworks are not produced in a 'typical' factory, again for safety reasons. Teams of 1, 2 or 3 employees work in small huts which are geographically separated on the site. If there is an explosion, the hut roof blows upwards and the sides outwards; only a limited number of people are at risk. Gunpowder is delivered in small quantities to each hut on a regular basis, and finished products are taken away for storage elsewhere. Transport is by rubber-wheeled hand carts; there are no petrol-driven vehicles within the confines of the production area. The amount of gunpowder and fireworks that can be stored in any one building and on any one site is regulated and restricted. Standard hire secondary storage facilities near Gretna Green and in Staffordshire.

Standard cannot physically distribute all its fireworks itself during October. It has to hire capacity from independent carriers. Standard delivers large loads to the carriers who then take the fireworks (in small packages) to the retailers. Co-ordinating this network is critical for success. In 1994 there were problems with one carrier who was simply unable to deliver the packages on time; given the tight deadlines, this constituted a crisis for Standard.

Managing the cash flow is also critical. The bulk of Standard's inward cash flow is in November; by February the cash reserves have been spent and the overdraft then grows steadily and remorselessly until the following November. There is some limited flexibility in that low-cost fireworks can be manufactured early in the cycle, leaving the most expensive ones until the end.

Looking ahead, it is not inconceivable that resins could replace gunpowder in fireworks, in which case many of the current production constraints would disappear. Production in factory units could be more mechanized. Another opportunity concerns the new millennium, New Year 1999/2000. If people decide to celebrate with fireworks it will markedly change the pattern of deliveries for one year. Manufacturing and delivery would probably not fit conveniently in the spare capacity weeks of November and December, particularly as the pre-Christmas period is traditionally very busy for both carriers and shops.

Efficiency and effectiveness in resource allocation and management

It is important to consider both efficiency and effectiveness measures in relation to the allocation and deployment of resources. An examination of the way in which resources are employed and managed in the production and marketing of existing products and services can be used to search for improvements. Savings in time and costs (without threatening quality) lead to higher productivity, higher profits and the freeing up of resources which can be deployed elsewhere. This is essentially a search for greater efficiency.

At the same time it is also useful to consider whether resources are being allocated to those products, services and activities which are most important for the organization as a whole and for the achievement of its objectives. This analysis is applicable at organizational, divisional and business unit level – wherever there is an opportunity cost of the resources in question. If resources are finite and limited to the extent that choices have to be made concerning which products to concentrate resources on and which to give low priority to, then the opportunity cost of the resources should be considered. If growth or profitability or both are important objectives, the resources should be allocated to those products and services which can best fulfil the objectives. This is an assessment of effectiveness. However, as discussed above, it is important to ensure that sufficient resources are allocated to development programmes that will lead to growth and profits in the future.

If decisions are made to alter resource allocations and concentrate them in different areas, issues of managing change arise; these are considered in Chapter 22. It should be appreciated that particular business units, products and services are likely to have their champions within the organization. Resource reductions in favour of alternative products may be resisted by certain managers. Their ability and willingness to resist change pressures from higher management will be related to their power bases and their ability to influence decisions. These issues also are considered in Chapter 22.

It is now appropriate to consider in more detail how resources are allocated to managers and how policies influence the way that resources are used. Put simplistically, managers are allowed certain resources, which represent costs to the organization, and are then expected to use them to generate revenues and profits. The budgeting process determines how many of what resources managers are allocated. Their agreed objectives and targets concerning particular products and services determine how the resources are further deployed, and established policies influence the way they are deployed and managed.

Policies, procedures, plans and budgets

Policies

Policies are designed to guide the behaviour of managers in relation to the pursuit and achievement of strategies and objectives. They can guide either thoughts or actions or both by indicating what is expected in certain decision areas. Over time they establish the way that certain tasks should normally be carried out, and place constraints upon the decision-making freedom that managers have. In this respect they imply that the implementation of strategies formulated by strategic leaders is a planned activity, and recognize that managers may at times wish to make changes and pursue objectives which are personally important to them. Policies, therefore, should be related to stated objectives and strategies and assist in their implementation; at the same time they should not restrict managers to the extent that they are unable to make incremental and adaptive changes when these are appropriate or necessary. Managers should be offered sufficient inducements to comply with organizational policies, and sanctioned when they fail to comply without justification.

Policies need not be written down or even formulated consciously. They may emerge as certain behaviour patterns become established in the organization and are regarded as a facet of values and culture. A policy can exist simply because it is the perceived way that something has always been done. Policies are particularly significant in the case of recurring problems or decisions as they establish a routine and consistent approach.

Policies can be either advisory, leaving decision makers with some flexibility, or mandatory, whereby managers have no discretion. Koontz and O'Donnell (1968) suggest that mandatory policies should be regarded as 'rules' rather than policies. They argue that mandatory policies tend to stop managers and other employees thinking about the most efficient and effective ways to carry out tasks and searching for improvements. Policies should guide rather than remove discretion.

Koontz and O'Donnell further argue that advisory policies should normally be preferred because it is frequently essential to allow managers some flexibility to respond and adapt to changes in both the organization and the environment. Moreover, mandatory policies are unlikely to motivate managers whilst advisory guides can prompt innovation.

The creation and use of policies

It has already been mentioned that policies may be created both consciously and unconsciously.

The main stated policies are those which the managers of the company draw up in relation to their areas of discretionary responsibility. Certain key policies will be established by the overall strategic leader and will be filtered down the organization. It is important that when general managers create policies for their divisions and business units, and functional managers for their departments, there is some consistency between them.

Some policies will be forced on the company by external stakeholders. Government legislation upon contracts of employment, redundancy terms and health and safety at work all affect personnel policies, for example. The design of certain products will have to meet strict criteria for safety and pollution. The fabric used for airline seats in the UK must be fire-resistant, and there are similar restrictions upon the type of foams that can be used in furniture. Car engines must be designed to meet certain emission regulations. In some cases financial policies can be dictated by powerful shareholders or bankers.

It is useful, then, if the major functional areas of the business are covered by explicit policies which are known to all employees who will be affected by them. Where they exist in this form they provide a clear framework in which decisions can be made; and they also allow people to understand the behaviour patterns that are expected of them in particular circumstances. However, the

Visit the website:
http://www.
itbp.com

policies should not be too rigid and prevent managers making important change decisions. Changes in strategies may require changes of policy if they are to be implemented successfully.

Examples of functional policies

Policies can exist for any functional task undertaken by the organization, and consequently the following examples are merely indicative.

In **finance** the dividend policy discussed in Chapter 12 constitutes one example. Similarly there may be policies for assessing the viability of proposed investments and ranking a set of alternatives. Where the firm has a financial strategy of investing cash balances on a short-term basis there may well be policies and criteria for evaluating appropriate opportunities.

Personnel policies would include the following:

- ❑ the type and qualification of employees for particular jobs
- ❑ the recruitment activities and procedures which will take place
- ❑ the training and development of particular skills and competences in relation to specified jobs
- ❑ communicating to employees how well (or poorly) the company is performing
- ❑ policies concerning overtime and bonuses.

Policies with regard to quality and meeting delivery dates are examples from the **operations** function. Policies may also establish who has the authority to change production schedules; and in a retail organization there are likely to be policies concerning the re-ordering of stock, the refilling of shelves, and the ways in which merchandise should be displayed both in-store and in the windows.

Marketing policies are related to the four components of the marketing mix: product, price, promotion and distribution. One product policy of a car manufacturer might establish which models are made in anticipation of sale and displayed in distributor showrooms and which ones are only made when orders have been placed for them. A pricing policy of certain retailers is to reduce prices to the level of their competitors when customers highlight the differential. A preference for advertising in certain magazines or the use of a particular layout would constitute examples of promotional policies. The willingness of Marks and Spencer to exchange goods on demand, regardless of whether they are faulty, is a merchandising policy.

Procedures

A procedure is a type of plan designed to establish the steps that employees should follow in carrying out certain, normally routine, tasks. If a customer complains, for example, there may be an established procedure for gathering the required information and dealing with the complaint. Where products fail inspection there may be procedures for establishing the cause. Algorithms, whereby a series of questions are posed and the answer to one question determines the next question asked, can be used to provide an appropriate framework for diagnosing faults. These again would constitute a formalized procedure.

In the same way that policies help clarify expectations, a well-conceived and straightforward procedure can ensure that the necessary action in certain circumstances is clear to everyone. In addition, procedures can provide a useful control mechanism.

Functional and single-use plans

When strategic planning was discussed in general terms in Chapter 14 and alternative approaches were considered, it was pointed out that the thinking process was often more important than the production of a definite rigid plan. The activities to be carried out by certain divisions, business units and functional managers must be clarified through a planning process if the resources required for their implementation are to be allocated efficiently. Certain functional activities, however, lend themselves to detailed planning and specific plans. The scheduling of production, of operator hours and of the receipt of supplies under a just-in-time (JIT) system are examples.

In addition there are single-use plans which are self-explanatory, designed to meet specific contingencies and generally detailed. The plan for the launch and development of a new product, the plans for the installation of a new piece of equipment, and the change-over plans linked to the implementation of a new organization structure are all examples of single-use plans. The value of single-use plans lies in forcing managers to set down the steps which are required to accomplish specific tasks and at the same time to examine the impact on all the people who are in some way affected. Techniques such as network analysis and Gantt charts (activity flow charts) can prove helpful in single-use planning.

Budgets

Budgets, quite simply, are plans expressed in numerical terms, usually in financial terms. They will indicate how much should be spent, by which departments, when, and for what purpose.

Pearce and Robinson (1985) distinguish between three types of budget. **Capital budgets** concern the allocation of resources for investment in buildings, plant and equipment. These new resources will be used to generate future revenues. **Sales budgets** reflect the anticipated flow of funds into the organization based on forecast sales; and **revenue or expense budgets** concern the operating costs that will be incurred in producing these products and services. Because of such factors as seasonal demand, the need to hold stock, and the fact that the final payment for goods and services is likely to occur after all operating expenses have been paid, the flows of cash in and out of the business need to be controlled through these budgets.

Budgeting the direct costs of producing certain products and services requires an estimate of the raw materials, components, labour and machine hours that are likely to be needed. Standard costing techniques usually form the basis of this, with analyses of any variances being used to measure both performance and the reliability of the standard costs.

People are a crucial strategic resource, and their physical contribution in terms of hours of work can be budgeted. Work study and other techniques will be used to establish the standard times required to complete particular tasks, which can then be costed. Whilst such standards, and the wage rates which are used to determine the payment for these inputs, are likely to be common throughout the organization, and in many cases agreed centrally, the selection and training of the people in question are likely to be decentralized. Whilst the skills and capabilities of staff should be considered when the budgets are quantified, the process of budgeting can be useful for highlighting weaknesses and deficiencies.

Developing from this, another expense which needs to be budgeted is training and management development programmes. This involves the utilization of funds which are currently available to improve the long-term contribution and value of people. Training and development should therefore be seen as an investment. However, the anticipated returns will be difficult to quantify, and as a result the investment techniques considered earlier may be of only limited use. Moreover, the contribution of people will also depend upon their commitment to the organization, which in turn will be influenced by the overall reward and incentives packages which are offered and the ability of the organization structure to harness and co-ordinate their various contributions.

The budgeting process

All managers who spend money, and whose departments consume resources, should ideally be given a budget. These budgets should represent agreed targets which relate closely to the manager's objectives, again agreed with his or her superior. In the same way that individual manager objectives contribute towards the objectives for departments, business units, divisions and ultimately the organization as a whole, individual budgets will be part of a master budget. Activities which constrain other activities, because they involve scarce resources for which demand exceeds supply capability, should be budgeted early.

Budgets and objectives are clearly related, and consequently resources should be allocated to those areas and activities in the organization which are seen as priorities. If important objectives are to be achieved, and priority strategies implemented, resources must be provided. Where growth and profits are important organizational objectives, those business units and products which are best able to contribute to their achievement should be funded accordingly. This approach suggests that the strategies being implemented have been formulated to satisfy corporate objectives, and personal objectives have been contained. However, the process of budgeting can facilitate the ability of managers to pursue personal objectives. Moreover, budgeting can be perceived as a technique for short-term financial management rather than a key aspect of strategy implementation. These contentions are expanded below.

Where resources are available and new developments are being considered, the previous record and contribution of managers is likely to have an influence. Rather than select strategies on merit and then allocate the most appropriate managers to implement them, the strategies championed by successful managers may be preferred.

Furthermore, the ability of certain managers to exercise power and influence over resource allocations within the organization, issues which are discussed in the next chapter, may result in allocations to areas and activities which potentially are not the most beneficial to the organization as a whole. Bower (1970) points out that where the objectives of the organization are difficult to agree and quantify, as is the case in many not-for-profit organizations, the political ability of managers to defend existing allocations and bid for additional resources grows in importance. Wherever this is evident, the resource allocation process becomes a determinant of the objectives and strategies pursued by organizations.

Flexibility

The budgeting process will normally take place on an annual basis, but as the targets will be utilized for regular performance reviews there should be scope to adjust budgets either upwards or downwards. Whilst sales and revenue budgets are by nature short term, capital budgets have long-term implications. Investments may be paid for in instalments, and their returns are likely to stretch over several years. The budgets, of course, are inter-related. Once capital investment decisions have been taken there are immediate implications for revenue to support them.

The allocation of resources to managers is dependent upon the strategies which the organization has decided to continue and develop, but adaptive changes require flexibility which must be accounted for. Where resources are limited and finite, strategic opportunities may be constrained. New alternatives may only be feasible if other activities are divested. Flexed budgets are designed to allow for changes in the level of activity, which might result from adaptive changes in functional and competitive strategies. Managers would realize that, if they were able to sell in excess of their targets, then resources would be found to facilitate increased production. The assumption would be that more sales equals more profit, which may well be true. However, if the implication is that resources would be diverted from other activities, issues of opportunity cost are again relevant; and the resources should only be diverted from activities which are either less profitable or strategically less important to the organization in the long term.

Zero-base budgeting

Where a traditional approach to budgeting is adopted, once the continued production of a product or service has been assumed or decided, demand prospects are forecast. Against these are set expense budgets based on standard costs. Overhead contributions are most probably adjusted for volume changes and inflation. Previous experiences are therefore carried forward and used as a base. With zero-base budgeting no previous experience is assumed, and every proposed activity must be justified afresh.

It was suggested earlier that many local authorities have, historically, sought to continue with existing service provisions, supplemented by new and additional services when resources could be found to fund them. Local authorities who make use of zero-base techniques start with the assumption that all services must be justified and priorities established on merit. Existing services

---

Continuous business success is built when the solid foundations are strong, open relationships throughout an organization. It is not built upon systems or management techniques – they are tools which will be used by people working well together for one another.

Businesses which nurture good, open relationships will encourage, welcome and survive change. Businesses driven by systems and characterized by fear and anxiety will do none of these things.

Change is about people. The management of change is therefore about the management of people.

Patrick Byrne, Group Chief Executive Officer, Waterford Wedgwood plc

might well be replaced rather than continued simply because they already exist, or better ways of providing the services might be found.

Under traditional budgeting methods it is easy to carry forward past inefficiencies which result in over-spending. Zero-base budgeting should prevent this and offer opportunities for reducing expenses by searching for improved efficiencies. Moreover, the establishment of priorities on merit can result in greater effectiveness, depending on the assessment criteria selected for evaluation.

Zero-based budgeting is conceptually very attractive as it distinguishes between high and low priority areas and constrains the pursuit of personal objectives by managers. Its implementation presents a number of difficulties, however, which often result in traditional budgeting being preferred. The most serious problems concern the administration, paperwork and time required to implement it effectively and establish priorities objectively. In large complex organizations the decision-making burden concerning low level priorities, which individually may not be very significant, can draw senior management attention away from the overall strategic needs of the organization. Finally zero-based budgeting implies that any job might be declared redundant at any time, and this causes both uncertainty and increased political activity.

Measurement and control systems

The need to measure and evaluate performance, and to make changes when necessary, applies at all levels of the organization. Budgets establish quantitative targets for individual managers, departments, business units and divisions. Progress against these targets can be measured through the information system; and the feedback should be both fast and accurate to enable any corrective actions to take place quickly. The ability of all these budget holders to achieve their targets will be useful when reviewing their futures. The system used by BTR is described in Case 21.2.

When establishing budgets and performance targets it is however important to ensure that the attention of managers is not focused too narrowly on only their areas of responsibility. Their contributions to other managers and their commitment to the overall interests of the organization are the sources of synergy. Whilst these measures of individual performances are crucial, the effectiveness of all functional, competitive and corporate strategies and their abilities to achieve corporate objectives are the ultimate measures.

Visit the website:
http://www.
itbp.com

The effectiveness of the contribution of such activities as research and development is difficult to assess, but this is no excuse for not trying.

Figure 21.1 summarizes these ideas and Fig. 21.2 charts a number of possible performance measures – those on the right focus on efficiency and reflect a financial control culture; those on the left are crucial indicators of a commitment to service, quality and excellence. The culture of the organization will dictate which measures are given priority. It has been pointed out earlier that establishing such excellence measures requires a real attempt to reconcile the different expectations of the stakeholders. Where there is no common agreement, the objectives and measures selected will reflect the relative power of the various stakeholders. In any case, commercial pressures invariably focus attention on resource management and efficiencies, which are easier to set and monitor. There is then always the danger that because efficiency measures are

BTR is an acquisitive and diversified conglomerate, and its strategy was outlined in Chapter 20, where it was also identified as a financial control company. BTR operates with several hundred profit centres directed by a head office with fewer than 50 staff and four regional offices.

> BTR ... allows its operations a large degree of autonomy within a carefully designed system of financial controls. The control system enables BTR to build its business both by investment in existing companies and through acquisitions, which it integrates rapidly and successfully.
>
> (BTR offer document for Hawker Siddeley)

The control system is built around two documents:

❑ *The Annual Profit Plans* These are fed through the regional office structure and ultimately approved by one designated main board director – because of the number of profit centres, the profit plans have to be spread amongst the whole board. The profit plan encapsulates corporate investment, and the objectives for each profit centre are negotiated to a level where they are thought to be achievable, but not too easily.

Profit centre general managers are delegated considerable autonomy whilst ever their targets are attained.

❑ *Monthly Management Reports* These contain some 17 pages of detailed analysis, with a strong emphasis on cash flow management. A working capital target of between 20 and 25% is set, and general managers are charged interest by the centre if they exceed their target.

The two documents characterize BTR's strong internal discipline, and they require that all profit centre managers are competent financially. The obvious attention to detail relies upon large quantities of carefully reported, accurate and honest information.

The efficiency aspects of the BTR system are clear; the attainment of potential internal synergies is less obvious.

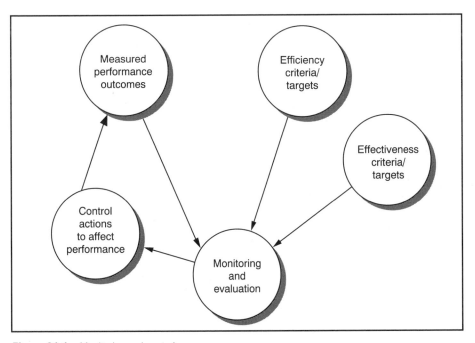

Figure 21.1 Monitoring and control.

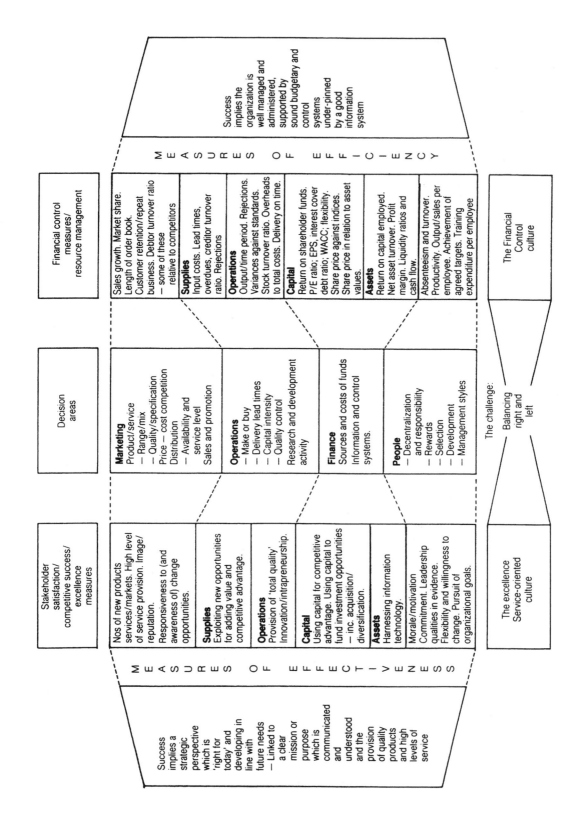

Figure 21.2 Some possible measures of performance.

possible, and often straightforward, they may become elevated in significance and, as a result, begin to be seen as the foundation for the objectives. In other words, measurement potential rather than stakeholder satisfaction dictates objectives.

Performance expectations

Arguably the central issue in measurement and control is what is communicated to managers in terms of performance expectations, and how they are rewarded and sanctioned for their success or failure to achieve their targets. The two issues are linked, and resources should be allocated to enable managers to perform as required and, at the same time, to motivate them.

Reed and Buckley (1988) argue that when this is handled effectively then strategy implementation through action plans can be proactive, and strategies can be adapted in line with changes in the environment. Where it is poorly thought through there is likely to be more reaction to events and external threats. Research indicates that this aspect of implementation is difficult to achieve, however.

Wernham (1984) contends that managers benefit from an appreciation of 'superordinate organizational goals' and the overall strategic perspective, and that any perceived internal inconsistencies between the performances expected of different managers can be demotivating. Communication and information systems should therefore seek to make managers aware about where the organization is going strategically and how well it is doing. Wernham's argument also implies that resource allocations and strategic priorities should be seen as fair and equitable, and that political activity to acquire or retain resources for the pursuit of personal objectives, or to support ineffective strategies, must be contained.

McMahon and Perrit (1973) have demonstrated that the effectiveness of managers in achieving their objectives is enhanced when the control levers are high, but Lawrence and Lorsch (1967) indicate that these controls also need to be loose and flexible if the environment is volatile.

It has been argued that resources are allocated through the budgeting process and that this establishes a quantitative short-term link between expectations and resources. It has also been argued that managers need to be aware of wider strategic issues, and that their attention should be focused on long-term strategies as well as short-term tactics and actions designed to bring immediate results. This necessitates that managers are aware of the key success factors for their products and business units, and of how their competitive environments are changing. Whilst it is important to achieve budget targets, it is also important that there is a continuing search for new ways of creating, improving and sustaining competitive advantage.

Reed and Buckley (1988) suggest that implementation can be made more effective by addressing the following issues:

❏ establishing the **strategic benefits** that the organization is hoping to achieve from particular strategic options – both immediate and long-term benefits
❏ clarifying the managerial actions which will be required if these benefits are to be attained, and using these as a basis for action plans
❏ incorporating the matching of resources with key success factors, and the development of sustainable competitive advantage, in the objectives and targets which are agreed with managers

❑ appraising and rewarding the ability of managers to contribute to the development of sustainable competitive advantage and not merely their ability to meet short-term budget targets
❑ ensuring that sufficient flexibility is built in.

These arguments emphasize that, whilst budgeting is essential for allocating resources on a short-term basis and progress against budget targets is a vital efficiency measure, organizational effectiveness also depends on longer-term flexibility. New developments and strategies, and improved ways of doing things, must also be considered. These may well involve changes in structures and policies as well as in the status of individual business units and managers. Issues in the implementation and management of change are the subject of Chapter 22.

The final section of this chapter looks at the deployment and commitment of resources to deal with crises.

Crisis avoidance and management

Crisis management concerns the management of certain risks and future uncertainties. Organizations should be ready to deal with both opportunities and surprises – resources should be managed to cope with unexpected and unlikely events in the organization's environment. E–V–R congruence again. It is important strategically because failure to deal effectively with crises can lead to losses of confidence, competitiveness, profits and market share.

Crisis management involves elements of planning and management. Planning constitutes crisis prevention or avoidance – the search for potential areas of risk, and decisions about reducing the risks. Management is being able to deal with crises if and when they occur.

The word *crisis* covers a number of different issues and events, and it includes a mixture of technical and managerial elements. Fires, fraud and computer failure are typical crises which might affect any organization almost any time. Poisoning scares or contamination with food products, and oil or chemical spillages, are foreseeable crises for particular companies. Major transport accidents, when they happen, are crises for the railway, shipping company or airline involved. Sometimes, but not always, the accident will prove to have been preventable. In relation to these there is an obvious logic in making contingency plans and being prepared.

In a different way, strategic changes can also lead to crises of confidence, particularly amongst employees. Rumours that a firm might be taken over often imply redundancies; falling sales and profits suggest possible cutbacks or closure. Good internal communications and openness are required to minimize the potential damage, especially as competitors might see these situations as competitive opportunities.

Decision areas

Simplified there are three decision areas in determining the crisis strategy:

1. Decisions concerning what can go wrong, the probability of it happening, and the impact it will have if it does happen.

2. Crisis planning. Decisions about investing in prevention in order to reduce or minimize the risk. Invariably this implies cost increases; and for this and other reasons less is often done than conceivably could be done.
3. Mechanisms for contingency management.

The decisions involve trade-offs between costs and risks in an attempt to find the best balance between 2 and 3. The successful management of crisis situations involves both awareness and the ability to deal effectively with unexpected change pressures.

Fire provides a useful example of these points. Fires are caused by such events as smoking, overheating machinery and electrical faults. All of these are predictable. The likelihood of a fire happening will differ from situation to situation, and the potential damage will similarly vary. Smoking can be banned and all conceivable safety measures can be invested in, if necessary, in order to minimize the risks. However these may not always be practical or affordable, and consequently detectors, sprinklers and fire doors to isolate areas are used as contingency measures. Nuclear power generation and airlines are examples of businesses which invest substantially in safety and prevention, often led by legislation. Situations are, however, frequently unclear. In 1991, following research after the 1985 fire on board a Boeing 737 at Manchester Airport, the Civil Aviation Authority ruled out the use of passenger smoke hoods on aircraft. The CAA argued they delayed the time required to evacuate an aircraft and thereby risked causing more deaths. The Consumers' Association is one group who disagreed, saying it was 'outraged' at the decision.

Crisis avoidance

Bartha (1995) suggests that many, but certainly not all, crises occur because they evolve gradually and nobody spots their progress. These potential crises can be prevented if organizations objectively monitor their environment and assess the emerging strategic issues. Consequently, an organization can develop a relative aversion to crises – as opposed to being crisis-prone – if it develops associated competencies in awareness, learning and stakeholder management. The challenge is to identify, assess, and deal with potential opportunities and threats before opportunities disappear (perhaps because they have been exploited by a competitor) or threats turn into crises. Another manifestation of an emerging threat would be a gap between the performance level expected of the organization by its stakeholders, especially its shareholders, and the actual performance level.

Visit the website: http://www. itbp.com

There are a number of elements involved in *scanning the environment.* Competitor activity should be monitored as far as possible; whilst their most recent actions and changes will be visible, the challenge is to determine future strategic changes before they are implemented. There should be constant contact with key stakeholders, such as customers, distributors and suppliers; and the organization should be aware of pending government legislation and

Remember chaos in time of order; watch out for danger and chaos while they are still formless.

Sun Tzu, some 2000 years ago

pressure group developments. The media can be a valuable source of information.

However the strategic challenge is not one of obtaining information, but rather discerning the important messages and separating out the key issues. Quite often it is necessary to synthesize snippets of information to create a meaningful pattern. The significance of the issue then needs determining and appropriate action plans initiated. Managerial judgement will be an important element.

Opportunities will emerge where the organization can build upon its strengths or tactically out-manoeuvre a rival; the crisis might occur if the opportunity is missed by the organization but picked up by a competitor. A potential threat can be present in a number of ways: new legislative restrictions, a disappearing market, financial difficulties for an important supplier or distributor. Information and triggers can be received anywhere in the organization at any time; making sure that their significance is appreciated and that they are channelled to those people, functions and businesses who could benefit is the next critical step. Communication systems are crucial, together with the ability of individual managers to take an organization-wide, or holistic, perspective.

The ability of managers to act upon the information will, in turn, depend upon organizational policies and the extent of their empowerment; their willingness to act will be affected by their personality, their competencies, their motivation and the reward/sanction system practised by the organization.

Crisis management

There are a number of identifiable steps in attempting to manage crises effectively:

❑ Initially it is necessary to identify the most obvious areas of risk.
❑ Following on from this firms should establish procedures and policies for ensuring risks do not become crises. Discussing possible scenarios, training sessions and actual rehearsals can all contribute, in addition to the investment in physical prevention.
❑ A crisis management team should be identified in advance, trained and prepared to step aside from all normal activities in the event of a crisis occurring. Experience suggests that the expertise required will be primarily communications and public relations, financial and legal. Clear leadership of the team by the strategic leader will be expected; and personnel, operations and marketing skills can be added as required. Secretarial support is sometimes overlooked.
❑ Building the team is one aspect of a planning process which should also cover how to get hold of key people over weekends and during holidays, how to restore critical facilities which might go down, and how to gain fast access to important regulatory bodies.
❑ Stakeholder analysis is another crucial aspect of the planning. It is vital to clarify which stakeholders are most likely to be affected by particular crises – and how. After a crisis customers either exhibit loyalty or switch to competitors; the confidence of distributors and the banks may also prove important. The media often play a significant role and their stance is likely to influence the confidence of other stakeholders. Where stakeholder perspectives and expectations differ it may be necessary to deal with each group on an individual basis.

In 1991 the insurance brokers Sedgewick showed that whilst 75% of Britain's largest companies claimed to have contingency plans for dealing with sudden crises when they occur, few had plans to cover the follow-up implications. Plans should also be in hand for re-launching products which might have to be withdrawn and for dealing with investors and possible litigation. 'Most companies only find out about the cost of a crisis once it's over'.

❏ Finally, a clear communications strategy is essential. Ethical issues may be involved, and the company will be expected to be co-operative, open, honest, knowledgeable and consistent. They must be seen to be in control and not attempting to cover-up. The media will want to know what has happened, why, and what the company intends to do about the situation. 'No comment' may well be interpreted as defensive or incompetent.

An effective information system will be required for gathering and disseminating the salient facts.

Strategies and examples

The most proactive strategy for crisis management can be compared with the notion of total quality management. The organization is looking for a culture where all employees think about the implications and risks in everything they do.

Reactions when a crisis has happened can prove to be effective or ineffective. Effective management is likely to mean that confidence is maintained and that there is no long-term loss of customers, market share or share price. Booth (1990) quotes research which indicates that this is more likely to happen in an open, flexible structure than it is in one which is bureaucratic.

Sandoz, the Swiss chemical company, was perceived as handling a crisis in 1986 ineffectively. Water used to fight a fire in a warehouse, possibly caused by arson, drained into the River Rhine because the local 'catch basins' were too small for the volume of water involved. The river was polluted. When pressed by the media Sandoz did not have important details readily available; and the company, the local authority and the Swiss government put out contradictory statements. Considerable ill-feeling was manifested against the company; and it has been suggested that the incident led to a medium-term loss of confidence in both Sandoz and the Swiss chemical industry.

Kabak and Siomkos (1990) offer a spectrum of four reactive approaches. At one extreme (and normally ineffective) is denial of responsibility, arguing the company is an innocent victim or that no harm has been done. Similarly some organizations will attempt to pin the blame on identified individuals (who possibly did make mistakes), or argue that the general public must share the risks. Where individual errors do lead to crises there may well be a lack of effective organizational control systems; and equally the public can only be expected to share the risk if they have available all the information required for decision making. Much of this is likely to be exclusive to the company, and quite possibly buried away in files.

A better, but still ineffective, approach is involuntary regulatory compliance. Exxon's reluctant acceptance of responsibility after their tanker *Exxon Valdez* ran aground and spilled oil off North Alaska in 1989 is given as an example. The incident was the result of human error rather than poor systems, but the company is still held accountable.

Kabak and Siomkos offer Perrier as an excellent example of the third strategy – voluntary compliance. Here there is a positive company response towards meeting its responsibilities. See Case 21.3. The incident highlights that even though companies may have crisis management strategies a number of unforeseen difficulties are likely to be encountered.

The other extreme strategy is the so-called super effort, whereby the company does everything it can, openly and honestly, and stays in constant touch will all affected stakeholders. In 1982 an extortionist succeeded in introducing cyanide to packs of Tylenol in America. Tylenol is manufactured by Johnson and Johnson and at the time it was the country's leading pain-killer with a 35% market share. Six people died.

All stocks were recalled immediately 'to contain the crisis and demonstrate responsibility'. The media were provided with constant up-to-date information. The product was re-launched in tamperproof containers and the associated heavy advertising featured the new containers rather than simply claiming the product was safe. The incident was costly, but market share was quickly regained. Some had suggested that Johnson and Johnson should drop the Tylenol brand name, but this was resisted. Interestingly the name *Townsend Thoresen* has been dropped by its parent company, P & O, after the ferry, *Herald of Free Enterprise*, capsized off Zeebrugge in 1987.

Whilst there is little argument against the logic of planning ahead of a crisis, some organizations are cautious about the extent to which one should attempt to plan.

> *The scale of the Bhopal [Union Carbide chemical plant in India] disaster [gas leak in 1984] was unimaginable. There is simply no way anyone could have anticipated it.*
>
> (Union Carbide Director of Corporate Communications quoted in Nash (1990)).

Whilst the extent and magnitude of a disaster may be unexpected, events like Bhopal are predictable, often because there have been similar incidents in the past. Union Carbide argued that they tried to be as honest as they could, but they were limited by the lack of hard facts from a remote area of India. Nash comments that the organization appreciated the need to act quickly and develop effective communications, but, after the event, remained sceptical about establishing rigid guidelines, arguing that one can never be certain in advance about the actual nature and detail of any crisis.

Crisis proneness and crisis aversion

It is unrealistic to think that a 'perfect' organization which is successful, seen as successful, and unaffected by crises, can be created. But most organizations could manage their resources more efficiently and more effectively and, as a result, be less prone to crises. Attention to these issues has become increasingly important as environments have become more turbulent and unpredictable.

A crisis-prone organization is likely to feature a number of the following characteristics:

❑ Specialist functions which operate within closed boundaries and which do not think holistically.

❑ A tendency to look inwards more than outwards, possibly exacerbated by

In 1989 Perrier was the world leader in the fast-growing market for bottled water. In the UK, for example, the Perrier brand accounted for over one-third of the market for sparkling water, which represented 20% of the whole market. Perrier also own Buxton, which is second to Evian in the still water segment. The name 'Perrier' had become synonymous with bottled water.

In February 1990 minute traces of benzene were discovered in a sample during routine tests in North Carolina, America. The trace, six parts per billion, did not represent any discernible health risk. Within one week every Perrier brand world-wide had been withdrawn from sale. This amounted to 160 million bottles in 110 countries.

> *Even if it is madness, we decided to take Perrier off the market everywhere in the world. I don't want the least doubt, however small, to tarnish our product's image of quality and purity.*
> (Gustave Leven, then Chairman, Perrier)

(Leven, 77 years old in 1990, had built Perrier from a run-down business to world leadership over 40 years. He retired later in 1990.)

> Perrier had created crisis management strategies some years earlier ... 'Everyone knew what they were supposed to do ... in spite of this we never, ever, imagined a world-wide withdrawal. We'd never dreamed of a problem of such magnitude'. Only Tylenol had previously been withdrawn on such a scale; and in that crisis people had died.

Actions in the UK

Local tests were arranged as soon as news spread from the USA. The tests took a normal 48 hours, and benzene was again found in the sample. Unfortunately during this period a Perrier spokesman in Paris speculated prematurely that a greasy rag might have introduced the wrong cleaning fluid onto bottling equipment. Moreover, when the world-wide withdrawal was announced to the world's press in Paris – rather than local press conferences – the room was too small for the press and television crews attending.

On the following day advertisements appeared around the world, explaining the situation, and clarifying what people, including retailers, should do. The 24-hour emergency telephone network in the UK 'received mostly friendly calls'.

A major problem in the UK concerned the disposal of all the water and the further disposal or recycling of the bottles. A large proportion of the stocks were in the distinctive Perrier green glass, which, recycled, has few alternative uses.

The source of the contamination was quickly traced to a filter at the bottling plant in France, a filter used to purify carbon dioxide being added to the water. This revelation suggested that Perrier is not 100% naturally carbonated, although the label on the bottles stated 'naturally carbonated natural mineral water'. It transpired that the gas used is collected underground with the water and added back after purification. Only the gas, not the water, is purified. Nevertheless the publicity caused Sainsbury's to refuse to stock Perrier for a period after it was re-launched in April 1990.

One month after the re-launch Perrier was already selling at half its previous volume; and market leadership was quickly regained. The world-wide cost was estimated to be £125 million.

Competitors had not attempted to exploit the situation, possibly believing they might spread a scare by association and affect the market for all bottled water.

It has been suggested that the very popularity of Perrier had caused the problem. Demand world-wide had put pressure on the supply side. Some years earlier, and before the increased consumer awareness and concern with health issues, the problem would probably have been contained on a smaller scale.

The balance of opinion seems to be that Perrier got the big decisions right. It adopted a worst case scenario, acted fast, and spoke out honestly.

Shortly after the crisis Perrier was bought by Nestlé.

Sources: Butler, D (1990) Perrier's painful period, *Management Today*, August; Caulkin, S (1990) Dangerous exposure, *Best of Business International*, Autumn.

internal conflicts. Competitive energy is directed against colleagues instead of competitors; managers do not trust each other.

❑ A strong and rigid belief in present – or even past-systems, ways of doing things and competitive paradigms. A reluctance to embrace the need for change.

❑ Communication systems which do not flow horizontally to co-ordinate the various parts of the organization.

❑ An inability to correctly interpret signals and issues – leading to an inability to share and learn important information. This information can relate to external opportunities and threats, or internal strengths which could be exploited elsewhere in the organization.

❑ A willingness to bend or break rules to achieve short-term targets and personal objectives without thinking sufficiently about the longer-term impact or the effect on other parts of the organization.

It will be appreciated that these characteristics reflect the organization culture and the manifestations of power and influence. Inappropriate behaviour patterns will create a situation where potential crisis issues are either missed, ignored, underestimated or dealt with inappropriately. A real crisis does occur; in some instances, the organization will actually create the crisis. The long-term situation is made worse when an organization, having somehow dealt with a crisis, fails to learn and make itself less crisis-prone for the future.

Crisis aversion demands both single-loop and double-loop learning. Programmed responses to perceived events, the acceptance of current operating practices, norms and policies, can be speedy and efficient. They can reflect the organization's ability to share and learn and to benefit from its experiences. However, there is an important distinction between 20 years of accumulated learning and one year's experiences repeated 20 times over. The danger signals are present when 'we've seen it all before; this is the way we do it here' is utilized too readily and without checking the current circumstances. Double-loop learning demands that managers question why things are done in a particular way, paying attention to environmental changes whose impact will require more than a programmed response.

A crisis management framework

Companies succeed if they meet the needs and expectations of their stakeholders; companies which fail to meet these needs and expectations, long term, must be in trouble and they may collapse. Perception of relative success and failure is critical. Companies who are succeeding need to be recognized for this. Companies who are not succeeding will want to cover up their weaknesses if they can.

Visit the website:
http://www.
itbp.com

The simple matrix illustrated in Figure 21.3 is based on these premises. Companies which satisfy their stakeholders, and are seen to do so, are classified as crisis avoiders. Crisis prone organizations fail on both counts. Companies with a strong reputation they do not wholly deserve are termed 'thin high profile' as the situation is likely to be very fragile and fluid. The fourth quadrant contains 'unsung heroes', companies whose reputation does not do justice to their real achievements.

It is worth considering which quadrant the following three companies should be placed in.

Crisis avoidance and management

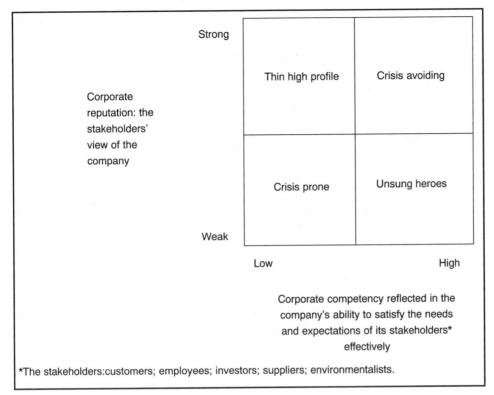

Figure 21.3 A crisis management framework.

Body Shop has seen its share price and price to earnings ratio fall in recent years as it has faced increasing competition internationally. In 1996, disillusioned with City investors, Body Shop looked at the viability of reprivatization, but concluded it would not be an appropriate strategy to follow. Nevertheless its customers and employees remain loyal and supportive, and the company's reputation as an environmentally-concerned organization also remains strong.

In 1995 **Shell,** one of Europe's most successful and respected companies, was forced to change an important strategic decision following a high-profile campaign by a leading pressure group. Shell had chosen to sink its redundant Brent Spar oil platform in deep seas some 150 miles west of Scotland. It had reached an agreement with the UK government that, scientifically, this was the most appropriate means of disposal for the platform. Greenpeace objected and protesters boarded the platform, claiming it still contained 5000 tonnes of oil which would eventually be released to pollute the sea. The ensuing and professionally orchestrated publicity fuelled public opinion, and there were protests in a number of European countries, including attacks on petrol stations in Germany. Shell backed down and agreed to investigate other possibilities for disposal. The UK government expressed both anger and disappointment with this decision. Independent inspectors later proved that Greenpeace's claims were gross exaggerations – the residual oil was much, much less than 5000 tonnes. The press concluded: 'Shell went wrong in spending too much time convincing government of the case for sea-bed dumping, but not attaching enough importance to consulting other stake-holder groups'. Shell had been made to appear socially irresponsible, even though the ethics of the Greenpeace campaign are questionable.

Again in 1995, **Yorkshire Water** was criticized on a number of occasions by its customers, provoked by the threat of rota cuts and a very visible road tankering operation to bring water into threatened areas of the county. Essential though it was, given the genuine and severe drought experienced, this operation upset residents who were affected by the noise of the lorries. There were definite technical issues such as the amount of water leaking from the infrastructure, combined with the past failure of the company to remedy this problem, and concerns over environmental damage as water was diverted out of rivers. However, many of the difficulties faced by the company were the result of poor public relations. The company's request to companies to restrict water use (and thus restrict manufacturing) was not well received. The statement by the managing director that he had not bathed in several weeks, subsequently proved not to be wholly accurate, was really another PR disaster. Similarly, positive statements that £50 million was being committed for new infrastructure investment were overshadowed in just two days by the announcement of strong profits and a 10% increase in dividend. The company's share price, however, held up throughout the crisis, perhaps explaining why the company was accused of placing its shareholders ahead of its customers.

Summary

In this chapter we have considered a number of issues in the way that resources are allocated and controlled. Resources are required for strategy implementation, and their availability is a determinant of the feasibility of a particular strategic option. However, the existence of resources does not guarantee the effective implementation of strategies. In addition resources must be flexible to allow incremental and adaptive change.

The way that resources are used and managed is also important. Policies are designed to guide the use of resources by managers; and budgets are used to allocate resources for particular activities and tasks. Budgets, however, are often short term in scope, and the measurement of performance against budget targets may be more an evaluation of efficiency than of longer-term strategic effectiveness.

Specifically we have:

- considered how policies, functional strategies and action plans constitute the operational aspects of strategy implementation, and provide a means of measuring performance discussed the need for corporate resource allocation to divisions, business units and functional departments, based on opportunity cost and designed to lead to the achievement of the overall corporate objectives
- pointed out that the appropriate style of allocating corporate resources may be influenced by the rate of growth of the organization
- examined the interrelationships between functions and illustrated the need to consider their interdependences when allocating resources
- distinguished between policies, procedures, functional plans and budgets
- explored the role of budgeting in the allocation of resources, highlighting the thinking behind zero-base budgeting
- considered a number of issues under-pinning measurement and control systems
- identified the main issues in crisis avoidance and management, and considered why some organizations are more crisis prone than others.

Checklist of key terms and concepts

You should feel confident that you understand the following terms and ideas:
* How strategies are made operational
* Corporate and functional resource planning
* Policies
* Budgets
* Efficiency and effectiveness issues in measurement and control
* Crisis avoidance and management.

Questions and research assignments

Text related

1 Should top management policies be essentially broad and general, and lower level policies narrow, explicit and rigid? Why? Why not?

2 What are the contributions and limitations of budgeting and the measurement of performance against budgets in the implementation of strategy and the monitoring of strategic effectiveness?

Research and assignment based

3 For an organization that you are familiar with, ascertain the main stated policies for finance, production, personnel and marketing.

How are these policies used? How were they created? How do they rate in terms of the principles of good policies discussed in the text?

4 Ascertain the budgeted resources and targets allocated to one manager you are able to interview.

What measures of performance are utilized?

What feedback is provided? What does the manager do with the feedback?

What do you believe is the personal impact of the budget and measures of performance on the manager? Is he or she motivated? Rewarded or sanctioned for success or failure?

5 By contacting either a local councillor or a financial executive ascertain how planning and budgeting is managed in your local authority. What have been the priority areas in the past? What are the current priorities? How have the changes in priority been decided?

6 In November 1991 (event: 13 November; Press reports: 14 November) SmithKline Beecham withdrew Lucozade from shops in the UK following a contamination alert.

Research the incident and assess how effectively the crisis was handled.

7 In 1984 Unilever launched a major new washing powder in several European countries; the product was branded Persil Power in the UK, Omo Power in the rest of Europe. Procter and Gamble quickly retaliated with evidence that the manganese granules included in Power damaged certain clothes after a number of washes. What happened in the so-called European Soap War? Which Unilever stakeholders were most affected? Least affected? How significant were publicity and public relations in influencing the final outcome?

Recommended further reading

The following two books are useful references on the conversion of strategies into operational and functional plans:

Murdick, RG, Eckhouse, RH, Moor, RC and Steiner, GA (1979) Strategic Planning, *Free Press*, Chapters 11–13. Zimmerer, TW (1976) *Business Policy: A Framework for Analysis*, Grid.

Barton, L (1993) *Crisis in Organizations: Managing and Communicating in the Heat of Chaos*, South-Western, is an excellent introduction to crisis management.

References

Bartha, P (1995) Preventing a high-cost crisis, *Business Quarterly*, Winter.

Booth, S (1990) Dux at the Crux, *Management Today*, May.

Bower, JL (1970) *Managing the Resource Allocation Process: A Study of Corporate Planning and Investment*, Division of Research, Harvard Business School.

Done, K (1992) Winter of despair, spring of hope *Financial Times* 17 February.

Kabak, IW and Siomkos, GJ (1990) How can an industrial crisis be managed effectively? *Industrial Engineering*, June.

Koontz, H and O'Donnell, C (1968) *Principles of Management*, 4th edn, McGraw-Hill.

Lawrence, PR and Lorsch, JW (1967) *Organisation and Environment*, Richard D Irwin.

McMahon, JT and Perrit, GW (1973) Toward a contingency theory of organisational control, *Academy of Management Journal*, **16**.

Nash, T (1990) Tales of the unexpected, *The Director*, March.

Pearce, JA and Robinson, RB (1985) *Strategic Management*, 2nd edn, Richard D Irwin.

Reed, R and Buckley, MR (1988) Strategy and action: techniques for implementing strategy, *Long Range Planning*, **21** (3).

Sedgwick (1991) Research quoted in de Jonquières, G (1991) Taking the drama out of a crisis, *Financial Times*, 14 November.

Seed, AH (1983) New approaches to asset management, *Journal of Business Strategy*, Winter.

Wernham, R (1984) Bridging the awful gap between strategy and action, *Long Range Planning*, **17**.

22

Issues in Strategic Change Management

In this chapter we look at various issues and problems in the management of change. It is stressed that organizations must be reactive to external change pressures and proactive in seeking to take advantage of opportunities and shape their environment if they are to be effective strategically. Cultural and power considerations are important variables in the management of change.

Learning objectives

After studying this chapter you should be able to:

- describe the major forces for change and types of change situation
- explain why people frequently resist change
- summarize alternative ways of overcoming resistance
- identify a number of different approaches to the planned management of change
- contrast planned change with emergent change in a learning organization
- assess the importance of power and how it is used in change situations
- describe ways in which managers can improve their political effectiveness in organizations.

Introduction

> There is nothing more difficult to take in hand, more perilous to conduct, or more uncertain in its success than to take the lead in the introduction of a new order of things.
>
> *(Machiavelli)*

> In this race ... you run the first four laps as fast as you can – and then you gradually increase the speed.
>
> *(William Weiss, CEO, Ameritech)*

Organizations and managers face change on a continuous basis, especially in volatile environments. Some changes are reactions to external threats; others are proactive attempts to seize opportunities and manage the environment. Organizations should seek to obtain and maintain a congruence between their environment, values and resources, making changes when there are pressures from either the environment or their resources. It is crucial that organizations seek to create and sustain competitive advantage, and wherever possible innovate to improve their competitive position. This implies a readiness to change within the organization and the ability to implement the proposed changes.

At times there will be a perceived need to try and change values and culture. In the last decade of the twentieth century the pressures for change in a wide cross-section of businesses are clearly visible. Food manufacturers and distributors are affected by changing consumer attitudes to their diets and by the public reaction and concern to the growing awareness of incidences of food

Don't forget to visit the website: http://www.itbp.com

poisoning. Building societies and banks are responding to changes in the competitive regulations which directly affect them, generally seeing the changes as opportunities. The water authorities and electricity industries have followed a number of other corporations into privatization, which has forced major changes of strategy, resource management and culture. Organizations within the umbrella of the National Health Service are responding to new proposals and legislation on controls and performance measures. Some National Health Service employees see the changes as threats; others as opportunities.

Effective organizations must be able to **manage change,** with managers and employees supportive rather than resistant or hostile. When strategies change, there are often accompanying changes in structures and responsibilities, and people are clearly affected. Kotter and Schlesinger (1979) and Waterman (1987) suggest that most companies or divisions need to make moderate organizational changes at least every year, with major changes every four or five years.

Whilst organizational changes can be reactive and forced by external change, effective strategic management really requires **learning.** Managers must be aware of their environment, assessing trends and deciding in advance what should be done about perceived opportunities and threats. Planning activities and systems should ensure that the future is considered, and the resultant plans should encompass the implementation aspects of any proposed changes and the need to be flexible to accommodate unexpected changes. Moreover, innovation should be possible within the organization. Managers should be constantly looking for ways of being more effective and able to proceed with appropriate changes.

Ideally the organization will seek to develop a culture where people do not feel threatened when they are constantly asked to question and challenge existing behaviours and acknowledged ways of doing things – and change them. A culture which sees innovation and change as normal; a culture that is ideal for dealing with the competitive chaos which characterizes many industries and markets. A culture where people do not automatically ask: 'Who is already doing this?' when somewhere proposes an innovative change. This cannot happen without strong strategic leadership which fosters, encourages and rewards intrapreneurial and innovative contributions from managers and other employees throughout the organization.

A culture such as this will frequently be based around a working atmosphere of creativity and fun; people must enjoy doing things differently and originally, actively looking for new competitive opportunities, instead of simply copying others.

A change culture is highly desirable for many organizations but very difficult to achieve.

Hence the implementation of change requires:

❏ **a perceived need for change** – this can originate with either the strategic leader or managers throughout the company who are aware of the possibilities
❏ **the necessary resources** – which involves aspects of competency as well as physical resources, and the ways in which managers use power to influence the allocation and utilization of resources
❏ **commitment** – the culture of the organization will influence the extent to which managers are responsive and innovative.

Figure 22.1 takes the concept of E–V–R congruence and restates the idea from the perspective of effective change management. The **environment** provides

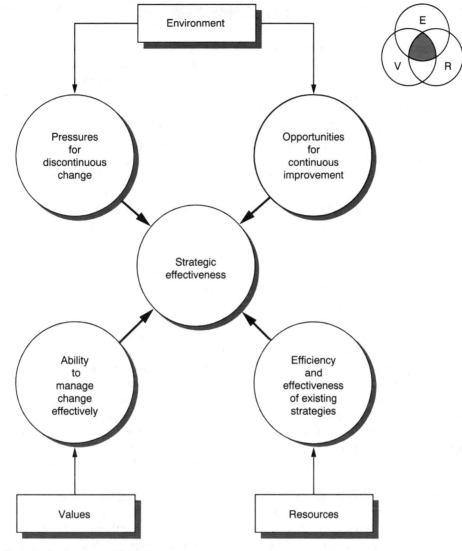

Figure 22.1 Strategic effectiveness and E–V–R congruence.

opportunities for organizations to benefit from innovation and continuous improvement; on other occasions the environment will encourage more dramatic, discontinuous change. This pressure can take the form of a threat (major environmental disturbance) or an opportunity (whereby the organization, 'seeing the future' ahead of its rivals, can shape its environment). The relative strength of the organization's **resources** is reflected in the success of existing strategies; **values** dictate the ability of the organization to manage change effectively. Strategic effectiveness demands congruency. Case 22.1 charts the story of Apple Computers over some 20 years and shows how the company has enjoyed mixed fortunes. Sometimes highly innovative and successful, Apple has also been affected by competitor initiatives which have changed the personal computer industry in dramatic ways.

Apple was started in 1976 by two young entrepreneurs, Steven Jobs and Stephen Wozniak, who began by making personal computers in a garage. In 1983 the company's turnover, from essentially one model – the distinctive Apple computer – was approaching $1 billion. At this stage in the company's development Wozniak had already left and Jobs had been quoted as saying that he was no longer able to do what he most enjoyed – working with a small group of talented designers to create new innovative products. To overcome his frustration with an increasingly bureaucratic organization Jobs had formed a new team of designers and set about developing the company's second major product, the Apple Macintosh, away from corporate headquarters and the production plant. The Macintosh was regarded as very user friendly and featured an illustrated screen menu and a handheld mouse unit for giving instructions. It was launched in 1984 and sold immediately.

John Sculley was appointed Apple President in 1983 and took over executive control. His initial priorities were to co-ordinate product development activities, which he felt were fragmented, and to integrate these developments with existing programmes. To achieve this, power was centralized more than it had been in the past and was supported by formalized reporting procedures and new financial control systems.

Sculley was regarded as being more marketing oriented than Jobs, and their business philosophies clashed. Jobs resigned in 1985, together with a number of other key employees, deciding to concentrate his efforts on the development of sophisticated personal computers for university students in a small, entrepreneurial organization environment.

Despite the increased business discipline, Sculley attempted to preserve important aspects of the original Apple culture. Informal dress codes, a 'fun working environment' and elaborate celebrations when targeted milestones are reached were all considered important. Apple retained a structure with few layers of management, few perks and few status-carrying job titles.

Sculley's challenge was to move the company away from an informal and entrepreneurial management style to a more functional and later (1988) a divisionalized structure, whilst retaining the important aspects of the culture. In addition Sculley felt that Apple needed to be repositioned in the market in order to overcome the competitive threats from the Far East.

With new versions of the Macintosh, Apple moved from an education and home computer base into a business computer company which also sold to schools and universities. Apple was a major innovator in desk-top publishing, pioneering the market in advance of competition from IBM and Xerox.

Apple prospered in the late 1980s, but its strategy began to appear inappropriate for the recession and the 1990s. Apple had concentrated on, and succeeded with, high-margin products which were substantially differentiated. However, Sculley claimed Apple's ideas were being copied and used in cheaper rival products – Apple began a legal action against Microsoft, alleging that its *Windows* software used ideas from the Macintosh. Moreover personal computers have become more of a commodity product in a maturing market. Although Apple has sold 22 million Macintosh's, the continued success of Microsoft has been very damaging to the company.

In 1991 Apple agreed a series of strategic alliances, mostly with IBM, historically its main rival. The alliances concentrated on areas where Apple lacked either development skills or the ability to fund the research and development independently. New personal computer technology and operating systems software were key areas. Cultural and other differences between Apple and IBM have led to their alliances being relatively unsuccessful.

Coincidental with its agreements with the global IBM Apple's culture had actually been changing. Empowerment, flexibility and freedom remained important, but 'there had to be more discipline. Our cost structure was out of line.

Continued

We did not know how to meet schedules. We were a benevolent company that sponsored people to work on things they were interested in' (Sculley).

Apple reduced the prices of its existing products, hoping for higher volumes which would more than compensate for the lower margins, and introduced a range of cheaper, lower-performance Macintosh's. In terms of new products Apple was arguably two years late with its lap-top computer. Other new products concentrated on personal electronics devices and included electronic books and a notebook computer. In 1993 Apple launched *Newton*, a $7 \times 4\frac{1}{2}''$ black box with a $5 \times 3''$ screen; users jot down ideas on the screen and draw sketches as they talk and think, and record notes and appointments. The machine can translate the images, store and organize. In addition, electronic data, such as a map, can be input. Sales of the Newton were disappointing and it has failed to live up to Apple's early expectations.

As market shares and gross margins fell during the early 1990s, Apple's pre-tax profits and share price were both erratic. Sculley, the Newton product champion, was accused of neglecting the main hardware products to push the new idea, and his position was threatened. Sculley was in fact replaced by Michael Spindler in 1993, an internal promotion, but, three years later, Spindler also left. The new strategic leader, Gil Amelio, joined Apple from National Semiconductor in 1996. After his departure Sculley commented: 'I don't think anyone can manage Apple'.

Amelio decided to halve the Macintosh product range (responsible for 80% of Apple's revenue) in order to reduce costs and help restore profitability. This controversial cut would radically affect Apple's strategy of market segmentation. In addition, six varieties of its software operating system would be consolidated into one, which Apple would also seek to license to other manufacturers.

The company was also to be restructured into seven profit-centre divisions: four for different hardware products, plus software, service and Internet – the Macintosh is an ideal machine for creating Internet products.

Amelio recognized that cultural change was again an issue – he believed from one where 'employees felt free to question, and even defy, management decisions' to a more conventional style. Product managers would no longer be 'free to veto the strategic leader'.

Apple's core competency is still its ability to make technology easy to use and Amelio argues that it needs to exploit this in ways which allow it to move further away from the cut-throat personal computer market and capitalize upon the new opportunities which will emerge as more and more people world-wide gain access to computers. Currently just 9% of the world's population has access.

Apple's new Macintosh operating system, called Copland, and due around the end of 1996, has been predicted 'to make Windows 95 seem as quaint and feeble as DOS' because of its radical new ability to organize, track and retrieve stored data and files.

A final comment from founder Steve Jobs (in *Fortune*, 19 February 1996):

If I were running Apple I would milk the Macintosh for all its worth – and get busy on the next great thing. The PC wars are over. Done. Microsoft won a long time ago.

Issues in the management of change

It was mentioned in the introduction that organizations face change pressures from the environment, and the significance, regularity and impact of these pressures will be determined by the complexity and volatility of the environment. At the same time managers may see opportunities and wish to adapt existing strategies. There are therefore a number of forces which encourage change, and a variety of different change situations. Change, though, affects people, their jobs and responsibilities and their existing behaviour patterns. It can also lead to changes in the underlying culture of the organization. For these reasons people may be wary or even hostile. This is increasingly likely if they fail to understand the reasoning behind the proposed changes and if they personally feel that they are losing rather than gaining from the changes. The various forces for change, the reasons why people resist change, and an outline framework for the effective management of change are considered in this section.

Forces for change

Five major forces for change are as follows.

❑ *Technical obsolescence and technical improvements* Technical change pressures can stem from outside the organization in the form of new developments by competitors and the availability of new technologies which the organization might wish to harness. Internal research and development and innovatory ideas from managers can generate technical change internally. In high technology companies and industries, and particularly where product life cycles are becoming shorter, this can be a very significant issue. Some organizations follow product strategies built around short life cycles, product obsolescence (both physical and design) and persuading customers to replace the product regularly. A number of service businesses also find this a useful strategy.

❑ *Political and social events* Many of these change pressures will be outside the control of the firm, but companies will be forced to respond. In the mid-to-late 1980s there was considerable pressure on companies not to trade with South Africa, and in the late 1980s increased public awareness of environmental issues began to place pressure on certain firms. Government encouragement for the use of lead-free petrol, in the form of both media coverage and price advantages from lower taxation, forced car manufacturers to respond. New cars are capable of running on both leaded and lead-free petrol; conversion kits for older cars have had to be developed.

❑ *The tendency for large organizations and markets to become increasingly global* Whilst this again has provided opportunities and new directions of growth for many organizations, others have been forced to respond to changing competitive conditions. The growing incidence of joint ventures and strategic alliances, discussed in Chapter 16, is a feature of this.

❑ *Increases in the size, complexity and specialization of organizations* The growth of organizations, linked to internal changes of structure, creates pressure for further changes. Large complex specialist organizations have made increasing use of information technology in their operations, introducing automation and JIT systems. These create a need for greater specialist expertise from both managers and other employees, possibly necessitating training and changes in their jobs. Effective use of these technological opportunities also requires greater co-operation and co-ordination between functions and managers.

❑ *The greater strategic awareness and skills of managers and employees* Able and ambitious managers, and employees who want job satisfaction and personal challenges, need opportunities for growth within the organization. These can be promotion opportunities or changes in the scope of jobs. Such changes require both strategic development and growth by the company, and appropriate styles of non-autocratic leadership.

From considering these general change forces we now briefly mention a num-

Visit the website:
http://www.
itbp.com

ber of issues which have a significant contemporary impact on the competitive activity of organizations.

The current dynamics of change

The strategic environment, especially competitive forces, determines how proactive and change oriented an organization must be if it is to be effective. Whilst the forces and their relative intensity vary between industries and organizations, Peters (1989) suggests that several factors require that most organizations must be receptive to the need for change. Specifically he highlights the following.

❑ The general dynamics and uncertainty of world economies.
❑ Time horizons, which he argues can be a strategic weapon in the face of uncertainty. It was discussed earlier how successful retailers are using information technology to monitor demand changes very quickly and to build distribution systems which allow them to respond to changes. As product life cycles shorten, the development time for new products must also be cut.
❑ Organization structures must be designed to enable decisions to be made quickly.
❑ Quality, design and service – which must be responsive to customer perceptions and competitor activities – are essential for competitive advantage.

Levels of change

Change decisions can be categorized in terms of their significance to the organization and the appropriate level of intervention, see Table 22.1. The five levels form a vertical hierarchy, and it is crucial to clarify and tackle needs and problems appropriately. If the problem is one of operating efficiencies, then the intervention should be at functional strategy level – but this alone would be inadequate for dealing with higher order needs. As one ascends the hierarchy the challenges and difficulties increase – as we saw in Chapter 4, changing the culture of the organization can be slow and problematical. Structural changes can sometimes be difficult to implement as well, particularly where individuals perceive themselves to be losing rather than benefiting.

Need	Level of change	Approaches/tactics
New mission; different 'ways of doing things'	Values; culture; styles of management	Organizational development
New corporate perspective/ strategy	Objectives; corporate strategy	Strategic planning
	Organization structure	New organization design
Improved competitive effectiveness (existing products and services)	Competitive strategies; systems and management roles	Empowerment; management by objectives; performance management; job descriptions; policies
		Business process re-engineering
Improved efficiencies	Functional strategies; organization of tasks	Method study; job enrichment

Table 22.1
Levels of change

In recent years the recession-hit high street banks have introduced major changes in an attempt to protect and consolidate their profits, and these have systematically moved up to the highest level. A variety of approaches have been used to improve productivity and reduce costs, but this alone was inadequate. The services provided to customers have been reviewed, resulting, for example, in new branch interiors and the introduction of personal bankers and specialist advisers. These changes have been linked to re-structuring, the closure of some small branches, job losses and increased market segmentation of business clients. More recently the banks have re-thought their corporate strategies, having pursued growth through diversification and overseas expansion during the early 1980s. Concentration on core activities is now preferred. During the 1990s the cultural focus has seen a reduced emphasis on image and marketing and a return to the more productive utilization of assets, harnessing information technology, in order to improve margins.

Case 22.2, National Power, categorizes the changes which followed privatization. Concentration is again preferred to diversification.

Types of change

Summarizing these points, Daft (1983) specifies four basic types of change which affect organizations:

❏ **Technology**   production processes
❏ **The product or service** the output of the business
❏ **Administrative changes** structure; policies; budgets; reward systems
❏ **People**   attitudes; expectations; behaviour

Invariably a change in one of these factors will place demands for change on one or more of the others.

When an organization decides to launch a new product it may also need to invest in new technology, modify its existing production plant and either acquire people with, or train existing employees in, the new skills required.

Major changes in the strategic perspective, say the acquisition of a similar sized firm, will force changes in the organization structure, which in turn necessitates changes in jobs and behaviour patterns.

However necessary the changes may be, and however ready the organization might be to implement them, the outcomes will not necessarily be positive for everyone affected.

The change process

Change frequently disrupts normality. Job security seems threatened; existing behaviour patterns and values are questioned; people are required to be more flexible and to take more risks. Whilst the organization may be facing strong external pressures it is unrealistic to expect managers and other employees not to query or resist the need to change. This is particularly true if individuals feel threatened, or perceive themselves to be losing out rather than benefiting or not being rewarded in some way for co-operating.

It is important to encourage people to recognize the need for change, the benefits, and the external threats from not changing. Managed change should be planned and evolutionary, although some organizations have attempted to

National Power is the larger of the two electricity **generating** companies created when the industry was privatized in 1991. The rival company is Powergen. Electricity **distribution** to domestic and business customers is the responsibility of 12 regional companies which were sold to private shareholders.

The privatization necessitated a series of changes which affected the whole organization:

Culture	Prior to privatization electricity generation was seen as bureaucratic and committee-led. Engineers and engineering considerations took priority over the interests of customers. The new culture is more commercial and entrepreneurial, service receives high priority and managers are empowered.
Corporate strategy	There has been a switch of emphasis from coal-fired stations to gas; and some coal-burning stations have already been closed. In addition more imported coal is being used, which increased the impact on the British coal industry. When the industry was nationalized political interests and pressures

protected the domestic coal industry.

Nuclear power stations, incidentally, were excluded from the privatization programme until 1996.

Structure	National Power was organized into 35 separate power stations, each a profit centre. The station managers were made more accountable.
Competitive strategy	A monopoly has been replaced by two rival generating companies who compete for the same business.

In the new competitive market anyone may seek a licence to generate electricity and sell it into the distribution system.

The prices offered by the generating companies are determined mainly by competitive forces now operating in the market place.

Functional strategies	Cost cutting to improve productivity. The number of jobs was reduced from 16,000 to 15,000 at privatization and further reductions followed.

become more flexible such that people not only accept change, but constantly seek new opportunities for change and improvement. Although change can be speedy and dynamic – normally when it is forced by powerful external influences – managing change positively in a growth situation, taking advantage of opportunities rather than responding to threats, requires that the process begins gradually and on a limited scale, and then spreads. Advancement needs consolidation and learning. The innovation stage, which can easily go wrong, requires that the change agents (who will not always be the strategic leader) find powerful and influential allies and supporters. Time and effort must be invested in explaining, justifying and persuading. Trial and error leads to incremental learning. Early supporters should be visibly rewarded for their commitment, and this will encourage others and begin to consolidate the changes. Conservative people are inevitably going to be late joiners; and some older people, together with those who are very set in their ways, are likely to be laggards. Because changes can be slow to take off they often appear to be failing once the process is well under way. This will renew opposition and resistance. During the process it is important to continue to monitor the environment. The programme may need amendment if circumstances alter.

Resistance to change

There are a number of reasons why change pressures might be resisted, and certain circumstances where the implementation of change will have to be planned carefully and the needs of people considered.

❑ Some resistance can be expected where people have worked out ways of doing things which are beneficial to them in terms of **their** objectives and preferences. They may see change as a threat. Similarly, when people have mastered tasks and feel in control of their jobs and responsibilities, they are likely to feel relatively safe and secure personally. Again change may be perceived as a threat to their security, although the aim might be to ensure the security of the organization as a whole.

❑ Resistance to 'sideways change' (expanding certain activities whilst contracting elsewhere) is likely unless the people affected are fully aware of the reasons and implications.

❑ Where particular policies, behaviour patterns and ways of doing things have been established and accepted for a long time and in effect have become part of the culture of the organization, change will require careful implementation. The need for change may not be accepted readily.

❑ It is not unusual for people to have some fear of the unknown and to feel comfortable with situations, policies and procedures they know. Awareness and understanding is therefore an important aspect of change.

❑ The organization itself, or particular managers, may resist external pressures if the change involves considerable expense, investment in new equipment and the associated risks. This issue can be exacerbated where there has previously been substantial investment in plant and equipment which technically is still satisfactory. Although demand may be falling there may be a reluctance to sell or close.

❑ Resistance is likely to be forthcoming where there are perceived flaws or weaknesses in the proposal. Change decisions may be made by the strategic leader and then delegated for implementation. Managers who are closer to the market may have some justified reservations if they have not been consulted during the formulation process.

The opposition may be to the change itself, or to the proposed means of implementation. Both can and must be overcome if changes are to be implemented successfully.

Casualties are, however, possible and sometimes inevitable. Some people will leave because they are uncomfortable with the changes.

Kotter and Schlesinger (1979) have identified six ways of overcoming resistance to change, and these are described in Box 22.1. They suggest that each method has both advantages and disadvantages and can be appropriate in parti-

---

Remember, it is not always the man on the shopfloor who opposes change. It can be the second or third tier of management who are the most reactionary.

Sir Peter Gibbings, Chairman, Anglia Television

Box 22.1
SIX WAYS OF OVERCOMING RESISTANCE TO CHANGE

Education and communication

Education and communication should help people understand the logic and the need for change. A major drawback can be the inherent time delays and logistics when a lot of people are involved. It also requires mutual trust.

Participation and involvement

The contention is that people will be more supportive of the changes if they are involved in the formulation and design. Again it can be time consuming; and if groups are asked to deliberate and make decisions there is a risk that some decisions will be compromises leading to suboptimization.

Facilitation and support

This can involve either training or counselling but there is no guarantee that any resistance will be overcome.

Negotiation and agreement

Negotiation and agreement are normally linked to incentives and rewards. Where the resistance stems from a perceived loss as a result of the proposed change, this can be useful, particularly where the resisting force is powerful. However, offering rewards every time changes in behaviour are desired is likely to prove impractical.

Manipulation and co-optation

This encompasses covert attempts to influence people, for example by the selective use of information and conscious structuring of events. Co-optation involves 'buying-off' informal leaders by personal reward or status. These methods are ethically questionable, and they may well cause grievances to be stored for the future.

Explicit and implicit coercion

The use of threats can work in the short run but is unlikely to result in long-term commitment.

Source: Kotter, JP and Schlesinger, LA (1979) Choosing strategies for change, *Harvard Business Review*, March–April.

---

cular circumstances. Issues raised by some of these alternatives are developed further in this chapter. Organizational development is considered as an approach to gaining support through active participation by managers on a continuous basis; manipulative approaches are discussed as a 'machiavellian' use of power and influence. In the next section we consider a number of general aspects in the management of change before specific strategies are discussed in more detail.

Implementing change: a general overview

Effective change occurs when managers and employees modify their behaviour in a desired or desirable way, and when the important changes are lasting rather than temporary.

No positive changes will occur within a company unless the Chief Executive realizes that people are basically opposed to change. A climate for change must be created in people's minds.

Changes need to be planned and everyone must be reassured that these changes will be for the betterment of the company, its employees, customers and shareholders.

Changes have therefore to be managed against a set of objectives and to a timetable.
Jacques G. Margry, Group Chief Executive, Parker Pen Ltd

Lewin (1947) contends that permanent changes in behaviour involve three aspects: unfreezing previous behaviour, changing, and then refreezing the new patterns. These three stages are crucial if changes in culture are required.

Unfreezing is the readiness to acquire or learn new behaviour. People are willing to accept that existing strategies and ways of doing things could be improved and made more effective. Normally this needs a trigger such as declining sales or profits, or the threat of closure or acquisition.

Change occurs when people who perceive the need for change try out new ideas. The changes could be introduced gradually or they may be more dramatic. Choosing the appropriate change strategy once the need is clarified may involve the selection of one from a number of alternatives, and consequently there are opportunities for involving the people who are most likely to be affected. Power structures are likely to be altered and consequently resistance might be evident from certain people.

Particularly where the pressures for change are significant, and the likely impact of the changes will be dramatic and felt widely throughout the organization, the change strategy will need a champion. Organizations in difficulty quite often appoint a new strategic leader to introduce fresh ideas and implement the changes. Newcomers are unlikely to be associated with the strategies which now need changing. Similarly, general managers might be moved to different business units when strategic changes are necessary

Refreezing takes place when the new behaviour patterns are accepted and followed willingly. People are supportive and convinced of the wisdom of the changes; ideally the new approaches become established within the culture. Rewards are often influential in ensuring that refreezing does in fact take place.

Throughout the change process it is important that people are **aware** of why changes are being proposed and are taking place, and that they **understand** the reasons. The key issues are participation, involvement and commitment.

Margerison and Smith (1989) suggest that the management of change exhibits four key features:

❏ **dissatisfaction** with the present strategies and styles
❏ **vision** of the better alternative – a clear picture of the desired state which can be communicated and explained to others (this again emphasizes the need for a champion of the change)
❏ a **strategy** for implementing the change and attaining the desired state
❏ **resistance** to the proposals at some stage.

Force field analysis
Lewin (1951) has proposed that changes result from the impact of a set of driving forces upon restraining forces. Figure 22.2 illustrates Lewin's theme of

---

A nursing team in a geriatric hospital wanted the seats of the toilets raised for the comfort of their patients. Hospital management was silent to their pleas. The team re-presented their request and argued that the change would reduce the amount of laundry and in turn the laundry bills. The proposal was approved and implemented.

Anecdote told by Christine Hancock, General Secretary, Royal College of Nursing

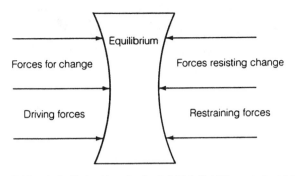

Figure 22.2 Force field analysis. Derived from Lewin, K (1951) *Field Theory in Social Sciences*, Harper & Row.

a state of equilibrium which is always under some pressure to change. The extent to which it does change will depend upon whether the driving forces or the restraining forces prove to be stronger. The driving forces, which may be external or internal in origin, are likely to have economic aspects. There may be a need to increase sales, to improve profitability, to improve production efficiencies, to generate new forms of competitive advantage. Corporate, competitive and functional strategies may appear in need of change, but existing strategies may have people who are loyal and committed to them. People will be affected and may feel concerned. Any resistance will constitute a restraining force, seeking to abandon or modify the change proposals.

Although the driving forces will be concerned with improving organizational efficiency and effectiveness, the opposition is more likely to stem from personal concerns than from disagreement that improved efficiency and effectiveness are desirable. Lewin suggests that the driving forces are based more on logic and the restraining forces on emotion. However, people who are aware of the situation may seek to argue their opposing case in relation to the relative ability of the change proposal to achieve the required improvements. As a result the ensuing debate concentrates on these issues. The opponents may choose not to be honest and open about their personal fears, feeling that their arguments must concentrate on the economic issues. When this happens the decision, whatever it might be, has not encompassed important underlying behavioural issues.

Effective managers of change situations will be clearly aware of both the driving forces and the real restraining forces. They will seek to strengthen the justifications by communication and explanation and diffuse opposition by exploring the likely impact with the people affected. Box 22.2 summarizes a number of important issues for the effective management of change. In this section we have looked generally at the issues which affect and underpin the management of change. Lewin's force field analysis is particularly helpful for establishing a holistic view of the change situation in terms of cause and likely effect. From this a clearer strategy for implementing the change can emerge. A number of strategies are explored in the following section. Where the extent of the change is substantial, and changes in culture are involved, it is important to ensure that the new behaviour patterns are permanent rather than temporary.

Visit the website:
http://www.
itbp.com

Box 22.2
ISSUES IN EFFECTIVE CHANGE MANAGEMENT

- ❏ Change programmes must be championed.
- ❏ There needs to be a clear purpose to which people can subscribe ... which can be justified and defended.
- ❏ The change proposals will not be backed by everyone.
- ❏ Managers must decide how much to communicate and when – there are dangers in both inadequate information provision and in being too open and candid.
- ❏ Senior managers must take responsibility; whilst empowerment is important, people still need effective leadership.
- ❏ Effective change management frequently involves well-led teams and may require process or even structural change.

- ❏ Creating and broadcasting early successes speeds up the process, especially as programmes often lose momentum part-way through.
- ❏ Setbacks must be anticipated and managed, and the momentum maintained.
- ❏ It is dangerous to 'claim victory' too quickly; the changes must become anchored in the culture.
- ❏ The feelings of people who might be hurt by the changes must not be overlooked.

Sources: Eccles, T (1994), *Succeeding With Change*, McGraw-Hill and Kotter, JP (1995), Why transformation efforts fail, *Harvard Business Review*, March–April.

Strategies for implementation and change

It is possible to view implementation as an activity which follows strategy formulation – structures and systems are changed to accommodate changes in strategy. However, implementation, instead of following formulation, may be considered in depth at the same time as the proposed strategy is thought through and before final decisions are made. This is more likely to happen where a number of managers, especially those who will be involved in implementation, are consulted when the strategy is evaluated. Strategies, as has been pointed out earlier, may evolve from the operation of the organization structure. Where managers are encouraged to be innovatory and make incremental changes, elements of trial and error and small change decisions are often found. Implementation and formulation operate simultaneously; the changes are contained rather than dramatic and resistance may similarly be contained. Innovatory organizations can develop change orientation as part of the culture. People expect things to change regularly and accept changes.

To many, uncertainty is a shadow of the unknown, to be avoided; far better, as we are stuck with an uncertain world, is to look upon it as the spice of life.

Sir Peter Holmes, Chairman, Shell UK

Teach people that change is inevitable and, if embraced, can be fun.

Leslie Hill, Chairman and Chief Executive, Central Independent Television plc

Bourgeois and Brodwin (1984) have identified five distinct basic approaches to strategy implementation and strategic change.

❑ The strategic leader, possibly using expert planners or enlisting planning techniques, defines changes of strategy and then hands over to senior managers for implementation. The strategic leader is primarily a thinker/planner rather than a doer.

❑ The strategic leader again decides major changes of strategy and then considers the appropriate changes in structure, personnel, and information and reward systems if the strategy is to be implemented effectively. Quinn (1988) contends that the strategic leader may reveal the strategy gradually and incrementally as he or she seeks to gather support during implementation. This theme is developed later in this section.

In both these cases the strategic leader needs to be powerful as both involve top-down strategic change.

❑ The strategic leader and his or her senior managers (divisional heads, business unit general managers or senior functional managers) meet for lengthy discussions with a view to formulating proposed strategic changes. All the managers are briefed and knowledgeable, and the aim is to reach decisions to which they will all be committed. Strategies agreed at the meetings are then implemented by the managers who have been instrumental in their formulation. Whilst this approach involves several managers it is still primarily centralized.

❑ The strategic leader concentrates on establishing and communicating a clear mission and purpose for the organization. He or she seeks to pursue this through a decentralized structure by developing an appropriate organization culture and establishing an organization-wide unity of purpose. Whilst the strategic leader will retain responsibility for changes in the strategic perspective, decisions concerning competitive and functional strategy changes are decentralized to general and functional managers who are constrained by the mission, culture, policies and financial resources established by the strategic leader.

❑ Managers throughout the organization are widely encouraged to be innovative and come up with new ideas for change. The strategic leader establishes a framework for evaluating these proposals – recognizing that those which are accepted and resourced result in increased status for the managers concerned.

These basic approaches highlight a number of general themes and ideas which are considered below.

Ideas for change can start at the bottom of the organization rather than always at the top; and change can be seen as both a clearly managed process and the incremental outcome of the decisions taken in an innovative change-oriented organization where managers are empowered.

Top-down strategic change

A number of approaches can be involved in drawing up the strategic plans for the organization, but changes in strategy are ultimately centralized decisions. This approach can be both popular and viable as long as the strategies which

The management of Change within *any* company usually fails for only one reason: an inadequate understanding on the part of top management of how much continuing effort – in years, not months – is needed from all senior managers on the basis of personal, engaged, hands-on commitment rather than just soothing memoranda. Without the willingness for this engagement, do not even think of embarking on the harnessing of Change to bring positive results within any company.

Sir Colin Marshall, Chairman, British Airways plc

are selected can be implemented effectively. It was mentioned earlier that resistance can be expected if managers who are charged with carrying out changes in strategy feel that there are flaws in the proposals. It is important to ensure that the appropriate level of consultation takes place during formulation.

Capable managers are needed throughout the organization to deal with operational issues, and the quality of the information systems which underpin the planning is a crucial issue. The approach is attractive to strategic leaders who are inclined more towards the analytical aspects of strategy than they are towards behavioural issues.

Quinn's incremental model

Whilst Quinn's model is another primarily top-down approach it suggests a high degree of political skill on the part of the strategic leader, who appreciates the difficulties involved in implementing change. These skills are discussed in detail towards the end of the chapter.

Quinn (1988) argues that the hardest part of strategic management is implementation as transition and change impacts structures and systems, organization culture and power relationships. The strategic leader is critical in the process because he or she is either personally or ultimately responsible for the proposed changes in strategy, and for establishing the structure and processes within the organization.

Quinn's approach is as follows.

❑ The strategic leader will develop his or her own informal information and communication channels, both within and external to the organization, and will draw on this as much as using the formal systems.
❑ The strategic leader must generate **awareness** of the desired change with the appropriate managers within the organization. This involves communication and cultural issues.
❑ The strategic leader will seek to legitimize the new approach or strategy, lending it authority, if not, at this stage, credibility.
❑ He or she will then seek to gather key supporters for the approach or strategy.
❑ The new strategy may be floated as a minor tactical change to minimize resistance, and possibly keep the ultimate aim unclear. Alternatively the strategy may be floated as a trial or experiment.
❑ Opposition will be removed by, for example, ensuring that supporters chair key committees, and that stubborn opponents are moved to other parts of the organization.
❑ The strategy will be flexible so that incremental changes can be made in the light of the trials. There will be a strong element of learning by doing, so that any unexpected resource limitations, such as a shortage of key skills, will be highlighted.

❑ Support for the change will harden.
❑ The proposals will be crystallized and focused.
❑ Finally, the proposed changes will be formalized and ideally accepted within the organization. This should involve honest evaluation and attempts to improve upon the original ideas. It is particularly important to look ahead and consider how the new strategy might be developed further in the future.

Quinn's approach incorporates an appreciation of the likely impact upon people and the culture, and pragmatically searches for a better way of doing things once the decision to change has been made

Empowerment and change

To sustain a culture of change, employees must be empowered, but, as we saw in Chapter 12, not everyone is comfortable with added responsibilities and accountability. They are risk-averse, and again, resistance can be expected. It would seem inevitable that change-focused organizations will be happy to see such people leave, for while they stay they constitute barriers to change. They actively seek to prevent changes which may be essential for the future of the business. Unfortunately many of these people are likely to be very experienced and knowledgeable; their underlying expertise is valuable. Their expertise might also be useful – at least temporarily – to a competitor, and for this reason there may be a reluctance to release them.

Empowerment cannot succeed without an appropriate reward system to support it. Financial rewards will remain important, but they are not the complete answer. People must not be rewarded simply because they are holding down a particular job or position; part of their pay must be based on their measured contribution. Outstanding performers must be rewarded for their continuing efforts, and, of course, as organizations are increasingly 'flattened', with fewer layers in the hierarchy, a series of promotions no longer provides the answer.

Empowered middle managers are critically important for the effective management of strategic change, but all-too-often they are hostile because of fear and uncertainty in a culture of blame. Mistakes are not tolerated, and people are reluctant to take risks. Such managers are portrayed as villains, when really it is the organizational climate which is making them victims. Change and empowerment will only happen when managers are not afraid to 'unfreeze and learn'.

Organizations can benefit from developing people, building their abilities and self-confidence and then providing them with greater stimulation and challenge. Success will yield the opportunity to take on more responsibility. Initially the organization motivates them but they become increasingly self-motivated. Part of their reward package is their enhanced reputation in a successful business, together with increased informal power and influence. They develop the ability to foster and champion innovation and change – strategic changes which they *own*.

A culture of innovation and gradual but continuous change will impact mainly on competitive and functional strategies – the lowest two levels of the hierarchy featuredin Table 22.1 earlier. Clearly they also support corporate strategic changes which may themselves be emergent in nature or the outcome of either a visionary or a planning mode of strategy creation.

Discontinuous change and strategic regeneration

We have seen how powerful environmental issues such as deregulation, globalization, lower trade barriers and economic recessions have combined in the 1990s to place enormous change pressures on companies. The individual significance of these issues will vary from year to year, but, in aggregate terms, the outcome is an increasingly turbulent and uncertain business environment for most organizations, private and public sector, manufacturing and service, large and small, profit-seeking and not-for-profit.

Companies have responded. Many have sought to manage their assets and strategic resources more efficiently and effectively – again the lowest two levels of the change hierarchy. Some have restructured; others have radically changed their processes through business process re-engineering.

However, continuous improvement to an organization's *competitive* capabilities, essential as it is, will not always be sufficient to meet these pressures.

Tom Peters (1992) argues that for some companies the challenge is 'not just about a *programme* of change ... strategies and structures need to change perpetually'. Peter Drucker (1993) agrees and contends that 'every organization must prepare to abandon everything it does'. Both authors are implying wholesale corporate renewal or reinvention, which we have earlier termed strategic regeneration.

Successful regeneration requires both an external and an internal focus. Externally organizations must search for new product, new service and new market opportunities, working with suppliers, distributors and customers to redefine markets and industries. Internally structures, management styles and cultures must be capable of creating and delivering these products and services. Innovation is dependent on processes and people. Strategic awareness, information management and change are critically important if the organization is to outperform its competitors.

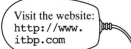

Visit the website:
http://www.
itbp.com

Achieving this position may require *simultaneous* changes to corporate strategies and perspectives, organization structures and styles of management. In order to implement strategic regeneration, Goss *et al.* (1993) insist that companies must be able to change their *context* – 'the underlying assumptions and invisible premises on which their decisions and actions are based'. Their 'inner nature or being' must be altered. Managers must learn how to think strategically, and be open to new paradigms and perspectives. The requirement is that they change 'what the company is' and not simply the things it does. Companies are being challenged with changing all the levels of the change hierarchy simultaneously, a huge and complex task for any organization.

High street banks, for example, have been forced to adopt a new paradigm. They have recognized that they are not simply a home for secure savings and current accounts, but diversified financial services institutions. The changes – visible to all of us who are bank customers – have clearly involved strategies, structure and culture, and they have proved painful.

Incremental change at the competitive and functional level, trying harder and searching for improvements, must appear to offer an easier, less painful route. The fundamental question is: alone, is it enough to meet the strategic demands of the contemporary business environment?

Some of the international companies featured in this book have clearly attempted to tackle these important challenges. British Airways (BA) realized in the 1980s that, contrary to much popular opinion at the time, airline customers are willing to pay extra for service. The challenge lies in defining that service and differentiating successfully. BA has consequently changed its strategies, structure and culture and become one of the most profitable airlines in the world. The changes at British Airways have proved successful, but they are not yet complete. The alliances described in Case 9.4, in particular the strategic investment in US Air, have yet to become as profitable as the core business; and in June 1996 BA and American Airlines announced an important, new code-sharing and ticketing alliance, but it would be subject to approval from the British and US regulatory authorities.

General Electric (GE) of the USA is another example. The regeneration philosophy and programme at GE is described in Case 22.3. General Electric has successfully reduced waste and improved efficiencies and competitive strategies. The first step of basically maintaining output levels whilst reducing assets (thus improving return on capital employed) has been achieved; the future challenge lies in re-generating the company and creating new growth from the reduced size. This subtle change of emphasis requires new values. The culture becomes one of challenging at the frontiers of technology and competition – discontinuous changes to create new futures ahead of competitors. It is different from a culture of benchmarking, productivity gains, process re-engineering and continuous improvement.

Hamel (1994) contends strategic regeneration needs vision and persever-ance. Companies must invest resources in an attempt to set the new 'competi-tive high ground' first by changing the key success factors. This inevitably implies time and risk, and it must be a managed and understood process. Speculative investment in the long-term must be risky because *spending pre-cedes understanding;* companies are heading into unknown territory. How-ever, companies which choose to avoid the risk, and rely instead on monitoring and copying competitors (such that *understanding precedes spending*) may be caught out.

Hamel cites three important barriers to effective strategic regeneration. First, too many senior managers in an industry have related, often industry-specific, backgrounds, and this inhibits their creative thinking. Secondly, there are political pressures to maintain the status quo from managers who feel threatened personally – an issue we look at next. Thirdly, the sheer difficulty of creating new competitive strategies in industries which are changing dynamically, continuously and chaotically.

Organizational development and innovation

The basic underlying theme of organizational development (OD) is that developing an appropriate organizational culture will generate desirable changes in strategy.

Beckhard (1969) defined OD as effort which is 'planned, organization-wide, and managed from the top, designed to increase organizational effectiveness and health through planned interventions in the organization's processes, using behavioural science knowledge'.

OD is, in essence, planned cultural change. The model which has been used to provide the structure for this book shows strategic leadership and culture as being central to both strategic awareness and decision making. The appreciation

Case 22.3
STRATEGIC REGENERATION AT GENERAL ELECTRIC

John F (Jack) Welch became Chief Executive Officer at General Electric (GE) in 1981. His structural vision was summarized earlier, in Case 19.4. This case describes 'one of the most far reaching programmes of innovation in business history'.

The programme involves three stages:

(i)   Awakening   the realization of the need for change.

(ii) Envisioning   establishing a new vision and harnessing resources.

(iii) Re-architecting the design and construction of a new organization.

❑ Although Welch is the identified strategic leader, several committed senior managers worked together to drive through the cultural changes.

❑ GE has been restructured, and clear progress has been made ... but the process of change continues. The implementation of the programme is not yet complete.

GE in the early 1980s – the need for change
The company had sound assets, reflected in a strong balance sheet, but it was seen as bureaucratic and heavily focused on the USA. It was not 'technologically advanced' and it clearly needed a more international perspective.

Specific problems were diagnosed:

❑ Revenue growth was slow. GE's core business (electrical equipment) was particularly slow.

❑ As a result, expensive investments were creating cash flow problems.

❑ Poor productivity was causing low profit margins.

❑ Innovation was limited.

❑ Decision making was slow.

❑ Negative internal politics was rife.

Awakening
Welch realized his first challenge was to determine which managers offered the greatest potential as 'transformational leaders', agents of discontinuous change.

He then sought to clarify and articulate the extent of the need for change, focusing on the above weaknesses. Resistance took three forms:

❑ Technical – A reliance on existing bureaucratic systems and a fear of the unknown; a distrust of international expansion.

❑ Political – A desire to protect existing power bases, especially where the strategic value of the particular business was declining.

❑ Cultural – an unwillingness to accept competitive weaknesses – over-confidence from past successes.

Changes
❑ Welch forced people to benchmark competitors' performance standards and achievements, rather than rely only on internal measures and budgets.

❑ He also took control of external corporate communications and

❑ Radically changed GE's approach to management training and development. Rigid rules and procedures about how things should be done were abolished.

Envisioning
A new vision was developed gradually during the mid- to late 1980s, and it finally became encapsulated in a matrix. Highlights of the new vision are featured in Table 22.2 opposite.

Welch saw the technical, political and cultural systems as three strands of a rope which must be changed and re-aligned together.

Re-architecting
At the heart of the vision is an 'organization without boundaries' and with an emphasis on internal and external linkages and architecture. Information must flow freely. People must be in a position – and willing – to act quickly. 'A large organization with the speed, flexibility and self-confidence of a small one.'

Continued

Table 22.2   Highlights of GE's corporate vision

	Strategy	Structure	Management style
Technical	Focus on market (segments) where the company can be No. 1 and No. 2

Prioritize high growth industries | Decentralized

Foster the sharing of best practises, pull down internal boundaries | Different reward systems for different businesses, dependent on needs

Continuous training and development |
| **Political** | Foster internal and external alliances to harness synergy potential | Flatter, open structure to remove power bases

Cross-function and cross-business development teams

Empowerment to lowest levels of management | Flexible reward systems

'360 degree evaluations' from superiors, peers and subordinates |
| **Cultural** | Speedy change to strategies

Intrapreneurial, innovative, incremental and adaptive change – as a result of – learning from upward, downward and lateral communications | Corporate values but individual business cultures and styles | Track attitudes and values

Commitment to customers and quality – and outperforming competitors |

A number of boundaries had to be removed as part of the implementation process:

(i) Vertical/hierarchical. Management layers were removed. Welch introduced performance incentives for many more managers and employees; in the past GE had focused on only senior executives.
(ii) Horizontal/internal walls. Cross-functional project teams were created.
(iii) External. There was a new emphasis on the whole supply or added value chain; alliances were forged with suppliers; customer satisfaction levels were tracked.

Removing these boundaries clearly required radical changes to the ways in which people worked together, made decisions and carried out tasks. Welch believed the changes must be inspired from the top and that any senior managers who resisted the new style 'would have to go'.

Adapted from: Tichy, NM (1993), Revolutionize your company, *Fortune*, 13 December.

In 1995, NBC, a General Electric subsidiary, was anxious to win the television rights for the Sydney Olympic Games in the year 2000.

Pre-empting its competitors, NBC:

❑ Bid jointly for the Sydney games and the next Winter Olympics in Salt Lake City.
❑ Presented the International Olympic Committee (IOC) with take-it-or-leave-it figure before any bids had been invited.
❑ Included both cable and network television in its bid.

When the idea (and the huge sum of money involved) were put to CEO Jack Welch, he took just half an hour to back the proposal. NBC executives spent the next 48 hours flying around the world to place their proposals before key IOC members; a deal was agreed and signed, all within a week.

The IOC commented that the reaction of NBC's rivals afterwards was one of 'disappointment but a reluctant admiration for the initiative NBC took'.

by managers of the effectiveness of the current match between resources and the environment, their ability and willingness to make adaptive changes to capitalize on environmental changes, and the formulation and implementation of major changes in corporate strategy are all influenced by the culture of the organization and the style of strategic leadership. Hence it is crucial for the strategic leader to develop the appropriate culture for the mission and purpose he or she wishes to pursue. OD helps to develop a co-operative and innovative culture.

The aim of OD is to establish mechanisms which encourage managers to be more open, participative and co-operative when dealing with problems and making decisions. Specifically the objectives are:

❏ improved organizational effectiveness and, as a result
❏ higher profits and better customer service (in its widest context)
❏ more effective decision making
❏ the ability to make and manage changes more smoothly
❏ increased innovation
❏ reduced conflict and destructive political activity
❏ greater trust and collaboration between managers and business units.

Organized OD programmes involve activities such as team-building and collaborative decision making, bringing managers together and encouraging them to share and discuss problems and issues. The thinking is that when managers learn more about the problems which face the organization as a whole, and about other managers who may have different technical or functional perspectives, they become more aware of the impact of the decisions they make. In addition, if they collaborate and share responsibilities, they are more likely to feel committed to joint decisions.

Whilst one aim is to change the attitudes and behaviour of people in organizations, OD can also allow and encourage the same people to initiate and implement changes through their discussions. Establishing the programmes is likely to involve outside experts who can be seen as objective. OD programmes are not normally a response to specific problems but rather a general approach to the management of change in the longer term.

Given that one idea behind OD is collaboration and collective responsibility, a key theme is the reduction of conflict between managers, functions, business units or divisions within the organization. A reduction in the use of manipulative styles of management, or dysfunctional political activity, whereby managers pursue personal goals in preference to the wider needs of the organization, is also implied. Functional and dysfunctional political activity is explored in the last section of this chapter where we look at the bases and uses of power by managers.

The essential pre-requisite for an effective change of direction is to create a climate throughout the organization where change is regarded positively. Professor Hague, when he was at Manchester Business School, made the following remark which I have always remembered: 'The successful manager will expect and understand change; the outstanding manager will anticipate and create it.'

Once the right climate exists, change must be preceded and accompanied by effective and honest communication, meaningful consultation and sound decision making. It is not easy and requires genuine top management commitment.

Tom W Cain, ex-Director, Human Resources, The Channel Tunnel Group Ltd

Power and influence: introductory comments

The management of change requires that managers have the requisite power to implement decisions and that they are able to exert influence. There are several bases of power, both organizational and individual, which constitute resources for managers. The processes they adopt for utilizing these power bases, their styles of management, determine their success in influencing others. The ability of managers to exert power and influence is manifested in a number of ways, including:

- ❏ budgets
- ❏ rewards
- ❏ organization structure and positions
- ❏ promotions and management development
- ❏ information systems
- ❏ symbols of power and status.

Power and politics

Managers who regularly attempt to get things done, both with and through other people, and introduce changes have the problem of generating agreement, consent or at least compliance with what should be done, how and when. Typically opinions and perspectives will differ. Disagreements may or may not be significant, and can range from the polite and friendly to those involving threats and coercion. Each side, quite simply, is attempting to influence the conduct of the other. In this section we consider the power resources which managers are able to use and how they might use them.

Checkland (1986) defines organizational politics as the process by which differing interests reach accommodation. These accommodations relate to the dispositions and use of power and influence, and behaviour which is not prescribed by the policies established within the organization. It will be shown later that political activity by managers in order to influence others, and ensure that their decisions and strategies are carried out, is essential. Politics can be legitimate and positive, although it can also be more negative and illegitimate. In the latter case managers are seeking to influence others in order to achieve their personal goals. This is often described as machiavellianism and is discussed at the end of this section.

The relative power of the organization

The need for change is affected by the relative power and influence of external stakeholders in relation to the organization. Powerful customers, powerful suppliers, and changes in government legislation would all represent potential threats and demands for change. In turn, the management and implementation of change is affected by the relative power of the organization. Some proposed strategies can be implemented because the organization possesses the appropriate power to acquire the resources which are needed and to generate consumer demand. Others may not be feasible.

At the same time the decisions taken within organizations concerning changes of corporate, competitive and functional strategies are influenced by the disposition of relative power between functions, business units or divisions, and the ways in which managers seek to use power and influence.

Internal and external sources of power are discussed further in the Key Reading 22.1 based on the work of Mintzberg (1983).

Political activity

Farrell and Petersen (1982) classify political activity in terms of three dimensions:

❑ legitimate or illegitimate
❑ vertical or lateral
❑ internal or external to the organization.

For example, a complaint or suggestion by an employee directly to a senior manager, bypassing an immediate superior, would be classified as legitimate, vertical and internal. Discussions with fellow managers from other companies within an industry would be legitimate, lateral and external – unless they involved any illegal activities such as price fixing. Informal communications and agreements between managers are again legitimate, whilst threats or attempts at sabotage are clearly illegitimate.

Power and politics are key aspects of strategy implementation because they can enable managers to be proactive and to influence their environment rather than being dominated and manipulated by external events. The issues affect managers at all levels of the organization and decisions concerning both internal and external changes.

The bases of power

Seven bases of manager power were introduced and described in Chapter 4: reward; coercive; legitimate; personal; expert; information; and connection. The extent to which managers and other employees in organizations use each of these sources of power is a major determinant of corporate culture

Reward and coercive power (the ability to sanction and punish) are two major determinants of employee motivation, and both can be very significant strategically. Thompson and Strickland (1981) argue that motivation is brought about primarily by the reward and punishment systems in the organization; and Blanchard and Johnson (1982) suggest that effective management involves three key aspects: establishing clear objectives for employees, and rewarding and sanctioning performance against objectives appropriately. Strategic leaders who dominate their organizations and coerce their senior managers can be effective, particularly when the organization is experiencing decline and major changes in strategy are urgently required

Legitimate power is determined primarily by the organization structure, and consequently changes of structure will affect the power, influence and significance of different business units, functions and individual managers.

Personal power, which can lead to the commitment of others to the power holder, can be very important in incremental changes. Managers who are supported and trusted by their colleagues and subordinates will find it easier to introduce and implement changes.

Expert power can also be useful in persuading others that proposed changes in strategy are feasible and desirable. Whilst expert power may not be real, and instead be power gained from reputation, it is unlikely that managers who genuinely lack expertise can be successful without other power bases. Moreover, expertise is job related. An expert specialized accountant, for example, may lose

Visit the website:
http://www.
itbp.com

KEY READING 22.1

INTERNAL AND EXTERNAL SOURCES OF POWER

Mintzberg (1983) contends that it is essential to consider both internal and external sources of power, and their relative significance, when assessing the demands for, and feasibility of, certain strategic changes.

The organization's stakeholders will vary in terms of their relative power and the ways in which they exert influence. The interests of the owners of the firm, for example, are legally represented by the board of directors. Whilst large institutional shareholders may exert considerable influence over certain decisions, many private shareholders will take no active part. Employees are represented by external trade unions, who again may or may not exert influence.

The power relationships between the firm and its stakeholders are determined by the importance and scarcity of the resource in question. The more essential and limited the supply of the resource, the greater the power the resource provider has over the firm. According to Mintzberg these external power groups may be focused and their interests pulled together by a dominant power, or they may be fragmented.

Where there are very strong external influences, the organization may seek to establish close co-operation or mutual dependence, or attempt to reduce its dependence on the power source. The relationship between Marks and Spencer and many of its suppliers is a good example of mutual dependence of this nature. Marks and Spencer have encouraged many of their clothing suppliers to invest in the latest technology for design and manufacturing in order that they can both succeed against international competition. Marks and Spencer are typically the largest customer of their suppliers, buying substantial quantities as long as both demand and quality are maintained. However, it is important that their suppliers are aware of fashion changes because they bear the risk of over-production and changes in taste.

Internal power is linked to the structure and configuration of the organization. Following from the issues discussed in Chapter 20, it is clear that the relative power of the strategic apex, middle management, operators, technocrats and support staff needs to be assessed.

Internal power is manifested in four ways:

❑ the personal control system of the strategic leadership
❑ rules, policies and procedures
❑ political activities external to these two factors
❑ cultural ideologies which influence decision makers.

External and internal power sources combine to determine a dominant source of power at any time, and Mintzberg suggests six possibilities.

❑ A **key external source**, such as a bank or supplier, or possibly the government as, say, a key buyer of defence equipment – the objectives of the source would normally be clearly stated and understood.
❑ **The operation of the organization structure**, and the strategies and activities of general and functional managers who are allocated the scarce resources: the relative power of business units is influenced by the market demand for their products and services, but generally external sources exert indirect rather than direct influence; functional managers can enjoy power if they are specialists and their skills are in short supply.
❑ **Strong central leadership.**
❑ **Ideologies**: certain organizations, such as charities or volunteer organizations, are often dominated by the underlying ideologies related to helping others.
❑ **Professional constraints**: accountants' and solicitors' practices, for example, have established codes of professional practice which dictate and influence behaviour. On occasions this can raise interesting issues for decision makers. A frequently used example is the television journalist or news editor working for the BBC or ITN and able to influence reporting strategies and policies. When assessing sensitive issues does the person see himself or herself as a BBC or ITN employee or as a professional journalist, and do the two perspectives coincide or conflict?
❑ **Active conflict** between power sources seeking dominance: whilst this can involve either or both internal and external sources it is likely to be temporary, as organizations cannot normally survive prolonged conflict.

The dominant source of power becomes a key feature of the organizational culture, and a major influence on manager behaviour and decision making.

Source of the basic arguments: Mintzberg, H (1983) *Power In and Around Organizations*, Prentice-Hall.

expert power temporarily if he or she is promoted to general manager. Consequently an important tactic in the management of change is to ensure that those managers who are perceived to be expert in the activity or function concerned are supportive of the proposed changes.

Information and related **connection power** are becoming increasingly significant as information technology grows in importance.

Invisible power

These seven power bases are all visible sources. There is, in addition, invisible power. One source of invisible power is the way in which an issue or proposal is presented, which can influence the way it is dealt with. Managers who appreciate the objectives, perspectives and concerns of their colleagues will present their ideas in ways that are likely to generate their support rather than opposition. Second, membership of informal, but influential, coalitions or groups of managers can be a source of power, particularly if the people involved feel dependent on each other. Third, information which would create opposition to a decision or change proposal might be withheld. In the same way that access to key information can be a positive power source, the ability to prevent other people obtaining information can be either a positive or a negative source of power.

Lukes (1974) has identified three further important aspects of power, namely:

- ❏ the ability to prevent a decision, or not make one
- ❏ the ability to control the issues on which decisions are to be made
- ❏ the ability to ensure that certain issues are kept off agendas.

The use of such power by individuals can inhibit changes which might be in the long-term best interests of the organization.

Political effectiveness

Hayes (1984) contends that effective managers appreciate clearly what support they will need from other people if proposed changes are to be carried through, and what they will have to offer in return. In such cases they reach agreements (or accommodations) which provide mutual advantages. It is important for the organization as a whole that general and functional managers are effective and politically competent if personal objectives are to be restrained and undesirable changes, championed by individual managers, prevented. Problems can occur where some managers are politically effective and able to implement change, and others are relatively ineffective and reach agreements with other managers whereby their personal interests, and the interests of the organization, are adversely affected.

Allen *et al.* (1979) and Dixon (1982) point out that certain sources of personal power are essential for managers who are effective politically and able to influence others. In addition they suggest certain tactics for managing change. These are featured in Table 22.3. It is important that managers are perceived by others to have expertise and ability, and it is useful if they have a reputation built on past successes. Depending on the relative power of outside stakeholders, such as suppliers or customers, external credibility can also prove valuable. It is essential to have access to information and to other powerful individuals and groups of managers.

Bases of personal power		
Expertise	Particularly significant where the skill is in scarce supply It is possible to use mobility, and the threat of leaving, to gain support for certain changes of strategy – again dependent upon the manager's personal importance to the firm	**Table 22.3** Political power bases and tactics
Assessed stature	A reputation for being a 'winner' or a manager who can obtain results. Recent successes are most relevant	
Credibility	Particularly credibility with external power sources, such as suppliers or customers	
Political access	Being well known around the organization and able to influence key groups of managers	
Control over information	Internal and external sources Information can be used openly and honestly or withheld and used selectively – consequently it is crucial to know the reliability of the source	
Group support	In managing and implementing change it is essential to have the support of colleagues and fellow managers	

Political tactics to obtain results

Develop liaisons	As mentioned above, it is important to develop and maintain both formal and informal contacts with other managers, functions, and divisions Again it is important to include those managers who are most powerful
Present a conservative image	It can be disadvantageous to be seen as too radical an agent of change
Diffuse opposition	Conflicts need to be brought out into the open and differences of opinion aired rather than kept hidden. Divide and rule can be a useful strategy
Trade-off and compromise	In any proposal or suggestion for change it is important to consider the needs of other people whose support is required
'Strike while the iron is hot'	Successful managers should build on successes and reputation quickly
Research	Information is always vital to justify and support proposals
Use a neutral cover	Radical changes, or those which other people might perceive as a threat to them, can sometimes be usefully disguised and initiated as minor changes. This is linked to the next point
Limit communication	A useful tactic can be to unravel change gradually in order to contain possible opposition
Withdraw strategically	If things are going wrong, and especially if the changes are not crucial, it can be a wise tactic on occasions to withdraw – at least temporarily

Politically successful managers understand organizational processes and they are sensitive to the needs of others.

Effective political action brings about desirable and successful changes in organizations – it is functional. Negative political action is dysfunctional, and can enable manipulative managers to pursue their personal objectives against the better interests of the organization.

The strategic leader needs to be an effective politician.

Source: Allen, RW, Madison, DL, Porter, LW, Renwick, PA and Mayes, BT (1979) Organizational politics: tactics and characteristics of its actors. *California Management Review,* 22, fall; Dixon, M (1982) The world of office politics, *Financial Times,* 10 November.

It can be a disadvantage for a manager to be perceived as a radical agent of change, as this can arouse fear and uncertainty, possibly leading to opposition, in others. As discussed earlier, it can sometimes be valuable to implement a change of strategy gradually and incrementally, allowing people to make adaptive changes as the learning experience develops. At the same time it is important to ensure that opposition is manifested and brought out into the open rather than being allowed to develop without other people being aware.

Managers who are effective and successful politically, and able to implement their decisions and proposed changes, will generally appreciate and understand organizational processes and be sensitive to the needs of others. It is extremely useful if the strategic leader is an able politician. The type and incidence of incremental changes in strategies throughout the organization will also be affected by the political ability of managers. Those with ability will be instrumental in introducing changes. Where the strategic leader wishes to encourage managers to be adaptive and innovative it is important to consider the political ability of the managers concerned. Political ability relates to the use of power and influence in the most appropriate way in particular circumstances. This is the subject of the next section.

Uses of power and influence

MacMillan (1978) argues that introducing and implementing change frequently requires the use of power and influence, which he examines in terms of the control of situations and the ability to change people's intentions. Where a person wishes to exercise control over the behaviour of other people, either within the organization or external to it, he or she has two basic options. First, he can **structure the situation** so that others comply with his wishes; second, by communicating with other people, he can seek to change their perceptions so that they see things differently and decide to do as he suggests. In other words he succeeds in **changing their intentions.** Both of these approaches are categorized as strategies of manipulation.

Where a manager is concentrating on structuring the situation he or she is using certain power bases as enabling resources; where he or she is attempting to change intentions he or she is seeking to use influence. Power, in particular personal power, is again important as a source of influence.

The outcome from both the situational and intentional approaches can be either positive or negative. When the effect is positive the other people feel that they are better off as a result of the changes; the effect is negative if they feel worse off.

MacMillan identifies four tactics in relation to these points.

Inducement Inducement implies an ability to control the situation, and the outcome is perceived as beneficial by others involved. A large retail organization with several stores might require managers to be mobile as a condition of their employment, and reward them with improved status, salary increases and relocation expenses every time they move. The situation is controlled; ideally the managers concerned feel positive about the moves.

Coercion The situation is again controlled, but the outcome is perceived negatively. In the above situation the same managers might be threatened with no further promotions unless they agreed to certain moves within the company.

Persuasion The manager does not try to control or change the situation but argues that the other people can or will benefit by behaving in certain ways. The desired outcome is positive. People might be persuaded to agree to a change which is not immediately desirable by suggestions that future rewards will be forthcoming.

Obligation Obligation is another intentional tactic, but the outcome is negative. People are persuaded to behave in a certain way by being made to feel that they have an obligation. It might be suggested that people

❑ owe the company something for the money that has been invested in their previous training, or
❑ owe particular managers a favour for something which has happened in the past, or
❑ are obligated to the group of people that they have been working with for some years and should not let them down.

In particular cases, individual managers may or may not have a number of alternative tactics to select from. Tactics which have positive outcomes must normally be preferable to those which cause negative feelings if both are available and likely to yield the desired results. At times managers whose power bases are limited and who need speedy results may have little option but to coerce or obligate people. Kanter (1983) emphasizes that successful managers of change situations are able to keep their power invisible both during and after the change. Participation in the change is then perceived to stem from commitment or conviction rather than from power being exercised over people. Kanter contends that it is very important for middle managers in organizations to be skilful in managing change as they implement the detailed strategies, and that it is important for strategic leaders to ensure that they have support from their middle managers for the overall corporate strategy.

Organizational politics and culture

We have seen earlier that culture broadly encapsulates manifest actions and behaviours and underlying beliefs, and that effective cultural change must include both. Where this happens, there will be willing support for, and compliance with, the change. Without a change in beliefs, compliance will be reluctant. Strong, political managers who oppose the changes will show either covert or even overt non-compliance, their choice reflecting their style and power.

Bartlett and Ghoshal (1995) argue that the radical and forced downsizing of the early 1990s has left many companies with a context of 'compliance, control, contract and constraint'. Behaviours have changed, but not beliefs; elements of the old culture remain to create confusion. The challenge for these companies is one of creativity and innovation; they must find ways of adding new values for competitive advantage, which will require a context of support, trust and liberation, and a willingness to accept stretching objectives, alongside appropriate control disciplines.

Organizational politics and ethics

It is clear that managers can use political behaviour both for and against the best interests of the organization; at the same time, they can also behave either ethically or unethically. Positive and ethical behaviour is required to satisfy all the stakeholders effectively; negative politics, whilst ethical, implies that internal stakeholders (maybe even individual managers and functions) receive priority over external stakeholders. Positive politicking which is unethical may well appear successful in the short term, but possibly with a long-term downside risk. Where negative politics combine with unethical behaviour, there is likely to be corruption.

Machiavellianism

Machiavellianism is the term often used to describe coercive management tactics. Marriott (1908), translating Machiavelli's book *The Prince* written in the sixteenth century, uses the expression to cover 'the ruthless use of power, particularly coercive power, and manipulation to attain personal goals'. Whilst coercive power can be used effectively by managers it may not always be easy to justify, especially if other alternatives are available. Coercion may not be practical on a repeat basis; and any fear of threats not carried out quickly recedes.

Jay (1967), however, contends that Machiavelli also offers much useful advice for ethical managers. Basing his arguments on Machiavelli's views on strategies and tactics for annexing and ruling nations, Jay argues that chief executive strategic leaders should concentrate their efforts outside the organization, developing and strengthening the strategic perspective. In order for them to feel able to do this, the internal structure and systems must be sound and effective, and managers must be supportive of proposals from the top. General and functional managers should be free to operate and feel able to make certain changes, but their overall power should be contained. They should exercise leadership, which is based on power. This power yields the freedom to decide how things should be done. Managers, though, should be afraid to pursue personal goals against the interest of the organization as a whole. Achieving this requires a clear awareness of what is happening throughout the organization and the appropriate punishment of offenders. Successful managers, of course, should be rewarded.

Pearce and DeNisi (1983) stress that most organizations are managed partially by informal coalitions or groupings of managers superimposed on the formal structure. It is particularly important that managers in key positions in the organization, those in charge of important resources or responsible for products upon which the profits or reputation of the organization depends, are

---

Machiavelli recommended that vanquished foes should be eliminated, but counselled that quite often only the King or Chief needs to be sacrificed; those spared will soon fall into line through fear.

Research into hostile takeovers and acquisitions in the UK between 1990 and 1994 shows that within one year of the take-over 70% of the chairmen of the acquired businesses had left; 57% of the chief executives left within two years.

known to be committed and loyal to the strategic leader. Moreover, any informal and powerful coalitions which develop should also be supportive. To achieve both these it may be appropriate for the strategic leader to remove or switch senior managers occasionally as a reminder of his or her overall power. This is particularly likely to happen after an acquisition, during a re-structuring exercise, or on the appointment of a new strategic leader.

Strategic coalitions can be a major force behind strategy formation, especially where the overall strategic leader is relatively weak. An effective leader will therefore seek to use coalitions which already exist, and encourage the formation of other loyal ones.

In considering the feasibility of changes and how to implement them, it is very important to examine the underlying political abilities and behaviour within the firm: who has power, how it is manifested, how it is used. Without taking these into account, implementation is likely to prove hazardous.

Checklist of key terms and concepts

You should feel confident that you understand the following terms and ideas:

- ★ Types of change situation
- ★ Lewin's force field analysis
- ★ Unfreezing, changing and refreezing behaviour
- ★ Quinn's model of incremental change
- ★ Strategic regeneration
- ★ Organizational development
- ★ Organizational politics
- ★ Visible and invisible power
- ★ Machiavellianism.

Summary

In this chapter we have explored a number of issues involved in the effective management of change. These are synthesized in Figure 22.3. It has been emphasized that, in volatile environments in particular, organizations face constant pressures for change. Some organizations are proactive and seek to manage their environments; others are reactive and changes are forced on them. However powerful the economic forces for change, people who are affected by the proposed changes are likely to resist them. The management of change is influenced by the relative power of external forces and of managers and groups of managers inside the organization. Power may arise in a number of ways and different managers are more able than others to use their power to influence and affect the behaviour of others.

Specifically we have:

- described the major forces for change and types of change situation, and the most common reasons why people resist change
- summarized six ways of overcoming resistance
- considered Lewin's work on the forces for and against change, and his arguments concerning the stages involved in achieving permanent changes in behaviour
- discussed the five basic approaches to the management of change summarized by Bourgeois and Brodwin, exploring in greater depth the notion of top-down strategic change, Quinn's incremental model, empowerment and continuous change, discontinuous change and strategic regeneration; and organizational development and innovation
- highlighted the significant role of power and political activity
- reviewed the seven bases of power introduced in Chapter 4 and introduced the idea of invisible power
- considered the relative importance of external and internal power
- discussed how managers might seek to be effective politically, and how power and influence can be used to achieve results with either positive or negative connotations
- concluded briefly with some ideas developed from the sixteenth-century writings of Machiavelli.

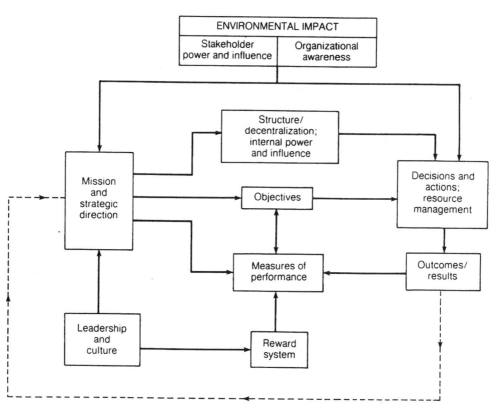

Figure 22.3   The strategic change process.

Questions and research assignments

Text related

1 Describe an event where you have personally experienced forces for change, and discuss any forces which were used to resist the change. What tactics were adopted on both sides?

2 Describe a strategic leader (any level in an organization of your choice) whom you consider to be a powerful person.

   What types of power does he or she possess?

3 Describe a manager whom you believe is successful at using organizational politics. On what observations and experiences are you basing your decision? How might you measure political effectiveness and the elements within it?

4 As a manager, what are your personal power bases? How politically effective are you? How could you increase your overall power and improve your effectiveness?

Library and assignment based

5 Select an industry or company and ascertain the forces which have brought about changes in the last ten years. How proactive/reactive have the companies been, and with what levels of success?

6 Analyse the news broadcasts of both the BBC and ITN and evaluate whether their reporting of industrial and business news is similar or dissimilar. Are they reporting to inform or to persuade about, say, the merits or demerits of government policy? To what extent are they constrained by government?

Recommended further reading

For a short and straightforward introduction to the management of change, see Plant, R (1989) *Managing Change and Making It Stick,* Fontana. A more detailed introduction can be found in Basil, DC and Cook, CW (1983) *The Management of Change,* McGraw-Hill. In addition Mintzberg (1983) and Argyris, C (1985) *Strategy, Change and Defensive Routines,* Pitman, are useful general texts.

Readers who are specifically interested in organizational development are referred to Beckhard R (1969) and Schein, EH and Bennis, WG (1967) *Personal and Organisational Change Through Group Methods*, John Wiley.

MacMillan IC (1978) provides a useful perspective on politics and change. Jay's book *Management and Machiavelli* (originally published in 1967, and reissued recently) is also thought provoking on this topic.

References

Allen, RW, Madison, DL, Porter, LW, Renwick PA and Mayes, BT (1979) Organisational politics: tactics and characteristics of its actors, *California Management Review,* **22,** fall.

Bartlett, C and Ghoshal, S (1995) Rebuilding behavioural cotext: turn process re-engineering into people rejuvenation, *Sloan Management Review,* autumn.

Beckhard, R (1969) *Organisation Development: Strategies and Models,* Addison-Wesley.

Blanchard, K and Johnson, S (1982) *The One Minute Manager,* Morrow.

Bourgeois, LJ and Brodwin, DR (1984) Strategic implementation: five approaches to an elusive phenomenon, *Strategic Management Journal,* **5**.

Checkland, PB (1986) The politics of practice. Paper presented at the IIASA International Round-table 'The Art and Science of Systems Practice', November.

Daft, RL (1983) *Organisation Theory and Design,* West.

Dixon, M (1982) The world of office politics, *Financial Times,* 10 November.

Drucker, P (1993) *Managing in Turbulent Times*, Butterworth-Heinemann.

Eccles, T (1994) *Succeeding With Change*, McGraw-Hill.

Farrell, D and Petersen, JC (1982) Patterns of political behaviour in organisations, *The Academy of Management Review,* **7**(3), July.

Goss, T, Pascale, R and Athos, A (1993) The Reinvention roller coaster: risking the present for a powerful future, *Harvard Business Review*, November–December.

Hamel, G (1994), Competing for the Future, Economist Conference, London (June).

Hayes, J (1984) The politically competent manager, *Journal of General Management*, **10**(1), autumn.

Jay, A (1967) *Management and Machiavelli,* Holt, Rinehart & Winston.

Kanter, RM (1983) The middle manager as innovator. In *Strategic Management* (ed. RG Hamermesch), John Wiley.

Kotter, JP (1995) Why transformation efforts fail, *Harvard Business Review*, March–April.

Kotter, JP and Heskett, JL (1992) *Corporate Culture and Performance,* Free Press.

Kotter, JP and Schlesinger, LA (1979) Choosing strategies for change, *Harvard Business Review,* March–April.

Lewin, K (1947) Frontiers in group dynamics: concept, method and reality in social science, *Human Relations,* **1**.

Lewin, K (1951) *Field Theory in Social Sciences,* Harper & Row.

Lukes, S (1974) *Power: A Radical View,* Macmillan.

MacMillan, IC (1978) *Strategy Formulation: Political Concepts,* West.

Margerison, C and Smith, B (1989) Shakespeare and management: managing change, *Management Decision,* **27**(2).

Marriott, WK (1908) Translation into English of *The Prince* written by N Machiavelli in the 1500s.

Mintzberg, H (1983) *Power In and Around Organisations,* Prentice-Hall.

Pearce, JA and DeNisi, AS (1983) Attribution theory and strategic decision making: an application to coalition formation, *Academy of Management Journal,* **26**, March.

Peters, T (1989) Tomorrow's companies: new products, new markets, new competition, new thinking, *The Economist,* 4 March.

Peters, T (1992), *Liberation Management – Necessary Disorganization for the Nanosecond Nineties*, Macmillan.

Quinn, JB (1988) Managing strategies incrementally. In *The Strategy Process: Concepts, Contexts and Cases* (eds JB Quinn, H Mintzberg and RM James), Prentice-Hall.

Thompson, AA and Strickland, AJ (1981) *Strategy and Policy: Concept and Cases,* Business Publications.

Waterman, RH Jr (1987) *The Renewal Factor,* Bantam.

23
Final Thoughts

In these last few pages we attempt to synthesize the main ideas from this book in order to reinforce the key ideas.

Many organizations are now operating or competing in dynamic, turbulent, uncertain, 'chaotic' environments. This is partly the result of industries and markets becoming ever more global; it is also driven by continual improvements in technology, which, amongst other things, causes product, service and strategic life cycles to shorten. In turn this means organizations must act, react and change more quickly. Some of these changes will be continuous and emergent, as vigilant, responsive organizations seize opportunities and innovate ahead of their rivals. In 1996, for example, airlines in the USA began to exploit the potential of the Internet to help reduce the incidence of empty seats. No airline wants to discount prices whilst ever there is a chance of full-price ticket sales; but it is easy to hold out for too long and not fill aeroplanes – resulting in lost revenue which cannot be recouped. The Internet is being used by American Airlines to auction last-minute seats for both money and the air miles passengers have accumulated.

Don't forget to visit the website: http://www. itbp.com

Other changes will be discontinuous and imply changes in competitive paradigms. Technology can both create and destroy industries, markets and windows of opportunity; breakpoints – or switches to new competitive rules and agendas – happen increasingly frequently. Organizations cannot ignore this reality and the pressures they bring.

Selected organizations, such as Coca-Cola and Walt Disney, continue to survive these breakpoints – sometimes actually creating them – and, as a result, they thrive, grow and prosper. They are recognized around the world and they exploit their competencies and their reputation. They create E–V–R (environment–values–resources) congruency and sustain it with carefully managed change. Again in 1996 Levi Strauss, the leading manufacturer of jeans and other casual clothes, announced that if its cash flow was healthy, it intended to pay a bonus of one full year's salary to every employee as a celebration of the new millennium in the year 2000. Not only was this excellent publicity, it should generate employee commitment to the company for a number of years. These organizations are truly entrepreneurial, but they are exceptional. We can learn from their actions, strategies and behaviours, although it will remain difficult to fully explain all the reasons for their success. Simply attempting to copy their behaviour is not an adequate answer to the challenges facing organizations.

Other companies grow more steadily and uncertainly; they never seem to have the same command over their environment. But, nonetheless, they do survive, partly with innovation, partly with contingent reaction. Others survive for some period of time, but then decline as they lose E–V–R congruency. Some organizations only survive with a change of leadership, style and culture. And, of course, some businesses disappear every year, some to takeover, others to liquidation. There are also important lessons to be learnt from their relative demise.

In looking at strategic effectiveness and success, we can take two related, but distinct, perspectives. The first concerns success: what reasons lie behind the relative prosperity of our most successful organizations, those which continue to add value for their customers, differentiate their products and services, and control their costs? The second perspective concerns survival and environmental management: what factors distinguish a crisis-averse from a crisis-prone organization? The latter will typically lurch from problem to problem, difficulty to difficulty, crisis to crisis, never really managing its environment. It is fashionable, in my opinion, to talk about competitiveness, competitive advantage and success; it is less fashionable, but equally important – and in many cases, more relevant – to explore the issues behind crisis aversion. Too many organizations hover on the narrow line which separates survival from failure.

Strategic success

Figure 23.1 summarizes our earlier arguments about strategic competency and competitive success. Organizations must add value – and continue to find new ways of adding fresh value – for their customers. They achieve this by developing, changing and exploiting core technological competencies. This exploitation involves organizational processes and capabilities, together with strong linkages with other companies in the supply chain, in order to create differentiation and effective cost control. The situation is always fluid; organizations cannot assume that currently successful products, services and competitive

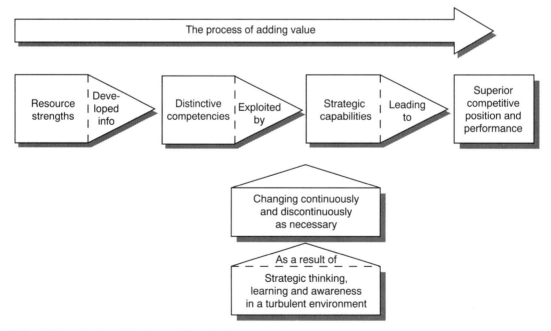

Figure 23.1　Adding value for sustained competitive advantage.

strategies will be equally successful in the future. They must be changed at appropriate times. In turn, this requires competency in awareness, thinking and learning. Realizing which competencies are most important for long-term success, concentrating attention on them, developing them and measuring the desired improvements is a critically important task for the strategic leader.

All the time, companies should carry out efficiently those activities which are essential for creating a distinctive or differentiated competitive position, and avoid incurring unnecessary costs by providing non-essential values. This implies that they clearly understand their markets, their customers and the key success factors they must meet – their defined competitive strategy. Moreover, they should constantly seek improvement by driving their operating efficiencies.

These activities will be encapsulated in the organization's functional strategies, as illustrated in Figure 23.2. The diagram highlights that these functional strategies must (a) fit a defined, clear competitive strategic position and (b) complement each other to achieve internal synergy. Where they fail to complement each other the company's competitive position will inevitably be weakened. The outcome will be a strong competitive position which can only be sustained by innovation and improvement – and sometimes by the move to a new competitive paradigm. Managing these changes effectively is very dependent upon the style and approach of the strategic leader and the culture and values of the organization. These arguments accord with the latest ideas of Michael Porter (1996).

Taking the logic a stage further: where the organization's various competitive strategies are also complementary, based around a fitting heartland of activities to which the corporation can add value, the organization will be able to maintain a strong corporate portfolio.

Given the critical emphasis on complementarity and sustained strategic fit at the heart of Figure 23.2, our earlier arguments about the importance of strategic awareness and learning to co-ordinate activity and change are reinforced.

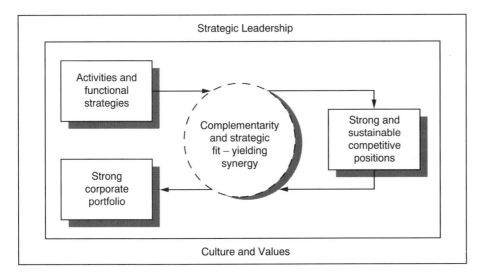

Figure 23.2 Strategic success through complementary activities.

Strategic failure

It is, however, all too easy for currently successful firms to lose their edge and their competitive advantage. Miles and Snow (1994) argue that there are four main reasons for this:

- ❏ A lack of awareness and a failure to be alert to new opportunities and threats
- ❏ Retaining a belief in a successful competitive paradigm for too long. Market leaders seem particularly prone to do this; they tend to rely on *continuous* change to retain their leadership
- ❏ An unwillingness to accept the need for structural or cultural change, and
- ❏ Poor judgement, causing a company to make poor, inappropriate decisions.

The crisis-averse organization

Figure 23.3 highlights that an organization must meet the needs and expectations of all its stakeholders if it is to survive. It is vital to retain customers; new customers then bring new business rather than merely replace others who have been lost or neglected. Employee support and commitment is essential for delivering the competitive quality and service that customers demand. To achieve this, they must be motivated and rewarded. And, of course, financial targets must be met to ensure shareholder loyalty.

Achieving these outcomes is dependent upon aspects of both strategy and structure, which in turn depend upon effective strategic leadership. A sound, appropriate, communicated and shared purpose and vision should be manifested in appropriate, feasible and desirable corporate and competitive strategies. These must be:

- ❏ implemented with a high level of customer service
- ❏ improved continuously, and
- ❏ changed to new corporate and competitive paradigms at appropriate times and opportunities.

We have already seen that this demands environmental awareness and the ability of the organization to respond to change pressures and to external strategic disturbances. Whilst we talk about an organization-wide response, the real challenge lies with individual managers and employees, who are closest to customers, suppliers and distributors. Innovative people drive functional-level improvements which can strengthen competitiveness. But they must be empowered and committed – issues of structure, style and implementation. The 'hard' aspects of strategy – leadership, vision and ideas – must be supported by the 'soft' people aspects.

Visit the website:
http://www.
itbp.com

People and process issues determine whether managers and other employees support and facilitate change, or inhibit the strategic changes that are necessary for survival. Egan (1993) adopts the term 'shadow side' of organizations to embrace issues of culture, complexity, politics, power, personal objectives and the ability of the organization to deal with the range of strategic issues and paradoxes we introduced in Chapters 1 and 2. They can be positive or negative influences. Where they are negative, the organization is likely to be more crisis-prone; for the organization to be crisis-averse, they must be largely

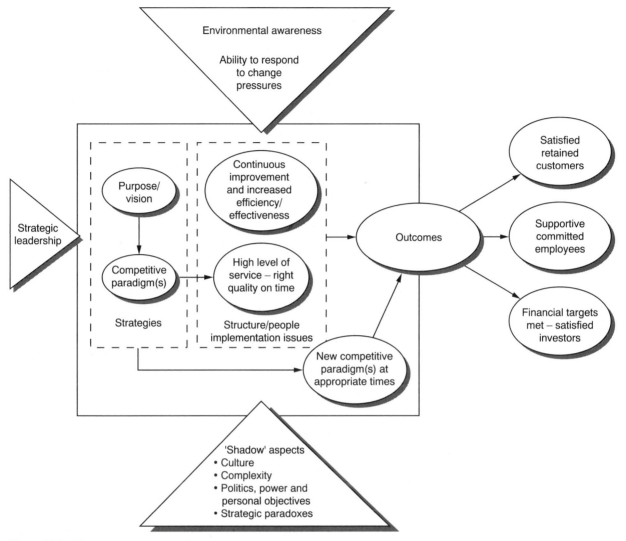

Figure 23.3 The crisis-averse organization.

positive. Organizations must find ways of empowering their employees,
harnessing their commitment and promoting organizational learning if the
'shadow side' is to make a positive contribution to strategic management and
change.

Human resource issues

Organizations are systems which comprise people who are trying to act
purposefully rather than thrash around without any real purpose (Checkland,
1981). However, people differ in their perspective and perceptions. They use
their personal meaning systems to interpret events, actions, opportunities and
threats and to decide upon responses. Whilst their personal strengths must be

captured and exploited, organizational information systems should ensure that they work within the parameters of the corporate purpose, vision and policies, and that their initiatives and contributions are shared and understood.

The new technological revolution and the increase in globalization has forced change on organizations everywhere, regardless of their type, size and sector. Few are unscathed. Some have embraced change positively and willingly; others more reluctantly. Those who have failed to change have probably been sold or liquidated. One outcome is a more flexible, but slimmed-down workforce.

On the positive side, many managers and employees are better educated. They are IT-literate, knowledge-workers in a knowledge-based society. Some of them possess scarce skills. In some organizations people have become less constrained and more empowered, willing to be creative and show initiative in a more open, less-hierarchical firm. And finally: information often flows more horizontally and freely, enriching and speeding up decision making.

But this, clearly, is not the case everywhere.

Many workers are now part-time and 'peripheral', as opposed to 'core'. When re-engineering their processes and changing their structures too many companies have gone too far. They have downsized but not 'rightsized'. Important skills and competencies have been lost. Linked to this, strategies of focusing on core activities and competencies, and divesting those which are non-core, have created an increasing incidence of strategic alliances and networks. Managing these networks effectively demands new capabilities, which many organizations have yet to develop fully. People feel under greater pressure and stress; there is more fear and insecurity. 'Hard' as distinct from 'soft' human resource strategies are practised in many companies, and many employees, instead of committing themselves to a single company, look to switch organizations and industries as they take more control of their working lives, and this despite the widespread managerial unemployment and insecurity.

Sadly, many large organizations, composed of very intelligent people, are still slow to respond to change pressures, and, when they do, their behaviour is often ponderous. Individuals can, and often do, act dynamically and entre-preneurially; yet many organizations have still to work out how to capture the intelligence and learning in order to facilitate the change process. This is the paradox of the large organization learning how to behave like the archetypal small business.

The challenge of embracing both the hard and soft elements of strategic management in order to increase strategic awareness and manage strategic change more effectively remains a major challenge for many organizations. It is a challenge that is more likely to intensify than to disappear.

References

Checkland, PB (1981) *Systems Thinking, Systems Practice*, John Wiley.

Egan, G (1993) *Adding Value: A Systematic Guide to Business-driven Management and Leadership*, Jossey-Bass.

Miles, RE and Snow, CC (1994) *Fit, Failure and the Hall of Fame: How Companies Succeed or Fail*, Free Press.

Porter, ME (1996) What is strategy? *Harvard Business Review*, November– December.

An Introduction to the Case Studies

The main text featured over 100 short cases and examples which have generally been written to illustrate specific points and strategic issues. The 11 full-length case studies which follow will provide readers with an opportunity to develop a deeper insight into strategic awareness and strategic change management in manufacturing and service businesses, large conglomerates and small, entrepreneurial companies, the profit-seeking and not-for-profit sectors. To a large extent they feature instantly-recognizable organizations with which students should feel comfortable. Every case covers a range of issues, but each one has a central theme. The accompanying chart lists these issues and shows how the cases have been chosen and ordered sequentially in terms of their key issues to follow the chapters of this book. The first case, The National Trust, can readily be used very early in a course as it covers basic strategic principles and issues at a straightforward level. Virgin comes at the end because it covers the widest range of issues; it could very easily be used part-way through a course, possibly in conjunction with

Thorn-EMI. It is, therefore, not essential that the cases are read or studied in this order; it is also clearly possible for strategy teachers to substitute or supplement any of the cases with ones they have written or prefer. Whilst market and financial data are included wherever it is seen as appropriate, the cases have been written to illustrate strategic issues and provoke discussion of these issues rather than as a vehicle for extensive quantitative analyses. A set of indicative questions is included at the end; they are not necessarily the only appropriate questions. Equally, lecturers may well prefer to focus on only selected aspects of the case.

Most of the cases have been produced with the support and encouragement of the organizations involved; in many instances they cover a range of topics but they are not fully comprehensive of all the strategic issues faced by the company concerned. They have all been written to foster discussion; they should not be taken as representative of either good or bad management practice.

Strategic management case studies

Key:
- ✓✓✓ Central theme
- ✓ Issue in the case
- (✓) Peripheral, support issue

	Chapter	National Trust	Elm	British Tourist Authority	Lilliput Lane A	Tesco	Thorn-EMI	Sony	Edward Macbean and James B Hunter	Hanson A	Hanson B	Virgin
1/2	Strategic management principles	✓✓✓										
2	Strategic competencies	✓										
3	Strategic leadership	✓	✓✓✓	(✓)	✓		(✓)	✓	✓	✓	✓	✓
4	Culture and values	✓	✓	✓	✓			✓	✓	(✓)		✓
5	Objectives and stakeholder expectations	✓	✓	✓✓✓	✓			✓		✓		✓
6	Strategic success and performance measures	✓	✓	✓			✓					
7	Strategic failure	(✓)	(✓)	(✓)								
Interlude	E–V–R congruence; synergy	✓	✓	✓			✓	✓		✓		✓
8	Environmental analysis			✓				✓		✓		
9	Competition and competitive advantage					✓	✓	✓				✓
10	Adding value		✓	✓	✓✓✓	✓	✓	✓				✓
11	Competitive advantage through people			✓	✓							
12	Financial strategy								✓	✓		✓
13	Competitive advantage and information				✓✓✓	✓✓✓						
14	Strategy creation						✓	✓		✓	✓	✓✓✓
15	Strategic alternatives					✓✓✓	✓✓✓	✓✓✓				
16	Strategic growth (and alliances)		(✓)	✓		✓	✓	✓✓✓	✓	✓		✓
17	Consolidation and recovery			✓			✓		✓			✓
	Management buy-outs					✓	✓		✓✓✓			
18	Strategy evaluation					✓	✓	✓		✓		✓
19	Organization structure					✓	✓	✓		✓		✓
20	Corporate management style					✓	✓	✓		✓✓✓	✓	✓
21	Strategic resource management						✓		✓✓✓	✓		✓
22	Strategic change management						✓		✓✓✓	✓	✓✓✓	✓

The National Trust

This case study is a longer version of Case 1.2 in the main text. It explains the work, the objectives and the performance of The National Trust, and concludes with an examination of the Trust in terms of E–V–R (environment–values–resources) congruence.

This version of the case was written by John L Thompson in 1996 with the earlier co-operation of the National Trust. It is for classroom discussion and should not be taken to reflect either effective or ineffective management.

Introduction

As we move into the twenty-first century, it will become increasingly important to safeguard the country's heritage, enabling us to understand and enjoy it, and passing it on to future generations.
Prime Minister John Major, 1995.

The National Trust, in essence, holds countryside and buildings in England, Wales and Northern Ireland *'for the benefit of us all'*. Trust properties include woodlands, coastal paths, nature reserves and country parks; sites of archaeological interest; castles and country houses, some associated with famous people such as Sir Winston Churchill and Rudyard Kipling; abbeys and priories; lighthouses; and even whole villages and hamlets. In 1995 these amounted to some 240,000 hectares, over 550 miles of coastline, 200 houses, 160 gardens, 25 industrial monuments and 1000 designated ancient monuments, many of which are open to the public. Some 250 properties charge an entry fee; more than 10 million visitors per year are recorded at properties where admission fees are charged, and millions more visit the open countryside free of charge. The most popular property, measured by the number of visitors, was Fountains Abbey and Studley Royal in North Yorkshire.

The National Trust, which is independent of government despite the 'national' in the name, is now over 100 years old. Founded in 1895 by a group of individuals concerned with conservation and preservation of the countryside and important buildings, the National Trust now boasts two-and-a-quarter million members. The two million figure was reached in October 1990. The growth of membership was particularly dramatic during the 1980s. The first thousand was reached in 1926, increasing to 10,000 in 1946, 100,000 in 1961 and one million in 1981. Members pay an annual subscription in return for free entrance to Trust properties and a variety of support publications. Initially the Trust concentrated on looking after land and ancient buildings; country houses have been included since 1934. The Trust is also heavily dependent on the annual contribution of 30,000 people who work voluntarily in a number of ways. Their contribution is estimated at 1.7 million hours work.

To celebrate its centenary in 1995, the Trust launched Project Minerva, a lifelong learning programme linked to conservation for both adults and children. Minerva includes discovery days, study bases and environmental activity centres, and it reflects the Trust's increasing emphasis on learning in recent years.

The Trust was formally incorporated by Act of Parliament in 1907. It has a constitution and legislation enables it to acquire property and hold it is as either 'inalienable' or 'alienable'. That part which the Trust formally declares 'inalienable', usually the important core of an estate, cannot by law be sold.

For this reason it is not valued in the Trust's balance sheet. It has been estimated that the current market value, hypothetically, would exceed £2 billion. Land, however, can, and frequently is, leased to farmers in return for an annual rent.

The mission and objectives

In simple terms, the purpose of the National Trust is the preservation of historic houses and beauty spots in England, Wales and Northern Ireland, keeping them open for the Nation.

The 1907 Act of incorporation states ...

promoting the permanent preservation, for the benefit of the Nation, of lands and tenements (including buildings) of beauty or historic interest, and as regards lands, for the preservation (so far as is practicable) of their natural aspect features and animal and plant life.

Given this mission and the 'inalienable property' constraint the time scale is clearly infinite and in fact the planning period for certain gardens is 100 years.

Conservation and preservation, however, costs money; revenues must be generated. The primary sources are members' subscriptions and the fees paid by non-member visitors, in addition to rents (see Appendix for details). This implies accessibility, which could result in damage if there are too many visitors. Light, humidity and the passage of time are all enemies to old properties and their furnishings; so too are curious fingers and thundering feet. **Hence there is an important potential conflict between conservation and access.**

During the late 1980s and early 1990s, for example, gardens have been more popular with visitors than country houses. While the Trust is generally happy to see more visitors at its various properties – enjoying them and at the same time contributing to their upkeep – occasionally a certain stage is reached where it is felt that more visitors would conflict with the preservation needs of the property *and the brakes need to be applied*. To prevent over-use and damage the Trust has selectively introduced policies to restrict entry, but these are exceptional rather than general practice. They have taken the form of direct controls (fixed numbers at any one time, say a half-hour period)

and indirect influence such as reduced marketing, higher admission prices and limited car parking availability. These restrictions have taken precedence over the thought of investing more resources to make the most popular properties even more enjoyable in order to attract increasing numbers of visitors and generate additional revenues. Generally the commercialism of many privately owned estates and houses is avoided by the National Trust. There are no safari or theme parks in the grounds. Activities like practising farmyards, mainly for children, are as far as the Trust is happy to go.

Instead attention has focused on the revenue potential of shops, restaurants and holiday cottages (National Trust Enterprises) and publications. In 1994–1995 National Trust Enterprises made a financial contribution of £6.2 million from a turnover of £38.8 million (16%); a further £2.9 million was provided through additional advertising and sponsorship. Donations and investment income are other significant sources of funds. These are discussed in greater detail later in the case.

In the main the National Trust takes over properties where no-one else can or will, mainly the latter, responding to need, rather than specifically seeking to acquire identified houses and gardens. The objectives are, therefore, more concerned with the preservation and improvement of properties already owned rather than the acquisition of new ones. There is, though, a clear long-term objective of acquiring some 900 miles of 'threatened' British coastline. This is almost half of the total of 2000 miles of coastline; and the project, Enterprise Neptune, which itself has been running for 25 years is over half way to its target. The rate of coastline acquisition depends on the success of the support fund raising.

Administration

The Trust has a head office executive staff comprising the Director-General, Martin Drury, the Deputy Director-General and Directorates for Estates, Finance, The Regions, Legal Affairs, Public Affairs, National Trust Enterprises and Personnel. The previous Director-General, Sir Angus Stirling, retired in 1995 after 12 years in office; he had presided over the important surge in membership. In addition there are 16 regional offices which are directly responsible for the properties in their regions. This executive operates within, and reports to, an elaborate committee structure of honorary non-executives.

The ruling committee is the Council, which is made up of 52 members, half of these nominated by organizations interested in, and appropriate to, the Trust's activities such as the Victoria and Albert Museum, the National Gallery, the Council for British Archaeology, the Royal Agricultural and Royal Horticultural Societies, the Ramblers' Association and various other protection and conservation agencies. The other half are elected by the members and come from all parts of the country. The Council itself has an Executive Committee which appoints, among others, a Finance and a Properties Committee and 16 regional committees. The Executive Committee 'reviews and carries out policies required to pursue the principles laid down by Council'. The Council, incidentally, is not bound by decisions taken at the Annual General Meeting of National Trust members. This was evidenced at the end of the 1980s when the Council did not adopt an AGM decision in favour of banning hunting on National Trust lands. In fairness only a small minority of members actually voted, either for or against.

Since the mid-1980s the senior executives of the Trust have operated with a management board which meets fortnightly. Prior to this, control was more directly hierarchical. These senior managers are responsible to all main committees of non-executives.

Staff in regional offices, guided and constrained by head office staff, will put forward proposals and plans to the various committees for approval. In general the Properties Committee considers property management issues in terms of policy, and issues papers on such subjects as the care of historic buildings, forestry and archaeology, whereas the Finance Committee approves the annual budget and accounts. When an acquisition is recommended by regional staff, the Properties Committee will evaluate the merit of the proposal and the Finance Committee the financial implications. Both pass their recommendations to the Executive Committee for the final decision.

Regional offices

The 16 regional offices are directly responsible for the maintenance and improvement of existing properties, and they will also be involved in potential new acquisitions. Each property has a managing agent who is charged with drawing up an annual plan or budget for repairs, maintenance and possible investments in say a larger car park or better sales kiosk facilities. Revenues from admission charges for non-members and all associated sales of publications and so on are estimated to arrive at a subsidy figure. In the main this subsidy will be provided from general funds, made up of such things as members' subscriptions and profits from retail activities.

A head office committee of senior staff reviews the management and finances of individual properties, roughly every five years on a continuing cycle. If any growing deficit or subsidy requirement is seen as being in need of close examination, then a number of options will be considered, such as:

- ❏ the potential (if desirable) for attracting more visitors, say by working through tourist authorities
- ❏ additional marketing activity by the Trust itself to target the property at defined market segments or niches
- ❏ new uses for the property, such as rallies, wedding receptions and outdoor concerts
- ❏ higher entry fees; and
- ❏ lower staff costs.

The constraint of not threatening conservation by commercialism is ever-present in discussions, but is, apparently, rarely a real issue because of the culture and values held by the Trust's employees both nationally and regionally.

New projects

New projects, such as new exhibition material, better presentations, or better visitor facilities can be financed from a special fund introduced a few years ago by the Trust's Finance Director. Regions can apply for investment funding if they can demonstrate that the projected return on the capital is likely to exceed a particular target. This fund is seen as a revolving fund, on the grounds that monies should be repaid within a relatively short space of time. Whilst the objective of the investment should primarily be to improve quality in the form of enjoyment from the visit, the financial return is utilized as a constraint.

Finance

A more detailed summary of income and expenditure in 1994–1995 is appended to this case, but the following table provides a breakdown of the percentages of the various contributions – excluding grants – to the Trust's income.

	1995 %	1990 %
Subscriptions	44	40
Rents (farms, etc.)	15	16
Admission fees	7	11
Investment income	21	22
Profit from Enterprises	10	7
Produce sales	2	2
Gifts	1	2

Two points are worth noting. First, the increasing significance of members' subscriptions, balanced by the corresponding reduction in admission fees. Second, the growing contribution from National Trust Enterprises.

In addition the Trust receives grants from government departments, conservation agencies and individuals, together with legacies, appeal proceeds and the sale of leases. The magnitude of these varies every year, often quite substantially. Ordinary income does not cover on-going expenditures; grants and legacies are critical.

The National Trust is Britain's leading charity in terms of both total incomes and total voluntary contributions. Its scope is so wide it can appeal to all five National Lottery distributors.

Investments

The National Trust holds and invests substantial funds, the majority of which have been donated over the years to support the upkeep of particular properties. In 1995 over £400 million was invested, comprising:

❑ The Capital Endowment Funds, endowments tied to specific properties, and required before the properties were acquired by the Trust. This is discussed below. Only the interest, not the capital, from this fund can be spent.

❑ The Defined Purpose Funds, gifts and donations tied to specific repair and maintenance projects and/or specified properties. Both the interest and the capital can be spent.
❑ The General Fund, cash which can be used as the Trust chooses. As highlighted earlier this is typically the annual subsidizing of those properties (in reality, most of them) which cannot be self-funded.

Wherever possible investment policies are linked to relevant time horizons. Funds designated for repairs are often earning short-term returns; capital endowment funds are invested for the optimum long-term benefits.

The acquisition of new properties

The National Trust only agrees to take on new properties if an endowment (calculated by a formula) to cover maintenance for the next 50 years is in place. Present owners, conservation agencies and the government, through the Department of the Environment and the National Heritage Memorial Fund, are the traditional sources of endowment funds.

The National Trust accepts that sometimes they underestimate the funding which will be required, and consequently the endowment covers only a percentage of the 50 years. Wage inflation has proved difficult to forecast over 50 years; depreciation is unpredictable, though not markedly relevant; most significant has been the march of scientific knowledge which results in ever higher standards being set by the state, and expected by the public, in hygiene, security and accommodation. Higher targets for maintenance and improvement often prove expensive.

When the National Trust acquires a property it seeks to decorate and furnish it as closely as possible to the way Trust employees believe the original owners would themselves have had it. This requires extensive knowledge of period preferences and tastes, and it can also again prove difficult and expensive. Where the most recent owners have views on the way the property should be presented these are encapsulated into a 'Memorandum of Wishes', but this is not legally binding.

Funds are also boosted continually by donations and legacies, and by fund raising, usually tied to specific appeals. Enterprise Neptune, to cover the cost of acquiring and looking after threatened coast-line, has been on-going for 25 years. As additional funds are raised more can be accomplished in this long-term project. There was a successful Trees and Gardens Storm Disaster Appeal following storm damage in 1990. The Lake District Appeal is another long-term venture to cover the cost of improving paths and preserving facilities, often utilizing volunteer labour. These are just a sample of many special appeals.

Measuring success

Measuring the success of the National Trust is a complex issue, and the various stakeholders and interest groups are likely to have differing views on the most appropriate measures, and on priorities.

❏ The Trust would argue that the main measure of success is the standard of preservation achieved, although this is clearly and inevitably subjective.

Other measures support the achievement of preservation standards:

❏ first, the number of members, including those who renew their subscriptions and those who join for the first time. The growth figures would suggest the Trust is successful, and this is logically linked to

❏ the ability to meet public expectations. The National Trust believe that their members and visitors are, in the main, seeking period authenticity – the property presented as it would have been lived in originally – rather than 'museum collections' say covering several generations, or activities for children. Resources are committed to achieving this type of presentation.

Clearly there is support for the way the National Trust market their properties. Were they to change their policies in any significant way they may well lose existing supporters but at the same time appeal to different market segments.

❏ The number, and particularly the substance, of complaints. The Trust argue that they treat all complaints seriously.

❏ The ability to generate new funds and endowments to enable them to take on additional properties where necessary.

In addition the National Trust has to measure the extent of any damage and decay at properties and react accordingly. There is, as highlighted earlier, a penalty for attracting too many visitors.

The Trust also has a number of key financial yardsticks which are measured on a monthly basis. Where figures fall below trigger thresholds remedial actions are implemented.

Environment–values–resources

The major environmental influences (the Trust's stakeholders), the National Trust's core skills and competencies and the manifest values of the Trust and its employees are listed below.

Stakeholders and interested parties

These include:

❏ Members and visitors – 'represented' at the AGM and by Committee members.
❏ Donors of properties. Many are motivated by genuine altruism, a wish to spread the enjoyment of their inheritance. Their wishes are sought and often followed; and visitors often find their interest in a property is enhanced if they know that the donor or a descendant, frequently related to the family which may have owned the property for centuries, is still resident.
❏ Conservation agencies.
❏ Ramblers' associations.
❏ Government. Government provides some financial support and legislates about certain requirements. Increasingly the National Trust may be affected by European legislation.
❏ Financial benefactors – although in some cases it must be debatable whether the financial support is directed at the specific properties rather than the work of the National Trust as a whole.
❏ Employees – whose values and orientations, as well as their expertise, are likely to be an important issue when they are appointed.
❏ The nation itself (as opposed to the state).

Core competencies and capabilities

The National Trust recognize that to be successful they must develop and preserve expertise in a number of areas:

- Property management. As well as the general maintenance and upkeep of properties the land resources must be managed effectively, and this includes the commercial lease arrangements with farmers and so on.
- Expertise in arts, furnishings and in the ways that people historically have lived and kept their properties. Many National Trust members are themselves experts and connoisseurs.
- Public relations and marketing. Attracting the most appropriate visitors and providing them with an enjoyable, satisfying visit. In addition running the National Trust shops both profitably and in keeping with the desired image of the Trust. Generally high-quality merchandise is sold at premium prices.
- Financial skills, including the management of a sizeable investment portfolio, together with an understanding of the fundamentals of economics. Yields do rise and fall, but the National Trust is substantially dependent on the returns from its various investments.

Values

- The National Trust feel that a high moral tone is appropriate for all their activities.
- The themes of preservation and improvement are dominant, but financial accountability and responsibility cannot be overlooked.
- The Trust also seeks to be educational where it is appropriate. Involving children is seen as important, but it is encouraged mostly at specific sites selected for their location, intrinsic interest and the 'resilience of the fabric'.
- Generally, Trust staff also share an 'ethos' which combines the feeling of working for a good cause, a degree of identification with its purpose and principles, and a certain readiness (typically shared by people who work for other charities) to accept rewards which may be less than employees of many manufacturing and service businesses would normally receive.

The Future

While the National Trust can cover its on-going expenses and acquire those new properties which both the Committees and staff feel it should take over, then its policies, which have emerged incrementally over a long period through a democratic,

if potentially bureaucratic organizational structure, need not change dramatically.

The dilemma comes when the National Trust cannot meet its expenses from current activities, supplemented by external grants, appeal proceeds and legacies. Membership fees could be increased substantially, but members are under no obligation to pay them. Other than in their first or early years of membership, members frequently and happily regard a proportion of their annual fee as a subsidy. They could save money by paying at individual properties when they visited, but of course they would not receive the Trust's directory, magazines and details of new properties and developments.

Admission charges could be raised, but this is likely to deter visitors, and, in fact, is more likely to be used when a property is too popular and conservation needs are threatened.

Support commercial activities, shops, restaurants, publications and holiday cottages are all capable of growth as long as they do not conflict with the values and culture of the Trust. However, these activities remain relatively small in relation to the Trust's total income.

Questions

1 What are the objectives of the National Trust?
   What are the inherent conflicts?
   How do you feel the objectives would be prioritized by the major stakeholders?
2 Do you think the performance measures used by the National Trust are wholly appropriate?
   If not: what measures should be adopted either instead of, or in addition to, those used?
3 Assess the National Trust in respect of E–V–R congruence. What, if any, changes are required if the National Trust is to enjoy congruence in the early years of the new millennium?
4 What opportunities for change are available to the Trust?
   What would constitute appropriate change?
   Do other charities pose any threats?
   Where are the main constraints to change?

Appendix

The National Trust outline income and expenditure, 1994–1995

	£m	£m	Comparative figures for 1986 £m
Ordinary income			
Membership fees	41.8		16.8
Rents from land leases, etc.	14.5		
Admission fees	7.4		14.0
Other property income, e.g. produce sales	1.7		
Investment income	20.2		8.3
Profit from National Trust Enterprises	9.1		N/A
Gifts	1.2		
	95.9		
Capital receipts			
Appeals and tied gifts	3.0		3.7
Grants and contributions	16.6		
Legacies	24.5		8.7
Sales of leases	1.6		
Others	1.0		
	46.7	142.6	
On-going property expenditure			
Property maintenance	45.7		
Property management	13.9		
Conservation and advisory services	4.5		
Membership and recruitment	6.9		
Publicity and fund raising	6.7		
Administration	4.6		
	82.3		
Capital works and projects			
Capital works	38.5		
New acquisitions	6.8		
	45.3		
Total expenditure		127.6	
Comprising total expenditure on property	109.4		55.8
non-property expenditure	18.2		
Total Income less total expenditure		15.0	
Represented by:			
retentions in tied funds	10.0		
retentions for future expenditure	5.0		

Note: Total expenditure less ordinary income is 31.7, representing a capital funding requirement.

Elm Limited

The case describes the development, from scratch, of a fairly large SME manufacturing business and the key role played by a highly motivated electronics engineer and two colleagues. The case indicates the problems of trying to develop such a business and the role played, both positive and negative, by the strong willed entrepreneurial founder.

This case study forms part of a series of case studies developed on behalf of Scottish Enterprise to highlight the role of the entrepreneur in the creation and development of a business.

It was prepared by John Anderson of Price Waterhouse under the supervision of Frank Martin, University of Stirling as a basis for class discussion rather than to illustrate either effective or ineffective handling of a management situation.

Copyright © Scottish Enterprise 1995.

Introduction

Raj Samuel switched the overhead projector off. Any comments? Raj looked around the room. There was a stunned silence. Not one of the directors wanted to make the first move.

Raj had just presented his ten-year vision 'to grow Elm to a £100 million company by the year 2004'. He had outlined the targets for the growth of Genus, the OEM business, and had talked excitedly about the prospects for a new range of products to be developed jointly with a Japanese company he had established a relationship with.

The newer directors, Paul, Derek and Frank, looked excited. Ross and Tony, however, had seen this before.

Tony is becoming increasingly concerned about the general management of the company. It is growing too quickly and he feels that he does not have the experience of running anything but a small company. Everyone seems to be firefighting and dealing with an increasing number of quality problems. No-one is in control.

Ross feels that the company has become something far bigger than he had originally expected and is already uncomfortable with the thought that he is responsible for 75 employees. There is also the issue of signing yet another bank guarantee.

Neither Ross nor Tony want to dampen Raj's enthusiasm, after all they would not be there now if it were not for his drive and determination. Nevertheless, they feel that they need to sit down with Raj and Chan (the company's external Malaysian investor), and talk frankly about their fears and set out formal action plans to ensure that Elm gets at least some of the way to the £100 million.

Historical overview

Elm as a sideline

Elm was founded in 1982 by three friends, Raj Samuel, Tony Llewelyn and Ross McKemmie, who had all worked with the same family-owned electronics company based in Glasgow, CT Ltd. CT was beginning to show signs of running into difficulties, and Tony had recently been made redundant. Raj and Ross also saw that their future employment was in jeopardy. Elm was set up initially to provide an additional source of income and potential security, and was run from Ross McKemmie's home.

At the outset work was sourced from a family contact that Raj Samuel had in Malaysia, K.H. Chan. Elm designed and manufactured (through a sub-contractor) burglar alarm systems and energy saving devices for hotels on behalf of Chan. The income from this business became sufficient to support the founders and Raj and Ross then left CT to work full-time at Elm and Tony then joined them.

Elm for real

Raj Samuel saw an opportunity to take advantage of the problems that their former employer was having and to pick up work from its existing customer base. Elm concentrated its efforts in this area on one sector: temperature controls for OEM refrigeration case manufacturers, such as Fosters, Sadia and Craig Nicholl (now Hussman). The approach that Raj took was to work at developing a strong relationship with potential customers so that Elm was not seen merely as a supplier but also a partner who was able to work on joint developments and act as a solution provider. However, it took until 1984 to get the first order from Craig Nicholl, which was then followed by orders from Fosters, Sadia and Hubbards, all of which were customers of the family company.

At the stage where this new business began to take off, the founders decided to withdraw from the sub-contract work for Chan. Nevertheless, Chan continued his support for Elm, maintaining his investment in the company and continuing to guarantee the bank facilities.

By 1986, Elm was achieving sales of some £260,000 from OEM case manufacturers which supplied UK supermarkets. In essence, what Elm had achieved was the replacement of traditional electro-mechanical temperature controls in refrigeration cases with electronic temperature controls. However, they were not alone as four competitor companies were also operating in the market: Woodlay, JKL, CDK Electronics, and Tetronic.

The birth of Genus

Raj, however, saw that there was scope for developing more sophisticated control mechanisms because of the electronic nature of the new generation of temperature controllers. He foresaw an ability to link each case electronically to provide a centralized monitoring function, but to do this Elm would need to be independent of the OEM case manufacturers. Elm would still supply the temperature controllers to the case manufacturers, but could potentially benefit from developing a relationship with the end user – the supermarket.

Raj Samuel got an introduction to a technical manager at Gateway through a contact at Hussman (formerly Craig Nicholl). By listening to the technical manager, Raj discovered that one of Elm's competitors, Woodlay, was the established leader for control systems – 'they were the Hoover of control systems'. However, the control systems were supplementary to the controllers built into the original cases and Elm began to develop an alternative alarm and control system using existing controllers which the supermarkets had already bought and installed. A similar concept had been tried successfully by JKL but was specific to Safeway. Raj saw an opportunity to develop a generic system capable of being used by any supermarket, and the Elm Genus system was born.

The first Genus sale was made to Gateway in 1988 and over the next two years Elm successfully sold Genus to Marks and Spencer, Safeway, Tesco and Waitrose in the UK and to Quinnsworth in Ireland, and by 1991 had a turnover of almost £3 million.

Rapid growth through product development

For Elm the Genus system had become the main part of its business, although the manufacture of controllers for OEMs still continued. Woodlay were taken by surprise since they had held their dominant position for so long, and JKL could not respond because of the significant investment in the Safeway specific control system. Raj Samuel's obsession with customer service led to the creation of separate account managers for each customer. He explained to customers that 'every time you fall there will be an Elm person to catch you'. This move coincided with the decisions taken by supermarkets to downsize their engineering functions, even though supermarkets were becoming more complex. Through the use of account managers who were in continuous contact with the end user and able to determine their changing needs, Elm developed Genus to control not only the refrigerated display units but also the heating, ventilation and air conditioning. In view of the high proportion of operating costs of a supermarket that energy comprises, the efficient co-ordinated control of such equipment was able to provide the supermarket with an effective cost-saving tool.

In order to demonstrate its commitment to developing Genus with its customers, Elm set up its own engineering function with both hardware and software engineers. This commitment, while relatively expensive, enabled Elm to work so closely with its customers that it became an integral part of the store design and refit planning teams. This resulted in Elm products being specified by the supermarkets. The refrigeration contractors, Rayan Jayborg, Waithes, General Refrigeration, Westwood and Hussman therefore came straight to Elm at the outset of any new-build or refit, and the company's growth continued apace.

The company's product range has successfully grown to comprise:

❑ Genus – supermarket control system.
❑ Gas detection system – an add-on to Genus to detect leaks in refrigeration systems.
❑ 'Plastic chicken' – an add-on to Genus for Marks and Spencer used to monitor conditions in chiller cabinets.
❑ OEM controllers – individual controllers and panels for case manufacturers.

However, not all new product developments have been successful. In 1991, Elm set up a new subsidiary, The Tanoki Corporation Limited, to develop and market stand-alone thermometers for the consumer and gift markets which was based on a modification to existing thermometers used in refrigeration cases. It became apparent that the company had no experience in consumer markets and the business was abandoned in 1992. Elm lost nearly £200,000 in this abortive venture.

Vision 2004

However, Raj continued to have big plans for Elm. Further market penetration of Genus in the UK was possible, as was the possibility of overseas expansion, and he believed that this would be easiest to achieve in Europe and Scandinavia. His frequent globe-trotting had led to a developing relationship with a Japanese company with an innovative inverter. Raj had already had preliminary discussions with this company with a view to forming a joint venture in Scotland to manufacture products under licence and to market them throughout Europe. Although there would be minor applications in supermarkets, Raj saw an enormous potential market which basically would comprise any user of electric motors. His vision had now become to grow Elm into a £100 million company by the year 2004.

The founders

Raj Samuel (Selvarai)

Raj Samuel helped found Elm when he was 31. Born in Malaysia, he followed a well-trodden educational path and came to the UK to attend university after leaving school. Raj graduated with an electrical engineering degree from Glasgow University in 1978. During summer vacations Raj worked for the Nardini family in Largs, servicing and repairing refrigeration equipment. After graduating he was offered a place at Hull University to study for an MSc in refrigeration but did not take it up and joined a Glasgow-based family-owned electronics company, CT Ltd, instead, where he met his co-founders Tony Llewelyn and Ross McKemmie.

Raj Samuel 'always had ambition for achievement', although not necessarily to have his own business. His father had moved from India to Malaysia and as well as pursuing a career in the civil service had created significant wealth as a property developer. The influence and support of Chan, a family friend in Malaysia and a very wealthy businessman, has also been significant.

Raj is married with two children. His wife accepts the long hours that he has had to put in during the life of Elm. To Raj 'the business is 24 hours'. In the early days of Elm Raj drove between 70,000 and 100,000 miles a year. As the sales force was built up, this reduced to 30,000 then to an average annual mileage of 12,000. However, he now flies some 250,000 miles a year, twice a week to London to see customers and once a month to the Far East to develop new business ideas. 'I don't waste time on the road any more'. Raj says that he has never had a sleepless night and 'can switch off from Elm at will'. However as soon as he gets up in the morning he is thinking about Elm and uses his 'showertime' which can be anything up to an hour, to plan out his day in response to the previous day's events.

Ross McKemmie

Ross McKemmie was 38 when Elm was established. Son of a Glasgow banker, Ross was educated at

Hutcheson's Grammar School and he too obtained an electrical engineering degree from Glasgow University. He entered the Scottish Electrical Training Scheme and joined Edgecom Peebles (now NEI) as a designer. After a year he went to South Africa with another group company where he worked for four years as an electrical engineer. After getting married he returned to Glasgow in 1973 to work for CT Ltd as a designer. Over the next few years Ross was involved in the design of a very wide range of electronic devices and had also trained Raj, who subsequently had joined CT.

In contrast to Raj's desire for achievement Ross had no such ambitions: 'I would have been happy to retire at CT'. Ross reported to Tony Llewelyn at the time that the three founders were thinking about Elm, and when Tony was made redundant Ross began to worry about his own position.

Ross had agreed to set up Elm, based in his son's bedroom, to carry out work for Chan, whilst he and Raj were still employees of CT. Both Ross and Raj could see the problems growing with their employers and Raj persuaded Ross that they should take Elm seriously. Ross finally had a major disagreement with the family board members about the way the company was run and resigned. Ross decided to pursue the Elm opportunity as it was 'easier to do than to hawk myself round the marketplace'. He also believed that having his own business could make him rich.

Tony Llewelyn

An engineering and economics graduate of Cambridge in 1973, Tony Llewelyn joined Siemens AG in Germany as project engineer where he was involved in the design of electrical equipment including motors, drive control systems and switchgear. Tony was seconded to Siemens India in 1977 to manage

Exhibit 1   Elm Limited
Profit and loss account information

	31.12.1994	31.12.1993	31.12.1992	31.12.1991	31.12.1990	31.12.1989	31.12.1888	31.12.1987	31.12.11986
Turnover	6,895,149	4,666,530	3,976,692	2,938,385	1,884,551	1,048,850	795,328	427,900	260,017
Cost of sales	(5,335,915)	(3,481,938)	(2,900,507)	(2,191,215)	(1,335,694)	(786,016)	(591,599)	(330,245)	(193,134)
Gross profit	1,559,234	1,184,592	1,076,185	747,170	548,857	262,834	203,729	97,655	66,883
Administrative expenses	(1,301,247)	(893,216)	(847,131)	(507,412)	(449,843)	(186,415)	(161,108)	(86,213)	(65,718)
Other operating income	–	17,911	8,023	18,529	12,500	12,046	8,954	5,691	3,088
Operating profit	257,987	309,287	237,077	258,287	111,514	88,465	51,575	17,133	4,253
Exceptional items	32,150	(99,000)[1]	–	–	–	–	–	–	–
Interest payable	(100,514)	(85,570)	(104,007)	(51,102)	(19,326)	(32,588)	(17,364)	(6,351)	(5,504)
Profit/(loss) on ordinary activities before taxation	189,623	124,717	133,070	207,185	92,188	55,877	34,211	10,782	(1,251)
Taxation	(49,422)	(49,358)	(15,758)	(64,322)	(25,566)	(9,153)	(8,631)	–	–
Profit on ordinary activities after taxation	140,201	75,359	117,312	142,863	66,622	46,724	25,580	10,782	(1,251)
Extraordinary items after taxation	–	–	(90,294)[2]	–	–	–	–	–	–
Profit for the financial year	140,201	75,359	27,018	142,863	66,622	46,724	25,580	10,782	(1,251)
Dividends	–	–	–	–	–	–	(3,150)	–	–
Retained profit	140,201	75,359	27,018	142,863	66,622	46,724	22,430	10,782	(1,251)
Number of employees	84	68	58	45	28	16	13	11	10

Notes to profit and loss account information:
1. Exceptional items relates to slow-moving and obsolete stock being written off.
2. The company wrote off a trading intercompany balance of £10,294 from its subsidiary company, The Tanoki Corporation Limited, which ceased trading on 31 December 1992. The company owned 99% of the share capital of the company and as a result wrote off its investment in that company of £80,000.

Exhibit 2   Elm Limited

Balance sheet information

	31.12.1994	31.12.1993	31.12.1992	31.12.1991	31.12.1990	31.12.1989	31.12.1988	31.12.1987	31.12.1986
Fixed assets									
Intangible assets	–	–	–	–	–	22,500[3]	–	–	–
Tangible assets	908,553	590,977[1]	560,061[1]	203,351	101,908	65,093	36,121	13,154	14,082
Investments	3,200	–	–	80,000[2]	–	–	–	–	–
	911,753	590,977	560,061	283,351	101,908	87,593	36,121	13,154	14,082
Current assets									
Stocks	944,700	659,300	642,941	405,313	231,948	148,420	101,600	45,000	31,175
Debtors	1,332,382	1,005,484	419,069	766,431	307,353	287,754	156,348	119,564	65,342
Investments	46,776	31,188	15,600	–	–	–	–	–	–
Cash	25,232	348	26,976	71	7,098	50,214	510	180	110
	2,349,090	1,696,320	1,104,586	1,171,815	546,399	486,388	248,458	164,744	96,627
Creditors: amounts falling due within one year	(2,192,134)	(1,322,296)	(863,206)	(924,779)	(433,899)	(387,954)	(229,613)	(144,548)	(86,709)
Net current assets	156,956	374,024	241,380	247,036	112,500	98,434	28,845	20,196	9,918
Total assets less current liabilities	1,068,709	965,001	801,441	532,387	214,408	186,027	64,966	33,350	24,000
Creditors: amounts falling due after more than one year	(509,397)	(545,415)	(465,373)	(219,988)	(46,475)	(84,861)	(11,897)	(3,156)	(4,588)
Provision for liabilities and charges Deferred taxation	(7,901)	(8,376)	(217)	(3,566)	(1,963)	(1,818)	(445)	–	–
	551,411	411,210	335,851	308,833	165,970	99,348	52,624	30,194	19,412
Capital and reserves									
Called up share capital	50,001	50,001	50,001	50,001	50,001	50,001[4]	30,000	30,000	30,000
Profit and loss account	501,410	361,209	285,850	258,832	115,969	49,347	22,624	194	(10,588)
	551,411	411,210	335,851	308,833	165,970	99,348	52,624	30,194	19,412

Notes to balance sheet information:

1. Significant level of fixed asset additions during 1992, principally new premises at a cost of approximately £380,000.
2. Investment in 99% of issued share capital of The Tanoki Corporation Limited, a company incorporated in Scotland. Note 2 to profit and loss account information shows subsequently written off in 1993.
3. R&D costs capitalized during 1989. Accounting policy subsequently changed in 1990 to immediate write off of all R&D expenditure.
4. A further 20,001 shares were allotted as fully paid as a bonus issue out of reserves. Shareholding now:

Raj Samuel	11,667	(was 7000)
Ross McKemmie	11,667	(was 7000)
Tony Llewelyn	11,667	(was 7000)
K H Chan	15,000	(was 9000)
	50,001	(was 30,000)

a contract with a state-owned electrical company. His role became less technical and more commercial, and he was responsible for customer liaison and commercial negotiation as well as technical support and training. In 1979 he returned to the UK and joined CT Ltd as a senior hardware design engineer. His role developed to include responsi-bility for all new product design and management of the design team, which included Ross McKemmie and Raj Samuel. Tony was made redundant by CT prior to the formation of Elm and worked as a design engineer for another small electrical engineering company before agreeing to join Ross and Raj at Elm. He was then 37.

Management

At the start of Elm the three founders were equal partners and shared in the management of the company. They naturally tended towards their areas of experience and interest and Raj took on the sales and customer service role, Ross the technical design role and Tony the production and administration role. This very democratic management process lasted until 1988 when, following a review by a national firm of management consultants, Raj was formally appointed managing director, with Tony as his key lieutenant and production director.

With the growth of the company, Raj had moved from being involved in almost everything and doing a lot of detailed work to more of a strategist: 'I do the thinking and someone else will do the work'. By 1990, Raj was thinking on a grander scale and his plans now covered a two-year period rather than a two-week period. However, he felt that as the company was successful and growing at a faster and faster rate, the rest of the people were not keeping pace with him and inevitably was becoming more dictatorial in style – 'there was no time to bring everyone along'. Ross and Tony seemed to accept this change in Raj – 'we trusted him'.

Gradually key managers were appointed and made Directors of the company. The board now comprises:

Raj Samuel — Chairman and Managing Director
Tony Llewelyn — Production Director
Ross McKemmie — Director (no functional responsibility)
Frank Hay — Technical Director
Paul Woodman — Sales Director
Derek Gardner — Service Director
K.H. Chan — Director (non-executive)

There is also a non-executive financial consultant, Bill Niven, who helps to advise on financial matters, although Chan, who is himself an accountant by training, provides most of the advice on finance. Indeed, from the very start of Elm he has insisted on proper management accounts as part of a formal management process within the company. The financial profile for Elm Limited for the period 1986–1994 is provided as Exhibits 1–3.

The way ahead

It was clear from the management meeting that the Vision 2004 plan, as outlined by Raj Samuel, had to be addressed quickly if Elm was to remain on course. For Ross and Tony, the problems seemed equally as real as the opportunities. What appeared to be needed was a period of analysis to determine just what Vision 2004 entailed and the likely shape of Elm to carry it off.

Exhibit 3 Elm Limited
Financing information

	31.12.1994	31.12.1993	31.12.1992	31.12.1991	31.12.1990	31.12.1989	31.12.1988	31.12.1987	31.12.1986
Cash at bank and in hand	(25,232)	(348)	(26,976)	(71)	(7,098)	(50,214)	(510)	(180)	(110)
Bank overdraft	770,703	361,181	345,069	261,731	–	122,696	72,300	52,892	29,526
Bank loans	422,962	491,037	443,335	100,000	–	–	–	–	–
Other loans	–	–	–	108,947	27,269	84,863	–	–	–
Hire purchase/ finance leases	194,186	102,768	40,801	66,927	36,581	14,736	16,694	3,156	4,588
Net external finance	1,362,619	954,638	802,229	537,534	56,751	172,081	88,484	55,868	34,004

Questions

1 Using appropriate strategic frameworks and concepts, evaluate the nature of the strategic problems now facing the management team at Elm.

   Based on this evaluation, what would be your preferred course of action?

2 Identify the causes of the main strategic and managerial issues facing Elm.

3 What longer-term issues face Elm?

4 What are the main strategic lessons which can be learned from the development of this company and, in particular, the role of Raj Samuel?

5 Which theories of leadership might be useful for evaluating the contribution of Raj Samuel to the development of Elm?

6 How would you classify the entrepreneurial style and strategy of Raj Samuel?

The British Tourist Authority (BTA)

This case study describes the purpose, activities, strategy and structure at the British Tourist Authority.

It has been written to illustrate the environment–values–resources model and its applicability for providing a framework to examine strategic change pressures and implications; and to explore priorities, objectives and performance measures in a not-for-profit organization with multiple stakeholders.

The case can also be used to provoke discussion on the importance of the tourist industry for the UK and the role of the BTA in relation to this. In this respect the strategic issues of adding value and external architecture are particularly relevant.

It is a full-length version of Case 6.1 in the main text.

This version of the British Tourist Authority was written by John L Thompson in 1996 with the earlier co-operation of the BTA for the purpose of class discussion. It should not be taken to reflect either effective or ineffective management.

Tourism and Britain

Travel and tourism accounts for one-third of the UK's invisible earnings and 4% of UK gross domestic product; the UK is the second largest exporter of invisibles in the world. Over 1.5 million people are employed full-time in the industry, more than work in the National Health Service. When part-time jobs are included, over 10% of the working population are part of the industry. Between 1985 and 1992 industry revenues grew by almost 13% per year. Although spending by overseas visitors in 1993 was 19% higher than in 1992, spending grew by just 4% in 1994.

In 1994 domestic and overseas tourists spent £24.5 billion on accommodation (37% of total spending), eating out (23%), shopping (18%), travel within the UK (14%), entertainment (4%) and other services (4%) – but British business people and tourists spend even more abroad. In 1992 there was a total account deficit of £3.4 billion; in 1993 this rose to a deficit of £3.7 billion.

In 1951 UK residents took a total of 26.5 million 'long holidays', defined as personal stays in excess of four nights. Twenty-five million of these were taken in the UK; 1.5 million abroad. By 1965 the respective figures were 35 million, 30 million and 5 million. The number of holidays taken has continued to rise steadily, but the percentage constituted by 'holidays at home' has fallen, reaching an all-time low of 58% in 1993. In this year 23.5 million holidays were taken overseas – supplemented by 13 million other overseas visits – and 32.5 million in the UK. At the same time Britain attracted 19.3 million overseas tourists, who spent an estimated total of £9.2 billion.

These figures place Britain fifth in the league of world earners from tourism, behind, for example, USA (first), France, Italy and Spain. Visitors to Britain come from all round the world; the leading country sources are:

1. USA   – not only the largest number; American visitors tend to stay longer and spend more than the average European tourist
2. France   – a few years ago the leading source
3. Germany
4. Ireland
5. Holland.

In 1980 Britain earned 6.7% of world tourist

spending; by 1993 this had fallen to 4.3%, representing a steady decline in market share. However this has been turned around again, and in 1995 Britain earned 5% of the world total.

Tourism:

❏ creates jobs
❏ boosts local communities and
❏ projects a positive image of the country, both at home and abroad.

The industry continues to offer enormous growth potential, but visitors must be persuaded to come, and, ideally, encouraged to come at particular times and travel around rather than focus on London and its various busy attractions. Over 80% of all UK tourism activity is concentrated in England; Scotland and Wales are clearly more popular with domestic holidaymakers.

The figures below in Table 1 indicate the relative popularity of the UK's paid attractions in 1992, 1993 and 1994; aggregate figures of this nature cannot distinguish between home and overseas visitors. Exhibits 1 and 2 highlight the seasonal and regional pattern of visitors from overseas.

Both Alton Towers and Madame Tussaud's are owned by the international media and communications conglomerate, Pearsons; by contrast with the figure for the Natural History Museum, 6.3 million visitors were recorded at the British Museum in 1992. The British Museum still offers free admission.

Research by the British Tourist Authority (BTA) (published in 1994) indicates clearly that visitors from different countries have differing tastes and expectations. Americans, for example, told researchers that to them Britain means 'bobbies, barristers, Big Ben and Westminster Abbey', and they want it to stay

this way. Many Japanese perceive Britain to be 'too masculine', represented by 'heroic castles'. As a result, a recent BTA promotional campaign in Japan has been designed to create a 'softer and more feminine feel – quaint country house hotels, green landscapes and Laura Ashley'. The theme of taking afternoon tea has proved particularly successful.

Exhibit 1   Overseas visitors to the UK: 1992

Month	Number	Percent of total		Hotel occupancy levels	
				England inc. London	London only
January	1200	6.5		21	30
February	966	5.0	18	28	40
March	1179	6.5		31	42
April	1648	9.0		36	50
May	1594	8.5	26.5	41	46
June	1655	9.0		44	50
July	2038	11.0		52	58
Aug	2430	13.0	33.5	51	56
September	1721	9.5		48	51
October	1483	8.0		42	51
November	1235	6.5	22.0	32	46
December	1385	7.5		27	37
	18,534				

Exhibit 2   Domestic and overseas tourism in the UK: 1994 regional popularity

Percent of trips spent in	UK residents	Overseas visitors
Scotland	7.5	6.9
Northern Ireland	1.0	0.4
Cumbria	2.5	1.2
Northumbria	2.7	1.7
Yorks & Humbs	8.2	3.6
North West	7.6	4.4
Wales	8.6	2.7
Heart of England	8.7	5.2
East Midlands	6.7	2.6
East Anglia	9.0	5.2
West Country	13.3	5.7
South England	9.3	7.1
South East	7.0	7.9
London	7.9	45.4

Table 1   Numbers of visitors to UK paid attractions, 1992–1994

Position in 1994		1992 million	1993 million	1994 million
1	Alton Towers	2.50	2.62	3.01
2	Madame Tussaud's	2.27	2.45	2.63
3	Tower of London	2.24	2.33	2.41
4	St Paul's Cathedral	1.40	1.90	1.90
5	Natural History Museum	1.70	1.70	1.63
12	London Zoo	0.94	0.86	1.05
16	Roman Baths, Bath	0.90	0.89	0.87

The BTA believes there are 'disturbing signs that Britain's competitive position in the international tourism market is facing new challenges' and that Britain's loss of market share could and should be tackled with more public money. However, the deployment and targeting of investment and publicity is a complex issue. The industry is fragmented and includes major, successful and profitable holiday companies, airlines and hotel chains, together with important attractions in both the public and private sectors and a multitude of small businesses. It spans the profit-seeking sectors of both manufacturing and service and not-for-profit organizations like the National Trust.

The UK tourist industry can be thought of as a mosaic of independent yet inter-dependent parts. Unfortunately the quality and standards of the component parts vary markedly. One challenge for the industry is to bring every part up to 'world class standards'.

The role of the British Tourist Authority

The BTA looks to co-ordinate some of the marketing efforts of the various organizations in the leisure and tourism industry and generally promote Britain to the rest of the world.

> *Our role is to be a catalyst, co-ordinator and champion of this sector ... we continue to attract substantial private sector funding for a wide range of joint projects.*
>
> (Adele Biss, Chairman, 1993–1996)

As a catalyst, the BTA has influence rather than power, and other organizations are the main beneficiaries of its efforts.

The logic behind the existence of the BTA is the need for a 'central message' about the UK, together with the desirability of some central control of standards. Private sector companies in the industry compete with each other and they have individual objectives, which inevitably differ from those of the BTA. Nevertheless there are many opportunities for joint ventures and promotions.

In 1993 Peter Brook, the National Heritage Secretary, the Ministry to which the BTA reports, stated in parliament that the BTA performs a function which the private sector cannot:

> *Overseas promotion is difficult to organize and the returns to individual businesses may be small and unpredictable – not worth the investment. The industry, unaided, would not put sufficient money and effort into overseas promotion. The tourism industry is particularly fragmented; it covers many sectors and it is not in the direct interest of any one private sector company to promote Britain as a destination.*

The BTA employs staff in London and in offices overseas. There is a central executive of five and a Board of external appointees, some of whom are from major tourism and leisure businesses. Current members include Sir John Egan (Chief Executive, British Airports Authority) and the Hon. Rocco Forte, ex-Chairman of Forte plc. Sir Colin Marshall, Chairman of British Airways, served on the Board until early 1993.

The stated mission of the BTA is 'to strengthen the performance of Britain's tourist industry in international markets by encouraging people to visit Britain and encouraging the improvement and provision of tourist amenities and facilities'.

At the end of the 1980's, external pressures resulted in strategic and structural changes at BTA, which have had important implications for the role and values of the staff – issues discussed later in the case.

Specifically the BTA:

❏ promotes Britain (selectively) to foreign tourists, attempting to make available to them the information they need to make 'informed decisions'.

The English, Wales and Scottish Tourist Boards are primarily responsible for promoting UK holidays to UK residents

❏ receives (from government), raises (through joint ventures with private industry) and spends money in order to accomplish this

❏ seeks to influence the products offered by providers and the quality of their service.

It is clearly arguable that given the number of jobs created and sustained by tourism, it makes economic sense for Britain to at the very least seek to keep pace with world market growth and arrest the relative decline in popularity. However, the impact of such *aggregate* growth must be considered in respect of *specific* timings (seasonality), destinations and attractions. London, Stratford, Bath and York remain the most popular places, although David Bowie's birthplace in Bromley is proving attractive to the growing number of visitors from eastern

Europe. If visitor numbers rise by 50% by the year 2001, in line with projections for the global industry, would the industry be able to cope? An alternative case could be made for concentrating less on numbers and more on innovative ways of adding new values to increase spending per head. This implies improving the quality and range of facilities on offer, a key task of the English Tourist Board rather than the BTA.

This debate raises a number of points. For example, it touches on the issue of the delicate balance between commercial exploitation on the one hand and preservation and conservation on the other. The UK's heritage, marketed effectively, will attract tourists and generate a substantial cash flow, some of which can be used to help meet the costs of preservation. At the same time, too many visitors, not controlled properly, will damage both the environment and the heritage.

A second issue concerns access to the UK by air. British Airways argues that a fifth terminal at Heathrow is essential in the next few years if the UK is to be able to cope with projected demand for air travel in and out of the country. A similar case has been put forward in support of a fifth runway in the south east, to supplement the two at Heathrow and the

ones at Gatwick and Stansted. Environmentalists and affected residents are likely to oppose both propositions.

Should the BTA be active in these issues, and if so, how?

The funded agencies

The government, since 1992 specifically the Ministry for National Heritage, provides grant-in-aid to the BTA and three National Boards: the English Tourist Board, which has headquarters in the same London building as the BTA and the same Chairman, the Scottish Tourist Board and the Wales Tourist Board. The respective figures for 1992–1993 were:

	£ million
British Tourist Authority	30.9
English Tourist Board	16.2
Scottish Tourist Board	10.1
Wales Tourist Board	9.5

Exhibit 3 provides a summary of BTA's income and expenditure since 1988, highlighting how trading surpluses have turned into operating losses and

Exhibit 3 British Tourist Authority finanical highlights

	Year ended							Projection	
	31.3.1989 £'000	31.3.1990 £'000	31.3.1991 £'000	31.3.1992 £'000	31.3.1993 £'000	31.3.1994 £'000	31.3.1995 £'000	31.3.1996 £ million	31.3.1997 £ million
Income									
Grant-in-aid	23,700	25,630	27,510	29,225	30,865	32,220	33,200	34.5	35.5
Publicity, consultancy, research	13,315	13,252	12,902	13,671	14,207	15,578	15,493		
Earnings from cash resources	539	397	314	522	928	360	406		
Total Income	37,554	39,279	40,726	43,418	46,000	48,158	49,131		
Expenditure									
Staff costs	8,284	8,234	7,768	8,480	9,655	9,513	9,668		
Exceptional cost – redundancy programmes					1,110	602	1,062		
Marketing and publicity	13,238	13,775	15,075	17,724	19,063	21,180	19,892		
Publications	4,759	4,573	3,134	2,351	2,684	2,677	3,367		
Overseas offices	5,497	5,322	6,155	6,299	6,222	6,324	7,091		
Other operational activities	4,696	5,421	7,166	8,196	7,022	7,316	7,119		
Depreciation	559	572	535	460	443	403	443		
Total expenditure	37,033	37,897	39,833	43,510	46,199	48,015	48,642		
Operating surplus after tax and other extraordinary items	498	33	791	(183)	(258)	89	439		
Retained surplus carried forward	2,919	2,952	3,743	3,560	3,302	3,391	3,830		

Table 2 English Tourist Board – grant-in-aid

Year	£ Million
1990–1991	14.9
1991–1992	15.1
1992–1993	16.2
1993–1994	13.9
1994–1995	11.3
1995–1996	10.0

back to profits. Whilst the grant-in-aid for the BTA has been increasing, that for the English Tourist Board, responsible for the quality of provision in England and for internal promotions, has declined. The BTA grant-in-aid is projected to rise from £32.2 million (1993–1994) to £35.5 million in 1996–1997. Over the same period the English Tourist Board is due to experience a fall. See Table 2.

The Scottish and Wales Tourist Boards have not had to cope with similar reductions. The government believes the quality and promotional work in England is better handled by 11 separate regional tourist boards.

The English Tourist Board (ETB), similar to those for Scotland and Wales:

❏ works closely with agencies and voluntary bodies in the fields of heritage, arts, sports and the countryside
❏ seeks to promote good service and value for money and develop the products visitors want to buy.

The ETB, for example, examines and awards Crowns to hotels throughout the UK, and it has parallel award schemes for lodges and self-catering accommodation.

In pursuing its objectives the ETB works in partnership with:

❏ leading hotel chains
❏ thousands of small companies and independent businesses
❏ hundreds of local authorities
❏ the 11 regional tourist boards – England is divided geographically into discrete regions for development and promotional purposes
❏ 15 government departments
❏ a wide array of related agencies and local tourist organizations.

The regional tourist boards and the ETB work together on promotions and publicity (such as brochures promoting the Lake District and its attractions say) and locally they focus on specific initiatives, generally seeking additional funding from members of the tourism industry. An example would be the development of new heritage sites with co-ordinated private and public sector sponsorship. In 1992–1993 the 11 boards in aggregate were funded as follows:

	£'000
Commercial members subscriptions	1,790
Local Authority subscriptions	1,982
English Tourist Board	6,758
Externally raised income	12,726
	23,256

Consequently, a substantial proportion of ETB promotional funds are allocated through the regional boards, which are not immune from commercial realities. In 1992–1993 the Thames and Chilterns Board went into voluntary liquidation, and its efforts were absorbed by neighbouring areas which simply re-drew their boundaries.

The British Tourist Authority

BTA's financial record

See Exhibits 3 and 4. In 1990 the number of visitors to the UK reached an all-time high of 18 million; they spent a record total of £7.8 billion. In 1991 the uncertainty which followed the Gulf conflict caused both the number of visitors and spending to fall. The BTA and the industry worked hard to turn the situation around, and both measures have been improved. In 1993 the ratio between total visitor expenditure and grant-in-aid was equal to the corresponding figure for 1990; but the figures take no account of inflation. The situation is always made more complex when sterling devalues over a period. Currency depreciation attracts more visitors but increases the relative cost of overseas promotions.

Over this period the proportion of expenditure on people, as opposed to promotions, has fallen;

and in the last few years there have been redundancy programmes at both the BTA and ETB. During the 1990s it has become increasingly necessary for the funded agencies to justify their existence and quantify their achievements. Some of the benefits must remain intangible; the sheer existence and visibility of the BTA has various indirect and long-term benefits for the UK as a whole, not simply tourism, and it helps many private sector companies to themselves be viable and profitable for the economy. But the BTA cannot use an argument such as this as a shield; it is not defensible for it to be essentially a 'publishing house doing a job which really belongs in the private sector'.

The Authority has been particularly successful in generating financial contributions from commercial partners in a variety of promotional joint ventures.

The 1992–1993 target of £18 million was surpassed by £3 milllion, to which can be added £5 million extra support in kind, in the form of airline tickets and free hotel accommodation for important opinion leaders. However, it has been commented that the BTA 'needs to pay more attention to travel companies' views on how their contributions should be spent'.

All marketing projects require a contribution from joint venture partners, the exact amount varying between projects and depending also on the type of partner and their ability to pay. BTA has strict targets to meet in respect of external joint marketing if it is to continue to minimize the scale of irrecoverable VAT; and their significance is likely to increase further in the future.

Figure 1 shows the key flows of money in the tourist industry system.

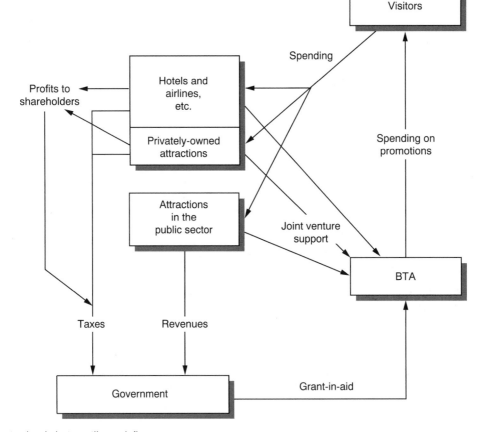

Figure 1   The tourism industry outline cash flow.

Exhibit 4

Spending in the UK by overseas visitors			BTA grant-in-aid		Amount spent per £ of grant-in-aid
Year	Visitors (millions)	Spending £ billion	Year	£'000	£
1989	17.0	7.0	1988/1989	23,700	295
1990	18.0	7.8	1989/1990	25,630	304
1991	17.13	7.38	1990/1991	27,510	268
1992	18.54	7.9	1991/1992	29,225	270
1993	19.5	9.38	1992/1993	30,865	304
1994	21.0	9.92	1993/1994	32,220	308

Activities

The BTA:

❏ publishes a wide range of literature, including directories, on holiday opportunities, hotels and so on, in a number of languages
❏ operates a number of travel centres which, amongst other things, issue British Rail and London theatre tickets, and provide help with accommodation and bureau de change facilities, sometimes franchised to specialist operators
❏ administers a world-wide network of offices which provide information to prospective visitors, co-ordinate promotions, and gather market intelligence. It is important for short- and long-term planning that specific needs and expectations are identified.

Exhibit 5 lists the offices.

Leadership

There have been a number of changes of leadership at the BTA in the 1990s.

William Davis, a millionaire publisher, who had been part-time Chairman for three years, left the organization in 1993. There had been disagreement with the government over funding, and on 22 May 1993 *Today* newspaper quoted Davis as saying:

❏ There is no long-term strategy in the UK for tourism.
❏ The industry is not taken seriously by government.
❏ The switch of reporting relationship from the Department of Trade and Industry to Environment and subsequently to National Heritage has not been wholly helpful.

Exhibit 5 BTA offices world-wide

North America:	USA	New York
		Atlanta
		Chicago
		Los Angeles
		Miami
	Canada	Toronto
Northern Europe		Frankfurt
		Amsterdam
		Brussels
Nordic region		Stockholm
		Copenhagen
Southern Europe		Paris
		Madrid
		Rome
		Milan (representative)
Africa		Johannesburg
Australasia		Sydney
		Auckland
Asia		Singapore
		Tokyo
		Osaka (representative)
Ireland		Dublin

There is representation – without an office which is open to the public – in the following locations:

Buenos Aires, Rio de Janiero, Caracas, Oslo, Lisbon, Prague, Budapest, Gurgaon (India), Seoul, Taiwan, Hong Kong, Mexico

Promotions take place in some 65 countries world-wide

Davis was replaced in June by Adele Biss in the two-days-a-week post which also encompasses chairing the English Tourist Board. Her salary was reported at £35,000 per year for a three-year term. Ms Biss had built a successful career and business in public relations, she was a non-executive director of British Rail and in the past she had held a senior marketing post at Thomson Holidays.

The full-time Chief Executive, Michael Medlicott, also left in April 1993 to join Delta Airlines. He was replaced temporarily by his deputy, Alan Jefferson, an expert in marketing, who had been with the BTA for many years. Ms Biss was in her late forties, but Jefferson was already over 60 years of age.

Towards the end of 1993 Jefferson retired and was succeeded by Anthony Sell, who joined from the Thomas Cook Group, where he was based in Paris as the Managing Director for Continental Europe. Prior to this Sell has been President of Boosey and Hawke's clarinet manufacturing company in France.

Adele Biss completed her three-year term and then stepped down in May 1996. Her replacement was David Quarmby, who had recently (March 1996) resigned as joint managing director at J. Sainsbury. Quarmby would spend three days a week chairing the BTA and ETB; his salary was estimated to be £54,000 per year.

BTA objectives

The BTA has agreed the following long-term objectives:

(i)   Maximize the benefit to the economy of tourism to Britain from abroad.
(ii) Ensure that the Authority makes the most cost-effective use of resources in pursuing its objectives.
      Resources, of course, are constrained by grants and the ability to agree joint venture projects; and therefore the benefits generated are inevitably limited. With more money benefits could be increased – but when do they become less cost-effective to create?
(iii) Identify what visitors want and stimulate improvements in products and services to meet their needs.
(iv) Encourage off-peak tourism.
(v)   Spread the economic benefit of tourism more widely, and particularly to areas with tourism

potential and higher-than-average levels of unemployment.

These last three objectives may well prove contradictory. Moreover there will always be considerable elements of subjectivity and value judgement in establishing priority areas.

Measures of corporate performance

The BTA could be judged to be successful if visitors (business people and tourists) come to Britain, if they come both off-season as well as in season [objective (iv)], if they spend increasing amounts of money whilst they are here, if they spend in the preferred places [objective (v)], and if they go home and tell other people to come – and over a period this increases the number of visitors and their expenditure [objective (i) explicitly and objective (iii) implicitly].

These are all measures of effectiveness, whilst objective (ii) specifically addresses resource efficiency. However there is a problem of cause and effect. Whilst the criteria listed above can all be measured, the net contribution of the BTA cannot be so easily ascertained. Tourists and business people would still come, regardless of the existence of the BTA. The cause and effect of BTA initiatives is very difficult to ascertain without extensive and expensive tracking studies.

It is believed implicitly that the activities undertaken around the world contribute to corporate objectives and performance, but often it is the activities (efficiencies) which are measured rather than the outcomes. Are particular promotions actually implemented? Are planned brochures published? Are desirable workshops and seminars attended?

The Scottish Tourist Board, for example, measures and monitors, amongst other things:

❏ income as a percentage
  of expenditure
❏ the number of strategic   } efficiency
  reports produced
❏ advertising cost per brochure
❏ direct mail response rate
❏ jobs created through
  financial assistance   } effectiveness
  programmes.

Since 1991 the BTA has engaged in an active

programme of measuring cost effectiveness. Acti-vites have been split: public information services; advertising; missions and exhibitions. The extra spending generated where BTA has been involved has been compared with the direct costs incurred. Studies have indicated a range of outcomes from £4 to over £50 for each £1 spent by BTA.

Effectiveness measures

Specifically we are concerned with added value, the extra contribution the BTA makes to the British economy. Visitors who otherwise would not have come to the UK, or who would have come but stayed for a shorter period. Visitors who would have come peak season rather than off-season and who may have stayed in London for the whole of their visit. There have been deliberate attempts to track these issues.

A 1993 assessment of BTA's information service in New York indicated that it generates £35 in overseas tourism expenditure for every £1 spent by BTA. Most enquiries concern theatres, accommodation and the English weather! A free 1-800 number has been introduced for handling American enquiries, substantially sponsored by United Airlines, Hertz and Mount Charlotte Thistle Hotels, who pay for a commercial message as soon as the phone number is answered.

The Japanese 'afternoon tea' promotion, mention-ed earlier, consisted of newspaper advertisements inviting people to attend a series of tea parties with well-known celebrities – a privilege they had to pay for. The advertising was partly funded by British Air-ways and KNT Tours, a Japanese tour operator. One thousand people were selected by lottery from 18,000 applicants. Tracking studies confirm 50 people have booked holidays as a direct result of the promotion; given the Japanese typically spend over £500 per person per visit to the UK, it can be assumed that £250,000 has been generated from £10,000 BTA costs.

Joint ventures

BTA's alliances, partnerships and commercial deals range from paid-for directory entries to complex joint venture projects. In 1993, for example, BTA's office in Singapore arranged for BA, Qantas and Singapore Airlines to jointly sponsor a Travel Austra-lia Britain Seminar in that country. UK suppliers

were brought face-to-face with over 200 travel agents from 12 countries in the Asia Pacific region. An extra £2 million of revenue for the UK suppliers is estimated to be the outcome.

Research – see Exhibit 6

Finding out exactly what different visitors want, and using this to develop carefully targeted promotional campaigns, is a critical role for the BTA. Research in 1993 in the Republic of Ireland clarified that the separate brand identities of England, Scotland and Wales are more important than an image of 'Britain'. This, and other findings, led to distinctive and specially targeted promotions to three ABC1 groups: young couples, families with cars and peo-ple aged 45 and over. The response rate was four times that of previous promotions and a 20% increase in business is projected.

The BTA annual survey of foreign visitors, pub-lished in March 1994, indicated that:

❑ The perception that Great Britain offers 'value for money' improves when sterling devalues; store, meal and transport prices are all a feature of this.
❑ There is general dissatisfaction with the cost of hotels which are perceived as 'offering poor value and not living up to expectations'.

  If prices were lower, demand would increase from both UK residents and overseas visitors.

  In 1995 the Department of National Heritage announced that it would use benchmarking to try and improve the standards of UK hotels.
❑ There is some dissatisfaction, particularly with French and Italian tourists, with the inability of British people to speak their language.

One outcome has been a campaign for VAT reduc-tion on tourism activities and accommodation. Most

Exhibit 6

Examples of research activities

❑ attitude surveys of overseas visitors
❑ tourist price indices around the world
❑ visitor spending surveys – focus on priority markets
❑ London visitors
❑ visitors to (and their spending at) exhibitions
❑ selected surveys abroad into what people want from any proposed visit to Britain

of the European Union – the exceptions are Denmark and the UK – operates a favourable VAT rate for hotels, theatres and leisure attractions.

Research has also highlighted the following needs:

❏ more airport runway capacity in the south east
❏ more lower-cost accommodation in London
❏ a more tourist-friendly attitude amongst certain sectors of the retail industry.

Other research has shown that 25% of all visitors to the UK had visited a BTA office abroad. Typically the offices overseas deal with some 1.5 million enquiries each year; the London base handles a further 600,000.

Campaigning

A final role of BTA is campaigning on key issues. For example, when London Bus Ltd was privatized and split into ten separate, regional bus companies, there was a real danger that each company would adopt new and distinctive liveries. London has had red buses for 60 years and BTA research clarified that they are perceived as being peculiarly British and should be retained. The BTA-led campaign has proved successful; the Minister for Tourism, Stephen Dorrell, is insisting that all buses on main routes through the capital must remain red.

Environment and key success factors

The BTA, as has already been established, is heavily dependent on grant-in-aid, which, recently, has been increasing by lower percentage amounts – roughly in line with reduced inflation. BTA continues to lobby government for more generous treatment.

The government, for its part, and as a major stakeholder, will always have a view on what the BTA should be achieving, and at any time it is likely to have preferred 'target' markets. These priorities will change periodically. Japan has been a favourite in recent years – but progress has been constrained in the short-term by the number of flights and seats available on air routes from Tokyo.

The government, anxious to improve the overall effectiveness and impact of the BTA, brought in PA Management Consultants to review their operations. The PA report, in July 1989, recommended strategic changes which emphasized further decentralization and a greater devolution of resources and responsibilities to the 22 overseas offices. Aspects of the implementation of this report are considered later in the section on resources. In the 1990s some offices have been closed and new ones opened.

Tourism generally faces an uncertain future. Competition is global; holiday tastes and preferences change; events like the 1991 Gulf War have a profound effect on selected destinations; and changes in the relative value of sterling also have an impact.

Different stakeholders have different time horizons. The objectives of BTA, as detailed above, are long-term, although there are specific annual targets. On the other hand the government has much shorter time horizons, and thereby seeks to influence resource allocations. Similarly, joint venture partners, like airlines and the major hotel chains, are most keen to invest in projects when they are experiencing unexpected low volumes, and again will be seeking short-term benefits. It becomes questionable how long-term the strategy can be. The broad directions can be established, but short-term changes and projects seem inevitable.

The role of the BTA is more *influential* than *powerful*. BTA needs the support of its various stakeholders, and must persuade them of the value and creativity of its projects and new ventures.

Finally there is an environmental lobby, keen to 'protect certain areas', to consider. The BTA states clearly that it will 'seek to ensure that its policies take account of the need to conserve and enhance Britain's built heritage, landscape and environment, sporting, cultural and artistic strengths'.

Effectiveness requires that the BTA is able to target the areas with the greatest potential (in a changing world) in the future. This must depend upon the quality of market intelligence and the ability of staff world-wide to spot, and capitalize upon, new opportunities. As highlighted above, it also requires that the BTA is able to forge appropriate joint marketing and promotion ventures in order to capitalize on these opportunities. This in turn will depend upon the ability of BTA to deliver quality in its promotional efforts, and be perceived to be doing this by prospective partners.

Values

In order to achieve these key success factors, staff need to be marketing and service oriented, and able to mount 'value-for-money' promotions – ones with a measurable return. Historically, though, many of the staff have not been recruited for their ability to be marketing oriented and commercial in outlook; other values have been of equal importance, a point developed in the next section. Given this fact, and a programme of staff reduction, these recent changes have proved challenging.

BTA must also be committed to improving the service orientation of tourist providers in the UK, but here again it can only influence. BTA has no direct power.

Adele Biss has commented that the UK needs:

❏ a stronger focus on quality standards and
❏ more energetic promotion and better marketing.

She believes that these requirements demand:

❏ greater commitment from government
❏ better partnerships between members of the industry and government and
❏ more effective exploitation of the possible linkages and synergy between the BTA and the English, Scottish and Wales Tourist Boards.

Effectiveness aspects of these issues will remain difficult to measure.

At the same time BTA should be seeking to help those providers least able to help themselves in terms of international marketing. Arguably, the major airlines and hotel chains, frequently keen to support joint promotions, really do not need the help of the BTA, however welcome joint ventures are. BTA, in theory, 'intervenes only where the industry lacks resources to deal with market obstacles and only where intervention is likely to be effective'. Success in establishing the most appropriate priorities is subjective.

The BTA strategy is basically risk averse. Efforts are spread globally, rather than key markets selected and targeted. France, in comparison, targets some ten key markets. The BTA strategy is useful for when preferences change, but the drawback is that insufficient funds may be being allocated to certain markets to have any real impact. It is a question of losing opportunities because priorities change, or because of inadequate funding in selected areas. BTA

also has a policy of pioneering in new and emerging markets. Joint venture partners, on the other hand, are more likely to want to invest in instant success. Could their interests and priorities clash?

The BTA is aware of the need for on-going cultural change to support the structural changes discussed below. The increasing marketing orientation is being developed, but further opportunities and potential benefits must still exist.

The corporate culture will need to reflect social and environmental values in order that the Authority is perceived as a desirable place to work. Personal development and organizational effectiveness will be bound together ...
(in short) *... an achievement and supportive culture.*

Resources

Historically, however, the BTA has been perceived as an élitist organization, albeit a QUANGO. For their staff there has always been the opportunity to travel abroad; and for many years recruitment focused on bright graduates who can be good ambassadors for Britain, offering them security of tenure with civil service conditions and salaries. Their general ability to communicate and promote has been seen to be as important as marketing orientation and commitment to commercial activity and profit.

The restructuring which followed the PA report has demanded a more commercial focus within the offices around the world, but, having regard to the minor and fragmented presence overseas, there remains an argument that true decentralization may not prove to be either feasible or cost effective in the long-run. In addition, 'spiralling costs' of the overseas offices continue to mean new pressures to reduce staff and advertising.

The 1992–1993 BTA annual report states that 100 posts had been lost over four years in London, but there had been an increase of 30 overseas. Jobs have also been lost at the English Tourist Board (42 out of 139 posts were declared redundant in 1992–1993); and publicity, sales and distribution activities which were previously a common service to the two Boards have been absorbed by BTA staff. In 1993–1994 the BTA employed – on average for the year – 168 people in London and 178 overseas, 20 fewer (mostly in London) than a year earlier. There appears to always be some reliance on temporary agency staff and people on short-term contracts. The BTA is committed to ensuring that the costs of its London office do not exceed 15% of total operational running costs.

For the moment, there is still a reliance on centrally driven planning influenced by overseas managers, with a resultant delegation rather than devolution. Some changes of orientation have been required both in London and overseas. If a successful attitude change to more commercialism and financial accountability, together with a change-oriented culture, cannot be fully achieved, there might be an argument to return to more centralization, and with greater reliance on representatives and local people rather than BTA-staffed offices. It has been recognized that the suggested changes in culture and attitude require that the reward and promotion systems are re-evaluated. The civil service pay and conditions were never intended to meet this kind of scenario.

The measurement of effective performance, particularly in relation to environmental issues and values clearly presents a challenge for BTA. The contribution of the staff is irrevocably linked to these and is consequently also in need of careful evaluation in a changing world.

Questions

1 Identify the major stakeholders of the BTA and clarify the relationships.

   How important is it for BTA specifically to act as a champion to ensure the smooth running of the network of interested parties?

2 Who do you believe should be responsible for promoting Britain as a tourist centre – a publicly-funded body or the private sector businesses who benefit financially?

   Should the BTA be anything more than a catalyst?

   What is needed for BTA to fulfil its role effectively?

   How might the government ensure the country as a whole and particularly the multitude of small businesses in the tourism industry – are major beneficiaries rather than the major benefits going to, say, the large and powerful hotel and airline companies?

3 Clarify the main roles of the BTA.

   Where do you believe BTA can make its most important contribution?

4 List the performance measures covered in the case study.

   Can you think of other suitable measures?

   How difficult do you believe it is to carry out the tracking required to measure effectiveness?

5 Using the latter sections of the case study, do you believe the BTA is achieving E–V–R congruence?

6 Do you think the country gets value for money from organizations like the BTA?

Lilliput Lane (A)

Lilliput Lane, based on the edge of the English Lake District, manufactures a range of miniature plaster cottages which are marketed to customers throughout the world, many of whom are committed collectors.

This case study traces the early growth of the company in the 1980s, its subsequent setbacks, a successful turnaround, followed by a flotation and sale in the 1990s.

It focuses on the issues of strategic leadership, stakeholder expectations, core competencies, adding value, diversification and focus strategies.

Lilliput Lane A has been written 1995 by John L Thompson for the purpose of class discussion. It should not be taken to reflect either effective or ineffective management. Lilliput Lane was reproduced in *Small Business and Enterprise Development*, vol. 2, no. 2, 1995, John Wiley.

Introduction

At the beginning of September 1994 it was announced that the Lilliput Group was to be sold to an American company, Stanhome, which markets and distributes consumer products, giftware and collectibles. Stanhome's best-known range of collectibles is the Precious Moments series. The bid valued Lilliput at £37.2 million; in November 1993 the company had been floated with a value of £31.4 million.

Lilliput, based at Skirsgill, near Penrith, on the edge of the English Lake District, is one of the UK's leading manufacturers of collectibles. Its main product is a range of some 180 high-quality, hand-painted miniature cottages and other buildings. Following early growth in the 1980s – the company was founded in 1982 – Lilliput enjoyed mixed fortunes. During the 1990s, however, and following the disposal of non-core activities, rationalization, recapitalization and the appointment of a new strategic leader, profits have grown significantly.

The cottages are marketed through 2400 retail outlets in the UK and exported to 44 countries. There is an important and active Collectors' Club with over 70,000 members world-wide.

The following extract, taken from company promotional literature, summarizes the philosophy on which the success has been built:

A cottage is a home, but to some it is a living thing which breathes and grows. It has a personality and character all of its own. Like every living thing the cottage needs to be nurtured, protected, loved and respected and every generation leaves its mark, however small, on the life of the building.

Many factors determine the character and personality of a cottage, the style of architecture, the materials used in its construction, the dictates of its environment, old age and decay, but mostly the area of the country from which it originates. As you travel around Great Britain you will notice many old buildings with similar features and overall appearance which have evolved a quite different look and character to cottages only a few miles away.

Each cottage was originally built to meet the needs of the family who were to occupy it and as the family grew, so did the cottage. The cottage was built and designed by the people who were to live in it, country folk who used their skills and crafts together with materials which were close at hand. This has given Britain an architectural heritage which is amongst the most varied and beautiful in the world.

Communities built using methods proved and improved by generations of their own craftsmen. Where stone was found that was used – flint, rubble, Cotswold or dressed stone. Wood is used in some form on almost every building, but in the once densely wooded areas of England and the Welsh borders it produced the spectacular timber framed buildings which we marvel at today. Clay was used in many different ways, in cob walls, wattle and daub panels or shaped into bricks and tiles and then fired. Roofs were covered in a number of different local materials, thatch, slate, stone flags, pantiles, claytiles or even heather.

The cottages which we at Lilliput Lane have chosen for our collection, are hidden away in the countryside behind high hedgerows, down farm tracks, in valleys or woods or high in the hills; the twentieth century has passed them by. Only after months of research do our sculptors discover these sometimes long forgotten homes. They will then take up to a hundred photographs before they are ready to magically create, in wax to minute scale, a three-dimensional cottage; every brick, tile and leaf faithfully captured as a true reflection of the original building.

The cottage then embarks on a long painstaking journey through the workshops and studios at Lilliput Lane. Complex moulds are made, then many painted samples are produced by our master-painters before we decide upon exactly the right colour combination for each miniature masterpiece. Finally every sculpture is exquisitely painted in Lilliput Lane's studios by one of our team of talented artists to the very highest standard. We do not compromise on quality. Every piece is rigorously inspected many times which assures our collectors that they are receiving a model perfect in every way.

Over 15 million pieces have been sold since the company was started. The founder, David Tate, has suggested that many people 'see their ideal home, or their ideal retirement home, in many of the models'.

The early years

Lilliput Lane Ltd was founded in 1982 by the families of Yorkshireman David Tate and Anthony Barnes to manufacture and market hard plaster cast (gypsum amorphite), hand-painted miniature cottage models 'unsurpassed in quality of workmanship and design'. Barnes left the organization in 1985. Tate had had to re-mortgage his house and sell most of his possessions to raise his share of the capital. Although both partners originally 'invested everything they had', the company was substantially dependent on long-term loans from their bankers and Lazard Ventures.

David Tate left school at 16 'with no qualifications', and subsequently spent 13 years in the Army – half of this in public relations work – and seven years in the fibreglass industry. For a short while he was also a self-employed sculptor and mould maker. He was 37 years old in 1982. His interest in cottages had begun much earlier, when, as a boy, he spent his school holidays with family relations in Bedfordshire. The Army taught him the technicalities of glass-fibre moulding and other skills which he later used to develop a revolutionary new system for enabling small, intricate objects to be moulded in one piece.

The company began at Skirsgill with 12 people in low-cost premises when Tate was offered the lease on a privately-owned but semi-derelict group of red sandstone buildings sited on a disused eighteenth-century farm. Tate was introduced to the owner by Penrith Council, anxious to promote industrial development. Neighbours on the emerging industrial site included a horsebox manufacturer and a builder of wooden houses. The company's headquarters today are on the same estate, where cows still graze just over the boundary wall and the view takes in the nearby Pennine Hills. The site has both the look and feel of a true cottage industry.

For the first six months, David Tate, his wife and two daughters 'lived in a rented damp cottage and slept on the floor. The whole family worked 18 hours a day, 7 days a week' on the original range of 14 models. The business enjoyed some early success with small sales through gift shops, and it has subsequently grown into Penrith's largest employer. It was first profitable in 1983–1984.

Between 1984 and 1987, and following a favourable reception at an important trade fair, sales grew rapidly from £318,000 to £4.1 million (see Exhibit 1). Two further production sites, again in Cumbria, were opened. The fast, demand-driven growth, reinforced by the ever-present need to recruit and quickly train new people – by late 1986 the number of employees had risen to 350 (see Exhibit 2) – led to some slack cost management. Profit before interest and tax, 13.5% of sales in 1985, fell back to 6.9% in 1987. Cashflow difficulties, realized as early as the 1983–1984 trading year, intensified.

At the end of 1984, the company's auditor, William Dodd, agreed to invest a substantial sum of money in the business – and at the same time he became company Chairman. 'It was time to match artistic impression with more formalized business organization'. Output continued to grow rapidly.

Diversification strategies

Dodd was ambitious for Lilliput Lane to grow and sometime later the company decided to diversify, partly by acquisition, in order to expand its product range. It has been said, with hindsight, that this decision represents the time when the company 'stopped thinking about what its business was about, and what market it was in'.

Exhibit 2 Lilliput Lane

	Number of employees
30.9.1983	24
30.9.1984	47
30.9.1985	86
30.9.1986	229
30.9.1987	453
30.9.1988	483
30.9.1989	641
30.9.1990	663
5.1.1992	577
3.1.1993	472
31.3.1994	c. 600

Exhibit 1 Lilliput Lane
Profit and loss account highlights

	Lilliput Lane	Turnover			Profit/loss before interest and tax
		Lilliput Group			
		Total	Continued activities	Discontinued activities	
	£'000	£'000	£'000	£'000	£'000
12 months to					
30.9.1983	123				(4)
30.9.1984	318				24
30.9.1985	793				107
30.9.1986	2138				133
30.9.1987	4124				285
30.9.1988		6450	5898	552	413
30.9.1989		9109	8294	815	(421)
30.9.1990		12,145	11,080	1065	(367)
15 months to					
5.1.1992		15,162	15,162		1427
12 months to					
3.1.1993		13,581			2129
31.12.1993		16,506			3075

In June 1987, a new company, Lilliput Group, was incorporated and it acquired the shares of Lilliput Lane. Later the same year Lilliput formed three new subsidiaries.

First, Land of Legend, to manufacture resin demons and fantasy models. A new production process was implied. Considerable learning was needed to catch up and match the quality of the leading resin manufacturers such as Border Fine Arts, which is also located on the edge of Cumbria, but specializes in animals and birds.

The second subsidiary, Lilliput Creations, was established to acquire, in January 1988, the Albany Fine China Company Ltd with borrowed cash. Albany manufactured large and expensive fine bone china pieces. 'The finest bone china studies available world-wide', ranging from a lady in period costume at £300 to large animals at £16,000. Again this was another new production process and a niche business which was difficult to expand. The resin business was based in Stoke-on-Trent; Albany's factory was in Worcester.

Lilliput Lane began to change its behaviour, style and culture from that of a small company. Some managers left, the company was restructured and overheads grew. The two new subsidiaries were never profitable, with the following recorded losses:

Trading year	Trading loss
1987–1988	£ 64,000
1988–1989	£635,000
1989–1990	£677,000

These trading losses, and the extra borrowing they had created, proved costly to Lilliput Group. A very high debt ratio meant recapitalization and rationalization were essential. In the event Albany was sold for cash in July 1990, and in August 1990, Lilliput's interests in Land of Legend were wholly demerged. William Dodd left the company to concentrate on Land of Legend which has prospered on its own.

The core business

Meanwhile, throughout the 1980s, the core miniature cottage business prospered. With constant innovation in production methods, the quality and aesthetic appearance of the models improved. Overseas sales and markets were developed – see Exhibit 3 – and the third subsidiary to be formed in 1987 was Lilliput Inc., an American distribution network based in Columbia, Maryland. Special ranges were developed for the American market and for selected European countries. New plants were opened in the Lake District and by the early 1990s Lilliput operated two sites in Penrith, one for production and one for warehousing and distribution, supported by factories in Workington and later Carlisle.

In 1988 Lilliput received the Queen's Award for Export, and in both 1987 and 1988 the company was a shortlisted finalist in the CBI Business Enterprise Awards. The 1987 winner was Body Shop International, and fellow-finalists in 1988 included Amstrad, Sock Shop and Iceland Frozen Foods. Also in 1988 David Tate was awarded the MBE for his contribution to local employment in Cumbria.

Exhibit 3 Lilliput Lane
World-wide sales (continuing operations)

	12 months to			15 months to	12 months to
	30.9.88 £'000	30.9.89 £'000	30.9.90 £'000	5.1.92 £'000	3.1.93 £'000
Sales	5898	8294	11080	15162	13581
Of which:					
UK	4910	5901	7519	10250	8132
USA	564	1836	2680	3694	4043
Cont'l Europe	230	286	543	888	906
Rest of world	194	271	338	330	500

Refinancing and turnaround

By 1989, due substantially to the fast growth and the losses of the two diversified subsidiaries, Lilliput's debt ratio had risen to 75% – see Exhibit 4. At its height the company's total indebtedness amounted to £5 million. The company turned to Lazard Ventures and other investment groups for help. The North of England Venture Fund (NEV) and Lazards agreed to invest £1.2 million in new equity – but there were strings. First the divestments described above. Second the appointment of new directors, some non-executive, but particularly John Russell as chairman and chief executive. Although William Dodd left, David Tate remained committed and he had a particular expertise to offer. He took the title of technical director with responsibility for research into new manufacturing techniques and the development of new models.

Although Tate has always retained an interest in product design, his most significant contribution over the years has been in technical innovation and production methods. A series of creative ideas has improved both the products and productivity. In addition he has continued to travel widely and internationally, speaking frequently at Collectors' Club promotional events. Tate is an extrovert who has rationalized his new role and who enjoys the adora-tion and respect he receives from collectors all round the world. Lilliput's collectors still see Tate as the organization, and, for example, queue willingly for his personal signature on one of their pieces. His public relations contribution is of enormous value.

John Russell is a chartered accountant who had worked in consultancy and for the Burton Group (14 years) and Courtaulds (10 years). The new strategic leader sought to:

❏ reduce the level of working capital required by more efficient stock control and cash collection
❏ improve production, productivity and production planning systems
❏ invest in new information technology to improve decision making. A total investment of £500,000 was made, and this has contributed substantially to reductions in production lead times and inventories
❏ overhaul internal communications, and
❏ cultivate and extend Lilliput's Collectors' Club – the real reason why the turnaround has been sustained.

Effective control of the Collectors' Club has also been dependent on the new information technology.

Commenting upon the information technology, John Russell said he saw it as 'simply spending on

Exhibit 4 Lilliput Lane
Balance sheet highlights

	At 30.9.88	At 30.9.89	At 30.9.90	At 5.1.92	At 3.1.93	At 31.12.93
	£'000	£'000	£'000	£'000	£'000	£'000
Total fixed assets	1388	2409	2009	1843	1862	1801
Net current assets*	1179	68	656	833	1149	3585
Provisions	(31)		(17)	(26)	(8)	
Creditors falling due after 1 year	1189	1885	2000	1465	664	662
Shareholders' funds†	1347	592	648	1185	2339	4724
*Current assets and liabilities						
Stocks	1174	1554	1692	716	416	858
Debtors	1694	2202	2393	1734	2020	2145
Cash	105	25	47	803	1244	4021
Short-term creditors	1794	3713	3476	2420	2531	3439
†Shareholders' funds						
Share capital	524	524	1700	1700	1700	1163
Share premium account	226	226	140	140	140	2286
Reserves (i.e. profit & loss account)	597	(158)	(1192)	(655)	499	1275

necessities, like pencil and paper used to be ... most small companies are terrified of the idea of spending on IT. If being in big business has taught me one thing, it is that the biggest problem affecting small businesses is that they think small'.

In 1991, after two loss-making years, Lilliput was again trading profitably. Growth and success continued.

Most of the production and administrative staff at Lilliput are young; many of them are teenagers. The management team is also relatively a young one; Russell and Tate are the elder statesmen. There are five other executive directors, all aged between 35 and 40 in 1994. Four of them worked for the company prior to the recapitalization. The average age of the 11 senior (non-director level) managers was 39 in 1994; five had been appointed since 1990.

The Lilliput products

The product range

The majority of Lilliput's products are models of vernacular architecture, indigenous to clearly identifiable countries and regions. Many models are copies of actual buildings; others are 'summaries of a style'. The English Collection, with individual regional sub-sets, is the largest of the ten discrete product groups. The full set is listed in Table 1.

The English Collection represents 70% of total UK sales, and also sells well in Europe and America. The Dutch, French, German and American Collections are marketed primarily in their respective countries as a means of market entry, but they can be obtained by special order through UK retailers.

The majority of pieces are produced in unlimited numbers in response to demand in the form of firm orders. However to reinforce the collectability of Lilliput cottages:

❑ there is an on-going programme of introductions and retirements
❑ certain large, high-price models are produced with a finite maximum, and
❑ there is an annual collectors' piece available only to members during the relevant year.

As a result there is a free secondary market where pieces which have been retired trade at premium prices.

Table 1   The Lilliput Lane collections

Collection	Description
English	A diverse collection of cottages and other buildings, sub-divided into four geographic regions, to reflect different architectural styles
Classics	Relatively new small-scale miniatures
Scottish	Scottish cottages and castles
Welsh	Distinctive Welsh houses
Irish	Typical Irish buildings
American Landmarks	Typical rural American buildings. Unlike all the other collections these are sculpted in America by a local artist, but manufactured solely in the UK.
Dutch	Amsterdam street scenes
French	French regional pieces
German	Again regional pieces, with an emphasis on castles (schlosses)
Christmas	Selected pieces given a snow effect.

The products fit into a number of clear price bands, and Lilliput's policies for new product launches and for retirements are designed to maintain these bands. Some 50 pieces, for example, are priced below £20.00 in the UK, and a further 50 are priced between £20.00 and £30.00.

New products are normally launched in February and July; retirements are announced six months in advance, which normally creates a surge in demand for the threatened pieces. Secondhand prices tend to rise almost immediately after a product is withdrawn.

Customers

People generally buy Lilliput pieces either as gifts or as collectibles. Gift purchases are often made on impulse by individuals buying either for themselves or buying presents for others. Clearly this market is very competitive with a wide variety of often quite different products available at comparable prices. Success depends on allotted retail space, retailer support and point-of-sale material.

The collectibles market embraces people who prefer collecting new products to antiques. Moreover Lilliput pieces are generally more readily available than most antiques, they are likely to be cheaper and the amateur enthusiast is not worried about being 'ripped off' with fakes. This market, which is far more developed in the US than the UK, is served by the Collectors' Club. Lilliput aims, not unexpectedly, to persuade gift buyers to become collectors, who tend to buy more pieces – and to purchase the more expensive ones in the range.

Because the UK is more reliant on the gift market, sales are most buoyant in the pre-Christmas period. It is quite normal for the company to have to close its order book for the calendar year at around the end of September.

Distribution

In the UK, Lilliput's products are sold through around 2400 outlets, most of which are china and glass specialists, gift shops, department stores or jewellers. H. Samuel, Lawley's (the retail division of Royal Doulton), House of Fraser and John Lewis Partnership together account for a quarter of the sales in the UK. The number of outlets in any individual town or city is carefully regulated.

Few stores stock the whole range, or even the majority of it, concentrating on the most popular pieces. Lilliput's own sales force targets the stores which are most likely to assist in building the number of collectors. Members of the Collectors' Club receive regular information bulletins from the company, including information on launches and retirements, but they buy the majority of their pieces from high street retailers, either off-the-shelf or by special order. Lilliput has a gift shop on-site in Skirsgill, where it displays an example of every model ever produced, but sells only those which are currently available in stores elsewhere. There is no direct distribution to individual customers and no mail order system. The store really caters for members of the Collectors' Club who come from around the world to visit the company's headquarters. There are organized tours on a daily basis, which allow collectors to meet the people who make the cottages, especially the artists who provide the finishing touches. Developments are underway on the Skirsgill site to create a proper 'Lilliput area' and thus augment the visitors' experience. A Collectors' Club cottage is being built using a traditional frame structure and thatch.

In the US over 40% of the sales are achieved through specialist collectibles stores.

The Collectors' Club

An organized club is now both typical and essential for products which are marketed as collectibles. Lladro porcelain and Caithness paperweights – both more expensive products – and David Winter Cottages, Lilliput's main direct rival, for example, all have clubs. Members are 'really committed; they are like train spotters'.

The Lilliput Collectors' Club was formed in 1986, and during 1993 it grew rapidly from 58,000 to 68,500. In 1994 it has been growing at a rate of 1000 a month. Some 40,000 of the members live in the UK with another 20,000 plus in America. The remainder are mostly in Canada, New Zealand, Australia and Continental Europe. The Club has active branches in the UK, USA, Canada and New Zealand. Members, who pay an annual fee, receive a free piece when they join, the right to buy an annual Collectors' piece, a quarterly magazine called 'Gulliver's World' and a catalogue of special merchandise available only to them. The magazine contains features on the company, its products and the actual cottages from which the models have been developed.

The Club costs Lilliput over £1 million in administration and carefully targeted promotions every year, but it is entirely self-financing. The Club organizes regional evening events and an annual trade fair, where, for example, members can buy plaster blanks, fresh from the mould, receive help and tuition and paint their own cottage. In addition retired pieces are auctioned privately. Typically the annual fairs are held in the grounds of a stately home and they attract up to 15,000 collectors. Medieval jousts and similar events provide the entertainment and David Tate invariably attends. Members from the USA also come to the UK for organized tours which take them to the actual cottages which have been sculpted.

Although there is an active secondary market for Lilliput cottages, particularly in the USA, both the company and the Collectors' Club remain detached. The record sale so far appears to be a model of an old Cornish Tin Mine – a very early piece which retailed at under £10 before its retirement – which was sold for £1600 at the 1993 Collectors' Fair.

It is estimated that purchases made by club members amount to 65% of Lilliput's total sales revenue each year. Members own, on average, 21 pieces, and typically they will buy three new pieces every year and receive two more as gifts.

International Sales

Some 40% of sales are now outside the UK. The company's international strategy has been to, first, open an American subsidiary, Lilliput Lane Inc., which is based in Maryland but also has an outlet in Chicago. Lilliput Lane (UK) sells products to Lilliput Lane Inc. on an arm's length basis; prices in the USA are generally higher than those prevailing in the UK partly because the collectibles market is more established. While Lilliput has been successful in America, William Dodd's entry strategy of high price/exclusive image has inhibited growth. The company has found it difficult to reposition itself with lower prices in order to replicate the market position it enjoys in the UK.

Second, Lilliput has appointed dedicated distributors in countries with large populations of British expatriates, namely Canada, Australia and New Zealand, who 'enjoy rural reminders'. There are also well-established distributors in Italy and Japan. Elsewhere a mix of distributors and agents is used. In the 1990s Continental Europe has shown growth potential, with sales growing by 40% in 1992–1993, and it is believed to offer exciting future prospects.

Competition

On the face of it, barriers to entry are not very great. You get a mould, pour plaster in and paint it!
But what we have is a strong brand and market awareness. Our research suggests that people think our business is ten times as big as it is.

(John Russell)

There are estimated to be some 130 competing manufacturers of miniature model cottages, but of course many of these will be one-person businesses with substantially localized demand. Lilliput's most visible rival is David Winter Cottages, which is the trading name for The Studios and Workshops of John Hine, and whose turnover is 50% greater. Winter has 50,000 American members in its Collectors' Guild, and half of these are known to be active speculators in the secondary market. The company was started two years before Lilliput, and its product range features more limited editions and generally higher prices. On occasions Winter is known to have withdrawn existing models from sale and destroyed all stock pieces and the moulds in order to encourage the collectability. Like Lilliput it has no direct role in the secondary market. One piece, the

only known surviving copy of a Provençal cottage, launched and withdrawn in 1981, has sold at auction for $42,000. Its original price was £7.50. In 1992 the complete collection of past and present models, a total of 146 pieces – half are still freely available – was estimated to be worth upwards of $200,000.

David Winter Cottages are reputed to be the third most popular collectible in America, behind Lladro porcelain (Spanish) and the Precious Moments collection of whimsical cherub-like creatures distributed by Stanhome's Enesco subsidiary.

Like Lilliput, David Winter pays considerable attention to detail, but the cottages feature a different style and range of colours. There are also certain different specialist ranges, including, for example, a set of Dickensian buildings. David Winter is based in Hampshire, and again it is housed in a true 'cottage-industry' setting. The company began with few full-time employees and relied on some 2000 home workers for painting; later 100 full-timers were employed.

Research and development

Active research and development is seen as an important aspect of Lilliput's competitive strength and distinctiveness. The company, for example, has designed all its own tooling for producing thin one-piece moulds for manufacturing the most detailed models. Some pieces include intricate features such as small archways, which present particular problems for this type of modelling.

Research and new product development encompasses the sculpting of proposed new models. Prior to this, as highlighted earlier, numerous photographs and illustrations of actual buildings are used to finalize a design which is then built out of wax. Normally a number of alternatives will be built; each individual prototype can take up to three weeks to sculpt. A Kentish oasthouse, now discontinued, contained 7500 identifiable roof slates. Aesthetic appeal, accuracy and the need for simplicity in order to minimize production difficulties are all seen as critical variables. Before production begins a number of colour combinations will also be tested and a 'production master' selected. The company strives very hard to accurately replicate the original style, materials and colouring, and consequently the whole design process can easily absorb six months, start to finish.

Production

The vertically integrated production process includes a number of distinct phases.

(i) Mould making

The finally selected wax sculpture is used to produce a number of identical masters, traditionally from resin, each of which is subsequently used to produce a number of rubber moulds. Moulds have finite lives, dependent on the size of the piece, its detail and complexity and the relative ease with which plaster casts can be removed. Lilliput Lane's mould making is innovative and new materials such as polyurethane and softer rubber compounds are constantly tried out. The quality of the mould affects productivity, rejection rates and the final aesthetic appearance of the model; it is a competency which the company believes gives it a competitive advantage. Once a model is retired all the relevant tooling is destroyed.

(ii) Casting

A specialist liquid plaster is poured into the moulds – a number of identical moulds will be fitted into a special tray – and allowed to set. The small team of casters is substantially empowered and rewarded well for high quality and high throughput. Their work is repetitive; and the continuous removal of the models from their rubber moulds in an undamaged state can be tiring. Models are rejected for a blemish the size of a pin-prick.

(iii) Fettling

After demoulding the plaster cast is inspected for any faults or discrepancies, and any rough surfaces and edges are fettled smooth.

(iv) Dipping

The next stage, another Tate innovation, is to immerse the model in a paint tank containing a basic background colour, which also acts as a seal. The shade selected for each model will be the most predominant of its finished colours in terms of surface coverage. Certain models are dipped twice; the finish of the plaster, smooth or stippled, on different parts of the model affects colour retention and can be used in conjunction with multiple dipping to bring out different shades of stone colours.

At this stage in the process the *direct* costs incurred will generally be less than £1.00. Lilliput's most expensive model – which retails at £450.00 – has cost approximately £5.00 at this stage. The real value – and costs – is added in painting. Because of the relatively low direct costs incurred, Lilliput holds a predetermined level of stocks of most of the models in this semi-finished state.

All these processes are centred on the company's main site in Penrith. For most of the year orders will be satisfied with a delivery time of no more than 28 days. Lilliput does not hold stocks of finished goods in any quantity, although clearly some are held to support the on-site shop.

(v) Painting

The dipped models out of stock are finished when retail orders are received and batched into an appropriate quantity. Painting takes place at all of the company's sites – Penrith, Workington and Carlisle. In the past Lilliput has also utilized a number of experienced home workers, but this practice has recently been discontinued. Reasons include the added costs and potential delays involved in delivering and collecting.

Most of the painters, who comprise over half the total workforce, are female and relatively young. They need 'a good eye and a steady hand' and they sit in small groups, sometimes facing each other across tables, painting up to ten models of the same cottage at any one time. The painting rooms are well-lit and exhibit a friendly atmosphere. The painters can talk to each other and they are encouraged to respond to visitors. Collectors who visit the Penrith site are shown round the painting rooms and they inevitably want to talk directly with the artists.

Painters copy the production master, but they are free to put on the colours in any order they wish. Typically they will paint one colour onto several pieces, allowing them to dry properly before applying the next colour. Each painter has a personal style, and each finished piece, whilst appearing basically the same as the others, will in some small, subtle way be unique.

Speed, accuracy and efficiency are critical. The simplest models can be finished by an experienced painter in just a few minutes, with perhaps only 30 seconds of actual painting time involved; the most complex pieces take several hours. Product planning and development always takes account of the likely painting time, which is related directly to the total cost and the eventual price band. A vicarage, which retails at £14.00, takes seven-and-a-half minutes to paint; a Welsh Lodge priced at £50.00 requires thirty-three-and-a-half minutes.

Training can take up to six months to complete, and productivity-based bonus schemes, linked to both quality and quantity, are used extensively. A painter's work load and remuneration is determined by her current efficiency rating – how long it takes her to paint particular pieces in relation to the predetermined standard times. Experienced painters enjoy efficiencies comfortably over 100%; the average at Penrith is just over 90%. The bonus schemes are undoubtedly successful, but the organization is beginning to question whether they are the most appropriate reward system for a workforce they would like to see being highly flexible. The company would, for example, like its casters to also do the fettling, and for painters to put on the baize bases and pack the finished models. These changes would reduce unpopular wage differentials between departments and help reduce the risk of repetitive strain injury for the painters.

(vi) Finishing and packing

The completed models are inspected visually and a piece of baize and an identification label are fixed to the base. Lilliput inspects its products but relies more on a culture of 'right first time' rather than post-production inspection. Every cottage is sandwiched between two small 'bean bags' or pillows filled with polystyrene chips (an invention of Lilliput Lane for which the company is seeking a patent) and individually packed in its own box. A small certificate, replicating a set of title deeds, accompanies every model.

To reinforce the idea of collectability it is normal for a small booklet illustrating all the pieces in a particular range also to be packed in the box.

People

The relative importance of the workforce in the production of Lilliput cottages can be seen in the following breakdown of costs for 1992–1993:

		£ '000
	Turnover	13,581
Less:	Cost of sales	6960
	Including:	
	Wages and salaries	5372*
	Distribution costs	2576
	Administration costs	1916
Leaving:	Profit before interest and tax	2129

*Representing an average of 434 manufacturing employees, 38 in management and office administration and 23 in the USA.

The painters comprise the majority of the production employees. In 1994 the following figures applied:

Site	Number of painters	Current painting capacity	
Skirsgill	55	75	Supported by
Carlisle	45	65	20 casters
Workington	160	180	

If the company needed to expand quickly, a number of options are open to it. It could, for example, readily acquire a suitable location on the eastern side of Penrith; Skirsgill is on the west. The young employees typically live locally.

Its main people issues are:

❑ flexibility
❑ the ease with which productivity-based wage differentials can widen and cause resentment, giving rise to
❑ the risk of absenteeism
❑ constant natural wastage and the need to balance demand with a supply of *trained* labour. It was highlighted earlier that painters in particular require up to six months training; they have to be recruited in advance of the need for their skills. Demand, of course, is seasonal and Lilliput Lane tries to minimize its stocks of finished cottages.

The flotation

In 1993, with the company solvent and profitable, a flotation was announced. Lilliput had been turned around successfully and could boast a number of strengths:

❏ The active and growing Collectors' Club.
❏ The quality of the products – authentic reproduction, colouring and finishing.
❏ Strong promotional material and high levels of customer service.
❏ The range covered a wide variety of price points, from around £10.00, for a simple cottage, to £450.00 for the most expensive piece, a hamlet based on two Suffolk villages.
❏ The brand name and its world-wide level of recognition.
❏ A set of clear objectives and accompanying strategies:
  • to sustain the collectability of the products world-wide, and build the Lilliput Lane brand
  • to concentrate marketing around the Collectors' Club, and
  • to develop the product range and provide marketing support to retailers in order to maintain a competitive advantage.

(Float prospectus)

Europe was seen to offer important opportunities, and future acquisitions were 'not ruled out' if and when they are appropriate.

The time seemed appropriate for the main backers, NEV and Lazard Ventures, to realize their investment. In 1993 NEV and Lazards held 50% of the issued ordinary shares; David Tate and his family retained 29.9%; Tate's fellow directors held a further 14%. The total share capital was split as follows:

	£'000	
9.8 million ordinary shares		split as
5 pence ordinary shares	229	detailed
0.05 pence deferred ordinaries	2	above
Deferred shares	319	mostly NEV
Redeemable preference shares	1150	and Lazards
Total issued share capital	1700	

The flotation would take place in late November 1993, when 2,222,214 new ordinary shares would be issued to supplement the existing 9,814,823 ordinaries and deferred ordinaries.

A proportion (51.7%) of the enlarged equity would then be offered for sale at 135 pence per share.

Afterwards, and assuming the sale was successful, the existing leading investors would retain the following shareholdings:

David Tate and family	16.5% of the equity
Other directors	6.3%
NEV	12.7%
Lazard Ventures	10.5%
Total	46.0%

The company was being valued at £31.4 million; £16.5 million of new money was being raised. It was estimated that the major shareholders, in particular NEV, Lazards and David Tate, would receive £13.5 million. Tate would personally receive some £5 million.

The 2.22 million new shares would generate exactly £3 million for the company, of which £1.47 million would be used to buy out the deferred and redeemable preference shares issued in 1990. After accounting for dealer costs, approximately £1 million would remain as investment capital for Lilliput Lane.

Initial enquiries indicated a strong interest from members of the Collectors' Club, who could now own part of the company behind their hobby. As many as 4.2 million of the 12 million ordinary shares could be held back for priority investors, namely Lilliput retailers and employees. In the event their interest in investing was over-estimated, and only 1 million shares needed to be clawed back.

At the time of the flotation Lilliput was estimating pre-tax profits of £3 million for the trading year to the end of December 1993. Earnings per share were forecast at 9.3 pence, showing a P/E ratio of 14.5. The *Investor's Chronicle* regarded the issue as 'worth considering for a medium-term investment'.

When the results were finally announced in March 1994, profits slightly exceeded £3 million; sales had grown to £16.5 million. UK sales, comprising 60% of total revenue, had increased by 25%; in the US (representing 27% of turnover) sales growth had been a more modest 10%.

Cash reserves in early 1994 stood at £4 million, and John Russell, still the Chairman and Chief Executive, commented 'Lilliput was looking for an acquisition where it could use its skills in marketing

744 Strategic management case studies

collectible products'. The lines, however, 'must be complementary and not imply diversification'.

Lilliput Lane began to discuss a possible merger with Border Fine Arts, whose products (mainly wildlife figures) were already distributed in the USA by Lilliput Lane Inc. Border Fine Arts was also involved in discussions with Enesco, the collectibles and giftware subsidiary of the US company, Stanhome. Stanhome specializes in marketing and distributing a range of consumer products; Enesco's best-known product is Precious Moments, the second most popular collectible in the USA.

Meanwhile, the share price fluctuated:

December 1993	115 pence
February 1994	140 pence
March 1994	130 pence (results announced)
July 1994	90 pence
Early September 1994	90 pence.

It has been argued that the stock market did not fully understand the nature of Lilliput's business.

In September 1994 it was announced that Stanhome was making a recommended cash offer of 160 pence per share for the Lilliput Group. Following the acquisition, Lilliput would stand alone within Stanhome's Enesco subsidiary. Lilliput was now being valued at £37.2 million. Russell would receive £1 million for his shareholding, and Tate a further £6 million. The company's venture capitalists could bow out with a handsome profit, a solid reward for their continued support over several years of mixed fortunes.

Enesco imports most of its products from the Far East, especially China, where Precious Moments are made. Another Enesco range, growing quickly in popularity in the 1990s, is Cherished Teddies, a range of small plaster teddy bears, also manufactured in China.

The fact that Lilliput actually manufactures in the UK is seen as important by Stanhome, especially for building sales in the Far East. Another benefit from the acquisition for the American company is a

foothold in Europe, which would be strengthened further if Enesco also acquire Border Fine Arts. In the past Lilliput has relied on outside carriers to distribute its products from the Penrith warehouse. Distribution represents another large slice of its costs and Enesco is reviewing the distribution strategy for all its products throughout Europe. Should Lilliput Lane now think to invest in its own distribution system? Lilliput would also benefit from reduced distribution costs in America; the Chief Executive of Lilliput Lane Inc. had resigned earlier in 1994 and he had not been replaced when the bid was announced.

What of David Tate? Tate had remained loyal to the company he founded 12 years earlier, accepting a new role when John Russell took over the strategic leadership, and he was now a rich man. He has vowed to continue working for the company. 'I've made a lot of money ... but what would I do if I retired now? I'd go mad sitting at home.'

Questions

1 In what ways does Lilliput Lane **add value** for its customers?

   Identify the most significant core competencies and strategic capabilities involved.

   Use Porter's 5-Force industry model to assess the company's competitive position.

2 Identify and prioritize the company's main stakeholders. How have they been rewarded for their support of the organization? How do you feel the interests of the key stakeholders might be best served in the future?

3 Critically evaluate the strategy of diversification pursued in the 1980s. In your opinion, do you believe the strategy failed because it was poorly conceived or poorly implemented?

   What are the lessons for the future?

4 Would you describe David Tate as an **entrepreneur**?

   Is Lilliput Lane **entrepreneurial**?

   How dependent do you feel Lilliput Lane still is on the continued involvement of David Tate?

Tesco

This case has two themes:

❏ the use of information technology by Tesco to strengthen its competitiveness and
❏ the role of information technology in forging strategic linkages between Tesco and its distributors and suppliers.

Information technology has both reduced costs and strengthened Tesco's competitiveness by improving its overall level of customer service.
The case is designed to be used in conjunction with Chapters 10 and 13.
This version of the Tesco case has been written in 1996 by John L Thompson with the co-operation of Tesco for the purpose of class discussion. It is not intended that it should be taken as a reflection of either effective or ineffective management.

Introduction

In the mid-1990s Tesco has overtaken Sainsbury's to become the market share leader for UK groceries. By the 1960s Tesco had become successful with a policy of 'pile it high, sell it cheap', the philosophy of the founder, John Cohen. Tesco concentrated at that time on relatively small supermarkets close to town centres. The shops offered only a basic level of comfort and service. In the 1970s it became apparent that future growth and prosperity required a new strategy. Tesco appeared to have too many small stores, poor warehousing and stock control and weak administration systems. The strong concentration on price was limiting the total service, and strategically implied a focus, rather than a broad appeal. Desiring a strong market presence, Tesco sought to reposition itself. The new strategy would be based on quality and service in a pleasant shopping environment, together with competitive prices.

In the 1970s Tesco had some 600 stores. This number was systematically reduced to 337 in 1987 through a series of closures and new openings of single-storey units with car parking. Redesigned new superstores have been built in carefully selec-ted locations and a further 57 stores were acquired in 1994 when Tesco bought the Scotland-based Wm. Low Group. In 1995 Tesco had 519 stores in the UK plus 105 Catteau stores in France and 44 Global stores in Hungary. The UK stores comprise:

❏ superstores
❏ compact stores – smaller supermarkets
❏ metros – town centre stores designed to serve specific local needs, and
❏ express stores – convenience stores adjacent to a petrol forecourt.

The total product range of some 17,000 food and non-food items is available in only the largest stores; the smaller ones carry just 3000 lines. Products are sourced from around the world, although British goods are used whenever it is possible and appropriate. Three of Tesco's eight stated objectives relate specifically to the stores and product range:
  Tesco is committed to

❏ offering customers the best value for money and the most competitive prices
❏ improving profitability through investment in efficient stores and distribution depots, in productivity improvements and in new technology

❑ working closely with suppliers to build long-term business relationships based on strict quality and price criteria.

The early Tesco stores (the company was founded in the 1930s) concentrated on canned and processed foods – fresh foods were added in the late 1970s. In addition Tesco has invested in scanning technology and distribution systems. The aim was to be at the forefront of retail technology, and use information technology (IT) for competitive advantage as well as cost savings. Tesco looks to have sufficient product on the shelves to cover a maximum day's sales without needing substantial on-site warehousing. It is both cheaper and easier to restock shelves outside peak shopping hours. Implementation of the IT strategy has required close co-operation with suppliers.

> *Every opportunity must be taken for retailers, suppliers and manufacturers to work closer together. We must move further away from the old retailer-versus-supplier arguments and accept that, if we are to grow, we can only do this together and on the basis of co-operation and mutual understanding.*
> (Lord MacLaurin, Chairman since 1985)

Before discussing the utilization of information technology by Tesco, an introduction to the key success factors for supermarket retailing and supply chain management in the 1990s is provided as background information.

Key success factors for supermarket retailing

Successful supermarket chains must satisfy certain key success factors:

❑ The location of the stores is critical. Easy access for cars, and sufficient parking places, is essential. In addition, new out-of-town shopping developments provide important opportunities.
❑ The product range. Larger stores, quite simply, offer wider ranges.
❑ Product availability. Shelves must be stocked and quickly replenished. However large stocks in stores are costly, and in-store 'warehousing' must inevitably be at the expense of selling space.
❑ Competitive prices – which in turn depends in part on controlling costs.

If customers visit the store regularly, and buy more items, then the retailer's turnover and profits will both increase.

The cost of distributing grocery products from the point of manufacture to the retail outlet accounts for between 12 and 20% of their value. These costs can be reduced by investment in IT, which may be used to reduce both transport and inventory costs. Seizing this opportunity requires close co-operation between the manufacturers and the retailer, and, quite often, a linked contribution from specialist distributors. IT has also allowed retailers to offer additional services, such as 'cashpoint banking' when switch cards are being used for payment. More recently Tesco has been a pioneer of loyalty or frequent purchase cards. Tesco's Clubcard has a magnetic strip which records a customer's purchases and awards a credit for use with future purchases.

The increasing predominance of retailer own-brand food products has increased the need for close co-operation between the store chain and its suppliers, and an expectancy that the retailer would develop expertise in *food* technology. Food legislation makes the retailer responsible for the composition and quality of products marketed under its brand name. Tesco was a late starter with own-brand products, but it has since developed one of the largest food technology departments in the country and been a pioneer of ethical product labelling.

The importance of distribution

Effective distribution can reduce costs whilst improving the overall level of service. The distribution or supply chain encapsulates the storage, handling and movement of goods from the point of manufacture to the point of sale. This distribution can be direct from the manufacturer to the individual retail stores, and 15 years ago some 90% of grocery products were moved this way. A large Tesco store would see between 50 and 60 different lorries every day, each dropping off just a portion of its load. Now 90% of products are distributed via intermediate warehouses, and a store will be fully supplied every day by three large container lorries. Depots, though, must be able to give the stores a fast response time if the system is to be effective. This changeover has led to enormous savings and benefits, but it has only been possible through harnessing the potential of IT.

The intermediate warehouse may be run by the retailer; it is more likely that it will be run for the retail chain by a specialist distribution company. Distribution to the warehouse is known as *primary distribution*; the movement on to the retail stores is designated *secondary distribution*. Primary distribution is still normally provided by manufacturers.

Tesco utilizes 18 regional warehouses for the secondary distribution of all its products in the UK. These comprise:

❏ eight multi-temperature food warehouses for frozen, chilled and ambient short-life foods
❏ five dry grocery centres for canned and long-life foodstuffs
❏ one national centre for Home 'n' Wear
❏ two bonded centres for wines and spirits
❏ two centres for slow-moving items.

Multi-temperature composite warehouses (described in detail later in the case and an invention of Tesco) require very specialized skills, and consequently Tesco utilizes the services of expert distributors to run seven out of its eight. The whole of the North of England, from a line drawn westwards from The Wash, together with Scotland, is served by three warehouses, all run by Glass Glover. The sites, all near motorway junctions, are at Doncaster, Middleton (in Lancashire) and Livingston, which is between Glasgow and Edinburgh. Glass Glover specializes in food warehousing, and Tesco's business constitutes over 40% of its revenue. Although it also provides similar facilities for Littlewoods, Asda, Leo and Safeway, Tesco is substantially its major customer. However, Tesco's other warehouses are run by National Freight Corporation (2), Hunter Distribution and Hays Distribution, and in these cases, Tesco is only a relatively small client.

There are a number of advantages to using such specialists:

❏ The skills required are different from those needed to run a successful retail chain.
❏ The retailer is better able to focus on its core skills and competencies.
❏ Cost savings – it is likely that there will be improved efficiencies and productivity. In addition the capital investment in the facilities and the trucks is provided by the distributor.

❏ The stores, quite frequently located in expensive, prime sites, are not required to carry any unnecessary stocks.

The contractor's purpose is clear and unequivocal – to provide a cost-effective, high service level, distribution system. Success requires close cooperation (utilizing IT), mutual understanding and trust. Given this, distribution, stock control and replenishment becomes a single, integrated system.

Key success factors for supply chain management

There are five critical factors:

❏ Automated data capture in stores using electronic point-of-sale (EPOS) – examined in detail in the next section.
❏ Electronic data interchange (EDI) for the rapid transmission of sales and stock data, order confirmations and delivery schedules. EDI requires that the computer systems of the retail chain and its suppliers are linked directly. EDI is also described in greater detail later.
❏ Pre-planning with suppliers. This implies that basic schedules are agreed in advance but that arrangements are sufficiently flexible to take account of demand changes which were not forecast.
❏ Decision support systems to help forecasting, planning and inventory management.
❏ Streamlined distribution to utilize these links and the improved information to achieve high levels of service cost effectively.

All the technology to achieve this is available; the challenge is one of implementation and achieving the potential. The systems require substantial investment; the benefits will only be achieved if retailers are able to establish network arrangements with their suppliers. In addition, and very significantly, the impacts upon people must be tackled.

Information technology on this scale implies that decisions concerning product ranges for stores, shelf layouts and stock levels, and replenishment orders are centralized. Store managers and staff may be empowered in respect of the *customer care and service* that they provide, but they will not control the product and stock decisions. In addition the multi-temperature warehouses with large frozen sections have been described as the 'coal mines of the 1990s'.

Electronic point-of-sale

EPOS systems rely on products being bar coded at source, which again requires co-operation with suppliers. Check-out systems scan the bar code. This provides an instant record of sales and stock movements out of the store, data which can be used for several purposes:

❏ stock replenishment from the warehouse
❏ analysing actual against forecast sales to monitor and modify orders with suppliers
❏ evaluating profitability. The central computer will contain information on the margin and relative profitability of every item, and this can be added to the sales data. Sales may be increasing, for example, but these additional sales may be of the company's least profitable products (*this cost and margin information is not normally made available to individual store managers*)
❏ make decisions concerning which products to boost and promote and which ones to drop. Every time a new product is added to a store's range, something has to give way for it.

Another benefit of bar coding and EPOS is the elimination of the need to price every single product. The price can be displayed where the products are shelved; the EPOS system inputs the price once the bar code is read. This means that products can be put out onto shelves very quickly after they are received into the store. (This benefit is clearly available to Tesco and the other food supermarkets. For retailers such as Boots and WH Smith it is available only for certain products. In the case of cassettes and compact discs with their ranges of different prices, for example, every individual item has to be priced separately.) In addition, price changes can be implemented rapidly. By the end of 1992 every Tesco store had up-to-date scanning technology.

IT and the supply chain key success factors

IT can be utilized to strengthen the link between the retail chains and their customers in a number of ways. Sophisticated models have been developed to predict demand patterns for individual stores (and possible new locations) by capturing data on the size and dispersion of the local population, age groupings, incomes, socio-economic groupings and car ownership. Clubcard purchasing information is captured at the point of sale and stored in a database for tracking exactly what individual, identifiable customers are buying. This information and forecasting can be used to target particular customer groups and to provide the 'right' range of products. This in turn provides a high level of customer service, and at the same time it should improve the retailer's profitability. Forecasts can be updated and modified with EPOS information.

It was stated earlier that IT offers the potential to both speed up stock replenishment and reduce the costs of distributing the products. If costs are to be reduced throughout the supply chain, the information must be shared and suppliers kept informed of changing trends. If a retailer used sales information purely to generate orders to its suppliers – and over a period of time demand fluctuated – the suppliers would only be able to meet demand quickly if they held high levels of stock. For short-life products this is often impractical. Moreover they would be required to interpret the changing orders they were receiving from the retailers to try and clarify any changing trends. Their interpretation may well be different from that of the retail buyers, and this could be a recipe for waste or lost opportunity. The suppliers could either over- or under-estimate demand changes and change their production schedules accordingly. If the retailers share their forecasting and interpretations the total system can be run more effectively. EDI enables suppliers and retailers to be in constant contact. Initial forecasts can be provided together with an anticipated schedule of orders. This can be up-dated on a constant basis. Suppliers should then be able to meet demand without undue waste.

IT can also be used to minimize duplication. The fewer times that actual deliveries and the support documentation need to be checked, the speedier and cheaper is the system.

Finally IT systems can also monitor warehouse efficiencies – space and vehicle utilization, delivery times linked to route planning etc.

The Tesco supply chain

Electronic data interchange (EDI)

Tesco supplies its 500 stores mostly from 18 regional warehouses. These depots handle some 17,000 food lines together with household, health and beauty products and wines and spirits. These are sourced from 2,500 different suppliers. In the past, linking 2,500 suppliers and 500 stores has implied a large volume of paper orders and paper invoices. The switch to linked computer systems began in the early 1980s, when most deliveries were still direct to the stores. The changeover began with the centralization of Tesco's purchasing from its major suppliers. Sales representatives were no longer required to call on stores and collect their orders. In 1986 Tesco first began to transmit orders electronically via Tradanet.

Tradanet is an EDI service operated by International Network Services Ltd, and it requires that Tesco's suppliers join Tesco in subscribing to the system. Each user has an electronic computer link into the system, and within the system each has both a 'post box' and a 'mail box'. In other words, a user can transmit information (such as an order or an invoice) into the system via its post box. This is then instantaneously switched to the mail box of the intended recipient. Information is received by periodically checking the mailbox and it can again be integrated into the recipient's internal information system for immediate action. Over a period of time both Tesco and its suppliers are in a position to learn how to maximize the benefits offered by such a system of fast and reliable information transfer.

The initial suppliers who pioneered the system with Tesco were Birds Eye (Unilever), Coca-Cola, Colman's, Nestlé, Schweppes and Spillers Foods. By the early 1990s three-quarters of Tesco's long-life products and over half of their short-life products were handled via the Tradanet system. The vast majority of Tesco's purchase orders is now dealt with centrally.

Composite distribution

EDI has been developed in parallel with composite, multi-temperature food warehouses and trucks,

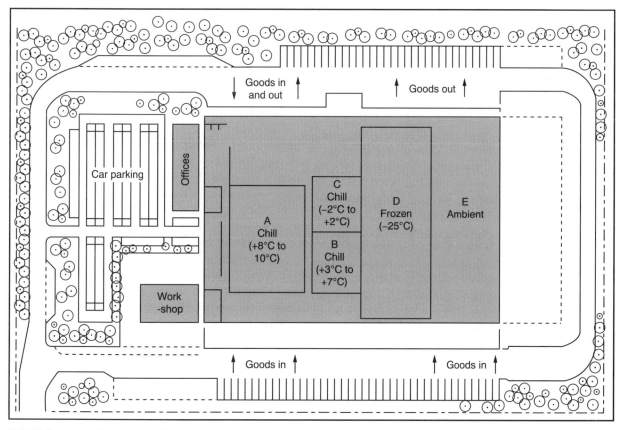

Exhibit 1   Layout of a composite distribution centre.

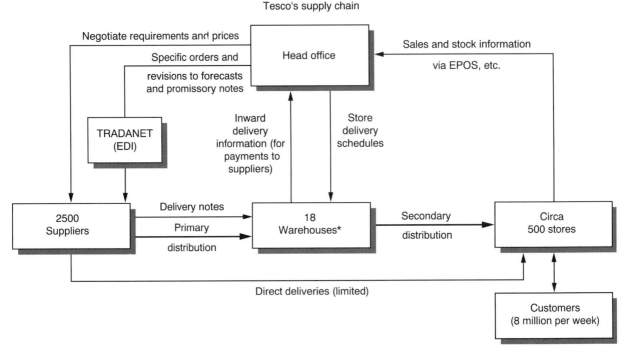

Tesco's supply chain

* Eighteen regional warehouses of which eight are multi-temperature composite food warehouses.
Many are run for Tesco by independent, specialist distribution companies.

Exhibit 2   Tesco's supply chain.

which can accommodate the need for storing and transporting different food products at different temperatures. Frozen foods need to be kept at approximately −20°C; cold chilled fresh meat and fish is handled at 0°C; fresh produce and provisions should be retained between +5 and +10°C. Grocery products such as biscuits, breakfast cereals, cakes and crisps should be kept at ambient temperature. Historically this has required five different types of truck.

Exhibit 1 illustrates a typical Tesco composite distribution warehouse. The total size is in the order of 25,000 square feet, and each section can be managed individually to take account of the different handling and operating procedures that are necessary. Tesco pioneered these warehouses, opening the first one in 1988. Each of the eight existing warehouses serves about 50 stores in a defined region using specialized vehicles. A composite distribution trailer contains flexible bulkhead partitions and can be utilized as one, two or three sections at different temperatures. The coolest compartment would be at −20°C, the middle at 0°C and the third would be at +10°C.

The Tesco system

See Exhibit 2.

Tesco's central buying division negotiates supply terms and prices with suppliers, and agrees a target schedule. In reality they are selling shelf space, and Tesco will generally look to stock a brand leader, their own-label variant and possibly one other alternative. For long-life products a 13-week rolling forecast is provided; for fresh goods it varies between one and six weeks. Where the number of weeks is very small, the forecast is broken down into individual days. The system is suitably sophisticated: when a supplier is unable to promise to meet Tesco's asking requirements, the orders can be immediately recycled to an alternative, competing supplier. Tesco has now gained sufficient experience and its forecasts, updated continually with EPOS data, provide an accurate estimate of likely demand. Tesco and its suppliers are both seeking to be profitable, and to reduce any unnecessary costs, and perceive it is in their mutual interest to share information.

Suppliers are mainly asked to deliver to Tesco's various warehouses, and consequently a fresh food supplier will have just eight delivery points. The actual orders are increasingly transmitted by EDI. Tesco argue that these new systems have meant lower costs and greater certainty for suppliers, and in turn lower prices for Tesco.

Suppliers on EDI send a delivery note ahead of the delivery itself, allowing Tesco to deal quickly with any shortages that might arise. Some products are received into warehouses for holding in stock for a limited period; other deliveries are sorted for immediate onward movement. Each store supplied by the warehouse has its own cages in each section of the warehouse, and the goods are placed in these cages to await loading and transfer. Quality and quantity are both checked thoroughly at the goods inwards points of the warehouse; and unpacking to allow fast and easy shelving in the stores themselves is often another service carried out within the warehouse.

Once a delivery has been scanned and the quality approved, Tesco send a promissory note electronically to the supplier. This in effect promises to pay for what Tesco has received; and sometime later payment can also be made by electronic funds transfer. The significance of this is that suppliers are not required to send any invoices, which takes out of the system a need for Tesco to carry out a further checking procedure. The onus is handed back to the suppliers to ensure that they are being paid for exactly what they think they have supplied to Tesco.

In the stores, portable data capture machines are used for checking shelf stock levels, and this information is transmitted back to head office to supplement the EPOS data. Replenishment needs, together with any revisions to products and stocks, are calculated centrally and the details are communicated to the stores, the warehouses and the suppliers. The system transmits data to the warehouses in the form of printed labels, which are run off on the warehouse computer. Each label represents a case of a determined size, of a particular product, which is to be delivered to an identified store. When a delivery from a supplier has been unloaded the labels are merely transferred to the boxes as they are checked off and then moved to the appropriate cages for each store. Stocked items are removed from inventory using similar procedures.

Short-life food products are normally distributed to the stores in full container loads between midnight and 8 am. It is anticipated that these will then be sold that day. This accounts for most produce, provisions, and fresh meat, poultry and fish. There are likely to be two deliveries each day to the largest stores. Approximately 60% of the anticipated daily requirements will be delivered before the store opens; the remaining 40% sometime during the day. Long shelf-life products are delivered separately between 8 am and 8 pm to spread out the demands for unloading and shelving. These would typically cover expected demand on the following day.

The networking and inter-dependency

Tesco does not just provide orders. Central buyers agree forecast expectations with suppliers, followed later by call-offs or definite confirmations. This enables suppliers to plan more effectively, but in return they are required to deliver quickly ex-stock. Before EDI, orders were delayed for at least 24 hours in the post; faster movement of information means shorter supply times.

As suppliers have systematically joined Tesco's network, which is sometimes described as a 'community', they have been provided with considerable early support by Tesco. Seminars are used to *'inform suppliers of EDI, to clarify Tesco's objectives, and to tell them about future plans. EDI is not just for orders and invoices, but to broadcast forecast information, and receive up-to-date product information'*. The emphasis is on sharing. *'Retailers and suppliers need to work closely together to achieve their common aim of providing an excellent service to customers ... suppliers are no longer dependent purely on their own forecasting. There are fewer surprises, and both partners develop a better understanding of each other's business.'*

The system can only work effectively when there is common agreement about such factors as case sizes, volumes and weights, and no deviation in practice. Suppliers must deliver in an agreed format, and essentially exactly as Tesco expects their supplies. Cases and individual products must all be correctly bar-coded. Tesco is dependent upon this at the point of check-out in the stores.

If Tesco can be more effective in communicating with suppliers than our competitors, then our business partnerships are strengthened and we get a better service, the benefits of which we pass on to our customers.

A summary of the benefits

There are a number of benefits from Tesco's supply chain, arising from the utilization of IT and collaboration with their suppliers. The main ones are as follows:

❑ It facilitates the achievement of the 'right' good at the 'right' place, at the 'right' time, and at the 'right' price.

❑ Daily deliveries to reduce stockholding in stores
   In 1994, for example, Tesco was able to add 35,000 square feet of sales space to existing stores by cutting out in-store stockrooms.

❑ In turn this enables a wider overall product range.

❑ It is easier for Tesco to deal with a large number of suppliers, including those based overseas.

❑ Products should reach the stores in better condition than in the past.

❑ Own-label products can be easily integrated into the system, which is in the interests of Tesco, the suppliers who manufacture for them, and customers.

❑ The likelihood of stock-outs and the consequent loss of sales is minimized.

❑ The wastage rates for short shelf-life products are reduced.

❑ The improved efficiencies and productivity generate a stronger cash flow and improved profits for both Tesco and their suppliers. Some of these benefits will be passed on to customers in the form of lower prices.

Clearly Tesco, in common with many other leading retailers, has become increasingly dependent on information technology. Exhibit 3 features the McFarlan Grid, which considers the relative significance of IT for a company's current and future competitiveness; it is appropriate at this stage to decide where Tesco would currently fit.

Operational dependency on information technology		
High	IT Systems vital for the ongoing operations of the business. Certain activities have become dependent upon IT.	Current operations are dependent on IT; Future IT developments can and will be harnessed to both improve efficiency and provide (greater) competitive advantage. IT may well alter the competitive strategy.
Low	IT systems useful for cost savings and efficiency. The organization is not using IT for competitive advantage.	The organization is not dependent on IT but uses it for efficiency and effectiveness. Future development could be important in the formulation of new strategies.
	Low	**High**

Strategic importance of developments in information technology

Exhibit 3   The strategic importance of information technology (developed from McFarlan, F.W. (1984) Information technology changes the way you compete, *Harvard Business Review*, May/June).

The full potential of networked supply chain management has not yet been achieved by any retailer, and future opportunities and challenges await the leaders.

In the USA in the 1990s, Efficient Customer Response (ECR) has captured retailers' attention. ECR fosters stronger links between supermarkets, their suppliers and their suppliers' suppliers because the purchase of a particular item at a supermarket checkout automatically triggers a replenishment decision at the supplier's warehouse together with orders for fresh ingredients, cans, bottles, labels further up the line. The outcome is a reduction in inventory plus the reduced likelihood of a stockout. Information management (concerning what customers are actually buying) enables changing trends to be spotted quickly. Retailers are essentially handing over the responsibility for stock replenishment to their suppliers. Whilst Tesco and other leading UK retailers have expressed interest in ECR, their inventory management systems were already far superior to those of the US supermarket groups. Moreover, because of the high incidence of own-label goods in the UK, Tesco is also its own supplier for many of its products. *'ECR is now being carefully examined for the further benefits that it might bestow.'*

Questions

1 How does EDI impact upon the retailing industry structure?

   (Michael Porter's industry analysis [See Chapter 9] provides an ideal framework for tackling this question.)

2 Using the McFarlan Grid:, to what extent has the grocery retailing industry become strategically dependent upon information technology?

   (McFarlan's analysis was briefly covered in Chapter 13, The original 'McFarlan grid' was introduced in: McFarlan FW (1984), Information Technology Changes the Way You Compete, *Harvard Business Review*, May/June.

   The grid has been revised and refined by McFarlan in later works, but the original ideas are perfectly satisfactory for the purposes of this exercise.)

3 Does Tesco appear to have taken the appropriate steps to forge effective alliances within the supply chain?

4 How might Tesco utilize IT and its supplier network to strengthen its competitiveness further in the future?

Thorn-EMI

> This case study looks at how Thorn-EMI has changed from a relatively diverse manufacturing and service business into a more focused service organization over a ten-year period.
>
> The case examines the relative success and the key success factors for the company's two core businesses, music and rentals. The role of the company's strategic leadership is examined.
>
> The case opens a discussion on what might happen to Thorn-EMI in the future.
>
> This case study was written by John L Thompson in 1995 from a variety of published sources and Thorn-EMI Annual Reports for the purpose of class discussion. It should not be taken to reflect either effective or ineffective management.

Introduction

In 1995 Thorn-EMI is an international company with a turnover exceeding £4 billion. Appendix 1 provides a five-year financial summary. It concentrates on carefully selected consumer-oriented *service* businesses where it enjoys both global scope and a strong market position. Its recent strategy has been to build world-class competitive strengths, partially achieved through appropriate cost-cutting, whilst dramatically rationalizing its portfolio of activities. Historically Thorn-EMI has competed as a manufacturer, most notably in the lighting and defence industries, but it has systematically divested most of these interests.

Thorn-EMI is one of the world's leading music companies, along with **Polygram** (majority-owned by Philips of the Netherlands and focused on music and filmed entertainment), the US **Time Warner**, the world's largest media and entertainment company, **Sony** of Japan (the electronics giant which absorbed CBS and Columbia Pictures), **Bertelsmann/RCA** of Germany (publishing company, owner of Doubleday and active in record and book clubs) and **MCA Music**, until recently a subsidiary (along with Universal Pictures) of Matsushita/JVC, another Japanese electronics giant. In the UK music industry, Thorn-EMI and Polygram vie for market leadership. Their annual market shares are in the 20–25% range, varying with the relative success of album releases by their major artists, whose fortunes can often rise and fall. Warner and Sony Music enjoy shares of around 10% each. In music publishing in the UK, Thorn-EMI leads jointly with Warner Chappell. Both have 20% market shares; Polygram Music has 11%. For 1994–1995, Soundscan (US) estimate EMI's US market share at 9%, placing it sixth. Time Warner leads with 23%. The vital US market is three times the size of the UK market and the largest in the world (Japan, 50% bigger than the UK, is the second largest with the UK third, closely followed by Germany and France). Recent estimates for the $33 billion global music market give Time Warner leadership with a 14% share. EMI, Polygram, Sony and Bertelsmann all have some 10–11%; MCA has 6%. Music is now Thorn-EMI's largest business – see Appendix 2. It is profitable and premium-rated, but by nature it is a risky industry.

The second-largest business is specialist equipment rentals (consumer household electrical products in the main) and associated activities. Thorn-EMI has been described as the only worldwide specialist in this field, with again a 15% share of the global market. This business is less profitable than music, but it is perceived as 'solid' and less risky. The third key business is retailing. Thorn-EMI is a leading retailer of music-based products in the UK; its HMV shops are also to be found in the USA, Canada, Australia, Japan, Hong Kong and Ireland.

In March 1995 Thorn acquired the Dillons chain of specialist bookshops from the Receiver of Pentos, its parent company. A fourth division encompassing security and electronics products was largely divested in early 1995.

In 1995 the company faces a number of key strategic issues. One concerns how the music business might be expanded further, possibly implying related diversification – book publishing was being suggested as an option worth considering even before the acquisition of Dillons. A second concerns the structure of the organization as a whole. Music is run from headquarters in New York; the rest of the businesses are controlled from London. At the Annual General Meeting in July 1995 it was announced that Thorn-EMI was investigating ways of splitting the company into two separate businesses; HMV would stay with Music. Given its recent growth in profitability, an inevitable third issue is the potential for take-over bids.

The development of Thorn-EMI

The music interests developed around the original HMV (His Master's Voice) label, owned by EMI – the initials stood for Electric and Musical Industries. HMV has been a major player in the recorded music business from its very beginnings. EMI grew and diversified but in the 1970s it came close to financial collapse. The company had invented the world-beating EMI brain scanner but seriously underestimated the extent of the resources required to market such an innovative product. In 1979 EMI was merged with Thorn, a well-known manufacturer in the lighting and electrical industries. The subsequent history of Thorn-EMI can be split into a number of stages.

Between 1979 and 1983 Sir Richard Cave (the chairman) set about integrating the two businesses into a cohesive whole; his declared aim was to create a leading company in selected industry sectors, information technology, entertainment and leisure. In 1983 Thorn-EMI bought Software Sciences. This specialist company had been founded in 1970 by Colin Southgate, who had begun his working life as an actuary, and he now joined Thorn-EMI.

Sir Richard Cave retired and was succeeded as chairman and chief executive by Thorn-EMI's managing director, Peter Laister. The new strategic leader saw Thorn-EMI's future as a global high-technology company, and in 1984 he agreed the purchase of Inmos.

Inmos had been set up in 1978 with funding from the then Labour government's National Enterprise Board. The intention was to give the UK a valuable presence in the fiercely competitive world semiconductor industry. Inmos was to design and manufacture high added value memory chips. Initially the company was reliant on American expertise and it invested in state-of-the-art production facilities. The revolutionary transputer chip was invented but the company was unable to raise the development capital required. Thorn-EMI, heavily dependent on consumer oriented businesses, agreed to buy Inmos from Mrs Thatcher's government for £125 million in September 1984. In that year Inmos enjoyed a small trading profit, but it was losing money by the first quarter of 1985 and it was not profitable again until 1988. The main problems came from defective chips, which had been delivered to customers before the acquisition by Thorn-EMI, and worldwide over-supply, which was driving down prices. Inmos was eventually sold in December 1988 to Thomson-SGS, the French micro-electronics group, for £108 million. Thorn-EMI had invested some £300 million in Inmos in four years and now retained a 10% share.

Meanwhile, in 1985, Laister had been replaced after a boardroom coup. Colin Southgate (later Sir Colin), who had joined the Thorn-EMI main board in 1984, became managing director (1985) and later chief executive (1987) and chairman (1989). He remains the strategic leader in 1995 as Executive Chairman. He is supported by a strong board of directors, which includes the heads of the two main divisions, EMI Music and the rentals business, and several strong non-executives.

In 1985, Thorn-EMI, labelled a 'lumbering giant' by some commentators, was a diversified conglomerate which comprised the following activities:

❏ Consumer electronics – television manufacture (Ferguson brand).
❏ Domestic appliances and heating products (including such brands as Kenwood kitchen appliances).
❏ Rental and retail of consumer products (DER, Radio Rentals, Rumbelows, and so on).

❑ Music.
❑ Film-making and screen entertainment.
❑ Lighting.
❑ Electronics, information technology and tele-communications.
❑ Semi-conductors (Inmos).

Southgate has been reported as believing that 'Thorn had tried to be all things to all men in all areas'. He felt it needed stronger focus.

Strategic problems and changes in the mid/late 1980s

Southgate, then, felt that Thorn-EMI faced two critical strategic dilemmas. First, there was a lack of focus on the perceived core businesses; second, the company was not big enough in most of its markets to gain all the potential economies of scale. Southgate feared that without drastic changes Thorn-EMI's growth would slow down, earnings would fall and the business could well become an acquisition (and break-up) target.

The company was competing in too many marketplaces and as a result the corporation was not able to add sufficient value in all the subsidiary businesses. Many of Thorn-EMI's markets were becoming increasingly global in scope; the perspective of a UK-based company which exported, rather than a global organization, was inappropriate.

Southgate was instrumental in initiating a strategy of greater focus, and he started a major divestment programme which involved the sale of over 60 subsidiary companies in three years, 1985–1988, with another 20 following in the next five years. These included such diverse businesses as property, telecommunications, instruments, film and video production and distribution (Elstree Studios), EMI cinemas and television manufacturing. Ferguson was sold to Thomson in 1987 for £90 million; simply 90% of its sales were in the UK while its major competitors were more international in scope. The sales ran parallel to an acquisition programme aimed at bolstering the selected core businesses. The number of companies bought is much lower than the number sold, but some of the acquisitions have been strategically very significant.

Sir Colin Southgate has therefore concentrated on acting as a *corporate* strategic leader and relied heavily on support and strong leadership from the heads of the remaining divisions.

Thorn-EMI was concentrating on businesses where it believed it could achieve an important world market share.

Appendix 3 charts the response of the stock market to the varying, but generally improving, fortunes of Thorn-EMI.

By 1988 Thorn-EMI had been consolidated into four groups:

❑ *Rental and retail* – Radio Rentals, DER, Rumbelows and the HMV Music shops in the UK, together with related interests abroad.
❑ *Technology* – primarily software and security systems.
❑ *Consumer and commercial* – based on lighting and Kenwood appliances.
❑ *Music*.

Thorn-EMI spent £371 million in 1987 to acquire the US rental specialist, Rent-A-Center, a national chain of owned and franchised outlets, and began to invest to increase the number of branches. Having bought a Swedish rental business from leading rival Granada in 1986, Thorn-EMI bought five more continental electronic rental companies from Granada in 1987. The total investment was some £60 million. Vallances, a Yorkshire-based electrical goods distributor was bought to supplement the Rumbelows high street stores.

The technology division operated in three areas: software, security and electronics. Notably these businesses were primarily targeted at niche markets, mostly but not exclusively, in the UK. Software Sciences was involved in various activities, including, for example, retail EPOS (electronic point of sale) systems; Marks and Spencer was an important customer. Security included building security and fire protection. Electronics had an important base in defence, but had expanded into ticketing systems for such customers as British Rail and London Underground.

Lighting spanned the automotive, industrial and consumer markets (the Mazda brand) and it was retained as a core activity in the 1980s because it fitted the requirements of a business which was profitable and in which Thorn-EMI believed it could build a global presence. By early 1989, and following a number of acquisitions, Thorn-EMI owned lighting companies in West Germany, Sweden,

France and Italy (joint venture). A major acquisition in the USA had been sought. One important buy was the French company, Holophane, which manufactures pressed glass products for automobile lighting together with light fittings. However Europe does not have standard voltages and light fittings, with the UK particularly out of alignment, leading to some fragmentation.

The kitchen appliances business, Kenwood, was divested in 1989. A management buy-out realized £55 million, with Thorn-EMI retaining an 8% stake.

Throughout the 1960s and 1970s EMI had consistently been the UK market leader for popular music albums and singles with a market share of around 20%. Artists such as Cliff Richard and The Beatles had ensured growth and prosperity. EMI was linked with the American Capitol label and consequently distributed the music of artists like The Beach Boys in the UK. Stronger competition, particularly from Polygram, and a failure to maintain the relative strength of the artist roster saw album market share fall to around 13% in 1987 – at this time EMI's share of the now less important singles market was some 8%. A determination to regain clear UK market leadership and become a force in the world music industry resulted in a number of key strategic acquisitions which are discussed later.

The strategy from 1989

In 1989 Southgate clarified that lighting, music and the rental of electronic and white goods would be Thorn-EMI's three core businesses for the future. All had international potential.

A year later **lighting** was made a candidate for divestment. Southgate explained that the underlying strategy of focus and international presence was consistent; simply the company no longer believed it could become a global player in lighting, the original Thorn business founded by Sir Jules Thorn in 1928. Thorn was strong in the provision of light *fittings*, but weak in light *sources* – the bulbs and tubes which go in the fittings. Moreover the light source business was again too heavily dependent on the UK.

In November 1990 the first part of lighting (the loss making lamp bulbs and tubes company) was sold to General Electric of America for £69 million. The remainder of lighting (fittings) was disposed of

through a management buy-out in 1993. This raised £162 million, with Thorn retaining a 10% share.

The fittings arm of Thorn Lighting competed on quality products, high levels of service, innovation and new product development. Efficient cost management and productivity were critical in a competitive market. To succeed the company had to win tenders for major industrial, commercial and public amenity lighting schemes, such as new airports and the channel tunnel, and the associated new terminals.

Table 1 shows the relative profitability of the Lighting Division in its last five years.

The software business was sold in 1991, and in 1992 the Rumbelows shops were partially converted from retail to rental. Thorn-EMI's retail activities were now being focused more on the HMV music and video shops.

Thorn-EMI had obtained a substantial minority shareholding in Thames Television, which it was rumoured to have offered for sale in early 1990. However, in February 1991, Thames shares owned by BET were bought by Thorn-EMI at a 'very favourable price', and Thorn was now in overall control with a 59% stake. Shortly afterwards Thames lost its regional commercial television franchise in the government's new bidding system; Thorn-EMI sold its shareholding to Pearson in 1993.

Thorn-EMI in 1995

Thorn-EMI consists of four businesses or divisions.

EMI Music, based in New York, itself comprises 65 record companies and 23 music publishing companies with operations in 37 countries. EMI Music is vertically integrated, the implications of which are discussed in a later section of this case study, and includes:

❏ artist and repertoire development – the acquisition and development of future talent

Table 1 Thorn Lighting, 1988–1993

Year £m.	Turnover £m	Operating profit £m
1988/1989	440.4	39.4
1989/1990	537.8	32.7
1990/1991	478.0	(1.9)
1991/1992	343.7	12.6
1992/1993	346.7	15.2

❑ studio recording

❑ production facilities, primarily compact disc pressing in the UK, USA, Holland, Australia and South Africa

❑ marketing and distribution – direct to HMV and other outlets

❑ promotional and music videos

❑ the 'ownership, management and exploitation of copyrights in songs and other compositions' – including the management of royalty earnings from EMI-owned music being used for films and television programmes and commercials. EMI's extensive back catalogue of recorded music is particularly valuable here.

At the heart of the **Thorn Group** are the rentals businesses. The philosophy of this division is one of providing access to a range of household products to those customers who cannot afford, or choose not, to buy outright. These products now include televisions, videos and stereos, white goods (washing machines, refrigerators, etc.), furniture, jewellery (USA only), computers, portable telephones and pagers. A variety of formats are targeted at selected niches world-wide, and customer options include long- and short-term hire, rent-to-own, rental with a purchase option and hire purchase. Thorn is also active in interactive in-room guest services and television systems for hotels. This is a business which requires heavy investment, but, managed well, delivers a strong cash flow.

HMV is a specialist retailer of recorded music and associated products. A few years ago the chain consisted of 40 UK-based stores; now there are 200, based in the UK, USA, Japan, Australia, Canada, Hong Kong and Ireland. 50% of the sales are generated outside the UK. **Dillons** comprised 149 shops when it went into receivership in 1995; on the announcement of the acquisition, analysts predicted that Thorn-EMI would 'cherry pick' and not keep open those stores with high rents or poor locations. In the end, 100 stores were retained, with the rest reverting to the receiver. Dillons is the second largest specialist bookseller in the UK; Waterstones, owned by WH Smith, is market leader.

TSE – Thorn Security and Electronics was formed in 1992 to co-ordinate a number of technology-related businesses. Historically the division exploited specialist competencies originally developed in defence-related industries,

Table 2 Thorn-EMI businesses

Division	1986	1995
	Percent of turnover	
EMI Music	15	49
Thorn Group	26	35
HMV	2	11
Other activities (TSE and discontinued)	57	5

later transferred to civilian applications. The division as a whole, or the businesses individually, was available for sale at the right price since 1989. Many businesses, accounting for the major part of TSE's turnover, have been divested; in 1994–1995, for example, ones manufacturing electron tubes, automation engineering products, defence electronics and fire detection systems were sold. Two of the three remaining in 1995 respectively produce and market transactions (ticketing) systems and credit/bank card security systems (based on patented magnetic 'watermark' technology); the third, the Central Research Laboratories, has recently invented an electronic fingerprint identification system.

During the divestment process, some negotiations have failed. Southgate has a reputation for holding on for the right deal; his strategy for TSE has always been 'to work our way out over time' and continue investing in the businesses to make sure operational improvements are achieved. Some analysts, however, believed Thorn's failure to quickly divest all the businesses reflected a weakness in the strategy.

The relative importance (in terms of turnover) of each business is shown in Table 2 and compared with the situation in 1986.

The music business

Figure 1 illustrates the value of linking the recording and marketing of music with music publishing. EMI records, presses, distributes and retails popular and classical music in a vertically integrated supply chain; the company is also a world leader in music publishing, enabling the long-term exploitation of

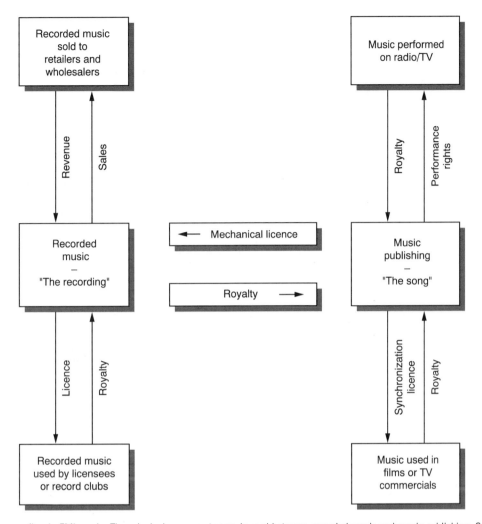

Figure 1 Revenue flow in EMI music. The principal revenue streams in, and between, recorded music and music publishing. Source: Thorn-EMI Annual Report.

the performing rights associated with compositions and recordings. Table 3 illustrates the breakdown of the costs and margins involved in a compact disc and highlights that EMI 'owns' every part of the added value chain except the artist him- or herself, who, of course, would normally be tied to the company by contract. On occasions these contracts will be geographically specific, rather than globally exclusive, and maybe cover the whole world except North America; another company would hold the American rights.

The marketing of new music, even from established artists, is inevitably risky. Performers, particularly if they write their own songs, may well be late

delivering their new material; success with a previous album is no guarantee that a new album will sell. However both back catalogue and compilations, and music publishing, provide a more stable and dependable source of revenue and earnings. Their relative importance for Thorn-EMI are illustrated in Table 4. Re-released back catalogue records also carry lower royalties to the artists.

The stability arises from two factors: first, multiple sources of income, and second, the breadth and depth of catalogue material owned by EMI and its major rival, Warner Chappell. It is additionally beneficial that these copyrights generally last for several years, with some songs and recordings able

Table 3 Breakdown of the price of a compact disc.

	£
Manufacturing	1.05*
Artist royalties	0.88
Publisher's royalties	0.44*
Recording producer	0.44*
Distribution/promotion	4.66*
Retail margin	3.25*
Tax	2.27
Total	12.99

*Denotes EMI involvement in the operation.
Source: *Financial Times*.

Table 4 EMI Music Revenues, 1992

	Percentage of sales	Return on sales (percent)
Recorded music	86	
comprising		
New releases	52	5
Back catalogue	34	10
Music publishing	14	36
comprising		
Mechanical	8	
Performance	4	
Synchronization	2	

Classical music represents some 20%, popular music 80%

to earn reproduction royalties over several decades. There are three key ways that song copyrights can be licensed to yield music publishing revenues.

1. Mechanical royalties are paid when a song or composition is reproduced and sold as a record, cassette, compact disc or video. This is an international business, with collection agencies around the world. Mechanical royalties account for the largest share of EMI's music publishing revenues, and they are clearly boosted whenever EMI contracts a new recording artist or song writer who becomes successful.

2. Performance royalties arise when the composition or song is performed anywhere in public, say in a theatre or as part of a radio or television broadcast. Again, there are collection agencies around the world.

3. Income from the utilization of the material as part of say a film soundtrack or a cinema or television commercial. In recent years music has played an increasingly important role in films and commercials, making this the fastest growing source of music royalties. Classical music has been used in a whole range of commercials, a factor linked to its generally increasing popularity. When music is used in film soundtracks, there is, of course, additional revenue from the sale of the associated album. These revenues are known as synchronization royalties.

Following a number of strategic acquisitions – described below – EMI Music Publishing controls over 800,000 musical compositions and songs and covers all types and ages of music.

EMI Music in the 1980s

In the 1980s EMI's main star artists were waning in popularity and they had not been effectively replaced (Table 5).

In addition, whilst EMI's market share was relatively stable, the company's position of UK market leader was taken by the fast-growing Polygram.

Table 5 The Relative Success of EMI's main artists, 1989, 1990. Source: BPI

Year	Artist	Best position(s) in the UK top 100 album charts
1989	Tina Turner	8
	Queen	17
	Cliff Richard	38 and 86
	Kate Bush	39
	Paul McCartney	56
	Duran Duran	65
1990	Nigel Kennedy (*Vivaldi's Four Seasons*)	12

In 1989 EMI's top single was *Something's Gotten Hold of My Heart* by Marc Almond and Gene Pitney.

Table 6 Album market shares, UK. Source: BPI

| Year | Recording company: | | | | |
	EMI	Chrysalis	Virgin	Polygram	WEA
1984	14.6	2.9	7.0	12.5	9.2
1985	13.4	3.3	8.0	14.5	12.2
1986	13.8	2.9	7.3	14.8	13.2
1987	13.2	2.2	7.1	15.2	12.8
1988	12.6	2.8	7.7	16.1	12.6
1989	12.7	2.5	8.2	16.1	14.8
1990	15.3	2.9	7.7	23.2	12.8

WEA, owned by Time Warner, was beginning to threaten the number two slot. During this decade the value of the UK singles market, at trade prices, rose from £50 million to £80 million; at the same time, partly the result of the emergence of compact discs around the middle of the decade, album sales (vinyl LPs, cassettes and compact discs combined) grew from £200 million to £600 million. Album market share was critical. See Table 6.

Comparable market share figures for singles were: Polygram 20% in 1990 (14% in 1984); EMI 13% (9%), Chrysalis 4% (3%), Virgin 7% (7%) and WEA 10% (11%). Whilst the singles market is much smaller than albums, singles can be vitally important for supporting new albums and for launching new artists.

Throughout the 1980s EMI Music's Chief Executive (Bhaskar Menon) and the Finance Director were based in Los Angeles; the Managing Director and the world-wide administrative centre were in London. Menon was a deliberate man who liked details. He had a deep and profound understanding of the business, but he was a conservative decision maker. EMI had become sluggish and reactive, values inappropriate for a fickle and fashion-oriented industry. The division was big, but its profitability was disappointing. Margins overall were in the region of 5%, and the company was losing money in America, a critically important but notoriously difficult market for UK music companies to conquer. Bhaskar Menon retired in 1989, to be replaced by Jim Fifield, who had joined the company a year earlier. Fifield declared he would double the profit margin in three years. His ambitions were pursued through a programme of rationalization, restructuring and strategic acquisitions in both music publishing and record production.

The new Chief Executive

Colin Southgate head-hunted Jim Fifield to EMI Music. Fifield, an American, had built his early career in General Mills, where he had focused on their retail operations, but from 1985–1988 he was President and Chief Executive Officer of CBS/Fox Video. In his first year he received a total remuneration package of some £13 million, which included a substantial 'signing-on fee'. In 1994 his basic salary was £2 million, supplemented by a cash and shares bonus of £5 million, making him 'the highest paid man in the music business'. By contrast in 1994, Sir Colin Southgate received a remuneration package of less than £1 million. Under Fifield the headquarters of EMI Music, including all corporate administration, has been switched to New York.

After declaring he would double EMI Music's profit margin from 5 to 10% within three years Fifield later set himself a target of 13% for the business.

Jim Fifield is extremely energetic and pragmatic, a marked contrast to his predecessor. He wears 'exotic ties and trendy glasses'. Commentators have pointed out that in the last few years Sir Colin Southgate has also switched from horn-rimmed spectacles to contact lenses and they have mused about a culture change driven down from the very top of the organization. More conservative values, of course, remain far more appropriate for the less fashionable rentals business.

A new 'attitude and focus' in EMI Music has been attributed to Fifield, who has championed substantial investments in information technology and management information systems. Declaring 'I will only work for something that is fun' he has set about transforming the company's repertoire, its stable of artists and an acknowledged key success factor, partially by restructuring and decentralization and partly through acquisitions.

Fifield, who has been described as an 'archetypal numbers man' claims to work with six key managerial principles:

❑ never settle for anything but the best
❑ focus on the future not the past
❑ take risks
❑ succeed as a team
❑ build on strengths and
❑ speak out – 'silence is not golden'.

Strategic acquisitions

In 1989 Thorn-EMI bought SBK Entertainment for $337 million, primarily to obtain its music publishing business. The deal was begun when SBK approached EMI with a view to buying EMI's music publishing arm. SBK had acquired its song collection by buying 250,000 song copyrights at a price of $130 million from CBS in 1986; these rights were earning annual royalties of $37 million world-wide. CBS itself had obtained the copyrights from a variety of different film studios and they included such titles as *Singin' in the Rain* and *Somewhere Over the Rainbow*. EMI already held the copyright to over 300,000 songs and compositions, and this acquisition put them alongside Warner Chappell as joint global market leaders. They each held 12% of the world market, measured by revenues. EMI's portfolio included compositions from David Bowie, Chris de Burgh, Kate Bush, Dire Straits, Carole King, Barry Manilow, Paul McCartney and Queen, some of whom, but not all, also recorded for EMI.

SBK had been founded by two American entrepreneurs, Martin Bandier and Charles Koppelman, who also discovered the folk rock singer, Tracy Chapman, whose first album, released in 1988, sold 7 million copies. SBK held the rights to her songs, but, because they did not own a recording business, she recorded for WEA. As a result of her success Bandier and Koppelman had the ambition of owning a record company, and this they now set up in a joint venture with EMI Music. This 50:50 arrangement was immediately successful; in its first year four albums – out of 20 released – reached the coveted Number 1 slot in the charts.

This 50:50 joint venture format in America was repeated with alliances between EMI and Enigma, a heavy metal label, and with IRS, a rock label. The Enigma agreement was later discontinued as it failed to work smoothly. Fifield's belief was that alliances of this nature preserved the entrepreneurial spirit of individual, repertoire-focused labels, each of which had a separate image and identity which made them uniquely attractive to particular artists. EMI's contribution is the vitally important international production and distribution network that small, independent labels need access to, but cannot afford to own.

In addition, and in accordance with the alliance objectives, EMI Music in America was split into three separate businesses, based on labels: Manhattan, EMI-America and Capitol. In the UK the company divided itself into EMI and Parlophone. The decentralized businesses/labels were all profit-accountable and charged with attracting new talent. EMI companies quickly signed new artists such as the rap singer, MC Hammer and country star Garth Brooks. EMI has subsequently bought the remaining 50% of SBK Records and absorbed the label into EMI-America; there were some redundancies. The challenge is finding a structure which permits devolution, empowerment and entrepreneurialism – attractive to the company's recording artists – with cost control in a competitive and uncertain industry. Koppelman is now head of EMI Music Group, North America; Bandier is head of EMI Music Publishing.

There were, though, disappointments. Fifield sought to acquire Geffen Records, founded by David Geffen and holding an 8% share of the US market, but he was beaten by MCA. In 1990 EMI Music Publishing added Filmtrax, which was bought for $93 million. Filmtrax owned the copyright to some 140,000 titles yielding annual royalties of $9.5 million.

Acquiring Chrysalis

Chrysalis, like Virgin, had grown into one of the UK's best-known independent record companies. Chrysalis, growing with the success of such artists as Jethro Tull, Blondie and Spandau Ballet, had expanded into studio recording, music publishing and television programming and had diversified more significantly when it acquired MAM in 1985. MAM's core activity was the management of international artists, but it had diversified differently into hotel management, juke boxes and amusement machines. The merger was successful, but Chrysalis hit financial difficulties when it tried to establish a serious presence in the US record industry. The US investment demanded more cash injections than had been initially budgeted. Chris Wright, Chrysalis' chairman (and one of the two original founders of the business), concluded with hindsight that Chrysalis had sought to create an organizational infrastructure in the USA, when what was crucially required was chart successes. Could the latter be achieved without the former?

In 1989 Chrysalis needed a cash injection, which,

although the company was now quoted, was not readily forthcoming. It was rumoured that 50% of Chrysalis *Records* would be sold to Bertelsmann, with whom Chrysalis already had distribution agreements. In the event EMI Music bought 50% for £46 million, with an option to buy the remainder by 1999. The second half was bought for a further £31 million three years later; Chrysalis still needed cash.

Fifield acquired a number of currently successful artists, in particular Sinead O'Connor and Billy Idol and a very valuable back catalogue. Chrysalis retained its independence as a label, but its operations and administration were absorbed. There were several redundancies.

The big acquisition: Virgin

If Chrysalis could provide EMI with a useful new repertoire and back catalogue, Virgin could provide an invaluable supplement. Virgin Music, again a vertically integrated company, was bigger than Chrysalis. Unlike its smaller rival it had remained profitable whilst successfully also penetrating America. However it was still too small to be classified as 'first division' in the global music industry. During the very late 1980s and early 1990s most independent labels the size of Chrysalis and Virgin have been absorbed by one of the leading global players. Virgin's artists included Genesis, Phil Collins, Janet Jackson, UB40, Simple Minds, Meat Loaf and The Rolling Stones, and there were 25,000 song copyrights. Virgin Music had grown and prospered with the 'visionary' Richard Branson at the forefront, backed by his cousin Simon Draper, Virgin's respected and key A and R person, and Ken Berry, 'the strategist'. Berry had been with Virgin for some 20 years, and he had been credited as their 'first person to handle accounts and bookkeeping'. He was popular with artists because he was 'willing to market and develop acts, not on quarterly statements, but based on their long-term career'. By the early 1990s Branson had lost interest in the music industry; his passion now was his airline. Draper felt stale. Branson was willing to sell at the right price; a deal would provide investment capital for Virgin Atlantic Airways. In the past, Branson had approached EMI with a view to buying its music business.

Branson negotiated with a number of the leading international music companies, but finally, and after fourteen months of protracted negotiations, he agreed to sell to Sir Colin Southgate for £510 million, financed by a rights issue. This was in 1992. Virgin had tangible assets of just £3 million – Virgin did not own any manufacturing or distribution – and the figure represented 1000 times Virgin Music's recent after tax earnings. Commentators queried the wisdom of such a high price for a number of key managers and a well-known repertoire. EMI, though, believed there was enormous synergy potential from blending its global structure with Virgin's repertoire. Moreover, Fifield had a reputation as a shrewd cost-cutter and he would be able to achieve savings. This he duly delivered, implementing at Virgin a strategy he had pursued already at EMI. Artists who were not contributing or who had passed their peak were dropped. 80 jobs went in the UK and a further 80 in the USA in two tranches. The merging of the two businesses was assisted by Ken Berry agreeing to stay on and run Virgin within EMI. Richard Branson has also retained the title 'President for Life' of Virgin Music.

Towards the end of 1994 Berry took on additional responsibilities for the whole of EMI Music's International interests. He was seen to have an 'iron grip on the business along with the intuitive understanding needed to deal effectively with artists'.

EMI Music in 1994

Thorn-EMI's Annual Report for 1993–1994 declared 'record results for the sixth consecutive year' in respect of EMI Music. Fifteen albums world-wide had each sold in excess of 2 million copies; EMI Records in the UK had received the Queen's Award for Export Achievement. Virgin Music had contributed £90 million out of a total of £246 million operating profits, and was the UK's top record label with six Number One albums. 'The performance (of Virgin) continues to exceed expectations'. £90 million was £10 million higher than EMI's target expectations for Virgin, itself a figure described as 'optimistic' by analysts; a year earlier Virgin had achieved just £21 million operating profit.

EMI believed the integration of the two companies had succeeded in preserving the cultural and artistic independence of Virgin whilst enabling its artists to benefit from EMI's stronger international structure and network. With hindsight the acquisition of Virgin is generally acknowledged to be a major coup for Thorn-EMI.

During the year EMI Music agreed to collaborate with Warner Music, Sony and Polygram in the development of a new music television channel, and invested in a digital cable radio venture in order 'to capitalize on the pace of change in the industry'. The company also acquired the largest independent German recorded music company.

EMI Music's artist roster now includes an array of 'yesterday's stars' with their valuable back catalogue recordings (including The Beatles, The Rolling Stones, The Beach Boys, Cliff Richard, Tina Turner and Diana Ross), artists still capable of chart-topping releases, such as Garth Brooks and Phil Collins, and new talent like Blind Melon and Smashing Pumpkins. *The Beatles Live At The BBC* album was particularly successful late in 1994. In addition EMI records Frank Sinatra, who has made a successful comeback in the 1990s with his duet albums, easy listening music from artists such as Brian May and orchestral classics conducted by Simon Rattle and other renowned musicians. It is noticeable that the repertoire includes several leading American artists instead of being focused heavily on the UK.

EMI also owns a number of Christian music labels.

Retailing

Music Retailing in the UK can be classified in four main categories:

❑ Specialist multiples – EMI's HMV Music stores and those branded Our Price and Virgin but controlled by the WH Smith Group.
❑ Non-specialist multiples – Boots, Woolworths, WH Smith.
❑ Independents.
❑ Mail order and record clubs.

Smith's in total accounts for some 30% of the market, followed by Woolworth's (15%) and HMV with a 13.5% market share. HMV sells recorded music, videos and other related entertainment products; the basic strategy is one of mixing superstores with a range of smaller satellite stores in defined geographic regions in order to provide an appropriately comprehensive coverage. The superstores feature appearances by leading artists and they champion special regional promotions.

The competitive strategies of the major retailers are built around:

❑ Competitive (or low) prices – a feature of W H Smith stores and Woolworth's.
❑ A wide range of stock – Virgin and HMV, whose largest superstores are reputed to offer the widest and deepest range in the UK.
❑ Service – again a feature of HMV, who are clearly not alone with this.
❑ Location.
❑ The ambience of the stores.

EMI Music owns a strong distribution network for its products within the UK, covering all important wholesalers and retailers. HMV imports directly from the USA and relies on several independent wholesalers for products from other key record companies and countries.

In 1993 HMV attempted to purchase the third largest US record retailer, Camelot, but failed.

The acquisition of Dillons

The retail chain Pentos had grown rapidly in the 1980s under the leadership of Terry Maher, its founder, chairman and chief executive. In the late 1980s/early 1990s, Pentos (now comprising Dillons, Rymans [stationery and office equipment] and Athena [posters, cards, and so on]) followed an aggressive expansion strategy. Pentos entered into a number of 'reverse premium' agreements with landlords, accepting cash advances for taking on long-term leases at high rents. The slow pick-up after the recession left the group unable to generate enough cash to meet its overheads. Maher was ousted by institutional shareholders in late 1993. Sometime later Thorn-EMI enquired about the possibility of acquiring Dillons, but was rebuffed. When Pentos went into receivership Sir Colin Southgate struck decisively and a deal was agreed within days. Thorn agreed to pay £36 million for the Dillons stores it wanted; up to another £20 million would be required to settle outstanding debts with suppliers. Maher, who would have liked to buy back Dillons himself, was infuriated and claimed the price was too low. The underlying strength and *competitive strategy* of Dillons had never been questioned when Pentos went into receivership; the group's problems with Athena and Rymans had been more worrying.

Dillons would be absorbed by HMV. After all, there are some similarities between music and book retailing. Both feature best sellers, which, at least for a number of months, sell in large numbers. At the same time stores need to stock huge numbers of slow movers which can turn over at the rate of just one a month or even less. Effective IT systems are needed to control such stocks.

The Thorn Group – the rentals business

Mike Metcalf has been chief executive of the Thorn Group since 1991; he is also a member of the main Thorn-EMI Board. In his early forties, he is ten years plus younger than both Sir Colin Southgate and Jim Fifield. He is an ex-finance director, and he has been described as more sober than Southgate and Fifield.

In 1991 the rentals business had a number of strategic problems.

❏ Rent-A-Center, the important American acquisition of the 1980s, was under Federal investigation; the company had been accused of strong-arm debt collection using 'guns and gangs of Hell's Angels'.

Rent-A-Center was exonerated in 1993 but there was still some risk the bad publicity would stick.
❏ Radio Rentals, Thorn's main UK high street rental chain and the market leader, was being out-performed by its key rival, Granada.
❏ The rentals business was, in effect, triple brand-ed, with Radio Rentals, DER and Multibroadcast all offering essentially the same service. Thorn had not used its acquisitions to establish clearly differentiated brands and consequently its overheads were unnecessarily high.

DER and Multibroadcast have since been replaced as brands and the stores relaunched.
❏ Rumbelows, which sold rather than rented, household appliances and electrical goods, had no real competitive advantage; it was too small a chain and it was being out-performed by market leader Dixons. Dixons had a 12% market share; Rumbelows just 2%. Rumbelows had traditionally concentrated on high street sites whilst many of its rivals had also developed out-of-town. Rum-belows had lost £50 million in the last three years.

In 1992 the 450 Rumbelows stores were partially switched to a rental format, concentrating on low-cost rentals such as the re-rental of appliances which a previous customer had returned. 800 jobs were lost and over 150 stores closed. In 1986, Rumbelows'

television rental accounts had been transferred to Radio Rentals with the loss then of 650 jobs.

In February 1995 Thorn announced the remaining 285 Rumbelows stores were to be closed within the next three months with the loss of a further 2500 jobs. Losses had continued at £12 million per year. Sir Colin Southgate commented: 'electrical retailing is a mayhem market in which no-one makes any money either in or out of town'.

A month later, Escom, Germany's second largest PC manufacturer and retailer, agreed to take on the leases of 231 ex-Rumbelows stores. Rumbelows' employees were encouraged to apply for jobs. Escom's computers were already sold through Rumbelows outlets; the deal would elevate the German company to the position of the UK's largest specialist high street PC retailer.

In the UK, Metcalf has also established a single administration and distribution centre for the whole business, inaugurated a warehouse sales operation for ex-rental equipment (a strategy copied from Granada), and introduced a rent-to-own format in the UK. Rent-to-own is the traditional format in the USA, whereas historically the UK has been mainly rent-to-rent. With rent-to-own, as with conventional hire purchase and credit sales, a customer rents an article and, after paying a certain number of instal-ments, becomes the owner. Unlike hire purchase, however, there is no down payment and the custo-mer can cancel the agreement or exchange the product for a different one at any time and without penalty. In addition, customers enjoy free repair services for the duration of the contract. In the US the industry has been accused of charging 'unsophi-sticated customers' two or three times the usual retail price for rent-to-own contracts.

As part of his strategy to create multiple brands targeted at distinct market segments, Metcalf intro-duced Fona (cash sales and rent-to-own and based on Thorn's successful Danish chain, where it is market leader in electrical retailing) and Crazy George's, radical format stores, piloted in Birming-ham, which offer credit sales without traditional credit checks.

However, again in 1995, Thorn has abandoned its UK experiment with Fona; the 36 stores are being closed. Whilst electrical *retailing* has been problem-atic, rental business in late 1994/early 1995 has been buoyant.

Table 7   The Thorn Group product/country/access matrix

Product	Country
Televisions Videos Hi-fi equipment White goods Telephones Personal computers	UK, Europe Asia Pacific, USA
Furniture	USA, UK, France, Australia, New Zealand
Jewellery	USA only

Access format	Country
Credit sales	UK and Europe
Rent-to-own	Global; the only access format offered in the USA
Rent-to-rent Rent with purchase option*	The world other than USA

*The rent with purchase option includes a wide variety of access opportunities, each tailor-made to suit individual countries and market niches

Table 8   **Selected access options**

Outlet	Selected access option
Radio Rentals	Option-2-Own – a premium rental charge provides for eventual ownership
Fona, Denmark	Easyown – similar; a credit sale leading to ownership
Crazy George's	New Buy Scheme – for customers disbarred from normal credit. A conditional sale agreement, no deposit, no credit checks. Weekly payments.
Rent-A-Center	Rental purchase – weekly payments and free servicing
Remco	Customer's Choice – monthly payments; targeted at more affluent customers who elect to pay large monthly slices and who can terminate the rental in favour of buying the product at any time for an overall lower charge
Radio Rentals Australia	Rent-Try-Buy – payments reduce the equity that customers eventually need to buy the product outright, which they are free to do at any time.

In 1992 Thorn also acquired Remco for $55 million. Remco could add 64 stores in Houston, Dallas, Chicago and North Carolina to the growing Rent-A-Center chain which then boasted 1100 outlets and a 25% US market share. Thorn is now market leader in both the UK and US, and it enjoys a market share of somewhere between 25 and 60% in each of the 19 countries (including 12 in Europe) in which it competes.

Service in the rentals industry is based on three key factors:

❏ the product range
❏ access options
❏ service support.

Table 7 illustrates the Thorn product/country/access matrix and Table 8 features a selection of the service options.

Key success factors

❏ Flexibility – of access formats and rental systems, together with the flexibility to change from one system to another or up-grade the product/-

model. Some customers, for example, see rental as an ideal opportunity for trying out a new product (such as high-definition television or CD-Rom system) before making a purchase commitment.

In the UK Thorn have pioneered purchase options within rental agreements.

❏ To accomplish this flexibility, strong linkages with product manufacturers/suppliers are essential.

❏ High levels of service, with minimum financial commitment, supported with advice on products and options. After-rental servicing is vital as word-of-mouth is a critical aspect of marketing.

In the mid-1990s the prospects for the Thorn Group have been described as 'modest', but, on the other hand, this is a relatively safe and stable business as long as a company succeeds with the key success factors. Other important strategic issues for Thorn are the extent of the capital tied up at any time and the lack of any real synergy with EMI Music.

The future

Analysts have calculated that the value of Thorn-EMI split into two separate and independent businesses would be in the order of £6.5 billion, £2 billion higher than the value of the group in 1994. In September 1995, when the shares stood at over 1500 pence each, Thorn-EMI was valued at £6.55 billion. However, there must always be some value in size and diversity.

For a period Thorn-EMI suggested a split was unlikely – and, if the right acquisition could be found, a move into book publishing, to complement Dillons, more realistic. However at the 1995 Annual General Meeting Sir Colin Southgate commented:

> We have concluded that demerger, if it can be achieved in an acceptable way, is in the best long-term interests both of the businesses that currently constitute Thorn-EMI and the shareholders. Demerger would permit the management of each group to develop its individual strengths and pursue opportunities which each judges appropriate to its future growth. Furthermore, by demerging, the value of these businesses would be more fully recognized.
>
> We are, therefore, considering proposals which, if implemented, would lead to the demerger of the Group ... at present we believe that any demerger would separate the Rental business from the rest of the Group. There would then be two publicly quoted companies.

Demerger requires the consent of 22 different national tax regimes.

There must, though, continue to be questions concerning the future of the music business. Most of the world's important independent record labels have now been absorbed by the majors; acquiring new repertoire is always going to be uncertain; once cost cutting and rationalization has been achieved, organic growth becomes vital for expanding the business.

One major boost for the record industry in the UK was provided in 1994 when the Monopolies and Mergers Commission ruled that compact discs (relatively more expensive than in other key markets in the world) were not being priced at exorbitant levels. However, throughout the 1980s and early 1990s many music buyers have systematically replaced their vinyl record collections with CDs, readily buying up 'greatest hits' albums based on back catalogue material. Has this opportunity peaked? Mini compact

discs (minidiscs) and digital compact cassettes (DCCs), rival new formats, wait in the wings, but will either have the impact that the launch of CDs had? At the same time, though, there must be considerable potential for exploiting EMI Music's back catalogue in multimedia products such as CD-Rom.

Sir Colin Southgate has commented (in an interview for the *Daily Telegraph*, November 1993) that, with hindsight, he would have:

❏ speeded up the disposals programme and
❏ attempted to cut back dividends to provide more cash for investment.

He also reflected that he had not been as hard on certain managers as perhaps he should have been.

He remains unconvinced about any need to link hardware and software in the entertainments industry. Sony (with Columbia Pictures and CBS Records) and Matsushita (Universal Pictures and MCA) have tracked a different route. Time Warner appear to side with Thorn-EMI on this issue; Polygram are 75% owned by Philips. Southgate argues that consumer electronics companies must gain the support of the whole music industry for any new formats and that film companies will license the music *they want to use* regardless of who owns the copyright. Time Warner 'unites content and distribution' to take their intellectual property and copyright material direct to their audiences. Thorn-EMI, meanwhile, has deliberately chosen not to enter into videos, video games and computer games software, and, having come out of film making and cinemas, declared it has no intention of returning.

What of the possibility of a take-over bid for Thorn-EMI?

> Thorn's management has spent 10 years cleaning up the group and [recent, 1995] results prove they've done a good job comments one leisure analyst. But they've also made it more attractive to predators.

Possible names which have been suggested include entertainment groups such as Disney and Viacom, which owns MTV, the global music video channel. Both corporations could usefully add music to their existing interests in films and television, and thereby become a more direct competitor for Time Warner. Other names to appear as possibly interested bidders are News Corporation, Microsoft and Seagram, which bought MCA from Matsushita in 1995. Given the ownerships of the large music companies, Thorn-EMI is realistically seen as the only possible acquisition. Was a company like Disney to bid successfully, it seems likely that the rentals business and Dillons would be seen as peripheral and Thorn-EMI broken up.

The last section of this case study provides a brief picture of Thorn-EMI's two main rivals in the music industry: Polygram and Time Warner.

Two leading competitors

Polygram

Polygram was formed in 1972 when the Dutch company Philips merged its record interests with those of the German company, Siemens, following a successful ten-year alliance. Siemens contributed Deutsche Grammophon, a leading classical music label, and Polydor; Philips contributed the Philips, Fontana and Mercury labels. The new Polygram quickly added to these by acquiring Decca and London to create additional synergy and savings. In 1989 Philips bought out the Siemens' shareholding; equity sales, partly to finance acquisitions, have resulted in Philips' shareholding being subsequently reduced to 75%.

Key independents acquired more recently are: Island in 1989, A & M in 1990, and Motown in 1993, this after a two-year distribution arrangement. Polygram entered music publishing in 1986 and film, video and television production in 1987. There were some moderately successful releases, but the real breakthrough came with *Four Weddings and a Funeral* in 1994, the leading UK box office earner of all time. The film cost $5 million to make; it has so far grossed over $250 million at the box office. Polygram manufactures compact discs but obviously not hardware, relying on the Philips link. Thirty per cent of Andrew Lloyd Webber's Really Useful Group was purchased in 1991, and Polygram also owns Britannia Music, the leading music mail order company which alone accounts for 8% of recorded music sales in the UK.

Leading artists include: INXS, Abba, Bon Jovi, Bryan Adams, The Cure, Elton John, Sting, U2 and Chris de Burgh together with the Motown back catalogue of Diana Ross, Lionel Richie, The Four Tops, Smokey Robinson and Stevie Wonder.

Polygram provides over 50% of the world's karaoke software and enjoys a substantial presence in the Far East, especially Japan and Hong Kong. As

Table 9   Polygram revenues, 1993

Popular music	69%
Classical music	12%
Films and videos	9%
Music publishing; license fees	10%
Europe	52%
North America	23%
Far East, including Japan	20%
Rest of the world	5%

well as being a major market for karaoke, Japan is also the world's largest classical music market. Polygram has subsidiaries in 30 countries, and, like Thorn-EMI, believes that a world-wide distribution network is essential for success. Table 9 provides a breakdown of Polygram revenues in 1993.

Polygram is now aiming to 'transform itself into a global entertainment company, to take advantage of the opportunities in multi-media'. Music and film production and distribution will remain at the heart of the business.

Film distribution is a targeted growth area; Polygram may have a strong presence in certain countries, including the UK, but it is thin elsewhere.

In January 1995 Polygram acquired – for £100 million – ITC Entertainment, formed in 1984 by Lord Grade. ITC owns the rights to some 350 feature films together with vintage television series such as The Prisoner and Thunderbirds, both of which enjoyed successful repeat showings in the UK in 1994. ITC thus provides valuable back catalogue material and access into US television syndication.

Time Warner

Time Warner is the world's largest media and entertainment company, and it is focused on software. With music, plus videos, magazines and books, it is the biggest holder of copyrights in the world. It is diversified, mainly in related businesses, with music contributing some 25% of global revenues (1994–1995). The company was created in 1990 when Time Inc. merged with Warner Communications; the vast majority of its earnings come from the USA.

Time Warner is the world leader in television ***programming***; in addition it owns the HBO (Home Box Office) network, which is accessed both domestically and through hotel television sets, and important cable TV interests. Recent investments have given Time Warner the 'finest collection of cable properties anywhere in the world'. The company is a major film producer through Warner Brothers and Lorimar, controlling all the distribution of its own films. Time Warner owns movie theatres. With titles like *Fortune, Time* and *Life*, Time Warner is a leading publisher; it also markets Time-Life books and owns the US Book-of-the-Month Club mail order network.

The acquisition by Time Warner of the smaller but innovatory Turner Broadcasting (announced in September 1995) will dramatically enhance its already strong programming interests. Turner owns Cable News Network, best-known for CNN Headline News, and cable entertainment businesses in Latin America, Europe, Asia and the Caribbean. It also owns a baseball team, the Atlanta Braves. Amongst other related interests being brought together, ownership of Yogi Bear and Flintstones programmes (Turner) will be added to Warner's Bugs Bunny!

The key music labels are Warner, Elektra and Atlantic, consolidated as WEA. Warner Chappell is a joint world leader, with EMI Music Publishing, owning 900,000 copyrights, including songs from Prince, Madonna and Elton John. Major recording artists are Simply Red, Madonna, Chris Rea, Enya, Rod Stewart, Prince and Eric Clapton. Madonna has been used as a springboard to exploit the potential synergies from linking book and music publishing.

Content is seen as a much lower risk industry than cable television, which is operating at the leading edge of the emerging multimedia technology – and it is subject to government regulation. Time Warner and Thorn-EMI have different views on the long-term feasibility of separating content and distribution. Time Warner's chairman, Gerald Levin, has commented: 'creative material is not created in isolation from its audience, nor from the question of whether it will make money. The value to creative content comes when it is going through the largest number of channels world-wide. The money is made on the distribution side, not the content'. In contrast with Thorn-EMI, Levin also believes that owning distribution brings an entertainment company closer to its ultimate customers and consequently acts as an important driver back down the value chain.

Time Warner, finally, has sizeable shareholdings in Atari (computer games) and the Six Flags Corporation, which runs a number of entertainment theme parks in the USA.

Appendix 1 Thorn-EMI five-year summary, 1991–1995

For the years to 31 March	1995 £m	1994 £m	1993 £m	1992 £m	1991 £m
Results					
Turnover					
Continuing operations	4329.0	3829.0	3643.0	3198.7	2974.8
Discontinued operations	178.3	462.2	809.3	755.7	685.5
	4507.3	4292.1	4452.3	3954.4	3660.3
Operating profit					
Cont. operations – normal	458.5	385.9	314.0	221.8	223.5
Cont. operations – exceptional	(126.9)				
	331.6	385.9	314.0	221.8	223.5
Discont. operations	(3.1)	(3.4)	65.3	59.3	72.2
	328.5	382.5	379.3	281.1	295.7
Exceptional items					
Profits (losses) on businesses disposed or terminated	(35.3)	(14.5)	(30.3)	(15.3)	(78.1)
Cost of fundamental reorganizations and restructuring	–	–	(23.4)	(91.9)	–
Profits (losses) on disposal of fixed assets	9.7	(3.2)	1.8	19.1	10.1
Profit before finance charges	302.9	364.8	327.4	193.0	227.7
Finance charges	(31.8)	(38.3)	(53.9)	(62.3)	(67.4)
Profit on ordinary activities before taxation	271.1	326.5	273.5	130.7	160.3
Taxation on profit on ordinary activities	(157.6)	(121.6)	(107.8)	(70.2)	(75.1)
Profit on ordinary activities after taxation	113.5	204.9	165.7	60.5	85.2
Minority interests	(6.8)	(3.1)	5.9	7.3	(1.5)
Profit attributable to members of the Holding Company	106.7	201.8	171.6	67.8	83.7
Key statistics					
Net cash flow from operating activities	938.8	740.7	678.6	620.5	661.1
Capital expenditure:					
property, plant, equipment and vehicles	214.3	150.4	143.7	140.1	160.0
Rental equipment	437.9	370.1	311.8	292.5	330.0
Total capital expenditure	652.2	520.5	455.5	432.6	490.0
Basic earnings per ordinary share	25.0p	48.2p	43.6p	20.5p	27.2p
Adjusted fully diluted earnings per ordinary share	61.9p	52.5p	50.8p	40.1p	46.9p
Dividends per ordinary share	36.5p	34.0p	32.0p	30.1p	29.3p
International proportion of operating profit before operating exceptional items	76.1%	74.5%	65.2%	64.5%	73.9%
turnover (cont'g operations)	9.1%	8.7%	7.7%	9.7%	
Return on sales (continuing operations)	10.6%	10.1%	9.3%	7.66%	8.5%
Debt: shareholders' funds (inc. minority interests)	55.2%	57.2%	154.9%	109.5%	98.6%
Debt: capital employed	35.6%	36.4%	60.8%	52.3%	49.6%

(continued overleaf)

For the years to 31 March	1995 £m	1994 £m	1993 £m	1992 £m	1991 £m
Employment of capital					
Music publishing copyrights	379.5	400.6	392.2	273.0	269.7
Property, plant, equipment and vehicles	709.6	502.6	558.5	502.9	501.7
Rental equipment	691.6	656.2	664.3	655.2	659.6
Fixed asset investments	52.3	131.8	142.1	122.5	119.6
Stocks and debtors, excluding taxation and interest	1017.1	1062.7	1192.6	1107.0	1129.9
Investments: own shares	38.8	18.2	–	–	–
Creditors and provisions, excluding borrowings, taxation and dividends and interest payable	(1683.5)	(1475.6)	(1627.1)	(1422.6)	(1285.1)
Operating assets	1205.4	1296.5	1322.6	1238.0	1395.4
Deferred taxation	(17.2)	(18.9)	(22.1)	(22.7)	(36.6)
Corporate taxation	(53.8)	(8.4)	(29.1)	(33.8)	(39.9)
Dividends and net interest payable	(113.2)	(110.4)	(100.4)	(93.6)	(84.5)
	1021.2	1158.8	1171.0	1087.9	1234.4
Capital employed					
Share capital	106.9	106.6	102.2	81.4	77.5
Share premium account	899.8	894.5	755.0	250.1	159.8
Profit and loss account	469.6	532.8	479.5	446.1	477.2
Other reserves	625.0	574.1	574.1	574.1	596.1
Goodwill	(1517.5)	(1372.9)	(1458.2)	(847.5)	(710.6)
Convertible unsecured loan stock	–	–	–	211.5	–
Shareholders' funds	583.8	735.1	452.6	715.7	600.0
Minority interests	74.1	2.1	6.8	15.0	21.6
Net borrowings	363.3	403.4	711.6	357.2	612.8
	1021.2	1158.8	1171.0	1087.9	1234.4

Source: Thorn-EMI Annual Reports

Appendix 2 Thorn-EMI – turnover and profit by division, 1991–1995

	Turnover (£'M To 31 March)				
	1995	1994	1993	1992	1991
Music	2189.0	1760.5	1507.3	1128.6	1016.2
Rental	1589.4	1484.2	1387.5	1371.8	1255.9
HMV	503.2	403.9	323.2	261.8	207.4
TSE	47.4	407.7	425.0	436.5	495.3
Discontinued operations	178.3	208.4			
UK	1371.3	1562.2	1903.7	1918.0	
USA	1293.0	1237.3	1051.7	818.5	
Rest of Europe	1207.0	1153.0	1200.3	931.1	
Asia Pacific	525.0	252.8	226.2	205.7	
Rest of World	111.0	86.8	70.4	81.1	
Operating profit (£'M to 31 March)					
Music	294.9	246.1	196.9	125.1	102.7
Rental	152.4	129.2	115.3	105.9	119.4
HMV	14.0	6.1	2.6	1.3	4.1
TSE	(2.8)	(11.6)	1.5	13.2	62.5
Discontinued operations	(3.1)	11.7			

*These operating profit figures are before an Extraordinary Charge of £126.9 million.

Sources: Thorn-EMI Annual Reports and the *Financial Times*.

Appendix 3 Thorn-EMI share prices, 28 Jan. 1985 to 30 Jan. 1995

High Value	1,134.00p	28.04.1994		Low Value	312.81p	26.07.1985		
1985	Jan	416.44	Feb	430.84	Mar	382.86	Apr	402.05
	May	450.03	Jun	342.56	Jul	312.81	Aug	368.17
	Sep	342.56	Oct	352.15	Nov	404.93	Dec	382.86
1986	Jan	373.26	Feb	428.92	Mar	478.81	Apr	480.73
	May	454.83	Jun	445.23	Jul	428.92	Aug	467.30
	Sep	438.51	Oct	431.80	Nov	453.87	Dec	449.07
1987	Jan	546.94	Feb	584.36	Mar	599.72	Apr	663.05
	May	677.44	Jun	729.26	Jul	728.30	Aug	635.22
	Sep	670.72	Oct	422.20	Nov	518.16	Dec	542.14
1988	Jan	550.78	Feb	540.23	Mar	564.69	Apr	602.60
	May	604.51	Jun	610.75	Jul	622.75	Aug	608.35
	Sep	605.47	Oct	633.30	Nov	617.95	Dec	597.80
1989	Jan	677.44	Feb	672.64	Mar	671.68	Apr	660.17
	May	675.52	Jun	737.89	Jul	806.02	Aug	820.41
	Sep	780.11	Oct	684.16	Nov	714.86	Dec	735.01
1990	Jan	733.09	Feb	668.80	Mar	652.49	Apr	620.83
	May	691.83	Jun	740.77	Jul	690.87	Aug	630.42
	Sep	563.25	Oct	596.84	Nov	624.67	Dec	649.61
1991	Jan	612.19	Feb	672.64	Mar	688.00	Apr	688.96
	May	678.40	Jun	711.02	Jul	723.50	Aug	764.76
	Sep	762.84	Oct	769.56	Nov	745.57	Dec	712.94
1992	Jan	791.63	Feb	776.27	Mar	730.00	Apr	843.00
	May	835.00	Jun	830.00	Jul	732.00	Aug	666.00
	Sep	789.00	Oct	819.00	Nov	833.00	Dec	852.00
1993	Jan	815.00	Feb	842.00	Mar	888.00	Apr	849.00
	May	874.00	Jun	915.00	Jul	952.00	Aug	1006.00
	Sep	941.00	Oct	938.00	Nov	923.00	Dec	1009.00
1994	Jan	1091.00	Feb	1093.00	Mar	1053.00	Apr	1134.00
	May	1025.00	Jun	1020.00	Jul	1040.00	Aug	1041.00
	Sep	1007.00	Oct	978.00	Nov	979.00	Dec	1032.00
1995	Jan	1018.00						

Footnote: The relative success of Thorn-EMI's shares changed markedly during 1995. By September the traded price exceeded 1500 pence for the first time ever.

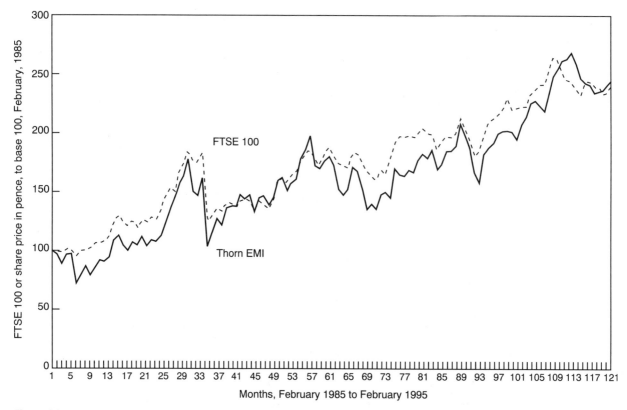

Figure A1   Thorn-EMI Share Price against FTSE 100 (both to base 100, February, 1985). Source: Datastream.

Questions

1 Evaluate Sir Colin Southgate's declared focus strategy for Thorn-EMI. Do you believe this was the correct path for the company to follow? How and why has the strategy been changed during implementation?

2 How successful has the strategy been? What criteria are you using to evaluate this success?

   Evaluate the strategic position of Thorn-EMI in 1995.

3 Review Thorn-EMI's three main businesses in respect of key success factors
   • related core competencies
   • strategic issues facing the company in 1995.

4 In your opinion, which corporate strategic options are most appropriate, desirable and feasible for Thorn-EMI at the end of 1995?

   (The issues raised by this question must take account of Thorn-EMI's declared intentions, but an objective evaluation of the alternatives is nevertheless possible).

The Sony Corporation

Sony, 50 years old in 1996, became renowned throughout the world as an innovatory, pioneering company with an international presence and reputation in the consumer electronics industry. Sony is now an acknowledged leader in a number of very competitive and dynamic industries where no single company enjoys a dominant market share.

Sony has always sought to develop unique products rather than copy other companies. Although profitable, profitability *per se* has not been the driving objective. Sony has invested in research and development at a rate above the average for both its industry and for Japan. Technologists are seen as a critically important resource and allowed freedom to work within relatively open-ended briefs.

However, the company has come under enormous pressure as it has struggled to remain a leader in the changing world of consumer electronics, and, as a result, there have been major changes in its strategies and structure in the 1990s.

This case study traces the growth, development, successes and setbacks of The Sony Corporation. It encapsulates issues of corporate and competitive strategies, structural evolution and the Japanese style of management. Sony's recent strategy of diversification into the American entertainment industry is examined in detail.

This version of The Sony Corporation case study was written by John L Thompson in 1996 for the purposes of class discussion. It should not be taken to reflect either effective or ineffective management.

Introduction

Sony is at a critical point in its development as a global corporation as it celebrates its fiftieth birthday in 1996. The success of recent strategic changes are likely to have a major impact upon whether Sony restores its lost prosperity or declines to become a business legend.

The increasing significance of computers and communications equipment in consumer electronics, reinforced by the continuing convergence of computing, telecommunications and electronic entertainment in a range of new multimedia products, have forced consumer electronics companies like Sony to focus their thinking and research on emerging technologies rather than concentrating on the innovatory development of new product variants. The conventional audio-visual products which have been at the heart of Sony's growth and development are now overshadowed by the latest developments in multimedia technology. To compete effectively in the late-1990s, Sony realized that

it had to transform itself from a company which was dependent on the analogue technologies of conventional audio-visual products to one with competencies in digital technology which it could use to develop a range of new products for the multimedia age.

History and product developments*

Humble beginnings

Sony Corporation, begun in Japan after the end of World War II, is much younger than its major Japanese rivals. In 50 years it has become established as a

*This section on the early history of Sony has been developed in part from The Sony Corporation case study (1986) in Quinn JB, Mintzberg H and James RM (1988) *The Strategy Process: Concepts, Contexts and Cases*, Prentice-Hall. Other material has been obtained from a variety of newspaper and journal articles.

market leader in the production of specialist electronic products in an environment of rapid technological change, economic growth and a global willingness to accept new technology.

Sony's corporate history has been built around core competencies in technological innovation and miniaturization and the development of quality products and quality systems which have led to high levels of differentiation. Early growth was organic and initially competition was limited. Today's competitors have typically followed Sony into the markets it pioneered. The successful targeting of innovators and early adopters generated healthy profit margins which were re-invested in the company, especially in research and development.

The founder of Sony was Masaru Ibuka, who gathered together a group of engineers 'to develop some sort of electronics laboratory or enterprise'. He had previously owned and managed a factory supplying electronic instruments for the war effort, and he was now keen 'to do something that no other company had done before'. In the 1940s and 1950s Japanese companies were not perceived to be innovators or leaders in technology, but rather businesses which were very skilled at copying Western technology. From these humble beginnings, a truly innovatory company with a world-wide reputation and presence has emerged.

The new enterprise had little capital, a limited track record and no definite ideas. Essentially the managers just had aspirations to apply the knowledge of the founder in the development of consumer products. Ibuka's first invention for the consumer market was an electric rice cooker manufactured from aluminium. It failed to sell. The electric element burnt the rice at the bottom of the pot whilst failing to cook the rice at the top.

To generate a stronger cash flow to fund further developments the company started repairing and modifying wartime radio sets. The company was already earning revenue from electronic instruments such as voltmeters which were still being manufactured and sold to the new peacetime markets.

From the beginning Sony developed as an independent company; it was not a member of a Japanese keiretsu or business network. Shortly after the company was started Ibuka was joined by a close wartime friend, Akio Morita, who initially combined a part-time post at the Tokyo Institute of Technology

with his time at the company. Unlike Ibuka, Morita was a member of a leading Japanese Samurai family. Morita was expected to forge his career in the family business, which was brewing sake. He had been trained in business skills from an early age. However, at university, he had proved himself to be a very talented electronics engineer. Whilst Ibuka was passionate about inventing, Morita was a more realistic businessman who understood finance and marketing. The two friends proved to have valuable, complementary skills.

In 1946 Ibuka successfully persuaded Morita's father to allow Akio to join his business on a full-time basis. Morita Snr actually invested in the business and eventually became the company's largest shareholder. The company was formally incorporated as Tokyo Telecommunications Engineering Company (TTK) in May 1946, and valued at ¥198,000, which approximated to US$500. TTK's next inventions were an electrically heated cushion and a resonating sound generator (for sending and receiving Morse code) which offered superior audio facilities to competing machines. The quality was high, and the American Occupation Forces were amongst the early customers. Although the products were relatively sophisticated the production facilities were housed in run-down, leaky premises. TTK also succeeded in obtaining contracts to convert and modernize all the equipment belonging to the Japanese Broadcasting Network. Noticeably there were still no breakthroughs with products for the theoretically targeted consumer market. Ibuka then saw an early American reel-to-reel tape recorder in one of the offices belonging to the Occupation Forces.

Tape recorders – the first consumer product

Ibuka realized the potential of the machine and purchased the Japanese patent rights immediately. He was convinced TTK had the requisite skills to design and produce a good quality tape recorder. One major stumbling block proved to be a shortage of plastic in Japan, from which TTK could manufacture the reel-to-reel tapes. Import regulations prohibited the acquisition of plastic from abroad. TTK tried cellophane, rice paper and finally a specially calendered paper with a smooth surface and which could be coated with magnetic powder. They overcame the inherent drawbacks in the paper tape by building superior quality into the circuitry, recording head and amplification system. Although it needed both patience and money TTK became the first company in the world to manufacture the complete range of tapes and recorders, including the component parts. Altogether this implied 12 different basic technologies.

Their first recorder, weighing 100 lbs, was introduced into the market in 1949. Several months passed though before the first unit was actually sold – to the Japanese equivalent of a pub. Realistically the device was too heavy, too bulky, too complex and too expensive. Once they realized why the market was slow and hesitant, Ibuka and his colleagues concentrated on reducing both the size and weight, and sought ways of halving the cost. Their main competition was from 3M, which was already a well-established and successful American corporation. 3M's magnetic tape, branded with the Scotch name, was a superior product which TTK sought to franchise. 3M were only willing to grant the franchise if TTK stopped manufacturing the hardware.

Transistor radios

Ibuka went to America in 1952 in search of new market opportunities for his smaller, cheaper tape recorder. It was on this visit that he began to realize the future potential for transistors, an invention patented by Western Electric of the USA. He returned home and told his engineers that they were going to use transistors to build radios – radios that would not need electricity for power and which were small enough for individuals to carry around easily. Current 'portable' models were the size of a typical briefcase, weighed over 10 lbs., and needed the batteries changed every few hours. Ibuka conceptualized a pocket-sized model and took up the challenge of developing the technology.

TTK had to licence the patent from Western Electric at a cost of $25,000. Protracted negotiations with the Japanese Ministry of International Trade and Industry (MITI) for the release of this amount of foreign currency imposed a nine month delay. The transistor patent was granted in 1954.

Increasing sales of their lighter, cheaper tape recorders enabled TTK to invest in a research programme for transistors. Their aim was to achieve satisfactory yields of the high frequency transistors which were needed if radios were to be manufac-

tured at a commercial cost. Early transistors were utilized in such products as hearing aids, which operated at much lower frequencies. Nevertheless TTK were beaten by Texas Instruments in the race to be first with a portable radio utilizing high frequency transistors. However in August 1955 TTK were also able to display a small portable radio. Its size was 8″ × 4″ × 1.1/2″. The production target for the first year was 10,000, and they actually achieved 8000.

Ibuka's team concentrated on making an even smaller model, despite critics who argued that any further reduction in size would have to be at the expense of sound quality. TTK's greatest challenge lay in convincing their component suppliers that size reductions were achievable. TTK formed research alliances with a number of their suppliers and offered them technical help and expertise. Existing components were often straight copies of Western technology, a typical Japanese strategy at that time. Perseverance was rewarded in March 1957 when TTK was first to market with a pocket radio. The radio was marginally bigger than a normal shirt pocket, and consequently TTK started producing and marketing shirts with slightly larger pockets!

The company was renamed Sony at around this time. The new name had been derived from the Latin *sonis*, meaning sound. Ibuka and Morita believed the name to be simple, recognizable and easily pronounced in most languages. The name Sony quickly became a generic for transistor radios, and Sony enjoyed an early technology lead of between two and three years. Later product developments included transistorized short-wave and FM receivers.

Consolidation and growth

Sony was growing into a very sound company, diversified into a number of related areas and with markets around the world as well as in Japan. Its reliance on the Japanese government (for aid) and banking system was minimal. Ibuka and Morita were firmly in control and able to make quick decisions. Rapid expansion drove Sony to poach senior managers from other Japanese companies, an unusual practice in that country, and one which was frowned upon. But Sony was clearly not a typical Japanese business.

A new director of research was recruited from MITI, where he had previously worked for over 25 years. A printing company manager was appointed and given a totally free hand to turn around a struggling semi-conductor factory. An ex-jet pilot and talented opera baritone, Norio Ohga, was employed firstly as a music consultant. After his retirement from active stage work he became head of the tape recorder business and some years later he succeeded Akio Morita as chief executive of the whole Sony Corporation. It was Ohga who championed Sony's entry into the music and entertainments industries in the 1980s. One executive remarked: 'I never knew what hidden abilities I had until I came to Sony'.

Sony's workforce grew tenfold in the 1950s and fourfold in the 1960s. In the mid-1990s Sony employs 138,000 people around the world (see Exhibit 5). The business was controlled through firm budgeting and production control systems – but within these constraints employees were given considerable freedom and empowerment. Creativity was encouraged. Workers were provided with homes by the company, a normal Japanese practice. These homes, though, were small, prefabricated houses, whereas most large Japanese companies would house their workers in dormitories. Also unusually Sony employees were given responsibility for their own residences.

Working practices

Production was organized in small cells, each a specialized unit with full control over its own work and with responsibility for monitoring its own output. Internal co-operation between cells was encouraged and fostered. The cells formed an inter-connected and inter-dependent network. Each cell had a second cell as its main supplier and a third cell as its main customer. The role of management was to assist the cells, helping them solve problems, setting overall goals, and praising superior performances.

New employees, regardless of their background, education and intended functional role, would spend several months on a production line. Ibuka and Morita believed it was important that all employees should understand the company's products, working practices and culture. It was also typical for Sony to switch people between jobs every few years. Frequently workers would move from an engineering to a production role, and vice versa. Rewards and bonuses were given to groups of workers rather than to individuals.

Employees were encouraged to be innovative *'in the interests of the company'* and not to be afraid to make mistakes – as long as they did not make the same mistake twice. Young employees were deliberately given heavy work loads and considerable responsibility. New managers all had corporate mentors.

Sony motivates executives not with special compensation systems, but by giving them joy in achievement, challenge, pride and a sense of recognition.

Television – an important new product

Sony began to use transistors in new consumer products, introducing the world's first transistorized television in 1959, the world's first transistorized video tape recorder in 1961, and the world's first micro-television in 1962.

In 1960 Sony established a subsidiary in the USA, and Akio Morita moved with his family to New York. Sony's managers felt they needed to know the US market by intuition and not be reliant on published statistics. Sony Corporation of America was subsequently developed into one of US's highest quality companies, renowned for both its products and after-sales service.

By the mid-1960s colour television was becoming established in the USA. The standard technology, which had been pioneered by RCA, was known as the 'shadow mask' system. A triangle of three electron guns created a grid of colour dots to produce the colour image. Sony did not want to copy this widely licenced US invention, and sought to develop a system based on a line (rather than a triangle) of electron guns in the television tube. Early trials were not successful, and not for the first time Sony appeared to some to be investing in a dream. Morita commented: 'If we wait and develop a unique product, we may start several years later, but we will be stronger than all the others in ten years'.

After several setbacks, and considerable frustration, Sony's new 'Trinitron' system was ready in 1967. Trinitron was a totally unique concept, using a single gun and a three striped beam system. Its

competitive advantage was that the colour reproduction was superior to the RCA system. By Spring
1968 the new Sony televisions were in the shops,
priced competitively, and within a year Trinitron
dominated the small-screen (12″) market in Japan.
Success in America, and systematically the rest of
the world, followed almost automatically and
inevitably. Production of Trinitron colour sets began
in America in 1972 and in Britain in 1975.

Later, in the 1980s, Sony was the first company to
develop a high-definition television standard. This
innovation prompted a defensive competitive reaction in Europe. The European Commission founded
an industrial consortium to develop a rival
standard.

Video recorders

Video tape recorders had been in existence since
the mid-1950s, but they were used primarily by the
professional broadcasters. A number of Japanese
companies, together with leading American electronics corporations, all produced models. Philips
(of Holland) dominated the market in Europe. Sony
made a deliberate decision not to enter the professional video market. Instead Ibuka decided that
Sony should manufacture less-expensive commercial video recorders. Some time later he also
decided that Sony should seek to develop videos for
use in the home.

It was his vision and innovatory zeal that led to
Sony's early predominance in the home video tape
recorder market, but it was not a lead they were
able to sustain.

Sony's high-quality commercial system, the U-
Matic format, was launched in 1972. U-Matic
machines and tapes were both bigger than the VHS
systems that are commonplace today, but much
smaller than the existing professional systems. U-
Matic machines used a single recording head and
tapes enclosed in cassettes – professional machines
normally had four heads and used reel-to-reel tapes.
Because of its high quality, U-Matic survived for a
number of years after smaller systems were
available.

Sony pioneered home video with the Betamax
format in 1976. Betamax cassettes were also larger
than the VHS format which was developed by Japan
Victor Corporation (JVC), a subsidiary of Matsushita,
under a patent agreement with Sony. Sony had
invited Matsushita to join them with the Betamax
format, but their suggestion had been declined. The
early VHS tapes offered twice the recording time of
Betamax, but Sony stuck with Betamax because of its
superior reproduction quality. They believed that this
advantage would guarantee success and consumer
preference. They misjudged the market and their
competitors. Most Japanese and American consumers preferred the smaller and cheaper VHS system.

Although relatively slow to take-off, the video tape
recorder reached a penetration level of 25% of
households by the mid-1980s. Sony gave up on
Betamax for the domestic market and instead
produced VHS recorders and tapes, but never
achieved a substantial market position. In 1990, for
example, Sony had a 1% UK market share for video
recorders and a 6% share of the blank tapes market.
Betamax was always a more popular format in the
broadcasting sector of the market, where Sony still
enjoys an 80% market share.

There were a number of lessons for Sony. Not
only had they failed to understand the needs and
preferences of their customers, they had failed to
promote their system effectively. JVC, on the other
hand, had been willing to share their technology
and had entered alliances with owners of software –
namely the studios who owned the rights to feature
and television films which could be released on
video. These lessons were instrumental in strategic
decisions made by Sony in the 1980s.

The Sony Walkman

The Walkman is probably Sony's best-known product, and its launch in 1979 heralded the restoration
of Sony's reputation and innovatory leadership. The
Walkman introduced a new dimension to the way
people listened to the radio and to pre-recorded
music and 'changed the lifestyle of a generation'.
The original Walkman was a compact cassette player
with small earphones to enable highly portable
listening without annoying or inconveniencing
other people. Over 50 million sets were sold within
the first 10 years. It is useful when walking and
jogging and on trains and aeroplanes. The concept
was later extended to a variety of different models,
including waterproof and sandproof sets, radio
receivers, special versions for children, compact
disc players, and, in 1988, video playback systems
using Sony's new 8 mm video cassettes.

The idea for the Walkman had come from Ibuka and Morita. Morita knew that young people liked to listen to music constantly, often wanting to play it at a loud volume, and that their tastes and preferences were frequently very personalized. He also played golf fanatically and believed that an individual cassette player would appeal to a whole range of sportsmen and women. His assumptions were correct this time. The Walkman was successful from the day it was launched.

Other products and competition

Sony launched its Mavica all-electronic still picture camera in Japan in 1981. Marketing in America and Europe followed some years later. Mavica records the images on small magnetic discs, rather than film, and they can be viewed on home television screens instead of using slides or photographs. Hard copy printing systems are available for people who also want a physical photograph.

These systems have so far failed to make major inroads into the popularity of film cameras, despite the dramatic success of hand-held video camera-recorders. These cameras have become increasingly compact during the 1980s, making use of 8-mm video cassettes which can be transferred onto VHS format for viewing on domestic televisions. This market is very lucrative but very competitive and increasingly dynamic, with several major Japanese electronics companies involved.

Sony launched the first miniaturized camcorder in June 1989. It weighed just 1.5 lbs, and it was one-quarter the size of existing camcorders. Within six months both Matsushita and its JVC subsidiary had introduced lighter models. Within a further six months there was additional competition from Canon, Sanyo, Ricoh and Hitachi. Sony introduced two new models in Summer 1990. One was the lightest then available; the other had superior technical features.

Japanese competitors such as Matsushita (which also incorporates Panasonic branded products), Hitachi and Toshiba are all older and larger than Sony. Although their product ranges are not identical they are all diversified and active internationally. A number of these Japanese companies have, for example, diversified into consumer white goods (washing machines, refrigerators, and so on), which

Sony has deliberately ignored. There are, in addition, many other smaller Japanese competitors. Sony also experiences competition from a variety of US and European producers, with certain companies successful in particular markets but perhaps less successful across the spectrum of the global consumer electronics industry. The major European competitors are AEG, Bosch, GEC, Philips and Thomson SA, which acquired Ferguson in the UK from Thorn-EMI. Amstrad is a competitor for certain products only. No single competitor enjoys wide market dominance, although there are market leaders for different products. The dynamism of the market, with short product life cycles and constant innovation, means that positions of leadership may well prove transient. Sony has always marketed its products creatively around the world, sometimes appearing more like a home producer than a Japanese company. Exhibit 1, which features examples of the humorous copy used in a number of radio and television advertisements in the UK, is included to illustrate that Sony is not a typical Japanese company. The advertisements all featured the instantly recognizable voice of John Cleese and date back to the late 1970s, early 1980s. It has also been claimed that many Americans actually believe that Sony is an American company.

In the early 1980s Sony formed an alliance with Philips to develop and launch compact disc players and CDs. At that time Philips had a substantial shareholding in Polygram, one of the leading recording companies, but not the controlling interest which it has today. Initially the record companies in America and Europe were cautious about releasing their music on the new format; and this hostility had a formative effect on Sony's future diversification strategies. Sony and Philips still earn royalties for every CD that is sold.

Sony also competes in sectors of the global computer industry, which again involves several leading Japanese players such as Hitachi and Fujitsu, and many American and European businesses. The American competitors range from the giant IBM through a number of medium-sized businesses to several small and very entrepreneurial hardware and software companies. Sony has targeted particular niches and focused carefully.

Sony pioneered the 3.5″ floppy disc which quickly proved more robust and popular than its 5.25″ predecessor. The disc, launched in 1980, was

Exhibit 1   Sony Radio and Television advertisements featuring John Cleese used in the UK in the late 1970s, early 1980s.

Good Evening.

Good Evening Sir.

I'd like to buy a Sony Trinitron Family Size Colour Television set please.

Well, this is an off-license Sir.

I see. Well do you have anything else that would give me really bright, clear, colourful pictures?

How about a gallon of creme de menthe? That'd put you on the way.

But would the pictures be really sharp?

Hmm – not really!

And is it reliable?

Well, you don't get the pictures immediately and there's always the danger your head'll fall off.

Oh, I think the Sony'll be better then. I'll try a TV shop.

Well, why did you come here in the first place?

I wanted to annoy you.

(Shop door bell)

Ring

Good afternoon.

Good afternoon Sir. Can I help you?

Yes, I'm looking for a colour television – what about this one?

Ah, the Sony Trinitron 1810.

Now, does it give a nice fuzzy picture and break down a lot?

No, no, the Trinitron system means a very sharp, reliable ...

Oh well, are the colours muddy and nasty?

No Sir, they're very bright. It's a feature ...

It's for my wife you see.

Oh – doesn't she like television?

Oh yes, but I don't like her.

Ah well, now, this little Ruritanian set's a real shocker.

Really, really. I still like the look of this Sony Trinitron you know.

Oh.

Yes, I'll take it.

But I must warn you ... it's not really right for you.

I know, but it's all right. I'll smash it up a bit. Do you sell mallets?

Sony the electronics people have asked me to tell you that they've just opened a fish and chip shop in Regent Street where you can wander in and play with the fish to your heart's content.

Sorry, sorry, that's quite wrong. I got confused – er – it's not a fish and chip shop, its a TV, Stereos and Radio showroom – sorry – I got a bit muddled there – I'm doing an ad for some fish and chip shops next – sorry – er.

Sony have a magnificent showroom and not a fish and chip shop in Reggent Street – sorry Regent Street – so if you want to go in and examine and operate stereo equipment, but not Halibut and Rock Salmon or anything fishy like that, go to 134 Regent Street. Sorry about the muddle.

Look I am frightfully sorry to bother you but some awfully nice people called Sony have agreed to pay me some money if I'll tell you they've a terribly nice showroom in Regent Street where you can just wander in and play with all the Sony Stereo and TV and Radio equipment and listen to the quadraphonic demonstration without being pestered by anyone, just to see if you like anything, you see.

It's at 134 Regent Street.

There, I've told you.

I've told them.

Cash register

Thank you.

---

far more successful for Sony than its early word-processor, for which it was actually designed. This floppy has become the industry standard, and in the 1990s Sony retains 25% of the world market. Until the early 1980s Sony manufactured semi-conductors for incorporation in its own consumer products, and then, realizing the potential for sharing its technology, sold them externally. Sony has been a pioneer and market leader for several specialized components and has also introduced a successful range of high-powered workstations.

Exhibit 2 provides a summary of Sony's product range in 1996. Exhibit 3 analyses the breakdown of Sony's sales by product and geography for the period 1973 to 1996. In the tables the category 'other products' mainly comprises computers and computing equipment together with Sony's chemicals activities. These businesses are essentially suppliers of necessary materials and represent vertical integration.

Lean manufacturing

Sony have seen lean manufacturing as another competitive weapon, and as both a supplement to, and partial replacement for, continuous innovation and new product developments. The improvements are still being sought, and are still happening, but for a number of products the speed of change has slowed down.

Lean manufacturing was necessary because the consumer electronics industry has become increasingly mature. At the same time it is this maturity, and the ability to slow down the rate at which new products and major product improvements are launched, that has facilitated lean manufacturing.

Exhibit 2 The Sony corporation. 1996 product range

Percentage breakdown of sales in 1996			
15%	**Video equipment**	–	A leading manufacturer for broadcast and professional use. Domestic VCRs, digital camcorders, 8 mm camcorders, video disk players, laserdisc players, still image video cameras and tapes. Video tape.
20%	**Audio equipment**	–	CD players, hi-fi and mini systems, radio cassette players and radios, personal stereos (Walkman series). DAT systems and car stereos. Audio tape.
17%	**Television sets**	–	Including HD TB and giant monitors.
29%	**Other products**	–	Semi-conductors. Electronic components. Computers and associated equipment (including games machines, PCs, laptops, disk drives and floppy disks). Cellular telephones.
19%	**Music and entertainment**	–	Sony Music Entertainment – CD and cassette software.
	Filmed entertainment	–	Columbia Pictures Tri-Star Pictures

Lean manufacturing systems imply some inflexibility, and are therefore preferable when products are not being constantly changed and updated.

Lean manufacturing describes manufacturing systems which are designed to reduce lead times and costs. They are likely to require investment in information technology but not necessarily the most advanced manufacturing technology. 'Lean' implies simpler systems, often based on just-in-time principles, and greater reliance on a network of inter-dependent suppliers. It is these arrangements which reduce the flexibility. In 1992, for example, Sony reduced the lead-time for manufacturing a video recorder by two thirds.

Typically parts are ordered firmly just 48 hours before they are needed. This is only practical if suppliers are integrated into Sony's value chain and if product cycles are relatively long. Although relatively inflexible for substantive product changes, such systems can be made very flexible for responding to changing consumer demand patterns. Facelifts, such as new housings, which are still changed frequently, can be accommodated without undue difficulty.

Overseas subsidiaries

Sony developed an extensive international business for three main reasons:

1. Sony lacked the domestic sales and distribution networks of its leading Japanese competitors and therefore looked to establish both production plants and sales networks around the world and close to its important markets
2. Sony wanted to be an innovatory pioneer for consumer electronics products and realized early in its history that it would be important to enjoy close proximity to its markets in order to understand and satisfy their disparate needs
3. The strength of the Japanese yen. When Sony was first incorporated the exchange rate was over 350 yen to the US dollar; in mid 1996 the rate was 108 yen to $1. When Sony built its UK plant in South Wales in 1974 £1.00 exchanged for 650 yen. In 1996 the rate is in the order of 170 yen to £1.00.

Sony's first production plant outside Japan was built in Taiwan in 1967. In 1972 Sony began manufacturing in San Diego, California. Europe followed in 1973 with a plant in Spain. Sony began producing televisions at Bridgend in South Wales in 1974, and this remains its only British manufacturing plant. The extent of Sony's operations in each European country tends to be focused. For example audio equipment is manufactured in France, magnetic tape in Italy and CD equipment in Austria. Countries like Malaysia (colour televisions,

The Sony Corporation

Exhibit 3 The Sony Corporation

Analysis of turnover by sector

Product sales (%)	(Financial years)		
	1973	1977	1981
Video equipment	6	14	27
Audio equipment*	12	12	7
Televisions	41	33	23
Tape recorders and radio*	27	20	17
Other products	14	21	26

*From1982 these categories were consolidated.

Product sales (%)	(Financial years)					
	1982	1987	1988	1989	1990	1991
Vvideo equipment	43	31	29	27	26	25
Audio equipment	23	31	31	26	25	
Televisions	23	21	20	16	15	16
Other products	11	17	17	15	15	15
Music and filmed entertainment			3	16	19	20

Product sales(%)	(Financial years)				
	1992	1993	1994	1995	1996
Video equipment	23	21	18	18	15
Audio equipment	25	24	23	23	20
Televisions	16	16	17	18	17
Other products	18	20	22	23	29
Music and filmed entertainment	18	19	20	18	19

Analysis of turnover by geography (selected years only)

	1973	1977	1981	1987	1991
Japan	53	39	29	34	26
USA	26	30	27	27	29
Europe	11	15	20	24	28
Rest of World	10	16	24	15	17

audio and video equipment) and Thailand (semi-conductors and magnetic tape) have more than one plant and a more diverse range of products.

Sony now has plants in America and in all major European and Far Eastern countries. Altogether there are over 600 subsidiaries, and over 70% of Sony's sales are outside Japan. In comparison the overseas sales percentages for three of Sony's main Japanese rivals are: Matsushita, 45%; Toshiba, 31%; and Hitachi, 24%.

The following sections chart how the innovative, successful and influential Sony began to lose its way.

Diversification into music and entertainments

Sony's diversification into the American music and entertainments industries was based on the following premise. To 'guarantee', or at least consolidate, the future potential for the permanently changing and improving consumer electronics hardware and gadgetry, Sony must be confident that the major entertainment companies would release their films and music in suitable formats. Sony therefore chose to integrate vertically and, by acquisition, secure a substantial presence in the entertainment software business.

In January 1988 Sony paid US$2.2 billion to buy CBS Records. This was followed in November 1989 with the purchase of Columbia Pictures (Columbia and Tri-Star studios) from Coca-Cola. See Exhibit 4 for a summary of the previous acquisition of Columbia by Coca-Cola. This acquisition cost $3.4 billion but Sony took on an additional $1.6 billion in debts. At the time, this constituted the largest ever overseas take-over by a Japanese company. CBS became Sony Music and Columbia was renamed Sony Pictures Entertainment. There was some cross-synergy potential with the increasingly important pop music videos and the release of film music albums.

Table 1 shows how the hardware-software linkages were to be created.

Sony was followed into America by Matsushita, which acquired MCA, owners of a recording business and Universal Studios, for $6.1 billion. Toshiba bought a stake in Time-Warner. Some critics argue that the Japanese 'have been mugged' and paid over-the-odds. Others have commented that Sony has been allowed to buy 'a significant part of America's soul'. Matsushita did not keep MCA for very long and re-sold it to Seagram, the Canadian drinks manufacturer. Matsushita tried unsuccessfully to run MCA from Japan; it was less willing than Sony has been to devolve significant power to foreign managers. The Toshiba/Time-Warner link has proved lucrative for the development of digital video technology.

Sony's gamble concerns the future and its ability to derive the potential synergy it claims is there. There is certainly no universal agreement that the synergy is anything other than imaginary. The hardware and software businesses are, quite simply, different. It is a question of technology versus creativity; and the key success factors are not the same. Some analysts, who disagree with the change of direction, have argued that the money would have been better invested in information technology.

Exhibit 4   Coca-Cola's acquisition of Columbia Pictures

In March 1982 the managements of the Coca-Cola Company and Columbia Pictures Industries Inc. agreed Columbia should become a subsidiary of Coca-Cola. The news was greeted with mixed feelings and the New York Times summarized many commentators' opinions: ' .... may be a mistake. To make a conglomerate of a company that has succeeded because it has stayed with its speciality is a dubious strategy'. At the time the Coca-Cola drink held a 25% share of the American soft drinks market, and it represented some 70% of the corporation's sales. The company had developed additional products for existing and related markets, namely Tab(sugar-free Coke, 1963) and Fanta (fizzy orange juice, 1960); and it manufactured and distributed tea, coffee, wine and natural fruit juices. Products were sold in 135 countries around the world, including China and Russia.

Coca-Cola had been looking for possible acquisitions in the food, health care and entertainment industries to enable it to grow more quickly than inflation. Any acquisition must not involve high technology (no experience) or require heavy capital investment in plant. Whilst looking for suitable companies Coca-Cola concluded that health care was becoming too high tech and that food companies did not offer a profit margin as good as its existing business. Columbia proved attractive because it was involved in home entertainments (cable TV and video), growth of which should be good for the Coca-Cola drink. In addition it had a reputation for successful films (Kramer versus Kramer, The China Syndrome and Close Encounters in the recent past), and it had an extensive film library of past productions which were undervalued in the balance sheet given their home movie potential.

Coca-Cola argued that potential synergy existed because both companies were experienced in mass consumer markets and world-wide operations, and both appealed significantly to young people. But were these sufficient grounds for synergy?

In 1986 David Puttnam, British producer of Chariots of Fire and The Killing Fields joined Columbia, but left the following year. He departed two months after Coca-Cola signed an agreement with Tri-Star Pictures, another film and TV company in which they had built a 33% stake, whereby the entertainment interests of both organizations were formed into a separate independent company, 80% owned by Coca-Cola and managed by Tri-Star executives.

Commentators contended that one reason behind this move was the reality that Wall Street was increasingly favouring pure rather than conglomerate businesses. In truth Columbia had always been profitable through the 1980s, but the key success factors for soft drinks and motion pictures were significantly different, and synergy proved elusive. Soft drinks, whatever their brand name, have certain similarities, and the emphasis must be upon effective marketing to build and maintain a market image. Films are often very different from each other.

By mid-1989 the film company was called Columbia Pictures Entertainment, and Coca-Cola held 49% of the equity. When Sony of Japan offered to buy Columbia Pictures, Coca-Cola was said to be 'demanding a high price for its shares'.

Table 1 The synergy between Sony's hardware and new software products

Film and recording studios	Cameras, broadcasting and recording equipment all provided by Sony.
	Sony also manufacture all the blank recording tape and films required.
Film and music production	Sony would determine the films and music which would be produced – and, critically, control the release formats.
	Sony also gained control over 12 television stations and the Columbia libraries, including 3000 film titles and 20,000 recorded television shows. These TV shows alone provide Sony with an annual income of $100 million.
Consumer hardware	At the time Sony manufactured: High definition televisions; Video recorders; The range of Walkman products covering audio cassettes, CDs and videos (8mm format); CD and Hi-Fi equipment.
Consumer software	Sony manufacture the film, video tape, compact discs and cassettes upon which the software will be released.
	There are, quite simply, several outlets for a single piece of recorded material.
	Additional opportunities for Sony lie in computer games based upon their movies and designed for high definition television and the Sony Play Station; and in the future in digital video discs which are seen as the replacement for video tape.

The inherent risks

There were three areas of risk for Sony.

The management risk concerned Sony's ability to manage an American acquisition. Sony was innovatory but managed by engineers. CBS and Columbia are 'people businesses'. Rather than try and manage the acquisitions from Tokyo, Sony decided early on to decentralize the business and recruit experienced Americans to control the companies. The entertainments businesses were controlled wholly from Hollywood until 1995. Although Akio Morita's brother was chairman of Sony America, American born Mickey Schulhof was the chief executive until he resigned in 1995. When he left, Schulhof had worked for Sony for 21 years; unusually for a foreigner, he had been appointed to the main Sony Board in 1989. Producers Peter Guber and Jon Peters, who had recently made the box-office successes Batman and Rain Man, were brought in by Schulhof at a cost to Sony of $200 million.

As it has become an increasingly global corporation, Sony has recruited more European and American managers to support the Japanese leadership. The integration of the different cultures is not perceived to be a problem. 'Sony's culture is heterogeneous and is strengthened by a continuous injection of new people and ideas.'

In reality the Japanese have accepted that the Americans must be given a free hand with the entertainments businesses, and that they must be given sufficient capital. Although it cannot have been easy for Sony to delegate such authority and responsibility, they have nevertheless done it. As a consequence the hardware and software businesses have so far been run as separate, independent businesses.

The second risk was *the political risk*. Would there be a hostile reaction from the US public? Sony was well established and well known in the USA, thanks to the past efforts of Morita, and consequently this has not proved to be a major concern.

Third was the significant and still unresolved *strategic risk*. Did Sony need to go into the software business? Did it pay too high a price, and could it recoup its investment? Is the synergy potential real or imagined? Could Sony succeed where Coca-Cola had failed?

Peter Guber has commented that Sony in Tokyo did not use the expression synergy, but nevertheless expected that Sony Entertainments would find ways of marrying the technology resources of the electronics businesses with entertainments. In this respect a new film should ideally be accompanied by a soundtrack produced by Sony Music. Cinemas will use Sony's digital sound equipment, which is said to be superior to Dolby systems. Depending on the film Sony will manufacture related video games based on the movie's characters.

Two main arguments against the synergy between hardware and software have been put forward. First, Sony must still make its hardware freely available to all software producers. Second, the decision by retailers to stock particular software formats, and the decision of consumers to buy, can only be influenced and not controlled by Sony.

The outcome – so far

Filmed entertainment

Sony acquired a film studio which had previously been very successful with such films as Lawrence of Arabia and Bridge Over the River Kwai. Sony also inherited Hook, directed by Stephen Spielberg at a cost of $62 million. It recouped $250 million at the box office. Sony allowed Columbia an annual film budget of $700 million, which was above-average for the industry and brought immediate criticisms of over-spending.

In December 1992 Sony concluded an exclusive long-term deal with Barbara Streisand to cover her music and film work. Streisand already recorded on CBS. This followed a similar deal with Michael Jackson in 1991, mainly covering music.

Sony have brought out a number of major box office (and consequentially, financial) successes, including Bugsy (Warren Beatty), Prince of Tides (Barbara Streisand), My Girl, A League of their Own (Madonna), Little Women, Legends of the Fall, Philadelphia (Tom Hanks), Jumanji (Robin Williams), The American President (Michael Douglas) and Sense and Sensibility (Emma Thompson). There has been one major disaster and box office failure: Last Action Hero with Arnold Schwarzenegger. Sony's films accounted for 15% of US cinema box office receipts in 1990, achieving an even higher proportion for a short period of time, but by 1994 they had fallen below 10%. At this time Sony was earning an average revenue of $18 million per film; Paramount Studios was averaging $55 million. Nevertheless high budget films continued to be made, leading to accusations that they were driving up the already high production costs. These comments caused Jon Peters to resign.

His departure was followed by that of Peter Guber in October 1994. One month later Sony wrote 265 billion yen (£1.67 billion) off the value of Sony Pictures Entertainment, commenting: 'the business has not provided adequate returns. Additional funding will be needed to attain acceptable levels of profitability'. It has been estimated that Sony had at this stage already invested $4.6 billion on top of the $3.4 billion it paid to acquire Columbia Pictures.

A Morgan Stanley analyst in London commented in 1994:

If there is a moral to this story, it is that Japanese electronics groups do not make good parents for Hollywood movie studios.

Television films began to take priority over high budget feature films, less attention was placed on finding elusive synergies and the relative success of the movie studios improved in 1995. Nevertheless, Schulhof left Sony at the end of the year and he was not replaced. His number two would continue with the same responsibilities but now report to the new strategic leaders Nobuyuki Idei and Norio Ohga in Japan (the succession of Norio Ohga and Nobuyuki Idei to the senior positions in Sony is described later in the case). Wall Street interpreted this to mean that Sony would be willing to sell at the right price.

Music

The music business was generally more stable and profitable that the movie studios; Sony's leading artistes, in particular Michael Bolton, Mariah Carey, Oasis and Bruce Springsteen, continued to deliver successful albums. However Michael Jackson's popularity fell back when he was accused of being involved with a minor, and Sony lost George Michael when he demanded to be released from his contract.

Product disappointments: the mini-disc and DCC

These two new formats for recorded music were both launched towards the end of 1992. By this time vinyl records were almost forgotten and, in certain countries including the UK, CDs were outselling audio cassettes.

Mini-disc is a small (2.5") compact disc which sells for roughly the same price as a conventional

CD. It was invented by Sony, as were the new mini-disc players. Mini-discs are not compatible with existing CD equipment. There is no loss of quality, there is random access (instant track selection), and blank discs can be bought for home recording. These blanks cost 40% of the pre-recorded disc price. They are ideal for Walkman-sized players.

Digital compact cassettes (DCC) were developed jointly by Philips and Matsushita. Philips designed the hardware, Matsushita the software. DCC offers CD-quality sound reproduction (a marked improvement on standard audio cassettes) at the same price as a standard CD. DCCs contain a spare track for recording additional data, such as biographical details of the artistes, which can be viewed on both special LCD and normal TV screens. The new DCC players will also play standard cassettes, as the two formats are the same size, but DCCs cannot be played on existing audio equipment. Philips and Matsushita saw this as a major advantage as the average person owns some 60 audio cassettes. Blanks are available. The major disadvantage was the existing drawback of standard cassettes – random access and track selection is not possible. In addition, the fear of piracy was greater for DCCs than mini-disc.

Nevertheless, the six leading record companies world-wide (including Sony Music) all agreed to release music on DCC. Initially only Sony and EMI Music were willing to support mini-disc, with the others looking to protect their existing CD sales for the time-being. It seemed unlikely that they would not support mini-disc if consumers were enthusiastic about the new format. After all, mini-disc players were cheaper than DCC players, and Sony was able to offer a combined CD/mini-disc player in 1994.

Initially consumers were reluctant to commit themselves to either product until there were clear indications of leadership. Could both formats succeed, or must there be a winner? Technical superiority alone would not guarantee success. In the event, both have failed to really take off. Some 750,000 mini-disc players have been sold, but most of these are in Japan; it continues as a niche market product. DCC was relatively less successful.

Changes in strategic leadership

Globalization was always a personal crusade of Akio

Morita. Now over seventy he retains only a peripheral involvement from his home in Hawaii, but he still exerts influence. Morita retired as Chief Executive Officer in 1989 (he was succeeded by Norio Ohga who had been Chief Operating Officer since 1982) but stayed active with the title of Chairman. Partially paralysed by a stroke in 1993 he relinquished this last position in 1995. Morita speaks perfect English and is highly Westernized. He was the public face of Sony, especially in America. He believed that Sony should be a good and ethical corporate citizen everywhere it operates, and he, like Ibuka, believed that the pursuit of profit is not the principal objective. Sony's plants have always been designed to fit into their local communities. In Alsace, for example, Sony inherited a vineyard with a piece of land that they bought. They continued to make wine, labelled Chateau Sony!

Morita frequently incorporated a strong element of intuition in his decision making. Ibuka was the same. Their executive successor, Norio Ohga, had a more considered style. According to Sony, however, his accession would have no effect on the basic culture. Sony would continue to 'operate rapidly and efficiently whilst placing strong emphasis on the long-term development of people and technology'.

Morita believed that Sony's commitment to innovation was deeply embedded in the culture of the organization world-wide. He argued that there were three essential features:

Creativity in technology	Sony is committed to high standards for the technical engineering within its products
Creativity in product planning	This technology must be harnessed to design useful, attractive and user-friendly products
Creativity in marketing	The organization must commit resources to ensure that customers are persuaded to buy Sony's products.

Interestingly Sony's Betamax video was characterized by the first two of these – but Sony failed to persuade the market that it was superior to the VHS format. The Walkman was a supremely successful example of effective product planning and marketing, but it was still harnessing 'old' technology.

Ohga himself was 65 years old in 1994; he had undergone a coronary bypass operation three years earlier. In 1995 he elected to step back and nominated Nobuyuki Idei to succeed him. Idei was currently the Chief Operating Officer, but, unlike Ibuka, Morita and Ohga, his background was not in engineering. He was essentially a marketing person who had worked for Sony for over 30 years. Typically he is perceived to be 'un-Japanese' and he speaks fluent English and French. Idei was determined to implement change in the once-mighty Sony whose performance had recently been deteriorating. In the year ended March 1995 Sony made a pre-tax loss for the first time in its history.

He stated that his main role would be to 'turn Sony into a company which can identify with a new generation of consumer electronics users – the digital dream kids'. There was to be an increased research and development emphasis on software, networks and information technology and new products relevant for the digital age.

The *Financial Times* (19 July 1996) commented that 'Sony, a young maverick company up to the 1980s, had become the sprawling, bureaucratic organization from which its founders sought to differ'. Idei was also determined to continue with the structural changes he had begun in 1994.

New products for the mid-1990s

Digital video

Similar to the way in which the CD replaced the vinyl record, digital video is predicted to replace the videocassette players and tapes which prospered in the 1980s. Digital video discs (DVD) and players (DVP) play digitized images onto a screen and are seen as an ideal format for computer-linked interactive video, the multimedia dream. As was the case with video, authorship of the technical standard is seen as critical as it will bring lifelong royalties, marketing advantages, power and influence. For digital video, the hardware/software challenge demands that the hardware and data formats meet the needs of the so-called information superhighway, including music and film makers, and the personal computer, telecommunications, cable television and satellite broadcasting industries. For Sony this

represents a philosophical shift. The last major Sony breakthroughs, the Walkman and the compact disc, were driven largely by the needs and preferences of customers; digital video will be producer-driven because of the complex array of interested parties.

Sony chose to develop digital video with its CD-partner, Philips. By 1993 it was clear that Sony-Philips was in competition with an alliance between Toshiba and Time-Warner. Sony's DVD was single-sided and could store over 2 hours of video. Toshiba's super-density disc was double-sided and offered greater storage capacity, equivalent to seven and a half normal CDs. Sony was convinced its costs and prices would be lower and that these issues would outweigh the capacity issue. However by early 1995 Sony and Philips were largely isolated, supported in the main by Mitsumi, Ricoh and Teac who all manufacture floppy disc drives. Hitachi, Pioneer, Mitsubishi, Thomson and, most critically, Matsushita/JVC supported the rival alliance. Initially Sony and Philips were determined to carry on with their own DVD, but in September they 'accepted the inevitable' and adopted the rival format.

The PlayStation

Sony's PlayStation is one of a new generation of 32-bit computer games systems, which are far faster and more graphic than their predecessors, the 16-bit systems. Sony, which was already active in games software, entered the hardware market in September 1995 with a high quality but competitively priced product and immediately took market share away from the two industry leaders, Sega and Nintendo. Sony's strategy was to price low to seize share and use this to boost sales of its more profitable and highly innovative games. The Sony PlayStation achieved sales of 3.2 million units in its first year, two million of these in trend-setting Japan.

Personal computers

The case described earlier how Sony became a major player in the computer floppy disc industry; it also manufactured several other computer components. In November 1995 Idei announced a new strategic alliance with Intel to develop a new range of personal computers and associated software. Intel, the world-leader for semi-conductor products, would provide the main circuit boards for a computer which will offer exceptionally high quality sound and graphics, ideal for multimedia applications.

Idei saw this as an essential development for Sony to exploit digital video. The PC industry is still growing, and, although it is very crowded and competitive, there are real opportunities for truly distinctive new products. The Sony PCs are to be launched first in the discerning American market, with Japan and Europe following on later.

Structural changes

In the 1980s Sony's international strategy was one of 'global localization'. Sony aimed to be a global company presented locally, and this involved devolving authority away from Tokyo and expanding manufacturing and R & D around the world. The typical large Japanese company had established both production and distribution networks around the world but had sought to remain centralized, with power firmly located in Japan.

Sony, however, divided the world into four – Europe, America, Asia and Japan – and created four organizations which *should* be virtually self-sufficient, and ultimately locally financed, independent businesses. In this respect Sony was seeking to become 'Japan's first truly global company'. The plan involved the systematic transfer abroad of all the functions required to 'perform the entire life cycle' of its products, namely design and development, engineering, production, marketing and sales. Sony already owned its own chains of retail outlets for consumer products in selected major markets. Sony was looking to devolve investment decisions, R & D, product planning and marketing. 'Changes can be implemented quicker when everything is on the spot.'

Sony created seven business groups in 1983 (this was later extended to 23) to co-ordinate the production and marketing of particular products around the world. With the exception of entertainments activities, the co-ordinating power remained in Tokyo. Structurally, Sony companies in the UK, France, Spain etc. theoretically reported to Sony Europe, based in Cologne, and with a Swiss chairman.

With the exception of entertainment the structure was designed to work as follows. Strategic decisions were all to be made centrally in Tokyo; operational decisions, concerning such issues as pricing and production, would be devolved to regional managers. Research and development at the basic development level remained centralized in Tokyo; local centres would concentrate on adaptations for local needs. Staff would be transferred between countries.

In theory, then, only corporate strategic issues should be referred back to Tokyo. These included requests for capital for investment to build a new factory and permission to alter the structure. In practice managers by-passed the regional layers and contacted Tokyo for advice and guidance on operational matters. The actual practice and culture lagged behind the theory, and Sony became overburdened by administration, rather than an organization that was quickly responsive. It had 'drifted from a paragon of creativity and entrepreneurial spirit to a bloated bureaucracy'.

When the strategic leaders decided that a different form of decentralization was required to deal with the global/local issues, they acted quickly and decisively.

In Spring 1994 Sony, with the exclusion of the American entertainments businesses, was divided up into eight separate divisions; these were not of equal size. They were to be called companies and they would enjoy considerable autonomy and power. Each would have its own President and would be responsible for design, manufacturing and marketing. The three largest companies were: consumer audio-visual products; components; and recording media and energy (batteries). The other five were: broadcast products (equipment); business and industrial systems (work stations); telecommunications (including mobile phones); mobile electronics (for cars); and semi-conductors.

The changes proved to be successful but Sony decided to modify the structure further in Spring 1996 to reflect its changing strategic emphasis. Eight companies became ten. A new one was formed to cover personal computers and information technology. The large audio-visual company was split into three. Telecommunications and mobile electronics were combined into a single company. Four new R & D laboratories would support information technology and semi-conductors. In addition, Sony created a new Executive Board to oversee corporate strategy, to integrate the companies effectively, and to foster learning and sharing.

Financial outcomes

Exhibits 5 and 6 provide summaries of key information from Sony's profit and loss accounts (1973 to
1996) and balance sheets (1986 to 1995). The data
shows that Sony has never been hugely profitable
(some, but not all, of its major Japanese rivals have
been more profitable), and that until the 1990s it
has experienced steady growth. The impact of the
American acquisitions in the late 1980s is clearly
illustrated in the 1994 and 1995 figures. Sony's
once-high R & D expenditure was reduced to
approximately 6%, which is actually typical for
Japanese electronics companies. The figures should,
however, be treated cautiously. The published
figures will incorporate adjustments for profits and
losses on currency fluctuations and therefore not
reflect pure trading successes. The figures are in
Japanese yen, and, given the continual revaluations
of the exchange value of the yen, were the accounts
to be restated in the currencies of the countries in
which Sony traded, the company's growth would
have been more marked. A proportion of the stated
long-term debt is in the form of Japanese bonds
carrying a 1% rate of interest.

The first major setback was in the 1991/1992
trading year when the parent company in Japan
reportedly lost money and relied upon Sony's
international businesses. Considerable income falls
were experienced in chemicals and magnetic tapes;
electronic parts and products held up satisfactorily
in the global recession. Sony's music and entertainments businesses also performed relatively well
in that year. Sales of consumer electronics reflected
the effect of the recession in the 1992/3 results,
when rising debt forced a reduction of capital
expenditures. Sales began to pick up in 1993/4 but
profits slumped after the film studio write-offs in
the USA. New strategies and products have brought
about a restoration in sales revenue for 1995/6 but
profits remain below those of earlier years.

Have Sony's fortunes been turned around with
the strategic and structural changes introduced by
the new strategic leader? How much more change
will be required to sustain the renewed growth and
prosperity?

Questions

1 Describe and evaluate the early strategies which
   made Sony a successful and innovative company.
       Can the recent changes to the corporate
   strategy and structure be justified strategically?
2 How would you evaluate Sony's track record as
   an innovative company?
3 Provide a strategic audit of Sony in the early
   1990s.
       How do you think Sony will now develop
   during the mid/late 1990s?
4 How does Sony compare and contrast with the
   typical Japanese corporation?

Exhibit 5

Sony Corporation profit and loss summary, 1972–1996 (m¥)

	12 Months to 31.10.			12 Months to 31.10.86.	17 Months to 31.3.88.	1989	1990	1991	Year ended 31.3				
	1973	1978	1982						1992	1993	1994	1995	1996
Turnover	314,000	534,900	1,114,000	1,325,000	1,431,000	2,145,329	2,879,856	3,616,517	3,822,000	3,879,000	3,610,000	3,827,000	4,593,000
Profit before tax	49,159	52,378	85,542	76,405	73,497	165,516	227,429	264,591	197,177	92,561	102,162	(220,900)	138,200
Profit after interest and tax	24,503	22,991	39,671	35,368	33,536	70,340	100,453	112,193	120,121	36,260	15,298	(293,000)	N/A
Expenditure on R & D	N/A	N/A	N/A	N/A	N/A		180,000	142,000	165,000	206,000	N/A	N/A	N/A
Average number of employees	20,600	27,112	43,126	47,600	60,500	78,900	95,600	112,900	N/A	N/A	N/A	130,000	138,000

Exhibit 6

Sony Corporation balance sheet summary 1985–1995 (m¥)

	12 Months To 31.10.1986	17 Months To 31.3.1988	1989	1990	1991	Year ended 31.3			
						1992	1993	1994	1995
Total fixed assets and investments	476,014	789,856	931,000	2,168,000	2,369,000	2,589,000	2,411,000	2,246,000	2,077,000
Total current assets	974,130	1,077,000	1,434,000	2,202,000	2,234,000	2,358,000	2,110,000	2,024,000	2,147,000
Total current liabilities	628,294	944,271	1,119,000	1,996,000	2,105,000	2,052,000	1,734,000	1,408,000	1,609,000
Net assets	821,850	922,585	1,246,000	2,374,000	2,498,000	2,895,000	2,787,000	2,862,000	2,615,000
Equity capital & reserves	606,392	650,346	911,800	1,430,000	1,476,000	1,537,000	1,428,000	1,330,000	1,008,000
Long-term loans	144,000	196,000	221,000	646,000	695,000	885,000	880,000	984,000	906,000
Long-term provisions	71,458	76,239	113,200	298,000	327,000	473,000	479,000	548,000	701,000
Total capital employed	821,850	922,585	1,246,000	2,374,000	2,498,000	2,895,000	2,787,000	2,862,000	2,615,000

Edward Macbean and James B Hunter

The case details the development of an ailing business under the direction of Jim Hunter who leads a management buy-out and turnaround of a clothing manufacturer for eventual sale to a larger company.

The case highlights the crucial role of the key entrepreneur – Jim Hunter – and his 'vision' for the business.

This case study forms part of a series of case studies developed on behalf of Scottish Enterprise to highlight the role of the entrepreneur in the creation and development of a business.

It was prepared by Ian T Long under the supervision of Frank Martin, University of Stirling as a base for class discussion rather than to illustrate either effective or ineffective handling of a management situation.

Copyright © Scottish Enterprise 1995

Introduction

Edward Macbean & Co. Ltd. was first established in 1876 and manufactured horse blankets from premises in Howard Street, Glasgow. Later the company diversified into macintosh raincoats, fishermen's oilskins and waxed cotton garments. Pursuit of quality and excellence in the design, development and manufacture of specialized protective clothing led to the company's present market positioning as an undisputed sector leader in the UK. The company had a succession of owners and was the subject of a management buy-out in 1987 led by JB Hunter. Macbean has grown to a £7m turnover high tech protective clothing specialist. It now has a growing presence in the European marketplace through a joint venture with a Dutch partner and German and Swiss marketing agreements. The company was acquired by a larger group in 1994 and JB Hunter became a millionaire and director of The Hollas Group plc.

Background details

In 1962, Edward Macbean & Co. Ltd was acquired by the Tootal organization and moved to premises of 1000 square metres in Kirkintilloch next door to the rapidly developing company, John McGavigan Ltd. In 1982 the company was acquired by Peter Deal and Associates, a London-based investment company, for £116,000. At that time, the business had 22 employees, was turning over £200,000 per annum and had an order book that accumulated to about seven days and was declining. The company was then selling to small retailers, angling shops, and so on.

During 1982, JB Hunter was appointed as sales director by Peter Deal Associates. Hunter recognized the potential of the specialized foul weather protective clothing market and moved the company's marketing focus from small retailers to big, blue chip organizations. These included British Rail, Police Forces, the Ministry of Defence, local authorities and the Post Office. By 1983 Jim Hunter was managing director. By 1987 he had grown the business to a turnover of £1.1 million and profit before tax of £43,000 p.a.

Despite prestigious orders, Peter Deal Associates were not willing to invest in new technology and premises. This prompted Jim Hunter to head a management buy-out team that paid £232,000 for

the entire ordinary shareholding of Edward Macbean & Co. He moved the company from 10,000
square ft of poor-quality premises in Kirkintilloch
and acquired a prestigious 30,000 square ft refurbished factory in Cumbernauld new town. Hunter's
vision was to build the company into a European
market leader.

In 1989 Macbean entered into a successful joint
venture with a Dutch company. As he gained experience of the European markets, he rapidly
realized that to exploit the potential for European
growth required a substantial increase in financial
resources. He estimated this to be in the order of
£2–3 million.

By February 1993 turnover had reached £6.8
million and pre tax profit £550,000. Investment in
leading technology equipment and in training
Macbean's 300 people had paid off as planned. At
this time Macbean had a few acquisition proposals
by larger groups and in 1994 Hunter sold out to The
Hollas Group plc for £4.5 million. He became a
director, responsible for the Group's European
operations, and a millionaire.

The financial detail on Edward Macbean & Co. for
the period 1987–1993 is provided as Exhibit 1.

Today Macbean considers itself to be a model of
manufacturing and marketing excellence, based on
a talented management team. This has been built
on a belief that good business is done with high regard for people; as customers, employees and colleagues. Most importantly, Macbean has been built
by virtue of the entrepreneurial drive, enthusiasm
and vision of Jim Hunter.

The entrepreneur: James B Hunter

Jim Hunter was born in Edinburgh in 1946, and was
educated at Parsons Green primary school and
Portobello secondary school, with further voca-
tional education in book keeping and accounts
administration and mathematics. He studied decision making and management by objectives at
Dundee College of Technology and Dundee College
of Education, and is a Fellow of the Institute of
Directors and of the Institute of Sales and Marketing
Management.

He first worked for Companies House and then
spent nine years working for Tyne Textiles in Fell-
ing, Tyne and Wear, in sales and marketing. He describes this role as one involving 'marketing vision
and entrepreneurial positivism'.

In 1982 he was headhunted to join Macbean as
Sales Director and later became Chief Executive and
Chairman, collecting numerous business awards on
the way.

Hunter attributes the success of Macbean to hard
work, a splendid team and 'a philosophy which is
based extensively on quality'. This ethos of hard
work and total commitment to quality in all operational areas comes from Hunter. It is his own energy, enthusiasm and talent for motivating and
encouraging staff that generates the high level of
commitment from everyone in the company. Hunter
believes his company's strongest asset is its people,
and this is demonstrated by his commitment to
employee training, to total quality management
programmes and to investment in the latest
technology.

Jim Hunter has always believed in the need for a
chief executive to display strong leadership qualities
and entrepreneurial flair. He is an extrovert and a
cosmopolite, and networks extensively to achieve
an in-depth understanding of the protective
clothing industry structure and trends. His vision is
to make Macbean the world-wide leader in the foul
weather protective clothing market.

Hunter believes in leading by example displaying
a high level of energy and drive and he expects the
same kind of input from all employees. Because he
is quick to understand situations and solve problems, he lacks patience with those who are slower
and more hesitant. In terms of his own management
input, he believes in a hands-on approach and as a
result he becomes involved in issues which could be
solved without his input. He consciously maintains
a 'family image' in the company; operating a bus
service morning and night for employees. Christmas
bonus, Easter eggs, chocolates at the summer break,
and so on. He presents them all individually and
personally.

Jim Hunter displays many of the classic attributes
of 'an entrepreneur'. He is ambitious, he uses money as a way of keeping score, he is competitive and
takes carefully calculated risks. Rather than reactive
post-event behaviour, Hunter displays a proactive
approach, making it happen before others know that
the game has started. He works hard at developing
the image of a strategic thinker and that of a formidable tactician. His own ambition is inextricably

Exhibit 1   Management buy-out

In June 1987 Jim Hunter headed a management buy-out team through a new parent company JB Hunter Group Ltd., (formerly Hunter and Maley Ltd). The team paid £232,000 for the entire ordinary share capital. The company relocated to Cumbernauld to 30,000 sq. ft of floorspace and sold its deteriorating Kirkintilloch premises.

The financing details are as follows:

Equity Funding

	£
47,760 ordinary shares at £1.00 each	47,760
184,240 (11% cumulative redeemable preference shares of £1.00 each)	184,240

The main shareholders on 4th June 1987 (buyout date) were

JB Hunter Chairman (Managing Director)	17,920
J. Maley (Production Director)	9,600
Other Management	4,480
	32,000
The Strathclyde Region Pension Fund (via Dunedin Ventures)	15,760
Total ordinary Shareholding	47,760

A member of the management team left the company on 24.3.88 and transferred 1100 shares to JB Hunter and 1000 to J. Maley.

   J. Maley resigned as a Director on 3.5.90 and his shareholding of 10,600 shares was divided between JB Hunter (Chairman and Managing Director) – 5370 and the Strathclyde Pension Fund – 4430 and the balance of 800 shares to other members of the management team. JB Hunter now owned 51% of the ordinary share capital.

   The 184,240 11% Redeemable Preference Shares were redeemable at par in five equal instalments commencing 30th June 1990.

Borrowings

In 1987, a bank term loan of £324,000 was raised to purchase a new factory of 30,000 sq. ft., backed by a letter of guarantee from Cumbernauld Development Corporation under the mortgage guarantee scheme. The loan is repayable over 15 years with interest charged quarterly at 1% over bank base rate. In 1989, the company raised a term loan of £55,000 for a computer aided design system. This was repayable over 7 years at 1.25% above base. A further term loan of £120,000 was raised in 1990 to purchase a computer aided cutting system. This was repayable over 7 years. Interest was 1.25% over base. This expenditure gave Macbean a significant competitive advantage such that the company became the UK sector leader.

Bank overdraft

In 1988 the bank overdraft facility was £150,000 and this was increased to £275,000. The overdraft peaked at £650,000 during the financial year ended 26th February 1993.

Financial performance summary

	Pre Buyout 1987	£000s 1988	1989	1990	1991	1992	1993
Turnover	1156	1664	3079	2879	3346	5505	6848
Profit before tax	43	281	121	(136)	71	262	550
Fixed assets	96	508	634	657	1155	1033	1074
Net current assets/(liab)	14	134	174	(10)	(104)	101	335
Called up share capital	25	232	232	232	195	158	121
Shareholders funds	56	325	428	302	572	637	913

Note:
In 1988, the profit before tax figure of £281,000 includes exceptional items of £249,000 relating to grants and profit on disposal of property.

   Macbean achieved rapid growth in both turnover (+492%) and Profit before Tax (+1179% between 1987 and 1993) which was funded primarily through a declining equity base as a direct result of the redemption of preference shares and a bank overdraft facility which was restricted by the Bank because of the high level of gearing and the earlier overtrading position within the Company.

linked with his company's growth. He devotes enormous amounts of time and effort to customer relations and to internal company relations. By force of his own personality, energy, infectious enthusiasm and 'entrepreneurial positivism', he has grown an indifferent little company into a recognized competitive force in the European marketplace.

The management team

When the buy-out was constructed the two central players were JB Hunter and John Malley. Later Brian Mercer and J.D. Woods joined the company as Finance Director and Sales Director respectively. Anne Marie Hunter also worked in the company and replaced John Malley as production director. An organizational chart for Macbean & Co. is provided as Exhibit 2.

The industry sector

The Scottish Textile Industry displayed the following statistics between 1990 and 1992:

- ❏ 45,013 currently employed (1991)
- ❏ gross output £1679.5 million (1990)
- ❏ total exports of £445.2 million (1992)
- ❏ exports 24% of sales (1990)
- ❏ 966 manufacturing worksites (1991)
- ❏ value added per employee £14,970 (1991)

The Scottish Textiles Industry was not performing well during Macbean's rapid growth. In 1993 Kurt Salmon Associates (economic consultants) saw the then current situation in the European market as follows:

consumption showing modest growth, imports growing faster than exports, stagnating production and declining employment, high industry fragmentation, changing international environment,

Exhibit 2

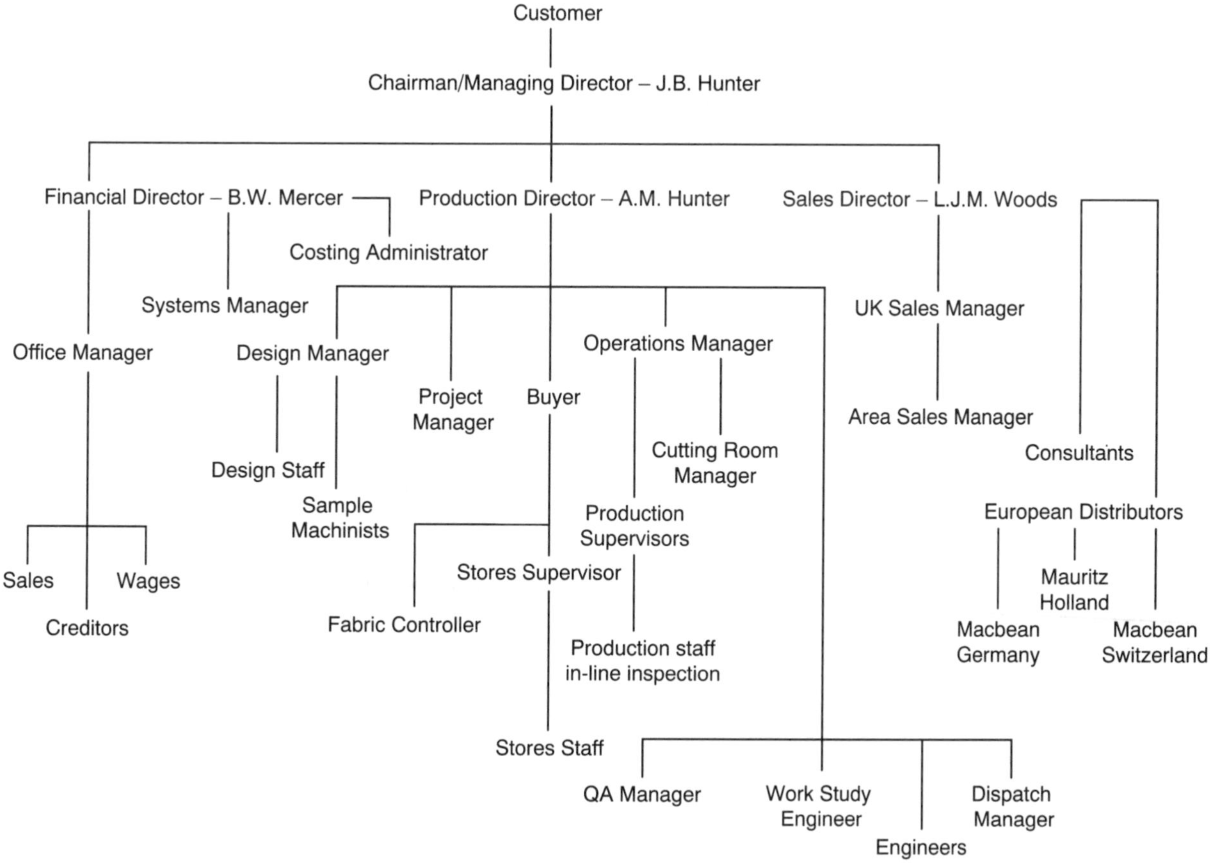

changing consumer preferences, changing distribution channels and relationships.

Of these, internationalization and changing distribution channels were seen as the most important.

In 1995, the Performance Outerwear segment of the Scottish Textiles sector contains only eight companies in the +100 employee category:

❏ Annis Protective Wear
❏ Glenmore Glasgow
❏ W.L. Gore & Associates
❏ Ilasco Ltd.
❏ Edward Macbean & Co.
❏ The North Face
❏ Sunderland of Scotland Ltd.
❏ Weatherguard Leisure Wear.

Macbean 'straddled' two segments of the market, CMT (cut, make and trim) and Workwear, and effectively developed a unique 'niche' in all weather protective clothing for utilities, the MOD, the Post Office, etc. Hunter developed the niche by building ever closer relationships with customers to the point where materials selection, design, customization and quality overrode price as a purchasing factor. No competitor matched that strategy and Macbean had virtually created a unique market where it was the only supplier of the highest quality product. Hunter had 'bucked the trend' in the industry.

The business story

This is a business which has its roots in the later part of the nineteenth century. The firm's pedigree is both a fascinating and proud one, with quality being the watchword then just as it is today.

When Edward Macbean founded his company in Victorian Glasgow, horses were the preferred mode of transport, and from its inception in 1876, the business was well known for the excellence of its horseblankets. As the horse was replaced by the car, Macbean diversified into rainproof garments designed both for day wear and for field sports. They were also highly suited to those who wanted to brave the elements in the new motorized transport!

While this change in manufacturing emphasis certainly ensured continued prosperity for Edward Macbean & Co. Ltd, it was the company's venture into protective clothing for the fishing industry which really set the scene for the product portfolio which is supplied by the modern day company.

Jim Hunter, the company Chairman and Managing Director, believes very strongly that one of the most powerful links between this flourishing modern business and that 19th century horse-blanket manufacturer is the company's continuous quest for quality in everything it tackles from the establishment of excellent supplier–customer relations, to good staff relations within the company, to the quality control system which operates for each and every garment.

When Edward Macbean made horseblankets, every one made was clearly identifiable and traceable back to the person who had made it; not necessarily because there might be faults in the product, but because there was a real pride in the job.

The company follows the same principles today. Every garment can be traced right back to the person who made it. Quality control is stringent. Macbean's commitment to quality led them to become the first manufacturing company in their industry in Europe to gain BS5750 part 1, International Standard ISO 9001, and European Standard EN 29001.

Hunter is impatient with the notion that, somehow, Scottish based firms are not really operating in the European marketplace. It is, he feels, a dangerous notion in terms of Scotland's manufacturing and industrial future:

We are Europeans and the sooner it is accepted that Europe is our domestic market the better.

This is one company which did not sit around waiting for the single market. Hunter was in there flying the flag for Scottish business long before many others had even thought about what it was supposed to mean. Macbean's are now looking to markets in the USA and the Pacific Basin, where Hunter sees enormous potential.

The modern history of the company really began in 1960, when Macbean was taken over by Tootal and later, in the 1980s when Tootal had taken the decision to get out of the manufacturing sector in the UK. Macbean's was sold to Peter Deal Associates, a London based company which Hunter reveals paid £116,000 for the business. It was at this point that Hunter joined the business, being head hunted from Tyne Textiles. He had a proven track record of accountancy and sales in the textiles industry and joined in 1982. Hunter admits that very shortly after his move he began to have very serious doubts about the wisdom of his decision. These misgivings were not without foundation, and after a number of unsuccessful attempts to secure investment in technology from the parent company, Hunter led a successful management buy-out in 1987. With hindsight, although Hunter does not see himself as a man who looks backwards, his initial move proved to be the right one. Hunter asserts that his is a 'people business' and that the success of the company stems directly from the people who work within the organization. He is right of course; nevertheless, colleagues on the Board and in the workforce alike, will, when asked about the remarkable success of Macbean's, single out Hunter for praise as a man with sterling leadership qualities. The workforce is given the full credit due to it for the quality of the product which it manufactures and for its part in winning the string of accolades which the company has enjoyed in the years since the management buy-out.

Macbean's respect for the 'people side' of the business is also strikingly evident in the relationships it has formed with its clients and distributors. The company stresses the importance of forming real partnerships with its clients, in building up a close and mutually beneficial relationship with them over a period of time. The service Macbean offers its customers is very much a customized one.

Sales Director Len Woods, who is the linchpin of the company's UK and European marketing wing, comments:

we are not interested in manufacturing a garment and then trying to sell it. Instead we would rather look closely into what a client really needs. What are the conditions to which a garment will be subjected? What type of fabric will provide the best protection for the job? All of these things need to be considered before we even begin to make the product.

While there can be no doubt that people are central to this company's business success, high technology also has had its very important part to play. Hunter has not been afraid to invest. 'You must speculate to accumulate' is one of the epigrams with which his colleagues must be very familiar and Hunter believes that all too many of the businesses in this country suffer from too much money being taken out of them and very little being put back in.

The capital investment in 'state of the art technology' at Macbean is enormous. As a result of massive expenditure on computerized cutting equipment which will examine fabrics electronically before they are passed for production, and in computer aided design and production systems, Macbean's has reached new levels of operating efficiency in manufacture. The resulting savings are passed on to the customer. When Hunter led the buy-out back in the 1980s, his ambition was to build the company until it was the best in its field in Europe and was recognized as such. At the time, the company exported none of its products. The company now sits comfortably at the top of the tree in European terms. It employs a workforce of around 300 people, has a turnover of nearly £7 million, and exports now account for 35% of turnover. 'But you can't achieve that kind of success without a clear mission statement, a strategic plan for the business and for the people who are working within that business', Hunter stresses.

There are staff appraisals every year with no exceptions. The Board appraises Hunter and he consistently outperforms the tasks that are allocated to him. It does after all take a certain grit and determination, energy and drive, to lead the kind of air-travel-oriented business life which has become his lot. Marketing in Europe, the USA and the Pacific Rim takes its toll but it keep Macbean at the top.

The original mission statement has been superseded by the company's plans to become a world leader in its sector. With the original plan well underway and significant success in Europe, the team now has its sights set on world supremacy in the protective clothing market. There is absolutely no doubt in Hunter's mind, that Macbean is well on the way to earning the same plaudits on the worldwide stage that they have been getting in Europe. It is a matter of supreme confidence in his products and in the people who are working with him. The company's aim to lead the world in the design and manufacture of protective clothing will not happen overnight and it certainly won't come without a great deal of hard work and investment. Again Hunter stresses that he and his team are afraid of neither, the company's pro-active attitude to the forging of new links overseas has resulted in the successful formation of a series of partnerships and joint ventures – initially on the continent of Europe. Hunter is a man with a global perspective, and his next move may well be into Malaysia. He made his first visit there about five years ago and has high hopes of forming a partnership in that region before too long. He is seeking a bigger stage for his business and fully appreciates that cultural differences will play a large part in Macbean's 'world view'.

When asked what it takes to be a good operator on the international business scene, he cites understanding as the chief quality required: 'spend time with people', he advises, 'get to know the cultural differences which may have a bearing on any transaction you hope to make ... you must work closely with people to develop products and to develop the marketplace'.

Macbean is involved in a number of joint ventures with European partners; for example Mauritz Holland, who with Macbean helped develop the market in the Netherlands, Belgium and expansion into Switzerland and Scandinavia. These relationships have been extremely beneficial to all parties concerned – not simply in terms of the distribution agreements, but in the kinds of support which arrangements of this nature can offer a Scottish company in general as it breaks new territory for its products.

Macbean Deutschland opened in 1994 just outside Frankfurt. Another joint venture, this company's brief is more on the sales and marketing side of Macbean's activities and Hunter predicts that it will be an invaluable part of Macbean's European strategy.

When Hunter looked at the changing marketplace nearly ten years ago, he realized that when the British market was saturated he would have to look for new business.

We have not reached saturation point yet in the UK ... you must constantly be looking for new business and far too often companies rest on their laurels and become complacent. A business is like the pendulum of a clock, when it stops in the middle you're dead. You have to be advancing all the time.

For Jim Hunter, Macbean has been a success story. Taking a job in a company which he found to have a very limited future, he simply turned it round and created a profitable business. From there he developed the business further and put together an imaginative and innovative management buy-out, sold assets, restructured the operations and 'took on' Europe. He needed additional capital to grow the business and deliberately avoided dilution of his own stake and control; indeed he increased his stake to 51%. Having done this, he invested in technology and by clever cash management supported the company's rapid growth from its own resources and with limited external funding.

Having sold the company, Hunter is still involved in heavy international travelling and still at the forefront of customer relations and big deals. Somehow, though, he appears to be missing the shop floor, the people and perhaps being master of his own destiny. He is personally wealthy now, a change because for years, apart from a good salary, he took little out of the business, and a divorce relieved him of any personal wealth which might have countered dilution of his shareholding.

With some irony he reflects on the sale:

I had a choice – go with the venture capital people, raise millions, invest more personal money and perhaps still lose control of what happens at Cumbernauld, or sell to a group with synergy which would build on Macbean's international success. I did not have the personal wealth to lever a big venture capital deal and therefore took the 'sale' option. It seemed at the time to provide the best deal for everyone, for the employees, for the management team and for me personally.

Asked if, with hindsight, he would have done anything differently he responded:

No – probably not, but I would certainly like to do it all again.

Questions

1 Assess the entrepreneurial style and characteristics of James Hunter.
2 Evaluate the turnaround strategies followed by Hunter.
3 Is Macbean well-placed to develop further now that James Hunter has left the organization?
   How would you evaluate the legacy he has left behind?

Hanson (A)

The Hanson (A) case is divided into three sections:

1. The development of Hanson and the major acquisitions
    'Hansonizing': The Hanson strategy
2. Changes in the 1990s to the earlier strategy
    Non-events and failed acquisition attempts
3. A profile of Lord James Hanson.

The case stops in 1992 and invites discussion on the key issues which affect the future development prospects.
  Hanson (A) is particularly useful for provoking discussion on:

■ Diversification strategies and synergy
■ Acquisition and asset sales
■ Business objectives
■ The contribution to the National economy of acquisitive diversifiers who split up companies.

Hanson (A) was written in 1993 by John Thompson for the purpose of class discussion. It should not be taken to reflect either effective or ineffective management.

Introduction

For the year ended 30 September 1992 Hanson plc reported the first ever decline in its pre-tax profits in nearly 30 years of trading. Exhibit 1 charts the growth of the company from 1965.

The fall has been attributed to two main causes. Firstly the costs of borrowing to acquire Beazer, the building company and the most recent (1991) of a long series of major acquisitions. Secondly, the world economic recession. Hanson is heavily involved in construction and basic industries in the US and the UK. Exhibit 2 provides a summary of the main balance sheet and profit and loss data for the period 1988–1992, and also analyses Hanson's 1991–1992 results by activity, showing which sectors have shown increases and which ones have declined.

Hanson's considerable success has been based on squeezing additional value from acquired assets, which have normally been under-performing companies bought at attractive prices. However many of these businesses are in cyclical industries and consequently they offer few opportunities for growth during a recession.

The growth and success of Hanson plc has been created wholly by Lord James Hanson (Chairman) and his partner, Lord Gordon White (the Deputy Chairman), who have worked together since the mid-1960s. In 1992 Hanson was 70 years of age, White a year younger. Both men indicated they had no plans to retire for a number of years, but some arrangements for their succession have been put in place. Lord White worked exclusively in America, controlling Hanson's US interests; Hanson himself splits his time between the UK and the USA but essentially runs the UK businesses.

It has been suggested that White was skilful at acquiring sleepy companies, whilst Hanson is expert at transforming them into immensely strong performers.

Exhibit 1   Hanson (UK and USA)

Year YE 30.9	Sales (£ million)	Profit before tax (£ million)	Value of shareholders' funds (£ million)
1966	9.1	0.4	1.2
1967	11.8	0.6	1.8
1968	19.5	1.2	4.1
1969	48.5	2.2	5.3
1970	47.1	2.4	7.6
1971	28.8	2.9	7.7
1972	36.4	4.5	16.6
1973	51.7	8.2	31.1
1974	71.1	10.4	33.5
1975	75.7	12.1	48.6
1976	322.2	19.2	57.5
1977	477.4	24.4	67.2
1978	604.6	26.1	74.9
1979	658.0	31.2	107.0
1980	684.3	39.1	120.7
1981	855.9	49.7	165.1
1982	1148.3	60.4	188.5
1983	1484.0	91.1	428.9
1984	2382.3	169.1	410.3
1985	2674.5	252.8	1124.8
1986	3772.0	408.0	
1987	6682.0	741.0	1879.0
1988	7396.0	880.0	2339.0
1989	6998.0	1064.0	1086.0
1990	7153.0	1285.0	2834.0
1991	7691.0	1319.0	3325.0
1992	8798.0	1286.0	4224.0

Formation and early development

In 1964 James Hanson, then in his early 40s, was the controlling director of Oswald Tillotson, a distributor of commercial vehicles based in Yorkshire. Hanson had been born in Huddersfield, where his family ran a successful transport business; and he had trained as an accountant. Prior to Tillotson's he had run businesses in the UK and Canada.

In 1964 Tillotson was acquired by the Wiles Group, a recently quoted agricultural services business, also based in Yorkshire. In 1965 Hanson became Chairman of Wiles, and he quickly began a long series of diversifications, acquisitions and divestments in Britain and the USA. The name of Wiles was changed to Hanson Trust in 1969, and sometime later this was shortened to Hanson plc.

Exhibits 3 and 4 provide details of the major acquisitions in the UK and the USA, respectively.

Hanson and White had known each other for several years but their business partnership really began in 1963. Gordon White was then the owner of a printing company based in Hull, but he was frustrated by the pressures of selling into a very competitive and diverse market. He fancied buying another company, but his resources were inadequate. Hanson introduced him to Lloyds Bank, who provided the necessary finance. Sometime later White suggested their business interests should be fused, and they duly were.

Hanson and White have worked together closely since the mid-1960s, and have jointly masterminded the growth and strategic development of the business. Initially their investments and acquisitions were exclusively in the UK, but in 1973 the partners crossed the Atlantic. They have deliberately concentrated on English-speaking countries.

The first acquisitions in the UK

Although Hanson's acquisitions have been in diverse industries from the outset there was normally a strategic logic in the purchases. The strategy has, however, changed and evolved over time.

After Hanson acquired Scottish Land Development (1967) and Jack Olding (1969), and merged the two companies, they became the leading distributors of construction equipment in the UK. This strategy of acquiring related businesses in order to create critical mass, attain scale economies and build market share set a pattern which has been repeated in other industries.

Hanson entered the agriproducts (agricultural products) industry in 1968 when they acquired West of England Sack Holdings, but this has never become a major interest in the UK.

Hanson invested in the manufacturing of basic products for the first time also in 1968. They bought Butterly Brick, who were renowned for their high-quality facing bricks, and who had successfully developed technology for lowering costs in kiln operations. Butterly also made lightweight aggregates – materials which are mixed with cement to make concrete. After acquiring National Star Brick and Tile (1971), Castle Bricks (1972) and London Brick (1984) Hanson became the UK's leading brick manufacturer. During the 1980s Hanson has built a strong position in the building materials industry in the USA.

Exhibit 2 Hanson PLC

	1988	1989	Year ended 30.9 (£m) 1990	1991	1992
Extracted items from the balance sheet 1988–1992					
Total fixed assets	1476	2414	5057	6199	9146
Investments	178	957	704	429	191
Current assets –					
Stock and work-in-progress	1071	988	984	992	1318
Debtors	1227	1157	1126	1192	1441
Cash and investments	3860	5309	6883	7771	8445
Total current assets	6158	7454	8993	9955	11204
Total current liabilities	2463	3269	4226	4751	6386
Net current assets	3695	4185	4767	5204	4818
Net assets	5349	7556	10528	11832	14155
Share capital and reserves	2339	1086	2834	3325	4224
Long-term loans and provisions	3010	6470	7694	8507	9931
Total capital employed	5349	7556	10528	11832	14155
Extracted items from profit and loss account 1988–1992					
Trading income	7396	6998	7153	7691	8798
Interest received	373	531	856	941	844
Interest charges	287	330	638	741	777
Published pre-tax profits	880	1064	1285	1319	1286
Less: published tax	204	251	314	284	197
Preference dividends	8	2	–	–	–
Ordinary dividends	260	335	499	529	265
Add: extraordinary items	445	288	29	71	–
Retained earnings	853	764	501	577	824
Published earnings per share (pence)	17.46	20.66	20.28	21.55	22.62

Hanson in 1992

Sales: £8.8 billion (up 14%)   Pre-tax profits £1.29 billion (down 2%)

Geographic analysis

	Sales (£m)	Trading profits (£m)
UK	4014	467
USA	3642	567
Rest of world	1055	78
	8711	1112

(Remaining sales and profits from discontinued operations)

Main activities	Sales (£m)	Trading profit (£m)	Profit trend, 1991–92
Industrial products (mainly USA)			
– Coal mining	1011	157	Down
– Chemicals	543	116	Down
– Materials handling	258	42	Down
– Gold mining	106	29	Down
– Others	802	86	Up
Consumer products			
– Imperial Tobacco (UK)	2980	280	Up
– Others (mainly USA)	650	100	Up
Building products			
– Aggregates	1120	81	Down
– Forestry & Lumber	221	69	Up
– Housebuilding	338	45	First profits
– Others	677	72	Up

Exhibit 3 Hanson's major UK acquisitions

Company	Date	Businesses	Cost (£m)	Value of disposals (£m)
Scottish Land Development	1967	Construction equipment distribution	0.7	
West of England Sack Holdings	1968	Agricultural sack hirers	3.1	
Butterley	1968	Brick manufacturing	4.7	
Jack Olding	1969	Construction equipment distribution	1.7	
National Star Brick & Tile	1971	Brick manufacturing	1.4	
Castle Brick	1972	Brick manufacturing	2.7	
BDH Engineers	1973	Engineering	12.2	11.0
Henry Campbell	1978	Linen & synthetic yarns	4.9	
Lindustries	1979	Linen & synthetic yarns + engineering & polymers	27.0	49.3 (by 1990)
Berec	1982	Ever Ready batteries	95.0	1983: $ 60 million*
United Gas Industries	1982		19.0	
UDS	1983	Allders retailing etc.	260.0	263.1
London Brick	1984	Brick manufacturing	245.0	33.0
Imperial Group	1986	Tobacco, foods, brewing & restaurants	2800.0	2340.0
Consolidated Gold Fields	1989	Mining	3300.0	2654.0
Beazer	1991	Building (incl. 2nd largest US aggregates business)	351.4	

*The rest of Berec (later renamed British Ever Ready) was sold in 1992.

Exhibit 4 Hanson's major US acquisitions

Company	Date	Businesses	Cost ($m)	Value of disposals ($m)
J Howard Smith	1973	Animal feedstuffs	32.0	
Carisbrook Industries	1975	Speciality textiles and machinery	36.0	22.8
Hygrade	1976	Meat processing and packing	32.0	165.5 (by 1989)
Interstate United	1977	Food service & vending	30.0	99.8 (by 1985)
Templon Spinning Mills	1978	Speciality textiles	7.25	
McDonough	1981	Footwear, hand tools, building materials	185.0	52.5
US Industries	1984	Varied	532.0	200.0
SCM	1986	Office equipment (Smith-Corona) + paints, chemicals, foods	930.0	1585.0
Kaiser	1987	Cement	250.0	274.0
Kidde	1987	Conglomerate, including Security systems etc.	1500.0	734.2
Stuart Anderson	1988	Restaurants	20.0	11.4
Peabody	1990	Mining (coal)	1200.0	
Cavenham Forest Products	1990	Forestry etc.	1300.0*	

*Cavenham was acquired in a swap arrangement for part of Consolidated Gold Fields (UK).

The move to the USA

The first US purchase was J. Howard Smith, an animal feedstuffs company, which Hanson renamed Seacoast Products. This was followed by the related acquisitions of Hygrade Food Products (meat processing) in 1975, and Interstate United in 1977. This company was active in food service, specifically serving meals in cafeterias in schools, factories and hospitals, and in vending machines.

The year 1975 saw a diversification into textiles. Carisbrook Industries, which manufactured speciality textiles and machinery, was followed by a series of related acquisitions on both sides of the Atlantic.

* * * *

Most of Hanson's early acquisitions were bought at favourable prices, often for a figure below the asset value of the business. Their post-purchase rationalization and cost cutting strategies quickly generated an improved cash flow – which increased Hanson's profits and earnings per share, and helped fund further acquisitions. In the USA Hanson concentrated on companies which were happy to be bought out.

From the mid-1970s the acquisitions started to involve businesses which were already diversified and multi-product. Hanson was always willing and happy to sell those parts of the business which did not fit with existing Hanson interests or appear to make strategic sense to him. He was also keen to divest the least profitable parts of the companies he acquired, together with any businesses which offered little opportunity for adding further value and improving profits. Exhibits 3 and 4 include summary details of the money Hanson has recouped from the various business and asset sales.

In the UK Hanson preferred to use new equity for his acquisitions, supported by the occasional rights issue and cash from asset sales. Cash was more normal in America.

Selected major acquisitions

This section analyses a number of important Hanson acquisitions throughout the 1980s and into the 1990s. The hostile purchase of Imperial Group is looked at in greatest detail as it provides an excellent illustration of 'Hansonizing', as the Hanson strategy of the 1980s has been christened.

McDonough

McDonough, bought for $185 million in 1981, spanned three quite different industries.

The Endicott Johnson subsidiary both imported and manufactured footwear, owning ten factories. The company had 689 shops, and leased space in department stores, across America, concentrating on the 'popular price' ranges. In addition the company provided shoes to some 18,000 independent retailers.

McDonough also owned cement and ready-mix concrete businesses in Texas. These two activities were linked, with 35% of the cement sales going to the ready-mix business. The cement company contributed just 10% of McDonough's profits but Hanson sold it immediately for over $50 million.

The third interest was hand tools, with manufacturing based in West Virginia. The brand name was Ames and the products included lawn, garden and industrial tools. The business, which was over 200 years old, serviced independent distributors nation-wide.

Berec

Acquired in 1982 for £95 Berec was a battery manufacturer, and Hanson capitalized upon its well-known brand and renamed the company British Ever Ready. In 1980–1981 Berec's pre-tax profits had fallen to £10.5 million from £17 million a year earlier – in 1977 they had peaked at £29 million. The company's main rival, Duracell, was developing new battery technology and gaining market share every year. Duracell were pioneering long-life batteries in ever smaller cases whilst Berec was still investing in new capital equipment to support increasingly obsolete technology.

Hanson's take-over bid prompted an acrimonious battle which featured hostile press advertising by both companies. After the acquisition Hanson cut Berec's head office staff from 550 to 75, reduced the number of management layers from nine to three, and sold the research and development facilities and the Continental manufacturing plants to Duracell. These sales recouped $60 million. Over a longer period the blue-collar workforce was reduced by two-thirds. Profits increased almost immediately. Research spending has been kept low and Duracell has been perceived to be more innovative and has strengthened its market dominance. Nevertheless Ever Ready has successfully introduced Gold Seal batteries to compete with Duracell.

Hanson sold Ever Ready in April 1992 'to help finance further acquisitions'.

UDS

UDS was a collection of retail chains bought for £260 million in 1983. Sequentially most of the company, including John Collier and Richard Shops, has been sold, with the single exception of Allders, duty free shops and department stores. Hanson recouped in excess of the £260 million purchase price, and Allders has always proved profitable.

US Industries

This US conglomerate cost Hanson $532 million in 1984. The corporation consisted of 30 subsidiary companies and included the manufacture of equipment for the motor industry, building materials, lighting, furniture and furnishings, and clothing. Parts of the business have been sold in seven separate transactions between 1984 and 1990.

Imperial Group

Hanson won control of Imperial Group in 1986 for £2.8 billion, its largest acquisition to date. The bid had been unwelcome to the Imperial Group directors who had encouraged shareholders to accept a rival offer from white-knight bidder, United Biscuits. Imperial had fought the Hanson bid aggressively, using mass media advertising as well as direct communications with shareholders. Their theme was that Hanson's style of management was not so much 'hands off' (decentralized – see later) as 'sell off', and they quoted selected facts about the earlier Berec deal. Imperial advertisements featured the sale of the advanced projects division, Berec's major research and development facility, the sale of two European operations to a major competitor, the 'slashing' of capital expenditure by 50%, battery prices being increased by 33% over four years, well above the rate of inflation, 40% of the UK workforce being made redundant, and a 20% loss of market share between 1981 and 1985. The company was bought in 1982.

Shareholders, however, believed the company's future would be safer in Hanson's hands. Imperial, like the other major tobacco companies, had diversified extensively as cigarette smoking declined in the face of adverse publicity and health scares. Arguably they had diversified too much too quickly, and had stretched both their management and their cash. Howard Johnson in the USA (the hotel and restaurant chain) had proved a major drain on resources, appearing to require management skills which Imperial did not have. This business had already been sold earlier in the 1980s, and, in fairness, the group was already being turned around by a new chief executive. Return on capital employed, which had hovered around 10% throughout most of the 1970s, had risen to 20% by the mid-1980s.

In the financial year ended October 1985 Imperial Group sales amounted to £4.92 billion with pretax profits of £235.7 million. Approximately half of the sales and half of the profits were contributed by the tobacco interests.

Hanson acquired the following businesses and brands when it bought the Group:

Tobacco	The existing John Player and Wills businesses and including the Embassy, Golden Virginia and St. Bruno brands
Foods	Ross Frozen Foods, Young Seafoods, Golden Wonder Crisps, HP and Lea & Perrin Sauces
Brewing	Courage – including John Smith and Harp Lager
Hotels	Anchor Hotels
Restaurants	Happy Eater Roadhouses, Welcome Break Motorway Service Areas
Shops	Finlays Newsagents.

Divestments

In 1986 the remaining hotels and restaurants were sold to Forte (then Trusthouse Forte) for £186 million. The sale was subject to approval from the Monopolies and Mergers Commission which investigated the effect of linking the Happy Eater chain and the Welcome Break Services with Forte's Little Chef restaurants.

Hanson maintains that brewing was the one activity he really intended to keep, but that he received an offer (from Elders IXL of Australia) 'he simply could not refuse' in the interests of his shareholders. Courage was sold for £1.4 billion in 1986.

Also in 1986 Hanson sold Golden Wonder to Dalgety for £87 million; £1.7 billion (out of a purchase price of £2.8 billion) was thus recouped in the year of purchase.

Two years later HP and Lea & Perrin was sold to the major French food group, BSN, for £199 million. The sale of Ross Frozen Foods and Young Seafoods brought in another £335 million.

After two years Hanson had recouped over £2 billion, and he still retained all the tobacco interests. Under Imperial tobacco had been run as two businesses, Players and Wills, with separate sales forces, factories and head offices (in Nottingham and Bristol respectively). Hanson rationalized the business into one company, combining the sales and marketing and retaining just two from the existing five factories. There are now fewer brands. Since 1986 staffing has been reduced by 46% without any loss of output, and operating costs have fallen by 25%. Productivity and profits have increased significantly, but market share in the UK has declined. Limited investment in state-of-the-art manufacturing technology has been directed at making Imperial the lowest cost producer in Europe.

SCM

The American conglomerate SCM proved to be another controversial purchase. The company cost $930 million in 1986. The acquisition was fought aggressively in America and legal actions were involved. Early disposals of pulp and paper, paints and foods businesses recovered $935 million in the year of purchase. By 1990 SCM divestments had earned $1.6 billion for Hanson.

After the initial divestments Hanson retained Smith-Corona typewriters and the profitable SCM specialist chemicals businesses. A majority stake in Smith-Corona was floated controversially in 1989. The share price collapsed shortly after the flotation as the company struggled against intensifying Japanese competition. Stockholder lawsuits ensued, and these took two years to settle. Lord Gordon White has insisted that the shares were priced appropriately and that the Japanese were dumping.

Kaiser

After earlier selling McDonough's cement business Hanson bought Kaiser in March 1987 for $250 million. Kaiser was the fifth largest cement business in America, and market leader in California. Hanson has since sold a number of the Kaiser cement plants.

Northwest Terminals and Montana City Plant were sold for $50 million shortly after the acquisition. Hanson then agreed to sell a 42.8% stake in Kaiser's Indonesian cement company to Mitsubishi Mining and Cement of Japan. The October 1987 sale of the San Antonio (Texas) plant was followed in February 1988 by the sale of the Lucerne Valley Plant in Southern California. This last sale was again to Mitsubishi and it recovered $195 million.

Hanson had again earned back more than the purchase price and still retained a key plant in Northern California. Hanson commented that it was holding on to plants which had contributed over half of Kaiser's 1986–1987 profits.

Consolidated Gold Fields/Cavenham Forest Products

Consolidated Gold Fields cost Hanson £3.3 billion

in 1989, and the acquisition included a 49% stake in Newmont Mining, the largest gold producer in America, and the whole of Gold Fields, another US mining business. Hanson now owned more gold in the ground than any other company outside South Africa.

After the purchase Hanson flagged that he was not looking for any long-term involvement and that he would be happy to sell any parts. Initial negotiations failed to result in any sales and some press articles speculated that the failure to recover a proportion of the investment might prove to be a limiting factor in Hanson's future development.

In October 1990 Hanson announced that it was swapping its stake in Newmont for Cavenham Forest Products, 85% of which was owned by Sir James Goldsmith. Goldsmith stated that he regarded the exchange as a long-term investment and an opportunity to retire from active business.

Cavenham comprised US timberland and sawmills together with oil and gas interests. Cavenham was valued at $1.3 billion, but as Goldsmith was himself renowned as an expert dealer in assets, it seemed unlikely that there would be any significant potential gain from selling off parts of the group. However the company was profitable and enjoyed a sound cash flow. Moreover Hanson's Newmont stake was estimated to be worth $300 million less than Cavenham's assets.

There have been further sales of Consolidated assets, and to date over £2.5 billion has been recouped.

Peabody

When Hanson bought Consolidated Gold Fields, its Newmont Mining subsidiary already owned part of Peabody Coal, the second largest coal producer in America. Hanson developed an interest in this business and acquired the whole of Peabody before Newmont was traded.

In January 1993 Hanson agreed another swap arrangement, this time with Santa Fe Pacific, the US railroads and minerals group. The exchange involved Hanson's remaining gold mining interests, specifically Gold Fields, which it had always wanted to divest, and Santa Fe's coal mining and aggregates businesses. The deal required approval from the US Internal Revenue Service. The coal mines would be amalgamated with Peabody, the aggregates business with Beazer.

Coal has become Hanson's fastest growing business interest and represents 30% of its capital employed.

Coal will continue to be an important long-term source of energy in the US and new technologies will increase its efficiency as a low-cost fuel.

(Lord White, January 1993)

Beazer

Hanson paid £350 million in 1991 to buy the Beazer building and construction business in a friendly acquisition. However it also took on debts of £1.1 billion. Servicing this debt had given Beazer cash flow problems. The business, which included Koppers, the second largest aggregates company in America, fitted in well with Hanson's existing interests. Hanson was able to reduce Beazer's financing charges immediately and thereby improve its profitability. Long-term Hanson hopes to benefit in both the UK and the USA when investment in building and the infrastructure goes up after the economic recession.

The Hanson strategy

Throughout this period of growth Hanson's strategy has been based upon three essential principles:

(i) The key objective of a business is the maximization of shareholder value.
(ii) Many companies fail to do this, and are therefore run badly.
(iii) Such companies are often good buys because their assets can be made to create more value for shareholders.

Lord Hanson, interviewed in *The Treasurer* (June 1987), highlights three pillars in his company's success:

❑ Hanson has selected countries and businesses very carefully
❑ they have sought to identify the key individual(s) who are essential for the success of the company. They have then sought to instil in them Hanson's important financial disciplines and to motivate them to produce results; and
❑ they have looked after both their shareholders and their customers. Hanson argues: 'Look after these and everything else falls into place. You can

raise shareholder capital, your businesses are healthy, you can borrow for expansion. At the same time your employees have confidence in the knowledge that their jobs are securely based'.

After acquisition Hanson's main target is unnecessary overheads and waste. It is, for example, usually quite straightforward to either close or reduce the existing head office of the newly acquired business. The directors of the business may or may not stay once Hanson has bought the company – if they do stay they will not be offered a seat on the main Hanson Board and they will have to achieve Hanson's new targets and expectations. In general Hanson believes that in the case of under-performing, sleepy companies, middle management is likely to be stronger than the most senior management, and that control of the business should be handed over to them.

Acquisitions

A typical Hanson purchase will be characterized by recent poor results. Quite often these will feature high gross margins (indicating sound products or services which enjoy market demand) but a much reduced pre-tax profit figure resulting from high, and probably excessive, overheads and high interest charges.

Hanson also looks at the amount of capital employed in the business, relative to its turnover, arguing that in many cases some of this capital could be taken out or better utilized. A final indicator of a potentially good buy is a market position which does not reflect the potential suggested by the company's assets, brands and reputation.

Hanson maintains a small but permanently active 'tracking team' for evaluating the current progress and worth of a large number of possible future acquisitions. Part of the secret is knowing the right moment to strike, and being ready and able to act when the opportunity arises. One ex-member of this team is Greg Hutchings, who left Hanson in 1983 to become chief executive of the equally acquisitive FH Tomkins, the company which thwarted Hanson's bid for RHM in 1992.

Hanson believes the strategy can be applied successfully in a wide range of industries, including services; and on the strength of this conviction Hanson has diversified into a number of unrelated areas. Earlier sections of this case have shown how Hanson acquired businesses in construction, bricks, textiles, animal foods and meat processing, pulp, gold, coal and chemicals. For many years Hanson concentrated on consumer oriented businesses in manufacturing, service and distribution. Cyclical businesses have also been attractive targets; but those which require expensive research and development with 'a prospect of a return sometime or never' (Lord Hanson) have been avoided.

The case has also described how Hanson divests companies and business units when they are not appropriate for their strategy. In the main businesses in competitive industries, and those which require investment, are sold, and mature, slow growth companies retained.

The outcome

Exhibit 2 confirms that in the early 1990s the majority of Hanson's profits stem from mature industries. Despite the lack of growth potential in such mature industries, the restructuring strategy pursued by Hanson has generated a high and consistent growth in group profits.

It could also be argued that Hanson has avoided industries where they might not understand the key success factors. In particular Lord White was anxious to avoid any real downside risk – where the risk of failure outweighs the benefits of success. Lord Hanson has suggested that White always look for trouble with prospective deals, and that as a result the company has undoubtedly missed out on potentially good deals.

Earnings per share (the key measure for shareholders) are maximized when business units achieve the highest possible sustainable return on capital employed. Earnings per share can be improved by increasing returns from existing capital resources, or by maintaining earnings whilst reducing the capital employed to produce them. These themes explain the thinking behind the Hanson strategy.

Hanson, in common with certain other acquisitive diversifiers, is not necessarily committed to staying in particular industries once the opportunities for increasing returns have been exploited. A restructuring strategy, like the one pursued by Hanson, dictates that businesses should be sold once their earnings cannot be increased any further. The money from their sale should be reinvested in companies with greater potential. Through most of the history of Hanson, profits in the acquired

businesses have soared very quickly after purchase. Costs, work-forces and investment programmes have been reduced as Hanson does not rely on organic growth within the businesses. Once profits stagnate, as for example they did at both Smith-Corona and Ever Ready, the companies are often available for sale.

Shareholders in companies like Hanson expect to see constantly increasing returns and speedy turnarounds; and consequently Hanson is thought to only take a prospective acquisition seriously if the cost is realistically recoverable in under four years – from a mixture of asset sales and improved profits. In fact Hanson expects the company to be profitable in the first year after purchase. Although earnings per share could be enhanced by preferring debt financing to increased equity, Hanson are fundamentally risk-averse and anxious to maintain a relatively low debt ratio.

Although Hanson seeks market share and critical mass in industries, in order to achieve economies of scale, they are not necessarily looking to be global players in these industries. Hanson has commented that he is not interested, for example, in being a major brick manufacturer in America or in having an involvement in garden tools in the UK.

Structure and control

Structurally, therefore, the focus is on profit centres rather than products. Business units are decentralized and given 'demanding but realistic' targets to achieve. Hanson maintains only a small head office of around 20 staff who concentrate on policy and financial control. There are few layers of management and short lines of communication.

Managing directors of the businesses are given considerable independence as long as they achieve their agreed targets. 'Royal visits' to the factories from either Hanson or White are very rare. Capital investments in excess of £500 or $1000 have to be approved by either Hanson or White. Within these financial constraints businesses can adapt their competitive and functional strategies. There is a very strong emphasis on cash flow, and budgets are 'intentional rather than hopeful' – managers must intend to achieve them. Profits will be reinvested in the businesses which earn them, but only if they can produce further increases in profits. Hanson has a philosophy of 'earn before you spend'.

Weekly and monthly financial returns are sent to London (head office) for scrutiny, and each company holds a monthly board meeting. Budgets are produced initially in mid-summer, and agreed with the main Board, and they are then reviewed in the following February after four months trading – the financial year runs from October to September. The revised targets are the ones the companies and their managers *must* achieve.

Hanson motivates its managers with both a stick and a carrot. Unit managers are required to accept personal responsibility for achieving their targets and for the success of their business. 'Managers are not required to walk on water, but they are required to produce what they promised' (Lord Hanson, quoted in the *Financial Times*, 22 August 1990). If they exceed their budget targets they can earn substantial bonuses.

The UK and US arms of Hanson are run as separate businesses with separate Treasuries. Different rules for borrowing and acquisition apply, with most US purchases being financed by debt, which is frequently secured against the value of the assets being acquired. The UK Head Office acts as a holding company. There are, however, very strong information flows between the USA and London.

Taxation management

A final important aspect of Hanson's strategy and success has been an ability to manage company funds and transactions globally in such a way that tax is avoided (legally) as much as possible. Hanson are reputed to be masters at this. Between 1985 and 1994 Hanson paid, on average, 22% of its profits in UK corporation tax and its USA equivalent. The highest percentage over the period was 28% (in 1993); the lowest, 15% in 1992. The prevailing tax rates were 35% in the UK and 34% (plus State taxes) in the USA.

A new strategy?

Some commentators have argued that Hanson 'cannot behave in the 1990s as it did in the 1980s', when it appeared to have a golden touch and built up a formidable reputation as well as a strong and successful business. There will be fewer opportunities to acquire and break-up companies; and consequently Hanson will have to focus on running the businesses it owns if it is to maintain profits growth.

In February 1992 Hanson announced that in the future the company would concentrate on running and expanding the group's core businesses and making further disposals of periphery activities. Hanson would no longer be a trader in assets, and instead would be dedicated to building and managing selected businesses.

By the early 1990s Hanson was involved in a variety of diverse industries, seven of which were designated core:

Hanson businesses in the early 1990s

UK	USA
Core businesses	**Core businesses**
Aggregates and bricks	Cement and aggregates
Tobacco	Chemicals
	Coal Mining
Other businesses	Forestry
Food	Crane manufacture
Textiles	(Grove)
Batteries (divested	
1992)	**Other businesses**
Retailing	Shoes
	Garden tools
	Electrical fittings and goods

Hanson argued that its future strategy would involve further acquisitions of suitable companies which could be bolted on to existing core activities. The managing directors of the individual core businesses would be encouraged to follow the lead of Hanson head office, and seek-out and cost potential buys. Justifiable organic growth might also be funded. In the past such internal investment has been rare. The other businesses would be retained, sold or floated off, the choice depending upon the opportunities for each one.

Although these changes have been implemented, Hanson has not switched over exclusively to the new strategy. Opportunistic acquisitions are still considered. In 1992, for example, Hanson bid for UK foods company, Ranks Hovis McDougall. When challenged about how this fitted in to the newly-declared strategy, Hanson commented that buying RHM was still consistent with their stated objective of maximizing the value of the business for its shareholders.

In addition Hanson's chief executive in the UK, Derek Bonham, stated: '*Core* means a significant market sector which we think is capable of responding to our management style. It does not mean that such a business will never be sold, nor that the existing list of core businesses cannot be extended'.

Hanson's failure to acquire RHM provoked some analysts to comment that the company might be losing its touch. RHM was not Hanson's only recent disappointment.

Non-events and failed acquisition attempts

In 1985 Hanson's £147 million bid for Powell Duffryn was rejected by that company's shareholders, and at this time such an occurrence was unusual. However the situation began to change in 1990.

In 1990 Hanson expressed an interest in buying PowerGen from the UK government. PowerGen was the smaller of two electricity generating companies to be created when the industry was privatized. Contrary to previous Hanson practice, electricity generating involves high technology supported by research and development. In addition, it was speculated that Hanson would have to adopt a much more hands-on style of management with PowerGen. Had it bought the company PowerGen would have constituted the largest business in the Hanson portfolio, but Hanson withdrew.

In 1992 Hanson also discussed buying at least part of the Canary Wharf development in London's Docklands, after the owners, Canadian company Olympia and York, went into receivership. Hanson again withdrew.

In between these two forays Hanson had bought a stake in ICI. In all three instances, but especially with ICI, Hanson's move had attracted considerable attention and publicity, much of it adverse.

ICI – a bridge too far?

In May 1991 Hanson paid £240 million for a 2.8% shareholding in ICI. ICI is a global business in chemicals and pharmaceuticals. Once this was made public it fuelled an immediate controversy concerning whether Hanson intended to bid for the whole company, and what its longer-term intentions might be. It was acknowledged that ICI was under-performing and that more value could be squeezed from its assets. A combination of Hanson and ICI would, though, constitute a truly global force. Hanson quickly denied that a bid was in the offing, claiming that ICI's shares were priced attractively and that this was merely a strategic investment.

However it was known that in 1988 Lord Hanson had approached ICI Chairman Sir Denys Henderson and proposed that Hanson should acquire a 20% stake in ICI together with boardroom representation. This suggestion had been rejected. Since 1988 ICI's profits have declined, and Hanson believed that this was only partially the result of the economic recession.

Henderson opposed Hanson's intervention openly and vociferously. He complained that Hanson 'does not care about building businesses ... ICI is not a box of chocolates that can be unwrapped and sold off one-by-one'. ICI analysts and their advisers effectively turned Hanson's style and results inside-out in their defence against a possible bid, and the publicity this created has probably tarnished the Hanson image, possibly for ever.

The speculation attracted interest and comment from various other stakeholders. The banking community questioned how Hanson could finance such an acquisition, speculating that it would require £11 billion. Hanson had, at the time, £7 billion debts, but £7 billion in reserves and investments. Possibly additional borrowings of some £6 billion would be required. Hanson's assets would certainly support this, but it would leave the company very highly geared. Moreover, would the banks actually lend Hanson this amount of money? Acquiring ICI by issuing Hanson shares would certainly lead to a dilution of earnings.

The regulatory authorities would have to be involved, and probably the issue would be dealt with in Brussels by the European Commission rather than solely in the UK by the Monopolies and Mergers Commission. Trade unions called for the immediate involvement of the MMC in order to slow things down. Opposition Labour MPs demanded that the government should express their opposition, but the government was non-commital.

Other analysts commented that, like PowerGen, this would require a different style of management with a more involved Head Office. Nevertheless few denied that ICI could benefit from Hanson's tight financial management for improving its efficiencies. Some asset sales would be inevitable if Hanson was to avoid a major involvement in the highly speculative, research-driven, pharmaceuticals industry.

Hanson never actually bid and later sold their shares for a substantial profit. ICI announced a major restructuring, involving splitting the corporation into two separate businesses (for details of this split see Case 19.2 in the main text).

The bid for Ranks Hovis McDougall – RHM

Hanson made a hostile £780 million cash bid for RHM in October 1992. RHM is involved in milling, bakeries and grocery products. The company is the UK's second largest baker and it had already rationalized its bakeries in the face of intense competition.

Four years earlier RHM had successfully fought off a bid from a leading New Zealand bakery business. In 1989 a consortium involving Sir James Goldsmith became the company's largest shareholder with a 28.5% stake, but these shares had been sold in 1991.

Between 1988 and 1992 both sales and profits had declined, and arguably the company looked vulnerable with a depressed share price. Had Hanson timed it right? Hanson was bidding 220 pence per share. The current price was 175 pence, but three years earlier the shares were trading for 465 pence.

Despite their newly-declared strategy it was assumed that Hanson would look to sell the RHM packaged grocery companies. When such businesses had been acquired with the purchases of Imperial and SCM they had been sold at the first suitable opportunity. In any case if RHM could be acquired for a relatively low price the parts might well be worth more than the whole.

RHM opposed the Hanson bid, and after considering their response the RHM Chairman declared an intention to split the company into three separate businesses, namely flourmilling and baking, grocery and speciality products and cakes (notably the Mr Kipling brand). RHM also announced the agreed purchase of a bakery business from Dalgety for £28 million. By this time the share price had risen to 246 pence. Hanson's reaction was that this confirmed there really was strategic logic in what they did – but added that they felt RHM's approach to splitting up the company was 'clumsy'.

At the end of the same month a rival bidder appeared. F.H. Tomkins, run by Greg Hutchings, previously an acquisition specialist at Hanson, bid £935 million. Tomkins is another diversified conglomerate, whose portfolio includes Smith and Wesson handguns and lawnmowers. Early in November Hanson withdrew from the competition, only the second time it had ever lost a hostile take-over battle.

The *Financial Times* stated: 'Regarded as the consummate deal maker of the 1980s Hanson has failed to pull off a number of big deals in the 1990s'.

Lord James Hanson

Who is the man behind the business which is 'feared, loathed, admired and praised?'
(Financial Times, 22 August 1990)

The company's head office overlooks the gardens of Buckingham Palace, and Hanson's own office is said to resemble a well-appointed living room. It is characterized by wood panelling, plush carpeting and shelves full of photographs of his family and friends. Easy listening music plays in the background. But this 'furnace' (as it has been described by Hanson executives) is the source of the energy and power which drives the company.

James Hanson was born in Huddersfield, and, after military service, he initially joined his family transport business. When the haulage industry was nationalized in 1948 James crossed the Atlantic, and, in partnership with his brother, founded Hanson Haulage in Canada. This business was sold in the early 1960s and James Hanson returned to Yorkshire to take a controlling interest in Oswald Tillotson, a distributor of commercial vehicles. The development of Hanson plc from this stage has already been described. James Hanson was knighted in 1976 and made a peer in 1983.

Hanson has been described as socially confident and charming, impeccably dressed and skilled at dealing with people. He is loyal to his employees, and, in turn, inspires their loyalty. He has a temper, though, which is occasionally evident if he is challenged.

He is reported to be anxious that Hanson plc should behave ethically, and that it should enjoy a positive image and reputation. There have been instances where these concerns have been tested. For example, Hanson was once forced on to the defensive at an Annual General Meeting when it was highlighted that the company had invested £12 million in racehorses without shareholder approval. Lord White is a fanatical racegoer and Hanson plc, using the Ever Ready brand name, has sponsored the Derby.

Unlike Lord White, who has a high social profile, James Hanson has allegedly few interests outside work. Before he started Hanson in the 1960s he earned a reputation as something of a playboy, but for many years he has led a settled family life. He moves between his houses (in London, Berkshire, Los Angeles and Palm Springs), living in America for a considerable part of each year. Hanson was popular with Mrs Thatcher, but it has been said their friendship cooled after he once chose to arrive at Chequers in his private helicopter.

Proud of his Yorkshire origins Hanson says that in business he has been cautious and followed 'basic North-country business sense ... you do not over-borrow'. One measure of success he jokes about is the fact that bankers now visit the company, whereas in the early days Hanson and White always had to visit the bank manager. Generally Hanson is likely to buy businesses by spending its cash, and then borrowing to replenish the reserves. Hanson believes in borrowing money but always paying it back on time. Companies which succeed in doing this can always borrow more.

Hanson plc is unquestionably a very personal business which has always been dependent on Lords Hanson and White, their long-standing friendship and their ability to work together. A former director has described the Hanson culture as 'a solar system, with everyone circling around the sun in the middle, James Hanson. Employees are encouraged to work within clear parameters and not to expect regular promotion'.

Lord Hanson believes that he has been a successful strategic leader because he has:

❏ ensured he has stayed informed
❏ wanted to actually do things in business
❏ deployed his not inconsiderable energy into making things happen
❏ been able to inspire others to do things
❏ stayed responsive to change pressures.

The future

James Hanson was 70 in January 1992, with Gordon White due to reach the same age in 1993. On his 69th birthday Hanson had announced that he and White intended to stay active in the company until 1997. Some commentators suggested they believe in their own immortality and indispensability.

Succession, though, has not been wholly ignored. Hanson's son, Robert, is a main board member, together with the husband of one of Hanson's nieces. In 1992 a new chief executive post was created in the UK and filled by Derek Bonham. David Clarke has acted as chief executive in America for some time.

But where does Hanson plc go next? The bottom line has always taken precedence over size, but companies like Hanson grow primarily by constantly acquiring new businesses. However as a take-over specialist grows ever-larger, their targets also need to get bigger if they are to maintain any momentum. What size and type of business constitutes a suitable acquisition for Hanson in the 1990s? Does this requirement explain the dalliance with ICI?

When profits fell for the first time in 1992, Hanson's share price, 40% above the FT all-share index in 1990, also fell to a premium of just 20%. If these trends were to continue any substantial acquisition funded by equity is likely to dilute earnings. However, the decline in profits and fortune may be solely due to the recession, in which case Hanson's profits will bounce back up when the economy grows again. Others believe Hanson and White have lost their way a little in recent years, although acknowledging that the Beazer purchase was 'classic Hanson'. These critics contend that Hanson and White will be unable to 'turn the clocks back to their glory days'.

Could Hanson plc conceivably become an acquisition and break-up target itself? Or will it always be able to find a suitable deal? Mainland Europe must offer new potential opportunities, especially with the single market in place. However, issues of corporate ownership and governance mean friendly acquisitions are more likely than hostile take-overs to be a feature of a European expansion strategy.

Questions

1 Describe and evaluate the key aspects of the Hanson strategy during the 1970s and 1980s.
    How did Hanson plc evolve through acquisitions?
    Assess the strategic position at the end of the 1980s.
2 What are the limitations to this strategy?
3 Is the declared new strategy more appropriate for the 1990s?
4 Does 'Hansonizing' provide lessons for other companies?
5 Describe and assess Hanson's style of management.
6 If you were a shareholder in Hanson how would you evaluate the company's future prospects?
7 What contribution to the National economy does a company like Hanson make?

Hanson (B)

Hanson (B) is a continuation from the A case. It discusses the changes to the company and its corporate strategy after 1992. It has been written to provoke discussion on four further important strategic issues:

❑ strategic life cycles
❑ the diversification versus focus argument
❑ the rationale for the financial control style of corporate management
❑ strategic leadership succession.

Hanson (B) was written in 1996 by John L Thompson for the purposes of class discussion. It should not be taken to reflect either effective or ineffective management.

Introduction

For over 25 years from the mid-1960s, led by Lord Hanson in the UK and Lord White in the USA, Hanson grew relentlessly. The company's profits and share price continued to climb every year, and Hanson shares out-performed the FTSE All-Share index. However, the company's fortunes changed in the early 1990s when Hanson suffered its first ever profits decline.

The graphs below (source: FT Extel) show how the FTSE All-Share index grew by nearly 50% between 1990 and 1995; Hanson shares declined by 3%. During 1995 the index grew by 15%; Hanson shares were now falling at a rate of 5%. Exhibits 1 and 2 provide a summary of the key balance sheet and profit and loss account figures for the 1991–1995 period.

At the beginning of 1996 Hanson announced that the company was to be split into four separate businesses.

What had happened to the company which had successfully carried through 35 agreed acquisitions and six hostile takeovers – disposing of some 40 businesses and failing with 15 other hostile bids

Share price (pence)

Log scale

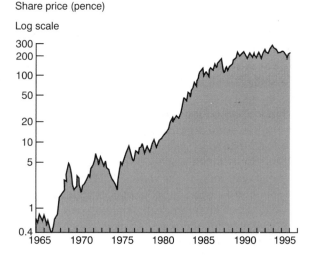

Share price relative to the FT-SE-A All-Share Index

Log scale

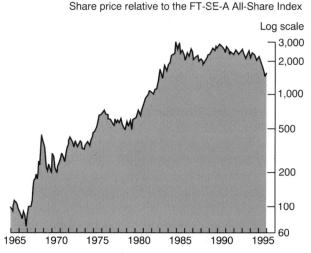

Exhibit 1 Hanson PLC – extracted items from the balance sheet 1991–1995

	Year ended 30.9.				
	1991 £m.	1992 £m.	1993 £m.	1994 £m.	1995 £m.
Total fixed assets	6199	9,146	12,195	11,386	12,968
Investments	429	191	236	221	203
Current assets					
– Stock and work-in-progress	992	1,318	1,746	1,184	1,028
– Debtors	1192	1,441	1,813	1,930	2,015
– Cash and investments	7771	8,445	8,067	6,815	7,419
Total current assets	9955	11,204	11,626	9,929	10,462
Total current liabilities	4751	6,386	7,065	6,704	10,377
Net current assets	5204	4,818	4,561	3,225	85
Net assets	11,832	14,155	16,992	14,832	13,256
Share capital and reserves	3,325	4,224	3,953	4,598	3,623
Long-term loans and provisions	8,507	9,931	13,039	10,234	9,633
Total capital employed	11,832	14,155	16,992	14,832	13,256

Exhibit 2 Hanson PLC – Extracted items from the Profit & Loss Account 1991–1995

	Year ended 30.9.				
	1991 £m.	1992 £m.	1993 £m.	1994 £m.	1995 £m.
Trading income	7691	8798	9760	11,199	11,390
Interest received	941	844	619	325	397
Interest charges	741	777	600	545	604
Published pre-tax profits	1319	1286	1016	1346	1275
Less: published tax	284	197	282	281	260
ordinary dividends	529	265	551	597	1181
Retained earnings	577	824	183	468	(166)
Published earnings per share (pence)	21.55	22.62	14.91	20.60	19.61

over the same 30-year period? Was there any convincing argument for retaining Hanson as a single Anglo-American entity? Was the diversified conglomerate strategy, practised superbly by Hanson, itself no longer appropriate? Or: had Hanson individually run out of inspiration and opportunity? How much was strategic leadership an issue in the change of fortunes and the decision to demerge?

> The purpose of life and the purpose of a job is to enjoy the adventure … while the numbers are important, if business is not fun, it is not worth doing.
>
> *Lord White of Hull, 1923–1995*

The main strategic changes, 1993–1995

During the early 1990s Hanson implemented a number of important acquisitions whilst following its declared strategy of focusing on (and building) selected core businesses. There were several strategic disposals at the same time. It appeared that Hanson had regained its touch with a new sense of direction and a modified strategic approach.

Acquisitions

In June 1993 Hanson bought a waste disposal business, **Econowaste**, from Tarmac. Econowaste was involved with waste site management and waste haulage and it was to be incorporated into ARC, the quarrying business Hanson had acquired with Cavenham Forest Products. Hanson was now the third largest landfill operator in the UK.

One month later Hanson bought the American company **Quantun Chemicals** for $3.2 billion, its largest ever American acquisition. The bid was a friendly one; and Quantum would join Hanson's SCM Chemicals business. Quantum is one of America's largest bulk chemical manufacturers, focusing on plastics products, but competing in nine distinct market segments. It holds two market leaderships, six second places and one third position in these nine segments.

Afterwards the 'strike' was described as a 'classic Hanson deal' as it was concluded virtually at the end of a major recession in the chemicals industry. Consequently the price was favourable to Hanson. Sales, prices and profits have all risen since 1993. Taking just one example, polyethylene prices rose gradually from 29 to 52 cents per pound (although more recently they have fallen back again) and it was claimed that Hanson's profits increased (or decreased) by $40 million for every one cent price change. Hanson has successfully refinanced Quantum's debts and reduced its interest charges and invested selectively in a number of subsidiary activities.

In July 1994 there was another agreed bolt-on acquisition in the UK. **Scholes**, the UK electrical installation equipment manufacturer, was bought for £96.1 million to link with Crabtree, which it had acquired with Berec (Ever Ready) and retained when most of the rest of the Berec businesses had been divested. Analysts saw the acquisition as defensive, in the face of strengthening European competition in the UK market. Combined, Scholes and Crabtree would have a 23% share of the UK circuit protection market, equal to that of the current market leader, the French company Schneider.

Hanson bought Exxon Coal's **Carter Mining** subsidiary for $360 million in October 1994. Carter would join Peabody Coal; both companies mine low sulphur, clean-burning coal.

Hanson's energy interests were boosted in July 1995 when it bought the profitable electricity *distribution* company **Eastern Electricity**. Eastern was one of the largest RECs (regional electricity companies) to emerge from the privatization of the electricity industry in the UK. At an agreed price of £2.3 billion, it was Hanson's largest acquisition in the UK since Consolidated Gold Fields in 1989. It was the first major deal to be implemented by the new chief executive, Derek Bonham.

Eastern, led by a highly respected management team, brought with it a shareholding in the National Grid (which would have to be sold) and two gas-fired power stations. Eastern had diversified more than most of the other RECs, and was supplying gas to a range of industrial and commercial customers, including McDonald's. Hanson quickly expressed an interest in buying additional power stations from the electricity *generators*, particularly National Power.

Geographic expansion

Hanson established an office in Hong Kong in March 1994, with the brief of searching out new opportunities in the Asia Pacific region. Previously Hanson had concentrated almost exclusively on activities in the UK and the USA. Lord Hanson's son, Robert, then aged 33, was put in charge of the new venture. It was assumed that the most likely developments would be joint ventures for Peabody Coal, SCM Chemicals, Imperial Tobacco and Cavenham Forest Products.

Imperial Tobacco now has a joint venture production unit in China, and in 1995 Hanson began to actively pursue investment opportunities in power generation projects in India, Indonesia and China.

Disposals

Hanson continued to seek disposal opportunities for non-core businesses and when, in December 1993, 11 disparate companies were sold to a management buy-out team for £90 million, Hanson's earnings from corporate divestments in 1993 reached £250 million. The trend continued in the following year, when, for example, Seven Seas, the UK vitamins manufacturer, was sold for £150 million.

In 1994 Hanson's housebuilding activities in the UK (Beazer) and USA were floated off as independent businesses to raise some £550 million.

Thirty-four assorted American businesses were demerged as an independent company, US Industries, in February 1995; the new head was David Clarke, who had been the chief executive of Hanson's operations in the USA and Lord White's apparent successor. These businesses had accounted for 17% of group turnover in 1994, and 15% of pre-tax profits. They included various household and leisure products, including bath and lighting goods, windows, automotive components, office furniture and shoes, as well as Hanson's remaining shareholding in Smith-Corona office equipment.

Later in the same year Hanson announced it had plans to float Suburban Propane, a subsidiary of Quantum, in the USA and to break up Cavenham Forest Products for sale in a number of lots. Altogether these disposals should realize a further £1.5 billion.

Outcomes

The various Hanson businesses performed with different levels of success in the 1990s. Coal mining saw profits fall in both 1992 and 1993 when there was a major coal strike in the USA. Profits doubled the following year, but the trend was generally downwards. Profits for Hanson's total energy interests were boosted by the acquisition of Eastern Electricity.

Chemicals profits fell in 1992, stabilized in 1993 and grew in 1994 and 1995, especially after the acquisition of Quantum. They began to fall back again in early 1996 as another recession bit.

Tobacco profits have risen throughout the period; forestry products grew for three years but fell in 1995. Aggregates followed two years of falling profits with two years of growth.

The following table summarizes the situation in 1995:

Activity	Turnover £ million	Operating profits £ million
Chemicals	2020	591
Tobacco	3570	348
Energy	3500	460
Bricks, aggregates and associated products	2300	286

Structurally Hanson included businesses which are important and valuable cash generators: aggregates and particularly tobacco. However, Hanson is also entrenched in industries which are notoriously cyclical: chemicals and natural resources. This raises two important questions. Which businesses was the cash generation supporting? And: given Hanson's long history of strong dividends, was investment capital being channelled to the most appropriate opportunities?

Changes in strategic leadership

The 1992–1993 annual report clarified that Derek Bonham was the most likely candidate to succeed Lord Hanson as Chairman of Hanson plc when he stepped down; his retirement was being planned for early 1997, the year when he would be 75 years old. To this end, Bonham, who was 50 years old, was promoted to the position of Deputy Chairman; he had been the UK chief executive since April 1992.

In 1995 Christopher Collins, the husband of Lord Hanson's niece, became Vice Chairman of Hanson plc at the age of 55. At the same time, Hanson's son Robert was given the post Collins relinquished, that of Corporate Development Director.

The *Financial Times* reported that some investment managers 'were unhappy with the corporate structure ... the business was meeting a dead end ... succession was a problem ... Hanson Jr was not the City's choice'.

Bill Landuyt, a 40-year-old American who was currently Finance Director for Hanson and based in the UK, returned to the USA in 1995 to replace David Clarke as Head of US Operations.

Clarke had been mentored by Lord White; he was seen as a similarly entrepreneurial deal-maker. Both Bonham and Landuyt were accountants, as was Lord Hanson by profession. The latest appointments were taken to reflect a general drift to internally-driven growth with less reliance on the large acquisitions which had characterized Hanson in the 1980s, and which were proving to be increasingly difficult to find and implement in the 1990s.

The following comment sums up Hanson's new dilemma:

> *Hanson was an acquisition-driven company. The people who are the likely successors are not acquisition people – they are operating people. If Hanson remains in its current form, who will do the acquisition strategy?*

The death of Lord White

When Lord White died in August 1995 his role had already been largely wound down to that of consultant to the company he had helped to found and develop. The growth and prosperity of Hanson owed much to White, especially after he began the American operations in 1973. Under his stewardship and with his deal-making Hanson had become the largest foreign corporate investor in the USA. One obituary commented: 'the great White shark was able to merge his own unique deal-making instincts with an environment more favourable to predators than in any other era'.

Plans to demerge

Five months after the death of Lord White, in January 1996, Lord Hanson announced his intention to split the corporation into four separate companies. Existing investors would receive shares in all the new businesses; clearer details of the demerger would emerge in the next few months. Had Hanson himself learned the benefits of demerger from the ICI/Zeneca split which followed Hanson's shareholding incursion into ICI – a foray which began a wave of hostile comment and publicity and which arguably tarnished the Hanson reputation permanently?

Lord Hanson argued that 'demerger is an exciting and radical move' and the *Financial Times* agreed. Commenting that this was 'as bold a move as any of Hanson's large take-overs' the FT quoted one large investor as saying: 'We always thought Lord Hanson would want to go out with a bang and this is the right thing to do for shareholders'.

Nevertheless, Hanson had always been expert at finding new opportunities for reducing waste and costs and for adding value to the businesses it acquired. The four new businesses would have few opportunities for adding extra value. Moreover, would they each need a corporate head office, a 'luxury' Hanson had been careful to restrict? Analysts also assumed that both debt costs and taxation rates would increase when the benefits of Hanson corporate ownership were lost. These had been important sources of competitive advantage for Hanson.

Whilst suitable bolt-on acquisitions for each business might now be easier to find and integrate, the smaller companies might themselves be more vulnerable to take-over. The whole Hanson had seemed generally resistant to a hostile bid as it was accepted that any predator who attempted to buy Hanson and then divest Imperial Tobacco or the US chemicals businesses would face huge capital gains tax demands.

The US chemicals businesses would be the first to demerge; they would begin trading as an independent American company called Millennium Chemicals on 1 October 1996. The other businesses would follow systematically in the following few months. It was predicted that some £4 billion long-term loans would remain; these had to be allocated to the businesses. It appeared they would be divided as follows: chemicals, £1.4 billion; tobacco and energy, £1.2 billion each; building activities, £0.2 billion.

The final section of this case briefly considers the prospects for the new companies.

Millennium Chemicals

Very profitable in 1994 and 1995, the chemicals business was performing less well in the early months of 1996 with the onset of another industry recession. Growth was forecast again for 1997, however. The new Chairman and Chief Executive of Millennium was to be Bill Landuyt.

In the main, Millennium comprises two different chemicals companies, SCM and Quantum, both of which are medium-sized in their differently volatile sectors of the industry. Quantum specializes in plastics, and arguably has not invested in the latest technology for all its key markets. SCM's main product is titanium dioxide, which provides the white pigment for a variety of coatings products used in the paper and paints industries. Earlier in the 1990s this sector had been plagued by over-capacity, but a resurgence of demand had brought back the profits. SCM has invested in new technology and plant to become the second largest producer, behind Du Pont and ahead of ICI Tioxide. The third, and smallest, Millennium business is Gildco, a niche producer which makes turpentine-based fragrances and flavours.

Imperial Tobacco

At face value Imperial Tobacco returned an operating profit of £348 million on a turnover of £3.57 billion in 1995, a rate of 9.7%. However, when excise duties are removed, turnover drops to £780 million, showing a profitability ratio of 45%. Given that the business employs capital of just £54 million, its return on capital employed is 650%. Derek Bonham was to be the new Chairman; the chief executive would be Gareth Davis rather than Ron Fulford who had been largely responsible for turning the business around and who had elected to retire.

Imperial Tobacco holds the number two spot in the UK market, but it has recently increased its sales force from 400 to 450 and is thought likely to replace Gallahers as the market leader. Hanson's main brands are JPS (John Player Specials) and Embassy; Gallahers, owned by American Brands, owns the Benson and Hedges and Silk Cut brands. Imperial has an estimated 38% share of the UK market which in aggregate terms is declining by approximately 2% per year.

Since it acquired the business, Hanson has dramatically improved its productivity (which trebled between 1987 and 1995) and made it the most efficient and lowest cost cigarette manufacturer in Europe. Nevertheless, it ranks only 22nd among world producers; BAT (British American Tobacco), the world leader and a company which, for historical reasons, does not manufacture in the UK, makes 20 times as many cigarettes.

Imperial's real growth prospects are outside the UK. The relative contribution of exports has grown from 5 to 15% in the 1990s. Western Europe, Eastern Europe and East Asia are all prospects for further expansion. Although Imperial has a joint venture in China it has yet to develop production plants overseas.

The current tax burden is just 11 percent; experts predict this will at least double once it is outside Hanson. Imperial could either become a take-over target or perhaps look to acquire another tobacco manufacturer. One possibility might be Gallahers if American Brands would sell it.

Energy

The launch name for the energy businesses was still to be confirmed in Summer 1996. However it was clear that the company would have a joint listing in the UK and USA. Derek Bonham will again be the Chairman and there will be joint chief executives, one for each main business.

Peabody is the world's largest private sector coal manufacturer; its main uncertainty is the possibility of healthcare liabilities in the USA for black lung disease.

The profitable Eastern Electricity is seeking to expand its generating capacity to obtain synergy with its distribution activities. In 1996 it was awaiting the outcome of a Monopolies and Mergers Commission report concerning its desire to acquire power stations from National Power.

Hanson (Building)

Hanson's bricks and aggregates businesses are the ones chosen to retain the Hanson name. Lord Hanson will chair the company until 1997, when he will

be replaced by Christopher Collins. Andrew Dougal, who succeeded Bill Landuyt as Hanson Finance Director, is the chief executive. The company inherits almost no debt and will again enjoy a joint UK/USA listing.

Hanson is the UK's largest brick manufacturer with 30% of the market. Recently it has been expanding into Europe with the acquisition of Belgium's leading brick company.

Hanson is one of the world's largest quarry operators, supplying rock, sand and gravel to the construction industries in the UK and the USA. ARC (second in the UK market behind Tarmac, and with an 18% share) has low overheads and is a cash generator along the lines of tobacco.

The new Hanson will also inherit Grove, the world's leading manufacturer of cranes, Hanson Electrical which manufactures a range of products from plugs to switchgear, and Hanson's 12.5% shareholding in National Grid – which it has to sell and which should yield in the order of £400 million. Grove and Hanson Electrical could be offered for sale, with the resulting income used to buy new aggregates businesses to seize market leadership.

Questions

1 Did the acquisitions and disposals in the 1990s suggest that Hanson had rediscovered its deal-making skills? Did they fit Hanson's declared new strategy of concentrating on core activities?

2 Did the decision to change the structure of Hanson follow logically from the corporate strategy it was pursuing?

   How would you evaluate the prospects for the four new businesses?

3 Was the demerger decision the most appropriate for the company and its shareholders? Was it a defensive reaction to circumstances? Did it suggest that Lord Hanson was being astute, creative and proactive – or that maybe he simply did not want to leave behind the business he had created?

4 Does the conglomerate diversification strategy have a future?

Virgin

This case highlights how Virgin grew into and then expanded from a music company to become an international leisure business which later diversified into air travel by starting its own airline, Virgin Atlantic. The case then traces how music and retailing were largely divested leaving Virgin a much more focused business. It also discusses how Virgin was launched on the stock exchange and later re-privatized.

It is the study of the growth of an entrepreneurial company and how the need for cash to fund expansion affected the strategic development.

Virgin cannot be separated from its founder and chairman, Richard Branson. Consequently it is also the study of the motivation and style of a charismatic strategic leader and his impact upon the culture and strategy of an organization.

Virgin can usefully be studied alongside the Thorn-EMI case.

Case 1.3 in the main text provides an introduction to Virgin Atlantic.

This version of the Virgin case was written in 1996 by John L Thompson for the purpose of class discussion. It should not be taken to reflect either effective or ineffective management.

History and development

Richard Branson was born in 1950. His father was a barrister and his grandfather a High Court judge. He attended public school, at Stowe; and it was here, at the age of 16, that he started the business that would eventually become Virgin.

Branson's first commercial venture was the *Student* magazine, designed for students world-wide, and with the aim of 'putting the world to rights'. Sales of 100,000 were claimed. The magazine, and the advertising on which it depended, were sold from a public telephone kiosk at Stowe school.

The magazine's success was patchy, and to generate a stronger cash flow Branson started selling popular records by mail order, using the *Student* to promote the venture. Certain records were normally sold only in selected London stores, and Branson saw an opportunity in making these more freely available to young people throughout the country. Cash was required with every order, and the records bought from wholesalers once a suitable size batch (for discounted prices) could be purchased. However, a number of record companies became suspicious of the venture and Branson had to change tactics and buy only through selected small record shops. The business was named Virgin because Branson saw himself as 'commercially innocent'.

The business expanded after Branson left school, but the prolonged postal strike in the early 1970s threatened its viability. In 1971 Richard Branson, together with his school friend and *Student* partner, Nick Powell, decided to take the lease on a small shop unit in Oxford Street, London, and sell records direct to the public. The partners were joined by a distant cousin of Branson's, Simon Draper, who had come to England from South Africa. Draper started as the record buyer for Virgin, but eventually became Branson's number two and the initial strength behind the enormously successful music business.

The profits from the first store, supplemented by a loan from one of his aunts, allowed Branson to diversify and start a small recording studio in a country house.

Real growth took place after a young musician, Mike Oldfield, approached Branson. Oldfield was an instrumentalist who had been experimenting in the search for a new sound, but whose demonstration tapes had been rejected by several well-known record companies. Branson and Draper saw an opportunity and decided to take the risk. They released Oldfield's music under the title *Tubular Bells*. The first record eventually sold 10 million copies and provided Virgin with its first real cash flow.

Expansion continued steadily through the mid-1970s as new artistes were signed and new stores opened. The company was growing at some 20% per year. In May 1977 Virgin signed the controversial punk rock band, the Sex Pistols, and their immediate success provided another growth surge. Virgin signed the Sex Pistols after they had had two previous contracts with EMI and A & M cancelled within a six-month period. Advertisements for their records were refused by the television companies.

In 1978 Draper became Managing Director of Virgin Records (as the music division was then called) and Branson ceased to have a day-to-day operational involvement.

The period from the late 1970s to the early 1980s was a difficult one for Virgin, which found its earlier growth hard to sustain. Virgin needed new artistes with true success potential, and this problem was compounded when the whole industry experienced a recession in 1980. Virgin had attempted to penetrate the significant and lucrative American market, but failed. For several other countries Virgin simply licensed its artistes to other companies, but knew this would not be appropriate for establishing a real presence in America. Initially it attempted to run its own US operation to push UK artistes with seconded British personnel.

There were now 16 record stores which were reported to be trading at a loss because of inadequate management control. Retailing demands an attention to detail as well as creative flair and risk taking, which were Branson's main strengths. An attempt to start a new London magazine to rival *Time Out* proved unsuccessful and was closed down. Branson's long-standing partner, Nick Powell, left the organization in 1981. Virgin's image was deteriorating.

Consultants recommended that Virgin should develop complementary activities and Branson determined that the company should become more professional with a clearer strategy and supportive structure. Related music and retailing activities, together with selected parts of the communications industry, were targeted because of the clear potential for synergy. Unrelated small enterprises and Virgin Atlantic Airways (begun in 1984) carried a different level of risk. The airline increasingly became Branson's main interest.

In 1982 Virgin signed Boy George and Culture Club and a third growth surge was provided for the music business. Branson recruited Don Cruickshank as Managing Director of Virgin (the central holding company) in 1984. Cruickshank, an accountant with an MBA who had previously been general manager of the *Sunday Times*, represented a more professional management style than had been previously associated with Virgin.

In 1983 Virgin was offered the opportunity to buy Our Price Records for £1 million, but was unable to raise sufficient cash. The company was sold to retail rival WH Smith instead.

However, by 1985 Virgin had become the 15th largest private company in the UK with a turnover of £150 million and pre-tax profits of £12 million. For many years Virgin had been restricted by its bank to an overdraft limit of £3 million, but was now able to borrow £25 million from City institutions (in the form of convertible preference stock) to fund further growth. Fundamentally Branson believed in organic growth rather than acquisition.

The continuing need for additional funding persuaded Branson that the time was right for Virgin to become a public company.

Flotation and re-privatization

Prior to the flotation in November 1986 Branson, Draper and a third director, Ken Berry, who was deputy to Simon Draper at Virgin Music, purchased certain Virgin assets and formed a new private company, Voyager, which provided an umbrella for amalgamating Virgin Atlantic Airways, the related holiday business and a variety of small enterprises. A new managing director, again with an MBA and experience in the travel industry, was appointed. These activities, which were essentially unrelated to the mainstream Virgin entertainment businesses, were regarded as too volatile to be floated as part of Virgin.

The Virgin shares were sold by tender, with prospective investors invited to offer to buy a particular maximum number at a certain price. The price was struck at 140 pence, which valued the company at £240 million. Branson, Draper and Berry had retained 63% of the shares, and control. Some 60,000 small shareholders bought in to Virgin but the institutions were less enthusiastic. After expenses the flotation raised £55 million, half of which was injected immediately into Virgin. The remainder went to the directors, with Branson investing most of his £20 million share into Voyager.

Some of the money invested in Virgin was directed towards securing the elusive US presence. The company had learnt from its previous failure and now sought to establish a more permanent business with both US artistes and locally recruited executives. Branson made no secret of the fact that he expected it would take a number of years before the venture turned in its first profits. The investment in the USA, and Virgin's increasing dependency on revenues from the USA, provoked Cruickshank into joking that Branson would have to moor his houseboat in mid-Atlantic. (For many years Branson ran Virgin's head office from a houseboat moored on a canal in West London.) Branson recognized the value of the back catalogue owned by EMI Music, a subsidiary of Thorn-EMI, and contemplated how he might acquire the company to establish Virgin properly amongst the largest companies in the industry. It was rumoured in Autumn 1987 that Virgin would bid for the whole of Thorn-EMI and divest the non-related businesses. However the stock market crash in October 1987 saw Virgin's share price marked down from 160 to 83 pence almost overnight; and Branson's opportunity to acquire EMI had vanished.

Meanwhile Branson caused unease in the City when his first attempt to cross the Atlantic by balloon ended with an emergency landing. (Branson has set world records for trans-Atlantic crossings by both hot-air balloon and power boat.) Institutional investors were concerned with succession in the company if anything went seriously wrong. In a number of other ways Virgin settled uncomfortably as a public company. Branson, together with most of his colleagues, enjoyed an informal style of management; for example, they tended to dress casually rather than formally. They also claimed that they found it difficult to explain the uncertainties of the pop music business to City analysts. In reality the links with the institutions were mainly forged by Cruickshank (who arguably did feel at ease), but inevitably Branson and Draper had to involve themselves.

Virgin felt that its real value was not being recognized by the City and that this was reflected in a low share price. It had introduced more robust management controls and was concerned to demonstrate that they were genuinely committed to 'the bottom line' and the interests of shareholders. Initially Virgin's shares had traded above the offer price, but once they fell below it they underperformed against the FT All-Share index.

Being public is incredibly time consuming ... every single thing has to be vetted by lawyers. You are tied up in tape.

Around 50% of our time was spent worrying about going to stockbrokers' meetings, analysts' meetings, institutional meetings ... and worrying about the next quarter's results ... rather than planning for the long term.

We thought: 'Let's try to get out of this'.

(Richard Branson, quotation summarized from material included in: *Richard Branson and the Virgin Group*, Manfred Kets de Vries, Insead-cedep, 1989.)

Virgin announced a fall in profits of 22% when it declared half-year results early in 1988, and this drove the share price down further.

If anything goes wrong in a public company, it goes wrong very publicly and happens very quickly – and everybody panics and pulls the rug out.

(Richard Branson, quote taken from *Richard Branson and the Virgin Group*, op cit.)

The US music business was losing some £2–3 million on a turnover of £16 million, and Branson, who was perhaps too honest about the situation, commented that it would take another two years to move into profits. Branson also announced that the Directors would buy back the 37% of the shares they did not have at the offer price of 140 pence.

The buy-back was completed in July 1988, and required a £182 million syndicated loan. One positive benefit to emerge from the period when Virgin was a quoted company was that the City insisted on sound control systems. They expected, for example, that Virgin would know the weekly turnover of each of its stores. These systems had been strengthened, and Virgin was therefore a sounder business when it was re-privatized.

Exhibit 1 Virgin management – financial analysis for the five years before re-privatization (figures in £ millions)

	12 months to 31.1.1984	12 months to 31.1.1985	18 months to 31.7.1986	12 months to 31.7.1987	12 months to 31.7.1988
Turnover	99.6	152.8	312.2	299.7	377.0
Profit before Interest and tax	11.2	14.2	23.1	34.5	17.7
Interest	1.1	2.2	6.2	3.5	8.5
Earnings	4.1	6.6	9.3	16.9	1.0
Profit after extraordinary items	4.1	5.2	7.5	21.5	(3.9)
Fixed assets	14.5	45.4	78.8	55.8	74.4
Current assets	37.7	51.2	100.4	167.6	194.0
Current liabilities	35.8	50.4	67.7	68.5	78.6
Net assets	16.4	46.2	111.5	154.9	189.8
Equity	5.3	10.8	33.3	74.9	70.8
Loan capital	11.1	35.4	78.2	80.0	119.0

Exhibit 2 Comparison of Virgin management with the total leisure industry

	Leisure industry co. average 12 months to 30.6.1988	Virgin 12 months to 31.7.1988
Return on net assets (%)	16.5	9.3
Return on equity (%)	13.8	1.4
Stock-days	42	40
Debtor days	51	125
Creditor days	56	70
Interest cover – times	2.7	1.7
Sales/employee – £'000	68 .4	153.6

Branson's problem now, though, would be funding the continued expansion of Virgin. Prior to going public he had often experienced difficulty in extending his overdraft facility.

Sometime later Don Cruickshank left Virgin (in 1996 Don Cruickshank is Director-General of OFTEL, the telecommunications regulatory authority).

Exhibits 1 and 2 summarize the financial results for Virgin for the mid-1980s, and provide a comparison of Virgin's performance with that of the total leisure industry in 1988.

Joint ventures

As one source of money Branson has entered a series of joint ventures and sold minority interests in several of his subsidiary businesses.

The Virgin group of companies, which remained separate from Voyager, was split into three distinct divisions – music, retail and communications. Voyager still encapsulated the airline, the holiday company and a variety of other enterprises. Each division comprised a series of small, autonomous businesses. More recently Voyager has been renamed Virgin Travel Group.

At the end of the 1980s, Virgin consisted of some 200 subsidiaries. Each time a company expanded beyond a staff level of 80 Branson split it up and separated the people, perhaps into different premises. He believes this prevents impersonality and maintains motivation.

In October 1989 Fujisankei of Japan bought 25% of Virgin Music for £96 million. Virgin as a whole (including retailing and communications as well as music) had been valued at £248 million when it was re-privatized in 1988.

In December 1989 Virgin formed a joint venture with Telfos Holdings for the manufacture of computer tapes, videos and cassettes which would be sold under the Virgin label.

A joint venture with Marui of Japan followed in April 1990. Marui is a leading Japanese department store which caters mainly for young people. Virgin and Marui would jointly open a Megastore (multiple products Virgin shop) in Tokyo in September the same year.

May 1990 brought Branson's third alliance with a Japanese partner. Seibu Saison, owner of Inter-Continental Hotels, paid Branson £36 million for 10% of Virgin Atlantic Airways. Branson's commitment to people and the quality of their working life meant he felt comfortable doing business with the Japanese.

Exhibit 3   The Virgin group – situation summary for 1990/1991

	Virgin Music	Virgin Retail	Voyager Travel Holdings	Virgin Communications
Activities	Recording (80%) Music Publishing (18%) Studios (2%)	Megastores and Gamestores Europe and Japan	Virgin Atlantic (80%) Virgin Holidays (17%) Aviation Services (3%)	Computer games TV post-production Publishing and distribution
Turnover (£ million)	350	175	383	140
Pre-tax profit/(loss) (£ million)	18	(1*)	6.2	14
Outside Shareholders	Fujisankei (25%)	U.K: WH Smith (50%) Japan: Marui (50%) Europe: Consortium (20%)	Virgin Atlantic: Seibu Saison (10%) Voyager Hotels: John Laing (50%)	–

*Profits in UK and Japan subsidizing expansion into Europe.
Source: *Financial Times*, 21.2.1992.

However Branson bought back the Seibu Saison shareholding in November 1993, at which time he invested more of his own personal fortune in Virgin Atlantic.

Exhibit 3 summarizes the situation of Virgin and Virgin Atlantic in 1991. The joint ventures alone, however, were not going to see Branson through the recession. Divestment and further strategic alliances would follow.

Virgin music

Virgin Music mainly comprised the record label, recording studios and music publishing (finding opportunities for composers in recording, television, films and advertising). In addition Virgin held merchandising rights to sell a variety of products and publications at selected concert venues.

Virgin grew to become the 'largest second division' record company, smaller than the four majors (Warner, Sony, Polygram and EMI) and substantially bigger than most of the independent labels. Virgin's UK market share maximized at around 10% for singles, and 8% for LPs, cassettes and CDs. Over the years Virgin developed a reputation for picking 'winners', artistes whose recordings would prove successful; and during the late 1970s and 1980s it obtained contractual rights for the music of

Genesis, Phil Collins, Human League, Simple Minds and UB40 (amongst many others) in certain territories world-wide.

A record company contracts with an artiste to exploit his or her talent in exchange for royalty payments. Normally a fixed number of albums and a number of years are agreed. The most successful companies are able to spot artistes whose popularity will last for several albums (together with linked singles, of course) and several years, and balance 'yesterday's winners' with future potential in a varied and extensive portfolio. Virgin had around 100 contracted artistes on its various labels. In addition, Virgin enjoyed considerable success from a joint venture with EMI for a series of compilation albums in the series 'Now That's What I Call Music'. In the early 1980s Virgin acquired a number of small independent record companies.

Virgin's early expansion abroad was through licensing agreements. After its initial failure in the USA the company realized that it would be increasingly profitable if it exercised greater control over marketing and promotion, and systematically it switched over to controlled subsidiaries. The USA was, however, always the prime target, and by the late 1980s Virgin was trading profitably with a wholly-owned subsidiary employing experienced US staff. Ironically the company became profitable earlier than Branson had anticipated.

The sale of Virgin Music

By 1990 the total Virgin Group was experiencing cash problems again. This became more critical when the Gulf War hit airline revenues, and throughout 1991 it was speculated that Branson might be willing to sell all Virgin's music interests in order to support the retailing, communications and airline businesses.

During 1991 Sony, Polygram and Walt Disney all expressed interest before withdrawing from any negotiations. Bertelsmann (Arista and RCA labels) was also a serious contender. Since Branson's failed attempt to acquire EMI Music, Thorn-EMI's chief executive, Sir Colin Southgate, had more than once tentatively approached Branson. EMI had already bought Chrysalis Records, and the acquisition of Virgin would elevate it to a position alongside the world leaders. The early overtures had been rejected, and throughout 1991 Branson remained undecided about whether he would actually sell. Early in 1992 Branson was seriously interested in a deal. Negotiations with Southgate finally took six weeks, and Thorn-EMI agreed to buy Virgin Music for £560 million in cash. Southgate had wanted a deal involving both cash and shares, but Branson had demanded future compensation if Thorn's share price were to fall. The £560 million bought £3 million tangible assets, £507 million intangible assets (back catalogue material) and goodwill, and £50 million debt. The figure represented 1000 times Virgin's after-tax earnings in 1991.

Fujisankei received £120 million, Draper and Berry £70 million jointly and Branson £320 million. This allowed Branson to pay off all Virgin's remaining debt (£119 million) and support his airline further.

Perhaps not unexpectedly Simon Draper subsequently left the more formal and culturally different Thorn-EMI, but Ken Berry stayed and was instrumental as Thorn-EMI proved it could extract additional synergy from linking Virgin Music with EMI and Chrysalis (the relative success of Virgin Music after the acquisition is discussed in the Thorn-EMI case).

Branson had obtained cash to support that business activity which he now cared most about, and although Virgin had sold the business for which it was best known the company was still a diversified leisure group with strong businesses.

Virgin Retail

Branson's challenge from retailing was to succeed with his preferred style of informal, empowered management as the number of stores increased and in an industry characterized by detail and normally making extensive use of control systems backed by information technology. Virgin developed with three different retail formats: specialist record stores, megastores and department store concessions. In 1984 all the stores were redesigned by Conran to try and give them greater distinctiveness, promote additional business and strengthen the profit flow.

The single-product store format (mostly music plus some specialist games centres) was systematically extended to towns and cities throughout Britain. Whilst they made an impact in terms of market share their returns were perceived as inadequate. In 1988 Virgin agreed to sell 74 specialist record shops to WH Smith's Our Price Music.

Virgin's megastores sell popular and classical music, back catalogue records and tapes, blank tapes, videos, T-shirts, posters, hi-fi equipment, computer games, books and stationery. They have a much greater selling area than the original single-product music stores and they have been concentrated in major cities in Britain, Europe, Australia and the Far East. By 1992 there were 14 stores in Continental Europe and Australia.

In September 1991 Virgin and WH Smith formed a 50:50 partnership to manage and develop Virgin's UK chain of 12 megastores and seven games centres. WH Smith was providing both finance and retail expertise.

In November 1992 Branson announced his latest joint venture with Blockbuster Video, a Florida-based video rental company. The purpose was to extend the Virgin megastore format to every large city in the USA as well as further sites in Europe and Australia. Consequently this deal excluded Britain and Japan.

In simple terms Blockbuster bought an interest for an unnamed sum, and it was assumed that the two companies would jointly fund further expansion. Virgin and Blockbuster would jointly own the European stores and the one in Los Angeles (the first in the USA) on a 50:50 basis, but the new US units were to be 75% owned by Blockbuster. Virgin was to manage every megastore, and video rentals were to be added to the product range.

One year later the Virgin/WH Smith joint venture for megastores and games sold the games outlets; and in March 1994 the joint venture was absorbed into WH Smith's Our Price subsidiary. At this time there were 24 stores in the UK and Ireland. While the two brands remain separated on the high street, management has been integrated. WH Smith now owns 75% of the joint venture, Virgin the remainder. No money changed hands and the overseas megastores were not affected. Simon Burke, managing director of Virgin Retail, took over the strategic leadership of the combined operation. (The fortunes of WH Smith deteriorated in the mid-1990s and a new strategic leader was appointed. At this time the main WH Smith retail branches were underperforming but Our Price and the Waterstone's specialist bookstores were profitable.)

At the same time Virgin established another joint venture with a Hong Kong trading company, Wheelock, and it was speculated that a Hong Kong megastore would be opened. In the event, Virgin decided rents were too high and instead looked to Taiwan and China for expansion.

Virgin Communications

From 1981 Virgin diversified into a series of related communications activities. Branson felt they offered new opportunities and synergy for his existing businesses.

He began with the distribution of filmed entertainment, arranging, for example, with major film studios to manufacture and distribute video copies of their old and new feature films. A subsequent dalliance with film making itself was discontinued in 1986. Virgin also provided services such as editing to the television and video industries, and acquired a company which produced television commercials. The film distribution business was internationalized before being sold in 1989 for £50 million.

Virgin bought MGM Cinemas for £190 million in 1995; Branson believed he could find new and distinctive opportunities for adding value and differentiating. Branson has tested out a Virgin retail outlet in foyers and a premium-service cinema (as part of a multiple) with a personalized cloakroom, special snacks and waitresses serving drinks. Virgin only kept the largest MGM cinemas, including all the multiplexes, and sold the others for £83 million,

some of which has been invested in new cinema complexes.

Virgin entered broadcasting through an involvement in satellite television, and in November 1988 formed a partnership with the Italian television company, Videomusic. The aim was to strengthen its European satellite business which at the time was failing to generate sufficient advertising revenue. In 1991 Virgin was part of a consortium which bid for (but failed to win) the franchise for a regional independent television channel.

Virgin Radio began broadcasting in the UK on medium wave in April 1993. This is an independent national radio station with a brief to provide 'popular music from the last 25 years'. It is a joint venture between Virgin and TVam, previously the provider of breakfast television for the ITV network. Virgin has continually attempted, but failed, to acquire a national FM radio wavelength.

The fourth arm of Virgin Communications was publishing. Virgin acquired WH Allen, and was also active in the manufacture and distribution of computer software games – many through its own stores. Virgin offered computer versions of Monopoly and Scrabble, and, since 1989, had an agreement to distribute Japanese Sega games in the UK. Sega is number two to world leader Nintendo.

In 1994 Branson sold a 19.9% shareholding in Virgin Interactive Entertainment (VIE) to Blockbuster – in exchange for Blockbuster shares. VIE develops games software for, among others, Sega and Nintendo and has a lucrative licensing deal with Walt Disney for producing games which feature Disney film characters. Some time earlier 15% of VIE had been sold to Hasbro, the US toy company; and commentators began to speculate that VIE would eventually be floated as a separate company in the USA.

One major benefit for VIE is the 1993 merger between Blockbuster and Viacom, the US cable television company, which is developing rapidly in the field of multi-media.

Six months later Branson (together with other smaller shareholders) sold a further 55% of VIE to Blockbuster; Virgin received $125 million and retained a 10% stake in VIE.

Virgin Enterprises

This division was originally part of Voyager and embraced those entrepreneurial activities which could not be fitted elsewhere. If employees or outsiders attracted Branson's interest with a new good idea that was likely to prove profitable he has generally been willing to provide venture capital and establish new small companies within the Virgin group. Those with the ideas are normally given shares in the new business, but not in Virgin overall. Early successful examples included a traditional pub, night clubs and a business set up to develop an electronic synthesizer controller.

In September 1994 Virgin finalized an agreement with ICL (itself majority owned by Fujitsu) whereby ICL would manufacture Virgin-branded desktop, notebook and games computers for marketing through Virgin megastores and mail order.

Earlier that year Branson was part of a consortium which bid unsuccessfully against Camelot for the right to run the UK National Lottery.

In September 1994 Virgin launched a new range of externally-sourced consumer goods branded with the Virgin name. A new business, Virgin Retail Brands was established. The first product was Virgin Vodka, soon followed by Virgin Cola. Virgin Cola is mixed and canned by various companies from a concentrate produced by the Canadian company Cott, which also produces the concentrate for Sainsbury's Classic Cola. The timing was good; the cola market was expanding. Distribution through Tesco and a range of petrol forecourts was quickly secured; and Virgin used its own fleet of vans to collect supplies from cash and carry warehouses and deliver them to independent retailers. Virgin Cola was marketed as a quality product at a low price; Coca-Cola and Pepsi prices are higher, partly because of the money they spend to promote the brand. Branson's declared aim was world-wide coverage using independent distributors who would invest most of the funding required. Coca-Cola was sceptical about this new form of consumer goods network, commenting Branson was *either very brave or uninformed*. Virgin Cola made an immediate impact and seized market share, but its initial success has not been maintained.

1995 saw Virgin enter the financial services market with a 50:50 joint venture with Norwich Union. The first product was a personal equity plan sold direct over the phone; personal pension schemes and insurance plans would follow later. Characteristically Virgin planned to *undercut competitors and remove the jargon and gimmicks from the products*.

Virgin Atlantic Airways

Branson's business interest in a cut-price trans-Atlantic airline was triggered by a US lawyer, Randolph Fields, although his enthusiasm had earlier been stimulated by his mother, an ex-air stewardess. Simon Draper was sceptical. Fields originally hoped to operate a Boeing 747 service from London to New York which was exclusively business class, but he was refused a license. Branson typically set out to gather the information he needed to reach a decision, and within a matter of weeks he had committed himself.

A major aspect of Branson's approach was an assessment of Freddie Laker's Skytrain – why Laker had failed, and what lessons could be learned. (The demise of Laker Airways is described in Case 7.1 in the main text. Freddie Laker has reintroduced trans-Atlantic flights to Florida from Gatwick in 1996.). Branson agreed with many other analysts that Laker had attempted to grow too quickly, and determined that his airline would stay relatively small. He also felt that Laker had made a mistake with his choice of aeroplane. Laker had flown DC10s, which are smaller than Boeing 747 jumbo jets, and Branson believed that in a tight price competition the airlines with the most seats available would have an advantage. Laker's competitive advantage was based wholly on his low prices, which he was able to offer by providing only the most basic of services. When the major carriers retaliated by discounting, Laker's initial advantage was unsustainable. Learning from this Branson has ensured that Virgin Atlantic offers a high quality of service as well as competitive prices.

Branson quickly agreed the lease for a Boeing 747-200, and in Summer 1984 he began flights from London Gatwick to Newark, New Jersey (which services New York). He added a second plane to the fleet and introduced flights to Orlando and Miami (1986). In 1988 he received permission for a daily flight from Gatwick to Tokyo. British Airways had two flights every day from the preferred Heathrow airport. In 1991, after lengthy campaigning, Virgin was also allowed flight slots at Heathrow, competing directly with British Airways on several of its most profitable routes. Fields had parted company with Branson in 1985, arguing the rate of expansion was too slow.

Virgin Atlantic now flies to New York (Newark and JFK), Los Angeles, San Francisco, Washington, Athens, Tokyo and Hong Kong from Heathrow and from Gatwick to Boston, Miami, Orlando and Athens again. The Manchester–Orlando route was inaugurated in 1996; and in partnership with CityJet Virgin also flies from London City airport to Dublin and Brussels. Future planned destinations include Johannesburg, Singapore and Sydney.

Virgin launched three code-sharing partnership agreements (for through ticketing) in 1995 – with Delta Airlines of the USA, Malaysia Airlines and British Midland.

Virgin's aircraft fleet now includes nine Boeing 747s, three of these being the new 747-400 series, which offers a higher payload and lower fuel consumption per nautical mile than the earlier versions. In addition there are five Airbus A340s, the largest plane built by Airbus. All Virgin's aircraft are four-engined.

Virgin Atlantic was first profitable in 1986–1987 after early teething problems. When Branson had just two aircraft (from 1986 to 1990) he had no spare capacity and, for example, any need for prolonged maintenance inevitably meant long delays for passengers.

Exhibit 4 provides a financial summary for the period 1987 to 1995. The figures for Virgin Travel (the renamed Voyager Group) include both the airline and the associated Virgin Holidays activities; the holiday business has typically been the more profitable activity. Exhibit 4 also includes data on passenger numbers and market share achievements in the 1990s. Exhibit 5 compares Virgin with BA and the complete transport industry sector in 1991. Care should be taken when comparing Virgin's ratios with those of BA, as the latter company is so much bigger and has an extensive portfolio of profitable and less profitable routes around the world. In 1989 Branson recruited British Airways' Head of Central Marketing as an executive director, but he left after five days, commenting on a 'lack of systems and structure'.

During 1991 and 1992 the airline industry world-wide was hit hard by the economic recession following on from the business lost during the period of the Gulf War. For a period Branson became increasingly dependent on Virgin Travel's non-airline activities, and throughout much of 1992 Branson was reported to be seeking a partner willing to buy a 10–25% stake in Virgin Atlantic in order to help buy new aircraft and open up new routes. Nevertheless the expansion has continued.

The airline, of course, has provided excellent publicity opportunities, and self-publicity is a key feature of Branson's style of management.

From the beginning Branson decided to offer just two classes of travel, Business and Economy. He speculated that they should be named Upper Class and Riff Raff, but was talked out of the latter. His aim was *the highest quality of travel at the lowest cost for all grades of passenger*. Branson's strategy has always been to discount trans-Atlantic fares, but recently this has been in an environment of low price special fares offered by BA and all the major US carriers. Virgin has less freedom for low prices on the Tokyo route. Virgin, however, has a different fare structure, providing its own equivalent of other airlines' first class seats and service at traditional business class prices. Virgin calls this its Upper Class service; and it also provides free limousine transport to and from airports for these particular customers, who are also provided with lounges to very high standards at most airports. Economy passengers who pay full-fare rather than a specially discounted rate have a separate cabin. Legroom tends to be more generous on Virgin than on most other planes, and Branson has used his expertise in music and communications to pioneer new forms of in-flight entertainment, such as personal videos with a selection of films. The airline has won several awards for the quality of its services.

Branson has been involved in an acrimonious and protracted dispute with BA, whom he accused of discounting fares to uneconomic levels in order to force out any smaller competitors. He also alleged that BA poached his passengers and spread untrue stories about Virgin. In January 1993 BA 'apologized unreservedly' and agreed an out-of-court settlement of £610,000 plus costs. Branson had in turn provoked BA and its then chairman, Lord King, who once described him as a pirate. In response to this, Branson, with the media fully informed, dressed himself as a pirate and draped the Virgin logo over BA's model of Concorde, which is on public display at Heathrow.

Exhibit 4 Virgin Travel Group (renamed from Voyager Travel Holdings) financial results (figures in £ millions)

	12 Months to 31.7.1988	12 Months to 31.7.1989	12 Months to 31.7.1990	15 Months to 31.10.1991	12 Months to 31.10.1992	12 Months to 31.10.1993	12 Months to 31.10.1994	10 Months to 31.8.1995
Turnover	84.7	106.8	208.9	382.9	356.9	401.0	503.4	507
Profit before Interest and Tax (including Non-Trading Income)	12.5	11.6	13.5	12.6	(10.3)	5.5	1.05	38.1
Operating Profit	12.0	8.9	10.0	10.7	(9 4)	8.4	1.9	38.7
Interest	2.0	3.2	4.9	5.6	4.0	5.0	4.0	2.76
Profit before Tax	10.5	8.4	8.7	6.2	(14.5)	0.4	(2.98)	36.5
Fixed Assets	46.6	64.0	89.6	92.1	95.1	97.5	93.5	91.2
Current Assets	29.4	68.3	74.4	104.8	110.8	128	137.2	213.4
Current Liabilities	29.0	48.5	75.9	99.5	125.6	146.5	145.1	181.8
Net Assets	47.0	83.8	88.1	97.4	80.3	79.0	85.5	122.8
Equity	16.4	24.2	30.4	36.1	21.9	34.7	30.3	57.4
Loan Capital	30.6	59.6	57.7	61.3	58.4	44.3	55.2	65.4

Virgin Airways contribution								
Turnover	75.39	92.29	180.54	336.7	303.4	346.6	444	448
Exports (Included)	30.58	30.75	88.16	146.4	127.4	N/A	200	219.5
Profit Before Tax	10.14	7.19	7.57	0.7	(21.0)	(6.0)	(9.8)	31.6

Source: Company records.

Total passengers carried	
1990	906,199
1991	1,088,517
1992	1,232,983
1993	1,399,077
1994	1,694,871

Source: *CAA Annual and Monthly Operating & Traffic Statistics*.

Market Share				
Route	1991 %	1992 %	1993 %	1994 %
New York (JFK & Newark)	18	17.4	19.9	19.2
Florida (Miami & Orlando)	25.2	30.6	34.5	41.1
Los Angeles	25.8	22.3	23.8	24.1
Tokyo	16	17.3	18.3	16.6
Boston	15.3	19.7	23	24.6
San Francisco	–	–	–	15.2

Source: CAA Nett and Mutual Exchange Stats.

Exhibit 5 Comparison of Voyager Travel Holdings with British Airways and the total transport and freight industry

	Transport and freight industry company average	British Airways	Voyager
	12 months to 30.06.1991.	12 months to 31.03.1991	15 months to 31.10.1991
Return on net assets (%)	7.0	8.0	11.0
Return on equity (%)	4.4	9.9	13.7
Stock – days	22	3	5
Debtor days	67	58	38
Creditor days	88	100	48
Interest cover – times	1.8	1.8	2.0
Sales/employee – £'000	53.3	90.7	126.3

Branson's long-term risk must be that prolonged fare wars will make Virgin Atlantic's profits unsustainable. Flying in and out of Heathrow, of course, also brings Virgin into direct competition with the leading US carriers, who are also quite happy to offer special price promotions in order to increase their load factors.

Virgin has so far expressed no interest in following the hub-and-spoke strategies (several flights into and out of an important centre) of the major carriers.

In 1992 Dan-Air, which operated scheduled services within the UK and Europe together with holiday charter flights, was in financial difficulty. Branson discussed a rescue package but pulled out of negotiations in October because Dan-Air's 'financial needs were too great'. BA stepped in, and, after consideration by the Office of Fair Trading, took over Dan-Air. BA has retained the scheduled services but stopped the charter flights. Branson complained about BA's increasingly strong market position, a complaint renewed when BA announced its intended alliance with American Airlines in 1996.

In December 1992 Virgin expanded in Florida, with a new holiday airline, Virgin Vintage Air Tours. Branson uses restored DC3 Dakotas to fly from Orlando to Key West, and saw opportunities for expanding the service to include flights from Key West to Havana, and between Orlando and Miami and Los Angeles and Palm Springs.

Richard Branson

It is impossible to assess the development, strategy and success of Virgin without examining the style and contribution of Richard Branson. Branson began the company some 25 years ago and he still dominates every major move. Although perceived to be unconventional he is clearly astute, and he has become one of Britain's richest businessmen.

Branson is quietly-spoken and informal and he rarely wears a business suit. When Virgin was a public company it was commented that Branson was not very articulate when confronted by a room full of City analysts – a situation in which he clearly felt uncomfortable. His record of success has caused some outsiders to fear he was always looking to increase his own wealth and reputation rather than develop Virgin in the best interests of the shareholders. Branson is entrepreneurial and a risk taker – arguably it was the City's inability to relate to the risks he took, and to understand properly the risks inherent in the music business, that caused the rift between them to develop.

Yet despite his quiet manner Branson is an insatiable self-publicist. His exploits in crossing the Atlantic by both hot-air balloon and power boat are testimony both to his risk taking and his publicity seeking. When Virgin Atlantic was launched he invited the press to photograph him in his bath playing with a model aeroplane. He has also taken a personal interest in ventures unrelated to Virgin's businesses, launching, for example, Mates low-price condoms to help in the fight against AIDS.

The publicity has had a major impact. Branson is well known and easily recognized. Mrs Thatcher selected him to chair an independent committee to examine ways of clearing up the environment, on the grounds that he was a role model for young people. Branson has at the same time been able to direct the publicity for the benefit of Virgin. Before Virgin started flights to Tokyo Branson capitalized on his public image and gave numerous interviews in Japan.

Branson's management style

For many years Branson ran Virgin's head office with very few staff from a houseboat moored on a canal in West London. The various divisions and businesses operated from offices all over London. Virgin is genuinely decentralized, with each division comprising several autonomous small businesses. The atmosphere everywhere is casual, and pop music is normally being played. Branson's aim is to ensure that people relate to the business they work in, and feel part of something tangible and handleable. Virgin Atlantic is something of an exception and it is run from a more modern and formal office block near Gatwick airport.

Information flows and management are frequently informal (although there are effective control systems in place), and it tends to work. Branson himself scribbles endlessly in small notebooks which he keeps. He is renowned for travelling frequently on Virgin Atlantic, talking to passengers about their expectations and levels of satisfaction with Virgin's service, and making notes of his conversations. Many Virgin employees are given Branson's work and home telephone numbers and encouraged to ring with problems and queries they need help with. There is considerable delegation and empowerment.

If the staff are happy the business will prosper ...

You should never really criticize your staff. You should always be praising. If you praise somebody they are going to blossom.
    (Richard Branson, from *Richard Branson and the Virgin Group*, op cit.)

Branson gives away shares in new venture companies within the Virgin group, arguing that this actually costs nothing to do but it acts as a powerful motivator for creating growth and success.

An assessment

It is tempting to argue that Branson has been lucky. For example, he made his first fortune after Mike Oldfield turned up with *Tubular Bells*. However

Branson backed a project that other major record companies had already rejected. His success has been dependent upon his ability and willingness to seize opportunities which are offered to him. Randolph Fields provided the idea for Virgin Atlantic – Branson raised the money and took the risk. Branson's skill lies in taking other people's ideas and really developing them. He seems very astute at judging the implicit risks.

Initially Virgin's development was haphazard and directionless, with no clear strategy. The mail order business was initially seen as a means of raising money to support his student magazine. The record label and recording studio was hardly a natural progression from a record shop. However Branson has later proved very successful at developing one business out of another, and seeing linkages. This has fitted well with his desire to run Virgin as a conglomerate of small entrepreneurial businesses.

Branson has proved himself to be a ruthless negotiator of a good deal, belying the media image of the happy-go-lucky entrepreneur, or, as he was once described, a 'hippy capitalist'. But he remains more a deal maker than a detail man. This ability has been extremely valuable in establishing the series of strategic alliances and joint ventures which have enabled Virgin to continue expanding in recent years.

In the end one must question whether the Virgin group's diversification, and pursuit of ideas which interested Richard Branson, such as the airline, inhibited the development of the core Virgin company and ultimately necessitated the sale of Virgin Music. When Virgin became a public company the launch prospectus had stated: 'The Directors aim to develop Virgin into the leading British international media and entertainment group. Virgin will continue to expand those activities in which it has proven skills, knowledge and depth management'.

But if this was never achieved, did it really matter? Is business about growth and power, or about pursuing interesting challenges?

I never let accountants get in the way of ideas. You only live once, and you might as well have a fun time while you're living.
    (Richard Branson, from: Austin, T (1992) Return ticket, *Sunday Times Magazine*, 6 December)

Questions

1 What are the major strategic issues raised by the Virgin case?

2 What do you believe have been Richard Branson's objectives for his business interests?
Are the objectives consistent?
What strategies has he followed?
What difficulties has he encountered?

3 Do you believe Virgin and Virgin Atlantic are efficient and effective?

4 Apply the E–V–R (environment–values–resources) model to Virgin during the period it was a public company and to the Virgin businesses (Virgin Group and Virgin Atlantic) in the mid-1990s.

Author Index

Subject Index